THE CONTINENTAL PH
OF FILM READER

Also available from Bloomsbury

THE LANGUAGE OF FASHION
Roland Barthes

THE INTELLIGENCE OF EVIL
Jean Baudrillard

CINEMA I
Gilles Deleuze

CINEMA II
Gilles Deleuze

ERIC ROHMER: FILMMAKER AND PHILOSOPHER
Vittorio Hösle

MOVIES WITH MEANING
Daniel Shaw

MORALITY AND THE MOVIES
Daniel Shaw

THE RE-ENCHANTMENT OF THE WORLD
Bernard Stiegler

FILM FABLES
Jacques Rancière

THE CONTINENTAL PHILOSOPHY OF FILM READER

Edited by Joseph Westfall

Bloomsbury Academic
An imprint of Bloomsbury Publishing Plc

BLOOMSBURY
LONDON • OXFORD • NEW YORK • NEW DELHI • SYDNEY

Bloomsbury Academic
An imprint of Bloomsbury Publishing Plc

50 Bedford Square
London
WC1B 3DP
UK

1385 Broadway
New York
NY 10018
USA

www.bloomsbury.com

BLOOMSBURY and the Diana logo are trademarks of Bloomsbury Publishing Plc

First published 2018

British Library Cataloguing-in-Publication Data
A catalogue record for this book is available from the British Library.

ISBN: HB: 978-1-4742-7569-9
PB: 978-1-4742-7573-6

Library of Congress Cataloging-in-Publication Data
A catalog record for this book is available from the Library of Congress.

Typeset by Integra Software Services Pvt. Ltd.
Printed and bound in Great Britain

for O, E, and D—who love movies

The usefulness of theoretical books on cinema has been called into question (especially today, because the times are not right). Godard likes to recall that, when the future directors of the new wave were writing, they were not writing about cinema, they were not making a theory out of it, it was already their way of making films. However, this remark does not show a great understanding of what is called theory. For theory too is something which is made, no less than its object. For many people, philosophy is something which is not "made," but is preexistent, ready-made in a prefabricated sky. However, philosophical theory is itself a practice, just as much as its object. It is no more abstract than its object. It is a practice of concepts, and it must be judged in the light of the other practices with which it interferes. A theory of cinema is not "about" cinema, but about the concepts that cinema gives rise to and which are themselves related to other concepts corresponding to other practices, the practice of concepts in general having no privilege over others, any more than one object has over others. It is at the level of the interference of many practices that things happen, beings, images, concepts, all the kinds of events. The theory of cinema does not bear on the cinema, but on the concepts of the cinema, which are no less practical, effective, or existent than cinema itself. The great cinema authors are like the great painters or the great musicians: it is they who talk best about what they do. But, in talking, they become something else, they become philosophers or theoreticians—even Hawks who wanted no theories, even Godard when he pretends to distrust them. Cinema's concepts are not given in cinema. And yet they are cinema's concepts, not theories about cinema. So that there is always a time, midday-midnight, when we must no longer ask ourselves, "What is cinema?" but "What is philosophy?" Cinema itself is a new practice of images and signs, whose theory philosophy must produce as conceptual practice. For no technical determination, whether applied (psychoanalysis, linguistics) or reflexive, is sufficient to constitute the concepts of cinema itself.

Gilles Deleuze

CONTENTS

ACKNOWLEDGMENTS

A work of this magnitude naturally requires the cooperation and effort of a great many individuals and institutions. I would like to thank my home institution, the University of Houston-Downtown (UHD), for all of its support—moral, intellectual, and financial—including the funding of three Organized Research and Creative Activities grants, and one semester of Faculty Development Leave, with which I was able to move this book much closer to completion than I would otherwise have been able to do. In particular, I'd like to thank my colleagues in the Philosophy Program, Jeffrey Jackson and Andrew Pavelich, as well as my colleagues in Film Studies, Greg Getz and Chuck Jackson, for the many thoughtful exchanges about film. I'm extremely grateful to the many librarians—but especially those who assisted me regularly with my many Interlibrary Loan requests—of the W. I. Dykes Library at UHD. I would also like to thank Ed Hugetz, whose administrative support made all of the above grants possible, but who also engaged me more than once in lengthy, meaningful conversations about film, film history, and filmmaking.

I am profoundly grateful to the many students who have taken my film classes over the years, often enthusiastic but almost always unwitting accomplices in the development of many of the ideas that underlie various portions of this work. Some of the texts included herein simply would not have struck me as so exceptionally significant, were it not for the opportunity these students have afforded me to provide clear, concise explanations of these and related works. I have benefited immensely from their willingness to share their thoughts, their insights, and their favorite movies with me along the way.

I would like to thank everyone at Bloomsbury for shepherding this book from idea to print, including the Editorial Board and the anonymous readers for the press. More than anyone else, however, I would like to thank Frankie Mace. Her support, assistance, insights, and occasional camaraderie have had a greater influence upon the outcome of this book than almost any other single contribution—and, for that, I thank her. The book simply would not have been possible in this form without her help.

Naturally, any defects, failings, flaws, or oversights in the book are my own responsibility.

Finally, for tolerating an inordinate amount of time away—in body and in spirit—during the production of this book, as well as for all the old movies, I would like to thank my children. Without their frequently inexplicable love and support, nothing I do would ever get done—and nothing I do could ever be worth the doing. To them, I dedicate this book.

J. W.
Houston, TX, USA

Acknowledgments

The editor gratefully acknowledges the permissions granted by the various copyright holders to include selections from their copyrighted works in this reader:

Chapter 1: "The Birth of the Sixth Art," by Ricciotto Canudo, *Framework* 13 (1980), is reprinted with kind permission by *Framework.*

Chapter 2: Georg Lukács, "Thoughts on an Aesthetics of the Cinema," translated by Lance W. Garmer, in Richard W. McCormick and Alison Guenther-Pal, eds., *German Essays on Film*, New York: Continuum, 2004, pp. 11–16. Originally "Gedanken zu einer Ästhetik des Kinos," in Anton Kaes, ed., *Kino-Debatte. Texte zum Verhältnis von Literatur und Film 1909–1929*, Tübingen: Max Niemeyer Verlag, 1984, pp. 112–118.

Chapter 3: Republished with permission of Dover Publications, from *The Film: A Psychological Study*, by Hugo Münsterberg. Copyright © 1970; permission conveyed through Copyright Clearance Center, Inc.

Chapter 4: Rudolf Arnheim, *Film Essays and Criticism*, translated by Brenda Benthien. Copyright © 1997 by the Board of Regents of the University of Wisconsin System. Reprinted by permission of The University of Wisconsin Press.

Chapter 5: Andre Bazin, *What Is Cinema? Vol. 1.* Copyright © 2004 by the Regents of the University of California. Published by the University of California Press.

Chapter 6: "The Interchangeability of Continuity and Discontinuity" and "Mechanical Philosophy" are excerpted from the book *The Intelligence of a Machine*, by Jean Epstein, translated by Christophe Wall-Romana. Copyright © 2004 by Univocal Publishing.

Chapter 7: Republished with permission of Dover Publications, from *Theory of the Film: Character and Growth of a New Art*, by Béla Balázs. Copyright © 1970.

Chapter 8: "Romans in the Movies," "Garbo's Face," and "*Lost Continent*" from *Mythologies*, by Roland Barthes, translated by Annette Lavers. Translation copyright © 1972 by Jonathan Cape Ltd. Reprinted by permission of Hill and Wang, a division of Farrar, Straus and Giroux, LLC. From *Mythologies* by Roland Barthes, translated by Annette Lavers. Published by Jonathan Cape. Reprinted by permission of The Random House Group Limited.

Chapter 9: Copyright © 1974 by Northwestern University Press. All rights reserved. Originally published in French as a section of *Les Ecrits de Sartre: Chronologie, bibliographie commentée* (copyright © 1970 by Editions Gallimard). This is volume 2 of a two-volume edition of that work. "L'art cinématographique" by Jean-Paul Sartre, in *Les Ecrits de Sartre*, edited by Michel Contat and Michel Rybalka. Copyright © 1970 by Editions Gallimard, Paris.

Chapter 10: Extract from "Esquisse d'une psychologie du cinéma," by André Malraux. Copyright © 1946 Editions Gallimard, Paris.

Chapter 11: Roman Ingarden, *Ontology of the Work of Art*, translated by Raymond Meyer with John T. Goldthwait. Copyright © 1989 by the Ohio University Press. This material is used by permission of Ohio University Press, www.ohioswallow.com.

Chapter 12: From “The Film and the New Psychology” in *Sense and Non-Sense*. Originally published in French as *Sens et non-sense*. Copyright © 1948 by Les Éditions Nagel. This translation is based upon the revised third edition, issued by Nagel in 1961. English translation © 1964 by Northwestern University Press. First published in 1964 by Northwestern University Press. All rights reserved.

Chapter 13: From *The Enigmatic Body: Essays on the Arts* by Jean Louis Schefer, edited by Paul Smith. Copyright © 1995 by Cambridge University Press. Reprinted with permission of Cambridge University Press.

Chapter 14: Copyright © Serge Daney, 2007, “Postcards from the Cinema,” Berg Publishers, used by permission of Bloomsbury Publishing Plc.

Chapter 15: From *Filmosophy*, by Daniel Frampton. Copyright © 2006 by Columbia University Press. Reprinted with permission of the publisher.

Chapter 16: *The Mass Ornament: Weimar Essays*, by Siegfried Kracauer, translated and edited by Thomas Y. Levin. Copyright © 1995 by the President and Fellows of Harvard College.

Chapter 17: “A Dialectic Approach to Film Form” from *Film Forum*, by Sergei Eisenstein, translated by Jay Leyada. Copyright © 1949 by Houghton Mifflin Harcourt Publishing Company. Copyright © 1977 by Jay Leyada. Reprinted by permission of Houghton Mifflin Harcourt Publishing Company. All rights reserved.

Chapter 18: “The Work of Art in the Age of Mechanical Reproduction” from *Illuminations*, by Walter Benjamin, translated by Harry Zohn. Copyright © 1955 by Suhrkamp Verlag. Frankfurt A.M. English translation copyright © 1968 and renewed 1996 by Houghton Mifflin Harcourt Publishing Company. Reprinted by permission of Houghton Mifflin Harcourt Publishing Company. All rights reserved.

Chapter 19: Copyright © 1986, Max Horkheimer and Theodor Adorno, *Dialectic of Enlightenment*, Bloomsbury Publishing Inc.

Chapter 20: “Filmtransparente,” from: Theodor W. Adorno, Ohne Leitbild: Parva Aesthetica, in: ibid., Gesammelte Schriften. Herausgegeben von Rolf Tiedemann, Band 10: Kulturkritik und Gesellschaft I. © Suhrkamp Verlag Frankfurt am Main 1970. Alle Rechte bei und vorbehalten durch Suhrkamp Verlag Berlin.

Chapter 21: Copyright © Jacques Rancière, 2006, *Film Fables*, Bloomsbury Academic, and imprint of Bloomsbury Publishing Inc.

Chapter 22: *The Aesthetics and Psychology of the Cinema*, by Jean Mitry, translated by Christopher King. Copyright © 1997 by Indiana University Press. Reprinted with permission of Indiana University Press.

Chapter 23: Baudry, Jean-Louis, and Alan Willaims, “Ideological Effects of the Basic Cinematographic Apparatus” in *Film Quarterly,* Vol. 28, No. 2, Winter 1974–1975, pp. 39–47, © 1974 by the Regents of the University of California. Published by the University of California Press.

Chapter 24: Félix Guattari, "A Cinema of Desire" and "The Poor Man's Couch" in *Soft Subversions*, edited by S. Lotringer, pp. 143–166. Copyright © 1996 by Semiotext(e).

Chapter 25: From *Intimate Revolt: The Powers and Limits of Psychoanalysis*, Vol. 2, by Julia Kristeva, translated by Jeanine Herman. Copyright © 2002 by Columbia University Press. Reprinted with permission of the publisher.

Chapter 26: Slavoj Žižek, *The Fright of Real Tears*, published 2001 BFI Publishing reproduced with permission of Palgrave Macmillan.

Chapter 27: "Brigitte Bardot et le syndrome Lolita," by Simone de Beauvoir, in *Les Ecrits de Simone de Beauvoir*, edited by Claude Francis and Fernande Gontier. Copyright © 1979 by Editions Gallimard, Paris.

Chapter 28: Laura Mulvey, "Visual Pleasure and Narrative Cinema," *Screen*, Vol. 16, No. 3, 1975, pp. 6–18, by permission of Oxford University Press.

Chapter 29: *Alice Doesn't: Feminism, Semiotics, Cinema*, by Teresa de Lauretis. Copyright © 1984 by Teresa de Lauretis. Reprinted with permission of Indiana University Press.

Chapter 30: Republished with permission of Routledge, from *Bodies That Matter: On the Discursive Limits of "Sex,"* by Judith Butler. Copyright © 1993; permission conveyed through Copyright Clearance Center, Inc.

Chapter 31: "The Transgender Look," from *In a Queer Time and Place*. Copyright © 2005 by New York University. All rights reserved.

Chapter 32: *The Picture of Abjection: Film, Fetish, and the Nature of Difference*, by Tina Chanter. Copyright © 2008 by Tina Chanter. Reprinted with permission of Indiana University Press.

Chapter 33: Republished with permission of Fordham University Press, from *Clint Eastwood and Issues of American Masculinity*, by Drucilla Cornell. Copyright © 2009; permission conveyed through Copyright Clearance Center, Inc.

Chapter 34: Originally published in *Le cinéma ou l'homme imaginaire. Essai de l'anthropologie* (Les Editions de Minuit, 1956) and in the second edition, *Le cinéma ou l'homme imaginaire. Essai de l'anthropologie sociologique* (Les Editions de Minuit, 1978). English translation © 2005 by the Regents of the University of Minnesota.

Chapter 35: Monique Wittig, "Lacunary Films," *New Statesman* (July 15, 1966), p. 102, reprinted with permission of PMI Publishing.

Chapter 36: Jean-François Lyotard, "Acinema," *Wide Angle*, Vol. 2, No. 3, 1978, pp. 53–59 by permission.

Chapter 37: Michel Foucault, "Film and Popular Memory" in *Foucault Live*, ed. S. Lotringer, pp. 122–132. Copyright © 1996 by Semiotext(e).

Chapter 38: Jean Baudrillard, *Simulacra and Simulation* (Ann Arbor: The University of Michigan Press), pp. 43–48. Copyright © 1994 by The University of Michigan.

Chapter 39: Paul Virilio, *War and Cinema: The Logistics of Perception*, translated by P. Camiller, pp. 46–51 and 61–67. Copyright © 1989 by Verso.

Chapter 40: Originally published in *Cinema 2, L'Image-temps*. Copyright © 1985 by Les Editions de Minuit. English translation © 1989 by Athlone Press. US edition published by the University of Minnesota Press. © Gilles Deleuze, 2000 "Conclusions of Cinema II: The Time-Image," The Athlone Press, used by permission of Bloomsbury Publishing Plc.

Chapter 41: Giorgio Agamben, "Notes on Gesture," from *Means without End: Notes on Politics*. Translated by Vicenzo Binetti and Cesare Casarino (University of Minnesota Press, 2000), pp. 49–60.

Chapter 42: Reprinted from "On Evidence: *Life and Nothing More*, by Abbas Kiarostami" by Jean-Luc Nancy, translated by *Verena Andermatt Conley*, in *Discourse: Journal for Theoretical Studies in Media and Culture*, Vol. 21, No. 1. Copyright © 1999 Wayne State University Press, with permission of Wayne State University Press.

Chapter 43: From *Handbook of Inaesthetics*, Alain Badiou, translated by Alberto Toscano. Copyright © 2005 by the Board of Trustees of the Leland Stanford Jr. University for the translation; © 1998 by Editions du Seuil.

Chapter 44: Reprinted from "Cinema and Its Ghosts: An Interview with Jacques Derrida" by Antoine de Baecque and Thierry Jousse, translated by Peggy Kamuf, in *Discourse: Journal for Theoretical Studies in Media and Culture*, Vol. 37, No. 1. Copyright © 2015 Wayne State University Press, with the permission of Wayne State University Press.

Chapter 45: From *Technics and Time, 3: Cinematic Time and the Question of Malaise*, Bernard Stiegler. Copyright © 2011 by the Board of Trustees of the Leland Stanford Jr. University.

Epilogue: Giorgio Agamben. "The Six Most Beautiful Minutes in the History of Cinema" in *Profanations* (New York: Zone Books, 2007), pp. 93–94.

INTRODUCTION

I want to see the den of thinking men
Like Jean-Paul Sartre.
I must philosophize with all the guys
Around Montmartre,
And Montparnasse... Bonjour, Paris!
—*Funny Face* (1957)[1]

Bonjour, Paris! (and Berlin! and Rome! and London! and Ljubljana! and Moscow! and New York! and...)

Few things in this world are as captivating, as fascinating, as entertaining, as engrossing, as unsettling, as overwhelming, as life-changing, as inspiring, as simultaneously complex and oh-so-simple as philosophy—and *movies*.

Somewhat naturally, then, the philosophical inquiry into the cinema is a lively and engaging subfield of both philosophy and film studies, and the number of philosophers, filmmakers, and cinephiles who take the philosophy of film seriously seems only to increase with time. The relationship between film and philosophy is by its very nature a lopsided one—philosophy has, it would seem, a great deal more to say about film than film does philosophy. This is perhaps as it should be: no doubt, a film culture that was devoted more fully to the presentation, examination, explanation, or criticism of philosophical concepts would produce many fewer thoroughly entertaining movies. Philosophical films tend toward the expositive and the didactic, at least in the popular consciousness, and as such they are—exceedingly—unpopular, on the whole. The number of movies made with explicitly philosophical content is thus rather small; the number of such films that also function well as entertainment or art is much smaller.[2]

The philosophy of film, however, is not simply a concern for or interest in those films which participate in what we might call the genre of "philosophical" or "explicitly thoughtful" films, films that in one way or another take philosophy as their subject matter, such as

---

[1] *Funny Face* (USA, 1957). Directed by Stanley Donen. Produced by Roger Edens. Written by Leonard Gershe. Starring Audrey Hepburn, Fred Astaire, and Kay Thompson.

[2] There are, of course, some startlingly exceptional exceptions to this trend—most notably, the films of Ingmar Bergman, sometimes credited as a philosopher himself; perhaps also a selection of the middle and late works of Woody Allen (especially those of the late 1970s and 1980s). See Irving Singer, *Ingmar Bergman, Cinematic Philosopher: Reflections on His Creativity* (Cambridge, MA: The MIT Press, 2007) . And Sander Lee, *Woody Allen's Angst: Philosophical Commentaries on His Serious Films* (Jefferson, NC: McFarland & Co., 1997) . In addition, certain periods or movements in cinema history have also tended more toward the philosophical than others—the French New Wave, for example, or Dogme 95.

The Seventh Seal,[3] *My Dinner with Andre*,[4] or *Derrida*.[5] The philosophy of film is precisely that: the philosophy of *film*, of film *as such*, of *all* films—whether treated abstractly as an art form or art medium, or by way of the philosophical examination and exploration of one or more particular films. More often than not, philosophers of film—when they write about particular films (which they do not always do)—write about the same films you would find engage the interest of film theorists, film critics, film buffs, and moviegoers everywhere. (One recent book, for example, examines film philosophically by way of analyses of the films constituting the *Alien* and *Mission: Impossible* film franchises,[6] and *The Matrix*[7] was a film that inspired much philosophical interest.[8]) This is simply another way of saying that, although the philosophy of film depends upon a certain sort of knowledge of film, it does not require specialist knowledge thereof. Every philosophy of film has something to say about every possible movie, or aspect of the movies, if only in a general way.

Gathered together in the present volume are contributions to the philosophy of film made by thinkers participating in (and constituting) the Continental philosophical traditions. Some of the readings collected here are rather familiar among philosophers and students of philosophy; many of the philosophers whose work is anthologized in this book are well known, even outside of Continental circles. There are a number of philosophers, whose work is included here, are, however, much better known among Continental European philosophers and cinephiles than they are to readers elsewhere in the world. And I think it is the case that, even the more popular authors—Sartre, Beauvoir, Adorno, Foucault, Derrida, and so on—appear in a new light when their work focuses on questions surrounding the cinema, and when they are situated and read alongside other thinkers in the Continental philosophical traditions, thinkers who are likewise focused on cinematic questions. Film is *the* great art form of the twentieth (and, given all indications so far, twenty-first) century: a truly mass art form, a synthesis of art and technology and language and social discourse, a means of edification and propaganda and inspiration and confusion and beautification and corruption. The philosophers whose writings appear here have attempted, in their various ways, to address the questions that naturally arise from such a phenomenon as film—questions about the nature of film itself, and questions about the role and impact of film upon those who make films or view them. They address those questions in ways that are sometimes unfamiliar outside of the Continental philosophical traditions, although despite this unfamiliarity, their contributions to our thinking about, understanding, and experience of film can be of value not only to other Continental philosophers, but to anyone interested in film, or the philosophy of film. To broach some of the difficulties posed by the possibility of such unfamiliarity, however, it is helpful to have at least a basic understanding of what is meant both by "Continental philosophy," as well as the Continental philosophy of film.

---

[3] *Det sjunde inseglet* [*The Seventh Seal*] (Sweden, 1957). Directed and Written by Ingmar Bergman. Produced by Allan Ekelund. Starring Gunnar Björnstrand, Bengt Ekerot, Nils Poppe, Max von Sydow, Bibi Andersson, Inga Landgré, and Åke Fridell.

[4] *My Dinner with Andre* (USA, 1981). Directed by Louis Malle. Produced by George W. George and Beverly Karp. Written by and Starring Andre Gregory and Wallace Shawn.

[5] *Derrida* (USA, 2002). Directed by Kirby Dick and Amy Ziering Kofman. Produced by Amy Ziering Kofman. Starring Jacques Derrida.

[6] Stephen Mulhall, *On Film*, 2nd ed. (Abingdon: Routledge, 2008).

[7] *The Matrix* (Australia–USA, 1999). Directed and Written by The Wachowskis. Produced by Joel Silver. Starring Keanu Reeves, Laurence Fishburne, Carrie-Ann Moss, Hugo Weaving, and Joe Pantoliano.

[8] See, among others, Slavoj Žižek, "The Matrix: Or, the Two Sides of Perversion," in *The Matrix and Philosophy: Welcome to the Desert of the Real*, ed. William Irwin (Chicago: Open Court, 2002), pp. 240–266.

What is Continental philosophy?

Early in the twentieth century, Western philosophy split into two different and often opposed traditions, each with its own interests and methods. Some philosophers gravitated toward a preoccupation with logic and the intellectual foundations of highly quantitative disciplines such as the natural sciences and mathematics. Although this tradition has its origins in the writings of the German logician, Gottlob Frege, and the Austrian philosopher, Ludwig Wittgenstein, it quickly became the philosophical tradition characteristic of the Anglo-American world and, taking its name from the practice of logical analysis, it was dubbed "Analytic philosophy." On the other hand, taking their inspiration from Frege's contemporary, Edmund Husserl, as well as Husserl's star pupil, Martin Heidegger (and Husserl's and Heidegger's mutual appreciation of Continental European thinkers from Descartes to Nietzsche), other thinkers focused on the ambiguities present in any inquiry or intellectual investigation, and the things such ambiguities could tell us about human existence generally. This second approach—characteristic, since Husserl, of French and German philosophy, and a minority tradition in the Anglophone world—takes its name from its primary geography, and is called "Continental philosophy." In some philosophical communities, and particularly the English-speaking ones, Analytic and Continental philosophies are understood to be at cross purposes, and there has been a longstanding antagonism (especially in the United States) between professional philosophers who align themselves with one of the two camps, approaches, or schools. Not only has this led to widespread antipathy between the two approaches, but it also means that participants in one tradition seldom thoroughly read or understand the work promoted in the other. Every student and professor of philosophy who comes to understand philosophy in terms of this "divide," then, is cut off not only from a significant portion of his or her philosophical colleagues, but also from half of contemporary Western philosophy.

Various schools of thought also occur, of course, within each of these two major trends, and within the history of Continental philosophy we have seen the emergence of a wide variety of sometimes very different styles, methods, purposes, and presuppositions, typically owing their existence to the groundbreaking work of one or more of the major European philosophers of the nineteenth and early twentieth centuries (including, but of course not limited to, figures such as Hegel, Kierkegaard, Schopenhauer, Nietzsche, Marx, de Saussure, and Freud). Without delving deeply into the genealogies of these various movements, discovering in what ways and to which earlier thinkers they are connected, we might simply say that the scene of Continental philosophy—running from the post–Second World War period through the present day—is well characterized (even if not exhaustively so) by reference to six movements, fields, or schools: phenomenology, existentialism, Critical Theory or the Frankfurt School, psychoanalysis, French feminism, and postmodernism. These six sorts or subtypes within Continental thought do not always agree with, support, or confirm one another, despite their common historical, geographical, and cultural origins; nor would many Continental philosophers regard a six-member list as exhaustive of the Continental philosophical traditions. But this list does seem to provide a minimally broad base for the beginning of an inquiry.

"Continental philosophy," then, is as much an association of related perspectives and styles of thinking as it is a distinct and definable brand of philosophical discourse. Whether from within or without Continental philosophy, the precise meanings of the terms "philosophy" and "Continental philosophy" are contested matters. All the same, a precise definition is perhaps unnecessary here, and we might borrow a page from a volume of Analytic thought—although admittedly that of a Continental European, Wittgenstein—to suggest that, even in the absence of the possibility of a definition, we might perceive and understand the relationships that, when interwoven with one another, constitute Continental philosophy as a loose system of "family resemblances." Despite their differences, they do have a kind of kinship with one another. In addition, and perhaps most importantly, Continental philosophy as a field is characterized by an openness to and appreciation of sometimes vast differences in style, method, and subject matter. To deny the fluidity, difference, and even contradiction central to the Continental philosophical endeavor would be to deny Continental philosophy itself.

What is the Continental philosophy of film?

Much of the recent work in the philosophy of film has been done by Analytic philosophers, but there is nevertheless a long and substantial history of philosophical work on film that has been done within Continental philosophy, as well. This work, although not hidden, exactly, remains nevertheless largely underutilized by philosophers of film, underread and marginalized by the nature and scope of the contemporary scholarly discussion of the philosophy of film, if not also by an express desire on the part of some thinkers and theorists to keep it out of view. Naturally, some figures discussing film from within the Continental traditions have had greater and more prolonged exposure than others, but even these (Eisenstein, for example, or Arnheim, Bazin, and Barthes) have typically been presented—especially to students—outside of the Continental philosophical context that made their views possible and in which those views could be understood as part of a larger, ongoing, philosophical conversation about the nature of film. Where Continental philosophers of film have been read and acknowledged, it has almost exclusively been outside of the field of philosophy—in both its Continental and Analytic varieties—and as such has not been understood or applied to film(s) *philosophically*. This strange history of reception, especially in the English-speaking world and *most* especially in the field of film studies, has colored much of the response to Continental philosophies of film among Analytic philosophers.

Views on the Continental philosophy of film—what it is, what it does, its worthwhileness at all, and so on—vary among Analytic philosophers of film, but they are not on the whole positive. Certainly, the most vocal and renowned philosophers of film in the Analytic tradition have taken stances largely at odds with, if not explicitly opposed to, the views of some of the Continental philosophers included in this book. That is to be expected; disputation is in the nature of philosophy. In addition, however, it has often been suggested that there is something fundamentally wrongheaded about the entire Continental philosophical approach to film, and in addition, the view has been promulgated by some Analytic philosophers since at least the mid-1980s that Continental philosophy as such, or at least the Continental philosophy of film, is on the wane. Naturally, even Analytic philosophy is a diverse field with a variety of practitioners holding a variety of opinions, and any easy summary of the state of the reception of Continental philosophies of film by Analytic philosophers is an oversimplification. For the sake of clarity, however, and as a means of coming to better terms with what the Continental philosophy of film is, exactly, we might identify the two primary sorts of arguments against it as denials of its status either as (1) philosophy or (2) about film. I would like briefly to consider each of these in turn.

(1) *Continental philosophy of film is not (really) philosophy*. This argument is frequently made by the same philosophers who wish to deny that Continental philosophy as such is properly

philosophical, and it takes (as does that more general criticism) a variety of forms. We see the criticism perhaps most plainly (if also least subtly) presented in the relegation of the major Continental philosophers of film into the category of "film theory," a term made dubious by its use in opposition to other thinkers, almost uniformly Analytic in approach, whose work is understood to "count" as philosophy. In his essay, "Analytic Philosophy of Film," the philosopher Berys Gaut notes that, while the first philosophical study of film was that of Hugo Münsterberg (a psychologist by training) in 1915, "Munsterberg's work stands in splendid isolation: the real, sustained beginning of the subject stems from the early 1970s (including Cavell, Sparshott, Sesonske)." Gaut goes on to say that "we should note that with the exception of Munsterberg philosophers already confronted a large and developed subject, film theory, which conditioned the development of the philosophy of film, sometimes by providing a source of ideas, more often by providing an object of criticism."[9] Continental philosophers of film, on Gaut's view, are not only (increasingly properly) criticized by Analytic philosophers: the content of the criticism is to a large extent that the Continental philosophers of film are not engaged in philosophy at all. This is, on the one hand, an almost outright dismissal of the work of these Continental philosophers altogether. On the other hand, however, it is the beginning of an argument against the sort of work done by Continental philosophers of film, and this is where this first argument dovetails with the second.

(2) *Continental philosophy of film is not (really) about film.* While some Analytic philosophers of film, such as Gaut and, to a somewhat less polemical extent, Noël Carroll,[10] dismiss the Continental approaches to cinema altogether—predicting or observing or perhaps simply wishing that the popularity of Continental philosophy in the Anglophone world is ending—others seek to establish just what it is that Continental philosophers of film, or Continentally inspired film theorists, are getting wrong. While these thinkers typically fail to recognize that there is such a thing as the Continental philosophy of film, they nevertheless do sometimes acknowledge that key thinkers on film in the Continental traditions are philosophers. These philosophers are not understood to engage in philosophy properly speaking, however, but, when it comes to film, they promulgate what is called sometimes "contemporary film theory" (Gaut),[11] "Theory" (Carroll),[12] "Grand Theory" (Bordwell), or—most colorfully and admittedly acrimoniously—"SLAB Theory" (also Bordwell),[13] an acronym that refers to the significance of the writings of Ferdinand de Saussure (*S*), Jacques Lacan (*L*), Louis Althusser (*A*), and Roland Barthes (*B*) in Continental approaches to cinema. In general, such nomenclature—in addition to satisfying some derogating impulse—is meant to point out what these Analytic philosophers of film take to be the chief problem with Continental perspectives: they (especially Bordwell and Carroll) argue that, for the Continental "film theorist," the discussion of cinema only serves as a means of further asserting the truth of the theorist's particular ideological commitments. Thus, when Continental philosophers write about film, they do so—on this argument—only so as to write more about Saussure, Lacan, Althusser, Barthes, or others (Bordwell admits we might also have to add Claude Lévi-Strauss, Émile Benveniste, and Michel Foucault;[14] Carroll

[9] Berys Gaut, "Analytic Philosophy of Film: History, Issues, Prospects," *Philosophical Books* 38, no. 3 (1997), p. 145.
[10] See Noël Carroll, "Prospects for Film Theory: A Personal Assessment," in *Post-Theory: Reconstructing Film Studies*, eds. David Bordwell and Noël Carroll (Madison: University of Wisconsin Press, 1996), pp. 37–68.
[11] See Gaut, "Analytic Philosophy of Film."
[12] See Carroll, "Prospects for Film Theory."
[13] See David Bordwell, "Historical Poetics of Cinema," in *The Cinematic Text: Methods and Approaches*, ed. R. Barton Palmer (New York: AMS Press, 1989), pp. 369–398 . The admission of acrimony appears on p. 385.
[14] Ibid., pp. 395–396, n. 43.

includes figures such as Foucault, Julia Kristeva, Jacques Derrida, Gilles Deleuze, Jean-Louis Baudry, and Teresa de Lauretis[15]). "Real" philosophy of film—that is, the *Analytic* philosophy of film—is set forth as taking a different, film-centered approach to cinema, trying to understand each film in itself and as an instance of the socio-aesthetic phenomenon of film, but always on (the) film's own terms: never as a mere instance of ideology. Or so the criticism goes.

In general, I do not think it is useful to respond to the claim that Continental philosophy is not really philosophy, both because the term "philosophy" has been contested since the time of the Greeks (and thus what "counts" as philosophy is not easily settled), and because, when the charge is made against Continental philosophers that they are not engaged in the practice of philosophy, it is not typically made as a means of opening a discussion, but of closing one. It is a dismissal of the relevance of what Continental philosophers have to say before what they have said has been seriously considered, and is thus not a position that invites (or even tolerates) a Continental response.

The other arguments, however, merit at least preliminary consideration. And the replies to these arguments, from a Continental perspective if not also that of an uncommitted philosophical observer, are fairly obvious: although it is true that there are some theorists or philosophers who seek only and in a circular way to produce more justification for the ideologies to which they subscribe—assuming the truth of certain fundamental principles which are then "demonstrated" by their application to a movie or movies—it is hard to see how this is the case for the major Continental philosophers named by Gaut, Carroll, Bordwell, and others. Roland Barthes does not analyze various films as a means of supporting his commitment to the views of Roland Barthes; rather, he does so (at the very least) as a means of expressing those views. To be sure, many professional theorists and philosophers who consider themselves "Barthesians" engage in interpretations and analyses of film that begin from and conclude with the assertion of ideas first expressed by Barthes, but this seems neither dangerous to the continued practice of the philosophy of film nor a trait unique to students and scholars in the Continental traditions (the view that defines "philosophy" to be in accord only with *Analytic* philosophy, and then on this basis "proves" that Continental philosophy is not philosophy, "properly speaking," might be taken as a non-Continental case in point). Moreover, many of the thinkers named in the Analytic criticisms—certainly Saussure, Lacan, and Althusser—said nothing about film themselves. While their points of view are sometimes applied to cinematic concerns by others, it seems strange to cite the original thinkers as somehow productive of any perceived problems with this way (relatively widespread in both Continental and Analytic circles) of coming to film philosophically. "SLAB Theory" is not anything properly ascribed to the S, the L, the A, or the B of the acronym, and it seems rather unfair to hold the teachers accountable for the transgressions (if transgressions they be) of their students.

The real problem identified—if not accurately—by these Analytic critics is not with the Continental philosophers of film, but instead, with the use made of the writings of these Continental thinkers in the predominantly English-speaking worlds of film and literary studies. It has been, in general, English and film studies departments at (mostly American) universities that have produced the large number of deconstructions of films without any philosophical defense of deconstruction, for example, or film interpretations that rely upon psychoanalytic jargon in superficial, insular, and unjustified ways. One need not agree with any one Continental

---

[15] Carroll, "Prospects for Film Theory," p. 37.

philosopher on the question of film or on any other question—and, obviously, no one Continental philosopher could agree with all of the others—to see that there is a difference between the thoughtful application and the unthinking appropriation of another's views. And, without naming any particular writers, theorists, philosophers, or critics, we can quite simply note that Analytic philosophy has its own share of such misappropriations by relatively superficial disciples of great philosophers, as well. This seems, in fact, to be characteristic of the history of philosophy from the very beginning: one can recall Socrates' warning in Plato's *Apology*, for example, that any number of less thoughtful, less careful, less self-controlled borrowers of Socratic philosophy would certainly follow in his stead. It does not seem on that basis wise to side with the Athenians against the philosopher, even if ultimately we do not share his philosophical point of view.

In any case, it is the presupposition of this book that one need not provide a defense in advance of any of the philosophers whose writings are included here. Whether we agree or disagree with their views, we should all agree that their views stand (or fall) on their own merits, not by virtue of their status as "semiotic" or "psychoanalytic" or "Marxist" or "postmodern," and the reader is asked to allow these texts to have their say before he or she rejects (or affirms) their significance for the philosophy of film.

Within the context of Continental philosophy, on the other hand, the task of describing the contours of the field of the Continental philosophy of film seems, at first glance, relatively straightforward. One might simply list the six schools of thought identified above, and apply them specifically to film: Continental philosophy of film is the phenomenology of film, film existentialism, Critical Theory of film, and so on. And there is something entirely appropriate and accurate about this conception of Continental philosophy in general, and the Continental philosophy of film in particular: while Analytic philosophy has its origins in the interrelated approaches of a small group of likeminded thinkers committed, historically, to an ideal vision of disciplinary univocality comparable to that of the natural sciences (wherein, even though different scientists do not always agree, their goal does seem to be the production/discovery of knowledge with which every rational scientist ought to be able to agree), Continental philosophy is in general and of its essence a much more diverse field of endeavor. There are certainly ties that bind various members of the Continental tradition—or traditions—to one another, but these are far more often along the lines of influence, impact, and response than they are indicative of any association or agreement on fundamental issues. Which is to say that, for example, the existentialists, the psychoanalysts, and the Critical Theorists all owe a great debt to—and claim a certain sort of origin in—the works of Nietzsche. And yet, it is difficult to imagine three philosophical methodologies more disparate, or even contradictory, than these three—and even within each of these three movements, there are numerous different and disagreeing points of view on everything, including Nietzsche.

This means, among other things, that in general the Continental philosophy of film will not be able to be encompassed or encapsulated by a simple account or definition. We will have to make sense of the varying philosophical approaches to film within the Continental traditions, and within each Continental tradition, hoping (somewhat optimistically, I admit) that, in the end, a general sense of "the Continental philosophy of film" will become at least somewhat evident. In this sense, and to this end, an anthology of representative readings from a wide array of perspectives serves as a better introduction to the Continental philosophy of film than would a monograph or textbook all on their own. A reader such as this one affords us the opportunity to encounter the sometimes dizzying diversity of philosophical points of view on cinema within the Continental traditions in the words of the thinkers who helped to constitute those traditions, rather than hearing about them "secondhand," as it were. Reading the sometimes very different authors together, or at least alongside each other, allows us to see what connections we can see for ourselves.

That said, one cannot deny that there are some more general aspects or elements of the Continental philosophy of film which can and should be discerned and discussed. Almost all Continental philosophies of film situate film itself, as a sociocultural-aesthetic practice and institution, in history—noting the historicity of the concepts associated with film and the various roles film plays and has played in culture. Almost all Continental philosophies of film are radically aware of the ways in which cultural institutions like the cinema have established themselves at the center of discourse, privileging their own concerns over those of other, marginalized groups, as well as the myriad ways in which the institutions (and industry) of the cinema promote and encourage films to adopt a specific, marginalizing, pro-capitalist and misogynistic point of view. Almost all Continental philosophies of film recognize a strong correspondence, if not resemblance, between the external, technologically mediated, objective world of the cinema and the private, internal, psychologically subjective realm of human consciousness. Almost all Continental philosophies of film recognize the important role played by ambiguity in all human productions and interactions, including film, and thus are aware of the significance of silence, absence, nonsense, irony, fragmentation, and contradiction within cinematic works. While there are certainly some ways in which some non-Continental philosophers have touched upon one or more of these general aspects of film, they are at the base of Continental philosophical approaches to film—and thus can serve, if not as a definition, then at least as a sort of blurry line demarcating the concerns of Continental from non-Continental (Analytic) approaches.

The Continental philosophy of film reader

Although Continental philosophers have been writing about film for over a century, the present volume is the first anthology explicitly concentrated on texts in the Continental philosophy of film ever to be published. And as noted above, while a small number of Continental thinkers have made their way into the more popular academic consciousness, and thus have been read and anthologized more frequently than many others, it remains the case that they are never presented as representing a diverse Continental tradition of the philosophy of film, nor as anything but non-philosophical "film theory" or a curious philosophical minority position in an otherwise overwhelmingly Analytic field. This reader has been designed in large part to address this oversight, providing access for the first time in one place to a substantial, representative survey of the thinkers and traditions constituting the Continental philosophy of film. It is not meant to replace other perspectives, but rather as a necessary—and long-awaited—supplement to them.

Many of the works written in the Continental philosophy of film have not been read by English-speaking students of film philosophy or film theory, because they have not been included among the "standard" texts, readings, and authors in the field—as it is understood in the Anglo-American Analytic tradition. While most anthologies of film theory include selections from Arnheim, Eisenstein, Barthes, Bazin, Benjamin, and sometimes Deleuze, the overlap between this reader and those others is quite small. Other than these important contributions, the remainders of those readers are constituted by essays by philosophers in the Analytic tradition. This is typical of readers in the field.[16] At the same time, the most significant texts attempting an overview of Continental European philosophies of film deal with a significant number of the philosophers who have written on cinema and film in the Continental traditions, but they are not anthologies of primary sources.[17] This volume is situated in the resultant gap, between the major existing anthologies of primary sources (which skew in a decidedly Analytic direction) and the major texts on Continental philosophy of film (which are composed entirely of secondary sources). It is an anthology of primary source material by Continental thinkers on film, and it is the first of its kind. Although the works collected here are all substantial contributions to the philosophy of film, the philosophers who have authored them are not exclusively philosophers of film, which is to say that film is not every contributor's primary field of philosophical concern. In some cases, the texts included here are the only works on cinema their authors have written. In every case, however, the works included here are either significant contributions to the ongoing Continental philosophical conversation about film—or, by virtue of the content of the contribution or the philosophical insight of the contribution's author, in the opinion of this editor ought to be.

The reader is divided into six sections: "Foundations," "Phenomenology and Existentialism," "Marxism and Critical Theory," "Psychoanalysis," "Feminism and Gender Studies," and "Postmodernism." These correspond roughly to the six subfields of the Continental philosophy of film mentioned above, with the exception of the addition of a section on foundational texts in the field, and the combination of phenomenology and existentialism into a single section. Justifications for these differences from the model of the field set out before appear in the summary descriptions of those sections, below. Each of the six sections contains a number of chapters, and each chapter is constituted by one or more selections from one philosopher writing on film in that section. Each chapter begins with a brief introduction to the philosopher and the text, as well as a filmography of the films mentioned explicitly in that chapter. Viewing these films is not typically necessary for understanding the philosophers' points of view, but it is my hope that listing them in this fashion will assist the interested reader/viewer in organizing his or her film viewing to correspond more readily to the works to be read here. The philosophy of film is always to a certain extent an immersive process, over the course of which one generally views a great many films. Even if one is not watching the movies that these philosophers watched, one shares with them the (sometimes) critical appreciation for products of the seventh art that guides and inspires this work that they—and we—do.

---

[16] Among the major anthologies already in use in the field of film-philosophy are: Thomas E. Wartenberg and Angela Curran, eds., *The Philosophy of Film: Introductory Text and Readings* (Oxford: Blackwell Publishing, 2005); Noël Carroll and Jinhee Choi, eds., *Philosophy of Film and Motion Pictures: An Anthology* (Oxford: Blackwell Publishing, 2006); and Leo Braudy and Marshall Cohen, eds., *Film Theory and Criticism: Introductory Readings*, 8th ed. (Oxford: Oxford University Press, 2016).

[17] Two of the most significant works at the present time are: Ian Aitken, *European Film Theory and Cinema: A Critical Introduction* (Bloomington: Indiana University Press, 2001), and Felicity Colman, ed., *Film, Theory and Philosophy: The Key Thinkers* (Abingdon: Routledge, 2009) . Aitken's book is a monographic history of European film theory (including, in part, film-philosophy), whereas Colman's is an anthology of essays *about* but not *by* many of the key Continental thinkers.

Foundations

Every approach or method has its origins in originary perspectives which are not necessarily straightforwardly classifiable in the terms of that approach or method—they are the beginning, the foundations of the discipline, and as such they exist in a slightly different theoretical space from their successors. Which is not to say that such texts always occur chronologically prior to others in the field; just that, for whatever reason (chronological primacy is one, but there are others), they serve a foundational role with regard to the others. In the Continental philosophy of film, there are a considerable number of such texts, not all of which are included in this section (some of which, in fact, are included in other sections in this reader). In the case of this section, all of the texts included seek to answer—or, at least, to ask—very basic questions about the nature, function, or purpose of film, from the earliest (Ricciotto Canudo's effort to situate cinema among the arts) to more recent writings. Some of these selections have equally natural homes in other sections of the reader (Georg Lukács and Béla Balázs among the Marxists, Hugo Münsterberg and Rudolf Arnheim among the psychologists, Roland Barthes with the postmoderns), and other authors could just as easily have been included here (for example, Sergei Eisenstein, Serge Daney, Edgar Morin, or Gilles Deleuze). But what all of these texts have in common is that they serve as a basis for all the rest, the beginnings of any number of Continental philosophies of film.

Phenomenology and existentialism

Although phenomenology and existentialism are distinct traditions within twentieth-century Continental thought, they are historically related—existentialism coming about as a full-fledged philosophical methodology for the first time in the work of Jean-Paul Sartre, whose training and education was in Husserlian phenomenology—and, when it comes to the philosophy of film, we see that this relation in some ways amounts to the treatment of phenomenological and existentialist philosophies of film as instances of a single approach. I group the two together here. Among the chief concerns or interests of phenomenologists and existentialists with regard to the cinema are the relationship between the film image and the body (what is sometimes called the "film body," the film image as itself a visible, illuminated, or projected body), and the significance of film as an art medium, the simultaneous expression of the individuality of the artist and a particular art culture. Taken together, these concerns demand that we make sense not only of the process and products of the filmmaking art, but also—and just as importantly—with the ways in which film spectatorship can express and even transform the filmgoer. The cinema becomes, for these thinkers, an opportunity for a heightened experience of either the perceptual foundations of human consciousness, or the significance of art and mortality for human existence, or both.

Marxism and critical theory

Critical Theory—or the Frankfurt School—has its basis in a set of readings and socio-politico-economic applications of a series of fundamentally Marxist insights into the structure and function (or dysfunction) of late capitalist societies. The major Critical Theorists—including such figures as Walter Benjamin and Theodor Adorno—take an interest in culture, and the history of culture, which centralizes the role of economic exchange and systems of production, and which remains suspicious of all mass media given their potential for use as instruments of propaganda. These concerns appear in their thoughts on film and the cinema in the form of an interest in the technological origins and techniques of filmmaking as well as the technologies of film projection and distribution, the supportive role film has played historically in various governmental structures and institutions, and the significance of the changes wrought on Western culture by the rapid development of cinema into the dominant mass art form of the twentieth and twenty-first centuries.

Psychology and psychoanalysis

Psychoanalysis, based upon the views of Sigmund Freud and Jacques Lacan, pursues knowledge of human thought, activity, and cultural production in light of the structures and relations inherent to (and developed by and within) the conscious and subconscious mind in its varying subjective, self-reflective, intersubjective, interpersonal, and social instantiations or constructions. Psychoanalytic theory undergirds many different practices and fields, including some forms of clinical psychotherapy, but as a theoretical discipline, its most basic qualities and schemata are much more philosophical. Psychoanalytical approaches to film subject cinema to rigorous analysis informed by the fundamental elements involved in the development of personality and consciousness in both their Freudian and Lacanian forms. Cinematic tropes and styles, as well as the constitutive elements of various particular films, are presented and understood as indicative of the underlying impact of latent drives and desires, and implicit anxieties and aversions. Psychoanalytic approaches to film are among the most popularly known and frequently cited among Continental philosophies of film, in part it would seem due to the deeply Freudian-psychological underpinning of the contemporary West's self-understanding.

Feminism and gender studies

There is a long and significant history of feminist philosophy in the Continental tradition (going back at least as far as Simone de Beauvoir), and French feminist thought and theory have had a deep impact on the philosophy of film. Many theorists and philosophers of film working in the late twentieth and early twenty-first centuries have relied upon Continental feminist sources in coming to terms with the aesthetic power and social significance of film, and in their philosophies of film they have elucidated the essential role of feminist voices and directed readers' attention to questions of sex, gender, sexuality, transgenderism, and the like—and their suppression (if not near-total erasure) under patriarchy. Feminist philosophies of film focus on a variety of different aspects of film, although many have a basis in psychoanalysis.

Postmodernism

Although each of the subfields constituting the Continental philosophy of film is, as we have seen, diverse, none of them is quite as remarkably so as is postmodernism. It might be possible to say that postmodern philosophies have in common an overturning of the Enlightenment ideal of philosophical activity, including a distrust of overarching narratives (Lyotard), a commitment to uncovering the subtle ways in which power, distributed or diminished across a diverse and ever-changing social structure, both informs and creates culture (Foucault), and an awareness of the subtleties and ambiguities of language and a joyful desire to wield them in pursuit of a truth uncontained and unable to be contained in purely conceptual categories (Derrida), but this would just be to make a beginning in our understanding of the postmodern. Postmodern philosophies of film ask us to reconsider film's nature, as well as the purposes to which we put it, from the ground up—from the absolutely basic to the most complex. This will mean abandoning perhaps long held assumptions about the functionality of film, such as the view that a work of cinematic art is a communication or an expression of an individual artist, the filmmaker/director/*auteur*. In addition, postmodern philosophers of film—like their psychoanalytic colleagues—find often great significance in what general spectators (or even the filmmakers themselves) might consider minor, inconsequential, even unintended details. Such details, when interpreted well, have the potential to renew or even reverse our understandings of both film and philosophy itself.

SECTION ONE
FOUNDATIONS

CHAPTER 1
RICCIOTTO CANUDO

Ricciotto Canudo (1877–1923) was an Italian film theorist whose work contributed to—if not inaugurated—the French traditions of theoretical and philosophical approaches to film, film criticism, and film aesthetics. "The Birth of the Sixth Art" was originally published in French ("La Naissance d'une sixième Art") in Les Entretiens Idéalistes *in 1911.*

In "The Birth of the Sixth Art," Canudo establishes film as a potential sixth art form in addition to the "traditional" five arts of painting, sculpture, architecture, music, and poetry. These more traditional arts are further divided into the plastic arts (painting, sculpture, and architecture), on the one hand, and music and poetry, on the other. The distinguishing characteristic of the plastic arts, for Canudo as for others, is that they do not essentially involve motion or the passage of time; they are static, whereas music and poetry both occur only in time; they are impossible to conceive without a temporal component. (In a later essay, "The Birth of the Seventh Art," Canudo adds dance as a third art alongside music and poetry in opposition to the plastic arts, making dance the sixth art and film the seventh.) In any case, the crucial element here is that, for Canudo, the traditional arts fall into either one category or the other, characterized by what he dubs "the rhythm of space" (the plastic arts) or "the rhythm of time" (music and poetry, and later, dance). He suggests that film has the potential to become not only a sixth art, but one that draws evenly upon the histories of the arts associated with both the rhythm of space and the rhythm of time—something akin to a plastic art developing in time.

Cinematography has its technological origins in photography, of course, and so it is of some interest that Canudo denies the aesthetic potential of photography altogether: it simply cannot be an art, as a photograph can only ever be a direct reproduction of the visible world. Art, for Canudo, thus requires original creation—not simply reproduction. At the time of writing "The Birth of the Sixth Art," Canudo does not see anyone utilizing the cinematographic camera in anything but its merely photographic-reproductive capacity, leaving its aesthetic potential untapped. With the right sort of development, however, Canudo argues that film could take its place alongside painting, music, and the other arts as the first new art medium of the twentieth century.

The closest comparison Canudo can find to the case of film is the case of theater, which is not itself an art (according to Canudo, who appears subject to the long-standing classification of drama as a branch of poetry, rather than as an art all its own). All the same, he suggests that the great cultural significance of tragic poetry in ancient Greece was due at least in part to the manner in which the tragedians unified irony with spectacle, making a public show of the relationship between drama and farce (in the union of three tragedies and one comic satyr play in the competition at the Great Dionysia, for example). Modern theater has, in contrast, led with comedy rather than tragedy—and the result has been a dramatic failure. After remarking on the surprising and new possibilities occasioned by early film comedies, Canudo notes that in the cinema, we have "the first new theatre of our time." If film could transcend short and simple cinematic comedies, it might take advantage of its potential to provide us with the ironic spectacle we need—an ironic theater comparable only, it seems, to that of the ancient Greeks.

Continuing with the comparison to ancient Greek tragedy, and uniting this thought with his belief in the synthetic possibility of the cinematic art, Canudo suggests that we conceive of film as "painting in motion," "a modern pantomime," or a "new dance of manifestations": all ways of emphasizing his view of film as drawing from both the spatial and the temporal arts. When made spectacular, all of the arts—but especially the theatrical—grant their spectators an experience of communion with one another, what Canudo calls a "joyous unanimity," and which he identifies with the idea of the festival. The greatest promise of the cinematic art is in what Canudo takes to be its capacity for reinstituting the festival in modern cultural life, an opportunity for isolated modern individuals to experience that joyous unanimity characteristic of the ancient experience of the theater. And film offers modern culture a new festival in an entirely new—in fact, Canudo thinks, unforeseen and unforeseeable—way: through a succession of pictures presenting moods and objects in motion, that is, in the form of an event.

Filmography

- ***Cabiria*** (Italy, 1914). *Directed and Produced by* Giovanni Pastrone. *Written by* Gabriele d'Annunzio *and* Giovanni Pastrone. *Starring* Bartolomeo Pagano.

THE BIRTH OF THE SIXTH ART

Translated by Ben Gibson, Don Ranvaud, Sergio Sokota, and Deborah Young

I

It is surprising to find how everyone has, either by fate or some universal telepathy, the same aesthetic conception of the natural environment. From the most ancient people of the east to those more recently discovered by our geographical heroes, we can find in all peoples the same manifestations of the aesthetic sense; Music, with its complimentary art, Poetry; and Agriculture, with its own two compliments, Sculpture and Painting. The whole aesthetic life of the world developed itself in these five expressions of Art. Assuredly, a sixth artistic manifestation seems to us now absurd and even unthinkable; for thousands of years, in fact, no people have been capable of conceiving it. But we are witnessing the birth of such a sixth art. This statement, made in a twilight hour such as this, still ill-defined and uncertain like all eras of transition, is repugnant to our scientific mentality. We are living between two twilights: the eve of one world, and the dawn of another. Twilight is vague, all outlines are confused; only eyes sharpened by a will to discover the primal and invisible signs of things and beings can find a bearing through the misty vision of the *anima mundi*. However, the sixth art imposes itself on the unquiet and scrutinous spirit. It will be a superb conciliation of the Rhythms of Space (the Plastic Arts) and the Rhythms of Time (Music and Poetry).

II

The theatre has so far best realized such a conciliation, but in an ephemeral manner because the plastic characteristics of the theatre are identified with those of the actors, and consequently are always different. The new manifestation of Art should really be more precisely *a Painting and a Sculpture developing in Time*, as in music and poetry, which realize themselves by transforming air into rhythm for the duration of their execution.

The Cinematograph, so vulgar in name, points the way. A man of genius, who by definition is a miracle just as beauty is an unexpected surprise, will perform this task of mediation which at present seems to us barely imaginable. He will find the ways, hitherto inconceivable, of an art which will appear for yet a long time marvelous and grotesque. He is the unknown individual who tomorrow will induce the powerful current of a new aesthetic function, whence, in a most astonishing apotheosis, the *Plastic Art in Motion* will arise.

III

The Cinematograph is composed of significant elements, "representative" in the sense used by Emerson rather than the theatrical sense of the term, which are already classifiable.

There are two aspects of it: the *symbolic* and the *real*, both absolutely modern; that is to say only possible in our era, composed of certain essential elements of modern spirit and energy.

The *Symbolic aspect* is that of velocity. Velocity possesses the potential for a great series of combinations, of interlocking activities, combining to create a spectacle that is a series of visions and images tied together in a vibrant agglomeration, similar to a living organism. This spectacle is produced exactly by the excess of movement to be found in film, those mysterious reels impressed by life itself. The reels of the engraved celluloid unroll in front of and within the beam of light so rapidly that the presentation lasts for the shortest possible time. No theatre could offer half the changes of set and location provided by the Cinematograph with such vertigious rapidity, even if equipped with the most extraordinarily modern machinery.

Yet more than the motion of images and the speed of representation, what is truly symbolic in relation to velocity are the actions of the characters. We see the most tumultuous, the most inverisimilitudinous scenes unfolding with a speed that appears impossible in real life. This precipitation of movement is regulated with such mathematical and mechanical precision that it would satisfy the most fanatical runner. Our age has destroyed most earnestly, with a thousand extremely complex means, the love of restfulness symbolized by the smoking of a patriarchal pipe at the domestic hearth. Who is still able to enjoy a pipe by the fire in peace these days, without listening to the jarring noise of cars, animating outside, day and night, in every way, an irresistible desire for spaces to conquer? The cinematograph can satisfy the most impatient racer. The motorist who has just finished the craziest of races and becomes a spectator at one of these shows will certainly not feel a sense of slowness; images of life will flicker in front of him with the speed of the distances covered. The cinematograph, moreover, will present to him the farthest countries, the most unknown people, the least known of human customs, moving, shaking, throbbing before the spectator transported by the extreme rapidity of the representation. Here is the second symbol of modern life constituted by the cinematograph, an "instructive" symbol found in its rudimentary state in the display of "freaks" at the old fairgrounds. It is the symbolic destruction of distances by the immediate connaissance of the most diverse countries, similar to the real destruction of distances performed for a hundred years now by monsters of steel.

The *real aspect* of the cinematograph is made up of elements which arouse the interest and wonder of the modern audience. It is increasingly evident that present day humanity actively seeks its own show, the most meaningful re-presentation of its self. The theatre of perennial adultery, the sole theme of the bourgeois stage, is at last being disdained, and there is a movement towards a theatre of new, profoundly modern Poets; the rebirth of Tragedy is heralded in numerous confused open-air spectacles representing disordered, incoherent, but intensely willed effort. Suddenly, the cinematograph has become popular, summing up at once all the values of a still eminently scientific age, entrusted to Calculus rather than to the operations of Fantasy (*Fantasia*), and has imposed itself in a peculiar way as a new kind of theatre, a scientific theatre built with precise calculations, a mechanical mode of expression. Restless humanity has welcomed it with joy. It is precisely this theatre of plastic Art in motion which seems to have brought us the rich promise of the *Festival* which has been longed for unconsciously, the ultimate evolution of the ancient *Festival* taking place in the temples, the theatres, the fairgrounds of each generation. The thesis of a plastic Art in motion has recreated the *Festival*. It has created it scientifically rather than *aesthetically*, and for this reason it is succeeding in this age, although fatally and irresistibly moving towards the attainment of Aesthetics.

IV

The careful observer who seeks in every movement of the masses a meaning that is in some way eternal, simultaneously traditional and new, cannot fail to register the following considerations of a general psychological order.

At the cinematographic theatre, as at the fairground, men become children again. Performances take place between the two pathetic extremes of general emotivity: the *very touching* and the *very comical.* The posters contain and conjoin these two promises of heightened emotion. They should move swiftly, as in life, from one to the other. And a primal, childlike humanity forgets itself, allows itself to be transported into a whirlpool of ultra-rapid representations with an abandon hardly to be found in our prose theatre.

At the cinematograph theatre, everything is done to retain the attention, almost in suspension, to retain an iron hold on the minds of the audience bolted to the animated screen. The quick gesture, which affirms itself with monstrous precision and clockwork regularity, exhalts the modern audience used to living at an ever-increasing velocity. "Real" life is therefore represented in its quintessence, *stylized in speed.*

V

I move on now to a great aesthetic problem, which must be emphasized.

Art has always been essentially a stylization of life into stillness; the better an artist has been able to express the greater number of "typical" conditions, that is, the synthetic and immutable states of souls and forms, the greater the recognition he has attained. The cinematograph, on the contrary, achieves the greatest mobility in the representation of life. The thought that it might open the unsuspected horizon of a new art different from all pre-existing manifestations cannot fail to appeal to an emancipated mind, free from all traditions and constraints. The ancient painters and engravers of prehistoric caves who reproduced on reindeer bones the contracted movements of a galloping horse, of the artists who sculpted cavalcades on the Parthenon friezes, also developed the device of stylizing certain aspects of life in clear, incisive moments. But the cinematograph does not merely reproduce one aspect; it represents the whole of life in action, and in such action that, even when the succession of its characteristic events unravel slowly, in life, it is developed with as much speed as possible.

In this way cinematography heightens the basic psychic condition of western life which manifests itself in action, just as eastern life manifests itself in contemplation. The whole history of western life reaches to people in the dynamism characteristic of our age, while the whole of humanity rejoices, having found again its childhood in this new *Festival.* We could not imagine a more complex or more precise movement. Scientific thought with all its energy, synthesizing a thousand discoveries and inventions, has created out of and for itself this sublime spectacle. The cinematographic visions pass before its eyes with all the electrical vibrations of light, and in all the external manifestations of its inner life.

The cinematograph is thus the theatre of a new Pantomime, consecrated *Painting in motion*, it constitutes the complete manifestation of a unique creation by modern man. As the modern Pantomime, it is the new *dance of manifestations.*

Now, it is necessary to ask of the cinematograph, is it to be accepted within the confines of the arts?

It is not yet an art, because it lacks the freedom of choice peculiar to plastic *interpretation*, conditioned as it is to being the *copy* of a subject, the condition that prevents photography from becoming an art. In executing the design of a tree on a canvas, the painter expresses without any doubt, unconsciously and in a particular and clear configuration, his global interpretation of the vegetative soul, that is of all the conceptual elements deposited deep in his creative spirit by an examination of all the trees he has seen in his life; as Poe said, with the "eyes of dream." With that particular form he synthesizes corresponding souls and his art, I repeat, will gain in intensity in proportion to the artist's skill in *immobilizing* the essence of things and their universal meanings in a particular and clear configuration. Whoever contented himself with copying the outlines, with imitating the colors of a subject, would be a poor painter; the great artist extends a fragment of his cosmic soul in the representation of a plastic form.

Arts are the greater the less they *imitate*, and they *evoke* by means of a synthesis. A photographer, on the other hand, does not have the faculty of choice and elaboration fundamental to Aesthetics; he can only put together the forms he wishes to reproduce, which he really is not reproducing, limiting himself to cutting out images with the aid of the luminous mechanism of a lens and a chemical composition. The cinematograph, therefore, cannot today be an art. But for several reasons, the cinematographic theatre is the first abode of the new art—an art which we can just barely conceive. Can this abode become a "temple" for aesthetics?

A desire for an aesthetic organization drives entrepreneurs towards certain kinds of research. In an age lacking in imagination, such as ours, when an excess of documentation is everywhere, weakening artistic creativity, and patience games are triumphing over expressions of creative talent, the cinematograph offers the paroxysm of the spectacle: objective life represented in a wholly exterior manner, on the one hand with rapid miming, on the other with documentaries. The great fables of the past are retold, mimed by *ad hoc* actors chosen from the most important stars. What is shown above all is the appearance rather than the essence of contemporary life, from sardine fishing in the Mediterranean to the marvel of flying steel and the indomitable human courage of the races at Dieppe or the aviation week at Rheims.

But the entertainment makers are already experimenting with other things. It is their aim that this new mimetic representation of "total life" take ever deeper root, and Gabriele D'Annunzio has dreamed up a great Italian heroic pantomime for the cinematograph (*Cabiria*, TN). It is well known that there exist in Paris societies which organize a kind of "trust" for cinematographic spectacles among writers. Hitherto the theatre has offered writers the best chance of becoming rich quickly; but the cinematograph requires less work and offers better returns. At this moment hundreds of talented people, attracted by the promise of immediate and universal success, are concentrating their energies towards the creation of the modern Pantomime. And it will come out of their strenuous efforts and from the probable genius of one of them. The day such work is given to the world will mark the birthday of a wholly new art.

VI

The cinematograph is not only the perfect outcome of the achievements of modern science, which it summarizes wonderfully. It also represents, in a disconcerting but important way, the most recent product of contemporary theatre. It is not the exaggeration of a principle, but its most logical and ultimate development. The "bourgeois" dramatics, like all of our playwrights, should spontaneously acknowledge the cinematograph as their most discreet representative, and should in consequence ready themselves for its support by making use of it, because the so-called psychological, social drama, etc., is nothing but a degeneration of the original comic theatre, counterposed with the tragic theatre of fantasy and spiritual ennoblement, the theatre of Aristophanes and Plautus. Vitruvius, describing as an architect the many different sets used in ancient performances, talks about the solemnity of columns and temples of the tragic theatre, about the wood of the satyric theatre, and about sylvian adventures and the houses of the middle classes where the *commedias* took place. The latter were but the representation of daily life in its psychological and social aspects, that is, of customs and characteristics.

Shakespeare, who synthesized for the theatrical art the wild and artistic vigor of the great talents of his race, by his own predecessors, was himself the precursor of our "psychological" theatre. And above all he was the great dramatist of the theatre without music. This theatrical form is absurd when applied to tragedy (in this sense the very important, but not truly brilliant art of Racine and Corneille, undoubtedly more deeply tragic in a collective and religious sense, is an art of aberration). On the other hand, a theatre without music is not at all absurd if it represents an ephemeral life, everyday life, to capture some of its aspects without pretending, and in any case without being able to fix its "activity" in a profound sense. This is the reason, then, why comedy, from Aristophanes to Becque, or Porto-Riche to Hervieu, continues to exist and to be enjoyed, even in its altered form which has become "serious," called drama. The basis of such dramas is the portrayal of common contemporary life, and for this very reason this type of theatre is realistic, or as the Italians would call it, *rivista*. All our playwrights writing for the indoor theatre (as against the small band of new poets of the open-air theatre) mean to portray life as accurately as possible by copying it. Impresarios, theatre directors, take this principle to extremes, to the point of attributing more importance to a painstakingly photographic scenography than to the works themselves.

Now, all the cinematograph does is to exalt the principle of the representation of life in its total and exclusively exterior "truth."

It is the triumph of that artistic view called by Cézanne with sacred disdain: *l'oeil photographique*.

VII

The cinematograph, on the other hand, adds to this type of theatre the element of *absolutely accurate* speed, in this way inducing a new kind of pleasure that the spectator discovers in the extreme precision of the spectacle. In fact, none of the actors moving on the illusory stage will betray his part, nor would the mathematical development of the action lag for a fraction of a second. All movement is regulated with clockwork precision. The scenic illusion is therefore less engaging, in a sense less physical, but terribly absorbing. And this life, regulated as if by clockwork, makes one think of the triumph of modern scientific principle as a new Alviman, master of the mechanics of the world in Manichean doctrine.

The rapid communion of vital energies between the two opposite poles of the *very touching* and the *very comical* produces in the spectator a sense of relaxation. Everything which in real life presents itself as an obstacle, the inevitable slowness of movements and actions in space, is as if suppressed in the cinematograph. Moreover, the *very comical* soothes the mind, lightening existence of the weight of the somber social cape, imposed by the thousand conventions of the community and representing all kinds of hierarchies. The comic can suppress hierarchies, it can join together the most different beings, given an extraordinary impression of the mixture of the most separate universes, which in real life are irreducibly distinct from one another. Since the comic is essentially irreverent, it gives a deep sense of relief to individuals oppressed in every moment of their real lives by social discriminations, so emphatically present. This sense of relief is one of the factors of that nervous motion of contraction and expansion called laughter. Life is *simplified* by the grotesque which is nothing other than a deformation *per excessum* or *per defectum* of the established forms. The grotesque, at least in this sense, relieves life of its inescapable grimness and releases it into laughter.

Caricature is based on the display and masterful combination of the most minimal facets of the human soul, its weak spots, which gush forth from the irony of social life, which is itself, after all, somewhat ironical and insane. With irony, in the convulsive motion of laughter, caricature provokes in man this feeling of extreme lightness, because irony throws over its raised shoulders Zarathustra's "dancing and laughing" cape of many colors.

The ancients were able to perceive in irony the roots of Tragedy. They crowned their tragic spectacles in laughter, in the farce. Conversely, we precede rather than follow the dramatic spectacle with Farce, immediately upon the raising of the curtain, because we have forgotten the significance of some of the truths discovered by our forebears. Yet the need for an *ironic spectacle* persists. And the Farce of the Orestes Tetrology of Aeschylus, the Farce which could not be found, must have been originally immensely rich in humour to have been able to lighten the spirit of the elegant Athenian women oppressed by the sacred terror of Cassandra. Now I do not know of anything more superbly grotesque than the antics of film comics. People appear in such an extravagant manner that no magician could pull anything like them out of a hat; movements and vision change so rapidly that no man of flesh and blood could present so many to his fellows, without the help of that stunning mixture of chemistry and mechanics, that extraordinary creator of emotions that is the cinematograph. A new comic type is thus created. He is the man of blunders and metamorphoses who can be squashed under a wardrobe of mirrors, or fall head-first breaking through all four floors of a four-story building, only to climb up out of the chimney to reappear on the roof in the guise of a genuine snake.

The complexity of this new kind of spectacle is surprising. The whole of human activity throughout the centuries has contributed to its composition. When artists of genius bestow rhythms of Thought and Art on this spectacle, the new Aesthetics will show the cinematographic theatre some of its most significant aspects.

In fact the cinematographic theatre *is the first new theatre*, the first authentic and fundamental theatre of our time. When it becomes truly aesthetic, complemented with a worthy musical score played by a good orchestra, even if only representing life, real life, momentarily fixed by the photographic lens, we shall be able to feel then our first *sacred* emotion, we shall have a glimpse of the spirits, moving towards a vision of the temple, where Theatre and Museum will once more be restored for a new religious communion of the spectacle and Aesthetics. The cinematograph as it is today will evoke for the historians of the future the image of the first extremely rudimentary wooden theatres, where goats have their throats slashed and the primitive "goat song" and "tragedy" were danced, before the stone apotheosis consecrated by Lycurgus, even before Aeschylus' birth, to the Dionysian theatre.

The modern public possess an admirable power of "abstraction" since it can enjoy some of the most absolute abstractions in life. In the Olympia, for instance, it was possible to see the spectators fanatically applauding a phonograph placed on the stage and adorned with flowers whose shining copper trumpet had just finished playing a love duet... The machine was triumphant, the public applauded the ghostly sound of far away or even dead actors. It is with such an attitude that the public go to the cinematographic theatre. Moreover, the cinematograph brings, in the midst of even the smallest human settlement, the spectacle of distant, enjoyable, moving or instructive things: it spreads culture and stimulates everywhere the eternal desire for the representation of life in its totality.

On the walls of the cinematographic theatre at times one can see inscriptions commemorating the latest achievements of this prodigious invention which accelerates our knowledge of universal events and reproduces everywhere life and the experience of life since 1830 to the present day. Among the latest heroes are Regnault, Edison, Lumière, the Pathé brothers... But what is striking, characteristic and significant, even more than the spectacle itself, is the uniform will of the spectators, who belong to all social classes, from the lowest and least educated to the most intellectual.

It is desire for a new *Festival*, for a new joyous *unanimity*, realized at a show, in a place where together, all men can forge, in greater or lesser measure, their isolated individuality. This forgetting, soul of any religion and spirit of any aesthetic, will one day be superbly triumphant. And the Theatre, which still holds the vague promise of something never dreamt of in previous ages: *the creation of a sixth art, the plastic Art in motion*, having already achieved the rudimentary form of the modern pantomime.

Present day life lends itself to such victory.

The elder Franconi, last hero of the circus, mourned the already certain decadence of the circus, attributing it more to the passion for the cinematograph than to the circus-like performance of the music hall. The fact is that the collective psyche has been impressed by sports in which it takes part intensely, and with which it has complicated its own real existence, turning them into an industry more than anything else. Our age has therefore created various *heroic industries*, aviation being the most brilliant of them. Our sportsmen no longer regard sport merely as pleasure, the most impetuous, the healthiest of pleasures. A golden ring more rigid than iron, the business circle, holds them in an inescapable grip. Why then sit in a chair watching others do acrobatic exercises and somersaults, content with a very pale image of what life gives so lavishly in the shapes of a thousand modern sports?

Summing up, then, painting consists of the still representation of a gesture, an attitude, or a whole body of gestures and attitudes, or yet again of certain significant representations of living beings and of objects. But who could have dreamt of *successive series of pictures* strung together? A successive series of paintings, that is of certain moods of living beings and objects put together in an event—that is what life is, without doubt. Each passing minute composes, decomposes, transforms an incalculable number of pictures before our eyes. The successful cinematograph film can fix and reproduce them *ad infinitum*. In fixing them, it performs an action previously reserved to painting, or to that weak, merely mechanical copy of painting which is photography. By presenting a succession of gestures, of represented attitudes, just as real life does in transporting the picture from space, where it existed immobile and enduring, into time, where it appears and is immediately transformed, the cinematograph can allow us a glimpse of what it could become if a real, valid, directing idea could co-ordinate the pictures it produces along the ideal and profoundly significant line of a central aesthetic principle. We are able, therefore, to think of a plastic Art in motion, the sixth art. Who could have done it before now? No-one, because the spiritual development of mankind had not yet succeeded in experiencing such a strong desire for the conciliation of Science and Art, for the complex representation of life as a whole. The cinematograph renews more strongly every day the promise of such a great conciliation, not only between Science and Art, but between the Rhythms of Time and the Rhythms of Space.

CHAPTER 2
GEORG LUKÁCS

Georg (György) Lukács (1855–1971) was a Hungarian philosopher and literary critic, deeply influential in the development of Marxist theory as well as theories of the novel. "Thoughts on an Aesthetics of the Cinema" was originally published in German ("Gedanken zu einer Ästhetik des Kino") in the Frankfurter Zeitung und Handellsblatt *in 1913.*

Lukács begins by acknowledging that although the cinema has been viewed and evaluated in terms of its pedagogical potential and its economic value, it has not yet been discussed in aesthetic terms: no one, as far as Lukács was aware in 1913, had yet addressed the question of film's potential as art. However inaccurate the observation might technically have been (we have already seen that Ricciotto Canudo was thinking about at least the possibility of a cinematic art two years prior), it is the motivating impulse of Lukács' contribution: to come to terms with the artistic potential of the relatively new recording technology that was the cinema.

Despite the prevalence in early film criticism of references to the journalistic and otherwise educational possibilities of film (discussions of film's ability to tell stories or otherwise engage in the construction of narrative fictions or artistic imagery in motion seem in general to come later), Lukács focuses almost exclusively on a comparison between the cinema and the stage: film and theater as different, perhaps competing, media for the presentation of dramatic performance. This brings Lukács into conversation with much later trends in film philosophy than we might otherwise expect from a philosopher writing in early nineteen-teens. In any case, Lukács begins the comparison by quite straightforwardly noting that the cinema simply cannot replace the theater, as they are entirely different art media. It is this instructive comparison that is the heart of Lukács' argument.

The beginning of the comparison has everything to do with presence, and in particular, it seems, the relative degree of presence of the performers in any given performance. Given the very real bodily presence of stage actors in the theater, Lukács further notes that the nature of theatrical drama is such that those actors are always engaged in the performance of a necessity, in thrall to what we might call fate (or doom). The stage is a site of "absolute presence," he notes, wherein it is not only the case that the real bodies of real persons are present on the stage at all times during the performance, but that on the stage the performers enact an "inexorable necessity": they are so fully bound to be whatever they must be in the present moment, and to become whatever their being in the present moment entails, that it is as if, on the stage, there is neither past nor future. There is only the necessary, the present tense, such that in every moment on the stage the performers exhibit the unchangeability and undeniability of fate. Of course, this might seem odd, especially in comparison to the cinema, since the performers in a film are incapable of changing anything at all (they are, after all, merely recordings of performances), whereas on the stage it always remains possible for an actor to miss a cue, flub a line, and so on. But Lukács is trying to cut far more deeply into the core of the ideas and structures governing each of these art media, and his point is not that theatrical performance always runs smoothly—just that the idea of the theater is the idea of an unchanging fate becoming increasingly apparent to the characters in the play, and the audience in the theater, alike. The great stage performances make evident what was going to have had to happen all along, and in this sense any deviation from what has been foreordained is impossible.

The "essential characteristic of the cinema," however, according to Lukács, is the absence of such presence. Cinematic performances are conducted in the absence of the bodies of the performers, which is to say, of course, only that the actors are not engaged bodily in performance when moviegoers attend the screening of a given film. A past performance, recorded on film, is projected as light upon a screen: nothing more. This seems at first like a limitation, vis-à-vis the stage, until, as Lukács points out, we consider the fact that, unencumbered by real performing bodies, cinematic "performances" are likewise unencumbered by the ordinary laws governing the movements and display of such bodies. This absence not only enables film performers to engage in feats impossible for actors on the stage, but also enables the audience to view the performance in similarly theatrically impossible ways: to see one performer in one moment as distant, and in the next as extraordinarily near; to view a scene from multiple perspectives, even those (very high up, very low to the ground, etc.) impossible for human observers in real space; and so on. Far more essentially (and far more demonstrably) than theater on the stage, cinema presents us with the fantastic, of "a life without presence," and thus without fate or necessity. In this vein, then, Lukács suggests that, while the stage presents us with an inexorable necessity, the cinema shows us possibility restricted by nothing.

Given the fatedness of the theater, Lukács can say that what happens on the stage in any given moment does not really matter all that much: if a character is doomed to suffer, nothing that character says or does prior to that suffering can actually change the outcome. Thus, what matters most on the stage is not what is done, nor how, nor why it is done, but in the end, only the ultimate necessity driving everything in the world of theatrical presentation. The classical model of this structure, according to Lukács, is ancient Greek tragedy, and in tragedy, the particular thoughts or actions of any one character are inconsequential when compared with the fact (within the world of the play) that human beings are powerless in the face of fate or the gods. This contradicts the situation in the cinema, where—given the infinitude of possibility in the worlds presented on the screen—anything can happen, and thus the details of every action can take on heightened significance. If one conceives of the idea (or set of ideas) informing the development of a stage play as the soul of the piece, and the actual performance as their body, then what matters most of all on the stage is the soul—but on the screen, Lukács argues, it is as if there is no soul at all, only body. Bearing no relationship to fate, cinematic narratives place the "how" of any series of actions at the center of the viewer's attention, and films tend to focus on bodies overcoming (in dramatic films) or succumbing to (in comedies) various sorts of obstacles.

Lukács concludes his thoughts by noting that, at the time he wrote the piece, there were (in his estimation, at any rate) no great cinematic artists—but that they were sure to come, given the great aesthetic potential of cinematography. In addition, he notes that really only "grand tragedy" and "grand comedy" are well suited to the stage; anything else, anything "lesser," anything concerned with the deliberations and thoughts and actions of realistic people in mundane or everyday situations, fails to incarnate the necessity at theater's heart. Importantly, he notes that tragedy is not dramatic—that is, there ought to be no question of suspense, no possibility of an unforeseen future, on the tragic stage. Everything has been ordained. In the cinema, however, we can and should focus on the myriad ways in which one choice, one belief, one decision, one act can change the course of a life, or of many lives. This responsibility, coupled with the uncertainty characteristic of so many human decisions, is the essence of drama—and, Lukács argues, it is only really able to be well presented today in the cinema.

THOUGHTS ON AN AESTHETICS OF CINEMA

Translated by Lance W. Garmer

We never get out of the state of conceptual confusions; something new and beautiful has arisen in our days, yet, instead of accepting it as it is, people want to classify it by all possible means in old, unfitting categories, to strip it of its true meaning and value. People today conceive of the "cinema" as an instrument of visual instruction one moment and as new and cheap competition for the theater the next—thus, pedagogically on the one hand and economically on the other. Today only the smallest number of people, though, thinks that a new *beauty* is indeed a beauty and that rules and valuations of *aesthetics* are befitting it.

A well-known dramatist occasionally fantasized that the "cinema" (through perfection of technique and through perfected reproducibility of speech) could replace the *theater*. If this succeeds—so he says—there will no longer be an imperfect ensemble: the theater is no longer bound to the spatial dispersion of good acting abilities; only the best actors will play in the pieces and they will play only well, for people just do not make recordings of performances in which someone is indisposed. The good performance, though, will be something eternal; the theater will lose everything merely momentary; it will become a large museum of all truly perfected accomplishments.

This beautiful *dream*, though, is a big *error*. It oversees the fundamental condition for all stage effects: the effect of the actually present person. For the root of the theater's effect lies not in the words and facial expressions of the actor or in the events of the drama, but in the power with which a person, the living will of a living person, emanates immediately and without hampering guidance to an equally living crowd. The stage is absolute *presence*. The transience of its accomplishment is not a lamentable weakness, but rather a productive limit: it is the necessary correlate and the evident expression of the fateful in drama. For fate is that which is present in itself. The past is merely framing, in a *metaphysical* sense, something entirely purposeless. (If a pure metaphysics of drama were possible, one that no longer required a merely aesthetic category, then it would no longer know concepts such as "exposition," "development," etc.) And a future is entirely unreal and meaningless for fate: the death that concludes tragedies is the most convincing symbol for this. Through the drama's being portrayed, this metaphysical feeling acquires a great enhancement toward the immediate and evident: from the deepest truth of man and his place in the cosmos arises a self-evident reality. The "presence," the *Dasein* of the actor, is the most evident and thus deepest expression of the fated doom of the characters of the drama. For to be present, that is, to live really, exclusively and most intensely, is already in and of itself fate—except that so-called "life" never attains such an intensity of living that could elevate everything into the sphere of fate. For that reason, the mere appearance of a truly significant actor on the stage (such as that of Eleanora Duse) is itself, without great drama, already doomed by fate, already tragedy, mystery, and divine service. *Duse* is the fully present person in whom, according to Dante's words, the "essere" is identical with the "operazione." Duse is the melody of the music of fate that must resonate, regardless of the accompaniment.

The absence of this "presence" is the essential characteristic of the "cinema." Not because films are imperfect, not because the characters today must still move silently, but rather because they are only movements and deeds of people, but *not people.* This is not a shortcoming of the "cinema"; it is its limit, its *principium stilisationis.* In this manner, the eerily life-like images of the "cinema," identical in character to nature not only in their technique, but also in their effect, become by no means less organic and living than those of the stage, only they acquire a life of an entirely different sort; they become—in a word—*fantastic.* The fantastic, though, is not the opposite of living life, it is only a new aspect of it: a life without presence, a life without fate, without reasons, without motives, a life with which the innermost part of our soul will never become, nor can become, identical. And even if it—often—yearns for this life, the yearning is only for a strange abyss, for something far and internally distanced. The world of the "cinema" is a life without background and perspective, without difference of weights and of qualities. For only presence gives things fate and gravity, light and levity: it is a life without measure and order, without essence and value, a life without soul, of pure superficiality.

The temporality of the stage, the flow of events upon it is always something paradoxical: it is the temporality and the flow of great moments, something deeply quiet internally, nearly petrified, made eternal, precisely as a result of the torturously stark "present." Temporality and flow of the "cinema" is movement in itself, the eternal transience, the never-resting change of things. The *different basic principles* of composition on the stage and in the "cinema" correspond to these different concepts of time: the one is aloof toward everything metaphysically, everything empirically living, the other is so starkly, so exclusively empirically living and unmetaphysical that, indeed, another, entirely different metaphysics thereby arises through this, its most extreme intensification. In a word: the basic law of connection for stage and drama is inexorable necessity; for the "cinema," it is possibility restricted by nothing. The individual moments whose confluence brings about the temporal succession of "cinema" scenes are connected with one another only by their following one another immediately and without transition. There is no causality that would connect them with one another or, more precisely, their causality is inhibited or bound by no substantiveness. "Everything is possible": that is the worldview of the "cinema," and because its technique in every individual moment expresses the absolute (if only empirical) reality of this moment, the validity of the "possibility" as a category juxtaposed to "reality" is nullified; both categories are equated, they become an identity. "Everything is true and real, everything is equally true and equally real": the successions of images of the "cinema" teach this.

Thus, a new, homogenous and harmonic, uniform and varied world arises to which, in the worlds of literature and life, the fairy tale and the dream approximately correspond: great liveliness without an inner third dimension; suggestive connection by mere succession; austere reality attached to nature and the most extreme fantasia; the process of apathetic, of normal life becoming decorative. In the "cinema," everything that the romanticism of the theater had hoped—in vain—to achieve can be realized: the most extreme and least limited mobility of the characters, the complete vivification of the background, of nature and of the interior, of plants and of animals; a liveliness, though, that is by no means bound to the content and boundaries of normal life. For this reason, the Romantics attempted to force onto the stage the fantastic closeness to nature of their feeling for the world. The stage, though, is the realm of naked souls and fates; every stage is *Greek* in its innermost essence: abstractly clothed people walk onto it and perform their play of fate before abstractly grand, empty columned halls.

Costume, milieu, wealth and variety of external events are a mere compromise for the stage; at the truly decisive moment, they always become superficial and thus distracting. The "cinema" merely depicts actions, but not souls, and what happens to them is merely event, but not fate. Therefore—and only seemingly because of today's imperfection of technique—the scenes of the "cinema" are silent: the spoken word, the articulated concept are vehicles of fate; only in them and through them does binding continuity arise in the psyche of the people of the drama. The *revocation* of the *word* and, with it, of memory, of duty and of faithfulness to oneself and to the idea of one's own selfhood makes everything, if the non-verbal develops into a totality, light, sprightly and quickened, frivolous and terpsichorean. That which is of importance to the portrayed events is and must be expressed exclusively through occurrences and gestures; any appeal to the word is a downfall out of this world, a demolishing of its essential value. Through this, though, everything that ever overwhelmed the abstractly monumental weight of fate flourishes into a rich and abundant life: what happens on the stage is not even important, so overpowering is the effect of its fatefulness; in the "cinema," the "how" of events has a power that dominates everything else. The animate in nature here acquires artistic form for the first time: the rushing of the water, the wind in the trees, the tranquility of the sunset and the raging of the thunderstorm as occurrences of nature become art here (not, as in painting, through pictorial values fetched from other worlds). Man has lost his *soul*, yet gains his *body* in return; his greatness and poetry lie here in the way in which his strength or his skill overpower physical impediments, and comedy consists in his failure in the face of them. The characteristics of modern technique, fully without significance for every great art, will here have a fantastic and poetically enthralling effect. Only in the "cinema" has the automobile—to cite only one example—become poetic, such as in the romantically exciting event of a chase in racing autos. In this manner, even the normal activity of streets and markets here acquires a strong humor and an extremely powerful poetry: the child's naïve, animal glee over a successful prank or over the helpless fumbling of a ne'er-do-well is shaped in unforgettable form. In the theater, before the great stage of the great drama, we gather and attain our highest moments; in the "cinema," we are supposed to forget these, our highpoints, and to become irresponsible: the *child* that is alive in every person is liberated here and becomes lord over the psyche of the viewer.

The *fidelity to nature* of the "cinema," though, is not attached to our reality. The furniture moves in the room of a drunken person, his bed flies with him—he was able to grab onto the edge of his bed at the last moment and his shirt waves around him like a flag—out over the city. The balls with which a group of people wanted to bowl become rebellious and chase them over mountains and fields, swimming through rivers, jumping onto bridges and chasing them up steep stairs, until finally the pins also become living and fetch the balls. Purely mechanically, too, the "cinema" can become fantastic: when films are rolled in reverse and people get up from under racing autos, when a cigar stub becomes larger and larger by smoking until, at the moment of lighting, the untouched cigar is finally laid back into the box. Or one turns the films upside down and strange creatures move, suddenly darting from the ceiling to the depths and crawling around there like caterpillars. These are pictures and scenes from a world like that of *E. T. A. Hoffmann* or *Poe*, like that of *Arnim* or of *Barbey d'Aurevilly*—only their great author who would have interpreted and ordered them, who would have retrieved their merely technically accidental fantasia into the meaningful metaphysical and into pure style, has not yet come. What has so far come arose naively, often against the will of people, only from the spirit of the *technique* of the "cinema": an Arnim or a Poe of our days, though, would find an instrument ready for his scenic yearning, one as rich and as internally adequate as the Greek stage was for a *Sophocles.*

Granted: a stage for *recuperation* of the self, a place of amusement, at once of the most subtle and most refined, of the crudest and of the most primitive, and never one of edification and of elevation of any sort. Yet, precisely by these means, the truly developed "cinema," commensurate with its idea, can also open the way for *drama* (again: for truly great drama and not for what is today called "drama"). The invincible drive for amusement has virtually displaced drama from our stages: we can see everything on today's stage, from screenplay adaptations of trashy literature to heartfelt, anemic novellas or blustering, vacant brouhaha and ballyhoo—but not drama. The "cinema" can make a clear break here: more than the stage theater, it has in itself the ability to shape more effectively and, indeed, more gracefully everything that belongs in the category of amusement and that can be rendered obvious. No suspense of a theater piece can compete with the breathlessness of the tempo that is possible here; any closeness to nature in the nature brought to the stage is barely a shadow of what is attainable here and—instead of the crude truncations of souls that, because of the form of the stage drama, must inadvertently be measured against souls and must therefore be found repulsive—a world of intended and would-be soullessness arises, a world of the purely external: what was brutality on the stage can here become childlike, pure suspense, or grotesque. And when the popular literature of the stages has finally been slain—I am speaking here about a quite distant, yet all the more deeply desired goal of all who are seriously concerned with drama—then the stage will again be forced to cultivate that which is its actual calling: grand *tragedy* and grand *comedy.* And the amusement that was damned to crudity on the stage because its subject matter contradicted the forms of the drama stage can find an adequate form in the "cinema" that can be internally appropriate and thus truly artistic, even if it is quite rare in today's "cinema." And if the psychologists, refined and possessing talent for novellas, have been driven from both stages, then this can only be beneficial for the culture of the theater and a portent of clarity.

CHAPTER 3
HUGO MÜNSTERBERG

Hugo Münsterberg (1863–1916) was a German psychologist and an associate of William James, who spent most of his academic career in the United States, where he wrote one of the first book-length theoretical works on film. The Photoplay: A Psychological Study, *from which the reading presented here is a selection, was published in English in 1916 by D. Appleton & Company (New York).*

The first of the two selections from Münsterberg's book, "The Means of the Photoplay," deals with the ways in which cinema achieves its goals as an art and communications medium. Although we associate the motion pictures with precisely that—motion—it is of course only the illusion of movement; as has been widely observed, what we actually see when we view a film is a series of still images projected in such rapid succession that our minds produce the appearance of motion for us. This instantiates what is, for Münsterberg, an unusual relationship between the human spectator and the outer world: the basic forms of the outer world—space, time, and causality—are in some sense overcome by way of cinema. Instead of the forms of the outer world, cinema forces the spectator to adjust himself or herself to the forms of the inner world: rather than explaining movies in terms of space, time, and causality, we must do so in terms of attention, memory, imagination, and emotion. This is, ultimately for Münsterberg, the synthesis of aesthetic and psychological categories. Such a synthesis is required to make sense of both the technological-physical and spectatorial-psychological aspects of cinema and cinema-going, but it also results (as does stage theater) in the introduction of a distance from reality in film: the complete unreality of all events, as Münsterberg puts it.

One of the most overt means by which film instantiates a distance from reality is in divorcing the actions and movements of the actors from the sound of their speech (presuming, given the time at which Münsterberg was writing The Photoplay, *that film is a silent medium). This distancing does not, however, deny the corporeality of the actors' bodies, and in this, Münsterberg argues, it is like pantomime. Unlike pantomime, however, the screen actor remains realistic in his or her expressivenesss; in pantomime, the performer does not enact a feeling, thought, or emotion, but acts instead like someone who wants others to see how he feels. Thus, pantomimes exaggerate their facial expressions, gestures, and other body movements so as to make an unnatural show of whatever they are meant to express. Screen actors, on the other hand, do not have to do this—thanks in large part to the possibility of the close-up—and, thus, can engage in something more akin to natural expression. The silence of the screen actor, however, is a constant reminder of his or her complete unreality, and this serves to keep in the center of the cinemagoer's consciousness the fact that, in film, the actor's picture is substituted for the actor himself. Although the screen actor is embodied, the bodily space of the actor is eliminated to accommodate the two-dimensional projection of what Münsterberg dubs "light flitting immateriality."*

In addition to the spatial difference between two- and three-dimensional bodies, there is an additional temporal difference between cinema and the stage: on the stage (as in reality), time only flows forward. Each development in a stage drama (says Münsterberg) is aesthetically required to follow from what happens prior. But film does not function in this way. As a result of the possibility and practice of montage, a film can be distanced absolutely from time and causality: anything can happen on the screen at any point before or after any other thing. This does not mean, however, that film is free from rules or constraints. Quite the contrary: there are more rules governing the cinematic art than there are in the theater. It is simply that the rules governing the cinema are at a distance from the rules governing real life. Among them, perhaps even chief among them, are the need for unity of action (such that everything that happens in a film must be related to everything else that happens) and the need for unity of character (such that individual characters must remain consistent with themselves). Without these rules, cinema cannot hope to fulfill its function—and it is that function, and the incredible degree of success with which cinema is already fulfilling it in the early twentieth century, which is the subject of the second selection included here.

In "The Function of the Photoplay," Münsterberg tries to address the popularity of cinema as a means of getting into a discussion of film's function, psychologically and socially. He admits that part of its popularity stems from the historical fact that cinema tickets are less expensive than theater tickets, on the whole; this is not an original observation, as he notes, nor is it a philosophically interesting one, as it fails to touch upon the essence of film itself. Münsterberg also thinks that, given the fact that the images in a film are projected in rapid—"unnaturally" rapid—succession, film heightens the feeling of vitality in the spectator. In addition, he notes, the characters in film stories are simpler—because they cannot speak—and thus the cinema typically presents a stereotyped and common portrait of humanity. Münsterberg's recognition of this narrative simplicity, however, is not to be misunderstood as a criticism: rather, it is the simplicity of spectating at the cinema which affords viewers the experience of the ease of consumption and assimilation of a film. In eliminating the need to think too strenuously through the events of a film and thus seeming to present film narratives without the need for interpretation, as well as rendering the bodies of the actors and objects in a film immaterial for the audience, cinema gives us an experience of the superiority of mind over matter: everything in a film is intelligible, in every sense of the word. The result is, as Münsterberg writes, "a superb enjoyment which no other art can furnish us."

Films are thus both more enjoyable than the other arts in at least this one way, and more enjoyable because they are easier to view than other sorts of artworks. Going to the cinema is easy in a way that spectating the other arts is not. This ease makes the cinema, however, potentially dangerous and destructive both of individual character and of society—and Münsterberg rather straightforwardly supports some system of film censorship for this reason. Nevertheless, he thinks the best solution is not a censorial one, but rather to maintain a focus—in film viewership as well as film theory and film criticism—on the beneficial educational possibilities instantiated by the medium. Ultimately, he notes, there are far fewer outright corruptive forces working in film than there are uninteresting and insipid films, films which are destructive not in any direct manner but which destroy public standards for the cinema through their sheer number: the more bad movies we make, the more tolerant of bad movies the movie-going public becomes.

The insipidity of mainstream cinema today (or in Münsterberg's day) does not express an essential quality of film, he is quick to note, merely the result of the fact that the movies—like so much else in the twentieth century—are products of a certain sort of industry, which has goals that are something other than aesthetic. One might only reasonably expect film producers and filmmakers to make those films they think will be profitable (Münsterberg seems far less optimistic than Canudo was about the possibility of the film industry becoming one of the "heroic industries" of its own accord), but in this rather pragmatic expectation lies at least part of the solution, Münsterberg thinks. The situation in cinema today is the result, in part, of the public's general ignorance of aesthetic standards; bad movies are made because an ignorant public doesn't buy tickets to see good, aesthetically and intellectually demanding movies. What's needed here, Münsterberg argues, is an aesthetic education—something the movie-going public sorely needs, and which, he seems to suggest, the cinema itself (with its potential for mass pedagogy) might be able to provide.

Filmography

- ***The Battle Cry of Peace*** (USA, 1915). *Directed by* Wilfrid North *and* J. Stuart Blackton. *Produced by the* Vitagraph Company of America. *Written by* J. Stuart Blackton. *Starring* Charles Richman, L. Rogers Lytton, *and* James W. Morrison.
- ***The Old Homestead*** (USA, 1915). *Directed by* James Kirkwood, Sr. *Produced by* Daniel Frohman. *Written by* Hugh Ford *and* Denman Thompson. *Starring* Frank Losee, Creighton Hale, Denman Maley, Louise Huff, Mrs. Corbett, *and* Horace Newman.
- ***Ben Hur*** (USA, 1907). *Directed by* Sidney Olcott. *Produced by the* Kalem Company. *Written by* Gene Gauntier. *Starring* Herman Rottger *and* William S. Hart.

THE MEANS AND FUNCTION OF THE PHOTOPLAY

The Means of the Photoplay

We have now reached the point at which we can knot together all our threads, the psychological and the esthetic ones. If we do so, we come to the true thesis of this whole book. Our esthetic discussion showed us that it is the aim of art to isolate a significant part of our experience in such a way that it is separate from our practical life and is in complete agreement with itself. Our esthetic satisfaction results from this inner agreement and harmony, but in order that we may feel such agreement of the parts we must enter with our own impulses into the will of every element, into the meaning of every line and color and form, every word and tone and note. Only if everything is full of such inner movement can we really enjoy the harmonious coöperation of the parts. The means of the various arts, we saw, are the forms and methods by which this aim is fulfilled. They must be different for every material. Moreover the same material may allow very different methods of isolation and elimination of the insignificant and reënforcement of that which contributes to the harmony. If we ask now what are the characteristic means by which the photoplay succeeds in overcoming reality, in isolating a significant dramatic story and in presenting it so that we enter into it and yet keep it away from our practical life and enjoy the harmony of the parts, we must remember all the results to which our psychological discussion in the first part of the book has led us.

We recognized there that the photoplay, incomparable in this respect with the drama, gave us a view of dramatic events which was completely shaped by the inner movements of the mind. To be sure, the events in the photoplay happen in the real space with its depth. But the spectator feels that they are not presented in the three dimensions of the outer world, that they are flat pictures which only the mind molds into plastic things. Again the events are seen in continuous movement; and yet the pictures break up the movement into a rapid succession of instantaneous impressions. We do not see the objective reality, but a product of our own mind which binds the pictures together. But much stronger differences came to light when we turned to the processes of attention, of memory, of imagination, of suggestion, of division of interest and of emotion. The attention turns to detailed points in the outer world and ignores everything else: the photoplay is doing exactly this when in the close-up a detail is enlarged and everything else disappears. Memory breaks into present events by bringing up pictures of the past: the photoplay is doing this by its frequent cut-backs, when pictures of events long past flit between those of the present. The imagination anticipates the future or overcomes reality by fancies and dreams; the photoplay is doing all this more richly than any chance imagination would succeed in doing. But chiefly, through our division of interest our mind is drawn hither and thither. We think of events which run parallel in different places. The photoplay can show in intertwined scenes everything which our mind embraces. Events in three or four or five regions of the world can be woven together into one complex action. Finally, we saw that every shade of feeling and emotion which fills the spectator's mind can mold the scenes in the photoplay until they appear the embodiment of our feelings. In every one of these aspects the photoplay succeeds in doing what the drama of the theater does not attempt.

If this is the outcome of esthetic analysis on the one side, of psychological research on the other, we need only combine the results of both into a unified principle: *the photoplay tells us the human story by overcoming the forms of the outer world, namely, space, time, and causality, and by adjusting the events to the forms of the inner world, namely, attention, memory, imagination, and emotion.*

We shall gain our orientation most directly if once more, under this point of view, we compare the photoplay with the performance on the theater stage. We shall not enter into a discussion of the character of the regular theater and its drama. We take this for granted. Everybody knows that highest art form which the Greeks created and which from Greece has spread over Asia, Europe, and America. In tragedy and in comedy from ancient times to Ibsen, Rostand, Hauptmann, and Shaw we recognize one common purpose and one common form for which no further commentary is needed. How does the photoplay differ from a theater performance? We insisted that every work of art must be somehow separated from our sphere of practical interests. The theater is no exception. The structure of the theater itself, the framelike form of the stage, the difference of light between stage and house, the stage setting and costuming, all inhibit in the audience the possibility of taking the action on the stage to be real life. Stage managers have sometimes tried the experiment of reducing those differences, for instance, keeping the audience also in a fully lighted hall, and they always had to discover how much the dramatic effect was reduced because the feeling of distance from reality was weakened. The photoplay and the theater in this respect are evidently alike. The screen too suggests from the very start the complete unreality of events.

But each further step leads us to remarkable differences between the stage play and the film play. In every respect the film play is further away from the physical reality than the drama and in every respect this greater distance from the physical world brings it nearer to the mental world. The stage shows us living men. It is not the real Romeo and not the real Juliet; and yet the actor and the actress have the ringing voices of true people, breathe like them, have living colors like them, and fill physical space like them. What is left in the photoplay? The voice has been stilled: the photoplay is a dumb show. Yet we must not forget that this alone is a step away from reality which has often been taken in the midst of the dramatic world. Whoever knows the history of the theater is aware of the tremendous rôle which the pantomime has played in the development of mankind. From the old half-religious pantomimic and suggestive dances out of which the beginnings of the real drama grew to the fully religious pantomimes of medieval ages and, further on, to many silent mimic elements in modern performances, we find a continuity of conventions which make the pantomime almost the real background of all dramatic development. We know how popular the pantomimes were among the Greeks, and how they stood in the foreground in the imperial period of Rome. Old Rome cherished the mimic clowns, but still more the tragic pantomimics. "Their very nod speaks, their hands talk and their fingers have a voice." After the fall of the Roman empire the church used the pantomime for the portrayal of sacred history, and later centuries enjoyed very unsacred histories in the pantomimes of their ballets. Even complex artistic tragedies without words have triumphed on our present-day stage. "L'Enfant Prodigue" which came from Paris, “Sumurun” which came from Berlin, “Petroushka” which came from Petrograd, conquered the American stage; and surely the loss of speech, while it increased the remoteness from reality, by no means destroyed the continuous consciousness of the bodily existence of the actors.

Moreover the student of a modern pantomime cannot overlook a characteristic difference between the speechless performance on the stage and that of the actors of a photoplay. The expression of the inner states, the whole system of gestures, is decidedly different: and here we might say that the photoplay stands nearer to life than the pantomime. Of course, the photoplayer must somewhat exaggerate the natural expression. The whole rhythm and intensity of his gestures must be more marked than it would be with actors who accompany their movements by spoken words and who express the meaning of their thoughts and feelings by the content of what they say. Nevertheless the photoplayer uses the regular channels of mental discharge. He acts simply as a very emotional person might act. But the actor who plays in a pantomime cannot be satisfied with that. He is expected to add something which is entirely unnatural, namely a kind of artificial demonstration of his emotions. He must not only behave like an angry man, but he must behave like a man who is consciously interested in his anger and wants to demonstrate it to others. He exhibits his emotions for the spectators. He really acts theatrically for the benefit of the bystanders. If he did not try to do so, his means of conveying a rich story and a real conflict of human passions would be too meager. The photoplayer, with the rapid changes of scenes, has other possibilities of conveying his intentions. He must not yield to the temptation to play a pantomime on the screen, or he will seriously injure the artistic quality of the reel.

The really decisive distance from bodily reality, however, is created by the substitution of the actor’s picture for the actor himself. Lights and shades replace the manifoldness of color effects and mere perspective must furnish the suggestion of depth. We traced it when we discussed the psychology of kinematoscopic perception. But we must not put the emphasis on the wrong point. The natural tendency might be to lay the chief stress on the fact that those people in the photoplay do not stand before us in flesh and blood. The essential point is rather that we are conscious of the flatness of the picture. If we were to see the actors of the stage in a mirror, it would also be a reflected image which we perceive. We should not really have the actors themselves in our straight line of vision; and yet this image would appear to us equivalent to the actors themselves, because it would contain all the depth of the real stage. The film picture is such a reflected rendering of the actors. The process which leads from the living men to the screen is more complex than a mere reflection in a mirror, but in spite of the complexity in the transmission we do, after all, see the real actor in the picture. The photograph is absolutely different from those pictures which a clever draughtsman has sketched. In the photoplay we see the actors themselves and the decisive factor which makes the impression different from seeing real men is not that we see the living persons through the medium of photographic reproduction but that this reproduction shows them in a flat form. The bodily space has been eliminated. We said once before that stereoscopic arrangements could reproduce somewhat this plastic form also. Yet this would seriously interfere with the character of the photoplay. We need there this overcoming of the depth, we want to have it as a picture only and yet as a picture which strongly suggests to us the actual depth of the real world. We want to keep the interest in the plastic world and want to be aware of the depth in which the persons move, but our direct object of perception must be without the depth. That idea of space which forces on us most strongly the idea of heaviness, solidity and substantiality must be replaced by the light flitting immateriality.

But the photoplay sacrifices not only the space values of the real theater; it disregards no less its order of time. The theater presents its plot in the time order of reality. It may interrupt the continuous flow of time without neglecting the conditions of the dramatic art. There may be twenty years between the third and the fourth act, inasmuch as the dramatic writer must select those elements spread over space and time which are significant for the development of his story. But he is bound by the fundamental principle of real time, that it can move only forward and not backward. Whatever the theater shows us now must come later in the story than that which it showed us in any previous moment. The strict classical demand for complete unity of time does not fit every drama, but a drama would give up its mission if it told us in the third act something which happened before the second act. Of course, there may be a play within a play, and the players on the stage which is set on the stage may play events of old Roman history before the king of France. But this is an enclosure of the past in the present, which corresponds exactly to the actual order of events. The photoplay, on the other hand, does not and must not respect this temporal structure of the physical universe. At any point the photoplay interrupts the series and brings us back to the past. We studied this unique feature of the film art when we spoke of the psychology of memory and imagination. With the full freedom of our fancy, with the whole mobility of our association of ideas, pictures of the past flit through the scenes of the present. Time is left behind. Man becomes boy; today is interwoven with the day before yesterday. The freedom of the mind has triumphed over the unalterable law of the outer world.

It is interesting to watch how playwrights nowadays try to steal the thunder of the photoplay and experiment with time reversals on the legitimate stage. We are esthetically on the borderland when a grandfather tells his grandchild the story of his own youth as a warning, and instead of the spoken words the events of his early years come before our eyes. This is, after all, quite similar to a play within a play. A very different experiment is tried in "Under Cover." The third act, which plays on the second floor of the house, ends with an explosion. The fourth act, which plays downstairs, begins a quarter an hour before the explosion. Here we have a real denial of a fundamental condition of the theater. Or if we stick to recent products of the American stage, we may think of "On Trial," a play which perhaps comes nearest to a dramatic usurpation of the rights of the photoplay. We see the court scene and as one witness after another begins to give his testimony the courtroom is replaced by the scenes of the actions about which the witness is to report. Another clever play, "Between the Lines," ends the first act with a postman bringing three letters from the three children of the house. The second, third, and fourth acts lead us to the three different homes from which the letters came and the action in the three places not only precedes the writing of the letters; but goes on at the same time. The last act, finally, begins with the arrival of the letters which tell the ending of those events in the three homes. Such experiments are very suggestive but they are not any longer pure dramatic art. It is always possible to mix arts. An Italian painter produces very striking effects by putting pieces of glass and stone and rope into his paintings. The drama in which the later event comes before the earlier is an esthetic barbarism which is entertaining as a clever trick in a graceful superficial play, but intolerable in ambitious dramatic art. It is not only tolerable but perfectly natural in any photoplay. The pictorial reflection of the world is not bound by the rigid mechanism of time. Our mind is here and there, our mind turns to the present and then to the past: the photoplay can equal it in its freedom from the bondage of the material world.

But the theater is bound not only by space and time. Whatever it shows is controlled by the same laws of causality which govern nature. This involves a complete continuity of the physical events: no cause without following effect, no effect without preceding cause. This whole natural course is left behind in the play on the screen. The deviation from reality begins with that resolution of the continuous movement which we studied in our psychological discussions. We saw that the impression of movement results from an activity of the mind which binds the separate pictures together. What we actually see is a composite; it is like the movement of a fountain in which every jet is resolved into numberless drops. We feel the play of those drops in their sparkling haste as one continuous stream of water, and yet are conscious of the myriads of drops, each one separate from the others. This fountainlike spray of pictures has completely overcome the causal world.

In an entirely different form this triumph over causality appears in the interruption of the events by pictures which belong to another series. We find this whenever the scene suddenly changes. The process are not carried to their natural consequences. A movement is started, but before the cause brings its results another scene has taken its place. What this new scene brings may be an effect for which we saw no causes. But not only the processes are interrupted. The intertwining of the scenes which we have traced in detail is itself such a contrast to causality. It is as if different objects could fill the same space at the same time. It is as if the resistance of the material world had disappeared and the substances could penetrate one another. In the interlacing of our ideas we experience this superiority to all physical laws. The theater would not have even the technical means to give us such impressions, but if it had, it would have no right to make use of them, as it would destroy the basis on which the drama is built. We have only another case of the same type in those series of pictures which aim to force a suggestion on our mind. We have spoken of them. A certain effect is prepared by a chain of causes and yet when the causal result is to appear the film is cut off. We have the causes without the effect. The villain thrusts with his dagger—but a miracle has snatched away his victim.

While the moving pictures are lifted above the world of space and time and causality and are freed from its bounds, they are certainly not without law. We said before that the freedom with which the pictures replace one another is to a large degree comparable to the sparkling and streaming of the musical tones. The yielding to the play of the mental energies, to the attention and emotion, which is felt in the film pictures, is still more complete in the musical melodies and harmonies in which the tones themselves are merely the expressions of the ideas and feelings and will impulses of the mind. Their harmonies and disharmonies, their fusing and blending, is not controlled by any outer necessity, but by the inner agreement and disagreement of our free impulses. And yet in this world of musical freedom, everything is completely controlled by esthetic necessities. No sphere of practical life stands under such rigid rules as the realm of the composer. However bold the musical genius may be he cannot emancipate himself from the iron rule that his work must show complete unity in itself. All the separate prescriptions which the musical student has to learn are ultimately only the consequences of this central demand which music, the freest of the arts, shares with all the others. In the case of the film, too, the freedom from the physical forms of space, time, and causality does not mean any liberation from this esthetic bondage either. On the contrary, just as music is surrounded by more technical rules than literature, the photoplay must be held together by the esthetic demands still more firmly than is the drama. The arts which are subordinated to the conditions of space, time, and causality find a certain firmness of structure in these material forms which contain an element of outer connectedness. But where these forms are given up and where the freedom of mental play replaces their outer necessity, everything would fall asunder if the esthetic unity were disregarded.

This unity is, first of all, the unity of action. The demand for it is the same which we know from the drama. The temptation to neglect it is nowhere greater than in the photoplay where outside matter can so easily be introduced or independent interests developed. It is certainly true for the photoplay, as for every work of art, that nothing has the right to existence in its midst which is not internally needed for the unfolding of the unified action. Wherever two plots are given to us, we receive less by far than if we had only one plot. We leave the sphere of valuable art entirely when a unified action is ruined by mixing it with declamation, and propaganda which is not organically interwoven with the action itself. It may be still fresh in memory what an esthetically intolerable helter-skelter performance was offered to the public in "The Battlecry of Peace." Nothing can be more injurious to the esthetic cultivation of the people than such performances which hold the attention of the spectators by ambitious detail and yet destroy their esthetic sensibility by a complete disregard of the fundamental principle of art, the demand for unity. But we recognized also that this unity involves complete isolation. We annihilate beauty when we link the artistic creation with practical interests and transform the spectator into a selfishly interested bystander. The scenic background of the play is not presented in order that we decide whether we want to spend our next vacation there. The interior decoration of the rooms is not exhibited as a display for a department store. The men and women who carry out the action of the plot must not be people whom we may meet tomorrow on the street. All the threads of the play must be knotted together in the play itself and none should be connected with our outside interests. A good photoplay must be isolated and complete in itself like a beautiful melody. It is not an advertisement for the newest fashions.

This unity of action involves unity of characters. It has too often been maintained by those who theorize on the photoplay that the development of character is the special task of the drama, while the photoplay, which lacks words, must be satisfied with types. Probably this is only a reflection of the crude state which most photoplays of today have not outgrown. Internally, there is no reason why the means of the photoplay should not allow a rather subtle depicting of complex character. But the chief demand is that the characters remain consistent, that the action be developed according to inner necessity and that the characters themselves be in harmony with the central idea of the plot. However, as soon as we insist on unity we have no right to think only of the action which gives the content of the play. We cannot make light of the form. As in music the melody and rhythms belong together, as in painting not every color combination suits every subject, and as in poetry not every stanza would agree with every idea, so the photoplay must bring action and pictorial expression into perfect harmony. But this demand repeats itself in every single picture. We take it for granted that the painter balances perfectly the forms in his painting, groups them so that an internal symmetry can be felt and that the lines and curves and colors blend into a unity. Every single picture of the sixteen thousand which are shown to us in one reel ought to be treated with this respect of the pictorial artist for the unity of the forms.

The photoplay shows us a significant conflict of human actions in moving pictures which, freed from the physical forms of space, time, and causality, are adjusted to the free play of our mental experiences and which reach complete isolation from the practical world through the perfect unity of plot and pictorial appearance.

The Function of the Photoplay

Enthusiasts claim that in the United States ten million people daily are attending picture houses. Sceptics believe that "only" two or three millions form the daily attendance. But in any case "the movies" have become the most popular entertainment of the country, nay, of the world, and their influence is one of the strongest social energies of our time. Signs indicate that this popularity and this influence are increasing from day to day. What are the causes, and what are the effects of this movement which was undreamed of only a short time ago?

The economists are certainly right when they see the chief reason for this crowding of picture houses in the low price of admission. For five or ten cents long hours of thrilling entertainment in the best seats of the house: this is the magnet which must be more powerful than any theater or concert. Yet the rush to the moving pictures is steadily increasing, while the prices climb up. The dime became a quarter, and in the last two seasons ambitious plays were given before audiences who paid the full theater rates. The character of the audiences, too, suggests that inexpensiveness alone cannot be decisive. Six years ago a keen sociological observer characterized the patrons of the picture palaces as "the lower middle class and the massive public, youths and shopgirls between adolescence and maturity, small dealers, pedlars, laborers, charwomen, besides the small quota of children." This would be hardly a correct description today. This "lower middle class" has long been joined by the upper middle class. To be sure, our observer of that long forgotten past added meekly: "Then there emerges a superior person or two like yourself attracted by mere curiosity and kept in his seat by interest until the very end of the performance; this type sneers aloud to proclaim its superiority and preserve its self-respect, but it never leaves the theater until it must." Today you and I are seen there quite often, and we find that our friends have been there, that they have given up the sneering pose and talk about the new photoplay as a matter of course.

Above all, even those who are drawn by the cheapness of the performance would hardly push their dimes under the little window so often if they did not really enjoy the plays and were not stirred by a pleasure which holds them for hours. After all, it must be the content of the performances which is decisive of the incomparable triumph. We have no right to conclude from this that only the merits and excellences are the true causes of their success. A caustic critic would probably suggest that just the opposite traits are responsible. He would say that the average American is a mixture of business, ragtime, and sentimentality. He satisfies his business instinct by getting so much for his nickel, he enjoys his ragtime in the slapstick humor, and gratifies his sentimentality with the preposterous melodramas which fill the program. This is quite true, and yet it is not true at all. Success has crowned every effort to improve the photo-stage; the better the plays are the more the audience approves them. The most ambitious companies are the most flourishing ones. There must be inner values which make the photoplay so extremely attractive and even fascinating.

To a certain degree the mere technical cleverness of the pictures even today holds the interest spellbound as in those early days when nothing but this technical skill could claim the attention. We are still startled by every original effect, even if the mere showing of movement has today lost its impressiveness. Moreover we are captivated by the undeniable beauty of many settings. The melodrama may be cheap; yet it does not disturb the cultured mind as grossly as a similar tragic vulgarity would on the real stage, because it may have the snowfields of Alaska or the palm trees of Florida as radiant background. An intellectual interest, too, finds its satisfaction. We get an insight into spheres which were strange to us. Where outlying regions of human interest are shown on the theater stage, we must usually be satisfied with some standardized suggestion. Here in the moving pictures the play may really bring us to mills and factories, to farms and mines, to courtrooms and hospitals, to castles and palaces in any land on earth.

Yet a stronger power of the photoplay probably lies in its own dramatic qualities. The rhythm of the play is marked by unnatural rapidity. As the words are absent which, in the drama as in life, fill the gaps between the actions, the gestures and deeds themselves can follow one another much more quickly. Happenings which would fill an hour on the stage can hardly fill more than twenty minutes on the screen. This heightens the feeling of vitality in the spectator. He feels as if he were passing through life with a sharper accent which stirs his personal energies. The usual make-up of the photoplay must strengthen this effect inasmuch as the wordlessness of the picture drama favors a certain simplification of the social conflicts. The subtler shades of the motives naturally demand speech. The later plays of Ibsen could hardly be transformed into photoplays. Where words are missing the characters tend to become stereotyped and the motives to be deprived of their complexity. The plot of the photoplay is usually based on the fundamental emotions which are common to all and which are understood by everybody. Love and hate, gratitude and envy, hope and fear, pity and jealousy, repentance and sinfulness, and all the similar crude emotions have been sufficient for the construction of most scenarios. The more mature development of the photoplay will certainly overcome this primitive character, as, while such an effort to reduce human life to simple instincts is very convenient for the photoplay, it is not at all necessary. In any case where this tendency prevails it must help greatly to excite and to intensify the personal feeling of life and to stir the depths of the human mind.

But the richest source of the unique satisfaction in the photoplay is probably that esthetic feeling which is significant for the new art and which we have understood from its psychological conditions. *The massive outer world has lost its weight, it has been freed from space, time, and causality, and it has been clothed in the forms of our own consciousness. The mind has triumphed over matter and the pictures roll on with the ease of musical tones. It is a superb enjoyment which no other art can furnish us.* No wonder that temples for the new goddess are built in every little hamlet.

The intensity with which the plays take hold of the audience cannot remain without strong social effects. It has even been reported that sensory hallucinations and illusions have crept in; neurasthenic persons are especially inclined to experience touch or temperature or smell or sound impressions from what they see on the screen. The associations become as vivid as realities, because the mind is so completely given up to the moving pictures. The applause into which the audiences, especially of rural communities, break out at a happy turn of the melodramatic pictures is another symptom of the strange fascination. But it is evident that such a penetrating influence must be fraught with dangers. The more vividly the impressions force themselves on the mind, the more easily must they become starting points for imitation and other motor responses. The sight of crime and of vice may force itself on the consciousness with disastrous results. The normal resistance breaks down and the moral balance, which would have been kept under the habitual stimuli of the narrow routine life, may be lost under the pressure of the realistic suggestions. At the same time the subtle sensitiveness of the young mind may suffer from the rude contrasts between the farces and the passionate romances which follow with benumbing speed in the darkened house. The possibilities of psychical infection and destruction cannot be overlooked.

Those may have been exceptional cases only when grave crimes have been traced directly back to the impulses from unwholesome photoplays, but no psychologist can determine exactly how much the general spirit of righteousness, of honesty, of sexual cleanliness and modesty, may be weakened by the unbridled influence of plays of low moral standard. All countries seem to have been awakened to this social danger. The time when unsavory French comedies poisoned youth lies behind us. A strong reaction has set in and the leading companies among the photoplay producers fight everywhere in the first rank for suppression of the unclean. Some companies even welcome censorship provided that it is high-minded and liberal and does not confuse artistic freedom with moral licentiousness. Most, to be sure, seem doubtful whether the new movement toward Federal censorship is in harmony with American ideas on the freedom of public expression.

But while the sources of danger cannot be overlooked, the social reformer ought to focus his interest still more on the tremendous influences for good which may be exerted by the moving pictures. The fact that millions are daily under the spell of the performances on the screen is established. The high degree of their suggestibility during those hours in the dark house may be taken for granted. Hence any wholesome influence emanating from the photoplay must have an incomparable power for the remolding and upbuilding of the national soul. From this point of view the boundary lines between the photoplay and the merely instructive moving pictures with the news of the day or the magazine articles on the screen become effaced. The intellectual, the moral, the social, and the esthetic culture of the community may be served by all of them. Leading educators have joined in endorsing the foundation of a Universal Culture Lyceum. The plan is to make and circulate moving pictures for the education of the youth of the land, picture studies in science, history, religion, literature, geography, biography, art, architecture, social science, economics and industry. From this Lyceum "schools, churches and colleges will be furnished with motion pictures giving the latest results and activities in every sphere capable of being pictured."

But, however much may be achieved by such conscious efforts toward education, the far larger contribution must be made by the regular picture houses which the public seeks without being conscious of the educational significance. The teaching of the moving pictures must not be forced on a more or less indifferent audience, but ought to be absorbed by those who seek entertainment and enjoyment from the films and are ready to make their little economic sacrifice.

The purely intellectual part of this uplift is the easiest. Not only the news pictures and the scientific demonstrations but also the photoplays can lead young and old to ever new regions of knowledge. The curiosity and the imagination of the spectators will follow gladly. Yet even in the intellectual sphere the dangers must not be overlooked. They are not positive. It is not as in the moral sphere where the healthy moral impulse is checked by the sight of crimes which stir up antisocial desires. The danger is not that the pictures open insight into facts which ought not to be known. It is not the dangerous knowledge which must be avoided, but it is the trivializing influence of a steady contact with things which are not worth knowing. The larger part of the film literature of today is certainly harmful in this sense. The intellectual background of most photoplays is insipid. By telling the plot without the subtle motivation which the spoken word of the drama may bring, not only do the characters lose color but all the scenes and situations are simplified to a degree which adjusts them to a thoughtless public and soon becomes intolerable to an intellectually trained spectator.

They force on the cultivated mind that feeling which musical persons experience in the musical comedies of the day. We hear the melodies constantly with the feeling of having heard them ever so often before. This lack of originality and inspiration is not necessary; it does not lie in the art form. Offenbach and Strauss and others have written musical comedies which are classical. Neither does it lie in the form of the photoplay that the story must be told in that insipid, flat, uninspired fashion. Nor is it necessary in order to reach the millions. To appeal to the intelligence does not mean to presuppose college education. Moreover the differentiation has already begun. Just as the plays of Shaw or Ibsen address a different audience from that reached by the "Old Homestead" or "Ben Hur," we have already photoplays adapted to different types, and there is not the slightest reason to connect with the art of the screen an intellectual flabbiness. It would be no gain for intellectual culture if all the reasoning were confined to the so-called instructive pictures and the photoplays were served without any intellectual salt. On the contrary, the appeal of those strictly educational lessons may be less deep than the producers hope, because the untrained minds, especially of youth and of the uneducated audiences, have considerable difficulty in following the rapid flight of events when they occur in unfamiliar surroundings. The child grasps very little in seeing the happenings in a factory. The psychological and economic lesson may be rather wasted because the power of observation is not sufficiently developed and the assimilation proceeds too slowly. But it is quite different when a human interest stands behind it and connects the events in the photoplay.

The difficulties in the way of the right moral influence are still greater than in the intellectual field. Certainly it is not enough to have the villain punished in the last few pictures of the reel. If scenes of vice or crime are shown with all their lure and glamour the moral devastation of such a suggestive show is not undone by the appended social reaction. The misguided boys or girls feel sure that they would be successful enough not to be trapped. The mind through a mechanism which has been understood better and better by the psychologists in recent years suppresses the ideas which are contrary to the secret wishes and makes those ideas flourish by which those "subconscious" impulses are fulfilled. It is probably a strong exaggeration when a prominent criminologist recently claimed that "eighty-five per cent. of the juvenile crime which has been investigated has been found traceable either directly or indirectly to motion pictures which have shown on the screen how crimes could be committed." But certainly, as far as these demonstrations have worked havoc, their influence would not have been annihilated by a picturesque court scene in which the burglar is unsuccessful in misleading the jury. The true moral influence must come from the positive spirit of the play itself. Even the photo-dramatic lessons in temperance and piety will not rebuild a frivolous or corrupt or perverse community. The truly upbuilding play is not a dramatized sermon on morality and religion. There must be a moral wholesomeness in the whole setting, a moral atmosphere which is taken as a matter of course like fresh air and sunlight. An enthusiasm for the noble and uplifting, a belief in duty and discipline of the mind, a faith in ideals and eternal values must permeate the world of the screen. If it does, there is no crime and no heinous deed which the photoplay may not tell with frankness and sincerity. It is not necessary to deny evil and sin in order to strengthen the consciousness of eternal justice.

But the greatest mission which the photoplay may have in our community is that of esthetic cultivation. No art reaches a larger audience daily, no esthetic influence finds spectators in a more receptive frame of mind. On the other hand no training demands a more persistent and planful arousing of the mind than the esthetic training, and never is progress more difficult than when the teacher adjusts himself to the mere liking of the pupils. The country today would still be without any symphony concerts and operas if it had only received what the audiences believed at the moment that they liked best. The esthetically commonplace will always triumph over the significant unless systematic efforts are made to reënforce the work of true beauty. Communities at first always prefer Sousa to Beethoven. The moving picture audience could only by slow steps be brought from the tasteless and vulgar eccentricities of the first period to the best plays of today, and the best plays of today can be nothing but the beginning of the great upward movement which we hope for in the photoplay. Hardly any teaching can mean more for our community than the teaching of beauty where it reaches the masses. The moral impulse and the desire for knowledge are, after all, deeply implanted in the American crowd, but the longing for beauty is rudimentary; and yet it means harmony, unity, true satisfaction, and happiness in life. The people still has to learn the great difference between true enjoyment and fleeting pleasure, between real beauty and the mere tickling of the senses.

Of course, there are those, and they may be legion today, who would deride every plan to make the moving pictures the vehicle of esthetic education. How can we teach the spirit of true art by a medium which is in itself the opposite of art? How can we implant the idea of harmony by that which is in itself a parody of art? We hear the contempt for "canned drama" and the machine-made theater. Nobody stops to think whether other arts despise the help of technique. The printed book of lyric poems is also machine-made; the marble bust has also "preserved" for two thousand years the beauty of the living woman who was the model for the Greek sculptor. They tell us that the actor on the stage gives the human beings as they are in reality, but the moving pictures are unreal and therefore of incomparably inferior value. They do not consider that the roses of the summer which we enjoy in the stanzas of the poet do not exist in reality in the forms of iambic verse and of rhymes; they live in color and odor, but their color and odor fade away, while the roses in the stanzas live on forever. They fancy that the value of an art depends upon its nearness to the reality of physical nature.

It has been the chief task of our whole discussion to prove the shallowness of such arguments and objections. We recognized that art is a way to overcome nature and to create out of the chaotic material of the world something entirely new, entirely unreal, which embodies perfect unity and harmony. The different arts are different ways of abstracting from reality; and when we began to analyze the psychology of the moving pictures we soon became aware that the photoplay has a way to perform this task of art with entire originality, independent of the art of the theater, as much as poetry is independent of music or sculpture of painting. It is an art in itself. Only the future can teach us whether it will become a great art, whether a Leonardo, a Shakespeare, a Mozart, will ever be born for it. Nobody can foresee the directions which the new art may take. Mere esthetic insight into the principles can never foreshadow the development in the unfolding of civilization. Who would have been bold enough four centuries ago to foresee the musical means and effects of the modern orchestra? Just the history of music shows how the inventive genius has always had to blaze the path in which the routine work of the art followed. Tone combinations which appeared intolerable dissonances to one generation were again and again assimilated and welcomed and finally accepted as a matter of course by later times. Nobody can foresee the ways which the new art of the photoplay will open, but everybody ought to recognize even today that it is worth while to help this advance and to make the art of the film a medium for an original creative expression of our time and to mold by it the esthetic instincts of the millions. Yes, it is a new art—and this is why it has such fascination for the psychologist who in a world of ready-made arts, each with a history of many centuries, suddenly finds a new form still undeveloped and hardly understood. For the first time the psychologist can observe the starting of an entirely new esthetic development, a new form of true beauty in the turmoil of a technical age, created by its very technique and yet more than any other art destined to overcome outer nature by the free and joyful play of the mind.

CHAPTER 4
RUDOLF ARNHEIM

Rudolf Arnheim (1904–2007) was a German psychologist, aesthetician, film theorist, and film critic, whose groundbreaking work culminated in major writings on visual thinking and the relationship between art and visual perception. The increasing power and violence of the Nazi Party, and his growing reputation as a Jewish intellectual, led him to move to Italy in 1933 and then, later, to immigrate to the United States. The three essays included in this volume, however, were all published in German, while he lived in Germany. "Sound Film" ("Der tönende Film") was originally published in Die Weltbühne *in 1928; "The Sad Future of Film" ("Die traurige Zukunft des Films"), in* Die Weltbühne *in 1930; and "Sound Film Gone Astray" ("Tonfilm auf Abwegen"), in* Berliner Tageblatt *in 1932.*

Overall, in these three brief articles, Arnheim makes the case for silent film against sound film—primarily by way of articulating what he takes to be sound film's greatest flaws and failings, rather than advocating for the strengths or advantages of silent film. In the first article, "Sound Film," Arnheim interestingly notes that a large part of the problem of sound film lies in its increased ability to represent the world in something approximating its sensory fullness. Thus, he notes that the addition of sound recording makes film too realistic, turning film into what he calls "a spatial stage." When the figures on the screen produce sound, then it's the sounds they produce that come to the center of the spectator's attention. The visual images take second place to the sounds, in a way, prompting spectators to seek out the "sources" of the film's various sounds rather than to view the image before them. This inverts what Arnheim takes to be the proper cinematic privileging of the beauty of visual images over all else. Ultimately, Arnheim argues that sound film operates according to a different set of priorities and should be held to different aesthetic standards than silent film—and, thus, that sound film should not be allowed to replace silent film. That said, he does admit that it would be possible for sound film to replace another of the arts: the theater. "Canning theatre," as he says, might have the additional benefits of spurring innovation in cinematic technologies (he envisions the addition of stereoscopic features of some sort) and increasing access to the performances of the world's greatest actors. In essence, Arnheim argues here that, whatever sound film is, it isn't comparable to silent film as an art.

In the second of the articles collected here, "The Sad Future of Film," Arnheim continues his assault on sound film—no longer merely from the perspective of someone concerned about potential developments, but by way of an indictment of the film industry as a whole in its embrace of sound. He accuses the film industry of pursuing sound films at the expense of silent films for the sake of profit alone, following the audience's preference for unthinking entertainment instead of attempting to raise their standards with artistically worthwhile films. And in attempting to satisfy this relatively base desire as a means to increasing its own profit, the film industry not only encourages the production of lower quality films, it discourages the production of great films and the work of great film artists. Silent film—the artistic institution that made possible the great silent films, like those of Charlie Chaplin, Buster Keaton, or Greta Garbo, Arnheim notes—is not "ripe for replacement," and sound film is not simply the introduction of one more technological innovation at the cinema. Sound film (as he established in the earlier article collected here) seeks to overthrow the dominance of silent film, not to supplement it, and as such, Arnheim argues, silent film was "strangled" by its usurper. In short, silent film was an art form that had not yet matured, much less reached the end of its creative potential. Its time had not come. But, because audiences were willing to pay more for sound films than for their silent counterparts, the film industry effectively decided that the silent film era was over. Art makes gains, Arnheim seems to conclude, only by challenging the audience's expectations: sound film, as he sees it, does not challenge us because it was not intended to challenge us. Like future innovations in the movies which Arnheim predicts, color films and 3D, stereoscopic films, sound film simply entertains us—for a price.

In the last of Arnheim's articles collected here, "Sound Film Gone Astray," Arnheim very much picks up where he left off in "The Sad Future of Film." Having established in that article that sound film is inferior to silent film in large part because it does not wish to challenge its audience—because industry executives fear that aesthetically and intellectually challenging films might drive some potential purchasers of movie tickets to other means of entertainment—Arnheim here wants to address what it is that makes sound films "easier" than the silent films that came before. Ultimately, Arnheim argues, the difference lies very much in sound film's ability to use language (speech) to communicate the story. When you can simply have a character explain the plot points to another character (and thus, to the audience), you no longer need to engage in any meaningful visual communication at all. Silent film, on the other hand, had a much greater challenge to meet in order to accomplish even the most basic communicative project. Although intertitles were sometimes used to orient the audience within the narrative, there was the sense that they ought not to be used too extensively or with too much frequency; the view, Arnheim argues, was that the cinema is a visual medium, not a linguistic one. Thus, silent cinema had to become extremely creative in providing visual solutions to narrative problems—pantomime, innovative shots and camera angles, symbolic use of props and sets—and these were, when well employed, at the heart of a great silent film's greatness.

Sound film, Arnheim asserts, is inferior to silent film because the ability to use speech to explain characters, motivations, and events makes storytelling easier for the filmmaker. That increased ease causes the filmmaker to become more relaxed, perhaps even lazy, in producing a film, no longer having to confront what Arnheim calls "the fruitful problems of silent communication." Given the increased ease of filmmaking, as well as the overwhelming drive for profit in the film industry (and the potential for sometimes unbelievable return on the producers' initial investment in a film), there is no economic or corporate incentive to adopt again the unnecessarily difficult approach to filmmaking characteristic of silent film. Moreover, Arnheim argues, the "relaxation" characteristic of the making of a sound film infects all of the other participants in the filmmaking process, as well. Despite the fact that sound films rely heavily on dialogue, screenplays tend to be significantly less well written than stage plays written for the theater. While the silent film actor needed to employ a wide variety of performance skills in his or her work, the sound film actor need in most cases only be able to read his or her lines convincingly—which is to say that the main talent required of a sound film actor is comparable to that required of the stage actor. Given the obvious superiority of stage plays to screenplays, in general, Arnheim suggests that the great acting talents migrate away from the screen toward the stage, leaving screen roles to inferior actors—further lowering the general quality of sound films. And, despite the reserve of great acting talent left over from the silent film era, silent film actors were physical actors whose product was one element in a visual filmic image, something sound film almost always neglects in favor of speech. Thus, great silent film actors such as Buster Keaton or Anny Ondra find no place, or almost no place, in the world of sound film.

Arnheim gives us, by way of these three articles, a deep analysis of the differences between silent and sound film, written during the time when the transition from silent film dominance to sound film dominance is occurring. In addition, however, Arnheim eloquently laments the untimely demise of silent film. As an art form, he tells us, there was nothing like it before the advent of cinema—and, given what he sees in the early sound films, it is unlikely there will ever be any such art again.

Film Referenced in "Sound Film," "The Sad Future of Film," and "Sound Film Gone Astray"

- ***Die tönende Welle/Lichtspiel: Opus I*** [*The Sound Wave/Lightplay*] (Germany, 1921). *Directed by* Walter Ruttmann.
- ***The Gold Rush*** (USA, 1925). *Directed, Produced, Written by, and Starring* Charlie Chaplin. *Also starring* Mack Swain *and* Tom Murray.
- ***The Kiss*** (USA, 1929). *Directed by* Jacques Feyder. *Produced by* Metro-Goldwyn-Mayer. *Written by* Hanns Kräly. *Starring* Greta Garbo, Conrad Nagel, *and* Lew Ayres.
- ***Wild Orchids*** (USA, 1929). *Directed by* Sidney Franklin. *Produced by* Metro-Goldwyn-Mayer. *Written by* Hanns Kräly, Ruth Cummings, Willis Goldbeck, *and* Richard Schayer. *Starring* Greta Garbo, Lewis Stone, *and* Nils Asther.
- ***Anna Christie*** (USA, 1930). *Directed by* Clarence Brown. *Produced by* Clarence Brown, Paul Bern, *and* Irving Thalberg. *Written by* Frances Marion. *Starring* Greta Garbo.
- ***City Lights*** (USA, 1931). *Directed, Produced, Written by, and Starring* Charlie Chaplin. *Also starring* Virginia Cherrill.
- ***Parlor, Bedroom and Bath*** (USA, 1931). *Directed by* Edward Sedgwick. *Produced by* Buster Keaton. *Written by* C. W. Bell *and* Mark Swan. *Starring* Buster Keaton *and* Charlotte Greenwood.

SOUND FILM

Translated by Brenda Benthien

First of all: the people in the theater do not care whether the music accompanying a film is played by a live orchestra or by a machine. As far as that is concerned, sound film is the producers' private, calculated affair. All the same, the thrifty among us will be relieved to know that the music no longer has to be played anew every evening, and in the villages the barber's wife will not have to be coerced to appear Wednesdays and Saturdays at the horse-hair piano in the ballroom of the Golden Lion, for now the music will be provided up front by the distributor. We are afraid, though, that those flickering streaks of rain that used to hurt only our eyes will scrape incomparably painful welts across the musical accompaniment. And though it does not make any difference whether Harry Piel[1] skips a couple of obstacles in the provinces that he took in front of everybody's eyes in Berlin, how will the music suffer when it is ripped apart and taped together time and again by a careless film projectionist? But let us suppose that everything works out and the Tri-Ergon machine spits out an exemplary mountain landscape and an impeccable men's choir simultaneously: well then, that's nothing new, just a distressing form of competition for the common musicians.

Sound film has arrived, though, when the actor Paul Grätz appears in giant form on the screen—a bit confused, since he is probably not used to showing his face at that size in front of people, clothed as it is in nothing more than a few civilian facial expressions—and it has arrived when he talks to us. The *s* still sounds as if Paulie has forgotten to hook in his dentures, and blurry echoes swallow the voice as though it were surrounded by the four walls of an empty cathedral, but otherwise everything is just dandy. When the photographed Paulie, with a casualness which we are surprised at first to see in such a two-dimensional creation, opens his mouth to speak, nothing disgraceful happens; he has his voice in the right place, and it obeys the slightest twitch of his mouth. He stands before us now and talks, and in the face of this miracle we turn naive as a child. Weissgerber the violinist steps back with a bow, after performing a virtuoso piece before our very eyes and ears, and we break out into spontaneous applause, thinking we see how pleased he looks—and then we glance in fear and shame at our neighbor, but he has been applauding, too. The impression that this is not a copy but a living being is completely compelling. In the split second that this happens, however, film art abdicates its hard-won place back to the good old peepshow.

It is obvious that sound film gets under your skin far more than silent film. A boxing match, recorded with all its sounds, is just as exciting as a real one, and a loudly barking dog is more impressive than one that just snaps silently at the air. What a painful educational experience it is for your internal politics to hear glowing hot iron hiss as it's shoved by two half-naked men into a cylinder; and how clear everything suddenly becomes when you see Stresemann[2] in action, supernaturally large and at full volume.

[1] Director, author, producer, and actor, Piel (1892–1963), was the hero of countless extraordinarily popular action films in the twenties and thirties, often including wild animal stunt scenes which Piel himself performed.—*Trans.*

[2] Gustav Stresemann, the German Foreign Minister.—*Trans.*

But the advantages of sound film in the areas of instruction and journalism work as disadvantages on an artistic level. Let us outline what we mean by this:

First, when real sounds are emitted by the filmed virtuoso's violin, the visual picture suddenly becomes three-dimensional and tangible. The acoustics perfect the illusion to such an extent that it becomes complete, and thus the edge of the picture is no longer a frame, but the demarcation of a hole, of a theatrical space: the sound turns the film screen into a spatial stage! Now, a major and particular appeal of film lies in the fact that a film scene consists of the competition between division of the picture and movement within an area, and three-dimensional body and movement in space. Sound film does away with this aesthetically important double game almost entirely. Take the image of a singer with her accompanist; way up front sits the very large accompanist, and behind the grand piano we see the small upper body of the singer. The appeal of such a shot lies in the fact that the relative sizes are paradoxical to the contents of the event, since the singer is really the main character. If we see the same scene in a sound film and a song emits from the woman's mouth, the accompanist seems like a figure that has been coincidentally placed up front, which annoyingly blocks the center of the action. Rather than a pretty picture, we have a lopsidedly narrated event. For the sound has rendered the "treatment" dominant. The shot of a military band marching forward into the picture from far behind is similar. If now, way up front, the giant figure of an officer appears, behind whose wide back the marching band gradually disappears, it is a wonderful playing off of opposites, purely visually speaking. Suppose now, though, that I hear the military music playing at the same time; my interest remains with the band longer than it would if the scene were only represented visually. As soon as the first trumpeter disappears behind the officer's back, I would perceive the officer as a disturbance, and be tempted to shout, "Sir, step out of the way of my music!"

Second, it is not only that sound makes it nearly impossible to interpret two-dimensional pictures, but also that the producer cannot pay adequate attention to the beauty of the picture, since it is no longer only the visual, but now also the acoustic that is part of the composition. Thus Stresemann makes a speech, and when we force ourselves to look filmically, despite the sound, what do we see? A naked skull bobbing tiresomely back and forth, a monotonous facial expression, the same picture for minutes on end. Deathly dull! Or, if I am making a sound film recording of a violinist and his accompanist, and I show a close-up of the accompanist as soon as the piano has a solo, this pleasant visual change inevitably tears apart the acoustical progression of the musical piece with a jolt. This means that consideration for the unity of the sound demands that I also keep the picture unchanged—and that is very nearly identical to being boring. And if we forget about the impression the picture makes and take the scene as a material course of events, then it is not film and not sound film, but just plain old theater. And that is something we know already.

Third, film plays a superior game with realities in that it allows scenes whose contents are disparate to blur together, sets contrasting courses of events against each other at the speed of light, and unexpectedly changes perspectives and the sizes of objects. Therein lie its most important "musical" possibilities. Here the sound is inhibitive. It lends each scene so much importance—burdens it with naturalism—that it cannot compete with the dance of form which is running roughshod over all the contents. We look into the individual pictures as though we were looking into the doorless cars of a paternoster lift.[3] Things which were previously

---

[3] An old-fashioned elevator without doors.—*Trans.*

kept on the same footing and which flowed together effortlessly by means of common visual characteristics, despite all discrepancies in content, now stand, disjointed, next to each other.

The prospects are not very good. It seems rather questionable whether it will be possible for talented people to put aside such elementary faults and create a new artistic medium for themselves from the principles of sound film. Walter Ruttmann[4] and Edmund Meisel's picture revue "Sound Wave" (*Die tönende Welle*) uses primarily musical accompaniment and is on the whole not yet very courageous in its experimentation. It is certain, though, that the addition of sound will have about the same ennobling effect on the average feature film as the affixation of a curly tail might have on a realistic picture postcard of a dachshund: it will wag flirtatiously with its third dimension, thereby adding a great deal to the amusement of the public at large, and to the horror of the few who matter.

But sound film can replace theater. Imagine the film image in color, its spatial effects heightened even more—perhaps by a stereoscopic arrangement—its acoustic transmission even more improved upon, and it is difficult to see why we should continue wasting the energies of our great actors on a nerve-deadening dramatic series, or why the theater public, insofar as it sits more than ten yards away from the stage, should continue to know about the performance only by hearsay, or why people in the provinces, New York, and Singapore should be deprived of all the great acting the world has to offer!

Sound film as an improvement on opera glasses and as a means of "canning" theater—superb! Sound film as its own art form...?

---

[4] Abstract and documentary filmmaker best known for *Berlin—Symphony of a Big City* (1927), for which he employed rhythmic montage.—*Trans.*

THE SAD FUTURE OF FILM

Translated by Brenda Benthien

Film is not an art of the masses, except that it must amass a profit at the box office. Those who try to be lovers of both the people and art—a difficult double calling these days—have hailed film as the illustrated bible for the people. The esoteric pleasures of the art of printing are now to be surpassed by the (equally nutritional) visual instruction provided by the living picture, whose lessons are thought to be best suited to making an impression on the eye of the common man. The developments of the past two years have made this whole pious swindle painfully clear.

For the people would rather have pictures than a bible. They can be educated, but not these days—not so long as the work needed to earn their daily bread is either nonexistent or so overtaxing that the worker drops dead tired into bed at night. The discovery of living photography, of an easily manufactured picture of reality, fit in perfectly with the legitimate need of the employed, from the messenger boy up to the factory director, for distraction and amusement. Thus a cult of the image quickly arose, one that has since turned into a spiritual epidemic. Everywhere that there had been words—that is, thoughts—there was now raw, pointless viewing.

The film industry, as purveyor of such visual amusements, has never been in good stead with the film artists. Similarly, it became apparent that, to a certain modest degree, the desired product could be produced not only by untalented but also talented artists. Thus arose the flattering legend of the great artist as the darling of the people (whereas the sorriest local one-act play, *Little Karl Seeks Mother-in-Law*, has actually provoked the same gales of laughter as *Gold Rush*, the most melancholy film ever made). No sooner did sound film appear than bluff triumphed over quality, and from one day to the next the people's darlings saw their life's work in question. The wide country road of film art, whose lovely goal was becoming ever clearer in the distance, was closed for technical renovations, with a detour erected on a bumpy path over the fields. Chaplin became insecure and lost precious months, but finally remained resolute (*City Lights* has only synchronized music); Buster Keaton held his most recent premiere in a second-rate theater; the marvelous porcelain face of Anna May Wong emitted stupid girlish noises; and we fearfully await Greta Garbo's first talking films, *The Kiss*, *Wild Orchids*, and *Anna Christie*. One may welcome the appearance of sound film, but the unscrupulous strangulation of an entire branch of art, the violation of talented and inspired artists, remains a scandal. Silent film was not ripe for replacement. It had not lost its fruitfulness, but only its profitability. Especially when we understand that sound film is more than just an addition to silent film, that it is, rather, an artistic activity unto itself, we ought to reject the popular opinion that it represents an "advance," one automatically condemning the previous method to the compost heap. Sound film is not an advance, but a new thing entirely—and that is undoubtedly a mixed blessing.

The patron saint of the visual arts has switched over from Saint Luke to the electric company, and the results look it. The world public, just as powerful as it is uneducated, wants film to look more and more like reality. At the cinema they look for the sensation of the waxworks, the ventriloquist—the doll looks and talks like a man! Similarly, technicians see their task as being to conquer sound, color, and space, and they're going to reach their goal damned fast. We allowed silent film time to bring at least a couple of well-formed products into the world. From here on in, however, Progress will be in an even greater rush. It will trample the unhatched eggs of sound film with its seven-league army boots, and then it will be obvious to even the most well-meaning opportunist among film lovers that film's latest achievements cut a better figure in the patent registry than in the annals of art history.

It is touching and tragic to notice the current efforts of serious directors, actors, screenwriters, and aesthetes trying to discover the laws of sound film. Good possibilities present themselves, but the task will remain uncompleted. For no sooner will the final cinema-goer return from his well-earned summer holiday than color film will arrive. The heavens of art will positively darken and cloud over with poisonously beautiful tinctures; it will be our eyes again, for a change, which are subjected to atrocities, and the discordant Tobis[1] trumpets of the twilight of silent film will resound like sweet oboes in our memory.

Even if it should be possible to perfect the technology of colored film so that the color no longer controls the director, but the director the color—something that will take a long time, dragging out the production of more or less watchable sound films for another number of years—even then, nothing will have been gained. Rather, one of those qualities of the camera that makes film art possible will be lost again, since every artistic creation demands that distance from reality which Progress is trying to remove! Just as color film will render extraordinarily beautiful, substantial black-and-white effects impossible—most likely without offering anything else in their place—so the stereoscopic film will render the decorative separation of surfaces and the pictorial-symbolic use of perspective impossible, and the enlargement of the format will destroy the formative power of the frame. Finally, nothing will be left to the film camera but to confine its work to what Frank Warschauer in *Filmkunst* (the only good German film magazine) recently termed its sole task: namely the mechanical, life-like reproduction of art or non-art which is set up and acted out in the studio.

While it is still possible today to produce a high-quality film, without concessions, for a limited, elite audience (for instance, for the first-run cinemas of the big cities), this too will end with film's takeover by radio. Radio will assume the monopoly on film broadcasts, and the result will be a lowering of standards such as we have already observed of radio. After all, those high-quality musical, literary, and scientific broadcasts merely serve to amuse the few, and they place unreasonable demands on all those millions of listeners who don't understand a word of them, and still want to get something for their money!

[1] Tonbild Syndikat AG was a German production company founded in 1928 by a number of (primarily foreign) shareholders. Tobis took over European rights to UFA's Tri-Ergon sound system without using them. In 1929 Tobis joined with the Klangfilm company, which produced sound film machines and worked on their standardization. Tobis was taken over by the government in 1937 and produced propaganda films (among others) until 1945. After the war, a new company with the same name was founded and now distributes films in Germany.—*Trans.*

SOUND FILM GONE ASTRAY

Translated by Brenda Benthien

We met the arrival of sound film with distrust. It seemed, after all, that it would have to destroy all the exceptional qualities of silent film that we had loved. Then we became more hopeful, because we admitted that sound film would be able to replace the attractions that it destroyed with new ones of its own. Since then, it has become apparent that sound film desires to make as little use of these new possibilities as possible. It has destroyed, but without replacing anything.

It cannot be denied that, for the demanding cinema-goer, sound films are on the average duller than the silent ones were. Silent film, precisely because of its silence, was forced to be delightful. Inter-titles that were too long and too frequent were annoying to the mass public, who wanted to watch and not read, and so the director was forced to seek visual solutions, filmic ideas, for what was to be said but should not, and could not, be said. This was a situation not of artistic ambition, but of pure necessity. Thus it happened that even the average industrial film often included individual gripping scenes. The actor did not speak and still made himself understood, clever shots translated the situation, and the symbolic play with typical props created an attractive sign language.

Sound film has brushed aside nearly all of these fruitful communication difficulties. Theoretically, sound should only intervene where it has something new to offer the picture; it should not water down the visual with tiresome addenda. If we look at the pictures produced to date, we find these challenges met in only a few scenes of a few excellent films; the average film has relaxed so much that we feel inclined to yawn. The means of sound film are rich, but there is unfortunately no more pressure to use them. Art has become optional. To clarify the plot, one can talk as much as one pleases and as much as the foreign market can tolerate. The camera has nothing more to do than place the bearer of the voice, the actor, clearly before our eyes. Montage, which was the spice of the silent film, is now to be avoided, since the obvious need not be pointed out to us. The "long passage" has become fashionable: the scene floats slowly through the pictorial space. This has made camera direction less intelligent, less humorous. The shot has almost entirely lost its formative function and serves as a mere organ for reporting, as it did at the beginning of the silent film era. This situation did not have to be, but came to pass because the industry film works according to the comfortable principle of least resistance.

Since, in addition, the script writer's dialogue generally cannot compete with an average theater piece, the most certain point of attraction remains the acting talent. Sound films offer us the possibility of experiencing great actors' stage-quality performances through a magnifying glass, from an ideal orchestra seat, and yet at gallery prices. But the charm of the average actor has faded. This is particularly apparent with the actresses: now that more than a superficial "graphic" quality is required, those women who embodied a certain beauty appropriate to the image and movement of a silent film demonstrate an art of song and speech that does not amount to much more than third-rate provincial theater. When it comes to sound film, one cannot restructure human beings as easily as cinemas. Thus the past three years have given us the "talking tart" type, who considerably depreciates our enjoyment of film.

Music and song should have opened up a new field to film. The mistake began with the takeover of the theater operetta form. It was sound film that showed us how unnatural the style of a theater performance is. Colorfully made-up people move around in a showcase, gesticulating pushily and reciting overloudly—this is already so far from reality that no break in style is ever noticeable when the actors in a stage operetta suddenly begin to hop around choreographically and carry on with musical numbers in the middle of the so-called unstylized dialogue. Carried over to film, this process is insufferable; one can be convinced of the fact any day.

Film space, film set, and film acting are of such an intimate character that every opera-buffa ham seems unnatural, every sudden burst of song unfitting, every inserted dance crazy, as if the actor were having an attack of illness. This is true at least to the extent that it is impossible to create, and stick to, a superreal comprehensive style that determines the plot's pantomimic form to the last detail, as far as song and dance are concerned. The American silent film comedy can be taken here as a model: the music need only bring a strong, dance-like element to the sound film operetta. This element must make itself noticeable throughout—above and beyond the hackneyed interludes—and must be supported in its hyperreality by incidental music that characterizes the types of movements we have come to recognize in Mickey Mouse films.

It is particularly difficult to find a suitable speaking style for these films. We know of only two representative solutions till now: Chaplin parodied the human voice with a saxophone squawk in *City Lights*, and Buster Keaton, because he coincidentally speaks our language brokenly, came up with a very effective clown's jargon in the German version of *Parlor, Bedroom and Bath*. Eccentrics in the circus have always spoken brokenly, not so much to provide a foreign touch as from the correct feeling that someone in baggy pants and a plaster nose who leaps about like a goat cannot speak like a gentleman in a sports jacket.

In America the spoken word seems to burst open the grotesque style of the silent film era. Buster Keaton turns up in a society comedy of the usual kind and seems to have fallen from an alien planet, with his acrobatic mannerisms and his immobile face amongst the elegantly conversing gentlepeople of high society. He is entirely without antagonists and seems unnatural because his surroundings are too natural. It is much the same with our Anny Ondra.[1] She too is a small art object amidst the weather-beaten remains of the comic opera. She has something of Keaton's cold beauty and his acrobatic dancer's talent with his limbs. This unusual type of girl golem is a treasure which our industry does not know to appreciate. A true film operetta style of international proportions could be built up around this woman.

---

[1] Born Anna Sophie Ondrakowa in Poland in 1903, Anny Ondra was one of the greatest comedic stars of middle European films of the 1920s. She filmed in Prague, Berlin, and Vienna, and played the lead in Hitchcock's *Blackmail* in 1929.—*Trans.*

CHAPTER 5
ANDRÉ BAZIN

André Bazin (1918–1958) was a French film theorist and film critic. He is one of the most influential early film realists, a predecessor of auteur theory, and a cofounder of the influential French film journal, Cahiers du Cinéma. *He wrote numerous essays on film, a selection of which have been published in English translation under the title* What Is Cinema?, *a volume itself deeply influential on the development of American film philosophy (by way, initially, of its impact on the American philosopher Stanley Cavell in his book,* The World Viewed*). "The Ontology of the Photographic Image" was originally published in French ("Ontologie de l'image photographique") as a contribution to the volume* Les Problèmes de la Peinture *(Confluences; edited by Gaston Diehl) in 1945.*

Bazin begins the essay with the suggestion that the plastic arts, taken together, might best be understood as being inspired by what he calls a "mummy complex": that is, that the plastic arts are driven by a desire to preserve life in the face of (and in opposition to) the passage of time and, ultimately, death. Thus, he asserts that the first "sculpture" was, in fact, a mummy—the literal effort to preserve human physicality for the purposes of resurrected or eternal life. Clearly thinking of ancient Egypt, Bazin understands those most paradigmatic products of that long past culture—mummies, the pyramids (insofar as they were monuments and tombs)—to constitute an attempt to overcome time. While it is arguable whether pyramids are themselves works of art (and it seems inappropriate to say that mummies are, or were), Bazin connects this attempt to master and evade time with the transition from mummification to statuary. Rather than making an effort to preserve life for the dead, the sculptor offers us something else: not only a memorial to, but a representation of, life. Thus, sculpture and statuary serve as representatives in the present of life (and lives) past. The history of the plastic arts follows this trajectory one step further, Bazin argues, when art works begin to serve not so much as representatives, but as reminders, of the dead. When art is charged with the preservation of memory, we can immediately see two further developments. First, art works become constituents of an alternative, ideal world which runs parallel to but is essentially different from the real world; they are like the real persons and objects they resemble, but they are not those persons or objects themselves (in contrast, for example, to a mummy). Second, following directly from the first point, is that the plastic arts then can be understood as essentially concerned with resemblance, or to put it in Bazin's terms, realism.

The realist turn in the plastic arts centralizes reproduction as the essential task of the work of art (and the artist): the purpose of art, understood in this way, is to reproduce the world. Bazin takes one of the earliest reproductive technologies in the arts to be the Renaissance discovery and understanding of perspective in painting, which gave the painter the power to reproduce the illusion of three-dimensional space on a two-dimensional surface. This technological facilitation of the capacity to produce an illusion of depth is already, Bazin thinks, latent photography—the exploitation of perspective in Renaissance painting reveals already the roots of an artistic principle that will make photography possible, despite the fact that, in another sense, photography would have to await certain technological innovations before it could take its place among the arts.

All of the plastic arts after the turn toward perspective in painting are, Bazin argues, torn between two competing artistic tendencies. On the one hand, art strives for representation—the work of art offers us one thing standing in place of another, or symbolism, what Bazin calls "the aesthetic." On the other hand, art also strives for what Bazin calls "the psychological," reproduction, duplication of the world. Great artists strive to combine the two tendencies, he says, but such combination cannot resolve the natural tension between them. That said, with the invention of photography (and, later, cinematography), the obsession with likeness and with reproduction or duplication of the world (the psychological tendency in art) that had characterized painting for so long is finally fully satisfied. While a painting would always be influenced by the painter's style, and the painter's style always detracts from the painting's ability to be a "pure" and "simple" duplication of the world (a painting always only ever represents), works of photography and cinema are automatically produced by machines; the absence of the human hand is, in fact, what makes photographs and films such perfect reproductions of a visual scene. Painting is freed to pursue the furthest reaches of aesthetic style, leaving the mechanical work of world-duplication, resemblance, and straightforward likeness to photography and cinematography.

Given their automatic production, works of cinema and photography affect viewers like natural phenomena: when we see something reproduced in a photograph, we take ourselves in some very real and important sense to be seeing the thing reproduced, not merely an image of it. At no point, Bazin suggests, need the viewer of a photograph or the moviegoer take into account the possibly transformative effects of the artist's style in assessing the realism of the reproduction. This absence of style in the photographic image makes photography the most credible of the arts, he argues, forcing the viewer to accept that the person or object whose image is reproduced in the photo must actually have existed, at least at the time at which the photograph was taken. A painting—no matter how faithful the resemblance to the model—does not instill this kind of confidence in its viewer, nor should it. Thus, photography is able, more than painting or the other plastic arts ever could have been, to free the objects it reproduces from time and space in the reproduction. In Bazin's poetically funerary terms, photography embalms time.

Although cinematography shares most of these traits with photography, one essential difference which Bazin notes has to do with the fact that, by their very nature, the motion pictures are not merely pictures but also movement, in time. While photography is the art of mummifying moments, cinematography is not: the cinema captures time's passage, in real time, not merely the objects and images that constitute the visual basis of that passage. Thus, while the photographer provides us with the images of things, the cinematographer or filmmaker provides the image of the duration of things: photography embalms time, but the cinema is "change mummified." Insofar as the cinema is a visual medium with roots in photography, it helps to demonstrate that the introduction of photography was the most important event in the history of the plastic arts. Bazin concludes the essay, however, with the pregnant assertion that "cinema is also a language"—an idea that is treated in other of Bazin's writings.

THE ONTOLOGY OF THE PHOTOGRAPHIC IMAGE

Translated by Hugh Gray

If the plastic arts were put under psychoanalysis, the practice of embalming the dead might turn out to be a fundamental factor in their creation. The process might reveal that at the origin of painting and sculpture there lies a mummy complex. The religion of ancient Egypt, aimed against death, saw survival as depending on the continued existence of the corporeal body. Thus, by providing a defense against the passage of time it satisfied a basic psychological need in man, for death is but the victory of time. To preserve, artificially, his bodily appearance is to snatch it from the flow of time, to stow it away neatly, so to speak, in the hold of life. It was natural, therefore, to keep up appearances in the face of the reality of death by preserving flesh and bone. The first Egyptian statue, then, was a mummy, tanned and petrified in sodium. But pyramids and labyrinthine corridors offered no certain guarantee against ultimate pillage.

Other forms of insurance were therefore sought. So, near the sarcophagus, alongside the corn that was to feed the dead, the Egyptians placed terra cotta statuettes, as substitute mummies which might replace the bodies if these were destroyed. It is this religious use, then, that lays bare the primordial function of statuary, namely, the preservation of life by a representation of life. Another manifestation of the same kind of thing is the arrow-pierced clay bear to be found in prehistoric caves, a magic identity-substitute for the living animal, that will ensure a successful hunt. The evolution, side by side, of art and civilization has relieved the plastic arts of their magic role. Louis XIV did not have himself embalmed. He was content to survive in his portrait by Le Brun. Civilization cannot, however, entirely cast out the bogy of time. It can only sublimate our concern with it to the level of rational thinking. No one believes any longer in the ontological identity of model and image, but all are agreed that the image helps us to remember the subject and to preserve him from a second spiritual death. Today the making of images no longer shares an anthropocentric, utilitarian purpose. It is no longer a question of survival after death, but of a larger concept, the creation of an ideal world in the likeness of the real, with its own temporal destiny. "How vain a thing is painting" if underneath our fond admiration for its works we do not discern man's primitive need to have the last word in the argument with death by means of the form that endures. If the history of the plastic arts is less a matter of their aesthetic than of their psychology then it will be seen to be essentially the story of resemblance, or, if you will, of realism.

Seen in this sociological perspective photography and cinema would provide a natural explanation for the great spiritual and technical crisis that overtook modern painting around the middle of the last century. André Malraux has described the cinema as the furthermost evolution to date of plastic realism, the beginnings of which were first manifest at the Renaissance and which found a limited expression in baroque painting.

It is true that painting, the world over, has struck a varied balance between the symbolic and realism. However, in the fifteenth century Western painting began to turn from its age-old concern with spiritual realities expressed in the form proper to it, towards an effort to combine this spiritual expression with as complete an imitation as possible of the outside world.

The decisive moment undoubtedly came with the discovery of the first scientific and already, in a sense, mechanical system of reproduction, namely, perspective: the camera obscura of Da Vinci foreshadowed the camera of Niepce. The artist was now in a position to create the illusion of three-dimensional space within which things appeared to exist as our eyes in reality see them.

Thenceforth painting was torn between two ambitions: one, primarily aesthetic, namely the expression of spiritual reality wherein the symbol transcended its model; the other, purely psychological, namely the duplication of the world outside. The satisfaction of this appetite for illusion merely served to increase it till, bit by bit, it consumed the plastic arts. However, since perspective had only solved the problem of form and not of movement, realism was forced to continue the search for some way of giving dramatic expression to the moment, a kind of psychic fourth dimension that could suggest life in the tortured immobility of baroque art.[1]

The great artists, of course, have always been able to combine the two tendencies. They have allotted to each its proper place in the hierarchy of things, holding reality at their command and molding it at will into the fabric of their art. Nevertheless, the fact remains that we are faced with two essentially different phenomena and these any objective critic must view separately if he is to understand the evolution of the pictorial. The need for illusion has not ceased to trouble the heart of painting since the sixteenth century. It is a purely mental need, of itself nonaesthetic, the origins of which must be sought in the proclivity of the mind towards magic. However, it is a need the pull of which has been strong enough to have seriously upset the equilibrium of the plastic arts.

The quarrel over realism in art stems from a misunderstanding, from a confusion between the aesthetic and the psychological; between true realism, the need that is to give significant expression to the world both concretely and its essence, and the pseudorealism of a deception aimed at fooling the eye (or for that matter the mind); a pseudorealism content in other words with illusory appearances.[2] That is why medieval art never passed through this crisis; simultaneously vividly realistic and highly spiritual, it knew nothing of the drama that came to light as a consequence of technical developments. Perspective was the original sin of Western painting.

It was redeemed from sin by Niepce and Lumière. In achieving the aims of baroque art, photography has freed the plastic arts from their obsession with likeness. Painting was forced, as it turned out, to offer us illusion and this illusion was reckoned sufficient unto art. Photography and the cinema on the other hand are discoveries that satisfy, once and for all and in its very essence, our obsession with realism.

No matter how skillful the painter, his work was always in fee to an inescapable subjectivity. The fact that a human hand intervened cast a shadow of doubt over the image. Again, the essential factor in the transition from the baroque to photography is not the perfecting of a

[1] It would be interesting from this point of view to study, in the illustrated magazines of 1890–1910, the rivalry between photographic reporting and the use of drawings. The latter, in particular, satisfied the baroque need for the dramatic. A feeling for the photographic document developed only gradually.

[2] Perhaps the Communists, before they attach too much importance to expressionist realism, should stop talking about it in a way more suitable to the eighteenth century, before there were such things as photography or cinema. Maybe it does not really matter if Russian painting is second-rate provided Russia gives us first-rate cinema. Eisenstein is her Tintoretto.

physical process (photography will long remain the inferior of painting in the reproduction of color); rather does it lie in a psychological fact, to wit, in completely satisfying our appetite for illusion by a mechanical reproduction in the making of which man plays no part. The solution is not to be found in the result achieved but in the way of achieving it.[3]

This is why the conflict between style and likeness is a relatively modern phenomenon of which there is no trace before the invention of the sensitized plate. Clearly the fascinating objectivity of Chardin is in no sense that of the photographer. The nineteenth century saw the real beginnings of the crisis of realism of which Picasso is now the mythical central figure and which put to the test at one and the same time the conditions determining the formal existence of the plastic arts and their sociological roots. Freed from the "resemblance complex," the modern painter abandons it to the masses who, henceforth, identify resemblance on the one hand with photography and on the other with the kind of painting which is related to photography.

Originality in photography as distinct from originality in painting lies in the essentially objective character of photography. [Bazin here makes a point of the fact that the lens, the basis of photography, is in French called the "objectif," a nuance that is lost in English.—Trans.] For the first time, between the originating object and its reproduction there intervenes only the instrumentality of a nonliving agent. For the first time an image of the world is formed automatically, without the creative intervention of man. The personality of the photographer enters into proceedings only in his selection of the object to be photographed and by way of the purpose he has in mind. Although the final result may reflect something of his personality, this does not play the same role as is played by that of the painter. All the arts are based on the presence of man, only photography derives an advantage from his absence. Photography affects us like a phenomenon in nature, like a flower or a snowflake whose vegetable or earthly origins are an inseparable part of their beauty.

This production by automatic means has radically affected our psychology of the image. The objective nature of photography confers on it a quality of credibility absent from all other picture-making. In spite of any objections our critical spirit may offer, we are forced to accept as real the existence of the object reproduced, actually *re*-presented, set before us, that is to say, in time and space. Photography enjoys a certain advantage in virtue of this transference of reality from the thing to its reproduction.[4]

A very faithful drawing may actually tell us more about the model but despite the promptings of our critical intelligence it will never have the irrational power of the photograph to bear away our faith.

Besides, painting is, after all, an inferior way of making likeness, an *ersatz* of the processes of reproduction. Only a photographic lens can give us the kind of image of the object that is capable of satisfying the deep need man has to substitute for it something more than a mere approximation, a kind of decal or transfer. The photographic image is the object itself, the object freed from the conditions of time and space that govern it. No matter how fuzzy,

---

[3] There is room, nevertheless, for a study of the psychology of the lesser plastic arts, the molding of death masks for example, which likewise involves a certain automatic process. One might consider photography in this sense as a molding, the taking of an impression, by the manipulation of light.

[4] Here one should really examine the psychology of relics and souvenirs which likewise enjoy the advantages of a transfer of reality stemming from the "mummy-complex." Let us merely note in passing that the Holy Shroud of Turin combines the features alike of relic and photograph.

distorted, or discolored, no matter how lacking in documentary value the image may be, it shares, by virtue of the very process of its becoming, the being of the model of which it is the reproduction; it *is* the model.

Hence the charm of family albums. Those grey or sepia shadows, phantomlike and almost undecipherable, are no longer traditional family portraits but rather the disturbing presence of lives halted at a set moment in their duration, freed from their destiny; not, however, by the prestige of art but by the power of an impassive mechanical process: for photography does not create eternity, as art does, it embalms time, rescuing it simply from its proper corruption.

Viewed in this perspective, the cinema is objectivity in time. The film is no longer content to preserve the object, enshrouded as it were in an instant, as the bodies of insects are preserved intact, out of the distant past, in amber. The film delivers baroque art from its convulsive catalepsy. Now, for the first time, the image of things is likewise the image of their duration, change mummified as it were. Those categories of *resemblance* which determine the species of *photographic* image likewise, then, determine the character of its aesthetic as distinct from that of painting.[5]

The aesthetic qualities of photography are to be sought in its power to lay bare the realities. It is not for me to separate off, in the complex fabric of the objective world, here a reflection on a damp sidewalk, there the gesture of a child. Only the impassive lens, stripping its object of all those ways of seeing it, those piled-up preconceptions, that spiritual dust and grime with which my eyes have covered it, is able to present it in all its virginal purity to my attention and consequently to my love. By the power of photography, the natural image of a world that we neither know nor can know, nature at last does more than imitate art: she imitates the artist.

Photography can even surpass art in creative power. The aesthetic world of the painter is of a different kind from that of the world about him. Its boundaries enclose a substantially and essentially different microcosm. The photograph as such and the object in itself share a common being, after the fashion of a fingerprint. Wherefore, photography actually contributes something to the order of natural creation instead of providing a substitute for it. The surrealists had an inkling of this when they looked to the photographic plate to provide them with their monstrosities and for this reason: the surrealist does not consider his aesthetic purpose and the mechanical effect of the image on our imaginations as things apart. For him, the logical distinction between what is imaginary and what is real tends to disappear. Every image is to be seen as an object and every object as an image. Hence photography ranks high in the order of surrealist creativity because it produces an image that is a reality of nature, namely, an hallucination that is also a fact. The fact that surrealist painting combines tricks of visual deception with meticulous attention to detail substantiates this.

So, photography is clearly the most important event in the history of plastic arts. Simultaneously a liberation and an accomplishment, it has freed Western painting, once and for all, from its obsession with realism and allowed it to recover its aesthetic autonomy. Impressionist realism, offering science as an alibi, is at the opposite extreme from eye-deceiving

---

[5] I use the term *category* here in the sense attached to it by M. Gouhier in his book on the theater in which he distinguishes between the dramatic and the aesthetic categories. Just as dramatic tension has no artistic value, the perfection of a reproduction is not to be identified with beauty. It constitutes rather the prime matter, so to speak, on which the artistic fact is recorded.

trickery. Only when form ceases to have any imitative value can it be swallowed up in color. So, when form, in the person of Cézanne, once more regains possession of the canvas there is no longer any question of the illusions of the geometry of perspective. The painting, being confronted in the mechanically produced image with a competitor able to reach out beyond baroque resemblance to the very identity of the model, was compelled into the category of object. Henceforth Pascal's condemnation of painting is itself rendered vain since the photograph allows us on the one hand to admire in reproduction something that our eyes alone could not have taught us to love, and on the other, to admire the painting as a thing in itself whose relation to something in nature has ceased to be the justification for its existence.

On the other hand, of course, cinema is also a language.

CHAPTER 6
JEAN EPSTEIN

Jean Epstein (1897–1953) was a French-Polish critic, film theorist, and filmmaker working in France whose work—both cinematic and critical—made a significant impact on the French understanding of and approach to film. He is among the very first instances of the filmmaker-theorist-critic (other instantiations of which type include figures such as Sergei Eisenstein, Jean-Luc Godard, Andrei Tarkovsky, and François Truffaut), and his voluminous and diverse creative output is widely regarded as standing with Eisenstein near the head of that line. Although his perspective on film is relatively difficult to classify, he is nevertheless referenced by many later (especially French) philosophers of film, his views serving as something of a foundation upon which those later developments are built. Included here are two selections from Epstein's book, The Intelligence of a Machine, *which was originally published in French (*L'intelligence d'une machine*) by J. Melot in 1946.*

In the first selection, "The Interchangeability of Continuity and Discontinuity," Epstein situates cinema within the larger context of the question of the continuous (or discontinuous) nature of the world. He begins by noting—as many others have noted—that cinema transforms a discontinuity (many different still images) into a continuity (moving pictures). In general, he notes, we have trouble believing that the world around us might function in the same fashion, however: that the world might be fundamentally discontinuous seems out of accord with our empirical experience. It seems, in fact, that when individuals who are unfamiliar with the way in which movies are made come to learn that they are experiencing only an illusion of motion, they are typically surprised—in real life, continuity seems far more basic than discontinuity. Discontinuity seems, in fact, unnatural.

Epstein calls this everyday appearance of continuity in the world "superficial continuity." He calls it that, of course, in contrast to what we know of the world from the physical atomism of traditional physics: although continuity appears on the surfaces of things, when we examine them very closely we find that the material world is fundamentally composed of unbelievably small objects (atoms) at relatively great distances from one another. The atom shows us that there is no depth continuity, that every material object is always already in a state of discontinuity within itself. This, Epstein calls "intermediate discontinuity," to differentiate it from the superficial continuity we perceive in our everyday lives—and from yet another continuity. As our models of the material world progressed beyond Newton to Einstein (and beyond), we have found that, at least in some instances, it makes more scientific and observational sense to think of the subatomic universe as composed not of discontinuous atoms (or subatomic particles), but instead as fields of forces in overlapping relation. These fields make possible the existence of material objects and their interactions, which traditional physics describes: not matter themselves, these fields of forces nevertheless constitute the necessary physical precondition for matter, and Epstein thus calls this substrate of material existence "pre-material continuity." In describing these relations to us,

Epstein makes clear that there is no simple continuity or simple discontinuity; each is always in some ways implied or presupposed by the other.

Unlike the material world (according to Epstein's understanding of the state of science in 1946), the world of the cinema depends entirely upon the viewer: while it is true that a continuity appears to be produced from the discontinuity of still frames, this continuity is produced only in the viewer's mind, by way of a deficiency built into human sight. Cinematic continuity is an illusion—or, using Epstein's term, a ghost—presenting us with immobile discontinuities but knowing in advance that we will be unable to perceive them as anything but a mobile continuity. In (at least) this sense, cinematic continuity is a trick, or a lie.

That said, the discontinuity of the still frames produced by cinematography is itself imposed upon the world recorded on film by the camera. Thus, cinematography can be understood not to displace discontinuity once and for all with an illusory continuity, but instead to be a site of exchange and interchangeability between continuity and discontinuity—the apparent continuity of the world transformed into the immobile discontinuity of still photographic frames, which is in turn productive (through projection) of the mobile continuity apparent to the cinemagoer. Each of them, continuity and discontinuity, is equally basic, and thus neither is primordial where the cinema is concerned. Both the discontinuity of the still photographic frame (which appears to "freeze" time) and the continuity of the motion picture seem unnatural, in their own ways. Which leads Epstein to conclude that continuity and discontinuity are interchangeable modes of unreality: each is as good as the other, and neither presents us with reality itself. Following Francis Bacon, he calls continuity and discontinuity the twin "ghosts of the mind."

In addition to the superficial continuity of everyday empirical perception, Epstein notes that we experience another sort of continuity in the world—that known to mathematics, and evident in our perceptions of and thinking about quantity, sequence, shape, and so on. Given the unreality of both continuity and discontinuity, Epstein notes that both superficial continuity and mathematical continuity are ghosts of human intelligence: both require a human mind in order to exist (i.e., they do not exist in the unobserved world), and both are illusions imposed by that mind. Discontinuity, however, in all its perceivable forms—whether at the smallest physical level, which is only accessible through scientific models and high-powered microscopes, or as a product of photography or cinematography—is not a ghost of human intelligence. On the contrary, the necessity of technological intervention in perception or experience to make discontinuity perceptible makes discontinuity what Epstein calls a ghost of mechanical intelligence. Both are ghosts, but one of those ghosts is a product exclusively of nonhuman, machine minds. This leads us, naturally, to our second selection from Epstein's book.

In the second selection, "Mechanical Philosophy," Epstein takes up the possibility of machine psychology. He notes that all of our most frequently used instruments acquire what seem like psychological characteristics. Despite their material identicalness, machines are individuated in use in ways that are not the products of human intention: they can appear to be sluggish, or tired, or thoughtful, or stubborn, or to inhabit any number of other psychological states. Individualized machines often require their human users to find idiosyncratic techniques for engaging them in use; despite the fact that all well-functioning automobiles of the same make, model, and year ought to function in the very same ways, one may require certain techniques to insure satisfactory operation that others may not, and these differences do incline the users of those automobiles to grant them particularity and even individuality despite their machine natures. Of course, another way to describe the necessity of such techniques is to say that machines are often unpredictable (which, again, runs contrary to our basic conception of machines as lacking individuality), and Epstein suggests that it is meaningful at this point, when addressing the phenomenon of individuated machines, to think of their unpredictability in terms of freedom, or the will, or even the soul.

Equating soul with freedom, unpredictability, idiosyncrasy, and individuation, Epstein suggests that soul emerges from complex material organisms. In their organization and functionality, human bodies give rise to the idiosyncrasies and freedoms that incline us to think of human beings as each different from the others, despite material similarities. Machines, then, ought to be thought of as mechanical organisms—organized and functional bodies which can give rise to individuality, freedom, and ultimately soul (or intelligence)—if they are sufficiently complex. As spirit exists nowhere in particular in the body, as is widely acknowledged, bodies with spirits need not have any particular structure or constitution. Epstein gives us the example of a calculating computer, which performs mathematical algorithms with astonishing speed and without error. While it would be inaccurate to say that such a computer engaged in thinking of the sort of which human beings are capable, it is nevertheless reasonable, Epstein argues, to conceive of the computer as a thinking machine—exhibiting, not human intelligence, but intelligence of a sort: mechanical intelligence.

Following along the lines of his discussion of the computer, Epstein suggests that the cinematographic apparatus (not merely the movie camera, but the whole constellation of machines which, working together in the performance of complex tasks from filming to postproduction and projection) is a small society of machines form which a mind (of a sort) emerges. Bi-sensorial (both seeing and hearing, as it were) and characterized by specific rhythms of succession, the cinematographic apparatus relates to the world in both spatial (sensory) and temporal (sequential) terms. Operating in and upon time and space, the cinematographic apparatus is a mechanical organism from which, then, causation can emerge almost automatically. We then have, as Epstein sees it, a mechanical organism capable of operating causally in time and space in the production of original works (of art!), and from which a sort of intelligence emerges. For Epstein, this suggests that the cinematographic apparatus is comparable to a brain, the material correspondent (if there is one) to mind.

Mechanical thinking, as Epstein envisions it, is not the same as human thinking. Among other things, the thinking of the cinematograph is not conscious—Epstein does not suggest that movie cameras are self-aware, or could become self-aware, self-conscious, or even achieve consciousness in any meaningful sense. But as a kind of thinking, the mechanical thinking of the cinematographic apparatus will produce by way of thought a representation of the universe in which it can itself be situated as intelligence—and, Epstein notes, one way to refer to such an ideal representation is as a philosophy. The cinema (understood as the society of machines with an emergent mind, not as the sociocultural art institution) has, or will have, or should have, a philosophy all its own—a philosophy so distinct from any human philosophy that we must think of it as an antiphilosophy. This antiphilosophy would be, whatever else it is, the ideal representation of the universe as it appears from the perspective of the cinematograph itself.

THE INTELLIGENCE OF A MACHINE

Translated by Christophe Wall-Romana

I. The Interchangeability of Continuity and Discontinuity

A Kind of Miracle

As we know, a film comprises a large number of images juxtaposed on the filmstrip, and yet they are distinct and made somewhat dissimilar through the progressively modified position of the cinematographed subject. At a certain speed, the projection of this series of figures separated by short intervals of space and time produces the appearance of uninterrupted motion. Therefore the most striking wonder of the Lumière brothers' machine is precisely that it transforms a discontinuity into a continuity; that it allows for the synthesis of discontinuous and immobile elements into a mobile and continuous set; that it effects a transition between the two primordial aspects of nature which, ever since science and the metaphysics of science have existed, were strictly oppositional and mutually exclusive.

The First Semblance: Sensible Continuity

The scale at which our senses perceive the world, directly or indirectly, appears at first to be a rigorously coherent assemblage of material parts, in which the existence of an iota of nothingness, of any true discontinuity, seems so impossible that, in places where we do not know what there is, we have imagined a filler substance christened ether. Certainly, Pascal has demonstrated that the supposed horror of nature toward the void is a mirage, yet he did not dispel the horror that human intelligence feels toward the void, about which it can secure no sensorial experience.

Second Semblance: Discontinuity in the Physical Sciences

Since Democritus, and against this primitive conception of universal continuity, the theory of atomism has victoriously developed itself through the presupposition that matter is constituted of indivisible corpuscles distant from one another. While the atom, in spite of its presumed indivisibility, had to be subdivided into several kinds of electrons, today we still generally accept the hypothesis of a discontinuous material structure with gaps, a gaseous structure one might say, both in the infinitely large and the infinitely small, in which the solid elements only occupy a very small volume compared to the immense vacuums through which they circulate. Hence a galaxy is compared to star vapor, in the same way that the atom recalls a miniature solar system.

Underneath the solid world that we know pragmatically hide surprises of a scattered reality in which the proportion of what is, in comparison to that which is not at all nameable, can be depicted by a fly aloft in a space of nearly one cubic mile.

Third Semblance: Mathematical Continuity

While material particles may be conceived of as distinct, they cannot be independently considered since they all exert reciprocal influences on each other that explain the behavior of every single one of them. The network of these innumerable interactions, or field of forces, represents an intangible weave that, for the proponents of Relativity, fills the entire space-time continuum. In this new four-dimensional continuity, energy, which is everywhere virtual, condenses itself here and there into granules possessing a mass: these are the elementary components of matter.

Underneath material discontinuity—whether molecular, atomic or subatomic—we must then imagine a continuity, deeper and still more hidden, that we might call pre-material since it prepares and directs the quanta and probabilistic locations of mass, light and electricity.

The Transmutation of Discontinuity into Continuity: Denied by Zeno, but Accomplished by the Cinematograph

The most obscure aspects of this poetry are to be found in the transitions and overlaps from superficial continuity to intermediate discontinuity, and thence to pre-material continuity whose existence remains strictly mathematical. That the same reality is able to cumulate continuity and discontinuity, that a series without rupture might be a sum of interruptions, that the addition of immobilities might produce movement, is what reason has puzzled over since the time of the Eleatics.

Yet, the cinematograph seems to be a mysterious mechanism devoted to assessing the false truth of Zeno's famous argument about the arrow, devoted to analyzing the subtle metamorphosis of stasis into mobility, of gaps into wholes, and of continuity into discontinuity, a transformation every bit as astounding as the generation of life out of inanimate matter.

Continuity, a Make-Believe Discontinuity

Is it the recording device or the projector that produces this marvel? In truth, all of the figures in each of the images of the film, successively projected on screen, remain as perfectly immobile and separate as they were when they emerged in the sensitive layer of the film. The animation and confluence of these forms does not take place on the filmstrip, or in the lens, but only within humans themselves. Discontinuity becomes continuity only once it has entered the movie-viewer. It is a purely interior phenomenon. Outside the viewing subject there is no movement, no flux, no life in the mosaics of light and shadow that the screen always displays as stills. But within ourselves, we get an impression that is, like all the other data of the sense, an interpretation of the object, that is to say, an illusion, a ghost.

Poor Sight Is the Source of the Metaphysics of Continuity

This phantom of a non-existing continuity, we know it is caused by a deficiency of our sight. The eye possesses a power of discrimination narrowly limited in space and time. A row of dots very close to one another is perceived as a line, evoking the ghost of spatial continuity. And a sufficiently quick succession of distinct but only slightly different images generates, because of the eye's lack of speed and retinal persistence, a new, more complex, and imaginary space-time continuity.

Every movie therefore gives us a clear instance of a mobile continuity that is only made, in its deeper reality, of immobile discontinuities. Zeno was thus right to argue that the analysis of movement provides a set of pauses: he was wrong only in denying the possibility of this absurd synthesis that actually recomposes movement by adding stoppages together, and which the cinematograph produces thanks to the weakness of our sight. "The absurd is not impossible," Faraday noted. The natural consequence of phenomena is not necessarily logical: we understand as much when, by adding light to light, we see darkness generated by interferences.

Is Discontinuity the Actuality of an Unreal Continuity?

Our continuous sensorium, whose daily experience assures us of the existence of everything around us, but whose actuality scientific research invalidates as a whole, ends up being a lie, born, like the fallacious continuity of a movie, of the insufficiency of the discriminating power not only of our sight, but of all our senses. Hence, the charm of music, a tightly linked flux of harmonies, which we enjoy when listening to a symphony, results from the inability of our hearing to distinctly locate each vibration of each set of sound waves in time and space. Hence, the relative coarseness of the multiple senses regrouped under the label of touch also allows us to know neither the minute divisions nor the formidable swarming of the most miniscule components in the objects we manipulate. It is out of the shortcomings of our perceptions that all the false notions of matter without gaps, of a compact world, or of a full universe are born.

At all levels, continuity, whether visible, touchable, audible, or breathable, is merely a first and very superficial appearance which likely has its use, that is, its practical truth, but which also masks a subjacent organization of a discontinuous nature whose discovery has proved remarkably useful, and whose degree of reality can, and consequently must, be held as deeper for the same reasons.

Discontinuity, a Make-Believe Continuity

Where does this discontinuity, deemed more real, come from? For instance, in the cinematographic apparatus, where and how are the discontinuous images the viewer uses to create the film's subjective continuity recorded? These images are taken from the perpetually moving spectacle of the world—a spectacle that is fragmented and quickly cut into slices by the shutter that unmasks the lens, at each rotation, for only a third or a quarter of the time that rotation takes. This fraction of time is so short that the resulting photographs are as sharp as snapshots of still subjects. The discontinuity and immobility of cinematographic frames, considered in themselves, are thus a creation of the camera apparatus, a very inexact interpretation of the continuous and mobile aspect of nature—an aspect standing for actual reality.

While Humans, Through Their Senses, Are Organized to Perceive Discontinuity as If It Were Continuity, the Apparatus, on the Contrary, "Imagines" Continuity More Easily as Discontinuity

In such an instance, a mechanism proves to be endowed with its own subjectivity, since it does represent things the way they are perceived by the human gaze, but only by the way it sees them, with its particular structure, which then constitutes a personality. And the discontinuity of still images (still at least during the time of projection, in the intervals between their abrupt substitution), a discontinuity acting as a real foundation to the imaginary human content of the projected film as a whole, ends up, in turn, being but a ghost, conceived and thought-out by an apparatus.

First, the cinematograph showed us, in continuity, a subjective transfiguration of a truer discontinuity; then, the same cinematograph shows us, in discontinuity, an arbitrary interpretation of a primordial continuity. We can presume, therefore, that neither cinematographic continuity nor discontinuity truly exist, or, conversely, that continuity and discontinuity alternatively act as object and concept, their reality being merely a function through which one can substitute for the other.

Continuity: Reality of an Artificial Discontinuity?

The entire discontinuity of the currently accepted scientific doctrine is no less artificial and deceitful than the discontinuity and immobility of cinematographic frames. Bernard Shaw refused to believe in either electrons or angels, since he had never seen either. If seeing was enough, the existence of electrons could not be doubted since, indeed, we can see them today, and count and measure them. However, it is far from certain that they exist in a natural state, in the course of the evolution of phenomena. All that can be posited is that they show up as results—monstrous ones perhaps—under certain experimental conditions that infringe upon and disfigure nature.

If we isolate one image of an actor's performance in a film recording, it might show the tensed-up face of the hero, his mouth twisted, one eye closed and the other upturned in a grotesque expression. Yet, during both the shooting and the projection, the scene appears well acted, moving, and without the slightest trace of comedy. But the camera apparatus, by fragmenting the continuity of the gestures of a protagonist, cuts out a discontinuous image of the scene, which because of its very discontinuity, is false, and will regain its truth only when it reenters its original continuity during the projection.

In the same way, the powerful instruments used by physicists intrude within material, apparent or deep continuity, in order to cut it up into billions of pieces, and the result of this brutal surgery, of these firings and dismemberments, transmutations and explosions, are discontinuous aspects: atoms, protons, electrons, neutrons, photons, quanta of energy, etc., which perhaps, more than likely, did not exist before the destructive experiments on continuity. A spinthariscope, a cyclotron, or an electronic microscope extracts a few snapshots from out of the texture of the universe, transplanting them into space, fixing them in time—yet these winces of tortured nature have no more real signification than the happenstance of a comical expression attributed to the mask of a tragic actor.

We break a pane of glass, count its pieces, and proclaim: this pane of glass was composed of four triangular pieces, two rectangular ones and six pentagons, etc. This is the model of reasoning of all atomistics, indeed similar to that of Zeno. Nonetheless, it is clear that the pane of glass, before it splintered into pieces, was composed of no triangles, rectangles or pentagons, nor any other pieces, but was only the unity it constituted.

Reality: A Sum of Unrealities

Some analyses of light show it to have a granular, discontinuous structure. But it is impossible to demonstrate that this discontinuity existed prior to the investigative experiments that generated it, in the same manner that the camera apparatus invented a succession of pauses within the continuity of a movement. Other phenomena concerning light may be explained only if light is considered as an uninterrupted flux of waves, rather than a continuity of projectiles. Wave mechanics has not entirely succeeded in erasing this incomprehensible contradiction, by assuming that light rays have a double nature, immaterially continuous and materially discontinuous, formed of a corpuscle and a pilot wave, about which, all we can know is its mathematical formula, which determines the probabilities according to which the grain of light materializes here rather than there.

Confronted with an insoluble problem, an irreconcilable contradiction, we might do well to suspect that in fact, there is neither problem nor contradiction. The cinematograph instructs us that continuity and discontinuity, rest and movement, far from being two incompatible modes of reality, are two interchangeable modes of unreality, twin "ghosts of the mind" as Francis Bacon called them, seeking to purge knowledge at the cost of leaving nothing in it. Everywhere, sensible continuity and mathematical continuity, these ghosts of human intelligence, may substitute or be substituted for the discontinuity intercepted by machines—the ghost of mechanical intelligence. They are no more mutually exclusive than the colors of a disk and the whiteness that results when it spins. Continuity and discontinuity, rest and movement, color and whiteness, alternatively play the role of reality, which is here as elsewhere, never, nowhere, merely a function, as we will make clear later on.

II. Mechanical Philosophy

The Psychology of Machines

A driver who knows his car well speaks of it with the same terms a rider uses to speak of his horse. He calls is docile or reticent, soft or responsive, supple and reliable, or stubborn and touchy. He knows the best way to handle it to derive the maximum of efforts from it: at times he uses gentleness, at other times roughness; sometimes he gives it a rest, or lets it go and pushes it to the utmost, from the beginning to the end of a run. Two engines of the same brand and same series are rarely the same: each displays its own character through the particulars of its behavior. This is because the complexity of the inner structure and interactions of a mechanical organism leads to the individualization of the machine and impels, with regard to its overall working, a tinge of unpredictability which signals the very beginning of what we call, at varying degrees of development, freedom, will, or soul.

Depending on their complexity and subtlety, all instruments that require the attentive care of humans, so as to ensure their optimal use, acquire from this attention, albeit implicitly, certain psychological characteristics. And, as anyone can attest, it is a fact that a fountain pen becomes used to a certain penmanship with such attunement that it will not allow variation; a watch that faithfully kept time for twenty years in the father's pocket will stop working in a few days when handed down to his son, mindful as he may be, for even the watchmaker cannot restore the personal climate in which the mechanism has become accustomed to live.

Whether Mechanical or Organic, the Complexity of an Apparatus Creates Its Own Psychic Aspect

A cell is certainly a being, but a soul emerges only through a colony of cells, all the more clearly when the colony is constituted of numerous and better-differentiated elements within a cooperative whole of a higher organization. A spring, a cog, or a valve are only die-cast metal, but a community of gears and pistons, functionally assembled, displays tendencies, habits and whims that form a rudiment of mind—and this psychological aspect is all the more apparent when the mechanism has a complex structure and complex functions. At a certain degree of multiplicity and architectural and functional sophistication, machines routinely behave in such a way that humans, against their better judgment, must recognize a kind of habituation in them. It amounts to a convergence of sensibility and memory, and also implies some kind of choice and discernment about proper and improper working, that is to say, between good and evil, as well as some latitude, some fantasy—a trace of freedom by the system in response to the forces we impress upon it and within it. Hence the fundamental observation of Ribot who underlined the fact that the psyche emerges through the growth of the number of possible reactions among multiple nervous components, may be transposed into the inorganic world where it applies to the interplay of mechanical elements.

Linked to the Functioning of a Whole That We Cannot Easily Locate, the Spiritual Character is Foremost Ubiquitous

Seeking to recognize the slightest bit of spirit in a farm tractor might seem excessive. But, to begin with, what is spirit? We generally only agree upon what it seems not to be: it couldn't be material because we cannot exactly situate its insertion points in matter, nor can we fathom how it communicates with and commands matter. A good part of the human soul has been assigned residence in the brain, yet the heart, kidneys, liver, gallbladder and other still more mysterious organs have also claimed the honor of housing our invisible spirituality. The soul is everywhere in humans, and nowhere in particular. It results from the whole of organic function. Similarly, the personal character of a motor does not dwell exclusively in this or that part: carburetor or magneto, piston or cylinder head. This character is also an impalpable being, a global product of the activity of all mechanical organs.[1]

Much simpler figures also possess a characteristic aspect that we cannot connect to any of their parts, but to which the collaboration of all these parts is indispensable. Hence the essential virtue of a Euclidian triangle is that the sum of its angles equals two right angles. Where does the character of this species come from? Neither from one angle nor the other, nor from its sides or heights or surface: it is everywhere and nowhere, it is a spirit.

Beyond the Spirituality Common to All Superior Machines, the Cinematograph Develops Its Own Genius

Like any mechanism, and proportionally to its own degree of complexity, the cinematographic apparatus—in its multiplicity, comprising both camera and projector, sound recording and reproduction devices, and all their assemblies—possesses this personality that characterizes all superior objects, though in this case it might appear diffuse on account of the different contraptions through which it is implemented: thus it represents the collective personality of a small society of machines. However, beyond these characters of first individualization, a usual

[1] This is another convergence with Gilles Deleuze's thought, namely his notion of "the body-without-organs" in *A Thousand Plateaus*, trans. Brian Massumi (Minneapolis: University of Minnesota Press, 1987) .—*Trans.*

occurrence in the world of machines, the cinematograph displays its own genius loud and clear, of which no other mechanism has until now given such a pointed example.

Other systems born of the human mind, especially optical ones, have certainly reacted to it for a long time, allowing the human mind to reform and considerably develop its theories of the universe. Copernicus, Galileo, Kepler, Newton and Laplace were trained to rethink the world according to the images their astronomical telescopes delivered to them from the sky, in the same way that Spallanzani, Claude Bernard, and Pasteur were led to build or rebuild anatomy, physiology and pathology in accordance with the particular vision of their magnifying glasses and microscopes. Still, these enlarging lenses only multiply and transform—exclusively visual—uni-sensorial data that address only one category of the mind, optical extent [*étendue*]. Hence the modifications that these instruments propose to philosophical and scientific conceptions can only present themselves to intelligence by way of the spatial category in the same way as ordinary messages from a single sense, however important it may be: sight. For the researcher or the philosopher, a telescope can do nothing more than amplify the work of the external perception of an organ—an artificial super-eye that sees farther or closer or deeper, but does nothing else but look, unable as it is to mechanically combine data belonging to several rational categories. In other words, it cannot think.

The cinematograph differs from solely optical apparatuses firstly in that it gathers information pertaining to two distinct senses from the outside world, and secondly and foremost, in that, in and of itself, it presents this bi-sensorial data as arranged into specific rhythms of succession. The cinematograph is a witness that recounts a figure of sensible reality that is not only spatial but temporal, integrating its representations into an architecture whose relief presupposes the synthesis of two intellectual categories (extension and duration), a synthesis in which a third category emerges almost automatically: causation. Through this power of effective diverse combinations, the cinematograph, though it may be purely mechanical, proves to be more than an instrument of enlargement or replacement for one or several of the sense organs. Through this power, which is one of the fundamental characteristics of any intellectual activity among living beings, the cinematograph stands out as a substitute and annex of the organ in which the faculty that coordinates perceptions is generally located—the brain—the alleged center of intelligence.

No, the thinking machine is not exactly a utopia any longer; the cinematograph, like the computing machine, represents its first implementation, already working far better than a rough model. Leibniz, who obtained the notes and drafts left by Pascal, succeeded in working out the cog system that the Jansenist mathematician had invented without being able to make it function properly. Since then, evermore perfected, a purely mechanical device knows how to group the numbers it is provided in accordance with the fundamental algorithms of mathematics, not exactly in the same way the human mind does, but better, since it is errorless. Yet—one might object—this machine does not think. Then what is it actually doing when its work replaces the cerebral task of the calculator to perfection? We should recognize that a mechanical thinking exists alongside organic thought, and while it resembles organic thinking, we are only beginning to learn to activate this mechanical thinking that will expand in future robots and whose implementation is logically prescribed by the development of our civilization. This mechanical pre-thought would seem to be unconscious: but this presents an objection neither to its existence nor to its affiliation with the human soul, since today we agree that the latter is largely unknown to itself.[2]

The Philosophy of the Cinematograph

The cinematograph is among the still partially intellectual robots that, with two photo and electro-mechanical senses, as well as a photochemical recording memory, shapes representations—that is, thought—in which we discern the primordial framework of reason: the three categories of extension, duration, and causation. This would already be a remarkable result if cinematographic thought, as in the case of the calculating machine, were only mimicking human ideation. On the contrary, we know that the cinematograph inscribes its own character within its representations of the universe with such originality that it makes this representation not simply a record or copy of the conceptions of its organic mastermind [*mentalité-mère*], but indeed a differently individualized system, partly independent, comprising the seed of the development of a philosophy that strays far enough from common opinions so as to be called an antiphilosophy.

[2] The emphasis of Gilles Deleuze on the brain in the second volume of his two books on cinema, *The Time-Image*, is clearly beholden to Epstein. He cites Epstein's collected works (36 n.15) and refers directly to *The Mind of the Apparatus* (181). Gilles Deleuze, *Cinema 2: The Time-Image*, trans. Hugh Tomlinson and Robert Galeta (Minneapolis: University of Minnesota Press, 1989) .—*Trans.*

CHAPTER 7
BÉLA BALÁZS

Béla Balázs (1884–1949) was a German-Hungarian film theorist, librettist, screenwriter, and poet. He lived through a period of many and diverse technological developments in the arts, and made contributions across that diverse aesthetic spectrum—his participation in at least some of which was later elided in Germany because he was Jewish. Balázs spent much of the Second World War living in exile in the Soviet Union, because of his Marxist sympathies and his internationalist and cosmopolitan political views, views which sometimes appear even in his film theory and criticism. He is increasingly regarded as an important early voice in the development of film theory, screenwriting, and film technique. The selection included here is from his book, Theory of the Film: Character and Growth of a New Art, *originally published in Hungarian (*Filmkultúra [a film muveszetfilozofiaja]*) by Szikra Kiadas in 1948.*

This selection includes sections: "A New Form-Language," "Visual Culture," and "Der Sichtbare Mensch (The Visible Man)," the third of which is a lengthy quotation from an earlier book written by Balázs, Der Sichtbare Mensch, *published in German in 1924.*

In "A New Form-Language," Balázs describes the essential difference he observes in the early cinema between what he calls "photographed theater," and film art. While both appear as motion pictures and both use cinematographic technologies, photographed theater never breaks with the aesthetic conventions, principles, and rules of stage theater and thus, for Balázs, does not constitute a new art. Stage theater, he notes, adheres to three basic structural principles regarding the relationship between the spectator and the scene on stage: (1) the spectator always sees the whole space of the performance; (2) the spectator always sees the stage from a fixed distance; and (3) the spectator's angle of vision never changes. Most early cinema retains these structural elements, Balázs notes: even in cases when the distance between the camera and the objects or persons photographed changes from scene to scene, it remains constant within any given scene. This is different from the cinematic art, which is created (in Hollywood, by D. W. Griffith, according to Balázs) precisely by breaking with these three structural principles in light of the possibilities of the cinematographic technologies. Thus, in film understood as an independently creative art: (1) there is a varying distance between spectators (or the camera) and the scene, alternating over the course of a single scene between long and medium shots and close-ups; (2) there is a division of scenes into shots, such that the perspective of the camera shifts regularly depending upon the action; (3) camera angles can change frequently within scenes; and (4) there is the introduction—impossible on the stage—of montage, which Balázs compares to a mosaic of images. These are importantly stylistic innovations, not technological ones, despite the fact that they are only occasioned by developments within photographic and cinematographic technologies—as the fact of "photographed theatre" demonstrates. And these stylistic innovations can give spectators a new kind of access to the characters being performed for us in film art. This is especially clear in the case of the close-up, which allows the spectator access to the intimate secrets of the characters in a film without losing the intimacy and secrecy retained by the character (on the stage, such revelations of inner experience would require either broad gestural demonstrations or expository dialogue, both of which destroy the sense of the character having a private moment). Moreover, changing camera angles and camera positions (as well as camera movement) enable the film director not only to direct the actors and crew, but to direct the order and manner in which the spectators view the elements constituting the film. Ultimately, this means that every work of film art is already an interpretation.

In "Visual Culture," Balázs argues that every new art requires the development of new human faculties: that is, for an art to be truly new, it must demand of its spectators that they perceive and understand the art in a new way, unlike the ways in which they have perceived and understood earlier arts. Silent film, in both the absence of speech to sustain (and explain) the narrative and in its resultant reliance upon gesture, facial expression, cinematographic framing, and film editing, required a new way of viewing to be developed by film spectators. Balázs gives here a number of examples of individuals unfamiliar with film going to see a movie, only to discover that they were incapable of understanding what was happening therein. We have learned, as individuals and as a culture, to integrate the fragmented shots that make up a film into a coherent scene, and thus are able without any obvious effort at all to understand the relationship between the long shot of an actor and the close-up of the actor's face (whereas the Siberian girl Balázs mentions cannot help but see the movement from long shot to close-up as a sort of dismemberment, and she is horrified). More generally, Balázs argues that there is no real development within the art itself—once we've made the transition to film as an independent art medium, films remain what films have always been—but there is much potential for development in spectators' ways of viewing. As such, new techniques and technological advances do not make for great art, but they can occasion developments in the viewing culture which greaten the experience of the art for the spectator.

Finally, in "Der Sichtbare Mensch," Balázs continues with the notion that silent film created new possibilities for viewership, re-creating visual culture. In a brief introduction to this selection from his earlier work, he notes that much has changed in the cinema in the intervening time (between 1923 and 1948), most notably the advent of sound films. He admits he did not expect sound film so quickly and completely to overtake silent film, such that, by the 1940s, very few silent films were still being made. All the same, he argues that there is still something more than merely historically valuable about the earlier work, and proceeds to offer a lengthy selection from that book.

Balázs begins the section by noting that the invention of the printing press and the popularization of the printed book had the effect of making facial expressions illegible. He cites Victor Hugo's claim that the printed book has replaced the cathedral as the "carrier of the spirit of the people," adding that if it has done so, the printed book has also made possible a proliferation of opinions—such that the spirit of the people of such interest to Hugo has been fragmented into innumerable pieces. This widespread dissolution of what was once an unified aesthetic culture into a widely diverse culture of opinions and ideas—occasioned by the dominance of the printed word over other art media—created a culture of words and concepts which replaced the prior, visual culture of painting and sculpture (and, following Hugo, architecture). In such a conceptual culture, self-expression seems to be something most appropriately, completely, and authentically conducted by way of rational concepts communicated in language, and to the extent that culture has focused on words, individuals within the culture have lost much of the ability to express themselves, and understand the expressions of others, visually.

*The cinematographic camera, then, Balázs argues, reintroduces into a conceptual culture of the printed book the possibility of a new visual culture: as Balázs poetically puts it, the cinematographic camera gives us "new faces." The silence of the silent film makes linguistic expression impossible, or at the very least extremely unwieldy (intertitles can only do so much). Silent film requires of filmmakers (or, at least, film actors) that they learn to express themselves in gestures and facial expressions, and it requires of film spectators that they learn to understand this new mode of expression. Of course, silent gestures do not—*cannot*—express rational concepts; for that, you need words. Silent film can thus only express nonrational emotions and the inner experiences of the characters on screen. That this is not conceptual expression, however, does not make it inexpressive or incomplete, and Balázs compares the expressivity of the silent gestures in film to the expressivity of music, also nonconceptual and nonrational but not, for that reason, nonexpressive.*

Before the printed book, of course, painters and sculptors were able to create works of art without feeling the necessity of tying their creations to concepts. There was a visual culture that preceded the book; after the invention of the printed book, of course, painting and sculpture did not disappear, but they did become more conceptually and less visually expressive. When words replaced images as human beings' primary mode of self-expression, Balázs notes, human bodies lost their capacity for expression—they became "soulless and empty." When the soul learned to speak, the self became almost invisible. But in silent film, words recede, and with words, concepts. Silent film requires and enables humanity to become visible again. Expressive movement is more primitive than the spoken conceptual discourse, and it is both nonrational and nonconceptual. This does not, however, make it unclear. That silent, bodily expression that strikes modern audiences sometimes as ambiguous or unclear is the result, Balázs seems to say, of the loss of visual culture to conceptual culture. To the extent that film allows us to recapture the visual as a mode of self-expression, our ability to understand bodily gesture and facial expression will increase. Our thoughts and feelings are determined, at least in part, by the possibility of expressing them. As silent film increases our ability to express ourselves visually, so film can widen the human spirit itself.

THEORY OF THE FILM

Translated by Edith Bone

A New Form-Language

If the film had from its infancy produced specific new subjects, new characters, a new style, even a new art form, why then do I say that it was not yet a new art, but merely a photographic copy of a stage performance? When and how did cinematography turn into a specific independent art employing methods sharply differing from those of the theatre and using a totally different form-language? What is the difference between photographed theatre and film art? Both being equally motion pictures projected on to a screen, why do I say that the one is only a technical reproduction and the other an independently creative art?

The basic formal principle of the theatre is that the spectator sees the enacted scene as a whole in space, always seeing the whole of the space. Sometimes the stage presents only one corner of a larger hall, but that corner is always totally visible all through the scene in question, and everything that happens in it is seen within one and the same frame.

The second basic formal principle of the theatre is that the spectator always sees the stage from a fixed unchanging distance. True, the photographed theatre already began to photograph different scenes from different distances, but within one and the same scene the distance was never changed.

The third basic formal principle of the theatre is that the spectator's angle of vision does not change. The photographed theatre did change the perspective sometimes from scene to scene, but within one and the same scene the perspective never changed, any more than the distance.

These three basic formal principles of the stage are of course interconnected, they form the groundwork of dramatic style and means of expression. In this connection it makes no difference whether we see the scenes on the living stage or in photographic reproduction; nor does it matter whether the scenes presented are such as could not be shown on the stage at all, but only in the open air and by means of photographic technique.

It was these three basic principles of theatrical art that were discarded by the art of the film—it begins where the three principles no longer apply and are supplanted by new methods. These are:

1. Varying distance between spectator and scene within one and the same scene; hence varying dimensions of scenes that can be accommodated within the frame and composition of a picture.
2. Division of the integral picture of the scene into sections, or "shots."
3. Changing angle, perspective and focus of "shots" within one and the same scene.
4. Montage, that is the assembly of "shots" in a certain order in which not only whole scene follows whole scene (however short) but pictures of smallest details are given, so that the whole scene is composed of a mosaic of frames aligned as it were in chronological sequence.

This revolutionary innovation in visual artistic expression came about in the United States of America, in Hollywood, during the first world war. David Griffith was the name of the genius to whom we owe it. He not only created masterpieces of art, but an art that was totally new.

One of the specific characteristics of the art of the film is that not only can we see, in the isolated "shots" of a scene, the very atoms of life and their innermost secrets revealed at close quarters, but we can do so without any of the intimate secrecy being lost, as always happens in the exposure of a stage performance or of a painting. The new theme which the new means of expression of film art revealed was not a hurricane at sea or the eruption of a volcano: it was perhaps a solitary tear slowly welling up in the corner of a human eye.

A good film director does not permit the spectator to look at a scene at random. He leads our eye inexorably from detail to detail along the line of his montage. By means of such a sequence the director is enabled to place emphasis where he sees fit, and thus not only show but at the same time interpret the picture. It is in this that the individual creativeness of a film-maker chiefly manifests itself. Two films in which story and acting are exactly the same, but which are differently cut, may be the expression of two totally different personalities and present two totally different images of the world.

Visual Culture

The birth of film art led not only to the creation of new works of art but to the emergence of new human faculties with which to perceive and understand this new art.

It is a great pity that the scholars dealing with the arts have up to now concerned themselves chiefly with already existing works of art and not at all with the subjective faculties which, created through a dialectical interaction, enable us to see and appreciate the newly-emerging beautiful things. Although objective reality is independent of the subject and his subjective consciousness, beauty is not merely objective reality, not an attribute of the object entirely independent of the spectator, not something that would be there objectively even without a corresponding subject, even if there were no human beings on earth. For beauty is what we like—we know of no other beauty—and this human experience is not something independent, but a function changing with races, epochs and cultures. Beauty is a subjective experience of human consciousness brought about by objective reality; it has its own laws, but those laws are the universal laws of consciousness and to that extent of course not purely subjective.

The philosophy of art has in the past devoted little attention to the subject, the carrier of an artistic culture, whose sensibility and receptivity not only develop under the influence of the arts, but may actually be created by them. What is required is not merely a history of art but a history of art running to and linked with a history of mankind.

It is the purpose of this book to investigate and outline that sphere of the development of human sensibility which developed in mutual interaction with the evolution of the art of the film.

Film Culture

The evolution of the human capacity for understanding which was brought about by the art of the film, opened a new chapter in the history of human culture. Just as musical hearing and musical understanding develop under the influence of music, so the development of the material richness of film art leads to a parallel development of film vision and film appreciation. The forms of expression of the silent film developed gradually, but the rate of development was fast enough and together with it the public developed the ability to understand the new form-language. We were witnesses not only of the development of a new art but of the development of a new sensibility, a new understanding, a new culture in its public.

The Colonial Englishman

There is a story about an English colonial administrator, who, during the first world war and for some time after it, lived in a backward community. He regularly received newspapers and periodicals from home, thus knew of films, and had seen pictures of the stars and had read film reviews and film stories; but he had never seen a motion picture. As soon as he reached a place where there was a cinema, he went to see a film. A number of children around him seemed to enjoy it very much, but he was completely baffled by what he saw and was quite exhausted when at last the film came to an end.

> "Well, how did you like it?" asked a friend.
>
> "It was very interesting," he said, "but what was it all about?"

He had not understood what was going on, because he did not understand the form-language in which the story of the film was told, a form-language every town-dweller already knew at that time.

The Siberian Girl

This story was told to me by a friend in Moscow. A cousin had arrived on a visit from a Siberian collective farm—an intelligent girl, with a good education, but who had never seen a motion picture (this of course was many years ago). The Moscow cousins took her to the cinema and having other plans, left her there by herself. The film was a burlesque. The Siberian cousin came home pale and grim. "Well, how did you like the film?" the cousins asked her. She could scarcely be induced to answer, so overwhelmed was she by the sights she had seen. At last she said: "Oh, it was horrible, horrible! I can't understand why they allow such dreadful things to be shown here in Moscow!"

> "Why, what was so horrible then?"
>
> "Human beings were torn to pieces and the heads thrown one way and the bodies the other and the hands somewhere else again."

We know that when Griffith first showed a big close-up in a Hollywood cinema and a huge "severed" head smiled at the public for the first time, there was a panic in the cinema. We ourselves no longer know by what intricate evolution of our consciousness we have learnt our visual association of ideas. What we have learnt is to integrate single disjointed pictures into a coherent scene, without even becoming conscious of the complicated psychological process involved. It is amazing to what extent we have, in a couple of decades, learnt to see picture perspectives, picture metaphors and picture symbols, how greatly we have developed our visual culture and sensibility.

We Have Learned to See

Thus the new technique of the film camera produced a new way of presentation and a new way of telling a story. The new picture language was developed, polished and differentiated to an incredible degree in the course of some twenty years. We can almost measure this process by harking back twenty years, when we ourselves would probably not have understood films which are quite obvious to spectators to-day. Here is an instance. A man hurries to a railway station to take leave of his beloved. We see him on the platform. We cannot see the train, but the questing eyes of the man show us that his beloved is already seated in the train. We see only a close-up of the man's face, we see it twitch as if startled and then strips of light and shadow, light and shadow flit across it in quickening rhythm. Then tears gather in the eyes and that ends the scene. We are expected to know what happened and to-day we do know, but when I first saw this film in Berlin, I did not at once understand the end of this scene. Soon, however, everyone knew what had happened: the train had started and it was the lamps in its compartment which had thrown their light on the man's face as they glided past ever faster and faster.

Another example. A man is sitting in a dark room in gloomy meditation. The spectator knows from the previous scene that a woman is in the next room. We see a close-up of the man's face. Suddenly a light falls on it from one side. The man raises his head and looks towards the light with an expression of hopeful expectation. Then the light fades from his face and with it the expression of hope. He lowers his head in disappointment. Complete darkness falls slowly. It is the last shot of a tragic scene. No more is needed. What happened here? Every picture-goer knows and understands this language now. What happened was that the door of the next room opened for a moment, the woman came to the threshold of the lighted room, hesitated, but turned back and closed the door for ever. Even this "for ever" could be felt in the slow and complete darkening of the picture. Precisely the fact that no more was shown stimulated our imagination and induced the right mood in us. Therein lay its subtlety.

Why Are Old Films Funny?

To-day we understand not only the situation presented in a picture but every shade of its significance and symbolic implications. The rapidity of our evolution towards this new understanding can be measured by looking at old films. We laugh aloud, especially at the grimmest tragedies, and can scarcely believe that such antics could be taken seriously a mere twenty years ago. What is the reason for this? Other old works of art do not appear funny to us and we rarely feel like laughing even at the most naïve and primitive art.

The reason is that old art usually expresses the mentality of a bygone age in adequate form. But what we see in a film we relate to our own selves, it is not yet "history" and we laugh at our own recent selves. It is not yet a historical costume that can be beautiful and dignified, however strange it may be—it is merely the fashion of the last year but one which strikes us as comic.

Primitive art is the adequate expression of primitive taste and skill. The primitiveness of old films gives the impression of grotesque impotence. A spear in the hand of a naked savage is not as comic as a pike in the hands of a Home Guard. While a fifteenth-century Portuguese sailing-ship is a lovely sight, the early steam-engines and motor-cars are ridiculous because we see in them not something quite different, something no longer existent, but recognize a ridiculous, imperfect form of what is still in use to-day. We laugh at it as we laugh at the antics in the monkey-house—because the monkeys are like ourselves.

For the culture of the film has developed so rapidly that we still recognize our own selves in its clumsy primitiveness. It is for this reason that this culture is of so great an importance for us, this art which is accessible to millions of ordinary people.

Art Does Not Develop

We should realize that, while art has a history, it has no development in the sense of growth or increase in aesthetic values. We do not consider the paintings of Renoir or Monet more precious or perfect than those of Cimabue or Giotto. There is no development in the objective side of art but there is development on the part of those who enjoy art or are connoisseurs of art. Artistic *culture* has not only a history, it also has an evolution in a certain direction. Subjective human sensibility, the faculty of understanding and interpreting art, has demonstrably developed in continuous cultures, and when we speak of a development of subjective human faculties, we do not mean the development of aesthetic values. For instance the discovery and application of perspective in art did not in itself imply an increase in artistic values. The rules of perspective are learned in school to-day by every ungifted dauber, but that does not make him a greater artist than Giotto, who knew nothing of these rules. The former will not be a greater artist, but his visual sensibility, his culture will be on a higher level. The discovery of the rules of perspective drawing played a much greater part in the evolution of general human culture than in the evolution of art. It enriched the culture of the eye far more than that of painting. It did of course pervade the routine of painting, but it is much more important that it has come to be an indispensable element in the everyday life of civilized man.

Der Sichtbare Mensch (The Visible Man)

This chapter which deals with the visual culture developed through the silent film is taken from my book *Der sichtbare Mensch*. In it I hailed the silent film as a turning-point in our cultural history, not suspecting that the sound film would soon come to oust it. The truth which stated a then existing reality has remained true, but the reality it dealt with has bolted like a runaway horse and has made new observations and interpretations necessary. Nevertheless, this chapter may be of interest not merely as a chapter in the history of film theory. Nor does it perhaps retain its interest only because the picture still remains the essence of the film and its visual content. Lines of development are never rigidly set. They often proceed in a roundabout way, throwing the light of old knowledge on to new paths through dialectical interaction. Because I believe that we have now come to such a doubling back in the development of the film, when the already once accomplished and then again lost achievements of the silent film are about to be revalued and restored, I want to quote here what I wrote in 1923 about the silent film:

***

The discovery of printing gradually rendered illegible the faces of men. So much could be read from paper that the method of conveying meaning by facial expression fell into desuetude.

Victor Hugo wrote once that the printed book took over the part played by the cathedral in the Middle Ages and became the carrier of the spirit of the people. But the thousands of books tore the *one* spirit, embodied in the cathedral, into thousands of opinions. The word broke the stone into a thousand fragments, tore the church into a thousand books.

The visual spirit was thus turned into a legible spirit and visual culture into a culture of concepts. This of course had its social and economic causes, which changed the general face of life. But we paid little attention to the fact that, in conformity with this, the face of individual men, their foreheads, their eyes, their mouths, had also of necessity and quite concretely to suffer a change.

At present a new discovery, a new machine, is at work to turn the attention of men back to a visual culture and given them new faces. This machine is the cinematographic camera. Like the printing press, it is a technical device for the multiplication and distribution of products of the human spirit; its effect on human culture will not be less than that of the printing press.

For not to speak does not mean that one has nothing to say. Those who do not speak may be brimming over with emotions which can be expressed only in forms and pictures, in gesture and play of feature. The man of visual culture uses these not as substitutes for words, as a deaf-mute uses his fingers. He does not think in words, the syllables of which he sketches in the air like the dots and dashes of the Morse code. The gestures of visual man are not intended to convey concepts which can be expressed in words, but such inner experiences, such non-rational emotions which would still remain unexpressed when everything that can be told has been told. Such emotions lie in the deepest levels of the soul and cannot be approached by words that are mere reflexions of concepts; just as our musical experiences cannot be expressed in rationalized concepts. What appears on the face and in facial expression is a spiritual experience which is rendered immediately visible without the intermediary of words.

In the golden age of the old visual arts, the painter and sculptor did not merely fill empty space with abstract shapes and forms, and man was not merely a formal problem for the artist. Painters could paint the spirit and the soul without becoming "literary," for the soul and the spirit had not yet been confined in concepts capable of expression only by means of words; they could be incarnated without residue. That was the happy time when paintings could still have a "theme" and an "idea," for the idea had not yet been tied to the concept and to the word that named the concept. The artist could present in its primary form of manifestation the soul's bodily incarnation in gesture or feature. But since then the printing press has grown to be the main bridge over which the more remote interhuman spiritual exchanges take place and the soul has been concentrated and crystallized chiefly in the word. There was no longer any need for the subtler means of expression provided by the body. For this reason our bodies grew soulless and empty—what is not in use, deteriorates.

The expressive surface of our body was thus reduced to the face alone and this not merely because the rest of the body was hidden by clothes. For the poor remnants of bodily expression that remained to us the little surface of the face sufficed, sticking up like a clumsy semaphore of the soul and signaling as best it could. Sometimes a gesture of the hand was added, recalling the melancholy of a mutilated torso. In the epoch of word culture the soul learnt to speak but had grown almost invisible. Such was the effect of the printing press.

Now the film is about to inaugurate a new direction in our culture. Many million people sit in the picture houses every evening and purely through vision, experience happenings, characters, emotions, moods, even thoughts, without the need for many words. For words do not touch the spiritual content of the pictures and are merely passing instruments of as yet undeveloped forms of art. Humanity is already learning the rich and colorful language of gesture, movement and facial expression. This is not a language of signs as a substitute for words, like the sign-language of the deaf-and-dumb—it is the visual means of communication, without intermediary of souls clothed in flesh. Man has again become visible.

Linguistic research has found that the origins of language lie in expressive movement, that is, that man when he began to speak moved his tongue and lips to no greater extent than the other muscles of his face and body—just as an infant does to-day. Originally the purpose was not the making of sounds. The movement of tongue and lips was at first the same spontaneous gesturing as every other expressive movement of the body. That the former produced sounds was a secondary, adventitious phenomenon, which was only later used for practical purposes. The immediately visible message was thus turned into an immediately audible message. In the course of this process, as in every translation, a great deal was lost. It is the expressive movement, the gesture, that is the aboriginal mother-tongue of the human race.

Now we are beginning to remember and re-learn this tongue. It is still clumsy and primitive and very far removed as yet from the refinements of word art. But already it is beginning to be able sometime to express things which escape the artists of the word. How much of human thought would remain unexpressed if we had no music! The now developing art of facial expression and gesture will bring just as many submerged contents to the surface. Although these human experiences are not rational, conceptual contents, they are nevertheless neither vague nor blurred, but as clear and unequivocal as is music. Thus the inner man, too, will become visible.

But the old visible man no longer exists to-day and the new visible man is not yet in existence. As I have said before, it is the law of nature that unused organs degenerate and disappear, leaving only rudiments behind. The animals that do not chew lose their teeth. In the epoch of word culture we made little use of the expressive powers of our body and have therefore partly lost that power. The gesturing of primitive peoples is frequently more varied and expressive than that of the educated European whose vocabulary is infinitely richer. A few more years of film art and our scholars will discover that cinematography enables them to compile encyclopedias of facial expression, movement and gesture, such as have long existed for words in the shape of dictionaries. The public, however, need not wait for the gesture encyclopedia and grammars of future academies: it can go to the pictures and learn it there.

We had, however, when we neglected the body as a means of expression, lost more than mere corporal power of expression. That which was to have been expressed was also narrowed down by this neglect. For it is not the same spirit, not the same soul that is expressed once in words and once in gestures. Music does not express the same thing as poetry in a different way—it expresses something quite different. When we dip the bucket of words in the depths, we bring up other things than when we do the same with gestures. But let no one think that I want to bring back the culture of movement and gesture in place of the culture of words, for neither can be a substitute for the other. Without a rational, conceptual culture and the scientific development that goes with it there can be no social and hence no human progress. The connecting tissue of modern society is the word spoken and written, without which all organization and planning would be impossible. On the other hand fascism has shown us where the tendency to reduce human culture to subconscious emotions in place of clear concepts would lead humanity.

What I am talking about is only art and even here there is no question of displacing the more rational art of the word. There is no reason why we should renounce one sort of human achievement in favor of another. Even the most highly developed musical culture need not crowd out some more rational aspect of culture.

But to return to the simile of the bucket: we know that the wells that dry up are the wells from which no water is dipped. Psychology and philology have shown that our thoughts and feelings are determined *a priori* by the possibility of expressing them. Philology is also aware that it is not only concepts and feelings that create words, but that it is also the other way round: words give rise to concepts and feelings. This is a form of economy practiced by our mental constitution which desires to produce unusable things just as little as does our physical organism. Psychological and logical analysis has shown that words are not merely images expressing our thoughts and feelings but in most cases their *a priori* limiting forms. This is at the root of the danger of stereotyped banality which so often threatens the educated. Here again the evolution of the human spirit is a dialectical process. Its development increases its means of expression and the increase of means of expression in its turn facilitates and accelerates its development. Thus if then the film increases the possibilities of expression, it will also widen the spirit it can express.

Will this newly developing language of facial expression and expressive gesture bring human beings closer to each other or the contrary? Despite the tower of Babel there were concepts common to all behind the different words and one could also learn the languages of others. Concepts on the other hands, have, in civilized communities, a content determined by convention. A universally valid grammar was an even more potent unifying principle holding together the individuals who in bourgeois society were prone to become estranged and isolated from each other. Even the literature of extreme subjectivism used the common vocabulary and was thus preserved from the loneliness of final misunderstanding.

But the language of the gestures is far more individual and personal than the language of words, although facial expression, too, has its habitual forms and conventionally accepted interpretations, to such an extent that one might—and should—write a comparative "gesturology" on the model of comparative linguistics. Nevertheless this language of facial expression and gesture, although it has a certain generally accepted tradition, lacks the severe rules that govern grammar and by the grace of our academies are compulsory for us all. No school prescribes that you must express your cheerfulness by this sort of smile and your bad humor with that sort of wrinkled brow. There are no punishable errors in this or that facial expression, although children doubtless do observe and imitate such conventional grimaces and gestures. On the other hand, these are more immediately induced by inner impulses than are words. Yet it will probably be the art of the film after all which may bring together the peoples and nations, make them accustomed to each other, and lead them to mutual understanding. The silent film is free of the isolating walls of language differences. If we look at and understand each other's faces and gestures, we not only understand, we also learn to feel each other's emotions. The gesture is not only the outward projection of emotion, it is also its initiator.

The universality of the film is primarily due to economic causes—which are always the most compelling causes. The making of a film is so expensive that only very few nations have a home market sufficient to make film production pay. But one of the preconditions of the international popularity of any film is the universal comprehensibility of facial expression and gesture. Specific national characteristics will in time be permissible only as exotic curiosities and a certain leveling of "gesturology" will be inevitable. The laws of the film market permit only universally comprehensible facial expressions and gestures, every nuance of which is understood by princess and working girl alike from San Francisco to Smyrna. We now already have a situation in which the film speaks the only universal, common world language understood by all. Ethnic peculiarities, national specialities sometimes can lend style and color to a film, but can never become factors in causing the story to move on, because the gestures which convey the meaning and decide the course of the action must be uniformly comprehensible to every audience everywhere, otherwise the producer will lose money on the film.

The silent film helped people to become physically accustomed to each other and was about to create an international human type. When once a common cause will have united men within the limits of their own race and nation, then the film which makes visible man equally visible to everyone, will greatly aid in leveling physical differences between the various races and nations and will thus be one of the most useful pioneers in the development towards an international universal humanity.

CHAPTER 8
ROLAND BARTHES

Roland Barthes (1915–1980) was a French philosopher, literary theorist, and semiotician. He is well known for his wide-ranging interests in a variety of fields and methodologies, as well as his foundational work in semiology, structuralism, and post-structuralism. As a critic and theorist of culture—including popular culture—Barthes has much to say about the cinema. The reading included here is a set of three essays from his groundbreaking book, Mythologies, *a collection of essays written between 1954 and 1956, published in French by Éditions du Seuil in 1957.*

*The three essays included here are "Romans in the Movies," "Garbo's Face," and "*Lost Continent.*" Each of them begins with consideration of at least one aspect of one film (*Julius Caesar, Queen Christina, *and* Lost Continent, *respectively), and through analysis of signification therein, offers some more general conclusions about the nature of cinema.*

In "Romans in the Movies," Barthes gives serious consideration to the hairstyles given to the actors playing Romans in Joseph L. Mankiewicz's 1953 film, Julius Caesar. *All the men in the film, Barthes notes, wear bangs—different styles of bangs, to be sure, but always bangs. There are no bald men presented in the movie, despite the fact that there were bald Romans, and there is no diversity at all with regard to this one aspect of men's coiffure. Bangs are, in the film, the sign of Roman-ness; to wear them is to be marked as Roman in the film. As such, the actors can have any sort of appearance otherwise—they can be phenotypically non-Roman—and can speak any language or engage in any sort of activity: so long as they wear bangs, they are Romans. For a Frenchman, Barthes observes, this is somewhat ridiculous, as the cast is almost entirely American, and from the perspective of the Frenchman, according to Barthes, Americans still have an identifiable look. Thus, the fact that despite their overt non-Roman-ness the actors are presented as Romans by virtue of their bangs alone makes the significatory intention of the hairstyles transparent to French audiences, and thus laughable. (The only exception to this ridiculousness, Barthes says, is Marlon Brando.)*

In addition to hair, another sign exists in the film: sweat. Almost every character is sweating all the time throughout the film (Barthes suggests the effect is achieved with vaseline), and in the film, sweat is the sign of morality. Specifically, Barthes notes that most of the characters in Julius Caesar *are engaged in an internal struggle (over the assassination of Caesar, specifically), and we see that they are not motivated by hatred or bloodthirstiness precisely by the fact that it is difficult for them to justify to themselves this murder. To sweat is to think, Barthes says, and every character who is privy to the assassination plot is made to appear quite sweaty. The only character who doesn't sweat in the entire film is Caesar himself, for the obvious reason that he is the only one unaware of the plan to kill him. He does not think, does not engage in this internal dialogue, and as such, he does not sweat.*

From the use of these signs (bangs and sweat) in this film, Barthes concludes that we can learn something about the morality of the sign. He argues that a sign should always be either thoroughly intellectual and algebraic (such as the equivalence of a single flag with a whole regiment in Chinese theater), or deeply rooted in a secret inwardness, as (Barthes says) in the art of Konstantin Stanislavsky. What ought to be impermissible is the intermediary sign—such as the bangs and the sweat in Julius Caesar*—which takes on the character of a "degraded spectacle." Such signs confuse sign and signified, such that it is merely by the application of vaseline-sweat or a wig with bangs (rather than in performance, or in the aesthetic structure of the film) that the appearance of thought or Roman-ness is believed to be able to be achieved.*

In the second essay included here, "Garbo's Face," Barthes takes on one of the icons of the early American cinema, Greta Garbo. In particular, Barthes is interested in images of Garbo's face in close-up, presented almost as an object isolated from both the films in which she appeared as well as the rest of Garbo's person. Barthes notes that Garbo is from a different era, one in which, he asserts, faces signified more. In particular, he is fascinated with the presentation of Garbo's face in the film Queen Christina*, in which, Barthes notes, Garbo wears such heavy makeup that her face appears almost mask-like—the skin so white (and the makeup so heavy) that her face seems almost to be sculpted, or made of plaster. In this white face, Garbo's darkened eyes take on an extraordinary darkness, and vitality, in contrast to the paleness—a contrast he also notes is characteristic of Chaplin. But pursuing this image further, of the heavily made-up (and thus largely immobilized) face on screen, Barthes suggests that in* Queen Christina *(and other of Garbo's films), there is the temptation to transform her face into a mask: to make of Garbo's face not just one face, not just any face, but the very archetype of the human face. In this way, Barthes says that Garbo's face is in a way the Platonic Form of the human itself, and as such (and in* Queen Christina*, thanks in part to her character's cross-dressing), virtually sexless. Garbo's face, despite the fact that it is so exceptionally iconic, comes close to lacking any particularity at all.*

Garbo's face represents the moment in the history of cinema when cinema begins to move away from what Barthes calls "the Essential" (the actor as attempting to present the ideal, universal, and abstract) to "the Existential" (in which the actor attempts to present a real, particular, concrete individuality). Garbo's face remains very close to the Essential end of the spectrum; we can see a movement toward the Existential in the expressiveness of her eyes, but the mask-like impression her face gives in general is something very much like the idea of a face. Barthes suggests that a fitting contrast to Garbo's face in the cinema of the 1950s is the face of Audrey Hepburn, which is decidedly on the side of the Existential. Hepburn's face is full of idiosyncrasies and particularities which one could not include in any attempt at creating an archetypal Face. Or, as Barthes puts it, Garbo's face was an Idea; Hepburn's face was an Event.

Finally, in "Lost Continent," *Barthes turns his attention to the Italian documentary film,* Lost Continent, *from 1955. The film attempts a cinematic ethnological study of parts of Southeast Asia, and although the film is a documentary, Barthes argues that it is in an important sense false: it is, he argues, altogether too easy, too thoughtless, too naïve.* Lost Continent *gives no thought, he says, to the many historical or sociological issues surrounding ethnology—and especially surrounding European attempts to understand Asia. In addition, the film saturates the images in color. In this essay, Barthes argues that "to color the world" is always in some way to deny it. Between the film's easy thoughtlessness and its coloration of "the East," it presents a picture of Asia and Asians that is altogether too familiar in the West: of a culture that is formally exotic but is ultimately "really" very much like the West. It does this in particular, Barthes notes, in its treatment of Buddhism as simply an Eastern form of Christianity, eliding the meaningful differences between the two religious traditions in favor of the idea that all religions are basically the same.*

In addition, the depictions of fishermen and refugees in Lost Continent *present them as "essences," not as real, historically situated individuals, which is to say that the film presents the fishermen it presents merely as ciphers for the very basic, transcultural idea of "The Fisherman," and presents the refugees it presents as the natural product of "the East." Ultimately, Barthes charges* Lost Continent *with employing and encouraging a particularly dangerous exoticism with regard to Asia (an exoticism that leads directly to the sort of cultural imperialism Edward Said and others have called "Orientalism"). He concludes that the exoticism of* Lost Continent *and other comparable films and cultural products denies all situation to history, effectively denying the particularity, concreteness, and reality of Eastern cultures and people in favor of an easy Western stereotype. Ironically, Barthes notes,* Lost Continent *misses precisely what it ostensibly sets out to discover: it loses the continent it had hoped to find, traveling all the way from Europe to Asia only to repeat for its spectators the same myth of "the East" they had accepted all along.*

Filmography

- ***Queen Christina*** (USA, 1933). *Directed by* Rouben Mamoulian. *Produced by* Walter Wanger. *Written by* S. N. Behrman *and* Ben Hecht. *Starring* Greta Garbo *and* John Gilbert.
- ***Julius Caesar*** (USA, 1953). *Directed and Written by* Joseph L. Mankiewicz. *Produced by* John Houseman. *Starring* Marlon Brando, James Mason, John Gielgud, Louis Calhern, Edmond O'Brien, Greer Garson, *and* Deborah Kerr.
- ***Continente Perduto*** [*Lost Continent*] (Italy, 1955). *Directed by* Enrico Gras, Giorgio Moser, *and* Leonardo Bonzi. *Produced by* Leonardo Bonzi. *Written by* Mario Craveri *and* Enrico Gras.

ROMANS IN THE MOVIES

Translated by Richard Howard

In Mankiewicz's *Julius Caesar*, all the male characters wear bangs. Some (bangs, not characters) are curly, some straight, others tufted, still others pomaded, all are neatly combed, and bald men are not allowed, though Roman History has a good number to its credit. Those with scant hair don't get off so easily, and the hairdresser, the film's principal artisan, always manages one last lock which joins the frieze along the top of the forehead—of those Roman foreheads whose exiguity has ever indicated a specific mixture of power, of virtue, and of conquest.

What can it be which is attached to these persistent fringes? Quite simply, the announcement of Romanity. So that we see the Spectacle's mainspring exposed here: the *sign*. These frontal locks flood us with evidence, henceforth there can be no doubt we are in Ancient Rome. And this certitude is continuous: the actors speak, act, torment themselves, struggle with "universal" questions without ever losing, thanks to this little flag spread across their foreheads, their historical verisimilitude: their generality can even expand, quite safely, across the Ocean and down through the ages, merging with the Yankee lineaments of the Hollywood extras: no matter, everyone is reassured, installed in the tranquil certainty of an unequivocal universe where Romans are Roman by the most legible of signs, that bit of toupee over the forehead.

A Frenchman, to whose eyes American faces still retain something exotic, finds comical the mixture of these gangster-sheriffs with the little Roman fringe: rather like an excellent music-hall gag. It's because for us the sign functions to excess, discrediting itself by letting its purpose show. But that same fringe produced on the one naturally Latin forehead in the whole film, Marlon Brando's, "works" for us without earning a laugh, and it's not unlikely that a share of this actor's success is due to the perfect integration of Roman capillarity with the general morphology of the character. Conversely, Julius Caesar is incredible, with his Anglo-Saxon lawyer's phiz already familiarized by a thousand bit parts in thrillers and comedies, his compliant skull carefully raked by a stylist's hairpiece.

In the category of capillary significations, here is a subsign, that of nocturnal surprises: Portia and Calpurnia, wakened in the middle of the night, have ostensibly disheveled hair; the younger Portia's expressed by flowing locks, so that her disarray is, so to speak, primary; while the mature Calpurnia presents a more studied informality: a braid winds around her neck and hangs over her right shoulder, expressing the traditional sign of disorder, asymmetry. But these signs are at once excessive and absurd: they postulate a naturalness which they lack the courage to honor completely: they are not "open and above board."

Still another sign in this *Julius Caesar*: every face sweats unremittingly: workers, soldiers, conspirators all bathe their austere and tense features in an abundant perspiration (of vaseline). And the close-ups are so frequent that sweat here must be an intentional attribute. Like the Roman bangs or the midnight braid, sweat too is a sign. Of what? Of morality. Everyone sweats because everyone is arguing with himself about something; we are meant to be in a site of an agonizingly laborious virtue, i.e., in the very locus of tragedy, which perspiration is intended to represent. The populace, traumatized by Caesar's death, then by Mark Antony's arguments, the populace sweats, economically combining in this one sign the intensity of its emotion and the primitive nature of its condition. And the virtuous men, Brutus, Cassius, Casca, also perspire continually, thereby testifying to the enormous labor which virtue performs in them as they are about to give birth to a crime. To sweat is to think (which obviously is based on the postulate, quite proper to a populace of businessmen, that to think is a violent, cataclysmic operation of which thinking is the mildest sign). In the whole film, only one man fails to sweat, remains smooth-skinned, unperturbed, and watertight: Caesar. Of course, Caesar, the *object* of the crime, remains dry, for he doesn't know, *he doesn't think*, he alone must sustain the firm, polished texture of a judicial piece of evidence.

Here again, the sign is ambiguous: it remains on the surface yet does not renounce passing itself off as a depth; it seeks to make itself understood (which is praiseworthy) but at the same time presents itself as spontaneous (which is deceptive), it declares itself to be simultaneously intentional and irrepressible, artificial and natural, manufactured and yet discovered. Which serves to introduce us to a morality of the sign. The sign ought to present itself in only two extreme forms: either frankly intellectual, reduced by its distance to an algebra, as in the Chinese theater, where a flag signifies a regiment; or else deeply rooted, somehow invented on each occasion, presenting an inward and secret face, the signal of a moment and no longer of a concept (such, for instance, would be the art of Stanislavsky). But the intermediary sign (the bangs of Romanity or the perspiration of thought) betrays a degraded spectacle, one which fears the naïve truth as much as the total artifice. For if it is a good thing that a spectacle be created to make the world clearer, there is a culpable duplicity in confusing the sign with what is signified. And this is a duplicity peculiar to bourgeois art: between the intellectual sign and the visceral sign, this art hypocritically arranges an illegitimate sign, at once elliptical and pretentious, which it baptizes with the pompous name *natural*.

GARBO'S FACE

Translated by Richard Howard

Greta Garbo still belongs to that moment in cinema when the apprehension of the human countenance plunged crowds into the greatest perturbation, where people literally lost themselves in the human image as if in a philter, when the face constituted a sort of absolute state of the flesh which one could neither attain nor abandon. Some years earlier, Valentino's face caused suicides; Garbo's still participates in that same realm of *amour courtois* when the flesh develops certain mystical sentiments of perdition.

It is without a doubt an admirable face-as-object; in *Queen Christina*, a film shown again here in recent years, the star's makeup has the snowy density of a mask; it is not a painted face but a face in plaster, protected by the surface of its shadows and not by its lineaments; in all this fragile and compact snow, only the eyes, black as some strange pulp but not at all expressive, are two rather tremulous wounds. Even in its extreme beauty, this face not drawn but instead sculptured in something smooth and friable, which is to say both perfect and ephemeral, matches somehow Chaplin's flour-white complexion, those vegetally dark eyes, his totemic visage.

Now, the temptation of the total mask (the mask of antiquity, for example) may imply less the theme of secrecy (as is the case with the Italian half mask) than that of an archetype of the human face. Garbo produced a sort of Platonic idea of the human creature, which accounts for her own face being virtually sexless without being at all "dubious." It's true that the film (Queen Christina alternately a woman and a young cavalier) lends itself to this indeterminacy; but Garbo does not give any kind of travestied performance; she is always herself, frankly revealing under her crown or her wide-brimmed felt hats the same countenance of snow and solitude. Her nickname, Divine, probably intended to suggest less a superlative state of beauty than the essence of her corporeal person, descended from a heaven where things are formed and finished with the greatest clarity. She herself knew this: How many actresses have consented to let the crowd watch the disturbing maturation of their beauty? Not Garbo: the Essence must not degrade, her visage could never have any other reality than that of its intellectual perfection, even more than its plastic one. The Essence has gradually dimmed, progressively veiled by dark glasses, hooded capes, and various exiles; but it has never altered.

Still, in that deified countenance, something sharper than a mask appears: a sort of deliberate and therefore human relation between the curve of the nostrils and the superciliary arcade, a rare, individual function between two zones of the face; the mask is merely an addition of lines, the face is above all a thematic recall of the former to the latter. Garbo's face represents that fragile moment when cinema is about to extract an existential beauty from an essential beauty, when the archetype will be inflected toward the fascination of perishable figures, when the clarity of carnal essences will give way to a lyric expression of Woman.

As a moment of transition, Garbo's face reconciles two iconographic ages, assures the passage from terror to charm. We know that in our own moment we are at the other pole of this evolution: Audrey Hepburn's face, for instance, is individualized not only by its specific thematics (woman-as-child, woman-as-cat), but also by her person, by a virtually unique specification of the face, which has nothing essential left in it but is constituted by an infinite complexity of morphological functions. As a language, Garbo's singularity was of a conceptual order, Audrey Hepburn's of a substantial order. Garbo's face is an Idea, Hepburn's an Event.

LOST CONTINENT

Translated by Richard Howard

A film, *Lost Continent*, nicely illuminates the current myth of exoticism. It is a full-length documentary on "the East," whose pretext is some vague ethnographic expedition, an obviously false one, moreover, led by three or four bearded Italians in the Malay Archipelago. The film is euphoric, everything in it is easy, innocent. Our explorers are fine fellows, occupying their leisure with childish diversions: playing with a mascot bear cub (mascots are indispensable on any expedition: no polar film without a tame seal, no tropical reportage without its monkey) or comically spilling a dish of spaghetti on the boat-deck. Which is to say that these good ethnologists are hardly troubled by historical or sociological problems. Penetration of the East is never anything for them but a little boat trip on an azure sea under an essential sun. And this East, the very place which has today become the political center of the world, is shown here all smoothed out and gaily colored like an old-fashioned postcard.

The method of irresponsibility is clear: to color the world is always a way of denying it (and perhaps we should begin here with an inquiry into the use of color in films generally). Deprived of all substance, forced into the expedient of color, disembodied by the very luxuriance of the "images," the East is ready for the disappearing act our film has in readiness for it. Between the bear cub mascot and the comical spaghetti incident, our studio ethnologists will have no difficulty postulating an East formally exotic, in reality deeply resembling the West, at least the spiritualist West. Orientals have religions of their own? No problem, the differences are insignificant compared to the deep unity of idealism. Each rite is thereby at once specialized and eternalized, simultaneously promoted to the level of a fascinating spectacle and a para-Christian symbol. And if Buddhism is not literally Christian, that matters little enough since Buddhism too has nuns who shave their heads (a major theme in the pathos of all ceremonies of taking the veil), since it has monks who kneel and confess to their superior, and finally since, as in Seville, the faithful come and cover the god's statue with gold.[1] It is true that it is always the "forms" which emphasize the identity of all religions; but this identity, far from betraying them, exalts them, all to the credit of a superior catholicity.

We know that syncretism has always been one of the Church's major techniques of assimilation. In the seventeenth century, in this very East whose Christian predispositions *Lost Continent* has shown us, the Jesuits went very far in the ecumenicity of forms: it was the Malabar rites which the pope in fact ended by condemning. It is this very "all things are alike" which our ethnologists have hinted at: Orient and Occident, it is all the same, there are only differences in color, the essential is identical, which is the eternal postulation of man toward God, the absurd and contingent character of geographies in relation to this human nature, of which Christianity alone possesses the key. The legends themselves, all this "primitive" folklore whose foreignness seems to be constantly pointed out to us, has as its mission nothing but to

[1] A good example here of the mystifying power of music: all the "Buddhist" scenes are accompanied by a vague musical syrup, part American crooning and part Gregorian chant; in any case it is monadic (the sign of monocalism).

illustrate "Nature": the rites, the accidents of culture are never related to any specific historical order with an explicit social or economic status, but only with the great neutral forms of cosmic commonplaces (seasons, storms, death, etc.). If we are dealing with fishermen, it is never the mode of fishing that we are shown, but rather, drowned in the eternity of a chromatic sunset, a romantic essence of fisherman, described not as a worker dependent by his technique and his profits on a specific society, but rather as a theme of an eternal condition, that of a man far away and exposed to the dangers of the sea, the wife weeping and praying at home. It is the same for refugees, a long procession of whom is shown at the start of the film making their way down a mountain; futile, of course, to locate them: they are eternal essences of refugees, it is in the *nature* of the East to produce them.

All told, exoticism clearly shows here its true justification, which is to deny any and all situation to History. By affecting the Oriental reality of several good native signs, we carefully vaccinate the Oriental reality against any responsible content. A bit of "situation," as superficial as possible, provides the necessary alibi and disposes of any deeper experience. Confronting anything foreign, Order knows only two behaviors which are both forms of mutilation: either to acknowledge the Other as another Punch and Judy show or to render it harmless as a pure reflection of the West. In any case the essential thing is to deprive it of its history. We see that the "beautiful images" of *Lost Continent* cannot be innocent: it cannot be innocent to *lose* the continent which has been found again at Bandung.

SECTION TWO
PHENOMENOLOGY AND EXISTENTIALISM

CHAPTER 9
JEAN-PAUL SARTRE

Jean-Paul Sartre (1905–1980) was a French philosopher, playwright, and novelist, widely regarded as the founder and figurehead of the distinctively French school of Existentialism. Sartre's impact on Continental philosophy was enormous, but he was no less influential in the public sphere, having made philosophy—and, particularly, existentialist philosophy—a matter of relatively mainstream concern in France during his lifetime. "Motion Picture Art" is Sartre's sole contribution to the philosophy of film; it was originally published in French ("L'Art cinématographique") in Le Petit Havre *in 1931.*

Sartre's essay begins with a long quote from the memoirs of Anatole France, in which France notes that the turning point in his life—the dividing line between youth and adulthood—was going to the theater. He describes the experience in moving detail. Following this passage, Sartre notes, as an older generation was no doubt frequently noting, that contemporary youth (that is, the generation who were young adults in 1931) do not typically have this experience of the theater, or of any of the arts. Instead of the theater, the new generation has the cinema—and cinemagoing isn't the "event" that theatergoing was. One does not dress up for the movies, one can eat during the show, and at the time Sartre was writing, movies typically did not have set showtimes: the films ran continuously (with newsreels and perhaps a cartoon between showings), and audience members arrived at whichever point in the film at which they happened to arrive. As Sartre describes it, the typical moviegoer in France in 1931 would arrive mid-film, would watch the film through to the end, remain as the film was shown again, and then would leave at the point in the next showing when they had arrived in the last. The scene he describes is not an elegant or sophisticated one; rather, it's loud and busy, with people arriving and leaving all of the time. This means, among other things, that whatever role the cinema plays in culture, it does not play the role that the theater once did: going to the movies could never be emblematic of a young person's arrival at cultural maturity. The cinema is much more closely identified with the everyday life of ordinary people than that.

Sartre raises the question (a question that is clearly not his own, but is frequently asked in his time) as to whether, in the transition from an arts culture centered on the theater to one centered on the cinema, do we lose something important? And almost immediately, Sartre answers in the negative: although the cinema is in no way as majestic as the theater was and is, cinematographic art can penetrate much more deeply into the minds of the youth who enjoy it, thanks to its cultural proximity. Majesty, with all its ceremony and prestige, is distancing in a way that leaves the virtues and values of the theater in the theater. The cinema, on the other hand, is so close to so many that they cannot help but be influenced by it.

Given the potential cinema has for such immense and immediate influence over the youth, Sartre returns again to the very basic question: is film art? His answer to this question may strike twenty-first-century readers as somewhat naïve and short-sighted, but it is an affirmative one: film is an art, but it is a silent art. In other words, the art of film has to do with the images and actions already able to be displayed in silent film; although sound film had already been invented, and talking pictures were starting to be shown in France, Sartre insists that the sound aspect of film is not only inessential but temporary: sound film is a fad, he seems to argue, and it will not take long for audiences to see through the gimmick and demand artful, silent pictures once again. This is not, in fact, how things turned out—but it is unsurprising that Sartre shares the suspicion and skepticism of sound film that so many philosophers of the arts did at the time (recall, among other things, Rudolf Arnheim's articles on sound film, also from roughly this period). Nevertheless, whether in its silent or talking forms, film demonstrates it is an art by way of its capacity for displaying motion—and so we need not share Sartre's views on sound film in order to accept the rest of his argument.

Ultimately, Sartre argues that film is not (as it was widely viewed) simply recorded (or "canned") theater; it is a new art with its own aesthetic principles. It is a new development within the larger category, as Sartre understands it, of the arts of movement—a category in which he includes music, tragedy (or theatrical drama), and film. The arts of movement are characterized, according to Sartre, by their ability to give outward expression to the irreversibility of time: thus, in each of these arts, Sartre looks for the ways in which they exhibit a kind of fatalism, an inevitable march toward the end. Music does this by way of melody; tragedy, through the dramatic structure of the actions that constitute the play. Music is thus more abstract than theater, but both are highly intellectual arts—and, to that extent, discontinuous with everyday life.

Film, on the other hand and as we have already seen, is continuous with the everyday, the humdrum, the mundane. While cinematic narratives may depict extraordinary events or persons, as an art form, film does not require intellectual preparation to be viewed or understood. Like music and tragedy, film is a fatalistic art—but unlike its confrères, a film's inevitable ending is accessible without the necessity of abstract or philosophical thought (as Sartre notes of his cinematic experiences, this makes coming into the movie house at an arbitrary point in the narrative tolerable, since "you know the traitor will be punished and the lovers will get married"). The means by which the end is achieved in each of the arts of movement differs, however, and it is by way of these differing means that the three arts Sartre mentions attain their distinctiveness from one another.

Music achieves its end by way of what Sartre calls "thematic unity," the tying together (by way of the development and ultimate resolution of the melody's main theme) of disparate musical elements at work, and sometimes in tension with each other, throughout the musical work. A piece of music can thus exhibit a wide variety of different themes, each appearing perhaps only for a moment, perhaps for a longer time, but ever in contrast to the others: a sort of polyphony, as Sartre would have it. Tragedy, on the other hand, cannot display anything like music's thematic unity—since competing and merely momentary dramatic themes would make a play unwatchable or, at the very least, extremely difficult to understand (if not also, through the concomitant practical difficulty of changing sets and scenes, impossible to stage). The means by which tragedy achieves the unity that leads it to its aesthetic end is a unity of action, then, not of themes: every line, every movement, every characterization or vocalization on the stage must lend itself directly to the achievement of the work's goal. Everything extraneous or merely happenstance in the work must be removed, for the work to truly achieve tragic beauty.

By contrast to those two arts, cinema instantiates both the thematic unity of music and the unity of action of the tragedy. The latter it achieves in much the same way tragedy does, in the maintenance of a focus on the necessity of each moment in the film. But, unlike tragedy, cinema—with its capacity for momentary and multiple shots, instantaneous changes of scene or setting, or even individualized images in meaningful (but perhaps not narrative) succession such as those characteristic of montage—can also work with multiple, interwoven but perhaps not entirely connected, themes. It is this capacity for a synthesis novel in the arts which constitutes the distinctive potential for beauty in cinema, and which establishes beyond all doubt that film is an art.

Filmography

- ***Die Freudlose Gasse*** [*Joyless Street*] (Germany, 1925). *Directed by* Georg Wilhelm Pabst. *Produced by* Sofar-Film-Produktion. *Written by* Willy Haas. *Starring* Greta Garbo, Werner Krauss, *and* Asta Nielsen.
- ***Der heilige Berg*** [*The Holy Mountain*] (Germany, 1926). *Directed by* Arnold Fanck. *Produced by* Harry R. Sokal. *Written by* Arnold Fanck *and* Hans Schneeberger. *Starring* Leni Riefenstahl, Luis Trenker, *and* Frida Richard.
- ***Napoléon*** (France, 1927). *Directed, Produced, and Written by* Abel Gance. *Starring* Albert Dieudonné, Gina Manès, Antonin Artaud, *and* Edmond Van Daële.
- ***Finis Terræ*** (France, 1929). *Directed by* Jean Epstein. *Produced by* Serge Sandberg. *Written by* Jean Epstein. *Starring* Jean-Marie Laot *and* Ambroise Rouzic.

MOTION PICTURE ART

Translated by Richard McCleary

Thumb through the recollections of some contemporary or recently deceased writer, you will surely find a long and fond account of his first contact with the theater. "One whole day long I lived perturbed by fear and hope, consumed by fever, waiting for that unheard-of bliss which just one blow might suddenly destroy.... The day the play was due to be performed, I thought the sun would never set. Dinner (of which I swallowed not one mouthful) seemed endless, and I was in mortal terror of getting there late.... Finally we did arrive; the usher showed us into a red box.... The solemnity of the three opening knocks on the stage and the profound silence following them moved me deeply. The raising of the curtain really was for me a journey to another world."

Now those of you who forty years from now will write memoirs of their own will have a hard time finding comparable expectations and equally overwhelming emotions. That is because you have been going to movie houses since you were very small: many of you were already acquainted with motion pictures before you were five, for it is with motion pictures, not the theater, that one starts out today. Some of us perhaps can still remember the first film we saw, but usually these beginnings are lost in the haze of memory.

Thus that solemn initiation to the rites of the theater, that pomp, those three blows which mark not so much the raising of the curtain as the passage from childhood to adolescence—all that is gone. We hardly dress up to go to the movies; we don't think about going days ahead of time; we go there any time—in the afternoon, the evening, and for some months now in Paris even in the morning. You have no knowledge of that long wait in a half-empty and gradually filling theater, and of that "journey to another world" which Anatole France spoke about. But you push your way brusquely into a darkened house, still uncertain in the darkness, your eye fixed on the flashlight zigzagging in the usher's hand. The orchestra is playing and does not, as one might expect, stop for you. The picture has been on for a long time; the heroes are there, with their hands or legs going, caught in the thick of action. You are shown your seat; you slip in, bumping knees; you plump down in your seat without having the time to take off your coat. You watch the end of the film and then, after a fifteen-minute wait, the beginning. You don't mind: you know the traitor will be punished and the lovers will get married. Then at the precise moment the heroes reassume the positions you found them in, you get up, bump more knees, and go out without looking back, leaving the heroes frozen with their hands or legs going—perhaps eternally.

This is a very familiar art, an art mixed very closely with our daily life. We dash into movie houses, talk, laugh, and eat there. We have no respect for this popular art. It does not deck itself at all in that majesty which half entered into the pleasure our elders took in the art of the theater. It is good-natured and much closer to us.

Are we losers by the change? Should we regret the vanished solemnities?

If it could be shown that the motion picture really is an art, we would on the contrary need only congratulate ourselves on the change in our customs. It seems to me your total disrespect for motion picture art and your offhand way of dealing with it are much more worthwhile than a mixture of frozen admiration, troubled feelings, and sacred awe. You have heard far too often, unfortunately, that our great classical authors were "artists": you mistrust their fine phrases, which are the pretext for a thousand insidious questions. From your dealings with them, bit by bit and in spite of yourself, you do undoubtedly derive a benefit that you will later on appreciate. But it is good that in certain darkened houses which parents and professors know nothing about, you can find an unpretentious art which has not been dinned into your ears, which no one has dreamed of telling you was an art, concerning which, in a word, you have been left in a state of innocence. For this art will penetrate more deeply into you than the others, and it is this art which will gently shape you to love beauty in all its forms.

It remains to be shown that the motion picture really is an art. The same Anatole France whom we have seen so gently moved when he went to the theater was no doubt differently affected by his first encounter with the motion picture. He said, as a matter of fact, "The motion picture materializes the worst ideals of the masses.... The end of the world is not in the balance, but the end of civilization is."

These are very big words; we are going to see if they are justified. Someone will tell me that my investigation is inopportune: if by chance I were to persuade you that there are fine motion pictures, just as there are fine epistles by Boileau and fine funeral orations by Bossuet, you would not go to the movies any more. But that doesn't bother me. I know you will not take the things I tell you seriously, because to have you listen till the end of any speech they made you hear would be unprecedented. Perhaps it also seems ironic to discuss the beauty of mute art just when we are being invaded by talking pictures. But we ought not to pay too much attention to them. Pirandello used to say, and not without melancholy, that the motion picture resembles the peacock in the fable. He silently displayed his marvelous plumage, and everyone admired it. The jealous fox persuaded him to sing. He opened his mouth, gave forth with his voice, and uttered the cry you know about. But what Aesop doesn't say, or Pirandello either, is that after this experience the peacock undoubtedly returned without much urging to his muteness. I think the motion picture is in the process of earning the right to be silent.

So I come back to the question: I claim that the motion picture is a new art with its own laws and its own social means, that it cannot be reduced to theater, and that it should serve your cultivation in the same capacity as Greek or philosophy.

To put it briefly, what's new about motion pictures?

You know that each instant depends narrowly upon those which have preceded it; that any given state of the universe is absolutely explained in its anterior states; that there is nothing which is lost, nothing which is in vain; and that the present goes strictly toward the future. You know this because you have been taught it. But if you look within yourself, around yourself, you do not in the slightest feel it. You see movements arising which, like the sudden stirring of a treetop, seem spontaneous. You see others which, like waves upon the sand, are dying out, and in their dying seem to lose their vital force. It seems to you that the past is bound very loosely to the present, and that everything gets old in an aimless, sloppy, groping way.

Now the aim of the arts of movement is to give the irreversibility of time—the knowledge of which we gain from science, but the feeling of which we would be unable to bear if it inwardly accompanied all of our actions—an outward expression, awesome but still beautiful, in things themselves. There is something fatal in melody. The notes composing it crowd in upon and govern one another with a strict necessity. Similarly, our tragedy presents itself as a forced march toward catastrophe. Nothing in it can turn back: each line, each word, sweeps things a little farther on in this race to the abyss. There is no hesitation, no delay, no hollow phrase which gives a bit of rest; all the characters, no matter what they say or do, advance toward their end. Thus these lost voyagers who have set foot in the swamp's quicksand may struggle as much as they wish; each movement sinks them in a little deeper till they disappear completely.

But music is very abstract. Paul Valéry is right to see it as no more than "interchanging forms and movements." And tragedy, although less intellectual, is still very much so: with its five acts and very pronounced lines, it is still a product of reason, like number and all that is discontinuous.

At the movies the forward movement of the action is still inevitable, but it is continuous. There is no stopping point; the picture is all of a piece. Instead of the abstract and interrupted time of tragedy, one would say that here everyday duration, that humdrum of our lives, has suddenly thrown back its veils to stand forth in its inhuman necessity. At the same time, the motion picture is of all the arts the closest to the real world: real men live in real landscapes. The *Montagne sacrée* is a real mountain, and the sea in *Finis Terrae* is a real sea. Everything seems natural except that march toward the end which cannot be stopped.

If there were no more in the motion picture than this representation of fatality, a place would still have to be reserved for it among the fine arts. But there is more.

You will recall that imperative rule which still dominates the theater. The romantics relaxed it, but they were not able to get rid of it, because it is, as it were, what constitutes dramatic art. I want to talk about the third unity, the unity of action. If you take it in its broadest sense, it is applicable to all the arts: the artist must deal with his subject, never be diverted by extrinsic temptations, resist the pleasure of enhancing a development by adding useless touches, and never lose sight of his initial plan.

But this rule has a narrower sense which is applicable to the theater alone: in this sense, the action must be single, spare, and stripped of everything that would only add picturesqueness to the plot. In short, it must be a strict succession of moments so closely tied together that each of them alone explains the following—or better yet, a logical deduction from a few principles established from the start.

But the unity found in music is already different: the composer builds several themes into it. He begins by setting them forth independently while arranging imperceptible movements from one to the other. Then he subtly takes his themes up again, develops them, enlarges upon them, and weaves them into one another. And finally, in the last movement, he gives all these motifs a strict foundation by simply echoing some and bringing others to their most perfect fulfillment.

This unity, which could be called "thematic," could not possibly be appropriate to the theater: it was in vain that a German romantic tried to introduce it. A multiplicity of themes would as a matter of fact require, as it did in Jules Romains's *Donogoo*, the use of short quick scenes. Experience has shown that this technique tends to make people tired. Furthermore, no matter how short the scenes which follow one another in this way might be, they would still not be short enough: the effect of contrast and symmetry would often be lost; one could not leap from one to the other, indicate a resemblance, then come back to the first, insist on some characteristic, and so on in order to stress the more subtle correlations.

Now this is just what the motion picture does. The picture's universe is thematic, because skillful editing can always bring the most diverse scenes together and interweave them: we were in the fields and here we are in town; we thought we would stay in town and the next instant we were taken back to the fields. You know how much can be done with this extreme mobility. Think of Abel Gance's *Napoléon* and that stormy convention accompanied and emphasized by a storm on the Mediterranean. A wave swells and rises up, but before it has broken we are already far away on dry land, among the howling deputies. Robespierre gets up, he is about to speak, but we have left him; we are out on the high sea being tossed about in Napoleon's little boat. A brandished fist. A rolling wave. A threatening face. A waterspout. The two themes accentuate each other, expand upon each other, and finally merge together.

Sometimes, by means of what is technically called a "dissolve," the transition from one motif to another is steady, slow, and imperceptible; sometimes, as the need arises, swift and brutal. It is also possible to develop several themes simultaneously by means of the "multiple exposure." But there is another and much more elegant way to achieve this cinematographic polyphony. Suppose you want to unify two different motifs: all you have to do is use them to bring out a situation which is not reducible to either one but symbolizes the two together. Look what happens in the classic film, *La Rue sans joie*. In it Pabst shows the postwar destitution of the Viennese people and the dissolute debauchery of a few profiteers. These two themes co-exist for a long time without intermingling. Finally the two series of paths meet: one of the profiteers is driving along "the street without joy" on the way to a nearby dive where he is going to finish out the night; in that same street a wretched crowd is standing in line in front of the butcher shop. The profiteer's car brushes by these poor people and disappears; the two momentarily united themes reassume their independence. It seems that everything in all of this is natural and necessary—that it is just a meeting. But that is because you have not really seen the picture. The car's headlights sweep slowly over that bleak and shivering crowd, making hate-filled faces stand out, one by one, from the shadows. That blinding light, these blinking eyes, these squat and worn-out bodies, that powerful, sumptuous car, these gaping shadows; all of this, no doubt, is fated, but in a certain respect it has a stamp all its own: before it fades out, the episode throws a quick, sharp light on the whole picture.

Do not think that these situations, produced by a necessary chain of events yet nevertheless ambiguous and packed with meaning, are rare in motion pictures. On the contrary, motion pictures are what you might call their natural habitat. You'll find throngs of "sign-bearing" objects there, humble utensils on which a theme piled and rolled up onto itself is written in shorthand.

So go admire this supple yet unbending chain of images, this subtle knot wound through events packed full of meaning and determined by both mind and nature, this scattering of actions which makes room, all of a sudden, for striking and soon-broken unions, brief and fleeting flash backs, deep and hidden correspondences between each object and the rest—for such is the world of motion pictures. To be sure, pictures that stay unfailingly at this level are rare; but you will see no pictures that are completely lacking in beauty.

Now I say that you can find your way around this new world very well: you have acquired a certain ability to find your bearings in the mazes of its plots, its symbols, and its rhythms. I have seen cultured men who got lost in them because they had not been going to movie houses. But you who almost live in them, even though you may not be able yet to express your impressions or ideas, are completely at ease there: nothing escapes you; nothing fools you.

Your parents may rest assured; the motion picture is not a bad school. It is an art which seems easy but is really extremely hard and, if it is approached in the right way, very profitable; because by its nature it reflects civilization in our time. Who will teach you about the beauty of the world you live in, the poetry of speed, machines, and the inhuman and splendid inevitability of industry? Who, if not your art, the motion picture…

CHAPTER 10
ANDRÉ MALRAUX

André Malraux (1901–1976) was a French philosopher, novelist, and statesman. He was more influential, in France and internationally, as a writer than as a theorist—but his philosophical thoughts on the arts (including film) continue to grow in popularity, not least because they offer a different existential perspective on some of the same issues that so concerned his contemporaries, Jean-Paul Sartre and Simone de Beauvoir. "Sketch for a Psychology of the Moving Pictures" was originally published in French ("Esquisse d'une psychologie du cinéma") in Verve *in 1940.*

Malraux suggests, early in "Sketch for a Psychology of the Moving Pictures," that the history of Western art makes a decisive break after the baroque period—a break from its past, and a break with art as it was practiced and produced in the rest of the world. It was then, Malraux claims, that a commitment to reproduce the illusion of three-dimensionality in a two-dimensional medium really overtook art, and especially painting. After that moment, the future of the plastic arts—from painting through photography to cinema—is already written, in principle. Of course, as an art medium, photography faces all of the same problems that painting had always faced: it was a visually reproductive medium with no capacity for narrative.

Cinema's technological advance upon photography seems immediately to be the introduction of motion into the photograph images projected on the screen, but Malraux says that motion is not enough all by itself to produce narrative. Rather, in addition to the illusion of movement, cinematic narrative is only possible on the basis of the editing process. Without editing, and the division of continuity which it introduces into the film, fiction is impossible. What editing gives the cinema, Malraux argues, is the division of the film into what he calls "planes," and which we might think of as the various perspectives and points of view from which the figures in the film are seen by the moviegoer, or (alternatively) the various perspectives and points of view from which the figures in the film are projected. In either case, what we're talking about is film's capacity to show us an image from different angles and degrees of proximity.

Malraux says that, while the cinematic means of reproduction is moving photographs (a common starting point for philosophical or other analyses of film), the cinematic means of expression is a sequence of planes. Planes allow the film, he thinks, to be expressive—unlike a photograph. Ironically, for example, the size of the actors on the movie screen—and the fact that their sizes can change, depending upon the nature of the shot—allows the actors to express more genuine emotions than does the theater (the close-up, especially, frees the screen actor from the necessity of the large, demonstrative, over-the-top pantomime gestures necessary on the stage). Not despite but because of the cinematographic technology's intervention in the performance, coupled with the work of editing in post-production and, finally, the ways in which the actors' performances are differently enabled by the cinema, Malraux notes that the performances on the screen are truer to life than those on the stage. This, of course, in spite of the fact that, in theatrical performance, the real, living actors are in the same room as the audience—and in cinema, they are (necessarily) not. This radical increase in expressivity resides not in the actors' performances, per se, but in the way in which the introduction of planes into cinema by editing changes the actors' relations to the spectator, to us.

So far, Malraux has only addressed film as a visual medium—but, writing in 1940, he was well aware of sound film. Unlike some of the early philosophers of film, who saw in the talkie the end of film art, Malraux only claims that sound isn't a kind of perfection of film—providing silent film with something it lacks. Rather, when a film incorporates sound, it adds something to the visual character of the silent film—and becomes a new art thereby. The immediate forerunner of the sound film, Malraux claims, is in fact not the silent film—but the radio sketch. Misunderstanding the medium, early sound filmmakers produced what were effectively recorded stage plays, and Malraux notes, they were uniformly bad movies.

Although the radio sketch is the forerunner of the sound film, for Malraux, it is not the only art medium to which film can meaningfully be compared. We've already seen how he thinks cinema and theater line up against one another, and how poorly theater comes off in the comparison. But Malraux says toward the end of the essay that film's true rival is not the theater, but, given film's narrative capacity, the novel. He then proceeds to redescribe the novel in cinematic terms: the novelist, he notes, is a kind of "producer," and the most important moments the novelist "produces"—those where the greatness of the novel hangs in the balance—are in the transitions from narration to dialogue.

According to Malraux, dialogue in the novel serves one of three functions. First, dialogue can serve as exposition, explaining characters or elements of the plot to the reader. This mode of dialogue is rarely used in cinema, he notes, and it is the least cinematic mode of dialogue possible (since a film can simply show its audience; it does not have to tell them). Second, dialogue can help to bring out character—but, again Malraux thinks that this is done in cinema less by way of dialogue than by acting. And, third, dialogue is the stuff of the dramatic scene, the heart of the great novel and the great stage play, as well as of the (potentially) great sound film. This is what Malraux calls "essential dialogue," and he claims that it has only recently been discovered in cinema, and only infrequently employed. Although Malraux does not think that there have been any significant developments in film art since the era of silent films, it does seem that he suggests that the next such development could be in the incorporation and mastery of essential dialogue—a development that would begin with the presupposition of sound.

In lieu of such an artistic development, however, Malraux notes that the cinema of the 1940s is about myth. Film stars—especially female film stars, he says—are not actors, really. They're incarnated myths. Thus, while the stage actress achieves greatness as an actress when she can convincingly play a large number of roles, the film star achieves greatness as a star when she inspires a large number of screen roles to be written just for her. Instead of writing a great character and then finding an actress worthy of the role, the screenwriter begins with the idea of writing a movie wherein the star can be put on display—and none of the rest of the film really matters. The myth that is the film star is almost completely independent even of filmcraft: as Malraux notes, the best expression he had ever seen of the Chaplin Myth was in an unauthorized montage of clips from different Chaplin films he saw in Persia. Chaplin had nothing to do with the final product, and the "scenes" were not connected to each other in any way: but Chaplin the Myth shone clearly forth, all the same. Myth is exceedingly powerful, Malraux notes, more powerful than art, more powerful than politics. People love the myths they find gratifying, and they believe what they see in those myths. After making this point (one we will revisit in the film philosophy of the Frankfurt

School), Malraux concludes the essay with the somewhat ominous reminder that, whatever else it is, the cinema is an industry—an industry, we might add, that wields the power of myth.

Filmography

- ***Das Kabinet des Dr. Caligari*** [*The Cabinet of Dr. Caligari*] (Germany, 1920). *Directed by* Robert Wiene. *Produced by* Rudolf Meinert *and* Erich Pommer. *Written by* Hans Janowitz *and* Carl Mayer. *Starring* Werner Krauss, Conrad Veidt, *and* Friedrich Feher.
- ***Nosferatu*** (Germany, 1922). *Directed by* F. W. Murnau. *Produced by* Enrico Dieckmann *and* Albin Grau. *Written by* Henrik Galeen. *Starring* Max Schreck.
- ***Bronenosets Patyomkin*** [*The Battleship Potemkin*] (USSR, 1925). *Directed by* Sergei Eisenstein. *Produced by* Jacob Bliokh. *Written by* Nina Agadzhanova *and* Sergei Eisenstein. *Starring* Aleksandr Atonov, Vladimir Barksy, *and* Grigori Aleksandrov.
- ***Mat*** [*Mother*] (USSR, 1926). *Directed by* Vsevolod Pudovkin. *Produced by* Mezhrabpomfilm. *Written by* Nathan Zarkhi. *Starring* Vera Baranovskaya *and* Nikolai Batalov.
- ***Der blaue Engel*** [*The Blue Angel*] (Germany, 1930). *Directed by* Josef von Sternberg. *Produced by* Erich Pommer. *Written by* Carl Zuckmeyer, Karl Vollmöller, Robert Liebmann, *and* Josef von Sternberg. *Starring* Emil Jannings, Marlene Dietrich, *and* Kurt Gerron.
- ***Le Million*** [*The Million*] (France, 1931). *Directed and Written by* René Clair. *Produced by* Films Sonores Tobis. *Starring* Annabella, René Lefèvre, Jean-Louis Allibert, *and* Paul Ollivier.

SKETCH FOR A PSYCHOLOGY OF THE MOVING PICTURES

Had it befallen Giotto, or even Clouet, to travel round the world, all the paintings they set eyes on would have seemed of a more or less familiar order. Nor would they have had much trouble in establishing communication with Chinese or Persian fellow-artists. For all approached their task of *representing* the thing seen, in the same way, and dealt with the same set of problems.

Had Rubens or Delacroix made the same journey, all the paintings they set eyes on would have struck them as archaic; similarly their own works would have bewildered the non-European painters. For their methods of representation differed from those of the Asiatics. Chinese and Persian artists were ignorant of, or disdained, depth, perspective, lighting and expression. Europe had come to differ from the rest of the world in its idea of the function of painting. And, after the close of the baroque period, there was this fundamental cleavage between Western and all other arts, past and present: that the former devoted its researches to a three-dimensional world.

There were several reasons for this, which I shall deal with elsewhere.[1] Christianity had imported into a world that had known little else than representation of a more or less subtly symbolical nature, something hitherto unknown, which I would call "dramatic representation." Buddhism has scenes, but no drama; pre-Columbian American art, dramatic figures but no scenes. Even the decline of Christianity, far from weakening this occidental sense of the dramatic actually strengthened it, and at the same time heightened another sense, of which the sense of drama is only one of several manifestations—the sense of Otherness, that desire for volume and figures in bold relief which is peculiar to the West, and links up with its political conquest of the world. Europe replaces flat tone by relief, chronicles by history, tragedy by drama, saga by the novel, wisdom by psychology, contemplation by action—and, as a result, the gods by Man.

The criteria of present-day taste can only be misleading in this connexion; for a great deal of the best modern painting is, like the oriental, in two dimensions. The problem is not of an aesthetic order, but strikes deeper. It derives from culture itself, the relations between man and the outside world. At one pole of human expression are the mime, the actor and narrator in the *No* play, declaiming through their masks, Chinese and Japanese dancers; and, at the opposite extreme, a language tantamount to shorthand, the mysterious whisperings of a dark night, a face whose fugitive expression fills a twenty-foot screen…

The visitor to one of our national galleries, who has no feeling for painting as an art, gets an impression of a series of efforts (not unlike those of certain sciences) to *re-present* natural objects. To him a Rubens seems truer-to-life, and thus more convincing, than a Giotto; a Botticelli than a Cimabue; for he regards art as a means of reproducing the universe according to the data furnished by his senses. From the XIIIth Century up to the time of the baroque masters, there

[1] In my *Psychology of Art*.

was steady progress in the technique of exact resemblance. And European painting during that period was at once this "mirror held up to nature" and an effort to represent persons and things (especially fictional scenes) under the most evocative and engaging guise. It is the confusion between what we should call to-day the art of painting and the technique of representation, that leads the Sunday afternoon visitor to our galleries to say approvingly of such and such a figure (always a post-Renaissance work) that it seems almost to be "talking to you." It was the same confusion that led the Florentine populace to applaud Giotto's figures as being "truer than life;" and the enthusiasm of the Tuscans for the "new" Madonnas was not perhaps so very different from that which would ensue to-day were television suddenly to enter every home.[2]

But at the close of the baroque period came an event unprecedented in the annals of painting. Ceasing to search for new methods of representation, the painter turned away towards what art has come to mean for us to-day: a specialty of artists. Never again was a picture to draw enthusiastic crowds to view it. Line and colour were to become more and more the revelation of an inward vision. And while the secret flower of modern painting blossomed forth, the votaries of representation took to a frantic headlong quest of movement.

It was no "artistic" discovery that was to enable movement to be come by. What, with its gesturings like those of drowning men, baroque art was straining after was not a modification of the picture itself, but a picture-*sequence*. It is not surprising that an art so obsessed with theatrical effect, and made up of gestures and emotions, should end up in the cinema.

II

When photography came into its own in the middle of the nineteenth century, western painting formally made over two of its former spheres of action: the depiction of emotions and the "story." It became once more an art of pure form and was again, in certain instances, restricted to two dimensions.

For the purposes of an Identity Card the photograph is wholly adequate. But for representing life, photography (which within thirty years has evolved from a phase of primitive immobility to a more or less extravagant baroque) is inevitably coming up once more against all the old problems of the painter. And where the latter halted, it too had to halt. With the added handicap that it had no scope for fiction; it could record a dancer's leap, it could not show the Crusaders entering Jerusalem. And from the "likenesses" of the Saints to the most absurd historical fantasies, men's craving for pictures has always been directed quite as much to what they have not seen as towards what they know.

Thus the attempt, which had been carried on four centuries through, to capture movement was held up at the same point in photography as in painting; and the cinema, through enabling the photography of movement, merely substituted moving gesticulation for unmoving. If the great drive towards representation which came to a standstill in baroque art was to continue, somehow the camera had to achieve independence as regards the scene portrayed. The problem was not one of rendering the movements of a person within a picture, but of conveying tempo, the sequence of successive moments. It was not to be solved mechanically by tinkering with the camera, but artistically, by the invention of "cutting."

[2] Written in 1940.—*Ed.*

So long as the cinema served merely for the portrayal of figures in motion it was no more (and no less) an art than plain photography. Within a defined space, generally a real or imagined theatre stage, actors performed a play or comic scene, which the camera merely recorded. The birth of the cinema as a means of expression (not of reproduction) dates from the abolition of that defined space; from the time when the cutter thought of dividing his continuity into "planes" (close-up, intermediate, remote, etc.) and of shooting not a play but a succession of dramatic moments; when the director took to bringing forward the camera (and thus enlarging, when necessary, the figures on the screen) and moving it back; and, above all, to replacing the theatre set by an open field of vision, corresponding to the area of the screen, into which the player enters, from which he goes out, and which the director *chooses* instead of having it imposed on him. The means of reproduction in the cinema is the moving photograph, but its means of expression is a sequence of *planes*.

The tale goes that Griffith, when directing one of his early films, was so much impressed by the beauty of an actress in a certain scene that he had the camera brought nearer and a re-take made, which he incorporated in the final version of the picture. Thus the close-up was invented. The story illustrates the manner in which one of the great pioneers of filmcraft applies his genius to the problems of the moving picture, aiming less to influence the actor (by making him play, for instance, in a different way) than to modify the relation between him and the spectator (by increasing the volume of his face). It illustrates, too, a fact we are aware of but tend to overlook: that decades after the humblest photographer had formed the habit of photographing his clients full figure, half length or face only, as desired, the cinema took what was for it a bold, decisive forward step when it began registering half-length figures. For till then "planes" were an unknown quantity; the camera and field being static, the act of taking two figures half-length would have involved shooting the whole scene in the same manner.

Thus it was, by the adoption of variable planes, by this new freedom given director and cameraman in their dealings with the objective, that the cinema was endowed with possibilities of *expression*, that it was born as an *art*. Thereafter it was able to select the "shot" and co-ordinate significant "shots"; by selectivity to make up for its silence.

III

The talking picture was to modify the *data* of the problem. Not, as some have thought, by perfecting the silent picture. The talking picture was no more a bringing to perfection of its silent predecessor than was the elevator of the skyscraper. Modern cinema was not born of the possibility of making us hear what the characters of the silent film were saying, but of the joint possibilities of expression due to sound and picture acting in concert. So long as the talking picture is merely phonographic, it is as unsatisfactory as was the silent picture when it was mere photography. It rises to the rank of an art when the director understands that the forerunner of sound-cinema is not the gramophone record but the radio sketch.

When a group of artists presented on the radio the Trial of Joan of Arc, and the Session of Thermidor 9, their first task in each case was to compose an original work, the verbal structure of which was conditioned by the method of reproduction to be applied to it. There was no question of asking actors to read out passages from the *Moniteur*; they had to begin by selecting certain phases of the famous Session from the detailed report in the Gazette, and make a *montage* of them. For the record of the Session which has come down to us is, like all such *verbatim* reports, far too long to bear audition.

We are inclined to suppose that this selection leaves, in fact, no option; that there were certain outstanding moments in that eventful night when Robespierre fell, which every art alike is bound to utilize. Indeed at first sight one might conclude that in every complex of events, in every life, certain elements are of a nature to provide the raw material of art; the rest being so much lumber, amorphous and inert. This view is due to a confusion between the suggestive, significant, vitally "artistic" element and the historically memorable factor or remark. True, there are highlights in every chaos, but they are not necessarily the same highlights for every art. When Robespierre's voice is failing, the crucial fact for the radio may be that failing voice; for the cinema it may be, for instance, the gestures of a sentry intent at that moment on bundling some children out of the room, or fumbling for his tinder-box.

In the twentieth century we have for the first time arts that are inseparable from mechanical methods of expression; not only capable of being reproduced, but intended for mass-reproduction. Already the finest drawings can be adequately reproduced; before the century is out the same will probably be true of paintings. But neither drawings nor paintings were *made* to be reproduced; the artist had nothing of that sort in mind. Whereas what is enacted on a studio set by living actors is *per se* doomed to transience; it has less intrinsic value than a used engraving plate. It was *made* to be photographed, and for that end alone, just as a radio play is made to be recorded and then broadcast.

But the expressive range of recorded sounds, somewhat limited in the case of radio and gramophone records, becomes immense when the picture adds its visual counterpoint. The cinema in relief will be, when it comes, a technical advance; but the sound film stands to the silent as painting does to drawing.

At first it was so little recognized that sound was opening up a new field of expression that the talking film tended to bring the cinema back to where it had started, the moving picture at its crudest. Just as the first films were photographic records of stage effects and no more, so the early "talkies" aimed no higher than to be phonograph records of stage-plays. The dialogue was ready to hand, the footage suitable—and the result deplorable!

IV

The theatre in countries such as Russia, Germany and the United States, where it had kept its full vitality, had for twenty years been tending towards cinema. Great stage-managers were straining every effort to force a stage-play to become something more than a series of conversations. A play is—people talking; the aim of such men as Meyerhold was to *suggest* a world encompassing the dialogue. The talking film made it possible to add a complete setting to the dialogue, a real street or a fantastic background, the shadow of Nosferatu as well as sky and sea.

The life of the theatre is bound up with the expression of emotions, and the fact that its scope is limited to words and gestures made it seem, when faced with the competition of the talking picture, almost as handicapped as was the silent film.

A small head in an enormous auditorium, such is the stage actor; a film actor is an enormous head in a small auditorium. All to the advantage of the latter; for moments that the theatre could never render save by silence could, even on the silent screen, be implemented by the play of emotion writ large on a face.

Moreover, the size of the figures on the screen enables the actor to dispense with the gesticulation and other symbolic byplay needed by stage-acting if it is to take effect. Beside a good silent film it was the stage-play that had the air of being a dumb-show performance. Despite the microphone (indeed because of it) the hurried or breathless delivery of the cinema is truer to life than that of the best actor, if he is playing in a large theatre-hall.

The chief problem for the author of a talking film is to decide *when* his characters should speak. On the stage, remember, there is someone talking all the time... except during the intervals. The *entr'acte* is one of the great standbys of the dramatist. Things take place while the curtain is down, and he can convey them by allusions. To bridge these time-gaps the novel has the blank page between the parts; the theatre, the interval; the cinema, next to nothing.

A film director will retort that he has the division into sequences, each sequence ending on a fade-out, which suggests the lapse of time. That is so, but only relatively so; it suggests a lapse of time in which nothing occurs. (With some exceptions, special cases such as *The Blue Angel*, which call for individual analysis.) Unlike the time-gap of the interval during which all sorts of things may happen, that of the fade-out permits of scarcely any allusion to what has filled it, if that involves a change affecting any of the characters. The only methods of suggesting a long, eventful lapse of time in the film are bound to be symbolic devices (e.g. clocks, calendars with the dates fluttering past). On the other hand, while the stage-play can never move back in time, from a man's middle age to his youth, for instance, the film can manage this, though none too easily.

Roughly, the sequence is the equivalent of the chapter. The cinema has not those ampler divisions expressed by the parts of a book and the acts of a play. True, the silent film had parts; they are suppressed in talking films, and this is where the cutter comes up against one of his knottiest problems; for the "talkie" allows no gaps, continuity is the essence of its technique.

Because it has become narrative, its true rival is not the play but the novel.

V

The film can tell a story; there lies its power. So can the novel, and when sound films came in, the silent films had borrowed greatly from the novel.

A great novelist is a "producer" of sorts and we can analyse his methods from that angle; whether his aim be to tell a story, to depict or dissect characters, or to explore the meaning of life; whether his talent runs to copiousness as with Proust, or tends to crystallization as in Hemingway's case, he is bound to narrate—in other words, to epitomize, to stage-manage, to "present." What I mean by the "production" of a novel is the instinctive or deliberate selection by the author of the moments he sets store on and the methods used to make them salient.

With most writers the hall-mark of "production" is the transition from narrative to dialogue. Dialogue in the novel serves three purposes.

Firstly, that of exposition. This was the technique prevalent in England at the close of the nineteenth century; the method of Henry James and Conrad. It tends to obviate the absurd convention of the novelist's omniscience, but replaces it by another still more palpable convention. The cinema uses that sort of dialogue as sparingly as possible; likewise the modern novel.

Secondly, to bring out character. Stendhal aimed at bringing out Julien Sorel's character far more by his acts than by his way of speaking; but in the twentieth century what I may call "tone of voice" came to rank high in the novelist's technique. It became a method of expressing personality, indeed a vital element of character. Proust hardly seems to see his characters, but he has a blind man's adroitness in making them speak; one feels that many scenes from his books would, if well read, be more effective on the radio, where the actor is invisible, than in the theatre. But the cinema, like the theatre, attaches less importance to dialogue; for the acting should suffice to bring a character to life.

Lastly, there is the *essential* dialogue, that of the dramatic "scene." This calls for no further development. It is what every great artist makes of it: suggestive, terse, impassioned; whether it emerges in sudden, splendid isolation (as in Dostoievsky) or is linked up with the scheme of things (as in Tolstoy). For all great writers it is the supreme method of energizing narrative, gripping the reader; it enables them to conjure up scenes before his eyes, adding the third dimension.

The cinema has recently discovered this sort of dialogue, and owes much of its present vigour to it. In the most modern pictures the director switches over into dialogue after long passages of silent film, exactly as a novelist breaks into dialogue after long stretches of narrative.

The novelist has another weapon to his armoury; he can imbue a critical moment in his character's career with the prevailing atmosphere, the climate of the outside world. Conrad uses this device all but systematically, and Tolstoy owes to it one of the finest romantic scenes in literature, the wounding of Prince Andrew at Austerlitz. The Russian cinema used it ably in its great period; but it is dropping out of use as box-office receipts mount up.

The novel seems, however, to retain one notable advantage over the cinema: it can delve into the inner consciousness of a character. Nevertheless, the modern novelist seems less and less disposed to analyse his characters in their hours of crisis; and, moreover, such a dramatic psychology as Shakespeare's and, to a great extent, that of Dostoievsky, in which the secrets of the heart are conveyed by acts or veiled avowals, can be no less artistically effective, no less revealing, than complete analysis. And, finally, the element of mystery in every character left partly unexplained, if it be conveyed as, thanks to the marvelous expressiveness of the human face it can be, on the screen, may well serve to give a work of art that curious *timbre*, as of a lonely voice seeking an explanation of life's riddle, which endows certain memorable reveries (Tolstoy's magnificent short novels, for example) with their compelling majesty.

VI

These pages are a series of reflexions on a method of expression; they have no necessary connexion with the industry which aspires to set the whole world dreaming of a *milieu* whose atmosphere seems to a French mind approximately that of our Paris Boulevards at the close of the Second Empire. From the puerile beginnings of the silent film to its apogee, the cinema seemed to have made vast strides; what has it achieved since then? It has perfected lighting and technique, but it has made no outstanding discoveries in the field of art.

By "art" I mean here the expression of significant relations between human beings, or between minds and things. Some of the best silent films, Germanic and Scandinavian, realized these possibilities. The American cinema of 1940, followed by that of other countries, is concerned above all—naturally enough from a commercial point of view—with enhancing its entertainment value. It is a form not of literature but of journalism. And yet, as journalism, it is constrained to have recourse to an element from which art cannot be permanently banned: the element of the Myth. For a full decade the cinema has been dallying with the Myth.

Symptomatic of this game of hide-and-seek that has been going on is the relation between scenarios and film-stars, especially the female stars. A screen star is not by any manner of means an actress who goes in for film work. She is a person capable of a modicum of dramatic competence, whose face expresses, symbolizes, incarnates, a collective instinct. Marlene Dietrich is not an actress as Sarah Bernhardt was an actress; she is a myth, like Phryne. The Greeks gave their instincts vague biographies; thus do modern men who invent for theirs successive life-stories, as the myth-makers invented, one after the other, the labours of Hercules.

So true is this that the film artists themselves are vaguely conscious of the myths they incarnate, and insist on scenarios that bear them out. Thanks to close-ups the public knows them as it never knew its stage idols. And the artlife of the film-star takes a different course from that of the stage idol; a great actress is a woman who can incarnate a large number of different rôles; the star, a woman who can give rise to a large number of scenarios built to her measure.

The dumb-show performances of an earlier age grafted countless adventures on to certain characters of the Italian *commedia*. And cinema-goers know well that, however much a scenario-writer attempts to create original characters, the actor always imposes his own personality on them. In former days there was a "Pierrot" series: "Pierrot Takes to Stealing," "Pierrot on the Gallows," "Pierrot Drunk," and "Pierrot in Love." So now we have Greta Garbo the Queen, Greta the Courtesan; Marlene the Spy, Marlene the Harlot; Stroheim at Gibraltar, Stroheim at Belgrade, Stroheim at the Front; Gabin in the Foreign Legion, Gabin as a Pimp. And so forth. But the perfect example is Charlie Chaplin. I saw in Persia a film that has no existence, called *Charlie's Life*. Persian picture-shows are given in the open; on the walls surrounding the enclosure sat black cats watching. The Armenian exhibitors had made a *montage* of all the Charlie "shorts" and done the job with skill. The film ran to a considerable footage and the result was breath-taking. It was the myth pure and unadulterated; it had a huge success.

What the actor thus demonstrates holds good probably for the scenario as well. *The Ring of the Nibelungs* is a famous myth; René Clair's international success, *The Million*, a rejuvenation of the Cinderella fairy-tale; there is an element of myth in *Potemkin*, in *The Mother*, in *Caligari*, in *The Blue Angel*, in the great Swedish pictures, in all Chaplin's films. Amongst other modern myths, Justice (in its individual or collective forms) and Sex are far from having outlived their appeal.

The cinema is addressed to the masses; and, for good or evil, they love the myth. A fact that war brings home to us; the parlour strategist is a far less common figure in wartime than the mythmonger who assures us "on good authority" that the enemy chop children's hands off. The lies of journalism and sensational magazine articles batten on the myth.

The myth begins with Sexton Blake, but it ends with Christ. The masses are far from invariably preferring what is best for them; still, on occasion, they are drawn to it. How much did the crowds who listened to St. Bernard's preaching understand? But what they did understand, at the moment when that unaccustomed voice struck deep into the secret places of their hearts, was well worth understanding…

Also, we must never forget—the cinema is an industry.

CHAPTER 11
ROMAN INGARDEN

Roman Ingarden (1893–1970) was a Polish aesthetician, ontologist, and phenomenologist, primarily known outside of Poland for his work on literature and the arts. He was a student of Edmund Husserl, although he ultimately rejected Husserlian phenomenology for his own, realist approach, which seeks to unify phenomenology and ontology. The selection included here appeared under this heading, "The Film," in his book, Ontology of the Work of Art (Untersuchungen zur Ontologie der Kunst, *published in German in 1961), which was originally published in French ("Le temps, l'espace et le sentiment de réalité") in* Revue Internationale de Filmologie *in 1947.*

"The Film" addresses the relationship between film and reality, and in so doing discusses both the relationship between the spectator and the film and the ways in which film compares to the other arts. At the heart of Ingarden's philosophy of film is his notion of the "habitus of reality," the impression of reality given by a work of art that inspires spectators to relate to the things, characters, and events in the work as if they were real—while knowing the whole time, of course, that they are appreciating a fiction. This forces the filmmaker to walk a very thin line when making a film, between producing a work that is altogether too unbelievable for anyone to relate meaningfully to it, on the one hand, and a work that is so inseparable from reality that the spectator cannot see it as a fiction at all, on the other.

Ingarden begins by establishing a distinction between the artistic film (any film with a fictional narrative) and the news film. In watching a news film, Ingarden notes, the spectator thinks that what they are seeing are the events or persons concerned, themselves: it is not a reenactment, certainly not a fiction, not even an interpretation, but instead, the spectator watches the new film as if reality has been recorded directly onto the film. With an artistic film, however, everyone knows that the things and persons presented are not real. Of course, real actors and real things are filmed—the cameras are pointed at and recording images of real things—but these things are not what they are presented as in the film itself (the actor is not the same person as the character he or she plays, for example). Because of the impression of reality that the actors are able to give us in their performances, as well as the coherence of the world of the film presented by the film as a whole (in, at least, good films), spectators can relate to the fictional characters—emotionally, intellectually, etc.—as if they were real, while knowing they are not. Film is incapable of presenting the things themselves; film, rather, presents only the aspects—the images, impressions, expressions—of those things. Thus, in the aesthetically successful film, mere phantoms take on the habitus of reality.

The spectator's job, then, is to determine the natures of the "objectivities" presented in a film, and Ingarden thinks that this is done somewhat differently in silent and sound films. In silent film, the only access the spectator has to the things and persons presented in the film is what Ingarden calls a "pictorial process," that is, the sequence of still photographs that make up the film strip and, when projected in a movie house, ultimately produce the experience of motion on the screen familiar to all moviegoers. In sound film, in addition to the visual access common to silent film, the spectator also has aural access to whatever the film makes audible. On Ingarden's view, the sound film can do this in two ways: by way of presenting the voices and incidental sounds of objects whose images are presented in the film, or by way of music. Good sound films, Ingarden thinks, employ both. Whether a film is silent or a talkie, however, the cinema is only possible by way of a collaboration between different arts: painting, literature, theater, and music, at the very least. As Ingarden notes, however, there are immense difficulties and challenges in attempting to harmonize the many diverse artistic elements of a film. Understanding film's relationship to those other arts helps us to see just what sort of collaboration (and comparisons) he has in mind.

The photographic origins of cinematography centralize the visual image in any aesthetic consideration of film, and Ingarden's analysis is no exception: film is in some respects one of the so-called "spatial arts," that is, those arts, like painting, which achieve their artistic ends through the organization of (in this case) the visual field. The chief difference between painting and cinema, of course, has to do with the possibility of motion in the latter: while something is always happening in a film, paintings present events at a halt—one moment, frozen in time. Of course, not every painting presents an event; still-lifes, landscapes, portraits, and so on are often meant much more straightforwardly as mere depictions of forms or essences rather than events. On Ingarden's view (articulated in greater detail in the section of Ontology of the Work of Art *devoted to "The Picture"), paintings that depict frozen moments—what he calls "literary paintings"—have three strata of signification: (1) the visual aspects of whatever is being depicted, reconstructed according to whatever technique or tradition within which the painter works; (2) the presented objects themselves (whereas the first stratum is the method by which the painter presents whatever is presented, the second stratum consists of the objects being presented themselves); and (3) the presented life situation, within which the presented objects take on whatever meaning they have for the moment captured and represented in the painting. On this view, then, a painting can be seen as a somewhat complex method for presenting a narrative by way of a single moment within that narrative's timeframe—and cinematic frames certainly do this, to some extent. Nevertheless, the fundamental difference between painting and film must now also be evident: while a literary painting is by its very nature limited to a single moment in time, a film is not. For Ingarden, this indicates that film shares something fundamental with literature, as well.*

If film and literature are both arts which can present narrative sequences over the course of time, it is also the case that literature can only ever do so by way of the mediation of language. This is simply to say, for Ingarden, that if a novelist or poet wishes to present an object to the reader, they cannot do so directly; they must describe the object in words, which then stand in for the presented object in the process of reading. This mediating quality of language is not essential to film, however—not even to sound film—since the fundamental aesthetic principle of film is that everything must be shown. When the characters in a good film speak, speech is simply one more aspect of the world presented in the film, and in this sense is not mediating as in literature, but instead is a part of the object (the character) that is presented. Other uses of language in cinema—such as narration, or intertitles (in silent films)—stand outside the presented world of the film as a part of the mode of presentation itself. Naturally, a film can attempt to use language in a more literary way—the mediating quality of extensive narration or exposition, for example—but Ingarden thinks such films have failed as films precisely to the extent that they force the filmgoer to become a "reader" instead.

Film, then, stands on the borderline of literature and painting—bearing traits in common with both, but identical to neither. Another art that might seem similarly situated, at first, is theater, but Ingarden makes very clear that, on his view, the stage play is very much on the side of (if not a species of) literature. In the stage play, the characters speaking present almost everything that is presented; to be sure, the language of the stage play serves a mediating function in the presentation of the world of the play. In film, however, as in painting, the figures presented (whether they speak or not) are elements within the whole world that is presented by non-linguistic means. (This is true even of characters within works of literature, for Ingarden, who although constantly mediated by language in their presentation are nevertheless not typically the presenters themselves; that is, literary dialogue is a part of the object presented in a work of literature, not the mode of presentation itself.) Although Ingarden suggests that early sound films suffered from their perceived similarity to stage plays (and thus, were too much driven by language, and not nearly enough by the visual image), over time it has become apparent that, if a film is to be a good film, the characters presented in the film should not talk too much. A character should speak only when speech is the most realistic action for that character in the life situation in which they find themselves. Otherwise, Ingarden warns, the habitus of reality is threatened; a film in which the characters say things that real people in their situations would not say (typically for expository benefit) is an unbelievable film.

Finally, Ingarden examines the relationship between cinema and music. Ultimately, he asserts that music is an appropriate supplement to film because of the ways in which both arts organize the flow of time. This is a different sort of analysis than those Ingarden conducts of painting and literature, in large part because music is not a representational art. What music can and must do, however, is manage the listener's experience of time in the musical work. Music organizes time according to tone and tempo, he says, as opposed to anything as objective as measure. Thus, the time of music is always already colored by affect and expressivity. Ingarden thinks that this is true of filmic time, as well: time in a film is much less about objective measurement than it is about mood and pacing (many quick cuts and rapid camera movements, for example, make a scene move more quickly—even if it is objectively longer than other, slower scenes). Film then functions as a kind of visual music, at least where time is concerned, and music is thus a natural fit with film. Every film will require its own special music, of course, as the phenomenon of the film score seems to reflect. And Ingarden will go so far as to say that even a silent film is incomplete without music; music is not a mere supplement to the film, but a true complement which can bring to fruition and greater effect the presentation of temporality latent in the film. This means, however, that the film's visual images ought to be produced with music in mind, and thus that the spatial organization of the film ought to complement its temporal organization. The flow of the opening and closing of spaces in the film's visual aspect takes on something of a musical character which can be made evident and even heightened by the right score.

Only film, Ingarden thinks, can bring such disparate arts as painting, literature, theater, and music together to such harmonious effect. Harmony is not guaranteed, however, and it is in his belief that a film is a good film only when it achieves such harmony in its presentation that Ingarden establishes what could be read as an aesthetic criterion for the cinema. Without the proper complementarity and organization, a film would descend into cacophony—and such disharmony is antithetical to and destructive of whatever beauty is possible in film.

Filmography

- ***Romance Sentimentale*** [*Sentimental Romance*] (France, 1930). *Directed and Written by* Grigori Aleksandrov *and* Sergei M. Eisenstein. *Produced by* Léonard Rosenthal. *Starring* Mara Griy.
- ***Sous les toits de Paris*** [*Under the Roofs of Paris*] (France, 1930). *Directed and Written by* René Clair. *Produced by* Films Sonores Tobis. *Starring* Albert Préjean *and* Pola Illéry.
- ***City Lights*** (USA, 1931). *Directed, Produced, Written by, and Starring* Charlie Chaplin. *Also starring* Virginia Cherrill.
- ***Fantasia*** (USA, 1940). *Directed by* Samuel Armstrong, James Algar, Bill Roberts, Paul Satterfield, Ben Sharpsteen, David D. Hand, Hamilton Luske, Jim Handley, Ford Beebe, T. Hee, Norman Ferguson, *and* Wilfred Jackson. *Produced by* Walt Disney *and* Ben Sharpsteen. *Written by* Joe Grant *and* Dick Huemer. *Starring* Leopold Stokowski *and* Deems Taylor.
- ***Goupi mains rouges*** [*It Happened at the Inn*] (France, 1943). *Directed and Written by* Jacques Becker. *Produced by* Charles Méré. *Starring* Fernand Ledoux, Robert Le Vigan, Georges Rollin, *and* Blanchette Brunoy.
- ***Hamlet*** (UK, 1948). *Directed, Produced, Written by, and Starring* Laurence Olivier.

THE FILM

Translated by Raymond Meyer with John T. Goldthwait

The Habitus *of Reality*

We sometimes speak of the "film" as an art. By that we do not mean "film" in the sense of the ribbon of celluloid that is covered with a series of "pictures." Rather, what we have in mind is a special kind of spectacle, that is produced on a screen by means of that ribbon of film and a projection apparatus and is shown to spectators. I intend to concern myself here with this kind of spectacle. Among the spectacles of this kind, however, I shall single out for examination one particular type, the "artistic" film, leaving out of consideration both journalistic and scientific films.

Now, in what does the difference between the kinds of film spectacles that have been opposed to one another consist? The news film shows the spectator certain real things and the events and processes taking place through the participation of those things. This happens, of course, by means of the projection of certain "pictures" upon the screen. Consequently, the spectator does not deal directly with persons, things, and processes, but merely with their "likenesses." However, when the spectator apprehends these likenesses, he involuntarily directs his attention to the originals of these likenesses. He sees in the pictures the persons and things themselves, without being explicitly aware that these objects are not, strictly speaking, present themselves to him. He forgets, so to say, that he has before him mere likenesses, and it seems to him that he is seeing, for example, the participants at the Yalta Conference and the happenings that once really took place there. This state of affairs is fundamentally different from the situation in the case of an "artistic" film, even if one disregards for the time being the artistic or aesthetic value of the latter. Things and persons presented in such a film play, for example, in Chaplin's *City Lights* or René Clair's *Sous les Toits de Paris*, do not belong, strictly speaking, to the real world. We cannot encounter them in the street and have dealings with them directly, as we obviously can with the authors of these films or with the actors. They are mere phantoms of a very special kind, characters out of a "story"—and everything that happens to them, all events in which they take part, do not take place in the real world, in which, for example, the events of the last war took place, which we all witnessed and participated in. The events in which they participate are likewise from the completely different world of fiction; they are events from a novel or some other kind of literary work, with the sole difference that they are not told of with words, but instead are shown. Even when these persons say something, what we are concerned with is not a narration or a report about what they are saying; rather, their words themselves are presented.[1]

[1] There is another difference between the manner in which the spoken words are presented and the way in which the persons and things presented in the film-picture are presented. But we need not concern ourselves with this difference here.

The fact that the persons and things presented in the film play are not real is not in contradiction with the circumstance that real objects—people, puppets, things, or mere "decorations"—are photographed in order to produce the corresponding "pictures" on the ribbon of film. For just as in the theater it is not the real actor—Moissi, say, or Kainz—who forms an element of the play performed, but the person whom he "plays," Hamlet, or Rosmer (from Ibsen's *Rosmersholm*), in the same way real actors do not take part in the play presented in the film, but only certain—at bottom fictional—persons, things, and their fates.

When we view the objectivities presented in the film play we can sometimes forget that they are merely fictional objectivities belonging to the world of fantasy, which only pretend to be real. Sometimes we see in them not merely certain realities that have somewhere formed parts of our world, but rather—for example, in "historical" dramas—certain real personalities known to us from history, such as Queen Christina of Sweden or Peter the Great, as well as real happenings in which these once took part or which they underwent. The illusion brought about by the film then is then so perfect that one forgets that in actuality the merely presented objectivities are not at all that which they only pretend to be. Finally, it can also happen that they are only shown to us for the purpose of evoking in us, at least to a certain extent, the impression that we are dealing with real people and real events, for otherwise their fictional fates would leave us quite cold and indifferent. In point of fact, however, they do move us, and that is also their purpose. Nevertheless, none of us, as spectators of a film play, really believes that we are dealing with real persons and real happenings. Nor are they such; they are only fictions, fantasy figures, and phantoms, that only give the illusion of being real. If the degree and the kind of suggestions that they exercise on the spectator oversteps a certain limit, if the illusion of reality loses the character of illusion and the character of reality becomes absolutely predominant, then the film play ceases to be a work of art, and changes into a news report, as is the case, for example, in the weekly "newsreel." The impression which an "artistic" motion picture evokes in the spectator becomes transformed into the interest and the sympathy with which we respond to real happenings, and in its activity goes beyond all that a play can and should bring forth in the spectator.

This can be illustrated with an example. In a film play, a hero of the story presented was supposed to undergo a surgical operation. In order to achieve the greatest possible impression upon the spectator, an actual operation on a sick person was filmed. But, as it happened, the surgeons encountered great difficulties in the course of the operation. An unforeseen complication, a strong and dangerous hemorrhage, occurred and for a time appeared to greatly endanger the patient, so that it was all the physicians could do to save the patient's life. This all took place with such "realism" that it was believed that the film would make a strong, perturbing impression on the spectators, and would thereby achieve a great aesthetic success. But while the actual effect was indeed great, it was of an entirely different kind than had been expected. The spectators simply protested. They were so deeply disturbed by experiencing a human being in real danger of death that they no longer wanted to look at the film. What happened? There came a moment when the unexpected consternation coming clearly to expression in the behavior of the physicians and the grisly details of the operation translated the spectators into the attitude of real, serious belief in the reality of what was happening. They could no longer regard the processes being shown them as a mere artistic presentation, and with that there disappeared not only the purely aesthetic effect, but also all desire to witness such a grave turn of human fortune.

What happened was something similar to what occurred in the case of the radio broadcast in the United States, some years after the war, in which an alleged invasion of the Earth by Martians was announced. In other words, the artistically fashioned illusion of reality was transformed for the listeners into an actual reality in which nothing could any longer be recognized as illusory, and at some particular moment the listeners changed their attitude, their mode of attending. Instead of listening to a radio production and receiving it aesthetically, they were truly terrified and reacted to the radio show with real deeds in order to escape from the danger. They turned to the authorities for information or in order to take measures for saving or defending themselves. Their manner of behavior no longer had anything in common with an aesthetic reaction. The radio broadcast had to be broken off, in order to forestall a general panic.

The question arises: By what means does the cinematographic art produce that illusion of reality without showing a "true" reality? This problem is not easy to solve. It is even much more difficult to solve than for a literary work of art. For the moment we shall confine ourselves to establishing that there is no film art work which would not tend to give the illusion of reality, without evoking in the spectator the complete conviction that what is presented in the film is indeed real. It is, by the way, not even necessary that the persons, things, and happenings presented in the film pretend to be real by feigning to be something known to us from history or from our own lives. An artistically made film does not necessarily have to be an "historical" film. The *habitus* of reality can also occur where that which is presented in the film seems to form a unique world of its own, without being related to what we are acquainted with outside the film. How far this peculiarity of the world presented in the film, and its independence from what we know through our daily experience, can go—that, too, is a problem the solution of which requires special reflections that are much too difficult for us to undertake here. But just posing this problem presupposes awareness of the specificity of the world presented in the film. Thus, what is important here is merely that we be aware of the difference between the world presented in the film and the real world.

But not all film plays that show the spectator objects and happenings which are unreal and only appear real are "works of art" in the specific sense of the term. For not all possess an artistic value. In order to have such a value, they must fulfill certain further conditions. Determining these conditions, however, requires a number of preparatory considerations that cannot all be brought forward here. Hence I will limit myself to some introductory remarks.

The Film on the Borderline between the Arts

It must first of all be made clear which particular structural moments distinguish the film play from the works of other arts. To this end, it is especially important that the silent film be distinguished from the sound film. The first offers us a drama in which the sole medium of presentation is a multiplicity of photographically reconstructed visual aspects.[2] The spectator

[2] I am disregarding here the interpolated texts with which in an earlier day silent films were usually provided; they constitute a different medium of information about the presented objectivities, so that when they occur one is no longer dealing with a silent film in the pure sense. It was believed, and is to some extent still believed today, that without the interpolated texts it would be impossible to present cinematographically a fully understandable world. But whether this belief is correct is another question.

has to experience these aspects, in order to apprehend, in their changes and transformations, the objectivities brought to appearance through them. To a great degree, this apprehension resembles that which takes place in the viewing of a picture, with the essential difference, however, that it is not a matter of an immobile picture, but instead—if one might put it this way—of a pictorial process, in which ever new reconstructed aspects succeed one another and bring about the illusion of a transformation to the presented objects. By utilizing all the data that a given film provides by means of reconstructed aspects, we can attempt to understand everything that occurs in the presented world, and especially what takes place within the persons who attain to appearance in the film. In this way we can apprehend the plot of the drama and understand its deeper meaning. In a sound film, the auditory perception of the sounds, and especially the words spoken by the presented persons (perhaps also the sounds made by animals), helps us to achieve this end. The sound film usually contains yet another important factor apprehensible by auditory perception, namely music, which can exercise various other functions in the whole of the sound film.[3] However, it can exercise them properly only if it does not form an independent whole existing purely for itself, but is instead an essential component of the particular film play. Then it is composed in a quite special way and is subordinated in its own particularities to the requirements of the film play, only together with which it forms an artistic, organically structured whole.

The completely "silent" film is an ideal that has never yet been fully realized. It is even questionable whether the silent film as such does not manifest definite limits of presentability that can be crossed only in quite rare cases. Here we encounter the problem of the possibility and of the construction of "abstract" films. For an absolutely "silent" film is already in a certain sense an "abstract" film, since of that which is to be concretely presented it exhibits only what can be constituted by means of purely visual, photographically reconstructed aspects, while it "abstracts" from all non-visual, concrete, quasi-perceptual aspects.

However, interesting though the silent film may be in its specific nature, and important though the problems of the possibilities of its realization may be, the fact remains that the sound film already exists, and that today it is almost the only kind of film that is shown. The sound film presents us with quite special problems, both with respect to its structure and with regard to the artistic possibilities that it opens up.

If we confine ourselves to the sound films which realize the possibilities of the art of the film, we can say that the film play is a work of art that lies on the borderline between different arts, the collaboration of which results in a formation of a quite special kind. On the one hand, it approaches the literary work of art of one or another genre; on the other hand, it is related to the picture, or better, to a multiplicity of pictures that merge one into the other. However, it is also close to the theatrical play, although differing from it in important ways. Finally, the film play contains essential moments of the musical work, leaving aside the fact that it is often combined with a musical work, especially a work of program music, and forms with it a whole of a higher order.

---

[3] Zofia Lissa published an interesting book on these functions with the title *Muzyka I film, stadium z pogranicza ontologii, estetyki I psychologii muzyki filmowej* (Music in the film: a study on the borderlines of ontology, aesthetics, and psychology of film music) (Lvov: Nakt. Księgarni Lwowskiej, 1937). [In addition to the work mentioned, and since the publication of the German original of the present translation, Prof. Lissa has also published *Estetyka muzyki filmowej* (Aesthetics of music in the film) (Cracow: Polskie Wydawn. Muzyczne, 1964), available in German translation as *Ästhetik der Filmmusik* (Berlin: Henschelverlag, 1965).]

Considering the same problem from another point of view, one can say that, on the one hand, the film play belongs to the works of temporal art, but on the other hand contains essential moments of spatial art. It is a work of presentational art, but at the same time contains in itself moments of art consisting of a synthesis of pure qualities of different fundamental kinds, and it contains them in higher measure, the more it embodies the ideal of the abstract film. It is, then, an extraordinarily rich and complex formation, a polyphonic work in which very different qualitative moments cooperate and lead to harmonies and disharmonies of various kinds. The problems of the artistic structuring of a whole produced synthetically from these heterogeneous qualities, that also embodies artistic values of its own, are extraordinarily numerous and complex. In order to determine what they are even provisionally, it is necessary to penetrate somewhat deeper into the details of the film work's structure.

On the Borderline between Literature and Painting

The basic element of the film play and also the factor that makes it an art of a special kind, is that which is decisive for its essential kinship with the picture as a work of art. In both cases certain visual aspects, which are reconstructed on the screen with the help of patches of color or of light and shadow, make possible the quasi-perceptual presentation of Objects that have been made visible, of things, of people, and of events. But a picture that is a static phenomenal presentation of certain objects and of the events taking place at a definite point of time through the participation of those objects, which events are, as it were, brought to a halt. In contrast, the film play presents the continuous unfolding of certain processes in their successive phases, as well as the dynamic production of events in which presented people and things take part. And this presentation takes place with the help of a series of visual aspects merging fluidly one with the other, which are mentally, consciously experienced by the spectator, and which, in their being so experienced, permit him to apprehend the presented objects.

In a film play something is always happening. This is so in a double sense: (a) in the stratum of presented objects something constantly happens with the persons and things, and even the processes taking place change in their course; (b) in the stratum of reconstructed aspects, the contents of these aspects and their succession change continually; some appear while others pass by and vanish.

Because of this continuous happening in the objectual stratum, the film play most nearly resembles the kind of pictures which earlier I called pictures with a literary theme. As I demonstrated, a picture of this kind contains three different strata: (a) the stratum of the aspects, which are reconstructed using a certain technique (of the particular painter or of an entire artistic movement), (b) the stratum of presented objects, (c) the stratum of the presented life situation, of an event, in which the presented objects, and especially certain persons, take part. A picture of this kind always shows only a single moment of a process, but also intimates certain earlier and maybe also certain future phases of the process, which must be guessed by the viewer. And this guessing—if it is to become fully conscious—can only unfold in a literary formation, in a sentence. Just this fact is the reason why I speak here of a literary theme of the picture. In contrast, a film shows at least the most important stages of its development, which make its complete unfolding understandable. The film does not confine itself to presenting merely a single situation that is taken out of a whole story and is thus made static. This mode of successive presentation of a multiplicity of phases of that which takes place in the presented world, and which, at least in principle, could just as well be set forth in words, determines the close kinship between the film play and the literary work. The film narrates, as it were, that which takes place in the world of presented objectivities,[4] but it does it with the help of a multiplicity of pictures fluidly merging one with the other and not with the help of linguistic formations (I am disregarding, of course, the words of the persons presented in the film which are reproduced by a recording). Both the means and the procedures used for presentation are different in the two cases.

In the literary work of art, the elements of the presented world are, so to say, created and determined in their details by the twofold stratum of the language. It is also the language that determines and suggests to the reader the aspects in which the presented objects in the literary work of art are exhibited. It is, so to speak, the mediator between the reader and the presented quasi-real world of the work, and gives him an interpretation of it. It permits him to intend the presented objects, to keep them before his mind's eye, and to visualize them more or less vividly, without, however, making immediate contact with them possible for him. This mediating character of language can be clearly felt especially when a mediator of a peculiar kind appears: the narrator. A narrator appears in a very great number of literary works, but neither is he necessary for the literary work as such, nor does he stand in contradiction with its essential nature. However, language as such cannot be lacking in a literary work. In contrast to this, the mediating role of language is not indispensable in the film—and the more so that of the narrator. Not language, but a multiplicity of flowing visual aspects, reconstructed photographically or graphically, constitutes here the proper—and in the silent films the only—means of presentation, which gives the spectator access to the phenomenally appearing presented world. In his mental experiencing of these aspects, the spectator ceases to see the screen, and in its place sees in an almost perceptual manner things and people which conduct themselves in a certain way in the presented space.

If these aspects were identical with the originally experienced aspects that one experiences in sensory perceiving, then one would simply see things and people in real space. But in the film they are always *aspects*, which, despite the far-reaching tendency to achieve a faithful reconstruction of perceptual aspects, deviate from the latter in various respects, since the technique of reconstruction results in certain distortions. The essential and principal point of the affinity of the two types of aspects lies in the fact that both have as their bases a multiplicity of sense data which essentially distinguish themselves by their special aliveness and actuality from the data that we have in the case of intuitive imaginings, no matter how vivid these may be. With justification one could say, then, that the things and people presented in the film are not simply imagined, but rather really seen by the spectator, although it is not a matter of a straightforward perceptual seeing. In consequence of the distortions to which the aspects reconstructed in the film are subjected, the character of the immediate, "personal" own presence of the object—as it occurs in perception—is only apparent in the film, and thus the objects presented in the film are only phantoms, that merely feign to be "personally" themselves present. However, the reconstructed aspects' foundation of sense data has the effect that what in point of fact is only a pure illusion appears to the spectator almost in its own selfhood and takes on the character or the phenomenal *habitus* of a reality.

---

[4] These objectivities are, of course, those objects from a fictional story of which we spoke earlier. They must not be confused with real objects that were photographed for the purposes of the film play.

This appearance of reality is further strengthened by certain characteristic features of the film play. The individual presented things and persons move in a way that is independent of the spectator and apparently autonomous, and they comport themselves like real beings. This conduct comprehends not only what one can see, but also, in the sound film, all that can be heard, such as tones, noises, spoken words, etc. In particular, the presented people in general behave physically in a way completely similar to that of real people. In their gestures, their facial expressions, and their movements, various changes take place that express their mental states and processes. Consequently, the spectator is not just a witness of their physical behavior, but also has access to their mental life, almost in the same way as in daily life, provided, of course, that he himself acts appropriately. There appear before him not merely human bodies, but people, physical beings, endowed with a mental life and psychical character qualities. He understands their emotions, their yearning and their love, or their hatred and their resentment. He penetrates into their plans and the realization of their expectations; to a certain degree, he knows what mental images they are having and can understand their thoughts. Thus, he apprehends their actions not merely from the outside, but also from within, and grasps their meaning. He thus arrives at what is intrinsically peculiar to their activities and their souls. For their part, the character of a subject, which they have, and the spontaneity of their action in interpersonal conflicts strengthen the character of autonomy and consequently the character of (apparent) reality of what one "sees" and understands in the film. And one begins to live with the fictive figures and their fortunes, almost as in daily life, although never so directly and concretely as in the theatrical play, but on the other hand more concretely and intuitively than in a purely literary work of art.

Despite all affinity of the film play with the literary work of art, the factor of language is completely lacking in the silent film, while in the sound film it constitutes only a supplementary means of presentation. The fact that even in the sound film the chief means of presentation is a multiplicity of flowing aspects, is the basic principle of composition of the film play. In it, everything in the presented world must either be determined in the content of the aspects or be expressed mediately by what is presented visually. If the sound film is made in accordance with this principle, then the language occurring in the film must be the living speech of the persons appearing in the film. It then belongs to their behavior and thus also to what is presented in the film, although it is at the same time that which presents linguistically. In contrast, the texts that are often interpolated in a film, as well as the speech of the narrator who is sometimes introduced into films, are an alien element in relation to presented world, which is, so to speak, only joined onto the film play from the outside.

Thus the film play is situated on the borderline between two arts that are completely different from one another: literature and painting. At first glance, it appears that in a good film play everything takes place exactly as in a stage play. As a consequence, the art of the film initially struck out on a false path and imitated the theater. In the theater, too, there is ordinarily no narrator; here the "dramatis personae" are shown to us directly in what befalls them and in their physical behavior, the latter permitting us to have commerce with and to understand their mental processes and states. In the theater also, the spoken words and speeches are happenings in the presented world. Lastly, in both cases the words spoken spontaneously by the persons contribute significantly to the character of reality of the presented persons and happenings. And yet the two kinds of play differ essentially from one another.

Apart from the different ways of reconstructing the aspects, the essential difference between the plays of the two types consists in the fact that in the theater the words spoken, and thus realized, as it were, by the figures constitute the essential means of presentation, while all that which we can *see* in the stage play (όψεως χόσμος) is only an ancillary means, a supplementary factor, of presentation and also, in a certain sense, of the presented world. The stage play is a borderline instance of literature and is closer to it than the sound-film play. In the latter, the roles of the two means of presentation are radically changed. Here the factor of the visible, of the visual aspects and of the visually given qualities of the presented world, becomes the primary means of presentation, while the spoken words and everything else audible are only a supplementary factor that helps us to understand what is not presentable in a purely visual way, and that also contributes significantly to the full concreteness of the presented world—which in itself is not a silent world—even if only in a secondary and supplementary fashion. In all cases where a factor of the play—in the theater or in the film—stands in conflict with the fundamental principle of its structure, it proves, in its aesthetic apprehension, to be something unnecessary, something dispensable, or even to be a disturbing element. Thus every long speech, every tirade, even every long dispute, that is acceptable, or at worst still tolerable in the stage play, especially when the play is written in verse, is in the film play something intolerable, boring and often disturbing to the unity of the play.[5] If the spoken word is fashioned in consonance with the fundamental principle of the film play's composition, then it is only a component of the behavior of the figure to which form is given, only a supplement of the gesture, indeed, it is sometimes almost this gesture itself. In film, the figures often speak with one another in half-sentences, even in half-words, a way of speaking that belongs essentially to their behavior, while these utterances could not be called fragmentary. But everything that goes beyond that has the effect of unnecessary declamation.

Of course, the spoken word is never a gesture in the strict sense. For the gesture, like every behavioral means of expression, does nothing other than express just that which is itself not audible or visible. That is, it externalizes what is interior and makes mental phenomena or at least their specific qualities at all apprehensible. In contrast, the word always *means* something,[6] and if it is a normal formation, it also always designates an object. Only when it is pronounced, and in a tone bearing "manifestation qualities,"[7] does it express something. Without meanings there are no words, and a fortiori, no sentences. There are, however, many sentences and

---

[5] Thus Shakespeare's *Hamlet*, for example, even with such a good actor as Olivier, would have been wholly intolerable as a film if the complete Shakespearean text had been preserved. This is also true, for example, of the dramas of Grillparzer, or even those of Ibsen.

[6] When they speak of meaning in contradistinction to expression, linguists are often inclined to cite the works of Karl Bühler, especially his *Sprachtheorie* (Theory of language) (Jena: Fischer, 1934), as the source of this distinction. However, Kazimierz Twardowski in his monograph *Zur Lehre von Inhalt und Gegenstand der Vorstellungen* (Toward a theory of the content and the object of mental presentations) (Vienna, 1894) had already distinguished the different functions of language. Edmund Husserl subsequently elaborated this distinction much more deeply—see "Investigations" II and V in *Logical Investigations* [2 vols., translated by J.N. Findlay (New York: Humanities Press, 1970); first published in German as *Logische Untersuchungen*, 2 vols. (Halle an der Saale: Max Niemeyer, 1900; 2nd ed. 1913–1921)]. Finally, I also concern myself with linguistic formations and functions of language in the fifth chapter of my book: *The Literary Work of Art: An Investigation on the Borderlines of Ontology, Logic, and Theory of Literature. With an Appendix on the Functions of Language in the Theater*, trans. George G. Grabowicz (Evanston, IL: Northwestern University Press, 1973). (Hereafter cited as *The Literary Work.*) [First published in German as *Das literarische Kunstwerk: Eine Untersuchung aus dem Grenzgebiet der Ontologie, Logik und Literaturwissenschaft* (Halle an der Saale: Max Niemeyer, 1931; 2nd ed., Tübingen: Max Niemeyer, 1960; 3rd ed., 1965). Polish translation by Maria Turowicz, *O dziele literackim: Badania z pogranicza ontologii, teorii jezyka I filozofii literatury* (Warsaw: Państwowe Wydawnictwo Naukowe, 1960).]

[7] See *The Literary Work*, pp. 60–61.

other linguistic formations that express nothing mental, for example, printed mathematical theorems or functional equations. But for the word used in the film, it is important that it always be uttered. Every linguistic formation fashioned in the spirit of the film play performs its expressive function very powerfully and precisely by intimately fitting in with the behavior of the one speaking. The meaning of such a linguistic formation is, so to speak, very condensed. Through its meaning it only complements the presented situation with moments which cannot be brought to presentation in visual aspects, which also enter into the course of happenings as essential elements of it, and without which the action would consist merely of *disiecta membra* and would be not only incomprehensible to the spectator, but also could not be followed by him. So used, words do not draw the spectator's attention to themselves and do not divert it from the movement of the plot. Rather they permit him better to become absorbed in this movement, to apprehend it not just from the outside, but also in its inner sense.

If the spoken word is used in the film play in the way indicated, one does not violate the fundamental principle that in a film everything must be shown. For the spoken words (or other sound formations) also are shown in their concrete sound and form a component part of the physical behavior of the persons presented. They must, however, be such that they are in conformity with the aforementioned principle. They may occur there, and there only, where the presented reality would not be self-sufficient without them, and where their meaning or expressive function delineate what cannot be shown but yet somehow belongs essentially to which is in a certain sense artificial—generally fulfills its expression function and its function of establishing mutual understanding between the speakers. It is efficacious and also economical: It says that and only that which is indispensable in a given situation, and helps human beings to develop their activity. Through its use in the film, incompleteness and incomprehensibility of the presented action are avoided. And thereby are also avoided the deformation and violation of the reality to be presented, which would of necessity result from the elimination of everything human behavior that is not directly visible. An excessive volubility of the presented persons—assuming, of course, that it is not intended as a caricature—not only disturbs and bores the spectator, but also works against the unfolding of the character of reality of the presented world because it seems unnatural. If, however, speech is lacking in a film where it is indispensable, then this not only has a destructive effect on the developing plot, but also weakens the *habitus* of reality of the presented world, inasmuch as by its absence the film is deprived of moments which are essential to the continued development of the plot. It belongs to the normal relations between humans that they speak with one another. The presented persons must therefore be understood in their behavior not merely by the spectator, but also by their partners, for otherwise there would arise misunderstandings between them which would make their cooperation impossible.

Consequently, the completely silent film does not belong to the presentation of collaborative human actions and of human conflicts. One can successfully make such a film only when what is presented contains no interpersonal situations or actions, that is, when the film brings to presentation either an individual human in solitude or an extra-human world (for example, mountain ranges seen from an aircraft). It is thus no accident that at least some films have this new facet of an affinity with literary works, namely that certain linguistic phenomena, seized in their concrete liveliness and reconstructed with that same liveliness, belong to their natural whole. The limits of what is presentable, set by the fully silent film, are thereby broken through, and at the same time language in the sound film is accorded a collaborative role in the reconstruction of the presented world. But if the film play as a whole is to remain a cinematographic phenomenon par excellence, then this role may be conferred only on linguistic formations which belong to the behavior of the presented persons the action. These words then do not exceed the natural function of speech. Living speech—as opposed to the language in literary texts, (from which results the demand for the elimination of every interpolated text), and which do not overstep the boundaries within which they only complement what is presented by aspects. Language's role of an ancillary means of presentation must also be maintained where the objectual units constituted with the help of linguistic meanings are of decisive importance for the plot's tight coherence.

Film and music

In certain cases, where the word does not suffice for the disclosure of mental states which are not expressible in visual aspects,[8] or where speech by the persons taking part in the action would not be appropriate, music is used to assist in the presentation of these states in the film play. Music can collaborate in two different ways in cinematographic presentation. Either the musical structures belong to the presented world itself and appear within it in order to influence certain processes and events taking place there,[9] or else they occur outside the world presented in the film as an accompanying phenomenon.

In the latter case, the musical structures are a factor that remains outside the presented world—just as do, for example, interpolated texts—but they assist in the constitution of the presented world, and in the disclosure of facts in this world that are not brought to appearance by other means of presentation. This is the case, for instance, in Eisenstein's *Romance sentimentale*.[10] The general mood of this film is significantly codetermined and complemented by the mood of the music. But no one in the presented world plays the music; it comes from somewhere outside this world, yet without it this world could not be apprehended and understood in its unique emotional coloring.

There are, however, much deeper grounds for music's contribution to the constitution of the presented world and also for its being closely bound up with this world. The film play, like the stage play or any literary work, is temporally extended, and is so in a double sense: first, what

[8] Even the extreme behaviorists concede that, in addition to a person's visible behavior, which expresses his mental states, there is also behavior apprehensible through other senses, for example, through hearing, touch, etc. There is a certain parallelism between the domain of the mental and the means of expression in different kinds of behavior. There are also, as it appears, mental facts that express themselves in different kinds of behavior, that can thus be apprehended both through visual and through auditory perception. The study of this parallelism, as well as of the different intimate relations between mental facts and the many expressive phenomena, forms an important foundation for the development of the artistic film.

[9] As in the film *The Advocate*, for example, in which a lawyer has to defend his daughter's fiancé, who is accused of a murder. At a certain moment the viewer observes the mental exertion of the lawyer, who is trying to think himself into and to immerse himself in the situation in which the murdered man found himself, in order to discover how the perpetrator of the murder could have committed it. At this moment the music starts up, which expresses the lawyer's mental effort, but this music belongs to the presented world: The lawyer sits down at a piano and begins to play.

[10] Of this film *The Oxford Companion to Film*—edited by Liz-Anne Bawden (New York and London: Oxford University Press, 1976)—says: "Finally a firm offer from Paramount [to Eisenstein] came while Alexandrov and Tissé were working in Paris on *Romance sentimentale* (1930). (Eisenstein allowed his name to be attached to this film at the producer's stipulation, but it held no interest for him and he had little or no hand in its making.)" (p. 224) Eisenstein, with his collaborators Grigori Alexandrov and Edvard Tissé, was on a tour to study film technique outside the USSR.

runs its course in the presented world takes place in presented time[11] (for example, during a few summer months)—and there is no film play in which the phenomenon of concrete time does not occur; second, in the sense that the film play itself, as a peculiar process of the unfolding of certain phenomena (aspects, logemes, etc.) has its own phases and "movements," which, in the same sense as in a musical work, do not merely have as a natural consequence a general time structure, but also lead to the structuring of different particular forms of concretely organized time.

The time in a musical work of art is a structure and phenomenon that is determined exclusively by tone formations and their arrangement.[12] This happens in a twofold way. On the one hand, because the works' different time phases themselves (its moments) bear a qualitative coloring, which results from the purely musical filling-out of a given phase of the work and is codetermined by the qualitative coloring of the earlier moments and sometimes also by those moments of the work that are coming, and that announce their coming. Through this specific coloring the different phases or moments of the work distinguish themselves from one another. Moreover, the time immanent in the work possesses new qualitative determinations that give more precise form to its structural particularities. They are of a still different nature.

Among other things the concrete time appearing in the work (and not merely the time of the work) is distinguished by different structurings and peculiar phenomena. It is a slower or faster developing and passing of the musical formations that are contained in it; it has a rhythm which is peculiar to it, a fact that is connected with a different size of the units of time, of the moments, which contain in a single musical present more or less complex musical phenomena and motifs internally joined with one another.[13] As a result of a greater multitude of musical phenomena which are contained and condensed in them, they appear to be, so to speak, "longer." At the same time, however, they appear to develop much more rapidly, and they do so as a result of the greater condensation of the phenomena contained in them and of their sequence itself. And in this more rapid succession, the individual moments of time acquire a greater "brevity" (paradoxical though this may sound!). And conversely, moments that combine different musical structurings which they contain in a less intimate way, and that do not distinguish themselves through especially great condensation of the musical phenomena they contain, appear to be shorter in themselves; but as a result of this lesser condensation and liveliness, they appear to unfold more slowly, so that the succession of such moments of musical phenomenal time appears to draw itself out longer. Precisely as a consequence of that, the musical formations contained in this time appear to become longer.

What I have called the "organization" of time in the musical work rests on such a determination of the units of time by musical formations and their determinately ordered succession, as well as on the particular qualitative form of the succession and of the unfolding of the work's temporal phases. It is different from work to work in approximately the same measure as these works differ from one another in their musical formations. However, one can also distinguish among these different organizations of time certain general types and certain rankings, such as are designated, for example, by the terms *presto*, *andante*, *largo*, and so on.

---

[11] With regard to the time of the presented world, see *The Literary Work*, § 36.

[12] On this point, see the analyses carried out in the essay on the musical work.

[13] That is why we find that there is something like a "measure" in music. But one must be cautious and should not identify the musical measure with what I have called a unit of time without going into the matter more deeply. It is, however, probable that there are close relationships between the two.

This organization of time, which constitutes itself exclusively with the help of purely acoustic phenomena, can, remarkably enough, also appear on temporally extended objectivities that are not built up of acoustic formations. Thus one can—and in fact must—broaden the concept of music by recognizing musical phenomena also in those instances where the material leading to the organization of time is constituted by determinations that are fundamentally different from all acoustic phenomena. It is exactly this which, among other things, takes place in the film play.

The rhythmic determinations of the movements shown purely visually in the film play, as well as the peculiar rhythmic characteristics and the whole dynamic of the processes which are developed in the plot, the finer traits of the events, their slow succession or the accumulation of catastrophes in short segments of time—all this is a phenomenon of a specifically musical kind and is most intimately connected with the constitution of these or those types and forms of concrete time in the film play. The purely tonal music that, according to the incorrect customary expression, "accompanies" the multiplicity of "pictures" shown in the film fulfills—if it is correctly composed—various functions in the film play. In particular, this music realizes in the tonal material those forms, or at least similar ones, of the organization of time which the cinematographic play itself predetermines, firstly in a pure visual fashion. It is also possible that the music constitutes that form of the organization of time which is a counterpart or a complement to the temporal organization constituted by the film play itself in its phases.

Without the collaboration of music, the fact that the film play engages with the domain of concrete time would of itself be sufficient to make of the film play something mutilated in itself, something lacking the full realization of a determination that it bears in itself in a certain potentiality, or that it determines without, however, being able, with its own purely visual means, to fully embody that determination. That is the reason why from the first beginnings of the art of film, the need was felt to let music somehow participate in the spectacle, without prior reflection on what the proper role of music is with regards to the film play. Thus, at first pieces of music were played, the mood of which seemed to be in agreement with the content of the film, just to fill the acoustic emptiness of the silent film with something, not to mention that it was necessary to cover over the noises of the projector. Only the gradual development of the sound film taught us to understand wherein the organic connection between music and the film play lies. Thus we have ascertained that for every film a quite special piece of music must be created, in order to realize a particular coordination of these two factors and to build a whole out of both of them. In this whole, both of these factors are coordinated with one another or are dependent on one another. Consequently, either one artist must create both, or else there must be an ideal understanding between the composer and the film maker. However, it seems to me that we have not yet fully grasped the musical character of the film play.

The organization of space and the music of transformation

The organization of time in the film play, which is essentially complemented by the temporal organization of the musical work, is closely connected with the organization of the space presented in the film—or at least ought to be. This space is something that cannot be lacking in a film play. This is a consequence of the fact that the fundamental factor of the film's structure is a multiplicity of reconstructed visual aspects of things and people. Leaving aside purely abstract films that bring no bodies whatever to presentation,[14] every picture possesses its three-dimensional presented space, in which the things and bodies presented in it are located, and of which they take up or fill out a portion. This space brought to appearance in the picture—just like the time presented in the film—is a concrete and not an abstract or purely mathematical space. And it is—like that time—organized to a certain extent by the bodies located in it. This occurs through the placement and the motion of the bodies situated in it. On their selection and their position in relation to one another depends the shape of the "empty," transparent space between them. And this space, which is delimited by the surfaces of the things located in it, and, on the other hand, the shape of those spaces that are taken up by those bodies, together form the concrete space presented in the film. The changing distribution of the masses in this space introduces a specific dynamic into the film play. This space is also a special object of aesthetic apprehension by the spectator, and can offer him various aesthetically valuable and active particularities. In this space there is always a certain structure of empty and filled spaces and also a hierarchy of its parts, all of which offers moments that of themselves extend into the domain of architecture. In the film all this undergoes different kinds of transformations as soon as the bodies located in the space begin to move. In this way begins the play of the masses positioned in various ways in the space, and the play of the empty spaces.[15] The movements of the bodies, which have their rhythm and a dynamic of their unfolding, determine both the time presented in the film as well as the presented space, and emphasize in it certain accents that stand out. On the one hand, these accents divide the time into periods and qualitatively determined moments and give time a particular form, but on the other hand they emphasize in concrete space certain precisely outlined or only indistinctly delineated parts (spaces and places), as well as different directions of orientation, lines, and parts of surfaces, etc., all of which taken together introduce a certain heterogeneity into the concrete space.

If we take note of the fact that diverse structurings of the organization of space are developed in different phases of the film, and that the one structuration is transformed into another, that we witness the opening and closing of different spaces in the course of time, of streets, squares, and valleys, for example, which unfold, recede or come closer, spread out or draw together, then we understand that in this domain there are a special rhythm and peculiar effects of the dynamics of transformation, which are all intimately joined with the organization of time, and which constitute in the interior of the presented world a peculiar music of movement and of transformation, with respect to which the ordinary purely tonal music makes up only a particular special case. No art other than that of the film is capable of combining these transformations of organized space, made visible one after the other, so well with music, and of uniting to such a high degree concrete space and concrete time. Further, no other art is capable, to the degree possible to the film, of showing the fortunes of human beings so deeply embedded in concrete time and concrete space.

The literary work of art, of course, has at its disposal the means to situate humans and their fortunes in presented space. It also possesses the means to give form to this space in various ways, according to how this space is understood, but also according to the conception of the

---

[14] Incidentally, I have seen only one such film, which in its first part approached this idea of the abstract film: Walt Disney's *Fantasia*, in London in 1948.

[15] Cf., for example, the French film *Goupi mains rouge*, especially the scene in which one of the heroes, fleeing from the police, climbs a tree from which he finally falls to his death.

bodies located in the space. It has, finally, the means to utilize the particular structuring of the presented space in order to better express the mental and emotional life and the inner structure of the persons presented in the work, or to make a harmonious counterpart to a given human type and to the events taking place in the work. But all this is a merely intentional objectivity that is created and determined by the medium of language, and that is at most indicated in potential aspects in which these objectivities are exhibited. Only the film (especially the three-dimensional film) can effectively show this space and visually present the complete unfolding of its different structurings (something impossible in the theater which makes use of immovable "scenery"), in order to create in this way a unique visible music of the transformation of things and of living persons in a spatial world as well as the space into which they are projected, and finally to envelop all this in the motifs and the rhythmic form of the tonal music that organically belongs to the particular film play.

Thus my assertion is confirmed, that the film play stands on the borderline between many different arts, and that there is an extraordinary multiplicity of heterogeneous moments in it which can be joined in very many ways with one another into an organically unified whole. This happens, of course, only when the film in question is a true work of art. For if it is only a collection of heterogeneous elements that are inimical to one another, then it forms an intolerable cacophony, as was often the case with the first silent films, which were combined with quite randomly selected music.

But in order to surpass this stage of cacophonous conglomerations, in order to create works that, despite all the inner diversity of their elements, are coherent, harmoniously constructed works of art, which harbor within themselves an astonishing multiplicity of moments, the cinematographic art must overcome difficulties and obstacles that are much greater than in the other arts. And this assertion holds good all the more when one considers that it is a matter here of an art whose works cannot come into existence without the harmonious collaboration of different artists, and indeed of artists who, despite the differences among their activities, must understand one another and must influence and support each other in their artistic intentions.

What kind of principles of artistic structuring allow the fashioning of works of art that are coherent, internally coalescent, and, despite all the multiplicity of their moments, internally unitary—that is a problem whose treatment transcends the limits of this essay, but also the limits of what we have thus far learned from our artistic experience. Here we are undoubtedly only "enroute" to that goal, and perhaps even only at the very beginning of the road. But every successful film teaches us something new and is a new means for foreseeing further possibilities that at the present time are only suggested by the multitude of film plays. In order to really attain to the experiential knowledge which reveals itself here as a possibility, perhaps it will be useful to examine also the news film, and the documentary and scientific film, which all show or make accessible to us areas of reality which are not accessible to us in our usual, often superficial and summary, everyday experience. But that is a new facet of this complex of problems that cannot be discussed more fully here.

Revue Internationale de Filmologie, Paris 1947.

CHAPTER 12
MAURICE MERLEAU-PONTY

Maurice Merleau-Ponty (1908–1961) was a French phenomenologist, deeply influenced by Martin Heidegger and at times closely associated with Jean-Paul Sartre, but for whom, in contrast to those thinkers, perception and the body became the focal points of his work. "The Film and the New Psychology" is Merleau-Ponty's only work in the philosophy of film, and was originally published in French ("Le cinéma et la nouvelle psychologie") in Merleau-Ponty's book, Sense and Non-Sense *(*Sens et non-sens*; Gallimard) in 1948.*

Merleau-Ponty begins the essay by explaining a fundamental difference between two approaches in psychology, classical psychology and gestalt psychology (what, in the essay, he calls "the new psychology"). Of the many differences between them, Merleau-Ponty begins with their differing accounts of perception. Classical psychology, as he understands it, treats the sensory field (in the first case that Merleau-Ponty considers, the visual field) as the sum of individual sensations. A perceiving individual gathers a great deal of visual data over the course of even a few moments. Those data are then gathered into something like a mosaic, Merleau-Ponty suggests, and this mosaic is what we what we see by way of visual perception. Importantly, the classical psychological model of visual perception makes the individual elements of the visual scene primary; only after other (non-perceptive) parts of the mind compile the acquired sense data do we "see" whole objects.

In the new psychology, however, the whole object is the primary phenomenon perceived. Only after there is a perception of the whole (or the "gestalt") is the mind able to analyze the experience and divide it into its component elements. Thus, on the new psychology, visual perception reorganizes the sense stimuli, and instead of a mosaic, we have something more like a system of configurations: I see a whole object, which only then can be understood in terms of its visual aspects in space. Merleau-Ponty goes on to note that sight is not the only sense that operates in this way; it is common to all human perception. With hearing, we are dealing with temporal rather than spatial phenomena, but the gestalt perspective remains the same. A melody, Merleau-Ponty says, is not simply the sum of its notes—any more than an image is the sum of its individual visible aspects. Music is a powerful reminder of the fact that, at least from a certain perspective, perception of the whole is more natural than perception of isolated elements. Perception of forms, Merleau-Ponty writes, is our spontaneous way of seeing.

Given its understanding of perception, then, it makes sense that classical psychology teaches that there are five distinct senses. Each accumulates sense data separately, and those data are aggregated to form a complex sensory image of the whole. But the new psychology posits a total way of perceiving with one's whole being, not five separate organs or faculties of sense. The gestalt theory of perception argues that, when perceiving anything, the singular structure of the thing speaks to all of our senses at once. We cannot organize discrete sense data into a mosaic impression because we do not begin with discrete sense data; we begin with a complex perceptual phenomenon that is not only the whole being perceived, but is that whole across all possible sensory perceptions—it is heard, and seen, and touched, etc., all at once, all as one.

Thus, classical psychology must conclude that we cannot see objects—we only see perceptual aspects. The perception of objects requires the intervention of intelligence and memory. For the classical psychologist, perception is always a deciphering of sense data by the rational mind. But on the new psychology, objects are all we see. Perception is of a gestalt, a whole phenomenon. For the classical psychologist, we must organize the world in thought before we can even begin to perceive it; for the gestalt psychologist, however, we perceive the world before we think about it. While I think by way of my intelligence, for Merleau-Ponty, I perceive the world from something more basic, my existential (and psychological) perspective. But I do not will my perspective; it is there, always already underlying my thoughts, perceptions, and actions. Thus, my perspective is, he notes, older than my intelligence. The situation from which I think and the point of view of my thinking is more fundamental than my thoughts ever could be.

This remains true, for Merleau-Ponty, with regard to our relationships with and knowledge of other people, as well. On the classical psychological model, there is always a distinction between inner feelings (which are entirely subjective, and accessible only to the subject him- or herself) and outer expressions—behavior, conduct, etc. One's "true feelings" are thus always hidden from others, such that they are left to interpret one's behavior and choose whether to trust whatever one says about oneself and one's feelings in their efforts to come to know one. But for the new psychologist, feelings are not hidden; feelings are themselves manifest primarily in types of behavior or forms of conduct. Thus, from this perspective, each of us has direct access to other people's feelings, character, personality, and so on. We can know other people, if we perceive them as the being or structure they are in the world.

Given everything he has said so far, Merleau-Ponty thinks that the new psychology presents us with the best theoretical approach to cinema yet devised. A film is not merely the sum of its constituent images, as if looking through the film strip at each individual still frame might, once they all were seen, give us the movie. No, the film is a whole phenomenon—a gestalt—the individual constitutive elements of which can only be understood after the whole has been perceived. This understanding of film operates not only at the level of the film frame, Merleau-Ponty thinks, but also at more complex stages of the process of uniting cinematic images into a film. Citing the famous experiment of Soviet filmmaker Lev Kuleshov (for which Vsevolod Pudovkin also claimed credit), Merleau-Ponty points out that the meaning of an image in a film depends entirely upon the images that immediately precede and succeed it. (Kuleshov photographed the actor Ivan Mosjoukine wearing an ambiguous expression on his face, and then inserted it into a film strip after three different images—a bowl of soup, a corpse, and a woman resting. Audiences regularly reported that Mosjoukine's expression was different in the three images, depending upon which of the three objects he was "looking at." This phenomenon of audience response, which demonstrates something fascinating about the nature of filmic meaning, is called the "Kuleshov Effect.") For Merleau-Ponty, the Kuleshov Effect proves that the succession of scenes in a film creates a whole new reality—it is not simply the combination of all those objects and persons filmed. A film takes on a rhythm of its own by way of the sequence and duration of the shots that make it up, and that rhythm must also come into some sort of relationship with the rhythm of the sounds of the film (if it is a sound film), creating yet another new organization and a new whole. Yet another level of meaning is added to a sound film (and yet another new gestalt is created) when the characters speak. Merleau-Ponty agrees explicitly with the views set forth by André Malraux on the role of language and music in film, and specifically, the three sorts of dialogue that are possible within film and the importance of integrating whatever music is heard into the structure of the film.[1] *Malraux is arguing for the production of films that are coherent wholes beyond the sum of their parts; Merleau-Ponty is suggesting that it is only a film that is perceived as a coherent whole which can be found to have any significant relation to its parts at all.*

By way of concluding his essay, Merleau-Ponty raises the question of the meaning of film. He acknowledges that each film tells a story, and notes that, while there are ideas and facts in a film, these are just the raw materials of the art—the film does not "mean" any idea or any fact. This undermines, among other things, any overtly ideological (including psychoanalytical) interpretation of a film that suggests the film is meant simply to convey a message. The meaning of a film, Merleau-Ponty argues, is incorporated into its rhythm. Like a gesture, the film means nothing in itself. This is possible, ultimately, because a film is not thought by the viewer: it is perceived. The film is a gestalt which is perceived primarily as a whole, and the film presents characters—other human beings—who are themselves gestalts. The persons presented in a film are not presented by way of their thoughts; in fact, they could not be so presented (unlike as in literature, where presentation of a character's thoughts and inner feelings is commonplace).

The new psychology and phenomenology are aligned in a wide variety of ways, not the least important of which is their agreement that consciousness is thrown into the world, subject to the gaze of others. Phenomenology and existentialism both try to get us to see the phenomena for which they give an account, not to explain those phenomena. And perhaps most especially by way of this effort we can see why Merleau-Ponty thinks that film is a perfect fit for both phenomenology and the new psychology. He goes so far as to say that phenomenological and/or existential philosophy is "movie material," by which he does not mean that there is any influence in either direction (he does not think the movies produce movements in philosophy, nor that philosophy inspires the production of any films), but instead that the filmmaker and the philosopher share a perspective on the world. It is from this common perspective from which they both live and think that the philosopher and the filmmaker produce the works they do produce, each at least an analog—if not also a collaborator—with the other.

Filmography

- ***The Broadway Melody*** (USA, 1929). *Directed by* Harry Beaumont. *Produced by* Irving Thalberg *and* Lawrence Weingarten. *Written by* Norman Houston *and* James Gleason. *Starring* Charles King, Anita Page, Bessie Love, *and* Jed Prouty.
- ***On Borrowed Time*** [*L'Etrange sursis*] (USA, 1939). *Directed by* Harold S. Bucquet. *Produced by* Sidney Franklin. *Written by* Alice D. G. Miller *and* Frank O'Neill. *Starring* Lionel Barrymore, Cedric Hardwicke, *and* Beulah Bondi.
- ***Here Comes Mr. Jordan*** [*Défunt recalcitrant*] (USA, 1941). *Directed by* Alexander Hall. *Produced by* Everett Riskin. *Written by* Sidney Buchman *and* Seton I. Miller. *Starring* Robert Montgomery, Eveyln Keyes, Claude Rains, Rita Johnson, *and* Edward Everett Horton.

[1] For more on Malraux' views, see Chapter 8 of the present volume.

- ***Premier de cordée*** (France, 1944). *Directed by* Louis Daquin. *Produced by* Jacqueline Jacoupy. *Written by* Alexandre Arnoux. *Starring* Irène Corday *and* André Le Gall.
- ***Espoir: Sierra de Teruel*** [*Man's Hope*] (Spain-France, 1945). *Directed by* Boris Peskine *and* André Malraux. *Produced by* Roland Tual *and* Edouard Corniglion-Molinier. *Written by* Max Aub *and* Antonio del Amo. *Starring* Andrés Majuto *and* Nicolás Rodríguez.

THE FILM AND THE NEW PSYCHOLOGY

Translated by Hubert L. Dreyfus and Patricia Allen Dreyfus

Classical psychology considers our visual field to be a sum or mosaic of sensations, each of which is strictly dependent on the local retinal stimulus which corresponds to it. The new psychology reveals, first of all, that such a parallelism between sensations and the nervous phenomenon conditioning them is unacceptable, even for our simplest and most immediate sensations. Our retina is far from homogeneous: certain parts, for example, are blind to blue or red, yet I do not see any discolored areas when looking at a blue or red surface. This is because, starting at the level of simply seeing colors, my perception is not limited to registering what the retinal stimuli prescribe but reorganizes these stimuli so as to re-establish the field's homogeneity. Broadly speaking, we should think of it not as a mosaic but as a system of configurations. Groups rather than juxtaposed elements are principal and primary in our perception. We group the stars into the same constellations as the ancients, yet it is *a priori* possible to draw the heavenly map many other ways. Given the series:

ab cd ef gh ij
.. ..

we will always pair the dots according to the formula a-b, c-d, e-f, etc., although the grouping b-c, d-e, f-g, etc. is equally probable in principle. A sick person contemplating the wallpaper in his room will suddenly see it transformed if the pattern and figure become the ground while what is usually seen as ground becomes the figure. The idea we have of the world would be overturned if we could succeed in seeing the intervals between things (for example, the space between the trees on the boulevard) as *objects* and, inversely, if we saw the things themselves—the trees—as the ground. This is what happens in puzzles: we cannot see the rabbit or the hunter because the elements of these figures are dislocated and are integrated into other forms: for example, what is to be the rabbit's ear is still just the empty interval between two trees in the forest. The rabbit and the hunter become apparent through a new partition of the field, a new organization of the whole. Camouflage is the art of masking a form by blending its principal defining lines into other, more commanding forms.

The same type of analysis can be applied to hearing: it will simply be a matter of temporal forms rather than spatial ones. A melody, for example, is a figure of sound and does not mingle with the background noises (such as the siren one hears in the distance during a concert) which may accompany it. The melody is not a sum of notes, since each note only counts by virtue of the function it serves in the whole, which is why the melody does not perceptibly change when transposed, that is, when all its notes are changed while their interrelationships and the structure of the whole remain the same. On the other hand, just one single change in these interrelationships will be enough to modify the entire make-up of the melody. Such a perception of the whole is more natural and more primary than the perception of isolated elements: it has been seen from conditioned-reflex experiments, where, through the frequent association of a piece of meat with a light or a sound, dogs are trained to respond to that light or sound by salivating, that the training acquired in response to a certain series of notes is simultaneously acquired for any melody with the same structure. Therefore analytical perception, through which we arrive at absolute value of the separate elements, is a belated and rare attitude—that of the scientist who observes or of the philosopher who reflects. The perception of forms, understood very broadly as structure, grouping, or configuration should be considered our spontaneous way of seeing.

There is still another point on which modern psychology overthrows the prejudices of classical physiology and psychology. It is a commonplace to say that we have five senses, and it would seem, at first glance, that each of them is like a world out of touch with the others. The light or colors which act upon the eye do not affect the ears or the sense of touch. Nevertheless it has been known for a long time that certain blind people manage to represent the colors they cannot see by means of the sounds which they hear: for example, a blind man said that red ought to be something like a trumpet peal. For a long time it was thought that such phenomena were exceptional, whereas they are, in fact, general. For people under mescaline, sounds are regularly accompanied by spots of color whose hue, form, and vividness vary with the tonal quality, intensity, and pitch of the sounds. Even normal subjects speak of hot, cold, shrill, or hard colors, of sounds that are clear, sharp, brilliant, rough, or mellow, of soft noises and of penetrating fragrances. Cézanne said that one could see the velvetiness, the hardness, the softness, and even the odor of objects. My perception is therefore not a sum of visual, tactile, and audible givens: I perceive in a total way with my whole being; I grasp a unique structure of the thing, a unique way of being, which speaks to all my senses at once.

Naturally, classical psychology was well aware that relationships exist between the different parts of my visual field just as between the data of my different senses—but it held this unity to be a construction and referred it to intelligence and memory. In a famous passage from the *Méditations* Descartes wrote: I say that I see men going by in the street, but what exactly do I really see? All I see are hats and coats which might equally well be covering dolls that only move by springs, and if I say that I see men, it is because I apprehend "through an inspection of the mind that I thought I beheld with my eyes." I am convinced that objects continue to exist when I no longer see them (behind my back, for example). But it is obvious that, for classical thought, these invisible objects subsist for me only because my judgment keeps them present. Even the objects right in front of me are not truly seen but merely thought. Thus I cannot *see* a cube, that is, a solid with six surfaces and twelve edges; all I ever see is a perspective figure of which the lateral surfaces are distorted and the back surface completely hidden. If I am able to speak of cubes, it is because my mind sets these appearances to rights and restores the hidden surface. I cannot see a cube as its geometrical definition presents it: I can only think it. The perception of movement shows even more clearly the extent to which intelligence intervenes in what claims to be vision. When my train starts, after it has been standing in the station, I often "see" the train next to mine begin to move. Sensory data are therefore neutral in themselves and can be differently interpreted according to the hypothesis on which my mind comes to rest. Broadly speaking, classical psychology made perception a real deciphering of sense data by the intelligence, a beginning of science, as it were. I am given certain signs from which I must dig out the meaning; I am presented with a text which I must read or interpret. Even when it takes the unity of the perceptual field into account, classical psychology remains loyal to the notion of sensation which was the starting point of the analysis. Its original conception of visual data as a mosaic of sensations forces it to base the unity of the perceptual field on an operation of the intelligence. What does *gestalt* theory tell us on this point? By resolutely rejecting the notion of sensation it teaches us to stop distinguishing between signs and their significance, between what is sensed and what is judged. How could we define the exact color of an object without mentioning the substance of which it is made, without saying, of this blue rug, for example, that it is a "woolly blue"? Cézanne asked how one is to distinguish the color of things from their shape. It is impossible to understand perception as the imputation of a certain significance to certain sensible signs, since the most immediate sensible texture of these signs cannot be described without referring to the object they signify.

Our ability to recognize an object defined by certain constant properties despite changes of lighting stems, not from some process by which our intellect takes the nature of the incident light into account and deduces the object's real color form it, but from the fact that the light which dominates the environment acts as *lighting* and immediately assigns the object its true color. If we look at two plates under unequal lighting, they will appear equally white and unequally lighted as long as the beam of light from the window figures in our visual field. On the other hand, if we observe the same plates through a hole in a screen, one will immediately appear gray and the other white; and even if we *know* that it is nothing but an effect of the lighting, no intellectual analysis of the way they appear will make us see the true color of the two plates. When we turn on the lights at dusk, the electric light seems yellow at first but a moment later tends to lose all definite color; correlatively, the objects, whose color was at first perceptibly modified, resume an appearance comparable to the one they have during the day. Objects and lighting form a system which tends toward a certain constancy and a certain level of stability—not through the operation of intelligence but through the very configuration of the field. I do not think the world in the act of perception: it organizes itself in front of me. When I perceive a cube, it is not because my reason sets the perspectival appearances straight and thinks the geometrical definition of a cube with respect to them. I do not even notice the distortions of perspective, much less correct them; I am at the cube itself in its manifestness through what I see. The objects behind my back are likewise not represented to me by some operation of memory or judgment; they are present, they *count* for me, just as the ground which I do not see continues nonetheless to be present beneath the figure which partially hides it. Even the perception of movement, which at first seems to depend directly on the point of reference chosen by the intellect is in turn only one element in the global organization of the field. For, although it is true that, when either my train or the one next to it starts, first one, then the other may appear to be moving, one should note that the illusion is not arbitrary and that I cannot willfully induce it by the completely intellectual choice of a point of reference. If I am playing cards in my compartment, the other train will start moving; if, on the other hand, I am looking for someone in the adjacent train, then mine will begin to roll. In each instance the one which seems stationary is the one we have chosen as our abode and which, for the time being, is our environment. Movement and rest distribute themselves in our surroundings not according to the hypotheses which our intelligence is pleased to construct but according to the way we settle ourselves in the world and the position our bodies assume in it. Sometimes I see the steeple motionless against the sky with clouds floating above it, and sometimes the clouds appear still and the steeple falls through space. But here again the choice of the fixed point is not made by the intelligence: the looked-at object in which I anchor myself will always seem fixed, and I cannot take this meaning away from it except by looking elsewhere. Nor do I give it this meaning through thought. Perception is not a sort of beginning science, an elementary exercise of the intelligence; we must rediscover a commerce with the world and a presence to the world which is older than intelligence.

Finally, the new psychology also brings a new concept of the perception of others. Classical psychology unquestioningly accepted the distinction between inner observation, or introspection, and outer observation. "Psychic facts"—anger or fear, for example—could be directly known only from the inside and by the person experiencing them. It was thought to be self-evident that I can grasp only the corporal *signs* of anger or fear from the outside and that I have to resort to the anger or fear I know in myself through introspection in order to interpret these signs. Today's psychologists have made us notice that in reality introspection gives me almost nothing. If I try to study love or hate purely from inner observation, I will find very little to describe: a few pangs, a few heart-throbs—in short, trite agitations which do not reveal the essence of love or hate. Each time I find something worth saying, it is because I have not been satisfied to coincide with my feeling, because I have succeeded in studying it as a way of behaving, as a modification of my relations with others and with the world, because I have managed to think about it as I would think about the behavior of another person whom I happened to witness. In fact, young children understand gestures and facial expressions long before they can reproduce them on their own; the meaning must, so to speak, adhere to the behavior. We must reject that prejudice which makes "inner realities" out of love, hate, or anger, leaving them accessible to our single witness: the person who feels them. Anger, shame, hate, and love are not psychic facts hidden at the bottom of another's consciousness: they are types of behavior or styles of conduct which are visible from the outside. They exist *on* this face or *in* those gestures, not hidden behind them. Psychology did not begin to develop until the day it gave up the distinction between mind and body, when it abandoned the two correlative methods of interior observation and physiological psychology. We learned nothing about emotion as long as we limited ourselves to measuring the rate of respiration or heartbeat in an angry person, and we didn't learn anything more when we tried to express the qualitative and inexpressible nuances of lived anger. To create a psychology of anger is to try to ascertain the *meaning* of anger, to ask oneself how it functions in human life and what purpose it serves. So we find that emotion is, as Janet said, a disorganizing reaction which comes into play whenever we are stuck. On a deeper level, as Sartre has shown, we find that anger is a magical way of acting by which we afford ourselves a completely symbolic satisfaction in the imagination after renouncing effective action in the world, just as, in a conversation, a person who cannot convince his partner will start hurling insults at him which prove nothing or as a man who does not dare strike his opponent will shake his fist at him from a distance. Since emotion is not a psychic, internal fact but rather a variation in our relations with others and the world which is expressed in our bodily attitude, we cannot say that only the signs of love or anger are given to the outside observer and that we understand others indirectly by interpreting these signs: we have to say that others are directly manifest to us as behavior. Our behavioral science goes much farther than we think. When unbiased subjects are confronted with photographs of several faces, copies of several kinds of handwriting, and recordings of several voices and are asked to put together a face, a silhouette, a voice, and a handwriting, it has been shown that the elements are usually put together correctly or that, in any event, the correct matchings greatly outnumber the incorrect ones. Michelangelo's handwriting is attributed to Raphael in 36 cases, but in 221 instances it is correctly identified, which means that we recognize a certain common structure in each person's voice, face, gestures and bearing and that each person is nothing more nor less to us than this structure or way of being in the world. One can see how these remarks might be applied to the psychology of language: just as a man's body and "soul" are but two aspects of his way of being in the world, so the word and the thought it indicates should not be considered two externally related terms: the word bears its meaning in the same way that the body incarnates a manner of behavior.

The new psychology has, generally speaking, revealed man to us not as an understanding which constructs the world but as a being thrown into the world and attached to it by a natural bond. As a result it re-educates us in how to see this world which we touch at every point of our being, whereas classical psychology abandoned the lived world for the one which scientific intelligence succeeded in constructing.

* * * *

If we now consider the film as a perceptual object, we can apply what we have just said about perception in general to the perception of a film. We will see that this point of view illuminates the nature and significance of the movies and that the new psychology leads us straight to the best observations of the aestheticians of the cinema.

Let us say right off that a film is not a sum total of images but a temporal *gestalt*. This is the moment to recall Pudovkin's famous experiment which clearly shows the melodic unity of films. One day Pudovkin took a close-up of Mosjoukin with a completely impassive expression and projected it after showing: first, a bowl of soup, then, a young woman lying dead in her coffin, and, last, a child playing with a teddy-bear. The first thing noticed was that Mosjoukin seemed to be looking at the bowl, the young woman, and the child, and next one noted that he was looking pensively at the dish, that he wore an expression of sorrow when looking at the woman, and that he had a glowing smile for the child. The audience was amazed at his variety of expression although the same shot had actually been used all three times and was, if anything, remarkably inexpressive. The meaning of a shot therefore depends on what precedes it in the movie, and this succession of scenes creates a new reality which is not merely the sum of its parts. In an excellent article in *Esprit*, R. Leenhardt added that one still has to bring in the time-factor for each shot: a short duration is suitable for an amused smile, one of intermediate length for an indifferent face, and an extended one for a sorrowful expression.[1] Leenhardt drew from this the following definition of cinematographic rhythm: "A certain order of shots and a certain duration for each of these shots or views, so that taken together they produce the desired impression with maximum effectiveness." There really is, then, a cinematographic system of measurements with very precise and very imperious requirements. "When you see a movie, try to guess the moment when a shot has given its all and must move on, end, be replaced either by changing the angle, the distance, or the field. You will get to know that constriction of the chest produced by an overlong shot which brakes the movement and that deliciously intimate acquiescence when a shot fades at the right moment." Since a film consists not only of montage (the selection of shots or views, their order and length) but also of cutting (the selection of scenes or sequences, and their order and length), it seems to be an extremely complex form inside of which a very great number of actions and reactions are taking place at every moment. The laws of this form, moreover, are yet to be discovered, having until now

[1] *Esprit*, 1936.

only been sensed by the flair or tact of the director, who handles cinematographic language as a man manipulates syntax: without explicitly thinking about it and without always being in a position to formulate the rules which he spontaneously obeys.

What we have just said about visual films also applies to sound movies, which are not a sum total of words or noises but are likewise a *gestalt*. A rhythm exists for sounds just as for images. There is a montage of noises and sounds, as Leenhardt's example of the old sound movie *Broadway Melody* shows. "Two actors are on stage. We are in the balcony listening to them speak their parts. Then immediately there is a close-up, whispering, and we are aware of something they are saying to each other under their breath...." The expressive force of this montage lies in its ability to make us sense the coexistence, the simultaneity of lives in the same world, the actors as they are for us and for themselves, just as, previously, we saw Pudovkin's visual montage linking the man and his gaze to the sights which surround him. Just as a film is not merely a play photographed in motion and the choice and grouping of the shots constitutes an original means of expression for the motion picture, so, equally, the soundtrack is not a simple phonographic reproduction of noises and words but requires a certain internal organization which the film's creator must invent. The real ancestor of the movie soundtrack is not the phonograph but the radio play.

Nor is that all. We have been considering sight and sound by turns, but in reality the way they are put together makes another new whole, which cannot be reduced to its component parts. A sound movie is not a silent film embellished with words and sounds whose only function is to complete the cinematographic illusion. The bond between sound and image is much closer, and the image is transformed by the proximity of sound. This is readily apparent in the case of dubbed films, where thin people are made to speak with the voices of fat people, the young have the voices of the old, and tall people the voices of tiny ones—all of which is absurd if what we have said is true—namely, that voice, profile, and character form an indivisible unit. And the union of sound and image occurs not only in each character but in the film as a whole. It is not by accident that characters are silent at one moment and speak at another. The alternation of words and silence is manipulated to create the most effective image. There are three sorts of dialogue, as Malraux said in *Verve* (1940). First may be noted expository dialogue, whose purpose is to make the circumstances of the dramatic action known. The novel and the film both avoid this sort of dialogue. Then there is *tonal* dialogue, which gives us each character's particular accent and which dominates, for example, in Proust where the characters are very hard to visualize but are admirably recognizable as soon as they start to talk. The extravagant or sparing use of words, their richness or emptiness, their precision or affectation reveal the essence of a character more surely than many descriptions. Tonal dialogue rarely occurs in movies, since the visible presence of the actor with his own particular manner of behaving rarely lends itself to it. Finally we have dramatic dialogue which presents the discussion and confrontation of the characters and which is the movies' principal form of dialogue. But it is far from continuous. One speaks ceaselessly in the theater but not in the film. "Directors of recent movies," said Malraux, "*break into* dialogue after long stretches of silence, just as a novelist breaks into dialogue after long narrative passages." Thus the distribution of silences and dialogue constitutes a metrics above and beyond the metrics of vision and sound, and the pattern of words and silence, more complex than the other two, superimposes its requirements upon them. To complete the analysis one would still have to study the role of music in this ensemble: let us only say that music should be incorporated into it, not juxtaposed to it. Music should not be used as a stopgap for sonic holes or as a completely exterior commentary on the sentiments or the scenes as so often happens in movies: the storm of wrath unleashes the storm of brass, or the music laboriously imitates a footstep or the sound of a coin falling to the ground. It should intervene to mark a change in the film's style: for example, the passage from an action scene to the "inside" of the character, to the recollection of earlier scenes, or to the description of a landscape. Generally speaking, it should accompany and help bring about a "rupture in the sensory balance," as Jaubert said.[2] Lastly, it must not be another means of expression juxtaposed to the visual expression. "By the use of strictly musical means (rhythm, form, instrumentation) and by a mysterious alchemy of correspondences which ought to be the very foundation of the film composer's profession, it should recreate a sonorous substance beneath the plastic substance of the image, should, finally, make the internal rhythm of the scene physically palpable without thereby striving to translate its sentimental, dramatic, or poetic content" (Jaubert). It is not the job of words in a movie to add ideas to the images, nor is it the job of music to add sentiments. The ensemble tells us something very precise which is neither a thought nor a reminder of sentiments we have felt in our own lives.

What, then, does the film *signify*: what does it mean? Each film tells a *story*: that is, it relates a certain number of events which involve certain characters and which could, it seems, also be told in prose, as, in effect, they are in the scenario on which the film is based. The talking film, frequently overwhelmed by dialogue, completes this illusion. Therefore motion pictures are often conceived as the visual and sonic representation, the closest possible reproduction of a drama which literature could evoke only in words and which the movie is lucky enough to be able to photograph. What supports this ambiguity is the fact that movies do have a basic realism: the actors should be natural, the set should be as realistic as possible; for "the power of reality released on the screen is such that the least stylization will cause it to go flat" (Leenhardt). That does not mean, however, that the movies are fated to let us see and hear what we would see and hear if we were present at the events being related; nor should films suggest some general view of life in the manner of an edifying tale. Aesthetics has already encountered this problem in connection with the novel or with poetry. A novel always has an idea that can be summed up in a few words, a scenario which a few lines can express. A poem always refers to things or ideas. And yet the function of the pure novel or pure poetry is not simply to tell us these facts. If it were, the poem could be exactly transposed into prose and the novel would lose nothing in summary. Ideas and facts are just the raw materials of art: the art of the novel lies in the choice of what one says and what one does not say, in the choice of perspectives (this chapter will be written from the point of view of this character, that chapter from another's point of view), in the varying tempo of the narrative; the essence of the art of poetry is not the didactic description of things or the exposition of ideas but the creation of a machine of language which almost without fail puts the reader in a certain poetic state. Movies, likewise, always have a story and often an idea (for example, in *l'Etrange sursis* the idea that death is terrible only for the man who has not consented to it), but the function of the film is not to make these facts or ideas known to us. Kant's remark that, in knowledge imagination serves the understanding, whereas in art the understanding serves the imagination, is a profound one. In other words, ideas or prosaic facts are only there to give the creator an opportunity to seek out

[2] Ibid.

their palpable symbols and to trace their visible and sonorous monogram. The meaning of a film is incorporated into its rhythm just as the meaning of a gesture may immediately be read in that gesture: the film does not mean anything but itself. The idea is presented in a nascent state and emerges from the temporal structure of the film as it does from the coexistence of the parts of a painting. The joy of art lies in its showing how something takes on meaning—not by referring to already established and acquired ideas but by the temporal or spatial arrangement of elements. As we saw above, a movie has meaning in the same way that a thing does: neither of them speaks to an isolated understanding; rather, both appeal to our power tacitly to decipher the world or men and to coexist with them. It is true that in our ordinary lives we lose sight of this aesthetic value of the tiniest perceived thing. It is also true that the perceived form is never perfect in real life, that it always has blurs, smudges, and superfluous matter, as it were. Cinematographic drama is, so to speak, finer-grained than real-life dramas: it takes place in a world that is more exact than the real world. But in the last analysis perception permits us to understand the meaning of the cinema. A movie is not thought; it is perceived.

This is why the movies can be so gripping in their presentation of man: they do not give us his *thoughts*, as novels have done for so long, but his conduct or behavior. They directly present to us that special way of being in the world, of dealing with things and other people, which we can see in the sign language of gesture and gaze and which clearly defines each person we know. If a movie wants to show us someone who is dizzy, it should not attempt to portray the interior landscape of dizziness, as Daquin in *Premier de cordée* and Malraux in *Sierra de Terruel* wished to do. We will get a much better sense of dizziness if we see it from the outside, if we contemplate that unbalanced body contorted on a rock or that unsteady step trying to adapt itself to who knows what upheaval of space. For the movies as for modern psychology dizziness, pleasure, grief, love, and hate are ways of behaving.

* * * *

This psychology shares with contemporary philosophies the common feature of presenting consciousness thrown into the world, subject to the gaze of others and learning from them what it is: it does not, in the manner of the classical philosophies, present mind *and* world, each particular consciousness *and* the others. Phenomenological or existential philosophy is largely an expression of surprise at this inherence of the self in the world and in others, a description of this paradox and permeation, and an attempt to make us *see* the bond between subject and world, between subject and others, rather than to *explain* it as the classical philosophies did by resorting to absolute spirit. Well, the movies are peculiarly suited to make manifest the union of mind and body, mind and world, and the expression of one in the other. That is why it is not surprising that a critic should evoke philosophy in connection with a film. Astruc in his review of *Défunt récalcitrant* uses Sartrian terms to recount the film, in which a dead man lives after his body and is obliged to inhabit another. The man remains the same *for himself* but is different *for others*, and he cannot rest until through love a girl recognizes him despite his new exterior and the harmony between the *for itself* and the *for others* is reestablished. The editors of *Le Canard enchainé* are annoyed at this and would like to send Astruc back to his philosophical investigations. But the truth is that both parties are right: one because art is not meant to be a showcase for ideas, and the other because contemporary philosophy consists not in stringing concepts together but in describing the mingling of consciousness with the world, its involvement in a body, and its coexistence with others; and because this is movie material *par excellence.*

Finally, if we ask ourselves why it is precisely in the film era that this philosophy has developed, we obviously should not say that the movies grew out of the philosophy. Motion pictures are first and foremost a technical invention in which philosophy counts for nothing. But neither do we have the right to say that this philosophy has grown out of the cinema which it transposes to the level of ideas, for one can make bad movies; after the technical instrument has been invented, it must be taken up by an artistic will and, as it were, re-invented before one can succeed in making real films. Therefore, if philosophy is in harmony with the cinema, if thought and technical effort are heading in the same direction, it is because the philosopher and the moviemaker share a certain way of being, a certain view of the world which belongs to a generation. It offers us yet another chance to confirm that modes of thought correspond to technical methods and that, to use Goethe's phrase, "What is inside is also outside."

CHAPTER 13
JEAN LOUIS SCHEFER

Jean Louis Schefer (b. 1938) is a French scholar and writer, both influential and prolific in a wide variety of fields including philosophy, art history, and film theory. Although less well read in the Anglophone world than he is in France, Schefer's work—especially his important book on film, The Ordinary Man of the Cinema*—has had a significant influence on other philosophers, including the works on cinema of such thinkers as Gilles Deleuze and Jacques Rancière. The selection in this volume is from* The Ordinary Man of the Cinema, *originally published in French (*L'homme ordinaire du cinéma; *Gallimard) in 1980.*

Schefer begins by noting that it is in the nature of cinema always to be oriented toward a spectator: it is a certain sort of spectacle. Unlike other spectacles, however, the cinema presents us with the case of a machine representing action to a theater full of immobile bodies. This representation has the character of embodying a particular experience of time, movement, and images, lending a voice to memory. Film lends memory a voice, for a mostly passive audience, by producing in the spectators the effects of memory. That is, film is not a memory—but watching a film produces many of the same effects as having a memory. This, Schefer thinks, accounts for how we remember film events in the same way that we remember real events, and that our memories of film events can get mixed up with our memories of our own real lives, such that we cannot by memory alone determine whether something remembered actually happened to us or was simply something we saw happen in a movie. The reverse side of this potential for confusion, however, is the potential of projecting ourselves into the film action, such that we can take pleasure in becoming immersed in a film.

Schefer's understanding of film depends largely on his understanding of the film spectator and, as such, he devotes a fair amount of time to explaining the nature of the spectator as he understands it. As we've already noted, the film viewer is typically immobile, full of memories, and in the world. This makes the viewer, at least in these three respects, the opposite of the film or the film world, which is memoryless and composed merely of the presentation of affects. Whatever reality the film world might possess, it gets from its relationship with the viewer, and that relationship is primarily one of illusion: while the film has no memories (film is not memory), it produces the effects of memory in the viewer's mind—and, at the same time, the illusion that the memories are in fact, secretly, the viewer's own. This is not to say that the viewer at any point confuses him- or herself with the characters on the screen. Rather, it's that there is always something unexpressed in the viewer which corresponds to something unexpressed in the film. Human beings, as they live their lives, find that the unexpressed increases within them—there is simply more that is thought, more that is left unsaid, more possibilities unpursued, and so on, as time passes. Film cannot express such inexpression, however, except as bodies in action, since that is the only thing that cinema really depicts. But film bodies remain unreal bodies: they are projected light, lack memory, and have no solidity. Film bodies, Schefer argues, are affects through and through.

Insofar as there is anything real in cinema, it is provided by the spectator: a memory mixed with images and experiences. Film, then, while lacking that reality in itself, can provide the spectator with a new experience of their perspective—a new experience of time and memory. In general, memory situates us alongside time in a unique way. Schefer calls it an "aporistic duration": something remembered is an object of thought which I can neither think (because it is not an object in the present) nor remove from thought (because it is remembered). The passions one has felt endure in memory—not over time, exactly, but by way of their intensity and power. And the power of passions remembered endures by way of the remnants of images. Thus, memory "writes" the experience of an entire life—and cinema allows memory to separate that experience from the world. The cinema creates within us a final chamber, within or alongside memory, wherein the temporality of the film, the film's passage through time, is absent. All that is left in the mind of the viewer, corresponding (but not identical) to real memory, are lingering filmic images. Tied to each of those images is a passion which, by way of its lingering in the viewer's mind, retains something of its power. In this, we see that, for Schefer, film is not the realization of desire—it is not wish fulfillment—but is instead the legitimation of desire.

Film, then, gives us nothing of its own, but reflects what is already within the viewer back to us. The film is like a mirrored surface, from which the feelings and affects of the characters it depicts are thrown back to the viewer, and which in this way throw the viewer away from the film world back into him- or herself (and reality, which the film world lacks). Film becomes in this way affects without a purpose, without a destination or a world, affects without the reality affects might need to inform a life. They are affects playing out a scene, as it were, and although they construct a world (the film world), that world is not real. It's a world populated by film bodies, disguised bodies the shape and look of which represent their fates. Schefer gives us many examples, two of which are Fred Astaire's top hat and cane, and Cary Grant's suit. Both of these costuming choices in fact do much, much more than merely maintain the historical integrity of the film world. (Schefer notes that Grant's suit "is both his ignorance of danger and the deferral of his fear," and this seems in a certain way quite right: the "Cary Grant" character must wear a suit, and that suit must situate him on the borderline of ignorance and temporary courage.) In any case, Schefer notes that film bodies give us the film world in between gestures (he has both silent and sound films in mind). Film bodies, as visual representations of affects, express a certain relationship to the unreal world from which they emanate by way of the movements of those bodies on screen. The affective presentation that is movement in film is never finished, despite the fact that every film ends, because the affects endure beyond the duration of the film—by way of the film images left lingering in the minds of the viewers, for whom the whole thing ultimately feels like memory.

In the end, Schefer argues that it is not the film world which draws the spectator into the film: it's the new affects, presented within the film world as bodies in motion but representative of that film world only in the mind of the viewer. The film body is never granted solidity by the film, whether that body is presented as a mere aggregation of gestures in an instructive costume, or as a body overlapped by a distinct and audible voice (in sound film). The voice, Schefer argues, adds not stability but anxiety to the film body; like operatic music, he notes, the human voice cannot hide the truth of the body—that it is visible, but vulnerable—even in the artificial environs of the film world. Film is, thus, unrealistic: necessarily, and aesthetically, so. The truth of film lies not in the correspondence of its images to real objects, nor in the correspondence of the narratives it employs to real-life events. Rather, as he says repeatedly throughout the selection, the truth of film is in the individual spectator alone—in a real mind wherein the illusion of memory can be intangibly embodied in fragments of a film image which, by way of their power to endure, can legitimate the very real (if altogether ordinary) desires of very real (if altogether ordinary) human beings.

Filmography

- ***La Passion de Jeanne d'Arc*** [*The Passion of Joan of Arc*] (France, 1928). *Directed by* Carl Theodor Dreyer. *Produced by the* Société Générale des Films. *Written by* Joseph Delteil *and* Carl Theodor Dreyer. *Starring* Renée Jeanne Falconetti.
- ***La Chienne*** (France, 1931). *Directed and Written by* Jean Renoir. *Produced by* Pierre Braunberger *and* Roger Richebé. *Starring* Michel Simon, Janie Marèse, *and* Georges Flamant.
- ***Little Caesar*** (USA, 1931). *Directed by* Mervyn LeRoy. *Produced by* Hal B. Wallis *and* Darryl F. Zanuck. *Written by* Francis Edward Faragoh, Robert Lord, *and* Darryl F. Zanuck. *Starring* Edward G. Robinson, Douglas Fairbanks, Jr., *and* Glenda Farrell.
- ***La Grande Illusion*** [*Grand Illusion*] (France, 1937). *Directed by* Jean Renoir. *Produced by* Réalisations d'Art Cinématographique. *Written by* Jean Renoir *and* Charles Spaak. *Starring* Jean Gabin, Dita Parlo, Pierre Fresnay, *and* Erich von Stroheim.
- ***They Live by Night*** (USA, 1948). *Directed by* Nicholas Ray. *Produced by* John Houseman. *Written by* Charles Schnee *and* Nicholas Ray. *Starring* Cathy O'Donnell, Farley Granger, *and* Howard Da Silva.
- ***A Streetcar Named Desire*** (USA, 1951). *Directed by* Elia Kazan. *Produced by* Charles K. Feldman. *Written by* Tennessee Williams. *Starring* Vivian Leigh, Marlon Brando, Kim Hunter, *and* Karl Malden.
- ***Fortini/Cani*** (Italy, 1976). *Directed by* Jean-Marie Straub *and* Danièle Huillet. *Produced by* Straub-Huillet. *Written by and Starring* Franco Fortini. *Also starring* Luciana Nissim *and* Adriano Aprà.

THE ORDINARY MAN OF THE CINEMA

Translated by Paul Smith

The ordinary man of the cinema makes a preliminary and redundant announcement: the cinema isn't my profession.[1] I go to the cinema for entertainment, but by chance I also learn something there apart from what a film will tell me (a film won't teach me that I'm mortal—it will, perhaps, teach me a trick of time, about the expansion of bodies in time, and about the improbability of it all. In fact, I'm always less the film's reader and more like its totally submissive servant, and also its judge). What I learn there is the astonishment of being able to live in two worlds at once.

So it's a being without qualities that's speaking now. I want to say just this: I don't have the necessary qualities to speak about cinema except insofar as I'm in the habit of going quite often. This habit should probably have taught me something?—naturally. But what?—about films, about myself, about our whole species, about memory.

So, what this "ordinary man" can say arises not from some fixed discourse (which would have to do with the transmission of a knowledge) but from a writing (a research whose object isn't a polished construction, but the enigma of an origin). The only origin I can speak of, publicly ask myself about, is primarily tied to an elucidation of the visible, an explanation not of its constitution but of the certainty that it only exists with such power because it opens up and names within us a whole world; and of the certainty that we are in some way the genesis and the momentary life of this world that's suspended from a collection of artifices.

So, I'm writing about a particular experience of time, movement, and images.

But this still has to satisfy certain ideational conditions. I don't intend to write a theoretical essay about film. It's more a matter of lending a voice, however briefly, to a memory, to the spectacle of its effects, and to render a certain threshold tangible. In the end, I'm calling upon a spectator's "knowledge." That's *my* knowledge, and so immediately some part of my own life is at stake.

A machine whirls, representing simultaneous actions to the immobility of our bodies; it produces monsters, even though it all seems delicious rather than terrible. In fact, however awful it really is, it's always undeniably pleasurable. But perhaps it's the unknown, uncertain, and always changing linkage of this pleasure, this nocturnal kinship of the cinema, that asks a question of both memory and signification; the latter, in the memory of film, remains attached to the experience of this experimental night where something stirs, comes alive, and speaks in front of us.

So for this spectator the cinema is primarily something completely different than what most film criticism reflects. The meaning that comes to us (and reaches us by dint of our being a sounding board for the effects of images and their depth, and insofar as we organize the whole future of these images and sounds into affect and meaning) is a very special quality of signification made tangible. And it's irremediably linked to the conditions of our vision; or,

[1] Given the "autobiographical" nature of these texts, I have kept Schefer's gendered pronouns.—*Trans.*

more exactly, linked to our experience (to the quality of this nocturnal vision, appearing as the threshold of reception and the condition for the existence of those images—and, perhaps, to our very first experience of seeing them).

If the cinema, apart from its constant renewal in every film and each projection, can be defined by its peculiar power to produce effects of memory, then we know—and have known for several generations—that through such memory (in this case, through precise images) some part of our lives passes into our recollection of films that might be totally unrelated to the contents of our lives.

So there was (first of all, immediately, like a residual humus that retains images) a sentiment of persistent strangeness born in "my" cinema, and I wanted to account for it. I wanted to make it apparent. It's not likely that my experience of film is an entirely isolated one. Indeed, rather than the illusion of movement or mobility in filmic objects, the illusion proper to the cinema is that this experience and this memory are solitary, hidden, secretly individual, since they make an immediate pact (story, pictures, affective colors) with a part of ourselves that lives without expression; a part given over to silence and to a relative aphasia, as if it were the ultimate secret of our lives—while perhaps it really constitutes our ultimate subjecthood. It seems that in this artificial solitude a part of us is porous to the effects of meaning without ever being able to be born into signification through language. We even recognize there—and to my eyes this is the imprescriptible link between film and fear—an increase in the aphasia of feelings in our social being (the cinema acting upon every social being as if upon one solitary being). The fear that we live out at the cinema (the first knowledge a child takes from the cinema, or that "colors" his experience) isn't unmotivated, in fact—it's just disproportionate: I've thought for some time now that *we fear* this latent aphasia because it has already cut into us.

I'm far from denying the pleasure of cinema. But I need to make something about it more explicit (at very least, its ambiguity). Briefly, this pleasure isn't simple enjoyment; it is, I think, the visible basis for all the aesthetic pleasure we take in the image's definition—that's the basis for what's sometimes called our "imaginary projection" into filmic action. The pleasure is in the enjoyment of our moral being, which is why (for me) it's so close to its opposite—fear (which is the result of a simulated realization of affects which live deprived of an object). The reality of these sentiments is our subjection to a world that's actually their derision. I maintain that this can be called an experience, to be spoken of seriously.

Suddenly, within these forms, in these unities of sound and vision where I have no place and of which I remain just a spectator, I find myself trying to identify what might be their essential counterbalance… in the end, to discover to what absence any form relates.

Unpredictably, every human form (every imitation of a destiny) responds to the expression (the necessity or the abeyance of expression) of the feelings that define humanity.

So it's not that we're projecting our lives onto forms or beings, agents of a part of identity that's the missing link in every living being, or the secret that's not fixed in an image but that keeps it alive outside of images. It's rather that the unexpressed increases within the living being as we live—that is, it never ceases to substitute actions for the possibility of contemplating nothingness.

But these feelings, relying on a notion of the lonely profundity proper to our species, cannot be represented in the cinema except by way of *bodies in action*. To support them, those bodies have to be new to the point of indicating the reflexivity of actions—not their power of transition or their material resolution in the world. Such reflexivity can only augment the invisible world, and that's what an action is properly destined to do. (Which means that an action isn't an event. The strongest captivation of the image is finally that world; all causality in this universe of images is shut up inside a body of enigmas, as if by a suspicion of signification.)

Perhaps such a "being without qualities" can state a truth here, ask a question, make a proposition whose goal is not to endorse an image of man in terms of any of the usually elaborated theoretical notions. That would constitute an unreasonable alteration of the image by allowing contents to enter in (the relationships of contents to representations are always precisely experiments and not representations).

So, what we might try to grasp is this: there's probably nothing, in the name of any knowledge, that we could envisage about forms or that could be said about cinema which, by theoretical strategies, would accord with or verify the protocols of anthropological content. In the cinema we are dealing with a new experience of time and memory which alone can form an experimental being.

The cinema, in that we're a part of it, doesn't compose or organize any particular structure of alienation—it's more a matter of the structure of a realization and the appropriation of some *real*, not of some *possible*. The real we're talking about here is what's already and momentarily alive in the form of the spectator. Not a momentary, suspended life, but a memory mixed with images and experiential sensations: we should, then, question the function of the scenario not as the object of a desire to exist but as the *store of affects* within this being whom I describe as being "without qualities." Similarly, the ironic structure of film is an anthropological lure. And what's more, the dream here is not the realization of a desire, but we should understand it rather—more essentially—as the *legitimization* of desire.

Of course, all this presupposes no knowledge, but at most a certain usage, the habit of a *usage within the invisible part of our bodies*. I'm alluding to that part of ourselves whose nativity is, as it were, put back into our hands for use at our own discretion. The part that, having no reflection, desperately dedicates itself to transforming its own obscurity into a *visible world*.

So the only knowledge presumed here is just that of the use of our own memory: in the end, memory teaches us nothing but the manipulation of time as an image, made possible by the purloining of our actual bodies. This doesn't respond to some theory or other, but only to a paradoxical experience—that is, to an aporistic duration (the relation of an object of thought to something that refuses itself to thought in its very activity). So it is experience itself that is the source of aporias. From then on things can't emerge from some hidden meaning, but rather from this difficult and vacillating relationship between things and their secret (and thus *our* secret, like a photo of our complete "body" that can't be developed in the realm of the visible).

So the duration of passions (what Kierkegaard used to call the character of an alternative man) can be measured only by the remnants of images—not by their cinematic duration, but by the power they have to remain, repeat, or recur. This is quite close to what defines the image's transformation into a mnesic double—that is to say, into that sort of trace or guarantee that's intrinsic to the movement of disappearance or effacement in phenomena.

The cinema and filmic images don't mobilize for me any (technical or theoretical) knowledge as such: that kind of knowledge is inessential as far as I'm concerned. The cinema is perhaps the only domain of signification that I believe cannot have *a subject for the operations of its science.*

It is an art which awakens a memory, mysteriously tied to the experience of a profundity of feeling (but also the very particular life of isolated phenomena).

This is also echoed in Dreyer's words: "What I want to obtain is a penetration to my actors' profound thoughts by means of their most subtle expressions.... [Falconetti] had taken off her make-up... and I found... a rustic woman, very sincere, who was also a woman who had suffered."[2]

That memory doesn't evoke so much as write the experience of an entire life that it induces into separation from the world. As if we went to the cinema in order to annihilate the film bit by bit (with a few retained images) by way of the sentiments it makes us feel; and as if this mass of affects progressively summoned chains of images back to the light and to the color of feelings.

I wanted to explain how the cinema stays within us as a final chamber where both the hope and the illusion of *an interior history* are caught: because this history doesn't unfold itself and yet can only—so feebly does it subsist—remain invisible, faceless, without character, but primarily without duration. Through the resilience of their images we acclimatize all these films to an absence of duration and to that absence of a scene where interior histories might become possible.

So this chamber exists within us, where, in the absence of any object, we torture the human race, and from which the feeling or anticipated consciousness of the sublime mysteriously and incomprehensibly arises.

None of this locates the grip or anchoring of feeling within a film. Film is perhaps just a sort of mirrored surface that appears to us as such only at the moment when we are thrown away from it by the feelings or affects that it gives birth to: it only gives birth to them by simulating them in characters, through "bits of men" who have to die in order to assure the perpetuity of what's outside them.

So the sight of all this makes me take leave of myself; that's to say, take leave of the most uncertain center of myself; it makes me find some semblances of identity that then hunt me down again like a center waiting to be encircled.

So, it's not quite a merchandise (a sort of sexual merchandise), nor is it quite a pole of projection that I find in the cinema. Rather, acting out a scene there, I find affects (not quite feelings, just the stirring of feeling, tied to impossible actions), affects without a destination—that is, without a world (there's no world that preconditions this coloring of affects); affects playing out a scene—by some unbreakable alliance, playing *the visible interior of a species*. So far as the spectacle of visible man is concerned (though he's not any particular structure of enjoyment—he's simply an unknown being), it would be necessary to know that affects constitute a world—possibilities of action somewhere else, and immediately an ineluctable destiny.

Could the techniques of cinema have a finality that, in all conscience or with a little clarity, I might reduce to the production of effects? Here, all the played-out simulations are basically imperfect (or simultaneously shown to be simulations), parallel to the production of effects. What attracts me to the perfection of this world isn't its illusion; it's the illusion of a center I will never be able to approach. This illusion *has* no center but is a mechanism for the elision of objects. All in all, its bodily movements aren't gratuitous—they constitute the spectacle itself, with its freedom removed. Furthermore, it's the affects themselves, and not signification (which here is the deferral of their liaison), that construct an anterior world, a

---

[2] From "Carl Dreyer," in *Interviews with Film Directors*, ed. A. Sarris (New York: Bobbs-Merrill, 1967), 112–13. Falconetti is the stage actress whom Dreyer cast as the heroine of his *Passion of Joan of Arc* (1928).—*Trans.*

world subsisting without proportions begged or borrowed from the real. By an elementary alchemy, objects are only as privileged as they are here because they're so rare (selected) and dependent; they're not the components of the cinematic universe that we would recognize by their resemblance to all the things we've ever touched, seen, or coveted. They're woven from an altogether different material. We desire them because they constitute a fate. The dressing gown in *Little Caesar*, Fred Astaire's top hat and cane, Ketty's watch in *They Live by Night* (whose dial is never seen but that still tells us the wrong time of that nocturnal love and shows us the curse of adolescents oppressed by a crime in the distant shadow of their lives); or Cary Grant's suit, which is both his ignorance of danger and the deferral of his fear—here I project not a sovereign consciousness but a disguised body, dressed from the start in a prism of minor passions, sequences of gestures, words, and lighting.

In films the body (in any situation) is only desirable because of the hope that its clothes can be worn, but at the same time that it can carry away with it all the worldly light in which it has bathed. The initial hallucination in which we mimicked gestures (for example, von Stroheim's little stereotypes in *La Grande Illusion*) managed to induce, in place of our bodies and like an airy chimera, the same stiffness we saw in the actor, the same pleasure in details; or it managed to teach us that the cinematic body is one that lives "in detail" (just as Bichat's old man dies "in detail").[3] What we couldn't regain was the peculiarity of a world residing in the transitions between gestures. We'd been struck, for example, by the fact that all action is accomplished in a single, sketchy movement; that a man never gets to the end of the track, but that his action is nonetheless complete because the whole world (at any given moment) can be no more than the consciousness of his escape, and because nothing escapes signification (which might be the very peculiarity of this universe). Endowed with mobile proportions, affected by changing causes, this is still only an *intended* world.

And burlesque, wasn't that in its way simply the blow-up of a single detail of our own lives? Or perhaps the entire life of something we could get to know and that would then live alone in the world (as alone as the perpetual life of a scar on the skin, a ridiculous hat on the same head, or a leg that was forever in plaster). This is a reflexivity and a perception of action which reaches a body and determines its spectacle. This is why burlesque is so frightening: those bodies are already more guilty than they are clumsy; they're just a brief, gesticulatory reprieve from our waiting for hell.

The world and its shadows rise up before our eyes, initiating in us the experience of those unrepeatable movements.

Two trees that the camera shoots from a distance, around which it begins to film, which it then shoots in an incomplete pan where the trees are successively the center and the periphery: this grouping of trees, in Straub and Huillet's *Fortini/Cani*, isn't made from trees alone, because these particular ones could only be reflections, and also because the very distance from the world we can never approach subsists within them. And this bouquet of trees is not simply all that distance preserved. Those trees, caught in a slow and brusquely sublime movement, are unnamed and unknown affects; they are a sort of silent, rigid, and delicate contouring of the most unknown emotion. And why—unless it's because all our own movement is suspended from that sight—can we do no more than register that this is sublime?

---

[3] Bichat was a nineteenth-century medical scientist and author of *Recherches psychologiques sur la vie et la mort*; among other things, the book minutely records the experience of death. Schefer has written an article on Bichat—*Trans.* [See Jean Louis Schefer, "Remarques sur un usage du corps," *L'Ecrit du temps* 8/9 (67–83).—*JW*]

Poe, in *Eureka*, speaks of the genesis of matter in which attraction and repulsion separate atoms: there, the soul is the product of their repulsion.[4] It is also by the unconsciousness, the ignorance of these systems of luminous dots sifting bodies and remaining encrusted on their faces, that the birth of feelings unrelated to our lives is accompanied. And blindly, across this bridge of trembling light, we enter this world. First of all, film isn't constituted in more or less perfect scenes, nor by obvious, admitted decors (such as those in *A Streetcar Named Desire*, which are just theater sets filmed in close-up), nor by the points and displacements of perspective that reveal them to me; nor are any of them either credible or *invraisemblable*: this world, beyond its artificial sets and shots in front of which I might remain incredulous—and can therefore get away with being badly done—doesn't install me within the truth of the story; it has already made me enter into the truth and strangeness of whole new affects—which, by dint of the fact that their qualities are unheard of, and because their relations to objects are unknown, easily dominate me.

I don't believe in the reality of film (and its verisimilitude is unimportant); and yet, because of that, I'm its ultimate truth. The truth is verified in me alone, but not by final reference to reality; it is, first of all, only a change in the proportions of the visible whose final judge I will doubtless be, though I'll also be its body and its experimental consciousness.

No kind of assurance is ever added to the image, no finishing touches are given to a pluperfect image of solidity; indeed, what's added is the anxiety of the human voice (and perhaps only a hint that it can signify). From the voice I retain only certain qualities—smoothness or roughness—or its particular composition, astonishingly produced by Michel Simon in *La Chienne*; and I hear behind it, behind its memory, nothing but a feeble burbling, an incoherence, something like the bankrupt monologue of a lover's protestation. The voices in this film—those of Simon and Janie Marèze—are neither real nor copied; they're simply the truth of a given scene. The voice of Marèze is stereotyped (it's "stamped" as the historical representation of a social class, attached to the irony of the characters who choose it, or the irony of a "type"). Simon's voice is not of a particular class; it's an invention and a mixture that begins to constitute the sonorous volume of his character. This is all laid bare in the conversation scene, in the impossible confidences that precede the murder: the vocal tissue imports only the "culture" that precisely allows him to appear as an imbecile in the place where he lives. In this I can hear the beginnings of the jocular tone that is always a strain in this actor's voice, the foundation he exploits—the strange, bleating tone of an old woman through which some emotion is always transferred along with the proper distancing of the voice from the role itself, from its utterances, and from the actor's body: this is the whistle and the toothy sound that characterize the actor's place of origin, the "accent" of Genevan Protestants. The tissue and composition of this voice are played out in the character (Legrand) as nostalgia for a place where he doesn't belong—the distance of the bleating voice and the raised accent suddenly lend him the air of a mental case. It's like listening to an opera—I can hear only the feeble strain of what the voice signifies, what protestation it makes through the totally instrumental singing that, at the height of its artifice, cannot disguise the blinding truth of the body, of that sudden apparition of visible man, trembling like a wet dog.

---

[4] Edgar Allan Poe, *Eureka: A Prose Poem*, ed. R. Benton (Hartford: Transcendental Books, 1973): "... *attraction* and *repulsion*. The former is the body; the latter the soul: the one is material; the other spiritual, principle of the Universe... attraction and repulsion are the sole properties through which we perceive the Universe" (37).—*Trans.*

CHAPTER 14
SERGE DANEY

Serge Daney (1944–1992) was a French film and television critic, co-founder of the magazine Trafic, *out of which critical and journalistic work he constructed a philosophy of the film image. His writings and ideas about film were hugely influential on a great number of French filmmakers, film theorists, and philosophers of film, but his writings have not been widely available in English translation. The essay included here, "The Tracking Shot in* Kapo,*" is among the last things Daney wrote before his death. It was originally published in French ("Le travelling de Kapo") in* Trafic *in 1992.*

In what might seem like a surprising admission from the author of a work ostensibly about the 1960 film, Kapò, *by Gillo Pontecorvo, the first sentence of Daney's essay includes the film on a list of movies he has never seen. Everything he knows about Kapò, Daney says, he learned at the age of 17 by reading a review of the film by Jacques Rivette in* Cahiers du cinèma. *Rivette's review excoriates Pontecorvo's film on the basis of a single (infamous) shot: a tracking shot which reframes the image of the dead body of a suicide, a woman who threw herself against the electrified barbed wire of a Nazi concentration camp during the Second World War. Daney notes that, even as a teenager, he agreed with Rivette, that there was something wrong with the choice to use such a shot in this context; in fact, Daney says that this was his first conviction as a future film critic.*

In his lifelong effort to come to terms with Kapò, *and to make sense of his almost automatic (and initially ungrounded) agreement with Rivette about the tracking shot, Daney comes to make a distinction between beautiful films and just films. A beautiful film, he claims, tries to effect an aesthetic experience for the audience. Beautiful films try to present, or re-present, beauty; they seek to entertain us, perhaps, to amuse us, to impress us with its grace and form. A just film, on the other hand, attempts to approach "the limits of a distorted humanity," as Daney puts it. Which is to say that a just film seeks to make the audience aware of some injustice, something inhumane in the human present or past which should be remembered, and learned from, and never repeated. While beautiful films have at their center something beautiful, or something beautifully filmed, just films present their audiences with ugliness—and, in particular, an ugliness in which the audience is to at least some degree (by virtue of their humanity, if nothing else) complicit. The summary version of Daney's (following Rivette) criticism of* Kapò *is that, depicting the Holocaust, it nevertheless is trying to be beautiful. By contrast, Daney suggests that Alain Resnais' Holocaust film,* Night and Fog, *is trying not to be beautiful but to be just.*

Daney refers to the suggestion of Jean-Louis Schefer, that there are films that watch us—especially as children, Daney adds. In contrast to beautiful films, just films judge us. We are judged by the piles of corpses in Night and Fog, *he says; we are called to account. Even after the film is finished, the brain functions something like a film projector, projecting the images over and over again for us in our minds—like a memory, like conscience. Such a film presents us with scenes in which we, the viewers, are not present, but which seem entirely to be about us: each of us, individually, personally. A film like* Night and Fog *makes the viewer feel responsible, and encourages the viewer to redefine humanity itself in light of this responsibility. In this way, a film can be a second birth for the viewer, Daney says, as another of Resnais' films,* Hiroshima mon amour, *was for him. Between* Night and Fog *and* Hiroshima mon amour, *Resnais was the filmmaker who awakened Daney to the cinema in his youth, a maker of just rather than beautiful films. At least, this is true of the early Resnais; Daney notes that Resnais' later cinematic works do not have the same effect on him as those earlier films, which show us humanity attempting to survive and come to terms with the genocidal and atomic catastrophes of the Second World War. (In his later years, Daney says, his interest in Resnais' films wanes; he turns instead to the films of Roberto Rossellini and Jean-Luc Godard.)*

In contrast to Resnais' Night and Fog, *and in a completely different way than in Pontecorvo's* Kapò, *Daney notes another film that sets out to depict the camps—the documentary footage, filmed by George Stevens, of the liberation of the camps at Duben and Dachau by American troops. Stevens shoots the camps in color, and to Daney's eye, aims for beauty rather than justice. Stevens' footage tries to make the vision of the camps into art. This seems to draw the Stevens footage much closer to Pontecorvo's film than Resnais', and Daney seems to suggest as much, as both the Stevens footage and* Kapò *are trying to be beautiful. But there is one important distinction, Daney thinks: both because he is an American, not a European, and because he is coming to the camps at the moment of their liberation, rather than after years of reflection, Stevens' cinematic gaze has a kind of innocence. He cannot see the evil of the camps for what it is, and naïvely seeks beauty there.*

Resnais, however, making his film over a decade later, cannot pretend to be innocent. In the place of innocence, Daney says, Resnais' gaze is characterized by a kind of necrophilia: a love of death. Such cinematic necrophilia can have a noble and an ignoble side. In Resnais' case, the noble side, we see the filmmaker in search of a greater proximity to death—coupled with the jouissance of "the just distance," which is to say, Resnais' film tries to get as close as possible to death in the camps so as to judge humanity for its crimes. The ignoble side of the necrophiliac gaze, however, revels in a different sort of jouissance: it tries to make the camps beautiful, and in so doing provides a justification for their existence (something noted, and famously condemned, by Theodor Adorno). Daney—again, deeply influenced here by Rivette—is disgusted with such attempts to beautify evil, and says he much prefers crass concentration camp pornography, even, to the "artistic" pornographic approach taken in such films as Kapò *and* The Night Porter.

Kapò *tries to present the camps to us in motion, infusing the images of death with a kind of life, beautifying the ugly, justifying the unjust. In so doing, Pontecorvo must fill in whatever gaps might exist in the history of images, must transition from moment to moment seamlessly (as in the tracking shot), must provide continuity in pursuit of the spectator's appreciation and enjoyment. But in a film like* Night and Fog, *both the spectator and the image are stilled: motion ceases, some images are unavailable, and the only movement the spectator really experiences is the repeated projection of those images of evil in his or her own mind. With this contrast in mind, Daney compares* Kapò *to Kenji Mizoguchi's film,* Ugetsu, *which he says pretends not to see death. Whereas Pontecorvo beautifies death unflinchingly, bringing the spectator along for the ride, Mizoguchi's film pretends not to see death. Death is thus, in Mizoguchi, never something to enjoy. This shows, Daney says, that Mizoguchi fears death and war, whereas Pontecorvo, who tries to find beauty in the desperate suicide of a victim of the Holocaust, does not. Daney identifies Pontecorvo's approach with the traditional approach to cinema, seeking always motion and beauty; he identifies Mizoguchi's approach (like Resnais') with modern cinema, more aware of and open to stillness and justice in beauty's stead. Cinema oscillates between the two, traditional and modern, sometimes favoring the one, and then shifting to favor the other. Unlike traditional cinema, however, modern cinema is cruel: it forces the filmgoer to witness pain and war and death, without trying to make them beautiful.*

Filmography

- ***Nana*** (France, 1926). *Directed by* Jean Renoir. *Produced by* Pierre Braunberger. *Written by* Pierre Lestringuez *and* Jean Renoir. *Starring* Catherine Hessling *and* Werner Krauss.
- ***The Unknown*** (USA, 1927). *Directed by* Tod Browning. *Produced by* Irving G. Thalberg. *Written by* Waldemar Young. *Starring* Lon Chaney, Norman Kerry, *and* Joan Crawford.
- ***Oktyabr': Desyat' dney kotorye potryasli mir*** [*October: Ten Days that Shook the World*] (USSR, 1928). *Directed and Written by* Grigori Aleksandrov *and* Sergei Eisenstein. *Produced by* Sovkino. *Starring* Vladimir Popov, Vasili Nikandrov, *and* Layaschenko.
- ***Le Jour Se Lève*** [*Daybreak*] (France, 1939). *Directed by* Marcel Carné. *Produced by* Robert *and* Raymond Hakim. *Written by* Jacques Prévert. *Starring* Jean Gabin, Jules Berry, *and* Arletty.
- ***Bambi*** (USA, 1942). *Directed by* David Hand. *Produced by* Walt Disney. *Written by* Perce Pearce.
- ***Roma città aperta*** [*Rome, Open City*] (Italy, 1945). *Directed by* Roberto Rossellini. *Produced by* Guiseppe Amato, Ferruccio De Martino, Roberto Rossellini, *and* Rod E. Geiger. *Written by* Sergio Amidei *and* Federico Fellini. *Starring* Aldo Fabrizi, Anna Magnani, *and* Marcello Pagliero.
- ***Louisiana Story*** (USA, 1948). *Directed and Produced by* Robert J. Flaherty. *Written by* Robert J. Flaherty *and* Frances H. Flaherty. *Starring* Joseph Boudreaux, Lionel Le Blanc, E. Bienvenu, *and* Frank Hardy.
- ***Le Sang des bêtes*** [*Blood of the Beasts*] (France, 1949). *Directed and Written by* Georges Franju. *Produced by* Paul Legros. *Narrated by* Georges Hubert *and* Nicole Ladmiral.
- ***Limelight*** (USA, 1952). *Directed, Produced, and Written by* Charlie Chaplin. *Starring* Charlie Chaplin *and* Claire Bloom.
- ***Ugetsu*** (Japan, 1953). *Directed by* Kenji Mizoguchi. *Produced by* Masaichi Nagata. *Written by* Matsutarō Kawaguchi *and* Yoshikata Yoda. *Starring* Masayuki Mori, Machiko Kyō, *and* Kinuyo Tanaka.
- ***Shin Heike Monogatari*** [*The Taira Clan Saga*] (Japan, 1955). *Directed by* Kenji Mizoguchi. *Produced by* Masaichi Nagata. *Written by* Masashige Narusawa, Kyûchi Tsuji, *and* Yoshikata Yoda. *Starring* Ichikawa Raizō VIII, Yoshiko Kuga, *and* Michiyo Kogure.
- ***Nuit et Brouillard*** [*Night and Fog*] (France, 1956). *Directed by* Alain Resnais. *Produced by* Anatole Dauman. *Written by* Jean Cayrol. *Narrated by* Michel Bouquet.
- ***Anatomy of a Murder*** (USA, 1959). *Directed and Produced by* Otto Preminger. *Written by* Wendell Mayes. *Starring* James Stewart, Lee Remick, Ben Gazzara, Arthur O'Connell, Eve Arden, *and* Kathryn Grant.
- ***Hiroshima mon amour*** (France, 1959). *Directed by* Alain Resnais. *Produced by* Samy Halfon *and* Anatole Dauman. *Written by* Marguerite Duras. *Starring* Emmanuelle Riva *and* Eiji Okada.

- ***Das indische Grabmal*** [*The Indian Tomb*] (Germany–France–Italy, 1959). *Directed by* Fritz Lang. *Produced by* Artur Brauner. *Written by* Thea von Harbou, Fritz Lang, *and* Werner Jörg Lüddecke. *Starring* Sabine Bethmann, René Deltgen, Jochen Brockmann, Valéry Inkijinoff, *and* Claus Holm.
- ***Pickpocket*** (France, 1959). *Directed and Written by* Robert Bresson. *Produced by* Agnès Delahaie. *Starring* Martin LaSalle.
- ***Rio Bravo*** (USA, 1959). *Directed and Produced by* Howard Hawks. *Written by* Jules Furthman *and* Leigh Brackett. *Starring* John Wayne, Dean Martin, *and* Ricky Nelson.
- ***La Dolce Vita*** (Italy, 1960). *Directed by* Federico Fellini. *Produced by* Guiseppe Amato *and* Angelo Rizzoli. *Written by* Federico Fellini, Ennio Flaiano, Tullio Pinelli, *and* Brunello Rondi. *Starring* Marcello Mastroianni *and* Anita Ekberg.
- ***Kapò*** (Italy, 1960). *Directed by* Gillo Pontecorvo. *Produced by* Franco Cristaldi *and* Moris Ergas. *Written by* Gillo Pontecorvo *and* Franco Solinas. *Starring* Susan Strasberg, Didi Perego, *and* Laurent Terzieff.
- ***Psycho*** (USA, 1960). *Directed and Produced by* Alfred Hitchcock. *Written by* Joseph Stefano. *Starring* Anthony Perkins, Vera Miles, *and* John Gavin.
- ***Merrill's Marauders*** (USA, 1962). *Directed by* Samuel Fuller. *Produced by* Milton Sperling. *Written by* Samuel Fuller *and* Milton Sperling. *Starring* Jeff Chandler.
- ***La battaglia di Algeri*** [*The Battle of Algiers*] (Italy–Algeria, 1966). *Directed by* Gillo Pontecorvo. *Produced by* Rizzoli. *Written by* Gillo Pontecorvo *and* Franco Solinas. *Starring* Jean Martin, Saadi Yacef, Brahim Haggiag, *and* Tommaso Neri.
- ***Week-end*** [*Weekend*] (France, 1967). *Directed and Written by* Jean-Luc Godard. *Produced by* Athos Films. *Starring* Mireille Darc *and* Jean Yanne.
- ***Il portiere di notte*** [*The Night Porter*] (Italy, 1974). *Directed by* Liliana Cavani. *Produced by* Robert Gordon Edwards *and* Esa De Simone. *Written by* Liliana Cavani, Italo Moscati, Barbara Alberti, *and* Amedeo Pagani. *Starring* Dirk Bogarde *and* Charlotte Rampling.
- ***Ilsa, She Wolf of the SS*** (Canada, 1975). *Directed by* Don Edmonds. *Produced by* Herman Traeger. *Written by* Jonah Royston. *Starring* Dyanne Thorne *and* C. D. Lafleuer.
- ***Salò o le 120 giornate di Sodoma*** [*Salò, or the 120 Days of Sodom*] (Italy–France, 1975). *Directed by* Pier Paolo Pasolini. *Produced by* Alberto Grimaldi. *Written by* Sergio Citti *and* Pier Paolo Pasolini. *Starring* Paolo Bonacelli, Giorgio Cataldi, Umberto P. Quintavalle, *and* Aldo Valletti.
- ***Hitler, ein Film aus Deutschland*** [*Hitler: A Film from Germany*] (France–UK–Germany, 1977). *Directed and Written by* Hans-Jürgen Syberberg. *Produced by* Bernd Eichinger. *Starring* Heinz Schubert.
- ***Holocaust*** (USA, 1978). *Directed by* Marvin J. Chomsky. *Produced by* Robert Berger *and* Herbert Brodkin. *Written by* Gerald Green. *Starring* James Woods, Meryl Streep, *and* Michael Moriarty.
- ***La Vie est un Roman*** [*Life Is a Bed of Roses*] (France, 1983). *Directed by* Alain Resnais. *Produced by* Philippe Dusart. *Written by* Jean Gruault. *Starring* Vittorio Gassman, Ruggero Raimondi, Geraldine Chaplin, *and* Fanny Ardant.
- ***Je vous salue, Marie*** [*Hail, Mary*] (France, 1985). *Directed and Written by* Jean-Luc Godard. *Produced by* Sara Films. *Starring* Myriam Roussel, Thierry Rode, Philippe Lacoste, Manon Andersen, *and* Juliette Binoche.

- ***Au revoir les enfants*** (France, 1987). *Directed, Produced, and Written by* Louis Malle. *Starring* Gaspard Manesse, Raphael Fejtö, Philippe Morier-Genoud, *and* Francine Racette.
- ***The Last Temptation of Christ*** (USA, 1988). *Directed by* Martin Scorsese. *Produced by* Barbara De Fina *and* Harry Ulfland. *Written by* Paul Schrader. *Starring* Willem Dafoe, Harvey Keitel, Barbara Hershey, Harry Dean Stanton, *and* David Bowie.

THE TRACKING SHOT IN *KAPO*

Translated by Paul Grant

Among the many films I've never seen there is not only *October*, *Le jour se lève*, and *Bambi*, but the obscure *Kapo* as well. A film about the concentration camps shot in 1960 by the leftist Italian Gillo Pontecorvo, *Kapo* was by no means a landmark in the history of cinema. Am I the only one who has never seen this film but has never forgotten it? I haven't seen *Kapo* and yet at the same time I have seen it. I've seen it because someone showed it to me—with words. This movie, whose title—functioning as a kind of password—has accompanied my life of cinema, I know it only through a short text: the review written by Jacques Rivette in the June 1961 issue of *Cahiers du cinéma*. It was the 120th issue and the article was entitled "On Abjection." Rivette was 33 and I was 17. I had probably never uttered the word "abjection" in my life.

Rivette didn't recount the film's narrative in his article. Instead he was content to describe one shot in a single sentence. The sentence, engraved in my memory, read: "Just look at the shot in *Kapo* where Riva commits suicide by throwing herself on electric barbed wire: the man who decides at this moment to track forward and reframe the dead body in a low-angle shot—carefully positioning the raised hand in the corner of the final frame—deserves only the most profound contempt." Therefore a simple camera movement could be the *one* movement not to make. The movement one must—*obviously*—be abject to make. As soon as I read those lines I knew the author was absolutely right.

Abrupt and luminous, Rivette's text allowed me to give voice to this particular form of abjection. My revulsion had found the words to express itself. But there was more. This revolt was accompanied by a feeling both less pure and less clear: a sense of relief in realizing that I had just obtained my first conviction as a future critic. Over the years, "the tracking shot in *Kapo*" would become my portable dogma, the axiom that wasn't up for discussion, the breaking point of any debate. I would definitely have nothing to do or share with anyone who didn't immediately *feel* the abjection of "the tracking shot of *Kapo*."

At the time this type of refusal was common. Looking at the raging and exasperated style of Rivette's article, I sensed that furious debates had already taken place and it already seemed obvious to me that cinema was the echo box of all polemic. The war in Algeria was ending, and because it hadn't been filmed, it brought suspicion to bear upon any representation of history. Everybody seemed to understand that things such as taboo figures, criminal aptitudes, and forbidden cuts existed—especially in cinema. Godard's famous expression that a tracking shot was a "moral affair" was one of those truths that could no longer be questioned. Not by me anyway.

Rivette's article was published in *Cahiers du cinéma*, three years prior to the end of the yellow period. Did I sense that the text couldn't have been published in any other magazine, that it belonged to *Cahiers* just as, later on, I would belong to it? In any case I found my family. Therefore it wasn't out of pure snobbery that I'd been buying *Cahiers* for the last two years, and that my friend from *lycée* Voltaire, Claude D., and I shared our amazed commentary. It wasn't pure caprice if at the beginning of every month I pressed my nose against the window of the modest bookshop on Avenue de la République. Seeing that beneath the yellow border, the black and white picture on the cover of *Cahiers* had changed was enough to set my heart racing. But I didn't want the shop-keep to tell me whether or not there was a new issue. I wanted to find out for myself and then coolly buy the magazine, in a neutral voice, as if I was buying a notepad. It never even occurred to me to subscribe: I liked the anxious wait. Whether buying, writing for, or editing *Cahiers*, I could always hang around out front since it was "my place."

There were a handful of us at the *lycée* Voltaire who were surreptitiously recruited into cinephilia. The date: 1959. The word "cinephile" was still cheerful, although it already had the pathological connotations and the stale aura that would little by little discredit it. As for me, I immediately despised those who were too normal and sneered at the "cinemathèque rats" we were on the verge of becoming—guilty of living cinema passionately and life by proxy. At the dawn of the 1960s, the world of cinema was still an enchanted one. On the one hand it had all the charms of a *parallel* counter-culture. On the other it had the advantage of already being developed with a heavy history, recognized values, Sadoul's typos (that insufficient bible), jargon, persistent myths, battles of ideas, and wars between magazines. The wars were almost over and we were certainly arriving a little late, but not so late that we couldn't nourish the tacit project of making this *whole* history, which wasn't even as old as the century, our own.

Being a cinephile meant simply devouring *another* education parallel to that of the *lycée*, with the yellow *Cahiers* as the common thread and a few "adult" *passeurs* who, with conspiratorial discretion, showed us that indeed there was a world to discover, and maybe nothing other than *the* world to live in. Henri Agel—a literature teacher at *lycée* Voltaire—was one of these peculiar *passeurs*. To spare himself, as well as us, the burden of Latin lessons, he would put to a vote whether to spend an hour on Titus Livius or watch movies. The pupils who chose the movies often left the decrepit cine-club pensive and feeling tricked. Out of sadism and probably because he had the prints, Agel showed little movies designed to seriously open the students' eyes: Franju's *Le sang des bêtes* and in particular Resnais' *Nuit et brouillard*. Through cinema I learned that the human condition and industrial butchery were not incompatible and that the worst had just happened.

I imagine Agel, who wrote "Evil" with a capital E, enjoyed watching the effects of this particular revelation on the teenagers' faces. There had to be a degree of voyeurism in his brutal way of transmitting, via the cinema, this gruesome and unavoidable knowledge that we were the first generation to fully inherit. Christian but not proselytizing, and a rather elitist militant, Agel was *showing*. It was one of his talents. He was showing because it was necessary, and because the cinematic culture at the *lycée*, for which he was campaigning, also meant a silent classification of students: those who would never forget *Nuit et brouillard* and the others. I wasn't one of the "others."

Once, twice, three times, depending upon Agel's whims and the number of sacrificed Latin lessons, I watched the famous piles of dead bodies, hair, glasses, and teeth. I listened to Jean Cayrol's despondent commentary recited by Michel Bouquet along with Hanns Eisler's music, which seemed ashamed of itself for existing. A strange baptism of images: *to comprehend at the same time that the camps were real and that the film was just*. And to understand that cinema (alone?) was capable of approaching the limits of a distorted humanity. I felt that the distances set by Resnais between the subject filmed, the subject filming, and the subject spectator were, in 1959—as in 1955—the only ones possible. Was *Nuit et brouillard* a "beautiful" film? No, it was a *just* film. It's *Kapo* that wanted to be a beautiful film and wasn't. And I'm the one who would never quite see the difference between the just and the beautiful—hence my rather "workaday" boredom in front of beautiful images.

Already captivated by cinema, I didn't need to be seduced as well. And there was no need to talk to me like a baby. As a child I never saw *any* Disney movies. Just as I went directly to communal school, I was proud to have been spared the infantile and clamorous kindergarten showings. Worse: animated movies for me would always be something other than cinema. Even worse: animated movies would always be something of an enemy. No "beautiful image," especially drawn, would match the emotion—fear and trembling—before *recorded* things. All of this, which is so simple, and took me years to formulate simply, began to come out in front of Resnais' images and Rivette's text. Born in 1944, two days before D-Day, I was old enough to discover *my* cinema and *my* history at the same time. A strange history that for a long time I believed I was sharing with others, before realizing, rather late, that it was well and truly mine.

What does a child know? Especially this child, Serge D., who wanted to know everything except that which concerned him? What absence *from the world* will later require the presence *of images of the world*? I know of few expressions more beautiful than Jean-Louis Schefer's in *L'homme ordinaire du cinéma* when he speaks of "the films that have watched our childhood." It's one thing to learn to watch movies "professionally"—only to verify that movies watch us less and less—but it is another to live with those movies that watched us grow up and saw us—prematurely hostage to our coming biographies—already entangled in the snare of our history. For me, *Psycho*, *La Dolce Vita*, *The Indian Tomb*, *Rio Bravo*, *Pickpocket*, *Anatomy of a Murder*, *The Taira Clan*, or *Nuit et brouillard*, in particular, are unlike any other films. To the rather brutal question "Does this watch you?" all of them answer yes.

The corpses in *Nuit et brouillard* and then two years later those in the opening shots of *Hiroshima mon amour* are among those "things" that watched me more than I saw them. Eisenstein tried to produce such images, but it was Hitchcock who succeeded. It's only one example, but how can I ever forget the first meeting with *Psycho*? We snuck into the Paramount Opera theater without paying and the movie was terrorizing in the most normal way. Then, near the end of the film, my perception slides upon a scene, a careless montage out of which only grotesque props emerge: a cubist robe, a falling wig, and a brandished knife. From the collectively experienced fear follows a calm of resigned solitude: the brain functions as a second projector allowing the image to continue flowing, letting the film and the world continue without it. I can't imagine a love for cinema that does not rest firmly on the stolen present of this "continue on without me."

Who hasn't experienced this state or known these screen memories? Unidentified images are engraved in the retina; unknown events inevitably happen and spoken words become the secret code of an impossible self-knowledge. Just as Paulhan speaks about literature as an experience of the world "when we are not there" and Lacan speaks about "that which is missing from its place," these moments "neither seen nor taken" are the primitive scene of the lover of cinema, the scene *in which he wasn't present and yet it was entirely about him*. The cinephile? He who in vain keeps his eyes wide open but will tell no one that he *couldn't* see a thing; he who prepares himself for a life as a professional "watcher," as a way to make up for his tardiness, as slowly as possible.

Thus my life had its zero point, its second birth, which was experienced as such and immediately commemorated. The year is well known, again 1959. It is—coincidentally?—the year of Duras' famous "you saw nothing at Hiroshima." My mother and I left *Hiroshima mon amour*, both of us staggered—we weren't the only ones—because we never thought that cinema was capable of "that." On the subway platform I finally realized that to the tedious question I could never answer—"What are you going to do with your life?"—I had just found a response. "Later," one way or another, it would be cinema. And I never kept any details of this cinema-birth from myself: *Hiroshima*, the platform of the metro station, my mother, the now closed *Agricultures* theater and its seats will often be remembered as the legendary set of the good origin, the one you choose for yourself.

Resnais is the name that links this primitive scene in three acts over two years. It's because *Nuit et brouillard* was possible that *Kapo* was born obsolete and that Rivette could write his article. However, before becoming the prototype of the "modern" filmmaker, Resnais was just another *passeur*. If he was revolutionizing "cinematic language" (as we used to say), it's because he took his *subject* seriously and because he had the intuition, almost the luck, to recognize this subject among all the others: nothing less than the human species coming out of the Nazi camps and the atomic trauma, disfigured and ruined. There has always been something strange in the fact that later on I became a bored spectator of Resnais' other films. It seemed to me that his attempts to revitalize a world whose illness he alone had registered in time were destined to produce nothing but uneasiness.

Therefore I won't make the journey of "modern" cinema with Resnais, but rather with Rossellini. Nor will the moral lessons be memorized and conjugated with Resnais but instead with Godard. Why? First, because Godard and Rossellini spoke, wrote, and thought out loud while the image of Saint Alain Resnais freezing in his anoraks and begging us—rightly but in vain—to believe him when he said that he wasn't an intellectual started to get on my nerves. Was I "avenging" myself for the importance of two of his movies at the beginning of my life? Resnais was the filmmaker who kidnapped me from childhood or rather made me a *serious* child for three decades. And he is precisely the one with whom, as an adult, I would never share anything. I remember that at the end of an interview—for the release of *La vie est un roman*—I thought it a good idea to tell him about the shock I experienced with *Hiroshima mon amour*. He thanked me stiffly, as if I had just complimented him on his new raincoat. I was offended, but I was wrong: the films that have watched our childhood can't be shared, not even with their author.

Now that this story has come full circle and I've had more than my share of the "nothing" to be seen at Hiroshima, I inevitably ask myself: could it have been different? Facing the camps, was there any other possible justness besides the anti-spectacular *Nuit et brouillard*? A friend recently brought up the George Stevens' documentary made at the end of the war, which was buried, exhumed, and then shown on French television not so long ago. It is the first movie to record the opening of the camps in color, and the colors transform it—*without any abjection*—into art. Why? Is it the difference between color and black and white, between America and Europe, between Stevens and Resnais? What's amazing in Stevens' film is that it's the story of a journey: the daily progression of a small group of soldiers and filmmakers wandering across a destroyed Europe, from the ravaged Saint-Lô to Auschwitz, which nobody had foreseen and that totally overwhelms the entire crew. And then a friend tells me that the piles of dead bodies have a strange beauty which make her think of this century's great paintings. As always, Sylvie Pierre was right.

What I understand today is that the beauty of Stevens' film is due less to the justness of the distance than to the *innocence* of the gaze. Justness is the burden of the one who comes "after," innocence the terrible grace accorded to the first to arrive, to the first one who simply makes the cinematic gesture. It took me until the mid-1970s to recognize in Pasolini's *Salo*, or even in Syberberg's *Hitler*, the other sense of the word "innocent": not so much the not-guilty but he one who in filming evil doesn't think evil. In 1959, as a young boy paralyzed by his discovery, I was already caught in the collective guilt. But in 1945, perhaps it was enough to be American and to witness, like George Stevens or Corporal Samuel Fuller at Falkenau, the opening of the real gates of the night, camera in hand. One had to be American—that is to say, to believe in the fundamental innocence of the spectacle—to make the German population walk by the open tombs, to *show* them what they were living next to, so well and so badly. It took ten years before Resnais could sit down at the editing table and fifteen years before Pontecorvo made this one little move too many that revolted us, Rivette and I. Necrophilia was the price of this "delay" and was the erotic body double of the "just" gaze—the gaze of a guilty Europe, Resnais' gaze, and consequently mine.

This is how my story began. The space that Rivette's sentence opened was truly mine, as the intellectual family of *Cahiers du cinéma* was already mine. But I realized that this space wasn't so much a vast field as a narrow door. On the noble side was the *jouissance* of the just distance and its reverse, sublime necrophilia or necrophilia sublimated. On the not so noble side was the possibility of a completely other *jouissance* unable to be sublimated. It's Godard who, showing me videotapes of "concentration camp porn" tucked away in his video collection at Rolle, was surprised that nothing had been said about these films and that no interdiction had been pronounced. As if their creators' cowardly intentions and their viewers' trivial fantasies somehow "protected" them from censorship and indignation. Evidence that in the domain of sub-culture, the silent claim of an obligatory interlacing of executioners and victims was persisting. I was never really upset about the existence of these films. I had for them—just like any openly pornographic films—the almost polite tolerance one has for the expression of a fantasy that, so naked, claims only the sad monotony of its necessary repetition.

It's the other pornography that always revolted me: the "artistic" pornography of *Kapo*, or, a little later, *The Night Porter*, and other retro films of the 1970s. To this consensual after the fact aestheticization, I would prefer the obstinate return of the non-images in *Nuit et brouillard* or the unfurling drives of *Ilsa, She Wolf of the S.S.*, which I wouldn't see. At least these films had the honesty to acknowledge the impossibility of telling a story, the stopping point in the course of history, when storytelling freezes or runs idle. So we shouldn't be speaking about amnesia or repression but rather about foreclosure. Later I would learn the Lacanian definition of foreclosure: a hallucinatory return to the real of something upon which it was impossible to place a "judgment of reality." In other words: since filmmakers hadn't filmed the policies of the Vichy government, their duty fifty years later wasn't to imaginarily redeem themselves with movies like *Au revoir les enfants* but to draw the contemporary portrait of the good people of France who, from 1940 to 1942 (and that includes the Vel' d'Hiv raid), didn't budge. Cinema being the art of the present, their remorse is of no interest.

This is why the spectator who I was before *Nuit et brouillard* and the filmmaker who tried to show the unrepresentable with this film were linked by a complicit symmetry. Either it's the spectator who is suddenly "missing from his place" and is stilled while the film continues, or it's the film which, instead of "continuing," folds back onto itself and onto a temporarily definitive "image" that allows the spectator to continue believing in cinema and the subject-citizen to live his life. Spectator-stilled, image-stilled: cinema entered adulthood. The sphere of the visible had ceased to be wholly available: there were gaps and holes, necessary hollows and superfluous plenitude, forever missing images and always defective gazes. The spectacle and the spectator stopped playing every ball. It is thus having chosen cinema—supposedly "the art of moving images"—that I began my cinephagic life under the paradoxical aegis of a first *image-stilled*.

This still protected me from strict necrophilia and I never saw any of the rare films or documentaries "on the camps" that came after *Kapo*. The matter was settled for me with *Nuit et brouillard* and Rivette's article. For a long time I have been like the French authorities, who, still to this day, in the face of any resurgence of anti-Semitism, urgently broadcast Resnais' film as if it is part of a secret arsenal that, whenever evil returns, can indefinitely apply its virtues of exorcism. If I didn't apply the axiom of the "tracking shot in *Kapo*" only to films that were exposed to abjection by their subject, it was because I was tempted to apply it to *every* film. "There are things," wrote Rivette, "that must be approached with fear and trembling. Death is undoubtedly such a thing, and how does one, at the moment of filming such a mysterious thing, avoid feeling like an impostor?" I agreed.

Since there are only a few films in which nobody dies, there were many occasions to fear and tremble. Indeed certain filmmakers weren't impostors. Again, in 1959, Miyagi's death in *Ugetsu* nailed me to the seat of the Studio Bernard theater. Mizoguchi filmed death as a vague fatality that one *saw* could and could not happen. The scene is memorable: in the Japanese countryside ravenous bandits attack travelers and one of them kills Miyagi with a spear. But he almost does it inadvertently, teetering, moved by a bit of violence or an idiotic reflex. This event seems so accidental that the camera almost misses it, and I'm convinced that all spectators of *Ugetsu* have the same crazy, almost superstitious idea that if the camera hadn't been so slow the event would have happened "out of frame," or who knows, it might not have happened at all.

Is it the camera's fault? In dissociating the camera-movement from the actors' gesticulations, Mizoguchi proceeded in precisely the opposite manner of *Kapo*. Instead of an embellishing glance, this was a gaze that "pretended not to see," that preferred not to have seen and thus showed the event taking place *as an event*, that is to say, ineluctably and obliquely. An absurd and worthless event, absurd like any accident and worthless like war—a calamity that Mizoguchi never liked. An event that doesn't concern us enough to even move past it, shameful. I bet that at precisely this moment, every spectator of *Ugetsu absolutely* knows the absurdity of war. It doesn't matter that the spectator is a westerner, the movie Japanese, and the war medieval: it's enough to shift from pointing with the finger to showing with the gaze for this knowledge—the only knowledge cinema is capable of, as furtive as it is universal—to be given to us.

Opting so early for the panoramic shot in *Ugetsu* instead of the tracking shot in *Kapo*, I made a choice whose gravity I would only measure ten years later, amidst the late and radical politicization of *Cahiers* after 1968. If Pontecorvo, the future director of *The Battle of Algiers*, is a courageous filmmaker with whom I share by and large the same political beliefs, Mizoguchi seemed to have lived solely for his art and to have been a political opportunist. So where is the difference? Precisely in the "fear and trembling." Mizoguchi is scared of war for different reasons than Kurosawa: he is appalled by little men hacking each other apart for some feudal virility. It's this fear, this desire to vomit and flee, which issues the stunned panoramic shot. It's this fear that makes this moment just and therefore able to be shared. Pontecorvo neither trembles nor fears: the concentration camps only revolt him ideologically. This is why he can inscribe himself in the scene with the worthless but pretty little tracking shot.

I realized that most of the time cinema oscillated between those two poles. With even more substantial directors than Pontecorvo, I often stumbled upon this smuggler's way of adding extra parasitic beauty or complicit information to scenes that didn't need it. It was thus that the wind blowing back the white parachute, like a shroud, over a dead soldier's body in Fuller's *Merrill's Marauders* troubled me for years. However, not as much as Ana Magnani's revealing skirt after she is shot dead in *Rome, Open City*. Rossellini was also hitting "below the belt," but in such a new way that it would take years to know towards which abyss it was taking us. Where does the event end? Where is the cruelty? Where does obscenity begin and where does pornography end? I knew these were questions constitutive of the "post-camp" cinema. A cinema that I began to call, because we were the same age, "modern."

This modern cinema had one characteristic: it was *cruel*; we had another: we accepted this cruelty. Cruelty was on the "good side." It was cruelty that said no to academic "illustration" and destroyed the counterfeit sentimentalism of a wordy humanism. Mizoguchi's cruelty, for instance, of showing two irreconcilable movements together, producing an unbearable feeling of "not helping someone in danger." A modern feeling *par excellence*, coming fifteen years before the long tracking shots in *Weekend*. An archaic feeling as well since that cruelty was as old as cinema itself, like an index of what was fundamentally modern in cinema, from the last shot in *Limelight* to Browning's *The Unknown*, and up to the end of *Nana*. How could one forget the slow, trembling tracking shot that the young Renoir hurls towards Nana lying on her bed, dying of smallpox? How is it that some people see in Renoir a crooner of the good life when he was one of the few filmmakers, right from the beginning, who was capable of finishing someone off with a tracking shot?

Actually, cruelty was within the logic of my journey at the combative *Cahiers*. André Bazin, who already theorized cruelty, had found it so closely linked to the essence of cinema that he almost made it "its thing." Bazin, the lay saint, liked *Louisiana Story* because you could see a bird eaten by a crocodile in real time and in one shot: cinematic proof and forbidden editing. Choosing *Cahiers* was choosing realism and, as I would discover, a certain contempt for imagination. To Lacan's formula "Do you want to watch? Then watch this" there was already the response of "Has it been recorded? Well then I have to watch it," even and especially when "it" was painful, intolerable, or completely invisible.

For this realism was two-faced. If modern filmmakers were showing a world surviving through realism, it was with a completely other realism—one more "realistic"—that movie propaganda in the 1940s had collaborated with the lies and foreshadowed death. This is why in spite of all it was fair to call the former realism, born in Italy, "neo." It was impossible to love the "art of the century" without seeing this art working with the madness of the century and being worked by it. Contrary to the theater, with its collective crises and cures, cinema, with its personal information and mourning, had an intimate relation with the horror from which it was barely recovering. I inherited a guilty convalescent, an old child, and a tenuous hypothesis. We would grow old together but not eternally.

Conscientious heir, a model *ciné-fils*, with the "tracking shot in *Kapo*" as a protective charm, I didn't let the years go by without some apprehension: what if the talisman lost its power? I remember a course I was teaching at Censier where I distributed Rivette's text to my students and asked for their impressions. It was still a "red" period when some students were trying to glean a bit of the political radicalism of '68 from their professors. It seemed that out of consideration for me the most motivated of them consented to see "On Abjection" as an interesting historical, but slightly dated document. I wasn't insistent with them, and if I ventured to repeat the experience with students today, I wouldn't be so concerned as to whether or not they understood the tracking shot, but I would have my heart set on knowing that they saw some *trace* of abjection. To be honest, I'm afraid they wouldn't. A sign that not only are tracking shots no longer a moral issue, but that the cinema is even too weak to entertain such a question.

Thirty years after the repeated projections of *Nuit et brouillard* at the *lycée* Voltaire, concentration camps—which served as my primitive scene—have ceased to be held in the sacred respect in which Resnais, Cayrol, and many others maintained them. Returned to the historians and the curious, the question of the camps is from now on linked with their work, their divergences, and their madness. The foreclosed desire, which returns "like a hallucination in the real," is evidently the one that should never have returned. It is the desire that no gas chambers, no final solution, or, at the most, no camps ever existed: revisionism, Faurissonism, negationism, sinister and last -isms. Film students today are not only inheriting the tracking shot in *Kapo*, but also an uncertain transmission, a poorly defined taboo, in brief just another round in the worthless history of the tribalization of the same and the fear of the other. The image-stilled has ceased to operate; the banality of evil can animate new, electronic images.

In contemporary France there are enough symptoms surging forth for someone of my generation to look back on the history he was given and notice the landscape he grew up in, a landscape that is both tragic and comfortable. Two political dreams defined by Yalta: American and Communist. Behind us was a moral point of no return symbolized by Auschwitz and the new concept of "crimes against humanity." Ahead of us, the unthinkable, almost reassuring, nuclear apocalypse. What had just ended lasted more than forty years. I belonged to *the first generation* for which racism and anti-Semitism had fallen definitively into the "dustbin of history." The first and only generation? The only one in any case which cried out so easily against fascism ("fascism will not pass!") because it seemed a thing of the past, once and for all, null and void. A mistake to be sure, but a mistake that didn't stop us from living very well during the "thirty glorious years," but in quotation marks. Naïve to be sure, acting as if Resnais' elegant necrophilia in the so-called "aesthetic" field would eternally keep any intrusion "at a distance."

"No poetry after Auschwitz," said Adorno, before rethinking this now famous formula. "No fiction after Resnais," I could have echoed before abandoning this slightly excessive idea. "Protected" by the shockwave produced by the discovery of the camps, did we now believe humanity had fallen into the inhuman only once with no chance of it happening again? Had we really bet that for once the worst was over? At this point did we hope that what wasn't yet called the Shoah was the *unique* historical event "thanks" to which *the whole of* humankind was "exiting" history in order to look at it from above and instantly recognize the worst face of its own possible fate? It seems we had.

But if "unique" and "the whole of" were too much and if humankind didn't inherit the Shoah as the *metaphor* of what it was and is capable of, then the extermination of the Jews would remain a Jewish story and also—in order of importance with regards to guilt, *by metonymy*—a very German story, a French story, and consequently an Arab story, but not very Danish and almost not Bulgarian at all. The "modern" imperative to articulate the image-stilled and pronounce the embargo on fiction responded to—within cinema—the possibility of the metaphor. The history of telling another story another way where "humankind" was the only character and the first anti-star. The history of giving birth to *another* cinema "which would know" that to give the event back to fiction too early is to take away its uniqueness, because fiction is this freedom which dissolves and opens itself beforehand to an infinity of variations and the seduction of true lies.

In 1989, while visiting Phnom Penh and the Cambodian countryside for *Libération*, I caught a glimpse of what genocide—that is, auto-genocide—"looked like" when left without any images and almost no trace. Ironically, I saw the proof that cinema was no longer intimately linked to human history by the fact that, unlike the Nazi executioners who filmed their victims, the Khmer Rouge left behind only photographs and mass graves. Because another genocide—the Cambodian genocide—was left both imageless and unpunished, a retroactive effect of contagion occurred: the Shoah itself was rendered relative. Return of the blocked metaphor to the active metonymy, return of the image-stilled to the viral analogue. It went very quickly: in 1990 the "Romanian revolution" was frivolously indicting indisputable murderers for "illegal possession of firearms *and* genocide." Does everything need to be repeated? Yes everything, but this time without cinema—hence the mourning.

Undoubtedly we *believed* in cinema, which is to say we did everything not to believe it. That's the whole history of the post-'68 *Cahiers* and its impossible rejection of Bazinism. Of course it wasn't about "sleeping in the image-bed [*plan-lit*]" or upsetting Barthes by confusing the real and the representation. We knew too much not to put the spectator in the signifying concatenation or to locate the tenacious ideology beneath the false neutrality of technology. Pascal Bonitzer and I were even a little brave when we shouted in cracking voices before an amphitheater packed with excited leftists that a film could no longer be "seen" but had to be "read." It was a laudable effort to be on the side of the non-duped, laudable and, in my case, in vain. There always comes a moment when you have to pay your debt to the cash-box of sincere belief and *dare to believe in what you see*.

Of course you're not obligated to believe in what you see—it can even be dangerous—but you're not obligated to hold on to cinema either. There has to be some risk and some virtue, that is, some value, in the act of showing something to someone who is capable of seeing it. Learning how to "read" the visual and "decode" messages would be useless if there wasn't still the minimal, but deep-seated, conviction that *seeing* is superior to not seeing, and that what isn't seen "in time" will never really be seen. Cinema is an art of the present. If nostalgia doesn't suit it, it's because melancholy is its instantaneous double.

I remember the vehemence with which I said this for the first and last time. It was at a film school in Teheran. In front of the invited journalists, Khemais K. and myself, there were rows of boys with budding beards and rows of black sacks—probably the girls. The boys were on the left and the girls on the right, all in accordance with the apartheid. The most interesting questions—those from the girls—came to us on furtive little slips of paper. And seeing those girls so attentive and so stupidly veiled, I gave way to a rage with no particular object; it was directed less towards them than to all the powers that be, and for whom the visible is primarily what is read, i.e. what is permanently suspected of betrayal and reduced with the assistance of a chador or a police of signs. Encouraged by the unusual moment and place, I delivered a sermon in favor of the visual before a veiled audience who agreed.

Late anger, terminal anger. For the age of suspicion is well and truly over. One is only suspicious when a certain idea of truth is at stake. Nothing like that really exists today except among creationists and bigots, those who attack Scorsese's *Last Temptation of Christ* or Godard's *Marie*. The images are no longer on the side of the dialectical truth of "seeing" and "showing"; they have entirely moved over to the side of promotion and advertising, which is to say the side of power. It's therefore too late not to begin working on what's left: the golden and posthumous legend of what cinema once was, of what it was and what it could have been.

> Our work will be to show how individuals, gathered together in the dark, were stoking their imagination to warm up their reality—that was silent cinema; to show how they have let the flame go out to the rhythm of social conquest, satisfied to maintain only a very small fire—this is the talkie and the television in the corner of the room.

When he decided upon this program—just recently, in 1989—Godard the historian could have added "Alone, at last!"

As for me, I remember the exact moment when I knew that the axiom of "the tracking shot in *Kapo*" should be revisited and the homemade concept of "modern cinema" revisited. In 1979, French television broadcast *Holocaust*, the American mini-series by Marvin Chomsky. We had come full circle, and I was sent back to square one. If in 1945 the Americans allowed George Stevens to make his astonishing documentary, they never broadcast it because of the cold war. Unable to "deal" with that story, which after all is not theirs, the American entrepreneurs of entertainment temporarily abandoned it to European artists. But with that story, *like every story*, they reserved the *right to buy it*, and sooner or later Hollywood and the television machine would dare to tell "our" story. It would tell it very carefully but it would sell it to us as another American story. So *Holocaust* would become the misfortunes that tear apart and destroy a Jewish family: there would be extras looking a little too fat, good performances, generic humanism, action, and melodrama. And we would sympathize.

It would therefore be only in the form of the American docu-drama that this history could escape the cine-clubs and could, via television, concern this servile version of the "whole of humanity" that is the global TV audience. The simulation-*Holocaust* was certainly no longer confronting the strangeness of a humanity capable of a crime against itself, but it remained obstinately incapable of bringing back the singular beings—each with a story, a face, and a *name*—who made up this history, who were the exterminated Jews. Rather it would be graphic art—Spiegelman's *Maus*—that later dared to make this salutary act of re-singularization. Graphic art and not cinema since it's true that American cinema hates singularity. With *Holocaust*, Marvin Chomsky brought back, modestly and triumphantly, our perennial aesthetic enemy: the good old sociological program with its well-studied cast of suffering specimens and its light-show of animated police sketches. We had come full circle and we had truly lost. The proof? It was around this time that Faurissonian tracts started to circulate in France.

It took me twenty years to go from *my* "tracking shot in *Kapo*" to this irreproachable *Holocaust*. I took my time. The "question" of the camps, of my prehistory, would still and forever be put to me, but *no longer really through cinema*. Yet it was with cinema that I had understood in what respect this history concerned me and in which *form*—one tracking shot too many—it had appeared to me. We must remain faithful to the face that once transfixed us. And every "form" is a face that looks at us. This is why, even if I feared them, I never believed those at the *lycée* cine-club who condescendingly attacked those poor "formalist" fools who were guilty of preferring *jouissance* of the "form" to the "content" of films. But only he who has been struck early enough by *formal violence* will end up realizing—at the end of his life—how this violence also has an "essence." And the moment will always come early enough for him to die cured, having traded the enigma of the singular figures of his history for the banalities of a "cinema as reflection of society" and other serious questions without answers. The form is desire, the essence but the background when we are no longer here.

These were my thoughts a few days ago while watching a music video on television that languorously interlaced famous singers with famished African children. The rich singers ("We are the world, we are the children!") were mixing their image with the image of the starving. In fact they were taking their place, replacing them, erasing them. Dissolving and mixing stars and skeletons in a kind of figurative flashing where two images try to become one, the video elegantly carried out this electronic communication between North and South. Here we have, I thought, the present face of abjection and the improved version of my tracking shot in *Kapo*. These are the images I would like at least *one* teenager to be disgusted by or at least *ashamed* of. Not merely ashamed to be nourished and rich, but ashamed to be seen as someone who *has to be aesthetically seduced* where it is only a matter of conscience—good or bad—of being a human and nothing more.

I realized that my entire history is there. In 1961 a camera movement aestheticized a dead body and thirty years later a dissolve makes the dying and the famous dance together. Nothing has changed, neither I—forever incapable of seeing in this a carnivalesque dance of death, medieval and ultra-modern—nor the predominant conceptions of consensual beauty. The form has changed a bit, though. In *Kapo*, it was still possible to be upset with Pontecorvo for inconsiderately abolishing a distance he should have "kept." The tracking shot was immoral for the simple reason that it was putting us—he as a filmmaker and I as a spectator—in a place where we did not belong. Where I anyway could not and did not want to be, because he "deported" me from my real situation as a spectator-witness, forcing me to be part of the picture. What was the meaning of Godard's formula if not that *one should never put oneself where one isn't nor should one speak for others*?

Imagining Pontecorvo's gestures deciding upon and mimicking the tracking shot with his hands, I am even more upset with him because in 1961 a tracking shot still meant rails, a crew, and physical effort. Yet I have more trouble imagining the movements of the person responsible for the electronic dissolve of "We are the World." I imagine him pushing buttons on a console, with the images at his fingertips, definitely cut off from what or whom they represent, incapable of suspecting that someone could be upset with him for being a slave to automatic gestures. That person belongs to a world—television—where, alterity having more or less disappeared, there are no longer good or bad ways to manipulate images. These are no longer "images of the other" but images among others on the market of brand images. And this world, which no longer revolts me, which provokes only lassitude and uneasiness, is precisely the world "without cinema." That is to say, without this feeling of belonging to humanity via *a supplementary country called cinema*. And then I clearly see why I have adopted cinema: so it could adopt me in return and could teach me to ceaselessly touch—with the gaze—that distance between myself and the place where the other begins.

Of course this story begins and ends with the camps because they are the limit that was awaiting me at the beginning of my life and at the end of my childhood. Childhood: it will have taken me a lifetime to win it back.This is why (message to Jean-Louis Schefer) I will probably end up seeing *Bambi*.

CHAPTER 15
DANIEL FRAMPTON

Daniel Frampton is a British philosopher of film, founding editor of the journal, Film-Philosophy. *His signature contribution to the philosophy of film, however, is his book,* Filmosophy, *in which he synthesizes the phenomenology of film (as practiced by Maurice Merleau-Ponty and Vivian Sobchack) with the post-structuralist approach of Gilles Deleuze. In addition to offering a sustained articulation of Frampton's own views,* Filmosophy *is also a valuable resource for those interested in the history and development of the Continental philosophy of film; the first half of the book moves through that history at length (although from Frampton's own perspective). Included here is the introduction to* Filmosophy, *which was originally published in English (Wallflower Press) in 2006.*

Frampton begins his book with the notion of the film world, a notion he sees permeating the history of the philosophy of film and film studies in general. The film world, he notes, is not reality—but it is related to reality (a "cousin" of reality, he calls it), and a large part of the relation has to do with the fact that we, as filmgoers, live in the film world (when we are viewing a film) as if it were a second world. Our capacity for inhabiting fictional worlds (whether they are of the cinematic or literary or other sorts) indicates, to Frampton, that aesthetic thinking is a basic element of human being: we are, whatever else we are, the sort of thing that creates, views, and inhabits the worlds created by works of art.

The parallel that the film world creates alongside the lived reality of human experience, however, poses a challenge to reality—or, at least, to our views of reality. This is something more than the notion of the film world we see in earlier thinkers, like Stanley Cavell and V. F. Perkins, for both of whom, Frampton argues, the film world is a "new" world only to the extent that it is a recording of reality. While he asserts that this has always been true of film, it has not always been so clearly true of film as it is today, with the introduction of new technologies that enable the digital manipulation of the film image. In addition to the grandiose settings and fully CGI characters we are familiar with in large-scale, big-budget motion pictures today, film images are regularly manipulated on a much smaller scale in a variety of ways (the first example in the selection included in this volume is from the film Contact, *in which the movement of one of Jodie Foster's eyebrows is altered in post-production to change her facial expression—and thus the emotional character of the scene). The effect of such technologies on works of the cinematic art makes evident that an entirely new conception of film is needed.*

This new conception—which Frampton, in his Filmosophy, *seeks to provide—begins with the recognition that film is neither a mere recording of the real nor something totally unreal, but instead that film* uses *the real. A film constitutes a world, but one that interacts with, employs, and manipulates the real world to its own ends. Both the realist (Bazin, Cavell) and anti-realist (Eisenstein) theories of film subordinate the film world to the real world such that films become entirely dependent upon and subservient to reality. What Frampton proposes is nothing less than the elevation of the film itself over, or at least up to the same level, as reality: the film world is related to but distinct from the real world, and thus merits consideration on its own ground, rather than the constant comparison to reality Frampton thinks we find in traditional film theory.*

As a means of creating an entirely new world—sometimes quite dramatically and completely so, as in Avatar*; sometimes, much more subtly so, as in* Casablanca*—film is comparable, Frampton argues, to a mind. The analogy between films and minds is not new to Frampton (it is at least as old as Münsterberg's* The Photoplay*), but it is seldom taken up as earnestly as Frampton does so, insisting that we re-conceive film as "its own imagination," both the thought of the world as well as the thinker who thinks that thought. A film is thus both a kind of thinker (a mind) and a kind of thought. It is in this insight that Frampton's unique take on film comes into its own.*

Filmosophy—the neologism Frampton coins to name his conception of film—is both a theory of film-being (what the film is) and film form (how the film is what it is). Conceiving film as a thinker or a mind, Frampton dubs the film-being "filmind," and the primary activity of filmind—film form, or the manner in which filmind is itself—he calls "film-thinking." He insists that filmosophy is not "an empirical description of film," but is instead one useful theoretical lens through which to view a film, one that avoids the pitfalls of some more traditional perspectives in film studies. Conceiving of film as its own mind, as the mind that thinks itself—however counterintuitive—prevents us from having to address thorny questions of authorial intention in film, and even evades the question of authorship altogether (which, given the essentially collaborative nature of the film art, is a particularly difficult question to resolve). Filmind, then, is the party responsible for everything that occurs within or even constitutes the film, and is identical with the film itself. Everything from the aspect ratio to the run time to the dialogue to the appearance of any given actor to random events transpiring in the background is understood by filmosophy to be the intentional thought of the filmind, and thus as relevant to any understanding or interpretation of the film.

Film-thinking, then, is the activity associated with filmind which produces the thoughts (perceived by the spectator as shots in the film) that constitute the film. On the one hand, film-thinking is the fact of film world creation, the film's responsibility for creating the film world. On the other hand, the film is also responsible for the refiguring of the film world it has created—whether that take the form of editing, changing camera angles, distance, and camera movement, or some of the more technologically sophisticated interventions such as digital manipulation and CGI animation. By way of his accounts of film-thinking, both in this selection and in his book as a whole, Frampton reiterates the extent to which filmind is responsible for everything the filmgoer experiences in and by way of the film.

If the images on the screen are effectively the thoughts of the filmind which is responsible for the creation of the film, then the ways in which those thoughts are projected—the manner in which a given shot is shot, or in which a scene is filmed, or a film written, and so on—come to be of central importance to any interpretation of the film. Frampton calls this style, and he says that style should be understood as "the dramatic intention" of the film. By this, he means to say that every film image is intentional in the phenomenological sense: each image is more than a mere presentation, but is saying something about whatever is presented. Every image constituting the film is thus not merely an object to be interpreted, but is always already itself an interpretation. With this in mind, Frampton calls for nothing less than the reinvention of the language of film description—something he attempts, for his part, with such neologisms as "filmind," "filmosophy," and "film-thinking"—so as to elevate the image from its secondary status in film studies. What is unique, and uniquely valuable, about film is its capacity for the presentation of moving images, not its ability to engage in narrative storytelling. While many (perhaps most) philosophers of film treat the narrative and dialogue as the primary elements of the film which both require interpretation and suggest a philosophical aspect of film, Frampton insists that it is not in the ways in which film is superficially like philosophy that we can find its philosophical possibilities. Instead, it is in film's ability to project thoughts as images, without the intermediary (and possibly constraining) influence of language, that we begin to see a philosophical possibility in film. With this possibility in mind, we not only find philosophy in film; we find that film is itself a possible medium for engaging in the work of philosophy.

Filmography

- ***Rear Window*** (USA, 1954). *Directed and Produced by* Alfred Hitchcock. *Written by* John Michael Hayes. *Starring* James Stewart *and* Grace Kelly.
- ***L'Odeur de la papaye verte*** [*The Scent of Green Papaya*] (France, 1993). *Directed and Written by* Tran Anh Hung. *Produced by* Christophe Rossignon. *Starring* Tran Nu Yên-Khê.
- ***To Vlemma tou Odyssea*** [*Ulysses' Gaze*] (Greece, 1995). *Directed by* Theo Angelopolous. *Produced by* Phoebe Economopolous, Eric Heumann, *and* Giorgio Silvagni. *Written by* Theo Angelopolous, Tonino Guerra, Petros Markaris, Giorgio Silvagni, *and* Kain Tsitseli. *Starring* Harvey Keitel.
- ***The Usual Suspects*** (USA, 1995). *Directed by* Bryan Singer. *Produced by* Kenneth Kokin, Michael McDonnell, *and* Bryan Singer. *Written by* Christopher McQuarrie. *Starring* Stephen Baldwin, Kevin Pollack, Gabriel Byrne, Benicio del Toro, *and* Kevin Spacey.
- ***Contact*** (USA, 1997). *Directed by* Robert Zemeckis. *Produced by* Robert Zemeckis *and* Steve Starkey. *Written by* James V. Hart *and* Michael Goldenberg. *Starring* Jodie Foster *and* Matthew McConaughey.
- ***Fight Club*** (USA, 1999). *Directed by* David Fincher. *Produced by* Art Linson, Ceán Chaffin, *and* Ross Grayson Bell. *Written by* Jim Uhls. *Starring* Brad Pitt *and* Edward Norton.
- ***Star Wars: Episode 1—The Phantom Menace*** (USA, 1999). *Directed and Written by* George Lucas. *Produced by* Rick McCallum. *Starring* Liam Neeson, Ewan McGregor, Natalie Portman, *and* Jake Lloyd.

FILMOSOPHY

In the summer of 1896 Maxim Gorky attended a screening of the Lumière Cinematograph in Nizhi-Novgorod, Russia, and famously recorded his experience of this early silent black and white projection for a local newspaper:

> Last night I was in the Kingdom of Shadows. If you only knew how strange it is to be there. It is a world without sound, without colour. Everything there—the earth, the trees, the people, the water and the air—is dipped in monotonous grey. Grey rays of the sun across the grey sky, grey eyes in grey faces, and the leaves of the trees are ashen grey. It is not life but its shadow, it is not motion but its soundless spectre.[1]

A hundred years later, on the DVD of *Contact*, Jodie Foster offers her own commentary on the making of the film, and at one point talks about a simple conversation scene between her character and her love interest, played by Matthew McConaughey. Foster points out, with not a little shock, the fact that the director, Robert Zemekis, had digitally readjusted her facial expression at one point. Zemekis had removed her eyebrow movement in a way to make her character react differently to McConaughey. Foster seemed obviously annoyed—not only that her original performance was deemed unsuitable, but that her person had almost been violated by a digital effect: "Stop fooling with my face!" she says.

Both Gorky and Foster are illustrating a simple fact about cinema: that it has never been, and is definitely becoming less and less, a simple and direct reproduction of reality. Cinema is a world of its own—whether a grey soundless shadowy world, or a fluidly manipulatable one. This film-world is a flat, ordered, compressed world; a world that is subtly, almost invisibly organized. A world that is a *cousin* of reality. And the multiplicity of moving-image media in the twenty-first century means that this film-world has become the second world we live in. A second world that feeds and shapes our perception and understanding of reality. So it seems especially important that we get to grips with the moving image, that we come up with a sufficient range of conceptual frameworks by which to understand it. Because before we can confidently argue a sociology of the cinema we must have an adequate range of moving image philosophies. That is, before we can talk confidently about the social *effects* of film we first must study the personal *affects* of film—how film affects us directly, emotionally. And both philosophers and film theorists have been doing this since cinema was invented. They have realized that how we engage with film informs and reflects how we engage with reality—and that the nature of aesthetic experience, as a form of knowledge, is as valid as rational thought. For Immanuel Kant aesthetic judgment is not a conceptual, intellectual judgment: we are necessarily aesthetic beings with a natural aesthetic emotion and a practical appetite, a rational need, for emotions such as wonder and pleasure. The brain is mobilized by the eye; beauty

[1] Maxim Gorky (1996) "Nizhegorodski Listok," in *In the Kingdom of Shadows: A Companion to Early Cinema*, ed. C. Harding and S. Popple (London: Cygnus Arts Press, 1996), p. 5.

lies in the eye of the beholder; therefore if beauty is removed, we are removed—that is how important aesthetics is to philosophy. We are not aesthetic beings only during some sort of "contemplation" in front of art works; we are thinking aesthetically all the time—framing our friends, meditating on vistas, even while watching television. And the validity of this aesthetic thinking is being proved ever more important in this visually saturated age.

But forget culture and theories and philosophies for just for a moment, and think of film, just film—think simply of the personal experience of film: what does it present that we find interesting and thoughtful? What kind of world does it show? Why is it both strange and familiar? What does its separateness and its closeness reveal? We all enjoy film fictions—these unmessy, streamlined stories—partly because we live a bad wondering script that seems to take a lifetime to get going (perhaps we all secretly want to live a film-life). And I am quite happy to admit that going to the cinema can be a classic wish for escape—a daydream drug. The expectation as you arrive and take your seat is part of the pleasure: it is an expectation of enjoyment, of gaining knowledge, of aesthetic rejuvenation, of spectacle and forgetting. And the cinema's darkness seems very necessary for the full encounter between film and filmgoer: we lose our bodies and our minds take over, working alone, locked to the film-world.

And when I leave the cinema I personally often feel drained and confused, almost disconnected, if only for a few moments. Reality now appears random, structureless, chaotic. This blinking return from another world is an experience in itself—bearings are found and sustenance is sought (usually at the nearest pub). It takes time for the film to leave my head; and it takes time for reality to become real again—time for my mind and body to re-adjust. But some films have a longer, lingering effect: not always an altering, transfiguration of reality, but a gentle continuing inhabitation of our perceptions. Life outside the cinema is released, illuminated, freed-up. Time is elongated and movements magnified—my perceptions become images: my eyes become cameras, unafraid to lock onto faces or scenes or moments. Film reveals reality, exactly by showing a distorted mirror of it. Film transforms the recognizable (in a small or large way), and this immediate transfiguration provokes the idea that our thinking can transform our world. The feeling when you step out of the cinema can result in a new realization, a change, "a little knowledge." Why do we feel this way? What does film do to create this feeling? It appears that film, in some of its forms, can rejig our encounter with life, and perhaps even heighten our perceptual powers. Cinema allows us to re-see reality, expanding our perceptions, and showing us a new reality. Film challenges our view of reality, forcing a phenomenological realization about how reality is perceived by our minds.

It is the unique way that film takes and refigures reality that seems to be behind this effect on the filmgoer. But do we always need to start with questions about cinema's "relationship to reality" in order to understand film? Writers always pose the relationship, but then find they need to stretch it out of all recognition. For example, for the mysterious early French theorist Yhcam, writing in 1912, film presents "an improbably realism."[2] Writing six years later, Emile Vuillermoz, a French music critic by profession, noted that cinema seems to produce a "superreality" which may be "more intense than the truth."[3] Just because cinema usually shows

[2] Yhcam, "Cinematography," in *French Film Theory and Criticism: A History/Anthology, 1907–1939, Volume I: 1907–1929*, ed. Richard Abel (Princeton, NJ: Princeton University Press, 1988 [1912]), p. 69 . Yhcam was pseudonym, and the writer's real identity is still not established.

[3] Emile Vuillermoz, "Before the Screen: Hermes and Silence," in Abel (ed.), *French Film Theory and Criticism, Volume 1* (1988 [1918]), p. 158.

us a recognizable world does not mean we have to work out "why it isn't a copy of reality," but how it is a new reality, *a new world*. The epistemological difference is the key here—and, for a filmmaker like Vsevolod Pudovkin, the key to understanding film as art: "Between the natural event and its appearance on the screen there is a marked difference. It is exactly this difference that makes the film an art."[4] In one sense the world "taken" by film is immediately transfigured, but it might also be argued that it is only a certain cinematic slice of the world that appears, that when the camera is turned-over a certain kind of reality pushes its way to the front, like a star-struck wannabe. This *cinematic reality* was noted by the German theorist Walter Benjamin, who saw that "a different nature opens itself to the camera than opens to the naked eye."[5]

In his 1971 book *The World Viewed* the American philosopher Stanley Cavell reminds us that part of the reason we enjoy cinema so much is simply because we have a natural wish to see the world recreated and retold in its own image. For Cavell, cinema is about artists reorganizing pictures of reality as best they can: film is a succession of "automatic world projections" given significance by "artistic discoveries of form and genre and type and technique"; the film-artist simply masters and deploys these "automatisms" as creatively as they can.[6] The poetry of film, for Cavell, is "what it is that happens to figures and objects and places as they are variously moulded and displaced by a motion-picture camera and then projected and screened."[7] This remoulded world exists beyond us (and perhaps reflects our estrangement from our own world): "The 'sense of reality' provided on film is the sense of *that* reality, one from which we already sense a distance."[8] Cavell's film-world is a distant copy of reality, a reality that is reorganized by the artist. He continues by asking whether film is a recording of a past performance, or a performance of an always present recording. Are we seeing things that are not "present"? How can this be if we accept that the film itself is present? Cavell's first conclusion is that the reality in film "is present to me while I am not present to it; and a world I know, and see, but to which I am nevertheless not present… is a world past."[9] It is only a hundred or so pages later that he reconsiders this position: "the world created is neither a world just past nor a world of make-believe. It is a world of an immediate future."[10] It is in this sense that Cavell seems to find a world existing in passing, a world neither now nor then, but new.

An author with a similar outlook to Cavell is the English film theorist V. F. Perkins. For Perkins, film subtly alters the reality it records, changing time and space relations, yet the end product is a "solid world which exists in its own right."[11] But Perkins argues that many early theorists were unable to assign recorded action any artistic worth, and that film can only shape what it first must record. The obvious point to make here is that nowadays it is

---

[4] Vsevolod I. Pudovkin, *Film Technique and Film Acting* (New York: Grove, 1960), p. 86.

[5] Walter Benjamin, "The Work of Art in the Age of Mechanical Reproduction," trans. Harry Zohn, in *Illuminations* (London: Pimlico, 1999), p. 230 . [See Chapter 18 of the present volume.—*JW*]

[6] Stanley Cavell, *The World Viewed: Reflections on the Ontology of Film*, enlarged edition (Cambridge, MA: Harvard University Press, 1979), p. 105.

[7] Stanley Cavell, (1983) "The Thought of Movies," in *Philosophy and Film*, ed. Cynthia A. Freeland and Thomas E. Wartenberg (New York: Routledge, 1995), p. 21.

[8] Cavell, *The World Viewed*, p. 226.

[9] Ibid., p. 23.

[10] Ibid., p. 129. For a writer such as Susanne K. Langer film is "an eternal and ubiquitous present," creating an ever-changing "future" or "destiny" within "an endless Now"; *Feeling and Form: A Theory of Art Developed from Philosophy in a New Key* (London: Routledge, 1953), p. 415.

[11] V. F. Perkins, *Film as Film* (Harmondsworth, Middlesex: Penguin, 1972), p. 69.

hard to find a film that *does not* include some images of places or people that were never in front of the camera (digital stand-ins, imaginary backdrops, computer-designed buildings). Film is no longer a question of automatic photography—even without considering the classic artistry of the simple choice of angle, exposure, and so forth—and to *generalize* that the film-world is a simple copy of reality seems limiting. Modern computer-generated imagery not only makes Perkins' statement from 1972 that everything that happens on the screen in a live-action picture "has happened in front of the camera" historical, but also demands of us a great re-thinking of the cinematic image.[12] It is exactly this possible fluidity of the film image—this new digitally manipulatable film image—that might make us realize that we need (and in fact have always needed) a new conception of film.

Yes film *uses* the real; but it takes it and immediately moulds it and then refigures it and puts it back in front of the filmgoer as interpretation, as re-perception. Film recording technology automatically changes reality, and the filmmaker artistically refigures reality. For a start, film flattens reality, a notion Cavell characterizes as "the ontological equality of objects and human subjects in photographs."[13] Characters and buildings and vistas and objects are no longer real, no longer part of nature, but part of cinema. Locking all film to reality disenfranchises the possibilities of film poetry by *conceptually* limiting the routes of film style and world. To get the most out of film, we might acknowledge that film is not *of* the world, film *is* a world (a new world). Film is not simply a reproduction of reality, it is its own world with its own intentions and creativities. Cinema is the projection, screening, showing, of *thoughts of the real.*

The argument of this book is premised upon the idea that film presents a unique world, almost a future-world (not least because the film's "experience" of its people and objects feels "new"). Film is its own world with its own rules (and philosophy should certainly learn from its fluid re-situating of experience and knowledge). This creation of a new (immaterial, possible) world is even acknowledge by some fictions: *The Usual Suspects*, the film itself, seems to immediately "think" the precise worlds recounted by the character Verbal.[14] Part of the project of this book is to question the *conceptual* link between cinema and reality (while simultaneously pushing the transfiguring effect cinema can have on our understanding and perception of reality). There is no doubt that most cinema starts with a recording of reality, but the argument here is that the filmgoer would be impoverished by understanding cinema only in relation to the reality it records. It will surely become more and more tiring to continually compare and contrast the increasingly fluid world of cinema to our own reality.

Film might now be understood as creating its *own* world, *free* to bring us any scene or object it wishes. Film becomes less a reproduction of reality than a *new* reality, that merely sometimes looks like our reality (can be different like film noir, or different like the other world of *Star Wars: Episode 1—The Phantom Menace*). Film is not transparent, but dependent on the film's *beliefs* as regards the things it portrays. The continual comparison to "the real" has handicapped film studies, has disallowed a radical reconceptualization of film-being. Contemporary cinema has given us an endlessly animatable film-world that can be whatever it likes, go anywhere, think anything—"gigantic visions of mankind crushed by the juggernaut of war and then

---

[12] Ibid., p. 67.

[13] Cavell, *The World Viewed*, p. 72.

[14] The film philosopher Homer Simpson incisively commented on this as he began to tell a story in *The Simpsons*: "Listen closely, as my words will conjure up pictures as clear as any television program."

blessed by the angel of peace may arise before our eyes with all their spiritual meaning," as Hugo Münsterberg noted in 1916.[15] This powerful film-world reveals itself in any form—and so the spiritual metaphors can go on: maybe there is a God and she is busily thinking our world. Perhaps our enjoyment of the experience of film stems from our wish to be part of a perfect world, created by an "absolute mind"? Film's different reality (film's re-thinking of reality-like objects) creates its own (more formal) question of subjectivity and objectivity. For instance, while Münsterberg argued that film is pre-eminently *a medium of subjectivity*, André Bazin understood cinema as "objectivity in time."[16] There may be no possible objective view of the real world, but the view of the film-world is the only one available, and thus "objective"—yet the images of film also often appear to be "subjective."

For Münsterberg the film-world is a complete transfiguration of the real world. Film moves away from reality, and towards the mind. It is the mind that creates this transfiguration, recreating the world in its own form. Film should therefore be seen as its own imagination (*even* when it initially looks normal and realistic). Films have a different space, a space that resembles reality, but flat and bordered. The frame of film makes for a rational space—a decided, intended space—with rational and non-rational thinkings. Film is another world, a new world, an organized world, a constructed world, a world thought-out, and as filmgoers we usually enjoy being swamped by this "artificial intelligence." Benjamin intuitively understood the difference between life and cinema: "an unconsciously penetrated space is substituted for a space consciously explored by man."[17]

Through cinema man was able to control reality. Film can thus be seen as an incredibly unique and therefore important link between man and world: film becomes the *explanation* of our position in the world—film acts out an interaction with a world, which thus becomes a mirror for us to recognize *our* interaction with our world. This acting out is a kind of intention, a kind of thought. The film-world is an ordered and thought-out world—characters meet and move on and love and die and find themselves, all in about two hours flat. The philosopher Gilles Deleuze found that cinema resembled a higher, spiritual life: "the domain of cold decision, of absolute determination (*entêtement*), of a choice of existence."[18] The creation of this film-world is set and immovable and thus untouchable, unchangeable—it is unwavering intention, decision, choice, belief: a filmic kind of thought.

Filmosophy is a study of film as thinking, and contains a theory of both film-being and film form. The "filmind" is filmosophy's concept of film-being, the theoretical originator of the images and sounds we experience, and "film-thinking" is its theory of film form, whereby an action of form is seen as the dramatic thinking of the filmind. In a sense filmosophy can

---

[15] Hugo Münsterberg, *The Photoplay: A Psychological Study* (New York: D. Appleton, 1916), p. 102. Münsterberg was a German-American psychologist and philosopher, who died the same year that *The Photoplay* was published. [See Chapter 3 of the present volume.—*JW*]

[16] André Bazin, *What is Cinema?, Volume 1*, selected and trans. Hugh Gray, preface by Jean Renoir (Berkeley: University of California Press, 1971), p. 14.

[17] Benjamin, "The Work of Art in the Age of Mechanical Reproduction," p. 230. [See Chapter 18 of the present volume.—*JW*]

[18] Gilles Deleuze, "The Brain is the Screen: Interview with Gilles Deleuze on *The Time-Image*," trans. Melissa McMahon (1998 [1989]), in Réda Bensmaïa and Jalal Toufic, eds., *Gilles Deleuze: A Reason to Believe in this World* (1998), special issue of *Discourse: Jurnal for Theoretical Studies in Media and Culture* 20, no. 3, p. 48.

therefore be understood as an extension and integration of theories of both para-narrational "showing" and mise-en-scène aesthetics. *Filmosophy proposes that seeing film form as thoughtful, as the dramatic decision of the film, helps us understand the many ways film can mean and affect.* There are two aspects to contemporary film that provoked the idea of filmosophy: that both the unreliable narrator and non-subjective "point of view" shot are becoming more and more common, and that it has become digitally malleable and free to show virtually anything. To *creatively* and *positively* handle these new forms film studies needs a conception of film-world creation, and a descriptive language of film style, that are both adaptable and poetic.

The filmind is not an empirical description of film, but rather a *conceptual* understanding of the origins of film's actions and events. That is, the filmgoer can decide to use it as part of their conceptual apparatus while experiencing a film—they would then see the film *through* this concept. Filmosophy conceptualizes film as an organic intelligence: a "film being" thinking about the characters and subjects in the film. Yet the concepts of the filmind and film-thinking are not intended as replacements for the concepts of "narrator" and "narration," but are simply proposals that reflect the limits of the idea of "the narrator" and the restrictive and literary nature of theories of "narration" (the former is incapable of accounting for the creation of film-worlds, and the latter is limited in that it traditionally only handles that which cannot be attributed to character-narrators). The filmind is not an "external" force, nor is it a mystical being or invisible other, it is "in" the film itself, it is *the film* that is steering its own (dis)course. The filmind is "the film itself."

There are two aspects to the filmind: the creation of the basic film-world of recognizable people and objects, and the designing and refiguring this film-world. This re-creational designing and refiguring is here called "film-thinking." One particular sentence in Deleuze's *Cinema* is helpful in understanding film-thinking: "It is the camera, and not a dialogue, which *explains* why the hero of *Rear Window* has a broken leg (photos of the racing car, in his room, broken camera)."[19] The film surveys the tenement courtyard before returning to Jeffries, asleep in his chair, his leg in a cast, at which point it then moves through his apartment to show the photo of the crashing racing car and a smashed camera. Film-thinking is thus the action of film form in dramatizing the intention of the filmind. Importantly, filmosophy does not make a direct analogy between human thought and film, because film is simply different to our ways of thinking and perceiving: as we have noted, film seems at once subjective and objective in its actions of form. Rather there is a functional analogy: film's constant, never-ending "intent" and attitude to its characters and spaces is here conceptualized as a (new kind of) "thinking." Phenomenological metaphors of human perception would limit the meaning possibilities of film (the camera would then be "another character," and any non-human-like actions of the camera would be signs of excessiveness or reflexivity). Film-thinking resembles no one single kind of human thought, but perhaps the functional spine of human thinking—film-thinking seems to be a combination of idea, feeling and emotion.

Filmosophy is designed as an organic philosophy of film. The filmind allows the filmgoer to experience the film as a drama issuing from itself, rather than taking them further outside the experience to the actions of authors, directors or invisible narrators. The concept of the filmind also means that the whole film is intended, making all formal moves important or possibly

[19] Gilles Deleuze, *Cinema 1: The Movement-Image*, trans. Hugh Tomlinson and Barbara Habberjam (Minneapolis: University of Minnesota Press, 1985 [1983]), p. 201.

meaningful, enlarging the experience of film, and helping the filmgoer *relate* to the formal twists and turns of film. And the concept of film-thinking is organic in two further senses: that it binds form to content, and that it also evolves smoothly into a language of describing film that positively affects the experience of the filmgoer. An organic relation of concept to film to language to experience (to philosophy). The concept of film-thinking bonds form to content by making style part of the action: the experience of film becomes in some sense "organic" because style is tied to the story with natural, thoughtful, humanistic terms of intention that make film forms dramatic rather than technical. In filmosophy form is not an appendix to content, but simply more content itself (just of a different nature).

How a person is "shot" can now be seen not just as "relating" to that person in an indirect, metaphorical way, but a *becoming* of that person's character, or perhaps a thinking of the film's idea of that person. When a film frames a person that act of framing creates a way of seeing that person (as central or peripheral or close-up). The filmgoer sees that person via the film's thinking of that person—this thinking is simply the action of form as dramatic intention. This effect is enhanced by the filmgoer's understanding of film's actions as emotional thinkings—through this engagement they merge with the film a little more fully, because their natural aesthetic thinking links more directly with the film. The filmgoer experiences film more intuitively, not via technology or external authorship, but directly, as a thinking thing. In making "style" integral to the film's thinking (and not an addendum to its "main content work"), filmosophy hopes to widen and deepen the experience of the filmgoer. Film form is always there, and thus necessarily part of the actions and events, and filmosophy simply, holistically, bonds film's actions to dramatically thoughtful motives and intentions. Film style is now seen to be the dramatic intention of the film itself.

The most obvious result of reconceptualizing film as thinking is a change in how we talk about film. First of all it does a necessary job of highlighting the worth and important of image and sound, something simply missing, in direct terms, from a lot of film writing. The concepts of filmosophy advance on this "match" between film and filmgoer by providing a more "suitable" rhetoric derived from the concept of film-thinking. One of the heartfelt aims of the book is to popularize the possibilities of film (of all moving sound-images) by reinventing the language of its description. Too little is written about the power and impact of images—the writing on film that reaches the public is almost exclusively led by plot and acting and cultural references. My argument is that reconceptualising film as thinking will hopefully allow a more poetic entry to the intelligence of film. Filmosophy does not just offer a *linking* of thinking to film (not just an interest in making the comparison), but an analysis of film as its own kind of thought. It is not merely a question of resolving the puzzle of what makes film be, because it is just as important how we construct its theory, its *language of image description*, and its role for interpretation.

Perhaps the study of film and philosophy should die in order to be reborn. It is the linking "and" that not just separates the two disciplines but disfigures the balance. Like literary theorists in the 1970s, philosophers are turning from Socrates to fiddling about with a video player (and probably not getting a picture). And all that many of them really want to do is simply brighten up a lecture by showing a few scenes from a classic movie or two. These philosophers are simply concerned with how some films *contain* stories and characterizations that helpfully *illustrate* well-known philosophical ideas. But cinema is more than a handy catalogue of philosophical problems, and to say that film can only present ideas in terms of story and dialogue is a narrow, literary view of film's possible force and impact. If the starting point for these philosophers is "what can film do *for philosophy*?," how long will it take for them to realize what film *offers* philosophy?

So much writing within the area of "film and philosophy" simply ignores cinematics and concentrates on stories and character motivations. It only takes one character to say "man is not an island" for somebody to jump up and declare the film philosophical (if someone were to recount a moral fable while doing a jig, then that could be claimed to be "dance as philosophy"). These are writings that rely much too heavily on the set subjects of academic philosophy, adding the two disciplines together like oil and water: film "plus" philosophy. Much of this writing takes the form of philosophy offering its services to film, that is, taking a paternal, patronizing, condescending stance: the film does not realize what philosophical problem lies within it, philosophy shall show the real, hidden worth of film (to help philosophy). Like academic SAS squads they come in to sort out the mess left by film studies. This is an infecting of film by philosophy. These writers are very simply and effectively *using* film to teach philosophy courses—using film to illustrate philosophy's classic problems and questions. Their attention is only on the story of the film (dialogue and plot outlines and character motivations), and the film is then quickly left behind while they elaborate on the problem. These classical problems of dried-up philosophy departments are *forced* onto film stories—they may as well simply make up a story of a friend of a friend instead of making some readers believe they are *actually telling us something about film*. In a sense they encourage yet another wave of film students to ignore the moving sound-image and concentrate on characters and story.

But the survival of a new-born interdisciplinary subject depends on how well it does actually create a *new* type of study (one that can then continue the revolution by being nomadic in *its* future travels). There is no doubt that film offers dramas that can play as putty in the hands of philosophers. Some film stories do play-out well-known philosophical ideas, and it is most probably philosophers that are best suited to understanding them, but films are more than this, and carry more than dialogue and plot. Some of these writers also still use staid, literary terms, borrowed from those 1970s literature departments, and these exterior (non-site-specific) concepts steer analyses away from the forms of film—whereas studying film for its own (site-specific, cinematic) philosophical worth should open interesting future questions. Philosophy needs to work *for* film studies to re-balance the weight of writings that search films for philosophical illustrations. Working *through* film philosophically, rather than applying philosophy to film, reveals film to be much more "philosophical" than the latter method could ever produce. As Deleuze writes: "I was able to write on cinema, not by right of reflection, but when philosophical problems led me to seek answers in cinema, which itself then relaunched other problems."[20]

So part of the argument of this book is that the questions film philosophy has posed—about how film transfigures its subjects, how it communicates ideas, how it resembles memory and dream and poetry, how it beautifully and gracefully mingles with our minds—can find direction and illumination in the work of filmosophy, and its two main concepts: the filmind and film-thinking. With this incursion of film-thinking into the subject of film philosophy we have new forms of philosophical film to discuss. Where before some were content to write about films that "contained" philosophical musings or problems, now certain films can be

[20] Deleuze, "The Brain is the Screen," p. 49.

understood as "thinking philosophically." Then we can ask: how *Ulysses' Gaze* thinks about landscape and humanity; how *Fight Club* thinks about the self and psychosis; how *The Scent of Green Papaya* thinks about love.

Focusing, editing, camera movement, sound, framing—all "think" a certain relation to the story being told. Of course there are no shapes and colours to *specific* ideas, or else film would be reduced to language. Philosophy produces ideas in the precise sense, and film is a poetical thinking that achieves a different kind of philosophicalness; a languageless thinking that Wittgenstein saw as impossible in everyday talk. And it is we who complete the thoughts of film, who decide, if we so wish, on the ideas to be gained from a film. Filmosophy ultimately aims to release the image from its secondary position in human interaction—by realizing the thoughtful capacity of film. In moving towards an understanding of just what can be thoughtfully achieved cinematically, filmosophy attempts to find the *philosophical* in the movements and forms of film. If this is a new kind of thinking, what does it mean for our thinking, and what can film philosophically imagine? What are the philosophical implications of understanding film in this way? How has philosophy attempted to think with images? How might we practically apply film-thinking to current philosophical problems and discussions? How might we utilize this nonconceptual thinking for philosophy? Philosophy should thus make of film a companion in concept-creation. Film possibly contains a whole new system of thought, a new episteme—perhaps the new concepts of philosophy might even find their paradigms in cinema. Philosophy is not just a subject, but a practice, a creative practice, and film provides a philosopher such as Deleuze with as much conceptual creation as science and philosophy itself: "Cinema is one type of image. Between different types of aesthetic image, scientific functions and philosophical concepts, there are currents of mutual exchange, with no overall primacy of any one field."[21] We need to recognize that film can add a new kind of thought to philosophy, which can be helped by the full understanding of imagistic thinking. In turn, philosophy then becomes *another kind of film*.

Filmosophy does not aim to be a solution to film studies, but should be used and changed and adapted alongside other perspectives and interpretive schemas—a purely filmosophical reading of a film is only a partial reading, one to be added to other insights and approaches. This book is consciously designed as a provocation, a manifesto almost: hopefully it should create questions, but also possibilities of application. In this sense it aims to open a new conversation (about film as thinking), one to be argued with, and discussed, and extended where necessary. "Filmosophy" is not a difficult word to arrive at, and echoes the neologisms of the 1920s—as Ricciotto Canudo wrote in 1923: "Cinegraphy, cineology, cinemania, cinephilia and cinephobia, cinepoetry and cinoedia, cinematurgy, cinechromism—the list goes on. Only time and chance will tell what terminology will stay with us."[22]

[21] Gilles Deleuze, "Doubts About the Imaginary," trans. Martin Joughin, in *Negotiations: 1972–1990* (New York: Columbia University Press, 1995 [1986]), p. 64.

[22] Ricciotto Canudo, "The Birth of a Sixth Art," trans. Ben Gibson, Don Ranvaud, Sergio Sokota and Deborah Young, in Abel (ed.), *French Film Theory and Criticism, Volume 1* (1988 [1911]) p. 296–297. [See Chapter 1 of the present volume.—*JW*]

SECTION THREE
MARXISM AND CRITICAL THEORY

CHAPTER 16
SIEGFRIED KRACAUER

Siegfried Kracauer (1889–1966) was a German sociologist, cultural critic, writer, and film theorist who lived and worked in Germany (until 1933), France, and the United States. He was friends with Theodor Adorno early in his career, deeply influenced by his reading of Karl Marx somewhat later, and is frequently associated with the Frankfurt School of Critical Theory. In film studies, he is perhaps most well known for his book, published in English in 1947, From Caligari to Hitler: A Psychological History of German Film. *The reading included here is an essay, "Cult of Distraction: On Berlin's Picture Palaces," originally published in German ("Kult der Zerstreuung") in the* Frankfurter Zeitung *in 1926; it was also included in his collection,* Der Ornament der Masse *(*The Mass Ornament*), published by Suhrkamp in 1963.*

Kracauer begins by noting that the "picture palaces" in Berlin are not movie theaters: in some ways much more than that, the mass theaters being built in Berlin in the 1920s are, rather, "palaces of distraction." Everything about them is characterized by a superficial sort of splendor, from the entertainments they provide to the architectural ornamentation of the buildings themselves. Such superficiality suits them, however; as Kracauer notes, they are in fact tasteful edifices. The entertainment program is not simply cinematic in nature, however, which is perhaps the most substantial difference between the picture palaces and movie theaters: movie theaters show films exclusively, and as such attract audiences of cinephiles. The picture palaces, however, follow what Kracauer identifies as "the American style," situating the film within a larger, self-contained show—a "total artwork of effects," as it were, including both the film as well as live performances of pantomime, ballet, and the like. Thus, between the architecture, the live performance, and the film, Berlin's picture palaces raise distraction to the level of culture—for the masses. They are Berlin's response to the demand for mass culture.

As populations have risen, Kracauer notes, different places within Germany have responded differently to the concomitant rise in a desire for mass culture: for entertainments that require relatively little of the spectator, and promise much by way of amusement, distraction from the difficulties of everyday (often industrial) life. In the provincial industrial centers (outside of the city), the masses are too overwhelmed to create their own way of life: most industrial workers find their workdays too exhausting then to engage in further labor during their limited leisure time. In these communities, then, all culture is a sort of "hand-me-down" culture from the upper classes: their outdated rubbish, Kracauer says, becomes the culture and entertainment to which the working class has access. Contrariwise, in those larger provincial towns in which industry does not dominate, traditional cultural forces are too strong for the working masses to have a say in cultural production. The cultural interests of the working class are denigrated and denied by the bourgeois middle class as "low-brow" and unsophisticated.

Berlin, however, was a city of four million people in 1926. This created the possibility of a homogeneous, cosmopolitan audience for mass culture—to which everyone could be expected to have more or less the same reaction. Unlike the provincial population centers, then, Berlin is an ideal ground for the development of mass culture. Kracauer notes that some have said that the Berliners are "addicted to distraction," but he argues that this is a bourgeois criticism, indicative of the same negative attitude toward working-class amusements as can be found in the provincial towns. The mass theaters—picture palaces—built in Berlin are designed to keep attendees focused always on the peripheral, always looking for whatever stimulus is coming next. This state of perpetual distraction leaves no room for audiences to pause, reflect on what they have seen, and contemplate its aesthetic or social value. Such entertainment leaves audiences forever on the surfaces of things, but this superficiality is sincere, Kracauer asserts. Mass culture is not a trick perpetuated by the middle or upper classes; it is an authentic attempt to meet the sincere cultural demands of the growing, concentrated, urban working class.

In meeting this cultural demand, the picture palaces succeed where the so-called "high" arts—literature, drama, music—fail. These higher art forms only perpetuate outdated aesthetic forms meant to fulfill a different audience altogether; the great practitioners and creators of those arts have moved on, and so those works in these media produced for popular consumption are not only anachronistic, but completely derivative of the greater works of a prior era. The sincere superficiality of the picture palaces, however, has the potential to re-present the reality the mass audience experiences every day back to them, aestheticized: the fragmented, self-contradictory, distracted entertainment re-presents the genuine disorder characteristic of late modern society. Unfortunately, Kracauer notes, altogether too many of the picture palaces rely too heavily upon a sort of integration of the various elements of the shows they present, a "gluing together" of the fragments that would otherwise empower mass audiences by way of genuine mass culture. The false integration does just enough, however, in presenting a total program, to rob the distraction they provide of its potential for meaning: a reflection of the "uncontrolled anarchy" of the modern world.

CULT OF DISTRACTION: ON BERLIN'S PICTURE PALACES

Translated by Thomas Y. Levin

The large picture houses in Berlin are palaces of distraction; to call them *movie theaters [Kinos]* would be disrespectful. The latter are still abundant only in Old Berlin and in the suburbs, where they serve neighborhood audiences, and even there they are declining in number. Much more than such movie houses or even the ordinary theaters, it is the picture palaces, those optical fairylands, that are shaping the face of Berlin. The *UFA palaces* (above all, the one at the Zoo), the *Capitol* built by Poelzig, the *Marmorhaus*, and whatever their names may be, enjoy sellouts day after day. The newly built *Gloria-Palast* proves that the style these palaces have initiated is still developing in the same direction.[1]

Elegant surface splendor is the hallmark of these mass theaters. Like hotel lobbies, they are shrines to the cultivation of pleasure; their glamor aims at edification. But while the architecture does perhaps bombard the patrons in its attempt to create an atmosphere, it in no way relapses into the barbaric pomposity of Wilhelminian secular churches—like the Rhinegold, for example, which seeks to give the impression that it harbors the Wagnerian Nibelungen treasure. Instead, the architecture of the film palaces has evolved into a form that avoids stylistic excesses. Taste has presided over the dimensions and, in conjunction with a refined artisanal fantasy, has spawned the costly interior furnishings. The *Gloria-Palast* presents itself as a baroque theater. The community of worshipers, numbering in the thousands, can be content, for its gathering places are a worthy abode.

The programs, too, display a well-wrought grandiosity. Gone are the days when films were allowed to run one after another, each with a corresponding musical accompaniment. The major theaters, at least, have adopted the American style of a self-contained show, which integrates the film into a larger whole. Like the program sheets which have expanded into fan magazines, the shows have grown into a structured profusion of production numbers and presentations. A glittering, revue-like creature has crawled out of the movies: *the total artwork [Gesamtkunstwerk] of effects.*

This total artwork of effects assaults all the senses using every possible means. Spotlights shower their beams into the auditorium, sprinkling across festive drapes or rippling through

[1] Hans Poelzig (1869–1936) was one of the founders of the modern movement in German architecture. He designed the Grosses Schauspielhaus for Max Reinhardt in Berlin (1919), with its famous "stalactite dome," as well as the "Capitol" cinema in Berlin (1925), the "Deli" cinema in Breslau (1926), and the "Babylon" cinema in Berlin (1928–1929). He also made the Expressionist sets for the second version of Paul Wegener's film *Golem* (1920). For more material on the Berlin film palaces (including extensive photographic documentation), see Rolf-Peter Baacke, *Lichtspielhausarchitektur in Deutschland: Von der Schaubude bis zum Kinopalast* (Berlin: Frolich und Kaufmann, 1982); and Heinz Frick, *Mein Gloria Palast: Das Kino vom Kurfürstendamm* (Munich: Universitats Verlag, 1986). For information on respective developments in America, see Douglas Gomery, "Towards a History of Film Exhibition: The Case of the Picture Palace," *Film Studies Annual*, part 2 (Pleasantville, N.Y.: Redgrave, 1977), 17–26 .—*Trans.*

colorful, organic-looking glass fixtures. The orchestra asserts itself as an independent power, its acoustic production buttressed by the responsory of the lighting. Every emotion is accorded its own acoustic expression and its color value in the spectrum—a visual and acoustic kaleidoscope that provides the setting for the physical activity on stage: pantomime and ballet. Until finally the white surface descends and the events of the three-dimensional stage blend imperceptibly into two-dimensional illusions.

Alongside the legitimate revues, such shows are the leading attraction in Berlin today. They raise distraction to the level of culture; they are aimed at the masses.

* * *

The masses also gather in the provinces, but there they are subjected to a pressure that does not allow them the spiritual and cultural *[geistig]* fulfillment appropriate to their number and real social significance. In the industrial centers where they appear in great numbers, they are so overburdened as workers that they are unable to realize their own way of life. They are handed down the rubbish and outdated entertainment of the upper class, which, despite its repeated claims to social superiority, has only limited cultural ambitions. In contrast, in the larger provincial towns not dominated primarily by industry, the traditional forces are so powerful that the masses are unable to shape the cultural and spiritual *[geistig]* structure on their own. The bourgeois middle classes remain segregated from them, as if the growth of this human reservoir meant nothing, and thus they maintain the illusory claim that they are still the guardians of culture and education. Their arrogance, which creates sham oases for itself, weighs down upon the masses and denigrates their amusements.

It cannot be overlooked that there are *four million* people in Berlin. The sheer necessity of their circulation transforms the life of the street into the ineluctable street of life, giving rise to configurations that invade even domestic space. The more people perceive themselves as a mass, however, the sooner the masses will also develop productive powers in the spiritual and cultural domain that are worth financing. The masses are no longer left to their own devices; rather, they prevail in their very abandonment. Refusing to be thrown scraps, they demand instead to be served at laid-out tables. There is little room left for the so-called educated classes, who must either join in the repast or maintain their snobbish aloofness. Their provincial isolation is, in any case, at an end. They are being absorbed by the masses, a process that creates the *homogeneous cosmopolitan audience* in which everyone has the *same* responses, from the bank director to the sales clerk, from the diva to the stenographer. Self-pitying complaints about this turn toward mass taste are belated; the cultural heritage that the masses refuse to accept has become to some extent merely a historical property, since the economic and social reality to which it corresponded has changed.

* * *

Critics chide Berliners for being *addicted to distraction*, but this is a petit bourgeois reproach. Certainly, the addiction to distraction is greater in Berlin than in the provinces, but the tension to which the working masses are subjected is also greater and more tangible; it is an essentially formal tension, which fills their day fully without making it fulfilling. Such a lack demands to be compensated, but this need can be articulated only in terms of the same surface sphere that imposed the lack in the first place. The form of free-time busy-ness necessarily corresponds to the form of business.[2]

A correct instinct will see to it that the need for entertainment is satisfied. The interior design of movie theaters serves one sole purpose: to rivet the viewers' attention to the peripheral, so that they will not sink into the abyss. The stimulations of the sense succeed one another with such rapidity that there is no room left between them for even the slightest contemplation. Like *life buoys*, the refractions of the spotlights and the musical accompaniment keep the spectator above water. The penchant for distraction demands and finds an answer in the display of pure externality; hence the irrefutable tendency, particularly in Berlin, to turn all forms of entertainment into revues and, parallel with this tendency, the increasing number of illustrations in the daily press and in periodical publications.

This emphasis on the external has the advantage of being *sincere*. It is not externality that poses a threat to truth. Truth is threatened only by the naïve affirmation of cultural values that have become unreal and by the careless misuse of concepts such as personality, inwardness, tragedy, and so on—terms that in themselves certainly refer to lofty ideas but that have lost much of their scope along with their supporting foundations, due to social changes. Furthermore, many of these concepts have acquired a bad aftertaste today, because they unjustifiably deflect an inordinate amount of attention from the external damages of society onto the private individual. Instances of such repression are common enough in the fields of literature, drama, and music. They claim the status of high art while actually rehearsing anachronistic forms that evade the pressing needs of our time—a fact that is indirectly confirmed by the artistically derivative quality of the respective works. In a profound sense, Berlin audiences act truthfully when they increasingly shun these art events (which, for good reason, remain caught in mere pretense), preferring instead the surface glamor of the stars, films, revues, and spectacular shows. Here, in pure externality, the audience encounters itself; its own reality is revealed in the fragmented sequence of splendid sense impressions. Were this reality to remain hidden from the viewers, they could neither attack nor change it; its disclosure in distraction is therefore of *moral* significance.

But this is the case only if distraction is not an end in itself. Indeed, the very fact that the shows aiming at distraction are composed of the same mixture of externalities as the world of the urban masses; the fact that these shows lack any authentic and materially motivated coherence, except possibly the glue of sentimentality, which covers up this lack but only in order to make it all the more visible; the fact that these shows convey precisely and openly to thousands of eyes and ears the *disorder* of society—this is precisely what would enable them to evoke and maintain the tension that must precede the inevitable and radical change. In the streets of Berlin, one is often struck by the momentary insight that someday all this will suddenly burst apart. The entertainment to which the general public throngs ought to produce the same effect.

* * *

[2] Kracauer here plays with the ambiguity of *Betrieb*, which can mean both "enterprise" (business) and "activity" (hustle and bustle, busy-ness).—*Trans.*

Most of the time it does not, as is demonstrated in exemplary fashion by the programs of the large movie theaters. For even as they summon to distraction, they immediately rob distraction of its meaning by amalgamating the wide range of effects—which by their nature demand to be isolated from one another—into an "artistic" unity. These shows strive to coerce the motley sequence of externalities into an organic whole. To begin with, the architectural setting tends to emphasize a dignity that used to inhabit the institutions of high culture. It favors the lofty and the *sacred* as if designed to accommodate works of eternal significance—just one step short of burning votive candles. The show itself aspires to the same exalted level, claiming to be a finely tuned organism, an aesthetic totality as only an artwork can be. The film alone would be too paltry an offering, not primarily because one would want to increase the sheer quantity of distractions but because the show has pretensions to artistic form. The cinema has secured a standing independent of the theatrical stage, yet the leading movie theaters are once again longing to return to that stage.

This thespian objective of the movie theaters—an objective that may be considered symptomatic of Berlin social life as well—displays *reactionary* tendencies. The laws and forms of the idealist culture that haunts us today only as a specter may have lost their legitimacy in these movie theaters; nonetheless, out of the very elements of externality into which they have happily advanced, they are attempting to create a new idealist culture. Distraction—which is meaningful only as improvisation, as a reflection of the uncontrolled anarchy of our world—is festooned with drapery and forced back into a unity that no longer exists. Rather than acknowledging the actual state of disintegration that such shows ought to represent, the movie theaters glue the pieces back together after the fact and present them as organic creations.

This practice takes its revenge in purely artistic terms: the integration of film into a self-contained program deprives it of any effect it might have had. It no longer stands on its own, but appears as the crowning event of a type of revue that does not take into account its particular conditions of existence. The *two-dimensionality* of film produces the illusion of the physical world without any need for supplementation. But if scenes of real physicality are nevertheless displayed alongside the movie, the latter recedes into the flat surface and the deception is exposed. The proximity of action that has spatial depth destroys the spatiality of what is shown on the screen. By its very existence, film demands that the world it reflects be the only one; it should be wrested from every three-dimensional surrounding, or it will fail as an illusion. A painting, too, loses its power when it appears alongside living images. Nor should one fail to mention that the artistic ambitions behind the move to incorporate film into the pseudo-totality of a program are inappropriate, and hence remain unsuccessful. The result is at best *applied art [Kunstgewerbe]*.

But the movie theaters are faced with more urgent tasks than refining applied art. They will not fulfill their vocation—which is an aesthetic vocation only to the extent that it is in tune with its social vocation—until they cease to flirt with the theater and renounce their anxious efforts to restore a bygone culture. Rather, they should rid their offerings of all trappings that deprive film of its rights and must aim radically toward a kind of distraction that exposes disintegration instead of masking it. It could be done in Berlin, home of the masses—who so easily allow themselves to be stupefied only because they are so close to the truth.

CHAPTER 17
SERGEI EISENSTEIN

Sergei Eisenstein (1898–1948) was a Soviet filmmaker and film theorist. He has achieved nearly universal recognition and widespread acclaim for his pioneering use in film of montage, as well as adopting a theory of film that centralized the practice as essential to the nature of film. He was a film theorist before he was a filmmaker, and his understanding of the most basic elements constituting film owes a great deal to his reading of Hegel and Marx. The essay included here, "A Dialectic Approach to Film Form," was originally written in German in 1929, but left in untitled manuscript form. A portion of the essay was first published, in an English translation by Ivor Montagu, in Close-Up *in 1931, under the title "The Principles of Film Form." The selection included here is from the first complete version of the essay published, again in English translation, in the posthumous collection of Eisenstein's essays on film,* Film Form *(Harcourt, Brace, 1949).*

Eisenstein approaches cinema by way of art in general, and art in general by way of dialectic: as he notes right from the start of the essay, the origin of art—like philosophy—is in the representation (or projection) of the dialectical system of things. Philosophy constitutes the abstract projection; art, the concrete. On the dialectical model (which Eisenstein appropriates from Hegel, Marx, and some Marxists), things themselves must be understood as dynamic: they only are *insofar as they* are becoming *something new, by way of the overcoming of the antagonism between "thesis" and "antithesis" in "synthesis." Conflict, then, is the very basis of art (and philosophy). For Eisenstein, this can be seen both in art's social mission—where it must bring contradictions to the attention of the audience—and in the nature of art itself, where we see a contradiction between the natural existence of things and the transformation of things by way of a creative impulse. We might reconceive these elements of art's nature, as Eisenstein does, as Nature (or "organic form") and Industry (or "rational form"). In these terms, we can think of the dialectic of art as a conflict between the logic of organic form and the logic of rational form. Rhythm in art—whether in music, or poetry, or film—springs from this conflict. In the case of film in particular, this is the dialectical conflict of shot and montage.*

Although Eisenstein is rightly famous for the centrality of montage in his film theory and his films, he was not the first filmmaker to see the practice as centrally significant to filmmaking. Montage played such an important role in Soviet filmmaking in particular, on Eisenstein's view, that he thinks that addressing montage definitively would resolve all the problems of film as such. He identifies two basic principles underlying the understanding and use of montage in Soviet film, the epic principle (which he associates with the filmmaker, V. I. Pudovkin) and the dramatic principle (which he identifies with himself). According to the epic principle, montage unrolls an idea by way of individual shots: thus, there is an overall unity to the film that is both known and knowable from the outset, and which informs the significance of each shot as one step in a sequential explication or illustration of the idea. Eisenstein's dialectical and dynamic approach to film makes him extremely skeptical of such an approach. Rather, for Eisenstein's dramatic principle, montage is the production of an idea by way of the conflict or collisions of individual shots. On this approach to montage, Eisenstein further centralizes what he calls counterpoint, the conflict between one "vibration" (in tone or color) and the next. Cinema, he argues, is a dialectical synthesis of spatial counterpoint and temporal counterpoint, a complex and conflicted, dynamic phenomenon which he calls "visual counterpoint," in the case of silent film, or "audio-visual counterpoint," in the case of the sound cinema. Everything meaningful in film, for Eisenstein, springs from conflict—and montage is the vehicle and preserver of conflict in cinema.

As such, Eisenstein insists that the shot is not merely an element of montage, one piece among others (as it would have been, on Eisenstein's view, for Pudovkin). Rather, the shot is the cell or molecule of montage, he argues, montage at the microscopic level, as it were. Film is conflict, and always a dynamic interrelation of conflicts on at least three levels: (1) the conflict within the sub-titles (in silent film), which is primarily a linguistic or literary conflict; (2) the conflict within any given shot, between visual elements; and (3) the conflict between shots, that is, counterpoint. Furthermore, he notes, not only is there conflict within each of these three levels, but there is conflict between them, as well. Film, conceived as a conflict between different sorts of conflict, is at its heart a dynamic tension and synthesis—and, if Eisenstein is right about the nature of film, then there is no more appropriate approach for the film theorist or filmgoer than the (Hegelian-Marxist) dialectical one.

At least at the time of the writing of this essay, in the early 1930s, Eisenstein believes that there really has only been one successful film dramaturgy in use: a dramaturgy of the film-story. This approach treats film as an essentially narrative art, and understands and interprets it in what are essentially literary terms. Eisenstein's interest, however, is in developing a new approach to film, a dramaturgy of film-form—not to replace, but to complement, the existing approaches. This would require a great deal more attention to be paid to film images, rather than merely the dialogue and narrative structure: what is shown, and what is seen (or, in the case of sound film, seen and heard). Only on this basis, and necessary to this project, would be the construction of a film syntax: a way of "reading" the film images. It is in pursuit of the beginnings of such a syntax that Eisenstein closes the essay with a discussion of the various ways in which montage—the centerpiece of film form—functions in the Soviet cinema, perhaps especially (if not exclusively) in Eisenstein's films.

There are, Eisenstein asserts, two kinds of montage: visible montage and association montage. Visible montage occurs in terms of the images themselves, as they are seen in the film, and he thinks there are two basic ways in which we encounter visible montage, the logical and the illogical. Logical visible montage presents the audience with various elements of a moving object: it is in this sense the most basic sort of montage possible in film, as it really simply shows related and sequential shots of the same object or event over the course of the motion that defines it. Illogical visible montage, by contrast, superimposes different, unrelated events upon one another. (We might take a simple example, such as reading a book, to illustrate this contrast: logical visible montage might show us a woman, standing near a table with a book in her hand; then the pages of the book in close-up as it rests upon the table; then the woman, seated at the table, concentrated upon the book. We do not see the movement, but its trajectory is logical and implied by the images we do see in the order in which we see them. Contrariwise, illogical visible montage might show us the woman standing near the table, with the book; then the image of the woman's empty apartment; then a page of the book; then the sun, setting; then the woman, reading. There is no logical connection between the images that might imply movement, and yet the meaning of their interrelation in this particular sequence seems nevertheless filmic.)

Association montage is the sort of montage for which Eisenstein himself if best recognized, and in aesthetic terms, perhaps the most difficult to pull off successfully. Association montage brings into relation shots not by way of their visible relatedness, but by way of the emotional associations between them. This takes the subject of the film out of the realm of the merely visible or physical, and transposes it into the field of emotion. Eisenstein gives us a number of examples; one of the simplest and most moving is from his first feature-length film, Strike, *in which images of striking workers being killed are intercut with images of the butchering of a bull. What makes such montage so difficult, Eisenstein thinks, is that it always risks falling into empty literary symbolism. Unless the emotional association between the intercut shots is true, the montage ends up relying simply on the spectator's ability to construct a rational explanation for their concurrence—rather than presenting the spectator with two unrelated scenes the emotional resonance of which is great enough to overcome their visible unrelatedness. When successful, however, association montage liberates the action of the film from any specific time or place, making of it a truly universal art.*

Filmography

- ***Bronenosets Patyomkin*** [*Battleship Potemkin*] (USSR, 1925). *Directed by* Sergei Eisenstein. *Produced by* Jacob Bliokh. *Written by* Nina Agadzhanova *and* Sergei Eisenstein. *Starring* Aleksandr Antonov, Vladimir Barksy, *and* Grigori Aleksandrov.
- ***Stachka*** [*Strike*] (USSR, 1925). *Directed by* Sergei Eisenstein. *Produced by* Boris Mikhin. *Written by* Grigori Aleksandrov, Ilya Kravchunovsky, Sergei Eisenstein, *and* Valeryan Pletnyov. *Starring* Maksim Shtraukh, Grigori Aleksandrov, *and* Mikhail Gomorov.
- ***Bukhta smerti*** [*The Bay of Death*] (USSR, 1926). *Directed by* Abram Room. *Produced by* Goskino. *Written by* Boris Leonidov *and* Aleksei Novikov-Priboy. *Starring* V. Yaroslavtsev, A. Matsevich, *and* Vasili Lyudvinsky.
- ***Mat*** [*Mother*] (USSR, 1926). *Directed by* Vsevolod Pudovkin. *Produced by* Mezhrabpomfilm. *Written by* Nathan Zarkhi. *Starring* Vera Baranovskaya *and* Nikolai Batalov.
- ***Konets Sankt-Peterburga*** [*The End of St. Petersburg*] (USSR, 1927). *Directed by* Vsevolod Pudovkin *and* Mikhail Doller. *Produced by* Mezhrabpomfilm. *Written by* Nathan Zarkhi. *Starring* Aleksandr Chistiakov, Vera Baranovskaya, Ivan Chuvelev, *and* V. Obolenskii.
- ***Oktyabr': Desyat' dney kotorye potryasli mir*** [*October: Ten Days that Shook the World*] (USSR, 1928). *Directed and Written by* Grigori Aleksandrov *and* Sergei Eisenstein. *Produced by* Sovkino. *Starring* Vladimir Popov, Vasili Nikandrov, *and* Layaschenko.
- ***Rossiya Nikolaya II i Lev Tolstoy*** [*The Russia of Nikolai II and Lev Tolstoy*] (USSR, 1928). *Directed and Written by* Esfir Shub. *Produced by* Sovkino.
- ***Arsenal*** (USSR, 1929). *Directed, Produced, and Written by* Alexander Dovzhenko. *Starring* Semyon Svashenko, Mykola Nademsky, Amvroziy Buchma, *and* Les Podorozhnij.
- ***Zhivoy trup*** [*The Living Corpse*] (USSR, 1929). *Directed by* Fyodor Otsep. *Produced by* Mezhrabpomfilm *and* Prometheus-Film-Verleih und Vertriebs-GmbH. *Written by* Boris Gusman, Anatoli Marienhof, *and* Fyodor Otsep. *Starring* Vsevolod Pudovkin.

A DIALECTIC APPROACH TO FILM FORM

Translated by John Winge

In nature we never see anything isolated, but everything in connection with something else which is before it, beside it, under it, and over it.

GOETHE[1]

According to Marx and Engels the dialectic system is only the conscious reproduction of the dialectic course (substance) of the external events of the world.[2]

Thus:

The projection of the dialectic system of things
into the brain
into creating abstractly
into the process of thinking
yields: dialectic methods of thinking;
dialectic materialism—PHILOSOPHY.

And also:

The projection of the same system of things
while creating concretely
while giving form
yields: ART.

The foundation for this philosophy is a dynamic concept of things:
Being—as a constant evolution from the interaction of two contradictory opposites.
Synthesis—arising from the opposition between thesis and antithesis.

A dynamic comprehension of things is also basic to the same degree, for a correct understanding of art and of all art-forms. In the realm of art this dialectic principle of dynamics is embodied in

CONFLICT

as the fundamental principle for the existence of every art-work and every art-form.

---

[1] In *Conversations with Eckermann* (5 June 1825), translated by John Oxenford.
[2] Razumovsky, *Theory of Historical Materialism*, Moscow, 1928.

For art is always conflict:

(1) according to its social mission,

(2) according to its nature,

(3) according to its methodology.

According to its social mission *because*: It is art's task to make manifest the contradictions of Being. To form equitable views by stirring up contradictions within the spectator's mind, and to forge accurate intellectual concepts from the dynamic clash of opposing passions.

According to its nature *because*: Its nature is a conflict between natural existence and creative tendency. Between organic inertia and purposeful initiative. Hypertrophy of the purposive initiative—the principles of rational logic—ossifies art into mathematical technicalism. (A painted landscape becomes a topographical map, a painted Saint Sebastian becomes an anatomical chart.) Hypertrophy of organic naturalness—of organic logic—dilutes art into formlessness. (A Malevich becomes a Kaulbach, an Archipenko becomes a waxworks side-show.)

Because the limit of organic form (the passive principle of being) is *Nature*. The limit of rational form (the active principle of production) is *Industry*. At the intersection of Nature and Industry stands *Art*.

The logic of organic form *vs*. the logic of rational form yields, in collision,

the dialectic of the art-form.

The interaction of the two produces and determines Dynamism. (Not only in the sense of a space-time continuum, but also in the field of absolute thinking. I also regard the inception of new concepts and viewpoints in the conflict between customary conception and particular representation as dynamic—as a dynamization of the inertia of perception—as a dynamization of the "traditional view" into a new one.)

The quantity of interval determines the pressure of the tension. (See in music, for example, the concept of intervals. There can be cases where the distance of separation is so wide that it leads to a break—to a collapse of the homogeneous concept of art. For instance, the "inaudibility" of certain intervals.)

The spatial form of this dynamism is expression.
The phases of its tension: rhythm.

This is true for every art-form, and, indeed, for every kind of expression.

Similarly, human expression is a conflict between conditioned and unconditioned reflexes. (In this I cannot agree with Klages, who, *a*) does not consider human expression dynamically as a process, but statically as a result, and who, *b*) attributes everything in motion to the field of the "soul," and only the hindering element to "reason."[3] ["Reason" and "Soul" of the idealistic concept here correspond remotely with the ideas of conditioned and unconditioned reflexes.])

[3] Ludwig Klages, *The Science of Character*, translated by W.H. Johnston, London, George Allen & Unwin Ltd., 1929.

This is true in every field that can be understood as an art. For example, logical thought, considered as an art, shows the same dynamic mechanism:

> … the intellectual lives of Plato or Dante or Spinoza or Newton were largely guided and sustained by their delight in the sheer beauty of the rhythmic relation between law and instance, species and individual, or cause and effect.[4]

This holds in other fields, as well, e.g., in speech, where all its sap, vitality, and dynamism arise from the irregularity of the part in relation to the laws of the system as a whole.

In contrast we can observe the sterility of expression in such artificial, totally regulated languages as Esperanto.

It is from this principle that the whole charm of poetry derives. Its rhythm arises as a conflict between the metric measure employed and the distribution of accents, over-riding this measure.

The concept of a formally static phenomenon as a dynamic function is dialectically imaged in the wise words of Goethe:

> *Die Baukunst ist eine ertarrte Musik.*
> (Architecture is frozen music.)[5]

Just as in the case of a homogeneous ideology (a monistic viewpoint), the whole, as well as the least detail, must be penetrated by a sole principle. So, ranged alongside the conflict of *social conditionality*, and the conflict of *existing nature*, the *methodology* of an art reveals this same principle of conflict. As the basic principle of the rhythm to be created and the inception of the art-form.

Art is always conflict, according to its methodology.

Here we shall consider the general problem of art in the specific example of its highest form—film.

Shot and montage are the basic elements of cinema.

Montage

has been established by the Soviet film as the nerve of cinema.

To determine the nature of montage is to solve the specific problem of cinema. The earliest conscious film-makers, and our first film theoreticians, regarded montage as a means of description by placing single shots one after the other like building-blocks. The movement within these building-block shots, and the consequent length of the component pieces, was then considered as rhythm.

A completely false concept!

This would mean the defining of a given object solely in relation to the nature of its external course. The mechanical process of splicing would be made a principle. We cannot describe such a relationship of lengths as rhythm. From this comes metric rather than rhythmic

[4] Graham Wallas, *The Great Society, A Psychological Analysis*. Macmillan, 1928, p. 101.

[5] In *Conversations with Eckermann* (23 March 1829).

relationships, as opposed to one another as the mechanical-metric system of Mensendieck is to the organic-rhythmic school of Bode in matters of body exercise.

According to this definition, shared even by Pudovkin as a theoretician, montage is the means of *unrolling* an idea with the help of single shots: the "epic" principle.

In my opinion, however, montage is an idea that arises from the collision of independent shots—shots even opposite to one another: the "dramatic" principle.[6]

A sophism? Certainly not. For we are seeking a definition of the whole nature, the principal style and spirit of cinema from its technical (optical) basis.

We know that the phenomenon of movement in film resides in the fact that two motionless images of a moving body, following one another, blend into an appearance of motion by showing them sequentially at a required speed.

This popularized description of what happens as a *blending* has its share of responsibility for the popular miscomprehension of the nature of montage that we have quoted above.

Let us examine more exactly the course of the phenomenon we are discussing—how it really occurs—and draw our conclusion from this. Placed next to each other, two photographed immobile images result in the appearance of movement. Is this accurate? Pictorially—and phraseologically, yes.

But mechanically, it is not. For, in fact, each sequential element is perceived not *next* to the other, but on *top* of the other. For the idea (or sensation) of movement arises from the process of superimposing on the retained impression of the object's first position, a newly visible further position of the object. This is, by the way, the reason for the phenomenon of spatial depth, in the optical superimposition of two planes in stereoscopy. From the superimposition of two elements of the same dimension always arises a new, higher dimension. In the case of stereoscopy the superimposition of two nonidentical two-dimensionalities results in stereoscopic three-dimensionality.

In another field: a concrete word (a denotation) set beside a concrete word yields an abstract concept—as in the Chinese and Japanese languages,[7] where a material ideogram can indicate a transcendental (conceptual) result.

The incongruence in contour of the first picture—already impressed on the mind—with the subsequently perceived second picture engenders, in conflict, the feeling of motion. Degree of incongruence determines intensity of impression, and determines that tension which becomes the real element of authentic rhythm.

Here we have, temporally, what we see arising spatially on a graphic or painted plane.

What comprises the dynamic effect of a painting? The eye follows the direction of an element in the painting. It retains a visual impression, which then collides with the impression derived from following the direction of a second element. The conflict of these directions forms the dynamic effect in apprehending the whole.

I. It may be purely linear: Fernand Léger, or Suprematism.

II. It may be "anecdotal." The secret of the marvelous mobility of Daumier's and Lautrec's figures dwells in the fact that the various anatomical parts of a body are represented in

---

[6] "Epic" and "dramatic" are used here in regard to methodology of form—not to *content* or *plot*!

[7] See discussion in preceding essay. ["The Cinematographic Principle and the Ideogram," in *Film Form*, pp. 28–44.—*JW*]

spatial circumstances (positions) that are temporally various, disjunctive. For example, in Toulouse-Lautrec's lithograph of Miss Cissy Loftus, if one logically develops position A of the foot, one builds a body in position A corresponding to it. But the body is represented from knee up already in position A + a. The cinematic effect of joined motionless pictures is already established here! From hips to shoulders we can see A + a + a. The figure comes alive and kicking!

III. Between I and II lies primitive Italian futurism—such as in Balla's "Man with Six Legs in Six Positions"—for II obtains its effect by retaining natural unity and anatomical correctness, while I, on the other hand, does this with purely elementary elements. III, although destroying naturalness, has not yet pressed forward to abstraction.

IV. The conflict of directions may also be of an ideographic kind. It was in this way that we have gained the pregnant characterizations of a Sharaku, for example. The secret of his extremely perfected strength of expression lies in the anatomical and *spatial disproportion* of the parts—in comparison with which, our I might be termed *temporal disproportion*.

Generally termed "irregularity," this *spatial disproportion* has been a constant attraction and instrument for artists. In writing of Rodin's drawings, Camille Mauclair indicated one explanation for this search:

> The greatest artists, Michelangelo, Rembrandt, Delacroix, all, at a certain moment of the upthrusting of their genius, threw aside, as it were, the ballast of exactitude as conceived by our simplifying reason and our ordinary eyes, in order to attain the fixation of ideas, the synthesis, the *pictorial handwriting* of their dreams.[8]

Two experimental artists of the nineteenth century—a painter and a poet—attempted esthetic formulations of this "irregularity." Renoir advanced this thesis:

> Beauty of every description finds its charm in variety. Nature abhors both vacuum and regularity. For the same reason, no work of art can really be called such if it has not been created by an artist who believes in irregularity and rejects any set form. Regularity, order, desire for perfection (which is always a false perfection) destroy art. The only possibility of maintaining taste in art is to impress on artists and the public the importance of irregularity. Irregularity is the basis of all art.[9]

And Baudelaire wrote in his journal:

> That which is not slightly distorted lacks sensible appeal; from which it follows that irregularity—that is to say, the unexpected, surprise and astonishment, are an essential part and characteristic of beauty.[10]

---

[8] In the preface to Baudelaire's *Les fleurs du mal*, illustrated by Auguste Rodin, Paris, Limited Editions Club, 1940.

[9] Renoir's manifesto for *La Société des Irrégularistes* (1884) is thus synopsized by Lionello Venturi in his *Painting and Painters*, New York, Scribners, 1945; the original text can be consulted in *Les archives de l'Impressionisme*, edited by Lionello Venturi, Paris, Durand-Ruel, 1939, I, pp. 127–129.

[10] Charles Baudelaire, *Intimate Journals* (13 May 1856), translated by Christopher Isherwood. New York, Random House, 1930.

Upon closer examination of the particular beauty of irregularity as employed in painting, whether by Grünewald or by Renoir, it will be seen that it is a disproportion in the relation of a detail in one dimension to another detail in a different dimension.

The spatial development of the relative size of one detail in correspondence with another, and the consequent collision between the proportions designed by the artist for that purpose, result in a characterization—a definition of the represented matter.

Finally, color. Any shade of a color imparts to our vision a given rhythm of vibration. This is not said figuratively, but purely physiologically, for colors are distinguished from one another by their number of light vibrations.

The adjacent shade or tone of color is in another rate of vibration. The counterpoint (conflict) of the two—the retained rate of vibration against the newly perceived one—yields the dynamism of our apprehension of the interplay of color.

Hence, with only one step from visual vibrations to acoustic vibrations, we find ourselves in the field of music. From the domain of the spatial-pictorial—to the domain of the temporal-pictorial—where the same law rules. For counterpoint is to music not only a form of composition, but is altogether the basic factor for the possibility of tone perception and tone differentiation.

It may almost be said that in every case we have cited we have seen in operation the same *Principle of Comparison* that makes possible for us perception and definition in every field.

In the moving image (cinema) we have, so to speak, a synthesis of two counterpoints—the spatial counterpoint of graphic art, and the temporal counterpoint of music.

Within cinema, and characterizing it, occurs what may be described as:

visual counterpoint

In applying this concept to the film, we gain several leads to the problem of film grammar. As well as a *syntax* of film manifestations, in which visual counterpoint may determine a whole new system of forms of manifestation....

For all this, the basic premise is:

The shot is by no means an element of montage.
The shot is a montage cell (or molecule).

In this formulation the dualistic division of

Sub-title and shot
and
Shot and montage

leaps forward in analysis to a dialectic consideration as three different phases of one homogeneous task of expression, its homogenous characteristics determining the homogeneity of their structural laws.

Inter-relation of the three phases:

Conflict within a thesis (an abstract idea)—*formulates* itself in the dialectics of the sub-title—*forms* itself spatially in the conflict within the shot—and *explodes* with increasing intensity in montage-conflict among the separate shots.

This is fully analogous to human, psychological expression. This is a conflict of motives, which can also be comprehended in three phases:

1. Purely verbal utterance. Without intonation—expression in speech.
2. Gesticulatory (mimic-intonational) expression. Projection of the conflict onto the whole expressive bodily system of man. Gesture of bodily movement and gesture of intonation.
3. Projection of the conflict into space. With an intensification of motives, the zigzag of mimic expression is propelled into the surrounding space following the same formula of distortion. A zigzag of expression arising from the spatial division caused by man moving in space. *Mise-en-scène.*

This gives us the basis for an entirely new understanding of the problem of film form.

We can list, as examples of types of conflicts within the form—characteristic for the conflict within the shot, as well as for the conflict between colliding shots, or, montage:

1. Graphic conflict....
2. Conflict of planes....
3. Conflict of volumes....
4. Spatial conflict....
5. Light conflict.
6. Tempo conflict, and so on.

Nota bene: This list is of principal features, of *dominants*. It is naturally understood that they occur chiefly as complexes.

For a transition to montage, it will be sufficient to divide any example into two independent primary pieces, as in the case of graphic conflict, although all other cases can be similarly divided.... *Some further examples:*

7. Conflict between matter and viewpoint (achieved by spatial distortion through camera-angle)....
8. Conflict between matter and its spatial nature (achieved by *optical distortion* by the lens).
9. Conflict between an event and its temporal nature (achieved by slow-motion and *stop-motion*)

and finally

10. Conflict between the whole *optical* complex and a quite different sphere.

Thus does conflict between optical and acoustical experience produce:

sound-film,

which is capable of being realized as

audio-visual counterpoint.

Formulation and investigation of the phenomenon of cinema as forms of conflict yield the first possibility of devising a homogeneous system of *visual dramaturgy* for all general and particular cases of the film problem.

Of devising a *dramaturgy of the visual film-form* as regulated and precise as the existing *dramaturgy of the film-story.*

From this viewpoint on the film medium, the following forms and potentialities of style may be summed up as a film syntax, or it may be more exact to describe the following as:

a tentative film-syntax.

We shall list here a number of potentialities of dialectical development to be derived from this proposition: The concept of the moving (time-consuming) image arises from the superimposition—or counterpoint—of two differing immobile images.

I. *Each moving fragment of montage.* Each photographed piece. Technical definition of the phenomenon of movement. *No composition as yet.* (A running man. A rifle fired. A splash of water.)

II. *An artificially produced image of motion.* The basic optical element is used for deliberate compositions:

A. *Logical*

Example 1 (from *October*): a montage rendition of a machine-gun being fired, by cross-cutting details of the firing.

Combination A: a brightly lit machine-gun. A different shot in a low key. Double burst: graphic burst + light burst. Close-up of machine-gunner.

Combination B....: Effect almost of double exposure achieved by *clatter* montage effect. Length of montage pieces—two frames each.

Example 2 (from *Potemkin*): an illustration of instantaneous action. Woman with pince-nez. Followed immediately—without transition—by the same woman with shattered pince-nez and bleeding eye: impression of a shot hitting the eye....

B. *Illogical*

Example 3 (from *Potemkin*): the same device used for pictorial symbolism. In the thunder of the *Potemkin's* guns, a marble lion leaps up, in protest against the bloodshed on the Odessa steps.... Composed of three shots of three stationary marble lions at the Alupka Palace in the Crimea: a sleeping lion, an awakening lion, a rising lion. The effect is achieved by a correct calculation of the length of the second shot. Its superimposition on the first shot produces the first action. This establishes time to impress the second position on the mind. Superimposition of the third position on the second produces the second action: the lion finally rises.

> Example 4 (from *October*): Example 1 showed how the firing was manufactured symbolically from elements outside the process of firing itself. In illustrating the monarchist *putsch* attempted by General Kornilov, it occurred to me that his militarist *tendency* could be shown in a montage that would employ religious details for its material. For Kornilov had revealed his intention in the guise of a peculiar "Crusade" of Moslems (!), his Caucasian "Wild Division," together with some Christians, against the Bolsheviki. So we intercut shots of a Baroque Christ (apparently exploding in the radiant beams of his halo) with shots of an egg-shaped mask of Uzume, Goddess of Mirth, completely self-contained. The temporal conflict between the closed egg-form and the graphic star-form produced the effect of an instantaneous *burst*—of a bomb, or shrapnel....[11]

Thus far the examples have shown *primitive-psychological* cases—employing superimposition of optical motion *exclusively*.

> III. *Emotional* combinations, not only with the visible elements of the shots, but chiefly with chains of psychological associations. *Association montage*. As a means for pointing up a situation emotionally.

In Example 1, we had two successive shots A and B, identical in subject. However, they were not identical in respect to the position of the subject within the frame.... producing *dynamization in space*—an impression of spatial dynamics.... The degree of difference between the positions A and B determines the tension of the movement.

For a new case, let us suppose that the subjects of Shots A and B are not *identical*. Although the associations of the two shots are identical, that is, associatively identical.

This *dynamization of the subject*, not in the field of space but of psychology, i.e., *emotion*, thus produces:

emotional dynamization.

> Example 1 (in *Strike*): the montage of the killing of the workers is actually a cross montage of this carnage with the butchering of a bull in an abattoir. Though the subjects are different, "butchering" is the associative link. This made for a powerful emotional intensification of the scene. As a matter of fact, homogeneity of gesture plays an important part in this case in achieving the effect—both the movement of the dynamic gesture within the frame, and the static gesture dividing the frame graphically.

This is a principle subsequently used by Pudovkin in *The End of St. Petersburg*, in his powerful sequence intercutting shots of stock exchange and battlefield. His previous film, *Mother*, had a similar sequence: the ice-break on the river, paralleled with the workers' demonstration.

Such a means may decay pathologically if the essential viewpoint—emotional dynamization of the subject—is lost. As soon as the film-maker loses sight of this essence the means ossifies

[11] Examples of more primitive effects belong here also, such as simple cross-cutting of church spires, angled in mutual opposition.

into lifeless literary symbolism and stylistic mannerism. Two examples of such hollow use of this means occur to me:

> Example 2 (in *October*): the sugary chants of compromise by the Mensheviki at the Second Congress of Soviets—during the storming of the Winter Palace—are intercut with hands playing harps. This was a purely literary parallelism that by no means dynamized the subject matter. Similarly in Otzep's *Living Corpse*, church spires (in imitation of those in *October*) and lyrical landscapes are intercut with the courtroom speeches of the prosecutor and defense lawyer. This error was the same as in the "harp" sequence.

On the other hand, a majority of *purely dynamic* effects can produce positive results:

> Example 3 (in *October*): the dramatic moment of the union of the Motorcycle Battalion with the Congress of Soviets was dynamized by shots of abstractly spinning bicycle wheels, in association with the entrance of the new delegates. In this way the large-scale emotional content of the event was transformed into actual dynamics.

This same principle—giving birth to concepts, to emotions, by juxtaposing two disparate events—led to:

IV. *Liberation of the whole action from the definition of time and space.* My first attempts at this were in *October*.

> Example 1: a trench crowded with soldiers appears to be crushed by an enormous gun-base that comes down inexorably. As an anti-militarist symbol seen from the viewpoint of subject alone, the effect is achieved by an apparent bringing together of an independently existing trench and an overwhelming military product, just as physically independent.
>
> Example 2: in the scene of Kornilov's *putsch*, which puts an end to Kerensky's Bonapartist dreams. Here one of Kornilov's tanks climbs up and crushes a plaster-of-Paris Napoleon standing on Kerensky's desk in the Winter Palace, a juxtaposition of purely symbolic significance.
>
> This method has now been used by Dovzhenko in *Arsenal* to shape whole sequences, as well as by Esther Schub in her use of library footage in *The Russia of Nikolai II and Lev Tolstoy*.

I wish to offer another example of this method, to upset the traditional ways of handling plot—although it has not yet been put into practice.

In 1924–1925 I was mulling over the idea of a filmic portrait of *actual* man. At that time, there prevailed a tendency to show actual man in films only in *long* uncut dramatic scenes. It was believed that cutting (montage) would destroy the idea of actual man. Abram Room established something of a record in this respect when he used in *The Death Ship* uncut dramatic shots as long as 40 meters or 135 feet. I considered (and still do) such a concept to be utterly unfilmic.

Very well—what would be a linguistically accurate characterization of a man?

His raven-black hair...
The waves of his hair...
His eyes radiating azure beams...
His steely muscles...

Even in a less exaggerated description, any verbal account of a person is bound to find itself employing an assortment of waterfalls, lightning-rods, landscapes, birds, etc.

Now why should the cinema follow the forms of theater and painting rather than the methodology of language, which allows wholly new concepts of ideas to arise from the combination of two concrete denotations of two concrete objects? Language is much closer to film than painting is. For example, in painting the form arises from *abstract* elements of line and color, while in cinema the material *concreteness* of the image within the frame presents—as an element—the greatest difficulty in manipulation. So why not rather lean towards the system of language, which is forced to use the same mechanics in inventing words and word-complexes?

On the other hand, why is it that montage cannot be dispensed with in orthodox films?

The differentiation in montage-pieces lies in their lack of existence as single units. Each piece can evoke no more than a certain association. The accumulation of such associations can achieve the same effect as is provided for the spectator by purely physiological means in the plot of a realistically produced play.

For instance, murder on the stage has a purely physiological effect. Photographed in *one* montage-piece, it can function simply as *information*, as a sub-title. *Emotional* effect begins only with the reconstruction of the event in montage fragments, each of which will summon a certain association—the sum of which will be an all-embracing complex of emotional feeling. Traditionally:

1. A hand lifts a knife.
2. The eyes of the victim open suddenly.
3. His hands clutch the table.
4. The knife is jerked up.
5. The eyes blink involuntarily.
6. Blood gushes.
7. A mouth shrieks.
8. Something drips onto a shoe...

and similar film clichés. Nevertheless, in regard to the *action as a whole*, *each fragment-piece* is almost *abstract*. The more differentiated they are the more abstract they become, provoking no more than a certain association.

Quite logically the thought occurs: could not the same thing be accomplished more productively by not following the plot so slavishly, but by materializing the idea, the impression, of *Murder* through a free accumulation of associative matter? For the most important task is still to establish the idea of murder—the feeling of murder, as such. The plot is no more than a device without which one isn't yet capable of telling something to the spectator! In any case, effort in this direction would certainly produce the most interesting variety of forms.

Someone should try, at least! Since this thought occurred to me, I have not had time to make this experiment. And today I am more concerned with quite different problems. But, returning to the main line of our syntax, something there may bring us closer to these tasks.

While, with I, II, and III, tension was calculated for purely physiological effect—from the purely optical to the emotional, we must mention here also the case of the same conflict-tension serving the ends of new concepts—of new attitudes, that is, of purely intellectual aims.

> Example 1 (in *October*): Kerensky's rise to power and dictatorship after the July uprising of 1917. A comic effect was gained by sub-titles indicating regular ascending ranks ("*Dictator*"—"*Generalissimo*"—"*Minister of Navy—and of Army*"—etc.) climbing higher and higher—but into five or six shots of Kerensky, climbing the stairs of the Winter Palace, all with exactly the *same* pace. Here a conflict between the flummery of the ascending ranks and the "hero's" trotting up the same unchanging flight of stairs yields an intellectual result: Kerensky's essential nonentity is shown satirically. We have the counterpoint of a literally expressed conventional idea with the *pictured* action of a particular person who is unequal to his swiftly increasing duties. The incongruence of these two factors results in the spectator's purely *intellectual* decision at the expense of this particular person. Intellectual dynamization.

> Example 2 (in *October*): Kornilov's march on Petrograd was under the banner of "In the Name of God and Country." Here we attempted to reveal the religious significance of this episode in a rationalistic way. A number of religious images, from a magnificent Baroque Christ to an Eskimo idol, were cut together. The conflict in this case was between the concept and the symbolization of God. While idea and image appear to accord completely in the first statue shown, the two elements move further from each other with each successive image.... Maintaining the denotation of "God," the images increasingly disagree with our concept of God, inevitably leading to individual conclusions about the true nature of all deities. In this case, too, a chain of images attempted to achieve a purely intellectual resolution, resulting from a conflict between a preconception and a *gradual discrediting of it in purposeful steps.*

Step by step, by a process of comparing each new image with the common denotation, power is accumulated behind a process that can be formally identified with that of logical deduction. The decision to release these ideas, as well as the method used, is already *intellectually* conceived.

The conventional *descriptive* form for film leads to the formal possibility of a kind of filmic reasoning. While the conventional film directs the *emotions*, this suggests an opportunity to encourage and direct the whole *thought process*, as well.

These two particular sequences of experiment were very much opposed by the majority of critics. Because they were understood as purely political. I would not attempt to deny that *this form is most suitable for the expression of ideologically pointed theses*, but it is a pity that the critics completely overlooked the purely filmic potentialities of this approach.

In these two experiments we have taken the first embryonic step towards a totally new form of film expression. Towards a purely intellectual film, freed from traditional limitations, achieving direct forms for ideas, systems, and concepts, without any need for transitions and paraphrases. We may yet have a

synthesis of art and science.

This would be the proper name for our new epoch in the field of art. This would be the final justification for Lenin's words, that "the cinema is the most important of all the arts."

Moscow, April 1929

CHAPTER 18
WALTER BENJAMIN

Walter Benjamin (1892–1940) was a German literary theorist, cultural critic, and philosopher. His work is often reflective of his reading of Marx and Marxism, as well as German literary history and Jewish mysticism, among other influences. Although he was friends with a number of its members—perhaps most notably, Theodor Adorno—Benjamin's association with the Frankfurt School appears to have had as much to do with his profound influence on those thinkers (again, especially Adorno) as it does with any formal similarity between his writings and those of other Critical Theorists. The essay included here, "The Work of Art in the Age of Mechanical Reproduction," is one of the most important works in philosophical aesthetics, not only on the cinema, but in the twentieth century in general; it is widely read, and is among the greatest and most far-reaching aesthetic theories in the Continental tradition. Benjamin produced three versions of the essay: the German original ("Das Kunstwerk im Zeitalter seiner technischen Reproduzierbarkeit," unpublished until 1955), in 1935; a French translation ("L'Œuvre d'art à l'époque de sa reproduction mécanisée") by Pierre Klossowski in collaboration with Benjamin himself, in Zeitschrift für Sozialforschung *in 1936; and a final version in German in 1939, the basis for the English translation included here.*

Benjamin's primary interest in "The Work of Art in the Age of Mechanical Reproduction" is in the consequences of the advanced technical reproducibility of artworks for the production and consumption of art and culture in the early twentieth century, as well as the political uses and ramifications of mechanized art production, specifically, the significance of photography and film for European fascist and communist movements. He begins by addressing the technical reproducibility of art, noting that works of art have been reproducible since ancient times—both manually, as well as by way of various reproductive technologies. In ancient Greece and Rome, Benjamin notes, there were already the technologies of founding and stamping; these progress over the course of Western history through the woodcut, engraving, and etching, to printing and lithography, and finally photography and cinematography. Each of these, again, is discussed here in the first place in its capacity for mechanically reproducing works of art, and thus Benjamin asserts that, of the two major ramifications of technical reproducibility for art in the twentieth century, the first is the widespread and easy reproduction of works of art, photographic prints of paintings and the like. The second major ramification for art, however, has to do with what he sees initially in the cinema, and then somewhat later in photography, which is the art (in this case) of the film: the use of these technologies in the production of wholly new works of art, works of art that are by their very nature mechanically reproducible because they are mechanically produced.

The primary aesthetic difference between a manually produced and a mechanically reproduced work of art is in what Benjamin famously calls the artwork's "aura." For Benjamin, the aura of the work has to do with its unique presence in time and space: the fact that, for most traditional works of art, to exist is to exist in only one place at a time. This uniqueness in terms of presence grants the work—the "original"—a sort of authenticity that any copy would lack. In addition, that authenticity and uniqueness grant the original work authority over all copies. When a work is manually reproduced, of course, we are dealing either with a print or copy (when the reproduction is authorized by the artist) or a forgery, and in either case, the authenticity and authority of the original work—its aura—is without question. But when a work is mechanically reproduced, we find a somewhat different phenomenon occurring. No one could seriously try to convince anyone that a photographic reprint of the Mona Lisa *was in fact* the Mona Lisa*: there is no question of forgery here nor of copying in the traditional sense. Rather, the photographic reproduction of a particular painting seems to be the attempt to communicate something of the original to spectators at a distance, individuals who for whatever reason cannot come to be in the presence of the authentic and original work. A photograph of the* Mona Lisa *shows the real* Mona Lisa, *but lacks something of the unique presence, the authenticity, and authority of the original. In Benjamin's terms, this is to say that the aura of the work diminishes when it is communicated via mechanical reproduction.*

Benjamin establishes a further distinction among artworks in terms of the ways in which they are artworks, or perhaps better, the ways in which they are received and appreciated by spectators. Originally in the West, Benjamin argues, works of art served an exclusively religious or ritual function: whether we're thinking of paintings on prehistoric cave walls or the statue of the god in the Greek or Roman temple, works of art are produced with an awareness of a spiritual or sacred purpose and meaning in mind. Such artworks, whatever their aesthetic value, are treated with a degree of unapproachability, Benjamin notes, such that what matters most is that they exist in the time and place that they do—not whether anyone sees them. He calls this phenomenon the "cult value" of art, and sets cult value forth as the sort of relationship between a spectator and an artwork in which the aura of the work plays a significant, even essential, role. Mechanical reproducibility emancipates the work of art from ritual, and thus from cult value, and when it does so we see a concomitant shift in attention away from religious meaning and toward political significance. Such works of art are valued, not for their aura or inherent uniqueness, but rather to the extent that they can be experienced by multitudes: this shift is the shift, for Benjamin, from cult value to what he calls "exhibition value." And the best examples of works of art with exhibition rather than cult value are, for Benjamin, works of photography and film.

Early theories of film, he suggests, are characterized by an uncomfortable attempt to force ritual value onto the cinematic work. These theorists fail to recognize the transition in art culture from cult value to exhibition value, and so read (in a variety of different ways) ritual into the experience of film. Cult value requires the maintenance of an appropriate distance between the spectator and the artwork, as well as the artist and the spectator, and Benjamin notes that the more traditional, handmade arts—such as painting—manage this relatively well. Film is incapable of such distance, however. He compares the contrast between the painter and the cinematographer to that between a magician and a surgeon. The magician heals, when he or she heals, only by maintaining a natural distance: there is the laying on of hands, he notes, but there is also the absolute difference in authority between the faith healer and the healed. The surgeon, on the other hand, heals only by way of eliminating the distance between him- or herself and the patient, so much so that the surgeon literally penetrates the patient's body. While the painter maintains a respectful but authoritative distance from the world, the cinematographer penetrates that world—collapsing the distance, but also divesting him- or herself of the sort of "magical" authority the painter retains. In so doing, the filmmaker is able to represent in film something the painter is incapable of presenting in painting: everyday life.

Film, by its very nature, distracts the spectator constantly. The fact of cinematic motion, the movement from shot to shot and scene to scene, keeps the spectator ever seeking to reestablish his or her footing in the film—and ever expectant of what might be coming next. This means that one cannot contemplate a film (since contemplation, as Benjamin understands it, is the opposite of distraction), and that the spectator receives whatever he or she receives in film-watching while in a state of distraction. This makes film in particular among the arts quite susceptible to propagandistic uses (or abuses). In the Germany of the 1930s, in which Benjamin formulates and writes the essay, he sees the fascists using the cinema as a propaganda tool, providing audiences with an outlet for their frustrations and fears without enabling them to engage in a revolutionary transformation of the material conditions of their lives. Fascist propaganda films can give ordinary people the sense that they have expressed themselves and their needs, and yet property relations can be maintained. Such redirection, from revolutionary frustration to distraction, inevitably results in war, Benjamin writes, and at its worst, a state of perpetual war. Politics becomes aesthetic, in fascism, with public interest in political processes amounting to little more than entertainment value. An alternative model exists, however: according to Benjamin, communism offers the opposite structure, politicizing art instead of aestheticizing politics. And communist political art would, in the cinema as elsewhere, likely follow in the tradition of other revolutionary and avant garde art movements before it, seeking to cultivate public outrage rather than contentment with the status quo.

Filmography

- ***A Woman of Paris*** [French title: *L'Opinion publique*] (USA, 1923). *Directed, Produced, and Written by* Charlie Chaplin. *Starring* Edna Purviance.
- ***The Gold Rush*** (USA, 1925). *Directed, Produced, and Written by* Charlie Chaplin. *Starring* Charlie Chaplin *and* Mack Swain.
- ***Le Passion de Jeanne d'Arc*** [*The Passion of Joan of Arc*] (France, 1928). *Directed by* Carl Theodor Dreyer. *Produced by* Société Générale des Films. *Written by* Joseph Delteil *and* Carl Theodor Dreyer. *Starring* Renée Jeanne Falconetti.
- ***Misère au Borinage*** [*Misery in Borinage*] (Belgium, 1933). *Directed and Written by* Henri Storck *and* Joris Ivens.
- ***Tri pesni o Lenine*** [*Three Songs about Lenin*] (USSR, 1934). *Directed and Written by* Dziga Vertov. *Produced by* Mezhrapobfilm.
- ***A Midsummer Night's Dream*** (USA, 1935). *Directed by* Max Reinhardt *and* William Dieterle. *Produced by* Henry Blanke. *Written by* Charles Kenyon *and* Mary C. McCall, Jr. *Starring* Ian Hunter, James Cagney, Mickey Rooney, *and* Olivia de Havilland.

THE WORK OF ART IN THE AGE OF MECHANICAL REPRODUCTION

Translated by Harry Zohn

> Our fine arts were developed, their types and uses were established, in times very different from the present, by men whose power of action upon things was insignificant in comparison with ours. But the amazing growth of our techniques, the adaptability and precision they have attained, the ideas and habits they are creating, make it a certainty that profound changes are impending in the ancient craft of the Beautiful. In all the arts there is a physical component which can no longer be considered or treated as it used to be, which cannot remain unaffected by our modern knowledge and power. For the last twenty years neither matter nor space nor time has been what it was from time immemorial. We must expect great innovations to transform the entire technique of the arts, thereby affecting artistic invention itself and perhaps even bringing about an amazing change in our very notion of art.[1]
>
> —Paul Valéry, *Pièces sur l'Art*,"La Conquète de l'ubiquité," Paris.

Preface

When Marx undertook his critique of the capitalistic mode of production, this mode was in its infancy. Marx directed his efforts in such a way as to give them prognostic value. He went back to the basic conditions underlying capitalistic production and through his presentation showed what could be expected of capitalism in the future. The result was that one could expect it not only to exploit the proletariat with increasing intensity, but ultimately to create conditions which would make it possible to abolish capitalism itself.

The transformation of the superstructure, which takes place far more slowly than that of the substructure, has taken more than half a century to manifest in all areas of culture the change in the conditions of production. Only today can it be indicated what form this has taken. Certain prognostic requirements should be met by these statements. However, theses about the art of the proletariat after its assumption of power or about the art of a classless society would have less bearing on these demands than theses about the developmental tendencies of art under present conditions of production. Their dialectic is no less noticeable in the superstructure than in the economy. It would therefore be wrong to underestimate the value of such theses as a weapon. They brush aside a number of outmoded concepts, such as creativity and genius, eternal value and mystery—concepts whose uncontrolled (and at present

[1] Quoted from Paul Valéry, *Aesthetics*, "The Conquest of Ubiquity," translated by Ralph Manheim, p. 225. Pantheon Books, Bollingen Series, New York, 1964.—*Trans.*

almost uncontrollable) application would lead to a processing of data in the Fascist sense. The concepts which are introduced into the theory of art in what follows differ from the more familiar terms in that they are completely useless for the purposes of Fascism. They are, on the other hand, useful for the formulation of revolutionary demands in the politics of art.

I

In principle a work of art has always been reproducible. Manmade artifacts could always be imitated by men. Replicas were made by pupils in practice of their craft, by masters for diffusing their works, and, finally, by third parties in the pursuit of gain. Mechanical reproduction of a work of art, however, represents something new. Historically, it advanced intermittently and in leaps at long intervals, but with accelerated intensity. The Greeks knew only two procedures of technically reproducing works of art: founding and stamping. Bronzes, terra cottas, and coins were the only art works which they could produce in quantity. All others were unique and could not be mechanically reproduced. With the woodcut graphic art became mechanically reproducible for the first time, long before script became reproducible by print. The enormous changes which printing, the mechanical reproduction of writing, has brought about in literature are a familiar story. However, within the phenomenon which we are here examining from the perspective of world history, print is merely a special, though particularly important, case. During the Middle Ages engraving and etching were added to the woodcut; at the beginning of the nineteenth century lithography made its appearance.

With lithography the technique of reproduction reached an essentially new stage. This much more direct process was distinguished by the tracing of the design on a stone rather than its incision on a block of wood or its etching on a copperplate and permitted graphic art for the first time to put its products on the market, not only in large numbers as hitherto, but also in daily changing forms. Lithography enabled graphic art to illustrate everyday life, and it began to keep pace with printing. But only a few decades after its invention, lithography was surpassed by photography. For the first time in the process of pictorial reproduction, photography freed the hand of the most important artistic functions which henceforth devolved only upon the eye looking into a lens. Since the eye perceives more swiftly than the hand can draw, the process of pictorial reproduction was accelerated so enormously that it could keep pace with speech. A film operator shooting a scene in the studio captures the images at the speed of an actor's speech. Just as lithography virtually implied the illustrated newspaper, so did photography foreshadow the sound film. The technical reproduction of sound was tackled at the end of the last century. These convergent endeavors made predictable a situation which Paul Valéry pointed up in this sentence: "Just as water, gas, and electricity are brought into our houses from far off to satisfy our needs in response to a minimal effort, so we shall be supplied with visual or auditory images, which will appear and disappear at a simple movement of the hand, hardly more than a sign" (*op. cit.*, p. 226). Around 1900 technical reproduction had reached a standard that not only permitted it to reproduce all transmitted works of art and thus to cause the most profound change in their impact upon the public; it also had captured a place of its own among the artistic processes. For the study of this standard nothing is more revealing than the nature of the repercussions that these two different manifestations—the reproduction of works of art and the art of the film—have had on art in its traditional form.

II

Even the most perfect reproduction of a work of art is lacking in one element: its presence in time and space, its unique existence at the place where it happens to be. This unique existence of the work of art determined the history to which it was subject throughout the time of its existence. This includes the changes which it may have suffered in physical condition over the years as well as the various changes in its ownership.[2] The traces of the first can be revealed only by chemical or physical analyses which it is impossible to perform on a reproduction; changes of ownership are subject to a tradition which must be traced from the situation of the original.

The presence of the original is the prerequisite to the concept of authenticity. Chemical analyses of the patina of a bronze can help to establish this, as does the proof that a given manuscript of the Middle Ages stems from an archive of the fifteenth century. The whole sphere of authenticity is outside technical—and, of course, not only technical—reproducibility.[3] Confronted with its manual reproduction, which was usually branded as a forgery, the original preserved all its authority; not so *vis à vis* technical reproduction. The reason is twofold. First, process reproduction is more independent of the original than manual reproduction. For example, in photography, process reproduction can bring out those aspects of the original that are unattainable to the naked eye yet accessible to the lens, which is adjustable and chooses its angle at will. And photographic reproduction, with the aid of certain processes, such as enlargement or slow motion, can capture images which escape natural vision. Secondly, technical reproduction can put the copy of the original into situations which would be out of reach for the original itself. Above all, it enables the original to meet the beholder halfway, be it in the form of a photograph or a phonograph record. The cathedral leaves its locale to be received in the studio of a lover of art; the choral production, performed in an auditorium or in the open air, resounds in the drawing room.

The situations into which the product of mechanical reproduction can be brought may not touch the actual work of art, yet the quality of its presence is always depreciated. This holds not only for the art work but also, for instance, for a landscape which passes in review before the spectator in a movie. In the case of the art object, a most sensitive nucleus—namely, its authenticity—is interfered with whereas no natural object is vulnerable on that score. The authenticity of a thing is the essence of all that is transmissible from its beginning, ranging from its substantive duration to its testimony to the history which it has experienced. Since the historical testimony rests on the authenticity, the former, too, is jeopardized by reproduction when substantive duration ceases to matter. And what is really jeopardized when the historical testimony is affected is the authority of the object.[4]

---

[2] Of course, the history of a work of art encompasses more than this. The history of the "Mona Lisa," for instance, encompasses the kind and number of its copies made in the 17th, 18th, and 19th centuries.

[3] Precisely because authenticity is not reproducible, the intensive penetration of certain (mechanical) processes of reproduction was instrumental in differentiating and grading authenticity. To develop such differentiations was an important function of the trade in works of art. The invention of the woodcut may be said to have struck at the root of the quality of authenticity even before its late flowering. To be sure, at the time of its origin a medieval picture of the Madonna could not yet be said to be "authentic." It became "authentic" only during the succeeding centuries and perhaps most strikingly so during the last one.

[4] The poorest provincial staging of *Faust* is superior to a Faust film in that, ideally, it competes with the first performance at Weimar. Before the screen it is unprofitable to remember traditional contents which might come to mind before the stage—for instance, that Goethe's friend Johann Heinrich Merck is hidden in Mephisto, and the like.

One might subsume the eliminated element in the term "aura" and go on to say: that which withers in the age of mechanical reproduction is the aura of the work of art. This is a symptomatic process whose significance points beyond the realm of art. One might generalize by saying: the technique of reproduction detaches the reproduced object from the domain of tradition. By making many reproductions it substitutes a plurality of copies for a unique existence. And in permitting the reproduction to meet the beholder or listener in his own particular situation, it reactivates the object reproduced. These two processes lead to a tremendous shattering of tradition which is the obverse of the contemporary crisis and renewal of mankind. Both processes are intimately connected with the contemporary mass movements. Their most powerful agent is the film. Its social significance, particularly in its most positive form, is inconceivable without its destructive, cathartic aspect, that is, the liquidation of the traditional value of the cultural heritage. This phenomenon is most palpable in the great historical films. It extends to ever new positions. In 1927 Abel Gance exclaimed enthusiastically: "Shakespeare, Rembrandt, Beethoven will make films… all legends, all mythologies and all myths, all founders of religion, and the very religions… await their exposed resurrection, and the heroes crowd each other at the gate."[5] Presumably without intending it, he issued an invitation to a far-reaching liquidation.

III

During long periods of history, the mode of human sense perception changes with humanity's entire mode of existence. The manner in which human sense perception is organized, the medium in which it is accomplished, is determined not only by nature but by historical circumstances as well. The fifth century, with its great shifts of population, saw the birth of the late Roman art industry and the Vienna Genesis, and there developed not only an art different from that of antiquity but also a new kind of perception. The scholars of the Viennese school, Riegl and Wickhoff, who resisted the weight of classical tradition under which these later art forms had been buried, were the first to draw conclusions from them concerning the organization of perception at the time. However far-reaching their insight, these scholars limited themselves to showing the significant, formal hallmark which characterized perception in late Roman times. They did not attempt—and, perhaps, saw no way—to show the social transformations expressed by these changes of perception. The conditions for an analogous insight are more favorable in the present. And if changes in the medium of contemporary perception can be comprehended as decay of the aura, it is possible to show its social causes.

The concept of aura which was proposed above with reference to historical objects may usefully be illustrated with reference to the aura of natural ones. We define the aura of the latter as the unique phenomenon of a distance, however close it may be. If, while resting on a summer afternoon, you follow with your eyes a mountain range on the horizon or a branch which casts its shadow over you, you experience the aura of those mountains, of that branch. This image makes it easy to comprehend the social bases of the contemporary decay of the aura. It rests on two circumstances, both of which are related to the increasing significance of the masses in

[5] Abel Gance, "Le Temps de l'image est venu," *L'Art cinématographique*, Vol. 2, pp. 94 f, Paris, 1927.—*Trans.*

contemporary life. Namely, the desire of contemporary masses to bring things "closer" spatially and humanly, which is just as ardent as their bent toward overcoming the uniqueness of every reality by accepting its reproduction.[6] Every day the urge grows stronger to get hold of an object at very close range by way of its likeness, its reproduction. Unmistakably, reproduction as offered by picture magazines and newsreels differs from the image seen by the unarmed eye. Uniqueness and permanence are as closely linked in the latter as are transitoriness and reproducibility in the former. To pry an object from its shell, to destroy its aura, is the mark of a perception whose "sense of the universal equality of things" has increased to such a degree that it extracts it even from a unique object by means of reproduction. Thus is manifested in the field of perception what in the theoretical sphere is noticeable in the increasing importance of statistics. The adjustment of reality to the masses and of the masses to reality is a process of unlimited scope, as much for thinking as for perception.

IV

The uniqueness of a work of art is inseparable from its being imbedded in the fabric of tradition. This tradition itself is thoroughly alive and extremely changeable. An ancient statue of Venus, for example, stood in a different traditional context with the Greeks, who made it an object of veneration, than with the clerics of the Middle Ages, who viewed it as an ominous idol. Both of them, however, were equally confronted with its uniqueness, that is, its aura. Originally the contextual integration of art in tradition found its expression in the cult. We know that the earliest art works originated in the service of a ritual—first the magical, then the religious kind. It is significant that the existence of the work of art with reference to its aura is never entirely separated from its ritual function.[7] In other words, the unique value of the "authentic" work of art has its basis in ritual, the location of its original use value. This ritualistic basis, however, remote, is still recognizable as secularized ritual even in the most profane forms of the cult of beauty.[8] The secular cult of beauty, developed during the Renaissance and prevailing for three centuries, clearly showed that ritualistic basis in its decline and the first deep crisis which befell it. With the advent of the first truly revolutionary means of reproduction, photography, simultaneously with the rise of socialism, art sensed the approaching crisis which has become

---

[6] To satisfy the human interest of the masses may mean to have one's social function removed from the field of vision. Nothing guarantees that a portraitist of today, when painting a famous surgeon at the breakfast table in the midst of his family, depicts his social function more precisely than a painter of the 17th century who portrayed his medical doctors as representing this profession, like Rembrandt in his "Anatomy Lesson."

[7] The definition of the aura as a "unique phenomenon of a distance however close it may be" represents nothing but the formulation of the cult value of the work of art in categories of space and time perception. Distance is the opposite of closeness. The essentially distant object is the unapproachable one. Unapproachability is indeed a major quality of the cult image. True to its nature, it remains "distant, however close it may be." The closeness which one may gain from its subject matter does not impair the distance which it retains in its appearance.

[8] To the extent to which the cult value of the painting is secularized the ideas of its fundamental uniqueness lose distinctness. In the imagination of the beholder the uniqueness of the phenomena which hold sway in the cult image is more and more displaced by the empirical uniqueness of the creator or of his creative achievement. To be sure, never completely so; the concept of authenticity always transcends mere genuineness. (This is particularly apparent in the collector who always retains some traces of the fetishist and who, by owning the work of art, shares in its ritual power.) Nevertheless, the function of the concept of authenticity remains determinate in the evaluation of art; with the secularization of art, authenticity displaces the cult value of the work.

evident a century later. At the same time, art reacted with the doctrine of *l'art pour l'art*, that is, with a theology of art. This gave rise to what might be called a negative theology in the form of the idea of "pure" art, which not only denied any social function of art but also any categorizing by subject matter. (In poetry, Mallarmé was the first to take this position.)

An analysis of art in the age of mechanical reproduction must do justice to these relationships, for they lead us to an all-important insight: for the first time in world history, mechanical reproduction emancipates the work of art from its parasitical dependence on ritual. To an ever greater degree the work of art reproduced becomes the work of art designed for reproducibility.[9] From a photographic negative, for example, one can make any number of prints; to ask for the "authentic" print makes no sense. But the instant the criterion of authenticity ceases to be applicable to artistic production, the total function of art is reversed. Instead of being based on ritual, it begins to be based on another practice—politics.

V

Works of art are received and valued on different planes. Two polar types stand out: with one, the accent is on the cult value; with the other, on the exhibition value of the work.[10] Artistic

---

[9] In the case of films, mechanical reproduction is not, as with literature and painting, an external condition for mass distribution. Mechanical reproduction is inherent in the very technique of film production. This technique not only permits in the most direct way but virtually causes mass distribution. It enforces distribution because the production of a film is so expensive that an individual who, for instance, might afford to buy a painting no longer can afford to buy a film. In 1927 it was calculated that a major film, in order to pay its way, had to reach an audience of nine million. With the sound film, to be sure, a setback to its international distribution occurred at first: audiences became limited by language barriers. This coincided with the Fascist emphasis on national interests. It is more important to focus on this connection with Fascism than on this setback, which was soon minimized by synchronization. The simultaneity of both phenomena is attributable to the depression. The same disturbances which, on a larger scale, led to an attempt to maintain the existing property structure by sheer force led the endangered film capital to speed up the development of the sound film. The introduction of the sound film brought about a temporary relief, not only because it again brought the masses into the theaters but also because it merged new capital from the electrical industry with that of the film industry. Thus, viewed from the outside, the sound film promoted national interests, but seen from the inside it helped to internationalize film production even more than previously.

[10] This polarity cannot come into its own in the aesthetics of Idealism. Its idea of beauty comprises these polar opposites without differentiating between them and consequently excludes their polarity. Yet in Hegel this polarity announces itself as clearly as possible within the limits of Idealism. We quote from his *Philosophy of History*:

> "Images were known of old. Piety at an early time required them for worship, but it could do without *beautiful* images. These might even be disturbing. In every beautiful painting there is also something nonspiritual, merely external, but its spirit speaks to man through its beauty. Worshipping, conversely, is concerned with the work as an object, for it is but a spiritless stupor of the soul... Fine art has arisen... in the church..., although it has already gone beyond its principle as art."

Likewise, the following passage from *The Philosophy of Fine Art* indicates that Hegel sensed a problem here.

"We are beyond the stage of reverence for works of art as divine and objects deserving our worship. The impression they produce is one of a more reflective kind, and the emotions they arouse require a higher test.... "—G. W. F. Hegel, *The Philosophy of Fine Art*, trans., with notes, by F. P. B. Osmaston, Vol, I, p. 12, London, 1920.

The transition from the first kind of artistic reception to the second characterizes the history of artistic reception in general. Apart from that, a certain oscillation between these two polar modes of reception can be demonstrated for each work of art. Take the Sistine Madonna. Since Hubert Grimme's research it has been known that the Madonna originally was painted for the purpose of exhibition. Grimme's research was inspired by the question: What is the purpose of the molding in the foreground of the painting which the two cupids lean upon? How, Grimme asked further,

production begins with ceremonial objects destined to serve in a cult. One may assume that what mattered was their existence, not their being on view. The elk portrayed by the man of the Stone Age on the walls of his cave was an instrument of magic. He did expose it to his fellow men, but in the main it was meant for the spirits. Today the cult value would seem to demand that the work of art remain hidden. Certain statues of gods are accessible only to the priest in the cella; certain Madonnas remain covered nearly all year round; certain sculptures on medieval cathedrals are invisible to the spectator on ground level. With the emancipation of the various art practices from ritual go increasing opportunities for the exhibition of their products. It is easier to exhibit a portrait bust that can be sent here and there than to exhibit the statue of a divinity that has its fixed place in the interior of a temple. The same holds for the painting as against the mosaic or fresco that preceded it. And even though the public presentability of a mass originally may have been just as great as that of a symphony, the latter originated at the moment when its public presentability promised to surpass that of the mass.

With the different methods of technical reproduction of a work of art, its fitness for exhibition increased to such an extent that the quantitative shift between its two poles turned into a qualitative transformation of its nature. This is comparable to the situation of the work of art in prehistoric times when, by the absolute emphasis on its cult value, it was, first and foremost, an instrument of magic. Only later did it come to be recognized as a work of art. In the same way today, by the absolute emphasis on its exhibition value the work of art becomes a creation with entirely new functions, among which the one we are conscious of, the artistic function, later may be recognized as incidental.[11] This much is certain: today photography and the film are the most serviceable exemplifications of this new function.

VI

In photography, exhibition value begins to displace cult value all along the line. But cult value does not give way without resistance. It retires into an ultimate retrenchment: the human countenance. It is no accident that the portrait was the focal point of early photography. The cult of remembrance of loved ones, absent or dead, offers a last refuge for the cult value of the picture. For the last time the aura emanates from the early photographs in the fleeting

---

did Raphael come to furnish the sky with two draperies? Research proved that the Madonna had been commissioned for the public lying-in-state of Pope Sixtus. The Popes lay in state in a certain side chapel of St. Peter's. On that occasion Raphael's picture had been fastened in a nichelike background of the chapel, supported by the coffin. In this picture Raphael portrays the Madonna approaching the papal coffin in clouds from the background of the niche, which was demarcated by green drapes. At the obsequies of Sixtus a pre-eminent exhibition value of Raphael's picture was taken advantage of. Some time later it was placed on the high altar in the church of the Black Friars at Piacenza. The reason for this exile is to be found in the Roman rites which forbid the use of paintings exhibited at obsequies as cult objects on the high altar. This regulation devalued Raphael's picture to some degree. In order to obtain an adequate price nevertheless, the Papal See resolved to add to the bargain the tacit toleration of the picture above the high altar. To avoid attention the picture was given to the monks of the far-off provincial town.

[11] Bertolt Brecht, on a different level, engaged in analogous reflections: "If the concept of 'work of art' can no longer be applied to the thing that emerges once the work is transformed into a commodity, we have to eliminate this concept with cautious care but without fear, lest we liquidate the function of the very thing as well. For it has to go through this phase without mental reservation, and not as noncommittal deviation from the straight path; rather, what happens here with the work of art will change it fundamentally and erase its past to such an extent that should the old concept be taken up again—and it will, why not?—it will no longer stir any memory of the thing it once designated."

expression of a human face. This is what constitutes their melancholy, incomparable beauty. But as man withdraws from the photographic image, the exhibition value for the first time shows its superiority to the ritual value. To have pinpointed this new stage constitutes the incomparable significance of Atget, who, around 1900, took photographs of deserted Paris streets. It has quite justly been said of him that he photographed them like scenes of crime. The scene of a crime, too, is deserted; it is photographed for the purpose of establishing evidence. With Atget, photographs become standard evidence for historical occurrences, and acquire a hidden political significance. They demand a specific kind of approach; free-floating contemplation is not appropriate to them. They stir the viewer; he feels challenged by them in a new way. At the same time picture magazines begin to put up signposts for him, right ones or wrong ones, no matter. For the first time, captions have become obligatory. And it is clear that they have an altogether different character than the title of a painting. The directives which the captions give to those looking at pictures in illustrated magazines soon become even more explicit and more imperative in the film where the meaning of each single picture appears to be prescribed by the sequence of all preceding ones.

VII

The nineteenth-century dispute as to the artistic value of painting versus photography today seems devious and confused. This does not diminish its importance, however; if anything, it underlines it. The dispute was in fact the symptom of a historical transformation the universal impact of which was not realized by either of the rivals. When the age of mechanical reproduction separated art from its basis in cult, the semblance of its autonomy disappeared forever. The resulting change in the function of art transcended the perspective of the century; for a long time it even escaped that of the twentieth century, which experienced the development of the film.

Earlier much futile thought had been devoted to the question of whether photography is an art. The primary question—whether the very invention of photography had not transformed the entire nature of art—was not raised. Soon the film theoreticians asked the same ill-considered question with regard to the film. But the difficulties which photography caused traditional aesthetics were mere child's play as compared to those raised by the film. Whence the insensitive and forced character of early theories of the film. Abel Gance, for instance, compares the film with hieroglyphs: "Here, by a remarkable regression, we have come back to the level of expression of the Egyptians… Pictorial language has not yet matured because our eyes have not yet adjusted to it. There is as yet insufficient respect for, insufficient cult of, what it expresses."[12] Or, in the words of Séverin-Mars: "What art has been granted a dream more poetical and more real at the same time! Approached in this fashion the film might represent an incomparable means of expression. Only the most high-minded persons, in the most perfect and mysterious moments of their lives, should be allowed to enter its ambience."[13] Alexandre Arnoux concludes his fantasy about the silent film with the question: "Do not all the bold

[12] Abel Gance, *op. cit.*, pp. 100–1.—*Trans.*
[13] Séverin-Mars, quoted by Abel Gance, *op. cit.*, p. 100.—*Trans.*

descriptions we have given amount to the definition of prayer?"[14] It is instructive to note how their desire to class the film among the "arts" forces these theoreticians to read ritual elements into it—with a striking lack of discretion. Yet when these speculations were published, films like *L'Opinion publique* and *The Gold Rush* had already appeared. This, however, did not keep Abel Gance from adducing hieroglyphs for purposes of comparison, nor Séverin-Mars from speaking of the film as one might speak of paintings by Fra Angelico. Characteristically, even today ultrareactionary authors give the film a similar contextual significance—if not an outright sacred one, then at least a supernatural one. Commenting on Max Reinhardt's film version of *A Midsummer Night's Dream*, Werfel states that undoubtedly it was the sterile copying of the exterior world with its streets, interiors, railroad stations, restaurants, motorcars, and beaches which until now had obstructed the elevation of the film to the realm of art. "The film has not yet realized its true meaning, its real possibilities... these consist in its unique faculty to express by natural means and with incomparable persuasiveness all that is fairylike, marvelous, supernatural."[15]

VIII

The artistic performance of a stage actor is definitely presented to the public by the actor in person; that of the screen actor, however, is presented by a camera, with a twofold consequence. The camera that presents the performance of the film actor to the public need not respect the performance as an integral whole. Guided by the cameraman, the camera continually changes its position with respect to the performance. The sequence of positional views which the editor composes from the material supplied him constitutes the completed film. It comprises certain factors of movement which are in reality those of the camera, not to mention special camera angles, close-ups, etc. Hence, the performance of the actor is subjected to a series of optical tests. This is the first consequence of the fact that the actor's performance is presented by means of a camera. Also, the film actor lacks the opportunity of the stage actor to adjust to the audience during his performance, since he does not present his performance to the audience in person. This permits the audience to take the position of a critic, without experiencing any personal contact with the actor. The audience's identification with the actor is really an identification with the camera. Consequently the audience takes the position of the camera; its approach is that of testing.[16] This is not the approach to which cult values may be exposed.

---

[14] Alexandre Arnoux, *Cinéma pris*, 1929, p. 28.—*Trans.*

[15] Franz Werfel, "Ein Sommernachtstraum, Ein Film von Shakespeare und Reinhardt," *Neues Wiener Journal*, cited in *Lu* 15, November, 1935.—*Trans.*

[16] "The film... provides—or could provide—useful insight into the details of human actions.... Character is never used as a source of motivation; the inner life of the persons never supplies the principal cause of the plot and seldom is its main result." (Bertolt Brecht, *Versuche*, "Der Dreigroschenprozess," p. 268.) The expansion of the field of the testable which mechanical equipment brings about for the actor corresponds to the extraordinary expansion of the field of the testable brought about for the individual through economic conditions. Thus, vocational aptitude tests become constantly more important. What matters in these tests are segmental performances of the individual. The film shot and the vocational aptitude test are taken before a committee of experts. The camera director in the studio occupies a place identical with that of the examiner during aptitude tests.

IX

For the film, what matters primarily is that the actor represents himself to the public before the camera, rather than representing someone else. One of the first to sense the actor's metamorphosis by this form of testing was Pirandello. Though his remarks on the subject in his novel *Si Gira* were limited to the negative aspects of the question and to the silent film only, this hardly impairs their validity. For in this respect, the sound film did not change anything essential. What matters is that the part is acted not for an audience but for a mechanical contrivance—in the case of the sound film, for two of them. "The film actor," wrote Pirandello, "feels as if in exile—exiled not only from the stage but also from himself. With a vague sense of discomfort he feels inexplicable emptiness: his body loses its corporeality, it evaporates, it is deprived of reality, life, voice, and the noises caused by his moving about, in order to be changed into a mute image, flickering an instant on the screen, then vanishing into silence.... The projector will play with his shadow before the public, and he himself must be content to play before the camera."[17] This situation might also be characterized as follows: for the first time—and this is the effect of the film—man has to operate with his whole living person, yet forgoing his aura. For aura is tied to his presence; there can be no replica of it. The aura which, on the stage, emanates from Macbeth, cannot be separated for the spectators from that of the actor. However, the singularity of the shot in the studio is that the camera is substituted for the public. Consequently, the aura that envelops the actor vanishes, and with it the aura of the figure he portrays.

It is not surprising that it should be a dramatist such as Pirandello who, in characterizing the film, inadvertently touches on the very crisis in which we see the theater. Any thorough study proves that there is indeed no greater contrast than that of the stage play to a work of art that is completely subject to or, like the film, founded in, mechanical reproduction. Experts have long recognized that in the film "the greatest effects are almost always obtained by 'acting' as little as possible...." In 1932 Rudolf Arnheim saw "the latest trend... in treating the actor as a stage prop chosen for its characteristics and... inserted at the proper place."[18] With this idea something else is closely connected. The stage actor identifies himself with the character of his role. The film actor very often is denied this opportunity. His creation is by no means all of a piece; it

---

[17] Luigi Pirandello, *Si Gira*, quoted by Léon Pierre-Quint, "Signification du cinéma," *L'Art cinématographique*, op. cit., pp. 14–15.—*Trans.*

[18] Rudolf Arnheim, *Film als Kunst*, Berlin, 1932, pp. 176 f. In this context certain seemingly unimportant details in which the film director deviates from stage practices gain in interest. Such is the attempt to let the actor play without make-up, as made among others by Dreyer in his *Jeanne d'Arc*. Dreyer spent months seeking the forty actors who constitute the Inquisitors' tribunal. The search for these actors resembled that for stage properties that are hard to come by. Dreyer made every effort to avoid resemblances of age, build, and physiognomy. If the actor thus becomes a stage property, this latter, on the other hand, frequently functions as actor. At least it is not unusual for the film to assign a role to the stage property. Instead of choosing at random from a great wealth of examples, let us concentrate on a particularly convincing one. A clock that is working will always be a disturbance on the stage. There it cannot be permitted its function of measuring time. Even in a naturalistic play, astronomical time would clash with theatrical time. Under these circumstances it is highly revealing that the film can, whenever appropriate, use time as measured by a clock. From this more than from many other touches it may clearly be recognized that under certain circumstances each and every prop in a film may assume important functions. From here it is but one step to Pudovkin's statement that "the playing of an actor which is connected with an object and is built around it... is always one of the strongest methods of cinematic construction." (W. Pudovkin, *Filmregie und Filmmanuskript*, Berlin, 1928, p. 126.) The film is the first art form capable of demonstrating how matter plays tricks on man. Hence, films can be an excellent means of materialistic representation.

is composed of many separate performances. Besides certain fortuitous considerations, such as cost of studio, availability of fellow players, décor, etc., there are elementary necessities of equipment that split the actor's work into a series of mountable episodes. In particular, lighting and its installation require the presentation of an event that, on the screen, unfolds as a rapid and unified scene, in a sequence of separate shootings which may take hours at the studio; not to mention more obvious montage. Thus a jump from the window can be shot in the studio as a jump from a scaffold, and the ensuing flight, if need be, can be shot weeks later when outdoor scenes are taken. Far more paradoxical cases can easily be construed. Let us assume that an actor is supposed to be startled by a knock at the door. If his reaction is not satisfactory, the director can resort to an expedient: when the actor happens to be at the studio again he has a shot fired behind him without his being forewarned of it. The frightened reaction can be shot now and be cut into the screen version. Nothing more strikingly shows that art has left the realm of the "beautiful semblance" which, so far, had been taken to be the only sphere where art could thrive.

X

The feeling of strangeness that overcomes the actor before the camera, as Pirandello describes it, is basically of the same kind as the estrangement felt before one's own image in the mirror. But now the reflected image has become separable, transportable. And where is it transported? Before the public.[19] Never for a moment does the screen actor cease to be conscious of this fact. While facing the camera he knows that ultimately he will face the public, the consumers who constitute the market. This market, where he offers not only his labor but also his whole self, his heart and soul, is beyond his reach. During the shooting he has as little contact with it as any article made in a factory. This may contribute to that oppression, that new anxiety which, according to Pirandello, grips the actor before the camera. The film responds to the shriveling of the aura with an artificial build-up of the "personality" outside the studio. The cult of the movie star, fostered by the money of the film industry, preserves not the unique aura of the person but the "spell of the personality," the phony spell of a commodity. So long as the movie-makers' capital sets the fashion, as a rule no other revolutionary merit can be accredited to today's film than the promotion of a revolutionary criticism of traditional concepts of art. We do not deny that in some cases today's films can also promote revolutionary criticism of social conditions, even of the distribution of property. However, our present study is no more specifically concerned with this than is the film production of Western Europe.

---

[19] The change noted here in the method of exhibition caused by mechanical reproduction applies to politics as well. The present crisis of the bourgeois democracies comprises a crisis of the conditions which determine the public presentation of the rulers. Democracies exhibit a member of government directly and personally before the nation's representatives. Parliament is his public. Since the innovations of camera and recording equipment make it possible for the orator to become audible and visible to an unlimited number of persons, the presentation of the man of politics before camera and recording equipment becomes paramount. Parliaments, as much as theaters, are deserted. Radio and film not only affect the function of the professional actor but likewise the function of those who also exhibit themselves before this mechanical equipment, those who govern. Though their tasks may be different, the change affects equally the actor and the ruler. The trend is toward establishing controllable and transferrable skills under certain social conditions. This results in a new selection, a selection before the equipment from which the star and the dictator emerge victorious.

It is inherent in the technique of the film as well as that of sports that everybody who witnesses its accomplishments is somewhat of an expert. This is obvious to anyone listening to a group of newspaper boys leaning on their bicycles and discussing the outcome of a bicycle race. It is not for nothing that newspaper publishers arrange races for their delivery boys. These arouse great interest among the participants, for the victor has an opportunity to rise from delivery boy to professional racer. Similarly, the newsreel offers everyone the opportunity to rise from passer-by to movie extra. In this way any man might even find himself part of a work of art, as witness Vertoff's *Three Songs About Lenin* or Ivens' *Borinage*. Any man today can lay claim to being filmed. This claim can best be elucidated by a comparative look at the historical situation of contemporary literature.

For centuries a small number of writers were confronted by many thousands of readers. This changed toward the end of the last century. With the increasing extension of the press, which kept placing new political, religious, scientific, professional, and local organs before the readers, an increasing number of readers became writers—at first, occasional ones. It began with the daily press opening to its readers space for "letters to the editor." And today there is hardly a gainfully employed European who could not, in principle, find an opportunity to publish somewhere or other comments on his work, grievances, documentary reports, or that sort of thing. Thus, the distinction between author and public is about to lose its basic character. The difference becomes merely functional; it may vary from case to case. At any moment the reader is ready to turn into a writer. As expert, which he had to become willy-nilly in an extremely specialized work process, even if only in some minor respect, the reader gains access to authorship. In the Soviet Union work itself is given a voice. To present it verbally is part of a man's ability to perform the work. Literary license is now founded on polytechnic rather than specialized training and thus becomes common property.[20]

---

[20] The privileged character of the respective techniques is lost. Aldous Huxley writes:

> "Advances in technology have led... to vulgarity.... Process reproduction and the rotary press have made possible the indefinite multiplication of writing and pictures. Universal education and relatively high wages have created an enormous public who know how to read and can afford to buy reading and pictorial matter. A great industry has been called into existence in order to supply these commodities. Now, artistic talent is a very rare phenomenon; whence it follows... that, at every epoch and in all countries, most art has been bad. But the proportion of trash in the total artistic output is greater now than at any other period. That it must be so is a matter of simple arithmetic. The population of Western Europe has a little more than doubled during the last century. But the amount of reading—and seeing—matter has increased, I should imagine, at least twenty and possibly fifty or even a hundred times. If there were n men of talent in a population of x millions, there will presumably be 2n men of talent among 2x millions. The situation may be summed up thus. For every page of print and pictures published a century ago, twenty or perhaps even a hundred pages are published today. But for every man of talent then living, there are now only two men of talent. It may be of course that, thanks to universal education, many potential talents which in the past would have been stillborn are now enabled to realize themselves. Let us assume, then, that there are now three or even four men of talent to every one of earlier times. It still remains true to say that the consumption of reading—and seeing—matter has far outstripped the natural production of gifted writers and draughtsmen. It is the same with hearing-matter. Prosperity, the gramophone and the radio have created an audience of hearers who consume an amount of hearing-matter that has increased out of all proportion to the increase of population and the consequent natural increase of talented musicians. It follows from all this that in all the arts the output of trash is both absolutely and relatively greater than it was in the past; and that it must remain greater for just so long as the world continues to consume the present inordinate quantities of reading-matter, seeing-matter, and hearing-matter."
>
> *—Aldous Huxley, Beyond the Mexique Bay. A Traveller's Journal, London, 1949, pp. 274 ff. First published in 1934.*

This mode of observation is obviously not progressive.

All this can easily be applied to the film, where transitions that in literature took centuries have come about in a decade. In cinematic practice, particularly in Russia, this change-over has partially become established reality. Some of the players whom we meet in Russian films are not actors in our sense but people who portray *themselves*—and primarily in their own work process. In Western Europe the capitalistic exploitation of the film denies consideration to modern man's legitimate claim to being reproduced. Under these circumstances the film industry is trying hard to spur the interest of the masses through illusion-promoting spectacles and dubious speculations.

XI

The shooting of a film, especially of a sound film, affords a spectacle unimaginable anywhere at any time before this. It presents a process in which it is impossible to assign to a spectator a viewpoint which would exclude from the actual scene such extraneous accessories as camera equipment, lighting machinery, staff assistants, etc.—unless his eye were on a line parallel with the lens. This circumstance, more than any other, renders superficial and insignificant any possible similarity between a scene in the studio and one on the stage. In the theater one is well aware of the place from which the play cannot immediately be detected as illusionary. There is no such place for the movie scene that is being shot. Its illusionary nature is that of the second degree, the result of cutting. That is to say, in the studio the mechanical equipment has penetrated so deeply into reality that its pure aspect freed from the foreign substance of equipment is the result of a special procedure, namely, the shooting by the specially adjusted camera and the mounting of the shot together with other similar ones. The equipment-free aspect of reality here has become the height of artifice; the sight of immediate reality has become an orchid in the land of technology.

Even more revealing is the comparison of these circumstances, which differ so much from those of the theater, with the situation in painting. Here the question is: How does the cameraman compare with the painter? To answer this we take recourse to an analogy with surgical operation. The surgeon represents the polar opposite of the magician. The magician heals a sick person by the laying on of hands; the surgeon cuts into the patient's body. The magician maintains the natural distance between the patient and himself; though he reduces it very slightly by the laying on of hands, he greatly increases it by virtue of his authority. The surgeon does exactly the reverse; he greatly diminishes the distance between himself and the patient by penetrating into the patient's body, and increases it but little by the caution with which his hand moves among the organs. In short, in contrast to the magician—who is still hidden in the medical practitioner—the surgeon at the decisive moment abstains from facing the patient man to man; rather, it is through the operation that he penetrates into him.

Magician and surgeon compare to painter and cameraman. The painter maintains in his work a natural distance from reality, the cameraman penetrates deeply into its web.[21]

[21] The boldness of the cameraman is indeed comparable to that of the surgeon. Luc Durtain lists among specific technical sleights of hand those "which are required in surgery in the case of certain difficult operations. I choose as an example a case from oto-rhino-larynology;... the so-called endonasal perspective procedure; or I refer to the acrobatic tricks of larynx surgery which have to be performed following the reversed picture in the laryngoscope. I might also speak of ear surgery which suggests the precision work of watchmakers. What range of the most subtle muscular acrobatics is required from the man who wants to repair or save the human body! We have only to think of the couching of a cataract where there is virtually a debate of steel with nearly fluid tissue, or of the major abdominal operations (laparotomy)."—Luc Durtain, *op. cit.*

There is a tremendous difference between the pictures they obtain. That of the painter is a total one, that of the cameraman consists of multiple fragments which are assembled under a new law. Thus, for contemporary man the representation of reality by the film is incomparably more significant than that of the painter, since it offers, precisely because of the thoroughgoing permeation of reality with mechanical equipment, an aspect of reality which is free of all equipment. And that is what one is entitled to ask from a work of art.

XII

Mechanical reproduction of art changes the reaction of the masses toward art. The reactionary attitude toward a Picasso painting changes into the progressive reaction toward a Chaplin movie. The progressive reaction is characterized by the direct, intimate fusion of visual and emotional enjoyment with the orientation of the expert. Such fusion is of great social significance. The greater the decrease in the social significance of an art form, the sharper the distinction between criticism and enjoyment by the public. The conventional is uncritically enjoyed, and the truly new is criticized with aversion. With regard to the screen, the critical and the receptive attitudes of the public coincide. The decisive reason for this is that individual reactions are predetermined by the mass audience response they are about to produce, and this is nowhere more pronounced than in the film. The moment these responses become manifest they control each other. Again, the comparison with painting is fruitful. A painting has always had an excellent chance to be viewed by one person or by a few. The simultaneous contemplation of paintings by a large public, such as developed in the nineteenth century, is an early symptom of the crisis of painting, a crisis which was by no means occasioned exclusively by photography but rather in a relatively independent manner by the appeal of art works to the masses.

Painting simply is in no position to present an object for simultaneous collective experience, as it was possible for architecture at all times, for the epic poem in the past, and for the movie today. Although this circumstance in itself should not lead one to conclusions about the social role of painting, it does constitute a serious threat as soon as painting, under special conditions and, as it were, against its nature, is confronted directly by the masses. In the churches and monasteries of the Middle Ages and at the princely courts up to the end of the eighteenth century, a collective reception of paintings did not occur simultaneously, but by graduated and hierarchized mediation. The change that has come about is an expression of the particular conflict in which painting was implicated by the mechanical reproducibility of paintings. Although paintings began to be publicly exhibited in galleries and salons, there was no way for the masses to organize and control themselves in their reception.[22] Thus the same public which responds in a progressive manner toward a grotesque film is bound to respond in a reactionary manner to surrealism.

---

[22] This mode of observation may seem crude, but as the great theoretician Leonardo has shown, crude modes of observation may at times be usefully adduced. Leonardo compares painting and music as follows: "Painting is superior to music because, unlike unfortunate music, it does not have to die as soon as it is born.... Music which is consumed in the very act of its birth is inferior to painting which the use of varnish has rendered eternal." (Trattato I, 29.)

XIII

The characteristics of the film lie not only in the manner in which man presents himself to mechanical equipment but also in the manner in which, by means of this apparatus, man can represent his environment. A glance at occupational psychology illustrates the testing capacity of the equipment. Psychoanalysis illustrates it in a different perspective. The film has enriched our field of perception with methods which can be illustrated by those of Freudian theory. Fifty years ago, a slip of the tongue passed more or less unnoticed. Only exceptionally may such a slip have revealed dimensions of depth in a conversation which had seemed to be taking its course on the surface. Since the *Psychopathology of Everyday Life* things have changed. This book isolated and made analyzable things which had heretofore floated along unnoticed in the broad stream of perception. For the entire spectrum of optical, and now also acoustical, perception the film has brought about a similar deepening of apperception. It is only an obverse of this fact that behavior items shown in a movie can be analyzed much more precisely and from more points of view than those presented on paintings or on the stage. As compared with painting, filmed behavior lends itself more readily to analysis because of its incomparably more precise statements of the situation. In comparison with the stage scene, the filmed behavior item lends itself more readily to analysis because it can be isolated more easily. This circumstance derives its chief importance from its tendency to promote the mutual penetration of art and science. Actually, of a screened behavior item which is neatly brought out in a certain situation, like a muscle of a body, it is difficult to say which is more fascinating, its artistic value or its value for science. To demonstrate the identity of the artistic and scientific uses of photography which heretofore usually were separated will be one of the revolutionary functions of the film.[23]

By close-ups of the things around us, by focusing on hidden details of familiar objects, by exploring commonplace milieus under the ingenious guidance of the camera, the film, on the one hand, extends our comprehension of the necessities which rule our lives; on the other hand, it manages to assure us of an immense and unexpected field of action. Our taverns and our metropolitan streets, our offices and furnished rooms, our railroad stations and our factories appeared to have us locked up hopelessly. Then came the film and burst this prison-world asunder by the dynamite of the tenth of a second, so that now, in the midst of its far-flung ruins and debris, we calmly and adventurously go traveling. With the close-up, space expands; with slow motion, movement is extended. The enlargement of a snapshot does not simply render more precise what in any case was visible, though unclear: it reveals entirely new structural formations of the subject. So, too, slow motion not only presents familiar qualities of movement but reveals in them entirely unknown ones "which, far from looking like retarded rapid movements, give the effect of singularly gliding, floating, supernatural motions."[24] Evidently a different nature opens

[23] Renaissance painting offers a revealing analogy to this situation. The incomparable development of this art and its significance rested not least on the integration of a number of new sciences, or at least of new scientific data. Renaissance painting made use of anatomy and perspective, of mathematics, meteorology, and chromatology. Valéry writes: "What could be further from us than the strange claim of a Leonardo to whom painting was a supreme goal and the ultimate demonstration of knowledge? Leonardo was convinced that painting demanded universal knowledge, and he did not even shrink from a theoretical analysis which to us is stunning because of its very depth and precision...."—Paul Valéry, *Pièces sur l'art*, "Autour de Corot," Paris, p. 191.

[24] Rudolf Arnheim, *loc. cit.*, p. 138.—*Trans.*

itself to the camera than opens to the naked eye—if only because an unconsciously penetrated space is substituted for a space consciously explored by man. Even if one has a general knowledge of the way people walk, one knows nothing of a person's posture during the fractional second of a stride. The act of reaching for a lighter or a spoon is familiar routine, yet we hardly know what really goes on between hand and metal, not to mention how this fluctuates with our moods. Here the camera intervenes with the resources of its lowerings and liftings, its interruptions and isolations, its extensions and accelerations, its enlargements and reductions. The camera introduces us to unconscious optics as does psychoanalysis to unconscious impulses.

XIV

One of the foremost tasks of art has always been the creation of a demand which could be fully satisfied only later.[25] The history of every art form shows critical epochs in which a certain art form aspires to effects which could be fully obtained only with a changed technical standard, that is to say, in a new art form. The extravagances and crudities of art which thus appear, particularly in the so-called decadent epochs, actually arise from the nucleus of its richest historical energies. In recent years, such barbarisms were abundant in Dadaism. It is only now that its impulse becomes discernible: Dadaism attempted to create by pictorial—and literary—means the effects which the public today seeks in the film.

Every fundamentally new, pioneering creation of demands will carry beyond its goal. Dadaism did so to the extent that it sacrificed the market values which are so characteristic of the film in favor of higher ambitions—though of course it was not conscious of such intentions as here described. The Dadaists attached much less importance to the sales value of their work than to its uselessness for contemplative immersion. The studied degradation of their material was not the least of their means to achieve this uselessness. Their poems are "word salad" containing obscenities and every imaginable waste product of language. The same is true of their paintings, on which they mounted buttons and tickets. What they intended and achieved was a relentless destruction of the aura of their creations, which they branded as reproductions

---

[25] "The work of art," says André Breton, "is valuable only in so far as it is vibrated by the reflexes of the future." Indeed, every developed art form intersects three lines of development. Technology works toward a certain form of art. Before the advent of the film there were photo booklets with pictures which flitted by the onlooker upon pressure of the thumb, thus portraying a boxing bout or a tennis match. Then there were the slot machines in bazaars; their picture sequences were produced by the turning of a crank.

Secondly, the traditional art forms in certain phases of their development strenuously work toward effects which later are effortlessly attained by the new ones. Before the rise of the movie the Dadaists' performances tried to create an audience reaction which Chaplin later evoked in a more natural way.

Thirdly, unspectacular social changes often promote a change in receptivity which will benefit the new art form. Before the movie had begun to create its public, pictures that were no longer immobile captivated an assembled audience in the so-called *Kaiserpanorama*. Here the public assembled before a screen into which stereoscopes were mounted, one to each beholder. By a mechanical process individual pictures appeared briefly before the stereoscopes, then made way for others. Edison still had to use similar devices in presenting the first movie strip before the film screen and projection were known. This strip was presented to a small public which stared into the apparatus in which the succession of pictures were reeling off. Incidentally, the institution of the *Kaiserpanorama* shows very clearly a dialectic of development. Shortly before the movie turned the reception of pictures into a collective one, the individual viewing of pictures in these swiftly outmoded establishments came into play once more with an intensity comparable to that of the ancient priest beholding the statue of a divinity in the cella.

with the very means of production. Before a painting of Arp's or a poem by August Stramm it is impossible to take time for contemplation and evaluation as one would before a canvas of Derain's or a poem by Rilke. In the decline of middle-class society, contemplation became a school for asocial behavior; it was countered by distraction as a variant of social conduct.[26] Dadaistic activities actually assured a rather vehement distraction by making works of art the center of scandal. One requirement was foremost: to outrage the public.

From an alluring appearance or persuasive structure of sound the work of art of the Dadaists became an instrument of ballistics. It hit the spectator like a bullet, it happened to him, thus acquiring a tactile quality. It promoted a demand for the film, the distracting element of which is also primarily tactile, being based on changes of place and focus which periodically assail the spectator. Let us compare the screen on which a film unfolds with the canvas of a painting. The painting invites the spectator to contemplation; before it the spectator can abandon himself to his associations. Before the movie frame he cannot do so. No sooner has his eye grasped a scene than it is already changed. It cannot be attested. Duhamel, who detests the film and knows nothing of its significance, though something of its structure, notes this circumstance as follows: "I can no longer think what I want to think. My thoughts have been replaced by moving images."[27] The spectator's process of association in view of these images is indeed interrupted by their constant, sudden change. This constitutes the shock effect of the film, which, like all shocks, should be cushioned by heightened presence of mind.[28] By means of its technical structure, the film has taken the physical shock effect out of the wrappers in which Dadaism had, as it were, kept it inside the moral shock effect.[29]

XV

The mass is a matrix from which all traditional behavior toward works of art issues today in a new form. Quantity has been transmuted into quality. The greatly increased mass of participants has produced a change in the mode of participation. The fact that the new mode of participation first appeared in a disreputable form must not confuse the spectator. Yet some people have launched spirited attacks against precisely this superficial aspect. Among these, Duhamel has expressed himself in the most radical manner. What he objects to most is the kind of participation which the movie elicits from the masses. Duhamel calls

[26] The theological archetype of this contemplation is the awareness of being alone with one's God. Such awareness, in the heyday of the bourgeoisie, went to strengthen the freedom to shake off clerical tutelage. During the decline of the bourgeoisie this awareness had to take into account the hidden tendency to withdraw from public affairs those forces which the individual draws upon in his communication with God.

[27] Georges Duhamel, *Scènes de la vie future*, Paris, 1930, p. 52.—*Trans.*

[28] The film is the art form that is in keeping with the increased threat to his life which modern man has to face. Man's need to expose himself to shock effects is his adjustment to the dangers threatening him. The film corresponds to profound changes in the apperceptive apparatus—changes that are experienced on an individual scale by the man in the street in big-city traffic, on a historical scale by every present-day citizen.

[29] As for Dadaism, insights important for Cubism and Futurism, are to be gained from the movie. Both appear as deficient attempts of art to accommodate the pervasion of reality by the apparatus. In contrast to the film, these schools did not try to use the apparatus as such for the artistic presentation of reality, but aimed at some sort of alloy in the joint presentation of reality and apparatus. In Cubism, the premonition that this apparatus will be structurally based on optics plays a dominant part; in Futurism, it is the premonition of the effects of this apparatus which are brought out by the rapid sequence of the film strip.

the movie "a pastime for helots, a diversion for uneducated, wretched, worn-out creatures who are consumed by their worries..., a spectacle which requires no concentration and presupposes no intelligence..., which kindles no light in the heart and awakens no hope other than the ridiculous one of someday becoming a 'star' in Los Angeles."[30] Clearly, this is at bottom the same ancient lament that the masses seek distraction whereas art demands concentration from the spectator. That is a commonplace. The question remains whether it provides a platform for the analysis of the film. A closer look is needed here. Distraction and concentration form polar opposites which may be stated as follows: A man who concentrates before a work of art is absorbed by it. He enters into his work of art the way legend tells of the Chinese painter when he viewed his finished painting. In contrast, the distracted mass absorbs the work of art. This is most obvious with regard to buildings. Architecture has always represented the prototype of a work of art the reception of which is consummated by a collectivity in a state of distraction. The laws of its reception are most instructive.

Buildings have been man's companions since primeval times. Many art forms have developed and perished. Tragedy begins with the Greeks, is extinguished with them, and after centuries its "rules" only are revived. The epic poem, which had its origin in the youth of nations, expires in Europe at the end of the Renaissance. Panel painting is a creation of the Middle Ages, and nothing guarantees its uninterrupted existence. But the human need for shelter is lasting. Architecture has never been idle. Its history is more ancient than that of any other art, and its claim to being a living force has significance in every attempt to comprehend the relationship of the masses to art. Buildings are appropriated in a twofold manner: by use and by perception—or rather, by touch and sight. Such appropriation cannot be understood in terms of the attentive concentration of a tourist before a famous building. On the tactile side there is no counterpart to contemplation on the optical side. Tactile appropriation is accomplished not so much by attention as by habit. As regards architecture, habit determines to a large extent even optical reception. The latter, too, occurs much less through rapt attention than by noticing the object in incidental fashion. This mode of appropriation, developed with reference to architecture, in certain circumstances acquires canonical value. For the tasks which face the human apparatus of perception at the turning points of history cannot be solved by optical means, that is, by contemplation, alone. They are mastered gradually by habit, under the guidance of tactile appropriation.

The distracted person, too, can form habits. More, the ability to master certain tasks in a state of distraction proves that their solution has become a matter of habit. Distraction as provided by art presents a covert control of the extent to which new tasks have become soluble by apperception. Since, moreover, individuals are tempted to avoid such tasks, art will tackle the most difficult and most important ones where it is able to mobilize the masses. Today it does so in the film. Reception in a state of distraction, which is increasing noticeably in all fields of art and is symptomatic of profound changes in apperception, finds in the film its true means of exercise. The film with its shock effect meets this mode of reception halfway. The film makes the cult value recede into the background not only by putting the public in the position of the critic, but also by the fact that at the movies this position requires no attention. The public is an examiner, but an absent-minded one.

---

[30] Duhamel, *op. cit.*, p. 58.—*Trans.*

Epilogue

The growing proletarianization of modern man and the increasing formation of masses are two aspects of the same process. Fascism attempts to organize the newly created proletarian masses without affecting the property structure which the masses strive to eliminate. Fascism sees its salvation in giving these masses not their right, but instead a chance to express themselves.[31] The masses have a right to change property relations; Fascism seeks to give them an expression while preserving property. The logical result of Fascism is the introduction of aesthetics into political life. The violation of the masses, whom Fascism, with its *Führer* cult, forces to their knees, has its counterpart in the violation of an apparatus which is pressed into the production of ritual values.

All efforts to render politics aesthetic culminate in one thing: war. War and war only can set a goal for mass movements on the largest scale while respecting the traditional property system. This is the political formula for the situation. The technological formula may be stated as follows: Only war makes it possible to mobilize all of today's technical resources while maintaining the property system. It goes without saying that the Fascist apotheosis of war does not employ such arguments. Still, Marinetti says in his manifesto on the Ethiopian colonial war: "For twenty-seven years we Futurists have rebelled against the branding of war as antiaesthetic.... Accordingly we state:... War is beautiful because it establishes man's dominion over the subjugated machinery by means of gas masks, terrifying megaphones, flame throwers, and small tanks. War is beautiful because it initiates the dreamt-of metallization of the human body. War is beautiful because it enriches a flowering meadow with the fiery orchids of machine guns. War is beautiful because it combines the gunfire, the cannonades, the cease-fire, the scents, and the stench of putrefaction into a symphony. War is beautiful because it creates new architecture, like that of the big tanks, the geometrical formation flights, the smoke spirals from burning villages, and many others.... Poets and artists of Futurism!... remember these principles of an aesthetics of war so that your struggle for a new literature and a new graphic art... may be illumined by them!"

This manifesto has the virtue of clarity. Its formulations deserve to be accepted by dialecticians. To the latter, the aesthetics of today's war appears as follows: If the natural utilization of productive forces is impeded by the property system, the increase in technical devices, in speed, and in the sources of energy will press for an unnatural utilization, and this is found in war. The destructiveness of war furnishes proof that society has not been mature enough to incorporate technology as its organ, that technology has not been sufficiently developed to cope with the elemental forces of society. The horrible features of imperialistic warfare are attributable to the discrepancy between the tremendous means of production and

[31] One technical feature is significant here, especially with regard to newsreels, the propagandist importance of which can hardly be overestimated. Mass reproduction is aided especially by the reproduction of masses. In big parades and monster rallies, in sports events, and in war, all of which nowadays are captured by camera and sound recording, the masses are brought face to face with themselves. This process, whose significance need not be stressed, is intimately connected with the development of the techniques of reproduction and photography. Mass movements are usually discerned more clearly by a camera than by the naked eye. A bird's-eye view best captures gatherings of hundreds of thousands. And even though such a view may be as accessible to the human eye as it is to the camera, the image received by the eye cannot be enlarged the way a negative is enlarged. This means that mass movements, including war, constitute a form of human behavior which particularly favors mechanical equipment.

their inadequate utilization in the process of production—in other words, to unemployment and the lack of markets. Imperialistic war is a rebellion of technology which collects, in the form of "human material," the claims to which society has denied its natural material. Instead of draining rivers, society directs a human stream into a bed of trenches; instead of dropping seeds from airplanes, it drops incendiary bombs over cities; and through gas warfare the aura is abolished in a new way.

"*Fiat ars—perat mundus*," says Fascism, and, as Marinetti admits, expects war to supply the artistic gratification of a sense perception that has been changed by technology. This is evidently the consummation of "*l'art pour l'art*." Mankind, which in Homer's time was an object of contemplation for the Olympian gods, now is one for itself. Its self-alienation has reached such a degree that it can experience its own destruction as an aesthetic pleasure of the first order. This is the situation of politics which Fascism is rendering aesthetic. Communism responds by politicizing art.

CHAPTER 19
MAX HORKHEIMER AND THEODOR W. ADORNO

Max Horkheimer (1895–1973) and Theodor Adorno (1903–1969) were German philosophers and sociologists instrumental in the early years of the Frankfurt School. They are regarded alongside a select few others as essential figures in that school of thought, and they collaborated in the writing of one of the core texts of Critical Theory, Dialectic of Enlightenment. *Both Horkheimer and Adorno addressed issues of politics, society, and culture in light of the German experience leading up to, during, and following the Second World War—and both were outspoken critics of fascism and all forms of authoritarianism. The selection included here, "The Culture Industry: Enlightenment as Mass Deception" ("Kulturindustrie—Aufklärung als Massenbetrug") is from* Dialectic of Enlightenment, *which was first published in German under the title* Philosophical Fragments *(*Philosophische Fragmente*) by Social Studies Association, Inc., in New York in 1944; a revised edition under the final title,* Dialektik der Aufklärung, *was published by Querido Verlag in Amsterdam in 1947.*

Horkheimer and Adorno begin their work with a consideration of the matter of greatest general concern to them, the rise and development of mass culture in the modern West. All mass culture, they argue, is identical: that is, across the various mass entertainment media (at the time of the writing of this selection, that meant radio, film, and magazines), there is a uniform system of presentation and representation. None of these media pretend any longer to be art; to take one example, Horkheimer and Adorno note, no one blanches any longer at the notion that the "film industry" is just that: a business. In the field of mass culture, as in most of the rest of the late capitalist industry, both standardization and mass production have been achieved. Whether automobiles, bombs, or movies, they note, society can produce multiple copies of the same thing quickly and efficiently and in a way that turns a profit. The idea underlying such industry—that consumer products can be provided to the masses, but that this requires everyone to purchase the same things—is, Horkheimer and Adorno say, the rationale of domination itself.

Their emphasis on domination would seem to imply that the consumers of mass culture are overtaken by the producers in a way that ought to seem controlling or oppressive, and purveyors of mass culture regularly argue that they are merely meeting the demands of the public: the industry can only sell what its customers are willing to buy, after all. This common argument places responsibility for the nature, content, and quality of the products of mass culture on ordinary consumers, but Horkheimer and Adorno suggest that, in fact, public desire for mass culture is itself one product of the system of mass culture itself. Which is to say, ultimately, that underlying the notion of any given product of culture being available for participation or purchase by the masses, there is the sense that culture itself is now a product being sold to the masses: that culture is itself an industry, mass producing cultural products across the various media. The culture industry is not isolated in the world economy, however: it depends almost entirely upon larger industries (Horkheimer and Adorno name, specifically, steel, petroleum, electricity, and chemicals).

Operating like any other industry, the culture industry markets its products to potential customers, and Horkheimer and Adorno note that the marketing of culture is organized in the manner of all propaganda. Despite the fact that there is no real difference between the products of different brands, each brand sells itself as unique among its peers. Thus, they say, the differences between the automobiles produced by Chrysler and General Motors aren't actually that different from each other, despite what the car commercials and car salespersons might tell you. A false difference is introduced as a means of each brand attempting to sell more cars than the other. Likewise, Horkheimer and Adorno suggest, the differences between the films produced by the Warner Brothers and Metro-Goldwyn-Mayer are not terribly significant, yet the sole means they have to compete for customers is to suggest that those differences are essential and important. Among other strategies, the major brands engage in what Horkheimer and Adorno call "conspicuous production," making more and more blatantly extravagant investments in their own products as a means of drumming up business.

Because the culture industry is an industry, and operates according to industrial standards, the effort is always primarily to sell products—not to create challenging or surprising new artworks. Thus, in the film industry in particular, we find that most movies produced are formulaic and predictable; nothing new or surprising ever happens, and in fact the same set of standardized clichés are slotted into various films as the filmmakers see fit, so that we view the same characters or plot elements over and over again in different movies. Everything in the film serves the formula, and the formula serves the bottom line. One consequence of the film industry, they write, is that real life and the movies are becoming indistinguishable from one another for the average filmgoer. By this, of course, they do not mean to say that filmgoers have trouble knowing whether they are watching a movie or having those experiences in their real lives. Rather, they mean to say that the pace at which the motion picture moves from event to event in order to satisfy the formula (and keep audiences distracted, as noted by Kracauer) prevents audience members from being able to stop and reflect on anything after they have seen it—because, in that moment, there is yet another thing to see. To follow the story the filmgoer must maintain him- or herself in a constant state of distraction (as noted by Benjamin), and as such are left with no room for contemplation or imagination. Filmgoers become mere receptacles for whatever the filmmakers seek to deliver, and the individuality of any given filmgoer is almost entirely overcome by this standardized, homogenizing cultural process.

The constant pressure on filmmakers to make new movies using exclusively the old patterns results in what Horkheimer and Adorno, borrowing from Nietzsche, call "stylized barbarity." Each work relies upon its similarity to other works for its own identity, such that novelty and uniqueness disappear and imitation becomes absolute: only by way of being like successful works that have come before can a new work achieve cultural success. Nothing is left at this point but style, since both content and form are constructed according to industrial standards based on what has sold before; but in such a rigorously policed art environment, style becomes little more than a means of achieving obedience to the existing social hierarchy. Everyone survives in late modern capitalism—whether in the culture industry or in other aspects of society—by fitting in. To fail to conform to the standards or to the formulas in place is to be excluded from participation in society, and thus to become totally powerless. Such an environment encourages nothing but the constant reproduction of the same.

When everything produced by the culture industry is the same, then audiences become mere consumers, and cannot be asked to think for themselves (lest they realize the lack of difference and cease making new purchases). Thus, to avoid boredom and to maintain a distracted public, films and other mass media must introduce more and varied surprises—new but meaningless variations on the formulas in circulation—and, given their meaninglessness, these surprises add little but nonsense to culture. The only pleasure to be found in cultural products of this sort, then, is in not thinking—a sort of helplessness that results from the fusion of culture and entertainment. And the ramifications of the culture industry extend beyond the bounds of art and culture, for Horkheimer and Adorno. The passive distractedness encouraged—required—by the culture industry diminishes the significance of individuality itself. People believe more and more that things "just happen," rather than attempting to understand their origins and causes, and resistance to the status quo comes to seem pointless. In such a society, those who fail to abide by the standards in place are immediately labeled "outsiders," and become suspicious; this role falls to no one more completely than it does to the poor or otherwise socioeconomically "unsuccessful."

In the absence of a strong sense of individuality, we come to have no identity beyond our class identity: we are what we earn. And since there is a clear formula for success in the public consciousness, those who succeed are understood to be superior to those who do not, and those who do not succeed are blamed for their lack of success. In this, Horkheimer and Adorno see the abolition of sympathy in Western societies. At its most extreme, a society in which sympathy has been abolished refers outsiders to concentration camps, or exterminates them outright. Of all the mass media, they think radio is the most thoroughly overtaken by these cultural trends, and is thus the perfect entertainment medium for fascism. Film, on the other hand, although moving in the same direction as radio, remains somewhat less thoroughly dominated by the culture industry (at least, at the time of the writing of the selection), and so we find some films still exhibiting liberal tendencies in the face of the social homogenization and repression otherwise characteristic of late modern capitalism. Television, as Horkheimer and Adorno see it, is a synthesis of radio and film—and thus one step closer to the fascistic tendencies of radio than film is. Thus, if there is hope among the arts of the mass media for resistance to fascism and the recuperation of the notion of the individual in the West, it seems it would be in the cinema.

Filmography

- ***The Great Dictator*** (USA, 1940). *Directed, Produced, Written by, and Starring* Charlie Chaplin.
- ***Mrs. Miniver*** (USA, 1942). *Directed by* William Wyler. *Produced by* Sidney Franklin. *Written by* Arthur Wimperis, George Froeschel, James Hilton, *and* Claudine West. *Starring* Greer Garson *and* Walter Pidgeon.

THE CULTURE INDUSTRY: ENLIGHTENMENT AS MASS DECEPTION

Translated by John Cumming

The sociological theory that the loss of the support of objectively established religion, the dissolution of the last remnants of precapitalism, together with technological and social differentiation or specialization, have led to cultural chaos is disproved every day; for culture now impresses the same stamp on everything. Films, radio and magazines make up a system which is uniform as a whole and in every part. Even the aesthetic activities of political opposites are one in their enthusiastic obedience to the rhythm of the iron system. The decorative industrial management buildings and exhibition centers in authoritarian countries are much the same as anywhere else. The huge gleaming towers that shoot up everywhere are outward signs of the ingenious planning of international concerns, toward which the unleashed entrepreneurial system (whose monuments are a mass of gloomy houses and business premises in grimy, spiritless cities) was already hastening. Even now the older houses just outside the concrete city centers look like slums, and the new bungalows on the outskirts are at one with the flimsy structures of world fairs in their praise of technical progress and their built-in demand to be discarded after a short while like empty food cans. Yet the city housing projects designed to perpetuate the individual as a supposedly independent unit in a small hygienic dwelling make him all the more subservient to his adversary—the absolute power of capitalism. Because the inhabitants, as producers and as consumers, are drawn into the center in search of work and pleasure, all the living units crystallize into well-organized complexes. The striking unity of microcosm and macrocosm presents men with a model of their culture: the false identity of the general and the particular. Under monopoly all mass culture is identical, and the lines of its artificial framework begin to show through. The people at the top are no longer so interested in concealing monopoly: as its violence becomes more open, so its power grows. Movies and radio need no longer pretend to be art. The truth that they are just business is made into an ideology in order to justify the rubbish they deliberately produce. They call themselves industries; and when their directors' incomes are published, any doubt about the social utility of the finished products is removed.

Interested parties explain the culture industry in technological terms. It is alleged that because millions participate in it, certain reproduction processes are necessary that inevitably require identical needs in innumerable places to be satisfied with identical goods. The technical contrast between the few production centers and the large number of widely dispersed consumption points is said to demand organization and planning by management. Furthermore, it is claimed that standards were based in the first place on consumers' needs, and for that reason were accepted with so little resistance. The result is the circle of manipulation and retroactive need in which the unity of the system grows ever stronger. No mention is made of the fact that the basis on which technology acquires power over society is the power of those whose economic hold over society is greatest. A technological rationale is the rationale of domination itself. Automobiles, bombs, and movies keep the whole thing together until their leveling element shows its strength in the very wrong which it furthered. It has made the technology of the culture industry no more than the achievement of standardization and mass production, sacrificing whatever involved a distinction between the logic of the work and that of the social system. This is the result not of a law of movement in technology as such but of its function in today's economy. The need which might resist central control has already been suppressed by the control of the individual consciousness. The step from the telephone to the radio has clearly distinguished the roles. The former still allowed the subscriber to play the role of subject, and was liberal. The latter is democratic: it turns all participants into listeners and authoritatively subjects them to broadcast programs which are all exactly the same. No machinery of rejoinder has been devised, and private broadcasters are denied any freedom. They are confined to the apocryphal field of the "amateur," and also have to accept organization from above. But any trace of spontaneity from the public in official broadcasting is controlled and absorbed by talent scouts, studio competitions and official programs of every kind selected by professionals. Talented performers belong to the industry long before it displays them; otherwise they would not be so eager to fit in. The attitude of the public, which ostensibly and actually favors the system of the culture industry, is a part of the system and not an excuse for it. If one branch of art follows the same formula as one with a very different medium and content; if the dramatic intrigue of broadcast soap operas becomes no more than useful material for showing how to master technical problems at both ends of the scale of musical experience—real jazz or a cheap imitation; or if a movement from a Beethoven symphony is crudely "adapted" for a film sound-track in the same way as a Tolstoy novel is garbled in a film script: then the claim that this is done to satisfy the spontaneous wishes of the public is no more than hot air. We are closer to the facts if we explain these phenomena as inherent in the technical and personnel apparatus which, down to its last cog, itself forms part of the economic mechanism of selection. In addition there is the agreement—or at least the determination—of all executive authorities not to produce or sanction anything that in any way differs from their own rules, their own ideas about consumers, or above all themselves.

In our age the objective social tendency is incarnate in the hidden subjective purposes of company directors, the foremost among whom are in the most powerful sectors of industry—steel, petroleum, electricity, and chemicals. Culture monopolies are weak and dependent in comparison. They cannot afford to neglect their appeasement of the real holders of power if their sphere of activity in mass society (a sphere producing a specific type of commodity which anyhow is still too closely bound up with easygoing liberalism and Jewish intellectuals) is not to undergo a series of purges. The dependence of the most powerful broadcasting company on the electrical industry, or of the motion picture industry on the banks, is characteristic of the whole sphere, whose individual branches are themselves economically interwoven. All are in such close contact that the extreme concentration of mental forces allows demarcation lines between different firms and technical branches to be ignored. The ruthless unity in the culture industry is evidence of what will happen in politics. Marked differentiations such as those of A and B films, or of stories in magazines in different price ranges, depend not so much on subject matter as on classifying, organizing, and labeling consumers. Something is provided for all so that none may escape; the distinctions are emphasized and extended. The public is catered for with a hierarchical range of mass-produced products of varying quality, thus advancing the rule of complete quantification. Everybody must behave (as if spontaneously) in accordance with his previously determined and indexed level, and choose the category of mass product turned out for his type. Consumers appear as statistics on research organization charts, and are divided by income groups into red, green, and blue areas; the technique is that used for any type of propaganda.

How formalized the procedure is can be seen when the mechanically differentiated products prove to be all alike in the end. That the difference between the Chrysler range and General Motors products is basically illusory strikes every child with a keen interest in varieties. What connoisseurs discuss as good or bad points serve only to perpetuate the semblance of competition and range of choice. The same applies to the Warner Brothers and Metro Goldwyn Mayer productions. But even the differences between the more expensive and cheaper models put out by the same firm steadily diminish: for automobiles, there are such differences as the number of cylinders, cubic capacity, details of patented gadgets; and for films there are the number of stars, the extravagant use of technology, labor, and equipment, and the introduction of the latest psychological formulas. The universal criterion of merit is the amount of "conspicuous production," of blatant cash investment. The varying budgets in the culture industry do not bear the slightest relation to factual values, to the meaning of the products themselves. Even the technical media are relentlessly forced into uniformity. Television aims at a synthesis of radio and film, and is held up only because the interested parties have not yet reached agreement, but its consequences will be quite enormous and promise to intensify the impoverishment of aesthetic matter so drastically, that by tomorrow the thinly veiled identity of all industrial culture products can come triumphantly out into the open, derisively fulfilling the Wagnerian dream of the *Gesamtkunstwerk*—the fusion of all the arts in one work. The alliance of word, image, and music is all the more perfect than in *Tristan* because the sensuous elements which all approvingly reflect the surface of social reality are in principle embodied in the same technical process, the unity of which becomes its distinctive content. This process integrates all the elements of the production, from the novel (shaped with an eye to the film) to the last sound effect. It is the triumph of invested capital, whose title as absolute master is etched deep into the hearts of the dispossessed in the employment line; it is the meaningful content of every film, whatever plot the production team may have selected.

The man with leisure has to accept what the culture manufacturers offer him. Kant's formalism still expected a contribution from the individual, who was thought to relate the varied experiences of the senses to fundamental concepts; but industry robs the individual of his function. Its prime service to the customer is to do his schematizing for him. Kant said that there was a secret mechanism in the soul which prepared direct intuitions in such a way that they could be fitted into the system of pure reason. But today that secret has been deciphered. While the mechanism is to all appearances planned by those who serve up the data of experience, that is, by the culture industry, it is in fact forced upon the latter by the power of society, which remains irrational, however we may try to rationalize it; and this inescapable force is processed by commercial agencies so that they give an artificial impression of being in command. There is nothing left for the consumer to classify. Producers have done it for him. Art for the masses has destroyed the dream but still conforms to the tenets of that dreaming idealism which critical idealism balked at. Everything derives from consciousness: for Malebranche and Berkeley, from the consciousness of God; in mass art, from the consciousness of the production team. Not only are the hit songs, stars, and soap operas cyclically recurrent and rigidly invariable types, but the specific content of the entertainment itself is derived from them and only appears to change. The details are interchangeable. The short interval sequence which was effective in a hit song, the hero's momentary fall from grace (which he accepts as good sport), the rough treatment which the beloved gets from the male star, the latter's rugged defiance of the spoilt heiress, are, like all the other details, ready-made clichés to be slotted in anywhere; they never do anything more than fulfill the purpose allotted them in the overall plan. Their whole *raison d'être* is to confirm it by being its constituent parts. As soon as the film begins, it is quite clear how it will end, and who will be rewarded, punished, or forgotten. In light music, once the trained ear has heard the first notes of the hit song, it can guess what is coming and feel flattered when it does come. The average length of the short story has to be rigidly adhered to. Even gags, effects, and jokes are calculated like the setting in which they are placed. They are the responsibility of special experts and their narrow range makes it easy for them to be apportioned in the office. The development of the culture industry has led to the predominance of the effect, the obvious touch, and the technical detail over the work itself—which once expressed an idea, but was liquidated together with the idea. When the detail won its freedom, it became rebellious and, in the period from Romanticism to Expressionism, asserted itself as free expression, as a vehicle of protest against the organization. In music the single harmonic effect obliterated the awareness of form as a whole; in painting the individual color was stressed at the expense of pictorial composition; and in the novel psychology became more important than structure. The totality of the culture industry has put an end to this. Though concerned exclusively with effects, it crushes their insubordination and makes them subserve the formula, which replaces the work. The same fate is inflicted on whole and parts alike. The whole inevitably bears no relation to the details—just like the career of a successful man into which everything is made to fit as an illustration or a proof, whereas it is nothing more than the sum of all those idiotic events. The so-called dominant idea is like a file which ensures order but not coherence. The whole and the parts are alike; there is no antithesis and no connection. Their prearranged harmony is a mockery of what had to be striven after in the great bourgeois works of art. In Germany the graveyard stillness of the dictatorship already hung over the gayest films of the democratic era.

The whole world is made to pass through the filter of the culture industry. The old experience of the movie-goer, who sees the world outside as an extension of the film he has just left (because the latter is intent upon reproducing the world of everyday perceptions), is now the producer's guideline. The more intensely and flawlessly his techniques duplicate empirical objects, the easier it is today for the illusion to prevail that the outside world is the straightforward continuation of that presented on the screen. This purpose has been furthered by mechanical reproduction since the lightning takeover by the sound film.

Real life is becoming indistinguishable from the movies. The sound film, far surpassing the theater of illusion, leaves no room for imagination or reflection on the part of the audience, who is unable to respond within the structure of the film, yet deviate from its precise detail without losing the thread of the story; hence the film forces its victims to equate it directly with reality. The stunting of the mass-media consumer's powers of imagination and spontaneity does not have to be traced back to any psychological mechanisms; he must ascribe the loss of those attributes to the objective nature of the products themselves, especially to the most characteristic of them, the sound film. They are so designed that quickness, powers of observation, and experience are undeniably needed to apprehend them at all; yet sustained thought is out of the question if the spectator is not to miss the relentless rush of facts. Even though the effort required for his response is semi-automatic, no scope is left for the imagination. Those who are so absorbed by the world of the movie—by its images, gestures, and words—that they are unable to supply what really makes it a world, do not have to dwell on particular points of its mechanics during a screening. All the other films and products of the entertainment industry which they have seen have taught them what to expect; they react automatically. The might of industrial society is lodged in men's minds. The entertainments manufacturers know that their products will be consumed with alertness even when the customer is distraught, for each of them is a model of the huge economic machinery which has always sustained the masses, whether at work or at leisure—which is akin to work. From every sound film and every broadcast program the social effect can be inferred which is exclusive to none but is shared by all alike. The culture industry as a whole has molded men as a type unfailingly reproduced in every product. All the agents of this process, from the producer to the women's clubs, take good care that the simple reproduction of this mental state is not nuanced or extended in any way.

The art historians and guardians of culture who complain of the extinction in the West of a basic style-determining power are wrong. The stereotyped appropriation of everything, even the inchoate, for the purposes of mechanical reproduction surpasses the rigor and general currency of any "real style," in the sense in which cultural *cognoscenti* celebrate the organic precapitalist past. No Palestrina could be more of a purist in eliminating every unprepared and unresolved discord than the jazz arranger in suppressing any development which does not conform to the jargon. When jazzing up Mozart he changes him not only when he is too serious or too difficult but when he harmonizes the melody in a different way, perhaps more simply, than is customary now. No medieval builder can have scrutinized the subjects for church windows and sculptures more suspiciously than the studio hierarchy scrutinizes a work by Balzac or Hugo before finally approving it. No medieval theologian could have determined the degree of the torment to be suffered by the damned in accordance with the *ordo* of divine love more meticulously than the producers of shoddy epics calculate the torture to be undergone by the hero or the exact point to which the leading lady's hemline shall be raised. The explicit and implicit, exoteric and esoteric catalog of the forbidden and tolerated is so extensive that it not only defines the area of freedom but is all-powerful inside it. Everything down to the last detail is shaped accordingly. Like its counterpart, avant-garde art, the entertainment industry determines its own language, down to its very syntax and vocabulary, by the use of anathema. The constant pressure to produce new effects (which must conform to the old pattern) serves merely as another rule to increase the power of the conventions when any single effect threatens to slip through the net. Every detail is so firmly stamped with sameness that nothing can appear which is not marked at birth, or does not meet with approval at first sight. And the star performers, whether they produce or reproduce, use this jargon as freely and fluently and with as much gusto as if it were the very language which it silenced long ago. Such is the ideal of what is natural in this field of activity, and its influence becomes all the more powerful, the more technique is perfected and diminishes the tension between the finished product and everyday life. The paradox of this routine, which is essentially travesty, can be detected and is often predominant in everything that the culture industry turns out. A jazz musician who is playing a piece of serious music, one of Beethoven's simples minuets, syncopates it involuntarily and will smile superciliously when asked to follow the normal divisions of the beat. This is the "nature" which, complicated by the ever-present and extravagant demands of the specific medium, constitutes the new style and is a "system of non-culture, to which one might even concede a certain 'unity of style' if it really made any sense to speak of stylized barbarity."[1]

The universal imposition of this stylized mode can even go beyond what is quasi-officially sanctioned or forbidden; today a hit song is more readily forgiven for not observing the 32 beats or the compass of the ninth than for containing even the most clandestine melodic or harmonic detail which does not conform to the idiom. Whenever Orson Welles offends against the tricks of the trade, he is forgiven because his departures from the norm are regarded as calculated mutations which serve all the more strongly to confirm the validity of the system. The constraint of the technically-conditioned idiom which stars and directors have to produce as "nature" so that the people can appropriate it, extends to such fine nuances that they almost attain the subtlety of the devices of an avant-garde work as against those of truth. The rare capacity minutely to fulfill the obligations of the natural idiom in all branches of the culture industry becomes the criterion of efficiency. What and how they say it must be measurable by everyday language, as in logical positivism. The producers are experts. The idiom demands an astounding productive power, which it absorbs and squanders. In a diabolical way it has overreached the culturally conservative distinction between genuine and artificial style. A style might be called artificial which is imposed from without on the refractory impulses of a form. But in the culture industry every element of the subject matter has its origin in the same apparatus as that jargon whose stamp it bears. The quarrels in which the artistic experts become involved with sponsor and censor about a lie going beyond the bounds of credibility are evidence not so much of an inner aesthetic tension as of a divergence of interests. The reputation of the specialist, in which a last remnant of objective independence sometimes finds refuge, conflicts with the business politics of the Church, or the concern which is manufacturing the cultural commodity. But the thing itself has been essentially objectified and made viable before the established authorities began to argue about it. Even before Zanuck acquired her, Saint Bernadette was regarded by her latter-day hagiographer as brilliant propaganda for all interested parties. That is what became of the emotions of the character. Hence the style of the culture industry, which no longer has to test itself against any refractory material, is also the negation of style. The reconciliation of the general and particular, of the rule and the specific demands of the subject matter, the achievement of which alone gives essential, meaningful content to style, is futile because there has ceased to be the slightest tension between opposite poles: these concordant extremes are dismally identical; the general can replace the particular, and vice versa.

Nevertheless, this caricature of style does not amount to something beyond the genuine style of the past. In the culture industry the notion of genuine style is seen to be the aesthetic equivalent of domination. Style considered as mere aesthetic regularity is a romantic dream of the past. The unity of style not only of the Christian Middle Ages but of the Renaissance expresses in each case the different structure of social power, and not the obscure experience of the oppressed in which the general was enclosed. The great artists were never those who embodied a wholly flawless and perfect style, but those who used style as a way of hardening

[1] Nietzsche, *Unzeitgemässe Betrachtungen*, *Werke*, Vol. I (Leipzig, 1917), p. 187.

themselves against the chaotic expression of suffering, as a negative truth. The style of their works gave what was expressed that force without which life flows away unheard. Those very art forms which are known as classical, such as Mozart's music, contain objective trends which represent something different to the style which they incarnate. As late as Schönberg and Picasso, the great artists have retained a mistrust of style, and at crucial points have subordinated it to the logic of the matter. What Dadaists and Expressionists called the untruth of style as such triumphs today in the sung jargon of a crooner, in the carefully contrived elegance of a film star, and even in the admirable expertise of a photograph of a peasant's squalid hut. Style represents a promise in every work of art. That which is expressed is subsumed through style into the dominant forms of generality, into the language of music, painting, or words, in the hope that it will be reconciled thus with the idea of true generality. This promise held out by the work of art that it will create truth by lending new shape to the conventional social forms is as necessary as it is hypocritical. It unconditionally posits the real forms of life as it is by suggesting that fulfillment lies in their aesthetic derivatives. To this extent the claim of art is always ideology too. However, only in this confrontation with tradition of which style is the record can art express suffering. That factor in a work of art which enables it to transcend reality certainly cannot be detached from style; but it does not consist of the harmony actually realized, of any doubtful unity of form and content, within and without, of individual and society; it is to be found in those features in which discrepancy appears: in the necessary failure of the passionate striving for identity. Instead of exposing itself to this failure in which the style of the great work of art has always achieved self-negation, the inferior work has always relied on its similarity with others—on a surrogate identity.

In the culture industry this imitation finally becomes absolute. Having ceased to be anything but style, it reveals the latter's secret: obedience to the social hierarchy. Today aesthetic barbarity completes what has threatened the creations of the spirit since they were gathered together as culture and neutralized. To speak of culture was always contrary to culture. Culture as a common denominator already contains in embryo that schematization and process of cataloging and classification which bring culture within the sphere of administration. And it is precisely the industrialized, the consequent, subsumption which entirely accords with this notion of culture. By subordinating in the same way and to the same end all areas of intellectual creation, by occupying men's senses from the time they leave the factory in the evening to the time they clock in again the next morning with matter that bears the impress of the labor process they themselves have to sustain throughout the day, this subsumption mockingly satisfies the concept of a unified culture which the philosophers of personality contrasted with mass culture.

And so the culture industry, the most rigid of all styles, proves to be the goal of liberalism, which is reproached for its lack of style. Not only do its categories and contents derive from liberalism—domesticated naturalism as well as operetta and revue—but the modern culture monopolies form the economic area in which, together with the corresponding entrepreneurial types, for the time being some part of its sphere of operation survives, despite the process of disintegration elsewhere. It is still possible to make one's way in entertainment, if one is not too obstinate about one's own concerns, and proves appropriately pliable. Anyone who resists can only survive by fitting in. Once his particular brand of deviation from the norm has been noted by the industry, he belongs to it as does the land-reformer to capitalism. Realistic dissidence is the trademark of anyone who has a new idea in business. In the public voice of modern society accusations are seldom audible; if they are, the perceptive can already detect signs that the dissident will soon be reconciled. The more immeasurable the gap between chorus and leaders, the more certainly there is room at the top for everybody who demonstrates his superiority by well-planned originality. Hence, in the culture industry, too, the liberal tendency to give full scope to its able men survives. To do this for the efficient today is still the function of the market, which is otherwise proficiently controlled; as for the market's freedom, in the high period of art as elsewhere, it was freedom for the stupid to starve. Significantly, the system of the culture industry comes from the more liberal industrial nations, and all its characteristic media, such as movies, radio, jazz, and magazines, flourish there. Its progress, to be sure, had its origin in the general laws of capital. Gaumont and Pathé, Ullstein and Hugenberg followed the international trend with some success; Europe's economic dependence on the United States after war and inflation was a contributory factor. The belief that the barbarity of the culture industry is a result of "cultural lag," of the fact that the American consciousness did not keep up with the growth of technology, is quite wrong. It was pre-Fascist Europe which did not keep up with the trend toward the culture monopoly. But it was this very lag which left intellect and creativity some degree of independence and enabled its last representatives to exist—however dismally. In Germany the failure of democratic control to permeate life had led to a paradoxical situation. Many things were exempt from the market mechanism which had invaded the Western countries. The German educational system, universities, theaters with artistic standards, great orchestras, and museums enjoyed protection. The political powers, state and municipalities, which had inherited such institutions from absolutism, had left them with a measure of the freedom from the forces of power which dominates the market, just as princes and feudal lords had done up to the nineteenth century. This strengthened art in this late phase against the verdict of supply and demand, and increased its resistance far beyond the actual degree of protection. In the market itself the tribute of a quality for which no use had been found was turned into purchasing power; in this way, respectable literary and music publishers could help authors who yielded little more in the way of profit than the respect of the connoisseur. But what completely fettered the artist was the pressure (and the accompanying drastic threats), always to fit into business life as an aesthetic expert. Formerly, like Kant and Hume, they signed their letters "Your must humble and obedient servant," and undermined the foundations of throne and altar. Today they address heads of government by their first names, yet in every artistic activity they are subject to their illiterate masters. The analysis Tocqueville offered a century ago has in the meantime proved wholly accurate. Under the private culture monopoly it is a fact that "tyranny leaves the body free and directs its attack at the soul. The ruler no longer says: You must think as I do or die. He says: You are free not to think as I do; your life, your property, everything shall remain yours, but from this day on you are a stranger among us."[2] Not to conform means to be rendered powerless, economically and therefore spiritually—to be "self-employed." When the outsider is excluded from the concern, he can only too easily be accused of incompetence. Whereas today in material production the mechanism of supply and demand is disintegrating, in the superstructure it still operates as a check in the rulers' favor. The consumers are the workers and employees, the farmers and lower middle class. Capitalist production so confines them, body and soul, that they fall

[2] Alexis de Tocqueville, *De la Démocratie en Amérique*, Vol. II (Paris, 1864), p. 151.

helpless victims to what is offered them. As naturally as the ruled always took the morality imposed upon them more seriously than did the rulers themselves, the deceived masses are today captivated by the myth of success even more than the successful are. Immovably, they insist on the very ideology which enslaves them. The misplaced love of the common people for the wrong which is done them is a greater force than the cunning of the authorities. It is stronger even than the rigorism of the Hays Office, just as in certain great times in history it has inflamed greater forces that were turned against it, namely, the terror of the tribunals. It calls for Mickey Rooney in preference to the tragic Garbo, for Donald Duck instead of Betty Boop. The industry submits to the vote which it has itself inspired. What is a loss for the firm which cannot fully exploit a contract with a declining star is a legitimate expense for the system as a whole. By craftily sanctioning the demand for rubbish it inaugurates total harmony. The connoisseur and the expert are despised for their pretentious claim to know better than the others, even though culture is democratic and distributes its privileges to all. In view of the ideological truce, the conformism of the buyers and the effrontery of the producers who supply them prevail. The result is a constant reproduction of the same thing.

A constant sameness governs the relationship to the past as well. What is new about the phase of mass culture compared with the late liberal stage is the exclusion of the new. The machine rotates on the same spot. While determining consumption it excludes the untried as a risk. The movie-makers distrust any manuscript which is not reassuringly backed by a bestseller. Yet for this very reason there is never-ending talk of ideas, novelty, and surprise, of what is taken for granted but has never existed. Tempo and dynamics serve this trend. Nothing remains as of old; everything has to run incessantly, to keep moving. For only the universal triumph of the rhythm of mechanical production and reproduction promises that nothing changes, and nothing unsuitable will appear. Any additions to the well-proven culture inventory are too much of a speculation. The ossified forms—such as the sketch, short story, problem film, or hit song—are the standardized average of late liberal taste, dictated with threats from above. The people at the top in the culture agencies, who work in harmony as only one manager can with another, whether he comes from the rag trade or from college, have long since reorganized and rationalized the objective spirit. One might think that an omnipresent authority had sifted the material and drawn up an official catalog of cultural commodities to provide a smooth supply of available mass-produced lines. The ideas are written in the cultural firmament where they had already been numbered by Plato—and were indeed numbers, incapable of increase and immutable.

Amusement and all the elements of the culture industry existed long before the latter came into existence. Now they are taken over from above and brought up to date. The culture industry can pride itself on having energetically executed the previously clumsy transposition of art into the sphere of consumption, on making this a principle, on divesting amusement of its obtrusive naïvetés and improving the type of commodities. The more absolute it became, the more ruthless it was in forcing every outsider either into bankruptcy or into a syndicate, and became more refined and elevated—until it ended up as a synthesis of Beethoven and the Casino de Paris. It enjoys a double victory: the truth it extinguishes without it can reproduce at will as a lie within. "Light" art as such, distraction, is not a decadent form. Anyone who complains that it is a betrayal of the ideal of pure expression is under an illusion about society. The purity of bourgeois art, which hypostasized itself as a world of freedom in contrast to what was happening in the material world, was from the beginning bought with the exclusion of the lower classes—with whose cause, the real universality, art keeps faith precisely by its freedom from the ends of the false universality. Serious art has been withheld from those for whom the hardship and oppression of life make a mockery of seriousness, and who must be glad if they can use time not spent at the production line just to keep going. Light art has been the shadow of autonomous art. It is the social bad conscience of serious art. The truth which the latter necessarily lacked because of its social premises gives the other the semblance of legitimacy. The division itself is the truth: it does at least express the negativity of the culture which the different spheres constitute. Least of all can the antithesis be reconciled by absorbing light into serious art, or vice versa. But that is what the culture industry attempts. The eccentricity of the circus, peepshow, and brothel is as embarrassing to it as that of Schönberg and Karl Kraus. And so the jazz musician Benny Goodman appears with the Budapest string quartet, more pedantic rhythmically than any philharmonic clarinetist, while the style of the Budapest players is as uniform and sugary as that of Guy Lombardo. But what is significant is not vulgarity, stupidity, and lack of polish. The culture industry did away with yesterday's rubbish by its own perfection, and by forbidding and domesticating the amateurish, although it constantly allows gross blunders without which the standard of the exalted style cannot be perceived. But what is new is that the irreconcilable elements of culture, art and distraction, are subordinated to one end and subsumed under one false formula: the totality of the culture industry. It consists of repetition. That its characteristic innovations are never anything more than improvements of mass reproduction is not external to the system. It is with good reason that the interest of innumerable consumers is directed to the technique, and not to the contents—which are stubbornly repeated, outworn, and by now half-discredited. The social power which the spectators worship shows itself more effectively in the omnipresence of the stereotype imposed by technical skill than in the stale ideologies for which the ephemeral contents stand in.

Nevertheless the culture industry remains the entertainment business. Its influence over the consumers is established by entertainment; that will ultimately be broken not by an outright decree, but by the hostility inherent in the principle of entertainment to what is greater than itself. Since all the trends of the culture industry are profoundly embedded in the public by the whole social process, they are encouraged by the survival of the market in this area. Demand has not yet been replaced by simple obedience. As is well known, the major reorganization of the film industry shortly before World War I, the material prerequisite of its expansion, was precisely its deliberate acceptance of the public's needs as recorded at the box-office—a procedure which was hardly thought necessary in the pioneering days of the screen. The same opinion is held today by the captains of the film industry, who take as their criterion the more or less phenomenal song hits but wisely never have recourse to the judgment of truth, the opposite criterion. Business is their ideology. It is quite correct that the power of the culture industry resides in its identification with a manufactured need, and not in simple contrast to it, even if this contrast were one of complete power and complete powerlessness. Amusement under late capitalism is the prolongation of work. It is sought after as an escape from the mechanized work process, and to recruit strength in order to be able to cope with it again. But at the same time mechanization has such power over a man's leisure and happiness, and so profoundly determines the manufacture of amusement goods, that his experiences are inevitably after-images of the work process itself. The ostensible content is merely a faded foreground; what sinks in is the automatic succession of standardized operations. What happens at work, in the factory, or in the office can only be escaped from by approximation to it in one's leisure time. All amusement suffers from this incurable malady. Pleasure hardens into boredom because, if it is to remain pleasure, it must not demand any effort and therefore moves rigorously in the worn grooves of association. No independent thinking must be expected from the audience: the product prescribes every reaction: not by its natural structure (which collapses under reflection), but by signals. Any logical connection calling for mental effort is painstakingly avoided. As far as possible, developments must follow from the immediately preceding situation and never from the idea of the whole. For the attentive movie-goer any individual scene will give him the whole thing. Even the set pattern itself still seems dangerous, offering some meaning—wretched as it might be—where only meaninglessness is acceptable. Often the plot is maliciously deprived of the development demanded by characters and matter according to the old pattern. Instead, the next step is what the script writer takes to be the most striking effect in the particular situation. Banal though elaborate surprise interrupts the story-line. The tendency mischievously to fall back on pure nonsense, which was a legitimate part of popular art, farce and clowning, right up to Chaplin and the Marx Brothers, is most obvious in the unpretentious kinds. This tendency has completely asserted itself in the text of the novelty song, in the thriller movie, and in cartoons, although in films starring Greer Garson and Bette Davis the unity of the socio-psychological case study provides something approximating a claim to a consistent plot. The idea itself, together with the objects of comedy and terror, is massacred and fragmented. Novelty songs have always existed on a contempt for meaning which, as predecessors and successors of psychoanalysis, they reduce to the monotony of sexual symbolism. Today detective and adventure films no longer give the audience the opportunity to experience the resolution. In the non-ironic varieties of the genre, it has also to rest content with the simple horror of situations which have almost ceased to be linked in any way.

Cartoons were once exponents of fantasy as opposed to rationalism. They ensured that justice was done to the creatures and objects they electrified, by giving the maimed specimens a second life. All they do today is to confirm the victory of technological reason over truth. A few years ago they had a consistent plot which only broke up in the final moments in a crazy chase, and thus resembled the old slapstick comedy. Now, however, time relations have shifted. In the very first sequence a motive is stated so that in the course of the action destruction can get to work on it: with the audience in pursuit, the protagonist becomes the worthless object of general violence. The quantity of organized amusement changes into the quality of organized cruelty. The self-elected censors of the film industry (with whom it enjoys a close relationship) watch over the unfolding of the crime, which is as drawn-out as a hunt. Fun replaces the pleasure which the sight of an embrace would allegedly afford, and postpones satisfaction till the day of the pogrom. In so far as cartoons do any more than accustom the sense to the new tempo, they hammer into every brain the old lesson that continuous friction, the breaking down of all individual resistance, is the condition of life in this society. Donald Duck in the cartoons and the unfortunate in real life get their thrashing so that the audience can learn to take their own punishment.

The enjoyment of the violence suffered by the movie character turns into violence against the spectator, and distraction into exertion. Nothing that the experts have devised as a stimulant must escape the weary eye; no stupidity is allowed in the face of all the trickery; one has to follow everything and even display the smart responses shown and recommended in the film. This raises the question whether the culture industry fulfills the function of diverting minds which it boasts about so loudly. If most of the radio stations and movie theaters were closed down, the consumers would probably not lose so very much. To walk from the street into the movie theater is no longer to enter a world of dream; as soon as the very existence of these institutions no longer made it obligatory to use them, there would be no great urge to do so. Such closures would not be reactionary machine wrecking. The disappointment would be felt not so much by the enthusiasts as by the slow-witted, who are the ones who suffer for everything anyhow. In spite of the films which are intended to complete her integration, the housewife finds in the darkness of the movie theater a place of refuge where she can sit for a few hours with nobody watching, just as she used to look out of the window when there were still homes and rest in the evening. The unemployed in the great cities find coolness in summer and warmth in winter in these temperature-controlled locations. Otherwise, despite its size, this bloated pleasure apparatus adds no dignity to man's lives. The idea of "fully exploiting" available technical resources and the facilities for aesthetic mass consumption is part of the economic system which refuses to exploit resources to abolish hunger.

The culture industry perpetually cheats its consumers of what it perpetually promises. The promissory note which, with its plots and staging, it draws on pleasure is endlessly prolonged; the promise, which is actually all the spectacle consists of, is illusory: all it actually confirms is that the real point will never be reached, that the diner must be satisfied with the menu. In front of the appetite stimulated by all those brilliant names and images there is finally set no more than a commendation of the depressing everyday world it sought to escape. Of course works of art were not sexual exhibitions either. However, by representing deprivation as negative, they retracted, as it were, the prostitution of the impulse and rescued by mediation what was denied. The secret of aesthetic sublimation is its representation of fulfillment as a broken promise. The culture industry does not sublimate; it represses. By repeatedly exposing the objects of desire, breasts in a clinging sweater or the naked torso of the athletic hero, it only stimulates the unsublimated forepleasure which habitual deprivation has long since reduced to a masochistic semblance. There is no erotic situation which, while insinuating and exciting, does not fail to indicate unmistakably that things can never go that far. The Hays Office merely confirms the ritual of Tantalus that the culture industry has established anyway. Works of art are ascetic and unashamed; the culture industry is pornographic and prudish. Love is downgraded to romance. And, after the descent, much is permitted; even license as a marketable specialty has its quota bearing the trade description "daring." The mass production of the sexual automatically achieves its repression. Because of his ubiquity, the film star with whom one is meant to fall in love is from the outset a copy of himself. Every tenor voice comes to sound like a Caruso record, and the "natural" faces of Texas girls are like the successful models by whom Hollywood has typecast them. The mechanical reproduction of beauty, which reactionary cultural fanaticism wholeheartedly serves in its methodical idolization of individuality, leaves no room for that unconscious idolatry which was once essential to beauty. The triumph over beauty is celebrated by humor—the *Schadenfreude* that every successful deprivation calls forth. There is laughter because there is nothing to laugh at. Laughter, whether conciliatory or terrible, always occurs when some fear passes. It indicates liberation either from physical danger or from the grip of logic. Conciliatory laughter is heard as the echo of an escape from power; the wrong kind overcomes fear by capitulating to the forces which are to be feared. It is the echo of power as something inescapable. Fun is a medicinal bath. The pleasure industry never fails to prescribe it. It makes laughter the instrument of the fraud practiced on happiness. Moments of happiness are without laughter; only operettas and films portray sex to the accompaniment of resounding laughter. But Baudelaire is as devoid of humor as Hölderlin. In the false society laughter is a disease which has attacked happiness and is drawing it into its worthless totality. To laugh at something is always to deride it, and the life which, according to Bergson, in laughter breaks through the barrier, is actually an invading barbaric life, self-assertion prepared to parade its liberation from any scruple when the social occasion arises. Such a laughing audience is a parody of humanity. Its members are monads, all dedicated to the pleasure of being ready for anything at the expense of everyone else. Their harmony is a caricature of solidarity. What is fiendish about this false laughter is that it is a compelling parody of the best, which is conciliatory. Delight is austere: *res severa verum gaudium*. The monastic theory that not asceticism but the sexual act denotes the renunciation of attainable bliss receives negative confirmation in the gravity of the lover who with foreboding commits his life to the fleeting moment. In the culture industry, jovial denial takes the place of the pain found in ecstasy and in asceticism. The supreme law is that they shall not satisfy their desires at any price; they must laugh and be content with laughter. In every product of the culture industry, the permanent denial imposed by civilization is once again unmistakably demonstrated and inflicted on its victims. To offer and to deprive them of something is one and the same. This is what happens in erotic films. Precisely because it must never take place, everything centers upon copulation. In films it is more strictly forbidden for an illegitimate relationship to be admitted without the parties being punished than for a millionaire's future son-in-law to be active in the labor movement. In contrast to the liberal era, industrialized as well as popular culture may wax indignant at capitalism, but it cannot renounce the threat of castration. This is fundamental. It outlasts the organized acceptance of the uniformed seen in the films which are produced to that end, and in reality. What is decisive today is no longer puritanism, although it still asserts itself in the form of women's organizations, but the necessity inherent in the system not to leave the customer alone, not for a moment to allow him any suspicion that resistance is possible. The principle dictates that he should be shown all his needs as capable of fulfillment, but that those needs should be so predetermined that he feels himself to be the eternal consumer, the object of the culture industry. Not only does it make him believe that the deception it practices is satisfaction, but it goes further and implies that, whatever the state of affairs, he must put up with what is offered. The escape from everyday drudgery which the whole culture industry promises may be compared to the daughter's abduction in the cartoon: the father is holding the ladder in the dark. The paradise offered by the culture industry is the same old drudgery. Both escape and elopement are predesigned to lead back to the starting point. Pleasure promotes the resignation which it ought to help to forget.

Amusement, if released from every restraint, would not only be the antithesis of art but its extreme role. The Mark Twain absurdity with which the American culture industry flirts at times might be a corrective of art. The more seriously the latter regards the incompatibility with life, the more it resembles the seriousness of life, its antithesis; the more effort it devotes to developing wholly from its own formal law, the more effort it demands from the intelligence to neutralize its burden. In some revue films, and especially in the grotesque and the funnies, the possibility of this negation does glimmer for a few moments. But of course it cannot happen. Pure amusement in its consequence, relaxed self-surrender to all kinds of associations and happy nonsense, is cut short by the amusement on the market: instead, it is interrupted by a surrogate overall meaning which the culture industry insists on giving to its products, and yet misuses as a mere pretext for bringing in the stars. Biographies and other simple stories patch the fragments of nonsense into an idiotic plot. We do not have the cap and bells of the jester but the bunch of keys of capitalist reason, which even screens the pleasure of achieving success. Every kiss in the revue film has to contribute to the career of the boxer, or some hit song expert or other whose rise to fame is being glorified. The deception is not that the culture industry supplies amusement but that it ruins the fun by allowing business considerations to involve it in the ideological clichés of a culture in the process of self-liquidation. Ethics and taste cut short unrestrained amusement as "naïve"—naïveté is thought to be as bad as intellectualism—and even restrict technical possibilities. The culture industry is corrupt; not because it is a sinful Babylon but because it is a cathedral dedicated to elevated pleasure. On all levels, from Hemingway to Emil Ludwig, from Mrs. Miniver to the Lone Ranger, from Toscanini to Guy Lombardo, there is untruth in the intellectual content taken ready-made from art and science. The culture industry does retain a trace of something better in those features which bring it close to the circus, in the self-justifying and nonsensical skill of riders, acrobats and clowns, in the "defense and justification of physical as against intellectual art."[3] But the refuges of a mindless artistry which represents what is human as opposed to the social mechanism are being relentlessly hunted down by a schematic reason which compels everything to prove its significance and effect. The consequence is that the nonsensical at the bottom disappears as utterly as the sense in works of art at the top.

The fusion of culture and entertainment that is taking place today leads not only to a depravation of culture, but inevitably to an intellectualization of amusement. This is evident from the fact that only the copy appears: in the movie theater, the photograph; on the radio, the recording. In the age of liberal expansion, amusement lived on the unshaken belief in the future: things would remain as they were and even improve. Today this belief is once more intellectualized; it becomes so faint that it loses sight of any goal and is little more than a magic-lantern show for those with their backs to reality. It consists of the meaningful emphases which, parallel to life itself, the screen play puts on the smart fellow, the engineer, the capable girl, ruthlessness disguised as character, interest in sport, and finally automobiles and cigarettes, even where the entertainment is not put down to the advertising account of the immediate producers but to that of the system as a whole. Amusement itself becomes an ideal, taking the place of the higher things of which it completely deprives the masses by repeating them in a manner even more stereotyped than the slogans paid for by advertising interests. Inwardness, the subjectively restricted form of truth, was always more at the mercy of the outwardly powerful than they imagined. The culture industry turns it into an open lie. It has now become mere twaddle which is acceptable in religious bestsellers, psychological films, and women's serials as an embarrassingly agreeable garnish, so that genuine personal emotion in real life can be all the more reliably controlled. In this sense amusement carries out that purgation of the emotions which Aristotle once attributed to tragedy and Mortimer Adler now allows to movies. The culture industry reveals the truth about catharsis as it did about style.

The stronger the positions of the culture industry become, the more summarily it can deal with consumers' needs, producing them, controlling them, disciplining them, and even withdrawing amusement: no limits are set to cultural progress of this kind. But the tendency is immanent in the principle of amusement itself, which is enlightened in a bourgeois sense. If the need for amusement was in large measure the creation of industry, which used the subject as a means

[3] Frank Wedekind, *Gesammelte Werke*, Vol. IX (Munich, 1921), p. 426.

of recommending the work to the masses—the oleograph by the dainty morsel it depicted, or the cake mix by a picture of a cake—amusement always reveals the influence of business, the sales talk, the quack's spiel. But the original affinity of business and amusement is shown in the latter's specific significance: to defend society. To be pleased means to say Yes. It is possible only by insulation from the totality of the social process, by desensitization and, from the first, by senselessly sacrificing the inescapable claim of every work, however inane, within its limits to reflect the whole. Pleasure always means not to think about anything, to forget suffering even where it is shown. Basically it is helplessness. It is flight; not, as is asserted, flight from a wretched reality, but from the last remaining thought of resistance. The liberation which amusement promises is freedom from thought and from negation. The effrontery of the rhetorical question, "What do people want?" lies in the fact that it is addressed—as if to reflective individuals—to those very people who are deliberately to be deprived of this individuality. Even when the public does—exceptionally—rebel against the pleasure industry, all it can muster is that feeble resistance which that very industry has inculcated in it. Nevertheless, it has become increasingly difficult to keep people in this condition. The rate at which they are reduced to stupidity must not fall behind the rate at which their intelligence is increasing. In this age of statistics the masses are too sharp to identify themselves with the millionaire on the screen, and too slow-witted to ignore the law of the largest number. Ideology conceals itself in the calculation of probabilities. Not everyone will be lucky one day—but the person who draws the winning ticket, or rather the one who is marked out to do so by a higher power—usually by the pleasure industry itself, which is represented as unceasingly in search of talent. Those discovered by talent scouts and then publicized on a vast scale by the studio are ideal types of the new dependent average. Of course, the starlet is meant to symbolize the typist in such a way that the splendid evening dress seems meant for the actress as distinct from the real girl. The girls in the audience not only feel that they could be on the screen, but realize the great gulf separating them from it. Only one girl can draw the lucky ticket, only one man can win the prize, and if, mathematically, all have the same chance, yet this is so infinitesimal for each one that he or she will do best to write it off and rejoice in the other's success, which might just as well have been his or hers, and somehow never is. Whenever the culture industry still issues an invitation naïvely to identify, it is immediately withdrawn. No one can escape from himself any more. Once a member of the audience could see his own wedding in the one shown in the film. Now the lucky actors on the screen are copies of the same category as every member of the public, but such equality only demonstrates the insurmountable separation of the human elements. The perfect similarity is the absolute difference. The identity of the category forbids that of the individual cases. Ironically, man as a member of a species has been made a reality by the culture industry. Now any person signifies only those attributes by which he can replace everybody else: he is interchangeable, a copy. As an individual he is completely expendable and utterly insignificant, and this is just what he finds out when time deprives him of this similarity. This changes the inner structure of the religion of success—otherwise strictly maintained. Increasing emphasis is laid not on the path *per aspera ad astra* (which presupposes hardship and effort), but on winning a prize. The element of blind chance in the routine decision about which song deserves to be a hit and which extra a heroine is stressed by the ideology. Movies emphasize chance. By stopping at nothing to ensure that all the characters are essentially alike, with the exception of the villain, and by excluding non-conforming faces (for example, those which, like Garbo's, do not look as if you could say "Hello sister!" to them), life is made easier for movie-goers at first. They are assured that they are all right as they are, that they could do just as well and that nothing beyond their powers will be asked of them. But at the same time they are given a hint that any effort would be useless because even bourgeois luck no longer has any connection with the calculable effect of their own work. They take the hint. Fundamentally they all recognize chance (by which one occasionally makes his fortune) as the other side of planning. Precisely because the forces of society are so deployed in the direction of rationality that anyone might become an engineer or manager, it has ceased entirely to be a rational matter who the one will be in whom society will invest training or confidence for such functions. Chance and planning become one and the same thing, because, given men's equality, individual success and failure—right up to the top—lose any economic meaning. Chance itself is planned, not because it affects any particular individual but precisely because it is believed to play a vital part. It serves the planners as an alibi, and makes it seem that the complex of transactions and measures into which life has been transformed leaves scope for spontaneous and direct relations between man. This freedom is symbolized in the various media of the culture industry by the arbitrary selection of average individuals. In a magazine's detailed accounts of the modestly magnificent pleasure-trips it has arranged for the lucky person, preferably a stenotypist (who has probably won the competition because of her contacts with local bigwigs), the powerlessness of all is reflected. They are mere matter—so much so that those in control can take someone up into their heaven and throw him out again: his rights and his work count for nothing. Industry is interested in people merely as customers and employees, and has in fact reduced mankind as a whole and each of its elements to this all-embracing formula. According to the ruling aspect at the time, ideology emphasizes plan or chance, technology or life, civilization or nature. As employees, men are reminded of the rational organization and urged to fit in like sensible people. As customers, the freedom of choice, the charm of novelty is demonstrated to them on the screen or in the press by means of the human and personal anecdote. In either case they remain objects.

The less the culture industry has to promise, the less it can offer a meaningful explanation of life, and the emptier is the ideology it disseminates. Even the abstract ideals of the harmony and beneficence of society are too concrete in this age of universal publicity. We have even learned how to identify abstract concepts as sales propaganda. Language based entirely on truth simply arouses impatience to get on with the business deal it is probably advancing. The words that are not means appear senseless; the others seem to be fiction, untrue. Value judgments are taken either as advertising or as empty talk. Accordingly ideology has been made vague and noncommittal, and thus neither clearer nor weaker. Its very vagueness, its almost scientific aversion from committing itself to anything which cannot be verified, acts as an instrument of domination. It becomes a vigorous and prearranged promulgation of the status quo. The culture industry tends to make itself the embodiment of authoritative pronouncements, and thus the irrefutable prophet of the prevailing order. It skillfully steers a winding course between the cliffs of demonstrable misinformation and manifest truth, faithfully reproducing the phenomenon whose opaqueness blocks any insight and installs the ubiquitous and intact phenomenon as ideal. Ideology is split into the photograph of stubborn life and the naked lie about its meaning—which is not expressed but suggested and yet drummed in. To demonstrate its divine nature, reality is always repeated in a purely cynical way. Such a photological proof is of course not stringent, but it is overpowering. Anyone who doubts the power of monotony is a fool. The culture industry refutes the objection made against it just as well as that against the world which it impartially duplicates. The only choice is either to join in or to be left behind: those provincials who have recourse to eternal beauty and the amateur stage in preference to the cinema and the radio are already—politically—at the point to which mass culture drives its supporters. It is sufficiently hardened to deride as ideology, if need be, the old wish-fulfillments, the father-ideal and absolute feeling. The new ideology has as its objects the world as such. It makes use of the worship of facts by no more than elevating a disagreeable existence into the world of facts in representing it meticulously. This transference makes existence itself a substitute for meaning and right. Whatever the camera reproduces is beautiful. The disappointment of the prospect that one might be the typist who wins the world trip is matched by the disappointing appearance of the accurately photographed areas which the voyage might include. Not Italy is offered, but evidence that it exists. A film can even go so far as to show the Paris in which the American girl thinks she will still her desire as a hopelessly desolate place, thus driving her the more inexorably into the arms of the smart American boy she could have met at home anyhow. That this goes on, that, in its most recent phase, the system itself reproduces the life of those of whom it consists instead of immediately doing away with them, is even put down to its credit as giving it meaning and worth. Continuing and continuing to join in are given as justification for the blind persistence of the system and even for its immutability. What repeats itself is healthy, like the natural or industrial cycle. The same babies grin eternally out of the magazines; the jazz machine will pound away for ever. In spite of all the progress in reproduction techniques, in controls and the specialties, and in spite of all the restless industry, the bread which the culture industry offers man is the stone of the stereotype. It draws on the life cycle, on the well-founded amazement that mothers, in spite of everything, still go on bearing children and that the wheels still do not grind to a halt. This serves to confirm the immutability of circumstances. The ears of corn blowing in the wind at the end of Chaplin's *The Great Dictator* give the lie to the anti-Fascist plea for freedom. They are like the blond hair of the German girl whose camp life is photographed by the Nazi film company in the summer breeze. Nature is viewed by the mechanism of social domination as a healthy contrast to society, and is therefore denatured. Pictures showing green trees, a blue sky, and moving clouds make these aspects of nature into so many cryptograms for factory chimneys and service stations. On the other hand, wheels and machine components must seem expressive, having been degraded to the status of agents of the spirit of trees and clouds. Nature and technology are mobilized against all opposition; and we have a falsified memento of liberal society, in which people supposedly wallowed in erotic plush-lined bedrooms instead of taking open-air baths as in the case today, or experiencing breakdowns in prehistoric Benz models instead of shooting off with the speed of a rocket from A (where one is anyhow) to B (where everything is just the same). The triumph of the gigantic concern over the initiative of the entrepreneur is praised by the culture industry as the persistence of entrepreneurial initiative. The enemy who is already defeated, the thinking individual, is the enemy fought. The resurrection in Germany of the anti-bourgeois "Hans Sonnenstösser,"[4] and the pleasure felt when watching *Life with Father*, have one and the same meaning.

---

[4] The reference in Horkheimer and Adorno's German is to "Hans Sonnenstößer," a reference to *Hans Sonnenstösser's Hollen-fahrt* [*Hans Sonnenstösser's Trip to Hell*], a German play by Paul Apel. A typographical error in the English translation appears to have occurred, and in the English original reproduced here, the reference is to "Haus Sonnenstösser." I have corrected the error in accord with the German text, rather than preserving it exactly as it appeared in the English translation.—*JW*

In one respect, admittedly, this hollow ideology is in deadly earnest: everyone is provided for. "No one must go hungry or thirsty; if anyone does, he's for the concentration camp!" This joke from Hitler's Germany might shine forth as a maxim from above all the portals of the culture industry. With sly naïveté, it presupposes the most recent characteristic of society: that it can easily find out who its supporters are. Everybody is guaranteed formal freedom. No one is officially responsible for what he thinks. Instead everyone is enclosed at an early age in a system of churches, clubs, professional associations, and other such concerns, which constitute the most sensitive instrument of social control. Anyone who wants to avoid ruin must see that he is not found wanting when weighed in the scales of this apparatus. Otherwise he will lag behind in life, and finally perish. In every career, and especially in the liberal professions, expert knowledge is linked with prescribed standards of conduct; this can easily lead to the illusion that expert knowledge is the only thing that counts. In fact, it is part of the irrational planning of this society that it reproduces to a certain degree only the lives of its faithful members. The standard of life enjoyed corresponds very closely to the degree to which classes and individuals are essentially bound up with the system. The manager can be relied upon, as can the lesser employee Dagwood—as he is in the comic pages or in real life. Anyone who goes cold and hungry, even if his prospects were once good, is branded. He is an outsider; and, apart from certain capital crimes, the most mortal of sins is to be an outsider. In films he sometimes, and as an exception, becomes an original, the object of maliciously indulgent humor; but usually he is the villain, and is identified as such at first appearance, long before the action really gets going: hence avoiding any suspicion that society would turn on those of good will. Higher up the scale, in fact, a kind of welfare state is coming into being today. In order to keep their own positions, men in top posts maintain the economy in which a highly-developed technology has in principle made the masses redundant as producers. The workers, the real bread-winners, are fed (if we are to believe the ideology) by the managers of the economy, the fed. Hence the individual's position becomes precarious. Under liberalism the poor were thought to be lazy; now they are automatically objects of suspicion. Anybody who is not provided for outside should be in a concentration camp, or at any rate in the hell of the most degrading work and the slums. The culture industry, however, reflects positive and negative welfare for those under the administrators' control as direct human solidarity of men in a world of the efficient. No one is forgotten; everywhere there are neighbors and welfare workers, Dr. Gillespies and parlor philosophers whose hearts are in the right place and who, by their kind intervention as of man to man, cure individual cases of socially-perpetuated distress—always provided that there is no obstacle in the personal depravity of the unfortunate. The promotion of a friendly atmosphere as advised by management experts and adopted by every factory to increase output, brings even the last private impulse under social control precisely because it seems to relate men's circumstances directly to production, and to reprivatize them. Such spiritual charity casts a conciliatory shadow onto the products of the culture industry long before it emerges from the factory to invade society as a whole. Yet the great benefactors of mankind, whose scientific achievements have to be written up as acts of sympathy to give them an artificial human interest, are substitutes for the national leaders, who finally decree the abolition of sympathy and think they can prevent any recurrence when the last invalid has been exterminated.

By emphasizing the "heart of gold," society admits the suffering it has created: everyone knows that he is now helpless in the system, and ideology has to take this into account. Far from concealing suffering under the cloak of improvised fellowship, the culture industry takes pride in looking it in the face like a man, however great the strain on self-control. The pathos of composure justifies the world which makes it necessary. That is life—very hard, but just because of that so wonderful and so healthy. This lie does not shrink from tragedy. Mass culture deals with it, in the same way as centralized society does not abolish the suffering of its members but records and plans it. That it is why it borrows so persistently from art. This provides the tragic substance which pure amusement cannot itself supply, but which it needs if it is somehow to remain faithful to the principle of the exact reproduction of phenomena. Tragedy made into a carefully calculated and accepted aspect of the world is a blessing. It is a safeguard against the reproach that truth is not respected, whereas it is really being adopted with cynical regret. To the consumer who—culturally—has seen better days it offers a substitute for long-discarded profundities. It provides the regular movie-goer with the scraps of culture he must have for prestige. It comforts all with the thought that a tough, genuine human fate is still possible, and that it must at all costs be represented uncompromisingly. Life in all the aspects which ideology today sets out to duplicate shows up all the more gloriously, powerfully and magnificently, the more it is redolent of necessary suffering. It begins to resemble fate. Tragedy is reduced to the threat to destroy anyone who does not cooperate, whereas its paradoxical significance once lay in a hopeless resistance to mythic destiny. Tragic fate becomes just punishment, which is what bourgeois aesthetics always tried to turn it into. The morality of mass culture is the cheap form of yesterday's children's books. In a first-class production, for example, the villainous character appears as a hysterical woman who (with presumed clinical accuracy) tries to ruin the happiness of her opposite number, who is truer to reality, and herself suffers a quite untheatrical death. So much learning is of course found only at the top. Lower down less trouble is taken. Tragedy is made harmless without recourse to social psychology. Just as every Viennese operetta worthy of the name had to have its tragic finale in the second act, which left nothing for the third except to clear up misunderstandings, the culture industry assigns tragedy a fixed place in the routine. The well-known existence of the recipe is enough to allay any fear that there is no restraint on tragedy. The description of the dramatic formula by the housewife as "getting into trouble and out again" embraces the whole of mass culture from the idiotic women's serial to the top production. Even the worst ending which began with good intentions confirms the order of things and corrupts the tragic force, either because the woman whose love runs counter to the laws of the game plays with her death for a brief spell of happiness, or because the sad ending in the film all the more clearly stresses the indestructibility of actual life. The tragic film becomes an institution for moral improvement. The masses, demoralized by their life under the pressure of the system, and who show signs of civilization only in modes of behavior which have been forced on them and through which fury and recalcitrance show everywhere, are to be kept in order by the sight of an inexorable life and exemplary behavior. Culture has always played its part in taming revolutionary and barbaric instincts. Industrial culture adds its contribution. It shows the condition under which this merciless life can be lived at all. The individual who is thoroughly weary must use his weariness as energy for his surrender to the collective power which wears him out. In films, those permanently desperate situations which crush the spectator in ordinary life somehow become a promise that one can go on living. One has only to become aware of one's own nothingness, only to recognize defeat and one is one with it all. Society is full of desperate people and therefore a prey to rackets. In some of the most significant German novels of the pre-Fascist era such as Döblin's *Berlin Alexanderplatz* and Fallada's *Kleiner Mann, Was Nun*, this trend was as obvious as in the average film and in the devices of jazz. What all these things have in common is the self-derision of man. The possibility of becoming a subject in the economy, an entrepreneur or a proprietor, has been completely liquidated. Right down to the humblest shop, the independent enterprise, on the management and inheritance of which the bourgeois family and the position of its head had rested, became hopelessly dependent. Everybody became an employee; and in this civilization of employees the dignity of the father (questionable anyhow) vanishes. The attitude of the individual to the racket, business, profession or party, before or after admission, the Führer's gesticulations before the masses, or the suitor's before his sweetheart, assume specifically masochistic traits. The attitude into which everybody is forced in order to give repeated proof of his moral suitability for this society reminds one of the boys who, during tribal initiation, go round in a circle with a stereotyped smile on their faces while the priest strikes them. Life in the late capitalist era is a constant initiation rite. Everyone must show that he wholly identifies himself with the power which is belaboring him. This occurs in the principle of jazz syncopation, which simultaneously derides stumbling and makes it a rule. The eunuch-like voice of the crooner on the radio, the heiress's smooth suitor, who falls into the swimming pool in his dinner jacket, are models for those who must become whatever the system wants. Everyone can be like this omnipotent society; everyone can be happy, if only he will capitulate fully and sacrifice his claim to happiness. In his weakness society recognizes its strength, and gives him some of it. His defenselessness makes him reliable. Hence tragedy is discarded. Once the opposition of the individual to society was its substance. It glorified "the bravery and freedom of emotion before a powerful enemy, an exalted affliction, a dreadful problem."[5] Today tragedy has melted away into the nothingness of that false identity of society and individual, whose terror still shows for a moment in the empty semblance of the tragic. But the miracle of integration, the permanent act of grace by the authority who receives the defenseless person—once he has swallowed his rebelliousness—signifies Fascism. This can be seen in the humanitarianism which Döblin uses to let his Biberkopf find refuge, and again in socially-slanted films. The capacity to find refuge, to survive one's own ruin, by which tragedy is defeated, is found in the new generation; they can do any work because the work process does not let them become attached to any. This is reminiscent of the sad lack of conviction of the homecoming soldier with no interest in the war, or of the casual laborer who ends up by joining a paramilitary organization. This liquidation of tragedy confirms the abolition of the individual.

In the culture industry the individual is an illusion not merely because of the standardization of the means of production. He is tolerated only so long as his complete identification with the generality is unquestioned. Pseudo individuality is rife: from the standardized jazz improvisation to the exceptional film star whose hair curls over her eye to demonstrate her originality. What is individual is no more than the generality's power to stamp the accidental detail so firmly that it is accepted as such. The defiant reserve or elegant appearance of the individual on show is mass-produced like Yale locks, whose only difference can be measured in fractions of millimeters. The peculiarity of the self is a monopoly commodity determined by society; it is falsely represented as natural. It is no more than the moustache, the French accent, the deep voice of the woman of the world, the Lubitsch touch: finger prints on identity

---

[5] Nietzsche, *Götzendämmerung*, *Werke*, Vol. VIII, p. 136.

cards which are otherwise exactly the same, and into which the lives and faces of every single person are transformed by the power of the generality. Pseudo individuality is the prerequisite for comprehending tragedy and removing its poison: only because individuals have ceased to be themselves and are now merely centers where the general tendencies meet, is it possible to receive them again, whole and entire, into the generality. In this way mass culture discloses the fictitious character of the "individual" in the bourgeois era, and is merely unjust in boasting on account of this dreary harmony of general and particular. The principle of individuality was always full of contradiction. Individuation has never really been achieved. Self-preservation in the shape of class has kept everyone at the stage of a mere species being. Every bourgeois characteristic, in spite of its deviation and indeed because of it, expressed the same thing: the harshness of the competitive society. The individual who supported society bore its disfiguring mark; seemingly free, he was actually the product of its economic and social apparatus. Power based itself on the prevailing conditions of power when it sought the approval of persons affected by it. As it progressed, bourgeois society did also develop the individual. Against the will of its leaders, technology has changed human beings from children into persons. However, every advance in individuation of this kind took place at the expense of the individuality in whose name it occurred, so that nothing was left but the resolve to pursue one's own particular purpose. The bourgeois whose existence is split into a business and a private life, whose private life is split into keeping up his public image and intimacy, whose intimacy is split into the surly partnership of marriage and the bitter comfort of being quite alone, at odds with himself and everybody else, is already virtually a Nazi, replete both with enthusiasm and abuse; or a modern city-dweller who can now only imagine friendship as a "social contact": that is, as being in social contact with others with whom he has no inward contact. The only reason why the culture industry can deal so successfully with individuality is that the latter has always reproduced the fragility of society. On the faces of private individuals and movie heroes put together according to the patterns on magazine covers vanishes a pretense in which no one now believes; the popularity of the hero models comes partly from a secret satisfaction that the effort to achieve individuation has at last been replaced by the effort to imitate, which is admittedly more breathless. It is idle to hope that this self-contradictory, disintegrating "person" will not last for generations, that the system must collapse because of such a psychological split, or that the deceitful substitution of the stereotype for the individual will of itself become unbearable for mankind. Since Shakespeare's *Hamlet*, the unity of the personality has been seen through as a pretense. Synthetically produced physiognomies show that the people of today have already forgotten that there was ever a notion of what human life was. For centuries society has been preparing for Victor Mature and Mickey Rooney. By destroying they come to fulfill.

The idolization of the cheap involves making the average the heroic. The highest-paid stars resemble pictures advertising unspecified proprietary articles. Not without good purpose are they often selected from the host of commercial models. The prevailing taste takes its ideal from advertising, the beauty in consumption. Hence the Socratic saying that the beautiful is the useful has now been fulfilled—ironically. The cinema makes propaganda for the culture combine as a whole; on radio, goods for whose sake the cultural commodity exists are also recommended individually. For a few coins one can see the film which cost millions, for even less one can buy the chewing gum whose manufacture involved immense riches—a hoard increased still further by sales. *In absentia*, but by universal suffrage, the treasure of armies is revealed, but prostitution is not allowed inside the country. The best orchestras in the world—clearly not so—are brought into your living room free of charge. It is all a parody of the human society. You name it, we supply it. A man up from the country remarked at the old Berlin Metropol theater that it was astonishing what they could do for the money; his comment has long since been adopted by the culture industry and made the very substance of production. This is always coupled with the triumph that it is possible; but this, in large measure, is the very triumph. Putting on a show means showing everybody what there is, and what can be achieved. Even today it is still a fair, but incurably sick with culture. Just as the people who had been attracted by the fairground barkers overcame their disappointment in the booths with a brave smile, because they really knew in advance what would happen, so the movie-goer sticks knowingly to the institution. With the cheapness of mass-produce luxury goods and its complement, the universal swindle, a change in the character of the art commodity itself is coming about. What is new is not that it is a commodity, but that today it deliberately admits it is one; that art renounces its own autonomy and proudly takes its place among consumption goods constitutes the charm of novelty. Art as a separate sphere was always possible only in a bourgeois society. Even as a negation of that social purposiveness which is spreading through the market, its freedom remains essentially bound up with the premise of a commodity economy. Pure works of art which deny the commodity society by the very fact that they obey their own law were always wares all the same. In so far as, until the eighteenth century, the buyer's patronage shielded the artist from the market, they were dependent on the buyer and his objectives. The purposelessness of the great modern work of art depends on the anonymity of the market. Its demands pass through so many intermediaries that the artist is exempt from any definite requirements—though admittedly only to a certain degree, for throughout the whole history of the bourgeoisie his autonomy was only tolerated, and thus contained an element of untruth which ultimately led to the social liquidation of art. When mortally sick, Beethoven hurled away a novel by Sir Walter Scott with the cry: "Why, the fellow writes for money," and yet proved a most experienced and stubborn businessman in disposing of the last quartets, which were a most extreme renunciation of the market; he is the most outstanding example of the unity of those opposites, market and independence, in bourgeois art. Those who succumb to the ideology are precisely those who cover up the contradiction instead of taking it into the consciousness of their own production as Beethoven did: he went on to express in music his anger at losing a few pence, and derived the metaphysical *Es Muss Sein* (which attempts an aesthetic banishment of the pressure of the world by taking it into itself) from the housekeeper's demand for her monthly wages. The principle of idealistic aesthetics—purposefulness without a purpose—reverses the scheme of things to which bourgeois art conforms socially: purposelessness for the purposes declared by the market. At last, in the demand for entertainment and relaxation, purpose has absorbed the realm of purposelessness. But as the insistence that art should be disposable in terms of money becomes absolute, a shift in the internal structure of cultural commodities begins to show itself. The use which men in this antagonistic society promise themselves from the work of art is itself, to a great extent, that very existence of the useless which is abolished by complete inclusion under use. The work of art, by completely assimilating itself to need, deceitfully deprives men of precisely that liberation from the principle of utility which it should inaugurate. What might be called use value in the reception of cultural commodities is replaced by exchange value; in place of enjoyment there are gallery-visiting and factual knowledge: the prestige seeker replaces the connoisseur. The consumer becomes the ideology of the pleasure industry, whose institutions he cannot escape. One simply "has to" have seen *Mrs. Miniver*, just as one "has to" subscribe to

Life and *Time*. Everything is looked at from only one aspect: that it can be used for something else, however vague the notion of this use may be. No object has an inherent value; it is valuable only to the extent that it can be exchanged. The use value of art, its mode of being, is treated as a fetish; and the fetish, the work's social rating (misinterpreted as its artistic status) becomes its use value—the only quality which is enjoyed. The commodity function of art disappears only to be wholly realized when art becomes a species of commodity instead, marketable and interchangeable like an industrial product. But art as a type of product which existed to be sold and yet to be unsaleable is wholly and hypocritically converted into "unsaleability" as soon as the transaction ceases to be the mere intention and becomes its sole principle. No tickets could be bought when Toscanini conducted over the radio; he was heard without charge, and every sound of the symphony was accompanied, as it were, by the sublime puff that the symphony was not interrupted by any advertising: "This concert is brought to you as a public service." The illusion was made possible by the profits of the united automobile and soap manufacturers, whose payments keep the radio stations going—and, of course, by the increased sales of the electrical industry, which manufactures the radio sets. Radio, the progressive latecomer of mass culture, draws all the consequences at present denied the film by its pseudo-market. The technical structure of the commercial radio system makes it immune from liberal deviations such as those the movie industrialists can still permit themselves in their own sphere. It is a private enterprise which really does represent the sovereign whole and is therefore some distance ahead of the other individual combines. Chesterfield is merely the nation's cigarette, but the radio is the voice of the nation. In bringing cultural products wholly into the sphere of commodities, radio does not try to dispose of its culture goods themselves as commodities straight to the consumer. In America it collects no fees from the public, and so has acquired the illusory form of disinterested, unbiased authority which suits Fascism admirably. The radio becomes the universal mouthpiece of the Führer; his voice rises from street loud-speakers to resemble the howling of sirens announcing panic—from which modern propaganda can scarcely be distinguished anyway. The National Socialists knew that the wireless gave shape to their cause just as the printing press did to the Reformation. The metaphysical charisma of the Führer invented by the sociology of religion has finally turned out to be no more than the omnipresence of his speeches on the radio, which are a demoniacal parody of the omnipresence of the divine spirit. The gigantic fact that the speech penetrates everywhere replaces its content, just as the benefaction of the Toscanini broadcast takes the place of the symphony. No listener can grasp its true meaning any longer, while the Führer's speech is lies anyway. The inherent tendency of radio is to make the speaker's word, the false commandment, absolute. A recommendation becomes an order. The recommendation of the same commodities under different proprietary names, the scientifically based praise of the laxative in the announcer's smooth voice between the overture from *La Traviata* and that from *Rienzi* is the only thing that no longer works, because of its silliness. One day the edict of production, the actual advertisement (whose actuality is at present concealed by the pretense of a choice) can turn into the open command of the Führer. In a society of huge Fascist rackets which agree among themselves what part of the social product should be allotted to the nation's needs, it would eventually seem anachronistic to recommend the use of a particular soap powder. The Führer is more up-to-date in unceremoniously giving direct orders for both the holocaust and the supply of rubbish.

Even today the culture industry dresses works of art like political slogans and forces them upon a resistant public at reduced prices; they are as accessible for public enjoyment as a park. But the disappearance of their genuine commodity character does not mean that they have been abolished in the life of a free society, but that the last defense against their reduction to culture goods has fallen. The abolition of educational privilege by the device of clearance sales does not open for the masses the spheres from which they were formerly excluded, but, given existing social conditions, contributes directly to the decay of education and the progress of barbaric meaninglessness. Those who spent their money in the nineteenth or the early twentieth century to see a play or to go to a concert respected the performance as much as the money they spent. The bourgeois who wanted to get something out of it tried occasionally to establish some rapport with the work. Evidence for this is to be found in the literary "introductions" to works, or in the commentaries on *Faust*. These were the first steps toward the biographical coating and other practices to which a work of art is subjected today. Even in the early, prosperous days of business, exchange-value did carry use value as a mere appendix but had developed it as a prerequisite for its own existence; this was socially helpful for works of art. Art exercised some restraint on the bourgeois as long as it cost money. That is now a thing of the past. Now that it has lost every restraint and there is no need to pay any money, the proximity of art to those who are exposed to it completes the alienation and assimilates one to the other under the banner of triumphant objectivity. Criticism and respect disappear in the culture industry; the former becomes a mechanical expertise, the latter is succeeded by a shallow cult of leading personalities. Consumers now find nothing expensive. Nevertheless, they suspect that the less anything costs, the less it is being given them. The double mistrust of traditional culture as ideology is combined with mistrust of industrialized culture as a swindle. When thrown in free, the now debased works of art, together with the rubbish to which the medium assimilates them, are secretly rejected by the fortunate recipients, who are supposed to be satisfied by the mere fact that there is so much to be seen and heard. Everything can be obtained. The screenos and vaudevilles in the movie theater, the competitions for guessing music, the free books, rewards and gifts offered on certain radio programs, are not mere accidents but a continuation of the practice obtaining with culture products. The symphony becomes a reward for listening to the radio, and—if technology had its way—the film would be delivered to people's homes as happens with the radio. It is moving toward the commercial system. Television points the way to a development which might easily enough force the Warner Brothers into what would certainly be the unwelcome position of serious musicians and cultural conservatives. But the gift system has already taken hold among consumers. As culture is represented as a bonus with undoubted private and social advantages, they have to seize the chance. They rush in lest they miss something. Exactly what, is not clear, but in any case the only ones with a chance are the participants. Fascism, however, hopes to use the training the culture industry has given these recipients of gifts, in order to organize them into its own forced battalions.

Culture is a paradoxical commodity. So completely is it subject to the law of exchange that it is no longer exchanged; it is so blindly consumed in use that it can no longer be used. Therefore it amalgamates with advertising. The more meaningless the latter seems to be under a monopoly, the more omnipotent it becomes. The motives are markedly economic. One could certainly live without the culture industry, therefore it necessarily creates too much satiation and apathy. In itself, it has few resources itself to correct this. Advertising is its elixir of life. But as its product never fails to reduce to a mere promise the enjoyment which it promises as a commodity, it eventually coincides with publicity, which it needs because it cannot be enjoyed. In a competitive society, advertising performed the social service of informing the buyer about the market; it made choice easier and helped the unknown but more efficient supplier to dispose of his goods. Far from costing time, it saved it. Today, when the free market is coming to an end, those who control the system are entrenching themselves in it. It strengthens the firm bond between the consumers and the big combines. Only those who can pay the exorbitant rates charged by the advertising agencies, chief of which are the radio networks themselves; that is, only those who are already in a position to do so, or are co-opted by the decision of the banks and industrial capital, can enter the pseudo-market as sellers. The costs of advertising, which finally flow back into the pockets of the combines, make it unnecessary to defeat unwelcome outsiders by laborious competition. They guarantee that power will remain in the same hands—not unlike those economic decisions by which the establishment and running of undertakings is controlled in a totalitarian state. Advertising today is a negative principle, a blocking device: everything that does not bear its stamp is economically suspect. Universal publicity is in no way necessary for people to get to know the kinds of goods—whose supply is restricted anyway. It helps sales only indirectly. For a particular firm, to phase out a current advertising practice constitutes a loss of prestige, and a breach of the discipline imposed by the influential clique on its members. In wartime, goods which are unobtainable are still advertised, merely to keep industrial power in view. Subsidizing ideological media is more important than the repetition of the name. Because the system obliges every product to use advertising, it has permeated the idiom—the "style"—of the culture industry. Its victory is so complete that it is no longer evident in the key positions: the huge buildings of the top men, floodlit stone advertisements, are free of advertising; at most they exhibit on the rooftops, in monumental brilliance and without any self-glorification, the firm's initials. But, in contrast, the nineteenth-century houses, whose architecture still shamefully indicates that they can be used as a consumption commodity and are intended to be lived in, are covered with posters and inscriptions from the ground right up to and beyond the roof: until they become no more than backgrounds for bills and sign-boards. Advertising becomes art and nothing else, just as Goebbels—with foresight—combines them: *l'art pour l'art*, advertising for its own sake, a pure representation of social power. In the most influential American magazines, *Life* and *Fortune*, a quick glance can now scarcely distinguish advertising from editorial picture and text. The latter features an enthusiastic and gratuitous account of the great man (with illustrations of his life and grooming habits) which will bring him new fans, while the advertisement pages use so many factual photographs and details that they represent the ideal of information which the editorial part has only begun to try to achieve. The assembly-line character of the culture industry, the synthetic, planned method of turning out its products (factory-like not only in the studio but, more or less, in the compilation of cheap biographies, pseudodocumentary novels, and hit songs) is very suited to advertising: the important individual points, by becoming detachable, interchangeable, and even technically alienated from any connected meaning, lend themselves to ends external to the work. The effect, the trick, the isolated repeatable device, have always been used to exhibit goods for advertising purposes, and today every monster close-up of a star is an advertisement for her name, and every hit song a plug for its tune. Advertising and the culture industry merge technically as well as economically. In both cases the same thing can be seen in innumerable places, and the mechanical repetition of the same culture product has come to be the same as that of the propaganda slogan. In both cases the insistent demand for effectiveness makes technology into psycho-technology, into a procedure for manipulating men. In both cases the standards are the striking yet familiar, the easy yet catchy, the skillful yet simple; the object is to overpower the customer, who is conceived as absent-minded or resistant.

By the language he speaks, he makes his own contribution to culture as publicity. The more completely language is lost in the announcement, the more words are debased as substantial vehicles of meaning and become signs devoid of quality; the more purely and transparently words communicate what is intended, the more impenetrable they become. The demythologization of language, taken as an element of the whole process of enlightenment, is a relapse into magic. Word and essential content were distinct yet inseparable from one another. Concepts like melancholy and history, even life, were recognized in the word, which separated them out and preserved them. Its form simultaneously constituted and reflected them. The absolute separation, which makes the moving accidental and its relation to the object arbitrary, puts an end to the superstitious fusion of word and thing. Anything in a determined literal sequence which goes beyond the correlation to the event is rejected as unclear and as verbal metaphysics. But the result is that the word, which can now be only a sign without any meaning, becomes so fixed to the thing that it is just a petrified formula. This affects language and object alike. Instead of making the object experiential, the purified word treats it as an abstract instance, and everything else (now excluded by the demand for ruthless clarity from expression—itself now banished) fades away in reality. A left-half at football, a black-shirt, a member of the Hitler Youth, and so on, are no more than names. If before its rationalization the word had given rise to lies as well as to longing, now, after its rationalization, it is a straitjacket for longing more even than for lies. The blindness and dumbness of the data to which positivism reduces the world pass over into language itself, which restricts itself to recording those data. Terms themselves become impenetrable; they obtain a striking force, a power of adhesion and repulsion which makes them like their extreme opposite, incantations. They come to be a kind of trick, because the name of the prima donna is cooked up in the studio on a statistical basis, or because a welfare state is anathematized by using taboo terms such as "bureaucrats" or "intellectuals," or because base practice uses the name of the country as a charm. In general, the name—to which magic most easily attaches—is undergoing a chemical change: a metamorphosis into capricious, manipulable designations, whose effect is admittedly now calculable, but which for that very reason is just as despotic as that of the archaic name. First names, those archaic remnants, have been brought up to date either by stylization as advertising trade-marks (film stars' surnames have become first names), or by collective standardization. In comparison, the bourgeois family name which, instead of being a trade-mark, once individualized its bearer by relating him to his own past history, seems antiquated. It arouses a strange embarrassment in Americans. In order to hide the awkward distance between individuals, they call one another "Bob" and "Harry," as interchangeable team members. This practice reduces relations between human beings to the good fellowship of the sporting community and is a defense against the true kind of relationship. Signification, which is the only function of a word admitted by semantics, reaches perfection in the sign. Whether folksongs were rightly or wrongly called upper-class culture in decay, their elements have only acquired their popular form through a long process of repeated transmission. The spread of popular songs, on the other hand, takes place at lightning speed. The American expression "fad," used for fashions which appear like epidemics—that is, inflamed by highly-concentrated economic forces—designated this phenomenon long before totalitarian advertising bosses enforced the general lines of culture. When the German Fascists decide one day to launch a word—say, "intolerable"—over the loudspeakers the next day the whole nation is saying "intolerable." By the same pattern, the nations against whom the weight of the German "blitzkrieg" was thrown took the word into their own jargon. The general repetition of names for measures to be taken by the authorities makes them, so to speak, familiar, just as the brand name on everybody's lips increased sales in the era of the free market. The blind and rapidly spreading repetition of words with special designations links advertising with the totalitarian watchword. The layer of experience which created the words for their speakers has been removed; in this swift appropriation language acquires the coldness which until now it had only on billboards and in the advertisement columns of newspapers. Innumerable people use words and expressions which they have either ceased to understand or employ only because they trigger off conditioned reflexes; in this sense, words are trade-marks which are finally all the more firmly linked to the things they denote, the less their linguistic sense is grasped. The minister for mass education talks incomprehendingly of "dynamic forces," and the hit songs unceasingly celebrate "reverie" and "rhapsody," yet base their popularity precisely on the magic of the unintelligible as creating the thrill of a more exalted life. Other stereotypes, such as memory, are still partly comprehended, but escape from the experience which might allow them content. They appear like enclaves in the spoken language. On the radio of Flesch and Hitler they may be recognized from the affected pronunciation of the announcer when he says to the nation, "Good night, everybody!" or "This is the Hitler Youth," and even intones "the Führer" in a way imitated by millions. In such clichés the last bond between sedimentary experience and language is severed which still had a reconciling effect in dialect in the nineteenth century. But in the prose of the journalist whose adaptable attitude led to his appointment as an all-German editor, the German words become petrified, alien terms. Every word shows how far it has been debased by the Fascist pseudo-folk community. By now, of course, this kind of language is already universal, totalitarian. All the violence done to words is so vile that one can hardly bear to hear them any longer. The announcer does not need to speak pompously; he would indeed be impossible if his inflection were different from that of his particular audience. But, as against that, the language and gestures of the audience and spectators are colored more strongly than ever before by the culture industry, even in fine nuances which cannot yet be explained experimentally. Today the culture industry has taken over the civilizing inheritance of the entrepreneurial and frontier democracy—whose appreciation of intellectual deviations was never very finely attuned. All are free to dance and enjoy themselves, just as they have been free, since the historical neutralization of religion, to join any of the innumerable sects. But freedom to choose an ideology—since ideology always reflects economic coercion—everywhere proves to be freedom to choose what is always the same. The way in which a girl accepts and keeps the obligatory date, the inflection on the telephone or in the most intimate situation, the choice of words in conversation, and the whole inner life as classified by the now somewhat devalued depth psychology, bear witness to man's attempt to make himself a proficient apparatus, similar (even in emotions) to the model served up by the culture industry. The most intimate reactions of human beings have been so thoroughly reified that the idea of anything specific to themselves now persists only as an utterly abstract notion: personality scarcely signifies anything more than shining white teeth and freedom from body odor and emotions. The triumph of advertising in the culture industry is that consumers feel compelled to buy and use its products even though they see through them.

CHAPTER 20
THEODOR W. ADORNO

Theodor Adorno (1903–1969) was a German philosopher, social theorist, aesthetician, and musicologist, and an influential member of the Frankfurt School. His thoughts on politics, society, culture, and the arts have had a significant impact in philosophy, both within and outside of Critical Theory. His work continues to be the inspiration and object of much critical philosophical work being done on the arts today. While in "The Culture Industry," the selection from the last chapter and a collaboration with Max Horkheimer, Adorno's perspective is deeply shaped by his experience as a German living in exile in California during the Second World War, and thus is marked by a profound opposition to the fascistic potential of cinema, this second selection from Adorno (written in Germany twenty years after the end of the War) seems far more open to the possibility of film art. This essay, "Transparencies on Film," was originally published in German ("Filmtransparente: Notizen zu Papas und Bubis Kino") in Die Zeit *in 1966.*

Adorno begins the essay by making reference to the term "Daddy's Cinema," used by the French filmmaker and critic François Truffaut (in French, "le cinéma du papa") to criticize the big-budget, studio-produced feature films—films that tended to be heavy on dialogue and action, and eminently marketable. The films of which Truffaut is so critical are those which Adorno would characterize (and did characterize, with Max Horkheimer) as products of the "culture industry," mass art meant only to make a profit by reproducing the status quo. Opposed to Daddy's Cinema, we see what was called (somewhat disparagingly) "Kiddy's Cinema," a sort of filmmaking that embraces the incomplete, the unpolished, and the experimental—what me might today call "independent film" or "indie film." There is something liberating in the rawness and genuineness of such cinema, for Adorno, exactly the opposite of the studio film.

Ultimately, the difference between Daddy's Cinema and Kiddy's Cinema, according to Adorno, has to do with the relationship between film technique and society. And when it comes to technique, Adorno draws a sharp distinction between film and literature—a distinction that he applies directly to those instances in film where a character is adapted for the screen from a prior work of literature. Literature always mediates characters, he notes, in language and description, but also in terms of typeface and the other technologies of the book. As such, film adaptations of those characters never seem the same: in the cinema, characters are presented immediately, in images, rather than mediately in words. When words are used for the purposes of characterization in film, he adds, they always seem false. Film characters are shown, not described—neither by an omniscient, literary narrator, nor by themselves in expository dialogue. Film images seem more immediate than any verbal description could, and Adorno suggests that an even greater sense of immediacy could be achieved in film by way of improvisation—a technique which is entirely impossible in literature.

For Adorno, film effects the equation of technique and technology: the fact that the cinematic work is mechanically produced (per Benjamin) means that there is no "original" work of cinematic art, but this isn't to say that film is nothing but technique. Adorno notes that a number of film critics and film theorists suggest that technique is at the root of cinema, and that great films are made great by the effective deployment of various techniques. But he cites the example of Charlie Chaplin as one of an obviously great filmmaker who made films in a total ignorance of formal film technique. Whatever film is at its heart, it is not a merely or even essentially technical medium.

With regard to society and the social impact of film, Adorno notes that the intended ideologies in any given film do not always come through for audiences; independent films might inadvertently reinforce the status quo, and studio blockbusters might have revolutionary aspects. The ideology of the culture industry, to take Adorno's primary example, always has the potential to undermine itself in particular films or film showings: the depiction of a Parisian libertine, for example, might be intended to castigate and vilify the type, but only serve as an example for filmgoing youths of a new possibility which they imitate in their real lives. Whatever else is the case about film, however, Adorno insists that there is no way successfully to divorce the film image from some sort of social meaning. Films are always representational, and thus never purely aesthetic: there is always something in any given film image that cannot be explained away as a product of the artist's intention. Those irreducible elements are, Adorno writes, always concerned with society. On his view, no aesthetics of the cinema could exclude sociology absolutely, lest this irreducible social element of every film be neglected or misunderstood.

Given the irreducibly social nature of the cinema, the constitutive subject of a film is always a "we," a plural subject in which the aesthetic and the sociological converge. In this way, and in the inherently collaborative nature of filmmaking, film provides models for collective behavior. Film thus has an emancipatory potential, even if that potential in any given film goes mostly untapped. The films that constitute Daddy's Cinema give people what they want: they defend and perpetuate the status quo, reinforcing the socioeconomic and political structures presently in place. But conforming to the consumer's demands without any attempt at challenging or invoking thought in the filmgoer is a mode of consumer exploitation: Daddy's Cinema "gives the consumer what they want" because doing so prevents the consumer from ever becoming anything other than a consumer. In addition, the propagandistic potential of the cinema allows those in control of the means of production in society to project their will onto audiences or consumers. Every culture industry film is effectively an advertisement, for more or less particular elements which support the status quo. This explains, Adorno says, the increasing difficulty of distinguishing between the films we go to see and the previews for "coming attractions" that run before the films. Films are already advertisements for themselves. Every commercial film, he argues, is the preview for what Daddy's Cinema promises—enactment of the consumer's will in the world, or something like it—but never delivers. Although perhaps not yet fully realized, so-called Kiddy's Cinema presents an opportunity for a rawer, more dangerous, more genuine and thus potentially more liberating cinema.

Filmography

- ***Anything Goes*** (USA, 1936). *Directed by* Lewis Milestone. *Produced by* Benjamin Glazer. *Written by* Russel Crouse *and* Howard Lindsay. *Starring* Bing Crosby, Ethel Merman, Charlie Ruggles, Ida Lupino, *and* Grace Bradley.

- ***La Notte*** [*The Night*] (Italy, 1961). *Directed by* Michelangelo Antonioni. *Produced by* Emanuele Cassuto. *Written by* Michelangelo Antonioni, Ennio Flaiano, *and* Tonino Guerra. *Starring* Marcello Mastroianni, Jeanne Moreau, *and* Monica Vitti.
- ***Antithese*** (Germany, 1962). *Directed, Produced, Written by, and Starring* Mauricio Kagel.
- ***Der junge Törless*** [*Young Törless*] (Germany, 1966). *Directed by* Volker Schlöndorff. *Produced by* Franz Seitz. *Written by* Volker Schlöndorff *and* Herbert Asmodi. *Starring* Matthieu Carrière.

TRANSPARENCIES ON FILM

Translated by Thomas Y. Levin

Children when teasing each other in their squabbles, follow the rule: no fair copycat. Their wisdom seems to be lost on the all too thoroughly grown-up adults. The Oberhauseners attacked the nearly sixty-year old trash production of the film industry with the epithet: "Daddy's Cinema." Representatives of the latter in turn could come up with no better retort than "Kiddy's Cinema." This cat, as once again the saying goes among children, does not copy. How pathetic to pit experience against immaturity when the issue is the very immaturity of that experience acquired during the adolescence of the medium. What is repulsive about Daddy's Cinema is its infantile character, regression manufactured on an industrial scale. The sophistry of the defenders insists on the very type of achievement the concept of which is challenged by the opposition. However, even if there were something to that reproach—if films that did not play along with business really were in some ways clumsier than the latter's smoothly polished wares—then the triumph would be pitiful. It would only demonstrate that those supported by the power of capital, technological routine and highly trained specialists could do better in some respects than those who rebel against the colossus and thus must necessarily forego the advantages of its accumulated potential. In this comparatively awkward and unprofessional cinema, uncertain of its effects, is inscribed the hope that the so-called mass media might eventually become something qualitatively different. While in autonomous art anything lagging behind the already established technical standard does not rate, vis-à-vis the culture industry—whose standard excludes everything but the predigested and the already integrated, just as the cosmetic trade eliminates facial wrinkles—works which have not completely mastered their technique, conveying as a result something consolingly uncontrolled and accidental, have a liberating quality. In them the flaws of a pretty girl's complexion become the corrective to the immaculate face of the professional star.

It is known that in the Törless film large segments of Musil's early novel were incorporated into the dialogue almost unchanged. They are considered superior to the lines by the scriptwriters, which no living person would ever utter, and which in the meantime have been ridiculed by American critics. In their own way, however, Musil's sentences also tend to sound artificial as soon as they are heard, not read. This may be to some extent the fault of the novel which incorporates a type of rationalistic casuistry into the internal movement of its text under the guise of a psychology that the more progressive Freudian psychology of the period exposed as a rationalization. Nevertheless, this is hardly the whole point. The artistic difference between the media is obviously still greater than expected by those who feel able to avoid bad prose by adapting good prose. Even when dialogue is used in a novel, the spoken word is not directly spoken but is rather distanced by the act of narration—perhaps even by the typography—and thereby abstracted from the physical presence of living persons. Thus, fictional characters never resemble their empirical counterparts no matter how minutely they are described. In fact, it may be due to the very precision of their presentation that they are removed even further from empirical reality; they become aesthetically autonomous. Such distance is abolished in film: to the extent that a film is realistic, the semblance of immediacy cannot be avoided. As a result, phrases justified by the diction of narrative which distinguishes them from the false everydayness of mere reportage, sound pompous and inauthentic in film. Film, therefore, must search for other means of conveying immediacy: improvisation which systematically surrenders itself to unguided chance should rank high among possible alternatives.

The late emergence of film makes it difficult to distinguish between technique and technology as clearly as is possible in music. In music up to the electronic period, the intrinsic technique—the sound structure of the work—was distinct from its performance, the means of reproduction. Film suggests the equation of technique and technology since, as Benjamin observed, the cinema has no original which is then reproduced on a mass scale: the mass product is the thing itself. This equation, however, is problematic, in film as well as in music. Experts in cinematographic techniques refer to the fact that Chaplin was either unaware of or purposely ignorant of these techniques, being content with the photographic rendering of sketches, slapstick routines or other performances. This in no way lowers Chaplin's status and one can hardly doubt that he was "filmic." Nowhere but on the screen could this enigmatic figure—reminiscent of old-fashioned photographs right from the start—have developed its concept. As a consequence, it appears impossible to derive norms of criticism from cinematographic technique as such. The most plausible theory of film technique, and that which focuses on the movement of objects,[1] is both provocatively denied and yet preserved, in negative form, in the static character of films like Antonioni's *La Notte*. Whatever is "uncinematic" in this film gives it the power to express, as if with hollow eyes, the emptiness of time. Irrespective of the technological origins of the cinema, the aesthetics of film will do better to base itself on a subjective mode of experience which film resembles and which constitutes its artistic character. A person who, after a year in the city, spends a few weeks in the mountains abstaining from all work, may unexpectedly experience colorful images of landscapes consolingly coming over him or her in dreams or daydreams. These images do not merge into one another in a continuous flow, but are rather set off against each other in the course of their appearance, much like the magic lantern slides of our childhood. It is in the discontinuity of their movement that the images of the interior monologue resemble the phenomenon of writing: the latter similarly moving before our eyes while fixed in its discrete signs. Such movement of interior images may be to film what the visible world is to painting or the acoustic world to music. As the objectifying recreation of this type of experience, film may become art. The technological medium *par excellence* is thus intimately related to the beauty of nature (*tief verwandt dem Naturschönen*).

If one decides to take the self-censors more or less literally and confront films with the context of their reception, one will have to proceed more subtly than those traditional content analyses which, by necessity, relied primarily on the intentions of a film and neglected the potential gap between such intentions and their actual effect. This gap, however, is inherent in the medium. If according to the analysis of "Television as Ideology" film accommodates various layers of behavioral response patterns, this would imply that the ideology provided by the industry, its officially intended models, may by no means automatically correspond to those that affect the spectators. If empirical communications research were finally to look for problems which could lead to some results, this one would merit priority. Overlapping the

[1] Cf. Siegfried Kracauer, *Theory of Film: The Redemption of Physical Reality* (New York: Oxford University Press, 1960), pp. 41ff.

official models are a number of unofficial ones which supply the attraction yet are intended to be neutralized by the former. In order to capture the consumers and provide them with substitute satisfaction, the unofficial, if you will, heterodox ideology must be depicted in a much broader and juicier fashion than suits the moral of the story; the tabloid newspapers furnish weekly examples of such excess. One would expect the public's libido, repressed by a variety of taboos, to respond all the more promptly since these behavioral patterns, by the very fact that they are allowed to pass, reflect an element of collective approval. While intention is always directed against the playboy, the *dolce vita* and wild parties, the opportunity to behold them seems to be relished more than the hasty verdict. If today you can see in Germany, in Prague, even in conservative Switzerland and in Catholic Rome, everywhere, boys and girls crossing the streets locked in each others arms and kissing each other unembarrassed, then they have learned this, and probably more, from the films which peddle Parisian libertinage as folklore. In its attempts to manipulate the masses the ideology of the culture industry itself becomes as internally antagonistic as the very society which it aims to control. The ideology of the culture industry contains the antidote to its own lie. No other plea could be made for its defense.

The photographic process of film, primarily representational, places a higher intrinsic significance on the object, as foreign to subjectivity, than aesthetically autonomous techniques; this is the retarding aspect of film in the historical process of art. Even where film dissolves and modifies its objects as much as it can, the disintegration is never complete. Consequently, it does not permit absolute construction: its elements, however abstract, always retain something representational; they are never purely aesthetic values. Due to this difference, society projects into film quite differently—far more directly on account of the objects—than into advanced painting or literature. That which is irreducible about the objects in film is thus inherently concerned with society. There can be no aesthetics of the cinema, not even a purely technological one, which would not include the sociology of the cinema. Kracauer's theory of film which practices sociological abstention compels us to consider that which is left out in his book; otherwise antiformalism turns into formalism. Kracauer ironically plays with the resolve of his earliest youth to celebrate film as the discoverer of the beauties of daily life: such a program, however, was a program of *Jugendstil* just as all those films which attempt to let wandering clouds and murky ponds speak for themselves are relics of *Jugendstil*. By choosing objects presumably cleansed of subjective meaning, these films infuse the object with exactly that meaning which they are trying to resist.

Benjamin did not elaborate on how deeply some of the categories he postulated for film—exhibition, test—are imbricated with the commodity character which his theory opposes. The reactionary nature of any realist aesthetic today is inseparable from this commodity character. Tending to reinforce, affirmatively, the phenomenal surface of society, realism dismisses any attempt to penetrate that surface as a romantic endeavor. Every meaning—including critical meaning—which the camera eye imparts to the film would already invalidate the law of the camera and thus violate Benjamin's taboo, conceived as it was with the explicit purpose of outdoing the provocative Brecht and thereby—this may have been its secret purpose—gaining freedom from him. Film is faced with the dilemma of finding a procedure which neither lapses into arts-and-crafts nor slips into a mere documentary mode. The obvious answer today, as forty years ago, is that of montage which does not interfere with things but rather arranges them in a constellation akin to that of writing. The viability of a procedure based on the principle of shock, however, raises doubts. Pure montage, without the addition of intentionality in its elements, does not derive intention merely from the principle itself. It seems illusory to claim that through the renunciation of all meaning, especially the cinematically inherent renunciation of psychology, meaning will emerge from the reproduced material itself. It may be, however, that the entire issue is rendered obsolete by the insight that the refusal to interpret, to add subjective ingredients, is in itself a subjective act and as such *a priori* significant. The individual subject who remains silent speaks not less but more through silence than when speaking aloud. Those filmmakers ostracized for being too intellectual should, by way of revision, absorb this insight into their working methods. Nonetheless, the gap between the most progressive tendencies in the visual arts and those of film continues to exist, compromising the latter's most radical intentions. For the time being, evidently, film's most promising potential lies in its interaction with other media, themselves merging into film, such as certain kinds of music. One of the most powerful examples of such interaction is the television film *Antithèse* by composer Mauricio Kagel.

That, among its functions, film provides models for collective behavior is not just an additional imposition of ideology. Such collectivity, rather, inheres in the innermost elements of film. The movements which the film presents are mimetic impulses which, prior to all content and meaning, incite the viewers and listeners to fall into step as if in a parade. In this respect, film resembles music just as, in the early days of radio, music resembled film strips. It would not be incorrect to describe the constitutive subject of film as a "we" in which the aesthetic and sociological aspects of the medium converge. *Anything Goes* was the title of a film from the thirties with the popular English actress Gracie Fields; this "anything" captures the very substance of film's formal movement, prior to all content. As the eye is carried along, it joins the current of all those responding to the same appeal. The indeterminate nature of this collective "anything" (*Es*), however, which is linked to the formal character of film facilitates the ideological misuse of the medium: the pseudo-revolutionary blurring in which the phrase "things must change" is conveyed by the gesture of banging one's fist on the table. The liberated film would have to wrest its *a priori* collectivity from the mechanisms of unconscious and irrational influence and enlist this collectivity in the service of emancipatory intentions.

Film technology has developed a series of techniques which work against the realism inherent in the photographic process. Among these are soft-focus shots—a long outdated arty custom in photography—superimpositions, and also, frequently, flashbacks. It is about time to recognize the ludicrousness of such effects and get rid of them because these techniques are not grounded in the necessities of individual works but in mere convention; they inform the viewer as to what is being signified or what needs to be added in order to comprehend whatever escapes basic cinematic realism. Since these techniques almost always contain some expressive—even if commonplace—values of their own, a discrepancy arises between expression and conventional sign. This is what gives these inserts the appearance of *kitsch*. Whether it creates the same effect in the context of montage and extradiegetic associations has yet to be examined. In any case, such cinematographic divagations require particular tact on the part of the film-maker. The lesson to be learned from this phenomenon is dialectical: technology in isolation, which disregards the nature of film as language, may end up in contradiction to its own internal logic. Emancipated film production should no longer depend uncritically upon technology (i.e. the mere equipment of its profession) in the manner of a by no means still "new objectivity" (*einer keineswegs mehr neuen Sachlichkeit*). In commercial film production, however, the aesthetic logic inherent in the material is caught in a stage of crisis even before it is given a chance to really unfold. The demand for a meaningful relationship between technique, material and content does not mix well with the fetishism of means.

It is undeniable that Daddy's Cinema indeed corresponds to what the consumers want, or, perhaps, rather that it provides them with an unconscious canon of what they do not want, that is, something different from what they are presently being fed. Otherwise, the culture industry could not have become a mass culture. The identity of these two phenomena, however, is not so beyond doubt as critical thought assumes as long as it focuses on the aspect of production and refrains from empirical analyses of reception. Nevertheless, the favorite argument of the whole- and half-hearted apologists, that culture industry is the art of the consumer, is untrue; it is the ideology of ideology. Even the reductive equation of the culture industry with the low art of all ages does not hold up. The culture industry contains an element of rationality—the calculated reproduction of the low—which, while certainly not missing in the low art of the past, was not its rationale. Moreover, the venerable roughness and idiocy of such hybrids of *circenses* and burlesque so popular during the late Roman empire do not justify the revival of such phenomena after they have become aesthetically and socially transparent. Even if considered apart from its historical perspective, the validity of the argument for consumer-oriented art can be attacked in the very present. Its proponents depict the relationship between art and its reception as static and harmonious, according to the principle of supply and demand, in itself a dubious model. Art unrelated to the objective spirit of its time is equally unimaginable as art without the moment which transcends it. The separation from empirical reality which pertains to the constitution of art from the outset requires precisely that moment. The conformity to the consumer, on the contrary, which likes to masquerade as humanitarianism, is nothing but the economic technique of consumer exploitation. Artistically, it means the renunciation of all interference with the syrupy substance of the current idiom and, as a result, with the reified consciousness of the audience. By reproducing the latter with hypocritical subservience, the culture industry changes this reified consciousness all the more, that is, for its own purposes: it actually prevents that consciousness from changing on its own, as it secretly and, deep down, unadmittedly desires. The consumers are made to remain what they are: consumers. That is why the culture industry is not the art of the consumer but rather the projection of the will of those in control onto their victims. The automatic self-reproduction of the status quo in its established forms is itself an expression of domination.

One will have observed that it is difficult, initially, to distinguish the preview of a "coming attraction" from the main film for which one is waiting. This may tell us something about the main attractions. Like the previews and like the pop hits, they are advertisements for themselves, bearing the commodity character like a mark of Cain on their foreheads. Every commercial film is actually only the preview of that which it promises and will never deliver.

How nice it would be if, under the present circumstances, one could claim that the less films appear to be works of art, the more they would be just that. One is especially drawn to this conclusion in reaction to those snobbish psychological class-A pictures which the culture industry forces itself to make for the sake of cultural legitimation. Even so, one must guard against taking such optimism too far: the standardized Westerns and thrillers—to say nothing of the products of German humor and the patriotic tear-jerkers (*Heimatschnulze*)—are even worse than the official hits. In integrated culture one cannot even depend on the dregs.

CHAPTER 21
JACQUES RANCIÈRE

Jacques Rancière (b. 1940) is a French philosopher, aesthetician, and Marxist political theorist, who held the Chair of Aesthetics and Politics at the University of Paris VIII until his retirement in 2000. He has contributed much to the ongoing discussion in philosophical aesthetics of the significance of the political, and likewise to the political discussion of the meaning of aesthetics and the arts for sociopolitical life. The reading included here, "A Thwarted Fable" ("Une fable contrariée"*), is the prologue to Rancière's book,* Film Fables, *originally published in French (*Le Fable cinématographique*) by Éditions du Seuil in 2001.*

Rancière begins the reading with an extended presentation and discussion of the film theory of one of his predecessors in the history of French film philosophy, Jean Epstein. Epstein, Rancière argues, maintained that the cinema was not properly used when it is used for the telling of stories. Life itself is not about stories, Epstein insists, but instead about situations that are open in every direction—stories, that is to say, are always predetermined and directed toward a specific end. Real life is not. For Epstein, cinema has its origin in the "honest camera," a record of the material, visible world as it really is. In this art, then, for Epstein (according to Rancière), mere matter—prior to the phenomenon of appearance as experienced by the mind—is recorded on film, presenting objects in appearance again only for filmgoers in the audience. The sensible and intelligible thus become indistinguishable from one another in the cinema, on Epstein's view. Of course, many films are made by filmmakers with the express intention to produce a fictional narrative, but Epstein understands this quite critically: it is a nostalgia for old stories that has resulted in two of the greatest failings of the cinema as an art, he argues: (1) the talkies, which undermine the images at the heart of cinema, and (2) the Hollywood film industry, wherein filmmakers are little more than illustrators of scripts written according to standardized beliefs and narratives. Epstein's hope for the future of cinema, Rancière notes, is somewhat utopian, that film will eventually overcome its narrative excesses and return to its essence and origin in the honest image.

Despite the fact that Epstein's view has a certain sort of appeal, Rancière is clear that he thinks Epstein is wrong about the cinema: in the end, he says, Epstein describes an art of film that has never really existed. Put another way, Epstein produces a fable of film—the "honest camera"—which he himself draws from certain fables produced by and perpetuated in the cinema itself. And this phenomenon, the drawing of a fable from a preexisting fable, is something Rancière thinks is characteristic of the cinema. The three main figures of the cinema—the director, the audience, and the critic—all engage in this derivative fabulism: the director draws a cinematic fable from the screenplay; the audience, from their own memories; and the critic, from the idea of the commercial fiction that is film. Even the view countering Epstein's, which Epstein himself criticizes—the notion that the cinema empowers us to restore to ourselves the old stories—is a fable, an explanatory fiction.

For Rancière, art's originary power lies between activity and passivity, between pure creative activity (an expression of freedom) and the passive expressive power of the surfaces of things (which they exhibit without choosing to do so). In cinema, we find a fusion of these elements, with the director actively expressing his or her own creative vision by way of images recorded by a purely passive camera, capable only of producing a recording of the surfaces of the objects it photographs. This enables the cinematic camera—unlike in traditionally structured works of literary fiction or painting—to attend directly to gesture, to the "pure reasonless being" beneath conscious and intentional figuration. A filmmaker aware of this structure can remove him- or herself from the film only by way of a conscious effacement of style: an effort to allow things to express themselves on film. And this conscious self-effacement is at the heart of modern art, he thinks. One of the most notable achievements in modern art, in fact, is this synthesis of activity and passivity, uncharacteristic of traditional, figurative approaches: the modern artist can become actively passive.

Cinema is capable of this defiguration, or unstyling, but it faces a problem most of the other arts do not: in cinema, the apparatus of the art suppresses the active work of the artist, including the artist's active becoming-passive, we see burgeoning in more modern works and movements. The passivity of the camera can be employed for any purpose: the logic of representative, figurative art can be restored by the machine, for example, and as a result of this, the film director can end up serving economic, business ends (rather than aesthetic ones). In this way, moving in the opposite direction away from the effacement of style, we see style centralized in art, as marketing or branding. By way of its inherent and equal tendencies toward both activity and passivity, cinema makes possible both of these opposed ends: the film from which the director is effectively absent, and the film which is effectively but an advertisement for the director (or his or her corporate sponsors, or the dominant ideology). Both passive and active, cinema can be understood to thwart itself.

But this capacity for self-thwarting is seen throughout the history of cinema, Rancière notes, and is not always a bad thing. We see it in the burlesque body, most notably instantiated by Chaplin and Keaton, which is both superhumanly adept and a mere thing subject to other things; we see it in the same manner in certain action films, such as those of Takeshi Kitano, wherein the conflict between two individual's wills is established in the passive vulnerability to physics of their bodies. We see it in the films of Roberto Rossellini, where we find the extreme liberty of some characters coupled with their absolute subjection to a command, and in the films of Robert Bresson and Anthony Mann, in which what is visible in the image often contradicts the narrative meaning (as in Bresson) or the purportedly meaningful actions of the hero are cut off from what normally gives meaning to action (as in Mann's Westerns).

The same logic that operates here within a film operates on a more general cinematic level as well, abolishing the borders between genres or elements of film itself: the line is blurred between document and fiction, as it is between the politically committed film (produced to enact social or political change, a film with primarily instrumental value) and the "aesthetically pure" film (produced for its own sake, or for the sake of beauty or art). Rancière sees this playing out specifically in Humphrey Jennings' propaganda film, Listen to Britain, *wherein audiences are encouraged to join in the war effort by images of Britain in peacetime. And he sees it again in a different way in Chris Marker's* The Last Bolshevik, *which although a documentary, takes advantage of the opportunity to problematize the real itself—interspersing post-Soviet documentary footage with various other images, taken from both documentary and fiction films. But as in the Marker documentary, Rancière finds that the phenomenon of self-thwarting identifiable in film is not a problem so much as a gift: the thwarting nourishes a film, as in Marker, as often (and in the very same ways) as it undermines that film. Epstein's fable of film, like all film fables, is thwarted by the very nature of cinema itself—but this is only a problem for a theorist, such as Epstein, who seems to believe that cinema must be* one *thing. For Rancière, on the contrary, abandoning the feeling that we need to commit to one and only one model of cinematic art, and then to defend that model against anything that might thwart it, allows us to see that the thwarting so many theorists are concerned about is in fact not a problem for cinema:* it is *cinema.*

Filmography

- ***The Honor of His House*** (USA, 1918). *Directed by* William C. deMille. *Produced by* Jesse L. Lasky. *Written by* Marion Fairfax. *Starring* Sessue Hayakawa.
- ***Sherlock Jr.*** (USA, 1924). *Directed by and Starring* Buster Keaton. *Produced by* Joseph M. Schenk *and* Buster Keaton. *Written by* Clyde Bruckman, Jean Havez, *and* Joseph A. Mitchell.
- ***Bronenosets Patyomkin*** [*Battleship Potemkin*] (USSR, 1925). *Directed by* Sergei Eisenstein. *Produced by* Jacob Bliokh. *Written by* Nina Agadzhanova *and* Sergei Eisenstein. *Starring* Aleksandr Antonov, Vladimir Barksy, *and* Grigori Aleksandrov.
- ***Herr Tartüff*** [*Tartuffe*] (Germany, 1926). *Directed by* F. W. Murnau. *Produced by* Erich Pommer. *Written by* Carl Mayer. *Starring* Emil Jannings, Werner Krauss, *and* Lil Dagover.
- ***Chelovek s kinoapparatom*** [*Man with a Movie Camera*] (USSR, 1929). *Directed and Written by* Dziga Vertov.
- ***Staroye i novoye*** [*The General Line/Old and New*] (USSR, 1929). *Directed and Written by* Grigori Aleksandrov *and* Sergei M. Eisenstein. *Produced by* Sovkino. *Starring* Marfa Lapkina, M. Ivanin, Konstantin Vasilyev, *and* Vasili Buzenkov.
- ***M*** (Germany, 1931). *Directed by* Fritz Lang. *Produced by* Seymour Nebenzal. *Written by* Fritz Lang, Thea von Harbou, Adolf Jansen, *and* Karl Vash. *Starring* Peter Lorre.
- ***Modern Times*** (USA, 1936). *Directed, Produced, and Written by* Charlie Chaplin. *Starring* Charlie Chaplin *and* Paulette Godard.
- ***The Great Dictator*** (USA, 1940). *Directed, Produced, and Written by* Charlie Chaplin. *Starring* Charlie Chaplin *and* Paulette Godard.
- ***Listen to Britain*** (UK, 1942). *Directed and Written by* Humphrey Jannings *and* Stewart McAllister. *Produced by* Ian Dalrymple. *Starring* Chesney Allen, Bud Flanagan, *and* Myra Hess.
- ***Les Dames du Bois de Boulogne*** [*The Ladies of the Bois de Boulogne*] (France, 1945). *Directed and Written by* Robert Bresson. *Produced by* Raoul Ploquin. *Starring* Paul Bernard, Maria Casares, *and* Élina Labourdette.
- ***Roma città aperta*** [*Rome, Open City*] (Italy, 1945). *Directed by* Roberto Rossellini. *Produced by* Giuseppe Amato, Ferruccio De Martino, Roberto Rossellini, *and* Rod E. Geiger. *Written by* Sergio Amidei *and* Federico Fellini. *Starring* Aldo Fabrizi, Anna Magnani, *and* Marcello Pagliero.
- ***Germania anno zero*** [*Germany Year Zero*] (Italy, 1948). *Directed by* Roberto Rossellini. *Produced by* Salvo D'Angelo *and* Roberto Rossellini. *Written by* Roberto Rossellini, Max Kolpé, *and* Sergio Amidei. *Starring* Edmund Moeschke, Ernst Pittschau, Ingetraud Hinze, Franz-Otto Krüger, *and* Erich Gühne.

- ***They Live by Night*** (USA, 1948). *Directed by* Nicholas Ray. *Produced by* John Houseman. *Written by* Charles Schnee *and* Nicholas Ray. *Starring* Cathy O'Donnell, Farley Granger, *and* Howard Da Silva.
- ***Rear Window*** (USA, 1954). *Directed and Produced by* Alfred Hitchcock. *Written by* John Michael Hayes. *Starring* James Stewart, Grace Kelly, Wendell Corey, *and* Thelma Ritter.
- ***Moonfleet*** (USA, 1955). *Directed by* Fritz Lang. *Produced by* John Houseman. *Written by* Jan Lustig *and* Margaret Fitts. *Starring* Stewart Granger, George Sanders, Joan Greenwood, *and* Viveca Lindfors.
- ***While the City Sleeps*** (USA, 1956). *Directed by* Fritz Lang. *Produced by* Bert E. Friedlob. *Written by* Casey Robinson. *Starring* Dana Andrews, Rhonda Fleming, George Sanders, John Drew Barrymore, *and* Ida Lupino.
- ***Vertigo*** (USA, 1958). *Directed and Produced by* Alfred Hitchcock. *Written by* Alec Coppel *and* Samuel Taylor. *Starring* James Stewart *and* Kim Novak.
- ***Pickpocket*** (France, 1959). *Directed and Written by* Robert Bresson. *Produced by* Agnès Delahaie. *Starring* Martin LaSalle.
- ***Au hasard Balthazar*** (France, 1966). *Directed and Written by* Robert Bresson. *Produced by* Mag Bodard. *Starring* Anne Wiazemsky *and* François Lafarge.
- ***Mouchette*** (France, 1967). *Directed and Written by* Robert Bresson. *Produced by* Anatole Dauman. *Starring* Nadine Nortier, Jean-Claude Guilbert, Marie Cardinal, *and* Paul Hebert.
- ***Une femme douce*** [*A Gentle Woman*] (France, 1969). *Directed and Written by* Robert Bresson. *Produced by* Mag Bodard. *Starring* Dominique Sanda, Guy Frangin, *and* Jeanne Lobre.
- ***Le Tombeau d'Alexandre*** [*The Last Bolshevik*] (France, 1992). *Directed and Written by* Chris Marker. *Produced by* Michael Kustow. *Starring* Léonor Graser.
- ***Hana-bi*** [*Fireworks*] (Japan, 1997). *Directed and Written by* Takeshi Kitano. *Produced by* Masayuki Mori, Yasushi Tsuge, *and* Takio Yoshida. *Starring* Beat Takeshi, Kayoko Kishimoto, Ren Osugi, *and* Sunumu Terajima.

A THWARTED FABLE

Translated by Emiliano Battista

Cinema, by and large, doesn't do justice to the story. And "dramatic action" here is a mistake. The drama we're watching is already half-resolved and unfolding on the curative slope to the crisis. The real tragedy is in suspense. It looms over all the faces; it is in the curtain and in the door-latch. Each drop of ink can make it blossom at the tip of the pen. It dissolves itself in the glass of water. At every moment, the entire room is saturated with the drama. The cigar burns on the lip of the ashtray like a threat. The dust of betrayal. Poisonous arabesques stretch across the rug and the arm of the seat trembles. For now, suffering is in surfusion. Expectation. We can't see a thing yet, but the tragic crystal that will turn out to be at the center of the plot has fallen down somewhere. Its wave advances. Concentric circles. It keeps on expanding, from relay to relay. Seconds.

The telephone rings. All is lost.

Is whether they get married in the end really all you want to know? Look, really, THERE IS NO film that ends badly, and the audience enters into happiness at the hour appointed on the program.

Cinema is true. A story is a lie.[1]

In these lines, Jean Epstein lays bare the problem posed by the very notion of a film fable. Written in 1921 by a young man of twenty-four, they welcome, under the title *Bonjour cinéma*, the artistic revolution he believes cinema is bringing about. Jean Epstein sums up this revolution with remarkable brevity, in terms that seem to invalidate the very argument of this book: cinema is to the art of telling stories [*l'art des histoires*] what truth is to lying. Cinema discards the infantile expectation for the end of the tale, with its marriage and numerous children. But, more importantly, it discards the "fable" in the Aristotelian sense: the arrangement of necessary and verisimilar actions that lead the characters from fortune to misfortune, or vice versa, through the careful construction of the intrigue [*noeud*] and denouement. The tragic poem, indeed the very idea of artistic expression, had always been defined by just such a logic of ordered actions. And along comes this young man to tell us that this logic is illogical. Life is not about stories, about actions oriented towards an end, but about situations open in every direction. Life has nothing to do with dramatic progression, but is instead a long and continuous movement made up of an infinity of micro-movements. This truth about life has finally found an art capable of doing it justice, an art in which the intelligence that creates the reversals of fortune and the dramatic conflicts is subject to another intelligence, the intelligence of the machine that wants nothing, that does not construct any stories, but simply

---

[1] Jean Epstein, *Bonjour cinéma*, in *Écrits sur le cinéma* (Paris: Seghers, 1974) 86. A previous translation of this text, by Tom Milne, originally published in Afterimage 10 (Autumn 1981) 9–16, can be found in Richard Abel, ed. *French Film Theory and Criticism: A History/Anthropology, 1907–1939*, volume I: 1907–1929 (Princeton, NJ: Princeton University Press, 1988), 242.

records the infinity of movements that gives rise to a drama a hundred times more intense than all dramatic reversals of fortune. At the origin of the cinema, there is a "scrupulously honest" artist that does not cheat, that cannot cheat, because all it does is record. We mustn't confuse this recording with the identical reproduction of things in which Baudelaire had discerned the negation of artistic invention. Cinematographic automatism settles the quarrel between art and technique by changing the very status of the "real." It does not reproduce things as they offer themselves to the gaze. It records them as the human eye cannot see them, as they come into being, in a state of waves and vibrations, before they can be qualified as intelligible objects, people, or events due to their descriptive and narrative properties.

This is why the art of moving images can overthrow the old Aristotelian hierarchy that privileged *muthos*—the coherence of the plot—and devalued *opsis*—the spectacle's sensible effect. It isn't that the art of moving images provides access to an inner truth of the sensible that settles the quarrels for priority among the arts and among senses because it settles, first and foremost, the great quarrel between thought and sensibility. Cinema revokes the old mimetic order because it resolves the question of *mimesis* at its root—the Platonic denunciation of images, the opposition between sensible copy and intelligible model. The matter seen and transcribed by the mechanic eye, says Epstein, is equivalent to mind: a sensible immaterial matter composed of waves and corpuscles that abolishes all opposition between deceitful appearance and substantial reality. The eye and hand that struggled to reproduce the spectacle of the world, as well as the play that explored the most secret reaches of the soul, belong to the old art because they belong to the old science. In the writing of movement with light, fictional matter and sensible matter coincide: the darkness of betrayal, the poison of crimes, and the anguish of melodrama come into contact with the suspension of specks of dust, the smoke of a cigar and the arabesques of a rug. And this same writing reduces all of this to the intimate movements of an immaterial matter. That is the new drama to have found its artist in the cinema. Thoughts and things, exterior and interior, are captured in the same texture, in which the sensible and the intelligible remain undistinguished. Thought impresses itself on the brow of the spectator in "bursts of amperes," while love on the screen "contains what no love had contained till now: its fair share of ultra-violet."[2]

Admittedly, this is a way of looking at things that belongs to another time than our own, but there are many ways to measure the distance. One such way is nostalgia. It notes that, outside the faithful fortress of experimental cinema, the reality of cinema long ago relinquished the beautiful hope of becoming a writing with light that confronted the fables and characters of other ages with the intimate presence of things. The young art of cinema did more than just restore ties with the old art of telling stories: it became that art's most faithful champion. Cinema wasn't content just to use its visual power and experimental means to illustrate old stories of conflicting interests and romantic ordeals, it went further and put those at the service of restoring the entire representative order that literature, painting, and the theater had so deeply damaged. It reinstated plots and typical characters, expressive codes and the old motivations of pathos, and even the strict division of genres. Nostalgia indicts cinema's involution, which it attributes to two phenomena: the breakthrough of the talkies [*la coupure du parlant*], which dealt a severe blow to the attempts to create a language of images; the Hollywood industry,

[2] Epstein, *Bonjour cinéma* (Paris: Seghers, 1974) 91. Abel, *French Film Theory*, vol. I, 244.

which reduced directors to the role of illustrators of scripts based, for commercial reasons, on the standardization of plots and on the audience's identification with the characters.

At the other end of nostalgia is condescension. It tells us that if that dream is remote today, as it no doubt is, it is simply because it had never amounted to more than an inconsistent utopia. It just happened to synchronize with the great utopia of the times—with the aesthetic, scientific, and political dream of a new world where all material and historical burdens would find themselves dissolved in a reign of luminous energy. From the 1890s to the 1920s, this para-scientific utopia of matter dissolving itself in energy inspired both the symbolist reveries of the immaterial poem and the Soviet project of building a new social world. Under the guise of defining an art through its technical apparatus, Jean Epstein would have given us nothing more than his own particular version of the great ode to energy that his epoch sung and illustrated in myriad ways: in symbolist manifestoes à la Canudo and in futurist manifestoes à la Marinetti; in the simultaneist poems of Appolinaire and Cendrars to the glory of neon lighting and wireless communication, and in Khlebnikov's poems of transmental language; in the dynamism of dances à la Severini and in the dynamism of chromatic circles à la Delaunay; in Vertov's kino-eye, in Appia's stage lighting and designs, and in Loïe Fuller's luminous dances… Epstein wrote his poem about thought captured in bursts of amperes and love endowed with its fair share of ultra-violet under the spell of this utopia of a new electric world. He welcomed an art that no longer exists, for the simple reason that it never did. It is not our art, but it was not Epstein's either. It was not what filled the movie-theaters of his day, nor was it the art he himself made, in which he, too, told stories of ill-starred lovers and other old-fashioned heartbreaks. He hailed an art that existed only in his head, an art that was just an idea in people's heads.

It is by no means certain that condescension instructs us better than nostalgia. After all, what is this simple reality of the cinematographic art that condescension refers us to? How is this link between a technical apparatus for the production of visible images and a manner of telling stories forged? There is no shortage of theoreticians who have attempted to ground the art of moving images on the solid base of the means specific to it. But the means specific to yesterday's analogical machine and to today's digital machine have shown themselves equally suitable for filming both love stories and abstract dances and forms. It is only in the name of an idea of art that we can establish the relationship between a technical apparatus and this or that type of fable. *Cinema*, like *painting* and *literature*, is not just the name of an art whose processes can be deduced from the specificity of its material and technical apparatuses. Like painting and literature, cinema is the name of an art whose meaning cuts across the borders between the arts. Perhaps, in order to understand it, we should take another look at the lines from *Bonjour cinéma* and at the idea of art implied in them. Epstein pits the "real tragedy," that is, the "tragedy in suspense," against the old "dramatic action." Now, this notion of the tragedy in suspense is not reducible to the idea of the automatic machine inscribing the intimate face of things onto celluloid. It is something else altogether that Epstein identifies with the peculiar power of mechanical automatism: an active dialectic in which one tragedy takes form at the expense of another—the threat of the cigar, the dust of betrayal, or the poisonous power of the rug at the expense of the traditional narrative and expressive arrangements of expectation, violence, and fear. Epstein's text, in other words, undertakes a work of de-figuration. He composes one film with the elements of another. He is not describing an experimental film—real or imaginary—made expressly to attest to the power of cinema. We learn later that he has extracted this film from another film, from a melodrama by Thomas Harper Ince entitled *The Honour of His*

House, with Sessue Hayakawa, a fetish-actor of the period, in the lead role. Epstein extracts the theoretical and poetical fable that describes the original power of the cinema from the body of another fable, from which he erased the traditional narrative aspect in order to create another dramaturgy, another system of expectations, actions, and states of being.

The cinema-unity thus undergoes an exemplary split. Jean Epstein welcomes an art that restores the duality of life and fictions, of art and science, of the sensible and the intelligible, to their original unity. And yet, Epstein only arrives at this pure essence of the cinema by extracting a work of "pure" cinema from the filmed melodrama. This particular penchant for making a fable with another is not a fad of the period, but a constitutive fact of the cinema as experience, art, and idea of art. It is also a fact that puts cinema in a contradictory continuity with a whole regime of art. From Jean Epstein to today, making a film on the body of another is exactly what the three main figures spawned by the cinema have been doing all along—directors, who "film" scripts they themselves have nothing to do with, the audience, for whom cinema is a potpourri of mixed memories, and critics and cinephiles, who extract a work of pure plastic forms from the body of a commercial fiction. The same is true of those two encyclopedic works that attempt to sum up the power of cinema: Deleuze's *Cinema 1* and *2*, and Godard's *Histoire(s) du cinéma*, in eight episodes. These two works constitute an ontology of the cinema argued for with bits and pieces gleaned from the entire *corpus* of the cinematographic art. Godard offers as evidence for his theory of the image-icon the pure plastic shots he extracts from the functional images Hitchcock had used to convey the enigmas and affects of his fables. Deleuze builds his ontology on the claim that cinematographic images are two things in one: they are the things themselves, the intimate events of universal becoming, and they are the operations of an art that restores to the events of the world the power they had been deprived of by the opaque screen of the human brain. Deleuze's dramaturgy of ontological restitution, like Epstein's or Godard's dramaturgy of origin, depends on the same process of extracting from the details in the fiction. For Deleuze, Jeff's broken leg in *Rear Window* and Scottie's vertigo in *Vertigo* are embodiments of the "rupture of the sensory-motor schema" through which the time-image splits itself off from the movement-image. Deleuze and Godard both repeat Jean Epstein's dramaturgy, they both extract, after the fact, the original essence of the cinematographic art from the plots the art of cinema shares with the old art of telling stories [*l'art des histoires*]. Cinema's enthusiastic pioneer, its disenchanted historiographer, its sophisticated philosopher, and its amateur theoreticians all share this dramaturgy because it is consubstantial with cinema as an art and an object of thought. The fable that tells the truth of cinema is extracted from the stories narrated on its screens.

The substitution operated by Jean Epstein's analysis is not the work of youthful illusion. He presents a fable of the cinema that is consubstantial with the art of the cinematograph, though it was not a fable born with the cinema. The dramaturgy Jean Epstein grafted onto the cinematographic machine has come down to us because it is as much a dramaturgy of art in general as of the cinema in particular, because it belongs more to the aesthetic *moment* of cinema than to the distinctiveness of its technical means. Cinema as an artistic idea predated the cinema as a technical means and distinctive art. The opposition between the "tragedy in suspense" that reveals the intimate texture of things and the conventions of "dramatic action" was instrumental in pitting the young art of cinema against the outdated art of the theater. And yet, cinema inherited this opposition from the theater, where it was first played out in the time of Maeterlinck and Gordon Craig, Appia and Meyerhold. These playwrights and stage directors had already countered Aristotle's arrangement of incidents with the intimate suspense of the world. They were also the ones who taught the cinema to extract the tragedy in suspense from the body of old plots. It is quite tempting, in fact, to see Jean Epstein's "tragedy in suspense" as deriving from the "motionless tragedy" that, thirty years earlier, Maeterlinck had thought of extracting from Shakespeare's stories of love and violence: "The mysterious chant of the Infinite, the ominous silence of the souls and of God, the murmur of Eternity on the horizon, the destiny or fatality we are conscious of within us, though by what tokens none can tell—do not all these underlie King Lear, Macbeth, Hamlet? And would it not be possible, by some interchanging of the roles, to bring them nearer to us, and send the actors further off?... I have grown to believe that an old man, seated in his armchair, waiting patiently, with his lamp beside him; giving unconscious ear to all the eternal laws that reign about his house, interpreting, without comprehending, the silence of doors and windows and the quivering voice of the light, submitting with bent head to the presence of his soul and his destiny—an old man, who conceives not that all the powers of this world, like so many heedful servants, are mingling and keeping vigil in his room... or that every star in heaven and every fiber of the soul are directly concerned in the movement of an eyelid that closes, or a thought that springs to birth—I have grown to believe that he, motionless as he is, does yet live in reality a deeper, more human and more universal life than the lover who strangles his mistress, the captain who conquers in battle, or 'the husband who avenges his honor.'"[3]

The automatic eye of the camera so celebrated in *Bonjour cinéma* does no more than the poet of the "motionless life" dreamed up by Maeterlinck. Even the crystal metaphor Gilles Deleuze borrows from Jean Epstein is already there in the theoretician of symbolist drama: "Let but the chemist pour a few mysterious drops into a vessel that seems to contain the purest water, and at once masses of crystals will rise to the surface, thus revealing to us all that lay in abeyance there where nothing was visible before to our incomplete eyes."[4] Maeterlinck adds that this new poem about the sudden appearance of fabulous crystals in a liquid in suspension needs a new actor, a being that is not human, but closer in kind to the wax figures of a museum, and not the traditional actor with his old-fashioned feelings and means of expression. This android has enjoyed a not undistinguished life in the theater, from Edward Gordon Craig's Übermarionettes to Tadeusz Kantor's Theater of Death. The being of celluloid, whose "dead" chemical materiality jars with the actor's living gestures, is certainly one of its possible incarnations. Maeterlinck's description of the character who sits motionless beside his lamp conjures up for us a cinematographic shot; film directors, whether narrative or contemplative in temperament, have given this motionless character a great number of diverse incarnations.

But we are not so concerned here with the specific nature of the debt the film fable owes to symbolist poetics. It is not influence, or the fact of belonging to a particular lexical or conceptual universe, that leads Jean Epstein to work by extracting one fable from the body of another in Maeterlinck's wake and before Deleuze and Godard. The logic of a whole regime of art is implicated in the process. The work of de-figuration undertaking by Epstein was already being practiced by those nineteenth century art critics—Goncourt and others—who extracted from Rubens' religious scenes, Rembrandt's bourgeois ones, and Chardin's still-lives the same

---

[3] Maurice Maeterlinck, "The Tragical in Daily Life," in *The Treasure of the Humble*, trans. Alfred Sutro (London: George Allen, 1897) 98–9; 105–6.

[4] Maeterlinck, "The Tragical in Daily Life," 110.

dramaturgy of the painterly gesture and the adventures of pictorial matter being brought to the foreground while relegating to the background the painting's figurative content. The Schlegel brothers were already proposing this Romantic fragmentation, this process of picking apart old poems only to turn those parts into the seeds for new poems, in the texts they published in the *Athenäum* at the beginning of that century. The whole logic of the aesthetic regime of art finds its footing at this time.[5] This logic rejects the representative model of constructed incidents and expressive codes appropriate to the subjects and situations in favor of an originary power of art initially distributed between two extremes: a pure creative activity thenceforward thought to be without rules or models, and the pure passivity of the expressive power inscribed on the very surface of things, independently of every desire to signify or create. It confronts the old principle of form fashioning matter with the identity, at the core of this new regime, between the pure power of the idea and the radical impotence of sensible presence and of the mute writing of things. But this union of contraries, where the work required by the artistic idea and the originary power coincide, is the result of the long work of de-figuration that in the new work contradicts the expectations borne by the subject matter or the story, or that reviews, rereads, and rearranges the elements of old works. This process undoes the arrangements of fiction and of representational painting, and draws our attention instead to the painterly gesture and the adventures of matter lurking beneath the subject of figuration, to the glimmer of the epiphany and the splendor of pure reasonless being glowing just beneath the conflict of wills of the play or novel. It hollows out or exacerbates the gestures of expressive bodies, slows down or speeds up narrative progression, suspends or saturates meanings. The art of the aesthetic age wants to identify its unconditioned power with its contrary: the passivity of reasonless being, the specks of elementary particles, and the originary upsurge of things. Flaubert dreamed of writing a book without subject or matter, a book that would be held together by nothing more than its "style," though he himself realized that the only way to achieve this sovereign style, the pure expression of his artistic will, was to create its opposite: a book stripped of every trace of the writer's intervention and composed instead of the indifferent swirl of specks of dust and of the passivity of things with neither will nor meaning. This splendor of the insignificant had to be realized in the infinitesimal gap opened up at the heart of representative logic: in stories about individuals who help or thwart one another in the pursuit of their goals, these goals being, incidentally, of the most commonplace sort: seducing a woman, attaining a social position, earning money… The work of style was to affect the passivity of the empty gaze of reasonless things in its exposition of everyday actions, and it would only succeed in its task if it itself became passive, invisible, if it painstakingly effaced the difference between itself and the ordinary prose of the world.

Such is the art of the aesthetic age. It is an art that comes afterwards and undoes the links of representative art, either by thwarting the logic of arranged incidents through the becoming-passive of writing, or by refiguring old poems and paintings. This work presupposes all past art to be available and open to being reread, reviewed, repainted or rewritten at will. It presupposes also that anything and everything in the world is available to art. Banal objects, a flake peeling from a wall, an illustration from an ad campaign, are all available to art in their double resource: as hieroglyphs ciphering an age of the world, a society, a history, and,

---

[5] For a more elaborate discussion, please see my *The Politics of Aesthetics*, trans. Gabe Rockhill (London: Continuum Books, 2004), and *L'Inconscient esthétique* (Paris: Galilée, 2001).

inversely, as pure presences, as naked realities brought to light by the new-found splendor of the insignificant. The properties of this regime of art—identity of active and passive, elevation of everything to the dignity of art, work of de-figuration that extracts the tragedy in suspense from the dramatic action—are the properties Jean Epstein attributes to cinema. Cinema, in the double power of the conscious eye of the director and the unconscious eye of the camera, is the perfect embodiment of Schelling's and Hegel's argument that the identity of conscious and unconscious is the very principle of art. It is easy, then, to see how one may be tempted to conclude, with Epstein and others, that cinema is the dream come true of this regime of art. After all, it really does seem that Flaubert framed his micro-narrations like "film shots": Emma at the window absorbed in her contemplation of the bean props knocked down by the wind; Charles leaning out of another window and gazing distractedly at the laziness of the summer evening, at the skeins of cotton drying in the air and at the dirty water of an industrial river. Cinema seems to accomplish naturally the writing of *opsis* that reverses Aristotle's privileging of *muthos*. The conclusion, however, is false, for the very simple reason that cinema, being by nature what the arts of the aesthetic age had to strive to be, invariably reverts their movement. Flaubert's frames are the work of a way of writing that contradicts narrative plausibility and expectation by reaching for the dreamlike stasis of paintings. Painters and novelists had to work to make themselves the instruments of their becoming-passive; the mechanical apparatus, conversely, suppresses the active work involved in this becoming-passive. The camera cannot be made passive because it is passive already, because it is of necessity at the service of the intelligence that manipulates it. The camera-eye Dziga Vertov uses at the beginning of *Man with a Movie Camera* to explore the unknown face of things seems at first to illustrate Jean Epstein's claim. Just then, a cameraman enters the frame and installs the tripod of a second camera on top of the first, the instrument of a will that has prior access to the discoveries of the first and is free to arrange them into bits of celluloid appropriate for every use. The fact is that the mechanic eye lends itself to everything: to the tragedy in suspense, to the work of Soviet Kinoks, and not least to the illustration of old-fashioned stories of interest, heartbreak, and death. Those who can do everything are usually doomed to servitude. And indeed it turns out that the "passivity" of the machine that supposedly crowns the program of the aesthetic regime of art lends itself just as well to the work of restoring the old representative power of active form arranging passive matter that a century of painting and literature had struggled to subvert. At the end of the day, the whole logic of representative art finds itself restored, piece by piece, by this machine. And the artist who rules over the passive machine with a sovereign hand is, more than any other artist, doomed to transform his mastery into servitude, to put his art at the service of companies whose business is to control and cash in on the collective imaginary. In the age of Joyce and Virginia Woolf, of Malevich and Schönberg, cinema arrives as if expressly designed to thwart a simple teleology of artistic modernity, to counter art's aesthetic autonomy with its old submission to the representative regime.

We must not map this process of thwarting onto the opposition between the principles of art and those of a popular entertainment subject to the industrialization of leisure and the pleasures of the masses. The art of the aesthetic age abolishes all of these borders because it makes art of everything. The novel of the aesthetic age grew to maturity with the serial; its poetry beat to the rhythm of the masses; its painting adorned guinguettes and music halls. In Epstein's day, the new art of directing films drew inspiration from acrobatic feats and athletic performances. It was also in his day that one started seeing scraps of consumer goods hanging from picture rails or illustrating poems. There is no doubt that very early on pressure from the industry turned film directors into "craftsmen" who had to struggle to impress their logo on scenarios they were more often than not obliged to illustrate with actors not of their choosing. And yet, a basic law of the aesthetic regime of art is to come afterwards, to graft one's art onto a preexisting art and render its operations almost indiscernible from the prose of everyday stories and images. The film industry, in a sense, is only the most radical form of this law. It is true that today we seem more than willing to rehabilitate a cinema of craftsmen in the face of the impasses of an "auteur politics" whose culmination seems to be the aestheticism of publicity campaigns. Nobody needs to be prompted to reiterate Hegel's diagnosis that the work of the artist who does only what he wants succeeds in showing no more than the image of the artist in general. All we add today is that this image is bound in the end to be confused with the image of a name brand on a product.[6] If the art of cinema accepts to come after producers and scriptwriters and to illustrate the program they provide—which it invariably thwarts with its own logic—it isn't just because of the pressure the harsh laws of the market exert on it. It is also, and more importantly, because of an indecisiveness at the heart of its artistic nature. Cinema literalizes a secular idea of art in the same stroke that it actualizes the refutation of that idea: it is both the art of the afterwards that emerges from the Romantic de-figuration of stories, and the art that returns the work of de-figuration to classical imitation. Hence the paradoxical nature of the continuity between cinema and the aesthetic revolution that made it possible. Even though the basic technical equipment of the cinema secures the identity of active and passive that is the principle of that revolution, the fact remains that cinema can only be faithful to it if it gives another turn of the screw to its secular dialectics. The art of cinema has been constrained, empirically, to affirm its art against the tasks assigned to it by the industry. But the visible process by which it thwarts these tasks only hides a more intimate process: to thwart its servitude, cinema must first thwart its mastery. It must use its artistic procedures to construct dramaturgies that thwart its natural powers. There is no straight line running from cinema's technical nature to its artistic vocation. The film fable is a thwarted fable.

We must then call into question the idea of a continuity between the technical nature of the machine of vision and the forms of the cinematographic art. Filmmakers and theoreticians have been quick to suggest that the art of cinema attained its perfection there where its fables and forms succeeded in expressing the essence of the cinematographic medium. A few exemplary figures and propositions punctuate the history of this identification of form and fable: the burlesque automaton—whether Chaplinesque or Keatonian—that fascinated the generation of Delluc, Epstein, and Eisenstein before resurfacing at the core of André Bazin's film theory and inspiring systematizations being worked out today;[7] the gaze cast by Rossellini's camera at "non-manipulated things"; Bresson's theory and practice of the "model," which pits the truth of cinematographic automatism against the artifice of theatrical expression. It would be easy to show, however, that none of these dramaturgies properly belong to the cinema. Better yet, it would be easy to show that if they belong to cinema at all, it is because they put a thwarting

---

[6] Serge Daney has worked out the most rigorous form of this dialectic of art and commerce. See especially his: *L'Exercice a été profitable, monsieur* (Paris: P.O.L., 1993) and *La Maison cinéma et le monde* (Paris: P.O.L., 2001). I discuss these in my: "Celui qui vient après. Les antinomies de la pensée critique," *Trafic* 37 (2001) 142–50.

[7] Cf. Thérèse Giraud, *Cinéma et technologie* (Paris: PUF, 2001), which argues for the opposite thesis to the one I argue for here.

logic in motion. There are some brilliant pages in Bazin where he tries to demonstrate that Charlie's mime is the incarnation of cinematographic being, of the form silver nitrate prints on strips of celluloid.[8] But the burlesque automaton was an aesthetically constituted figure, a hero of the pure spectacle that flew in the face of traditional psychology, long before the advent of cinema. We might also add that its role in the cinema wasn't to be the embodiment of the technical automaton, but to make itself the instrument that derailed every fable, the equivalent, in the art of moving images, to the becoming-passive characteristic of the prose of the modern novel. The burlesque body is constantly shuttling between total impotence and absolute power, its actions and reactions are always overshooting or falling short of the mark. The best example here is the Keatonian hero, divided as he is between a look that spells defeat from the outset and a movement that nothing can stop. The Keatonian hero is always looking on as things slip right through his fingers, and he is also a moving body [*le mobile*] whose forward thrust knows no resistance, as in that scene in *Sherlock Junior* where he clears, in a straight line, all the obstacles in his way while sitting on the handlebars of a motorcycle whose driver has fallen off at the beginning of the course. The burlesque body cuts the links between cause and effect, action and reaction, because it throws the elements of the moving image into contradiction. This is why, throughout cinema's history, the burlesque body has been the preferred dramaturgic machine for transforming one fable into another. Today, we have Kitano using the mechanics of burlesque to turn the logic of the action film on its head. With acceleration, he turns the violent confrontation of wills into a pure mechanics of action and reaction divested of all expressivity; he then dissolves these automatic movements in pure contemplation by subjecting them to the inverse principle of distension, of a growing gap between action and reaction. The policemen at the end of *Hana-bi* have become pure spectators observing the suicide of their old colleague, perceptible only as a sound resonating in the indifference of sand and waves. Burlesque automatism drives the logic of the fable to what we might call, with Deleuze, pure optical and sound situations. But these "pure" situations are not the rediscovered essence of the image: they are the result of those operations whereby the cinematographic art thwarts its own powers.

At the risk of parting ways with Bazin and Deleuze, I would say that Rossellini's dramaturgy proves the same point: all of these "pure" situations result from a set of specific operations. Bazin argues that Rossellini, in the great fables of wandering he brings to the screen, realizes the fundamental vocation of the automatic machine to follow, ever so patiently, the minute signs that allow a glimpse into the spiritual secret of beings. Deleuze sees Rossellini as the director *par excellence* of the pure optical and sound situations that reflect the realities besetting Europe in the aftermath of the war, a time when individuals who had lost all their bearings were forced to confront situations they had no answers for. But the situations of narrative rarefaction Rossellini dramatizes on the screen are not situations indicative of the "impossibility to react," or of the inability to bear intolerable spectacles or coordinate gaze and

[8] André Bazin, "The Myth of Monsieur Verdoux," in *What is Cinema?*, vol. 2, trans. Hugh Gray (Berkeley: University of California Press, 1971) 104. "Before any 'character'... there exists a person called Charlie. He is a black-and-white form printed on the silver nitrate of film." Bazin's analysis does not limit itself to the onto-technological identification of the Chaplinesque character with cinematographic being, though that is one of its major concerns, hence his opposition to the "ideology" of *Modern Times* and *The Great Dictator*. Both these films, Bazin argues, destroy Charlie's "ontological" nature because they make Charlie Chaplin's hand and thought too visible.

action. They are experimental situations that Rossellini uses to superimpose onto the normal movement of narrative continuity another movement directed by a fable of *vocation*. In *Rome, Open City*, Pina tears herself free from a line of soldiers who clearly should have been able to restrain her and dashes after the truck driving away her fiancé. Originating in the mode of the burlesque movement only to end in a mortal fall, Pina's dash after the truck at once exceeds the visible of the narrative situation and of the expression of love. Similarly, the jump into the void that brings Edmund's wanderings to a close in *Germany Year Zero* exceeds every (non) reaction to Germany's material and moral ruin in 1945. These movements are not oriented towards a fictional end, nor have they been disoriented by an intolerable situation: they've been deflected by the imposition of another movement. Rossellini has transferred a dramaturgy of the call from the religious to the artistic level. That is what drives his characters from one mode of movement and gravitation to another mode, where they cannot but free-fall. Even if Rossellini achieves in that movement the coincidence of a fictional and a plastic dramaturgy, this unity of form and content is not the realized essence of the cinematographic medium, producing a "non-manipulated" vision of things; it is instead the product of a dramaturgy where the character's extreme liberty coincides with his or her absolute subjection to a command. The logic of the "rupture of the sensory-motor schema" is a dialectic of impotence and excessive power.

We reencounter this same dialectic in Bresson's "cinematography." Bresson had thought to sum it up with his well-known couple: the "passive" model who mechanically reproduces the gestures and intonations dictated by the director, and the director—painter—editor who uses the screen as if it were the blank canvas whereon to assemble the "pieces of nature" offered up by the model. Still, we need a more complex dramaturgy than this one to separate the art of the cinematographer from the stories he tells. A Bresson film is always the *mise-en-scène* of a trap and a hunt. The poacher (*Mouchette*), the rogue (*Au hazard, Balthazar*), the rejected lover (*Ladies of the Bois de Boulogne*), the jealous husband (*A Gentle Woman*), the thief and the chief of police (*Pickpocket*), all set their traps and wait for their victims to get caught. The film fable realizes its artistic essence by thwarting the scenarios concocted by these volitional agents. It's a mistake, however, to think that visual fragmentation and the passivity of the model do in fact thwart those scenarios, since what they actually do is erase the line between the hunter awaiting his prey and the director trying to surprise the truth of the "model." There must be, in other words, a counter-logic that opposes the visible complicity between these two hunters. What protects the prey from the hunter and the film fable from the story illustrated in Bresson is, first of all, a fleeing movement, a fall into the void. The door that slams shut as somebody opens a window and the flowing silk scarf in *A Gentle Woman*, or the girl who rolls down the slope time and again to the edge of the pond where she'll drown herself in *Mouchette*, mark the counter-movement, initial or final, by which the preys elude their hunters. The beauty of these scenes comes from how the visible contradicts narrative meaning: the veil gently suspended by the wind hides the fall of a suiciding body, the child playing at rolling down the slope both fulfills and denies the suicide of a teenager. That the authors thwarted by these scenes that Bresson himself added to the storyline are not obscure scriptwriters but Dostoevsky and Bernanos highlights all the more the counter-movement that keeps cinema from every simple effectuation of its visual essence. The role Bresson assigns to the voice in his films is the other part of this counter-effect logic. Far from being just the expression of the truth wrenched from the model, the so-called "white" voices of Bresson's films are, more radically, how cinema accomplishes the project of literature by inverting it. Literature, to thwart the arrangement of incidents and the conflict of wills, let itself be infiltrated by the great passivity of the visible. The addition of image to literature amounted to a subtraction of sense. Cinema, for its part, can only appropriate this power by reversing the game and hollowing out the visible with the word. That is the function of these "white voices" that melt together all the different intonations required by the classical expression of the characters. Paradoxically, it is this sound invention, and not the framing of the painter and the montage of the editor, that defines the art of the model representative of a "pure cinema." The counterpart of the image that cuts the literary narrative is this voice that simultaneously lends body to the image and subtracts from it. It is like a thwarted narrative voice in literature [*une parole littéraire contredite*]: neutrality of the narrative voice attributed to bodies it has disowned and that distort it in turn. Ironically, the voice that defines Bresson's cinematographic art was first imagined in the theater as the voice of the "third character," the Unknown or the Inhuman, Maeterlinck thought inhabited Ibsen's dialogues.

All these great figures of a pure cinema whose fables and forms would easily be deducible from its essence do no more than offer up the best examples of the film fable, split and thwarted: *mise-en-scène* of a *mise-en-scène*, counter-movement that affects the arrangement of incidents and shots, automatism separating image from movement, voice hollowing out the visible. Cinema can only make the games it plays with its own means intelligible to itself through the games of exchange and inversion it plays with the literary fable, the plastic form, and the theatrical voice. The texts gathered here attest to the multiplicity of these games, with no pretensions, of course, to exhausting the field of possibilities of the art of cinema. Some of the chapters show the paradoxes of the film fable at their most radical. This is the case, for instance, with Eisenstein's efforts to create a cinema that opposes the fables of old with its capacity to translate an idea—in his case, that of communism—directly into signs-images that convey new affects. It is also the case with Murnau's transposition of Molière's *Tartuffe* to the silent screen. Eisenstein's project governs *The General Line*, where he identifies the demonstration of the new art with the political opposition of the new and mechanized world of the kolkhozes to the old world of the peasants. But to bring it off, Eisenstein has to line the opposition with a more secret aesthetic complicity between the Dionysian figures of the new art and the trances and superstitions of old. Murnau manages his transposition of *Tartuffe* into silent film by transforming Molière's schemer into a shadow, and his conquest operation into the conflict of visibilities conducted by Elmire to dissipate the shadow haunting her husband. But then, it is the very power of the cinematographic shadow that Murnau must lay to rest in order to unmask the impostor. A more discrete thwarting of the text it brings to the screen can be found in Nicholas Ray's *They Live by Night*, where Ray imbues the visual fragmentation with the poetic powers of metonymy in order to undo the perceptive continuum created by the "stream of consciousness" that the novelist in the 1930s had used, inversely, to capture the sensory character of the moving image. Even the most classical of cinematographic forms, the ones most faithful to the representative tradition of carefully arranged incidents, clearly defined characters, and neatly composed images, are affected by this gap, evidence enough that the film fable belongs to the aesthetic regime of art. Anthony Mann's Westerns are a good example. There can be no doubt that Mann's Westerns are model representatives of that most coded of cinematographic genres, or that they obey all the fictional needs dictated by a narrative and popular cinema. And yet they too are inhabited by an essential gap. The meticulous precision that connects the hero's perceptions and gestures cuts his actions off from all those things—the stability of ethical values, and the frenzy of desires and dreams that transgress them—that normally give meaning to the action. Ironically, it is the perfection of the "sensory-motor schema" of action and reaction that causes problems for these tales of quarrels with desire and the law by substituting them with the confrontation between two perceptive spaces. A constant principle of what is known as *mise-en-scène* in the cinema is to supplement—and thwart—narrative continuity and the rationality of the goals by not aligning two visibilities, or two relationships of the visible to movements, either by means of visual reframings, or by means of the aberrant movements imposed by a character who simultaneously aligns himself with the scenario of the pursuit of goals and perverts it.

We should not be surprised to find here two other classical incarnations of this figure, namely the child (*Moonfleet*) and the psychopath (*M*, *While the City Sleeps*). The child in the cinema oscillates between two roles, traditionally playing either the victim of a violent world or the mischievous observer of a world that takes itself too seriously. In *Moonfleet*, Fritz Lang confronts these banal and representative figures with the aesthetic figure of the child director, who is determined to impose his own script and to mount the visual refutation of the narrative game of intrigues and the visual game of appearances that normally conspire to pigeonhole the child into the role of naïve victim. The obstinacy that exceeds every rational pursuit of goals is likewise the trait by which the psychopath, in the cinema, upsets the scenarios of the trap where the criminal is at once hunter and prey. In its aberration, this obstinacy mirrors the equality of action and passion where cinema metaphorizes itself. The murderer in *M* escapes visually because the automatism of his movements dovetails into the double trap set by the police and the mob that will in the end get the better of him. Unlike his pursuers, who trace circles on maps and post detectives on street corners, the murderer doesn't pursue a rational goal, he could not do something other than what he does. When he meets a child's gaze reflected in a shop window, he must pass from the insouciance of the anonymous *flâneur* to the automatism of the hunter, just as he must regain the image of a contented observer an instant later, as he stands side by side with another little girl. The shot of the murderer and his next victim looking happily at the window display of a toy shop belongs to the same counter-effect logic as the flowing scarf in *A Gentle Woman*, the rolls down the slope of *Mouchette*, the rectilinear trajectory of *Sherlock Junior*, the meticulous and indifferent gestures of James Stewart in Mann's Westerns, and the mythological elation of the bull's wedding in *The General Line*.

This same logic abolishes the borders between document and fiction, between the politically committed work and the pure work. The plastic extravagance of Eisenstein's communist film is part and parcel of the same dream that produced the indifferent "shot" of Emma Bovary gazing out of her window, and this indifference sometimes rubs off on the images of the politically committed documentary. This is the case in that moment of *Listen to Britain* when Humphrey Jennings' camera, positioned into the light, shows two characters in silhouette peacefully watching the sun set over the waves before a change of angle reveals their function and identity: they are two coastguards scanning the horizon for signs of the enemy. *Listen to Britain* is a limit example of the counter-effect characteristic of the film fable. Although meant to rally support for England's war efforts in 1941, the film never shows a country at war and mobilized militarily for its defense. Jennings only shows the soldiers during their moments of leisure: in a train compartment singing a song about distant lands, in a dance or concert hall, at a village procession. His camera slides seamlessly from one furtive image to another: a man at his window at night, holding a light with one hand and drawing the curtains with the other, a school courtyard where children dance in a circle, the two men watching the setting sun. The paradoxical political choice of showing a country at peace in order to win support for its war efforts succeeds because Jennings makes exemplary use of the paradox inherent to the film fable. The peaceful moments that make up the film—a face and light glimpsed behind a window, two men chatting as they watch the sunset, a song in a train, a dance contest—are nothing other than the moments of suspension that punctuate fiction films and that invest the constructed verisimilitude of the action and the story with the naked truth, the meaningless truth of life. The fable tends to intersperse these moments of suspension/moments of the real with action sequences. Jennings, by thus isolating them in this strange "documentary," highlights just how ambivalent this play of exchanges, between the verisimilar action characteristic of representative art and the life without reason emblematic of aesthetic art, really is.[9] The ordinary, the zero-degree of cinematographic fiction is for these two to complement one another, in order to provide a sort of double testimony to the logic of the action and the effect of the real. The artistic work of the fable, conversely, is to vary the values, to increase or diminish the gap, to invert the roles. The privilege of the so-called documentary film is that it is not obliged to create the *feeling* of the real, and this allows it to treat the real as a problem and to experiment more freely with the variable games of action and life, significance and insignificance. If this play is at its zero-degree in Jennings' documentary, it takes on an altogether different complexity when Chris Marker composes *The Last Bolshevik* by interlacing images from the post-Soviet present with various types of "documents": images of the imperial family in 1913 and those of a Stalin lookalike "helping" tractor drivers in their difficulties; the buried film-reports Alexander Medvekin shot from his film-train, the comedies he directed and which got brushed under the carpet, and the films he was obliged to make of the huge pageants put on by Stalinist athletes; the accounts gathered from interviews, the massacre on the Odessa steps of *Battleship Potemkin*, and Simpleton's lamentation on the stage of the Bolshoi Theater. Marker, by putting all of these in dialogue in the six "letters" to Alexander Medvekin that make up the film, can deploy better than all illustrators of made up stories the polyvalence of images and signs, the potential difference between values of expression—between the image that speaks and the one that silences, between the speech that conjures up an image and the one that is simply enigmatic—that make up, in contrast to the episodes of before, the new forms of fiction of the aesthetic age.

Documentary fiction invents new intrigues with historical documents, and thus it touches hands with the film fable that joins and disjoins—in the relationship between story and character, shot and sequence—the powers of the visible, of speech, and of movement. When Marker replays, under the shadow cast by the color images of restored Orthodox pomp, the "doctored" images of the massacre on the Odessa steps and images from Stalinist propaganda films, his work resonates with Godard's, who filmed, in the Pop age, the Maoist theatricalization of Marxism and, in the "Post-Modern" age, the fragments of the intermingled history of the cinema and the century. Marker also touches hands with Fritz Lang, who replays the same story of the chase for a psychopathic killer at two different ages of the visible: the first in *M*, where

[9] For a more detailed analysis of this film, please see: Jacques Rancière, "L'Inoubliable," in *Arrêt sur histoire*, eds. Jean-Louis Comolli and Jacques Rancière (Paris: Éditions du Centre Georges Pompidou, 1997) 47–70.

maps and magnifying glasses, inventories and drag-nets trap the murderer and prosecute him in a theatrical court; the second in *While the City Sleeps*, where all these accessories have disappeared and been replaced by a machine of vision, the television that places Mobley "face to face" with the murderer and transforms an imaginary capture into a weapon for a real capture. The TV monitor isn't the instrument of "mass consumption" that spells out the death of the great art. It is, more profoundly and also more ironically, the machine of vision that suppresses the mimetic gap and that thus realizes, in its own way, the new art's panaesthetic project of immediate sensible presence. This new machine doesn't annul the power of cinema, but its "impotence." It annuls the process of thwarting that has always animated its fables. The task of the director is then to invert, once again, the game where television "realizes" cinema. A longstanding lamentation in contemporary thought wants us to bear witness to the programmed death of images at the hands of the machine for information and advertisement. I have opted for the opposite perspective and have tried to show that the art and thought of images have always been nourished by all that thwarts them.

SECTION FOUR
PSYCHOLOGY AND PSYCHOANALYSIS

CHAPTER 22
JEAN MITRY

Jean Mitry (1907–1988) was a French filmmaker, film theorist, and film critic, and one of the first film aestheticians in France. He is much more widely read in his original French than in English translation, but his influence on other philosophers and theorists of film has been profound. Of particular significance is that Mitry was able to begin the process of moving serious discourse of film into academic and intellectual contexts, as opposed to solely popular discourse and the newspapers. The selection included here ("Psychologie du montage") is one chapter from his magnum opus, The Aesthetics of Psychology and the Cinema *(*Esthétique et psychologie du cinéma*), originally published in French in 1963.*

Mitry begins with a consideration of the relationship between images and signs. Cinema really only has value, he argues, to the extent that the images that constitute a film help to make a concrete reality. To do this, images must become signs—but they must fulfill a certain presignifying logic before they can do so. In themselves, images are concrete and objective; they are representations of real things. Only by way of the associations—between representations within an image, or between images—can signification take place. Thus, the logic of reality—the coherence of the relationships between the things in an image—must be fulfilled before that image can even begin to function as a sign; it is easy to see how signification advances upon the objective reality represented in any given film image, however, once we recognize that cinematography never simply records. There is always something subjective guiding the camera, guiding the production of any particular series of images. The view of the camera itself is an interpretation.

Mitry offers these observations in part to counter the rising popularity of figures in France like Jean Rouch, with his notion of "cinéma-vérité." The cinéma-vérité movement tried to remove any mitigating influences between the objective reality being filmed and the filming device (the camera), so as to provide audiences with a direct observation of reality. But, as Mitry points out, the process of observation always influences what is observed, and this is obviously true of the case of cinema, which requires the introduction of a cinematographic camera and camera crew into a scene of real life, while expecting those individuals who are filmed to act naturally, as if they are not being filmed. Now, aesthetically speaking, for a film like Rouch's to succeed, all it would need is to give the spectator the impression of truth—but that impression is precisely not reality. Any recording of reality is subjective, and, thus, on some level a fiction or an interpretation (or both). The only route to reality, Mitry says, is immersion in reality: not cinema.

Thus, while it is important for a film to fulfill the logic of the reality it presents, it is nevertheless the case that a film is always more than the images of the objects it has recorded: A filmmaker can describe an object simply by way of the technique he or she uses in filming and framing it, or a filmmaker can suggest what the image of the object means, interpreting it for viewers of the film. There are many film techniques by way of which these more significatory goals can be accomplished, and Mitry says that there are no good or bad techniques as such—just good and bad uses of techniques. Bad uses of a film technique submit the actions depicted to an idea, rather than allowing the images to tell their own stories; in this heavy-handedness, the director's direction can be felt by the audience, which is, for Mitry, always a failure in film. Good uses of a film technique submit the film to the demands of dramatic truth: actions are exploited as signs, meant to signify, to convey meaning. This makes keeping a clear distinction in mind between reality (the objects filmed) and pseudo-reality (the fictional representation produced by way of film editing) absolutely important. The dramatic truth of an image or a scene will have as much to do with the latter as it does the former.

Any given shot can either describe the objects presented within the frame, or suggest what those objects might mean, and Mitry insists that a film must make an effort to describe the objects it presents. The process of editing the film is a process of montage. Mitry is saying that montage ought to be used to analyze scenes or arrangements which have previously been established by way of simple description in the film, not to create a fictitious reality by way of editing without any grounding in concrete reality. He compares this distinction to that in the use of language between a poet and a novelist. The novelist, Mitry says, creates a fictitious reality, which he or she then hides behind. But a poet exploits the real world as his or her primary material, presenting his or her own subjective vision of the world—and, thus, what matters in poetry is not what the poet is saying, but how he or she says it. So, with film.

In the remainder of the essay, Mitry presents the task of film aesthetics as the determination of the psychological bases which justify a given filmmaker's formal choices in the particular context of that film. Working from a specific model of the human mind and sense perception, Mitry argues that we are incapable of paying attention to any one object for any length of time without a break. He notes that human perception never sees the entirety of any object: We perceive numerous details, and our attention shifts from detail to detail, until ultimately we construct "the whole" out of the details we remember. He notes further that our perception of duration functions in the same way: We have no continuous experience of duration; rather, our perception of the passage of time is likewise discontinuous. The construction of whole objects from isolated perceived details, and a causally charged flow of time from discrete moments of experience, is not unlike the way in which film provides audiences with the illusion of continuity: both take advantage of the structure of the human mind to pass the discontinuous off as the continuous. In a film, however, shots can be used by the filmmaker to guide our attention and, thus, intentionally produce ideas. Editing—montage—thus produces a feeling of continuity without giving us the sensation of the continuous.

Once again, Mitry notes that, if as we view the film, we find ourselves able to anticipate the action, we are experiencing the director's work in the film directly—and the impression of reality the film seeks to leave us with is destroyed. It is perceptual discontinuity alone that makes an aesthetic system possible, for Mitry, and thus the collaboration of the mind and montage which allows for cinema. We can be surprised in film, when a filmmaker frustrates our perceptual expectations—when we do not see or hear what we were expecting to see or hear—and, in those instances, film opens the possibility of the process of creating a film language. Novel approaches to cinematic structure and montage can be frustrating and difficult to understand at first, Mitry acknowledges, but with time, they can come to constitute one more element in our basic understanding of the possibilities of film technique, one more way in which the film image can become a sign.

Filmography

- ***Nanook of the North*** (USA, 1922). *Directed, Produced, and Written by* Robert J. Flaherty. *Starring* Allakariallak, Nyla, *and* Cunayou.
- ***Mat*** [*Mother*] (USSR, 1926). *Directed by* Vsevolod Pudovkin. *Produced by* Mezhrabpomfilm. *Written by* Nathan Zarkhi. *Starring* Vera Baranovskaya *and* Nikolai Batalov.
- ***Oblomok imperii*** [*Fragment of an Empire*] (USSR, 1929). *Directed by* Fridrikh Ermler. *Produced by* Sovkino. *Written by* Fridrikh Ermler *and* Ekaterina Vinogradskaya. *Starring* Emil Gal *and* Sergey Gerasimov.
- ***All Quiet on the Western Front*** (USA, 1930). *Directed by* Lewis Milestone. *Produced by* Carl Laemmle, Jr. *Written by* George Abbott. *Starring* Lew Ayres *and* Louis Wollheim.
- ***Prividenie, kotoroe ne vozvrashchaetsya*** [*The Ghost that Never Returns*] (USSR, 1930). *Directed by* Abram Room. *Produced by* Sovkino. *Written by* Valentin Turkin. *Starring* Boris Ferndinandov.
- ***Citizen Kane*** (USA, 1941). *Directed and Produced by* Orson Welles. *Written by* Herman J. Mankiewicz *and* Orson Welles. *Starring* Orson Welles, Joseph Cotten, *and* Dorothy Comingore.
- ***The Magnificent Ambersons*** (USA, 1942). *Directed, Produced, and Written by* Orson Welles. *Starring* Joseph Cotten, Dolores Costello, Anne Baxter, Tim Holt, Agnes Moorehead, Ray Collins, Erskine Sanford, *and* Richard Bennett.
- ***Shadow of a Doubt*** (USA, 1943). *Directed by* Alfred Hitchcock. *Produced by* Jack H. Skirball. *Written by* Thornton Wilder, Sally Benson, *and* Alma Reville. *Starring* Teresa Wright, Joseph Cotten, Macdonald Carey, Patricia Collinge, *and* Henry Travers.
- ***L'amore in città*** [*Love in the City*] (Italy, 1953). *Directed by* Federico Fellini, Michelangelo Antonioni, Alberto Lattuada, Carlo Lizzani, Francesco Maselli, Dino Risi, *and* Cesare Zavattini. *Produced by* Marco Ferreri *and* Riccardo Ghione. *Written by* Michelangelo Antonioni, Aldo Buzzi, Luigi Chiarini, Federico Fellini, Marco Ferreri, Alberto Lattuada, Luigi Malerba, Tullio Pinelli, Dino Risi, Vittorio Veltroni, *and* Cesare Zavattini.
- ***Mr. Arkadin*** (France–Spain–Switzerland, 1955). *Directed, Produced, Written by and Starring* Orson Welles.
- ***Moi, un noir*** [*I, a Negro*] (France, 1958). *Directed by* Jean Rouch. *Produced by* Pierre Braunberger *and* Roger Felytoux. *Written by* André Lubin. *Starring* Oumarou Ganda, Petit Touré, Alassane Maiga, Amadou Demba, Seydou Guede, Karido Faoudou, *and* Mademoiselle Gambi.
- ***Chronique d'un été*** [*Chronicle of a Summer*] (France, 1961). *Directed by* Jean Rouch. *Produced by* Anatole Dauman.

THE PSYCHOLOGY OF MONTAGE

Translated by Christopher King

The preceding remarks concerning rhythm and montage may be summarized as follows: the cinema has value only insofar as its images contribute to the development of a concrete reality. Moreover with this reality as its starting point, it must elevate these images to the level of *signs*; but only provided that the signs do not lose contact with the reality from which they derive and that they transcend the reality by signifying it rather than signifying beyond it.

We must never forget that the image—of necessity the image of something—is in its essence *objective* and *concrete*. It is only by association that it becomes a sign, a power; *but it is the power, not the image, which is abstract*. Yet, though the image is always subject to the personal vision and intentions of the director, it is at the level of its forms, not its essence; in its expressive purpose, not its actual existence.

It is therefore important that the logic of reality be fulfilled before any level of signification is achievable (and precisely so that this may be guaranteed). But fulfilling the logic of reality does not mean that the object must be presented in a way that is consistently objective, i.e., impersonal.

We should begin by taking issue with a school of thought which, thinking that it is possible to capture "true" reality, tries to turn the cinema into a tool of *scientific observation*, pure and simple, a machine for recording behavior. Granted, the cinema can be a scientific tool—within certain limitations. Fortunately, its conditions of existence prevent it from being this exclusively. When this is all it is, it is always to the detriment of art.

If the film is dealing with a dramatic action, then the supposed observation is merely the illusion of objectivity: the audience observes what it is meant to observe. However objective it may appear, this art form involves complete subjectivity. For which reason, the time and space of the drama must be respected and no obvious distortion or bias be allowed to intrude. However, it is an art just like any other. The more detailed the description of reality, the more the reality is damaged. We may try to confer on it all the appearances of objective reality (which is all well and good) but to speak of observation in this context is to beg the question.

Moreover, when the film is a document of life in the raw—since space must necessarily be fragmented into various fields of view—the view of the camera, guided by the cameraman, cannot help but be an arbitrary view, an interpretation of reality.

"True" reality cannot exist in art—any more in the cinema than in other art forms. What is recorded by the camera is never more than building bricks, contributing to the overall structure. It is not possible to film structures built up "objectively" since the very fact of recording the "reality" is already a subjective process, a choice. We shall see, moreover, that the same phenomenon pertains in our everyday behavior. As Pudovkin put it, "Film rearranges the elements of reality in its own way so as to make of them a new reality specific to it alone."

The most determined of the attempts to achieve an objective cinema—notably those of Jean Rouch—are obvious proof of this. In *Chronique d'un été*, Rouch follows up an investigation of several people from several different backgrounds. The intention—to record these people "in their living reality" is commendable, but what happens is that this "approximation of truth" has nothing to do with truth at all. Rouch goes into the people's homes with a microphone and a camera; he questions them and, at the moment they least expect it, he films them and is ingenious enough to believe that he has recorded them behaving "as they would in reality," whereas what he has done in fact is make them react to circumstances which he has contrived for them. The very fact of knowing that we are being observed, questioned and lined up in the viewfinder has the effect of making us assume (more or less unconsciously) an *attitude* of what we would like to be or what we think we are—which has nothing whatever to do with what we are: *being* is replaced by *acting*. Moreover, man is not an entity; his truth is made up of a series of multiple, contradictory appearances. For us to capture a single individual in his true reality, we would need an *invisible* camera filming him in his *everyday surroundings* for months on end. Anything else is self-delusion and all the more delusory for the fact that it is generally held to be true. In the example we have given, the actual presence of the "alien" interviewer would in itself be enough to alter the behavior of the subject (even though a familiarity might have developed between the subject and the interviewer).

The man who knows he is being observed is recorded no more objectively than is a path of electrons when a beam of light is projected onto them thereby changing the path. Nowhere is this more evident than in *Moi, un noir*. We know that after filming the life of some natives in Niger, down-and-outs living from hand to mouth in Treichville, a district of Abidjan, Jean Rouch asked one of them—Robinson—to comment freely on the images he had put together. Now, this commentary (which Jean Pouillon and Jean Carta take for a "series of thoughts about himself and his life, a gradual awakening of consciousness") is nothing more than an *attitude* which Robinson adopts through his own judgment of his own actions. He grants them the meaning he *would like* to see in them—that is all. What Marie Claire Wuilleumier[1] takes for an "apprenticeship to lucidity" is a good deal less lucid and a great deal more confused than she thinks. Robinson did not "discover something different within himself"; he made himself, with the best intentions, into a peep show. If he changed, it was not by *becoming* someone else but by acting as though he were someone else and accepting his own self-delusion, making himself out to be different from the person he actually was, with the effect that this "interior" documentary is even more mistakenly objective than more conventional documentaries. The "truth of testimony" is so elusive that it slips away just as we think we have it in our grasp. It would be wrong to deny the usefulness of such investigations; indeed, it is a psychological test of the highest possible value. And if we consider film from a strictly aesthetic point of view, it becomes immaterial whether Robinson's behavior is true or false as long as it gives the *impression* of being true: for this impression is all that matters. However, if we believe that we are capturing "real" truth when we film in this way, then decidedly we delude ourselves. This type of film does not help men to find themselves but, on the contrary, to arrange themselves when they most sincerely believe they are revealing themselves.

We can learn the same lesson exactly from an episode of Antonioni's *Amore in città*, a film with a suicide theme for which the director used the advice of some survivors of unsuccessful suicides. But, in this case, Antonioni is perfectly aware of how arbitrary his theme is; as he says,

[1] See *Esprit*, April 1959 and June 1960.

> Had I understood the complicated exhibitionism of this type of suicide, I would not have felt so bad about it. The majority were quite happy to have attempted suicide and be in front of the camera talking about it.... They wanted me to believe that they wished to die, that they had done the same thing more than once and that they considered themselves unlucky to have failed; moreover, that they were quite ready to try again were they ever to find themselves in the same situation again.
>
> I am sure this is not the case. I am sure they were not telling the truth, that they were exaggerating for some unaccountable reason of vanity or masochism. Such cases are more to do with psychology than ethics.[2]

Here also the well-intentioned critics had spoken of "real truth captured objectively and rigorously with all the precision of scientific observation." And scientific observation there is without a doubt, but for a psychologist or psychiatrist, not a collector of "real" truths, for then the truth under observation is doubly counterfeited: first by the individual being observed and second by the way the facts are reported—which does not mean that the films are any less interesting; they do, however, illustrate the crux of the problem.

Since any "recording" of reality is subjective, it follows that any method of reporting it is also subjective. Furthermore (has it been said often enough?), we can only capture a single aspect, a single feature, a single fleeting moment, a single "phenomenon from the external world." The only means of grasping "reality"—if only from the outside—without being forced to make an interpretation (unless it be our own—which is always assumed to be objective and true) is to go into the streets and look around; to be inside life and not inside the cinema looking at a work of art. Even so, this visual freedom is very limited: we can see only what is in front of our eyes, and we cannot be in places where we are not! The illusion that reality can be captured in all its reality, in its dimensions of time and space, is a trap for the unwary; to claim that reality is communicable through film is an example of either naïveté or self-delusion.

As Claude Roy so rightly put it, "To recreate reality, the cooperation of the imagination is required. The document (however authentic) is only a reflection. It is left to the poet to restore life itself (in the original sense of the word).... Poet, in the original sense—the *creator*, the Force whose insight discovers the truth more true than truth."[3]

Thus fulfilling the logic of reality does not mean choosing one method over others but, quite simply, making use of all the methods available. To appreciate the relative merits or demerits of a particular editing technique, we have only to compare two films which use the same technique with completely different results: *The Ghost That Will Not Return* by Abram Room and *Fragment of an Empire* by Friedrich Ermler (1927–28).

In the first, in which the action is set in a mining district in South America, a certain José has been condemned to several months in prison for his part in a revolutionary uprising. He is to be let out on parole. The sequence in question shows him waiting to be freed. We see him in his cell, grabbing hold of the bars and peering outside. Now, this same movement—i.e., this *same image*—is repeated ten times in succession, so that we become aware of a deeper *significance* than the mere fact of José's actions: the *idea* of impatience. Thus one movement, on its own, symbolically summarizes all the others. But the audience is supposed to see José *acting*

[2] *Cinema Nuovo*, March 15, 1954.

[3] In *L'Écran Français*, October 3, 1945.

in his cell. The concrete reality is thereby distorted and forced into an abstract representation which sucks the "life" out of it and turns it into nothing more than a *sign*. The freedom and spontaneity of José's actions are violated. The audience sees actions *worked out* by the director, not actions *experienced* by a character who is no more than a robot.

However, used subjectively, the same editing technique would have been perfectly acceptable. If we had seen José *remembering* past actions instead of *performing* present actions, we might have been able to identify the mechanics of the synthesis with the mechanics of José's memory (precisely what Ermler does in *Fragment of an Empire*, also known as *The Man Who Lost His Memory*). The film describes the gradual restoration of the consciousness of a Russian veteran of the First World War who, wounded in the head, recovers his memory some ten years later as the consequence of a series of emotional shocks. As he begins to make sense of his scattered, confused, and fleeting impressions, he remembers the events during which he was wounded. He sees the trenches again, the war, the tanks and the fighting. But the reality which he *reconstructs* does not conform with the reality he had actually experienced. Not only does he see himself as a soldier in his foxhole, but he *projects* himself into the attitudes and behavior of his superior officers, into those of the commanding officer of his detachment and of the colonel of the battalion, of the German soldier he has to kill, and of the Prussian officer in the trench opposite. To all intents and appearances, conforming in every way with actual reality, he is physically and psychologically *himself*. Thus the mental representation takes priority over the actual reality but in an entirely justified way. The symbolism of this sequence is in no way forced on the true reality; it becomes a substitute for it. However, it is justified only because it is presented as a memory and not as an objective representation.

When, later on, he becomes foreman in a factory, the hero has reason to discipline a troublemaker; we see him running to overpower the man. Now, when he launches himself at the criminal, we see in a short montage a sequence of jumbled images *not directly connected* with the fact being objectively reported: an explosion, a speeding fire engine, a motorboat, a running mob, a policeman directing traffic, a collapsing house, a statue of Lenin, etc. A random collection of images representing, in a few flashes, the character's motivating ideas: danger, the consequences of an accident, quick movement, order, and strong will. Yet these images in no way signify the action; they are not a substitute—they merely explain it. It is as though we were in communication with the hero's confused thoughts at the very moment in which we see him act.

Of course, this mental representation is quite arbitrary and, psychologically speaking, of questionable value. It is merely a symbolic representation which, though dispensable, nevertheless contributes a great deal to the dramatic action by providing an aesthetically valid translation of the mental reflexes and does not interrupt the rhythm. Quite the contrary, in fact: it accentuates it like contrapuntal harmony.

As we have said, there are no good or bad techniques—merely good or bad ways of using them. The same techniques are used in both the above films. In the first, they are disastrous because they are *against the grain*; in the second, they are effective because they are made to submit to the demands of the dramatic truth. In the first, where the action is *subordinate* to the idea, they conceptualize and fix the reality; in the second, the action is *exploited* for the purpose of *drawing* concepts from it without ever distorting the perceptual reality. We must agree with André Bazin in his criticism of yet another incorrect use of editing technique: "When the thematic structure of a particular scene depends on the simultaneous presence of two or more elements of the action, then montage is ruled out." Incidentally, instead of "elements of the action" we would prefer to say "fragmentation into successive shots," a fragmentation which becomes a contradiction in terms, as Bazin points out in a later passage:

> It is in no sense a matter of being obliged to revert to the single-shot sequence to repudiate the expression resources or the possible benefits to be gained from a change of shot.... When Orson Welles shoots certain scenes in *The Magnificent Ambersons* from a single setup whereas, in *Mr. Arkadin*, he uses an extremely truncated editing technique, it is merely a change of style which in no essential way alters the subject matter.... On the other hand, it would be hard to imagine the famous scene of the seal hunt in *Nanook* different from the way it is, showing us *in the same shot* the hunter, the hole, and then the seal. That the rest of the film be truncated in any way the director chooses is quite immaterial. It is necessary only that the spatial unity of the scene be respected at a moment when to disturb it would change the reality into a simple fictitious representation.... In other words, all that is needed to restore the reality of a narrative is for one of the shots, suitably chosen, to bring together those elements previously split up by montage. (*Qu'est-ce que le cinéma?*)

But no one denies that the unity of space must be respected. Filmmakers of any worth, facing the problem of representation of a *concrete* reality, have always adopted the course which Bazin advocates, however much they may try to submit that reality to fragmentation. Proof of this can be seen in the short sequence from *Mother* to which we referred earlier (Pudovkin being one of those directors who carried this type of fragmentation to its extreme). Before dividing this scene into a number of successive stages, he took care to show us *in the same shot* the mother, father, and clock; in other words, he "blocked" the protagonists (plotted the position of each element of the scene relative to the others), thereby defining the space of the drama and the location of the action, as Flaherty did in the episode of the seal hunt.

Granted, the sequence might have opened with a descriptive shot (as in *Mother*), in which case the fragmentation would have been merely the detailed breakdown of an already established unity. Yet it could just as easily have been introduced *afterward* to bring together, in the same *objective* space, a number of details whose relationship up until then might have been only hypothetical due to the fact that the montage had created a certain ambiguity through the absence of a spatial referent: a technique lending itself perfectly to the crime film or the suspense film, indeed any film whose purpose is to alarm, disturb, or surprise the audience.

However, Bazin's remarks would lead us to presume that the almost inevitable consequence of the montage principle is that Nanook, the seal, and the hole must be filmed in separate shots rather than a single shot; in other words, that a "pseudo-reality" must be generated—which is *absolutely wrong.*

It is a mistake Bazin makes quite frequently. Yet it seems that it is always in bad films that Bazin searches for examples of the stylistic traits he wishes to condemn or denigrate, so that in attempting to point out the demerits of a particular technique he most often is criticizing its misrepresentations or misinterpretations. Thus, while he cannot be faulted in his criticism of these misapplications, his generalizations almost always cause him to draw the wrong conclusions, leading him to hold the means of expression responsible for the misapplication (the resulting misunderstandings are endless!). What better example than the shot-reverse-shot technique, which invited his bitter condemnation? In the rare cases where this technique is used appropriately, Bazin gives his seal of approval; what point is there, then, in inveighing against the technique? Would it not be more to the point to use his invective against those who use the technique with no rhyme or reason? Less simple, perhaps, but how much more logical!

In any case, we must be careful not to confuse *real* space (divided into successive cuts or fragmentations) with pseudo-reality *manufactured* by editing, since editing does not in fact create any kind of reality—indeed is incapable of doing so. It merely creates relationships and determines ideas. This pseudo-reality is only a *fictional representation* (to borrow Bazin's terminology).

Indeed, though in limiting cases such as the "man committing suicide from the Pont de l'Alma," the reality is well and truly manufactured, the suggested idea is of a space no more abstract than if details of the same global space had been juxtaposed. It is a fictional space whose unreality is the product of our inability to relate these details to an objectively described place.

Look again at the example of *Nanook*. We saw the hunter, the hole, and the seal in the same frame. With their respective positions in the frame established, we are able to examine them *separately* because the spatial relationships created by editing have an automatic referent in our minds: the concrete reality of which we are already aware. However, if we had never seen Nanook, the hole, and the seal *in the same shot*, then our mental representation would be *fictional*, the product of *nonobjectified* relationships: a semiobjective, semisubjective *pseudo-reality*. And the effect of constructing a film in this way is to lose touch with reality. The elements in view may be perfectly concrete, but they assume the appearance of abstractions. As we have said, the development of ideas always takes place to the detriment of the visual data deprived of all living content and divorced from perceptual reality and from the associations of what they might become.

In another limiting case (*Nuremberg 1936–Berlin 1945*), the space-time relationship is pure abstraction. However, the huge gap between the two events is perceived as an ellipsis. In the pseudo-reality produced by the montage of news events, it is not space-time which is imaginary but the secondary reality (this is not important, however, since the purpose of films such as this is to provoke *ideas*, not represent actual reality).

To sum up: the impression of authentic reality does not depend on an effect of editing or nonediting any more than on the feeling of time or space produced by more or less subjective structures. It is essentially a matter of plotting the relative positions of each character in the drama. It is not a question of imagining these relationships but of *recording* them and therefore of revealing them—*describing* them, not suggesting them (suggestion being mainly concerned with the communication of *ideas*, not *facts*). No valid suggestion can exist without relying on facts *objectively* recorded beforehand—which is what we meant when we stated that "the logic of reality must be fulfilled before any level of signification is achievable" (and precisely so that it may be guaranteed). This "plotting of position" consists essentially in structuring the space of the drama and consequently in composing the image—less, however, in the plastic than in the dynamic sense: in distributing the forces in play according the dramatic actions and their associated significations.

It is clear that this organization of space has nothing at all to do with the impersonal objectivity we mentioned a while ago. Its apparent objectivity is merely one way of perceiving the world. Far from precluding suggestion, it intensifies it, reinforcing it with concrete facts. The idea which we infer from the sight of Nanook on his own, tugging at his fishing line, is intensified by the fact that we have already seen Nanook *actually* struggling with the seal in a *real* space. And the detail shots in *Mother* owe their intensity purely and simply to the fact that they are developing and building a scene whose concrete data have been presented to us from the outset. It is always a matter of analyzing or suggesting using a previously described scene as a *basis* rather than the construction of a fictitious reality which (at the risk of seeming repetitious) is not the purpose of montage. The same might be said of the Odessa Steps sequence and of Eisenstein's sign-images, which *become* signs and genuinely signify only insofar as they are integrated into a substantiated reality.

The fact remains that in the cinema the affective power of suggestion is always greater than that of description. Such is the case in the last image of *All Quiet on the Western Front*, where we are shown the hero trying to catch a butterfly resting on the edge of his trench. He crawls from the shelter of the trench and stretches out his arm. A closeup isolates his hand as it moves toward the insect. Suddenly it convulses, opens, and flops back motionless. Everyone can tell that he has just been killed.

We could just as easily have *seen* the lieutenant actually shot, been able to observe the fact objectively; yet (coming back to Eisenstein) through the allusion of the images we do not register the fact that the lieutenant has been killed: we react to the fact through the medium in which it is presented to us. In any event, though we are moved far more by what we imagine than by what we see, the imagination has to rely on tangible facts; it can never operate independently. Suggestion is merely one way of communicating what might have been revealed directly. And the image from *All Quiet on the Western Front* derives its value as a signifier entirely from the fact that we have seen previous scenes which enable us to appreciate the relationships between the various characters in the drama.

Elsewhere in *Notes of a Film Director*, Eisenstein has this to say:

> From the point of view of its dynamism, the work of art is a process causing the formulation of images in the audience's senses and intelligence. This is the essence of the truly living work of art, distinguishing it from stillborn works which communicate to the consciousness of the audience the represented effects of a creative process which has run its course, instead of involving it in the process as it takes place.... The strength of montage lies in that the emotions and reason of the audience are included in the creative process. The audience is forced to follow the road which the author followed in creating the image. The audience not only sees the elements of the representation; it also experiences the dynamic process of the emergence and formation of the image as it was experienced by the author. This is probably the highest degree of approximation there is to communicating to the audience the author's sensations and conception in the greatest possible completeness, to communicating them with "that power of physical truth" which was imposed on the author during the creative process, at the moment of his creative vision.... This method has one more strength in that it draws the audience into an act of creation during which his personality is not in the least dominated by that of the author but fully develops fusing itself with the conception of the author.... The image is the one intended and created by the author, recreated by the creative will of the audience.

This view is supported by Bergson in his remarks concerning the conditions necessary for the work of art: arranging it so that the audience's point of view coincides with that of the author, eliciting its complete attention in a kind of ecstatic communion after which it "accepts the concept suggested to it and sympathizes with the feelings contained in the expression."

Though this submission of self is, as we have said, the antithesis of self-abnegation and is merely an overwhelming sense of perfection, a state in which the effect of structuring these associations, these ideas, coincides with that of abandoning ourselves—which is Eisenstein's thesis—some critics have seen in this an aesthetic of domination and magic, an art which precludes all objectivity and critical examination and whose absolutism presenting only one meaning to the represented reality obstructs the audience's right to choose freely from the ambiguity of the world and its objects.

This sort of criticism, leveled most particularly by André Bazin, has a sound basis. It is associated in a sense with the ideas of alienation introduced by Berthold Brecht into the theater and finding its resolution in the dramatic use of depth-of-field as applied by Orson Welles. Suffice it to say, that this criticism is justified and acceptable only insofar as it is not used dogmatically and does not claim to replace an old aesthetic principle with a new one, since this comparison is merely a precise definition of two equally viable aesthetic principles (two codes of style—to be more accurate) with two completely separate purposes.

The contrast between the two underlines (as if it were necessary) the formal differences existing in film techniques between what in the cinema are the equivalents of the language of poetry and the language of the novel. All the evidence points to the fact that the rules governing each are not the same. Whatever the content of his prose, the novelist strives to retire behind his characters and behind the apparent authenticity which all his creative efforts have attempted to create or recreate. On the other hand, the poet expresses himself directly: *with* facts instead of *through* facts. The world is his poetic oyster. Instead of putting himself at the service of the world, he exploits it. He uses it as a primary material to be rehashed and served up in a different form. He transforms and therefore directs and orders: he organizes. What he reveals to me is *his* vision of the world and not an objective reality. And in this context, what interests me the audience is not so much what he shows me but the very personal way in which he does it, which gives me direct insight into him; I am able to sympathize—or even reject—his ideas and his way of seeing the world: the things he sees are of *secondary* importance. And, as we shall see further on, this is the only way that the cinema can be used in a *genuinely subjective* sense, with the subject as the artist and the "reality" a constant objectification of his thoughts.

Conversely, in narrative art, though the style of the narrator is important, what counts above all is what he shows me, what he communicates to me in the *most direct way possible*. The form of the narrative seeks to act as a mirror between the universe and me, whereas previously it had acted as a screen. The author is less interesting to me than his characters, which is why he must aspire to the greatest possible objectivity and present his characters as they are in the world, taking care not to reveal himself except *through* them.

We can illustrate the formal difference between these two techniques with a very simple example. Imagine that Peter is sitting at his desk; he is writing. Suddenly he looks up and begins to stare into space. He is daydreaming. Yet his eyes must necessarily be resting on something, so he is looking at—but not seeing—the lamp to one side of the desk.

If I show this scene in a shot close enough for Peter, the object of our interest, to have an important place in the frame but wide enough to include all the different objects arranged around him (a medium shot, for instance), the audience will understand perfectly that though Peter is looking at the lamp, he could just as easily be looking at his telephone or his pipe—or indeed anything. The act of looking is represented in its concrete psychological reality, according to its characteristic free will, what we could call psychological realism, the style of the novel or story. The author allows his character a certain latitude. He watches him living, while remaining outside.

If, on the other hand, I were to represent the scene as follows: (a) *Closeup*. Peter, sitting at his desk, is writing. Then he looks up with a faraway look in his eyes, which move to the right without seeming to fix on any particular object. Of course, we are not able to see what he is looking at; the objects on his desk are out of shot; (b) *Extreme closeup*. The lamp standing on the edge of his desk.

In this case, the lamp is *implied* in his look. Peter no longer has any freedom of action or free will. The only thing he can see is the lamp which I am *presenting* for him to see. It is I, the author, expressing myself, directing the action by making reality conform to a certain expressive purpose. I am not contradicting the authentic fact; I am not, exactly speaking, misrepresenting it; I am exploiting it, interpreting it, thereby forcing the audience to see with me, like me, in a way dictated by me. With the lamp becoming, thanks to me, the direct complement of Peter's view, the audience is no longer able to believe that Peter *might* potentially be capable of seeing something else since, like Peter, it is *capable* only of seeing the lamp. Thus I become the creative Force, the lyric or epic poet praising, redefining, transforming, exaggerating: I *order* reality more than *present* it; I present it as I intend people to see it. It is well and truly an art of domination, yet the audience is willing to accede to it all the more easily that it knows I am communicating *my* vision and not *the* world itself.

Needless to say, these are pure forms and there is nothing to prevent them, if need arises, from being alternated or mixed up during the course of the film. However, for Eisenstein, only the lyric form has meaning or communicates active power, which is why his aesthetic principles are really nothing more than statements of his stylistics—which have obvious relevance but could never claim to contain all possible forms of film expression. As much might be said for the form of the novel with which certain contemporary critics have tried to align present and future visual dialectics; and it is a truism that in the cinema most theorists have based their theories on prejudices and taboos as though, in literature, the style of Proust cannot be praised without condemning that of Péguy—and vice versa.

How convenient it would be to say—paraphrasing the definitions of logic—that aesthetics "is not concerned with content but with the way in which content is expressed." And this is not beyond the bounds of possibility so long as we mean aesthetics in the widest sense. However, since the way of saying something is always part of what it says, it would be impossible to formulate an aesthetic principle appropriate to all forms and all contents. Thus film aesthetics is really concerned with defining the reasons why one form is better than another because of a particular content or a particular intention; in other words, with determining the psychological bases which justify these forms in particular given circumstances.

Up to now, we have looked at the types of editing which in one way or another exploit the juxtaposition (or collage) of fixed shots. Before we pass on to camera movements, we should point out certain psychological phenomena relating to the perception of discontinuous elements.

"In the cinema," as Albert Laffay says, "permanence is intolerable."

> We must leap constantly from one viewpoint to the next, from one scale of size to the next. And yet this is still not enough. Once the angles and distances have been altered a certain number of times, like it or not the object has to change and the scene has to be shifted.... And yet, why should the audience, which, in the theater, is quite happy sitting in one place in front of the same unchanging perspective, wish to sprout wings in the cinema.... Doubtless because of the fact that since objects projected onto the screen are not really there, for us to believe (or half-believe) in them, they must be constantly changing or constantly being replaced.... That is one way of saying that the cinema is incapable of stopping to underline or articulate the associations of a *world*. Because of the very inadequacies of the objects it reveals to our eyes, through constant transposition, it inevitably describes a definite structure in which each object is what it is by virtue of the limitations imposed on it by all the others—specifically, the limitation of its place.[4]

A possible response to these subtle observations (in which, in our opinion, the author has been overzealous in dismissing the effect of shot changes on the fictional nature of the represented objects) might be that if the audience in the theater accepts the unity of the point of view, it is because the theater depends less on facts than on words, because speech is the main signifier, and because verbal mobility, acting as a substitute for action and describing the psychological mobility of the characters, transforms the immobility of the represented scenes and the immobility of the audience's eyes. Whereas in the cinema (even in talkies) words are of less importance than actions and actions must be followed in their constant mobility.

As regards movement, Jean Epstein's remarks would seem to be nearer the mark:

> In our normal world of all-too-stable solids, movement—because it is a relatively infrequent occurrence and, generally speaking, with a weak effect—appears distinct from the form in which it only intermittently occurs and without ever succeeding visibly in distorting it. By contrast, in film representation, movement appears to be intrinsic to form; it is form and it makes form, its form. Thereby a new empiricism—that of the cinema—requires the fusion of two first principles: that of form and that of movement, whose separation, until now, presented implicitly as an a priori fact, indispensable to the whole science of physics. The filmmaker considers form merely as the form of a movement. (*Le Cinéma du diable*)

But of paramount importance (and an aspect neglected by a great many theoreticians) is the fact that shot movement and discontinuity in editing appear in normal perception as one and the same thing. As René Zazzo points out so rightly, "empirically, the camera has discovered a mobility, that of psychological vision" (*Niveau mental et comprehension du cinéma*).

We know that our mind is incapable of concentrating without a break on a single object. Our attention relaxes and becomes confused. And though in everyday life we may have the impression of total constant perception, it is only because we are at the center of a homogeneous continuum and because at any moment we are capable of concentrating upon a specific feature of our surroundings. Yet though the act of perceiving is continuous, the object of our perception is discontinuous; the source of our frequent confusion is that the continuity

[4] In *La Revue du Cinéma*, April 1948.

of perception is related to perceived objects whose associations, at that moment understood as objective, are in fact (not just in our memories but also in the present) reconstructed and continually differentiated.

If I move within a particular place, a street for instance, I have the constant impression that I am seeing everything; and it is true that I have an overall view of events happening before my eyes; but I am seeing them, as it were, unconsciously. There must be something out of the ordinary to attract my attention in order that I may actually *see* each event in turn. Thus by shifting my attention successively from one detail to another, I see those details which seem to me essential: and it is these attention shifts, these fragmentary visions, which make up my global vision of the street. In recollection it is these details and they alone which spring to mind, evoking for me the distinctive features of the street, which then become the idea I form of it. Global vision is the effect of a succession of essential aspects chosen by our memories in the same way as, in the present, it is the effect of a sequence of impressions gathered haphazardly by our partially attentive perception. The same phenomenon pertains in our perception of duration. As Jean-Pierre Chartier points out,

> Just as we feel we are seeing the whole of our environment, whereas we are perceiving certain essential features, so we think we are aware of the complete duration in what we observe, whereas we can only be aware of essential moments from which we construct a duration (of the objects) to which we attribute the continuity of our awareness. We can see examples of this in our everyday lives: I leave a friend and start to make my way home following a familiar route; I climb the stairs and open my door. Between the time I leave my friend and the time I open the door, I will not have been particularly conscious of my surroundings. I retain only the images of my friend and my arrival. In the narrative convention of the cinema, the two images are merely juxtaposed and the intervening stage removed. The audience of a film feels that it is experiencing the narrative; it places the essential moments which the shot sequence presents to it in a continuous duration, with the help of the same movement which allows it to situate, within an actual duration, the real world of which it gradually becomes conscious throughout the discontinuous shifts of his attention. (*Art et réalité du cinéma*)

Thus film shots create, simply by their juxtaposition, an idea of space and an idea of time. Yet this fictional continuum is a concrete fiction similar in every respect to real space and time which is the effect of a permanent conceptualization—only the fragmentary features presented through our perceptual field having actual concrete validity.

And yet discontinuity in editing is more sudden than in real life, where the particular moments of attention are blended into the more or less general impression. Here also the film frame breaks up the transition from shot to shot as it severs the connection between what is represented and the rest of the field of view from which it has been chosen. To use M. Michotte's expression, from one shot to the next there is a kind of instantaneous "disappearance-creation." And as Henri Wallon indicates, "it can be said that in all the techniques of the cinema—contrary to what occurs in our perception (where everything is gradual, where everything depends on our moving)—there are shock effects" (*L'Acte perceptif et le cinéma*).

Moreover, in normal perception we are not aware of this fragmentation because it comes from us, from our situation in the world. In the cinema, on the other hand, it comes to us from the outside: it is the filmmaker making the shifts of attention on our behalf, decoding reality for us. And though in large part the purpose of the cinema is "to give us the illusion that we are present in real scenes taking place before us like everyday realities" (Bazin), its function is to replace life as we see and perceive it with a more intense and therefore more dense life. By retaining only selected moments, condensing space and time, film imposes on us a vision of the world organized toward a certain signification. To try to divest the cinema of this necessary and inevitable subjectivity is to ignore its true nature or even deny its value as art.

Yet if these shock effects exist, we may have reason to wonder, as Cohen-Séat suggests, "how the audience can accept without apparent distress such profound shocks to its perceptual system—whether or not it is already used to it" (*Problèmes du cinéma*). In our view, this shock is less real than apparent, particularly since it appears only after detailed examination during which it becomes overlooked that the perception of the film image can occur only in particular conditions, i.e., total darkness. Because nothing can be perceived beyond it, the image is not detached from anything. So, at least, it would appear. Successive moments of attention blended into an absence of perception replace the successive moments of attention blended into a vague perception.

It will be argued that because they are not compensated by any other (even unconscious) perception, shot changes are felt even more violently. Yet this is one of the effects of psychology upon which editing is based. If the shock effect did not exist, it would not be possible to make this kind of contrast. The (aesthetic) truth is that a shock from one shot to the next must not be felt as such. It must comply with the expressive needs and thus be felt as a collision of represented effects, objects, or actions. It is justified in this way, as an emotional shock, through the emotion it aims to express.

Within the discontinuous sequence of film shots, there is no discontinuity of either space, movement, or action—merely of point of view. The cutting from one shot to another restores the continuity of the actions and reestablishes the spatial unity. And in cutting from one location to another or one time sequence to another, our attention, guided by the story line and the dialectic of the narrative, finds no difficulty in rediscovering the unity of a world temporarily disunited.

We mentioned previously that in shot relationships there is not *one* but *several* spaces. By which we meant (and it must have been quite obvious to the reader) that whereas space in the theater never changes, in the cinema each shot involves *its own* representation, that is, the point of view and *specific dimension* created by the relationships between the represented space and the invariable frame lines. The "modulation of space" is nothing more than a constant interaction of the dimensional variety of the shots (or area encompassed by the shots) and the unity of the space in the field of vision. In other words, we perceive the *same* space according to constantly differentiated data or, to be more precise, we perceive variable data which enable us to *recognize* the same space and it is our perceptual constants which restore the balance. If, as Piaget assures us, these constants are the product of a perceptual activity already closely connected with intellectual compositions, it is obvious that spatial unity can be found only at the level of the intellect and that the process itself presupposes a certain way of thinking. R. Zazzo's tests have shown to what extent children can be confused by these differences of form and how difficult, even sometimes impossible, it is for them to recognize the same design presented under different conditions. However, this state of mind (whose various stages have been so admirably well documented by Piaget) is not found in cultured adults—only in children (or primitive people).

Even so, it is all too apparent that the editing of a series of fixed shots establishes a *feeling of continuity* but is unable, unlike moving shots, to create the *sensation* of the continuous, since this sensation is reconstructed intellectually and not perceived as such—which means that reality appears as though it were an idea or a memory; or, to put it another way, it appears *restructured*. Whence the impression of a ready-made reality, a kind of *presentification* rather than a present taking place and therefore of a world transcending the immediate experience. On the other hand, the moving camera provides, as we shall see further on, the feeling of a present in action, giving us the feeling that we might be able to have an effect on the world or, at least, play a part in altering its potentiality.

Of course, continuity in film cannot be created in the audience's mind except by direct appeal to its memory faculty (without which it would not be possible for it to have any perception whatever—not even of the simplest movement). We know that vision in the cinema (moving pictures) can be explained only by the persistence of images on the retina or, more exactly, the persistence of visual impressions on the cortex of the brain, a kind of short circuit (called the *phi* phenomenon) involving our immediate memory, as Wertheimer, David Katz, and Korte demonstrated between 1912 and 1915. "What film gives us," as Henri Wallon indicates,

> is a successive series of images relating to the same object, images which we must follow one by one in the order they are presented to us and which we must integrate in order to create the representation of the object from all its aspects, the representation of a location from all its angles or the representation of a person from all points of view. However, the succession of images is the succession of specific images which we must register and weld together using our memory—our intellectual memory, no doubt, but memory nonetheless. We must not lose track of the images because it is on their succession that the representation of the object, the identification of the location and characters and our understanding of the scenes depend. (*L'Acte perspectif et le cinéma*)

As for our "perceptual expectation," which, according to Henri Piéron, directs the way we act but presupposes a certain permanence of things, it cannot be held in suspense by the continuity of the film, whose changes of event are constantly varied and unexpected. At a pinch it can be followed for the duration of the sequence, duration then describing homogeneous time. But as Cohen-Séat points out so rightly,

> insofar as film signifies something, the changes of sequence or shot become part of the development of a single situation. They suggest an analytical vision, the revelation of one through another of the multiple aspects of a reality. The various shots are just so many points of view in the continuity of a unique sequence and time. Editing cleverly exploits and appeals to our expectation by introducing the ambition or desire to turn the object round and round. The change of shot merely confirms or fulfills this need.... Changing the camera axis and changing the shot give us the equivalent of a voluntary change of point of view and, by giving it a form, flesh out a vague attitude on the part of the audience. This is how the audience accepts the discontinuity of film time. (*Problèmes du cinéma*)

Yet, though the effects of editing are based on perceptual phenomena, it is clear that the order of the editing, indeed the editing itself, demonstrates an obvious intentionality which puts it in the realm of aesthetics. Editing is always the product of a sequence of scenes organized in such a way that their development becomes integrated into a formal narrative. Thus our perceptual expectation must be frustrated by the filmmaker in order that the element of surprise may constantly keep us at the alert as an audience. As Cohen-Séat points out,

> the point of view chosen to capture the sequence of the action is therefore the one with the greatest power of "revelation," the one most capable of maintaining the interaction of shock effects and, at the same time, the continuous tension of the dialectic. It is the perspective which in a real situation may be disregarded or may disappear and at the same time the perspective which the audience finds difficulty in anticipating because it is not even aware of its existence. (Ibid.)

In fact, the shot must never anticipate the action. Suppose, for instance, a café interior with a table and two empty chairs in the foreground and suppose, *some time later*, a couple (whom we have been expecting) enter the scene and sit down in the foreground, the mistake is obvious. It is tantamount to saying, "Look, this is where they come in." If the audience is able to anticipate the action, it means that the filmmaker is leading the events. It betrays his presence (which we should be able to ignore) and destroys the feeling which otherwise enables us to believe in what is being represented. Thus shot changes must be *dictated* by the action or by the movements of the characters. In this case it is the couple's entrance into the café. The field of view taking in the table and the empty chairs must be dictated by their movements. Then and only then can the camera move closer to them to film them in medium shot or closeup.

It is obvious that though they are dictated and justified in this way, shot changes must fulfill the requirements of the drama. In *The Shadow of a Doubt*, when the young girl comes down the stairs holding onto the banisters, though a closeup suddenly breaks the continuity of the movement to draw attention to the ring on her finger, it is clearly so as to emphasize the particular detail but also and *more especially* to show that her uncle has suddenly noticed the ring (which had belonged to one of the victims of the psychopath on the run from the police). All of a sudden the audience understands *for* him and at the same time, identifying psychologically with Uncle Charlie, understands that he sees that she has also understood. In other words, the shot changes are associated and identified with psychological movements relating to the characters in the drama or are determined by the audience's interest generated by the drama; once this has occurred, the fact that they are imposed becomes irrelevant, since they coincide with the audience's attention. Thus perceptual discontinuity and visual mobility become *potential* for an aesthetic system, a language.

This means that there can be no discontinuity in "film time." Discontinuity can exist only at the level of the image, i.e., at the level of the directly perceived forms, not the narrative structure. The near impossibility for perceptual expectation to exist is due to this discontinuity of forms of the representation and not to a pseudo-discontinuity of the represented. It is also connected with the fact that the audience, through the power of objects, can never dominate the scenes presented to it, since the director's art consists in making the scenes dominate the audience.

It would be wrong, however, to assume that in the cinema there is no perceptual expectation. Quite the contrary. However, it reveals itself differently from the way it does in reality, where the individual "centered in the world" is master of his actions. We have seen that audience participation is never more than an imaginary involvement, the projection of an imaginary self. Let us review all this in the light of perceptual expectation.

As we saw, perceptual expectation presupposes the capacity to move about. But—bearing in mind Weizsäcker's refutation of the classical division of sensory stimuli and motor responses—though it is not possible to make an arbitrary distinction between motor phenomena and perceptual phenomena, the association of a reflex movement with a perception cannot *effectively* be made except in terms of a specific need. According to Piaget, the stimuli-response relationship constitutes a general pattern linked to a signification and not a simple automatic association. The response becomes stable after several trial attempts and to the extent that it is reinforced by the repeated fulfillment of the need which guides and justifies it. It expresses the assimilation of the perceived data with an organized pattern. In the cinema, the response is not justified or commanded by any direct need or actual activity, except an essentially trivial fulfillment. Motivated by the perception of the represented actions and by their assimilation with the tendencies of the repressed Self, it is directly "transposed" onto an imaginary action similar to the hero's—becoming, as we have seen, the quasi-idealized projection of this "intentional" Self.

Now, to refer to Piaget,

> wherever there is association between movements and perceptions, the supposed association in fact consists in integrating the new element into a previous pattern of activity. Whether this previous pattern is in the nature of a reflex, as in the conditioned reflex or on even higher planes, it remains merely an assimilation, of such a kind that the bond of association is never just the simple facsimile of a ready-made relationship in external reality. (*Psychologie de l'intelligence*)

With these "ready-made" data existing here as the represented action, it is easy to see how movement, the stimuli-response bond generated by this action, inevitably becomes the carbon copy of the given relationship in the case that it is dealing with identification through simple imitation or mimicry. The organizing assimilation occurring in the association of perception and movement (whether real or imaginary) is fundamental to the process of projection-identification, upon which, as we have seen, the phenomena of participation are themselves based. In the circumstances, these are nothing more than transferred responses establishing expectation in normal perception; however, this transfer process shows how expectation becomes almost synonymous with participation.

If now we examine another side of the question, we can say in the general (rather than logical) sense of the word that association is the awareness of a relationship linking or uniting facts with no apparent or direct connection. In this regard, William James's law of coalescence, generating "association at the level of the action and syncretism at the level of the representation," is supported at all levels by film. Indeed, in any image, represented objects are simultaneously presented. Even separate and recognizably distinct, they are associated within a perceptual unity. No association from one to the other can possibly exist; they can only coincide. Relationships—what we take to be causal relationships—exist only between objects separated in time, together creating a kind of connective pattern which involves an organizing assimilation, a potential generalization. To put it another way, association involves repetition. However, for association to exist in the cinema, all that is needed is for term B to follow term

A. Once there is a potential logical relationship between the two terms, this immediately generates in the audience's mind an idea of causality. In other words, B is understood as the consequence of A, even if this is only temporarily valid. When it does not depend on the dramatic narrative, association is apparent in our minds because the objects represented are in the image of real objects. Just as in reality objects following each other are largely self-generating (apparently) in events presented successively by film, i.e., in shot relationships, our minds look for the causal link. They do so because they recognize—*think* they recognize or *want* to recognize—the image of the organizing patterns created by the causal links. *Seeing* in the cinema is not just recognizing the *object* but also comparing the film relationships with the relationships of real facts—interpreting the visual pattern as a repetition of known or tried patterns, however artificially created—which shows how accurate was Claparède's analysis (in *La Genèse de l'hypothèse* quoted by Piaget) which states that "repetition does not create association but association appears during the course of repetition (and only then) because association is the internal product of the assimilation ensuring the repetition of the external action."

It therefore follows that perceptual expectation in the cinema is based entirely upon patterns previously experienced in reality or else in film perception. Needless to say, all expectation is based upon previous experience; but in large measure, reality repeats this experience, whereas film does not or, if it does, does so according to constantly differentiated and unforeseen norms. Thus film expectation can be reduced to the comprehension of a series of relationships through simple assimilation, the associations remaining unfulfilled until the unfolding of the action confirms or denies them.

The mistake has no other consequences than incomprehension or confusion and expectation becomes a kind of artificial experience in a state of constant readjustment. A typical example of this is the marvelous sequence in *Citizen Kane*. During a celebration dinner in the reception room of the *Enquirer*, Kane announces his imminent departure for Europe. The sequence closes on Leland and Bernstein. They are talking in the foreground while Kane and the girls are shown dancing far in the background. At this moment, after a very quick and almost imperceptible fade to black, Bernstein moves toward the camera and crosses through the doorway of the room. The camera follows his movement. He goes down a corridor, walks up a few steps, and enters a huge storeroom, where crates containing statues and all kinds of objets d'art are stacked up. He shouts out: "Mr. Leland!… Mr. Leland!… I've just got a cable from Mr. Kane… from Paris…. It's just as well he's promised not to send any more statues!" He crosses over to Leland and the conversation continues (on another subject). In this way we learn that six months have elapsed between the dinner party and the receipt of the cable. Now, the *descriptive* continuity is such that we might believe that only a few moments have passed. The ellipsis is made through Bernstein's movement, from the reception room to the storeroom—but without any break in the continuity of the movement, without the makeshift transition from one shot to the next which we sometimes find in similar cases. The result is that the audience is at first confused because it does not appreciate the shorthand. It does not register the ellipsis—which is the opposite of the normal patterns on which it has based its thought processes. It is forced to make an effort and, if necessary, see the film a second time. Yet once the technique has been understood, it develops into a new associative form. From then on the audience will remember the new expression—not by remembering something experienced in reality but by remembering a form integrated into the language. It is clear that film is self-referencing, appealing to a certain culture, to a way of thinking, a cinematic *formula* in the same way that literature is self-referencing: Henri Bordeaux cannot be read in the same way as James Joyce.

For reasons similar to those we have just mentioned—returning form and content—we could never say that in the cinema there are long shots and closeups. There may well be if we take a tape measure or a stopwatch and measure them, but not when we *perceive them.* A shot lasts—or *should* last—only as long as is necessary for the expression of its content. Only through the duration of the content can the shot be perceived as a duration, i.e., the time of a movement or action. It is perceived as long only when it is *too long*, i.e., when it lasts longer than the time required by the meaning it is trying to communicate. In that case we are transferring our attention from the narrative duration—superseded in importance by the signification—to the actual duration of the shot, i.e., to "empty" time. If we accept Katz's formula, we find that "whenever we concentrate our attention on the passage of time it seems to get longer." Conversely, a shot is perceived as short when it is *too short*, i.e., when its brevity renders it incapable of achieving the meaning or expression it is supposed to be communicating. Or else, when the shot sequence is very fast (as in Hollywood-type montages) because "speed is all we can perceive in shots following each other in quick succession" (P. Fraisse). And if we can accept that a particular shot is longer or shorter than the previous one, it is only because we are registering a longer or shorter action in the content of the shot.

This brings us to an obvious crucial problem. An audience versed in the subtleties of film language will understand the meaning of a shot much more quickly than one less aware. It is certain that film form has trained us to think and structure more quickly. A silent film which seemed to have a fast rhythm when first shown now appears intolerably slow. We must therefore presume that the perfect film fulfills the greatest potential in the ideal audience.

We said that film rhythm is the rhythm *of* something. In the light of what we have said above, we may conclude that it is the rhythm of the represented action, i.e., the rhythm of an action formalized by its expression and subject to a slower or quicker tempo depending on the narrative structures. The relationships of time between the represented and its representation are significant in this respect. This is how the sequence from *Mother* we quoted reveals a representation time longer than the actual duration of the action—even though this is created using short shots. Time stretched in this way gives the narrative an impression of slowness despite the fact that the tempo of the shots is fast. On the other hand, a film created with shots representing a narrative duration longer than the representation time gives an impression of speed—however long each individual shot may be.

Determined and created by the action, rhythm is thus dependent on the successive relationships between the "time" of the form and the "time" of the content, since the representation time is always determined by the way in which the time of the objects is translated, i.e., by a certain intentionality from which the objects derive their meaning—the actual meaning of the film.

CHAPTER 23
JEAN-LOUIS BAUDRY

Jean-Louis Baudry (1930–2005) was a French novelist, film theorist, and member of the editorial board of the French literary magazine, Tel Quel. *He is perhaps most famous among film philosophers for his particular take on Apparatus Theory, following to some degree the theoretical approaches of Louis Althusser, Christian Metz, and Jacques Lacan, whereby he argued that ideology is essential to cinema. The essay included here is "Ideological Effects of the Basic Cinematographic Apparatus," originally published in French ("Effets idéologiques produits par l'appareil de base") in* Cinéthique *in 1970.*

Baudry draws a connection between the cinema and an association in Freud between the psyche and optics, between thinking and seeing. Of course, our everyday experience of visual perception inclines us to assert that "seeing is believing," as it were, that our eyes have direct access to objective reality. Scientific instruments, however, pose a problem for this commonsense understanding of vision: if something that can only be seen by way of a scientific instrument (such as a telescope, a microscope, etc.) is objectively real, but I cannot see it with "the naked eye," then there is a limitation on my ability to believe everything I see—or, at the very least, I am forced to acknowledge that natural human vision is not a direct conduit to objective reality. Baudry's point is that we must be very careful when talking about science, lest easy assumptions about the accessibility of reality to the mind by way of sense perception mask ideological aspects of scientific instruments (and the worldview that creates such instruments) themselves. Any technology which functions as if it is or can be a direct conduit to reality is a potential problem, with regard to the possibility of a hidden ideology.

Cinema, of course, also has a technological—and optical—base. A certain commonsense notion of the cinema suggests that it is the highest of the arts because it provides us, via the film image, with direct access to reality. For Baudry, however, this relationship is far more complicated and ambiguous—and must be understood. There is a gap between so-called "objective reality" and the camera, which filming can obscure; and there is a gap between the inscription of light on film (filming) and the projection on the screen, which that apparatus of projection (projector and screen) can likewise obscure. Cinema, on Baudry's view, then, is best understood as a work, in the sense of a process of transformation, on operation, that ultimately results in a certain sort of finished product (namely, the film). That finished product, existing on the other side of the work that is cinema, is totally cut off from objective reality by a double barrier: on the one hand, the camera mediates between objective reality and the series of recorded images that constitute the film; and on the other hand, the projector and screen mediate between that series of recorded images and the finished product, which is only ever screened for an audience.

This notion of the film as a series of images is central to Baudry's understanding of the essential differences between photography and cinema: ultimately photography relies on a conception of space and the arrangement of space developed in Renaissance painting. It's a conception dependent entirely upon the notion of perspective, and thus one that presupposes a specific point of view on the part of the spectator of the work of art: a single point of view, corresponding to a single subject who exists in some sort of relationship with the whole world—a focal or mediating point, as it were, between the world of the painting (or the photograph) and the spectator's own world; the point at which one world peers into and is informed and changed by another. This Renaissance idea of space presumes a continuity across and between these worlds. Cinema, however, deals essentially in discontinuity: each film image must differ at least slightly from the last in the series and from the next if the illusion of motion is to be achieved. Filming and editing are processes which deal in discontinuity; it is only in projection that (temporal) continuity is restored to the finished product. The paradox Baudry identifies here is well known: the illusion of continuity in the cinema depends entirely upon the real existence of a series of discontinuous images, yet that discontinuity must not present itself in the filmgoer's experience if the illusion of continuity is to be maintained. Film lives, then, for Baudry, on "the denial of difference."

Importantly, Baudry notes, the "language" of the unconscious also manifests itself as a broken continuity. The psychical world is one composed of fragmented images and isolated moments remembered, which must then (in self-reflection, or in analysis) be recomposed to constitute what we think of as the whole or authentic self. In this process, whether unconsciously in the psyche or visually in the cinema, difference is both essential and necessarily repressed, leaving only the relations between images—not the different images themselves. Movement and continuity are the visible expressions of these relations, in cinema, and they are on the surface of the filmgoer's primary experience of a film. Of course, a film is not composed entirely of static shots of objects in motion; in addition, although only discovered by filmmakers after a time, it is always possible for the camera (and thus the filmgoer's point of view) to move, too. Camera movements add a subjective dimension to movement in cinema, such that we cannot help but understand the images projected on the screen as intentional in the phenomenological sense: they are always already interpretations of the things they represent, in addition to being mere representations. In film, then, the viewing eye implies a thinking subject capable of shifting its attention from one object to another, and of incarnating attitudes about those objects.

The continuity of the film narrative, sustained by the repression of the visible differences between images in the series of images that constitute any film, does more than ground a good story, however: in addition, viewers of the film find their own subjectivity, their own psyches, reflected back to them in their experience of cinematic continuity. We relate to the film screen as to a mirror, Baudry suggests, referencing Jacques Lacan's notion of the "mirror stage," according to which subjectivity is first achieved in the infant by identification with a unified body seen reflected in a mirror. Looking into the mirror, the infant sees a "whole person," and in identifying with that body—despite his or her own (limited, and perhaps only liminally conscious) experience of him- or herself as discontinuous fragments (moods, thoughts, feelings, attitudes, intentions, etc.)—the infant succumbs to the image of him- or herself as a unified, integrated self, continuous across time and despite changes in his or her subjective states. Looking into the movie screen like a mirror, Baudry suggests, filmgoers can recapture something of this infantile experience Lacan describes: seeing the unified, transcendental subject in a film (the thinking perspective from which the many discontinuous elements of the film are "thought" as organically, continuously connected). Our sense of our own integrity and continuity as psychical beings can be reinforced in cinema, and we find ourselves then more and more seeking an impression of continuity there—cinematic narrative continuity ultimately can help us to retain the synthetic unity of the subject that is ourselves.

Filmography

- ***Chelovek s kinoapparatom*** [*Man with a Movie Camera*] (USSR, 1929). *Directed, Produced, and Written by* Dziga Vertov.
- ***Mediterranée*** (France, 1963). *Directed by* Jean-Daniel Pollet. *Produced by* Barbet Schroeder. *Written by* Philippe Sollers.

IDEOLOGICAL EFFECTS OF THE BASIC CINEMATOGRAPHIC APPARATUS

Translated by Alan Williams

At the end of *The Interpretation of Dreams*, when he seeks to integrate dream elaboration and its particular "economy" with the psyche as a whole, Freud assigns to the latter an optical model: "Let us simply imagine the instrument which serves in psychic productions as a sort of complicated microscope or camera." But Freud does not seem to hold strongly to this optical model, which, as Derrida has pointed out,[1] brings out the shortcoming in graphic representation in the area earlier covered by his work on dreams. Moreover, he will later abandon the optical model in favor of a writing instrument, the "mystic writing pad." Nonetheless this optical choice seems to prolong the tradition of Western science, whose birth coincides exactly with the development of the optical apparatus which will have as a consequence the decentering of the human universe, the end of geocentrism (Galileo).

But also, and paradoxically, the optical apparatus *camera obscura* will serve in the same period to elaborate in pictorial work a new mode of representation, *perspectiva artificalis*. This system, a recentering or at least a displacement of the center (which settles itself in the eye), will assure the setting up of the "subject"[2] as the active center and origin of meaning. One could doubtless question the privileged position which optical instruments seem to occupy on the line of intersection of science and ideological products. Does the technical nature of optical instruments, directly attached to scientific practice, serve to conceal not only their use in ideological products but also the ideological effects which they may provoke themselves? Their scientific base assures them a sort of neutrality and avoids their being questioned.

But already a question: if we are to take account of the imperfections of these instruments, their limitations, by what criteria may these be defined? If, for example, one can speak of a restricted depth of field as a limitation, doesn't this term itself depend upon a particular conception of reality for which such a limitation would not exist? Signifying productions are particularly relevant here, to the extent that instrumentation plays a more and more important role in them and that their distribution is more and more extensive. It is strange (but is it so strange?) that emphasis has been placed almost exclusively on their influence, on the effects they have as finished products, their content, the field of what is signified, if you like; the technical bases on which these effects depend and the specific characteristics of these bases have been ignored, however. They have been protected by the inviolability that science is supposed to provide. We would like to establish for the cinema a few guidelines which will need to be completed, verified, improved.

We must first establish the place of the instrumental base in the set of operations which combine in the production of a film (we omit consideration of economic implications). Between

[1] Cf. on this subject Derrida's work "La Scène de l'écriture," in *L'Ecriture et la Différence* (Paris: Le Seuil).

[2] The term "subject" is used by Baudry and others not to mean the topic of discourse, but rather the perceiving and ordering self, as in our term "subjective."—*Ed.*

"objective reality" and the camera, site of the inscription, and between the inscription and projection are situated certain operations, a *work*[3] which has as its result a finished product. To the extent that it is cut off from the raw material ("objective reality") this product does not allow us to see the transformation which has taken place. Equally distant from "objective reality" and the finished product, the camera occupies an intermediate position in the work process which leads from raw material to finished product. Though mutually dependent from other points of view, *découpage* [shot breakdown before shooting] and *montage* [editing, or final assembly] must be distinguished because of the essential difference in the signifying raw material on which each operates: language (scenario) or image. Between the two complementary stages of production a mutation of the signifying material takes place (neither translation nor transcription, obviously, for the image is not reducible to language) precisely where the camera is. Finally, between the finished product (possessing exchange value, a commodity) and its consumption (use value) is introduced another operation effected by a set of instruments. Projector and screen restore the light lost in the shooting process, and transform a succession of separate images into an unrolling which also restores, but according to another scansion, the movement seized from "objective reality."

Cinematographic specificity (what distinguishes cinema from other systems of signification) thus refers to a *work*, that is, to a process of transformation. The question becomes, is the work made evident, does consumption of the product bring about a "knowledge effect" [Althusser], or is the work concealed? If the latter, consumption of the product will obviously be accompanied by ideological surplus value.[4] On the practical level, this poses the question of by what procedures the work can in fact be made "readable" in its inscription. These procedures must of necessity call cinematographic technique into play. But, on the other hand, going back to the first question, one may ask, do the instruments (the technical base) produce specific ideological effects, and are these effects themselves determined by the dominant ideology? In which case, concealment of the technical base will also bring about a specific ideological effect. Its inscription, its manifestation as such, on the other hand, would produce a knowledge effect, as actualization of the work process, as denunciation of ideology, and as critique of idealism.

The Eye of the Subject

Central in the process of production[5] of the film, the camera—an assembly of optical and mechanical instrumentation—carries out a certain mode of inscription characterized by marking, by the recording of differences of light intensity (and of wavelength for color) and of differences between the frames. Fabricated on the model of the *camera obscura*, it permits the construction of an image analogous to the perspective projections developed during the Italian Renaissance. Of course the use of lenses of different focal lengths can alter the perspective of an image. But this much, at least, is clear in the history of cinema: it is the perspective construction of the Renaissance which originally served as model. The use of different lenses,

[3] [*Travail*, the process—implying not only "work" in the ordinary sense but as in Freud's usage: the dream*work*.—*Trans.*]

[4] Althusser opposes ideology to knowledge or science. Ideology operates by obfuscating the means by which it is produced. Thus an increase in ideological value is an increase in mystification.—*Ed.*

[5] Obviously we are not speaking here of investment of capital in the process.

when not dictated by technical considerations aimed at restoring the habitual perspective (such as shooting in limited or extended spaces which one wishes to expand or contract) does not destroy [traditional] perspective but rather makes it play a normative role. Departure from the norm, by means of a wide-angle or telephoto lens, is clearly marked in comparison with so-called "normal" perspective. We will see in any case that the resulting ideological effect is still defined in relation to the ideology inherent in perspective. The dimensions of the image itself, the ratio between height and width, seem clearly taken from an average drawn from Western easel painting.

The conception of space which conditions the construction of perspective in the Renaissance differs from that of the Greeks. For the latter, space is discontinuous and heterogeneous (for Aristotle, but also for Democritus, for whom space is the location of an infinity of indivisible atoms), whereas with Nicholas of Cusa will be born a conception of space formed by the relation between elements which are equally near and distant from the "source of all life." In addition, the pictorial construction of the Greeks corresponded to the organization of their stage, based on a multiplicity of points of view, whereas the painting of the Renaissance will elaborate a centered space. ("Painting is nothing but the intersection of the visual pyramid following a given distance, a fixed center, and a certain lighting."—Alberti.) The center of this space coincides with the eye which Jean Pellerin Viator will so justly call the "subject." ("The principal point in perspective should be placed at eye level: this point is called fixed or subject."[6]) Monocular vision, which as Pleynet points out, is what the camera has, calls forth a sort of play of "reflection." Based on the principle of a fixed point by reference to which the visualized objects are organized, it specifies in return the position of the "subject,"[7] the very spot it must necessarily occupy.

In focusing it, the optical construct appears to be truly the projection-reflection of a "virtual image" whose hallucinatory reality it creates. It lays out the space of an ideal vision and in this way assures the necessity of a transcendence—metaphorically (by the unknown to which it appeals—here we must recall the structural place occupied by the vanishing point) and metonymically (by the displacement that it seems to carry out: a subject is both "in place of" and "a part for the whole"). Contrary to Chinese and Japanese painting, Western easel painting, presenting as it does a motionless and continuous whole, elaborates a total vision which corresponds to the idealist conception of the fullness and homogeneity of "being,"[8] and is, so to speak, representative of this conception. In this sense it contributes in a singularly emphatic way to the ideological function of art, which is to provide the tangible representation of metaphysics. The principle of transcendence which conditions and is conditioned by the perspective construction represented in painting and in the photographic image which copies from it seems to inspire all the idealist paeans to which the cinema has given rise [such as we find in Cohen-Séat or Bazin].[9]

---

[6] Cf. L. Brion Guerry, *Jean Pellerin Viator* (Paris: Belles Lettres, 1962).

[7] We understand the term "subject" here in its function as vehicle and place of intersection of ideological implications which we are attempting progressively to make clear, and not as the structural function which analytic discourse attempts to locate. It would rather take partially the place of the ego, of whose deviations little is known in the analytic field.

[8] The perspective "frame" which will have such an influence on cinematographic shooting has as its role to intensify, to increase the effect of the spectacle, which no divergence may be allowed to split.

[9] See Cohen-Séat, *Essai sur les principes d'une philosophie du cinéma* (Paris: Corti) and Bazin, *What is Cinema?* (Berkeley & Los Angeles: University of California Press).—*Trans.*

Projection: The Difference Negated

Nevertheless, whatever the effects proper to optics generally, the movie camera differs from still photography by registering through its mechanical instrumentation a series of images. It might thus seem to counter the unifying and "substantializing" character of the single-perspective image, taking what would seem like instants of time or slices from "reality" (but always a reality already worked upon, elaborated, selected). This might permit the supposition, especially because the camera moves, of a multiplicity of points of view which would neutralize the fixed position of the eye-subject and even nullify it. But here we must turn to the relation between the succession of images inscribed by the camera and their projection, bypassing momentarily the place occupied by montage, which plays a decisive role in the strategy of the ideology produced.

The projection operation (projector and screen) restore continuity of movement and the temporal dimension to the sequence of static images. The relation between the individual frames and the projection would resemble the relation between points and a curve in geometry. But it is precisely this relation and the restoration of continuity to discontinuous elements which poses a problem. The meaning effect produced does not depend only on the content of the images but also on the material procedures by which an illusion of continuity, dependent on the persistence of vision, is restored from discontinuous elements. These separate frames have between them differences that are indispensable for the creation of an illusion of continuity, of a continuous passage (movement, time). But only on one condition can these differences create this illusion: they must be effaced as differences.[10]

Thus on the technical level the question becomes one of the adoption of a very small difference between images, such that each image, in consequence of an organic factor [presumably persistence of vision] is rendered incapable of being seen as such. In this sense we could say that film—and perhaps in this respect it is exemplary—lives on the denial of difference: the difference is necessary for it to live, but it lives on its negation. This is indeed the paradox that emerges if we look directly at a strip of processed film: adjacent images are almost exactly repeated, their divergence being verifiable only by comparison of images at a sufficient distance from each other. We should remember, moreover, the disturbing effects which result during a projection from breakdowns in the recreation of movement, when the spectator is brought abruptly back to discontinuity—that is, to the body, to the technical apparatus which he had *forgotten*.

We might not be far from seeing what is in play on this material basis, if we recall that the "language" of the unconscious, as it is found in dreams, slips of the tongue, or hysterical symptoms, manifests itself as continuity destroyed, broken, and as the unexpected surging forth of a marked difference. Couldn't we thus say that cinema reconstructs and forms the mechanical model (with the simplifications that this can entail) of a system of writing[11]

---

[10] "We know that the spectator finds it impossible to notice that the images which succeed one another before his eyes were assembled end-to-end, because the projection of the film on the screen offers an impression of continuity although the images which compose it are, in reality, distinct, and are differentiated moreover by variations in space and time." "In a film, there can be hundreds, even thousands of cuts and intervals. But if it is shown for specialists who know the art, the spectacle will not be divulged as such. Only an error or lack of competence will permit them to seize, and this is a disagreeable sensation, the changes of time and place of action." (Pudovkin, "Le Montage," in *Cinéma d'aujourd'hui et de demain* [Moscow, 1956]).

[11] [*Écriture*, in the French, meaning "writing" but also "schematization" at any given level of material or expression.—*Trans.*]

constituted by a material base and a counter-system (ideology, idealism) which uses this system while also concealing it? On the one hand, the optical apparatus and the film permit the marking of difference (but the marking is already negated, we have seen, in the constitution of the perspective image with its mirror effect).[12] On the other hand, the mechanical apparatus both selects the minimal difference and represses it in projection, so that meaning can be constituted: it is at once direction, continuity, movement. The projection mechanism allows the differential elements (the discontinuity inscribed by the camera) to be suppressed, bringing only the relation into play. The individual images as such disappear so that movement and continuity can appear. But the movement and continuity are the visible expression (one might even say the projection) of their relations, derived from the tiny discontinuities between the images. Thus one may assume that what was already at work as the originating basis of the perspective image, namely the eye, the "subject," is put forth, liberated (in the sense that a chemical reaction liberates a substance) by the operation which transforms successive, discrete images (as isolated images they have, strictly speaking, no meaning, or at least no unity of meaning) into continuity, movement, meaning; with continuity restored both meaning and consciousness are restored.[13]

The Transcendental Subject

Meaning and consciousness, to be sure: at this point we must return to the camera. Its mechanical nature not only permits the shooting of differential images as rapidly as desired but also destines it to change position, to move. Film history shows that as a result of the combined inertia of painting, theater, and photography, it took a certain time to notice the inherent mobility of the cinematic mechanism. The ability to reconstitute movement is after all only a partial, elementary aspect of a more general capability. To seize movement is to become movement, to follow a trajectory is to become trajectory, to choose a direction is to have the possibility of choosing one, to determine a meaning is to give oneself a meaning. In this way the eye-subject, the invisible base of artificial perspective (which in fact only represents a larger effort to produce an ordering, regulated transcendence) becomes absorbed in, "elevated" to a vaster function, proportional to the movement which it can perform.

And if the eye which moves is no longer fettered by a body, by the laws of matter and time, if there are no more assignable limits to its displacement—conditions fulfilled by the possibilities of shooting and of film—the world will not only be constituted by this eye but for it.[14] The movability of the camera seems to fulfill the most favorable conditions for the manifestation of the "transcendental subject." There is both fantasmatization of an objective reality (images, sounds, colors) and of an objective reality which, limiting its powers of constraint, seems equally to augment the possibilities or the power of the subject.[15] As it is said of consciousness—

[12] [Specular: a notion used by Althusser and above all by Lacan; the word refers to the "mirror" effect which by reflection (specularization) constitutes the object reflected to the viewer and for him. The body is the most important and the first of these objects.—*Trans.*]

[13] It is thus first at the level of the apparatus that the cinema functions as a language: inscription of discontinuous elements whose effacement in the relationship instituted among them produces meaning.

[14] "In the cinema I am simultaneously in this action and *outside* of it, in this space and out of this space. Having the power of ubiquity, I am everywhere and nowhere." (Jean Mitry, *Esthetique et Psychologie du Cinéma* (Paris: Presses Universitaires de France, 1965), p. 179 .)

[15] The cinema manifests in a hallucinatory manner the belief in the omnipotence of thought, described by Freud, which plays so important a role in neurotic defense mechanisms.

and in point of fact we are concerned with nothing less—the image will always be image *of* something; it must result from a deliberate act of consciousness [*visée intentionelle*]. "The word intentionality signifies nothing other than this peculiarity that consciousness has of being consciousness *of* something, of carrying in its quality of *ego* its *cogitatum* within itself."[16] In such a definition could perhaps be found the status of the cinematographic image, or rather of its operation, the mode of working which it carries out. For it to be an image of something, it has to constitute this something as meaning. The image seems to reflect the world but solely in the naive inversion of a founding hierarchy: "The domain of natural existence thus has only an authority of the second order, and always presupposes the domain of the transcendental."[17]

The world is no longer only an "open and unbounded horizon." Limited by the framing, lined up, put at the proper distance, the world offers up an object endowed with meaning, an intentional object, implied by and implying the action of the "subject" which sights it. At the same time that the world's transfer as image seems to accomplish this phenomenological reduction, this putting into parentheses of its real existence (a suspension necessary, we will see, to the formation of the impression of reality) provides a basis for the apodicity[18] of the ego. The multiplicity of aspects of the object in view refers to a synthesizing operation, to the unity of this constituting subject: Husserl speaks of " 'aspects', sometimes of 'proximity', sometimes of 'distance', in variable modes of 'here' and 'there', opposed to an absolute 'here' (which is located—for me—in 'my own body' which appears to me at the same time), the consciousness of which, though it remains *unperceived*, always accompanies them. [We will see moreover what happens with the body in the *mise-en-scène* of projection.—J. L. B.] Each 'aspect' which the mind grasps is revealed in turn as a unity synthesized from a multiplicity of corresponding modes of presentation. The nearby object may present itself as the same, but under one or another 'aspect'. There may be variation of visual perspective, but also of 'tactile', 'acoustic' phenomena, or of other 'modes of presentation'[19] as we can observe in directing our attention in the proper direction."[20]

For Husserl, "the original operation [of intentional analysis] is to *unmask the potentialities implied* in present states of consciousness. And it is by this that will be carried out, from the noematic point of view, the eventual *explication*, *definition*, and *elucidation* of what is meant by consciousness, that is, its *objective meaning*."[21] And again in the *Cartesian Meditations*: "A second type of polarization now presents itself to us, another type of synthesis which embraces the particular multiplicities of *cogitationes*, which embraces them all and in a special manner, namely as *cogitationes* of an identical self which, *active* or *passive*, lives in all the lived states of consciousness and which, through them, relates to all objects."[22]

Thus is articulated the relation between the continuity necessary to the constitution of meaning and the "subject" which constitutes this meaning: continuity is an attribute of the subject. It supposes the subject and it circumscribes his place. It appears in the cinema in the

---

[16] Husserl, *Les Méditations Cartesiennes* (Paris: Vrin, 1953), p. 28.
[17] Ibid., p. 18.
[18] [Apodicity, in phenomenological terminology, indicates something of an ultimately irrefutable nature. See Husserl, *op.cit.—Trans.*]
[19] On this point it is true that the camera is revealed as incomplete. But this is only a technical imperfection which, since the birth of cinema, has already in large measure been remedied.
[20] Ibid., p. 34, emphasis added.
[21] Ibid., p. 40.
[22] Ibid., p. 58.

two complementary aspects of a "formal" continuity established through a system of negated differences and narrative continuity in the filmic space. The latter, in any case, could not have been conquered without exercising violence against the instrumental base, as can be discovered from most of the texts by film-makers and critics: the discontinuity that had been effaced at the level of the image could have reappeared on the narrative level, giving rise to effects of rupture disturbing to the spectator (to a *place* which ideology must both conquer and, in the degree that it already dominates it, must also satisfy: fill). "What is important in a film is the feeling of continuity which joins shots and sequences while maintaining unity and cohesion of movements. This continuity was one of the most difficult things to obtain."[23] Pudovkin defined montage as "the art of assembling pieces of film, shot separately, in such a way as to give the spectator the impression of continuous movement." The search for such narrative continuity, so difficult to obtain from the material base, can only be explained by an essential ideological stake projected in this point: it is a question of preserving at any cost the synthetic unity of the locus where meaning originates [the subject]—the constituting transcendental function to which narrative continuity points back as its natural secretion.[24]

The Screen-Mirror: Specularization and Double Identification

But another supplementary operation (made possible by a special technical arrangement) must be added in order that the mechanism thus described can play its role effectively as an ideological machine, so that not only the reworked "objective reality" but also the specific type of identification we have described can be represented.

No doubt the darkened room and the screen bordered with black like a letter of condolences already present privileged conditions of effectiveness—no exchange, no circulation, no communication with any outside. Projection and reflection take place in a closed space and those who remain there, whether they know it or not (but they do not), find themselves chained, captured, or captivated. (What might one say of the function of the head in this captivation: it suffices to recall that for Bataille materialism makes itself headless—like a wound that bleeds and thus transfuses.) And the mirror, as a reflecting surface, is framed, limited, circumscribed. *An infinite mirror would no longer be a mirror.* The paradoxical nature of the cinematic mirror-screen is without doubt that it reflects *images* but not "*reality*"; the word reflect, being transitive,[25] leaves this ambiguity unresolved. In any case this "reality" comes from behind the spectator's head and if he looked at it directly he would see nothing except the moving beams from an already veiled light source.

---

[23] Mitry, *op. cit.*, p. 157.

[24] The lens, the "objective," is of course only a particular location of the "subjective." Marked by the idealist opposition interior/exterior, topologically situated at the point of meeting of the two, it corresponds, one could say, to the empirical organ of the subjective, to the opening, the fault in the organs of meaning, by which the exterior world may penetrate the interior and assume meaning. "It is the interior which commands," says Bresson. "I know this may seem paradoxical in an art which is all exterior." Also the use of different lenses is already conditioned by camera movement as implication and trajectory of meaning, by this transcendental function which we are attempting to define: it is the possibility of choosing a field as accentuation or modification of the *visée intentionelle*.No doubt this transcendental function fits in without difficulty the field of psychology. This, moreover, is insisted upon by Husserl himself, who indicates that Brentano's discovery, intentionality, "permits one truly to distinguish the method of a descriptive science of consciousness, as much philosophical and transcendental as psychological."

[25] It is always a reflection *of* something.—*Trans.*

The arrangement of the different elements—projector, darkened hall, screen—in addition from reproducing in a striking way the *mise-en-scène* of Plato's cave (prototypical set for all transcendence and the topological model of idealism[26]) reconstructs the situation necessary to the release of the "mirror stage" discovered by Lacan. This psychological phase, which occurs between six and eighteen months of age, generates *via* the mirror image of a unified body the constitution or at least the first sketches of the "I" as an imaginary function. "It is to this unreachable image in the mirror that the specular image gives its garments."[27] But for this imaginary constitution of the self to be possible, there must be—Lacan strongly emphasizes this point—two complementary conditions: immature powers of mobility and a precocious maturation of visual organization (apparent in the first few days of life). If one considers that these two conditions are repeated during cinematographic projection—suspension of mobility and predominance of the visual function—perhaps one could suppose that this is more than a simple analogy. And possibly this very point explains the "impression of reality" so often invoked in connection with the cinema for which the various explanations proposed seem only to skirt the real problem. In order for this impression to be produced, it would be necessary that the conditions of a formative scene be reproduced. This scene would be repeated and reenacted in such a manner that the imaginary order (activated by a specularization which takes place, everything considered, in reality) fulfills its particular function of occultation or of filling the gap, the split, of the subject on the order of the signifier.[28]

On the other hand, it is to the extent that the child can sustain the look of another in the presence of a third party that he can find the assurance of an identification with the image of his own body. From the very fact that during the mirror stage is established a dual relationship, it constitutes, in conjunction with the formation of the self in the imaginary order, the nexus of secondary identification.[29] The origin of the self, as discovered by Lacan, in pertaining to the imaginary order effectively subverts the "optical machinery" of idealism which the projection room scrupulously reproduces.[30] But it is not as specifically "imaginary," nor as a reproduction of its first configuration, that the self finds a "place" in the cinema. This occurs, rather, as a sort of proof or verification of that function, a solidification through repetition.

The "reality" mimed by the cinema is thus first of all that of a "self." But, because the reflected image is not that of the body itself but that of a world already given as meaning, one can distinguish two levels of identification. The first, attached to the image itself, derives from the character portrayed as a center of secondary identifications, carrying an identity which constantly must be seized and reestablished. The second level permits the appearance of the first and places it "in action"—this is the transcendental subject whose place is taken by the camera which constitutes and rules the objects in this "world." Thus the spectator identifies less with what is represented, the spectacle itself, than with what stages the spectacle, makes it seen, obliging

---

[26] The arrangement of the cave, except that in the cinema it is already doubled in a sort of enclosure in which the camera, the darkened chamber, is enclosed in another darkened chamber, the projection hall.

[27] Lacan, *Ecrits* (Paris: Le Seuil, 1966) . See in particular "Le Stade du miroir comme formateur de la function du je."

[28] We see that what has been defined as impression of reality refers less to the "reality" than to the apparatus which, although being of an hallucinatory order, nonetheless founds this possibility. Reality will never appear except as relative to the images which reflect it, in some way inaugurated by a reflection anterior to itself.

[29] We refer here to what Lacan says of identifications in liaison with the structure determined by an optical instrument (the mirror), as they are constituted, in the prevailing figuration of the ego, as lines of resistance to the advance of the analytic work.

[30] "That the ego be 'in the right' must be avowed, from experience, to be a function of misunderstanding." (Lacan, *op. cit.*, p. 637.)

him to see what it sees; this is exactly the function taken over by the camera as a sort of relay.[31] Just as the mirror assembles the fragmented body in a sort of imaginary integration of the self, the transcendental self unites the discontinuous fragments of phenomena, of lived experience, into unifying meaning. Through it each fragment assumes meaning by being integrated into an "organic" unity. Between the imaginary gathering of the fragmented body into a unity and the transcendentality of the self, giver of unifying meaning, the current is indefinitely reversible.

The ideological mechanism at work in the cinema seems thus to be concentrated in the relationship between the camera and the subject. The question is whether the former will permit the latter to constitute and seize itself in a particular mode of specular reflection. Ultimately, the forms of narrative adopted, the "contents" of the image, are of little importance so long as an identification remains possible.[32] What emerges here (in outline) is the specific function fulfilled by the cinema as support and instrument of ideology. It constitutes the "subject" by the illusory delimitation of a central location—whether this be that of a god or of any other substitute. It is an apparatus destined to obtain a precise ideological effect, necessary to the dominant ideology: creating a fantasmatization of the subject, it collaborates with a marked efficacity in the maintenance of idealism.

Thus the cinema assumes the role played throughout Western history by various artistic formations. The ideology of representation (as a principal axis orienting the notion of aesthetic "creation") and specularization (which organizes the *mise-en-scène* required to constitute the transcendental function) form a singularly coherent system in the cinema. Everything happens as if, the subject himself being unable—and for a reason—to account for his own situation, it was necessary to substitute secondary organs, grafted on to replace his own defective ones, instruments or ideological formations capable of filling his function as subject. In fact, this substitution is only possible on the condition that the instrumentation itself be hidden or repressed. Thus disturbing cinematic elements—similar, precisely, to those elements indicating the return of the repressed—signify without fail the arrival of the instrument "in flesh and blood," as in Vertov's *Man With a Movie Camera*. Both specular tranquility and the assurance of one's own identity collapse simultaneously with the revealing of the mechanism, that is of the inscription of the film-work.

The cinema can thus appear as a sort of psychic apparatus of substitution, corresponding to the model defined by the dominant ideology. The system of repression (primarily economic) has as its goal the prevention of deviations and of the active exposure of this "model."[33] Analogously one could say that its "unconscious" is not recognized (we speak of the apparatus and not of the content of films, which have used the unconscious in ways we know all too well). To this unconscious would be attached the mode of production of film, the process of "work" in its multiple determinations, among which must be numbered those depending on instrumentation. This is why reflections on the basic apparatus ought to be possible to integrate into a general theory of the ideology of cinema.

---

[31] "That it sustains itself as 'subject' means that language permits it to consider itself as the stagehand or even the director of all the imaginary capturings of which it would otherwise only be the living marionette." (*Ibid.*, p. 637.)

[32] It is on this point and in function of the elements which we are trying to put in place that a discussion of editing could be opened. We will at a later date attempt to make some remarks on this subject.

[33] *Mediterranée*, by J.-D. Pollet and Phillipe Sollers (1963), which dismantles with exemplary efficiency the "transcendental specularization" which we have attempted to delineate, gives a manifest proof of this point. The film was never able to overcome the economic blockade.

CHAPTER 24
FÉLIX GUATTARI

Félix Guattari (1930–1992) was a French psychoanalyst, philosopher, and political thinker. He trained in psychoanalysis under Jacques Lacan, and worked at La Borde, the clinic founded by another student of Lacan's, Jean Oury, for some time. Guattari was also a committed Marxist and was actively involved in political movements—which involvement led, after the 1968 student uprising in Paris, to his meeting the philosopher, Gilles Deleuze, with whom Guattari would collaborate on multiple works, including, perhaps most famously, Anti-Oedipus. *The selections included here are two essays of Guattari's on film and psychoanalysis, "A Cinema of Desire" and "The Poor Man's Couch." "A Cinema of Desire" was originally published in French in 1973. "The Poor Man's Couch" was originally published in French ("Le divan du pauvre") in* Communications *in 1975.*

In "A Cinema of Desire," Guattari opposes a possible future cinema rooted in his notion of desire, as opposed to the capitalist (or bureaucratic socialist) erotic cinema produced in the contemporary world. Of course, to understand this opposition, we must first understand what Guattari means by "desire," and how it relates to what he calls "eros." Power in any industrialized society relies upon the imposition of "reality" by a dominant semiology, such that words mean what the dominant ideology wants them to mean. Thus, although we might be led to believe that there is an opposition between pleasure and reality, it is rather an opposition of the principle of the dominant reality to the principle of licit pleasure. Eros functions within the bounds of what is permitted (licit) within a given semiological formulation of "reality." Desire, on the other hand, erupts somewhat more spontaneously from within the individual, unrelated to social codes, regulations, or the dominant language and modes of signification. As such, desire must try to maintain itself in the space between the dominant reality and licit pleasure—and it's a jealously guarded frontier, Guattari notes. Desire is so hunted down and so antagonized that it usually renounces its objects in favor of the established boundaries and limits. In focusing itself on the boundaries, free desire relinquishes itself to capitalist eros, a passion for the boundary. Industrialized societies impose such models of desire, which are always compatible with private ownership and according to which enjoyment is only possible in terms of possession.

Cinema, television, and the press have become instruments of this dominant reality, Guattari argues, with such media now mostly in the service of repression. But this is not to say that these media could not liberate—just that, in general, they do not. As we have already seen, the dominant reality is always enforced by way of signification, whether in terms of totalitarian power (which is always dominated by a single signifier), psychoanalysis (which understands everything in terms of the family triangle), or even structuralism (which offers as ultimate signifier a nameless God). A liberated desire would not signify, however, and would insist upon an asignifying semiotics. Cinematically speaking, this would permit cinema to escape questions of meaning—which is the direction in which cinema heads when exploited by capitalism or bureaucratic socialism. For Guattari, however, cinema's true effectiveness is in its pre- and asignifying components—in desire, which is prebodily and presignifying, which does not yet mean any one particular thing, and thus cannot be enacted or exploited by the dominant reality. Cinema, Guattari says, could be the machine of eros or the machine of liberated desire—and there is both social and psychic emancipation in the latter option.

*In "The Poor Man's Couch," Guattari turns his attention to the relationship between psychoanalysis and cinema. Picking up on the ideas at the conclusion of "A Cinema of Desire," Guattari notes that, while psychoanalysis can only ever focus on the individual or, at most, the family, cinema uses the whole social field and all of history. While film is, as he puts it, "a gigantic machine for modeling the social libido," psychoanalysis is reserved for the use of certain elites. That said, there are numerous similarities and points of comparison, starting with the fact that both cinema and psychoanalysis suspend the ordinary rules of communication. At the movies, you are not expected to act on the things you see or the feelings they inspire. Like psychoanalysis, this speech cut off from action exists in part to reinforce the dominant discourse. The best psychoanalytical strategy, Guattari notes, is silence—*écoute*—which makes of the analyst an analog to the (silent, observing and listening) filmgoer. This attentive silence works like a drug, transforming the subjectivity of the user while capturing the energy of desire and turning it against itself, providing a sort of catharsis that then prevents desire from disturbing the dominant social system.*

Within psychoanalysis, there is another contrast, between the orthodox Freudians and the Lacanians. The Freudians assume a certain social structure as the norm, and then designate all deviations from that norm to be perverse. But Lacanian structuralist psychoanalysis is meant to address what it takes to be Freudianism's abuses, abandoning the language of normality and perversity in favor of a semiotic understanding of the psyche. That said, Guattari argues, Lacanianism gets stuck in semiotic structures thereby—and as such gets no closer than Freud to desire. The struggles of desire never stay contained within any signifier; they always overflow the semiotic system in unpredictable ways. As such, Guattari disagrees with Lacan that the unconscious is structured like a language. Quite the contrary: the unconscious only takes on the appearance of a language when its multiplicity of voices and points of view are crushed by the dominant system.

Guattari asserts that psychoanalysis cannot really teach us anything about film—psychoanalysis does not understand the unconscious processes related to the production of film—but that there are things about the social field which film could teach the psychoanalysts. In film, the unconscious escapes the signifier, and we see the proliferation of desubjectivation and deindividuation which appear not to be as rare or isolated as psychoanalysis has held them to be. Film shows us that the self-conscious subject is not the norm, contra psychoanalysis, but instead one particular option in a field of possible subjectivities. Montage across different modes of asignifying expression—visual imagery, color, music, etc.—in particular frees film from the signifying grid so central to both Lacanian psychoanalysis and the dominating strategies of industrialized societies.

Psychoanalysis uses speech to dominate the inner world of the analysand: both analyst and analysand end up speaking the language of psychoanalysis, and do so as a means of bringing a modicum of control to the unconscious. Commercial film, on the other hand, does not inspire speech: no one speaks to or with the film, allowing the film instead to speak for everyone. In so doing, film has the power to reshape the unconscious—speaking on our behalf such that we identify ourselves with that voice. While psychoanalysis can alienate us from its own private, closed world and language, commercial cinema occupies the unconscious—it gives us our own world and language, but remolded, treating us (sometimes) like we are the puppet or the zombie to the dominating invader. Put another way, Guattari says that cinema turns us all into orphans for a moment—cut off from all that has come before for us—and in that moment, we can be changed. The drug that is commercial cinema can thus co-opt us for the dominant reality it serves, industrial capitalism or socialism. But here Guattari posits the possibility of a cinema that, resisting the urge to drug us, could have liberating potential. Such a cinema—a revolutionary cinema—is still able to be conceived, at least, whereas a revolutionary psychoanalysis, Guattari argues, is not.

A CINEMA OF DESIRE

Translated by David L. Sweet

The history of desire is inseparable from the history of its repression. Maybe one day a historian will try to write a history of "cinemas of desire" (the way one tells an audience who express their sentiments too excitedly to "stop their cinema"). But, at the very least, he would have to begin this history with classical antiquity! It could start with the opening of the first big theater of international renown, a theater for captive cinephiles: Plato's cave. It would have to describe the 2000 years or so of the Catholic church's monopoly of production and distribution, as well as the abortive attempts of dissident societies of production, such as the Cathar cinema of the 12th century, or the Jansenist cinema of the 17th, up to the triumph of the baroque monopoly. There would be color film in it: with 10th century stained-glass windows would be the silent cinema of the "bepowdered" and the Pierrots. A special place should be reserved for the big schools that transformed the economy of desire on a long-term basis, like that of courtly love, with its four hundred troubadours who managed to "launch" a new form of love and a new kind of woman. It would have to appreciate the devastating effects of the great consortia of romanticism and their promotion of an infantilization of love, while awaiting the saturation of the market by psychoanalytical racketeering with its standard shorts for miniaturized screens: the little cinema of transference, Oedipus, and castration.

Power can only be maintained insofar as it relies on the semiologies of signification: "No one can ignore the law." This implies that no one can ignore the meaning of words. Linguists like Oswald Ducrot insist on the fact that language is not simply an instrument of communication, but also an instrument of power.[1] The law, as the culmination of sexual, ethnic, and class struggles, etc., crystallizes in language. The "reality" imposed by the powers-that-be is conveyed by a dominant semiology. Therefore, one should not go from a principled opposition between pleasure and reality, between a principle of desire and a principle of reality, but rather, from a *principle of dominant reality* and a *principle of licit pleasure*. Desire is forced to maintain itself, as well as can be expected, in this space between reality and pleasure, this frontier that power jealously controls with the help of innumerable frontier guards: in the family, at school, in the barracks, at the workshop, in psychiatric hospitals and, of course, at the movies.

Thus, desire is so ruthlessly hunted down that it usually ends up renouncing its objects and investing itself and its guardians on these boundaries. The capitalist eros will turn into a passion for the boundary, it becomes the cop. While bumping on the all-too-explicit signs of the libido, it will take its pleasure from their hateful contemplation. "Look at this filth." It will become the gaze, the forbidden spectacle, the transgression, "without really getting into it." All the morals of asceticism and sublimation consist, in fact, of capturing the libido in order to identify and contain it within this system of limits. I don't mean, here, to oppose centralism with spontaneism, or the disciplines necessary for organizing the collectivity with the turbulence of

[1] Cf. J. L. Austin, *How to Do Things With Words* (Oxford: Clarendon Press, 1962).

the "natural" impulses; nor is it a matter of reducing this question to a simple case of morality or ideological strategy of dominant powers in order to better control the exploited... The dualities morality/instinct, culture/nature, order/disorder, master/slave, centrality/democracy, etc., appear to us to be insufficient as a way of accounting for this eroticization of the limits, at least in its contemporary evolution.

The development of productive forces in industrialized societies (it is true both for capitalism and bureaucratic socialism) involves an increasing liberation of the energy of desire. The capitalist system does not function simply by putting a flux of slaves to work. It depends on modeling individuals according to its preferences and, for this purpose, to propose and impose models of desire: it puts models of childhood, fatherhood, motherhood, and love in circulation. It launches these models the same way the automobile industry launches a new line of cars. The important thing is that these models always remain compatible with the axiomatic of capital: the object of love should always be an exclusive object participating in the system of private ownership. The fundamental equation is: enjoyment = possession. Individuals are modeled to adapt, like a cog, to the capitalist machine. At the heart of their desire and in the exercise of their pleasure, they have to find private ownership. They have to invest it with ideality: "production for production's sake." They can only desire the objects that the market production proposes to them; they must not only submit to the hierarchy, but even more, love it as such. To conjure up the dangers of class struggle, capitalism has tried hard to introduce a bourgeois owner into the heart of each worker. It is the prerequisite of his integration. Traditional models that attached the worker to his job, to his quarter, to his moral values, indeed to his religion (even if it be socialism) have all collapsed. The paternalistic model of the boss is no longer compatible with production, no more than that of the *pater familias* with the education of children. One now needs a deterritorialized worker, someone who does not freeze into professional experience, but who follows the progress of technology, indeed, who develops a certain creativity, a certain participation. Moreover, one needs a consumer who adapts to the evolution of the market.

For this reason, the problem raised is the transformation of traditional relations of production and other relations—familial, conjugal, educational, etc.... But if one relaxes the brakes too abruptly, then it is the machines of desire that risk flying off the handle, and breaking not only through the outdated frontiers but even the new ones the system wants to establish. The relations of production, formation, and reproduction oscillate between immobilist temptations and archaic fixations. The capitalist "solution" consists in pushing models that are at once adapted to its imperatives of standardization—i.e., that dismantle traditional territorialities—and that reconstitute an artificial security; in other words, that modernize the archaisms and inject artificial ones. In conditions such as these, from the angle of production, the worker will be deterritorialized; from the angle of relations of production, formation, and reproduction, he will be reterritorialized.

Cinema, television, and the press have become fundamental instruments of forming and imposing a dominant reality and dominant significations. Beyond being means of communication, of transmitting information, they are instruments of power. They not only handle messages, but, above all, libidinal energy. The themes of cinema—its models, its genres, its professional castes, its mandarins, its stars—are, whether they want to be or not, at the service of power. And not only insofar as they depend directly on the financial power machine, but first and foremost, because they participate in the elaboration and transmission of subjective models. Presently, the media, for the most part, functions in the service of repression. But they could become instruments of liberation of great importance. Commercial cinema, for example, entertains a latent racism in its Westerns; it can prevent the production of films about events like those of May '68 in France; but the Super-8 and the video-tape recorder could be turned into means of writing that are much more direct and much more effective than discourses, pamphlets, and brochures. As such it could contribute greatly to foiling the tyranny of the *savoir-écrire* that weighs not only on the bourgeois hierarchy but which operates also among the ranks of what is traditionally called the worker movement.

Beyond the signifier, beyond the illusion of a permanent reality. It's not a speculative option, but an affirmation: all reality is dated, historically and socially situated. The order of the real has nothing to do with destiny; one can change it. Let us consider three modern currents of thought, vehicles of three systems of signification: totalitarian systems, psychoanalysis, and structuralism. In each case, there is a certain keystone on which the organization of the dominant reality converges. A signifier dominates every statement of a totalitarian power, a leader, a church, or God. By right, all desire must converge upon it. No one can remain with impunity across "the line" or outside the church. But this type of libidinal economy centered on a transcendent object no longer corresponds exactly to the necessities of modern production, and it tends to be replaced by a more flexible system in developed capitalist countries. In order to form a worker, one must start in the cradle, discipline his Oedipal development within the family, follow him to school, to sports, to the cinema, and all the way to the juke-box.

Psychoanalysis, while borrowing its own model from this traditional type of libidinal economy, has refined and "molecuralized" it. It has to put to task new types of less obvious objects—objects that anyone can buy, so to speak. These objects are supposed to over-code all the *énoncés* of desire: the phallus and the partial objects—breast, shit, etc.... From then on, the despotism of the signifier no longer tends to concentrate on a leader or a God and to express itself on the massive scale of an empire or a church, but on that of the family itself reduced to a state of triangularity. The struggle between the sexes, generations, and social classes, has been reduced to the scale of the family and the self. The machine of familial power, rectified by psychoanalysis, functions by means of two primary parts: the symbolic phallus and castration, instruments of the alienation of woman and child. One recalls the tyrannical interrogation of Little Hans by his father under the supervision of Professor Freud. But before that, the mother's resistance must be subdued, compelling her to submit to psychoanalytical dogma. In fact, it never crosses her mind to object to her son's coming to join her in bed whenever he wants. The mother becoming the agent of phallic power, the attack on childhood is concentrated on the question of masturbation. One does not accuse him directly of masturbating; one imposes upon him the good, "castrating" explanation with regard to this question. One forces him to incorporate a particular system of signification: "What you desire—we know this better than you—is to sleep with your mother and to kill your father."

The importance of submitting the child to the Oedipian code—and this at an early age—does not result from a structural or signifying effect, separate from history or society. It depends on capitalism's inability to find other ways of providing the family with an artificial consistency. In archaic societies, the child was relatively free in his movements until his initiation. But in a capitalist society, initiation begins with the pacifier: the mother-child relationship tends to be more and more strictly controlled by psychologists, psychoanalysts, educators, etc. In its older formulation, power was maintained as a paradigmatic series—father-boss-king, etc., culminating in a discernible, incarnate, and institutionalized God. In its present formulation, incarnation is deterritorialized and decentered. It is everywhere and nowhere, and it depends on family models to arrange a refuge for it. But in their turn, the diverse psychoanalytic models of Oedipal triangulation appear too territorialized with regard to parental images and partial objects. Much more abstract, much more mathematical models of the unconscious have to be proposed.

Structuralism in psychoanalysis—as in other domains—can be thought of as an attempt to substitute a nameless God for the God of the church and the family. It proposes a transcendent model of subjectivity and desire that would be independent of history and real social struggle. From that moment, the conflict of ideas tends to be displaced anew. It leaves the psychoanalytical terrain of the family and the self for that of the semiotic and its applications in mass media. I cannot undertake here a critical analysis of structuralism; I only want to point out that, to my mind, such a critique should start by questioning the syncretic conception of the diverse modes of encoding. It seems to me indispensable, first of all, to avoid absorbing "natural" encodings, such as the genetic code, into human semiologies. One entertains the illusion that the "natural" order as well as that of the social arrangements (like structures of kinship) would be structured "like languages." Thus, one confuses the modes of encoding that I call *a-semiotic*—like music, painting, mathematics, etc.—with those of speech and writing. Second, it seems necessary to distinguish between the pre-signifying semiologies—for example, of archaic societies, the insane, and children—and fully signifying semiologies of modern societies that are all over-coded in the writing of social and economic laws. In primitive societies, one expresses oneself as much by speech as by gestures, dances, rituals, or signs marked on the body. In industrialized societies, this richness of expression is attenuated; all *énoncés* have to be translatable to the language that encodes dominant meanings.

It is also important to expose and insist on the independence of an a-signifying semiotics. It is this, in fact, that will allow us to understand what permits cinema to escape the semiologies of meaning and to participate in the collective arrangements of desire.[2]

If structuralism refuses to consider this independence, there can be no question of leaving the domain of signification—i.e., the signifier-signified duality. It tries, moreover, to systematically inject meaning into all signifying regimes that tend to escape it. (It will invent "relational significations" for science or, for the cinema, the unities of "iconomatic" significations, etc.) In putting the signifier and the signifying chains in the forefront, it substantiates the idea of keeping the contents at a secondary level. But in fact, it secretly transfers the normalizing power of language onto the signifier. Hence, in masking the possible creativity of a-signifying semiotic machines, structuralism plays into an order tied down to dominant significations.

When it is exploited by capitalist and bureaucratic socialist powers to mold the collective imaginary, cinema topples over to the side of meaning. Yet, its own effectiveness continues to depend on its pre-signifying symbolic components as well as its a-signifying ones: linkages, internal movements of visual images, colors, sounds, rhythms, gestures, speech, etc. But unlike the speech and writing that, for hundreds, indeed, thousands of years, has remained pretty much the same as a means of expression, cinema has, in a few decades, never ceased to enrich its technique. In this way, to catch up with these effects, the powers-that-be have tried to

[2] One must address in detail the role of a-signifying components vis-à-vis analogical ones: the fact, in particular, that the functioning as machines of deterritorialized signs "breaks" the effects of signification and interpretation, thwarts the system of dominant redundancies, accelerates the most "innovative," "constructivist," "rhizomatic" components.

increase the control they exercise upon it. The more it enlarges its scale of aesthetic intensities, the more the systems of control and censure have tried to subjugate it to signifying semiologies. As an a-signifying semiotic, how does cinema go beyond the structure of signifying semiologies? Christian Metz explains it better than I can; he shows that cinema is not a specialized language and that its *matter of content*[3] is undefined: "the breadth of its semantic fabric is a consequence of two distinct causes whose effects are cumulative. On the one hand, cinema encompasses a code—language, in the talkies—whose presence itself would be enough to authorize semantic information of the most varied type. Second, other elements of the filmic text, for example, images, are themselves languages whose matter of content has no precise boundaries."[4] Its matter of content extends so much more effectively beyond traditional encodings, since the semiotic alloy that composes its matter of expression is itself open to multiple systems of external intensities.

Its matters of expression are not fixed. They go in different directions. Christian Metz enumerates some of them, emphasizing that each has an intrinsic system of pertinent features:

- the phonic fabric of expression, that refers to spoken language (signifying semiology);
- the sonorous but non-phonic fabric that refers to instrumental music (a-signifying semiotic);
- the visual and colored fabric that refers to painting (mixed, symbolic, and a-signifying semiotic);
- the non-colored, visual fabric that refers to black and white photography (mixed, symbolic, and a-signifying semiotic);
- the gestures and movements of the human body, etc. (symbolic semiologies).

Umberto Eco has already pointed out that cinema does not bend to a system of double articulation, and that this had even led him to try to find a third articulation. But, doubtless, it is preferable to follow Metz who believes that cinema escapes all systems of double articulation, and, in my opinion, all elementary systems of significative encoding. The meanings in cinema are not directly encoded in a machine of intersecting syntagmatic and paradigmatic axes—they always come to it, secondarily, from external constraints that model it. If silent film, for example, had succeeded in expressing the intensities of desire in relation to the social field in a way that was much more immediate and authentic than that of the talkies, it was not because it was less expressive, but *because the signifying script had not yet taken possession of the image* and because, in these conditions, capitalism had not yet seized all the advantages it could take from it. The successive inventions of the talkies, of color, of television, etc., insofar as they enriched the possibilities of expressing desire, have led capitalism to take possession of cinema, and to use it as a privileged instrument of social control.

It is interesting, in this respect, to consider the extent to which television has not only not absorbed cinema, but has even subjected itself to the formula of commercial film, whose power, for this very reason, has never been so strong. In these conditions, the stakes of liberalizing pornographic film seems secondary to me. One remains here at the level of a sort

[3] Cf. Louis Hjelmslev, *Essais Linguistiques* (Paris: Editions de Minuit, 1971) and *Prolégomènes à une théorie du langage* (Paris: Minuit, 1971).

[4] Christian Metz, *Language and Cinema* (The Hague: Mouton, 1974); *Film Language, A Semiotic of the Cinema* (New York: Oxford University Press, 1974).

of "negotiation" with the contents that do not really threaten the established powers. On the contrary, these powers find it expedient to release the ballast on a terrain that does not threaten the foundations of established order. It would be completely different if the masses were at liberty to make the kind of film they wanted, whether pornographic or not. The miniaturization of material could become a determining factor in such an evolution.[5] The creation of private television channels by cable should be a decisive test; in fact, nothing guarantees us that what will develop, from the standpoint of the economy of desire, will not be even more reactionary than what is broadcast by national television. Whatever it is, it seems to me that all that tends toward limiting micropolitical struggles of desire to an eros cut off from all context is a trap. And this doesn't just hold true for the cinema.

The capitalist eros, we said, is always invested on the limit between a licit pleasure and a codified interdiction. It proliferates alongside the law; it makes itself the accomplice of what is forbidden; it channels the libido to the forbidden object that it only touches superficially. This economy of transgression polarizes the desiring production in a game of mirrors that cut it from all access to the real and catches it in phantasmic representations. In this way, desiring production never ceases to be separated from social production. Fantasized desire and the capitalist real which convert desire to "useful" work involve, apparently, two different types of arrangements. In fact, they involve two politics of desire that are absolutely complementary: a politics of re-enclosure on the person, the self, the appropriation of the other, hierarchy, exploitation, etc., and a politics of passive acceptance of the world such as it is.

Against the notions of eros and eroticism, I would like to oppose that of desire and desiring energy. Desire is not, like eros, tied down with the body, the person, and the law; it is no more dependent on the shameful body—with its hidden organs and its incestuous taboo—than to a fascination with and to myths about the nude body, the all-powerful phallus, and sublimation. Desire is constituted *before* the crystallization of the body and the organs, *before* the division of the sexes, *before* the separation between the familiarized self and the social field. It is enough to observe children, the insane, and the primitive without prejudice in order to understand that desire can make love with humans as well as with flowers, machines, or celebrations. It does not respect the ritual games of the war *between* the sexes: *it is not sexual*, it is transsexual. The struggle for the phallus, the threat of an imaginary castration, no more than the opposition between genitality and pre-genitality, normality and perversion, fundamentally concern it. Nothing essential leads to the subjugation of the child, the woman, or the homosexual. In a word, it is not centered on dominant significations and values: it participates in open, a-signifying semiotics, available for better or worse. Nothing depends here on destiny, but on collective arrangements in action.

In conclusion, I must say of the cinema that it can be both the machine of eros, i.e., the interiorization of repression, and the machine of liberated desire. An action in favor of the liberty of expression should therefore not be centered a priori on erotic cinema, but on what I will call a cinema of desire. The real trap is the separation between erotic themes and social themes; all themes are at once social and transsexual. There is no political cinema on the one hand and an erotic cinema on the other. Cinema is political whatever its subject; each time it represents a man, a woman, a child, or an animal, it takes sides in the micro-class struggle that concerns the reproduction of models of desire. The real repression of cinema is not centered

[5] The recent development of free radios on miniaturized FM transmitters would seem to confirm this tendency.

on erotic images; it aims above all at imposing a respect for dominant representations and models used by the power to control and channel the desire of the masses. In every production, in every sequence, in every frame, a choice is made between a conservative economy of desire and a revolutionary breakthrough. The more a film is conceived and produced according to the relations of production, or modeled on capitalist enterprise, the more chance there is of participating in the libidinal economy of the system. Yet no theory can furnish the keys to a correct orientation in this domain. One can make a film having life in a convent as its theme that puts the revolutionary libido in motion; one can make a film in defense of revolution that is fascist from the point of view of the economy of desire. In the last resort, what will be determinant in the political and aesthetic plane is not the words and the contents of ideas, but essentially a-signifying messages that escape dominant semiologies.

THE POOR MAN'S COUCH

Translated by Gianna Quach

Psychoanalysts are always a little suspicious of film, or rather, they have always been attracted to other forms of expression. But the reverse is not true. The covert advances of film into psychoanalysis have been innumerable, beginning with Mr. Goldwyn's proposition to Freud: $100,000 to put the famous loves on screen. This asymmetry is due, no doubt, not only to matters of respectability; it is tied, even more fundamentally, to the fact that psychoanalysis understands nothing of the unconscious processes involved in cinema. Psychoanalysis has sometimes tried to seize on the formal analogies between dream and film—for René Laforgue, cinema is a sort of collective dream; for René Lebovici, a dream to make spectators dream. Psychoanalysis has tried to absorb filmic syntagms into the primary processes, but it has never figured out its specificity and for a good reason: a normalization of the social imaginary that is irreducible to familialist and Oedipal models, even on those occasions when it puts itself deliberately at their service. Psychoanalysis now inflates itself in vain with linguistics and mathematics; yet it also continues trotting out the same generalities about the individual and the family, while film is bound up with the whole social field and with history. Something important happens in cinema where fantastic libidinal charges are invested—for example, those clustered around certain complexes that constitute the racist Western, Nazism, and the Resistance, the "American way of life," etc. Sophocles no longer holds his own in all this. Film has become a gigantic machine for modeling the social libido, while psychoanalysis will forever remain a small cottage industry reserved for selected elites.

One goes to the cinema to suspend the usual modes of communication for a while. All the constitutive elements of this situation lead to this suspension. Whatever alienating character the content or form of expression of a film may have, it aims fundamentally at reproducing a certain type of behavior that, for lack of a better term, I will call cinematographic performance.[1] Because film is capable of mobilizing the libido on this type of performance, it can be used to serve what Mikel Dufrenne has called a "house unconscious."[2]

Considered from the standpoint of unconscious repression, the cinematographic performance and the psychoanalytical performance ("the analytical act") perhaps deserve to be compared. For too long, belle époque psychoanalysis has persuaded us it was liberating the instincts by giving them a language; in fact, it never intended loosening the vice of the

[1] One could speak here of "film viewing-acts" in symmetry with the "speech-acts" studied by John Searle.

[2] "One offers you beautiful images, but in order to entice you: at the same time that you believe that you are having a treat, you absorb the ideology necessary to the reproduction of the relations of production. One dissimulates historical reality for you, one camouflages it under similitude of convention that is not just tolerable, but fascinating: so much so that you no longer even need to dream, nor have the right to do so, because your dreams could be nonconformist: one gives you the kind of packaged dream that disturbs nothing: tailormade fantasies, an agreeable phantasmagoria that puts you in tune with your unconscious, for it is understood that your consconscious [sic] must be given its due, from the time when you are knowledgeable enough to draw upon it and beg for it. Cinema today puts at your disposal a house unconscious perfectly ideologized." Mikel Dufrenne in *Cinema, Theory and Reading*. Paris: Klincksieck (1973).

dominant discourse except insofar as it reckoned on achieving even greater success than ordinary repression had ever done: to control, to discipline, to adapt people to the norms of a certain type of society. In the end, the discourse that is proffered in the analytical session is no more "liberated" than that served up in movie theaters. The so-called liberty of free association is only an illusion that masks a certain program, a secret modelization of statements (*énoncés*). As on the film screen, it is understood in analysis that no semiotic production of desire should have any effect on reality. The little playhouse of analysis and the mass analysis of film both proscribe the passage to action, to "acting out." Psychoanalysts, and even, in a way, filmmakers, would like to be considered as special beings beyond time and space: pure creators, neutral, apolitical, irresponsible… and in a sense, they may be right, they hardly have a hold on the process of control of which they are the agent. The grid of the psychoanalytical reading belongs today as much to the analyst as to the analysand. It is tailor made for all and sundry—"hey, you made a Freudian slip"—it integrates itself with intersubjective strategies and even perceptive codes: one proffers symbolic interpretations like threats, one "sees" the phallus, the returns to the maternal breast, etc. The interpretation is so obvious that the best, the most assured strategy, for an alerted psychoanalyst, continues to be silence, a systematically sanctioned silence: pure analytical *écoute*, floating attention. In truth, the emptiness of the *écoute* answers here to a desire emptied of all content, to a desire for nothing, to a radical powerlessness, and it is not surprising, under such conditions, that the castration complex has become the constant curative reference, the punctuation of every sequence, the cursor that perpetually brings desire back to the bottom line. The psychoanalyst, like the filmmaker, is "carried" by his subject. What one expects from both is the confection of a certain type of drug that, though technologically more sophisticated than the ordinary joint or pipe, nonetheless functions by transforming the mode of subjectivity of those who use it: one captures the energy of desire in order to turn it against itself, to anaesthetize it, to cut it off from the external world in such a way that it ceases to threaten the organization and values of the dominant social system. Yet, the psychoanalytic drug and the cinematographic drug are not the same; overall, they have the same objectives, but the micropolitics of desire they involve and the semiotic arrangements they rely on are completely different.

One could assume that these criticisms only aim at a certain type of psychoanalysis and are not concerned with the present structuralist current, insofar as it no longer affirms the reliance of interpretation on paradigms of content—as was the case with the classic theory of parental complexes—but rather on an interplay of universal signifiers, independent of any meanings they may carry. But can one believe structuralist psychoanalysis when they claim to have renounced shaping and translating the production of desire? The unconscious of orthodox Freudians was organized in complexes that crystallized the libido on heterogeneous elements: biological, familial, social, ethical, etc. The Oedipal complex, for example, apart from its real or imaginary traumatic components, was founded on the division of the sexes and age groups. One would think it was a matter, then, of objective bases in relation to which the libido had to express and finalize itself, with the consequence that, even today, questioning the "evidence" appears completely inappropriate to some. And yet, everyone knows about numerous situations in which the libido refuses these so-called *objective bases*, where it eschews the division of the sexes, where it ignores prohibitions linked to the separation of age groups, where it mixes people together, as if for the sake of it, where it tends to systematically avoid exclusive oppositions of subjective and objective, self and other. Orthodox psychoanalysts believe that it is only a matter of perverse, marginal, or pathological situations requiring interpretation and adaptation. Lacanian structuralism was originally founded in reaction to these "abuses," to this naïve realism, particularly regarding questions about narcissism and psychosis. It intended to radically break with a curative practice uniquely centered on reshaping the self. But in denaturalizing the unconscious, in liberating these objects from an all-too-constraining psychogenesis, in structuring them "like a language,"[3] it hasn't succeeded in breaking its personological moorings or opening up to the social field, cosmic and semiological flows of all kinds. One no longer submits these productions of desire to the whole battery of junk room complexes, yet one still claims to interpret each connection through the unique logic of the signifier. One has renounced summary interpretations of content ("the umbrella means…") and the stages of development (the famous "returns" to oral, anal stages, etc.). It is no longer a question of the father and the mother. Now one talks about the "name of the father," the phallus, and the great Other of the symbolic castration, yet without getting one step nearer to the *micropolitics of desire* on which is founded, in each particular situation, the social differentiation of the sexes, the alienation of the child. As far as we are concerned, the struggles of desire should not just be circumscribed in the domain of the signifier—even in the case of a "pure" signifying neurosis, like obsessional neurosis. They always overflow into somatic, social, and economic domains, etc. And unless one believes the signifier is found in everything and anything, one may as well admit that the role of the unconscious has been singularly restrained in order to consider it only from the angle of the signifying chains it activates. "The unconscious is structured like a language," Lacan tells us. Certainly. But by whom? By the family, the school, the barracks, the factory, the cinema, and, in special cases, by psychiatry and psychoanalysis. When one has fixed it, succeeded in crushing the polyvocity of its semiotic modes of expression, bound it to a certain type of semiological machine, then yes, it ends up being structured like a language. It remains fairly docile. It starts speaking the language of the dominant system, which is, moreover, not everyday language, but a special, sublimated, psychoanalyzed language. Not only has desire come to accept its alienation within the signifying chains, but it keeps demanding more and more signifier. It no longer wants to have anything to do with the rest of the world and its modes of semiotization. Any troubling problem will find there, if not its solution, at least a comforting suspension in the interplay of the signifier. Under such conditions, what becomes, for example, of the age-old alienation of women by men? For the signifier, as it is conceived by linguists, only neutral and innocent traces such as the opposition of masculine/feminine, and for the psychoanalysts, the mirages that play around the presence/absence of the phallus. In fact, for each type of linguistic performance, for each "degree of grammaticality" of an *énoncé*, there is a corresponding formation of power. The structure of the signifier is never completely reducible to pure mathematical logic; it is always partly bound by diverse, repressive social machines. Only then can a theory of universals, both in linguistics and economics, in anthropology and psychoanalysis, be an obstacle to any real exploration of the unconscious, i.e., *all kinds* of semiotic constellations, connections of flows, power relations and constraints that constitute the arrangements of desire.

Structuralist psychoanalysis doesn't have much more to teach us about the unconscious mechanisms mobilized by film at the level of its *syntagmatic organization* any more than

[3] With his theory of the little object *a*, Lacan came to treat partial objects as logico-mathematic entities ("There is a mathème of psychoanalysis").

orthodox psychoanalysis has at the level of its *semantic contents*. On the contrary, film could perhaps help us to better understand the *pragmatic of unconscious investments* in the social field. In fact, the unconscious does not manifest itself in cinema in the same way it does on the couch: it partially escapes the dictatorship of the signifier, it is not reducible to a fact of language, it no longer respects, as the psychoanalytical transfer continued to do, the classic locator-auditor dichotomy of meaningful communication. A question arises as to whether it is simply bracketed or whether there is any opportunity for reexamining the entirety of relations between discourse and communication. Communication between a discernible locator and auditor is perhaps only a particular case, an extreme case, of the discursive exercise. The effects of desubjectivation and deindividuation produced by the *énoncé* in cinema or in such arrangements as drugs, dreaming, passion, creation, delirium, etc., are perhaps not as exceptional as one would think in relation to the general case that "normal" intersubjective communication and "rational" consciousness of the subject object relationship is supposed to be. It's the idea of a transcendent subject of enunciation that is being questioned here, as well as the opposition between discourse and language (*langue*) or, even more, the dependence of diverse types of semiotic performance in relation to a so-called universal semiological competence. The self-conscious subject should be considered a particular "option," a sort of normal madness. It is illusory to believe there exists only *one* subject—an autonomous subject, centered on one individual. One never has to do with a multiplicity of subjective and semiotic modes of which film, in particular, can show how they are orchestrated, "machinated," and infinitely manipulated. But if it is true that the machinic expansion, the exaltation of the cinematographic unconscious, does not protect it—far from it—from contamination by the significations of power, the fact remains that, with it, things do not happen in the same way as with psychoanalysis or with even better-policed artistic techniques. And this all depends on the fact that it manifests itself through semiotic arrangements irreducible to a syntagmatic concatenation that would discipline it mechanically, structure it according to a rigorously formalized pattern of expression and content. Its montage of asignifying semiotic chains of intensities, movements, and multiplicities fundamentally tends to free it from the signifying grid that intervenes only at a second stage, through the filmic syntagmatic that fixes genres, crystallizes characters and behavioral stereotypes homogeneous to the dominant semantic field.[4]

This "excess" of the matters of expression over the content certainly limits a possible comparison between cinema and psychoanalysis with respect to repressing the unconscious. Both fundamentally lead to the same politics, but the stakes and the means they resort to are quite different. The psychoanalyst's clientele acquiesces to the whole enterprise of semiotic reduction, while cinema must permanently stay attuned to the social imaginary's mutations just to "stay in the race." It also has to mobilize a real industry, a multiplicity of institutions and powers capable of getting the better of the unconscious proliferation it threatens to unleash. Spoken language itself does not function in film the same way it does in psychoanalysis; it isn't the law, it constitutes but one way among others, a single instrument at the core of a complex semiotic orchestration. The semiotic components of film glide by each other without ever fixing or stabilizing themselves in a deep syntax of latent contents or in the

[4] One should take up again the analysis of Bettini and Cosseni, who distinguished the notion of iconicity from that of analogism: the filmic syntagmatic, in some way, "analogizes" the icons which are transported by the unconscious. See "La sémiologie des moyens de communications audio-visuals," *Cinema*. Paris: Klincksieck (1973).

transformational system that ends up with, on the face of it, the manifest content. Relational, emotive, sexual significations—I would prefer to say intensities—are constantly transported there by heterogeneous "traits of the matter of expression" (to borrow a formula that Christian Metz himself borrowed from Hjelmslev). The codes intertwine without one ever succeeding in dominating the others; one passes, in a continual back and forth, from perceptive codes to denotative, musical, connotative, rhetorical, technological, economic, sociological codes, etc....

Commercial cinema is nothing else but a simple, inexpensive drug. Its unconscious action is profound. More perhaps than that of psychoanalysis. First of all at the level of the session. Cinematographic performance affects subjectivity. It affects the personological individuation of enunciation and develops a very particular mode of conscience. Without the support of the other's existence, subjectivation tends to become hallucinatory; it no longer concentrates on *one* subject, but explodes on a multiplicity of poles even when it fixes itself on one character. Strictly speaking, it doesn't even concern a subject of enunciation in the usual sense—what is emitted by these poles is not simply a discourse, but intensities of all kinds, constellations of features of faciality, crystallizations of affects... It reaches the point where one no longer knows who is speaking or who is who.

The roles are much better defined in psychoanalysis, and the subjective transitivity much better controlled. In fact, one doesn't stop using the *discourse of the analyst*: one says what one thinks someone would like to hear, one alienates oneself by wanting to be worthy of the listener. In cinema, one no longer speaks; *it* speaks in one's place: the cinematographic industry uses the kind of speech it imagines one wants to hear.[5]

A machine treats you like a machine, and the essential thing is not what it says, but the sort of vertigo of abolition that the fact of being "machinized" provides for you. With people dissolving and things passing unwitnessed, one abandons oneself to a guilt-free world. While on the couch one pays to have a witness (preferably someone distinguished, someone of clearly higher standing than oneself) invest and control your most intimate thoughts and sentiments, at the movies one pays to be invaded by subjective arrangements with blurry contours in order to give in to adventures that, in principle, have no lasting effects. "In principle," because the modelization resulting from this cheap sort of vertigo is not without tell-tale traces: the unconscious finds itself populated by cowboys and Indians, cops and robbers, Belmondos and Monroes... It's like tobacco or cocaine; one cannot trace its effects (even if that were possible) unless one is already completely hooked.

But wasn't the psychoanalytical cure instituted precisely to avoid such promiscuity? Wasn't the function of interpretation and transfer to saturate and select the good and the bad in the unconscious? Isn't it the point that the patient be guided, helped by a safety net? Certainly. But in reality this net is more alienating than any other system of subjectivity-control. Upon leaving the movie house, one has to wake up and quietly put on one's own film reel (the entire social reality is devoted to it), while the psychoanalytic session, becoming interminable, overflows into the rest of life. Going to the movies, as one says, is an entertainment, while the analytical cure—and it is true even for neurotics—tends to be a sort of social promotion: it is accompanied by the sentiment that in the end one will be a specialist of the unconscious—a specialist, moreover, as bothersome for the whole entourage as any other specialists whatsoever, beginning with those of film.

[5] The psychoanalyst is somewhat in the position of the spectator at the cinema: he assists in the unfolding of a montage that one fabricates especially for him.

Alienation by psychoanalysis depends on the fact that the particular mode of subjectivation that it produces is organized around a subject-for-an-other, a personological subject, overadapted, overindebted to the signifying practices of the system. The cinematographic projection, for its part, deterritorializes the perceptual and deictic coordinates.[6] The semiotic taste buds of the unconscious haven't been titillated before the film, as a manufactured work, starts conditioning them to the semiologic paste of the system. The unconscious, as soon as it is exposed, becomes like an occupied territory. Cinema, in the end, has taken the place of ancient liturgies. Its function is to renovate, adapt, and assimilate the ancient gods of bourgeois familialism. The religion it serves borrows the language of "normal" communication that one finds in the family, at school, or at work. Even when it seems to give the "normal" character, a man, woman, or child a chance to speak, it is always, in reality, a reconstitution, a puppet, a zombie-model, an "invader" who is ready to be grafted onto the unconscious in order to dominate it. One doesn't go to the cinema with one's ego, one's childhood memories, the way one goes to a psychoanalyst. One accepts in advance that it robs us of our identity, our past and our future. Its derisive miracle is to turn us, for a few moments, into orphans: single, amnesiac, unconscious, and eternal. When, upon leaving, we take up our "daily" reflexes again, when we find the faces of our loved ones closed in on themselves again, we may be tempted to prolong the impression produced by the film, if it has touched us. It is even possible for a film to upset our whole existence. In truth, a film that could shake itself free of its function of adaptational drugging could have unimaginable liberating effects, effects on an entirely different scale from those produced by books or literary trends. This is due to the fact that cinema intervenes directly in our relations with the external world. And even if this exterior is contaminated by dominant representations, a minimal aperture could result from this intervention. Psychoanalysis suffocates us—with considerably luxury, it is true—it shuts off our relation to the external world in what is most singular, unpredictable, by projecting the cinema of interiority onto it. Whatever its stereotypes, its conformisms, cinema is overflowing with the richness of its expressive means. In this regard, everyone knows how the work of film is prolonged, sometimes directly, in that of the dream (I have shown that this interaction was all the stronger the weaker the film seemed to be).

Commercial cinema is undeniably familialist, Oedipian, and reactionary. But it is not intrinsically so, the way psychoanalysis is. It is so "on top of everything else." Its "mission" is not to adapt people to outdated and archaic elitist Freudian models, but to those implied by mass production. Even, it should be stressed, when they reconstitute archetypes of the traditional family. While its "analytic" means are richer, more dangerous, because more fascinating than those of psychoanalysis, they are, in fact, more precarious and more full of promise. And if one can imagine another film praxis being constituted in the future, a cinema of combat attacking dominant values in the present state of things, one can hardly see how a revolutionary psychoanalysis could possibly emerge.

---

[6] With television, the effect of deterritorialization seems attenuated, but perhaps it is still more underhanded: one bathes in a minimum of light, the machine is before you, like an amicable interlocutor, it's a family affair; in the Pullman car, one visits the abyssal profundities of the unconscious, then one switches to advertising and the news. The aggression is, in fact, even more violent than anywhere else; one bends unconsciously to the sociopolitical coordinates, to a type of moralization without which capitalist industrialized societies probably could not function.

In fact, the psychoanalytic unconscious (or the literary unconscious, since they derive one from the other) is always a secondhand unconscious. The discourse of analysis is shaped by analytical myths: individual myths themselves have to adapt to the framework of these reference-myths. Cinematic myths do not have at their disposal such a metamythic system, and the gamut of semiological means they do mobilize directly connects with the spectator's processes of semiotization. In a word, the language of cinema and audio-visual media is alive, while that of psychoanalysis has, for a long time now, spoken a dead language. One can expect the best or the worst from cinema. From psychoanalysis, nothing but a soothing yet hopeless purring. In the worst commercial circumstances, good films can still be produced, films that modify the arrangements of desire, that "change life," while, for quite some time now, there have been no worthwhile psychoanalytic sessions, discoveries, books.

CHAPTER 25
JULIA KRISTEVA

Julia Kristeva (b. 1941) is a Bulgarian-French philosopher and psychoanalyst. She is a Professor Emeritus at Paris Diderot University. Kristeva is widely regarded as among the most important psychoanalytic and feminist thinkers working in the late twentieth and early twenty-first centuries, and her work has had an immeasurable influence on both of those fields, as well as in Continental thought in general. The selection included here, "Fantasy and Cinema," is a chapter from her book, Intimate Revolt: The Powers and Limits of Psychoanalysis, *which was published originally in French (*La révolte intime: Pouvoirs et limites de la psychanalyse, tome 2*) by Fayard in 1997.*

In Intimate Revolt, *Kristeva is working with Lacanian categories and concepts to come to her own terms with the role of psychoanalysis in identity and culture. In this portion of the book, she is especially concerned with Lacan's notion of the imaginary (as opposed to the symbolic or the real), and she opens the chapter, "Fantasy and Cinema," with a consideration of the imaginary. She makes a fundamental connection, when she notes that the imaginary appears when introduced through fantasy—or through cinema. Fantasy is more than mere imagination; etymologically, Kristeva points out that the term has its origins in the ancient Greek words for light, and can come to mean representing oneself (bringing something about oneself into the light, for example). For Freud, she notes, fantasy is the intimate creation of representations—and it takes one of four different forms: diurnal fantasies are just daydreams, wherein we recount our desire to ourselves; subliminal fantasies are unconscious daydreams, and thus are less reflective of our conscious minds; unconscious fantasies, which are the origin of dreams, can lead to repression of desire followed by symptoms; and primal fantasies, technically a subtype of unconscious fantasies, but in any case fantasies about our origins which appear to recur from generation to generation and from person to person. A fantasy poses a particular reality that is distinct from perceptual reality—an illusion that is nevertheless the reality of an individual's desire—what we might call "psychical reality."*

Art is the favored place for formulating fantasies, Kristeva says, but not for realizing them. And a "society of the spectacle" (à la Guy Debord) such as our own, in which there seem to be images everywhere, is perhaps counterintuitively unfavorable to fantasies. Inundated with images which resonate with our fantasies, she argues, we remain unliberated: The stereotypes available in artistic and cultural products prevent us from creating our own imagery, and, thus, induce us to lose touch with our fantasies themselves. The loss of fantasy, however, threatens another loss, of inner depth itself. Although cinema, by way of the cinematic image, is the primary place where the contemporary imaginary appears, it remains the case that cinema also has the potential to destroy fantasy through the preponderance and stereotypicality of its images.

Kristeva introduces the idea of the specular at this point, following from Lacan's "mirror stage" (as discussed by Félix Guattari in its relation to film), the process of self-creation that depends upon the objectification of the self as a self in the perception of a unified being in reflection. The specular is, for Kristeva, the terminus of aggressions and anxieties, a place where aggressions and anxieties can be reforged into something more coherent with the rest of the self. And in presenting oneself to oneself in reflection (as if in a mirror), the specular is also a seducer. It transforms the drive into desire, Kristeva writes, and aggression into seduction. As the specular requires (self-)confrontation and reflection, it is the earliest point in the psyche at which we can find one identity speaking to another, and this basic interrelatedness is something we see regularly depicted in cinema, primarily by way of the depiction of sexual difference. Central to Kristeva's notion of the specular (as to Lacan's notion of the mirror) is that we do not see ourselves reflected back to us; we see a unified body which we interpret as reflective of ourselves.

Fantasy plays an enormous role here. Thus, Kristeva articulates the idea of the fascinating specular, a particular version of the specular which is (playing on the Disney imagery) both charming and maleficent at the same time. The fascinating specular is the intersection between the sight of a real object and fantasy, the seeing fantasy overlaid upon a visible object. This differs radically from what Kristeva calls the thought specular, which calls fantasy out for its illusory nature, leaving something else in its place. She cites the films of Jean-Luc Godard as examples of the thought specular, films which are not made up of images that convey information, but instead make the thought of the filmmaker evident through the sequencing and editing of the images in the film. Otherwise flat images are transformed into symptoms of a specific filmmaking subjectivity by way of the expression of desire. Some filmmakers are better at this than others, of course, but for Kristeva, among the very best are Sergei Eisenstein and Alfred Hitchcock.

There is, finally, also an ethical aspect to the relationship of fantasy to cinema, for Kristeva. One of the primary functions of the cinematic image, she notes, is to capture fear and appease it, restoring the fear (and the fearful individual) to the symbolic order. This cathartic function finds a psychic strategy for dealing with evil. And this association between evil and the image is not new; Kristeva compares the cinematic image to Augustine's notion of evil, as simultaneously articulating the imaginary and being appeased by it. In contrast to Augustine, Kristeva cites Debord as inscribing evil into the phenomenon of the cinematic spectacle as its natural conclusion: Evil is the end result of spectacle for Debord. The question for cinema, then, becomes: in depicting evil by way of the cinematic image, does cinema normalize it? The question almost has Arendtian roots. Is evil made more banal by a cinema in which horror, terror, fear, and so on are of the essence? Is there a cinematic means of addressing evil that is neither repression nor catharsis, both of which reinforce the dominant world order? Kristeva confesses that she does not know, but that she finds some hope in what she calls the "antifilm," a film which rather than seducing us tries to keep us at a distance. The antifilm presents evil, like other films, but in so doing the antifilm inspires neither deep thought nor horror nor complicity: the antifilm genuinely presents evil, and nevertheless makes us laugh at it. The best—and only—example Kristeva gives of this possibility is Charlie Chaplin's The Great Dictator, *and it is a fine example of a cinematic presentation of evil that maintains a distance between the film and the filmgoer such that, nevertheless recognizing the presence of genuine moral evil, can laugh at it—and, thus, refuse to normalize it. It is this Chaplinian possibility of the antifilm which is, for Kristeva, the best hope for cinema—and fantasy—in the future.*

Filmography

- ***Nosferatu, eine Symphonie des Grauens*** [*Nosferatu: A Symphony of Horrors*] (Germany, 1922). *Directed by* F. W. Murnau. *Produced by* Enrico Dieckmann *and* Albin Grau. *Written by* Henrik Galeen. *Starring* Max Schreck.

- ***The Great Dictator*** (USA, 1940). *Directed, Produced, and Written by* Charlie Chaplin. *Starring* Charlie Chaplin, Paulette Goddard, *and* Jack Oakie.
- ***Arsenic and Old Lace*** (USA, 1944). *Directed by* Frank Capra. *Produced by* Frank Capra *and* Jack L. Warner. *Written by* Julius J. *and* Philip G. Epstein. *Starring* Cary Grant.
- ***Psycho*** (USA, 1960). *Directed and Produced by* Alfred Hitchcock. *Written by* Joseph Stefano. *Starring* Anthony Perkins, Vera Miles, John Gavin, Martin Balsam, John McIntire, *and* Janet Leigh.
- ***Dr. No*** (UK, 1962). *Directed by* Terence Young. *Produced by* Harry Saltzman *and* Albert R. Broccoli. *Written by* Richard Maibaum, Johanna Harwood, *and* Berkely Mather. *Starring* Sean Connery, Ursula Andress, Joseph Wiseman, *and* Jack Lord.
- ***The Birds*** (USA, 1963). *Directed and Produced by* Alfred Hitchcock. *Written by* Evan Hunter. *Starring* Tippi Hedren, Rod Taylor, Jessica Tandy, Suzanne Pleshette, *and* Veronica Cartwright.
- ***Un homme et une femme*** [*A Man and a Woman*] (France, 1966). *Directed and Produced by* Claude Lelouch. *Written by* Pierre Uytterhoeven. *Starring* Anouk Aimée *and* Jean-Louis Trintignant.

FANTASY AND CINEMA

Translated by Jeanine Herman

At this point in my inquiry—the intimate as representation of the subject on the way to constitution and revolt—I am confronted with the imaginary. Consider this for a moment: suppose the imaginary offered the most immediate, most subtle, but also most dangerous access to the intimate. We cannot avoid the sense Lacan gives it: "That the imaginary is supported by the reflection of the same to the same is certain.... We have always imagined that being should contain a sort of plenitude of its own. Being is a body."[1]

But let me be clear. The imaginary, neither real nor symbolic, appears in all its logic—and risk—when introduced through fantasy (we all have fantasies, whether seductive or terrifying; this is inevitable). It also appears through cinema: we are a society of the image, it has been said often enough.

Organisms of Mixed Race (Didier, the Collage Man)

What is fantasy? The Greek root—*fae, faos, fos*—expresses the notion of light and thus the fact of coming to light, shining, appearing, presenting, presenting oneself, representing oneself.

When he uses the word *Phantasie*, Freud understands it as the intimate creation of representations, not the faculty of imagining in the philosophical sense of the word. German has another term for this: *Einbildungskraft*. Since then, the word "fantasy" has designated an imaginary scenario in which the subject depicts in a more or less distorted way the fulfillment of a desire, ultimately sexual. So at the outset the term in French does not at all indicate the field of the imagination but that of particular imaginary formations. Which ones? On this point, you would do well to consult *The Language of Psycho-Analysis* by Laplanche and Pontalis, which sums things up better than I can do here.[2]

But since I will guide you through this reading, I will remind you briefly of the distinction between diurnal fantasies, subliminal fantasies, unconscious fantasies, and, among the latter, primal fantasies. Diurnal fantasies are daydreams, those novels without an audience in which, in a more or less paradisiacal or infernal way, we recount our desire, in a counterpoint to our real destinies: our fairytales or nightmares.[3] There are unconscious daydreams with strong

---

[1] Jacques Lacan, *Le séminaire*, livre XX, "Encore" (1972–1973) (Paris: Seuil, 1975), pp. 77, 127.

[2] See Jean Laplanche and J.-B. Pontalis, *The Language of Psycho-Analysis*, trans. Donald Nicholson-Smith (London: Norton, 1973) . [Laplanche and Pontalis's definition of Phantasy: "Imaginary scene in which the subject is a protagonist, representing the fulfillment of a wish (in the last analysis, an unconscious wish) in a manner that is distorted to a greater or lesser extent by defensive processes. "Phantasy has a number of different modes: conscious phantasies or daydreams, unconscious phantasies like those uncovered by analysis as the structures underlying a manifest content, and primal phantasies."—*Trans.*]

[3] See Joseph Breuer and Sigmund Freud, *Studies on Hysteria*, in *SE*, vol. 2. [*SE* = *The Standard Edition of the Complete Psychological Works of Sigmund Freud*, trans. and ed. James Strachey (London: Hogarth, 1953–1974). —*JW*]

sexual connotations, reflexively conscious or not, which are the precursors of hysterical symptoms: these are unconscious subliminal fantasies.[4] Finally, unconscious fantasies in the strict sense—those linked to unconscious desires—are situated at the foundation of the progredient trajectory that ends in dream.[5] The impossibility of gaining access to this unconscious fantasy and the repression of the fantasy are the source of symptoms. Analytical work consists of making the fantasy conscious—formulating the phantasmatic narrative and interpreting it—in order to dissolve the symptom.

Freud's analysis of Dora's cough provides us with a classic example of unconscious fantasy linked to sexual desire. As you may recall, this young Viennese girl suffered from a cough that no traditional medical means could soothe. Freud revealed that at the origin of this symptom several sexual fantasies were hidden, notably this: as a child, Dora imagined her father's mistress performing fellatio on him, whom she thought to be impotent. This scenario, unacceptable to the subject herself, remained unconscious. What followed was the eroticization of the throat, tongue, and mouth, which was just as inadmissible for the subject and was transformed into neurotic spasms manifested by uncontrollable coughing. Note the way in which Freud manages to detect the fantasy. Naturally, like Lacan, he starts with language: Dora happily repeats that her father is "unfortunate" (*unvermöglich*). In German the word refers both to someone without money and someone without physical strength, which Freud deciphers as a man lacking sexual power. As you can see, the signifier for Freud is embodied immediately. Like Proust, Freud is a specialist in transubstantiation, but he hears flesh in the patient's associative speech, while Proust writes flesh in his metaphors and hyperbolic sentences. The difference is notable, but the intention is analogous: touching on the vibrations of desire with the word. The fantasy is precisely what emerges at the crossroads. In the same way, in another patient's hysterical fits, Freud discovers that her spasmodic movements mimic the gesture of both tearing off her clothes and putting them back on: active and passive, man and woman, replaying an unacceptable, repressed erotic scene.

Two details emerge when we try to enter the singular world of fantasy.

The first is this: although these scenes find their point of departure in childhood memories, they present us with a particular reality that is distinct from perceptual reality. The subject imagines something; he is having an illusion. But this illusion is nevertheless strong, steady, persistent, and subject to its own rigorous logic: it is the reality of his desire. The universe of fantasy prompts us to take seriously this other reality—psychical reality—which in a factual, efficient, pragmatic world we have a tendency to underestimate and diminish: "*Psychical* reality is a particular form of existence not to be confused with *material* reality."[6]

The second specificity is even more interesting: these illusory formations, these scenarios, the offshoots of our desires, are complex formations. They are transitional organisms, hybrid constructions between two psychical structures—between the conscious and the unconscious—that play with both repression and the return of the repressed. The pressure of sexual drives assures them a prepsychical, biological base, but they manifest themselves as narration, with syntax, grammar, logical construction, and a whole narrative setup. Thus in fantasy the mind's armature is in no way deficient but distortedly admits the subject's desire:

---

[4] See Sigmund Freud, "Hysterical Phantasies and Their Relation to Bisexuality" (1908), in *SE*, vol. 9.

[5] Sigmund Freud, *The Interpretation of Dreams*, in *SE*, vols. 4 and 5.

[6] Ibid., 5:620.

Dora loves her father; she also loves the woman who is his mistress, but she cannot admit this thought in her mind; she admits it only in the form of a painful symptom (inversion of the desired pleasure into pain) and on the level of an organ (the throat, coughing) rather than in its psychical representation. In other words, unconscious fantasy prompts us to think of psychical life as a life of multiple and heterogeneous strata, as a polyvalent, layered psychical apparatus: drive/preverbal representation/organic reaction/verbal representation/and so on. Freud never attributed fantasies solely to instinctual impulse (biology), or solely to symbolic formation (parental restrictions, religious and moral ideology, etc.), but always suggested an interdependence and translatability among all levels of psychical life. The fantasy as construction/crossroads is one of the favored examples of this work of translation: "We may compare them with individuals of mixed race who, taken all round, resemble white men, but who betray their coloured descent by some striking feature or other, and on that account are excluded from society and enjoy none of the privileges of white people."[7]

Then, while making distinctions among these various regimes of fantasy, Freud points out the close relationships between them. Whether they are conscious or unconscious, conscious fantasies in the pervert who can enact them, or delirious fears in the paranoiac who projects them onto others with a hostile meaning, or even erotic desires the psychoanalyst discovers behind the symptoms in the hysteric, the speaking, sexual subject is a subject of fantasies and subject to fantasies.[8]

Finally, Freud supposes the existence of far more archaic and profound fantasies, which he calls primal fantasies: these are scenarios concerning our origins, which he supposes go back through generations phylogenetically. A presubjective structure, the primal fantasy, like the fantasy of the primal scene, the fantasy of castration, and the fantasy of seduction, does not necessarily constitute a sedimentation of individual experiences but hereditary schemas. The child invents these scenarios, which he represses, but the invention is only an eternal return of hereditary schemas that have actually taken place in preceding generations and are mysteriously encrypted in the psyche: "Children in their phantasies are simply filling in the gaps in individual truth with prehistoric truth."[9]

If it is true that all fantasies have analogous structures and reflect unconscious fantasy, the subject's entire life would appear to be shaped by the phantasmatic. Literature and art are the favored places for the formulation of fantasies, not their realization. Thus the paroxysmal phantasmatic of Sade presents a hypertrophy of jouissance, particularly that provoked by violence and pain. In a more discreet way, the diaphanous and refined sensibility of Proust's *Remembrance of Things Past* is subtended by a phantasmatic of profanation (Mlle Vinteuil spitting on her father's portrait) and flagellation (Baron de Charlus in the brothel scene).[10] In another register, psychical uncertainty—am I a man or woman? and, more profoundly, am I human or inhuman?—is displayed in fantasies of metamorphosis or anamorphosis: thus Goya and his Caprices, inspired by the violence that Spain underwent during the postrevolutionary wars but also by the painter's depression and his loss of identity in the clutches of death.

---

[7] Sigmund Freud, "The Unconscious" (1915), in *SE* 14:191.
[8] On these questions, see Sigmund Freud, *Three Essays on the Theory of Sexuality* (1905).
[9] Sigmund Freud, *Introductory Lectures on Psycho-Analysis* (1915–1917) (New York: Norton, 1966), p. 461.
[10] On the development of this second scene, see chap. 4.

At times, social commentary makes almost no distinction between fantasy and reality. Thus a writer may find himself incriminated by horrors actually committed by executioners (e.g., Sade compared to a Nazi). We might think, on the contrary, that putting fantasies into (verbal or pictorial) form is our most subtle defense against acting out: to communicate one's fantasies by formulating them and commenting on them provides a jouissance that avoids the horror of translating them into action.

I can hear you asking: don't we inhabit a veritable paradise of fantasy today thanks to images in the media? Aren't we saturated with fantasies, stimulated to produce them and to become imaginary creators in turn?

Nothing is less certain.

The so-called society of the spectacle, paradoxically, is hardly favorable to the analysis of fantasies or even to their formation. The "new maladies of the soul" are characterized by a reining in, if not a destruction of, the phantasmatic faculty.[11] We are inundated with images, some of which resonate with our fantasies and appease us but which, for lack of interpretative words, do not liberate us. Moreover, the stereotype of these images deprives us of the possibility of creating our own imagery, our own imaginary scenarios.

Didier, a patient I have discussed at length elsewhere, was complaining of relationship problems and skin symptoms.[12] Over the years he had developed a technical discourse without managing to talk to me about his conflicts and desires: no dreams, no fantasies, or, if so, they were quickly dismissed. Learning that he was a painter in his spare time, I expressed interest, and soon enough he brought me reproductions of his works: collages of body parts and faces of stars set with paint and variously arranged. The patient's commentary was always very technical in nature: Rauschenberg, Jasper Johns, Andy Warhol, and so forth. I was the one to graft fantasy onto this: carnage, violence, murder on a background of the guilt he felt for provoking his mother's death by living as a bachelor, by not having a wife and children. A rejection followed, indicating Didier's initial aggression toward me. In the wake of this transference-countertransference, he would feel more free to talk.

By making his pictures, Didier set up operative fantasies that "operated." By that I mean, Didier managed to have a life that was satisfactory in appearance but stereotypical, as if operated by his operative fantasies: he had no interiority, he neither loved nor was loved, he had no contact with either himself or others and remained walled up in solitude and masturbation. On the other hand, the phantasmatic novels that followed the exhibition of the pictures opened up the true universe of his fantasies—aggressive and erotic—and allowed him to have a freer psychical life, a more complex sexual life, and more complex relationships. As long as he was in the picture, the unconscious fantasy was not solely or simply repressed; more gravely, it was not formed as a fantasy, the sexual drive flowing into a gesture without psychical representation. The role of language is essential for the formation of fantasies: without the possibility of telling them to someone (even if "I" do not use this possibility), "my" desires do not become fantasies but remain encysted at a prepsychical level and risk spilling over into somaticization and acting-out (from crime to drug addiction). With Didier, it was not only necessary to bring the repressed to consciousness; it was necessary

[11] See Julia Kristeva, *New Maladies of the Soul*, trans. Ross Guberman (New York: Columbia University Press, 1995).
[12] See the analysis of "the collage man," in ibid., pp. 22–26. See also chap. 9 of this book.

to create phantasmatic representation, to construct these psychical representations before analyzing them.

It has often been said how the society of the spectacle and certain aspects of the contemporary family (the lack of relationships, lack of authority, and so on) lead to phantasmatic poverty if not vacuity.[13] As a result, primal drives and fantasies, because they do not find psychical representation, seek the path to action or somaticization. Hence the banality of evil, the result of the inability to judge, certainly. But, even more, the impoverishment of fantasies, their reduction, their abolition threaten to abolish inner depth itself, this camera obscura that has constituted the psychical life of the speaking being for millennia. In this regard, art and literature are the allies of psychoanalysis; they open the verbal path to the construction of fantasies and prepare the terrain for psychoanalytical interpretation.

Fear and Specular Seduction

Now we come to the universe of the image that invades us through film and television: the cinematic image, the central place of the contemporary imaginary. A distinction should be made regarding the news or documentary images that fascinate us. Although not equivalent to our fantasies, these images do in fact resonate with them.

The cinema has assumed the universe of fantasy as a right: we may posit this to start, even if later we find that things are not so simple. For the cinema may also destroy fantasy: for example, when stereotypical, soap opera images reduce the viewer to a passive consumer, or, on the contrary, when so-called auteur cinema pulverizes fantasy and invents a veritable cinematic *écriture* with ambitions of conceptualizing the specular. But we can start by positing that a certain kind of cinema known as realist projects fantasies. Since the visible is the port of registry of drives, their synthesis beneath language, cinema as an apotheosis of the visible offers itself to the plethoric deployment of fantasies.

"Man walks in the image," St. Augustine said. But the cinematic image takes us (men, and women too, needless to say) for a ride. Movies that seduce or scare us, from *Arsenic and Old Lace* (Frank Capra, 1944) to *A Man and a Woman* (Claude Lelouch, 1966), from *Nosferatu* (Murnau, 1922) to *Doctor No* (Terence Young, 1962), have tapped into the fantasies of an era that is now that of cinema. So much so that the other arts, such as literature and painting, when they wish to preserve their specificity, take refuge in a maximal condensation—poetry, meditation, distortion, abstraction—in order to explore other regions of the imaginary, to keep us connected with these other regions.

Cinema—a certain cinema, an other cinema—shows this condensed and meditative mode of writing in the face of and as a stand-in for fantasies. We might call this second type of image the thought specular. Cinema—when it is great art, from Eisenstein to Godard and not a universal journalistic style or more or less dramatized stereotypes—seizes us precisely in this place.

Why does the visible lend itself to a primary and fragile synthesis of drives, to a more supple, less controlled, riskier representability of instinctual dramas, the games of Eros and Thanatos? Take "game" as a playful, regulated exchange (checkers, for example) but also as

[13] See Guy Debord, *The Society of the Spectacle* (1967), trans. Donald Nicholson-Smith (New York: Zone, 1994).

a space of adjustment, the free movement between two elements (the play of a window, for example). The voyeur makes a symptom of this first articulation of drives: he takes pleasure in the sadomasochism of an autoerotic, incestuous osmosis with an object from which he is not really detached. But we also know of other more standard, more indispensable, and in this sense more noble variants. Thus when a patient who is complaining of various forms of psychic and somatic ill-being does not manage either to grasp them or to communicate them through words, we suggest, instead of analysis or before analysis, a psychodrama. That is, we invite him to put his drives into play, to show them to us: gesture and image. The act of psychodrama is in large part a specular act: "one" shows oneself, "one" relies on the analyst's speaking action, before eventually becoming an "I" capable of deferring this action and this demonstration and acceding to the statement of a subject.[14]

To allow you to appreciate the role of the gaze in bringing about this initial specular synthesis at the borders of the sadomasochistic drive, I will give you two examples.

François was not yet a year old, and he spoke through echolalia: rhythms, intonations, variable intensities. He saw objects as so many embarrassing and accidental extensions of his body, which he still experienced as scattered. He allowed his voice to be recorded without protest: these were the recordings of the drama between expressions of sound and his breathing, choking, difficult adjustments between intensities and frequencies that were nevertheless already in the process of being organized by the first organizer that is rhythm. A few months later, objects began to exist for François; he saw them, hid them, lost them. He also saw the large tape recorder, and despite our attempt to keep the machine from impeding his movements, the simple fact of seeing it provoked his tears. It was as if the earlier vocalic dramas had been projected onto the visible object. The unbearable aspect of the vocalic apprenticeship requested by the adult, thus the rejection of the adult, tainted a visible object (the tape recorder) charged with representing the drive subjacent to the verbal function. The simplest echolalia took on a symbolic function, for it began to designate objects that were separate and that François henceforth saw as such. At that very moment, the drive, which previously was consumed in echolalia alone, was now represented by an object that had a metonymic relationship with the latter and became the "bad object." Even before the "mirror stage" that consolidates this dissociation, an object appears to the gaze as designatable, namable. The apprenticeship of language as a system of signs with a communicative function is precisely assured because this seen object has become possible, because the image is there from now on, the medium and tapping of aggression and anxiety.

In the current of friendship and love, dreams do not wait for the analyst's couch: they circulate like gifts. Antoine tells me that he often has the same nightmare: he is four years old, he is in the bathroom on his little potty. The excrement overflows and turns into a "big animal," something between a frog and a crocodile but with transparent skin, as if the membrane of an eye. Suddenly Antoine's father enters, sees the beast, and threatens to punish the son. We are faced with a terrifying montage of the anal drive, the autoerotic pleasure linked to maternal care of the sphincter, the incestuous desire for this invisible mother, and the subordination to the father for anal coitus. A montage also occurs between a phantasm of an anal penis and cloacal birth. Antoine gives birth to an object as if he were a woman, while at the same time

---

[14] See Paul-Claude Racamier, "En psychanalyse et sans séance," *Revue française de psychanalyse* 54 (1990): 1177, and idem, "Autour de l'inceste," *Gruppo* 7 (1991); see also his *Cortège conceptuel* (Paris: Apsygée, 1993), p. 21.

being this fecal object to which his mother gave birth. Onto this instinctual and desiring, ambiguous and reversible vector, the gaze of the father is grafted: the eye of the other, the eye of the third, the menacing and seductive paternal eye. You will note that in his dream there is a separation between the object, on the one hand—Antoine/waste/the expelling maternal body/Antoine's body caught in its autoerotic jouissance—and the paternal eye, on the other, which depicts the first instance of the separation with autoeroticism and the mother-child dyad. This separation, not yet made in the dream and no doubt in Antoine's unconscious, is carried out in and through visual representation, as well as in and through the symbolic prohibition that the father establishes. Antoine's dream presents us with a phantasmatic and oneiric conglomerate that has not yet constituted a subject detached from the other two instances of the familial triangle (father, mother). Why? Because it maintains, for the sake of a sadomasochistic and autoerotic pleasure, a lack of distinction between the paternal eye—the symbolic authority—and the ego-body-object. You will note that this lack of distinction is inevitably accompanied by another: a hesitation that Antoine manifests in his daily life over sexual difference and about which he complains to his close friends. Active or passive, seeing or seen, my eye and his eye, to be a man or to let himself be taken as an erotic object by the father (or by a given hierarchical superior but also, often, by the "superwomen" Antoine chooses as partners). The separation between these two registers (acted drive/representation; sadomasochistic body/paternal eye prefiguring the symbolic) initiates at once the autonomy of the subject and access to thought and language. But nothing guarantees that this separation will ever be clear and definitive in any of us. The dream, this cinema deprived of an audience, is there to remind us how dramatic and ever incomplete this apprenticeship of symbolism is in the precincts of the visible and the instinctual; how language is striated by the image itself and suspended at instinctual pleasure; and how these ambiguities command sexual indifferentiation, our endogenous psychical bisexualities, our polymorphisms. Whether nightmarish or delightful, the dream is always seductive: the specular is the primacy of pleasure that Antoine refuses himself in daily life, the mark of a jouissance that has not taken place, that will never take place enough in the waking order.

We are now in a position to define the specular as the final and very efficient depository of aggressions and anxieties and as brilliant purveyor-seducer. We can also define, with François and Antoine, specular seduction as a diversion of facilitation (rhythms, somatic waves, waves of color, erogenous excitations) toward this possible point of convergence where series of always incomplete images converge, in which "I" is finally constituted as identical to oneself.

The ultimate seduction, if it existed, would be the ideal mother, the one who holds up the ideal mirror in which "I" see myself, sure and autonomous, finally rid of the narcissistic throes of the "mirror stage" and the paradises, both perfumed and abject, where "I" depended on the mother, more or less indistinct from her. Yet it is the paternal eye—the eye of the Law—that takes over for this ideal mother and replaces her destabilizing seduction by a call to order. François and Antoine are the incestuous sons who need a strong paternal intrusion in order to detach themselves from the osmosis with their mothers. This terrifying father, who is nevertheless a seductive father, refers the very young narcissistic identity to its passive position of being a seduced, feminine, uncertain subject. In effect, Antoine had a hard time contenting himself with a single identity (with a single sexual identity, to start with), as the eye of paternal law demanded of him: he returned to his potty, in narcissistic instability, by offering himself as passive object to the father's gaze, as if he were the father's wife—another way of fusing with his mother. The seductive and terrifying specular endlessly celebrates our identity uncertainties. Keep this in mind: we find these archaic regions once again, surprisingly enough, in Sartre, who did not avoid associating the fate of thought and that of anality.[15]

Once installed in the specular, seduced by the image that the father holds out, seduced consequently by "my" image, "I" seduce others: "I" can entice others by addressing the aggressive drive as a desiring appeal to them. The specular transforms the drive into desire, aggression into seduction. It is at the specular that the diversion of the drive ends up, and it is from the specular that identificatory allure emanates, with its narcissistic mirage and its appeal to others. Chronologically, in the development of the child and, logically, in the functioning of the adult, the specular remains the most advanced medium for the inscription of the drive (in relation to sound or tactile material, for example). The specular is therefore also the earliest point of departure of the signs, narcissistic identifications, and phantasmatic trances of one identity speaking to another. Moreover, men and women find themselves in this knot of fear and seduction that the specular proposes in different ways. Cinema constantly offers a vision of this trial of sexual difference, as well as that of homosexuality, this collision with our impossible identities to the point of psychosis. I am thinking of the cinema that explores the specular, that reproduces it most closely to its untenable logic, or that preserves only its strident, discordant, ironic logic: Eisenstein, Hitchcock, Pasolini…

Fantasy and the Imaginary: the Specular

As we have just seen, fantasy in its visibility invents an instinctual montage and a drift toward meaning, language, thought. The most direct cinema, which projects more or less modified fantasies, seizes us in this place in our psychical lives where the imagination lets itself be controlled by fantasy, which I call the specular.

This point should be emphasized: what I see has nothing to do with the specular that fascinates me.

On the one hand, there is the gaze by which I identify an object, a face: mine, that of another. It offers me an identity that reassures me, for it delivers me from facilitations (*frayages*), unnamable fears (*frayeurs*), sounds prior to the name, to the image: pulsations, somatic waves, waves of colors, rhythms, tones. So-called intellectual speculation derives from this identifying, tenacious gaze: the hysteric knows something about this when, unable to find a sufficiently satisfying mirror, she finds herself in theory, a point of convergence of all sensible and senseless intentions, a shelter where "I" can know without seeing myself, for "I" have delegated to another (to philosophical contemplation) the concern of representing a (my) identity, as reassuring as it is false, because it blacks out fear, facilitation. So-called intellectual speculation socializes "me" and reassures others of "my" good intentions as far as sense and ethics go. But of my dreamed body it offers only what the doctor's speculum maintains: a deeroticized surface that "I" concede to him in the wink of an eye by which "I" make him believe that he is not another, that he has only to look as "I" would if "I" were him.

[15] See chap. 10 of this book, "Sartre: Freedom as Questioning."

On the other hand, there is a different gaze. In fact, when facilitation and fear burst into view this different gaze stops being simply reassuring, trompe-l'oeil, or the start of speculation and becomes—if you will—the fascinating specular, that is, at once charming and maleficent. Cinema seizes us here, precisely. This is its magic. At the intersection between the sight of a real object and fantasy, the cinematic image makes what is behind identification identifiable (and there is nothing more patently identifiable than the visible): the drive, not symbolized, not caught in the object, neither in the sign nor in language. Or, to put it bluntly, it conveys aggression. The fantasy is called on to find or recognize itself, to perpetuate or empty itself, based on the ability of the specular to distance itself from itself.

All specular is fascinating, because it bears the trace—in the visible—of this aggression, of this nonsymbolized, nonverbalized, and thus nonrepresented drive. But in certain images, fantasies are referred to as such; they exercise their power of fascination while at the same time mocking their fascinating specular. I propose the term the "thought specular" for the visible signs that designate fantasy and denounce it as such. This information no longer refers to the referent (or to the object) but to the attitude of the subject vis-à-vis the object. The cinema of Godard, which most everyone is familiar with, is the "thought specular": not images-information but signals captured, cut up, and arranged in such a way that the phantasmatic thought of the writer-director can be made out and invites you first to locate your own fantasies and then to hollow them out.

The Greek stoics distinguished the real object, or "referent," from what they called an "expressible," the *lekton*. I would say that what distinguishes the referent from the "expressible" (from the *lekton*) is that the latter is the expression of a desiring contract, this subjective alchemy that transforms a flat image (a denotative sign) into a symptom (a specular). There are no flat images in Godard; everything is thought specular, everything is a symptom: his, ours. But the sadness of this symptom is shattered in irony. The phantasmatic images themselves are never first degree; on the contrary, the fantasies seem boneless, dislocated, in the end there is only a certain music—logic, the movement that associates, displaces, condenses, and thereby judges: an unconscious judgment. We might call these supplementary bits of information "lektonic traces": it is essentially a matter of introducing supplementary displacements and condensations to the raw image, associating tones, rhythms, colors, figures—in short, putting into play what Freud called "the primary processes" (the "semiotic" in my terminology) underlying the symbolic, this primary seizure drives always in excess in relation to the represented and the signified.

That modern art—painting, sculpture, music—found its favored domain in the distribution of these lektonic traces (to the detriment of the image-sign of a referent) is something Matisse, Klee, Rothko, Schönberg, and Webern are there to remind us of. We call this imaginary "abstraction," wrongly. Nothing is closer to unconscious fantasy in its very logic, in its form if not content, displacing-condensing the semiotic energies of the pulsing, desiring body. We could certainly choose to decipher the mathematical calculations in the calculus of this specular, but this would be to ignore that it conceals facilitation and fear. As Philippe Sollers said in *Paradis*: "Writing comes from terror."[16] The imaginary as thought specular, by which I mean the imaginary filtering and hollowing out fantasy, comes from aggression, fear, pain inflicted or suffered, and it is expended as such. Since Sartre, Lacan, and Barthes (who dedicated his

[16] Philippe Sollers, *Paradis* (Paris: Seuil, 1981).

Camera Lucida to Sartre's *L'imaginaire*), we all know that the imaginary is not a reflection but a subjective synthesis: this is what phenomenology reveals. I will speak of this again in chapter eleven, when I reread Sartre's *L'imaginaire* (*The Psychology of Imagination*). I will simply point out an essential difference between what I am proposing here and the imaginary according to Sartre: namely, that I seek the specular in the imaginary, that is, the trace of fantasy.

Is this to say that the specular necessarily reveals evil, or could we even go so far as to maintain that evil structures the imaginary?

This is a step that I will happily take provided we extract evil from its moral connotations and submit it to the facilitations and fears already evoked. For all that, the cinema has a social function that does not allow us avoid the topic of ethics.

The Representable Conflict

Since its inception, cinema has not only projected the specular (imagination/fantasy) by making itself the bold revealer of our psychical lives, more seductively and more frighteningly than the other arts, but it has also assumed the power of thinking the specular. Thinking it in a way that is itself specular: using the visible, not evacuating fantasy but being protected from it while demonstrating it; not necessarily displaying it in its oneiric naïveté but exhibiting its main themes, its skeleton, its logic. With the effect of another pleasure: that of lucidity and thus laughter. Which is to say that the great filmmakers have always known to include the facilitation of fear in cinematic seduction, in explicit themes as well as the rhythm of images.

Thus Eisenstein wanted to express conflict, drama, the unbearable, even in the spatial organization of the cinematic mise-en-scène. Relentlessly, the Russian filmmaker pursued the project of conveying, with and beyond the image-referential sign, what I call a network of lektonic traces. In his seminar, he offered his students an evocative example: nothing less than the fundamental invisible, the primal scene, which moreover is illegitimate. Returning from the front, a soldier finds his wife pregnant. How should the objects, actors, and lines be distributed, Eisenstein wonders, in order to give shape, in the specular, to the conflictuality of the desire of knowing "where this child came from" and "how evil has functioned." To this end, the director advised his film students to present all the elements of the mise-en-scène according to a rigorous topology of the drama: that of a conflict between two spatial complexes. The meticulous organization of space, the placement of each object, the calculated intervention of each sound and each line of dialogue in a way that spatially inserts a subjacent conflict: here are the lektonic traces, the bones of the fantasy that must adjoin a "rhythmic," "plastic" dimension to what is too visible, an enigma that does not stare you in the face, in which the filmmaker's anxiety is encoded, which elicits that of the viewer more profoundly than the image-referential sign would. "All the elements must express the internal content of the drama spatially and temporally. Our solution (in the episode in question) consists in the clear confrontation of the two tendencies represented by two spatial complexes characterized differently—a straight forward, frontal tendency and an oblique, diagonal tendency"[17]....

Eisenstein's message in his seminar was clear: the drama, the conflict must be interiorized in every element of the visible; the slightest atom of the visible must be saturated with conflict and,

[17] See Sergei Eisenstein, *Complete Works*.

as he said, dramatic "rhythm." "It is only when one can hear the signifier (*Oboznacenije*) not as the cold sign of phenomena, but when one dynamically apprehends it in the innumerable multiplicities of its particular, ever-changing manifestations, that the signifier rids itself of its indirect character of plodding word play or deadly symbol" (4:60).

This concern for "rhythm" may vary from one filmmaker to another: "organic" in Eisenstein, "metric" in Pudovkin, "melodic" in Walt Disney: these at any rate are the distinctions established by Eisenstein himself.[18] But the filmmaker must always lie in wait for the conflict, at the borders of the unrepresentable.

To go a step further, in a less structural, more explicit perspective, we could maintain that this "organic drama" that Eisenstein aims for ultimately takes the form, quite simply, of represented horror. Might horror be the quintessential specular?

Doesn't Eisenstein's emphasis on the necessity of saturating the visibility of conflict (aggression, evil) evoke the detective novel or the horror film? Wouldn't Hitchcock, joining Eisenstein's rhythm to the vision of terror, be the quintessential filmmaker? The modern audience seems to think so: from the most sophisticated to the most common, we do not resist vampires or the massacres of the Far West. Catharsis, an adjustment necessary to all societies, no longer occurs through Oedipus, Electra, or Orestes but through *The Birds* or *Psycho*, if not simply the gunshots of any western or the alternating horror and embellishment of X-rated films. Moreover, the stupider it is, the better, for the filmic image does not need to be intelligent: what counts is that the specular presents the drive—aggression—through its direct signified (the object or situation represented) and encodes it through its plastic rhythm (the network of lektonic elements: sounds, tone, colors, space, figures), which has come back to us from the other without response and which consequently has remained uncaptured, unsymbolized, unconsumed.

But then another question arises: does specular seduction exist without fear? Is there a thought specular that is not melancholic irony or strident terror but pure seduction?

This seduction is what we dream of, with or without images: the radiant body, swelling music, the eye that serenely X-rays the interior of viscera, the camera coiled in the labyrinth of cavities as in a painting by Georgia O'Keeffe, blue-red-green lifting a flower on wings, on horseback.... Some of you have no doubt had these sorts of dreams, ecstasies, nocturnal or otherwise. I hope you have. On the other hand, if you want a character or a phantasmatic narrative to stage seduction, there is always Mozart. Don Juan remains the ideal specular hero: a seducer, because he is a master who defies the fathers, and a connoisseur of women, who counts them one by one until a thousand and three. He transforms the silent passion for his mother (as with Antoine, the patient mentioned earlier) into a series of mistresses and the passion for his father not into self-deprecation (like Antoine) but into reciprocal murder, always ambivalent: Law and transgression, terror and fascination. If the seductive specular required an emblem it would be Don Juan. But *Don Juan* is composed of music (Mozart) and text (Da Ponte and especially Molière). The visual arts do not dare confront this density of seductive fantasy that the image is afraid of making banal and unbearable. What would seduction passed through the sieve of thought specular be? I dream of an impossible film: Don Juan by Eisenstein and Hitchcock, with music by Schönberg. As you may remember, Schönberg

[18] See Sergei Eisenstein, *Beyond the Stars: The Memoirs of Sergei Eisenstein*, ed. Richard Taylor, trans. William Powell (Calcutta: Seagull, 1995).

sought the solution to the debate that he himself described as false between his Aaron and his Moses: between the jubilation of idol worshippers seduced by the golden calf (followers of the image?) and the divine threat exploding in thunder, imageless. For this is indeed the problem of the thought specular: how to remain in idolatry (fantasy) while at the same time exhibiting symbolic truth (the imageless divine thunder). Imagine the result! Invisible. An empty theater. But what terror, seduction, and lucidity!

Cinema and Evil

That the image is the primary recorder of our anxieties is not something humankind waited for Freud, Hitchcock, or Godard to notice. You will find the proof in one of the great geniuses of modern times: St. Augustine. Not only did he consider the image constitutive of the *mens*, that is, the symbolic order (the image was "irascible," with memory, sight, love, and will inscribed in it, as in the mind). But in addition, seeing the image as a support to the transcendental quest, even and especially if it is not the image of an identifiable object, he reversed a verse of Psalms, a marvelous gesture that I offer here for your reflection.

Psalms 39:6 says: "Surely every man walketh in a vain show; surely they are disquieted in vain: he heapeth up riches, and knoweth not who shall gather them."[19] Augustine substitutes this version: "Although man is vainly disquieted, yet he walks in an image." Translation: the imaginary captures fear, appeases it, and restores it to the symbolic order. Follow the ruse of the theologian and the use of the image by Christian, notably Catholic, monotheism: isn't the cinema the apogee of this Catholic astuteness that makes man in spite of his disquiet "walk in an image"? Christian art, in the half-light of churches, knows, multiplies, and exploits this fascination: calm reigns before images of hell. At least we hope so, if we rely on the pacifying virtue of the image. The image as compensation for anxiety and cultural project: this was already in Augustine. Isn't the media just a form of the vulgarization of a theological inhibition?

It is one thing however to say that evil—as nonsymbolized death drive—articulates the imaginary and that the imaginary appeases this evil ("man walks in an image," St. Augustine says); it is another thing to emphasize that evil is the end result of the spectacle. For this is indeed what happens in the society so well described by Guy Debord as a "society of the spectacle." By exhausting representation, being bored in representation, suffocating from its falseness in the ballet of those who govern us (and who trade planes for human rights, for example), by letting himself be invaded by representation, though he knows its strings, modern man comes up against the logic of fantasy. On the one hand, we ask the image to represent a desire for happiness, but, on the other, above all, we want it to represent its sadomasochistic flip side. Exhausted in the evening, we watch police dramas on television, and the crimes that we see appease us. I have just completed a metaphysical thriller myself that can be read with

[19] The Hebrew text, translated literally, says instead: "Although man walks in the image, yet he accumulates money in vain and he ignores who will collect it." This reflection should be compared to numerous texts that stigmatize "idols" and "the golden calf" and others that present man as a traveling "shadow" or "wind." The Vulgate as well as the Hebrew commentary compare the image to the idol and money: man is seduced by it; he struggles violently to accumulate it; although the term "disquiet" does not seem explicit in the Hebrew text, the Vulgate version makes it an intermediary between the image-idol and the idol-golden calf, which is certainly in the spirit of the Bible.

all the more ease since it is only a novel: the specular displays the sadomasochist repressed of the society of the spectacle.[20]

Having come to this point, we cannot avoid the ethical question I mentioned at the beginning: by displaying evil, does the cinema take part in another mystification, another banalization of evil? Actually, the risk does exist, but I think that it might also be something else. Provided what? Provided that, saturated with evil, the cinema does not only take us for a ride but makes us keep our distance. I am moving away from St. Augustine here and pleading the case for the man who "does not walk in an image."

Many have dreamed, along with Jean-Luc Godard, of the possibility of an antifilm, a spectacular that would not, at the outset, be deposited in the bank account of order. The burst of laughter remains the most salubrious means for such an operation: when the image, saturated with evil, also allows itself to laugh, identity collapses and all dictators are toppled. Charlie Chaplin, or specular shattering: he presents us with the successful order of embodied psychosis, but in such a way that evil is only representable insofar as you can laugh at it, with full knowledge of the facts. *The Dictator* opens a new era of the Western imaginary: "Although man walks in the image, he no longer walks."

The Chaplinian actor as well as the gap between sound and image, or the "impious dismantling of projection"[21] through camera movement itself (Godard, Bresson), hold the spectator—still plunged in fantasy—at a distance from fascination. It was no doubt inevitable that specular fascination should arrive at its perfect and total completion through cinema and that cinema itself should openly become the privileged place of sadomasochistic fantasy, so that fear and its seduction explode in laughter and distance. If it were not for this demystification, if it were content to revel in the naive presentation of evil, then cinema would be nothing else but a new Church.

As you can certainly sense, the contemporary stakes reside in this alternative: does cinema wish to be an exhibition of the sadomasochistic repressed in the spectacle, an authorized perversion, a banalization of evil? Or, on the contrary, its demystification?

I leave the question open: how can I do otherwise? Especially since the cinema is not really our subject: we have arrived here through the intermediary of intimacy in revolt and the imaginary that constitutes it, in order to examine the imaginary of demystification. And yet this seems impossible. But the wager has been made, notably by Roland Barthes, whose trajectory I will follow in the chapters to come. That demystification would lead us logically to Barthes will not surprise those of you who have read him.

---

[20] See Julia Kristeva, *Possessions*, trans. Barbara Bray (New York: Columbia, 1998).

[21] To use Stéphane Mallarmé's words in describing his project for a "démontage impie de la fiction" in *Oeuvres completes* (Paris: Gallimard, Bibliothèque de la Pléiade, 1945), p. 647.

CHAPTER 26
SLAVOJ ŽIŽEK

Slavoj Žižek (b. 1949) is a Slovenian philosopher and cultural critic. He is perhaps most widely known for his unique and challenging synthesis of Hegelian Marxism and Lacanian psychoanalysis in considerations of the individual, society, and culture, as well as his frequent willingness to incorporate considerations of popular cultural products and phenomena into otherwise academic, even esoteric, cultural analyses. This freedom from the traditional boundaries between so-called high and low culture has enabled Žižek to liberate psychoanalytic discourse from any unnecessary elitism associated with the academy—and has gained him a wide, and not exclusively academic, following. The selection included here, "The Strange Case of the Missing Lacanians," is the introduction to his book, The Fright of Real Tears: Krzyzstof Kieślowski between Theory and Post-Theory, *originally published in English by the British Film Institute in 2001.*

Žižek articulates a rift in contemporary film studies, between two camps identified loosely with the terms "Theory" and "Post-Theory." Theory, on this articulation, is the mostly Continental European approach to film (centralized in the present volume), with its many concomitant and sometimes disagreeing elements: phenomenology, psychoanalysis, Marxism, feminism, and so on. Post-Theory is, then, an approach incorporating either cognitivist or scientific understandings of both knowledge and objectivity, and has been spearheaded by such thinkers as David Bordwell and Noël Carroll. According to Žižek, Post-Theory grounds its identity (even nominally) in its opposition to Theory—and, specifically, to what it takes to be Theory's greatest excess, its reliance upon Lacanian psychoanalysis. Post-Theorists tend to agree, Žižek notes, that Theory refers to any number of imaginary or mythical entities as significant to film studies—entities like "the Gaze," for which the Post-Theorists assert there is no empirical evidence. Ironically, however, as Žižek points out, very few theorists of film are in fact Lacanians. In this text, he identifies only two—himself and Joan Copjec—and then makes passing reference to the existence of others, mostly in Slovenia. Rather, he notes, many Theorists engage with Lacan—but are not themselves Lacanian, as can be seen in their foundational criticisms of his psychoanalysis, mostly (as in the cases of Laura Mulvey and Kaja Silverman, according to Žižek) on feminist grounds. Thus, there is something of a further rift in film studies, on the side of Theory, between those who make ambiguous and often critical use of some of Lacan's ideas, and those who, like Žižek, fully endorse Lacan.

*The larger rift, however, between Theory and Post-Theory is just one instance of an even larger and longer term conflict in cultural studies, between those on the postmodernist or deconstructionist side, and those on the cognitivist side. This conflict has had many upsurges, including, famously, the de Man affair and the Sokal-*Social Text *affair. While these "affairs" might seem relatively modern phenomena to some (including their participants and instigators), Žižek notes that philosophical scandals are part of a very long tradition that stretches back at least as far as Socrates, and includes Fichte's resignation from his university post, as well as the intellectual revolutions originating in Darwin and Freud. A philosophical scandal, Žižek says,* *erupts whenever a philosophy disturbs the "substance of the communal being," that is, whenever a philosopher publicly calls the shared traditions and beliefs of a society into question. In most of these scandals, however, we find that the scandalous nature of the event distracts from the true nature of the conflict at hand, which is over the nature of the human in general. Ultimately, Žižek argues, the disagreement between Theory and Post-Theory is not so much a disagreement about film, but a disagreement about what it is to be human. Post-Theory demonstrates its lack of seriousness in this matter (Žižek thinks) in the ways in which its presentations of Theory and various associated thinkers are almost comical caricatures, rather than attempts in earnest to understand. Theory does have a tendency toward jargon, however, Žižek admits, and must rise to the challenge established by Post-Theory to delineate precisely where Theory ends and its jargonistic imitation begins.*

A large part of the conflict between the postmodernist Theorists and the cognitivist Post-Theorists, Žižek argues, has to do with the role and feasibility of psychoanalysis in cultural studies, including film studies. The Post-Theorists typically dismiss psychoanalysis outright, but there is another, accommodationist approach which Žižek finds even more dangerous: the view that says that psychoanalysis can do a little to help us understand some elements of culture or cinema, but never the essential. Presumably, Žižek is arguing here that, even in its dismissal of psychoanalysis, Post-Theory acknowledges that psychoanalysis is making a very fundamental claim about human being. In this vein, we can see how the rift between Theory and Post-Theory opens the possibility of a philosophical scandal of the sort Žižek sees as characteristic of the history of Western thought. The accommodationist approach is worse, because it does not even acknowledge the nature of the claims psychoanalysis is making—relegating it to one interpretive stance or tool among many. This compromise position is indicative of a larger and more disturbing general trend in cultural studies; however, the appearance of what Žižek calls a "radical apathy" at its heart. He observes that, more and more, everything has become neutralized—and thus nothing shocks or disturbs us anymore.

Most consequentially, there are certain "antinomies" or contradictions within cultural studies that receive very little if any attention, and thus result in problematic (if not hypocritical) positions. He offers two examples: the discoveries of quantum mechanics would seem to indicate that our understanding of the nature of the material world has been mistaken for quite some time, and yet the consequences of those discoveries for physics have been widely accepted without the development of a corresponding ontology of matter: we make use of the "new truths" without making sense of them. Likewise, he notes, the introduction of the notion of the unconscious into psychology by Freud resulted in the development of a variety of innovative philosophies and clinical practices, but many of us accept those changes without understanding their consequences for how we know: we use a radically altered concept of the mind without having developed a corresponding epistemology. This phenomenon, which appears both in the realm of individual consciousness as well as in culture, results in a radical split in language: we find, on the one hand, a jargonistic language of the specialist which almost no one understands, and on the other hand, a common sense language of everyday experience which remains uninformed by developments in knowledge.

This split is part of what is at work in the Theory/Post-Theory divide; perhaps one way of describing what the Post-Theorists are trying to observe about Theory is that most people (including the Post-Theorists) lack the theoretical tools they would need to incorporate the views of the Theorists in their worldviews, and that, in addition, many purported Theorists operate in a language so divorced from what most people can understand that there are ways in which they might as well be saying (or are believed, as by many Post-Theorists, to be saying) nothing. Žižek believes that there is a potential remedy to this split, and to these failures of culture and knowledge fully to understand relatively recent developments in cultural studies, however, and that is in turning to Lacan—not the Lacan criticized by some Theorists and dismissed by Post-Theory, but "another Lacan," which is to say, the Lacan of a more careful reading and appropriation of Lacan (Žižek's or Copjec's Lacan).

This "other Lacan" could help cultural studies to rationalize cinema theory in a way that was neither dismissive of Theory nor susceptible to its excesses. Although the selection included here does not further develop that suggestion, Žižek does indicate (and the rest of The Fright of Real Tears *demonstrates) that one route to a properly Lacanian understanding of cinema might go through an analysis of the cinematic works of the Polish filmmaker, Krzyzstof Kieślowski. Such a path would begin by examining one of the most basic seeming paradoxes in the study of Kieślowski's work, namely, that its rootedness in and appeal to the very specific culture of Poland, and more generally of Central Europe, is evident to anyone who views his films; but Kieślowski has achieved widespread, global, nearly universal acclaim, and the appeal of such distinctively Polish films to spectators, theorists, and critics living in so many different parts of the world—the universal appeal of such geographically and cultural specific films—is hard to understand. Trying to come to understand it—in Lacanian terms—might help us to see, Žižek suggests, how the work of Theory might continue, despite the criticisms and condemnations of Post-Theory, into the future.*

Filmography

- ***Dekalog*** [*Decalogue*] (Poland, 1989). *Directed by* Krzyzstof Kieślowski. *Produced by* Ryszard Chutkowski. *Written by* Krzyzstof Kieślowski *and* Krzyzstof Piesiewicz. *Starring* Artur Barciś et al.

THE STRANGE CASE OF THE MISSING LACANIANS

If this book had been published twenty-five years ago, in the heyday of "structuralist Marxism," its subtitle, undoubtedly, would have been "On Class Struggle in Cinema."

Let me begin by stating the obvious, with what in France they call *une verité de la Palice*: to put it in good old Maoist terms, the principal contradiction of today's cinema studies is the one between the deconstructionist/feminist/post-Marxist/psychoanalytic/sociocritical/cultural studies etc. approach, ironically nicknamed "Theory" (which, of course, is far from a unified field—the above chain is more a series of Wittgensteinian "family resemblances") by its opponents, and the so-called "Post-Theory," the cognitivist and/or historicist reaction to it. Here, however, we immediately encounter a paradox. Although Post-Theorists acknowledge the inner differences in the field of Theory (say, between the early *Screen* focus on interpellation, Gaze, suture, and the later more historicist-culturalist feminist orientation), they nonetheless emphasize a common Lacanian element as central. They even acknowledge that the only unity of their own project is negative, that of excluding (Lacanian) psychoanalysis—David Bordwell and Noel Carroll made it clear, in their introduction to the *Post-Theory* volume, that "[t]he unifying principle in this book is that all the research included exemplifies the possibility of scholarship that is not reliant upon the psychoanalytic framework that dominates film academia."[1] So who *are* these Lacanians? Post-Theorists like to emphasize that writers of Theory refer to mythical entities like the (capitalized) Gaze, entities to which no empirical, observable facts (like actual cinema viewers and their behavior) correspond—one of the essays in the *Post-Theory* volume actually has the Sherlock Holmesian title "Psychoanalytic Film Theory and the Problem of the Missing Spectator."[2] In the same vein, I would like to claim that, in the global field designated by Post-Theorists as that of Theory, we are dealing with a no less mysterious "case of the missing Lacanians": except for Joan Copjec, myself and some of my Slovene colleagues, I know of no cinema theorist who effectively accepts Lacan as his or her ultimate background. The authors usually referred to as Lacanians (from Laura Mulvey to Kaja Silverman) as a rule "engage with" Lacan: they appropriate some Lacanian concepts as the best description of the universe of patriarchal domination, while emphasizing that Lacan remained a phallogocentrist who uncritically accepted this universe as the only imaginable framework of our socio-symbolic existence. So, as a Lacanian, I seem to be caught in an unexpected double-bind: I am, as it were, being deprived of what I never possessed, made responsible for something others generated as Lacanian film theory. My response to this is, of course: what if one should finally give Lacan himself a chance? So, to continue in a Maoist vein, I am tempted to determine the opposition between the ambiguous reference to Lacan that has predominated in cinema studies and those

[1] David Bordwell and Noel Carroll, 'Introduction', in Bordwell and Carroll (eds), *Post-Theory* (Madison: The University of Wisconsin Press, 1996), p. xvi.

[2] Stephen Prince, 'Psychoanalytic Film Theory and the Problem of the Missing Spectator', in *Post-Theory*, pp. 71–86.

who fully endorse Lacan as the second, non-antagonistic contradiction of cinema studies, to be resolved through discussion and self-criticism.

My second *lapalissade* is that these struggles point towards a global and much more far-reaching crisis in cultural studies. What looms in the background is a whole set of dilemmas, from the purely epistemological to politico-ideological ones: do cultural studies provide an adequate instrument to counteract global capitalism, or are they simply the ultimate expression of its cultural logic? Will cognitive scientists and other representatives of the so-called "Third Culture" succeed in replacing cultural critics as the new model of "public intellectuals"? That is to say, the antagonism between Theory and Post-Theory is a particular case of the global battle for intellectual hegemony and visibility between the exponents of post-modern/deconstructionist cultural studies and, on the other hand, cognitivists and popularisers of hard sciences, a battle which caught the attention of a wide public first through the so-called de Man affair (where the opponents endeavored to prove the proto-Fascist irrationalist tendencies of deconstruction) and then through the Sokal-*Social Text* affair.

Such "affairs" or "scandals" should be taken much more seriously than is usually the case—they are part of a long tradition, consubstantial with philosophy itself. Did Socrates not cause a scandal which involved all—male, adult, free—citizens? Was this not the reason why he was condemned to death? Among later scandals one should mention at least the *Atheismusstreit* in Weimar in 1802, when Fichte, the German Idealist, had to resign his post because of his ethical teaching, which equated God with the ideal moral order of freedom and autonomy towards which humanity should strive (Goethe, the eternal conformist, interceded, imploring Fichte to compromise, and then raised his hands in despair at Fichte's stubborn attitude). So when some philosopher causes a scandal in the city, in his community, one should be wary of quickly dismissing it as a cheap affair of publicity that has nothing whatsoever to do with the inner truth of philosophizing per se—as if the proper attitude of a philosopher were to sit alone in the pose of Rodin's thinker (who, if one were to complete the statue in a post-modern way, should undoubtedly be revealed to sit on a toilet). A much more serious thing is at stake: to put it in Hegelian terms, a properly *philosophical* scandal erupts when some philosophy effectively disturbs the very substance of the communal being, what Lacan referred to as the "big Other," the shared implicit set of beliefs and norms that regulate our interaction.

The deception of "scandals" is not so much that they are superficial public events, but that they *displace* the true dimension of the conflict. Let us take the two great "scientific" scandals of the last two centuries: Darwin and Freud. The "scandal" of Darwin's discovery is not the notion that humanity emerged from the animal kingdom through the natural process of evolution; rather, it resides in the more uncanny notion that evolution is not a gradual progressive movement, but a radically contingent emergence of new species with no objective measure which would allow us to prioritize them. In a similar vein, what is really "scandalous" about the Freudian revolution is not the assertion of the central role of sexuality in human life, but, on the contrary, the assertion of the structurally *excessive and/or failed* character of human sexuality as opposed to animal mating.

And this holds more than ever for the most recent "philosophical" scandal, the so-called Sloterdijk affair, which exploded in Germany in 1999, when a majority in the liberal media accused Peter Sloterdijk, the author who first became known twenty years ago with his *Critique of Cynical Reason*, of promoting the renewed Nazi agenda of genetic breeding to create a superior race. Whatever one thinks of Sloterdijk, what he actually did was expose the inability of the predominant left-liberal ethical stance (best embodied in Habermas's ethics of communicative action) to cope with the new challenges posed by the digitalization of our daily lives and by the prospect of biogenetic interventions into the "substance" of the human individual. Ultimately, all this traditional stance can offer are variations on the motif of limits not to be violated (in total accord with the Catholic Church's reaction): how far are we allowed to go? Where should we stop? In short, this stance is reactive and protective: it accepts the inherited notion of "humanity," and then goes on to tackle the question: what limits should we impose on new technologies so that the essence of "humanity" will not be threatened? The real question to be addressed is exactly the opposite one: how do the new technologies compel us to redefine this very standard inherited notion of "humanity"? Is a person whose genome is exposed to technological manipulation still fully "human," and if yes, in what does his/her freedom reside? The true site of the scandal is thus again displaced: the need to rethink the very notion of what is human.

And, at a different level, the same goes for the so-called Sokal-*Social Text* affair. What was actually at stake in it? When Alan Sokal's essay for *Social Text* was revealed to be a parody, my first thought was: would it not be even simpler for a Lacanian to write an inverted parody, i.e. to imitate convincingly the standard scientistic commonsense critical rejection of post-modern deconstructionism? Then, after reading the book Alan Sokal co-wrote with Jean Brichmont, *Impostures intellectuelles*,[3] in which the two authors propose a detailed "serious" denunciation of the way selected "post-modern" authors (form Lacan to Baudrillard) refer to "hard" sciences, especially mathematics and physics, it suddenly struck me that this book, although meant to be taken seriously by its authors, already *is* this parody (does its characterization of opponents not as a rule amount to a caricaturalized version of what post-modern Theory is?). And the same goes for the large majority of the Post-Theory attacks on Theory: does what they describe as Theory, or what they attribute to Theory, not read as a comically simplified caricature of Lacan, Althusser, et al.? Can one really take seriously Noel Carroll's description of Gaze theorists? Nonetheless, there is, for precisely this reason, a positive function of Post-Theory for Theorists: Theory often does degenerate into jargon. Thus what we get in Post-Theory by way of a description of a Theory is not simply a misunderstanding or misreading. It confronts us with a certain deconstructionist "post-modern" ideology that accompanies Theory proper as its indelible shadow. In doing this, Post-Theory compels us to define in precise terms where we stand, and to draw—in an unabashedly Platonic way—a line of separation between Theory proper and its jargonistic imitation.

On 26 January 1999, Cardinal Medina Estevez presented to the public on behalf of the Vatican the new version of the Catholic Church's manual on exorcism, *De Exorcismis et supplicationibus quibusdam* (in Latin, but soon to be translated in modern languages). The interest of this volume resides in its reference to Freud: it emphasizes the need to distinguish between authentic possession by the Devil (when its victim fluently and inexplicably speaks unknown languages, violates physical laws, etc.) and phenomena that are merely expressions of the human mind taking a pathological turn—and in order to distinguish between the two, psychoanalysis can be of help. So when someone claims to be possessed by the Devil, one should first send him to an analyst to exclude the possibility that we are dealing with a mere subjective delusion. A similar constraining of the scope of psychoanalysis is often at work in so-

[3] Alan Sokal and Jean Brichmont, *Impostures intellectuelles* (Paris: Odile Jacob, 1997).

called "applied psychoanalysis"—psychoanalysis can explain a lot, like the psychic background of a work of art, but not its essence… This attitude is the falsest of them all, worse than any cognitivist outright rejection of psychoanalysis, which at least has the merit of pushing us to confront our own platitudes.

Some months before writing this, at an art round table, I was asked to comment on a painting I had seen there for the first time. I did not have *any* idea about it, so I engaged in a total bluff, which went something like this: the frame of the painting in front of us is not its true frame; there is another, invisible, frame, implied by the structure of the painting, which frames our perception of the painting, and these two frames do not overlap—there is an invisible gap separating the two. The pivotal content of the painting is not rendered in its visible part, but is located in this dislocation of the two frames, in the gap that separates them. Are we, today, in our post-modern madness, still able to discern the traces of this gap? Perhaps more than the reading of a painting hinges on it; perhaps the decisive dimension of humanity will be lost when we lose the capacity to discern this gap… To my surprise, this brief intervention was a huge success, and many following participants referred to the dimension in-between-the-two-frames, elevating it into a term. This very success made me sad, really sad. What I encountered here was not only the efficiency of a bluff, but a much more radical apathy at the very heart of today's cultural studies.

A little over 200 years ago, at the zenith of early modernity, Immanuel Kant grounded the greatest revolution in the history of philosophy in a shocking experience of the so-called antinomies of pure reason: with regard to the most fundamental questions of our existence, our reasoning unavoidably gets caught in a series of antinomies—the two opposed, mutually exclusive conclusions (there is God and there is no God; there is a free will and there is no free will) can both be demonstrated. For Kant, as is well known, the way out of this epistemological shock was through practical reason: when I am engaged in an ethical act, I resolve the antinomy in practice and display my free will.

Today, however, our experience confronts us with a different set of antinomies. But, these antinomies have lost their ability to shock us: the two opposed poles are simply left to coexist. Already in the 20s, the epistemological crisis generated by quantum mechanics was not really resolved: the predominant attitude of today's quantum physicists is: "Who cares about ontological questions concerning the reality of observed phenomena, the main thing is that the quantum formulae function!" And the same goes for the Freudian unconscious and other epistemological shocks: they are simply accepted and neutralized, and business goes on as usual. The personification of the contemporary subject is perhaps the Indian computer programmer who, during the day, excels in his expertise, while in the evening, upon returning home, lights a candle to the local Hindu divinity and respects the sacredness of the cow. What we encounter here is a certain radical split: we have the objectivized language of experts and scientists that can no longer be translated into the common language accessible to everyone, but is present in it in the mode of fetishized formulae that no one really understands, but which shape our artistic and popular imaginary (Black Hole, Big Bang, Superstrings, Quantum Oscillation). The gap between scientific insight and common sense is unbridgeable, and it is this very gap which elevates scientists into the popular cult-figures of the "subjects supposed to know" (the Stephen Hawking phenomenon). The strict obverse of this scientific objectivity is the way in which, in cultural matters, we are confronted with the multitude of lifestyles which cannot be translated into each other: all we can do is secure the conditions for their tolerant coexistence in a multicultural society.

The present book approaches these deadlocks at three levels. Through critical dialogue with cognitivist/historicist Post-Theory as well as with standard deconstructionist cinema theory, the first part endeavors to demonstrate that the reading of Lacan operative in the 70s and 80s was a reductive one—there is "another Lacan" reference to whom can contribute to the revitalization of the cinema theory (and of critical thought in general) today. This general approach is followed by an interpretation of the film-maker the very mention of whom triggers an immense aesthetic-ideological controversy: Krzysztof Kieślowski. Against the standard "post-modernist" as well as the now fashionable "post-secular" obscurantist readings, I endeavor to demonstrate how his work, the site of antagonistic ideological tensions, of the "class struggle in art," can be redeemed by a Lacanian approach....

Kieślowski definitely belongs to *Mitteleuropa*; if one is to look for the identity of this spectral entity, dismissed by many either as a purely geographic notion or as the product of reactionary nostalgia, one of the keys to it is a series of strange cultural phenomena from the turn-of-the-century novels of Karl May to the Irish folk-rock band The Kelly Family. Karl May's adventure novels (the most popular ones take place in an imagined American West, with the narrator Old Shatterhand—May himself in disguise—and the Apache chief Winnetou as their main heroes) were immensely popular throughout the entire twentieth century; in the mid-90s, the popularity of The Kelly Family's kitschy, family-values idealized "Irish" songs surpassed that of all of the main Anglo-American bands, with a key proviso: in both cases, *the success was geographically limited to the precise confines of "Central Europe"*: Germany, Austria, Poland, the Czech Republic, Hungary, Croatia and Slovenia. If nothing else, this shared image of the Other (of the imagined American West or Ireland) demonstrates that there *is* something to the notion of "Central Europe" as a common cultural-ideological space. Does this mean, however, that, in order to understand Kieślowski properly, we should locate him in the unique historical context of the disintegration of Middle European real socialism—in short, that only somebody well attuned to the life-world of Poland in the 80s (ultimately: only a Pole) can "really understand" Kieślowski?

The first thing that strikes the eye of the viewer aware of the historical circumstances in which *Decalogue*—the series of ten one-hour TV films, arguably Kieślowski's masterpiece—was shot, is the total absence of any reference to politics: although the series was shot in the most turbulent period of post-World War II Polish history (the state of emergency imposed by General Jaruzelski's *coup d'état* in order to curb Solidarity), one cannot but admire Kieślowski's heroic ascetism, his resistance to scoring easy points by spicing up the story with dissident thrills. Of course, it is not only legitimate, but also necessary, to inquire into the concrete social conditions within which Kieślowski accomplished the turn from socio-political concerns to more global ethico-religious ones: the fundamental lesson of dialectics is that universality as such emerges, is articulated "for itself," only within a set of particular conditions. (All great historical assertions of *universal* values, from Ancient Roman Stoicism to modern human rights, are firmly embedded in a *concrete* social constellation.) However, one should avoid here the historicist trap: this unique circumstance does not account for the "truth" and universal scope of the analyzed phenomenon. It is precisely against such hasty historicisers that one should refer to Marx's famous observation apropos of Homer: it is easy to explain how Homer's poetry emerged from early Greek society; what is much more difficult to explain is its universal appeal, i.e. why it continues to exert its charm even today. And, *mutatis mutandis*, the same goes for Kieślowski: it is easy to identify his "roots" in the unique moment of Polish socialism in decay; it is much more difficult to explain the universal appeal of his work, the way his films touch the nerves of people who have no idea whatsoever about the specific circumstances of Poland in the 80s.

Kieślowski is often (mis)perceived as a director whose work is falsified the moment one translates its content into the terms of a (social, religious, psychoanalytic) interpretation—one should simply immerse oneself in it and enjoy it intuitively, not talk about it, not apply to it the terms which irreparably reify its true content… Such a resistance to Theory is often shared by the artists who feel hurt or misunderstood by the theoretical explanations of their work, and who insist on the distinction between *doing* something and *describing* it, talking *about* it: the critic's or theorist's discourse about the anxiety or pleasure discernible in a work of art just talks about them, it does not directly *render* them, and in this sense it is deeply *irrelevant* to the work itself. However, in all fairness, one should bear in mind that the same distinction holds also for Theory itself: in philosophy, it is one thing to talk about, to report on, say, the history of the notion of subject (accompanied by all the proper bibliographical footnotes), even to supplement it with comparative critical remarks; it is quite another thing to work in theory, to elaborate the notion of "subject" itself.[4] The aim of this book is to do the same apropos of Kieślowski: not to talk *about* his work, but to refer to his work in order to accomplish the *work* of Theory. In its very ruthless "use" of its artistic pretext, such a procedure is much more faithful to the interpreted work than any superficial respect for the work's unfathomable autonomy.

[4] There is, of course, a homologous temptation at work in the counterpart of Theory, in *poetry*: if Theory can 'regress' into talk 'about' its topic (instead of practicing it), poetry can 'regress' into a kind of mental laziness, when, instead of enduring the effort to formulate a thought, we concede defeat by escaping into poetic pseudo-depth, into a bundle of metaphoric descriptions of what is otherwise a commonplace. A parallel to Freud's 'dream-work' might be of some help here: in the same way as the true desire of the dream does not reside in the latent dream-thought, but is articulated in the very work of translating/displacing the dream-thought into the manifest dream-text, a poem's true 'message' is not some meaning 'expressed' in the metaphoric poetic language, but resides in the very 'poetic' displacement of this meaning.

SECTION FIVE
FEMINISM AND GENDER STUDIES

CHAPTER 27
SIMONE DE BEAUVOIR

Simone de Beauvoir (1908–1986) was a French existentialist and feminist author, and women's rights activist. She was an accomplished novelist and philosopher, best known among contemporary philosophers as the author of the groundbreaking feminist treatise, The Second Sex. *In that work, as well as in a more general way in her earlier book,* The Ethics of Ambiguity, *Beauvoir extends or revises the existentialism of Jean-Paul Sartre to address the condition of the oppressed, and specifically, the situation of women in patriarchal societies. "Brigitte Bardot and the Lolita Syndrome" was first published in English translation in* Esquire *magazine in 1959, and it is Beauvoir's sole significant contribution to the philosophy of film and film criticism.*

Beauvoir begins her essay with the ironic observation that, although she is adored in America, Brigitte Bardot is disliked in her home country, France. Bardot's films—often centrally erotic in nature—are accused by the mothers of the young people who find them so appealing to have a perverting, corrupting influence. And, Beauvoir admits, a certain amount of prudery is normal. But the extremity of France's disapproval of Bardot is unusual. Sexuality is nothing new in cinema, of course, and Beauvoir contextualizes the Bardot phenomenon historically. Before 1930, sexuality in film was organized around a certain sort of eroticism the primary representative of which was "the vamp." The vamp was always a somewhat mysterious woman, acting to be sure on her own motives, but one who ultimately found her natural home in a relatively conventional relationship—a marriage—to a relatively conventional man. There was, thus, not only mystery but passivity at the heart of the vamp. Things change in the 1930s and 1940s, however, as the situation in Europe bent toward the Second World War: the vamp was replaced by a more wholesome figure, the girlfriend. Rather than outright eroticism, those films that centered on the girlfriend were invested in a kind of romantic sentimentalism.

After the end of the Second World War, and specifically, Beauvoir asserts, in 1947, we find a return in cinema to eroticism—but not to the vamp. This renewed eroticism took two distinct forms: the first was of a more basic sort, and focused in part on sheer physical attraction, the exemplars of which were women such as Marilyn Monroe, Sophia Loren, and Gina Lollobrigida, whose primary task on screen, Beauvoir indicates, was to put their bodies on display. But there was another new eroticism, and this last form is the one in which Beauvoir is centrally interested in this essay: the erotic hoyden, or tomboy, the "child-woman." There are many examples of this type to choose from, but Beauvoir includes among them Audrey Hepburn, Leslie Caron, and Bardot. The hoyden offers something new in cinema, responding to changing conditions in the post-War world. The adult woman shares the same world as men, Beauvoir notes, such that there is a newly demonstrable social equality between the sexes. This equality, this sameness, causes more traditional women to lose some of their erotic appeal for men of the era: there is a distance, Beauvoir notes, which is necessary for a certain sort of (male) erotic desire. What the adult woman loses by proximity and sameness, however, the hoyden gains: the difference in age between men and the child-woman—the paradigmatic literary instance of which is Nabokov's

Lolita—creates the distance these men need to actualize their desire. And of such erotic child-women, Bardot is the "perfect specimen."

Bardot's on-screen persona is characterized by an air of indifference, a perfect innocence without memory and without a past. Cinematically, she exists in a sort of mythical childhood, and her essential traits in film—especially in the films of Roger Vadim, which make her a star—include naiveté, instinctiveness, impulsiveness, temperamentality, changeableness, unpredictability. She is effectively a child in a woman's body, and even this body—which, Beauvoir observes, is only in accord with the conventions for female beauty from the front; from behind, Beauvoir notes, her appearance is quite androgynous—is situated somewhere between womanhood and prepubescent girlhood. Importantly, Bardot's motives in these films are never suspect: she is not perverse or rebellious, she is not immoral; she is amoral, somehow above or free from conventional morality. She has no rights or duties: she is pure inclination, simply doing as she pleases, and she does not suffer any negative consequences (in the films) for her unconventionality, which is disturbing to proponents of those conventions.

Thus, women committed to traditional mores cannot accept Bardot. While they might find it easy to tolerate an outright evil woman, Beauvoir says, they cannot tolerate a woman who situates herself beyond good and evil. This innocence is, thus, a threat: on film, Bardot eats what she wants and dresses how she wants (even in trousers!), and has sex when and with whom she wants; she does so, escaping the conventions of French femininity in the 1950s, by evading womanhood (as it was understood) altogether. The tomboy, the child-woman, the Lolita-esque nymphette, Bardot is despised by most Frenchwomen. The situation is slightly different, of course, with the average Frenchman. On Beauvoir's view, men find Bardot irresistibly sexually attractive ("a saint would sell his soul to the devil just to watch her dance"), and not least because her films give viewers the impression that she is not playing a character on screen: she is sharing herself, allowing her real self to be seen, by everyone. The earthliness of Bardot's appeal (opposed, for Beauvoir, to the divinity of Garbo) forces men to acknowledge the crudity of their desire. They see her on screen, they desire her in this self-consciously crude way, and then realize her actual unattainability—she is a movie star, and rich, and unable to be possessed—and, conflicted by their own impulses, they come to despise her, as well.

As noted before, Bardot's cinematic sexuality is neither mysterious nor passive: she is no vamp. She is not magical. Rather, she is erotically aggressive—"as much hunter as prey"—and this grants her, despite the inclination toward sexual objectification, a kind of dignity. The French, Beauvoir suggests, want almost exclusively to objectify women, and as such they have a much stronger dislike for Bardot than do Americans, who are (again, according to Beauvoir) better accustomed to sexual equality. In resisting that tendency toward passivity, toward objectifying sexual possession, Bardot has contributed to the debunking of myths of love and eroticism. In this, she is genuinely revolutionary. Beauvoir notes that, at the time of the writing of her essay in the late 1950s, Bardot had begun to move publicly toward reforming her reputation, with a greater conformity (on screen and off) to traditional morality. Audiences are split as to whether this development is a good one: those who want social morality fixed tend to favor it, she notes, whereas those who demand that our mores evolve with time (and Beauvoir certainly situates herself in this camp) find themselves somewhat disappointed by the incipient change. Conformity for popularity's sake, Beauvoir concludes, would mean a loss for both cinema and society.

Filmography

- ***The African Queen*** (UK–USA, 1951). *Directed by* John Huston. *Produced by* Sam Spiegel. *Written by* John Huston, James Agee, Peter Viertel, *and* John Collier. *Starring* Humphrey Bogart *and* Katharine Hepburn.
- ***Sommarlek*** [*Summer Interlude*] (Sweden, 1951). *Directed by* Ingmar Bergman. *Produced by* Allan Ekelund. *Written by* Ingmar Bergman *and* Herbert Grevenius. *Starring* Maj-Britt Nilsson *and* Birger Malmsten.
- ***The Barefoot Contessa*** (USA, 1954). *Directed, Produced, and Written by* Joseph L. Mankiewicz. *Starring* Humphrey Bogart, Ava Gardner, *and* Edmond O'Brien.
- ***Et Dieu … créa la femme*** [*And God Created Woman*] (France, 1956). *Directed by* Roger Vadim. *Produced by* Claude Ganz *and* Raoul Lévy. *Written by* Roger Vadim *and* Raoul Lévy. *Starring* Brigitte Bardot, Curd Jürgens, *and* Jean-Louis Trintignant.
- ***En enfeuillant la marguerite*** [*Plucking the Daisy/Please Mr. Balzac*] (France, 1956). *Directed by* Marc Allégret. *Produced by* Raymond Eger. *Written by* Marc Allégret *and* Roger Vadim. *Starring* Brigitte Bardot *and* Daniel Gélin.
- ***En cas de malheur*** [*In Case of Adversity/Love Is My Profession*] (France, 1958). *Directed by* Claude Autant-Lara. *Produced by* Raoul Lévy *and* Ray Ventura. *Written by* Jean Aurenche *and* Pierre Bost. *Starring* Jean Gabin, Brigitte Bardot, *and* Edwige Feuillère.
- ***Babette s'en va-t-en guerre*** [*Babette Goes to War*] (France, 1959). *Directed by* Christian-Jaque. *Produced by* Iéna Productions. *Written by* Raoul Lévy, Gérard Oury, *and* Michel Audiard. *Starring* Brigitte Bardot.
- ***Les liaisons dangereuses*** [*Dangerous Liaisons*] (France, 1959). *Directed by* Roger Vadim. *Produced by* Ariane Distributions *and* Astor Films. *Written by* Roger Vailland *and* Claude Brulé. *Starring* Jeanne Moreau, Gérard Philipe, Annette Vadim, *and* Madeleine Lambert.

BRIGITTE BARDOT AND THE LOLITA SYNDROME

Translated by Bernard Frechtman

On New Year's Eve, Brigitte Bardot appeared on French television. She was got up as usual—blue jeans, sweater and shock of tousled hair. Lounging on a sofa, she plucked at a guitar. "That's not hard," said the women. "I could do just as well. She's not even pretty. She has the face of a housemaid." The men couldn't keep from devouring her with their eyes, but they too snickered. Only two or three of us, among thirty or so spectators, thought her charming. Then she did an excellent classical dance number. "She *can* dance," the others admitted grudgingly. Once again I could observe that Brigitte Bardot was disliked in her own country.

When *And God Created Woman* was shown in first-run houses on the Champs-Elysées, the film which had cost a hundred and forty million francs, brought in less than sixty. Receipts in the USA have come to $4,000,000, the equivalent of the sale of 2,500 Dauphines. BB now deserves to be considered an export product as important as Renault automobiles.

She is the new idol of American youth. She ranks as a great international star. Nevertheless, her fellow-countrymen continue to shy away from her. Not a week goes by without articles in the press telling all about her recent moods and love affairs or offering a new interpretation of her personality, but half of these articles and gossip items seethe with spite. Brigitte receives three hundred fan letters a day, from boys and girls alike, and every day indignant mothers write to newspaper editors and religious and civil authorities to protest against her existence. When three young ne'er-do-wells of reputable families murdered a sleeping old man in a train at Angers, the Parent-Teachers' Association denounced BB to M. Chatenay, the deputy-mayor of the city. It was *she*, they said, who was really responsible for the crime. *And God Created Woman* had been shown in Angers; the young people had been immediately perverted. I am not surprised that professional moralists in all countries, even the USA, have tried to have her films banned. It is no new thing for high-minded folk to identify the flesh with sin and to dream of making a bonfire of works of art, books and films that depict it complacently or frankly.

But this official prudery does not explain the French public's very peculiar hostility to BB. Martine Carol also undressed rather generously in her hit films, and nobody reproached her, whereas almost everyone is ready to regard BB as a very monument to immorality. Why does this character, fabricated by Marc Allegret and particularly by Vadim, arouse such animosity?

If we want to understand what BB represents, it is not important to know what the young woman named Brigitte Bardot is really like. Her admirers and detractors are concerned with the imaginary creature they see on the screen through a tremendous cloud of ballyhoo. In so far as she is exposed to the public gaze, her legend has been fed by her private life no less than by her film roles. This legend conforms to a very old myth that Vadim tried to rejuvenate. He invented a resolutely modern version of "the eternal female" and thereby launched a new type of eroticism. It is this novelty that entices some people and shocks others.

Love can resist familiarity; eroticism cannot. Its role in the films dwindled considerably when social differences between the two sexes diminished. Between 1930 and 1940 it gave way to romanticism and sentimentality. The vamp was replaced by the girl friend, of whom Jean Arthur was the most perfect type. However, when in 1947 the cinema was threatened with a serious crisis, film-makers returned to eroticism in an effort to win back the public's affection. In an age when woman drives a car and speculates on the stock exchange, an age in which she unceremoniously displays her nudity on public beaches, any attempt to revive the vamp and her mystery was out of the question. The films tried to appeal, in a cruder way, to the male's response to feminine curves. Stars were appreciated for the obviousness of their physical charms rather than for their passionate or languorous gaze. Marilyn Monroe, Sophia Loren and Lollobrigida are ample proof of the fact that the full-blown woman has not lost her power over men. However, the dream-merchants were also moving in other directions. With Audrey Hepburn, Françoise Arnoul, Marina Vlady, Leslie Caron and Brigitte Bardot they invented the erotic hoyden. For a part in his next film, *Dangerous Connections*, Vadim has engaged a fourteen-year-old girl. The child-woman is triumphing not only in the films. In *A View from the Bridge*, the Arthur Miller play which has been a hit in the United States and a bigger one in England and France, the heroine has just about reached the age of puberty. Nabokov's *Lolita*, which deals with the relations between a forty-year-old male and a "nymphet" of twelve, was at the top of the best-seller list in England and America for months. The adult woman now inhabits the same world as the man, but the child-woman moves in a universe which he cannot enter. The age difference re-establishes between them the distance that seems necessary to desire. At least that is what those who have created a new Eve by merging the "green fruit" and "*femme fatale*" types have pinned their hopes on. We shall see the reasons why they have not succeeded in France as well as in the United States.

Brigitte Bardot is the most perfect specimen of these ambiguous nymphs. Seen from behind, her slender, muscular, dancer's body is almost androgynous. Femininity triumphs in her delightful bosom. The long voluptuous tresses of Mélisande flow down to her shoulders, but her hair-do is that of a negligent waif. The line of her lips forms a childish pout, and at the same time those lips are very kissable. She goes about barefooted, she turns up her nose at elegant clothes, jewels, girdles, perfumes, make-up, at all artifice. Yet her walk is lascivious and a saint would sell his soul to the devil merely to watch her dance. It has often been said that her face has only one expression. It is true that the outer world is hardly reflected in it at all and that it does not reveal great inner disturbance. But that air of indifference becomes her. BB has not been marked by experience. Even if she has lived—as in *Love Is My Profession*—the lessons that life has given her are too confused for her to have learned anything from them. She is without memory, without a past, and, thanks to this ignorance, she retains the perfect innocence that is attributed to a mythical childhood.

The legend that has been built up around Brigitte Bardot by publicity has for a long time identified her with this childlike and disturbing character. Vadim presented her as "a phenomenon of nature." "She doesn't act," he said. "She exists." "That's right," confirmed BB. "The Juliette in *And God Created Woman* is exactly me. When I'm in front of the camera, I'm simply myself." Brigitte was said not to bother to use a comb, but to do up her hair with her fingers. She was said to loathe all forms of worldliness. Her interviews presented her as being natural and unpretentious. Vadim went even further. He painted her as naïve to the point of absurdity. According to him, at the age of eighteen she thought that mice laid eggs. She was moody and capricious. At the gala performance of her film, *Please, Mr Balzac*, the producer waited in vain for her to show up. At the last minute, he informed the audience that she was not coming. She was described as a creature of instinct, as yielding blindly to her impulses. She would suddenly take a dislike to the decoration of her room and then and there would pull down the hangings and start repainting the furniture. She is temperamental, changeable and unpredictable, and though she retains the limpidity of childhood, she has also preserved its mystery. A strange little creature, all in all; and this image does not depart from the traditional myth of femininity. The roles that her script-writers have offered her also have a conventional side. She appears as a force of nature, dangerous so long as she remains untamed, but it is up to the male to domesticate her. She is kind, she is good-hearted. In all her films she loves animals. If she ever makes anyone suffer, it is never deliberately. Her flightiness and slips of behaviour are excusable because she is so young and because of circumstances. Juliette had an unhappy childhood; Yvette, in *Love Is My Profession*, is a victim of society. If they go astray, it is because no one has ever shown them the right path, but a man, a real man, can lead them back to it. Juliette's young husband decides to act like a male, gives her a good sharp slap, and Juliette is all at once transformed into a happy, contrite and submissive wife. Yvette joyfully accepts her lover's demand that she be faithful and his imposing upon her a life of virtual seclusion. With a bit of luck, this experienced, middle-aged man would have brought her redemption. BB is a lost, pathetic child who needs a guide and protector. This cliché has proved its worth. It flatters masculine vanity; it reassures mature and maturing women. One may regard it as obsolete; it cannot be accused of boldness.

But the spectators do not believe in this victory of the man and of the social order so prudently suggested by the scenario—and that is precisely why Vadim's film and that of another French director, Autant-Lara, do not lapse into triviality. We may assume that the "little rascal" will settle down, but Juliette will certainly never become a model wife and mother. Ignorance and inexperience can be remedied, but BB is not only unsophisticated but dangerously sincere. The perversity of a "Baby Doll" can be handled by a psychiatrist; there are ways and means of calming the resentments of a rebellious girl and winning her over to virtue. In *The Barefoot Contessa*, Ava Gardner, despite her licentiousness, does not attack established values—she condemns her own instincts by admitting that she likes "to walk in the mud." BB is neither perverse nor rebellious nor immoral, and that is why morality does not have a chance with her. Good and evil are part of conventions to which she would not even think of bowing.

Nothing casts a sharper light on the character she plays than the wedding supper in *And God Created Woman*. Juliette immediately goes to bed with her young husband. In the middle of the banquet, she suddenly turns up in a bathrobe and, without bothering to smile or even look at the bewildered guests, she picks out from under their very noses a lobster, a chicken, fruit and bottles of wine. Disdainfully and tranquilly she goes off with the loaded tray. She cares not a rap for other people's opinion. BB does not try to scandalize. She has no demands to make; she is no more conscious of her rights than she is of her duties. She follows her inclinations. She eats when she is hungry and makes love with the same unceremonious simplicity. Desire and pleasure seem to her more convincing than precepts and conventions. She does not criticize others. She does as she pleases, and that is what is disturbing. She does not ask questions, but she brings answers whose frankness may be contagious. Moral lapses can be corrected, but how could BB be cured of that dazzling virtue—genuineness? It is her very substance. Neither blows nor fine arguments nor love can take it from her. She rejects not only hypocrisy and reprimands, but also prudence and calculation and premeditation of any kind. For her, the future is still one of those adult inventions in which she has no confidence.

"I live as if I were going to die at any moment," says Juliette. And Brigitte confides to us, "Every time I'm in love, I think it's forever." To dwell in eternity is another way of rejecting time. She professes great admiration for James Dean. We find in her, in a milder form, certain traits that attain, in his case, a tragic intensity—the fever of living, the passion for the absolute, the sense of the imminence of death. She, too, embodies—more modestly than he, but quite clearly—the credo that certain young people of our time are opposing to safe values, vain hopes and irksome constraint.

That is why a vast and traditional-minded rear guard declares that "BB springs from and expresses the immorality of an age." Decent or unwanted women could feel at ease when confronted with classical Circes who owed their power to dark secrets. These were coquettish and calculating creatures, depraved and reprobate, possessed of an evil force. From the height of their virtue, the fiancée, the wife, the great-hearted mistress and the despotic mother briskly damned these witches. But if Evil takes on the colours of innocence, they are in a fury. There is nothing of the "bad woman" about BB. Frankness and kindness can be read on her face. She is more like a Pekingese than a cat. She is neither depraved nor venal. In *Love Is My Profession* she bunches up her skirt and crudely proposes a deal to Gabin. But there is a kind of disarming candour in her cynicism. She is blooming and healthy, quietly sensual. It is impossible to see in her the touch of Satan, and for that reason she seems all the more diabolical to women who feel humiliated and threatened by her beauty.

All men are drawn to BB's seductiveness, but that does not mean they are kindly disposed towards her. The majority of Frenchmen claim that woman loses her sex appeal if she gives up her artifices. According to them, a woman in trousers chills desire. Brigitte proves to them the contrary, and they are not at all grateful to her, because they are unwilling to give up their role of lord and master. The vamp was no challenge to them in this respect. The attraction she exercised was that of a passive thing. They rushed knowingly into the magic trap; they went to their doom the way one throws oneself overboard. Freedom and full consciousness remained their right and privilege. When Marlene displayed her silk-sheathed thighs as she sang with her hoarse voice and looked about her with sultry eyes, she was staging a ceremony, she was casting a spell. BB does not cast spells; she is on the go. Her flesh does not have the abundance that, in others, symbolizes passivity. Her clothes are not fetishes and, when she strips, she is not unveiling a mystery. She is showing her body, neither more nor less, and that body rarely settles into a state of immobility. She walks, she dances, she moves about. Her eroticism is not magical, but aggressive. In the game of love, she is as much a hunter as she is a prey. The male is an object to her, just as she is to him. And that is precisely what wounds masculine pride. In the Latin countries, where men cling to the myth of "the woman as object," BB's naturalness seems to them more perverse than any possible sophistication. To spurn jewels and cosmetics and high heels and girdles is to refuse to transform oneself into a remote idol. It is to assert that one is man's fellow and equal, to recognize that between the woman and him there is mutual desire and pleasure. Brigitte is thereby akin to the heroines of Françoise Sagan, although she says she feels no affinity for them—probably because they seem to her too thoughtful.

But the male feels uncomfortable if, instead of a doll of flesh and blood, he holds in his arms a conscious being who is sizing him up. A free woman is the very contrary of a light woman. In her role of confused female, of homeless little slut, BB seems to be available to everyone. And yet, paradoxically, she is intimidating. She is not defended by rich apparel or social prestige, but there is something stubborn in her sulky face, in her sturdy body. "You realize," an average

Frenchman once said to me, "that when a man finds a woman attractive, he wants to be able to pinch her behind." A ribald gesture reduces a woman to a thing that a man can do with as he pleases without worrying about what goes on in her mind and heart and body. But BB has nothing of the "easygoing kid" about her, the quality that would allow a man to treat her with this kind of breeziness. There is nothing coarse about her. She has a kind of spontaneous dignity, something of the gravity of childhood. The difference between Brigitte's reception in the United States and in France is due partly to the fact that the American male does not have the Frenchman's taste for broad humour. He tends to display a certain respect for women. The sexual equality that BB's behaviour affirms wordlessly has been recognized in America for a long time. Nevertheless, for a number of reasons that have been frequently analyzed in America, he feels a certain antipathy to the "real woman." He regards her as an antagonist, a praying mantis, a tyrant. He abandons himself eagerly to the charms of the "nymph" in whom the formidable figure of the wife and the "Mom" is not yet apparent. In France, many women are accomplices of this feeling of superiority in which men persist. Their men prefer the servility of these adults to the haughty shamelessness of BB.

She disturbs them all the more in that, though discouraging their jollity, she nevertheless does not lend herself to idealistic sublimation. Garbo was called "The Divine;" Bardot, on the other hand, is of the earth earthy. Garbo's visage had a kind of emptiness into which anything could be projected—nothing can be read into Bardot's face. It is what it is. It has the forthright presence of reality. It is a stumbling-block to lewd fantasies and ethereal dreams alike. Most Frenchmen like to indulge in mystic flights as a change from ribaldry, and vice-versa. With BB they get nowhere. She corners them and forces them to be honest with themselves. They are obliged to recognize the crudity of their desire, the object of which is very precise—that body, those thighs, that bottom, those breasts. Most people are not bold enough to limit sexuality to itself and to recognize its power. Anyone who challenges their hypocrisy is accused of being cynical.

In a society with spiritualistic pretensions, BB appears as something deplorably materialistic and prosaic. Love has been disguised in such falsely poetic trappings that this prose seems to me healthy and restful. I approve Vadim's trying to bring eroticism down to earth. Nevertheless, there is one thing for which I blame him, and that is for having gone so far as to dehumanize it. The "human factor" has lost some of its importance in many spheres. Technical progress has relegated it to a subordinate and at times insignificant position. The implements that man uses—his dwelling, his clothes, etc.—tend towards functional rationalization. He himself is regarded by politicians, brains-trusters, publicity agents, military men and even educators, by the entire "organization world," as an object to be manipulated. In France, there is a literary school that reflects this tendency. The "young novel"—as it calls itself—is bent on creating a universe as devoid as possible of human meanings, a universe reduced to shiftings of volumes and surfaces, of light and shade, to the play of space and time; the characters and their relationships are left in the background or even dropped entirely. This quest is of interest only to a small number of initiates. It has certainly not influenced Vadim, but he, too, reduces the world, things and bodies to their immediate presence. In real life, and usually in good novels and films, individuals are not defined only by their sexuality. Each has a history, and his or her eroticism is involved in a certain situation. It may even be that the situation creates it. In *African Queen*, neither Humphrey Bogart nor Katharine Hepburn, who are presented as aged and worn, arouses desire beforehand. Yet when Bogart puts his hand on Katharine's shoulder for the first time, his gesture unleashes an intense erotic emotion. The spectators identify themselves with the man, or the woman, and the two characters are transfigured by the feeling that each inspires in the other. But when the hero and heroine are young and handsome, the more the audience is involved in their history, the more it feels their charm. It must therefore take an interest in it. For example, in Ingmar Bergman's *Sommarlek*, the idyll which is related is not set in the past arbitrarily. As a result of this device, we witness the revels of two particular adolescents. The young woman, who has moved us and aroused our interest, evokes her youthful happiness. She appears before us, at the age of sixteen, already weighed down with her entire future. The landscape about her is not a mere setting, but a medium of communication between her and us. We see it with her eyes. Through the lapping of the waters and the clearness of the nocturnal sky, we merge with her. All her emotions become ours, and emotion sweeps away shame. The "summer trifling"—caresses, embraces, words—that Bergman presents is far more "amoral" than Juliette's adventures in *And God Created Woman*. The two lovers have barely emerged from childhood. The idea of marriage or of sin does not occur to them. They embrace with hesitant eagerness and unchaste naïveté. Their daring and jubilation triumphantly defy what is called virtue. The spectator does not dream of being shocked because he experiences with them their poignant happiness. When I saw *And God Created Woman*, people laughed during scenes. They laughed because Vadim does not appeal to our complicity. He "de-situates" sexuality, and the spectators become voyeurs because they are unable to project themselves on the screen. This partially justifies their uneasiness. The ravishing young woman whom they surprise, at the beginning of the film, in the act of exposing her nakedness to the sun, is no one, an anonymous body. As the film goes on, she does not succeed in becoming someone. Nonchalantly combining convention and provocation, Vadim does not deign to lure the audience into the trap of a convincing story. The characters are treated allusively; that of BB is loaded with too many intentions for anyone to believe in its reality. And the town of St-Tropez is merely a setting that has no intimate connection with the lives of the main characters. It has no effect on the spectator. In *Sommarlek*, the world exists; it reflects for the young lovers their confusion, their anxious desire, their joy. An innocent outing in a boat is as erotically meaningful as the passionate night preceding it and the one to follow. In Vadim's film, the world is absent. Against a background of fake colours he flashes a number of "high spots" in which all the sensuality of the film is concentrated: a strip-tease, passionate love-making, a mambo sequence. This discontinuity heightens the aggressive character of BB's femininity. The audience is not carried away once and for all into an imaginary universe. It witnesses without much conviction, an adventure which does not excite it and which is broken up by "numbers" in which everything is so contrived as to keep it on tenterhooks. It protects itself by snickering. A critic has written that BB's sexuality was too "cerebral" to move a Latin audience. This amounts to making BB responsible for Vadim's style, an analytical and consequently abstract style that, as I have said, puts the spectator in the position of a voyeur. The consenting voyeur who feeds on "blue films" and "peep shows," seeks gratifications other than the visual. The spectator who is a voyeur in spite of himself reacts with annoyance, for it is no fun to witness a hot performance cold-bloodedly. When BB dances her famous mambo, no one believes in Juliette. It is BB who is exhibiting herself. She is as alone on the screen as the strip-tease artist is alone on the stage. She offers herself directly to each spectator. But the offer is deceptive, for as the spectators watch her, they are fully aware that this beautiful young woman is famous, rich, adulated and completely inaccessible. It is not surprising that they take her for a slut and that they take revenge on her by running her down.

But reproaches of this kind cannot be levelled against *Love Is My Profession*, the film in which BB has displayed the most talent. Autant-Lara's direction, Pierre Bost's and Aurench's scenario and dialogue and Gabin's performance all combine to grip the spectator. In this context, BB gives her most convincing performance. But her moral reputation is none the better for it. The film has aroused furious protests; actually it attacks the social order much more bitingly than any of her early ones. The "amoralism" of Yvette, the heroine, is radical. She prostitutes herself with indifference, organizes a hold-up and has no hesitation about striking an old man. She proposes to a great lawyer a deal that threatens to dishonour him. She gives herself to him without love. Then she falls in love with him, deceives him and artlessly keeps him informed of her infidelities. She confesses to him that she has had several abortions. However, although the scenario indicates for a moment the possibility of a conversion, she is not presented as being unconscious of the nature of her behaviour and capable of being won over to Good, as defined by respectable folk. Truth is on her side. Never does she fake her feelings. She never compromises with what seems to her to be obviously true. Her genuineness is so contagious that she wins over her lover, the old unethical lawyer. Yvette awakens whatever sincerity and dynamism still remain in him. The authors of this film took over the character created by Vadim, but they charged it with a much more subversive meaning: purity is not possible in our corrupt society except for those who have rejected it or who deliberately cut themselves off from it.

But this character is now in the process of evolving. BB has probably been convinced that in France nonconformity is on the way out. Vadim is accused of having distorted her image—which is certainly not untrue. People who know BB speak of her amiable disposition, her kindness and her youthful freshness. She is neither silly nor scatter-brained, and her naturalness is not an act. It is nevertheless striking that recent articles which pretend to reveal the "real BB," "BB seen through the keyhole," "the truth about BB," mention only her edifying traits of character. Brigitte, we are told again and again, is just a simple girl. She loves animals and adores her mother. She is devoted to her friends, she suffers from the hostility she arouses, she repents of her caprices, she means to mend her ways. There are excuses for her lapses: fame and fortune came too suddenly, they turned her head, but she is coming to her senses. In short, we are witnessing a veritable rehabilitation, which in recent weeks has gone very far. Definitive redemption, for a star, comes with marriage and motherhood.

Brigitte speaks only faintly about getting married. On the other hand, she often declares enthusiastically that she adores the country and dreams of taking up farming.[1] In France, love of cows is regarded as a token of high morality. Gabin is sure of winning the public's sympathy when he declares that "a cow is more substantial than glory." Stars are photographed as much as possible in the act of feeding their chickens or digging in their gardens. This passion for the soil is appropriate to the reasonable bourgeoise that, as we are assured, Brigitte is bent on becoming. She has always known the price of things and has always gone over the cook's accounts. She follows the stock market closely and gives her broker well-informed instructions. During an official luncheon, she is said to have dazzled the director of the Bank of France with her knowledge. To know how to place one's money is a supreme virtue in the eyes of the French

[1] Written before Mademoiselle Bardot became Madame Charrier.

bourgeoisie. A particularly imaginative journalist has gone so far as to inform his readers that Brigitte has such a passion for the absolute that she may enter upon the paths of mysticism. Wife and mother, farmerette, businesswoman, Carmelite nun, BB has a choice of any one of these exemplary futures. But one thing is certain: on the screen she is already beginning to convert. In her next film, *Babette Goes to War*,[2] she will play a heroine of the Resistance. Her charming body will be hidden from us by a uniform and sober attire. "I want everyone under sixteen to be able to come and see me," she has been made to say. The film will end with a military parade in which Babette acclaims General de Gaulle.

Is the metamorphosis definitive? If so, there will still be a number of people who will be sorry. Exactly who? A lot of young people belong to the old guard, and there are older ones who prefer truth to tradition. It would be simple-minded to think that there is a conflict of two generations regarding BB. The conflict that does exist is between those who want *mores* to be fixed once and for all and those who demand that they evolve. To say that "BB embodies the immorality of an age" means that the character she has created challenges certain taboos accepted by the preceding age, particularly those which denied women sexual autonomy. In France, there is still a great deal of emphasis, officially, on women's dependence upon men. The Americans, who are actually far from having achieved sexual equality in all spheres, but who grant it theoretically, have seen nothing scandalous in the emancipation symbolized by BB. But it is, more than anything else, her frankness that disturbs most of the public and that delights the Americans. "I want there to be no hypocrisy, no nonsense about love," BB once said. The debunking of love and eroticism is an undertaking that has wider implications than one might think. As soon as a single myth is touched, all myths are in danger. A sincere gaze, however limited its range, is a fire that may spread and reduce to ashes all the shoddy disguises that camouflage reality. Children are forever asking why, why not. They are told to be silent. Brigitte's eyes, her smile, her presence, impel one to ask oneself why, why not. Are they going to hush up the questions she raised without a word? Will she, too, agree to talk lying twaddle? Perhaps the hatred she has aroused will calm down, but she will no longer represent anything for anyone. I hope that she will not resign herself to insignificance in order to gain popularity. I hope she will mature, but not change.

---

[2] Written before this film was released.

CHAPTER 28
LAURA MULVEY

Laura Mulvey (b. 1941) is a British feminist film theorist, and presently Professor of Film Studies at Birkbeck, University of London. Her work is widely read by philosophers of film, and she is perhaps most renowned for contributing to the movement in film studies toward psychoanalytic theory. Her single most famous work on film is the essay, "Visual Pleasure and Narrative Cinema," which is included here. It was originally published in English in Screen *in 1973.*

Mulvey takes as her starting point an examination of the pleasure we take in watching movies, and in particular, the pleasure we find in seeing the images presented in film themselves. She notes that much of the pleasure in cinematic looking has its origin in the cinematic representation of sexual difference: the ways in which women, specifically, are represented in film. Mulvey argues that we can see a sort of paradox in the phallocentric presentation of women in film: on the one hand, of course, phallocentrism marginalizes women. But at the same time, she notes, phallocentrism depends upon the image of woman as castrated—woman as essentially a lack, an absence or wound, in contrast to man—and thus, has at its center an image of woman. The dominant understanding of woman in Western culture has long been patriarchal, and Hollywood movies always reinforce the dominant system of values. Such films are in fact highly manipulative, structuring films so as to produce erotic pleasure in the presentation of the image of woman. In contrast to Hollywood movies, however, Mulvey suggests that alternative cinema might present the possibility of a cinema that is radical both aesthetically and politically.

Mulvey discusses scopophilia, the pleasure taken in looking, and notes that is a sort of pleasure based in the objectification of the other (the looked-at). Cinema is a voyeuristic medium, which aims to give the spectator the illusion that he or she is looking in on a private world. While the spectator might feel some urge to reveal him- or herself, an exhibitionist impulse, the cinematic context prevents the expression of that urge—and it is instead repressed, and ultimately projected onto the performer in the film. This dynamic tends to rigidify the distinction between looker and looked-at, subject and object, spectator and image. Drawing quite straightforwardly from the psychoanalytic tradition here, Mulvey reiterates a comparison made by earlier Lacanian theorists of film, that there is some sort of correspondence between the spectator in the cinema and Lacan's notion of the mirror stage of the formation of the subject. For Mulvey, the pleasure of looking in the context of cinema takes on two contradictory aspects: first, there is the scopophilic, mentioned above, which expresses the sexual instincts in the objectification of the image of a woman as a potential means to the gratification of desire; and second, there is the narcissistic, the ego libido, the identification with the screen (whether the image or the perspective on that image, the camera). Woman as image in film can be an object of desire for the spectator, but she can also be a threat, when the spectator identifies with her, seeing therein subjectivity within the image of what would otherwise be merely objectified—and thus finding in the image of woman the possibility of demasculinized subjectivity, or castration. As is undoubtedly obvious, the subject of cinematic looking—the spectator—is presumed to be heterosexual and masculine or male-

identified, a presumption on the basis of which Mulvey and other feminist film theorists take both film studies and psychoanalytic theory rightly to task.

The split in the pleasure taken in watching the film by the spectator, between scopophilia and narcissism, gives to cinema an entrenched bifurcation between the active (male) and the passive (female), between subjectivity and objectification. This instantiates a paradox at the very basis of commercial cinema: women are on the one hand indispensable to the film narrative; there are in fact very few films lacking a "leading lady." At the same time, however, on the other hand, whenever the image of woman appears on the screen, the forward motion of the narrative—the action—freezes, paralyzed in erotic contemplation of the objectified woman. The importance of woman for the traditional film is not inherent to the female character or even to the events of the story: rather, her importance is derived entirely from the effect she has on the male protagonist, how she makes him feel and how he acts as a result of those feelings. Women in film, then, are doubly objectified, by the other characters within the world of the film, and then by the spectators in the movie theater. For both sorts of cinematic subjects (protagonist and spectator), however, woman remains ever an object, a spectacle.

That spectacle has a great deal of erotic potential to slow, stop, or derail the movement of the plot, which is why the commercial film must find some way to move beyond the spectacular woman, to incorporate her into the narrative. As the narrative is driven by a heterosexually male-identified perspective, then, resolution of the problem of the image of woman in film is typically by means of the protagonist's ultimate possession of the female character, defusing both the promise (of the fulfillment of erotic desire) and the threat (of castration) she poses. She is destroyed by the hero, or she is married to him. In both of these cases, Mulvey argues that the film has demystified the woman by way of punishment, salvation, or both—and this resolves the problem in the (sadistic) satisfaction of the spectator's voyeuristic impulse. Alternatively, however, a film might fetishize woman instead—as, Mulvey notes, is characteristic of the films of Alfred Hitchcock and Josef von Sternberg. Neither approach to the objectification of women in Western culture—sadism or fetishism—is new to film, but film does offer for the first time the opportunity to combine the two approaches, the two looks, in a single work. Mulvey does not think, however, that cinema is condemned to such sexism: there is the potential in the medium to undermine both the voyeuristic/sadistic and fetishizing impulses. With regard to the former, she suggests that filmmakers make the camera evident in the film itself, which undermines the voyeuristic illusion of access to a private world. And with regard to the latter, Mulvey suggests that the film attempt to engage the audience dialectically—presenting woman to be seen in the film not only as object, but as the complex synthesis of subject and object all real human beings actually are.

Filmography

- ***Morocco*** (USA, 1930). *Directed by* Josef von Sternberg. *Produced by* Hector Turnbull. *Written by* Jules Furthman. *Starring* Gary Cooper, Marlene Dietrich, *and* Adolph Menjou.
- ***Dishonored*** (USA, 1931). *Directed and Written by* Josef von Sternberg. *Produced by* Paramount Pictures. *Starring* Marlene Dietrich *and* Victor McLaglen.
- ***Only Angels Have Wings*** (USA, 1939). *Directed and Produced by* Howard Hawks. *Written by* Jules Furthman. *Starring* Cary Grant, Jean Arthur, Thomas Mitchell, *and* Rita Hayworth.

- ***To Have and Have Not*** (USA, 1944). *Directed by* Howard Hawks. *Produced by* Howard Hawks *and* Jack L. Warner. *Written by* Jules Furthman *and* William Faulkner. *Starring* Humphrey Bogart, Walter Brennan, *and* Lauren Bacall.
- ***Rear Window*** (USA, 1954). *Directed and Produced by* Alfred Hitchcock. *Written by* John Michael Hayes. *Starring* James Stewart, Grace Kelly, Wendell Corey, *and* Thelma Ritter.
- ***River of No Return*** (USA, 1954). *Directed by* Otto Preminger. *Produced by* Stanley Rubin. *Written by* Frank Fenton. *Starring* Robert Mitchum *and* Marilyn Monroe.
- ***The Revolt of Mamie Stover*** (USA, 1956). *Directed by* Raoul Walsh. *Produced by* Buddy Adler. *Written by* Sydney Boehm. *Starring* Jane Russell, Richard Egan, Joan Leslie, *and* Agnes Moorehead.
- ***Vertigo*** (USA, 1958). *Directed and Produced by* Alfred Hitchcock. *Written by* Alec Coppel *and* Samuel Taylor. *Starring* James Stewart *and* Kim Novak.
- ***Marnie*** (USA, 1964). *Directed and Produced by* Alfred Hitchcock. *Written by* Jay Presson Allen. *Starring* Tippi Hedren *and* Sean Connery.

VISUAL PLEASURE AND NARRATIVE CINEMA

I Introduction

(a) A political use of psychoanalysis

This paper intends to use psychoanalysis to discover where and how the fascination of film is reinforced by pre-existing patterns of fascination already at work within the individual subject and the social formations that have moulded him. It takes as its starting-point the way film reflects, reveals and even plays on the straight, socially established interpretation of sexual difference which controls images, erotic ways of looking and spectacle. It is helpful to understand what the cinema has been, how its magic has worked in the past, while attempting a theory and a practice which will challenge this cinema of the past. Psychoanalytic theory is thus appropriated here as a political weapon, demonstrating the way the unconscious of patriarchal society has structured film form.

The paradox of phallocentrism in all its manifestations is that it depends on the image of the castrated woman to give order and meaning to its world. An idea of woman stands as linchpin to the system: it is her lack that produces the phallus as a symbolic presence, it is her desire to make good the lack that the phallus signifies. Recent writing in *Screen* about psychoanalysis and the cinema has not sufficiently brought out the importance of the representation of the female form in a symbolic order in which, in the last resort, it speaks castration and nothing else. To summarise briefly: the function of woman in forming the patriarchal unconscious is twofold: she firstly symbolises the castration threat by her real lack of a penis and secondly thereby raises her child into the symbolic. Once this has been achieved, her meaning in the process is at an end. It does not last into the world of law and language except as a memory, which oscillates between memory of maternal plenitude and memory of lack. Both are posited on nature (or on anatomy in Freud's famous phrase). Woman's desire is subjugated to her image as bearer of the bleeding wound; she can exist only in relation to castration and cannot transcend it. She turns her child into the signifier of her own desire to possess a penis (the condition, she imagines, of entry into the symbolic). Either she must gracefully give way to the word, the name of the father and the law, or else struggle to keep her child down with her in the half-light of the imaginary. Woman then stands in patriarchal culture as a signifier for the male other, bound by a symbolic order in which man can live out his fantasies and obsessions through linguistic command by imposing them on the silent image of woman still tied to her place as bearer, not maker, of meaning.

There is an obvious interest in this analysis for feminists, a beauty in its exact rendering of the frustration experienced under the phallocentric order. It gets us nearer to the roots of our oppression, it brings closer an articulation of the problem, it faces us with the ultimate challenge: how to fight the unconscious structured like a language (formed critically at the moment of arrival of language) while still caught within the language of the patriarchy? There is no way in which we can produce an alternative out of the blue, but we can begin to make a break by examining patriarchy with the tools it provides, of which psychoanalysis is not the only but an important one. We are still separated by a great gap from important issues for the female unconscious which are scarcely relevant to phallocentric theory: the sexing of the female infant and her relationship to the symbolic, the sexually mature woman as non-mother, maternity outside the signification of the phallus, the vagina. But, at this point, psychoanalytic theory as it now stands can at least advance our understanding of the *status quo*, of the patriarchal order in which we are caught.

(b) Destruction of pleasure as a radical weapon

As an advanced representation system, the cinema poses questions about the ways the unconscious (formed by the dominant order) structures ways of seeing and pleasure in looking. Cinema has changed over the last few decades. It is no longer the monolithic system based on large capital investment exemplified at its best by Hollywood in the 1930s, 1940s and 1950s. Technological advances (16 mm and so on) have changed the economic conditions of cinematic production, which can now be artisanal as well as capitalist. Thus it has been possible for an alternative cinema to develop. However self-conscious and ironic Hollywood managed to be, it always restricted itself to a formal *mise en scene* reflecting the dominant ideological concept of the cinema. The alternative cinema provides a space for the birth of a cinema which is radical in both a political and an aesthetic sense and challenges the basic assumptions of the mainstream film. This is not to reject the latter moralistically, but to highlight the ways in which its formal preoccupations reflect the psychical obsessions of the society which produced it and, further, to stress that the alternative cinema must start specifically by reacting against these obsessions and assumptions. A politically and aesthetically avant-garde cinema is now possible, but it can still only exist as a counterpoint.

The magic of the Hollywood style at its best (and of all the cinema which fell within its sphere of influence) arose, not exclusively, but in one important aspect, from its skilled and satisfying manipulation of visual pleasure. Unchallenged, mainstream film coded the erotic into the language of the dominant patriarchal order. In the highly developed Hollywood cinema it was only through these codes that the alienated subject, torn in his imaginary memory by a sense of loss, by the terror of potential lack in fantasy, came near to finding a glimpse of satisfaction: through its formal beauty and its play on his own formative obsessions. This article will discuss the interweaving of that erotic pleasure in film, its meaning and, in particular, the central place of the image of woman. It is said that analysing pleasure, or beauty, destroys it. That is the intention of this article. The satisfaction and reinforcement of the ego that represent the high point of film history hitherto must be attacked. Not in favour of a reconstructed new pleasure, which cannot exist in the abstract, nor of intellectualised unpleasure, but to make way for a total negation of the ease and plenitude of the narrative fiction film. The alternative is the thrill that comes from leaving the past behind without simply rejecting it, transcending outworn or oppressive forms, and daring to break with normal pleasurable expectations in order to conceive a new language of desire.

II Pleasure in looking/fascination with the human form

A The cinema offers a number of possible pleasures. One is scopophilia (pleasure in looking). There are circumstances in which looking itself is a source of pleasure, just as, in the reverse formation, there is pleasure in being looked at. Originally, in his *Three Essays on Sexuality*, Freud isolated scopophilia as one of the component instincts of sexuality which exist as drives quite independently of the erotogenic zones. At this point he associated scopophilia with taking other people as objects, subjecting them to a controlling and curious gaze. His particular examples centre on the voyeuristic activities of children, their desire to see and make sure of the private and forbidden (curiosity about other people's genital and bodily functions, about the presence or absence of the penis and, retrospectively, about the primal scene). In this analysis scopophilia is essentially active. (Later, in "Instincts and Their Vicissitudes," Freud developed his theory of scopophilia further, attaching it initially to pre-genital auto-eroticism, after which, by analogy, the pleasure of the look is transferred to others. There is a close working here of the relationship between the active instinct and its further development in a narcissistic form.) Although the instinct is modified by other factors, in particular the constitution of the ego, it continues to exist as the erotic basis for pleasure in looking at another person as object. At the extreme, it can become fixated into a perversion, producing obsessive voyeurs and Peeping Toms whose only sexual satisfaction can come from watching, in an active controlling sense, an objectified other.

At first glance, the cinema would seem to be remote from the undercover world of the surreptitious observation of an unknowing and unwilling victim. What is seen on the screen is so manifestly shown. But the mass of mainstream film, and the conventions within which it has consciously evolved, portray a hermetically sealed world which unwinds magically, indifferent to the presence of the audience, producing for them a sense of separation and playing on their voyeuristic fantasy. Moreover the extreme contrast between the darkness in the auditorium (which also isolates the spectators from one another) and the brilliance of the shifting patterns of light and shade on the screen helps to promote the illusion of voyeuristic separation. Although the film is really being shown, is there to be seen, conditions of screening and narrative conventions give the spectator an illusion of looking in on a private world. Among other things, the position of the spectators in the cinema is blatantly one of repression of their exhibitionism and projection of the repressed desire onto the performer.

B The cinema satisfies a primordial wish for pleasurable looking, but it also goes further, developing scopophilia in its narcissistic aspect. The conventions of mainstream film focus attention on the human form. Scale, space, stories are all anthropomorphic. Here, curiosity and the wish to look intermingle with a fascination with likeness and recognition: the human face, the human body, the relationship between the human form and its surroundings, the visible presence of the person in the world. Jacques Lacan has described how the moment when a child recognises its own image in the mirror is crucial for the constitution of the ego. Several aspects of this analysis are relevant here. The mirror phase occurs at a time when children's physical ambitions outstrip their motor capacity, with the result that their recognition of themselves is joyous in that they imagine their mirror image to be more complete, more perfect than they experience in their own body. Recognition is thus overlaid with misrecognition: the image recognised is conceived as the reflected body of the self, but its misrecognition as superior projects this body outside itself as an ideal ego, the alienated subject which, re-introjected as an ego ideal, prepares the way for identification with others in the future. This mirror moment predates language for the child.

Important for this article is the fact that it is an image that constitutes the matrix of the imaginary, of recognition/misrecognition and identification, and hence of the first articulation of the I, of subjectivity. This is a moment when an older fascination with looking (at the mother's face, for an obvious example) collides with the initial inklings of self-awareness. Hence it is the birth of the long love affair/despair between image and self-image which has found such intensity of expression in film and such joyous recognition in the cinema audience. Quite apart from the extraneous similarities between screen and mirror (the framing of the human form in its surroundings, for instance), the cinema has structures of fascination strong enough to allow temporary loss of ego while simultaneously reinforcing it. The sense of forgetting the world as the ego has come to perceive it (I forgot who I am and where I was) is nostalgically reminiscent of that pre-subjective moment of image recognition. While at the same time, the cinema has distinguished itself in the production of ego ideals, through the star system for instance. Stars provide a focus or centre both to screen space and screen story where they act out a complex process of likeness and difference (the glamorous impersonates the ordinary).

C Sections A and B have set out two contradictory aspects of the pleasurable structures of looking in the conventional cinematic situation. The first, scopophilic, arises from pleasure in using another person as an object of sexual stimulation through sight. The second, developed through narcissism and the constitution of the ego, comes from identification with the image seen. Thus, in film terms, one implies a separation of the erotic identity of the subject from the object on the screen (active scopophilia), the other demands identification of the ego with the object on the screen through the spectator's fascination with and recognition of his like. The first is a function of the sexual instincts, the second of ego libido. This dichotomy was crucial for Freud. Although he saw the two as interacting and overlaying each other, the tension between instinctual drives and self-preservation polarises in terms of pleasure. But both are formative structures, mechanisms without intrinsic meaning. In themselves they have no signification, unless attached to an idealisation. Both pursue aims in indifference to perceptual reality, and motivate eroticised phantasmagoria that affect the subject's perception of the world to make a mockery of empirical objectivity.

During its history, the cinema seems to have evolved a particular illusion of reality in which this contradiction between libido and ego has found a beautifully complementary fantasy world. In *reality* the fantasy world of the screen is subject to the law which produces it. Sexual instincts and identification processes have a meaning within the symbolic order which articulates desire. Desire, born with language, allows the possibility of transcending the instinctual and the imaginary, but its point of reference continually returns to the traumatic moment of its birth: the castration complex. Hence the look, pleasurable in form, can be threatening in content, and it is woman as representation/image that crystallises this paradox.

III Woman as image, man as bearer of the look

A In a world ordered by sexual imbalance, pleasure in looking has been split between active/male and passive/female. The determining male gaze projects its fantasy onto the female figure, which is styled accordingly. In their traditional exhibitionist role women are simultaneously looked at and displayed, with their appearance coded for strong visual and erotic impact so that they can be said to connote *to-be-looked-at-ness*. Woman displayed as sexual object is the *leitmotif* of erotic spectacle: from pin-ups to strip-tease, from Ziegfeld to Busby Berkeley, she holds the look, and plays to and signifies male desire. Mainstream film neatly combines spectacle and narrative. (Note, however, how in the musical song-and-dance numbers interrupt the flow of the diegesis.) The presence of woman is an indispensable element of spectacle in normal narrative film, yet her visual presence tends to work against the development of a story-line, to freeze the flow of action in moments of erotic contemplation. This alien presence then has to be integrated into cohesion with the narrative. As Budd Boetticher has put it:

> What counts is what the heroine provokes, or rather what she represents. She is the one, or rather the love or fear she inspires in the hero, or else the concern he feels for her, who makes him act the way he does. In herself the woman has not the slightest importance.

(A recent tendency in narrative film has been to dispense with this problem altogether; hence the development of what Molly Haskell has called the "buddy movie," in which the active homosexual eroticism of the central male figures can carry the story without distraction.) Traditionally, the woman displayed has functioned on two levels: as erotic object for the characters within the screen story, and as erotic object for the spectator within the auditorium, with a shifting tension between the looks on either side of the screen. For instance, the device of the show-girl allows the two looks to be unified technically without any apparent break in the diegesis. A woman performs within the narrative; the gaze of the spectator and that of the male characters in the film are neatly combined without breaking narrative verisimilitude. For a moment the sexual impact of the performing woman takes the film into a no man's land outside its own time and space. Thus Marilyn Monroe's first appearance in *The River of No Return* and Lauren Bacall's songs in *To Have and Have Not*. Similarly, conventional close-ups of legs (Dietrich, for instance) or a face (Garbo) integrate into the narrative a different mode of eroticism. One part of a fragmented body destroys the Renaissance space, the illusion of depth demanded by the narrative; it gives flatness, the quality of a cut-out or icon, rather than verisimilitude, to the screen.

B An active/passive heterosexual division of labour has similarly controlled narrative structure. According to the principles of the ruling ideology and the psychical structures that back it up, the male figure cannot bear the burden of sexual objectification. Man is reluctant to gaze at his exhibitionist like. Hence the split between spectacle and narrative supports the man's role as the active one of advancing the story, making things happen. The man controls the film fantasy and also emerges as the representative of power in a further sense: as the bearer of the look of the spectator, transferring it behind the screen to neutralise the extra-diegetic tendencies represented by woman as spectacle. This is made possible through the processes set in motion by structuring the film around a main controlling figure with whom the spectator can identify. As the spectator identifies with the main male protagonist, he projects his look onto that of his like, his screen surrogate, so that the power of the male protagonist as he controls events coincides with the active power of the erotic look, both giving a satisfying sense of omnipotence. A male movie star's glamorous characteristics are thus not those of the erotic object of the gaze, but those of the more perfect, more complete, more powerful ideal ego conceived in the original moment of recognition in front of the mirror. The character in the story can make things happen and control events better than the subject/spectator, just as the image in the mirror was more in control of motor co-ordination.

In contrast to woman as icon, the active male figure (the ego ideal of the identification process) demands a three-dimensional space corresponding to that of the mirror recognition, in which the alienated subject internalised his own representation of his imaginary existence. He is a figure in a landscape. Here the function of film is to reproduce as accurately as possible the so-called natural conditions of human perception. Camera technology (as exemplified by deep focus in particular) and camera movements (determined by the action of the protagonist), combined with invisible editing (demanded by realism), all tend to blur the limits of screen space. The male protagonist is free to command the stage, a stage of spatial illusion in which he articulates the look and creates the action. (There are films with a woman as main protagonist, of course. To analyse this phenomenon seriously here would take me too far afield. Pam Cook and Claire Johnston's study of *The Revolt of Mamie Stover* in Phil Hardy (ed.), *Raoul Walsh* (Edinburgh, 1974), shows in a striking case how the strength of this female protagonist is more apparent than real.)

C1 Sections III A and B have set out a tension between a mode of representation of woman in film and conventions surrounding the diegesis. Each is associated with a look: that of the spectator in direct scopophilic contact with the female form displayed for his enjoyment (connoting male fantasy) and that of the spectator fascinated with the image of his like set in an illusion of natural space, and through him gaining control and possession of the woman within the diegesis. (This tension and the shift from one pole to the other can structure a single text. Thus both in *Only Angels Have Wings* and in *To Have and Have Not*, the film opens with the woman as object of the combined gaze of spectator and all the male protagonists of the film. She is isolated, glamorous, on display, sexualised. But as the narrative progresses she falls in love with the main male protagonist and becomes his property, losing her outward glamorous characteristics, her generalised sexuality, her show-girl connotations; her eroticism is subject to the male star alone. By means of identification with him, through participation in his power, the spectator can indirectly possess her too.)

But in psychoanalytic terms, the female figure poses a deeper problem. She also connotes something that the look continually circles around but disavows: her lack of a penis, implying a threat of castration and hence unpleasure. Ultimately, the meaning of woman is sexual difference, the visually ascertainable absence of the penis, the material evidence on which is based the castration complex essential for the organisation of entrance to the symbolic order and the law of the father. Thus the woman as icon, displayed for the gaze and enjoyment of men, the active controllers of the look, always threatens to evoke the anxiety it originally signified. The male unconscious has two avenues of escape from this castration anxiety: preoccupation with the re-enactment of the original trauma (investigating the woman, demystifying her mystery), counterbalanced by the devaluation, punishment or saving of the guilty object (an avenue typified by the concerns of the *film noir*); or else complete disavowal of castration by the substitution of a fetish object or turning the represented figure itself into a fetish so that it becomes reassuring rather than dangerous (hence overvaluation, the cult of the female star).

This second avenue, fetishistic scopophilia, builds up the physical beauty of the object, transforming it into something satisfying in itself. The first avenue, voyeurism, on the contrary, has associations with sadism: pleasure lies in ascertaining guilt (immediately associated with castration), asserting control and subjugating the guilty person through punishment or forgiveness. This sadistic side fits in well with narrative. Sadism demands a story, depends on making something happen, forcing a change in another person, a battle of will and strength, victory/defeat, all occurring in a linear time with a beginning and an end. Fetishistic scopophilia, on the other hand, can exist outside linear time as the erotic instinct is focused on the look alone. These contradictions and ambiguities can be illustrated more simply by using works by Hitchcock and Sternberg, both of whom take the look almost as the content or subject matter of many of their films. Hitchcock is the more complex, as he uses both mechanisms. Sternberg's work, on the other hand, provides many pure examples of fetishistic scopophilia.

C2 Sternberg once said he would welcome his films being projected upside-down so that story and character involvement would not interfere with the spectator's undiluted appreciation of the screen image. This statement is revealing but ingenuous: ingenuous in that his films do demand that the figure of the woman (Dietrich, in the cycle of films with her, as the ultimate example) should be identifiable; but revealing in that it emphasises the fact that for him the pictorial space enclosed by the frame is paramount, rather than narrative or identification processes. While Hitchcock goes into the investigative side of voyeurism, Sternberg produces the ultimate fetish, taking it to the point where the powerful look of the male protagonist (characteristic of traditional narrative film) is broken in favour of the image in direct erotic rapport with the spectator. The beauty of the woman as object and the screen space coalesce; she is no longer the bearer of guilt but a perfect product, whose body, stylised and fragmented by close-ups, is the content of the film and the direct recipient of the spectator's look.

Sternberg plays down the illusion of screen depth; his screen tends to be one-dimensional, as light and shade, lace, steam, foliage, net, streamers and so on reduce the visual field. There is little or no mediation of the look through the eyes of the main male protagonist. On the contrary, shadowy presences like La Bessière in *Morocco* act as surrogates for the director, detached as they are from audience identification. Despite Sternberg's insistence that his stories are irrelevant, it is significant that they are concerned with situation, not suspense, and cyclical rather than linear time, while plot complications revolve around misunderstanding rather than conflict. The most important absence is that of the controlling male gaze within the screen scene. The high point of emotional drama in the most typical Dietrich films, her supreme moments of erotic meaning, take place in the absence of the man she loves in the fiction. There are other witnesses, other spectators watching her on the screen, their gaze is one with, not standing in for, that of the audience. At the end of *Morocco*, Tom Brown has already disappeared into the desert when Amy Jolly kicks off her gold sandals and walks after him. At the end of *Dishonoured*, Kranau is indifferent to the fate of Magda. In both cases, the erotic impact, sanctified by death, is displayed as a spectacle for the audience. The male hero misunderstands and, above all, does not see.

In Hitchcock, by contrast, the male hero does see precisely what the audience sees. However, although fascination with an image through scopophilic eroticism can be the subject of the film, it is the role of the hero to portray the contradictions and tensions experienced by the spectator. In *Vertigo* in particular, but also in *Marnie* and *Rear Window*, the look is central to the plot, oscillating between voyeurism and fetishistic fascination. Hitchcock has never concealed his interest in voyeurism, cinematic and non-cinematic. His heroes are exemplary of the symbolic order and the law—a policeman (*Vertigo*), a dominant male possessing money and power (*Marnie*)—but their erotic drives lead them into compromised situations. The power to subject another person to the will sadistically or to the gaze voyeuristically is turned onto the woman as the object of both. Power is backed by a certainty of legal right and the established guilt of the woman (evoking castration, psychoanalytically speaking). True perversion is barely concealed under a shallow mask of ideological correctness—the man is on the right side of the law, the woman on the wrong. Hitchcock's skilful use of identification processes and liberal use of subjective camera from the point of view of the male protagonist draw the spectators deeply into his position, making them share his uneasy gaze. The spectator is absorbed into a voyeuristic situation within the screen scene and diegesis, which parodies his own in the cinema.

In an analysis of *Rear Window*, Douchet takes the film as a metaphor for the cinema. Jeffries is the audience, the events in the apartment block opposite correspond to the screen. As he watches, an erotic dimension is added to his look, a central image to the drama. His girlfriend Lisa had been of little sexual interest to him, more or less a drag, so long as she remained on the spectator side. When she crosses the barrier between his room and the block opposite, their relationship is reborn erotically. He does not merely watch her through his lens, as a distant meaningful image, he also sees her as a guilty intruder exposed by a dangerous man threatening her with punishment, and thus finally giving him the opportunity to save her. Lisa's exhibitionism has already been established by her obsessive interest in dress and style, in being a passive image of visual perfection; Jeffries's voyeurism and activity have also been established through his work as a photo-journalist, a maker of stories and captor of images. However, his enforced inactivity, binding him to his seat as a spectator, puts him squarely in the fantasy position of the cinema audience.

In *Vertigo*, subjective camera predominates. Apart from one flashback from Judy's point of view, the narrative is woven around what Scottie sees or fails to see. The audience follows the growth of his erotic obsession and subsequent despair precisely from his point of view. Scottie's voyeurism is blatant: he falls in love with a woman he follows and spies on without speaking to. Its sadistic side is equally blatant: he has chosen (and freely chosen, for he had been a successful lawyer) to be a policeman, with all the attendant possibilities of pursuit and investigation. As a result, he follows, watches and falls in love with a perfect image of female beauty and mystery. Once he actually confronts her, his erotic drive is to break her down and force her *to tell* by persistent cross-questioning.

In the second part of the film, he re-enacts his obsessive involvement with the image he loved to watch secretly. He reconstructs Judy as Madeleine, forces her to conform in every detail to the actual physical appearance of his fetish. Her exhibitionism, her masochism, make her an ideal passive counterpart to Scottie's active sadistic voyeurism. She knows her part is to perform, and only by playing it through and then replaying it can she keep Scottie's erotic interest. But in the repetition he does break her down and succeeds in exposing her guilt. His curiosity wins through; she is punished.

Thus, in *Vertigo*, erotic involvement with the look boomerangs: the spectator's own fascination is revealed as illicit voyeurism as the narrative content enacts the processes and pleasures that he is himself exercising and enjoying. The Hitchcock hero here is firmly placed within the symbolic order, in narrative terms. He has all the attributes of the patriarchal superego. Hence the spectator, lulled into a false sense of security by the apparent legality of his surrogate, sees through his look and finds himself exposed as complicit, caught in the moral ambiguity of looking. Far from being simply an aside on the perversion of the police, *Vertigo* focuses on the implications of the active/looking, passive/looked-at split in terms of sexual difference and the power of the male symbolic encapsulated in the hero. Marnie, too, performs for Mark Rutland's gaze and masquerades as the perfect to-be-looked-at image. He, too, is on the side of the law until, drawn in by obsession with her guilt, her secret, he longs to see her in the act of committing a crime, make her confess and thus save her. So he, too, becomes complicit as he acts out the implications of his power. He controls money and words; he can have his cake and eat it.

IV Summary

The psychoanalytic background that has been discussed in this article is relevant to the pleasure and unpleasure offered by traditional narrative film. The scopophilic instinct (pleasure in looking at another person as an erotic object) and, in contradistinction, ego libido (forming identification processes) act as formations, mechanisms, which mould this cinema's formal attributes. The actual image of woman as (passive) raw material for the (active) gaze of man takes the argument a step further into the content and structure of representation, adding a further layer of ideological significance demanded by the patriarchal order in its favourite cinematic form—illusionistic narrative film. The argument must return again to the psychoanalytic background: women in representation can signify castration, and activate voyeuristic or fetishistic mechanisms to circumvent this threat. Although none of these interacting layers is intrinsic to film, it is only in the film form that they can reach a perfect and beautiful contradiction, thanks to the possibility in the cinema of shifting the emphasis of the look. The place of the look defines cinema, the possibility of varying it and exposing it. This is what makes cinema quite different in its voyeuristic potential from, say, striptease, theatre, shows and so on. Going far beyond highlighting a woman's to-be-looked-at-ness, cinema builds the way she is to be looked at into the spectacle itself. Playing on the tension between film as controlling the dimension of time (editing, narrative) and film as controlling the dimension of space (changes in distance, editing), cinematic codes create a gaze, a world and an object, thereby producing an illusion cut to the measure of desire. It is these cinematic codes and their relationship to formative external structures that must be broken down before mainstream film and the pleasure it provides can be challenged.

To begin with (as in ending), the voyeuristic-scopophilic look that is a crucial part of traditional filmic pleasure can itself be broken down. There are three different looks associated with cinema: that of the camera as it records the pro-filmic event, that of the audience as it watches the final product, and that of the characters at each other within the screen illusion. The conventions of narrative film deny the first two and subordinate them to the third, the conscious aim being always to eliminate intrusive camera presence and prevent a distancing awareness in the audience. Without these two absences (the material existence of the recording process, the critical reading of the spectator), fictional drama cannot achieve reality, obviousness and truth. Nevertheless, as this article has argued, the structure of looking in narrative fiction film contains a contradiction in its own premises: the female image as a castration threat constantly endangers the unity of the diegesis and bursts through the world of illusion as an intrusive, static, one-dimensional fetish. Thus the two looks materially present in time and space are obsessively subordinated to the neurotic needs of the male ego. The camera becomes the mechanism for producing an illusion of Renaissance space, flowing movements compatible with the human eye, an ideology of representation that revolves around the perception of the subject; the camera's look is disavowed in order to create a convincing world in which the spectator's surrogate can perform with verisimilitude. Simultaneously, the look of the audience is denied an intrinsic force: as soon as fetishistic representation of the female image threatens to break the spell of illusion, and the erotic image on the screen appears directly (without mediation) to the spectator, the fact of fetishisation, concealing as it does castration fear, freezes the look, fixates the spectator and prevents him from achieving any distance from the image in front of him.

This complex interaction of looks is specific to film. The first blow against the monolithic accumulation of traditional film conventions (already undertaken by radical film-makers) is to free the look of the camera into its materiality in time and space and the look of the audience into dialectics and passionate detachment. There is no doubt that this destroys the satisfaction, pleasure and privilege of the "invisible guest," and highlights the way film has depended on voyeuristic active/passive mechanisms. Women, whose image has continually been stolen and used for this end, cannot view the decline of the traditional film form with anything much more than sentimental regret.

CHAPTER 29
TERESA DE LAURETIS

Teresa de Lauretis (b. 1938) is an Italian feminist philosopher and writer, and Distinguished Professor Emerita in the History of Consciousness Department at the University of California, Santa Cruz. She works primarily in semiotics, including the semiotics of cinema, but is significantly influenced by other Continental philosophical perspectives including semiology and psychoanalysis. Her most widely read work in the philosophy of film is Alice Doesn't: Feminism, Semiotics, Cinema, *originally published in English in 1984. The selection included here, "Through the Looking-Glass: Women, Cinema, and Language," is the first chapter of that book—although the same material was published in a somewhat different form in* Yale Italian Studies *in 1980.*

Although more deeply influenced by semiotics than psychoanalysis, De Lauretis' point of view here owes much to Laura Mulvey's feminist and psychoanalytic take on the cinema. Following Mulvey, De Lauretis examines the paradoxical status of women in the West, and in particular in Western discourse and the arts. Culture originates in woman, she notes, and is founded on the dream of woman's captivity: capturing, taming, controlling, marrying the woman as a means of overcoming nature to found society. But at the same time, De Lauretis notes, women are all but absent from Western history and culture. This paradox is at least superficially resolved in the cinema: woman is absent from film insofar as she is a theoretical subject, but captive (and thus centrally present) in film as an historical subject. Which is to say that film does not typically present us with opportunities to identify with the point of view of a woman, but most films afford viewers many occasions to see the image of (the sexually objectified) woman.

De Lauretis understands cinema itself as a certain social technology, and she thinks that the history of theoretical perspectives on film reflect this understanding. In addition to being a certain sort of relation between the technical and the social, however, cinema also deals centrally with the question and construction of subjectivity. There is a development in the history of theories of film, then, which De Lauretis delineates along these lines: the treatment of film as essentially technologically distinct from other art forms and communication media takes its inspiration from the anthropological work of Claude Lévi-Strauss, and becomes a semiology of film. In response to what it takes to be the failings of film semiology, however, some film theorists turn away from the technical toward the social, and borrowing much from the work of Jacques Lacan, approach film psychoanalytically. De Lauretis herself takes neither of these approaches. Instead, she suggests that we might better understand film as at the intersection of the technical and the social, and that we ought to conceive of social being not as something static, but as dynamic and constructed day by day, an approach she ascribes to the semiotics of Umberto Eco. Following Eco, then, De Lauretis asserts that, although the individual is subject to social formations and codes (as the semiologists emphasize), the individual then reworks those codes and formations in light of his or her personal attitudes and experiences, resulting in a highly individualized version of the common structure. De Lauretis suggests that cinema is the "social apparatus" by way of which encounters between the technical and the social, the semiological and the psychoanalytical, take place.

Lévi-Straussian semiology and Lacanian psychoanalysis both presuppose a male-identified or masculine subject, De Lauretis explains, and both explain sexual difference in ways that presuppose what sexual difference means. They leave woman as the scene rather than the subject of sexuality. These similarities result in another situation Mulvey describes quite well: film spectators identify with the look of the camera, and thus with the masculine subject. Subjectivity itself comes to be seen as masculine, and women are thus left the sole role of object of man's desire. It is difficult for such a culture even to imagine a differently constituted (female) subject. Women themselves in such cultures identify both with the objectified image and the subjective look, instantiating a contradiction which could become the basis of a transgression of gender norms and the concomitant occasion for questioning those norms.

According to De Lauretis, the semiology of film confronted the realism that preceded it with an affirmation of cinematic codes and the social construction of reality. It reminds us that cinema is not simply a matter of turning the camera on and making a recording of whatever is seen. Likewise, after the rise of semiology in film studies, De Lauretis argues that psychoanalysis arrives to affirm the significance of the subject in contrast to the social constructivism of semiology and the scientism that can follow from the codification of film images or social behaviors. De Lauretis suggests, however, that we must now get beyond both semiology and psychoanalysis—language is not a unified field, she argues, with many changing discourses and multiple apparati—and she thinks that the way forward is semiotics, in something like Eco's sense. For Eco, meaning changes over time as new uses or interpretations arise. This creates a far more fluid and dynamic approach to meaning, which neither semiology nor psychoanalysis can accommodate on their own. Such an approach also opens up the possibility for a feminist critique, despite the fact that Eco's assumptions are largely productivist and masculinist, as with semiology and psychoanalysis. De Lauretis says, however, that in allowing the gap between the subjective camera and the objectified image to show itself fully, semiotics opens up a space for a critical woman. Such a woman would, in showing the contradictions discussed above, instantiate the difference between "woman" (as a rigidly organized signifier) and women. In so doing, she would open a space wherein the masculinist assumptions of semiology, psychoanalysis, and much of the history of film studies could be interrogated and overturned.

Filmography

- ***Letter from an Unknown Woman*** (USA, 1948). *Directed by* Max Ophüls. *Produced by* John Houseman *and* William Dozier. *Written by* Howard Koch *and* Max Ophüls. *Starring* Joan Fontaine *and* Louis Jourdan.
- ***Chung Kuo, Cina*** (Italy, 1972). *Directed by* Michelangelo Antonioni. *Produced by* RAI Radiotelevisione Italiana. *Written by* Michelangelo Antonioni *and* Andrea Barbato.
- ***Il portiere di note*** [*The Night Porter*] (Italy, 1974). *Directed by* Liliana Cavani. *Produced by* Robert Gordon Edwards *and* Esa De Simone. *Written by* Liliana Cavani, Italo Moscati, Barbara Alberti, *and* Amedeo Pagani. *Starring* Dirk Bogarde *and* Charlotte Rampling.

- ***Salò o le 120 giornate di Sodoma*** [*Salò, or the 120 Days of Sodom*] (Italy–France, 1975). *Directed by* Pier Paolo Pasolini. *Produced by* Alberto Grimaldi. *Written by* Sergio Citti *and* Pier Paolo Pasolini. *Starring* Paolo Bonacelli, Giorgio Cataldi, Umberto Paolo, Quintavalle, Aldo Valletti, Catarina Boratto, Elsa De Giorgi, Hélène Surgère, Sonia Saviange, *and* Inès Pellegrini.
- ***L'Empire des sens*** [*In the Realm of the Senses*] (France–Japan, 1976). *Directed and Written by* Nagisa Oshima. *Produced by* Anatole Dauman. *Starring* Eiko Matsuda *and* Tatsuya Fuji.

THROUGH THE LOOKING-GLASS: WOMEN, CINEMA, AND LANGUAGE

> From there, after six days and seven nights, you arrive at Zobeide, the white city, well exposed to the moon, with streets wound about themselves as in a skein. They tell this tale of its foundation: men of various nations had an identical dream. They saw a woman running at night through an unknown city; she was seen from behind, with long hair, and she was naked. They dreamed of pursuing her. As they twisted and turned, each of them lost her. After the dream they set out in search of that city; they never found it, but they found one another; they decided to build a city like the one in the dream. In laying out the streets, each followed the course of his pursuit; at the spot where they had lost the fugitive's trail, they arranged spaces and walls differently from the dream, so she would be unable to escape again.
>
> This was the city of Zobeide, where they settled, waiting for that scene to be repeated one night. None of them, asleep or awake, ever saw the woman again. The city's streets were streets where they went to work every day, with no link any more to the dreamed chase. Which, for that matter, had long been forgotten.
>
> New men arrived from other lands, having had a dream like theirs, and in the city of Zobeide, they recognized something of the streets of the dream, and they changed the positions of arcades and stairways to resemble more closely the path of the pursued woman and so, at the spot where she had vanished, there would remain no avenue of escape.
>
> Those who had arrived first could not understand what drew these people to Zobeide, this ugly city, this trap.
>
> Italo Calvino, *Invisible Cities*

Zobeide, a city built from a dream of woman, must be constantly rebuilt to keep woman captive. The city is a representation of woman; woman, the ground of that representation. In endless circularity ("streets wound about themselves as in a skein"), the woman is at once the dream's object of desire and the reason for its objectification: the construction of the city. She is both the source of the drive to represent and its ultimate, unattainable goal. Thus the city, which is built to capture men's dream, finally only inscribes woman's absence. The founding tale of Zobeide, fifth of the category "Cities and Desire" in Calvino's *Invisible Cities*, tells the story of the production of woman as text.

Invisible Cities is a sort of historical fiction, a postmodern *Decameron* in which Marco Polo, eternal exile and trader in symbols, recounts to Kublai Khan, emperor of the Tartars, the cities he has seen.[1] As the voices of Marco Polo and Kublai Khan in dialogue across continents and

[1] Italo Calvino, *Invisible Cities*, trans. William Weaver (New York: Harcourt Brace Jovanovich, 1974) from Italo Calvino, *Le città invisibili* (Turin: Einaudi, 1972). I have slightly altered Weaver's translation of p. 52 of the Italian edition.

centuries outline a vision of historical process sustained by a dialectic of desire, the whole text reproposes and reduplicates open-endedly the image of woman inscribed in the city of Zobeide. All the invisible cities described by Marco Polo to the Hegelian Khan have names of women, and, significantly, Zobeide is mentioned in *The Arabian Nights* as the name of a wife of the Caliph Harún-al-Rashid.

Woman is then the very ground of representation, both object and support of a desire which, intimately bound up with power and creativity, is the moving force of culture and history. The work of building and rebuilding the city, in a continuing movement of objectification and alienation, is Calvino's metaphor for human history as semiotic productivity; desire provides the impulse, the drive to represent, and dream, the modes of representing.[2] Of that semiotic productivity, woman—the dream woman—is both telos and origin. Yet that woman, because of whom the city is built, who is the foundation and the very condition of representation, is nowhere in the city, stage of its performance. ("This was the city of Zobeide, where they settled, waiting for that *scene* to be repeated *one night*. None of them, asleep or awake, ever saw the woman again.")

The city is a text which tells the story of male desire by performing the absence of woman and by producing woman as text, as pure representation. Calvino's text is thus an accurate representation of the paradoxical status of women in Western discourse: while culture originates from woman and is founded on the dream of her captivity, women are all but absent from history and cultural process. This is probably why we are not surprised that in that primal city built by men there are no women, or that in Calvino's seductive parable of "human" history, women are absent as historical subjects. This is also why I chose this text as a pre-text, a subterfuge, a lure, and an expedient with which to pose, from the impossible position of woman, the question of the representation of woman in cinema and language. Like cinema, the city of Zobeide is an imaginary signifier, a practice of language, a continuous movement of representations built from a dream of woman, built to keep woman captive. In the discursive space of the city, as in the constructs of cinematic discourse, woman is both absent and captive: absent as theoretical subject, captive as historical subject. The story of Zobeide therefore is a pretext to dramatize and to perform on my part the contradiction of feminist discourse itself: what does it mean to speak, to write, to make films *as* a woman? The following essay, then, is written on the wind, through the silence that discourse prescribes for me, woman writer, and across the chasm of its paradox that would have me at once captive and absent.

Recent critical speculation has been elaborating a theory of cinema as a social technology. Considering the cinematic apparatus as a historical and ideological form, it has proposed that the facts of cinema, and its conditions of possibility, should be understood as "a relation of the technical and the social."[3] Ironically, in view of the absence/captivity of woman as subject, and of the alleged feminine discomfort with technology, it has become apparent that such a relation cannot be effectively articulated without reference to a third term—subjectivity, or the construction of sexual difference—and that the questions of women, therefore, not only occupy a critical space within a historical materialist theory of the cinema, but directly concern its basic premises.

---

[2] I have discussed this at length in "Semiotic Models, *Invisible Cities*," *Yale Italian Studies* 2 (Winter 1978): 13–37.

[3] Teresa de Lauretis and Stephen Heath, eds., *The Cinematic Apparatus* (London: Macmillan, and New York: St. Martin's Press, 1980), p. 6.

As social beings, women are constructed through effects of language and representation. Just as the spectator, the term of the moving series of filmic images, is taken up and moved along successive positions of meaning, a woman (or a man) is not an undivided identity, a stable unity of "consciousness," but the term of a shifting series of ideological positions. Put another way, the social being is constructed day by day as the point of articulation of ideological formations, an always provisional encounter of subject and codes at the historical (therefore changing) intersection of social formations and her or his personal history. While codes and social formations define positions of meaning, the individual reworks those positions into a personal, subjective construction. A social technology—cinema, for example—is the semiotic apparatus in which the encounter takes place and the individual is addressed as subject. Cinema is at once a material apparatus and a signifying practice in which the subject is implicated, constructed, but not exhausted. Obviously, women are addressed by cinema and by film, as are men. Yet what distinguishes the forms of that address is far from obvious (and to articulate the different modes of address, to describe their functioning as ideological effects in subject construction, is perhaps the main critical task confronting cinematic and semiotic theory).

Whether we think of cinema as the sum of one's experiences as spectator in the socially determined situations of viewing, or as a series of relations linking the economics of film production to ideological and institutional reproduction, the dominant cinema specifies woman in a particular social and natural order, sets her up in certain positions of meaning, fixes her in a certain identification. Represented as the negative term of sexual differentiation, spectacle-fetish or specular image, in any case ob-scene, woman is constituted as the ground of representation, the looking-glass held up to man. But, as historical individual, the female viewer is also positioned in the films of classical cinema as spectator-subject; she is thus doubly bound to that very representation which calls on her directly, engages her desire, elicits her pleasure, frames her identification, and makes her complicit in the production of (her) woman-ness. On this crucial relation of woman as constituted in representation to women as historical subjects depend at once the development of a feminist critique and the possibility of a materialist, semiotic theory of culture. For the feminist critique is a critique of culture at once from within and from without, in the same way in which women are both *in* the cinema as representation and *outside* the cinema as subjects of practices. It is therefore not simple numerical evidence (women hold up half of the sky) that forces any theoretical speculation on culture to hear the questions of women, but their direct critical incidence on its conditions of possibility.

Two major conceptual models are involved in the current development of film theory, from classical semiology to the more recent metapsychological studies, and in its formulation of concepts of signification, symbolic exchange, language, the unconscious, and the subject: a structural-linguistic model and a dynamic, psychoanalytic model. In both cases, cinema being an apparatus of social representation, the relations of subjectivity, gender, and sexual difference to meaning and ideology are central to cinematic theory. The structural-linguistic model, which excludes any consideration of address and of the social differentiation of spectators (that is to say, it excludes the whole issue of ideology and the subject's construction in it), assumes sexual difference as simple complementarity within a "species," as biological fact rather than sociocultural process. The psychoanalytic model, on the other hand, does acknowledge subjectivity as a construction in language, but articulates it in processes (drive, desire, symbolization) which depend on the crucial instance of castration, and are thus predicated exclusively on a male or masculine subject.

In the two models under consideration, then, the relation of woman to sexuality is either reduced and assimilated to, or contained within, masculine sexuality. But whereas the structural-linguistic model, whose theoretical object is the formal organization of signifiers, assumes sexual difference as a preestablished, stable semantic content (the signified in the cinematic sign), the psychoanalytic model theorizes it in an ambiguous and circular way: on the one hand, sexual difference is a meaning-effect produced in representation; on the other, paradoxically, it is the very support of representation. Both models, however, contain certain contradictions which are produced textually and are thus historically verifiable, for they can be located in the theoretical discourses and in the practices that motivate them.[4] For example, as we shall see, the equation

woman : representation :: sexual difference : value in nature

(where woman as sign or woman as the phallus equals woman as object of exchange or woman as the real, as Truth) is not the formula of a naively or malignantly posited equivalence, but the end result of a series of ideological operations that run through an entire philosophical-discursive tradition. It is in these operations that a theory of the cinema must interrogate its models, as it interrogates the operations of the cinematic apparatus.

More and more frequently in the critical discourse on cinema the nexus representation/subject/ideology has been posed in terms of language, language thus becoming the site of their junction and articulation. Cinema *and* language. What relation does the *and* express? Classical semiology linked cinema and language in what could be called a metonymic relation: all sign systems are organized like language, which is the universal system of signs; and cinema is one system among others, a branch or sector of that multinational organization of signs. Recently, a theory of signifying practices based in psychoanalytic discourse has established between cinema and language something of a metaphoric relation: though realized in distinct practices and material apparati, both cinema and language are imaginary-symbolic productions of subjectivity, their differences being less relevant than their homologous functioning in/as subject processes.

I have used the words "metonymic" and "metaphoric" not inadvertently but as an ironic quotation, to underline the dependence on language common to the semiological and psychoanalytic reflections (evident in Metz's recent work), a dependence which heavily tilts the balance of the relation and instates an obvious hierarchy, the subordination of cinema to language. I would suggest, further, that just as metaphor and metonymy—in the linguistic framework—continually slide ("are projected," Jakobson says)[5] one onto the other, so are those discourses mutually implicated, convergent, and complicit; and insofar as they originate in a structural-linguistic model of language, they circumscribe a theoretical area of cinema *as* language, each representing one axis, one mode of discursive operation.

So I have set myself up to argue that the semiological and psychoanalytic discourses on cinema are, in some respect, similar; and from my rhetorical strategy (the pretext of a parable

[4] "Motivate" here is to be understood not as intentionality or design on the part of individuals who promote those discourses, but rather in the sense in which Marx describes the social determinations by which the capitalist, for example, is not a "bad" person but a function in a specific system of social relations.

[5] Roman Jakobson, "Closing Statement: Linguistics and Poetics," in *Style in Language*, ed. Thomas A. Sebeok (Cambridge, Mass: The MIT Press, 1960), p. 368.

about woman as representation) the reader might correctly infer that my argument will have something to do with woman. Semiotics tells us that similarity and difference are relational categories, that they can only be established in relation to some term of reference, which is thus assumed as the point of theoretical articulation; and indeed *that* term de-termines the parameters and the conditions of comparison. Should another term of reference be assumed, the relation and the terms of the relation would be differently articulated; the first relation would be disturbed, displaced, or shifted toward another relation. The terms, and perhaps the parameters and conditions of the comparison, would change, and so would the *value* of the "and," which in our case expresses the relation of cinema to language.

My term of reference and my point of enunciation (both of which, reader, are performative fictions) will be the absent woman inscribed in Calvino's city. Not unlike the city, cinematic theory is built in history, inscribed in historically specific discourses and practices; and while those discourses have traditionally assigned to woman a position of non-subject, the latter determines, grounds, and supports the very concept of subject and thus the theoretical discourses which inscribe it. Like the city of Zobeide, then, cinematic theory cannot disengage itself from the trouble caused by woman, the problems she poses to *its* discursive operations.

The hypothesis of classical semiology that cinema, like language, is a formal organization of codes, specific and non-specific, but functioning according to a logic internal to the system (cinema or film), apparently does not address me, woman, spectator. It is a scientific hypothesis and as such addresses other "scientists" in a closed economy of discourse. In building the city, the semiologist wants to know how the stones are put together to make a wall, an arcade, a stairway; he pretends not to care why any of these is being built or for whom. However, if asked about woman, he would have no doubt as to what woman was, and he would admit to dreaming about her, during the breaks from his research. Woman, he would say, is a human being, like man (semiology, after all, is a human science), but her specific function is reproduction: the reproduction of the biological species and the maintenance of social cohesion. The assumption implicit in his answer—that sexual difference is ultimately a question of complementarity, a division of labor, within the human species—is fully explicit in Lévi-Strauss's theory of kinship, which, together with Saussurian linguistics, historically constitutes the conceptual basis for the development of semiology.

The semiologist, of course, has read Lévi-Strauss as well as Saussure, plus some Freud and probably Marx. He has heard that the incest prohibition, the "historical" event instituting culture and found in all human societies, requires that women be possessed and exchanged among men to ensure the social order; and that although marriage regulations, the rules of the game of exchange, vary greatly throughout world societies, they all ultimately depend on the same kinship structures, which are really quite like linguistic structures. This, emphasizes Lévi-Strauss, becomes apparent only by applying the analytical method of structural linguistics to the "vocabulary" of kinship, i.e., by "*treating* marriage regulations and kinship systems *as a kind of language*."[6] One then understands that women are not simply goods or objects exchanged by and among men but also signs or messages which circulate among "individuals" and groups, ensuring social communication. Words too, like women, once had the value of (magical) objects; and to the extent that words have become common property, "la chose de tous," losing their character as values, language "has helped to impoverish perception and to strip it of its affective, aesthetic and magical implications." However, "in contrast to words, which have wholly become signs, woman has remained at once a sign and a value. This explains why the relations between the sexes have preserved that affective richness, ardour and mystery which doubtless originally permeated the entire universe of human communications."[7]

In sum: women are objects whose value is founded in nature ("valuables *par excellence*" as bearers of children, food gatherers, etc.); at the same time they are signs in social communication established and guaranteed by kinship systems. But it so happens that in positing exchange as a theoretical abstraction, a structure, and therefore "not itself constitutive of the subordination of women," Lévi-Strauss overlooks or does not see a contradiction that lies at the base of his model: for women to have (or to be) exchange value, a previous symbolization of biological sexual difference must have taken place. Women's economic value must be "predicated on a pre-given *sexual division* which must already be social."[8] In other words, at the origin of society, at the (mythical) moment in which the incest taboo, exchange, and thus the social state are instituted, the terms and items of exchange are already constituted in a hierarchy of value, are already subject to the symbolic function.

How can such remarkable oversight have occurred? Only, I suggest, as ideological effect of the discourses in which Lévi-Strauss's discourse is inscribed (as an "effect of the code")[9] and of the different semiotic values of the term "value" in the theoretical models upstream of Lévi-Strauss's theory: on the one hand the Saussurian model, which defines value entirely as a differential, systemic relation; on the other the Marxian notion of value, invoked to support the thesis—Lévi-Strauss's humanistic appeal—that women contribute to the wealth of a culture both as objects of exchange and as persons, as both signs and "generators of signs." Hence the confusion, the double status of woman as bearer of economic, positive value, and woman as bearer of semiotic, negative value, of difference.

The assimilation of the notion of sign (which Lévi-Strauss takes from Saussure and transposes to the ethnological domain) with the notion of exchange (which he takes from Marx, collapsing use-value and exchange-value) is not a chance one: it comes from an epistemological tradition that for centuries has sought to unify cultural processes, to explain "economically" as many diverse phenomena as possible, to totalize the real and, either as humanism or as imperialism, to control it. But the point is this: the universalizing project of Lévi-Strauss—to collapse the economic and the semiotic orders into a unified theory of culture—depends on his positing woman as the functional opposite of subject (man), which logically excludes the possibility—the theoretical possibility—of women ever being subjects and producers of culture. More importantly, though perhaps less evidently, this construction is founded on a particular representation of sexual difference implicit in the discourse of Lévi-Strauss.

So it is not a matter of proving or disproving his ethnological "data," the "real" conditions of women, their being or not being chattels or signs of masculine exchange in the real world. It is in his theory, in his conceptualization of the social, in the very terms of his discourse that women are doubly negated as subjects: first, because they are defined as vehicles for men's communication—signs of their language, carriers of their children; second, because women's sexuality is reduced to the "natural" function of childbearing, somewhere in between the fertility of nature and the productivity of a machine. Desire, like symbolization, is a property

---

[6] Claude Lévi-Strauss, *Structural Anthropology* (Garden City, New York: Doubleday, 1967), p. 60. My emphasis.
[7] Claude Lévi-Strauss, *The Elementary Structures of Kinship* (Boston: Beacon Press, 1969), p. 496.
[8] Elizabeth Cowie, "Woman as Sign," *m/f*, no. 1 (1978), p. 57.
[9] Jean Baudrillard, *The Mirror of Production* (St. Louis: Telos Press, 1975).

of men, property in both senses of the word: something men own, possess, and something that inheres in men, like a quality. We read:

> The emergence of symbolic thought must have required that women, like words, should be things that were exchanged. In this new case, indeed, this was the only means of overcoming the contradiction by which the same woman was seen under two incompatible aspects: on the one hand, as the object of personal desire, thus exciting sexual and proprietorial instincts; and, on the other, as the subject [*sic*] of the desire of others, and seen as such, i.e., as the means of binding others through alliance with them.[10]

Who speaks in this text? The syntactic and logical subject throughout is an abstract noun, "l'émergence de la pensée symbolique," and the verbs are impersonal in form as if a pure language—scientifically hypothetical, value-free, and subject-less—were speaking. And yet a speaking subject, a *masculine* subject of enunciation, has left his footprints. Consider the sentence: "the same woman was seen … as the object of personal desire, thus exciting sexual and proprietorial instincts." Barring a homogeneously homosexual society (from which Lévi-Strauss could not have descended), the personal desire and the sexual and proprietorial instincts must be those of men, who are then the term of reference for desire, sexuality, property.

And so that woman, seen as "the subject of the desire of others," is, lo and behold, the very same character running naked through the city's streets. But if we asked the semiologist about the dream woman, he would now say that she is just that—a dream, an imaginary fantasy, a fetish, a screen memory, a movie. By now, years have passed, and the semiologist has been reading Jacques Lacan and has forgotten Lévi-Strauss.

The city, he begins to think, is where the unconscious speaks, where its walls, arcades, and stairways signify a subject appearing and disappearing in a dialectic of difference. Upon entering the city, the traveler is taken up and shifted in the symbolic order of its layout, the disposition of its buildings and empty spaces through which the traveler pursues imaginary reflections, apparitions, ghosts from the past. Here and there the traveler seems to recognize a certain place, stops for a moment, sutured; but that place is already another place, unfamiliar, different. And so, moving through the city—made hundreds of years ago but always new to each entering traveler and in continuous metamorphosis like the ocean of Lem's *Solaris*—the newcomer becomes a subject.

This is an interesting city indeed, thinks the semiologist, as she continues to read. She wants to know whether the traveler, having become a resident, so to speak, a subject-in-process through the city, can do anything to change some of its blatantly oppressive aspects, for example to do away with ghettos. But she finds out that the city is ruled by an agency—The Name of the Father—which alone undergoes no metamorphosis and in fact oversees and determines in advance all urban planning.

At this point the semiotician goes back to reread Lévi-Strauss and realizes that Lacan's conception of language as the symbolic register is forged on the trace of Lévi-Strauss's formulation of the unconscious as the organ of the symbolic function:

[10] Lévi-Strauss, *Elementary Structures of Kinship*, p. 496.

> The unconscious ceases to be the ultimate haven of individual peculiarities—the repository of a unique history which makes each of us an irreplaceable being. It is reducible to a function—the symbolic function, which no doubt is specifically human, and which is carried out according to the same laws among all men, and actually corresponds to the aggregate of these laws .... The preconscious, as a reservoir of recollections and images amassed in the course of a lifetime, is merely an aspect of memory .... The unconscious, on the other hand, is always empty—or, more accurately, it is as alien to mental images as is the stomach to the foods which pass through it. As the organ of a specific function, the unconscious merely imposes structural laws upon inarticulated elements which originate elsewhere—impulses, emotions, representations, and memories. We might say, therefore, that the preconscious is the individual lexicon where each of us accumulates the vocabulary of his personal history, but that this vocabulary becomes significant, for us and for others, only to the extent that the unconscious structures it according to its laws and thus transforms it into language.[11]

No longer located in the psyche, the Lévi-Straussian unconscious is a structuring process, a universal articulatory mechanism of the human mind, the structural condition of all symbolization. Similarly, the Lacanian symbolic is the structure, the law which governs the distribution-circulation of signifiers, to which the individual, child or *infans* accedes in language, becoming a subject. In shifting the focus on to the subject, Lacan departs from Lévi-Strauss's structuralism, but the incest prohibition and structure of exchange guaranteed by the name (and the no) of the Father are still the condition—the structural condition—of the subject's rite of passage through culture. Thus, as Gayle Rubin observed, the same conceptual set underlies both theories:

> In one sense, the Oedipal complex is an expression of the circulation of the phallus in intrafamily exchange, an inversion of the circulation of women in interfamily exchange .... The phallus passes through the medium of women from one man to another—from father to son, from mother's brother to sister's son, and so forth. In this family Kula ring, women go one way, the phallus the other. It is where we aren't. In this sense, the phallus is more than a feature which distinguishes the sexes; it is the embodiment of the male status, to which men accede, and in which certain rights inhere—among them, the right to a woman. It is an expression of the transmission of male dominance. It passes through women and settles upon men. The tracks which it leaves include gender identity, the division of the sexes.[12]

It is that structure which Lacanian psychoanalysis holds responsible for the non-coherence or division of the subject in language, theorizing it as the function of castration. Again,

[11] Lévi-Strauss, *Structural Anthropology*, pp. 198–99. In this essay, entitled "The Effectiveness of Symbols," Lévi-Strauss interprets a Cuna incantation performed by the shaman to facilitate childbirth. Several of the terms used here by Lévi-Strauss return as metaphors in the language of Lacan's reading of the child's *fort-da* game described by Freud: "It is with his object [the spool, the object little a] that that infant leaps the boundaries of his domain transformed into holes, shafts, and with which he commences his incantation." Jacques Lacan, *Le Seminaire IX*; quoted by Constance Penley, "The Avant-Garde and Its Imaginary," *Camera Obscura*, no. 2 (Fall 1977), p. 30.

[12] Gayle Rubin, "The Traffic in Women: Notes on the 'Political Economy' of Sex," in *Toward an Anthropology of Women*, ed. Rayna R. Reiter (New York: Monthly Review Press, 1975), pp. 191–92.

as for Lévi-Strauss, the point of enunciation (and term of reference) of desire, drive, and symbolization is a masculine one. For, even though castration is to be understood as referring strictly to the symbolic dimension, its signifier—the phallus—can only be conceived as an extrapolation from the real body. When Lacan writes, for example, that "the interdiction against autoerotism, bearing on *a particular organ*, which for that reason *acquires the value of an ultimate (or first) symbol of lack (manque)*, has the impact of pivotal experience," there is no doubt as to which particular organ is meant: the penis/phallus, symbol of lack and signifier of desire.[13] Despite repeated statements by Lacan(ians) that the phallus is not the penis, the context of the terms I have emphasized in the quotation makes it clear that desire and signification are defined ultimately as a process inscribed in the male body, since they are dependent on the initial—and *pivotal*—experiencing of one's penis, of having a penis. In his discussion of *Encore*, Lacan's 1972–73 seminar devoted to Freud's question "What does a woman want?", Stephen Heath criticizes Lacan's "certainty in a representation and its vision," his pointing to Bernini's statue of Saint Teresa as the visible evidence of the *jouissance* of the woman.[14] Against the effective implications of the psychoanalytic theory he himself developed, Lacan runs analysis back into biology and myth, reinstating sexual reality as nature, as origin and condition of the symbolic. "The constant limit of the theory is the phallus, the phallic function, and the theorization of that limit is constantly eluded, held off, for example, by collapsing castration into a scenario of vision;" thus, in the supposedly crucial distinction between penis and phallus, Heath concludes, "Lacan is often no further than the limits of pure analogical rationalization."[15]

In the psychoanalytic view of signification, subject processes are essentially phallic; that is to say, they are *subject* processes *insofar* as they are instituted in a fixed order of language—the symbolic—by the function of castration. Again female sexuality is negated, assimilated to the male's, with the phallus representing the autonomy of desire (of language) in respect to a matter which is the female body. "Desire, as it detaches itself from need to assume its universal norm in the phallus, is masculine sexuality, which defines its autonomy by relinquishing to women the task of guaranteeing survival (survival of the species as well as satisfaction of the need for love)."[16]

The semiotician is puzzled. First, sexual difference is supposed to be a meaning-effect produced in representation; then, paradoxically, it turns out to be the very support of representation. Once again, as in the theory of kinship, an equivalence is postulated for two inconsistent equations. To say that woman is a sign (Lévi-Strauss) or that she is the real, or Truth (Lacan), implies that her sexual difference is a value founded in nature, that it preexists or exceeds symbolization and culture. That this inconsistency is a fundamental contradiction

---

[13] Jacques Lacan, "Pour une logique du fantasme," *Scilicet*, no. 2/3 (1970), p. 259; quoted by John Brenkman, "The Other and the One: Psycho-analysis, Reading, the *Symposium*," *Yale French Studies*, no. 55/56 (1977): 441; my emphasis.

[14] "Where the conception of the symbolic as movement and production of difference, as chain of signifiers in which the subject is effected in division, should forbid the notion of some presence from which difference is then derived; Lacan instates the visible as the condition of symbolic functioning, with the phallus as the standard of visibility required: seeing is from the male organ." Stephen Heath, "Difference," *Screen* 19, no. 3 (Autumn 1978): 52 and 54. See also Luce Irigaray's critique of this seminar, "Cosi fan tutti," in *Ce sexe qui n'en est pas un* (Paris: Minuit, 1977), pp. 84–101.

[15] Heath, "Difference," pp. 54 and 66. The ambiguity in the phallus/penis relation is emphasized by J. Laplanche and J.-B Pontalis. in *The Language of Psycho-Analysis*, trans. Donald Nicholson-Smith (New York: Norton, 1973), pp. 312–14. See also Anthony Wilden, "The Critique of Phallocentrism," in *System and Structure* (London: Tavistock, 1972).

[16] Lea Melandri, *L'infamia originaria* (Milan: Edizioni L'Erba Voglio, 1977), p. 25. My translation.

of both semiology and psychoanalysis, due to their common structural heritage, is confirmed by Metz's recent work.[17]

In *The Imaginary Signifier* Metz shifts his investigation from the semiological study of the cinematic signifier (its matter and form of expression), to the "psychoanalytic exploration of the signifier" (p. 46), to the signifier in cinema "as a *signifier effect*" (p. 42). The great divide, in this exploration, is the Lacanian concept of the mirror stage, which generates the ambiguous notion of "imaginary signifier." The term "signifier" has a double status in this text—which corresponds to the two sides of the inconsistency mentioned earlier—and thus covers up a gap, a solution of continuity in Metzian discourse from linguistics to psychoanalysis. In the first part of the essay, his use of the term is consonant with the Saussurian notion of signifier; he speaks in fact of signifiers as "coupled" to signifieds, of the script as "manifest signified," and of the "manifest filmic material as a whole," including signifieds and signifiers (pp. 38–40). Elsewhere, however, the cinema signifier is presented as a subject-effect, inaugurated in or instituted by the ego "as transcendental yet radically deluded subject" (p. 54): "At the cinema ... I am the *all-perceiving* ... a great eye and ear without which the perceived would have no one to perceive it, the *constitutive* instance, in other words, of the cinema signifier (it is I who make the film)" (p. 51). The filmic material as "really perceived imaginary," as already imaginary, and as object, becomes significant (becomes an imaginary signifier) to a perceiving subject in language. Metz thus abandons the signified as too naïve a notion of meaning (with which Saussure himself was never concerned) only to include, to subsume meaning in the signifier. The problem with this notion of meaning is that, being coextensive with the signifier as a subject-effect, meaning can only be envisaged as always already given in that fixed order which is the symbolic. In this sense Laplanche and Pontalis can say that "the phallus turns out to be the meaning—i.e., what is *symbolized*—behind the most diverse ideas;" as the signifier of desire, the phallus must also be its meaning, in fact the only meaning.[18] And so, caught between the devil and the deep blue sea, Metz in the last instance goes back to the equation of cinematic code(s) and language, now called the symbolic. He speaks of the "mirror of the screen, a symbolic apparatus" (p. 59) and of "inflections peculiar to the work of the symbolic such as the order of 'shots' or the role of 'sound off' in some cinematic sub-code" (p. 29). He returns, that is, to a systemic and linear notion of signification as approached by linguistics.[19]

The double status of the Metzian signifier—as matter/form of expression and as subject-effect—covers but does not bridge a gap in which sits, temporarily eluded but not exorcised, the referent, the object, reality itself (the chair in the theatre "in the end" is a chair; Sarah Bernhardt "at any rate" is Sarah Bernhardt—not her photograph; the child sees in the mirror "its own body," a real object, thus, henceforth, *known* to be its own image as opposed to the "imaginary" images on the screen, and so on, pp. 47–49). In the linguistic model, that gap, that

---

[17] Christian Metz, *Le signifiant imaginaire* (Paris: UGE, 1977). All page references hereafter are to the English translation by Ben Brewster, "The Imaginary Signifier," *Screen* 16, no. 2 (Summer 1975): 14–76, now reprinted in *The Imaginary Signifier* (Bloomington: Indiana University Press, 1981).

[18] Laplanche and Pontalis, p. 313.

[19] After stating that "the psychoanalytic itinerary is *from the outset a semiological one*" (p. 14), Metz then singles out linguistics and psychoanalysis as the sciences of the symbolic *par excellence*, "the only two sciences whose immediate and sole object is the fact of signification as such," which specifically explore, respectively, the secondary and the primary processes, and "between them... cover the whole field of the *signification-fact*" (p. 28). Where, then, does semiotics (or semiology) stand in relation to the fact of signification? What distinguishes the theoretical project of semiotics from those of linguistics and psychoanalysis?

substantial discontinuity between discourse and reality, can not be bridged nor can its terrain be mapped. On the contrary, the project of semiotics should be precisely such mapping: how the physical properties of bodies are socially assumed as signs, as vehicles for social meaning, and how these signs are culturally generated by codes and subject to historical modes of sign production. Lévi-Strauss retained the linguistic conceptual framework in his analysis of kinship and myth as semantic structures, and Lacan reinscribed that structuration in subject processes. That is why, finally, the psychoanalytic vision of cinema, in spite of Metz's effort, still poses woman as telos and origin of a phallic desire, as dream woman forever pursued and forever held at a distance, seen and invisible on another scene.

Concepts such as voyeurism, fetishism, or the imaginary signifier, however appropriate they may seem to describe the operations of dominant cinema, however convergent—precisely because convergent?—with its historical development as an apparatus of social reproduction, are directly implicated in a discourse which circumscribes woman in the sexual, binds her (in) sexuality, makes her the absolute representation, the phallic scenario. It is then the case that the ideological effects produced in and by those concepts, that discourse, perform, as dominant cinema does, a political function in the service of cultural domination including, but not limited to, the sexual exploitation of women and the repression or containment of female sexuality.

Consider the following discussion of the pornographic film by Yann Lardeau. The pornographic film is said relentlessly to repropose sexuality as the field of knowledge and power, power in the uncovering of truth ("the naked woman has always been, in our society, the allegorical representation of Truth"). The close-up in its operation of truth, the camera constantly closing in on the woman's sex, exhibiting it as object of desire and definitive place of *jouissance* only in order to ward off castration, "to keep the subject from his own lack": "too heavily marked as a term—always susceptible of castration—the phallus is unrepresentable .... The porno film is constructed on the *disavowal of castration*, and *its operation of truth is a fetishistic operation*."[20] Cinema, for Lardeau, is *pour cause* pornography's privileged mode of expression. The fragmentation and fabrication of the female body, the play of skin and make-up, nudity and dress, the constant recombination of organs as equivalent terms of a combinatory are but the repetition, inside the erotic scene, of the operations and techniques of the apparatus: fragmentation of the scene by camera movements, construction of the representational space by depth of field, diffraction of light, and color effects—in short, the process of fabrication of the film from découpage to montage. "It all happens as if the porno film were putting cinema on trial." Hence the final message of the film: "it is cinema itself, as a medium, which is pornographic."

> Dissociated, isolated (autonomized) from the body by the close-up, circumscribed in its genital materiality (reified), [the sex] can then freely circulate outside the subject—as commodities circulate in exchange independently of the producers or as the linguistic sign circulates as value independent of the speakers. Free circulation of goods, persons and messages in capitalism—this is the liberation effected by the close-up, sex delivered into pure abstraction.[21]

---

[20] Yann Lardeau, "Le sexe froid (du porno au dela)," *Cahiers du cinéma*, no. 289 (June 1978), pp. 49, 52, and 61. My translation.

[21] Ibid., pp. 51 and 54.

This indictment of cinema and sexuality in capitalism as apparati for the reproduction of alienated social relations is doubtless acceptable at first. But two objections eventually take shape, one from the other. First: as the explicit reference to the models discussed earlier is posed in terms critical of the linguistic model alone, while the Lacanian view of subject processes is simply assumed uncritically, Lardeau's analysis cannot but duplicate the single, masculine perspective inherent in a phallic conception of sexuality; consequently, it reaffirms woman as representation and reproposes woman as scene, rather than subject, of sexuality. Second: however acceptable it may have seemed, the proposition that cinema is pornographic and fetishistic resolves itself in the closure of syllogism; begging its question and unable to question its premise, such a critique is unable to engage social practice and historical change.

But, it may be counter-objected, the pornographic film is just *that* kind of social practice; it addresses, is made for, men only. Consider, then, the classical Hollywood narrative fiction film, even the sub-genre known as "the woman's film."

> Think again of *Letter from an Unknown Woman* and its arresting gaze on the illuminated body of Lisa/Joan Fontaine, the film the theatre of that .... With the apparatus securing its ground, the narrative plays, that is, on castration known and denied, a movement of difference in the symbolic, the lost object, and the conversion of that movement into the terms of a fixed memory, an invulnerable imaginary, the object—and with it the mastery, the unity of the subject—regained. Like fetishism, narrative film is the structure of a *memory-spectacle*, the perpetual story of a 'one time,' a discovery perpetually remade with safe fictions.[22]

Again and again narrative film has been exposed as the production of a drama of vision, a memory spectacle, an image of woman as beauty—desired and untouchable, desired *as* remembered. And the operations of the apparatus deployed in that production—economy of repetition, rhymes, relay of looks, sound-image matches—aim toward the achieved coherence of a "narrative space" which holds, binds, entertains the spectator at the apex of the representational triangle as the subject of vision.[23] Not only in the pornographic film, then, but in the "woman's film" as well, is cinema's ob-scenity the form of its expression and of its content.

The paradox of this condition of cinema is nowhere more evident than in those films which openly pose the question of sexuality and representation in political terms, films like Pasolini's *Salò*, Cavani's *The Night Porter*, or Oshima's *In the Realm of the Senses*. It is in such films that the difficulties in current theorization appear most evident and a radical reformulation of the questions of enunciation, address, and subject processes most urgent. For example, in contrast with the classic narrative film and its production of a fixed subject-vision, Heath asks us to look at Oshima's film as the film of the uncertainty of vision. It is, he writes, "a film working on a problem ... the problem of 'seeing' for the spectator."[24] By shifting to—and forcing on—the

---

[22] Stephen Heath, *Questions of Cinema* (Bloomington: Indiana University Press, 1981), p. 154.

[23] See, in particular, Stephen Heath, "Narrative Space," in *Questions of Cinema*, pp. 19–75.

[24] "*Empire of the Senses* is crossed by that possibility of a nothing seen, which is its very trouble of representation, but that possibility is not posed, as it were, from some outside; on the contrary, it is produced as a contradiction within the given system of representation, the given machine" (Heath, *Questions of Cinema*, p. 162). The thought is further developed in the following passage: "The order of the look in the work of the film is neither the thematics of

spectator the question of "the relations of the sexual and the political in cinema," by marking out the difficulties—perhaps the impossibility—posed by their articulation in representation, the film includes the spectator's view as divided, disturbs the coherence of identification, addressing a subject in division. Thus, it is compellingly argued, the struggle is still with representation—not outside or against it—a struggle in the discourse of the film and on the film.

It is not by chance that women's critical attention to cinema most often insists on the notions of representation and identification, the terms in which are articulated the social construction of sexual difference and the place of woman, at once image and viewer, spectacle and spectator, in that construction.

> One of the most basic connections between women's experience in this culture and women's experience in film is precisely the relationship of spectator and spectacle. Since women are spectacles in their everyday lives, there's something about coming to terms with film from the perspective of what it means to be an object of spectacle and what it means to be a spectator that is really a coming to terms with how that relationship exists both up on the screen and in everyday life.[25]

In the psychoanalytic view of film as imaginary signifier, representation and identification are processes referred to a masculine subject, predicated on and predicating a subject of phallic desire, dependent on castration as the constitutive instance of the subject. And woman, in a phallic order, is at once the mirror and the screen—image, ground, and support—of *this* subject's projection and identification: "the spectator *identifies with himself*, with himself as pure act of perception;" and, "as he identifies with himself as look, the spectator can do no other than identify with the camera."[26] Woman, here, cannot but be "cinema's object of desire," the sole imaginary of the film, "'sole' in the sense that any difference is caught up in that structured disposition, that fixed relation in which the film is centered and held, to which the times and rhythms and excesses of its symbolic tissue and its narrative drama of vision are bound."[27]

Like the city of Zobeide, those discourses specify woman in a particular natural and social order: naked and absent, body and sign, image and representation. And the same tale is told of cinema and its foundation: "men of various nations had an identical dream. They saw a woman running at night through an unknown city; she was naked, with long hair, and she was seen from behind ..." (for the female sex is invisible in psychoanalysis, and in semiology it does not exist at all). What this theory of the cinema cannot countenance, given its phallic premise, is the possibility of a different relation of the spectator-subject to the filmic image, of different meaning-effects being produced for and producing the subject in identification and

---

voyeurism (note already the displacement of the look's subject from men to women) nor the binding structure of a classic narrative disposition (where character look is an element at once of the form of content, the definition of the action in the movement of looks exchanged, and of the form of expression, the composition of the images and their arrangement together, their 'match'). Its register is not that of the 'out of frame', the *hors-champ* to be recaptured in the film by the spatially suturing process of 'folding over' of which field/reverse-field is the most obvious device, but that of the edging of every frame, of every shot, towards a *problem* of 'seeing' for the spectator" (ibid., p. 150).

[25] Judith Mayne, in "Women and Film: A Discussion of Feminist Aesthetics," *New German Critique*, no. 13 (Winter 1978), p. 86.

[26] Metz, "The Imaginary Signifier," pp. 51 and 52.

[27] Stephen Heath, "Questions of Property," *Cine-Tracts*, no. 4 (Spring-Summer 1978), p. 6.

representation—in short, the possibility of other subject processes obtaining in that relation. This very issue, the modalities of spectatorship, informs the debate, in avant-garde film practice and theory, around narrative and abstract representation, illusionist versus structural-materialist film; it also provides the context and a main focus of the feminist intervention.[28] As Ruby Rich puts it,

> According to Mulvey, the woman is not visible in the audience which is perceived as male; according to Johnston, the woman is not visible on the screen .... How does one formulate an understanding of a structure that insists on our absence even in the face of our presence? What is there in a film with which a woman viewer identifies? How can the contradictions be used as a critique? And how do all these factors influence what one makes as a woman filmmaker, or specifically as a feminist filmmaker?[29]

What one may make, as a feminist filmmaker, are films "working on a problem," in Heath's words. Such must be, provisionally, the task of the critical discourse as well: to oppose the simply totalizing closure of final statements (cinema is pornographic, cinema is voyeurist, cinema is the imaginary, the dream-machine in Plato's cave, and so on); to seek out contradictions, heterogeneity, ruptures in the fabric of representation so thinly stretched—if powerful—to contain excess, division, difference, resistance; to open up critical spaces in the seamless narrative space constructed by dominant cinema *and* by dominant discourses (psychoanalysis, certainly, but also the discourse on technology as autonomous instance, or the notion of a total manipulation of the public sphere, the exploitation of cinema, by purely economic interests); finally, to displace those discourses that obliterate the claims of other social instances and erase the agency of practice in history.

The importance of psychoanalysis for the study of cinema and of film is not to be denied. It has served to dislodge cinematic theory from the scientistic, even mechanistic enterprise of a structural semiology and urged upon it the instance of the subject, its construction and representations, in cinematic signification—just as the historical importance of semiology was to affirm the existence of coding rules and thus of a socially constructed reality there where a transcendental reality, nature (Bazin's "ontology of the image"), had been supposed to manifest itself. Yet nature does linger, if only as residue, in the semiological and psychoanalytic discourses; it lingers as non-culture, non-subject, non-man, as—in the last instance—base and support, mirror and screen of his representation. Thus Lea Melandri, in another context:

> Idealism, the oppositions of mind to body, of rationality to matter, originate in a twofold concealment: of the woman's body and of labor power. Chronologically, however, even prior to the commodity and the labor power that has produced it, the matter which was negated in its concreteness and particularity, in its "relative plural form," is the

---

[28] See, for example, Maureen Turim, "The Place of Visual Illusions"; Peter Gidal, "Technology and Ideology in/through/and Avant-Garde Film: An Instance"; and Jacqueline Rose, "The Cinematic Apparatus: Problems in Current Theory"; all in de Lauretis and Heath, pp. 143–86.

[29] Ruby Rich, in "Women and Film: A Discussion of Feminist Aesthetics," p. 87. Rich here refers to Laura Mulvey, "Visual Pleasure and Narrative Cinema," *Screen* 16, no. 3 (Autumn 1975): 6–18; and to Pam Cook and Claire Johnston, "The Place of Women in the Cinema of Raoul Walsh," in *Raoul Walsh*, ed. Phil Hardy (Edinburgh: Edinburgh Film Festival, 1974), pp. 93–109.

> woman's body. Woman enters history having already lost concreteness and singularity; she is the economic machine that reproduces the human species, and she is the Mother, an equivalent more universal than money, the most abstract measure ever invented by patriarchal ideology.[30]

The hierarchical setting up of "language" as universal model, which was the error of classical semiology, is also the structural heritage of Lacanian theory. In the former the language of linguistics was the privileged model for all signification systems and their "internal" mechanisms; in the latter the symbolic as phallic structure is taken as the primary model of subject processes. If and when either of those models is immediately transferred to the cinema, certain problems are voided and avoided, excluded from the theoretical discourse or disposed of within it. For example, the problem of materiality: while the material heterogeneity of the cinema in relation to language is readily asserted, the possibility that diverse forms of semiotic productivity, or different modes of sign production, may entail other subject processes has not been seriously considered.[31] Then there is the problem of the historicity of language, of cinema, and of the other apparati of representation; their uneven ratios of development, their specific modes of address, their particular relations to practice, and their combined, perhaps even contradictory effects on social subjects.

As I walk invisible and captive through the city, I keep thinking that the questions of signification, representation, and subject processes in cinema must be reformulated from a less rigid view of meaning than is fixed by Lacanian psychoanalysis; and that a materialist theory of subjectivity cannot start out from a given notion of the subject, but must approach the subject through the apparati, the social technologies in which it is constructed. Those apparati are distinct, if not disparate, in their specificity and concrete historicity, which is why their co-participation, their combined effect, cannot be easily assessed. Thus, for instance, while the novel, the cinema, and television are all "family machines," they cannot simply be equated with one another. As social technologies aimed at reproducing, among other things, the institution family, they do overlap to a certain degree, but the amount of overlap or redundancy involved is offset, precisely, by their material and semiotic specificity (modes of production, modalities of enunciation, of inscription of the spectator/interlocutor, of address). The family that watches together is really another institution; or better, the subject produced in the family that watches TV is not the same social subject produced in families that only read novels. Another example: the reworking of visual perspective codes into a narrative space in sound films, admirably analyzed by Stephen Heath,[32] certainly recreates some of the subject-effects of perspectival painting, but no one would seriously think that Renaissance painting and Hollywood cinema, as social apparati, address one and the same subject in ideology.

Language, no doubt, is one such social apparatus, and perhaps a universally dominant one. But before we elect it as absolutely representative of subjective formations, we ought to ask:

---

[30] Melandri, p. 27. My translation.

[31] Many have argued for Lacan's project as a materialist theory of language, and in particular a materialist rewriting of the idealist discourse on love from Plato on (see John Brenkman, "The Other and the One: Psychoanalysis, Reading, the *Symposium*"). But where a dialectic is certainly the movement of the subject's passage through language, and thus of its "personal" history, it is not at all clear to me whether that dialectic is a materialist or a Hegelian one; in a preestablished structural order, a logic of the signifier, that is always already determined for each entering subject, the personal history comes very close to being written with a capital H.

[32] Heath, *Questions of Cinema*, pp. 19–75.

what language? The language of linguistics is not the language spoken in the theatre, and the language we speak outside the movie theatre cannot be quite the same language that was spoken on Plymouth Rock. The point is too obvious to belabor. To put it briefly, after all the work done on the forming influence of visual codes like perspective, the still and motion cameras, and so forth, can one really think that the various forms of mechanical reproduction of language (visual and sound) and its incorporation into practically all apparati of representation have no impact on its social and subjective effects? In this respect, we should consider not only the question of internal speech in the film but also, reciprocally, the possible question of an internal sight or vision in language ("visible speech," *visibile parlare*, is the term of Dante's imaging, the inscription on the gates of Hell), both of which invoke the problematic of the relation of language to sensory perception, of what Freud called word-presentation and thing-presentation in the interplay of primary and secondary processes.[33]

If cinema can be said to be "a language," it is precisely because "language" *is* not; language is not a unified field, outside of specific discourses like linguistics or *The Village Voice*. There are "languages," practices of language and discursive apparati that produce meanings; and there are different modes of semiotic production, ways in which labor is invested in the production of signs and meanings. The types of labor invested, and the modes of production involved, it seems to me, are directly, materially, relevant to the constitution of subjects in ideology—class subjects, race subjects, sexed subjects, and any other differential category that may have political use-value for particular situations of practice at particular historical moments.

It has been said that, if language can be considered an apparatus, like cinema, producing meanings through physical means (the body, the articulatory and hearing organs, the brain), cinematic enunciation is more expensive than speech.[34] True enough. That observation is necessary to the understanding of cinema as a social apparatus (of questions of access, monopoly, and power) and underscores its specificity with respect to other signifying practices; but the single economic parameter is not sufficient to define its mode of semiotic production. The problem is not, or not just, that cinema operates with many different matters of expression and more "expensive," less available "machinery" than natural language. The problem is, rather, that meanings are not produced *in* a particular film but "circulate between social formation, spectator and film."[35] The production of meanings, I rephrase, always involves not simply a specific apparatus of representation but several. While each can be described analytically in its matters of expression or its social-economic conditions of production (e.g., the technological or economic modalities of, say, sound cinema), what is at issue is the possibility of accounting for their joint hold on the spectator and, *thus*, the production of meanings for a subject and/or of a subject in meaning across a plurality of discourses. If—to put it bluntly and circuitously—the subject is where meanings are formed and if, at the same time, meanings constitute the subject, then the notion of semiotic productivity must include that of modes of production. So "the question of how semantic values are constructed, read and located in history" becomes a most pertinent question.[36]

[33] See Paul Willemen, "Reflections on Eikhenbaum's Concept of Internal Speech in the Cinema," *Screen* 15, no. 4 (Winter 1974/5): 59–70; and "Cinematic Discourse: The Problem of Inner Speech," *Screen* 22, no. 3 (1981): 63–93; and Stephen Heath, "Language, Sight and Sound" in *Questions of Cinema*, pp. 194–220.
[34] Metz, in *The Cinematic Apparatus*, p. 23.
[35] Heath, *Questions of Cinema*, p. 107.

I have argued that a theory of cinema as a social technology, a relation of the technical and the social, can be developed only with a constant, critical attention to its discursive operations and from the awareness of their present inadequacy. I now want to suggest that cinematic theory must displace the questions of representation and subject construction from the procrustean bed of phallic signification and an exclusive emphasis on the signifier; that we must seek, that is, other ways of mapping the terrain in which meanings are produced. To this end, it may be useful to reconsider the notion of code, somewhat emarginated by current film theory after its heyday in semiology, and importantly redefined in Eco's *Theory of Semiotics*.

In the structural formulation of classical semiology, a code was construed to be a system of oppositional values (Saussure's *langue*, or Metz's code of cinematic punctuation) located upstream of the meanings produced contextually in enunciation and reception. "Meanings" (Saussure's signifieds) were supposed to be subsumed in, and in a stable relationship to, the respective signs (Saussure's signifiers). So defined, a code could be envisaged and described, like a structure, independently of any communicative purpose and apart from an actual situation of signification. For Eco this is not a code but, in fact, a structure, a system; whereas a code is a significant *and* communicational framework linking differential elements on the expression plane with semantic elements on the content plane or with behavioral responses. In the same manner, a sign is not a fixed semiotic entity (the relatively stable union of a signifier and a signified) but a "sign-function," the mutual and transitory correlation of two functives which he calls "sign-vehicle" (the physical component of the sign, on the expression plane) and "cultural unit" (a semantic unit on the content plane). In the historical process, "the same functive can also enter into another correlation, thus becoming a different functive and so giving rise to a new sign-function."[37] As socially established, operational rules that *generate* signs (whereas in classical semiology codes *organize* signs), the codes are historically related to the modes of sign production; it follows that the codes change whenever new or different contents are culturally assigned to the same sign-vehicle or whenever new sign-vehicles are produced. In this manner a new text, a different interpretation of a text—any new practice of discourse—sets up a different configuration of content, introduces other cultural meanings that in turn transform the codes and rearrange the semantic universe of the society that produces it. What is important to note here is that, in this notion of code, the content of the sign-vehicle is also a unit in a semantic system (but not necessarily a binary system) of oppositional values. Each culture, for example, segments the continuum of experience by "making certain units pertinent and understanding others merely as variants, 'allophones.'"[38]

> When it is said that the expression /Evening star/ denotes a certain large physical "object" of a spherical form, which travels through space some scores of millions of miles from the Earth, one should in fact say that: the expression in question denotes "a certain" corresponding *cultural unit* to which the speaker refers, and which she has accepted in the way described by the culture in which she lives, without having ever experienced the real referent. So much is this so that only the logician knows that the expression

---

[36] Paul Willemen, "Notes on Subjectivity," *Screen* 19, no. 1 (Spring 1978): 43.

[37] Umberto Eco, *A Theory of Semiotics* (Bloomington: Indiana University Press, 1976), p. 49.

[38] Ibid., p. 78. This is one reason why translation presents problems and why a film can be read so differently in different cultures or viewing situations; for example, Antonioni's controversial documentary on China, *Chung Kuo*, discussed by Eco in an interview with William Luhr in *Wide Angle* 1, no. 4 (1977): 64–72.

> in question has the same denotatum as has the expression /Morning star/. Whoever emitted or received this latter sign-vehicle thought that there were *two different things.* And she was right in the sense that the cultural codes to which she referred provided for two different cultural units. Her social life did not develop on the basis of things but on the basis of cultural units. Or rather, for her as for us, things were only known through cultural units which the universe of communication put into circulation *in place of things.*[39]

Even within a single culture, most semantic fields disintegrate very quickly (unlike the field of colors or kinship terms which have been studied systematically precisely because, in addition to being made up of highly structured cultural units, they have been, like syntax or phonemic structure, durable systems). Most semantic fields are constantly restructured by movements of acculturation and critical revision; that is, they are subject to a process of change due to contradictions within each system and/or to the appearance of new material events outside the system. Now, if cultural units can be recognized by virtue of their opposition to one another in various semantic systems, and can be identified or isolated by the (indefinite) series of their interpretants, then they can be considered to some extent independently of the systemic or structural organizations of the sign-vehicles.

The existence, or rather the theoretical hypothesis, of semantic fields makes it possible to envisage a non-linear semantic space constructed not by one system—language—but by the multilevel interaction of many heterogeneous sign-vehicles and cultural units, the codes being the networks of their correlations *across* the planes of content and expression. In other words, signification involves several systems or discourses intersecting, superimposed, or juxtaposed to one another, with the codes mapping out paths and positions in a virtual (vertical) semantic space which is discursively, textually and contextually, constituted in each signifying act. What distinguishes this notion of code is that both planes, expression and content, are assumed at once in the relationship of meaning. Thus it appears to be very close to the notion of cinematic apparatus as a social technology: not a technical device or *dispositif* (the camera, or the film "industry") but a *relation* of the technical *and* the social which involves the subject as (inter) locutor, poses the subject as the place of that relation. Only in this sense, according to Eco, can one speak of transformation of the codes, of the modes of production, of the semantic fields, or of the social.

Eco's emphasis is a productivist one: his view of sign production, and especially of the mode he calls invention, associating it with art and creativity, is from the perspective of the maker, the speaker, the artist, the *producer* of signs. But what about the woman? She has no access to the codes of the invisible city which represents her and absents her; she is not in the place of Eco's "subject of semiosis"—*homo faber*, the city builder, the producer of signs. Nor is she in the representation which inscribes her as absent. The woman cannot transform the codes; she can only transgress them, make trouble, provoke, pervert, turn the representation into a trap ("this ugly city, this trap"). For semiotics too, finally, the founding tale remains the same. Though now the place of the female subject in language, in discourse, and in the social may be understood another way, it is an equally impossible position. She now finds herself in the empty space between the signs, in a void of meaning, where no demand is possible and no code

[39] Eco, *A Theory of Semiotics*, pp. 65–66. The quotation has been slightly edited.

available; or, going back to the cinema, she finds herself in the place of the female spectator, between the look of the camera (the masculine representation) and the image on the screen (the specular fixity of the feminine representation), not one or the other but both and neither.

I have no picture of the city where the female subject lives. For me, historical woman, discourse does not cohere; there is no specific term of reference, no certain point of enunciation. Like the female reader of Calvino's text, who reading, desiring, building the city, both excludes and imprisons herself, our questioning of the representation of woman in cinema and language is itself a re-presentation of an irreducible contradiction for women in discourse. (What does speaking "as a woman" mean?) But a critical feminist reading of the text, of all the texts of culture, instates the awareness of that contradiction and the knowledge of its terms; it thus changes the representation into a performance which exceeds the text. For women to enact the contradiction is to demonstrate the non-coincidence of woman and women. To perform the terms of the production of woman as text, as image, is to resist identification with that image. It is to have stepped through the looking-glass.

As the reader by now has discovered, the title of this essay has little or nothing to do with Lewis Carroll's book or its heroine. It has, however, something to do with a text not cited directly, but whose presence here, as in much feminist writing, is due to our historical memory: Sheila Rowbotham's *Woman's Consciousness, Man's World.*[40] In Part I, also entitled "Through the Looking-Glass," Rowbotham describes her own struggle as a woman with and against revolutionary Marxism, which was dominated by what she calls the "male non-experience" of the specific material situation of women. She could be speaking for many others indeed when she says: "When women's liberation burst about my ears I suddenly saw ideas which had been roaming hopelessly round my head coming out in the shape of other people—women-people. Once again I started to find my bearings all over again. But this time we were going through the looking-glass together" (p. 25). Of many keen and moving passages I could cite, the following is particularly relevant to the conclusion of my essay:

> Consciousness within the revolutionary movement can only become coherent and self-critical when its version of the world becomes clear not simply within itself but when it knows itself in relation to what it has created apart from itself. When we can look back at ourselves through our own cultural creations, our actions, our ideas, our pamphlets, our organization, our history, our theory, we begin to integrate a new reality. As we begin to know ourselves in a new relation to one another we can start to understand our movement in relation to the world outside. We can begin to use our self-consciousness strategically. [pp. 27–28]

[40] Sheila Rowbotham, *Woman's Consciousness, Man's World* (Harmondsworth: Penguin Books, 1973).

CHAPTER 30
JUDITH BUTLER

Judith Butler (b. 1956) is an American philosopher and one of the world's foremost theorists of gender. She is the Maxine Elliot Professor of Comparative Literature at the University of California, Berkeley. She is best known for her theory of gender performativity, which she elaborated in her book, Gender Trouble: Feminism and the Subversion of Identity, *in 1990. Following on that work, she published* Bodies That Matter: On the Discursive Limits of "Sex" *in 1993, from which the selection included here is extracted. This selection, "Gender Is Burning," was originally published as a portion of Chapter 4 of that book. It is her sole contribution to the philosophical study of cinema.*

"Gender Is Burning" takes its title from, and takes as its subject matter, the documentary film (directed by Jennie Livingston), Paris is Burning, *which follows the lives of various Latinx, black, and transgender members of Harlem's drag ball culture in the 1980s. In this culture, Butler finds that the primary standard for judging a drag performance at a ball is "realness," a term which corresponds less to any notion of objective facticity than it does to an ability on the part of the individual engaged in the performance to compel a certain sort of belief. To be real, on this standard, is to be unable to be read—since a performance that can be read as a performance has failed as appearance. When what appears in the performance and what it means diverge from one another, then the performance can be read as artifice, and thus unreal.*

One individual upon whose ultimately tragic life story the film focuses is the transgender Latina performer, Venus Xtravaganza, for whom, Butler notes, gender serves as a vehicle for a "phantasmatic transformation" of other identity categories, and in particular, race and class. In the film, we learn that Venus wants to become a real woman, so as to find a man who can care for and protect her. This is, as Butler notes and as Venus herself admits, a fantasy of escaping the race- and class-based violence she has experienced: if only she could become a "real" woman, she could live a life more like that stereotypically identified with married, suburban white women. Interestingly, then, Butler sees in the drag ball culture Livingston documents in the film a series of subjects, like Venus Xtravaganza, whose subjectivity is constituted by the repetition and legitimation of certain sex, gender, racial, and class norms by which they have themselves been degraded in their lives: Venus performs heterosexual, cisgendered, white womanhood, despite the fact that the normative force of that identity in Western culture is at the heart of so much of her own suffering. Nevertheless, by performing those norms in the attempt to achieve realness, Venus and the other members of this community undermine them at the same time. The normative force of the identity Venus performs is grounded in a naïve cultural understanding of the relationship between anatomy and identity: to the extent that Venus can appear with that identity without being read as artificial, she demonstrates the falseness of that relationship. The norms are simultaneously legitimized and delegitimized thereby. The performative rearticulation of oppressive norms such as these means, Butler argues, that there is not a strict opposition between the dominant culture and resistance to that culture (or its dominance).

Having offered her understanding of the issues surrounding and emerging from gender in the film, Butler turns her attention to the film itself insofar as it is a film: to its form and function as cinema. In instances both specific and general with regard to the community Livingston filmed, Paris Is Burning *brings a sort of fame and recognition to a group of individuals for whom such things are the objects of a very real desire. This is particularly evident in the case of Venus Xtravaganza herself, whom the film in a way brings back to life after her murder in 1988: the fame Venus achieves by way of the film is simultaneously life giving and only after death. The camera, in fact, functions in general in the film, Butler argues, as the promise of "legendary" status: performers with only local renown, at best, can see the presence of the camera and a film crew as an opportunity to achieve national or international fame. Citing a review of the film by the black feminist theorist, bell hooks, Butler points out that, for some thinkers, the director's absence from the film contributes to the invisibility and normativity of the filmmaker's gaze: that the person through whom audiences are exposed to this largely poor, black, and Latinx drag ball community is not a member herself of that community instantiates a problem: the mostly oppressed, mostly minority community depicted in the film is depicted only from the perspective of an outsider, repeating the colonialist trope of the "innocent" ethnographic gaze.*

Ultimately, for Butler, the camera in Paris Is Burning *plays a phallic role, serving as an active instrument of transubstantiation for a group of individuals engaged always in the pursuit of some sort of transformation. Thus, by way of being filmed, someone like Venus can be transformed from male to female, from unknown to legendary, from vulnerable to protected, or even, again in Venus' case, from dead to alive. It is the camera, however, that controls these transformations in the film—the camera that controls the field of signification—and thus the camera (and whoever wields the camera, whether Livingston or a proxy for Livingston) that determines what the performances mean, and whether Venus (or any other performer) is "real." The film depicts Livingston's attempt to document one community's efforts to appropriate the dominant culture and use it to empower marginalized members of that culture, and in this effort, Butler thinks the film sometimes succeeds. It cannot achieve this goal, however, without implicating the audience, and thus a great deal depends upon the audience members' responses. To watch a film like* Paris Is Burning *is to enter into the logic of fetishization inherent both in this specific community and in the dominant culture at large, and this raises for the viewer the possibility of confronting his or her own performative experience of gender. If, after viewing the film, we conclude (or are encouraged by the filmmaker to conclude) that we are bearing witness simply to another exotic fetish, then the dominant gender ideals are reinforced and nothing changes for the marginalized. If, however, a film can contribute to the production of an ambivalence about the embodiment of gender ideals and norms, it opens a space for a critical response to and appropriation of those ideals and norms. Such an outcome would not only mitigate against some of hooks' concerns about the dominating attitude inherent in documentary filmmaking, but it would redeem the medium of documentary film by making newly evident its identity-transforming and revolutionary potential.*

Filmography

- ***Paris Is Burning*** (USA, 1990). *Directed and Produced by* Jennie Livingston. *Starring* Dorian Corey, Pepper LaBeija, Venus Xtravaganza, Octavia St. Laurent, Willi Ninja, Angie Xtravaganza, Freddie Pendavis, *and* Junior LaBeija.

GENDER IS BURNING

Paris Is Burning (1991) is a film produced and directed by Jennie Livingston about drag balls in New York City, in Harlem, attended by, performed by "men" who are either African-American or Latino. The balls are contests in which the contestants compete under a variety of categories. The categories include a variety of social norms, many of which are established in white culture as signs of class, like that of the "executive" and the Ivy League student; some of which are marked as feminine, ranging from high drag to butch queen; and some of them, like that of the "bangie," are taken from straight black masculine street culture. Not all of the categories, then, are taken from white culture; some of them are replications of a straightness which is not white, and some of them are focused on class, especially those which almost require that expensive women's clothing be "mopped" or stolen for the occasion. The competition in military garb shifts to yet another register of legitimacy, which enacts the performative and gestural conformity to a masculinity which parallels the performative or reiterative production of femininity in other categories. "Realness" is not exactly a category in which one competes; it is a standard that is used to judge any given performance within the established categories. And yet what determines the effect of realness is the ability to compel belief, to produce the naturalized effect. This effect is itself the result of an embodiment of norms, a reiteration of norms, an impersonation of a racial and class norm, a norm which is at once a figure, a figure of a body, which is no particular body, but a morphological ideal that remains the standard which regulates the performance, but which no performance fully approximates.

Significantly, this is a performance that works, that effects realness, to the extent that it *cannot* be read. For "reading" means taking someone down, exposing what fails to work at the level of appearance, insulting or deriding someone. For a performance to work, then, means that a reading is no longer possible, or that a reading, an interpretation, appears to be a kind of transparent seeing, where what appears and what it means coincide. On the contrary, when what appears and how it is "read" diverge, the artifice of the performance can be read as artifice; the ideal splits off from its appropriation. But the impossibility of reading means that the artifice works, the approximation of realness appears to be achieved, the body performing and the ideal performed appear indistinguishable.

But what is the status of this ideal? Of what is it composed? What reading does the film encourage, and what does the film conceal? Does the denaturalization of the norm succeed in subverting the norm, or is this a denaturalization in the service of a perpetual reidealization, one that can only oppress, even as, or precisely when, it is embodied most effectively? Consider the different fates of Venus Xtravaganza. She "passes" as a light-skinned woman, but is—by virtue of a certain failure to pass completely—clearly vulnerable to homophobic violence; ultimately, her life is taken presumably by a client who, upon the discovery of what she calls her "little secret," mutilates her for having seduced him. On the other hand, Willi Ninja can pass as straight; his voguing becomes foregrounded in het video productions with Madonna et al., and he achieves post-legendary status on an international scale. There is passing and then there is passing, and it is—as we used to say—"no accident" that Willi Ninja ascends and Venus Xtravaganza dies.

Now Venus, Venus Xtravaganza, she seeks a certain transubstantiation of gender in order to find an imaginary man who will designate a class and race privilege that promises a permanent shelter from racism, homophobia, and poverty. And it would not be enough to claim that for Venus gender is *marked by* race and class, for gender is not the substance or primary substrate and race and class the qualifying attributes. In this instance, gender is the vehicle for the phantasmatic transformation of that nexus of race and class, the site of its articulation. Indeed, in *Paris Is Burning*, becoming real, becoming a real woman, although not everyone's desire (some children want merely to "do" realness, and that, only within the confines of the ball), constitutes the site of the phantasmatic promise of a rescue from poverty, homophobia, and racist delegitimation.

The contest (which we might read as a "contesting of realness") involves the phantasmatic attempt to approximate realness, but it also exposes the norms that regulate realness as *themselves* phantasmatically instituted and sustained. The rules that regulate and legitimate realness (shall we call them symbolic?) constitute the mechanism by which certain sanctioned fantasies, sanctioned imaginaries, are insidiously elevated as the parameters of realness. We could, within conventional Lacanian parlance, call this the ruling of the symbolic, except that the symbolic assumes the primacy of sexual difference in the constitution of the subject. What *Paris Is Burning* suggests, however, is that the order of sexual difference is not prior to that of race or class in the constitution of the subject; indeed, that the symbolic is also and at once a racializing set of norms, and that norms of realness by which the subject is produced are racially informed conceptions of "sex" (this underscores the importance of subjecting the entire psychoanalytic paradigm to this insight).[1]

This double movement of approximating and exposing the phantasmatic status of the realness norm, the symbolic norm, is reinforced by the diagetic movement of the film in which clips of so-called "real" people moving in and out of expensive stores are juxtaposed against the ballroom drag scenes.

In the drag ball productions of realness, we witness and produce the phantasmatic constitution of a subject, a subject who repeats and mimes the legitimating norms by which it itself has been degraded, a subject founded in the project of mastery that compels and disrupts its own repetitions. This is not a subject who stands back from its identifications and decides instrumentally how or whether to work each of them today; on the contrary, the subject is the incoherent and mobilized imbrication of identifications; it is constituted in and through the iterability of its performance, a repetition which works at once to legitimate and delegitimate the realness norms by which it is produced.

In the pursuit of realness this subject is produced, a phantasmatic pursuit that mobilizes identifications, underscoring the phantasmatic promise that constitutes any identificatory move—a promise which, taken too seriously, can culminate only in disappointment and disidentification. A fantasy that for Venus, because she dies—killed apparently by one of her

[1] Kobena Mercer has offered rich work on this question and its relation to a psychoanalytic notion of "ambivalence." See "Looking for Trouble," reprinted in Henry Abelove, Michèle Barale, and David M. Halperin, eds., *The Lesbian and Gay Studies Reader* (New York: Routledge, 1993), pp. 350–59. Originally published in *Transition* 51 (1991); "Skin Head Sex Thing: Racial Difference and the Homoerotic Imaginary" in Bad Object-Choices, ed., *How Do I Look? Queer Film and Video* (Seattle: Bay Press, 1991), pp. 169–210; "Engendered Species," *Artforum* vol. 30, no. 10 (Summer 1992): pp. 74–78. See also on the relationship between psychoanalysis, race, and ambivalence, Homi Bhabha, "Of Mimicry and Man: The Ambivalence of Colonial Discourse" in *October* 28 (Spring 1984): pp. 125–133.

clients, perhaps after the discovery of those remaining organs—cannot be translated into the symbolic. This is a killing that is performed by a symbolic that would eradicate those phenomena that require an opening up of the possibilities for the resignification of sex. If Venus wants to become a woman, and cannot overcome being a Latina, then Venus is treated by the symbolic in precisely the ways in which women of color are treated. Her death thus testifies to a tragic misreading of the social map of power, a misreading orchestrated by that very map according to which the sites for a phantasmatic self-overcoming are constantly resolved into disappointment. If the signifiers of whiteness and femaleness—as well as some forms of hegemonic maleness constructed through class privilege—are sites of phantasmatic promise, then it is clear that women of color and lesbians are not only everywhere excluded from this scene, but constitute a site of identification that is consistently refused and abjected in the collective phantasmatic pursuit of a transubstantiation into various forms of drag, transsexualism, and uncritical miming of the hegemonic. That this fantasy involves becoming in part like women and, for some of the children, becoming like black women, falsely constitutes black women as a site of privilege; they can catch a man and be protected by him, an impossible idealization which of course works to deny the situation of the great numbers of poor black women who are single mothers without the support of men. In this sense, the "identification" is composed of a denial, an envy, which is the envy of a phantasm of black women, an idealization that produces a denial. On the other hand, insofar as black men who are queer can become feminized by hegemonic straight culture, there is in the performative dimension of the ball a significant *reworking* of that feminization, an occupation of the identification that is, as it were, *already* made between faggots and women, the feminization of the faggot, the feminization of the black faggot, which is the black feminization of the faggot.

The performance is thus a kind of talking back, one that remains largely constrained by the terms of the original assailment: If a white homophobic hegemony considers the black drag ball queen to be a woman, that woman, constituted already by that hegemony, will become the occasion for the rearticulation of its terms; embodying the excess of that production, the queen will out-woman women, and in the process confuse and seduce an audience whose gaze must to some degree be structured through those hegemonies, an audience who, through the hyperbolic staging of the scene, will be drawn into the abjection it wants both to resist and to overcome. The phantasmatic excess of this production constitutes the site of women not only as marketable goods within an erotic economy of exchange,[2] but as goods which, as it were, are also privileged consumers with access to wealth and social privilege and protection. This is a full-scale phantasmatic transfiguration not only of the plight of poor black and Latino gay men, but of poor black women and Latinas, who are the figures for the abjection that the drag ball scene elevates as a site of idealized identification. It would, I think, be too simple to reduce this identificatory move to black male misogyny, as if that were a discrete typology, for the feminization of the poor black man and, most trenchantly, of the poor, black, gay man, is a strategy of abjection that is already underway, originating in the complex of racist, homophobic, misogynist, and classist constructions that belong to larger hegemonies of oppression.

These hegemonies operate, as Gramsci insisted, through *rearticulation*, but here is where the accumulated force of a historically entrenched and entrenching rearticulation overwhelms

[2] See Linda Singer, *Erotic Welfare: Sexual Theory and Politics in the Age of Epidemic* (New York: Routledge, 1992).

the more fragile effort to build an alternative cultural configuration from or against that more powerful regime. Importantly, however, that prior hegemony also works through and as its "resistance" so that the relation between the marginalized community and the dominative is not, strictly speaking, oppositional. The citing of the dominant norm does not, in this instance, displace that norm; rather, it becomes the means by which that dominant norm is most painfully reiterated as the very desire and the performance of those it subjects.

Clearly, the denaturalization of sex, in its multiple senses, does not imply a liberation from hegemonic constraint: when Venus speaks her desire to become a whole woman, to find a man and have a house in the suburbs with a washing machine, we may well question whether the denaturalization of gender and sexuality that she performs, and performs well, culminates in a reworking of the normative framework of heterosexuality. The painfulness of her death at the end of the film suggests as well that there are cruel and fatal social constraints on denaturalization. As much as she crosses gender, sexuality, and race performatively, the hegemony that reinscribes the privileges of normative femininity and whiteness wields the final power to *re*naturalize Venus's body and cross out that prior crossing, an erasure that is her death. Of course, the film brings Venus back, as it were, into visibility, although not to life, and thus constitutes a kind of cinematic performativity. Paradoxically, the film brings fame and recognition not only to Venus but also to the other drag ball children who are depicted in the film as able only to attain local legendary status while longing for wider recognition.

The camera, of course, plays precisely to this desire, and so is implicitly installed in the film as the promise of legendary status. And yet, is there a filmic effort to take stock of the place of the camera in the trajectory of desire that it not only records, but also incites? In her critical review of the film, bell hooks raises the question not only of the place of the camera, but also that of the filmmaker, Jennie Livingston, a white lesbian (in other contexts called "a white Jewish lesbian from Yale," an interpellation which also implicates this author in its sweep), in relation to the drag ball community that she entered and filmed. hooks remarks that,

> Jennie Livingston approaches her subject matter as an outsider looking in. Since her presence as white woman/lesbian filmmaker is "absent" from *Paris Is Burning*, it is easy for viewers to imagine that they are watching an ethnographic film documenting the life of black gay "natives" and not recognize that they are watching a work shaped and formed from a perspective and standpoint specific to Livingston. By cinematically masking this reality (we hear her ask questions but never see her) Livingston does not oppose the way hegemonic whiteness "represents" blackness, but rather assumes an imperial overseeing position that is in no way progressive or counterhegemonic.[3]

Later in the same essay, hooks raises the question of not merely whether or not the cultural location of the filmmaker is absent from the film, but whether this absence operates to form tacitly the focus and effect of the film, exploiting the colonialist trope of an "innocent" ethnographic gaze: "Too many critics and interviewers," hooks argues, "... act as though she somehow did this marginalized black gay subculture a favor by bringing their experience to a wider public. Such a stance obscures the substantial rewards she has received for this work. Since so many of the black gay men in the film express the desire to be big stars, it is easy to

[3] bell hooks, "Is Paris Burning?" *Z* (June 1991): 61.

place Livingston in the role of benefactor, offering these 'poor black souls' a way to realize their dreams" (63).[4]

Although hooks restricts her remarks to black men in the film, most of the members of the House of Xtravaganza, are Latino, some of whom are light-skinned, some of whom engage in crossing and passing, some of who only do the ball, some who are engaged in life projects to effect a full transubstantiation into femininity and/or into whiteness. The "houses" are organized in part along ethnic lines. This seems crucial to underscore precisely because neither Livingston nor hooks considers the place and force of ethnicity in the articulation of kinship relations.

To the extent that a transubstantiation into legendary status, into an idealized domain of gender and race, structures the phantasmatic trajectory of the drag ball culture, Livingston's camera enters this world as the promise of phantasmatic fulfillment: a wider audience, national and international fame. If Livingston is the white girl with the camera, she is both the object and vehicle of desire; and yet, as a lesbian, she apparently maintains some kind of identificatory bond with the gay men in the film and also, it seems, with the kinship system, replete with "houses," "mothers," and "children," that sustains the drag ball scene and is itself organized by it. The one instance where Livingston's body might be said to appear allegorically on camera is when Octavia St. Laurent is posing for the camera, as a moving model would for a photographer. We hear a voice tell her that she's terrific, and it is unclear whether it is a man shooting the film as a proxy for Livingston, or Livingston herself. What is suggested by this sudden intrusion of the camera into the film is something of the camera's desire, the desire that motivates the camera, in which a white lesbian phallically organized by the use of the camera (elevated to the status of disembodied gaze, holding out the promise of erotic recognition) eroticizes a black male-to-female transsexual—presumably preoperative—who "works" perceptually as a woman.

What would it mean to say that Octavia is Jennie Livingston's kind of girl? Is the category or, indeed, "the position" of white lesbian disrupted by such a claim? If this is the production of the black transsexual for an exoticizing white gaze, is it not also the transsexualization of lesbian desire? Livingston incites Octavia to become a woman for Livingston's own camera, and Livingston thereby assumes the power of "having the phallus," i.e., the ability to confer that femininity, to anoint Octavia as model woman. But to the extent that Octavia receives and is produced by that recognition, the camera itself is empowered as phallic instrument. Moreover, the camera acts as surgical instrument and operation, the vehicle through which the transubstantiation occurs. Livingston thus becomes the one with the power to turn men into women who, then, depend on the power of her gaze to become and remain women. Having asked about the transsexualization of lesbian desire, then, it follows that we might ask more particularly: what is the status of the desire to feminize black and Latino men that the film enacts? Does this not serve the purpose, among others, of a visual pacification of subjects by whom white women are imagined to be socially endangered?

Does the camera promise a transubstantiation of sorts? Is it the token of that promise to deliver economic privilege and the transcendence of social abjection? What does it mean to eroticize the holding out of that promise, as hooks asks, when the film will do well, but the lives that they record will remain substantially unaltered? And if the camera is the vehicle for that

---

[4] Ibid., 63.

transubstantiation, what is the power assumed by the one who wields the camera, drawing on that desire and exploiting it? Is this not its own fantasy, one in which the filmmaker wields the power to transform what she records? And is this fantasy of the camera's power not directly counter to the ethnographic conceit that structures the film?

hooks is right to argue that within this culture the ethnographic conceit of a neutral gaze will always be a white gaze, an unmarked white gaze, one which passes its own perspective off as the omniscient, one which presumes upon and enacts its own perspective as if it were no perspective at all. But what does it mean to think about this camera as an instrument and effect of lesbian desire? I would have liked to have seen the question of Livingston's cinematic desire reflexively thematized in the film itself, her intrusions into the frame as "intrusions," the camera *implicated* in the trajectory of desire that it seems compelled to incite. To the extent that the camera figures tacitly as the instrument of transubstantiation, it assumes the place of the phallus, as that which controls the field of signification. The camera thus trades on the masculine privilege of the disembodied gaze, the gaze that has the power to produce bodies, but which is itself no body.

But is this cinematic gaze only white and phallic, or is there in this film a decentered place for the camera as well? hooks points to two competing narrative trajectories in the film, one that focuses on the pageantry of the balls and another that focuses on the lives of the participants. She argues that the spectacle of the pageantry arrives to quell the portraits of suffering that these men relate about their lives outside the ball. And in her rendition, the pageantry represents a life of pleasurable fantasy, and the lives outside the drag ball are the painful "reality" that the pageantry seeks phantasmatically to overcome. hooks claims that "at no point in Livingston's film are the men asked to speak about their connections to a world of family and community beyond the drag ball. The cinematic narrative makes the ball the center of their lives. And yet who determines this? Is this the way the black men view their reality or is this the reality that Livingston constructs?"[5]

Clearly, this *is* the way that Livingston constructs their "reality," and the insights into their lives that we do get are still tied in to the ball. We hear about the ways in which the various houses prepare for the ball, we see "mopping;" and we see the differences among those who walk in the ball as men, those who do drag inside the parameters of the ball, those who cross-dress all the time in the ball and on the street and, among the cross-dressers, those who resist transsexuality, and those who are transsexual in varying degrees. What becomes clear in the enumeration of the kinship system that surrounds the ball is not only that the "houses" and the "mothers" and the "children" sustain the ball, but that the ball is itself an occasion for the building of a set of kinship relations that manage and sustain those who belong to the houses in the face of dislocation, poverty, homelessness. These men "mother" one another, "house" one another, "rear" one another, and the resignification of the family through these terms is not a vain or useless imitation, but the social and discursive building of community, a community that binds, cares, and teaches, that shelters and enables. This is doubtless a cultural reelaboration of kinship that anyone outside of the privilege of heterosexual family (and those within those "privileges" who suffer there) needs to see, to know, and to learn from, a task that makes none of us who are outside of heterosexual "family" into absolute outsiders to this film. Significantly, it is in the elaboration of kinship forged through a resignification of the very

---

[5] Ibid.

terms which effect our exclusion and abjection that such a resignification creates the discursive and social space for community, that we see an appropriation of the terms of domination that turns them toward a more enabling future.

In these senses, then, *Paris Is Burning* documents neither an efficacious insurrection nor a painful resubordination, but an unstable coexistence of both. The film attests to the painful pleasures of eroticizing and miming the very norms that wield their power by foreclosing the very reverse-occupations that the children nevertheless perform.

This is not an appropriation of dominant culture in order to remain subordinated by its terms, but an appropriation that seeks to make over the terms of domination, a making over which is itself a kind of agency, a power in and as discourse, in and as performance, which repeats in order to remake—and sometimes succeeds. But this is a film that cannot achieve this effect without implicating its spectators in the act; to watch this film means to enter into a logic of fetishization which installs the ambivalence of that "performance" as related to our own. If the ethnographic conceit allows the performance to become an exotic fetish, one from which the audience absents itself, the commodification of heterosexual gender ideals will be, in that instance, complete. But if the film establishes the ambivalence of embodying—and failing to embody—that which one sees, then a distance will be opened up *between* that hegemonic call to normativizing gender and its critical appropriation.

CHAPTER 31
JACK HALBERSTAM

Jack Halberstam (b. 1961, also Judith Halberstam) is an American gender theorist working in a variety of interrelated fields, including feminism, queer theory, and transgender studies, and is Professor of American Studies and Ethnicity, Gender Studies, Comparative Literature, and English at the University of Southern California. Halberstam is the author of a number of works on issues related to gender, society, and culture, perhaps the most widely cited of which so far is Female Masculinity *(1998). The selection included here, "The Transgender Look," is Chapter 4 of Halberstam's book,* In a Queer Time and Place: Transgender Bodies, Subcultural Lives, *originally published in English in 2005.*

Halberstam engages here in an in-depth discussion of three films in which transgender characters figure prominently: The Crying Game, Boys Don't Cry, *and* By Hook or by Crook. *Before getting into the details specific to each film, however, Halberstam discusses the fact that contemporary cinema often depicts a fantasy of bodily fluidity by various means and in various genres (Halberstam's initial examples are all from action and science fiction films). This fantasy is most centralized, and best exemplified, however, in transgender film. Of the three films Halberstam identifies in this category,* The Crying Game *and* Boys Don't Cry *are alike in their use of affect to appeal to mainstream viewers: the audience member is granted access to the transgender gaze by way of an appeal to emotions understood to be universally human. There is something deeper going on in transgender film for Halberstam, however, having to do with the film's relationship to time. Whereas mainstream commercial cinema relies upon a fairly linear conception of time to ground the narrative, transgender film is always introducing (or on the cusp of introducing) a rift in the typical narrative fabric. When a trans character is identified in a film as trans, Halberstam notes, a rupture between distinct temporal registers is exposed. Audience members must reorient themselves in the temporality of the narrative, revisiting past moments in the film so as to reassess their perceptions and assumptions in light of the revelation of the character's transgender identity—and then must re-anticipate what is to come in the story. Trans characters are only sometimes visible as trans characters, and must sometimes even recede into that invisibility after having been identified as trans; this is a dynamic characteristic of both many transgender films and many transgender lives. And, thus, the transgender gaze as such, for Halberstam, depends upon a complex interaction of presence and absence (visibility/invisibility, appearance/disappearance, knowledge/ignorance/forgetting, etc.) which always takes place in and often ruptures simple notions of time and space. It is on this philosophical basis that Halberstam then examines the relative strengths and weaknesses of the three films.*

From the very start of the viewer's experience of The Crying Game*—that is, from the producers' request that movie theaters and patrons not give "the secret" away—the film constructs a mainstream viewer (someone who would not be "in the know") for itself. The transgender character in the film, Dil (Jaye Davidson), is famously revealed as anatomically male in an erotic scene with the film's protagonist, the straight white male Fergus (Stephen Rea), and it is this "secret" which was clearly meant, Halberstam points out, to "shock" moviegoers (if not quite* as traumatically as it shocks Fergus). Ultimately, however, Halberstam argues that The Crying Game cannot imagine the transgender gaze at all—Dil is only ever an object to be viewed (with alternating attraction and revulsion, and the attempt to understand precisely "what" Dil is), never a subject. We (and the camera) view the film only ever from Fergus' perspective, never from Dil's.

In shifting from The Crying Game to Boys Don't Cry, Halberstam notes that the success of the latter is due to its ability to seduce the viewer in its construction and sustaining of the transgender gaze. For Halberstam, the most cinematically successful moments of Boys Don't Cry are all involved in the dismantling of the chief convention of cinematic narrative, shot/reverse shot. Conventional film narratives offer a visual pleasure that, as Halberstam notes following Laura Mulvey, is always gendered. The subject (the protagonist, as well as the camera) are always stereotypically masculine, and women presented in the film are always presented as erotic objects. Constrained by this convention, which sutures the camera's point of view to the male gaze and thus cannot help but produce a sexist and heteronormative vision of human being, traditional cinema might seem to find alternatives to the dominant gender norms, but actually only reinforces the belief in the rightness of the traditional choices. (Thus Dil, at the end of The Crying Game, must be stereotypically masculinized and kept at a forced distance from Fergus for the narrative to resolve.) Boys Don't Cry, however, divorces the shot/reverse shot from the male gaze, which makes it possible for the look of the film not to become heteronormative: in this, it creates a transgender look. The transgender gaze so conceived is a look divided within itself, as Halberstam notes, a point of view from two places at the same time. In one scene in the film in particular, Brandon Teena (Hilary Swank) is depicted perceiving his own violent objectification from the perspective of the object and the perspective of a subjective observer. This unconventional use of shot/reverse shot opens the film to the possibility of a mode of seeing that does not simply objectify and fetishize the transgender body.

While Boys Don't Cry opens up some new possibilities for film, Halberstam points out that, in the end, the film abandons the transgender gaze for a universal humanism—when, after his sexual assault, Brandon is "restored" to the normative gender binary by his (at this point, her) girlfriend, Lana (Chloë Sevigny). Taking another approach altogether, however, is the final transgender film Halberstam examines, By Hook or by Crook. The protagonists of this film are individuals whose genders are never explained, or even addressed, within the film. This refusal to classify or problematize gender within the film universalizes queerness within the cinematic space, Halberstam argues, constructing a queer universe without ever objectifying queerness itself. Most movies with queer characters ultimately achieve mainstream audience identification by universalizing and humanizing those characters in terms of affect, as The Crying Game and Boys Don't Cry do to different extents. But this universalism undermines the project of queer subjectivity, adopting the straight gaze and making the argument that these characters are "just like us" (that is, just like straight men or women) instead. In its refusal to acknowledge the straight world, however, By Hook or by Crook resists the trap of liberal humanism. By Hook or by Crook thus presents gender ambiguity without explaining it (and thus deciding the ambiguity): transgender bodies are neither explained nor diluted in the film, just represented for what they are. Despite its relatively limited (commercial) success and its (apparently) niche market, By Hook or by Crook accomplishes a great deal more, cinematically, than either of the more commercially successful films, The Crying Game or Boys Don't Cry. For Halberstam, this accomplishment *is in fact one potential beginning for a genuinely queer cinema, and one successful model of an uncompromising transgender film.*

Filmography

- ***Walk on the Wild Side*** (USA, 1962). *Directed by* Edward Dmytryk. *Produced by* Charles K. Feldman. *Written by* John Fante *and* Edmund Morris. *Starring* Laurence Harvey, Capucine, Jane Fonda, Anne Baxter, *and* Barbara Stanwyck.
- ***Taxi Driver*** (USA, 1976). *Directed by* Martin Scorsese. *Produced by* Julia Phillips *and* Michael Phillips. *Written by* Paul Schrader. *Starring* Robert De Niro, Jodie Foster, Albert Brooks, Harvey Keitel, Leonard Harris, Peter Boyle, *and* Cybill Shepherd.
- ***Dead Ringers*** (Canada–USA, 1988). *Directed by* David Cronenberg. *Produced by* Marc Boyman *and* David Cronenberg. *Written by* David Cronenberg *and* Norman Snider. *Starring* Jeremy Irons *and* Geneviève Bujold.
- ***Terminator 2: Judgment Day*** (USA, 1991). *Directed and Produced by* James Cameron. *Written by* James Cameron *and* William Wisher. *Starring* Arnold Schwarzenegger, Linda Hamilton, *and* Robert Patrick.
- ***Basic Instinct*** (USA–UK–France, 1992). *Directed by* Paul Verhoeven. *Produced by* Alan Marshall. *Written by* Joe Eszterhaus. *Starring* Michael Douglas *and* Sharon Stone.
- ***The Crying Game*** (Ireland–UK–Japan, 1992). *Directed and Written by* Neil Jordan. *Produced by* Stephen Woolley. *Starring* Stephen Rea, Miranda Richardson, Jaye Davidson, *and* Forest Whitaker.
- ***Gazon maudit*** [*French Twist*] (France, 1995). *Directed by* Josiane Balasko. *Produced by* Pierre Grunstein *and* Claude Berri. *Written by* Josiane Balasko, Patrick Aubrée, *and* Telsche Boorman. *Starring* Victoria Abril, Josiane Balasko, *and* Alain Chabat.
- ***As Good as It Gets*** (USA, 1997). *Directed by* James L. Brooks. *Produced by* James L. Brooks, Bridget Johnson, *and* Kristi Zea. *Written by* Mark Andrus *and* James L. Brooks. *Starring* Jack Nicholson, Helen Hunt, Greg Kinnear, Cuba Gooding, Jr., Skeet Ulrich, *and* Shirley Knight.
- ***Face/Off*** (USA, 1997). *Directed by* John Woo. *Produced by* David Permut, Barrie M. Osborne, Terence Chang, *and* Christopher Godsick. *Written by* Mike Werb *and* Michael Colleary. *Starring* John Travolta *and* Nicolas Cage.
- ***The Brandon Teena Story*** (USA, 1998). *Directed by* Susan Muska *and* Greta Olafsdottir. *Produced by* Jane Dekrone.
- ***Boys Don't Cry*** (USA, 1999). *Directed by* Kimberly Peirce. *Produced by* Jeffrey Sharp, Eva Kolodner, *and* Christine Vachon. *Written by* Andy Bienen *and* Kimberly Peirce. *Starring* Hilary Swank *and* Chloë Sevigny.
- ***The Matrix*** (USA, 1999). *Directed and Written by* The Wachowskis. *Produced by* Joel Silver. *Starring* Keanu Reeves, Laurence Fishburne, Carrie-Anne Moss, Hugo Weaving, *and* Joe Pantoliano.
- ***The Sixth Sense*** (USA, 1999). *Directed and Written by* M. Night Shyamalan. *Produced by* Frank Marshall, Kathleen Kennedy, *and* Barry Mendel. *Starring* Bruce Willis, Toni Collette, Olivia Williams, *and* Haley Joel Osment.

- ***Girlfight*** (USA, 2000). *Directed and Written by* Karyn Kusama. *Produced by* Sarah Green, Martha Griffin, *and* Maggie Renzi. *Starring* Michelle Rodriguez.
- ***Romeo Must Die*** (USA, 2000). *Directed by* Andrzej Bartkowiak. *Produced by* Joel Silver *and* Jim Van Wyck. *Written by* Eric Bernt *and* John Jarrell. *Starring* Jet Li, Aaliyah, Isaiah Washington, Russell Wong, DMX, *and* Delroy Lindo.
- ***By Hook or by Crook*** (USA, 2001). *Directed, Written by, and Starring* Harry Dodge *and* Silas Howard. *Produced by* Steakhaus Productions.
- ***Southern Comfort*** (USA, 2001). *Directed and Produced by* Kate Davis.

THE TRANSGENDER LOOK

> Certain social groups may be seen as having rigid or unresponsive selves and bodies, making them relatively unfit for the kind of society we now seem to desire.
>
> —Emily Martin, *Flexible Bodies*

The potentiality of the body to morph, shift, change, and become fluid is a powerful fantasy in transmodern cinema. Whether it is the image of surgically removable faces in John Woo's *Face/Off*, the liquid-mercury type of slinkiness of the Terminator in *Terminator 2: Judgment Day*, the virtual bodies of *The Matrix*, or the living-dead body in *The Sixth Sense*, the body in transition indelibly marks late-twentieth- and early-twenty-first-century visual fantasy. The fantasy of the shape-shifting and identity-morphing body has been nowhere more powerfully realized recently than in transgender film. In films like Neil Jordan's *The Crying Game* (1992) and *Boys Don't Cry*, the transgender character surprises audiences with his/her ability to remain attractive, appealing, and gendered while simultaneously presenting a gender at odds with sex, a sense of self not derived from the body, and an identity that operates within the heterosexual matrix without confirming the inevitability of that system of difference. But even as the transgender body becomes a symbol par excellence for flexibility, transgenderism also represents a form of rigidity, an insistence on particular forms of recognition, that reminds us of the limits of what Martin has called "flexible bodies." Those bodies, indeed, that fail to conform to the postmodern fantasy of flexibility that has been projected onto the transgender body may well be punished in popular representations even as they seem to be lauded. And so, Brandon in *Boys Don't Cry* and Dil in *The Crying Game* are represented as both heroic and fatally flawed.

Both *The Crying Game* and *Boys Don't Cry* rely on the successful solicitation of affect—whether it be revulsion, sympathy, or empathy—in order to give mainstream viewers access to a transgender gaze. And in both films, a relatively unknown actor pulls off the feat of credibly performing a gender at odds with the sexed body even after the body has been brutally exposed. Gender metamorphosis in these films is also used as a metaphor for other kinds of mobility or immobility. In *The Crying Game*, Dil's womanhood stands in opposition to a revolutionary subjectivity associated with the Irish Republican Army (IRA), and in *Boys Don't Cry*, Brandon's manhood represents a class-based desire to transcend small-town conflicts and a predictable life narrative of marriage, babies, domestic abuse, and alcoholism. While Brandon continues to romanticize small-town life, his girlfriend, Lana, sees him as a symbol of a much-desired elsewhere. In both films, the transgender character also seems to stand for a different form of temporality. Dil seems deliberately removed in *The Crying Game* from the time of the nation and other nationalisms, and her performance of womanhood opens up a ludic temporality. Brandon in *Boys Don't Cry* represents an alternative future for Lana by trying to be a man with no past. The dilemma for the transgender character, as we have seen in earlier chapters, is to create an alternate future while rewriting history. In *Boys Don't Cry*, director Peirce seems aware of the imperative of queer time and constructs (but fails to sustain) a transgender gaze capable of seeing through the present to a future elsewhere. In experimental moments in this otherwise brutally realistic film, Peirce creates slow-motion or double-speed time warps that hint at an elsewhere for the star-crossed lovers that is located in both time and space.

The transgender film confronts powerfully the way that transgenderism is constituted as a paradox made up in equal parts of visibility and temporality: whenever the transgender character is seen to be transgendered, then he/she is both failing to pass and threatening to expose a rupture between the distinct temporal registers of past, present, and future. The exposure of a trans character whom the audience has already accepted as male or female, causes the audience to reorient themselves in relation to the film's past in order to read the film's present and prepare themselves for the film's future. When we "see" the transgender character, then, we are actually seeing cinematic time's sleight of hand. Visibility, under these circumstances, may be equated with jeopardy, danger, and exposure, and it often becomes necessary for the transgender character to disappear in order to remain viable. The transgender gaze becomes difficult to track because it depends on complex relations in time and space between seeing and not seeing, appearing and disappearing, knowing and not knowing. I will be identifying here different treatments of the transgenderism that resolve these complex problems of temporality and visibility.

In one mode that we might call the "rewind," the transgender character is presented at first as "properly" gendered, as passing in other words, and as properly located within a linear narrative; her exposure as transgender constitutes the film's narrative climax, and spells out both her own decline and the unraveling of cinematic time. The viewer literally has to rewind the film after the character's exposure in order to reorganize the narrative logic in terms of the pass. In a second mode that involves embedding several ways of looking into one, the film deploys certain formal techniques to give the viewer access to the transgender gaze in order to allow us to look *with* the transgender character instead of *at* him. Other techniques include ghosting the transgender character or allowing him to haunt the narrative after death; and doubling the transgender character or playing him/her off another trans character in order to remove the nodal point of normativity. *The Brandon Teena Story*, discussed in Chapter 2, provides an example of the ghosting technique, and in this film, Brandon occupies the space of the ghost; he literally haunts the film and returns to life only as an eerie voice recorded during a brutal police interrogation. Two other transgender films, Kate Davis's documentary *Southern Comfort* (2001) along with Harry Dodge and Silas Howard's feature film *By Hook or by Crook* (2001), work through the strategy of doubling. In *Southern Comfort*, the transgender man, Robert Eads, is in the process of disappearing as the film charts his decline and death from uterine and ovarian cancers. Robert is doubled by other male transgender friends, but also by his transgender girlfriend, Lola. By showing Robert to be part of a transgender community rather than a freakish individual, the film refuses the medical gaze that classifies Robert as abnormal and the heteronormative gaze that renders Robert invisible. Instead, *Southern Comfort* portrays Robert as a transgender man among other transgender people.

In *By Hook or by Crook*, transgenderism is a complex dynamic between the two butch heroes, Shy and Valentine. The two collude and collaborate in their gendering, and create a closed world of queerness that is locked in place by the circuit of a gaze that never references the male or the female gaze as such. The plot of *By Hook or by Crook* involves the random meeting of two trans butches and the development of a fast friendship. Shy tries to help Valentine, who has been adopted, find his mother, while Valentine introduces the lonely Shy, whose father has just died, to an alternative form of community. The dead or missing parents imply an absence of conventional family, and afford our heroes with the opportunity to remake home, family, community, and most important, friendship. As the story evolves into a shaggy-dog tale of hide-and-seek, we leave family time far behind, entering into the shadow world of queers, loners, street people, and crazies. Transgenderism takes its place in this world as a quiet location outside the storm of law and order, mental health, and financial stability. Unlike other transgender films that remain committed to seducing the straight gaze, this one remains thoroughly committed to the transgender look, and it opens up, formally and thematically, a new mode of envisioning gender mobility. In this chapter, I pay close attention to three versions of the "transgender film"—*The Crying Game*, *Boys Don't Cry*, and *By Hook or by Crook*—to track the evolution of a set of strategies (each with different consequences) for representing transgender bodies, capturing transgender looks, and theorizing transgender legibility.

Crying Games

> *crying—verb*: announce in public, utter in a loud distinct voice so as to be heard over a long distance; *noun*: the process of shedding tears (usually accompanied by sobs or other inarticulate sounds); *adj*.: conspicuously bad, offensive or reprehensible.
>
> —Oxford English Dictionary

When *The Crying Game* was released, the media was instructed not to give away the "secret" at the heart of the film—but what exactly was the film's secret? Homosexuality? Transsexuality? Gender construction? Nationalist brutalities? Colonial encounters? By making the unmasking of a transvestite character into the preeminent signifier of difference and disclosure in the film, director Jordan participates, as many critics have noted, in a long tradition of transforming political conflict into erotic tension in order to offer a romantic resolution.[1] I want to discuss *The Crying Game* briefly here to illustrate the misuse or simply the avoidance of the transgender gaze in mainstream films that purport to be about gender ambiguity. By asking media and audiences to keep the film's secret, then, *The Crying Game*'s producers created and deepened the illusion that the film would and could offer something new and unexpected. In fact, the secrecy constructs a mainstream viewer for the film and ignores more knowing audiences.

The Crying Game concerns a number of different erotic triangles situated within the tense political landscape of the English occupation of Northern Ireland. The film opens by animating one triangle that links two IRA operatives, Fergus and Jude, to the black British soldier, Jody, whom they must kidnap. Jude lures Jody away from a fairground with a promise of sexual interaction, and then Fergus ambushes Jody and whisks him away to an IRA hideout. The whole of the opening scene plays out to the accompaniment of "When a Man Loves a Woman." The song equates femininity with trickery, falsehood, and deceit, and it sets up the misogynist strands of a narrative that envision the white male as unknowing victim of feminine wiles. The first third of the film concerns the relationship between captors and captive, and particularly between the warmhearted Fergus and the winning Jody. Fergus and Jody bond and connect

---

[1] For an excellent discussion of the political contradictions of *The Crying Game*, see Shantanu Dutta Ahmed, "'I Thought You Knew!' Performing the Penis, the Phallus, and Otherness in Neil Jordan's *The Crying Game*" (1998).

over the picture of Jody's absent lover, Dil. After Jody dies in a foiled escape effort, Fergus leaves Ireland to escape the IRA and heads to England, where he becomes a construction worker. Fergus goes looking for Dil, and when he finds her, he romances her while seemingly unaware of her transgender identity. The last third of the film charts the course of Fergus's discovery of Dil's secret and his reentanglement with the IRA.

There are three major narrative strands in *The Crying Game*, all of which seem bound to alternative political identities, but none of which actually live up to their own potential. In the first strand, which involves the IRA, we'd expect to hear a critique of English colonialism, English racism, and the occupation of Northern Ireland by England. Instead, the film uses Jody to critique Irish racism and Fergus to delegitimize the IRA. The second narrative strand, which concerns the romance between Fergus and Dil, seems committed to a narrative about the "naturalness" of all types of gender expression, and here we expect to see the structures of heteronormativity exposed and the male gaze de-authorized. Instead, *The Crying Game* uses Dil's transvestitism only to re-center the white male gaze, and to make the white male into the highly flexible, supremely human subject who must counter and cover for the gender rigidity of the transvestite Dil (rigidity meaning that she cannot flow back and forth between male and female; she insists on being recognized as female) and the political rigidity of the IRA "fanatic" Jude. The triangulations that prop up each half of the film create the illusion of alternatives, but return time and again to the stable political format of white patriarchy. The third narrative strand has to do with cinematic time, and it projects an alternative ordering of time by positioning Dil as a character who seems to be able to cross back and forth between past, present, and future. When we first see Dil, she appears in a photograph representing Jody's past. When Fergus finally meets Dil, she represents his new present-tense life away from the IRA, and as the film winds down, Dil represents for Fergus a conventional future of marriage and family that awaits him when he obtains his release from jail, where he is "doing time." The seeming temporal fluidity of Dil is undercut, however, by the normative logic of the narrative's temporal drive, which seeks, through Fergus, to pin Dil down within the logic of heteronormative time.

Ultimately, the transgender character Dil never controls the gaze, and serves as a racialized fetish figure who diverts the viewer's attention from the highly charged political conflict between England and Ireland. The film characterizes Irish nationalism as a heartless and futile endeavor while depicting England ironically as a multicultural refuge, a place where formerly colonized peoples find a home. To dramatize the difference between Irish and English nationalism, the kidnapped black soldier, Jody, describes Ireland as "the only place in the world where they'll call you a nigger to your face." England, on the other hand, is marked for him by class conflicts (played out in his cricket tales), but not so much by racial disharmony. By the time Dil enters the film, about a third of the way in, England has become for Fergus a refuge and a place where he can disappear.

Disappearing is, in many ways, the name of the crying game, and the film plays with and through the fetishistic structure of cinema itself, with, in other words, the spectator's willingness to see what is not there and desire what is. In a series of scenes set in the gay bar, the Metro, where Dil performs, the viewer's gaze is sutured to Fergus's. In the first few scenes, the bar seems to be populated by so-called normal people, men and women, dancing together. But in the scene at the Metro that follows Fergus's discovery of Dil's penis, the camera again scans the bar and finds the garish and striking faces of the drag queens who populate it. Like

Fergus, we formerly saw bio men and women, and like Fergus, we suddenly see the bar for what it is: a queer site. And our vision, no matter how much we recognized Dil as transgender earlier, makes this abrupt detour around the transgender gaze along with Fergus. Indeed, *The Crying Game* cannot imagine the transgender gaze any more than it can cede the gaze to an IRA perspective. Here the revelation of a queer bar community sets up new triangulations within which the relationship between Fergus/Jimmy and Dil is now coded as homosexual. The homo context erases Dil's transsexual subjectivity, and throws the male protagonist into a panic that is only resolved by the symbolic castration of Dil when Fergus cuts Dil's hair. He does this supposedly to disguise Dil and protect her from the IRA, but actually the haircut unmasks her and serves to protect Fergus from his own desires.

If we recall the three definitions of "crying" with which I began this section, we will see that Jordan's film makes use of all of them in order to confirm the alignment of humanity with Fergus and otherness with Dil, Jody, and Jude. The first definition—"to announce in public, utter in a loud distinct voice so as to be heard over a long distance"—references the open secret of Dil's gender, and equates the "crying game" with the subtle interplay between being "out" and being "in." While Dil's secret is equated with dishonesty and sickening deceit (literally since Fergus/Jimmy vomits when he sees Dil's penis), the film makes no particular moral judgments about the secret that Fergus keeps from Dil—namely, his involvement in the death of her lover. Only Dil is shown to be playing the crying game and so it is her treacherous deceptions rather than his that must be punished. His punishment (jail time) is earned for his traitorous behavior of the nation rather than his betrayal of Dil. The second definition—"the process of shedding tears (usually accompanied by sobs or other inarticulate sounds)"—speaks to the potential for tragedy in and around the transgender figure. The tragic transgender, indeed, weeps because happiness and satisfaction, according to transphobic narratives, is always just out of reach. In this film, Dil cries when she thinks that Fergus is leaving her for Jude. Fergus uses Dil's tears to wipe her makeup off her face and begin the transformation from female to male that he says will be her cover from the violence of the IRA. By using her tears to erase her mask, the film once again creates a model of true humanity that is equated with gender and temporal stability. Dil's transformation from girl to boy matches up both sex and gender, past and present. The final definition of crying is "conspicuously bad, offensive or reprehensible," and ultimately this is the judgment that the film hands down on the transgender character and the fanatic IRA members.

Boys Don't Cry: Beyond Tears

Given the predominance of films that use transgender characters, but avoid the transgender gaze, Peirce's transformation of the Brandon story into the Oscar-winning *Boys Don't Cry* signaled something much more than the successful interpretation of a transgender narrative for a mainstream audience. The success of Peirce's depiction depended not simply on the impressive acting skills of Hilary Swank and her surrounding cast, nor did it rest solely on the topicality of the Brandon narrative in gay, lesbian, and transgender communities; rather, the seduction of mainstream viewers by this decidedly queer and unconventional narrative must be ascribed to the film's ability to construct and sustain a transgender gaze. Debates about the gendered gaze in Hollywood film have subsided in recent years, and have been replaced by much more flexible conceptions of looking and imaging that account for multiple viewers and perspectives. The range of subject positions for looking has been expanded to include "queer looks," "oppositional gazes," "black looks," and other modes of seeing not captured by the abbreviated structures of the male and female gaze (Hooks 1992; Gever 1993). But while different styles of looking have been accounted for in this expanded range, the basic formula for generating visual pleasure may not have shifted significantly. In other words, while different visual styles and pallets have helped to construct an alternative cinema, the structures of mainstream cinema have remained largely untouched. The success of *Boys Don't Cry* in cultivating an audience beyond the queer cinema circuit depends absolutely on its ability to hijack the male and female gazes, and replace them surreptitiously with transgender modes of looking and queer forms of visual pleasure.

In a gesture that has left feminist film theorists fuming for years, Laura Mulvey's classic essay, "Visual Pleasure and Narrative Cinema" argued, somewhat sensibly, that the pleasure in looking was always gendered within classic cinema. Mulvey went on to claim that within those classic cinematic narrative trajectories that begin with a mystery, a murder, a checkered past, or class disadvantage, or that advance through a series of obstacles toward the desired resolution in heterosexual marriage, there exist a series of male and female points of identification (Mulvey 1990). In other words, to the extent that cinema depends on the power to activate and attract desiring relations (between characters, between on-screen and offscreen subjects, between images and subjects, between spectators), it also depends on a sexual and gendered economy of looking, watching and identifying. The desiring positions within conventional cinematic universes tend to be called "masculine" and "feminine." While the masculine character in the film (whether or not that character is male or female) negotiates an obstacle course in order to advance toward a romantic reward, the feminine character waits at the course's end for the hero to advance, succeed, and arrive.[2] These gendered characters play their parts within a field of extremely limited and finite variation, and yet, because gendered spectators have already consented to limited and finite gender roles before entering the cinema, they will consent to the narrow range of narrative options within narrative cinema. Entertainment, in many ways, is the name we give to the fantasies of difference that erupt on the screen only to give way to the reproduction of sameness. In other words, as much as viewers want to believe in alternatives, the mainstream film assumes that they also want to believe that the choices they have made and the realities within which they function offer the best possible options. So for example, while gay or lesbian characters may appear within heterosexual romances as putative alternatives to the seemingly inevitable progression within adulthood from adolescence to romance to marriage to reproduction to death, the queer characters (say, Greg Kinnear in *As Good as It Gets*, or any and all lesbian characters in films about homo triangulations like *Basic Instinct*, *French Twist*, and so on) will function only to confirm the rightness of heterosexual object choice.

How does conventional narrative cinema allow for variation while maintaining a high degree of conformity? Sometimes the masculine character will be a woman (Barbara Stanwyck in *Walk on the Wild Side*; Michelle Rodriguez in *Girlfight*; Mercedes McCambridge in anything) and the narrative twist will involve her downfall or domestication. Sometimes the feminine

---

[2] The most sophisticated account of this narrative trajectory in cinema occurs in Teresa De Lauretis, *Alice Doesn't: Feminism, Semiotics, Cinema* (1984).

character will be a man (Jeremy Irons in *Dead Ringers*; Jet Li in *Romeo Must Die*) and the narrative will compel him to either become a male hero or self-destruct. And sometimes, as we saw in *The Crying Game*, the transgender character will be evoked as a metaphor for flexible subjecthood, but will not be given a narrative in his/her own right. But every now and then, and these are the instances that I want to examine here, the gendered binary on which the stability, the pleasure, and the purchase of mainstream cinema depend will be thoroughly rescripted, allowing for another kind of gaze or look. Here, I track the potentiality of the transgender gaze or the "transverse look," as Nick Mirzoeff describes it. Mirzoeff suggests that in an age of "multiple viewpoints," we have to think beyond the gaze. He writes about a "transient, transnational, transgendered way of seeing that visual culture seeks to define, describe and deconstruct with the transverse look or glance—not a gaze, there have been enough gazes already" (Mirzoeff 2002, 18).

While Mulvey's essay created much vigorous debate in cinema studies on account of its seemingly fatalistic perspective on gender roles and relations, the messenger in many ways was being confused with the message. Mulvey was not *creating* the gendered dynamics of looking, she was simply describing the remarkably restricted ways in which spectators can access pleasure. And so, for example, conventional narratives cannot conceive of the pleasure of being the image, the fetish, or the object of the gaze. Nor can they allow for the ways in which thoroughly scrambled gender relations might impact the dynamics of looking, at least not for long. Within conventional cinema, Mulvey proposed that the only way for a female viewer to access voyeuristic pleasure was to cross-identify with the male gaze; through this complicated procedure, the female spectator of a conventional visual narrative could find a position on the screen that offered a little more than the pleasure of being fetishized. Mulvey suggests that the female viewer has to suture her look to the male look. Others have talked about this as a form of transvestism—a cross-dressed look that allows the female spectator to imagine momentarily that she has the same access to power as the male viewer. The problem with the cinematic theory of masquerade, of course, is that it requires no real understanding of transvestism and of the meaning of male transvestism in particular. Mary Ann Doane, for example, in "Film and the Masquerade," simply theorizes all female subject positions as masquerade, and a hyperfeminine one (Doane 1990). In doing so, she misses the queer dimension of the masquerade. In a trenchant critique of Doane, Chris Straayer in *Deviant Eyes, Deviant Bodies* has described the appeal of the "temporary transvestite film" for mainstream viewers, and she claims that the popularity of these films has to do with "the appeasement of basic contradictions through a common fantasy of over-throwing gender constructions without challenging sexual difference."[3] But what happens when the transvestite narrative is not temporary, and when gender constructions are overthrown and sexual difference is shaken to its very foundations?

In the classic Hollywood film text, the camera looks from one position/character and then returns the gaze from another position/character, thereby suturing the viewer to a usually male gaze and simultaneously covering over what the viewer cannot see. This dynamic of looking is called shot/reverse shot and it occupies a central position within cinematic grammar. The shot/reverse shot mode allows for the stability of narrative progress, ensures a developmental logic, and allows the viewers to insert themselves into the filmic world by imagining that their access

[3] See Straayer's chapter, "Redressing the Natural: The Temporary Transvestite Film" (Straayer 1996).

to the characters is unmediated. The dismantling of the shot/reverse shot can be identified as the central cinematic tactic in *Boys Don't Cry*. In her stylish adaptation of the true-to-life story of Brandon, director Peirce self-consciously constructs what can only be called a transgender look. *Boys Don't Cry* establishes the legitimacy and the durability of Brandon's gender not simply by telling the tragic tale of his death by murder but by forcing spectators to adopt, if only provisionally, Brandon's gaze, a transgender look.[4] The transgender look in this film reveals the ideological content of the male and female gazes, and it disarms, temporarily, the compulsory heterosexuality of the romance genre. Brandon's gaze, obviously, dies with him in the film's brutal conclusion, but Peirce, perhaps prematurely, abandons the transgender look in the final intimate encounter between Lana and Brandon. Peirce's inability to sustain a transgender look opens up a set of questions about the inevitability and dominance of both the male/female and hetero/homo binary in narrative cinema.

One remarkable scene, about halfway through the film, clearly foregrounds the power of the transgender look, making it most visible precisely where and when it is most threatened. In a scary and nerve-racking sequence of events, Brandon finds himself cornered at Lana's house. John and Tom have forced Candace to tell them that Brandon has been charged by the police with writing bad checks and that he has been imprisoned as a woman. John and Tom now hunt Brandon, like hounds after a fox, and then they begin a long and excruciating interrogation of Brandon's gender identity. Lana protects Brandon at first by saying that she will examine him and determine whether he is a man or a woman. Lana and Brandon enter Lana's bedroom, where Lana refuses to look as Brandon unbuckles his pants, telling him, "Don't…. I know you're a guy." As they sit on the bed together, the camera now follows Lana's gaze out into the night sky, a utopian vision of an elsewhere into which she and Brandon long to escape. This is one of several fantasy shots in an otherwise wholly realistic film; Peirce threads these shots in which time speeds up or slows down through the film, creating an imagistic counternarrative to the story of Brandon's decline.

As Brandon and Lana sit in Lana's bedroom imagining an elsewhere that would save them from the impoverished reality they inhabit, the camera cuts back abruptly to "reality" and a still two-shot of Brandon in profile and Lana behind him. As they discuss their next move, the camera draws back slowly and makes a seamless transition to place them in the living room in front of the posse of bullies. This quiet interlude in Lana's bedroom establishes the female gaze, Lana's gaze, as a willingness to see what is not there (a condition of all fantasy), but also as a refusal to privilege the literal over the figurative (Brandon's genitalia over Brandon's gender presentation). The female gaze, in this scene, makes possible an alternative vision of time, space, and embodiment. Time slows down while the couple linger in the sanctuary of Lana's private world, her bedroom; the bedroom itself becomes an otherworldly space framed by the big night sky, and containing the perverse vision of a girl and her queer boy lover; and the body of Brandon is preserved as male, for now, by Lana's refusal to dismantle its fragile power with the scrutinizing gaze of science and "truth." That Lana's room morphs seamlessly into the living room at the end of this scene, alerts the viewer to the possibility that an alternative vision will subtend and undermine the chilling enforcement of normativity that follows.

---

[4] Patricia White has argued in "Girls Still Cry" (2001) that the gaze in *Boys Don't Cry* is Lana's all along. I think in the first two-thirds of the film, the gaze is shared between Lana and Brandon, but I agree with White that the film's ending transfers the gaze from Brandon to Lana's with some unpredictable consequences.

Back in the living room—the primary domestic space of the family—events take an abrupt turn toward the tragic. Brandon is shoved now into the bathroom, a hyperreal space of sexual difference, and is violently de-pantsed by John and Tom, and then restrained by John while Tom roughly examines Brandon's crotch. The brutality of John and Tom's action here is clearly identified as a violent mode of looking, and the film identifies the male gaze with the factual, the visible, and the literal. The brutality of the male gaze, however, is more complicated than simply a castrating force; John and Tom not only want to see the site of Brandon's castration but more important, they need Lana to see it. Lana kneels in front of Brandon, confirming the scene's resemblance to a crucifixion tableau, and refuses to raise her eyes, declining, again, to look at Brandon's unveiling.

At the point when Lana's "family" and "friends" assert their heteronormative will most forcefully on Brandon's resistant body, however, Brandon rescues himself for a moment by regaining the alternative vision of time and space that he and Lana shared moments earlier in her bedroom. A slow-motion sequence interrupts the fast and furious quasi-medical scrutiny of Brandon's body, and shots from Brandon's point of view reveal him to be in the grips of an "out-of-body" and out-of-time experience. Light shines on Brandon from above, and his anguished face peers out into the crowd of onlookers who have gathered at the bathroom door. The crowd now includes a fully clothed Brandon, a double, who returns the gaze of the tortured Brandon impassively. In this shot/reverse shot sequence between the castrated Brandon and the transgender one, the transgender gaze is constituted as a look divided within itself, a point of view that comes from two places (at least) at the same time, one clothed and one naked. The clothed Brandon is the one who was rescued by Lana's refusal to look; he is the Brandon who survives his own rape and murder; he is the Brandon to whom the audience is now sutured, a figure who combines momentarily the activity of looking with the passivity of the spectacle. And the naked Brandon is the one who will suffer, endure, and finally expire.

Kaja Silverman has called attention to cinematic suture in an essay of the same name, as "the process whereby the inadequacy of the subject's position is exposed in order to facilitate new insertions into a cultural discourse which promises to make good that lack" (Silverman 1983, 236). Here, in *Boys Don't Cry*, the inadequacy of the subject's position has been presented as a precondition of the narrative, and so this scene of the split transgender subject, which would ordinarily expose "the inadequacy of the subject's position," actually works to highlight the *sufficiency* of the transgender subject. So if usually the shot/reverse shot both secures and destabilizes the spectator's sense of self, now the shot/reverse shot involving the two Brandons serves both to destabilize the spectator's sense of gender stability and confirm Brandon's manhood at the very moment that he has been exposed as female/castrated.

Not only does *Boys Don't Cry* create a position for the transgender subject that is fortified from the traditional operations of the gaze and conventional modes of gendering but it also makes the transgender subject dependent on the recognition of a woman. In other words, Brandon can be Brandon because Lana is willing to see him as he sees himself (clothed, male, vulnerable, lacking, strong, and passionate), and she is willing to avert her gaze when his manhood is in question. With Brandon occupying the place of the male hero and the male gaze in the romance, the dynamics of looking and gendered being are permanently altered. If usually it is the female body that registers lack, insufficiency, and powerlessness, in *Boys Don't Cry*, it is Brandon who represents the general condition of incompleteness, crisis, and lack, and it is Lana who represents the fantasy of wholeness, knowledge, and pleasure. Lana can be naked without trauma while Brandon cannot; she can access physical pleasure in a way that he cannot, but he is depicted as mobile and self-confident in a way that she is not. Exclusion and privilege cannot be assigned neatly to the couple on the basis of gender or class hierarchies; power, rather, is shared between the two subjects, and she agrees to misrecognize him as male while he sees through her social alienation and unhappiness, recognizing her as beautiful, desirable, and special.

By deploying the transgender gaze and binding it to an empowered female gaze in *Boys Don't Cry*, director Peirce, for most of the film, keeps the viewer trained on the seriousness of Brandon's masculinity and the authenticity of his presentation as opposed to its elements of masquerade. But toward the end of the film, Peirce suddenly and catastrophically divests her character of his transgender look and converts it to a lesbian and therefore female gaze. In a strange scene following the brutal rape of Brandon by John and Tom, Lana comes to Brandon as he lies sleeping in a shed outside of Candace's house. In many ways, the encounter between the two that follows seems to extend the violence enacted on Brandon's body by John and Tom since Brandon now interacts with Lana *as if he were a woman*. Lana, contrary to her previous commitment to his masculinity, seems to see him as female, and she calls him "pretty" and asks him what he was like as a girl. Brandon confesses to Lana that he has been untruthful about many things in his past, and his confession sets up the expectation that he will now appear before Lana as his "true" self. Truth here becomes sutured to nakedness as Lana disrobes Brandon, tentatively saying that she may not know "how to do this." "This" seems to refer to having sex with Brandon as a woman. They both agree that his whole journey to manhood has been pretty weird and then they move to make love. While earlier Peirce created quite graphic depictions of sex between Brandon and Lana, now the action is hidden by a Hollywood dissolve as if to suggest that the couple are now making love as opposed to having sex. The scene is disjunctive and completely breaks the flow of the cinematic text by having Lana, the one person who could see Brandon's gender separate from his sex, now see him as woman. Moreover, the scene implies that the rape has made Brandon a woman in a way that his brutal exposure earlier in the bathroom and his intimate sex scenes with Lana could not. And if the scene seems totally out of place to the viewer, it apparently felt wrong as well to Hilary Swank. There are rumors that Swank and Peirce fought over this scene, and that Peirce shot the scene without Swank by using a body double. A close reading of the end of the scene indeed shows that the Brandon figure takes off his T-shirt while the camera watches from behind. The musculature and look of Brandon's back is quite different here from the toned look of Swank's body in earlier exposure scenes.

The "love" scene raises a number of logical and practical questions about the representation of the relationship between Brandon and Lana. First, why would Brandon want to have sex within hours of a rape? Second, how does the film pull back from its previous commitment to his masculinity here by allowing his femaleness to become legible and significant to Lana's desire? Third, in what ways does this scene play against the earlier, more "plastic" sex scenes in which Brandon used a dildo and would not allow Lana to touch him? And fourth, how does this scene unravel the complexities of the transgender gaze as they have been assembled in earlier scenes between Brandon and Lana? When asked in an interview about this scene, Peirce reverts to a tired humanist narrative to explain it and says that after the rape, Brandon could not be either Brandon Teena or Teena Brandon and so he becomes truly "himself," and in that interaction with Lana, Brandon "receives love" for the first time as a human being.[5] Peirce claims that Lana herself told her about this encounter and therefore it was true to life. In the context of the film, however, which has made no such commitment to authenticity, the scene ties Brandon's humanity to a particular form of naked embodiment that in the end requires him to be a woman.

Ultimately in *Boys Don't Cry*, the double vision of the transgender subject gives way to the universal vision of humanism; the transgender man and his lover become lesbians, and the murder seems to be simply the outcome of a vicious homophobic rage. Given the failure of nerve that leads Peirce to conclude her film with a humanist scene of love conquers all, it is no surprise that she also sacrificed the racial complexity of the narrative by erasing the story of the other victim who died alongside Brandon and Lisa Lambert. As discussed earlier, Philip DeVine, a disabled African American man, has in general received only scant treatment in media accounts of the case, despite the connection of at least one of the murderers to a white supremacist group (Jones 1996, 154). Now in the feature film, Philip's death has been rendered completely irrelevant to the narrative that has been privileged. Peirce claimed that this subplot would have complicated her film and made the plot too cumbersome, but race is a narrative trajectory that is absolutely central to the meaning of the Brandon murder. Philip was dating Lana's sister, Leslie, and had a fight with her the night he showed up at Lisa's house in Humboldt County. His death was neither accidental nor an afterthought; his connection to Leslie could be read as a similarly outrageous threat to the supremacy and privilege of white manhood that the murderers Lotter and Nissen rose to defend. By taking Philip out of the narrative and by not even mentioning him in the original dedication of the film ("To Brandon Teena and Lisa Lambert"), the filmmaker sacrifices the hard facts of racial hatred and transphobia to a streamlined romance.[6] Peirce, in other words, reduces the complexity of the murderous act even as she sacrifices the complexity of Brandon's identity.

In the end, the murders are shown to be the result of a kind of homosexual panic, and Brandon is offered up as an "everyman" hero who makes a claim on the audience's sympathies first by pulling off a credible masculinity, but then by seeming to step out of his carefully maintained manhood to appear before judge and jury in the naked flesh as female. By reneging on her earlier commitment to the transgender gaze and ignoring altogether the possibility of exposing the whiteness of the male gaze, *Boys Don't Cry* falls far short of the alternative vision that was articulated so powerfully and shared so beautifully by Brandon and Lana in Lana's bedroom. But even so, by articulating momentarily the specific formal dimensions of the transgender gaze, *Boys Don't Cry* takes a quantum leap away from the crying games, which continued in the past to locate transgenderism in between the male and female gazes and alongside unrelenting tragedy. Peirce's film, in fact, opens the door to a nonfetishistic mode of seeing the transgender body—a mode that looks with, rather than at, the transgender body and cultivates the multidimensionality of an indisputably transgender gaze.

---

[5] Interview by Terry Gross on *Fresh Air*, PBS Radio, March 15, 2001.

[6] In the review copy of the film I saw, *Boys Don't Cry* was dedicated "To Brandon Teena and Lisa Lambert." This dedication seems to have been removed later on, possibly because it so overtly referenced Philip's erasure.

Lovely and Confusing: By Hook or by Crook *and the Transgender Look*

> We feel like we were thrown almost every curve in the game. And we managed to make this thing by hook or by crook.
>
> —Harry Dodge and Silas Howard, *By Hook or by Crook* directors

By Hook or by Crook marks a real turning point for queer and transgender cinema. This no-budget, low-tech, high-concept feature, shot entirely in mini digital video, tells the story of two gender bandits, Shy and Valentine. Described by its creators as "utterly post-post-modern, a little bit of country and a little bit of rock and roll," the film conjures up the twilight world of two loners living on the edge without trying to explain or rationalize their reality.[7] The refusal to explain either the gender peculiarities of the heroes or the many other contradictions they embody allows directors Howard and Dodge instead to focus on developing eccentric and compelling characters. While most of the action turns on the bond between Shy and Valentine, their world is populated with a stunning array of memorable characters like Valentine's girlfriend, Billie (Stanya Kahn), and Shy's love interest, Isabelle (Carina Gia). The film also features fabulous guest appearances by queer celebrities like Joan Jett as a news interviewee, the late Kris Kovick typecast as a crazy nut in the park, and Machiko Saito as the gun store clerk. These cameos establish the world of *By Hook or by Crook* as a specifically queer universe and clearly mark a studied indifference to mainstream acceptance by making subcultural renown rather than Hollywood glamour into the most desirable form of celebrity.

Both *The Crying Game* and *Boys Don't Cry* relied heavily on the successful solicitation of affect—whether revulsion, sympathy, or empathy—in order to give mainstream viewers access to a transgender gaze. And in both films, a relatively unknown actor (Jay Davidson and Hilary Swank, respectively) performs alongside a more well-known actor (Stephen Rea and Chloe Sevigny, respectively); the relative obscurity of the transgender actors allow them to pull off the feat of credibly performing a gender at odds with the sexed body even after the body has been brutally exposed. *By Hook or by Crook* resists the seduction of crying games and the lure of sentiment, and works instead to associate butchness and gender innovation with wit, humor, and style. The melancholia that tinges *The Crying Game* and saturates *Boys Don't Cry* is transformed in *By Hook or by Crook* into the wise delirium of Dodge's character, Valentine. Dodge and Howard (Shy) knowingly avoid engaging their viewers at the level of sympathy, pity, or even empathy, and instead they "hook" them with the basic tools of the cinematic apparatus: desire and identification.

Dodge and Howard pioneer some brilliant techniques of queer plotting in order to map the world of the willfully perverse. As they say in interviews, neither director was interested in telling a story about "being gay." Nor did Dodge and Howard want to spend valuable screen time explaining the characters' sexualities and genders to unknowing audiences. In the press kit, Dodge and Howard discuss their strategy in terms of representing sexuality and gender as follows: "This is a movie about a budding friendship between two people. The

[7] Unless otherwise attributed, all quotes from directors Howard and Dodge are taken from the press kit for *By Hook or by Crook*, http://www.steakhaus.com/bhobc/.

fact that they happen to be queer is purposefully off the point. If you call them something, other than sad, rambling, spirited, gentle, sharp or funny… you might call them *'butches.'"* Instead of a humanist story about gay heroes struggling to be accepted, Dodge and Howard tell a beautifully fragmented tale of queer encounter set almost entirely in a queer universe. In other words, the heroes are utterly unremarkable for their queerness in the cinematic world that the directors have created. In this way, Dodge and Howard offer a tribute to the San Francisco subcultural worlds that they inhabit. As Howard remarks, "We've always hoped this project would reflect the creativity and actual valor of the community of people we came from. And I think it does. From the get-go, this movie had its roots in our extended family of weirdos in San Francisco."

In the film, Shy and Valentine visit cafes, clubs, shops, and hotels where no one reacts specifically to their butchness. This narrative strategy effectively *universalizes queerness* within this specific cinematic space. Many gay and lesbian films represent their characters and their struggles as "universal" as a way of suggesting that their film speaks to audiences beyond specific gay and lesbian audiences. But few do more than submit to the regulation of narrative that transforms the specific into the universal: they tell stories of love, redemption, family, and struggle that look exactly like every other Hollywood feature angling for a big audience. *By Hook or by Crook* actually manages to tell a queer story that is more than a queer story by refusing to acknowledge the existence of a straight world. Where the straight world is represented only through its institutions such as the law, the mental institution, or commerce, the queer cinematic world comes to represent a truly localized place of opposition—an opposition, moreover, that is to be found in committed performances of perversity, madness, and friendship. While some of Dodge's comments in the press notes imply a humanist aim for the project ("We wanted to make a film about people with big ideas and big dreams who end up dealing with the shadowy subtleties of human life"; "I want to make work that touches people's hearts…. I am interested in the human spirit"), the film resists the trap of liberal humanism (making a film about gays who are, in the end, just like everybody else). So *By Hook or by Crook* universalizes queerness without allowing its characters to be absorbed back into the baggy and ultimately heterosexist concept of the "human."

Different key scenes from the film build, capture, and sustain this method of universalizing queerness. In one scene soon after they meet, Shy and Valentine go to a club together. The club scene, filmed in San Francisco's notorious Lexington Bar, is a riotous montage of queer excess. The camera lovingly pans a scene of punky, pierced, tattooed, perverted young queers. The montages lasts much longer than necessary, signaling that the beauty and intrinsic worth of this world transcends its diegetic purpose. In *The Crying Game*, the bar scenes were used first to establish the credibility of Dil's womanhood and then, after she has "come out" to Fergus as male bodied, the bar scenes are used to cast her womanhood as incredible. So while *The Crying Game* casts the bar as a place of perversion and a primal scene of deception, Dodge and Howard situate the queer bar as central to an alternative vision of community, space, time, and identity. In the bar, Valentine dances wildly and ecstatically while Shy sits apart from the crowd watching. The camera playfully scans the bar and then lines up its patrons for quick cameos. Here, Dodge and Howard are concerned to represent the bar as both a space of queer community and a place of singularity. The singularity of the patrons, however, does not create the kind of transgressive exceptionalism that I discussed in Chapter 1; it instead reveals a difference to be a shared and collaborative relation to normativity rather than an individualist mode of refusal.

After watching Valentine dance, Shy gets up and steals Valentine's wallet before leaving. The theft of Valentine's wallet should create a gulf of distrust and suspicion between the two strangers, but in this looking-glass world, it actually bonds them securely within their underground existence. Shy uses Valentine's wallet to find out where she lives, and when Shy returns Valentine's wallet the next day, she is greeted like a long-lost brother—this has the effect of inverting the morality of the world represented in this film by the police. Other scenes deepen this refusal of conventional law and order. The two butches as wannabe thieves try to hold up a drugstore only to be chased off by an aggressive salesclerk; they try to scam a hardware store and, in a citation of Robert De Niro's famous scene from *Taxi Driver*, they pose with guns in front of the mirror in Shy's run-down motel room. All of these scenes show Shy and Valentine as eccentric, but gentle outlaws who function as part of an alternative universe with its own ethics, sex/gender system, and public space.

De Niro's taxi driver, muttering "you looking at me" as he pointed a loaded gun at his own mirror image, is a vigilante loner, a man turned inward and lost to the city he skims across in his yellow cab. But while De Niro's character accidentally hits a vein of humor with his mohawked "fuck you," Shy and Valentine deliberately ride butch humor rather than macho vengeance into the sunset. If the vigilante wants to remake the world in his image, the queer outlaws of *By Hook or by Crook* are content to imagine a world of their own making. When asked about the title of the film, Silas Howard responded: "The title refers to what is involved in inventing your own world—when you don't see anything that represents you out there, how can you seize upon that absence as an opportunity to make something out of nothing, by hook or by crook. We take gender ambiguity, for example, and we don't explain it, dilute it or apologize for it—we represent it for what it is—something confusing and lovely!"

The recent explosion of transgender films forces us to consider what the spectacle of the transgender body represents to multiple audiences. For some audiences, the transgender body confirms a fantasy of fluidity so common to notions of transformation within the postmodern. To others, the transgender body confirms the enduring power of the binary gender system. But to still other viewers, the transgender body represents a utopian vision of a world of subcultural possibilities. Representations of transgenderism in recent queer cinema have moved from a tricky narrative device designed to catch an unsuspecting audience off guard to truly independent productions within which gender ambiguity is not a trap or a device but part of the production of new forms of heroism, vulnerability, visibility, and embodiment. The centrality of the figure of Brandon in this drama of postmodern embodiment suggests, as I argued in Chapter 2, that we have a hard time thinking of seismic shifts in the history of representations separate from individual stories of transformation. The hopes and fears that have been projected onto the slim and violated body of one transgender loner in small-town Nebraska make clear the flaws of "representative history," and call for the kind of shared vision that we see in *By Hook or by Crook*—a vision of community, possibility, and redemption through collaboration.

Bibliography

Doane, M. A. "Film and the Masquerade: Theorizing the Female Spectator" (1982). In *Issues in Feminist Film Criticism*, edited by P. Erens, 41–57. Bloomington: Indiana University Press, 1990.

Gever, M., P. Parmar, and J. Greyson, eds. *Queer Looks: Perspectives on Lesbian and Gay Film and Video*. New York: Routledge, 1993.

Hooks, B. *Black Looks: Race and Representation*. Boston: South End Press, 1992.

Jones, A. *All S/he Wanted*. New York: Pocket Books, 1996.

Mirzoeff, N. "The Subject of Visual Culture." In *The Visual Culture Reader*, 3–28. New York: Routledge, 2002.

Mulvey, L. "Visual Pleasure and Narrative Cinema" (1975). In *Issues in Feminist Film Criticism*, edited by P. Erens, 28–40. Bloomington: Indiana University Press, 1990.

Silverman, K. "Suture." In *The Subject of Semiotics*. New York: Oxford University Press, 1993.

Straayer, C. *Deviant Eyes, Deviant Bodies: Re-Orientations in Film and Video*. New York: Columbia University Press, 1996.

CHAPTER 32
TINA CHANTER

Tina Chanter (b. 1960) is a British philosopher whose work on aesthetics and politics is deeply influenced by Continental thinkers in the psychoanalytical and feminist traditions. Her single most significant contribution to the philosophy of film is her book, The Picture of Abjection: Film, Fetish, and the Nature of Difference, *published originally in English by Indiana University Press in 2008. The text included here, "Concluding Reflections on the Necrophilia of Fetishism," is the last chapter of that work.*

Chanter begins the selection with some thoughts on identification in film. For much of the history of Continental philosophy of film, identification—the process by which the viewer comes to appropriate film subjectivity, either by way of identifying with a character's or the camera's point of view—has been situated alongside (objectifying) desire as one of the elements necessary to a philosophical (and psychoanalytical) understanding of cinema. Customarily, however, identification has been discussed somewhat abstractly as a synthesis of technical, narrative, and psychological processes—and, given that abstraction, the film viewer has been treated as a uniform entity of its own, individual differences between filmgoers, thus, becoming irrelevant to identification. A good or successful or effective film, then, puts the film viewers—all of the film viewers—in the same position, of identifying with the film, and identifying in the same way (with the protagonist's struggle, or with the camera's objectifying gaze, and so on). Chanter suggests, however, that this is an oversimplification. She notes that how we identify and understand ourselves has an impact on how (or when) we identify with film. This is because, in part, our understanding of our own identity has an impact on what we see and do not see when watching a film. (To take but one of her examples, what do we see when we see the relationship between the characters Sam [Dooley Wilson] and Rick [Humphrey Bogart] in Casablanca*? Those viewers with experience or awareness of the social marginalization characteristic of much of the African American experience see Sam's subordination to Rick as primary: Sam is Rick's employee and, at times, personal servant, and this does not seem independent of the racial difference between the men. Other viewers, however, predominantly white viewers, often see Sam and Rick as friends and equals. These are incompatible views, but which view we take has as much to do with our sense of our own personal identity as it does anything else.) Because all spectators do not view the film from the same existential or psychological position, it ceases to make sense to speak of the film viewer. And as such, film directors cannot sustain the belief that they are in control of the film's meaning for viewers of the film.*

Film seeks out viewer identification in order to produce a harmonious narrative—to have all the viewers "on the same page," as it were. This is the attempt to fulfill the fantasy of the film director, whose work leads him or her to seek control over the cinematic experience. D. W. Griffith directs The Birth of a Nation *as he does so as to have viewers identify with the point of view taken by the camera in the film, and the film fulfills its promise as one of the "great" films only by way of such identification. One of the consequences of such identification, however, is that the viewer is encouraged, thereby, to take a sympathetic attitude toward the Ku Klux Klan and an antagonistic one toward the "threat" of a racially diverse society. As Chanter notes, viewers who are critical of racism (and America's history of racism as perpetuated precisely but such groups as the Klan) simply do not identify with Griffith's camera. This fundamentally alters their experience of viewing the film, if it doesn't make viewing the film impossible altogether. In any case, the difference between what these two different viewers experience in viewing the film is at the very basic level of what they see, and what they do not see, therein.*

Disruptions of the process of identification, thus, have the potential to rearrange the ways in which we see what we see: They can perpetuate normative identifications, on the one hand, or move us beyond normative restrictions, on the other. Although Lacanians generally privilege language in their account of the organization of normative systems, Chanter follows Julia Kristeva in the view that language is always rooted in a pre-linguistic ordering of the world. It is on this pre-linguistic level that Kristeva situates her notion of abjection, which is at the heart of Chanter's philosophy of film.

For Chanter, as for Kristeva, a culture's identity is shaped by foundational fantasies, pre-linguistic representations of reality. When foundational fantasies become indistinguishable from language itself, however, then a culture must figure out how fantasies are enacted. In such cultures, however, investigation of foundational fantasies is particularly uncommon: The indistinguishability of fantasy and language grants linguistic relationships (between words and things) a sense of fixity and indubitability. This belief in the absolute fixity of meaning is the fetishization of language, whereby identity is established and ambiguity is exiled from understanding. An investigation of the process of fetishization, then, can loosen the grip of the fetish on language, allowing for an indeterminacy and, thus, a multiplicity of meaning. The abject is not an alternative to the fetish; however, it is the condition of the possibility of fetishization. When certain identities are fetishized, the establishment of these fetishes depends essentially upon the abjection of others: certain groups within the society or culture are abjected as insignificant, as non-subjects. To be abjected is to be determined impossible and meaningless within the system of possible meaning: should someone encounter an abject as an abject, the only possible response within the system is horror or disgust: a complete inability to comprehend. By investigating this response, however, one can open the possibility of changing the meanings of terms, undermining the fetish, and reconstituting the boundaries of the abject thereby.

The nature of abjection as ambiguous means that it is never clear who is abjected by what: abjection is prior to the subject/object distinction itself. It is, thus, also prior to, and thus unmarked by, sexual difference and the heterosexual imperative. From the perspective of the abject, the fixed terms of identity constitution within a culture are always later additions, fetishized and thus believed to be independent of one another. The abject demonstrates, however, that these identities are mutually dependent and mutually constitutive, such that they cannot exist except in a system of meaningful relation. Traditional cinematic identification, then, depends upon a fetishized misunderstanding of the nature of subjective identity construction. To the extent that film and culture in general opt to reinforce the fetish and denounce the abject, film privileges "dead" terms and identities—those which do not reflect the reality of subjectivity—in what Chanter calls necrophilia. Alternatively, however, abjection affords us the opportunity to reimagine the construction of fantasy—the imaginary—itself. In reconstituting the foundational fantasies of a culture, abjection can help us to reconstitute ourselves, and thus to redraw the boundaries of abjection, as well. Film can, then, subject us to new fantasies, and new conceptions of the subject itself.

Filmography

- ***The Birth of a Nation*** (USA, 1915). *Directed by* D. W. Griffith. *Produced by* D. W. Griffith *and* Harry Aitken. *Written by* D. W. Griffith *and* Frank E. Woods. *Starring* Lillian Gish, Mae Marsh, Henry B. Walthall, Miriam Cooper, Ralph Lewis, George Siegmann, *and* Walter Long.
- ***Casablanca*** (USA, 1942). *Directed by* Michael Curtiz. *Produced by* Hal B. Wallis. *Written by* Julius J. Epstein, Philip G. Epstein, *and* Howad Koch. *Starring* Humphrey Bogart, Ingrid Bergman, *and* Paul Henreid.
- ***The Crying Game*** (Ireland–UK–Japan, 1992). *Directed and Written by* Neil Jordan. *Produced by* Stephen Woolley. *Starring* Stephen Rea, Miranda Richardson, Jaye Davidson, *and* Forest Whitaker.
- ***Hollow Reed*** (UK–Germany–Spain, 1996). *Directed by* Angela Pope. *Produced by* Channel Four Films. *Written by* Paula Milne. *Starring* Martin Donovan, Joely Richardson, Ian Hart, Jason Flemyng, *and* Sam Bould.
- ***Secrets and Lies*** (UK, 1996). *Directed and Written by* Mike Leigh. *Produced by* Simon Channing Williams. *Starring* Timothy Spall, Brenda Blethyn, Phyllis Logan, Marianne Jean-Baptiste, Claire Rushbrook, Ron Cook, Lesley Manville, Elizabeth Berrington, Michele Austin, Lee Ross, Emma Amos, *and* Hannah Davis.
- ***Ma vie en rose*** [*My Life in Pink*] (Belgium, 1997). *Directed by* Alain Berliner. *Produced by* Carole Scotta. *Written by* Alain Berliner *and* Chris Vander Stappen. *Starring* Michèle Laroque, Jean-Phillippe Écoffey, Hélène Vincent, Georges Du Fresne, Daniel Hanssens, Laurence Bibot, Jean-François Gallotte, Caroliné Baehr, Julien Rivière, *and* Marie Bunel.

CONCLUDING REFLECTIONS ON THE NECROPHILIA OF FETISHISM

In the close-up of Ludovic applying lipstick and looking at his image in a mirror, Berliner withholds from his audience any visual cues that would render determinate the character's gender, thereby putting into question the normative assumptions typically in play as identifiers of gender, assumptions that will be interrogated systematically throughout *Ma vie en rose*. Cowie says:

> Identification… arises not with the visual view of a character but with a close-up of the character looking. The use of a full-face close-up can invoke a transitivist identification not merely because we can then see the face clearly, but more importantly because in filling the screen it also obscures the space and time of the narrative…. The transitivist identification with the image of the face is but a moment, and just like the mirror stage itself, it is no sooner constituted as identification than it is flipped over into identification in a chain of desire, and the figure of the Other intervenes. In the cinema it is the moment when movement, narrative, the shift to medium-shot from close-up, or to the object of the glance, breaks up the absorption in the image of the other and forces it to give way to the chain of signification, to the movement of desire which is figured. (1997, 105)

If identification arises with a close-up of the character looking, when that character is Ludovic, looking into a mirror and seeing the girl he wants to be, how does identification play out? The reflection in the mirror that Ludovic sees is his ideal ego, not the ego ideal or superego that admonishes him to identify as a boy. As the narrative unfolds, how viewers position themselves in relation to Ludovic's identification will depend in part on how critically they reflect on the heteronormative, binary fantasies that fuel the social order, defensive fantasies that abject the Ludovics of this world. In *Ma vie en rose* the assumption that male bodies entail masculine genders while female bodies entail feminine genders also proves to be constitutive of middle-class cohesion. Ludovic identifies as a girl, and cannot understand why his family and society frown upon his desire to wear his sister's clothes and red lipstick. Identificatory regimes can be made available for reconstitution when we discover ourselves as having identified with such a desire. *Ma vie en rose* encourages critical reflection on the necessity of such constitutive relationships. A transsexual who views the film will be likely to entertain a different relationship to gender assumptions than another viewer, just as those who gasp in surprise or horror when they see Dil's penis in *The Crying Game* will not see it in the same way as those who are, as it were, in the know. Yet Jordan works to undermine the certainty not only of those who did not "know," but also of those who claimed to "know." What exactly did they know, and how does such knowledge perpetuate sexual and racial binaries that continue to dictate the imaginary possibilities of those that are lovable and those that are not? The spectators who view *The Birth of a Nation* as aesthetically groundbreaking, while minimizing its racism, stand in a very different relation to its images than that of viewers who refuse to divorce its aesthetic achievements from its use of racial stereotypes. Those who read Sam in *Casablanca* as Rick's equal fail to see as significant—that is they fail to see at all—the fact that his character remains largely undeveloped and that he remains Rick's sidekick and subordinate. The invisible regimes of whiteness and heteronormative desire that orchestrate his subordinate status fail to signify. The ways in which spectators identify themselves in relation to racial, sexual, class, and nationalist regimes are not coincidental to what we will see and what we will not see. This suggests that the continued adherence to Christian Metz's contention that the spectator is "all-perceiving" (1982, 48) needs to be revisited. Commenting on Metz, Cowie says, "What is specific to the cinema as visual performance is that all the spectators see from the same position—everyone sees Garbo's face as a profile—but this point-of-view will be continually changing: now close-up, now long-shot, now from this character's position now from another's. In other words, the spectator's look is aligned with and made identical to another look, the camera's which has gone before it, and already 'organised' the scene" (Cowie 1997, 100). To say that "all the spectators see from the same position" is to obliterate the significance of the difference between someone who reads Dil as transgendered from the start, and someone who doesn't, a difference that depends on the position one takes in relation to prevailing foundational social fantasies of desire. The director who has organized the framing of the film is not in control of the meaning it takes on for its viewers, even if that director provides for ambiguous readings. There is more than one spectator, and some spectators will see what others fail to see. Metz posits an ideal spectator, while espousing a theory of cinema that adheres to the trope of disavowal, a trope that Rose identifies as an "exclusively male construction" (1986, 202). The terms in which Metz posits the spectator as ideal also covertly privilege whiteness, heterosexuality, and middle-class identity, at the same time as they tend to underline the passivity of the spectator. Even as he acknowledges that the spectator "constitutes the cinema signifier (it is I who make the film)," Metz construes the spectator as a "great eye and ear," in which "material is deposited," as the "place" in which a "really perceived imaginary accedes to the symbolic" (1982, 48–49). This reflects a more general tension in Metz's analysis between his attestation on the one hand that the "ego is already formed" (47) and his refusal of the idea on the other hand that "the psychical apparatus" is already "fully constituted" (47). Feminist theorists are among those to have emphasized that for Freud, not only must the ego be constituted, rather than assumed from the start, but that it continually elaborates itself in response to loss, through shifting identifications.[1] Yet these identifications are often explored either within the restrictive framework of castration theory and fetishism, or from a feminist framework that questions the trope of masculinist disavowal, but continues to privilege sexual difference over other differences. The attention Kristeva pays to the infant's abjection of and separation from the mother, which occurs prior to the infant's developing a capacity to signify its desire symbolically—prior to the subject's situating itself in relation to castration—opens up the possibility of attending to class, racial, and heteronormative power regimes not as secondary to sexual difference, but as mutually constitutive of one another. To say that such regimes are mutually constitutive of one another is not to say that all differences will signify equally for all subjects at all times, but to acknowledge that they will signify differentially and unequally for subjects, not in ways that necessarily reflect the social identity of spectators, but

[1] See Freud, "Mourning and Melancholia" (1953).

according to how spectators situate themselves in relation to dominant social norms. This differential operation of symbolic forms of cohesive identity has been consolidated precisely by the insistence of psychoanalytic theory that sexual difference is constitutive of taking up a meaningful position as a subject, and that it is therefore foundational to any meaning. When race theory takes over the trope of fetishism without critically addressing the psychoanalytic assumption that sexual difference is foundational to meaning, its insights continue to operate differentially around the question of sexual difference, even while making available for interrogation the elision of race by psychoanalytic theory.

If the trope of fetishism reemerges in the discourses of race theory and film theory, it does not do so without a significant recasting of its meaning. Thus, if Fanon retains fetishistic discourse, he radically recasts its meaning so that the racial connotations that appear in Freud, but tend to be repressed in standard, white, psychoanalytic theory, signify a history of colonialism. The racialized mapping and fragmentation of the corporeal schema that Fanon describes in terms of the historico-racial schema and the racial-epidermal schema has been rendered invisible by the dominant regimes of whiteness upheld by colonialism.[2] The corporeal mapping that Kristeva describes in relation to the mother's body has been repressed by the phallic, symbolic order of representation, which thereby subsumes it under the discourse of fetishism. When this repression and invisibility are interpreted by means of the fetishistic trope of disavowal, new forms of repression and invisibility are set in motion, this time in the name of feminist and race theory, which fail to mark themselves as masculinist and white.

If the abjection of subjects has been fetishized, sometimes precisely by theorists who attempt to address forms of social discrimination, it stands in need of demystification. Like the retaliatory maneuvers of Klein's projective identification, characteristic of the paranoid-schizoid position, and the reparative, creative responses characteristic of the depressive position, the play of abjection and transference/identification provides an interpretive tool that acknowledges the existence of multiple, sometimes conflicting, ways of splitting up the world. The defenses put in play in abjection are intended to safeguard subjects from greater threats (annihilation, nonexistence, nothingness). It should not surprise us that such defenses are liable to recuperation by fetishistic discourses, which in addition to their classic feature of disavowal—I know (that women are castrated/that blacks are inferior) but all the same (my fetish will cover over this deficiency)—consolidate difference according to a master discourse (patriarchy/whiteness). If abjection is a defensive response to the horror of disintegration or nonexistence—the threat is not limited to castration, rather my very being is threatened—it can follow the logic of projective identification, in which retaliation is projected outside, onto some other. Such logics operate by way of a refusal intended to cleanse the subject: I cannot be the bad object (disgusting, or impure), so you must be it. Works of art can perpetuate such logics, by acquiescing to available forms of marginalization, sustained by racist, homophobic, sexist, or classist fantasies. Or they can intervene in ways that disrupt and reorganize the social fantasies that fuel identifications legitimated by the symbolic order. As such, they can facilitate the work of reparation, by eliciting identifications against socially sanctioned norms.

While Metz wants to affirm the "permanent play of identification" (1982, 46) and sees the play of identification as definitive of "the cinematic situation in its generality, i.e. *the* code"

[2] See Fanon (1967) and Weate (2001).

(54), he also insists that "the spectator can do no other than identify with the camera" (49). Yet the spectator critical of the racism of *The Birth of a Nation* does not identify with the camera.[3] Metz is careful to say that it is the "film" that confers "its gift of 'ubiquity'" on the "all-powerful" subject (48) and the "camera" (49) with which the spectator identifies (49), but this privileging of technology, which he understands with reference to the trope of fetishism, must itself be treated with suspicion. It merely mystifies the choices made by the director not only in privileging certain shots over others or editing them in certain ways, but also in using them to build up a narrative that conforms to, or undercuts, foundational fantasies. Metz conflates an implied universal spectator with the subject of fetishism, whose knowledge that he is watching a film that he takes for reality is theorized in a way that, in Rose's words, makes sexual difference the "vanishing point" of the theory.[4] When the trope of disavowal is transferred to the discourse of race theory in a way that disavows sexual difference, racial difference, we might say, becomes the vanishing point of theory.

Film theory has tended to emphasize either the ways in which film facilitates identification, how it covers over any dissonance, to produce a harmonious narrative flow in keeping with the fantasy of the director, or how it disrupts that identification. When such disruptions have been the focus, as in Brechtian-inspired readings of film, whatever distanciation is explored tends to dislocate the pleasure of fantasy.[5] What matters, however, is how disruptions of affective identifications are effected that harbor the possibility of rearranging more permanently our ways of seeing. Film can play a part either in perpetuating normative identifications or in educating viewers to see differently through becoming invested in scenes, characters, and desires that move us beyond the normatively restrictive identifications of our daily lives. Their semiotic address can operate in tension with prevailing symbolic forms, alluding to an alternative symbolic. If film can elicit temporary, imaginary identifications that are dissonant with symbolically normative identifications, such identifications might have a lasting impact in rearranging the symbolic order. Yet even such interventions are susceptible to reification, will be liable to conform to rigid, doctrinaire beliefs, and must be ready to called, in their turn, to account.

No matter how metaphorically it functions, the name of the father remains the governing trope of psychoanalysis for Lacan—and the phallus remains its referent. The impetus behind this invocation of the phallus is concomitant with the priority accorded to symbolic meaning. Yet to assume such priority covers over the question of what legitimates symbolic meaning, who governs what is sanctioned as meaningful, and who is disqualified in advance as arbiters of meaning by a symbolic system that systematically evades the questioning of its own historically and socially established privilege.

---

[3] Cowie says, "The camera's look is not always or simply a look which is powerful, which knows and thus can control. It is sometimes a character's look, and it is this play of looks and the spectator's movement of identification between these looks which is one of the pleasures of cinema" (1997, 101). To be fair, Metz recognizes this formally by discussing not just the identification (which he calls primary in the context of cinema) with the camera, but also identification with characters (which he calls secondary).

[4] Rose has suggested that "sexual difference functions as the vanishing point" in the theories of Metz and Comolli (1986, 200). See also Lacan 1983, 47; Chase 1989, 82.

[5] As Kaja Silverman puts it, we are "far from being liberated of [the] assumption... that the pleasure of identifying with a fictional character always turns on the spectator's rediscovery of his or her preordained place within gender, class, and race. Secondary identification, in other words, is frequently equated with interpellation into the dominant fiction.... It logically follows... that only a cinema which thwarts identification can be truly transformative" (1996, 85).

To say, as Rose does, that the symbolic is inaugurated by the sense that "something is missing," and that words must be spoken only when the "first object is lost" (1986, 54), covers over a number of problems. What, precisely, is missing, and how does it come to be an object? How does a subject come to be a subject capable of representing an object as missing? How does an infant separate from the mother, and come to conceptualize itself as a subject? And how does the psychoanalytic account of language acquisition come to represent this necessary separation from the mother as only making sense as a function of the father? By explaining language as a function of the third, and by installing the paternal metaphor in the place of the third, Lacanian psychoanalytic theory consigns the mother to the status of the excluded other, who initiates the subject into the order of representation, but who is consigned to a past history that can never be adequately represented or spoken—except insofar as she is situated in relation to castration theory.

Rose's argument hinges on a shift in Lacan such that the fantasy of completion is no longer located in the imaginary but is now assigned to the symbolic: "there is no longer imaginary 'unity' and then symbolic difference or exchange, but rather an indictment of the symbolic for the imaginary unity which its most persistent myths continue to promote" (1986, 71). For Rose, if Lacan's early work is open to the same charge as Lévi-Strauss, namely that to define women as objects of exchange is to presuppose "the subordination which it is intended to explain" (69), Lacan moves away from the idea of women as objects of exchange in his later work. Woman is now "a category within language" (71), "constructed as an absolute category (excluded and elevated at one and the same time)" (71), but this status "as an absolute category and guarantor of fantasy… is false" (72). Yet to constitute woman as a category within language—even if the phantasmatic closure that she produces is illusory—is not to transform women's status as objects of exchange, as the guarantor of the possibility of meaning, but only to inoculate it from interrogation. To enclose women's generative capacity for representation within representation effectively closes off the possibility of questioning the legitimacy of this system of representation, while retaining the phantasmatic assurance of completion that women's imaginary castration accomplishes. The universalization of the language of disavowal, for which Freud can already be credited, has established a cultural monopoly.[6]

In Lacan's return to Freud, the game that is played by Ernst, Freud's eighteen-month-old grandson, is given peculiar importance as the staging of the acquisition of language. As such, it constitutes one of the primary sources of Lacan's elaboration of the symbolic. This essay, "Beyond the Pleasure Principle," is also one of the essays, along with Freud's "Negation," to have had a special importance for the Kleinians. The different emphases developed by Lacan on the one hand and Kristeva, following Klein and Isaacs, on the other hand, in their readings of Ernst's game, are therefore instructive for delineating their divergence, particularly around the question of the emergence of symbolic meaning. Lacan privileges the signifier, the object, the symbolic, or the phallic order, while Kristeva is more attentive to the pre-linguistic ordering of the world.[7] For the Kleinians, fantasies, and therefore also the splitting, schizoid mechanisms by means of which the infant attempts to control pleasure and pain, are operative from the beginning, prior to language.[8]

---

[6] W. J. T. Mitchell also comments, in the context of a discussion of Marxist criticism, commodity fetishism, and ideology, on the tendency to make "a fetish out of the concept of fetishism" (1986, 163).

[7] As Kristeva says, Lacan "emphasizes language and verbalization" and focuses on "the symbol" (2001, 174).

[8] See Kristeva 2001, 140–41. Also see Klein et al. 1989, 75.

According to Lacan "man thinks with his object… the signifier is the first mark of the subject" (1977b, 62). Lacan's emphasis is on "the world of words that creates the world of things" (Lacan 1977a, 65), or on the symbolic order (1991, 172, 179). He reads the significance of Freud's well-known account of the game Freud's grandson played, throwing and retrieving the spool, bobbin, or reel, accordingly (1953b). Whereas Freud had emphasized Ernst's pleasure in mastering his mother's absence, Lacan will understand Ernst's repetitive game as having revealed to us that "the moment in which desire becomes human is also that in which the child is born into language" (1977a, 103). In Freud's account, says Lacan, Ernst substitutes for "the painful tension engendered by the inevitable fact of the presence and absence of the loved object… the game, in which he himself manipulated the absence and presence in themselves and took pleasure in controlling them. He achieved it by means of a little reel at the end of a thread, which he threw away and pulled back" (1991, 172). For Freud, "the child makes up for the effect of his mother's disappearance by making himself the agent of it," but for Lacan, "this phenomenon is of secondary importance" (Lacan 1977b, 62). As we will see shortly, for Isaacs, on the contrary, this compensatory mastery remains of primary importance.

Drawing out what is "implicit" in Freud, Lacan focuses attention on language, on the symbolic, on the fact that this "game with the cotton-reel is accompanied by a vocalization" (1991, 172). "What is important" Lacan tells us "is not that the child said the words *Fort/Da*, which, in his mother tongue, amounts to *far/here*—besides, he pronounced them in an approximate fashion. It is rather that here, right from the beginning, we have a first manifestation of language. In this phonematic opposition, the child transcends, brings on to the symbolic plane, the phenomenon of presence and absence" (1991, 173). The absence of the mother is explained as a function of the father. "*Fort! Da!* It is precisely in his solitude that the desire of the little child has already become the desire of another, of an alter ego who dominates him and whose object of desire is henceforth his own affliction" (1977a, 104). Referring to Henri Wallon, Lacan specifies that the child's "vigilance" is aroused not when he sees his mother, the loved object, exit the room but "earlier, at the very point she left him, at the point she moved away from him" (1977b, 62). It is in the attempt to negotiate this "ever-open gap, introduced by… absence" (1977b, 62) that the child's back-and-forth game with the cotton-reel, accompanied by the sounds "oooh" and "aaah," expresses "self-mutilation" (1977b, 62). For "that which falls is" the "cotton-reel linked to itself by the thread… in which is expressed that which, of itself, detaches itself in this trial, self-mutilation on the basis of which the order of significance will be put in perspective. For the game of the cotton-reel is the subject's answer to what the mother's absence has created" (1977b, 62). The object, the cotton-reel, is understood as a mutilated part of the subject, an object that is linked to the child by the thread he holds. Lacan will give to this object the name "*petit a*" (1977b, 62). It is not the mother who is represented—or rather jettisoned—in the *objet petit a*, but a part of the self. The game of little Ernst is thereby understood as the overcoming of a split caused in the subject by the mother's departure (see 1977b, 63).

This splitting of the subject in turn is, according to Lacan, orchestrated by the castration complex, which retroactively "orientates the relations that are anterior to its actual appearance—weaning, toilet training, etc. It crystallizes each of these moments in a dialectic that has at its center a bad encounter" (1977b, 64).[9] Accordingly, we can see that Lacan's *petit a* comes to

[9] Constance Penley says: " 'Small object o' in Lacanian algebra stands not for the object of desire itself, but for the experience of separation, separation from all the things that have been lost from the body (for example, the mother's breast, which was once experienced as part of the infant's body" (1989, 24).

perform the work that is accomplished under the heading of castration. Kristeva's notion of abjection delineates the separation from the mother without recuperating it immediately in the name of the phallic, paternal signifier, and in doing so provides a space in which the imaginary of psychoanalysis can be rewritten in a way that opens up other avenues of interpretation, which do not necessarily follow the language of fetishistic disavowal. Just as for Lacan the object only comes to exist through its absence, so for Kristeva the mother only comes to be abjected through separation, through moving away. In contrast to Lacan's and Kristeva's derivation of an emerging sense of subjectivity from Hegelian particularity or "thisness," through differentiation, Isaacs understands what she calls "me-ness" on the basis of "sensations (and images)," which "give the phantasy a concrete bodily quality" (1989, 105). For Isaacs, the "earliest phantasies are built mainly upon oral impulses, bound up with taste, smell, touch" and so on (1989, 104). As Kristeva puts it, "The Kleinians' focus was on the experience of the drives underlying vision," preceding the "scopic hold" and prefiguring "the *Bejahung* [affirmation] of judgment that takes place before the gaze and immediately through taste" (2001, 172).

Where Lacan reads Ernst's game in terms of the "birth of the symbol" (1977a, 103), Isaacs reads it in terms of fantasy, emphasizing the child's "phantasied satisfaction of controlling his mother's comings and goings" (1989, 73). For Isaacs, as for Freud, "phantasies... are the 'mental expression' of an instinct" or "the psychic representatives of a bodily aim" (1989, 104). If for Lacan the compensatory pleasure Ernst takes in substituting for his mother's absence is of secondary importance, for Isaacs it is central. As she says, "forgoing... the satisfaction of an instinct," Ernst "compensated" for his mother's absence "by himself enacting the same disappearance and return with the objects within his reach" (1989, 73). For Isaacs, on discovering a mirror Ernst "delight[s] in making his own image appear and disappear in the mirror," confirming "his triumph in controlling feelings of loss, by his play, as consolation for his mother's absence" (Isaacs 1989, 73). In Kristeva's words,

> Isaacs concludes that the emergence of language is preceded, though not in a linear way, by a generic continuity in which the mastery of the presence or absence of the object, which culminates in the mastery of the appearance of the baby's own image, is a sine qua non for understanding language—which itself develops well before the active use of language. Her conclusion serves as a good introduction to what will become Lacan's "mirror stage," but here it is portrayed as a process of a heterogeneous negativity consisting of movements, fantasized acts, and verbalization, and only then of scopic images. (2001, 170)

For Lacan it is "the symbol" that "cancels the existing thing" and "opens up the world of negativity, which constitutes both the discourse of the human subject and the reality of his world in so far as it is human" (1991, 174). Recall that language, for Lacan, is manifested right from the start, whereas for Isaacs, words "are a late development in our means of expressing the inner world of our phantasy" (1989, 91), yet "[p]hantasy and reality-testing are both in fact present from the earliest days" (1989, 107). Fantasy, for Klein, in Kristeva's words, is "anchored in the drive" (2001, 172), while "the judgment of existence focused on reality" (172). Kristeva, who highlights Klein's proximity to Hyppolite, emphasizes the "asymmetry" (2001, 173) of these two stages, the first of which constitutes a kind of "*primary* symbolization" (2001, 172), neglected by Lacan. This is already "thinking" but "it does not appear... as such" (Kristeva

2001, 173). As Isaacs put it, "some measure of 'synthetic function' is exercised upon instinctual urges from the beginning… play creates and fosters the first forms of 'as if' thinking" (1989, 110–111).

For Klein and Kristeva, fantasy, a kind of primary symbolization, and negativity precede language; they are akin to what Freud calls "judgment[s] of attribution ('this *is* good or bad')" as opposed to judgments "of existence ('this *exists* in reality outside the scope of my representation')" (Kristeva 2001, 173). The birth of the subject proper emerges with the "judgment of existence," which

> Presumes that "I" rediscover in "my" memory (and thus that "I" attribute myself to "me"—who thus becomes a "subject") a representation that *belongs* to an object and that *de-sign-ates* an absent object for the subject that "I" have become. Put another way, the judging subject cannot exist without a lost object: by relying on memory, "I" can signify the object only as it is—lost for the "ego" who, as a result of losing the object, is held out as a "subject." The interaction between the judgment of existence and the judgment of attribution forms the basis of intelligence, in the sense of a symbolic thought that is distinct from the imaginary or from fantasy. (2001, 173)

When foundational fantasies, of race for example, inform collectivities in such a way as to have become all but indistinguishable from symbolic forms of thought, the work of identifying the various ways in which such fantasies are enacted becomes crucial. Not only do such fantasies help to shape our social realities, such that the availability of services can be based on racial myths of exclusion; they also help to shape our theories. To develop this thought, let me turn to Mike Leigh's *Secrets and Lies*, a film that Kalpana Seshadri-Crooks has discussed from a Lacanian perspective. My own reading of it, inspired by Kristeva, attends not only to the role of the absent father, but to the exclusionary racial fantasies that are rendered visible in the eruption of a crisis, precipitated by the redrawing of familial boundaries that Hortense's black skin represents.

When Mike Leigh in *Secrets and Lies* presents his audience with a series of photographic portraits, the fruit of Maurice's labor, he asks us to think about the difference between photography and film, and between commerce and art, as the inexorable unfolding of the narrative is interrupted by a sequence of photographic stills.[10] Presented as works in which Maurice, a commercial photographer, has revealed the inner truth of the clients who pay him to take their pictures, the stills prompt Leigh's audience to ask themselves what his film reveals about us. Tongue in cheek, Leigh plays with the idea that people resemble their dogs, presents us with a bickering couple, or with obsessive behavior. In the background of Leigh's exploration of the relationship between photography and film, one cannot help but detect a reflection on the status of "art" films in relation to their commercial success or their critical acclaim. *Secrets and Lies* garnered more awards and more recognition than Leigh's previous films, and it is thus ironic but fitting that he uses this film to reflect on the role of the business of commercial art, and whether or not its success is to be judged by how well it pleases its consumer. At the same time, despite the insistence of many reviewers that the film has nothing to do with race, the film raises some provocative questions about the mutual implication of race and class in one

[10] The actors whose photographs are taken in the stills appear in Mike Leigh's previous films. See Watson 2004, 130–31.

another. The culturally and economically circumscribed lives of Cynthia (Brenda Blethyn) and her daughter Roxanne (Claire Rushbrook) are nonetheless informed by a racist assumption that the family has not thought through until Hortense (Marianne Jean-Baptiste) appears on the scene. They might be poor, their horizons might be limited—but at least they are not black. In the moment that Cynthia reveals to Roxanne, to her brother Maurice (Timothy Spall), and to his wife Monica (Phyllis Logan) the identity of Hortense—that she is the daughter Cynthia had given up for adoption all those years ago—the horror registered on each of their faces tells its own story. What is so incomprehensible, so unacceptable? That Hortense is black, and therefore cannot be part of their family? That a transgression of racial boundaries has apparently taken place? That an adoption from long ago has come back to haunt the family? The return, not so much of the repressed, as of the real—that which has been excluded by Cynthia to make her life livable? That Cynthia has succeeded in rediscovering a daughter she had given up, while Monica has failed to give birth to the children she so desperately wants? That Hortense is not the person they took her to be, "a mate" of Cynthia's from work? What becomes all too visible is the invisibility, until this moment, of the whiteness cementing the family's relations.

Mike Leigh's *Secrets and Lies* confronts us with a world whose characters are hemmed in by the constrained horizons of a white working-class English family, whose aspirations to occupy the ranks of the lower middle classes are most keenly exhibited by Maurice and Monica. Hortense, more affluent, urbane, and genteel than the family that defensively asserts its boundaries in the face of the prospect that she might be one of them, is, most definitively, in a different class. Her black skin becomes a site of Cynthia's abjection, in the moment when Roxanne casts her mother to the ground like the fallen woman she is, calling her a whore not only because Hortense was born out of wedlock, but perhaps more significantly because her father must have been black. Ostensibly a way of designating Cynthia's alleged status as a fallen woman, the word "slag" is heavily burdened with racist overtones. If Cynthia is a whore according to conventional attitudes about the sanctity of marriage and female chastity, she is all the more so because Hortense is black. Cynthia is thrown to the ground because she is seen as having transgressed the racial boundaries between black and white. The unspoken racialized fantasy that informs the word "slag" is that which unites, perhaps unconsciously, Cynthia's extended family: to be a member of this collectivity, one has to be white. The unspoken myth of the black racist hovers in the background.

Race is precisely constitutive, here, of sexuality. If race functions to police the borders of sexuality, it also performs a constitutive function in the class identity of a white family, forced to confront its own assumption that to be white is, for them, a necessary part of what it means to be working class. Only when whiteness is challenged, only when it is made explicit by being called into question, does the pervasive constitutive role that race plays in white identities become available for critical analysis. When Cynthia's family is asked to accept a black person as one of them, the limits of what is tolerable and what is not come to the fore.

Kalpana Seshadri-Crooks reads the film in terms of the logic of suture and jokes, but in my view she does not acknowledge the extent to which the film consistently returns to the site of this "joke," which is performed repeatedly. While I think Seshadri-Crooks provides a brilliant and inspired analysis of race from a Lacanian point of view, I do not agree that *Secrets and Lies* sacrifices an "extended inquiry into the logic of racial knowledge and looking" by a limited mocking of our narrative compulsion.[11] This reading fails to capture the subtlety with which the film exposes the mundane working-class sensibility that functions as a horizon for the psychologically abusive relationship between Cynthia and Roxanne. If the similitude that Cynthia sees between herself and Hortense functions for us as a joke at all, the joke is reenacted in a different way when Hortense is nearly turned away on the doorstep by Monica, who assumes that her black skin signifies that she must have come to the wrong house, or when Roxanne pushes Cynthia to the floor, in a gesture that bespeaks her fallen status as miscegenator. The void around which Monica's assumption revolves, when she thinks that Hortense must have got the wrong address, or that she must be selling something, is not simply the absence of the father, but the impossibility of blacks entering a white neighborhood, the impossibility of Cynthia's mate from work being black, in short the impossibility of blackness that invisibly structures the imaginary of Monica's white social world. Cynthia has to assert her relation to Hortense no less than five times before the truth begins to sink in: "She's my daughter.... Maurice... it's me daughter... Hortense, sweet'eart... She's yer sister... That's 'er 'alf-sister, Paul," and finally, to Roxanne, "SHE'S YOUR SISTER!" This anxious reiteration of family ties underscores the disbelief with which her assertions of kinship are met, an anxiety that stems from the social taboo on race-mixing. When Cynthia reveals that Hortense is her daughter, she precipitates a family crisis, which results in Monica confessing her bitter disappointment at being childless, and her consequent envy of Cynthia. The impossibility of confronting a delayed sibling rivalry—an impossibility that is structured in complex ways—is at the heart of Roxanne's aggressive refusal to accept her mother's sudden introduction of Hortense as her daughter, as Roxanne's half-sister. Seshadri-Crooks overlooks this by insisting that the absent father is the site of impossibility around which the film's problematization of race functions.

When Seshadri-Crooks says, quoting Lacan (1978), that "the body must be understood in relation to the 'sexual reality' of the unconscious, which is the nodal point of desire [XI: 154]" (2000, 125), she subordinates the significance of her own reading of the trope of race in the film to the Lacanian scenario that relentlessly privileges sexual difference over race. By reading the film in terms of abjection I resist that privileging, and suggest that, if the body can only be "discerned... in time" and "only as a series of part objects" (Seshadri-Crooks 2000, 125), those part objects are not inevitably beholden to a phallic logic, but can be parsed out according to the unfixed and halting syntax of a maternal mapping, an excremental logic. The

[11] Kalpana Seshadri-Crooks (2000, 124). I would like to thank Kalpana Seshadri-Crooks for taking the time to respond to an earlier version of my discussion of *Secrets and Lies*. Seshadri-Crooks says that the impossibility of knowing the identity of Hortense's father "functions as a point where our suture as subjects of race is produced symptomatically even as we navigate between the secret and the lie. Any attempt to manufacture a narrative to cover over that lacuna becomes a lethal exposure of the effect of the signifier upon our unconscious.... However, this strategy is rather limited in that it questions our suturing to race through what is essentially a mockery of our narrative compulsion, rather than an extended inquiry into the logic of racial knowledge and looking" (124). She describes the scene in which Cynthia "referring to her other (white) daughter Roxanne, who is mostly rude or indifferent towards her, says that she believes that she shares more of a resemblance with Hortense than with Roxanne. She says: 'I'm more like you really,' etc. At this the audience invariably bursts into laughter." Seshadri-Crooks suggests that this scene is "coded for comic effect. This scene is 'too much' for the film, and thus the possibility of similitude 'across races' is turned into a joke. There is something anxiety-producing in the notion that this mother and her daughter may share certain similarities.... It is not so much similitude itself that is uncanny as the discovery of one's own surprise in encountering similitude. The unconscious logic of the joke can be stated thus: The subject of race runs into his/her own splitness with regard to race. We are surprised by ourselves. We thought we knew that people across races could bear similarities. Then why are we surprised into recognizing it? To encounter something about ourselves that we knew but hadn't recognized is uncanny" (124–25).

full force of this excremental, abject logic finds expression in the word "slag" that condemns Cynthia's symbolic transgression not only of sexual but also of racial taboos, a transgression underwritten by a white, masculinized, racial imaginary.

Hortense, the optometrist—whose job it is to help others see—provides a mirror for the various members of the family she claims as her own. She is the other who helps them break through their loneliness, their secrecy, and their lies.[12] In this sense she provides a counterweight to Maurice, the photographer, who frames people's lives according to the requirements of his commission—whether he is photographing a wedding or the scars of a victim of a car accident for insurance purposes. Yet the role Hortense plays is one that takes on transformative meaning only because her black skin has become the site of her white mother's abjection. While Cynthia, not Hortense, is pushed to the ground by Roxanne, Hortense is racialized by a series of gestures, from the time that Cynthia sees her black skin and assumes that this is a case of mistaken identity. At their first meeting, the color of Hortense's skin signals to Cynthia that there must have been a bureaucratic mistake. When Hortense arrives at the front door, Monica is unable to imagine that she might be Cynthia's invited guest. And when Roxanne casts her mother to the floor, Hortense looks on uneasily, aware that it is the color of her skin that accounts for the violence of Roxanne's reaction. Must racialized others be the ground on which those who have been able to assume the privilege of their white skin break through their racism? In the fantasized space of contemporary independent cinema, some directors are beginning to ask us to reflect on such questions, and are thereby returning us to the fantasized space of representation that enables our idealizations and identifications, asking us to rethink the ways in which some bodies are asked to carry the burden of racialization for the sake of others. If there is a sense in which Hortense could still be read in terms of the trope of fetishization that white culture resorts to in negotiating race, there is also a sense in which Mike Leigh examines the economy by which such a trope is produced. In his citation of racist myths, he explodes them.

In *Revolution in Poetic Language* Kristeva suggests that capitalist modes of production have created a situation in which linguistic theories tend to deal with the fetishized product of language, rather than the processes by which meaning is generated. "The capitalist mode of production has st[r]atified language into idiolects and divided it into self-contained, isolated islands—heteroclite spaces existing in different temporal modes (as relics or projections), and oblivious of one another" (1984, 13–14). The suggestion is that capitalist society has repressed the processes by which meaning is generated, codifying our experience according to the motives of the ruling classes, namely economic profit, and alienating us from other possible meanings. Any activity that doesn't conform to the useful—where the meaning of the term "useful" is restricted to the production of surplus value—is counted as irrelevant, rendering useless (within these terms) those forms of language that express any other values.

There is a truth to the fetishized linguistic entities—heteroclite islands—that have come to be the object of linguistic investigation. Yet this truth is produced by the historical circumstance of capitalism. By unfolding the process by which fetishization has occurred, we can loosen the grip of the fetish that language has become, and see how both the subject of capitalism and its objects have become reified. As Kristeva puts it, "capitalism eliminates

[12] Castoriadis 1987, 127. Also see 140–41. If for Fanon "the real Other for the white man... is the black man" (1967, 161), Hortense's blackness serves to reflect the identity of this white family back to them.

the free subject unified in his process, which Hegel was the last philosopher to summon," rendering it "a hypostasized subjectivity… cut off from the signifying and socio-historical process" (1984, 129–130). At stake in both the Cartesian question, how can I know that my ideas of the world conform to the reality of objects in the world, and the Kantian question, what must the world be like in order to be knowable, is the purity and priority of the judging I, whose unity is transhistorical. Despite Kant's Copernican revolution, the "I think" of the transcendental unity of apperception remains too close to a solipsistic Cartesian cogito, one that does not take itself to be situated in a historical world. For Hegel, both object and subject are historically constituted, and their constitution is not given once and for all. Like Hegel, rather than assuming the subject and the object as preexisting, Kristeva provides an account of how the subject comes to be a subject, or how the subject comes into relation with objects. For Kristeva, the process by which a subject becomes a subject, and thereby becomes capable of having objects, and in particular, how subjects are able to have a desiring relation to others, is embedded in historical relations. Kristeva steers a course between positing the subject on the one hand as transcendental ego, as originator of meaning, and on the other hand as embracing the chaos, delirium, or nonsense that would result from opting out of the symbolic altogether. She contests the theologization of the thetic by seeing it as a product of drives and facilitations, mapping the ways in which poetry, by way of mimesis, contests this theologization. Refusing to posit with Kant or Husserl "the judging 'I' as origin," Kristeva asks, "How is the thetic, which is a *positing* of the subject, produced?" (1984, 36). To construe the subject solely as symbolic would be to "reduce the subject to one of understanding" (1984, 27), to neglect the role of the imaginary in the signifying process that constitutes meaning, to enclose the subject in the ideality of its status as a judging subject, and to acquiesce to the repression of the corporeal materiality of the desiring subject.

Between 1974, when *Revolution of Poetic Language* appeared, and when Kristeva was still working through the impact of the events of May 1968, and 1996, a good deal had changed. In the course of time, the revolutionary ferment of Kristeva's work has considerably altered. *Tel Quel* had disintegrated, the Maoist inspiration of the Chinese Revolution proved not to be nearly as hopeful or productive as it once seemed, and the transformative impulse of the semiotic that Kristeva had tracked through the 1980s in *Powers of Horror: An Essay on Abjection*, *Tales of Love*, and *Black Sun* had considerably weakened.[13] If I insist on the importance of some of the insights contained in *Powers of Horror*, it is because I read them as mapping out in a provisional way not so much an alternative logic to the fetish, as the conditions of its possibility—the logic of abjection. As such, abjection also constitutes a site for the possible reworking of fetishism.

The logic of the fetish is one of substitution, a reiterated reification, in which the emergence of meaning is dependent on the stability of the terms being substituted for one another. In order for terms to be substituted for one another these terms need to have acquired a permanence: they need to exist as significant within a certain economy of meaning. How the set of meanings that signify as meaningful within a given system of signification came to be meaningful is not necessarily at issue within this system. The economic laws of substitution are not interrogated, so long as the series of substitutions depends upon keeping in the background or holding at bay the values that are assumed by a fetishistic economy—the logic of which generally does not present itself as available for questioning. Symbolic forms appear as fixed and static, but

[13] See Kristeva, *About Chinese Women*. See also Sara Beardsworth (2004) on what she calls the "1980s trilogy."

also as isolated and independent of one another, and the social fabric that they constitute is reproduced as if one form could stand for another metonymically, without either feeding into or disrupting the stability and integrity of the social whole. It is as if the shared unity of meaning characteristic of the social whole, whether this meaning is produced under the rubric of nation, or some other imagined unity, could stand as inherent, as if emergent categories such as class or gender or race could function as autonomous and self-sustaining parts of that social unit without impinging on one another. In the process of cultural and intellectual exchange, guaranteed not so much by the phallus as the circulation of the fetish, such concepts appear to be autonomous and self-evident. Interrogation of the practices of exchange reveals that their absolute autonomy is not merely compromised but impossible as such. The coherence of each socially salient category is only achieved through a rhetorical referentiality that appeals to other socially salient categories, and is inscribed in a history of dependence, inheritance, and alienation. This dependence is often implicit, covert, unconscious, or indirect, but is no less powerful for it. Circuits of meaning have been set in play in which the possibility of asking about multiple aspects of identity as constitutive of one another has been closed down in favor of their analytic definition and separation. Yet at the same time these circuits of meaning only operate by providing for one another mutual confirmation.

In order to ask intelligible or meaningful questions about the imaginary that informs the values of a patriarchal, capitalist, and postcolonial world, in order to interrogate the myths that determine and set in place the values it takes for granted, we need to have an account of both how those values are established, and how they legitimate themselves. What myths of origin are mobilized in order to confer on these values the appearance of self-evidence, and how might new myths enable the contestation of such self-evidence? What are the conditions of possibility for the predominance of fetishistic theories, and how are they upheld by the marginalization and subordination of certain others who are not recognized as subjects? How are certain groups or identities abjected as insignificant, as non-subjects, whose claims are not registered as valuable, or not capable of signifying? How do these non-subjects function as the illegitimate, prohibited ground on which objects, signs, values, and desires can signify and circulate in an exchange economy that presents itself as closed, but which derives its impetus from an outside that is constitutive of it, while failing to acknowledge it as constitutive? In what way do social systems that present themselves as self-legitimating remain vulnerable to being called to account?

Has language tailored not so much our thoughts as our desires, channeling them according to the ends of capitalism, imposing on subjects a pseudo-rationality that makes it difficult to imagine what we want outside the terms that capitalism formulates for us? Or is there a more fundamental alienation effected by language than the appearance it takes on under capitalism that cuts us off from the process by which symbolization comes to represent our experience? Perhaps, as Kristeva suggests in *Powers of Horror*, language itself is the ultimate fetish (1982, 37), because it takes the sign for the thing. Even though we know that the sign is not the thing, we act, think, and feel as if it is. "Je sais bien mais quand même."[14] We substitute the name for the thing, and take this sign as determinative of it. Is it, then, a particular mode of production—capitalist—that represses that which is not captured by the sign, that fetishizes

[14] It is worth noting that following this invocation of Mannoni, Kristeva adds an example that for some reason is missed out of the English translation (1992, 49).

language, or is it language itself? Is it that language in and of itself stabilizes, atomizes, or commodifies the processes by which subjects signify to themselves and to others? And what would be the difference? If language has become fetishized under capitalism, how could it be otherwise as long as capitalism survives?

In *Powers of Horror* Kristeva suggests that in addition to neurosis and psychosis, and the respective modes of negativity that articulate them, denial (*dénégation*) and repudiation (*forclusion*), there is another form of rejection. Abjection is based not upon the repression of a desired object, nor upon the repudiation of desire itself, but upon "exclusion" (1982, 6). As such, it has a different relation to the unconscious, and a different relation to castration. Kristeva develops the notion of abjection as subjacent not only to denial and repudiation, but also to the fetishistic logic of disavowal (*déni/Verleugnung*), with its "perverse dodges" (1982, 5). At the same time, abjection is "related to perversion" (1982, 15) in the sense that "it neither gives up nor assumes a prohibition" (1982, 15). Concerned not merely with the "fetishized product" as "object of want [*manque*]," abjection is implicated in the more fundamental possibility of there being any object at all, with the "recognition of the *want* [*manque*] on which any being, meaning, language, or desire is founded" (5). As the revelation to the subject that "all its objects are based merely on the inaugural *loss* that laid the foundations of its own being" (5), abjection is related to the separation of the subject (who is not yet a subject) from the mother (who is not yet the mother). For we are dealing with a point at which there is as yet no "secure differentiation between subject and object" (7).

Abjection, says Kristeva, is, "above all, ambiguity" (1982, 7). It is ambiguous with regard to the self and other, with regard to passivity or activity, neurosis or psychosis, and with regard to the boundaries it sets up, which are permeable. Is abjection something that I do to the other or to myself? Is it an act I engage in, or is it a state I suffer? It is not clear who is abjected by what, who is doing the abjection, and who is affected by it. In emphasizing the ambiguity of abjection, Kristeva takes up the tension contained in the Freudian libido, the life-and-death struggle between Eros and Thanatos, or the need to think desire in tandem with destructive forces. Abjection concerns both the pleasurable and the fascinating, dangerous, or horrific—that which threatens. One can also say that central to Kristeva's psychoanalytic understanding of desire is the suggestion that it assumes, rather than following, prohibition. The object of desire is desirable precisely as forbidden.[15] At the same time, however, Kristeva is interested in the instability of the incest prohibition, and therefore in the ways in which the symbolic function that is set up in its wake is liable to revision and transformation. It is precisely because abjection does not operate at the level of desire, but rather constitutes the rejection that desire presupposes, that its relation to prohibition is not straightforward, but perverse.

If the abject signals a structuring lack of the subject, but one that is not at first specified in relation to sexual difference, since it predates castration anxiety and the recognition of sexual differentiation, a space is opened up for this fundamental lack to be articulated in racial, ethnic, or class codes, and in terms that are as yet unmarked by any heterosexual imperative. What happens when a fear of the unnameable occurs not just at the individual level, as it does when Little Hans metaphorically writes the horse as his phobic object because he cannot find the

---

[15] In this way desire is structured in a way that parallels Foucault's discussion of sexuality, wherein the prohibition of sexuality contained in the repressive hypothesis functions as an incitement to discourse. Discourses of sexuality proliferate, far from being contained by their repression.

name for street sounds? What happens when a fear of the unnameable operates at the symbolic level to the point of a refusal to name what society finds impermissible? Or when the very paths along which desire is recognized as signaling an object are written in a symbolic whose imaginary forecloses the possibility of lesbian or gay or transgendered subjects of desire so as to make their objects unthinkable?

In *Hollow Reed*, according to Frank Donally (Jason Fleming), the only way to describe the sexuality of Martin and Tom is to cast it into the realm of animality from which ostensibly civilized, decent society has progressed. Frank's condemnation of homosexuality as animality is a transparent attempt to prejudice Oliver against his father. What happens when the symbolic system that orders sexual relations, and establishes sexual propriety, setting up the rules of who is allowed to couple with whom, partakes of a racialized imagery that it does not own?

With the revolutionary potential of the semiotic, Kristeva has helped to uncover the sense in which language can be rethought from the ground up, as it were, or how we can uncover its constitutive elements. By emphasizing the affective ways in which language is produced, by returning to the moments that make language necessary, by rethinking the infant's separation from the maternal breast, Kristeva provides some access to the formative processes that give rise to language. Extending the purview of Kristeva's inquiry one can ask after not merely the devaluation of maternity, but also the dehumanization of racialized others, not merely after the fetishization of language, but also the fetishistic forms of cultural theories. Like the necrophilia of archival, archaeological linguistic theorists who take their objects to be fixed according to an economy that endows them with value that is always already sanctioned and as such unavailable for interrogation, theorists of gender, race, and even film are prone to take their objects as given. This condemns them to the fate of reproducing cultural theories that both present themselves as relatively autonomous, and feed off the oppression implied in but neglected by other areas of cultural interrogation. By failing to question the model of fetishism that gets reiterated by apparently autonomous areas of cultural theory—that are in fact deeply implicated in one another—cultural theory neglects its conditions of possibility.

Kristeva accepts the account of castration that Freud and Lacan give as putting the "finishing touches on separation" (1984, 47), but also distances herself from it in her examination of the thetic as a "traversable boundary" (1984, 51). That is, she accepts that in order for a subject to be capable of representation, to acquiesce to the symbolic system in a signifying capacity, that subject must accomplish a separation, detaching itself from its dependence on the mother. She also accepts that the subject's entry into language "presupposes a decisive imposition of the phallic" and that the "subject must be firmly posited by castration" (1984, 50). Yet she insists that the thetic is "clearly distinct… from a castration imposed once and for all, perpetuating the well-ordered signifier and positing it as sacred and unalterable within the enclosure of the Other" (1984, 51).

While Kristeva distances herself in *Revolution in Poetic Language* from the idea of castration as "decisive" (1984, 50), that it is "imposed once and for all" (51), and from fetishism (62–67), it is not until *Powers of Horror* that this criticism acquires more substance. She sees the literary or poetic text as allowing the subject to "delv[e] into" the "constitutive process" or the process by which the "human being constitutes himself as signifying and/or social" (67). Her entire project is fueled by thinking through the possibility of revolutionary change, and asking how that which has been excluded from apparently self-legitimating systems can become available for questioning in a way that transforms those systems. "Under what conditions," she asks, does "'esoterism', in displacing the boundaries of socially established signifying practices, correspond to socioeconomic change, and, ultimately, even to revolution? And under what conditions does it remain a blind alley, a harmless bonus offered by a social order which uses this 'esoterism' to expand, become flexible, and thrive?" (16).

Not only is the imaginary in need of the symbolic, but just as crucially, the symbolic is sustained by the imaginary. So long as that imaginary is assumed to be phallic, so long as the symbols that cash out its value maintain the currency of an unexamined, monolithic fetishism that proves itself equally adaptable to race theory, feminist theory, class theory, and film theory, the possibilities of articulating radical challenges are limited. An imaginary that reinvents itself with apparently infinite malleability is supported by the incessant reproduction of the phallus as commodity. By interrogating the laws of the imaginary economy that sustain the symbolic production of the phallus as the only currency worthy of cultural accumulation, I have explored the repetitive and imitative gestures by which abjection is produced. It remains to be seen how capable the phallic economy proves to be in withstanding any investigation of the ways in which its imaginary shores up a symbolic system of exchange that depends on the unacknowledged production of dejects, a status that surreptitiously circulates between non-subjects, who overcome their own abjection by visiting it upon others.

Hollow Reed explores the hypocrisy of a society that is apparently willing to consider homosexuality, rather than child abuse, a sin. At the same time it explores the ramifications that Martyn's reluctance to admit his homosexuality have for those around him. Having gone through a divorce, his rejected ex-wife is in need of affirmation. Women are encouraged to believe that their worth is attested by their ability to find and keep a man, and Hannah (Joley Richardson) feels humiliated by her ex-husband's desertion of her for a gay partner, her sense of her femininity having been compromised. She is so desperate to avoid another failed relationship that she is willing to reconcile with her lover even after having discovered him abusing her child, wanting to believe that the abuse is over. In this context, Frank's violently abusive behavior represents a confirmation of his heteronormative manliness.

As he pins him up against the bathroom wall, Frank Donally (Jason Fleming), the abuser of nine-year-old Oliver (Sam Bould) in *Hollow Reed*, tells him that men like Oliver's father choose to be that way. Frank tells Oliver that the way gay men do it in bed is like dogs, like animals at the zoo. He tells him that he and Hannah, Oliver's mother, just want Oliver to be "normal," and assures him that he won't grow up homosexual like his father, that it can't be passed on through the genes. As Frank tries to poison Oliver's mind, ostensibly telling him that he doesn't have to worry about turning out like his father, but in fact warning him that he might do just that, Oliver stays mute, as he is throughout most of the film. By attempting to elicit Oliver's disgust at his father's gayness, Frank can represent himself as normal, safe, and conventional, while projecting on to Martyn (Martin Donovan), and thus denying, his own abjection of Oliver. Abusing or terrifying Oliver is a way of establishing control in a world in which he feels inadequate, a way of making him seem to himself a whole person, a way of venting his feelings of rage at his own abuse, without confronting them directly. He deflects them onto Oliver, continuing a chain of abjection. The social text of homophobia presents itself as available to him, and he draws upon it in order to facilitate his denial of his own aberrant behavior. I am not the one whose nature is excessive—it is you.

Desperate to remove his son from his abuser, Martyn determines to try to obtain legal custody of nine-year-old Oliver, despite the fact that he has no concrete evidence of the identity of the abuser. He might be aware that his ex-wife's lawyer will do all he can to parade his lifestyle as a gay man in front of the court, but nothing can prepare him for the humiliation he and his partner suffer, when it becomes all too obvious that, far from setting himself above abjection, the rhetoric of the legal system draws on its own perverted logic. The court battle, as Martyn had anticipated when he asked his partner, Tom (Ian Hart), to move out temporarily, is played out on the terrain of homophobia. Martyn's alleged inability to sustain a "normal" sexual relationship with his ex-wife comes into play as the lawyer does everything in his power to abject Martyn and Tom for being gay. Disgust is elicited by an indirect appeal to, or a re-inscription, of boundaries that are assumed to be fixed, naturalized, and immovable, through the intimation that gay lifestyles are in excess of the norm, that they cross the boundary separating humanity from animality. Frank is able to disguise his own cruelty to Oliver, displacing his self-contempt onto Martyn, in what Kristeva calls a "sublimating elaboration" (1982, 7), which accompanies his refusal to recognize his child-abuse as out of bounds. Devising strategies designed to cleanse themselves of what otherwise might have to be acknowledged as dirty, disgusting, or repugnant, dejects—those "by whom the abject exists" (1982, 8)—persist in territorializing in order to remake the rules and absolve or purify themselves, thus requiring others to become impure receptacles (see 1982, 10–12). The law itself cashes in on the implied excesses of Tom and Martyn's behavior that Frank's displacement elaborates. The convoluted logic of abjection, its ritualistic, obsessive, re-drawing of imaginary boundaries in the service of defensive postures, and the ways in which institutions sanction and uphold such logics without drawing out their complex processes of sublimation, has been the subject of the preceding meditation.

There are phenomena that should disgust us, but which do not, inured as we are to fundamentally racist, homophobic, sexist, and classist fabrics that constitute our normative identifications. To elicit disgust can be a political function of art, just as much as art can elicit disgust in ways that confirm, reiterate, and reproduce the foundational fantasies that govern our realities. Art can subject us anew to such fantasies, or it can provide a space in which we take our distance from them. Abjection can thus help to reconstitute us, and we can help to reconstitute abjection, in a process that is ongoing—in a process that should remain contestable, available for scrutiny, and subject to revision. By drawing out the symbolic implications of what we find disgusting, or beautiful, and why we make such judgments of taste, we can rework the imaginaries that have drawn the boundaries of revolt: we can redraw the boundaries of abjection. I have focused in particular on our discovery of ourselves as having identified with characters in particular moments that might have momentarily disrupted identifications we normally take for granted, and which might open up the possibility of rethinking the ground of such identifications. I have also focused on moments of abjection with which some of us identify, moments in which such identification can be cathartic. Such moments can result in the revolution of symbolic norms, in their renewal. Alternatively, the result can be a restoration of the symbolic without its rebirth, in which case abjection amounts to a purging of negativity that allows the symbolic to continue unchallenged and uninterrupted.

Works Cited

Sara Beardsworth, *Julia Kristeva: Psychoanalysis and Modernity*, ed. T. Chanter (Albany: State University of New York Press, 2004).

Cornelius Castoriadis, *The Imaginary Institution of Society*, trans. Kathleen Blamey (Cambridge, MA: MIT Press, 1987).

Cynthia Chase, "Desire and Identification in Lacan and Kristeva," in *Feminism and Psychoanalysis*, ed. Richard Feldstein and Judith Roof (Ithaca, NY: Cornell University Press, 1989).

Elizabeth Cowie, *Representing the Woman: Cinema and Psychoanalysis* (Minneapolis: University of Minnesota Press, 1997).

Frantz Fanon, *Black Skin, White Masks*, trans. Charles Lam Markmann (New York: Grove Press, 1967).

Sigmund Freud, "Beyond the Pleasure Principle," in *The Standard Edition of the Complete Psychological Works*, trans. James Strachey, Vol. 18 (London: Hogarth Press and the Institute of Psycho-analysis, 1953b).

Sigmund Freud, "Mourning and Melancholia," in *The Standard Edition of the Complete Psychological Works*, trans. James Strachey, vol. 14 (London: Hogarth Press and the Institute of Psycho-analysis, 1953m).

Susan Isaacs, "The Nature and Function of Phantasy," in *Developments in Psychoanalysis*, ed. Melanie Klein, Paul Heimann, Susan Isaacs, and Joan Riviere (London: Karnac Books and the Institute of Psycho-analysis, 1989).

Melanie Klein, Paula Heimann, Susan Isaacs, and Joan Riviere, *Developments in Psychoanalysis* (London: Karnac Books and the Institute of Psycho-analysis, 1989).

Julia Kristeva, *Powers of Horror: An Essay on Abjection*, trans. Leon S. Roudiez (New York: Columbia University Press, 1982).

Julia Kristeva, *Revolution in Poetic Language*, trans. Margaret Waller (New York: Columbia University Press, 1984).

Julia Kristeva, *Melanie Klein*, trans. Ross Guberman, *Female Genius*, Vol. 2 (New York: Columbia University Press, 2001).

Jacques Lacan, *Ecrits: A Selection*, trans. Alan Sheridan (London: Tavistock Publications, 1977a).

Jacques Lacan, *The Four Fundamental Concepts of Psycho-analysis*, ed. Jacques-Alain Miller, trans. Alan Sheridan (Hammondsworth, Middlesex: Penguin Books, 1977b).

Jacques Lacan, *Feminine Sexuality*, ed. Juliette Mitchell and Jacqueline Rose (New York: W.W. Norton, 1983).

Jacques Lacan, *The Seminar of Jacques Lacan. Book I: Freud's Papers on Technique, 1953–1954*, trans. John Forrester, ed. Jacques-Alain Miller (New York: W.W. Norton, 1991).

Christian Metz, *The Imaginary Signifier: Psychoanalysis and the Cinema*, trans. Celia Britton, Annwyl Williams, Ben Brewster, and Alfred Guzzetti (Bloomington: Indiana University Press, 1982).

W. J. T. Mitchell, *Iconology: Image, Text, Ideology* (Chicago: University of Chicago Press, 1986).

Constance Penley, *The Future of an Illusion: Film, Feminism and Psychoanalysis* (Minneapolis: University of Minnesota Press, 1989).

Jacqueline Rose, *Sexuality in the Field of Vision* (London: Verso, 1986).

Kalpana Seshadri-Crooks, *Desiring Whiteness: A Lacanian Analysis of Race* (New York: Routledge, 2000).

Kaja Silverman, *The Threshold of the Visible World* (New York: Routledge, 1996).

Garry Watson, *The Cinema of Mike Leigh: A Sense of the Real* (London: Wallflower Press, 2004).

Jeremy Weate, "Fanon, Merleau-Ponty and the Difference of Phenomenology," in *Race: Blackwell Readings in Continental Philosophy*, ed. Robert Bernasconi (Oxford: Blackwell, 2001).

CHAPTER 33
DRUCILLA CORNELL

Drucilla Cornell (b. 1950) is an American feminist philosopher and playwright whose work has made a significant impact on contemporary discussions of gender, politics, and the law, especially from Critical Theoretical and deconstructive standpoints. She is presently Professor of Political Science, Women's & Gender Studies, and Comparative Literature at Rutgers University. Her sole work in the philosophy of film is the book, Clint Eastwood and Issues of American Masculinity, *published originally in English in 2009. The text included here,* "Shooting Eastwood," *is the introduction to that book.*

Cornell's book takes as its twin foci the American actor and director, Clint Eastwood, and the types and tropes of American masculinity. The project of that book—as delineated (and instantiated in microcosm) in this selection—is to explore the latter by way of an examination of the former, or, alternatively, to treat the former as an especially interesting instance of and commentary upon the latter. Cornell explains that she thinks Eastwood is among the most exemplary ethical filmmakers of our time: he grapples, she says, with all of the most significant ethical issues of the day. Most of Eastwood's films, of course, deal in a central way with men, the lives and choices of men, and the idea, or competing ideas, of manliness. This was already evident in Eastwood's work as an actor, before he transitioned to film directing, and is perhaps most noted in his performances in a series of Western films, as well as his role as the iconic San Francisco police inspector, Harry Callahan, in the Dirty Harry *franchise. Eastwood's character in these films is an emblem of brute phallic force, Cornell argues, a typical instance of the "man-as-gun" film trope. As a result of this and similar roles, Eastwood has become identified with a certain sort of remorseless masculinity: he is a man with no qualms, a man with no uncertainty and no regrets, and a man who is totally incompatible with the domestic world associated stereotypically with women. While Cornell seems to agree that, by and large, this is a fair interpretation of the characters Eastwood typically portrayed as an actor, she notes that this idea of Eastwood as masculine icon has carried on even as Eastwood's own cinematic work has become more complex, and as Eastwood has transitioned from being a film actor to being almost exclusively a film director.*

At the center of Eastwood's directorial work, Cornell suggests, is the attempt to wrestle with, to understand, and ultimately to depict man as remorseful—in some ways, the antithesis of the Dirty Harry character. She sees this direction already emerging in Eastwood's first film as director, Play Misty for Me *(1971). Cornell argues that this film is among the first of a specific subgenre wherein obsessive femininity is presented as a danger to masculine survival (perhaps the most memorable film in which tradition is* Fatal Attraction *[1987]). Unlike that later film, however, in* Play Misty for Me *there is no glorification of the ultimate and inevitable destruction of the obsessive woman. Instead of showing the male character (also played by Eastwood) as victorious or even liberated by the death of his female antagonist, Cornell says that we see a man who has failed to understand women, and whose remorse over that failure is his defining quality. The cinematic exploration of masculine remorse continues throughout Eastwood's directorial corpus, achieving a previously unmatched intensity in a much later film,* Million Dollar Baby *(2004).*

Alongside (and sometimes by way of) this depiction of masculine remorse, according to Cornell, Eastwood's films repeatedly expose the vulnerability of man's phallic pretentions—and the hubris at the heart of the phallic fantasy of control. She sees this trait at the heart of Eastwood's A Perfect World *(1993). But it is also apparent in Eastwood's cinematic deconstruction of the Western genre, which becomes, under Eastwood's directorial care, an obsolete fantasy of masculine ideals. One might think immediately of one of Eastwood's most well-regarded films,* Unforgiven *(1992), where we see the issues of remorse, vulnerability, and hubris meet in the depiction of the male protagonist, but Cornell sees the deconstruction of the Western as the fantasy that was traditional American masculinity as well in films as diverse as* Bronco Billy *(1980) and* Space Cowboys *(2000), both of which she reads as the self-conscious ironizing of a certain conception of manhood.*

Cornell says that her approach to Eastwood's work might best be described as "shooting Eastwood," in the sense that she is "intentionally capturing and framing his work" along four related themes. The first of these is the way in which trauma impacts the community, and our shared ethical life. The second is the struggle with the possibility of evil inherent in each human being. The third, the power and danger of repentance and remorse. And the fourth, the relationship between narcissism and violence in masculine hubris. Ultimately, she argues, Clint Eastwood as a film director is engaged unceasingly in the struggle for ethical meaning, exploring the possibility of shared ideals after the apparent collapse of traditional moral systems after the Vietnam War. If we give up on the possibility of shared moral ideals, our notions of masculinity in particular and personhood in general become nothing more than parodies of themselves, as in the "Spaghetti Westerns" of Sergio Leone (in which, of course, Eastwood made his name as an actor): to have ethics at all, as well as ethical men, we must find our way back to common ideas of good and evil—or, at the very least, we must make an effort to find them. Cornell argues that Eastwood has surpassed Leone in this way, returning, as she says, "humanity to the face of the cowboy." While he may not be traditionally masculine or even traditionally heroic, the Eastwood man is one engaged in a constant struggle: with his own past and the remorse that follows, with his vulnerability as a man and a human being, with his temptations to believe he can control everything and reshape the world. In the end, success for this new model of manliness is not always found in ostensible victory over what confronts him: it is found more quietly, more personally, more poignantly, even, in the inner effort to make meaningful (if not always obviously accurate) judgments of right and wrong.

Filmography

- ***Dirty Harry*** (USA, 1971). *Directed by* Don Siegel. *Produced by* Don Siegel *and* Robert Daley. *Written by* Harry Julian Fink, R. M. Fink, *and* Dean Riesner. *Starring* Clint Eastwood, Andy Robinson, Harry Guardino, Reni Santoni, *and* John Vernon.
- ***Play Misty for Me*** (USA, 1971). *Directed by* Clint Eastwood. *Produced by* Robert Daley. *Written by* Jo Heims *and* Dean Riesner. *Starring* Clint Eastwood, Jessica Walter, Donna Mills, *and* John Larch.
- ***Bronco Billy*** (USA, 1980). *Directed by* Clint Eastwood. *Produced by* Dennis Hackin, Neil Dobrofsky, *and* Robert Daley. *Written by* Dennis Hackin. *Starring* Clint Eastwood *and* Sondra Locke.

- ***Tightrope*** (USA, 1984). *Directed and Written by* Richard Tuggle. *Produced by* Clint Eastwood *and* Fritz Manes. *Starring* Clint Eastwood, Geneviève Bujold, Dan Hedaya, Alison Eastwood, *and* Jennifer Beck.
- ***Fatal Attraction*** (USA, 1987). *Directed by* Adrian Lyne. *Produced by* Stanley R. Jaffe *and* Sherry Lansing. *Written by* James Dearden. *Starring* Michael Douglas, Glenn Close, *and* Anne Archer.
- ***A Perfect World*** (USA, 1993). *Directed by* Clint Eastwood. *Produced by* Mark Johnson *and* David Valdes. *Written by* John Lee Hancock. *Starring* Kevin Costner, Clint Eastwood, *and* Laura Dern.
- ***The Bridges of Madison County*** (USA, 1995). *Directed by* Clint Eastwood. *Produced by* Clint Eastwood *and* Kathleen Kennedy. *Written by* Richard LaGravenese. *Starring* Clint Eastwood *and* Meryl Streep.
- ***Space Cowboys*** (USA, 2000). *Directed by* Clint Eastwood. *Produced by* Clint Eastwood *and* Andrew Lazar. *Written by* Ken Kaufman *and* Howard Klausner. *Starring* Clint Eastwood, Tommy Lee Jones, Donald Sutherland, James Garner, Marcia Gay Harden, William Devane, Loren Dean, Courtney B. Vance, *and* James Cromwell.
- ***Million Dollar Baby*** (USA, 2004). *Directed by* Clint Eastwood. *Produced by* Clint Eastwood, Albert S. Ruddy, Tom Rosenberg, *and* Paul Haggis. *Written by* Paul Haggis. *Starring* Clint Eastwood, Hilary Swank, *and* Morgan Freeman.

SHOOTING EASTWOOD

Clint Eastwood has been acknowledged as one of this country's most original and provocative directors, but this classification fails to recognize the real depth of Eastwood's complex trajectory as a director. He grapples with all of the most significant ethical issues of our time: war, vengeance, the role of law, relations between the sexes, the meaning of friendship, and indeed with what it means to lead an ethical life as a good man in late modernity. Most of Eastwood's movies do focus on men—on a certain brand of manliness—but from the beginning of his directorial journey he has been more complicated than he has appeared, working with some of the most sophisticated literature that addresses the meaning of straight white maleness throughout the history of the United States.

Eastwood became famous for the Dirty Harry movies. Indeed, his famous phrase in the first film of the series—"Make my day," which is spoken as he stares down a suspect over the barrel of a.44 Magnum—has saturated the everyday vernacular of the English language, even appearing in American politics. Ronald Reagan famously used that phrase as a slogan in his election campaign. The projection of the image of magnum force is explicitly phallic in its identification of man with gun. We see the gun from the side, initially, in what seems like a frozen image; this goes on for a seemingly unbearable span of time, as we wait for the gun to be cocked and aimed. It is cocked, it's pointed, and we hear Clint Eastwood's voice before we even see his face: "But being this is a forty-four Magnum, the most powerful handgun in the world, and would blow your head clean off, you've got to ask yourself one question: 'Do I feel lucky?'"[1] It's not surprising, given these powerful images from the Dirty Harry movies, that Eastwood as an actor is identified by some of his critics as representing the perfect image of remorseless masculinity and the phallic power of the outlaw-hero who must never be drawn into the domestic world of women.

> Eastwood may spend large portions of a film pursuing a woman, and he may ride off with a woman at a film's conclusion, but if an Eastwood character is ever married in a film's "back story," he is inevitably estranged, divorced, or widowed. Because Eastwood's masculine presentation is incompatible with the daily frustrations and accommodations of conventional family life, a stable loving relationship becomes for his characters an unrepresentable element in an impossible past.[2]

The very power of these images, however, has taken even the most sophisticated authors down a wrong path when it comes to viewing Eastwood's complex engagement with violence and masculinity in his directorial trajectory. Indeed, in his first film as director, Eastwood begins to examine what it means for men to experience remorse—often through their own investment

[1] *Dirty Harry*. DVD, dir. Don Siegel, perf. Clint Eastwood (Warner Bros. Studios, 1971).

[2] Krin Gabbard, "'Someone Is Going to Pay'—Resurgent White Masculinity in *Ransom*," in *Masculinity: Bodies, Movies, Culture*, ed. Peter Lehman (New York: Routledge, 2001), p. 9.

in the saving power of phallic fantasy—and even when that fantasy is most mundanely played out in an actual sexual relationship.

Consider Eastwood's directorial debut, *Play Misty for Me* (1971),[3] a movie that has been identified as an originator of a particular genre of thriller in which obsessive femininity is shown as being the ultimate danger to masculine survival. But unlike some of the films to follow, such as *Fatal Attraction*, Eastwood breaks open the psychical fantasy of the women on whom these films are based. We do not have the traditional elements of the paradigm, in which a basically innocent man is lured by carnal temptations to a woman who is often portrayed as having phallic power—the "evil woman" in *Fatal Attraction* is a lawyer—and out-of-control female sexuality. In these movies, of course, the "good man" is restored to home and family while the "evil woman" is brutally killed. This brutality is seemingly necessary given her fantasized sexual potency, which incredibly withstands bullets and multiple knifings as in *Fatal Attraction*. In Eastwood's *Play Misty for Me*, however, the stereotype of masculine innocence is reworked and questioned, and there is no glorying in the death of the female antagonist. Although it is his first directed film, *Play Misty for Me* already highlights Eastwood's penchant for spinning the themes of a genre into a sort of commentary on the genre itself. Dave (Eastwood) explicitly plays out the perspective of a man's blindness to a woman's view of what goes on in a sexual relationship. The main character is, of course, a deeply troubled—in fact, psychotic—woman. However, unlike other later films in this genre, Eastwood plays this narrative not only for the thrill of suspense, but rather for the tragedy of Dave's failure to read the signs of her anguish, of her growing desperation—a failure premised on his inability to understand what it might mean for a woman to take on a sexual relationship with a man.

Indeed, remorse runs throughout the film. Eastwood devotes considerable time to Dave's attempt to make good on a relationship that he had, in his own mind, already failed. Here we see Eastwood grappling (as he will later in *The Bridges of Madison County*) with how to portray on film a scene of *lovemaking* rather than sex. In *Play Misty for Me* Dave seeks to win back the heart of his lost love, believing that she has rightly condemned him for his failures of attentiveness, sensitivity, and fidelity. Whatever one makes of the sentimentality of filming the two lovers in the forest with Roberta Flack's "First Time Ever I Saw Your Face" in the background, the opening of that scene is Dave's explicit sorrow at his betrayal of their relationship. Ironically, it is this remorseful focus that distracts him from what is going on in the other woman—for whom a one-night stand has turned into obsessive attachment. Even as the movie ends in his stalker's inevitable death, after her psychosis has run completely out of control, the last scene projects more than just her plummet into the ocean. It is not simply that he can finally be done with her. Instead, the film closes by acknowledging the horror of what has happened not only to Dave as the one who was stalked but also to Evelyn, as the tragic consequence of Dave's misreading her understanding of the meaning of sex.

By *Million Dollar Baby*, Eastwood's concern with remorse and repentance has become an obsession, which is expressed through a father's daily letters to a daughter who refuses even to open them and sends them back. But then as we have seen remorse, repentance, and moral repair are present in Eastwood's representations of masculinity from the very beginning of his career as a director. For now I would like to draw attention to another early film, *Tightrope* (1984), which was produced but not directed by Eastwood. In this film the Eastwood character

[3] *Play Misty for Me*, DVD, dir. Clint Eastwood, perf. Clint Eastwood, Jessica Walter (Universal Studios, 1971).

is a man deserted by his wife and abandoned as to be a single parent to his children. We will return to this film in more depth in Chapter 2, and will also explore my reasons for examining it in this book even though Eastwood did not direct the film, but for now I want to emphasize that *Tightrope* contradicts the critical implication that Eastwood characters are never portrayed in stereotypical domestic situations or in sustained romantic involvements with women. *Tightrope* opens with Wes Block (Eastwood) playing ball with his two girls, who convince him to adopt yet another stray dog to add to their nearly uncontainable menagerie. The chaos of Block's life as a single parent would seem to underscore the need for a mother or caretaker to care for the children while their father is away at work—but the woman who actually enters Block's life is far from the milk-toast good woman you would expect to save him. Beryl Thibodeaux is a fearless woman, even when facing Block's own terror at the perverted "dark side" of his own sexuality. She provides one of the most positive and affirmative images in film of a strong-willed feminist activist viewed as a potential lover. Rarely does Hollywood portray a sexy, witty feminist, who runs women's self-defense classes, as a desirable sex object expressly *because of* her strength and *because of* her feminism. Block does not need to "save" her; indeed, he ultimately catches the murderer only because *she* has effectively stalemated the murderer's attack.[4]

Eastwood maintains a focus on the vulnerability of men's phallic pretentions throughout his films. This focus runs through the various themes that he engages, including the so-called "masculine" responsibility to save others or to prevent them from being ensnared by a boyhood or manhood gone wrong. In *A Perfect World* (1993), Red Garnett (Eastwood) attempts to intervene in the fate of a young boy, but the ultimate failure of his effort underscores the hubris of control that lies at the heart of phallic fantasy.[5] Once again in this film we see a strong feminist character; this time it is Sally Gerber, who earns Garnett's respect during the manhunt that provides the film's dramatic tension, despite his initial sexist dismissal of her. As we come to fully understand the implications of Garnett's relationship with the escaped prisoner Butch, we see why he is so haunted by this case. At the end of the film, with Butch slowly dying in a field, the criminologist Sally Gerber attempts to comfort Garnett, telling him, "You know you did everything you could. Don't you?" Garnett responds, "I don't know nothin'. Not a damn thing." The echoes of these lines find us a long way from pretentions of a cocky, assertive masculinity.

What I am suggesting is that by reading Eastwood's involvement in these films against the grain of even his best critics, we can grapple with some of the most searing issues of masculinity that confront us in late twentieth and early twenty-first century America. Yes, Eastwood rides off into the sunset at the end of some of his films, a solitary figure with no need or promise for the complexity of a lasting connection, but he also struggles visibly with the contradictions of masculinity in relationships with both men and women.

This concern with the right relations between men and women (and, in the later Eastwood, between the generations) is a touchstone leading us to many of the dramatic high points in Eastwood's directed films. Eastwood comes into his own artistic position in the America after the closing of the frontiers, where the drama of the cowboy has an even more powerful hold on the imagination as American life transforms historical reality into pure fantasy. As Lee Clark

---

[4] *Tightrope*, DVD, dir. Richard Tuttle, perf. Clint Eastwood, Geneviève Bujold, prod. Clint Eastwood and Fritz Manes (Warner Bros. Studios, 1984).

[5] *A Perfect World*, DVD, dir. Clint Eastwood, perf. Clint Eastwood, Kevin Costner, Laura Dern (Warner Bros. Studios, 1993).

Mitchell has pointed out in his classic study, the Western genre itself was an elegy to what was never actually there except as a set of ideals for masculinity—and, indeed, for a kind of cultural and moral horizon that reminds the audience of what it means to be a man. As Mitchell writes,

> More generally, the central terms "West" and "Western," which have forged American cultural identity, are less self-evident than initial impressions might lead one to believe. Actual landscapes are everywhere recast in the Western, which conceives of setting not as authentic locale but as escapist fantasy. The West in the Western matters less as a verifiable topography than as space removed from cultural coercion, lying beyond ideology (and therefore, of course, the most ideological of terrains).
>
> The one aspect of the landscape celebrated consistently in the Western is the opportunity for renewal, for self-transformation, for release from constraints associated with an urbanized East. Whatever else the West may be, in whatever form it is represented, it always signals freedom to achieve some truer state of humanity.[6]

But Eastwood appears not only in the waning shadow of the cowboy mythos. He also comes to a generation traumatized in the aftermath of two world wars who has lost faith in the idea of progressive historical movement toward a better, more peaceful world—indeed, who has lost faith in the possibility of a world where shared meanings are essential to the aspiration for an ideal democracy founded on the rule of law.

In *Bronco Billy* (1980), Eastwood plays a cowboy who is past his time, one who is left only with the dreams of what it might have been to be a man in the "true West." He must actually live on as a performer of great deeds only in vaudeville acts.[7] Here, Eastwood clearly presents the cowboy (or at least one who still has the dream of living as a cowboy) anachronistically. Indeed, Bronco Billy poignantly struggles to live up to ideals of masculinity that are available to him only in his own parody of his fantasy of the West, his fantasy of himself as a cowboy. It is a story of a man out of sorts with his time.

Of course, Eastwood also has a more playful (and, indeed, ironic) relationship to the ideal of the cowboy, and as we shall see he understands it as both a fantasy and an allegory. In his later film *Space Cowboys* (2000), we see Eastwood explicitly and enjoyably featuring a friendship that has run a difficult life.[8] Four young men form lasting friendships as participants in an early military forerunner to NASA's space program. As Hawk Hawkins (Tommy Lee Jones) tells Frank Corvin (Eastwood) in an opening flashback (a device that Eastwood will develop and use more creatively in his later work as the black and white of memory and dream), someday—someday—the two of them will fly to the Moon. Unfortunately, Hawkins eventually plays too dangerously with his plane, destroying the expensive machine and leaving the men blacklisted by a government bureaucracy that wants men who conform and obey orders rather than those who cherish a desire to "shoot the moon."

Yet as fate has it, many years later the NASA program that did them in needs Corvin to unravel the outdated computer program of a Soviet satellite that has lost its orbit and is falling

---

[6] Lee Clark Mitchell, *Westerns: Making the Man in Fiction and Film* (Chicago: University of Chicago Press, 1996), pp. 4–5.
[7] *Bronco Billy*, DVD, dir. Clint Eastwood, perf. Clint Eastwood, Sondra Locke (Warner Bros. Studios, 1980).
[8] *Space Cowboys*, DVD, dir. Clint Eastwood, perf. Clint Eastwood, Tommy Lee Jones, Donald Sutherland, James Garner, Marcia Gay Harden (Warner Bros. Studios, 2000).

steadily to Earth. Corvin agrees to help, but only if he and his three comrades get to go into space, fulfilling the dreams of their youth. The film toys playfully with the various ideals of masculinity: Jerry O'Neill (Donald Sutherland) is the proudly strutting (if aging) stud, while Tank Sullivan (James Garner) finds it more than a little difficult to keep the stiff upper lip of a man who has made his way, as a preacher, to God. While at times this movie seems to feature men in a "boys-will-be-boys" fashion, always fighting and keeping their eyes out for young women, its spoofing and self-irony also underscores some of the deeper virtues, such as loyalty, trust, and courage, that make the film much more than simply a light, enjoyable comedy with four great actors making fun of themselves.

The four discover that the Soviet "communications satellite" actually houses an arsenal of nuclear weapons—and, tragically, no simple feat of engineering can avert the pull of gravity that is bringing the spacecraft down. Instead, Hawkins must sacrifice himself to pilot the rockets into space, out of range of Earth's gravitational pull. As it happens, Hawkins has been diagnosed with pancreatic cancer—and he has made it clear that he does not want to go down slowly, in the same painful manner that his wife did. Hawkins's current love interest, Sara Holland (Marcia Gay Harden), is one of Eastwood's feminist heroines—feminist, that is, in the sense that she is an engineer working in a predominantly male world. She is also a heroine for these men in that she actively supports their dream to shoot themselves to the Moon by travelling, at last, into space.

Hawkins is successful in his final mission, safely directing the missiles out of Earth's pull, and the badly damaged space shuttle returns to Earth without him. Facing a seemingly doomed final descent, the younger astronauts—and there has been much play between older and younger generations—throw open the hatch and parachute to safety. But in his final memorial to Hawkins, Corvin rejects all procedure and pilots the plane to what the "experts" and their manuals would call an impossible landing, because he knows that this would have been the move of his cocky, death-defying friend. Likewise, O'Neill and Sullivan refuse to bail out on the landing, confirming a profound fraternal loyalty that transcends considerations of safety or procedure. There is no question for them that Hawkins was the greatest pilot they had ever known; Hawkins would have landed the shuttle, and for this reason they know what they must do. They pay tribute to Hawkins's memory by living up to his unorthodox thinking about the relationship between a man and his machine.

For all of what may seem like a surface romantic sentimentality in this film, Eastwood is playing with all of the ironies inherent in masculinity, and the dramatic tension is not reducible to the outward play between four talented male actors. Indeed, Eastwood highlights in his own directorial fashion the fact that we can never just step out of that play because ideals of masculinity are embedded in it. When a writer or critic reviews such a rich body of work, she inevitably takes a perspective on it; and indeed, I am well aware that what I am offering my readers is very much my own take on Clint Eastwood as a director. I am, indeed, "shooting" Eastwood in that I intentionally capture and frame his work through four main themes.

The first is the horrifying impact of trauma on our shared ethical life. The second, related to the first, is Eastwood's struggle with evil as a possibility for each of us. The third is the powers of moral repair and repentance as well as the dangers implicit in them—dangers both to one's self and to others one may seek to save, whether from the abusive world that surrounds them or even from themselves. My fourth theme is the relationship between a masculine narcissism enforced through the terrifying threat of castration and the violence that inevitably inheres in the hubris of an exaggerated sense of control over one's self—and in the case of a nation-state, control over other nations and ethnicities.

All of these themes relate to the struggle for ethical meaning, which is oftentimes cast in the complex relation between ethics and law in that moral repair as a possible redemption from the hell of trauma and abuse, and this struggle will inevitably take us to the possibility or impossibility of a shared world of meanings and symbols. These symbols may be created by the victim as he or she seeks a more perfect world, a world that holds out hope for a "beyond" that is not inscribed with the endless repetition of anguish that is written upon a human being who has survived horrific trauma. A commonly expressed fear is that these shared ideals and allegories may so completely collapse that the ideals associated with masculinity, and indeed with ethical personhood, become so utterly vacated that they live on only as parody, as stylized performances without any cause for action. Such parodies were the Spaghetti Westerns of Sergio Leone—no doubt a great influence on Eastwood's own Westerns, but an influence, as we shall see, that he has clearly surpassed. Leone presents us with the living dead, fighters left with style but no standards, faces without souls. Yet Eastwood in his Westerns restores humanity to the face of the cowboy, implicitly stressing that even this face is not immune to the force and impact of trauma. His heroes, often enough, still have no name—but Eastwood reinterprets their namelessness as an identity *lost* in trauma rather than an absence of identity at all. Even if it were the case that wrong life could not be lived rightly (as Theodor Adorno once wrote) we are inevitably fated to make judgments of right and wrong. In Eastwood's directorial trajectory, the struggle to make judgments to hold onto ideals of right and justice—which in turn imply a complex relationship to law and the good man who supposedly upholds it—brings into vivid relief the drama of what we lose if we give up the struggle for ethical life and meaningful relationships, thinking it has already been lost.

SECTION SIX
POSTMODERNISM

CHAPTER 34
EDGAR MORIN

Edgar Morin (b. 1921) is a French philosopher, social theorist, and screenwriter working across disciplinary boundaries in a number of interrelated fields. He has long been affiliated with the Centre Nationale de la Recherche Scientifique (CNRS) in France. Despite certain points of comparison, and the recurring desire of some readers to think of him as such, Morin has long resisted classification as a postmodern or post-structuralist theorist. The text included here, "The Semi-imaginary Reality of Man," is a selection from his book, The Cinema, or The Imaginary Man. *It was originally published in French (*Le Cinéma, ou l'homme imaginaire: Essai d'anthropologie*) by Éditions Minuit in 1956. A second edition with a new preface by Morin was published in 1978.*

Central to Morin's idea in this text is his notion that the cinema has or is something like a mind. He notes that the cinema certainly reflects the human mind, as its predecessor, the cinematograph, reflected the world. But what Morin means about the cinema here is not that there are psychological truths embedded in film stories; rather, he says that a collective mind materializes in film, from a beam of light. That is to say that, what we see on the screen in the movie house is, in some important sense, itself a mind. Cinema is thus a joining of two minds: that on the screen and that of the spectator. While the spectator is, of course, an ordinary human being, cinema becomes something more than just stories woven in light-images: it is a "mind-machine," a "machine for thinking," a "quasi-robot."

The psyche of cinema, Morin argues, both engages with our perception of the real and helps to produce the imaginary. Like a human mind, then, it contains and projects as much truth as falsehood. Although there are some who turn to the cinema for something like history, or historical documentation, Morin suggests that film is less like history than it is like an historian: it is not history itself, but it tells us stories that we take for history. Rather than merely presenting (or representing) objective reality, film unites the objective reality of the world with a subjective vision of it. In this, film is constructed in the likeness of the human mind—and can in this way help us to understand the "inner theater" of the mind. Morin explains film's situation on the boundary between the objective and the subjective, or the real and the imaginary, in his suggestion that film incorporates both the respect for reality we find in photography with the subjectivity of painting, in shifting perspectives and camera angles, changing the viewer's approach to those photographed images. Cinema, Morin writes, is the world half-assimilated by the human mind. That film is a merging of the real and the imaginary puts it in a privileged position with regard to serving as a sort of mediator between human beings and the world. Morin notes that everything enters the human mind by way of the imaginary: even scientific and technological innovations begin as dreams.

Morin understands the human being to be simultaneously biological and psychological, on the one hand, and engaged in fantasy, on the other. Our biological nature gives us a certain set of drives and instincts which, although they guide our actions at some times, nevertheless are common to all human beings. To the extent that we act instinctively, we are just like everybody else, acting on the basis of our common nature. Human individuality, then, depends upon our ability to affirm ourselves as independent of our instinctive nature. If we are successful in this affirmation, those instincts play a smaller and smaller role in directing our lives; the animal instincts atrophy while the mental image of ourselves as free from biology grows more central.

For Morin, this is the production of what he calls "the double," a conception of the self, founded in the imaginary, which nevertheless has a significant impact on the reality of our lives. It is in one sense, of course, biological reality that is directly responsible for the production of a magical vision of the world—one originating itself in the imaginary—and this interweaving of imaginary and real, magical and biological, drives home the reality of a need that cannot be realized. The discourse between the individual and his or her imaginary double reflects the work the self does on itself, to improve by way of modeling real choices on an imaginary conception of the self, and this means that a substantial portion of our lives are lived elsewhere than reality. Another way to put this, of course, is to say that the reality of human being is semi-imaginary.

The dynamic Morin sees at work in cinema, and in the human mind, and in the interaction between the human mind and the film, is also at work in his general understanding of the relationship between the imaginary and the technical—or, as he puts it, between dreams and tools. Despite their obvious differences, Morin writes, the goal of both dreams and tools is the same: to make the human being the subject of the world. Of course, the two attempt to accomplish this goal in very different ways—dreams, through imaginary world-creation, and tools, through material manipulation—but all the same, they are not exactly at cross purposes. In addition, technical invention is always the result, he says, of an obsessive dream, and every dream is the unreal trying to fulfill a real need. Both individually and as a species, our dreams prepare for our technologies. Of all the human technological inventions, Morin thinks that the cinema is the one most emblematic and evocative of this relationship between dreams and tools: the cinema is a dream-technology, a machine the point of which is to satisfy imaginary needs. The cinema is, for Morin, a literal dream factory: it straightforwardly visualizes our dreams, projecting and objectifying them by industrial means for everyone to see and to share. And here, once again, we see the simultaneously objective and subjective representation, the semi-imaginary reality of (cinematic) human existence.

THE SEMI-IMAGINARY REALITY OF MAN

Translated by Lorraine Mortimer

The world was reflected in the mirror of the cinematograph. The cinema offers us the reflection no longer only of the world but of the human mind.

The cinema is psychic, Epstein has said. Its rooms are veritable mental laboratories where a collective mind materializes from a beam of light. The mind of the spectator performs tremendous, nonstop work, without which a film would be nothing but a Brownian movement on the screen, or at the most a fluttering of twenty-four images per second. Starting from this whirl of lights, two dynamisms, two systems of participation, that of the screen and that of the spectator, are exchanged, flow into one another, complete each other and join in a single dynamism. The film is that moment where two psyches, that incorporated in the film and that of the spectator, unite. "The screen is that place where active thought and spectatorial thought meet and take on the material appearance of being an action" (Epstein).

This symbiosis is possible only because it unites two currents of the same nature. "The mind of the spectator is as active as that of the filmmaker," says Francastel; in other words, it is a question of the same activity. And the spectator, who is all, is also nothing. The participation that creates the film is created by it. The nascent kernel of the system of projection-identification that radiates through the room is in the film.

Nascent mind, total mind, the cinema is so to speak a sort of mind-machine or machine for thinking, "mimic and rival brother of the intelligence" (Cohen-Séat), a quasi-robot. It has no legs, no body, no head, but the moment the beam of light flickers on the screen, a human machine is put into action. It sees in our place in the sense that "to see, is to... extract, read and select, transform," and, effectively, we see again on the screen "what the cinema has already seen." "The new gaze of the screen forces itself on our passive gaze."[1] Like a blender, the cinema processes perceptual work. It imitates mechanically—let us understand this word in its literal sense—what are no less appropriately called the psychic mechanisms of approach and assimilation. "An essential trait of the cinema is that it works for and on behalf of the spectator. It substitutes its investigation for ours."[2]

The psyche of the cinema not only elaborates our perception of the real, it also secretes the imaginary. Veritable robot of the imaginary, the cinema "imagines for me, imagines in my place and at the same time outside me, with an imagination that is more intense and precise."[3] It develops a dream that is conscious in many respects and organized in all respects.

---

[1] Jean Epstein, "The Senses 1(b)," trans. T. Milne, in *French Film Theory and Criticism*, vol. 1, *1907–1929*, ed. Richard Abel (Princeton, NJ: Princeton University Press, 1988), 244; and René Clair, "Rhythms," trans. Richard Abel, in the same volume, 368.

[2] Henri Wallon, "De quelques problèmes psycho-physiologiques que pose le cinéma," *Revue Internationale de Filmologie* 1, no. 1 (1947): 17.

[3] François Ricci, "Le cinéma entre l'imagination et la réalité," *Revue Internationale de Filmologie* 1, no. 2 (1947): 162.

Film represents and at the same time signifies. It remixes the real, the unreal, the present, real life, memory, and dream on the same shared mental level. Like the human mind, it is also as much lying as truthful, as mythomaniacal as lucid. It was only one moment—the moment of the cinematograph—this great open eye, "without prejudices, without morals, free from influence," that sees all, evades nothing in its field, that Epstein was speaking about.[4] The cinema, by contrast, is montage, that is, choice, distortion, special effects. "Images alone are nothing, only montage converts them into truth or falsehood." There are historical images, but cinema is not the reflection of history, it is at the very most historian: it tells stories that we take for History. It is impossible to recognize its faked documents, Constantine's false donation,[5] its Apocrypha. In its early days, the Passion Play of the villagers of Oberammergau was filmed on a New York skyscraper, the naval battle of Cuba in a bathtub, and the Boer War in a Brooklyn garden.

The field of the cinema has enlarged and shrunken to the dimensions of the mental field.

It is not pure chance if the language of psychology and that of the cinema often coincide in terms of projection, representation, field, and images. Film is constructed in the likeness of our total psyche.

To draw the whole truth from this proposition, we must turn it inside out, like a pocket; if the cinema is in the image of our psyche, our psyche is in the image of the cinema. The inventors of the cinema have empirically and unconsciously projected into the open air the structures of the imaginary, the tremendous mobility of psychological assimilation, the processes of our intelligence. Everything that can be said of the cinema goes for the human mind itself, its power at once conserving, animating, and creative of animated images. The cinema makes us understand not only theater, poetry, and music, but also the internal theater of the mind: dreams, imaginings, representations: *this little cinema that we have in our head.*

This little cinema that we have in our head is this time alienated into the world. We can see the human psyche in action in the real universe, that is, reciprocally, "reality seen through a brain and a heart" (Walter Ruttman).

In fact, the cinema indissolubly unites the objective reality of the world, as photography reflects it, and the subjective vision of the world, as painting called primitive or naive represents it. Naive painting orders and transforms the world according to psychic participation; it denies optical appearance; one minute it gives the same average size to characters situated at difference distances, the next, it substitutes a psychological appearance for optical appearance. It exaggerates or diminishes the dimensions of objects or beings to give them those of love, deference, contempt (and in that very way translates the sociological values attached to these representations); it ignores or transgresses the constraints of time and space, showing successive or geographically distant actions in the same space. Naive painting is thus guided by an immediate spirit that effects a humanization of vision on the picture itself. In the photograph, by contrast, things are left to their apparent dimensions and forms, lost in space, and enclosed in the uniqueness of the moment.

---

[4] Jean Epstein, "Le regard de verre," *Cahiers du Mois*, nos. 16–17 (1925): 11 [This became part of *Le cinématographe vu de l'Etna*, in *Écrits sur le cinéma*, vol. 1, *1921–1947* (Paris: Éditions Seghers, 1974), 136–37)—*Trans.*]; and Béla Balázs, *Theory of the Film: Character and Growth of a New Art*, trans. E. Bone (New York: Dover, 1970), 166.

[5] ["The Donation of Constantine" was a document that purported to be a deed of gift from the Emperor Constantine to Pope Sylvester. Appearing in the eighth century, it was only discredited as a forgery in the fifteenth.—*Trans.*]

The cinema participates in two universes, that of photography and that of nonrealist painting, or, rather, it unites them syncretically. It respects the reality, if we can put it this way, of the optical illusion; it shows things separated and isolated by time and space, and that was how it initially appeared as the cinematograph, that is, animated photography. But it ceaselessly corrects the optical illusion with the processes of naive painting: medium shots, close-ups. It ceaselessly reestablishes values in terms of care and expression, or else, like realist painting when it seeks to rediscover the meanings of primitive painting, it uses high-angle shots and low-angle shots. Most cinema techniques are responding to the same expressive needs as so-called primitive painting, but within the photographic universe.

The cinema, then, is the world, but half assimilated by the human mind. It is the human mind, but actively projected into the world in its work of elaboration and transformation, of exchange and assimilation. Its double and syncretic nature, objective and subjective, reveals its secret essence; that is, the function and the functioning of the human mind in the world.

The cinema allows us to see the process of the penetration of man in the world and the inseparable process of the penetration of the world in man. This process is first of all one of exploration; it begins with the cinematograph, which places the unknown world within arm's reach, or, rather, within reach of the eye. The cinema pursues and develops the exploratory work of the cinematograph. Perched on the horse's saddle, the airplane's engine, the buoy in the storm, the camera has become the omnipresent eye. It sweeps across the ocean depths and the stellar night equally well. Much more: this new remote-controlled gaze, endowed with all the powers of the machine, goes beyond the optical wall that the physical eye could not cross. Even before the cinematograph, Marey and Muybridge, succeeding in breaking down movement, were the first to bring about this surpassing of the visual sense. Since then, the cinema has extended this new empire in all directions. Beyond the optical wall, the eyes sees the movement of things that are apparently immobile (accelerated motion), and, above all, swept into microscopic and macroscopic infinity, it finally perceives the infrasensitive and the suprasensitive. Behind the telephoto lens, at the tip of the guided missile, the eye patrols, explores. Before man even broke away from the stratosphere, the telepathic eye made its way to the furthermost bounds of interplanetary no-man's-land. It is already impatient for the shores of the macrocosm, ready to take off, to be first on the moon. The cinema will precede us on the planets. But in the exploration of infinitely small worlds, it has already irresistibly and irreversibly left us behind.

Research of the microscopic world is mixed with scientific research itself:[6] microcinematography is truly ahead of the human mind.

So through all films, and through a veritable "supplement to the sense of sight," a "documentary deciphering of the visible world" is carried out. "Today, every fifteen-year-old child, in all classes of society, has a great many times seen the skyscrapers of New York, the ports of the Extreme-Orient, the glaciers of Greenland.... Filmed novels have rendered

[6] See Dr. Comandon, "Le cinematograph et les sciences de la nature," in *Le cinéma des origines à nos jours*, ed. H. Fescourt (Paris: Éditions du Cygne, 1932), cited by M. L'Herbier in *Intelligence du cinématographe* (Paris: Corrêa, 1946), 405; and Jean Painlevé, "Le cinéma au service de la science," *Revue des Vivants* (October 1931), also cited by L'Herbier, 403. See also the perspectives sketched by E.-J. Marey in *La photographie du mouvement* (Paris: G. Carré, 1892) . [See also E.-J. Marey, *La chronophotographie* (Paris: Gauthiers-Villars, 1899). Some of Marey's work has appeared in English, for example, *Movement*, trans. E. Pritchard (London: Heinemann, 1895), and *The History of Chronophotography* (Washington, DC: Smithsonian Institution, 1902) .—*Trans.*]

familiar to all children all the eternal emptiness that troubles the human soul, all the painful mysteries of life, of love and death."[7]

At the same time as it was beginning to collect materials for learning, the Lumière cinematograph was already imbuing them with Raymond Lulle's alchemical powder of projection and sympathy: cinematographic doubling was already a catalyst for subjectivity. The cinema goes further: all the things that it projects are already selected, impregnated, blended, semiassimilated in a mental fluid where time and space are no longer obstacles but are mixed up in one plasma. All the diastases of the mind are already in action in the world on the screen. They are projected into the universe and bring back identifiable substances from it. *The cinema reflects the mental commerce of man with the world.*

This commerce is a psychological-practical assimilation of knowledge or of consciousness. The genetic study of the cinema, in revealing to us that *magic* and, more broadly, *magical participation* inaugurate this active commerce with the world, at the same time teaches us that the penetration of the human mind in the world is inseparable from an imaginary efflorescence.

The spectrum analysis of the cinema completes the genetic analysis. It reveals to us the original and profound unity of knowledge and myth, of intelligence and feeling.

The secretion of the imaginary and the comprehension of the real, born from the same psyche in its nascent state, are complementarily connected in the midst of concrete psychological activity, that is, of mental commerce with the world.

Effectively, everything enters us, is retained, anticipated, communicates by way of images more or less inflated by the imaginary. This imaginary complex, which assures and disturbs participation at the same time, constitutes a placental secretion that envelops and nourishes us. Even in the state of wakefulness and even outside of any spectacle, man walks, solitary, surrounded by a cloud of images, his "fantasies." And not only in these daydreams: the loves that he believes to be of flesh and tears are animated postcards, delirious representations. Images slide between his perception and himself, they make him see what he wants to see. The substance of the imaginary is mixed up with our life of the soul, our affective reality.

The permanent source of the imaginary is participation. What can seem most unreal is born from what is most real. Participation is the concrete presence of man in the world: his life. Certainly, imaginary projection-identifications are apparently only its epiphenomena or deliriums. They carry all the impossible dreams, all the lies that man makes up for himself, all the illusions that he deceives himself with (spectacles, arts). Myths and religions are there to testify to their incredible unreality. Our feelings distort things, deceive us about events and beings. It is not by chance that sentiment signifies naïveté or weakness, that magic signifies error, helplessness, dupery.

But it is not only in the capacity of the reality of error or foolishness that we are envisaging the reality of the imaginary. We also want to remind ourselves that its myths are founded *in reality*; they even express the vital first reality of man. Magic, myth of all myths, is not only a myth. The analogy of the human microcosm to the macrocosm is also a biological truth; man is freed from the specializations and constraints that weigh upon the other animal species: he is the summation and battlefield of the forces that animate all living species; he is open to all the solicitations of the world that surrounds him, whence the infinite range of his mimicry and participation. Correlatively, human individuality is affirmed at the expense of specific

[7] H. Laugier, preface to G. Cohen-Séat, *Essai sur les principes d'une philosophie du cinéma* (Paris: PUF, 1946).

instincts that atrophy, and the *double* is the spontaneous expression of this fundamental biological affirmation. It is, then, the biological reality of man, self-determined individual and indeterminate microcosm, that produces the magical vision of the world, that is, the system of affective participation.

Without a doubt, individuality does not *practically* possess the powers of the double and does not practically embrace cosmic totality. *But the unreality of this myth, founded in reality, reveals to us the reality of the need that cannot be realized.*

This contradiction between the real being and his real need is unified by the concrete man, united not statically but in work. What can diversely be called human "personality," "consciousness," "nature," stems not only from practical exchanges between man and nature and social exchanges between men, but also from endless exchanges between the individual and his imaginary double, and from these anthropo-cosmomorphic exchanges, again imaginary, with things or beings in nature that man feels, sympathetically, participate in his own life. In the course of this ceaseless shuttle between the "I" that is another and the others that are in the "I," between the subjective consciousness of the world and the objective consciousness of the self, between the outside and the inside, the immediately objective self (double) is internalized, the internalized double atrophies and is spiritualized into soul; the immediately subjective macrocosm is objectivized to constitute the objective world subjected to laws.

Genetically, man is enriched in the course of all these imaginary transfers; the imaginary is the ferment of the work of the self on the self and on nature through which the reality of man is constructed and developed.

Thus the imaginary cannot be dissociated from "human nature"—from material man. It is an integral and vital part of him. It contributes to his practical formation. It constitutes a veritable scaffolding of projection-identifications from which, at the same time as he masks himself, man knows and constructs himself. Man does not exist totally, but this semi-existence is his existence. Imaginary man and practical man (*Homo faber*) are two faces of one "being of need," as D. Mascolo puts it. Let us say it another way, with Gorky: the reality of man is semi-imaginary.

Certainly the dream is opposed to the tool. The richness and proliferation of our dreams respond to our state of extreme practical indigence, sleep. At the moment of extreme insertion of the practical in the real, the technical appears and phantasms disappear to make way for the rational. But this contradiction is born of the unity of need: deprivation is the *need* itself from which compensating images spring up. Work is the need that drives away images and fixes itself on the tool.

The dream and the tool, which seem to contradict and despise one another, work along the same lines. The technical is used practically to give human form to nature and cosmic power to man. To the anthropo-cosmomorphism of the imaginary corresponds the anthropo-cosmomorphism of the practical, to the alienation and projection of human substance in dreams corresponds the alienation and projection in tools and work, that is, this long, uninterrupted effort to give reality to the fundamental need: to make man the subject of the world.

In fact, we cannot genetically dissociate imaginary participations with animals and plants from the domestication of animals and plants, the oneiric fascination of fire from the conquest of fire. In the same way, we cannot dissociate hunting or fertility rites from hunting or culture. The imaginary and the technical rely on one another, help each other. They always meet not only as negatives of each other but as mutual fermenting agents.

Thus, in the vanguard of the practical, *technical invention* only crowns an obsessive dream. All great inventions are preceded by mythical aspirations, and their novelty seems so unreal that trickery, sorcery, or madness are seen in them.

This is because, even in its extreme unreality, the dream is itself ahead of reality. The imaginary blends in the same osmosis the unreal and the real, fact and need, not only to attribute to reality the charms of the imaginary, but also to confer on the imaginary the capacities of reality. Every dream is an unreal fulfillment, but one that aspires to practical fulfillment. That is why social utopias foreshadow future societies, alchemy foreshadows chemistry, the wings of Icarus foreshadow those of the airplane.

We think we have sent the dream away into the night and reserved work for the day, but we cannot separate technology, the effective pilot of evolution, from the imaginary that precedes it, ahead of the world, in the oneiric fulfillment of our needs.

Thus the fantastic transformation and the material transformation of nature and man intersect and replace one another. Dream and tool meet and fertilize one another. Our dreams prepare for our technologies: a machine among machines, the airplane is born of a dream. Our technologies maintain our dreams: a machine among machines, the cinema has been taken over by the imaginary.

The cinema testifies to the opposition of the imaginary and the practical as to their unity.

Their opposition: like all fantasizing, films are proliferations of expectation, ectoplasms to keep the soul warm. That is what cinema is first of all: the disturbed image, given over to impotent desires and neurotic fears, its cancerous burgeoning, its morbid plethora. True life is absent, and it is only a substitute that keeps us company waiting for Godot. The world within arm's reach, man the subject of the world—it is only a program of illusion. Man the subject of the world is still only and will perhaps never be anything other than a representation, a spectacle—of the cinema.[8]

But at the same time, and in a contradictory way (and it is this concrete contradiction that we will have to analyze in the future), like every imaginary, the cinema is actual commerce with the world. Its kernel, which is imaginary projection-identification, is rich in all the riches of participation. It is the very kernel of our affective life, and the latter, at the kernel of the semi-imaginary and semipractical reality of man, is rich in its turn in human totality—*that is, in the work of production of man by man, by the humanization of the world and the cosmosization of man.*

The cinema is in its essence indeterminate, open, like man himself. This anthropological characteristic could seem to enable him to escape history and social determination. But anthropology, as we understand it, does not oppose eternal man to the contingency of the moment or historical reality to abstract man.

It is on the contrary in human evolution—that is, the history of societies—that we have wanted to grasp what there is too much of a tendency to consider as noumenal essences. So,

[8] The spectator is like God before his creation. It is immanent to him and confounds itself in him: effectively the spectator-God is the ride, the fight, the adventure. But at the same time, he transcends it, judges it: the ride, the adventure, the fight are only his own fantasies. So the all-powerful God is still impotent: to the extent that his creatures escape him, he is reduced to the role of supreme Voyeur, who participates in a clandestine fashion, in spirit, in the ecstasies and follies that unfold outside of him. To the extent that they are only his own fantasies, he cannot give them total reality, and thus himself accede to total reality. The spectator-God and the God-spectator cannot truly incarnate themselves and become embodied, and equally cannot give body outside of their mind to creation, which remains ectoplasm.

we have envisaged the aesthetic essence of the cinema, not as something transcendentally obvious, but in relation to magic. Reciprocally, the magical essence of the cinema appeared to us in relation to the aesthetic. This means that it is not the original magic that comes back to life in the cinema, but a reduced, atrophied magic, submerged in the higher affective-rational syncretism that is the aesthetic; it means the aesthetic is not an original human given—there was no Picasso of the caves exhibiting his prehistoric works to amateurs, and they are magical shadows that the Javanese Wayang made dance on the rock faces—but the evolutionary product of the decline of magic and religion. That means, in a word, that the very nature of the aesthetic, double consciousness, participating and skeptical at the same time, is historical.

Likewise, we have seen that the visual character of the cinema had to be considered in its historicity. The genesis of a language of the silent image, accompanied solely by music, has been able to be effected with ease and effectiveness only within a civilization where the preeminence of the eye has been progressively affirmed at the expense of the other senses, as much for the real as for the imaginary. While the sixteenth century is a time before seeing "hears and scents, inhales breaths and captures sounds," as L. Febvre showed in his *Rabelais*, the cinema reveals the decline of hearing (the inadequacy of the sound source in relation to visual sources, the approximations involved in dubbing, the schematization of sound mixing, and so on) at the same time as it establishes its empire from the concrete and analytic powers of the eye.[9] To connect the genesis of the cinema to the progress of the eye is by the same token to connect it to the general development of civilization and technology, to place it in that very moment that seems indifferent to it.

Much more directly, much more clearly still, the anthropology of the cinema places us at the very heart of historical actuality.

It is in fact because it is an anthropological mirror that the cinema necessarily reflects practical and imaginary realities, that is, also, the needs, communications, and problems of the human individuality of its century. So the various complexes of magic, affectivity, and reason, of the unreal and the real that constitute the molecular structure of films, take us back to contemporary social complexes and their components, to the progressions of reason in the world, to the civilization of the soul, to the magics of the twentieth century, legacies of archaic magic and the fetishistic fixations of our individual and collective life. We have already been able to observe the predominance of fiction or realist fantasy to the detriment of the fantastic and the documentary, the hypertrophy of the soul complex. In a later study, we will need to extend the analysis of, on the one hand, general trends and, on the other hand, differential, cultural, social, and national trends that are expressed in the cinema.

The anthropology of the imaginary, then, leads us to the heart of contemporary problems. But let us remember that that is where it started. The cinema is a mirror—the screen—but it is at the same time a *machine*, a device for filming and projection. It is the product of a machine era. It is even in the vanguard of mechanization. In fact the machine, which seemed to be limited to replacing human labor, is now spread throughout all sectors of life. It takes over from mental work—machines for calculating, thinking. It inserts itself into the heart of nonwork,

[9] In Japan, from the time of silent cinema to the beginning of sound cinema, the film's *phonographic narrative* played an equivalent role to that of the film as a whole. Films were accompanied by sound commentaries as important as vision itself. There were great star readers of great popularity. It is obvious that it is "the West" that is at the forefront of the civilization of the eye.

that is, of leisure. Omnipresent, it tends to constitute, as Georges Friedmann's analyses have shown, not only a set of tools, but a *new environment*, which from then on conditions the whole of civilization—that is, the human personality.[10] We are at the moment in history where man's inner essence is introduced into the machine, where, reciprocally, the machine envelops and determines the essence of man—better still, realizes it.

The cinema poses one of the key human problems of industrial mechanization, to take up another of Georges Friedmann's expressions. It is one of those modern technologies—electricity, radio, telephone, record player, airplane—that reconstitute, but in a practical way, the magical universe where remote-controlled action, ubiquity, presence-absence, and metamorphosis reign. The cinema is not content with providing the biological eye with a mechanical extension that allows it to see more clearly and further; it does not only play the role of a machine to set intellectual operations in motion. It is the mother-machine, genetrix of the imaginary, and, reciprocally, the imaginary determined by the machine. The latter has installed itself at the heart of the aesthetic that we thought reserved for individual artisanal creations: the division of labor, rationalization, and standardization command the production of films. This very word *production* has replaced that of creation.

This machine, dedicated not to the fabrication of material goods but to the satisfaction of imaginary needs, has created a dream industry. As a result, all the determinations of the capitalist system have presided over the birth and flourishing of the economy of the cinema. The accelerated genesis of the art of film cannot be explained apart from the fierce competition of the years 1900–1914; the subsequent improvements in sound and color were brought about by the difficulties of the Hollywood monopolies. More broadly, affective needs entered into the circuit of *industrial merchandise*. At the same time, we can foresee the object of our impending studies: the dream factory is a soul factory, a personality factory.

The cinema cannot be dissociated from the revolutionary movement—and the contradictions at the heart of this movement—that is sweeping civilization along. This movement tends toward universality: the powers of technology and the economy are deployed across the world market, and the theater of the universal movement of the accession of the masses to individuality is worldwide. The cinema industry is a typical industry, the merchandise that is film is typical merchandise of the world market. Its universal language and its universal art are the products of a universal gestation and diffusion. These multiple universalities converge on a fundamental contradiction between the needs of the masses and the needs of capitalist industry. This contradiction is at the heart of the content of films. But the result of this is that it returns us to the very heart of genetic anthropology, since the latter studies man, who realizes and transforms himself in society, man that *is* society and history.

Anthropology, history, sociology are contained, refer to one another, in the same total vision or genetic anthropology. The anthropology of the cinema is necessarily articulated upon its sociology and its history, on the one hand because, mirror of participation and human realities, the cinema is necessarily a mirror of the participation and realities of this century, and on the other hand because we have studied the genesis of the cinema as an ontophylogenetic complex. In the same way that the newborn recommences the historical development of the species modified by the particularity of its social environment—which is itself only one moment in the development of the species—so the development of the cinema recommences

[10] See Georges Friedmann, *Où va le travail humain?* (Paris: Gallimard, 1963).

that of the history of the human mind, but subject from the outset to the particularities of the environment, that is, what is inherited from the phylum.

Genetic anthropology, which grasps the cinema at its ontophylogenetic kernel, allows us just as much to illuminate its own ontogenesis by phylogenesis as the phylogenesis by its ontogenesis. Its effectiveness is double. We are present at the efflorescence of an art, the seventh by name, but at the same time we better understand the structures common to all art and this formidable unconscious reality within art that produces art. In return, it is this phylogenetic reality that allows us to better understand the seventh art.

Before our eyes, a veritable visitation of the virgin film by the human mind was brought about: the machine to reflect the world effected its own metamorphosis into a machine to imitate the mind. We have been able to see the irruption of the spirit into the crude world, Hegelian negativity at work, and the negation of this negation: the instant flourishing of magic, original humanity; then, through a shortcut blurred by the phylogenetic situation, all the psychic powers—feeling, soul, idea, reason—are incarnated in the cinematographic image. The world is humanized before our eyes. This humanization illuminates the cinema, but it is also man himself, in his semi-imaginary nature, that the cinema illuminates.

This is possible only because the *cinema* is a privileged subject for analysis. Its birth came about almost before our eyes: we can seize the very movement of its formation and its development as if under a laboratory lens. Its genesis has been quasi-natural: the cinema arose from the cinematograph outside of any conscious decision-making process, just as the cinematograph became fixed into spectacle outside of any conscious decision-making process. "The miracle of the cinema is that the progress of the revelations it offers us follows the automatic process of its development. Its discoveries educate us."[11] We have thus been able to be witness to an extraordinary unconscious product, nourished by an in-depth anthropo-historical (ontophylogenetic) process.

It is precisely these unconscious depths that offer themselves to our consciousness. It is because it is alienated in the cinema that the unconscious activity of man offers itself up to analysis. But the latter can apprehend these prodigious riches only if it captures the *movement* of this alienation.

Movement. This is the key word of our method: it is in *history* that we have considered the cinema; it is in its *genesis* that we have studied it; it is in relation to the psychic *processes* involved that we have analyzed it. We have brought everything back to movement. But we have also wanted to avoid considering movement as an abstract principle, an immovable key word; we have wanted to bring it back to man. At the same time, we have wanted to avoid considering humanity as a mystical virtue for humanists. We have also seen the magic of the cinema, the humanity of this magic, the soul of this humanity, the humanity of this soul in the *concrete processes* of *participation*.

Projection-identification allows us to bring fixed things and conceptual essences back to their human processes. All mass comes back to energy. Must we not Einsteinize in their turn the sciences of man, can we not explore those social *things* of which Durkheim spoke by applying to them an equivalent of the formula $E = MC^2$? To consider the sociological masses in

[11] Élie Faure, "Vocation du cinéma," in *Fonction du cinéma: De la cinéplastique à son destin social* (Paris: Éditions Gonthier, 1953), 73–74.

terms of the energy that produces and structures them is at the same time to show how energy becomes social matter. This is the genetic road already traced by Hegel and Marx. Participation is precisely the common site, at once biological, affective, and intellectual, of the first human energies. Doubling, a magical or spiritualist notion, appears to us as an elementary process of projection. Anthropo-cosmomorphism is not a kind of special faculty, proper to children and backward people, but the spontaneous movement of projection-identification. The latter is extended, refined, pursued in works of reason and technology, just as it is alienated in reifications and fetishes. The beginnings precisely allow us to see the processes of projection-identification in their real and observable productive work. They allow us to plunge, without getting lost, into the fundamental contradictions that define the cinema. They situate us at the crossroads of forces, at the live and active proton where individual and collective mental powers are involved; history, society, laws, pleasures, spectacle, communication, action.

And in the same way that the physicochemical sciences go by way of the energizing unity of matter to find the atomic and molecular complex proper to each body, so, finally, it is by returning to original energizing human sources *that this total complex can take shape, a complex whose particular constellations in the end give us this specificity of the cinema so searched for in the platonic sky of essences.*

This investigation is not finished, so our conclusion can only be an introduction to the study of what is to follow. Before envisaging the social role of the cinema, we must consider the contents of films in their triple reality that is anthropological, historical, and social, and always in the light of the processes of projection-identification. Once more, filmic material is privileged, precisely because it is at the limit of materiality, semifluid, in motion.

The time has come when sociological "extraspection" replaces and complements psychological introspection. The secret messages, the innermost depths of the soul are there, alienated, tapped in this imaginary that expresses universal needs as well as those of the twentieth century.

Of course from the time he appeared on earth, man has alienated his images, fixing them in bone, in ivory, or on the walls of caves. Certainly the cinema belongs to the same family as the cave drawings of Les Eyzies, of Altamira and Lascaux, the scribblings of children, the frescoes of Michelangelo, sacred and profane representations, myths, legends, and literature. *But never so incarnated in the world itself, never so much grappling with natural reality.* That is why we had to wait for the cinema for imaginary processes to be externalized so originally and totally. We can at last "visualize our dreams" because they have cast themselves onto real material.[12]

At last, for the first time, by means of the machine, in their own likeness, our dreams are projected and objectified. They are industrially fabricated, collectively shared.

They come back upon our waking life to mold it, to teach us how to live or not to live. We reabsorb them, socialized, useful, or else they lose themselves in us, we lose ourselves in them. There they are, stored ectoplasms, astral bodies that feed off our persons and feed us, archives of soul. We must try to question them—that is, to reintegrate the imaginary in the reality of man.

[12] Jean Tédesco, "Cinéma expression," *Cahiers du Mois*, nos. 16–17 (1925): 25.

CHAPTER 35
MONIQUE WITTIG

Monique Wittig (1935–2003) was a French feminist philosopher, novelist, and playwright. She was one of the first and most significant thinkers and writers in France to theorize a distinctively lesbian feminism, and is most famous in the English-speaking world for her claim, in her collection of essays The Straight Mind, *that lesbians are not women—because they do not satisfy the normative expectations placed upon women in straight, patriarchal society. The text included here is a brief essay, "Lacunary Films," originally published in English in* The New Statesman *in 1966.*

Wittig's essay is written largely in response to the films of Jean-Luc Godard, and the cinematic innovations and styles of Godard's films are foremost on her mind when she discusses what she calls "lacunary films." These films are lacunary—that is, characterized by empty spaces or gaps—because there is an essential discontinuity operating in them. Such films, according to Wittig, have no plot development, just several distinct events grouped together by way of the filmmaker's directorial and editing choices. In the depiction of people, she notes, we never see character—just mood. Of course, moods are variable and frequently change, and the depiction of them invites (and incites) all sorts of movement—making the depiction of mood especially cinematic. Importantly, however, mood can never be given "once and for all." There is no totality, no completion, no necessary or natural endpoint in the presentation of mood. Leaving plot and character behind in this way, Wittig argues, Godard turns discontinuity into a way of working on film—and a deeply untraditional one.

According to Wittig, then, Godard's films are made up of "pointless episodes," events unlinked by any inner logic. Godard juxtaposes them against one another, and this gives his films a sort of orderliness, but there is no development or progression—they are fundamentally discontinuous. As such, in addition to the absence of plot and character, these lacunary films portray no great human sentiments, and no single situation dominating the narrative: rather, Godard depicts a multiplicity of situations in mere succession. In evacuating the level of plot and character of any significance at all (in fundamental contrast to more traditional films), Godard forces viewers to seek out meaning only at the level of the film's images themselves. Wittig notes that this is a "wholehearted dedramatization," the elimination within or outside of the film of any sort of justification for anything that appears (or does not appear) there. In the absence of any distinction, then, between images and the events depicted by way of them, Godard ends up situating what in any other context would be considered differently meaningful elements in an equality of meaning and significance: death, a cup of coffee, love, the reading of a newspaper, and so on. In the absence of "greater significance," symbolism or the like, Wittig suggests that what ultimately comes to the fore in Godard's films is his "highly original rhythm." For Wittig, it is this stylish rhythm, coupled with the challenge to traditional cinema that the essential discontinuity of his films constitute, that make Godard a filmmaker with whom students, scholars, and viewers of film must contend.

Filmography

- ***Le Mépris*** [*Contempt*] (France–Italy, 1963). *Directed and Written by* Jean-Luc Godard. *Produced by* Georges de Beauregard, Joseph E. Levine, *and* Carlo Ponti. *Starring* Brigitte Bardot, Michel Piccoli, Jack Palance, Giorgia Moll, *and* Fritz Lang.
- ***Nicht versöhnt*** [*Not Reconciled*] (West Germany, 1965). *Directed by* Jean-Marie Straub. *Produced by* Produktion Straub-Huillet. *Written by* Jean-Marie Straub *and* Danièle Huillet. *Starring* Danièle Huillet, Heinrich Hargesheimer, Ulrich Hopmann, Henning Harmssen, Ulrich von Thüna, Ernst Kutzinski, Joachim Weiler, Georg Zander, Heiner Braun, Lutz Grubnau, Eva-Maria Bold, Hiltraud Wegener, Carlheinz Hargesheimer, Martha Staendner, *and* Karl Bodenschatz.

LACUNARY FILMS

> This a-rhetorical, broken speech....The units of speech... are—and must be—so perfectly mobile that by shifting them about at large in his poem, the author creates a kind of large animate body whose movement comes from perpetual change, not internal "growth."
>
> Roland Barthes, "Literature and the Discontinuous." *Critique* (1962)

Jean-Marie Straub calls his film *Nicht Versöhnt* a "lacunary film" quoting from Emile Littré: "Lacunary body, body composed of agglomerate crystals with spaces between them." It's a description which may reasonably be applied to the films of Jean-Luc Godard. They are lacunary in that their structure undergoes a process which operates at every level of the film and becomes a system: the process is discontinuity. Since it acts upon the development of the plot, we can no longer talk about plot development in discussing Godard's films, in which there is no single plot but several distinct events not necessarily linked one to another. This way of handling plot is contrary to that classical continuity of action which is a convention of French theatre, as it also is in those novels where the events recorded are joined together by links of necessity. Likewise films may be subordinated to a continuity of action and often are.

Discontinuity works decisively at the level of character. People are no longer regarded in terms of character but in terms of mood. Clearly this process offers rich possibilities for a film, since mood is by definition variable and an invitation to movement. Unlike those classical "characters" which are as fixed as we once thought the stars were, a character's mood can never be given once and for all. If we wished to represent this kind of film graphically so as to emphasise its discontinuity, instead of a straight line we would sometimes find a broken line, and at other times widening circles such that to get from one to another would require the jumps made by protons and negatrons travelling from one orbit to another inside an atom. This discontinuity, affecting as it does the whole structure of the film, has internal consequences of varying order and importance. The film offers itself as a sustained explosion. It doesn't try to convince you of its own validity. In this respect it's unlike those works which are spoken of as spontaneous, true, natural and so on. Here, for example, is Voltaire in the *Dictionnaire Philosophique*: Corneille, Molière, Racine, Boileau "are the only geniuses to have adorned French poetry in the *Grand Siècle*. Almost all the others lacked naturalness, variety, eloquence, precision and that secret logic which should lie behind all thought." This can't be said of Godard, who is readily reproached with being inconsequential, incoherent, uneven, boring. He turns absolute discontinuity into a way of working and this way of working upsets what I shall call, for want of a better phrase, those articulate or rhetorical systems we are more accustomed to, even in modern films. That is, we're accustomed to seeing character and events linked together in the cinema, whether character influences events or *vice versa*.

It's rather like a wave and its trough: now events ride on the crest of the wave and character represents the trough, now the positions are reversed—yet both are still tightly linked by some principle. They validate each other, both tending towards a final cause which keeps the film in suspense and validates it retrospectively. Events, character and dénouement, then, are based on a unique, fixed situation which underlies the whole structure of the film. You might say, without trying to be funny, that such films obey the convention of continuity of action, a convention as valid for modern works as for classical ones, for novels, plays and films alike. Littré defines "continuity of action" as "that convention which means that the main plot of a play should not be interrupted by any unnecessary episode."

Let me quote another opinion of Littré's:

> In *Le Médecin Malgré Lui*, Act Three, Scene Two—where two peasants come to ask Sganarelle for a remedy for their mother and he gives them cheese—is completely episodic. This is a sin against the continuity of action, although from another point of view it may be read as complementary to the portrait of the main character. As it stands, it could be cut from the scene without the audience realising that anything was missing.

This testifies to what the spectator is generally looking for in the cinema: the portrayal of a real character and a running plot unimpeded by pointless episodes. I can't help feeling that Godard's films are made up of the episodes Littré was so unhappy to find in Molière. What's more, these episodes are not linked by any inner logic. Yet the mere fact of choosing to juxtapose them is enough to give them an order, the order which I call discontinuous and which represents the way the film's sequences exist together. In this context, Godard simply isn't interested in what we normally think of as the psychology of his characters. He gives us pictures of characters in motion which reflect nothing more than moods. His films contain no great and eternal human sentiments. There is no main plot, no single situation, but rather a multiplicity of situations. The events have no necessary, inevitable connection one with another. Instead of a development, there is a succession. No more inner logic: the necessities of the work are no longer at the level of character or plot but of the film's images. It's not related events which justify the film: their forward march may be interrupted at any moment. In this kind of film nothing justifies anything, the film itself is not its own justification: it invents itself, it is absolute cinema. From a few items it produces a multiplicity—a delirium—of images.

We are faced with the exact opposite of what Brecht called Aristotelian dramaturgy, whose forms live on in many modern dramas. Godard's films make no effort to persuade the spectator to identify with their characters or acknowledge that before his eyes are the very finest specimens of the eternal human being, whose every feature is carefully drawn from nature. He makes no effort to please by offering a plot with only one possible development. And so we are involved in a wholehearted de-dramatisation. Death and the fortunes of love are treated in the same way as making a cup of coffee, reading the paper or getting up in the morning. These are facts. The way Godard juxtaposes them produces a highly original rhythm. This rhythm is characteristic not only of the relationships between the units of the film but also of those lacunary bodies, which similarly include spaces. Challenging both logic and rhetoric, Jean-Luc Godard's films might develop in many different ways: their progress is broken, interrupted. Fritz Lang remarks in Godard's *Le Mépris*: "it's logical that the illogical should go against logic." He is quoting—from a preface by Corneille.

CHAPTER 36
JEAN-FRANÇOIS LYOTARD

Jean-François Lyotard (1924–1998) was a French philosopher and literary theorist, one of the most important and influential postmodern thinkers alongside figures such as Gilles Deleuze and Jacques Derrida. He is particularly well known for his attempt at defining postmodernism in his essay, The Postmodern Condition *(*La Condition postmoderne*), published in 1979, where he noted that postmodernism is characterized by a skepticism with regard to all metanarratives. The text included here is the essay, "Acinema," originally published in French ("L'Acinéma") in* Cinéma: Théorie, lectures *(Klincksieck) in 1973.*

Lyotard begins by noting that cinematography—and filmmaking in general—is (more than just etymologically) a writing with movements. At every level of the film, movements abound, from the motion of objects represented in a shot, to the movement of the camera, to the movement caused by editing or cutting, to the large-scale movement effected by the script. Given this plethora of movements, and their tendency to multiply if left uninterrupted, Lyotard says that filmmaking is about knowing how to eliminate as many of those movements as is possible. Often, he argues, what is eliminated from a film is what is perceived by the filmmaker to be a mistake, something incongruous with the rest of the film the filmmaker is trying to make. Thus, cinematography is an incessant organizing of movements in accord with the rules of representation, of narrative, even of (film) music. The famed "impression of reality" which cinema seeks to achieve in the spectator's mind is, in fact, an "oppression of order," Lyotard argues, the enforcement of a nihilism of movements. Lyotard uses the word "nihilism" here to indicate that, in traditional, commercial filmmaking, no movement is treated as if it could be valuable in itself or for its own sake: rather, everything that appears in the film is left in the film (that is, is not eliminated from the film during editing) because the filmmakers believe its presence will eventuate in a return of some sort. Which is just another way of saying that, according to Lyotard, most films are made in pursuit of some sort of exchange: each element of the film is meant to contribute to the production of greater value, whether commercial (profit) or artistic.

Lyotard pursues this idea, of the productive, into an opposition with what he calls "the sterile." Using the example of striking a match, he notes that we can conceive of this simple event in either way: if we strike the match in order to light the stove in order to make coffee in order to remain alert on our way to work, then the striking of the match is productive: its value comes from what we can get in exchange for striking the match, in what returns. But Lyotard also notes that when a child strikes a match, it is typically not about return. Rather, the child delights in the sound of the match lighting, the smell, the flame, and the rapid incineration of the matchstick. The child enjoys the striking of the match for itself, in a pure eruption of jouissance, rather than for its exchange value. This is what Lyotard calls sterile; it produces nothing. (Here, Lyotard is thinking of Theodor Adorno's claim that fireworks are the perfect art, insofar as their value is in the sheer delight of witnessing the explosions; since everything is consumed thereby, there is nothing to exchange.) In order to maximize the exchange value of the film, commercial filmmakers do whatever they can to eliminate all of the useless, pointless—that is, unexchangeable—movements. Cinema thus comes to be organized almost entirely around the notion of return, either in the sense of profitability (box office returns) or the sense of good form (which is characterized by a commonality between all good films, a sameness that returns with each new instance of the form).

In opposition to this commercial pursuit of productive cinema, however, Lyotard suggests an alternative. He notes that two opposite impulses have come to characterize painting today: the pursuit of immobility, on the one hand, and the pursuit of excessive movement, on the other. Lyotard thinks that these poles are possible, and sometimes present, in cinema, as well—but that the pursuit of opposed poles would result in entirely unproductive, thoroughly sterile, films. Such an approach, if adopted by filmmakers, would result in the creation of a new, alternative cinema—so unlike the dominant cinema of today that Lyotard calls it an "acinema." Acinema situates itself at the two poles of immobility and excessive movement, which seems both contradictory and impossible, but which Lyotard argues are only incompatible for thought—not for emotion, and not in the film image. Emotion itself, he argues, should be reconceived as a motion moving toward its own exhaustion, that is, as an "immobilizing mobilization" or a tableau vivant. In film, of course, all duration is movement—movement from frame to frame, even if the frames are apparently identical—and yet a filmmaker could (and some filmmakers do; one might think here of someone like the Soviet filmmaker, Andrei Tarkovsky, for example) choose to eliminate from the shot or the scene any distracting difference.

Despite the fact that this runs counter to the tendency of commercial cinema (since a long, motionless shot seems unproductive, vain, and pointless), it remains a film, and it achieves the unity of opposites which is impossible for thought, both moving and unmoving at the same time. Such stillness in a film inevitably creates agitation in the spectator, however, thus shifting the movement from the image to the viewer of that image. The object of the viewer's cinematic desire also shifts, for Lyotard, from the represented object (as in commercial film) to the support for the representation itself—that is, to the screen. Acinema is, thus, as much about the apparatus and process of cinema itself as it is about anything represented within any given film. Acinema, a "cinema without cinema," is in the end the only cinema that is purely cinema, without reference to commercial value or cultural significance. Acinema would have whatever value it had in itself, not in exchange or return, and could thus only be appreciated for its own sake, an eruption or overflowing of jouissance in the spectator, like fireworks, enjoyed in the moment, without agenda or interest in return.

Filmography

- ***Joe*** (USA, 1970). *Directed by* John G. Avildsen. *Produced by* David Gil *and* Yoram Globus. *Written by* Norman Wexler. *Starring* Peter Boyle, Dennis Patrick, Audrey Claire, Susan Sarandon, K Callan, *and* Patrick McDermott.

ACINEMA

Translated by Paisley Livingston

The Nihilism of Convened, Conventional Moments

Cinematography is the inscription of movement, a writing with movements—all kinds of movements: for example, in the film shot, those of the actors and other moving objects, those of lights, colors, frame, and lens; in the film sequence, all these again plus the cuts and splices of editing; for the film as a whole, movements of the final script and the spatiotemporal synthesis of the narration (*découpage*). And over or through all these movements are those of the sound and words coming together with them.

Thus there is a crowd (nonetheless, a countable crowd) of elements in motion, a throng of possible moving bodies which are candidates for inscription on film. Learning the techniques of filmmaking involves knowing how to eliminate a large number of these possible movements. It seems that image, sequence, and film must be constituted at the price of these exclusions.

Here arise two questions that are really quite naive considering the deliberations of contemporary cine-critics: *which* movements and moving bodies are these? Why is it necessary to select, sort out, and exclude them?

If no movements are picked out we will accept what is fortuitous, dirty, confused, unsteady, unclear, poorly framed, overexposed… For example, suppose you are working on a shot in video, a shot, say, of a gorgeous head of hair à la Renoir; upon viewing it you find that something has come undone: all of a sudden swamps, outlines of incongruous islands, and cliff edges appear, lurching forth before your startled eyes. A scene from elsewhere, representing nothing identifiable, has been added, a scene not related to the logic of your shot, an undecidable scene, worthless even as an insertion because it will not be repeated and taken up again later. So you cut it out.

We are not demanding a raw cinema, as Dubuffet demanded an *art brut*. We are hardly about to form a club dedicated to the saving of rushes and the rehabilitation of clipped footage. And yet… We observe that if the mistake is eliminated it is because of its incongruity, and to protect the order of the whole (shot and/or sequence and/or film) while banning the intensity it carries. And the order of the whole has its sole object in the functioning of the cinema: that there be order in the movements, that the movements be made in order, that they make order. Writing with movements—cinematography—is thus conceived and practiced as an incessant organizing of movements following the rules of representation for spatial localization, those of narration for the instantiation of language, and those of the form "film music" for the sound track. The so-called impression of reality is a real oppression of orders.

This oppression consists of the enforcement of a nihilism of movements. No movement, arising from any field, is given to the eye/ear of the spectator for what it is: a simple *sterile difference* in an audiovisual field. Instead, every movement put forward *sends back* to something else, is inscribed as a plus or minus on the ledger book which is the film, *is valuable* because it *returns* to something else, because it is thus potential return and profit. The only genuine movement with which the cinema is written is that of value. The law of value (in so-called "political" economy) states that the *object*, in this case the movement, is valuable only insofar as it is exchangeable for other objects and in terms of equal quantities of a definable unity (for example, quantities of money). Therefore, to be valuable the object must move: proceed from other objects ("production" in the narrow sense) and disappear, but on the condition that its *disappearance makes room for still other objects* (consumption). Such a process is not sterile, but productive; it is production in the widest sense.

Pyrotechnics

Let us be certain to distinguish this process from sterile motion. A match once struck is consumed. If you use the match to light the gas that heats the water for the coffee which keeps you alert on your way to work, the consumption is not sterile, for it is a movement belonging to the circuit of capital: merchandise/match → merchandise/labor power → money/wages → merchandise/match. But when a child strikes the matchhead *to see* what happens—just for the fun of it—he enjoys the movement itself, the changing colors, the light flashing at the height of the blaze, the death of the tiny piece of wood, the hissing of the tiny flame. He enjoys these sterile differences leading nowhere, these uncompensated losses; what the physicist calls the dissipation of energy.

Intense enjoyment and sexual pleasure (*la jouissance*), insofar as they give rise to perversion and not solely to propagation, are distinguished by this sterility. At the end of *Beyond the Pleasure Principle* Freud cites them as an example of the combination of the life and death instincts. But he is thinking of pleasure obtained through the channels of "normal" genital sexuality: all *jouissance*, including that giving rise to a hysterical attack, or contrariwise, to a perverse scenario, contains the lethal component, but normal pleasure hides it in a movement of return, genital sexuality. Normal genital sexuality leads to childbirth, and the child is the *return* of, or on, its movement. But the motion of pleasure as such, split from the motion of the propagation of the species, would be (whether genital or sexual or neither) that motion which in going beyond the point of no return spills the libidinal forces outside the whole, at the expense of the whole (at the price of the ruin and disintegration of this whole).

In lighting the match the child enjoys this diversion (*détournement*, a word dear to Klossowski) that misspends energy. He produces, in his own movement, a simulacrum of pleasure in its so-called "death instinct" component. Thus if he is assuredly an artist by producing a simulacrum, he is one most of all because this simulacrum is not an object or worth valued for another object. It is not composed with these other objects, compensated for by them, enclosed in a whole ordered by constitutive laws (in a structured group, for example). On the contrary, it is essential that the entire erotic force invested in the simulacrum be promoted, raised, displayed, and burned in vain. It is thus that Adorno said the only truly great art is the making of fireworks: pyrotechnics would simulate perfectly the sterile consumption of energies in jouissance. Joyce grants this privileged position to fireworks in the beach sequence in *Ulysses*. A simulacrum, understood in the sense Klossowski gives it, should not be conceived primarily as belonging to the category of representation, like the representations which imitate pleasure; rather, it is to be conceived as a kinetic problematic, as the paradoxical product of the disorder of the drives, as a composite of decompositions.

The discussion of cinema and representational-narrative art in general begins at this point. Two directions are open to the conception (and production) of an object, and in particular, a cinematographic object, conforming to the pyrotechnical imperative. These two seemingly contradictory currents appear to be those attracting whatever is intense in painting today. It is possible that they are also at work in the truly active forms of experimental and underground cinema.

These two poles are immobility and excessive movement. In letting itself be drawn toward these antipodes the cinema insensibly ceases to be an ordering force; it produces true, that is, vain, simulacrums, blissful intensities, instead of productive/consumable objects.

The Movement of Return

Let us back up a bit. What do these movements of return or returned movements have to do with the representational and narrative form of the commercial cinema? We emphasize just how wretched it is to answer this question in terms of a simple superstructural function of an industry, the cinema, the products of which, films, would lull the public consciousness by means of doses of ideology. If film direction is a directing and ordering of movements it is not so by being propaganda (benefiting the bourgeoisie some would say, and the bureaucracy, others would add), but by being a propagation. Just as the libido must renounce its perverse overflow to propagate the species through a normal genital sexuality allowing the constitution of a "sexual body" having that sole end, so the film produced by an artist working in capitalist industry (and all known industry is now capitalist) springs from the effort to eliminate aberrant movements, useless expenditures, differences of pure consumption. This film is composed like a unified and propagating body, a fecund and assembled whole transmitting instead of losing what it carries. The diegesis locks together the synthesis of movements in the temporal order; perspectivist representation does so in the spatial order.

Now, what are these syntheses but the arranging of the cinematographic material following the figure of *return*? We are speaking not only of the requirement of profitability imposed upon the artist by the producer but also of the formal requirements that the artist weighs upon his material. All so-called good form implies the return of sameness, the folding back of diversity upon an identical unity. In painting this may be a plastic rhyme or an equilibrium of colors; in music, the resolution of dissonance by the dominant chord; in architecture, a proportion. Repetition, the principle not only of the metric but even of the rhythmic, if taken in the narrow sense as the repetition of the same (same color, line, angle, chord), is the work of Eros and Apollo disciplining the movements, limiting them to the norms of tolerance characteristic of the system or whole under consideration.

It was an error to accredit Freud with the discovery of the very motion of the drives. Because Freud, in *Beyond the Pleasure Principle*, takes great care to dissociate the repetition of the same, which signals the regime of the life instincts, from the repetition of the other, which can only be other to the first-named repetition. These death drives are just outside the regime delimited by the body or whole considered, and therefore it is impossible to discern *what* is returning, when returning with these drives is the intensity of extreme jouissance and danger that they carry. To the point that it must be asked if indeed any repetition is involved at all, if on the contrary something different returns at each instance, if the *eternal return* of these sterile explosions of libidinal discharge should not be conceived in a wholly different time-space than that of the repetition of the same, as their impossible copresence. Assuredly we find here the insufficiency of *thought*, which must necessarily pass through that sameness which is the concept.

Cinematic movements generally follow the figure of return, that is, of the repetition and propagation of sameness. The scenario or plot, an intrigue and its solution, achieves the same resolution of dissonance as the sonata form in music; its movement of return organizes the affective charges linked to the filmic "signifieds," both connotative and denotative, as Metz would say. In this regard all endings are happy endings, just by being endings, for even if a film finishes with a murder, this too can serve as a final resolution of dissonance. The affective charges carried by every type of cinematographic and filmic "signifier" (lens, framing, cuts, lighting, shooting, etc.) are submitted to the same rule absorbing diversity into unity, the same law of a return of the same after a semblance of difference; a difference that is nothing, in fact, but a detour.

The Instance of Identification

This rule, where it applies, operates principally, we have said, in the form of exclusions and effacements. The exclusion of certain movements is such that the professional filmmakers are not even aware of them; effacements, on the other hand, cannot fail to be noticed by them because a large part of their activity consists of them. Now these effacements and exclusions form the very operation of film directing. In eliminating, before and/or after the shooting, any extreme glare, for example, the director and cameraman condemn the image of film to the sacred task of making itself recognizable to the eye. The image must cast the object or set of objects as the double of a situation that from then on will be supposed real. The image is representational because recognizable, because it addresses itself to the eye's *memory*, to fixed references or identification, references known, but in the sense of "well known," that is, familiar and established. These references are identity measuring the returning and return of movements. They form the instance or group of instances connecting and making them take the form of cycles. Thus all sorts of gaps, jolts, postponements, losses, and confusions can occur, but they no longer act as real diversions or wasteful drifts; when the final count is made they turn out to be nothing but beneficial detours. It is precisely through the return to the ends of identification that cinematographic form, understood as the synthesis of good movement, is articulated following the cyclical organization of capital.

One example chosen from among thousands: in *Joe* (a film built entirely upon the impression of reality) the movement is drastically altered twice: the first time when the father beats to death the hippie who lives with his daughter; the second, when in "mopping up" a hippie commune he unwittingly guns down his own daughter. This last sequence ends with a freeze-frame shot of the bust and face of the daughter who is struck down in full movement. In the first murder we see a hail of fists falling upon the face of the defenseless hippie who quickly loses consciousness. These two effects, the one of immobilization, the other an excess of mobility, are obtained by waiving the rules of representation which demand real motion recorded and projected at 24 frames per second. As a result we could expect a strong affective charge to accompany them, since this greater or lesser perversion of the realistic rhythm responds to the organic rhythm of the intense emotions evoked. And it is indeed produced, but to the benefit, nevertheless, of the filmic totality, and thus, all told, to the benefit of order;

both arrhythmias are produced not in some aberrant fashion but at the culminating points in the tragedy of the impossible father/daughter incest underlying the scenario. So while they may upset the representational order, clouding for a few seconds the celluloid's necessary transparency (which is that order's condition), these two affective charges do not fail to suit the narrative order. On the contrary, they mark it with a beautiful melodic curve, the first accelerated murder finding its resolution in the second immobilized murder.

Thus the memory to which films address themselves is *nothing* in itself, just as capital is nothing but an instance of capitalization; it is an instance, a set of empty instances, which in no way operate through their content; *good* form, *good* lighting, *good* editing, *good* sound mixing are not good because they conform to perceptual or social reality, but because they are a priori scenographic *operators* which on the contrary determine the objects to be recorded on the screen and in "reality."

Directing: Putting In, and Out, of Scene

Film direction is not an artistic activity; it is a general process touching all fields of activity, a profoundly unconscious process of separation, exclusion, and effacement. In other words, direction is simultaneously executed on two planes, with this being its most enigmatic aspect. One the one hand, this task consists of separating reality on one side and a play space on the other (a "real" or an "unreal"—that which is in the camera's lens): to direct is to institute this limit, this frame, to circumscribe the region of de-responsibility at the heart of a whole which *ideo facto* is posed as responsible (we will call it *nature*, for example, or *society* or *final instance*). Thus between the two regions is established a relation of representation or doubling accompanied necessarily by a relative devaluation of the scene's realities, now only representative of the realities of reality. But on the other hand, and inseparably, in order for the function of representation to be fulfilled, the activity of directing (a placing in and out of scene, as we have just said) must also be an activity which unifies all the movements, those on *both sides* of the frame's limit, imposing here *and* there, in "reality" just as in the real (*réel*), the *same norms*, the same ordering of all drives, excluding, obliterating, effacing them *no less off* the scene than on. The references imposed on the filmic object are imposed just as necessarily on all objects outside the film. Direction first divides—along the axis of representation, and due to the theatrical limit—a reality and its double, and this disjunction constitutes an obvious repression. But also, beyond this representational disjunction and in a "pretheatrical" economic order, it eliminates *all impulsional movement, real or unreal, which will not lend itself to reduplication*, all movement which would escape identification, recognition, and the mnemic fixation. Considered from the angle of this primordial function of an exclusion spreading to the exterior as well as to the interior of the cinematographic playground, film direction acts always as a factor of *libidinal normalization*, and does so independently of all "content," be it as a "violent" as might seem. This normalization consists of the exclusion from the scene of whatever cannot be folded back upon the body of the film, and outside the scene, upon the social body.

The *film*, strange formation reputed to be normal, is no more normal than the *society* or the *organism*. All these so-called objects are the result of the imposition and hope for an accomplished totality. They are supposed to realize the reasonable goal par excellence, the subordination of all partial drives, all sterile and divergent movements, to the unity of an organic body. The film is the organic body of cinematographic movements. It is the ecclesia of images: just as politics is that of the partial social organs. This is why direction, a technique of exclusions and effacements, a political activity par excellence, and political activity, which is direction par excellence, are the religion of the modern irreligion, the ecclesiastic of the secular. The central problem for both is not the representational arrangement and its accompanying question, that of knowing how and what to represent and the definition of good or true representation; the fundamental problem is the exclusion and foreclosure of all that is judged unrepresentable because nonrecurrent.

Thus film acts as the orthopedic mirror analyzed by Lacan in 1949 as constitutive of the imaginary subject or *object a*; that we are dealing with the social body in no way alters its function. But the real problem, missed by Lacan due to his Hegelianism, is to know why the drives spread about the polymorphous body *must have* an object where they can unite. That the imperative of unification is given as hypothesis in a philosophy of "consciousness" is betrayed by the very term "consciousness," but for a "thought" of the unconscious (of which the form related most to pyrotechnics would be the economy sketched here and there in Freud's writings), the question of the production of unity, even an imaginary unity, can no longer fail to be posed in all its opacity. We will no longer have to pretend to understand how the subject's unity is constituted from his image in the mirror. We will have to ask ourselves how and why the *specular wall* in general, and thus the cinema screen in particular, can become a privileged place for the libidinal cathexis; why and how the drives come to take their place on the film (*pellicule*, or *petite peau*), opposing it to themselves as the place of their inscription, and what is more, as the support that the filmic operation in all its aspects will efface. A libidinal economy of the cinema should theoretically construct the operators which exclude aberrations from the social and organic bodies and channel the drives into this apparatus. It is not clear that narcissism or masochism are the proper operators: they carry a tone of subjectivity (of the theory of Self) that is probably still much too strong.

The Tableau Vivant

The acinema, we have said, would be situated at the two poles of the cinema taken as a writing of movements: thus, extreme immobilization and extreme mobilization. It is only for *thought* that these two modes are incompatible. In a libidinal economy they are, on the contrary, necessarily associated; stupefaction, terror, anger, hate, pleasure—all the intensities—are always displacements in place. We should read the term *emotion* as a *motion* moving toward its own exhaustion, an immobilizing motion, an immobilized mobilization. The representational arts offer two symmetrical examples of these intensities, one where immobility appears: the tableau vivant; another where agitation appears: lyric abstraction.

Presently there exists in Sweden an institution called the *posering*, a name derived from the *pose* solicited by portrait photographers: young girls rent their services to these special houses, services which consist of assuming, clothed or unclothed, the poses desired by the client. It is against the rules of these houses (which are not houses of prostitution) for the clients to touch the models in any way. We would say that this institution is made to order for the phantasmatic of Klossowski, knowing as we do the importance he accords to the tableau vivant as the near perfect simulacrum of fantasy in all its paradoxical intensity. But it must be seen how the paradox is distributed in this case: the immobilization seems to touch only the erotic object, while the subject is found overtaken by the liveliest agitation.

But things are probably not as simple as they might seem. Rather, we must understand this arrangement as a demarcation on both bodies, that of model and client, of the regions of extreme erotic intensification, a demarcation performed by one of them, the client, whose integrity reputedly remains intact. We see the proximity such a formulation has to the Sadean problematic of jouissance. We must note, given what concerns us here, that the tableau vivant in general, if it holds a certain libidinal potential, does so because it brings the theatrical and economic orders into communication; because it uses "whole persons" as detached erotic regions to which the spectator's impulses are connected. (We must be suspicious of summing this up too quickly as a simple voyeurism.) We must sense the price, beyond price, as Klossowski admirably explains, that the organic body, the pretended unity of the pretended subject, must pay so that the pleasure will burst forth in its irreversible sterility. This is the same price that the cinema should pay if it goes to the first of its extremes, immobilization: because this latter (which is not simply immobility) means that it would be necessary to endlessly undo the conventional synthesis that normally all cinematographic movements proliferate. Instead of good, unifying, and reasonable forms proposed for identification, the image would give rise to the most intense agitation through its fascinating paralysis. We could already find many underground and experimental films illustrating this direction of immobilization. Here we should begin the discussion of a matter of singular importance: if you read Sade or Klossowski, the paradox of immobilization is seen to be clearly distributed along the representational axis. The object, the victim, the prostitute, takes the pose, offering his or her self as a detached region, but *at the same time giving way and humiliating this whole person*. The allusion to this latter is an indispensable factor in the intensification, since it indicates the inestimable price of diverting the drives in order to achieve perverse pleasure. Thus representation is essential to this phantasmatic; that is, it is essential that the spectator be offered instances of identification, recognizable forms, all in all, matter for the memory: for it is at the price, we repeat, of going beyond this and disfiguring the order of propagation that the intense emotion is felt. It follows that the simulacrum's support, be it the writer's descriptive syntax, the film of Pierre Zucca whose photographs illustrate(?) Klossowski's *La Monnaie Vivante*, the paper on which Klossowski himself sketches—it follows that the support itself must not submit to any noticeable perversion in order that the perversion attack only what is supported, the representation of the victim: the support is held in insensibility or unconsciousness. From here springs Klossowski's active militancy in favor of representational plastics and his anathema for abstract painting.

Abstraction

But what occurs if, on the contrary, it is the support itself that is touched by perverse hands? Then the film, movements, lightings, and focus refuse to produce the recognizable image of a victim or immobile model, taking on themselves the price of agitation and libidinal expense and leaving it no longer to the fantasized body. All lyric abstraction in painting maintains such a shift. It implies a polarization no longer toward the immobility of the model but toward the mobility of the support. This mobility is quite the contrary of cinematographic movements;

it arises from any process which undoes the beautiful forms suggested by this latter, from any process which to a greater or lesser degree works on and distorts these forms. It blocks the synthesis of identification and thwarts the mnemic instances. It can thus go far toward achieving an *atarxy* of the iconic constituents, but this is still to be understood as a mobilization of the support. This way of frustrating the beautiful movement *by means of the support* must not be confused with that working through a paralyzing attack on the victim who serves as motif. The model is no longer needed, for the relation to the body of the client/spectator is completely displaced.

How is jouissance instantiated by a large canvas by Pollock or Rothko or by a study by Richter, Baruchello, or Eggeling? If there is no longer a reference to the loss of the unified body due to the model's immobilization and its diversion to the ends of partial discharge, just how inestimable must be the disposition the client/spectator can have; the represented ceases to be the libidinal object while the screen itself, in all its most formal aspects, takes its place. The film strip is no longer abolished (made transparent) for the benefit of this or that flesh, for it offers itself as the flesh posing itself. But from what unified body is it torn so that the spectator may enjoy, so that it seems to him to be beyond all price? Before the minute thrills which hem the contact regions adjoining the chromatic sands of a Rothko canvas, or before the almost imperceptible movements of the little objects or organs of Pol Bury, it is at the price of renouncing his own bodily totality and synthesis of movements making it exist that the spectator experiences intense pleasure: these objects demand the paralysis not of the object/model but of the "subject" client, the decomposition of his own organism. The channels of passage and libidinal discharge are restricted to very small partial regions (eye—cortex), and almost the whole body is neutralized in a tension blocking all escape of drives from passages other than those necessary to the detection of very fine differences. It is the same, though following other modalities, with the effects of the excess of movement in Pollock's paintings or with Thompson's manipulation of the lens. Abstract cinema, like abstract painting, in rendering the support opaque reverses the arrangement, making the client a victim. It is the same again though differently in the almost imperceptible movements of the Nō theater.

The question, which must be recognized as being crucial to our time because it is that of the staging of scene and society, follows: is it necessary for the victim to be in the scene for the pleasure to be intense? If the victim is the client, if in the scene is only film screen, canvas, the support, do we lose to this arrangement all the intensity of the sterile discharge? And if so, must we then renounce the hope of finishing with the illusion, not only the cinematographic illusion but also the social and political illusions? Are they not really illusions then? Or is believing so the illusion? Must the return of extreme intensities be founded on at least this empty permanence, on the phantom of the organic body or subject which is the proper noun, and at the same time that they cannot really accomplish this unity? This foundation, this love, how does it differ from that anchorage in nothing which founds capital?

Note

These reflections would not have been possible without the practical and theoretical work accomplished for several years by and with Dominique Avron, Claudine Eizykman, and Guy Fihman.

CHAPTER 37
MICHEL FOUCAULT

Michel Foucault (1926–1984) was a French philosopher and social theorist whose work on power and society has been deeply influential in a variety of disciplines and contexts around the world. Foucault turned his genealogical method (borrowed to a certain extent from Nietzsche) to a variety of social phenomena in the West, including imprisonment, health care, madness, sexuality, and history. He was, in addition, keenly interested philosophically in the arts, including painting, literature, and—to what seems a somewhat lesser extent—film. The text included here, "Film and Popular Memory," is an interview Foucault gave to Pascal Bonitzer and Serge Toubiana, originally published in French ("Anti-rétro: entretien avec Michel Foucault") in Cahiers du cinéma *in 1974.*

Bonitzer and Toubiana begin the interview by asking Foucault to address what they take to be a recent "retro" style in film and, in particular, a fondness in films of the 1960s and 1970s for the 1940s. For Europeans (and Americans, and many others), of course, this means in part a sort of nostalgia for or, at least, remembrance of the Second World War. This is certainly the specific cinematic interest in which Bonitzer and Toubiana are interested as they interview Foucault: the renewed interest in, interpretation and appropriation of the Second World War, and especially in the European experience of that war. They suggest that, from their point of view, three recent developments in France have led to the retro interest in this period in French and European history: a new approach to politics (most potently symbolized by the rise of French President Valéry Giscard d'Estaing), the new bourgeois attacks on orthodox Marxism, and the rise of political militants in Europe (including, presumably, the student protests of 1968). In particular, Bonitzer and Toubiana want to know what it is that, following the release of Marcel Ophüls' documentary about a French town during the German occupation, The Sorrow and the Pity, *overflowed into French culture—and French cinema—and occasioned the return of interest in the wartime (and occupied) France of the forties. Bonitzer and Toubiana thus see the cultural shift in France as having both a cinematic starting point and an effect on later filmmaking.*

Foucault begins by admitting that he does not think that the history of the war has ever really been written. Of course, what he means by this is somewhat ambiguous, given that even by 1974, numerous historians had addressed the topic of the Second World War. But in particular, it seems Foucault thinks that the history of the French people's experience of the war and the occupation has not been settled; it remains somewhat an open question, what happened and why. The openness and ambiguity are the result of a fight over popular memory, he asserts. Television and cinema can reprogram popular memory, according to Foucault, and if one controls people's memory, one controls their ability to respond to the past and develop into the future. Thus, although the conflict is not a thoroughgoing cinematic one, one of the primary battlefields is the cinema. The Sorrow and the Pity *depicts the French people as passive in the face of their Nazi occupiers. At stake in this depiction, then, is the very memory of the struggle—specifically here, the French Resistance—itself. When it is asserted in a high-minded way that "there are no heroes" in war, this may seem at first like the sort of thing to which any thoughtful individual might assent: war is so awful that it produces no victors of any sort. We might see in the expression a critique of the mythologization of war heroes, something performed today by the cinema, with figures (for Foucault) such as Burt Lancaster. There are no heroes of the war movie sort, but Foucault thinks that this is not the only interpretation of the claim possible: in saying "there are no heroes," we might be saying that there was no struggle. This is, of course, the direction taken by* The Sorrow and the Pity, *and the one Foucault, Bonitzer, and Toubiana all oppose: the notion that the French simply "rolled over" and let the Germans take their country.*

Foucault asks whether, in fact, one can make a film about a struggle without creating heroes. And, he goes on to note that what is of most interest to him is the construction of a common subject in all of these "retro" films, from The Sorrow and the Pity *forward. Ultimately, Foucault tries to remind us of the widespread disgust with war in general felt in France (and much of the rest of Europe) after the First World War. Rather than the precipitous decision not to oppose German occupation that many audiences see portrayed in these films, and which has started to take over the popular understanding of what happened, Foucault notes that it was in fact a very gradual return of the willingness to fight that, by the time of the Nazi occupation of France, resulted in the creation of the French Resistance. This movement—from disgust and disillusionment with war to the willingness to use violence in pursuit of justice—is the opposite of what these films show. This demonstrates, for Foucault, that these films might be different—might be differently made, and might be interpreted differently—if we watched them in light of history.*

Bonitzer and Toubiana then ask Foucault to address the seeming union of fascism and sex in two European films set in the 1940s: Lacombe Lucien *and* The Night Porter. *While the interviewers seem to understand the films as both evidence of a singular cinematic phenomenon, Foucault treats them separately: the introduction of eroticism into a fascist context is different in the one film than in the other. In* Lacombe Lucien, *the erotic humanizes the fascist character. Love and power are shown to have opposite effects, and the fascist character abandons his power in favor of love. In* The Night Porter, *however, there is an exchange established between love and power. What is eroticized in this film is the power the fascist character holds over others. Foucault wonders how Nazism has become so thoroughly eroticized in the popular imagination, given, as he notes, that it was originally associated with a kind of sexual prudery. And, he suggests that what we see in films such as* The Night Porter *is a return of the recognition of the power of seduction. He notes that no one loves the power exercised over them anymore, but that the figure of the Nazi allows a re-eroticization of precisely such dominating power in the popular imagination.*

This development in cinema accompanies a comparable development in public life. Until recently, Foucault says, power needed not to seem like power: democratic republics only exist by way of the invisibility of power relations, so that no one feels they are being controlled or dominated by another. Dictatorship is only superficially understood if we understand it as the situation of a power monopoly in the hands of one party; rather, Foucault argues, what dictatorship offers is the possibility of a wide dissemination of power amongst ordinary people. By way of joining the Nazi Party, or informing on one's neighbors, for example, any German could find himself able to exercise a great deal more power over others than anyone seems to possess in a democratic republic. In The Night Porter, *an emotional attachment to power is depicted such that, when there is an excess of power, it can be converted to love. Likewise, reciprocally, love converts power back into a total absence of power in that film—thus grounding a certain contemporary myth of the power relationships established in both fascism and the erotic.*

There is a battle going on for history, Foucault concludes, and the battleground is popular memory. If popular memory can be "reprogrammed" (as The Sorrow and the Pity *tries to reprogram it, so that the struggle of the Resistance is not remembered), then a new framework for interpreting the present can be instituted. And such a process, for good or ill, uses television and the cinema as two of its most important instruments. In this context, he understands the backward-looking appearance of the "retro" style in contemporary cinema as something other than historical documentation: it is, he says, the interpretation and reconstruction of history.*

Filmography

- ***Le Chagrin et la Pitié*** [*The Sorrow and the Pity*] (France, 1969). *Directed by* Marcel Ophüls. *Produced by* Télévision Rencontre, Norddeutscher Rundfunk, *and* Télévision Suisse-Romande. *Written by* Marcel Ophüls *and* André Harris.
- ***El coraje del pueblo*** [*The Courage of the People/The Night of San Juan*] (Italy–Bolivia, 1971). *Directed by* Jorge Sanjinés. *Produced by* Walter Achugar *and* Edgardo Pallero. *Written by* Óscar Soria. *Starring* Domitila de Chungara, Eusebio Gironda, Federico Vallejo, *and* Felicidad Coca García.
- ***Mein ganzes Leben lang*** [*My Whole Life Long/A Whole Life*] (East Germany, 1971). *Directed and Written by* Andrew *and* Annelie Thorndike. *Produced by* Deutsche Film.
- ***Les Camisards*** (France, 1972). *Directed by* René Allio. *Produced by* Éric Geiger. *Written by* René Allio *and* Jean Jourdheuil. *Starring* Philippe Clévenot, Jacques Debary, Gérard Desarthes, *and* Dominique Labourier.
- ***Lacombe Lucien*** (France, 1974). *Directed by* Louis Malle. *Produced by* Louis Malle *and* Claude Nedjar. *Written by* Louis Malle *and* Patrick Modiano. *Starring* Pierre Blaise *and* Aurore Clément.
- ***Il portiere di notte*** [*The Night Porter*] (Italy, 1974). *Directed by* Liliana Cavani. *Produced by* Robert Gordon Edwards *and* Esa De Simone. *Written by* Liliana Cavani, Italo Moscati, Barbara Alberti, *and* Amedeo Pagani. *Starring* Dirk Bogarde *and* Charlotte Rampling.

FILM AND POPULAR MEMORY

Interview conducted by Pascal Bonitzer and Serge Toubiana
Translated by Martin Jordan

Q: Let's start from the journalistic phenomenon of the "retro" style, the current fad for the recent past. Basically, we can put the question like this: how is it that films like Louis Malle's *Lacombe Lucien* or *The Night Porter*[1] can be made today? Why do they meet with such a fantastic response? We think the answer has to be sought on three levels:

(1) Giscard d'Estaing has been elected. A new kind of approach to politics, to history, to the political apparatus is coming into existence, indicating very clearly—in such a way that everyone can see it—that Gaullism is dead. So it's necessary, insofar as Gaullism remains very closely linked to the period of the Resistance, to look at how this is translated in the films which are being made.

(2) How is it possible for bourgeois ideology to attack the weak points of orthodox Marxism (rigid, economistic, mechanical—the terms don't matter much) which has for so long provided the only framework for interpreting social phenomena?

(3) Lastly, what does all this mean for political militants? Given that militants are consumers and sometimes also makers of films. The thing is, that after Marcel Ophuls' film *The Sorrow and the Pity*, the floodgates have been open. Something hitherto completely repressed or forbidden has flooded out. Why?

MF: I think this comes from the fact that the history of the war, and what took place around it, has never really been written except in completely official accounts. To all intents and purposes, these official histories are centered on Gaullism, which, on the one hand, was the only way of writing history in terms of an honorable nationalism; and, on the other, the only way of introducing the Great Man, the man of the right, the man of the old nineteenth-century nationalisms, as an historical figure. It boils down to the fact that France was exonerated by de Gaulle, while the right (and we know how it behaved at the time of the war) was purified and sanctified by him. What has never been described is what was going on in the very heart of the country from 1936, and even from the end of the 1914 war, up until the Liberation.

Q: So what has come about since *The Sorrow and the Pity* is some kind of return to truth in history. The point is really whether it is the truth.

MF: This has to be linked to the fact that the end of Gaullism means an end to this exoneration of the right by de Gaulle and by this brief period. The old right of Pétain and Maurras, the old reactionary and collaborating right, which disguised itself

[1] *Lacombe Lucien*, a film by Louis Malle, is the story of a French collaborator during the German occupation. *Night Porter*, a film by Liliana Cavani, is a sado-masochistic love story involving a former Nazi camp worker and prisoner.—*Ed.*

behind de Gaulle as best it could, now feels entitled to write its own history. This old right which, since Tardieu, had been upstaged both historically and politically, is now coming back into the limelight.

It openly supported Giscard. There's no longer any need for it to rely on disguises, it can write its own history. And among the factors which account for the present acceptance of Giscard by half of France (a majority of 200,000), we must not forget to include films like those we're discussing—whatever their makers' intentions. The fact that it's been possible to show everything has enabled the right to carry out a certain regrouping. In the same way that, conversely, it's really the healing of the breach between the national right and the collaborating right which has made these films possible. The two are inextricably linked.

Q: This history, then, is being rewritten both in the cinema and on television. It seems this rewriting of history is being carried out by film-makers who are thought of as more or less left-wing. This is a problem we should look at more closely.

MF: I don't think it's that simple. What I've just said is very schematic. Let's go over it again.

There's a real fight going on. Over what? Over what we can roughly describe as popular memory. It's an actual fact that people—I'm talking about those who are barred from writing, from producing their books themselves, from drawing up their own historical accounts—that these people nevertheless do have a way of recording history, or remembering it, of keeping it fresh and using it. This popular history was, to a certain extent, even more alive, more clearly formulated in the 19th century, where, for instance, there was a whole tradition of struggles which were transmitted orally, or in writing or songs, etc.

Now, a whole number of apparatuses have been set up ("popular literature," cheap books and the stuff that's taught in school as well) to obstruct the flow of this popular memory. And it could be said that this attempt has been pretty successful. The historical knowledge the working class has of itself is continually shrinking. If you think, for instance, of what workers at the end of the 19th century knew about their own history, what the trade union tradition (in the strict sense of the word) was like up until the 1914 war, it's really quite remarkable. This has been progressively diminished, but although it gets less, it doesn't vanish.

Today, cheap books aren't enough. There are much more effective means like television and the cinema. And I believe this was one way of reprogramming popular memory, which existed but had no way of expressing itself. So people are shown not what they were, but what they must remember having been.

Since memory is actually a very important factor in struggle (really, in fact, struggles develop in a kind of conscious moving forward of history), if one controls people's memory, one controls their dynamism. And one also controls their experience, their knowledge of previous struggles. Just what the Resistance was, must no longer be known…

I think we have to understand these films in some such way. Their theme is, roughly, that there's been no popular struggle in the 20th century. This assertion has been successively formulated in two ways. The first, immediately after the war, simply said: "What a century of heroes the 20th century is! There's been Churchill, de Gaulle, those chaps who did the parachuting, the fighter squadrons, etc.!" It amounted to saying: "There's been no popular struggle, because this is where the real struggle was." But still no one said directly, "There's been no popular struggle." The other, more recent formulation—skeptical or cynical, as you prefer—consists in proceeding to the blunt assertion itself: "Just look at what happened. Where have you seen any struggles? Where do you see people rising up, taking up rifles?"

Q: There's been a sort of half-rumor going around since, perhaps, *The Sorrow and the Pity*, to the effect that the French people, as a whole, didn't resist the Germans, that they even accepted collaboration, that they took it all lying down. The question is what all this finally means. And it does indeed seem that what is at stake is popular struggle, or rather the memory of that struggle.

MF: Exactly. It's vital to have possession of this memory, to control it, to administer it, tell it what it must contain. And when you see these films, you find out what you have to remember: "Don't believe all that you've been told. There aren't any heroes. And if there aren't any, it's because there's no struggle." So a sort of ambiguity arises: to start with, "there aren't any heroes" is a positive debunking of the whole war-hero mythology à la Burt Lancaster. It's a way of saying, "No, that's not what war is about." So your first impression is that history is beginning to reappear; that eventually they're going to tell us why we're not all obliged to identify with de Gaulle or the members of the Normandy-Niemen squadron, etc. But beneath the sentence "There are no heroes" is hidden a different meaning, its true message: "There was no struggle." This is what the exercise is all about.

Q: There's another phenomenon which explains why these films are so successful. The resentment of those who really did struggle is used against those who didn't. The people who formed the Resistance, watching *The Sorrow and the Pity* for example, see the passive citizens of a town in central France, and they recognize their passivity. And then the resentment takes over: they forget that they themselves did struggle.

MF: In my view, the politically important phenomenon is, rather than any one particular film, that of the series, the network established by all these films and the place—excuse the pun—they "occupy." In other words, the important thing is to ask: "Is it possible at the moment to make a positive film about the struggles of the Resistance?" Well, clearly the answer's no. One gets the impression that people would laugh at a film like this, or else quite simply wouldn't go to see it.

Q: Yes. It's the first thing to be brought up against us when we attack a film like Malle's. The response is always, "What would you have done, then?" And you're right; it's impossible to answer. We should be beginning to develop—how shall I put it—a left-wing perspective on all this, but it's true that one doesn't exist ready-made. Alternately, this restates the problem of how one is to produce a positive hero, a new type of hero.

MF: The problem's not the hero, but the struggle. Can you make a film about a struggle without going through the traditional process of creating heroes? It's a new form of an old problem.

Q: Let's go back to the "retro" style. From its own standpoint, the bourgeoisie has largely concentrated its attention on one historical period (the 40s) which throws into focus both its strong and weak points. For on the one hand, this is where it's most easily exposed (it's the bourgeoisie which created the breeding ground of Nazism or of collaboration with it); while on the other hand, it's here that it's currently trying to justify its historical behavior—in the most cynical ways. The difficulty is how to reveal what, for us, is the positive content of this same historical period—for us, that is, the generation of the struggles of 1968 or LIP.[2] Is the period of the Resistance really a weak point to be attacked, the point where some different kinds of ideological hegemony could emerge? For it's a fact that the bourgeoisie is simultaneously defensive and offensive about its recent history: strategically defensive, but tactically offensive because it's found this strong point from which it can best sow confusion. But do we have to be restricted (which is to be on the defensive) to simply re-establishing the truth about history? Isn't it possible to find some weak point where we might attack the ideology? Is this point necessarily the Resistance? Why not 1789 or 1968?

MF: Thinking about these films and their common subject, I wonder whether something different couldn't be done. And when I say "subject," I don't mean showing the struggles or showing they didn't exist. I mean that it's historically true that while the war was going on there was a kind of rejection of it among the French masses. Now where did this come from? From a whole series of episodes that no one talks about—the right doesn't, because it wants to hide them, and the left doesn't, because it's afraid of being associated with anything contrary to "national honor."

A good seven or eight million men went through the 1914–18 war. For four years they lived a horrifying existence, seeing millions upon millions of men die all around them. And what do they find themselves facing again in 1920? The right-wing in power, full-scale economic exploitation and finally an economic crisis and the unemployment of 1932. How could these people, who'd been packed into the trenches, still feel attracted by war in the two decades of 1920–30 and 1930-40? If the Germans still did, it's because defeat had reawakened such a national feeling in them that the desire for revenge could overcome this sort of repulsion. But even so, people don't enjoy fighting these bourgeois wars, with middle-class officers and these kind of benefits resulting from them. I think this was a crucial experience for the working class. And when in 1940, these guys tossed their bikes into the ditch and said, "I'm going home"—you can't simply say "They're scabs!" and you can't hide from it either. You have to find a place for it in this sequence of events. This non-compliance with national instructions has to be fitted in. And what happened during the Resistance is the opposite of what we're shown. What happened was that the process of repoliticization, remobilization and a taste for fighting reappeared little by little in the working class. It gradually reappeared after the rise of Nazism and the Spanish Civil War. Now what these films show is just the opposite process: namely, that after the great dream of 1939, which was shattered in 1940, people just gave up. This process did really take place, but as part of another, much more extended process which was going in the opposite direction: starting from a disgust with war, it ended up, in the middle of the occupation, as a conscious awareness of the need to struggle.

---

[2] LIP, a *cause célèbre* in France, involved the take-over by workers of a factory. Cf. A. Belden Field, *Trotskyism and Maoism: Theory and Practice in France and the United States*. (New York: Autonomedia, 1988)—*Ed.*

I think there was a positive political meaning to this noncompliance with the demands of the national armed struggles. The historical theme of *Lacombe Lucien* and his family takes on a new light if you look back to Ypres and Douaumont…

Q: This raises the problem of popular memory: of a memory working at its own pace, a pace quite detached from any seizure of central power or from the outbreak of any war…

MF: This has always been the aim of the history taught in schools: to teach ordinary people that they got killed and that this was very heroic. Look at what's been made of Napoleon and the Napoleonic wars…

Q: A number of films, including those of Malle and Cavani, leave off talking about history or the struggle over Nazism and fascism; usually, they talk instead, or at the same time, about sex. What's the nature of this discourse?

MF: But don't you make a sharp distinction between *Lacombe Lucien* and *Night Porter* on this? It seems that the erotic, passionate aspect of *Lacombe Lucien* has a quite easily identifiable function. It's basically a way of making the antihero acceptable, of saying he's not as anti as all that.

In fact, if all the power relations in his life are distorted, and if it's through him that they keep on running, on the other hand, just when you think he's distorting all the erotic relations, a true relationship suddenly appears and he loves the girl. On the one hand, there's the machinery of power which, starting with a flat tire, carries Lacombe closer and closer to something crazy. On the other hand, there's the machinery of love, which seems hooked up to it, which seems distorted, but which, on the contrary, has just the opposite effect and in the end restores Lucien as the handsome naked youth living in the fields with a girl.

So there's a fairly elementary antithesis between power and love. While in *Night Porter* the question is—both generally and in the present situation—a very important one: love for power.

Power has an erotic charge. There's an historical problem involved here. How is it that Nazism—which was represented by shabby, pathetic puritanical characters, laughably Victorian old maids, or at best, smutty individuals—how has it now managed to become, in France, in Germany, in the United States, in all pornographic literature throughout the world, the ultimate symbol of eroticism? Every shoddy erotic fantasy is now attributed to Nazism. Which raises a fundamentally serious problem: how do you love power? Nobody loves power any more. This kind of affective, erotic attachment, this desire one has for power, for the power that's exercised over you, doesn't exist any more. The monarchy and its rituals were created to stimulate this sort of erotic relationship towards power. The massive Stalinist apparatus, and even that of Hitler, were constructed for the same purpose. But it's all collapsed in ruins and obviously you can't be in love with Brezhnev, Pompidou or Nixon. In a pinch you might love de Gaulle, Kennedy or Churchill. But what's going on at the moment? Aren't we witnessing the beginnings of a re-eroticization of power, taken to a pathetic, ridiculous extreme by the porn-shops with Nazi insignia that you can find in the United States, and (a much more acceptable but just as ridiculous version) in the behavior of Giscard d'Estaing when he says, "I'm going to march down the streets in a lounge suit, shaking hands with ordinary people and kids on half-day holidays"? It's a fact that Giscard has built part of his campaign not only on his fine physical bearing but also on a certain eroticizing of his character, his stylishness.

Q: That's how he's portrayed himself on an electoral poster—one where you see his daughter turned towards him.

MF: That's right. He's looking at France, but she's looking at him. It's the restoration to power of seduction.

Q: Something that struck us during the electoral campaign, particularly at the time of the big televised debates between François Mitterand and Giscard, was that they weren't at all on the same level. Mitterand appeared as the old type of politico, belonging to the old left, let's say. He was trying to sell ideas, which were themselves dated and a bit old-fashioned, and he did it with a lot of style. But Giscard was selling the idea of power, exactly like an advertiser sells cheese.

MF: Even quite recently, it was necessary to apologize for being in power. It was necessary for power to be self-effacing, for it not to show itself as power. To a certain extent, this is how the democratic republics have functioned, where the aim was to render power sufficiently invisible and insidious for it to be impossible to grasp, to grasp what it was doing or where it was.

Q: Perhaps we have to talk about a certain powerlessness of traditional Marxist discourse to account for fascism. Let's say that Marxism has given an historical account of the phenomenon of Nazism in a deterministic fashion, while completely leaving aside what the specific ideology of Nazism was. So it's scarcely surprising that someone like Louis Malle, who's pretty familiar with what's going on on the left, can benefit from this weakness, and rush into the breach.

MF: Marxism has given a definition of Nazism and fascism: "an overt terrorist dictatorship of the most reactionary faction of the bourgeoisie." It's a definition that leaves out an entire part of the content and a whole series of relationships. In particular, it leaves out the fact that Nazism and fascism were only possible insofar as there could exist within the masses a relatively large section which took on the responsibility for a number of state functions of repression, control, policing, etc. This, I believe, is a crucial characteristic of Nazism; that is, its deep penetration inside the masses and the fact that a part of the power was actually delegated to a specific fringe of the masses. This is where the word "dictatorship" becomes true in general, and relatively false. When you think of the power an individual could possess under a Nazi regime as soon as he was simply S.S. or signed up in the Party! You could actually kill your neighbor, steal his wife, his house! This is where *Lacombe Lucien* is interesting, because it's one side it shows up well. The fact is that contrary to what is usually understood by dictatorship—the power of a single person—you could say that in this kind of regime the most repulsive (but in a sense the most intoxicating) part of power was given to a considerable number of people. The S.S. was that which was given the power to kill, to rape…

Q: This is where orthodox Marxism falls down. Because it's obliged to talk about desire.

MF: About desire and power…

Q: It's also where films like *Lacombe Lucien* and *Night Porter* are relatively "strong." They can talk about desire and power in a way which seems coherent…

MF: It's interesting to see in *Night Porter* how under Nazism the power of a single person is taken over and operated by ordinary people. The kind of mock trial which is set up is quite fascinating. Because on the one hand, it has all the trappings of a psychotherapy group, while in fact having the power structure of a secret society. What they re-establish is basically an S.S. cell, endowed with a judicial power that's different from, and opposed to, the central power. You have to bear in mind the way power was delegated, distributed within the very heart of the population; you have to bear in mind this vast transfer of power that Nazism carried out in a society like Germany. It's wrong to say that Nazism was the power of the great industrialists carried on under a different form. It wasn't simply the intensified central power of the military—it was that, but only on one particular level.

Q: This is an interesting side of the film, in fact. But what in our view seems very open to criticism is that it appears to say: "If you're a typical S.S. man, you'll act like this. But if, in addition, you have a certain inclination for the job, it will offer you incredible erotic experiences." So the film keeps up the seductiveness.

MF: Yes, this is where it meets up with *Lacombe Lucien*. Because Nazism never gave people any material advantages, it never handed out anything but power. You still have to ask why it was, if this regime was nothing but a bloody dictatorship, that on May 3, 1945, there were still Germans who fought to the last drop of blood; whether these people didn't have some form of emotional attachment to power. Bearing in mind, of course, all the pressuring, the denunciations… In *Lacombe Lucien*, as in *Night Porter*, this excess of power they're given is converted back into love. It's very clear at the end of *Night Porter*, where a miniature concentration camp is built up around Max in his room, where he starves to death. So here love has converted power, surplus power, back into a total absence of power. In one sense, it's almost the same reconciliation as in *Lacombe Lucien* where love turns the excess of power in which he's been trapped into a rustic poverty far removed from the Gestapo's shady hotel, and far removed, too, from the farm where the pigs were being butchered.

Q: So we now have the beginnings of an explanation for the problem you were posing at the start of our discussion: why is Nazism, which was a repressive, puritanical system, nowadays associated with eroticism? There's a sort of shift of emphasis: the central problem of power, which one doesn't want to confront head on, is dodged, or rather shoved completely into the question of sexuality. So that this eroticizing is ultimately a process of evasion, of repression…

MF: The problem's really very difficult and it hasn't been studied perhaps enough, even by Reich. What leads to power being desirable, and to actually being desired? It's easy to see the process by which this eroticizing is transmitted, reinforced, etc. But for the eroticizing to work, it's necessary that the attachment to power, the acceptance of power by those over whom it is exerted, is already erotic.

Q: It's that much more difficult since the representation of power is rarely erotic. De Gaulle or Hitler are not particularly seductive.

MF: True—and I wonder if the Marxist analyses aren't victims to some extent to the abstractedness of the notion of liberty. In a regime like the Nazi regime, it's a fact that there's no liberty. But not having liberty doesn't mean not having power…

There's a battle for and around history going on at this very moment which is extremely interesting. The intention is to reprogram, to stifle what I've called the "popular memory," and also to propose and impose on people a framework in which to interpret the present. Up to 1968, popular struggles were part of folklore. For some people, they weren't even part of their immediate concept of reality. After 1968, every popular struggle, whether in South America or in Africa, has found some echo, some sympathetic response. So it's no longer possible to keep up their separation, this geographical "quarantine." Popular struggles have become for our society, not part of the actual, but part of the possible. So they have to be set at a distance. How? Not by providing a direct interpretation of them, which would be liable to be exposed. But by offering an historical interpretation of those popular struggles which have occurred in France in the past, in order to show that they never really happened! Before 1968, it was: "It won't happen here because it's going on somewhere else." Now it's: "It won't happen here because it never has! Take something like the Resistance even, this glorious past you've talked about so much, just look at it for a moment… Nothing. It's empty, a hollow façade!" It's another way of saying, "Don't worry about Chile, it's no different; the Chilean peasants couldn't care less. And France too: the bulk of the population isn't interested in anything a few malcontents might do."

Q: When we react to all this—against it all—it's important that we don't limit ourselves to re-establishing the truth, to saying, about the Resistance, for example, "No, I was there and it wasn't like that!" If you're going to wage any effective ideological struggle on the kind of ground dictated by these films, we believe you have to have a much broader, more extensive and positive frame of reference. For many people this consists in reappropriating the "history of France" for instance. It was with this in mind that we undertook a close reading of *I, Pierre Rivière*; because we realized that, paradoxically enough, it was useful to us in understanding *Lacombe Lucien*, that their comparison was not unproductive. A significant difference between them, for example, is that Pierre Rivière is someone who writes, who commits a murder and who has a quite extraordinary memory. While Malle, on the other hand, treats his hero as a half-wit, as someone who goes through everything—history, the war, collaboration—without accumulating any experience. This is where the theme of memory, of popular memory, can help to separate off someone like Pierre Rivière from the character created by Malle (and Patrick Modiano, in *La Place de l'Etoile*).[3] Pierre Rivière, having no way of making his voice heard, takes the floor and is obliged to kill before he wins the right to speak. While Malle's character proves, precisely by making nothing of what has happened to him, that there's nothing worth the trouble of remembering. It's a pity you haven't seen *The Courage of the People*. It's a Bolivian film made with the explicit aim of becoming evidence on a criminal record. The characters in this film—which has been shown throughout the world (but not in Bolivia, thanks to the regime)—are played by the very people who were part of the real drama it re-enacts (a miner's strike and its bloody repression). They themselves take charge of their picture, so that nobody shall forget…

[3] Pierre Modiano, *La Place de l'Etoile* (Paris: Gallimard, 1968).—*Ed.*

There are two things going on in the cinema at the moment. On the one hand there are historical documents, which have an important role. In *A Whole Life*, for instance, they play a very big part. Or again, in the films of Marcel Ophuls, or of Harris and Sedouy, it's very moving to watch the reality of Duclos in action in 1936 or 1939. And on the other hand, there are fictional characters who, at a given moment of history, condense within themselves the greatest possible number of social relations, of links with history. This is why *Lacombe Lucien* is so successful. Lacombe is a Frenchman during the occupation, an ordinary Joe with concrete connections to Nazism, to the countryside, to local power, etc. And we shouldn't ignore this way of personifying history, of incarnating it in a character or a collection of characters who embody, at a given moment, a privileged relation to power.

There are lots of figures in the history of the workers' movement that aren't known; there are plenty of heroes in the history of the working class who've been completely driven out of memory. And I think there's a real issue to be fought here. There's no need for Marxism to keep on making films about Lenin. We've got plenty already.

MF: What you say is important. It's a trait of many Marxists nowadays—ignorance of history. All these people, who spend their time talking about the misrepresentation of history, are only capable of producing commentaries on texts. What did Marx say? Did Marx really say that? Look, what is Marxism but a different way of analyzing history itself? In my opinion, the left in France has no real grasp of history. It used to have one. At one time in the 19th century, Michelet might have been said to represent the left. There was Jaures, too, and after them there grew up a kind of tradition of left-wing, social democratic historians (Mathiez, etc.). Nowadays it's dwindled to a trickle; whereas it could be a formidable wave, carrying along writers, film-makers. True, there has been Aragon and *Les Cloches de Bâle*—a very great historical novel. But there are relatively few things, compared to what it could be like in a society where, after all, one can say that the intellectuals are more or less impregnated with Marxism.

Q: In this respect, the cinema offers something new: history captured "Live." How do people in America relate to history, seeing the Vietnam war on television every evening while they're eating?

MF: As soon as you start seeing pictures of war every evening, war becomes totally acceptable. That's to say, thoroughly tedious, you'd really love to see something else. But when it becomes boring, you put up with it. You don't even watch it. So how is this particular reality on film to be reactivated as an existing, historically important reality?

Q: Have you seen *Les Camisards*?

MF: Yes, I liked it very much. Historically, it's impeccable. It's well made, intelligent and it makes a lot of things clear.

Q: I think that's the direction we have to take in making films. To come back to the films we were talking about at the beginning—we must raise the question of the extreme left's confusion in the face of certain aspects of *Lacombe Lucien* and *Night Porter*, particularly the sexual one; and how this confusion can be of benefit to the right…

MF: As for what you call the extreme left, I find myself in considerable difficulty. I'm not at all sure that it still exists. Nonetheless, there really needs to be a thorough summing-up of what the extreme left has done since 1968, both negatively and positively. It's true that this extreme left has been the means of spreading a whole number of important ideas: on sexuality, women, homosexuality, psychiatry, housing, medicine. It's also been the means of spreading methods of action, where it continues to be of importance. The extreme left has played as important a role in the forms of activity as in its themes. But there's also a negative summing-up to be made, concerning certain Stalinist and terrorist organizational practices. And a misunderstanding, too, of certain broad and deeply-rooted processes which recently resulted in 13 million people backing Mitterand, and which have always been disregarded, on the pretext that this was the politics of the politicians, that this was the business of the parties. A whole heap of things have been ignored; notably, that the desire to defeat the right has been a very important political factor within the masses for a number of months and even years. The extreme left hasn't sensed this desire, thanks to a false definition of the masses, a wrong appreciation of what this will to win really is. Faced with the risks a co-opted victory would involve, it prefers not to take the risk of winning. Defeat, at least, can't be co-opted. Personally, I'm not so sure.

CHAPTER 38
JEAN BAUDRILLARD

Jean Baudrillard (1929–2007) was a French philosopher, photographer, and cultural theorist, who is among the very first and most significant postmodern philosophers of popular media culture, including film. He is perhaps most well known for his notion of "hyperreality," a state in which it is impossible for one to distinguish between the real and simulations of the real. This notion is potently explored in his book, Simulacra and Simulation *(*Simulacres et Simulation*), from which the text included here is a selection. "History: A Retro Scenario" was originally published in French ("L'Histoire: un scénario rétro") in* Simulacra and Simulation *by Éditions Galilée in 1981.*

Baudrillard notes that, in an earlier period in European history—immediately following the Second World War—the cinema was invaded and overwhelmed by myth. Myth had been chased from the real by the violence of history, and a new interest in what really happened, springing up all around. Myth hid, and survived in part because it was hidden. Today, however, history invades cinema in the same way that myth once did—but for the opposite reason. The pacified monotony of (Cold War) reality chases history off, seeking to let myth spring forth once again from within the real. Cinematically speaking, then, history is the contemporary filmgoer's myth, the lost referential, and history replaces myth on the movie screen. Movies today—that is, movies contemporary with Baudrillard's text, movies of the 1970s and early 1980s—try to be as realistic as possible. Fantasy, myth, and the imaginary have been pushed aside in favor of historical realism and verisimilitude.

Ultimately, Baudrillard argues, the great trauma of the contemporary age is the decline of strong referentials. By this, he means that the connection between the world of our discourse and the real world is weaker, and it grows ever less clear what is real and what is not. He suggests that this weakening reflects the "death pangs of the real and rational," and the beginning of the age of simulation—where everything seems always already to have been a copy or an illusion, with no real original in sight. This explains for Baudrillard the rise in popularity of "retro" cinema, which he argues is not an indication of a preference for or agreement with the ideas, movements, political parties, significant figures, etc., of prior eras: rather, he says that the retro fascination tries simply to resurrect the very general sense of those prior eras, when there was history. When our real lives no longer serve as a stable indicator of what has really happened, we look to art—and, today, film especially—to show us what is (or was) real. The retro fascination, then, treats almost all historical periods as equivalent, making no distinctions between them, with the exception of the immediately prior era, which it fetishizes. Thus, the retro movies of the 1970s and 1980s reflect a sort of fetishism of the Second World War and the post-War period (a phenomenon we also see Michel Foucault reflect on in his interview, "Film and Popular Memory," earlier in this section). History in cinema, then, is always a sort of nostalgia, according to Baudrillard—nostalgia for a lost referential. Ultimately, that is, history in cinema is reflective of a nostalgia for meaning.

Given these stakes—that we are seeking in our cinema to find the meaning we do not seem able to find in our real lives—we see that cinema makes the effort to get history exactly right, to make the cinematic experience as representative of reality as is possible. This results, however, in a disquieting perfection, Baudrillard says: we produce realistic films that are in fact more realistic than images or films from the era being reproduced actually were. The reproduction is too good, better than the original. This realism-more-real-than-reality is what Baudrillard calls the "hyperreal," and he thinks hyperreality is characteristic of contemporary historical cinema. Thus, cinema achieves an odd sort of improvement over its historical models—like androids to human beings, a pleasing simulacrum that nevertheless lacks the imaginary and thus is more lifeless than the original, cooler, colder although not unpleasant—and it becomes impossible to say that the films resemble anything that actually happened; they resemble nothing at all, in fact, instantiating instead just the form of resemblance itself.

In this vein, Baudrillard compares two filmmakers: Luchino Visconti and Stanley Kubrick. Visconti, he says, captures meaning and history in his films. There is a "sensual rhetoric," and an observable passion to them. They are technically less perfect than some other films, but this roughness adds to the sense of life within them. Kubrick, on the other hand, makes films, Baudrillard says, "like playing chess." Kubrick's films are perfect, or as near to perfect as human filmmakers can produce, but in achieving this perfection they lose the passion and meaning at the heart of more imperfect, more human films. We watch Visconti's films and get a sense that things mattered to the individuals depicted, and that these things matter—or ought to matter—to us. But watching Kubrick, we achieve a sort of placid, distant indifference that is about as far from meaning as is possible for cinema. And Kubrick is certainly more of the contemporary time than Visconti is.

Baudrillard argues, then, that we are living in an era of films without meaning. The most they can achieve is a sort of technical accuracy, and the "tactical value" of grouping together good writing with good performances, innovative cinematography, and so on. A meaningful film is more than the sum of its admirable elements, however. The trajectory of cinema's development is from the fantastic or mythical to the realistic, and from the realistic to the hyperrealistic. This is a trajectory established by a desire to achieve an absolute correspondence to the real, but this results in cinema being able only to copy itself ad infinitum, producing ever higher quality reproductions of its own past: reproductions which, by virtue precisely of their higher quality, seem somehow less real. Increasingly, Baudrillard concludes, we find our films have lost the mythical energy that once drove cinematic narratives. We are losing the fire, the life, at the heart of film, and thus find ourselves with a seamless and convincing cinema which is nevertheless meaningless to us all.

Filmography

- ***Senso*** (Italy, 1954). *Directed by* Luchino Visconti. *Produced by* Lux Film. *Written by* Carlo Alianello, Suso Cecchi d'Amico, Giorgio Bassani, Luchino Visconti, *and* Giorgio Prosperi. *Starring* Alida Valli *and* Farley Granger.
- ***Il Gattopardo/Le Guépard*** [*The Leopard*] (Italy, 1963). *Directed by* Luchino Visconti. *Produced by* Goffredo Lombardo *and* Pietro Notarianni. *Written by* Pasquale Festa, Campanile, Enrico Medioli, Massimo Franciosa, Luchino Visconti, *and* Suso Cecchi d'Amico. *Starring* Burt Lancaster, Claudia Cardinale, Alain Delon, Serge Reggiani, Mario Girotti, *and* Pierre Clementi.

- ***The Last Picture Show*** (USA, 1971). *Directed by* Peter Bogdanovich. *Produced by* Stephen J. Friedman. *Written by* Larry McMurtry *and* Peter Bogdanovich. *Starring* Timothy Bottoms, Jeff Bridges, Cybill Shepherd, Ellen Burstyn, Ben Johnson, Cloris Leachman, *and* Randy Quaid.
- ***Chinatown*** (USA, 1974). *Directed by* Roman Polanski. *Produced by* Robert Evans. *Written by* Robert Towne. *Starring* Jack Nicholson, Faye Dunaway, John Hillerman, Perry Lopez, Burt Young, *and* John Huston.
- ***Barry Lyndon*** (UK–USA, 1975). *Directed, Produced, and Written by* Stanley Kubrick. *Starring* Ryan O'Neal, Marisa Berenson, Patrick Magee, Hardy Krüger, Diana Koerner, *and* Gay Hamilton.
- ***Three Days of the Condor*** (USA, 1975). *Directed by* Sydney Pollack. *Produced by* Dino De Laurentiis. *Written by* Lorenzo Semple, Jr. *and* David Rayfiel. *Starring* Robert Redford, Faye Dunaway, Cliff Robertson, *and* Max von Sydow.
- ***1900*** (Italy, 1976). *Directed by* Bernardo Bertolucci. *Produced by* Alberto Grimaldi. *Written by* Franco Arcalli, Giuseppe Bertolucci, *and* Bernardo Bertolucci. *Starring* Robert De Niro, Gérard Depardieu, Dominique Sanda, Francesca Bertini, Laura Betti, Werner Bruhns, Stefania Casini, Sterling Hayden, Anna Henkel, Ellen Schwiers, Alida Valli, Romolo Valli, Stefania Sandrelli, Donald Sutherland, *and* Burt Lancaster.
- ***All the President's Men*** (USA, 1976). *Directed by* Alan J. Pakula. *Produced by* Walter Coblenz. *Written by* William Goldman. *Starring* Robert Redford *and* Dustin Hoffman.

HISTORY: A RETRO SCENARIO

Translated by Sheila Faria Glaser

In a violent and contemporary period of history (let's say between the two world wars and the cold war), it is myth that invades cinema as imaginary content. It is the golden age of despotic and legendary resurrections. Myth, chased from the real by the violence of history, finds refuge in cinema.

Today, it is history itself that invades the cinema according to the same scenario—the historical stake chased from our lives by this sort of immense neutralization, which is dubbed peaceful coexistence on a global level, and pacified monotony on the quotidian level—this history is exorcised by a slowly or brutally congealing society celebrates its resurrection in force on the screen, according to the same process that used to make lost myths live again.

History is our lost referential, that is to say our myth. It is by virtue of this fact that it takes the place of myths on the screen. The illusion would be to congratulate oneself on this "awareness of history on the part of cinema," as one congratulated oneself on the "entrance of politics into the university." Same misunderstanding, same mystification. The politics that enter the university are those that come from history, a retro politics, emptied of substance and legalized in their superficial exercise, with the air of a game and a field of adventure, this kind of politics is like sexuality or permanent education (or like social security in its time), that is, posthumous liberalization.

The great event of this period, the great trauma, is this decline of strong referentials, these death pangs of the real and of the rational that open onto an age of simulation. Whereas so many generations, and particularly the last, lived in the march of history, in the euphoric or catastrophic expectation of a revolution—today one has the impression that history has retreated, leaving behind it an indifferent nebula, traversed by currents, but emptied of references. It is into this void that the phantasms of a past history recede, the panoply of events, ideologies, retro fashions—no longer so much because people believe in them or still place some hope in them, but simply to resurrect the period when *at least* there was history, at least there was violence (albeit fascist), when at least life and death were at stake. Anything serves to escape this void, this leukemia of history and of politics, this hemorrhage of values—it is in proportion to this distress that all content can be evoked pell-mell, that all previous history is resurrected in bulk—a controlling idea no longer selects, only nostalgia endlessly accumulates: war, fascism, the pageantry of the belle epoque, or the revolutionary struggles, everything is equivalent and is mixed indiscriminately in the same morose and funereal exaltation, in the same retro fascination. There is however a privileging of the immediately preceding era (fascism, war, the period immediately following the war—the innumerable films that play on these themes for us have a closer, more perverse, denser, more confused essence). One can explain it by evoking the Freudian theory of fetishism (perhaps also a retro hypothesis). This trauma (loss of referentials) is similar to the discovery of the difference between the sexes in children, as serious, as profound, as irreversible: the fetishization of an object intervenes to obscure this unbearable discovery, but precisely, says Freud, this object is not just any object, it is often the last object perceived before the traumatic discovery. Thus the fetishized history will preferably be the one immediately preceding our "irreferential" era. Whence the omnipresence of fascism and of war in retro—a coincidence, an affinity that is not at all political; it is naive to conclude that the evocation of fascism signals a current renewal of fascism (it is precisely because one is no longer there, because one is in something else, which is still less amusing, it is for this reason that fascism can again become fascinating in its filtered cruelty, aestheticized by retro).[1]

History thus made its triumphal entry into cinema, posthumously (the term *historical* has undergone the same fate: a "historical" moment, monument, congress, figure are in this way designated as fossils). Its reinjection has no value as conscious awareness but only as nostalgia for a lost referential.

This does not signify that history has never appeared in cinema as a powerful moment, as a contemporary process, as insurrection and not as resurrection. In the "real" as in cinema, there was history but there isn't any anymore. Today, the history that is "given back" to us (precisely because it was taken from us) has no more of a relation to a "historical real" than neofiguration in painting does to the classical figuration of the real. Neofiguration is an *invocation* of resemblance, but at the same time the flagrant proof of the disappearance of objects in their very representation: *hyperreal*. Therein objects shine in a sort of hyperresemblance (like history in contemporary cinema) that makes it so that fundamentally they no longer resemble anything, except the empty figure of resemblance, the empty form of representation. It is a question of life or death: these objects are no longer either living or deadly. That is why they are so exact, so minute, frozen in the state in which a brutal loss of the real would have seized them. All, but not only, those historical films whose very perfection is disquieting: *Chinatown*, *Three Days of the Condor*, *Barry Lyndon*, *1900*, *All the President's Men*, etc. One has the impression of it being a question of perfect remakes, of extraordinary montages that emerge more from a combinatory culture (or McLuhanesque mosaic), of large photo-, kino-, historicosynthesis machines, etc., rather than one of veritable films. Let's understand each other: their quality is not in question. The problem is rather that in some sense we are left completely indifferent. Take *The Last Picture Show*: like me, you would have had to be sufficiently distracted to have thought it to be an original production from the 1950s: a very good film about the customs in and the atmosphere of the American small town. Just a slight suspicion: it was a little too good, more in tune, better than the others, without the psychological, moral, and sentimental blotches of the films of that era. Stupefaction when one discovers that it is a 1970s film, perfect retro, purged, pure, the hyperrealist restitution of 1950s cinema. One talks of remaking silent films, those will also doubtlessly be better than those of the period. A whole generation of films is emerging that will be to those one knew what the android is to man: marvelous artifacts,

[1] Fascism itself, the mystery of its appearance and of its collective energy, with which no interpretation has been able to come to grips (neither the Marxist one of political manipulation by dominant classes, nor the Reichian one of the sexual repression of the masses, nor the Deleuzian one of despotic paranoia), can already be interpreted as the "irrational" excess of mythic and political referentials, the mad intensification of collective value (blood, race, people, etc.), the reinjection of death, of a "political aesthetic of death" at a time when the process of the disenchantment of value and of collective values, of the rational secularization and unidimensionalization of all life, of the operationalization of all social and individual life already makes itself strongly felt in the West. Yet again, everything seems to escape this catastrophe of value, this neutralization and pacification of life. Fascism is a resistance to this, even if it is a profound, irrational, demented resistance, it would not have tapped into this massive energy if it hadn't been a resistance to something much worse. Fascism's cruelty, its terror is on the level of *this other terror that is the confusion of the real and the rational*, which deepened in the West, and it is a response to that.

without weakness, pleasing simulacra that lack only the imaginary, and the hallucination inherent to cinema. Most of what we see today (the best) is already of this order. *Barry Lyndon* is the best example: one never did better, one will never do better in… in what? Not in evoking, not even in evoking, in *simulating*. All the toxic radiation has been filtered, all the ingredients are there, in precise doses, not a single error.

Cool, cold pleasure, not even aesthetic in the strict sense: functional pleasure, equational pleasure, pleasure of machination. One only has to dream of Visconti (*Guépard*, *Senso*, etc., which in certain respects make one think of *Barry Lyndon*) to grasp the difference, not only in style, but in the cinematographic act. In Visconti, there is meaning, history, a sensual rhetoric, dead time, a passionate game, not only in the historical content, but in the mise-en-scène. None of that in Kubrick, who manipulates his film like a chess player, who makes an operational scenario of history. And this does not return to the old opposition between the spirit of finesse and the spirit of geometry: that opposition still comes from the game and the stakes of meaning, whereas we are entering an era of films that in themselves no longer have meaning strictly speaking, an era of great synthesizing machines of varying geometry.

Is there something of this already in Leone's Westerns? Maybe. All the registers slide in that direction. *Chinatown*: it is the detective movie renamed by laser. It is not really a question of perfection: technical perfection can *be part of* meaning, and in that case it is neither retro nor hyperrealist, it is an effect of art. Here, technical perfection is an effect of the model: it is one of the referential tactical values. In the absence of real *syntax* of meaning, one has nothing but the *tactical* values of a group in which are admirably combined, for example, the CIA as a mythological machine that does everything, Robert Redford as polyvalent star, social relations as a necessary reference to history, technical virtuosity as a necessary reference to cinema.

The cinema and its trajectory: from the most fantastic or mythical to the realistic and hyperrealistic.

The cinema in its current efforts is getting closer and closer, and with greater and greater perfection, to the absolute real, in its banality, its veracity, in its naked obviousness, in its boredom, and at the same time in its presumption, in its pretension to being the real, the immediate, the unsignified, which is the craziest of undertakings (similarly, functionalism's pretension to designating—design—the greatest degree of correspondence between the object and its function, and its use value, is a truly absurd enterprise); no culture has ever had toward its signs this naive and paranoid, puritan and terrorist vision.

Terrorism is always that of the real.

Concurrently with this effort toward an absolute correspondence with the real, cinema also approaches an absolute correspondence with itself—and this is not contradictory: it is the very definition of the hyperreal. Hypotyposis and specularity. Cinema plagiarizes itself, recopies itself, remakes its classics, retroactivates its original myths, remakes the silent film more perfectly than the original, etc.: all of this is logical, *the cinema is fascinated by itself as a lost object as much as it (and we) are fascinated by the real as a lost referent*. The cinema and the imaginary (the novelistic, the mythical, unreality, including the delirious use of its own technique) used to have a lively, dialectical, full, dramatic relation. The relation that is being formed today between the cinema and the real is an inverse, negative relation: it results from the loss of specificity of one and of the other. The cold collage, the cool promiscuity, the asexual nuptials of two cold media that evolve in an asymptotic line toward each other: the cinema attempting to abolish itself in the cinematographic (or televised) hyperreal.

History is a strong myth, perhaps, along with the unconscious, the last great myth. It is a myth that at once subtended the possibility of an "objective" enchainment of events and causes and the possibility of a narrative enchainment of discourse. The age of history, if one can call it that, is also the age of the novel. It is this *fabulous* character, the mythical energy of an event or of a narrative, that today seems to be increasingly lost. Behind a performative and demonstrative logic: the obsession with historical *fidelity*, with a perfect rendering (as elsewhere the obsession with real time or with the minute quotidianeity of Jeanne Hilmann doing the dishes), this negative and implacable fidelity to the materiality of the past, to a particular scene of the past or of the present, to the restitution of an absolute simulacrum of the past or the present, which was substituted for all other value—we are all complicitous in this, and this is irreversible. Because cinema itself contributed to the disappearance of history, and to the advent of the archive. Photography and cinema contributed in large part to the secularization of history, to fixing it in its visible, "objective" form at the expense of the myths that once traversed it.

Today cinema can place all its talent, all its technology in the service of reanimating what it itself contributed to liquidating. It only resurrects ghosts, and it itself is lost therein.

CHAPTER 39
PAUL VIRILIO

Paul Virilio (b. 1932) is a French urbanist philosopher and architect, whose theoretical work has focused largely on the cultural significance of technology. He is at the time of this writing a Professor of Philosophy at the European Graduate School. He has argued that modern society and culture have largely been organized around military technologies and war, both physically (in terms of architecture and organization) as well as ideally (in terms of the ideas that construct cultural and social identities). This view is set forth with particular reference to film in his book, War and Cinema, *originally published in French (*Guerre et cinéma*) by Cahiers du Cinéma in 1984. The text included here is Chapters 4 and 6 of that work.*

Virilio begins the first selection, "The Imposture of Immediacy," by noting the significant impact communications technologies have had on the modern experience of global geographical distances. It is commonly observed that the world is "shrinking" as a result of such technologies, and Virilio does not disagree, but the force of his point strikes a bit deeper than the popular saying might be understood to do. For Virilio, the shrinking of distances means, ultimately, that all the surfaces of the globe are directly present to one another at all times: which is not to say that traveling around the world is now like what traveling around the country once was for previous generations, but instead, that one need not travel around the world anymore. By way of the mediation of certain technologies, one can be wherever one is and somewhere else at the same time; one always already is at least potentially anywhere. He compares this relatively recent development to other, historical developments in the mediation of distance, from Halford Mackinder's Heartland Theory (which argues that one can achieve world dominance by way of strategic control of more limited areas—specifically in Mackinder's case, control of Eastern Europe would insure control of the "World Island," which consists of Europe, Asia, and Africa, control of which would then entail politico-military control of the whole world), to museum exhibitions of various artifacts gathered by colonial powers for display in their home countries, to the ever-developing innovations in transport, all the way to EPCOT Center at Disney World, where the various cultures and nations of the world are meant to be encountered at once by theme park guests. What these diverse examples have in common is their successful efforts to mediate distance by enabling individuals to encounter far-off places without having to engage in the effort typically required to travel there. In so doing, they effectively make the world smaller. Cinema, too, by bringing recorded images and sounds from elsewhere to every local movie house, can have something like this effect.

Having established this tendency in modern culture, Virilio considers the nature of war in such a highly technologically mediated age. Despite the widespread availability of literary, journalistic, and cinematic accounts of wartime, Virilio notes that the average soldier going to war for the very first time admits that he or she cannot imagine what it will be like. Many soldiers, he notes, relate up until the very moment of engagement with the enemy a relationship to battle that is too far removed—too distant—to be considered participation. He recalls an example from the philosopher of war, Carl von Clausewitz, of a soldier who looks on at a battle in which he has not yet engaged as if he were at a show. Updating the analogy for the twentieth century, Virilio maintains that modern war is like a living cinema. When one is observing or contemplating warfare from a distance (whether geographical or psychological), one is something like a spectator of this cinema; when one actually engages in combat, then one is very much like an actor (viewed in action by those spectators just mentioned). Perhaps the most difficult, and certainly the most complicated, viewpoint would be that of the survivor of such conflict: the survivor is at once an actor and a spectator, retaining a sense of his or her own activity alongside the spectatorial distance afforded by time.

Looking back on past wars, Virilio observes the popularity—increasing, in some places—of immersive cinematic shows at the real sites of real (past) battles. Whether this is the live Civil War reenactments so popular in some parts of the United States, or cine-historical light shows that project images of combat onto the abandoned battlements themselves, these shows attempt to provide spectators with something like the experience of the survivor: situating them simultaneously in the midst of and in reflection upon war. Naturally, such spectacles are nothing like war itself. But in making an effort to mediate the distance between the contemporary spectator and past combatants, they demonstrate both the ability to mediate between peacetime spectators and soldiers in wartime, and the desire those spectators have for such mediation.

Another aspect of Virilio's analysis is the interweaving of military and cinematic technologies. Cinematographic framing and focus, for example, are prefigured in the sniper or gunner's line of sight and the technologies invented to assist them in their targeting purpose. Central command uses maps upon which the movements of troops are displayed in something approximating real time, like the animated screens of the cinema. And advances in telecommunications allow war cabinets to remain at a distance from the war itself, observing actions on the ground from the safety of a significant remove—in some sense, the institution of the spectator as in command of the actor. Cinematic technologies depend upon military technologies; military movements depend upon cinematic techniques. The interrelation of the two, and the seeming cinematic nature of modern warfare, create an interdependence between the two that makes distinguishing easily between them in any absolute fashion difficult, if not impossible, to achieve.

Virilio discusses how, for instance, during the Blitz, the Luftwaffe not only dropped bombs on Britain, but made cinematographic recordings of the country as they flew over in their bombers, as a means of gathering military intelligence. The German bombers were literally both war and cinematographic machines. Moreover, realizing that this was what the Germans were doing, the British used the filming to their own advantage. The staged fake production sites in the manner of film sets, and they hid actual production either by way of clever camouflage or underground, an intentional misinformation campaign designed to influence command decisions on the German side (and, it seems, to a certain extent successfully). Virilio goes on to note that some of these same British sites were repurposed in the production of films in the decades following the Second World War, most famously, perhaps, Alien, *the producers of which wanted to keep various elements of the film secret from the prying eyes of curious entertainment journalists. In a more general sense, too, many later movies—especially those with military elements, such as* Dr. Strangelove *or* Star Wars*—incorporated actual parts of defunct military machines from the Second World War to give the technologies of their films an authentically martial feel.*

Ultimately, Virilio argues that the interrelatedness of war and cinema machines, and the exchangeability of war and cinematic techniques, results in the creation of a world wherein we must analyze reality in a cinematic way. Warfare today has opened a new "front," as it were, by way of television—such that modern war has made the journey from military secrecy (the First and Second World Wars) to the live broadcast (Vietnam, the Gulf War). When war is being fought on television sets in living rooms around the world, then everyone is "at" war. And when everything—war included—is staged for the cameras, then reality has become the sort of thing we cannot but observe, experience, and analyze as if it were a movie.

Filmography

- ***Outward Bound*** (USA, 1930). *Directed by* Robert Milton. *Produced by* Warner Brothers. *Written by* Sutton Vane *and* J. Grubb Alexander. *Starring* Leslie Howard, Douglas Fairbanks, Jr., Helen Chandler, Beryl Mercer, Dudley Digges, *and* Alec B. Francis.
- ***Around the World in 80 Minutes with Douglas Fairbanks*** (USA, 1931). *Directed by* Douglas Fairbanks *and* Victor Fleming. *Produced by* United Artists. *Written by* Robert E. Sherwood. *Starring* Douglas Fairbanks.
- ***The First of the Few*** (UK, 1942). *Directed by* Leslie Howard. *Produced by* Leslie Howard, George King, *and* John Stafford. *Written by* Henry C. James, Kay Strueby, Miles Malleson, *and* Anatole de Grunwald. *Starring* Leslie Howard *and* David Niven.
- ***To Be or Not to Be*** (USA, 1942). *Directed and Produced by* Ernst Lubitsch. *Written by* Melchior Lengyel *and* Edwin Justus Mayer. *Starring* Carole Lombard, Jack Benny, Robert Stack, Felix Bressart, *and* Sig Ruman.
- ***The Longest Day*** (USA, 1962). *Directed by* Ken Annakin, Andrew Marton, *and* Bernhard Wicki. *Produced by* Darryl F. Zanuck. *Written by* Cornelius Ryan, Romain Gary, James Jones, David Pursall, *and* Jack Seddon. *Starring* John Wayne, Henry Fonda, Robert Mitchum, Sean Connery, Eddie Albert, Curd Jürgens, Richard Todd, Richard Burton, Peter Lawford, Rod Steiger, Irina Demick, Gert Fröbe, Edmond O'Brien, *and* Kenneth More.
- ***Dr. Strangelove or: How I Learned to Stop Worrying and Love the Bomb*** (UK–USA, 1964). *Directed and Produced by* Stanley Kubrick. *Written by* Stanley Kubrick, Terry Southern, *and* Peter George. *Starring* Peter Sellers, George C. Scott, Sterling Hayden, Keenan Wynn, Slim Pickens, *and* Tracy Reed.
- ***Star Wars*** (USA, 1977). *Directed and Written by* George Lucas. *Produced by* Gary Kurtz. *Starring* Mark Hamill, Harrison Ford, Carrie Fisher, Peter Cushing, *and* Alec Guinness.
- ***Alien*** (UK–USA, 1979). *Directed by* Ridley Scott. *Produced by* Gordon Carroll, David Giler, *and* Walter Hill. *Written by* Dan O'Bannon. *Starring* Tom Skerritt, Sigourney Weaver, Veronica Cartwright, Henry Dean Stanton, John Hurt, Ian Holm, *and* Yaphet Kotto.
- ***Apocalypse Now*** (USA 1979). *Directed and Produced by* Francis Ford Coppola. *Written by* John Milius *and* Francis Ford Coppola. *Starring* Marlon Brando, Robert Duvall, *and* Martin Sheen.
- ***The Final Countdown*** (USA, 1980). *Directed by* Don Taylor. *Produced by* Peter Vincent Douglas. *Written by* Thomas Hunter, Peter Powell, David Ambrose, *and* Gerry Davis. *Starring* Kirk Douglas, Martin Sheen, Katharine Ross, James Farentino, Ryan O'Neal, *and* Charles Durning.

- ***Lightning Over Water*** (West Germany–Sweden, 1980). *Directed and Written by* Nicholas Ray *and* Wim Wenders. *Produced by* Road Movies Filmproduktion, Viking Film, Wim Wenders Productions, *and* Wim Wenders Stiftung.
- ***One from the Heart*** (USA, 1982). *Directed by* Francis Ford Coppola. *Produced by* Gray Frederickson *and* Fred Roos. *Written by* Armyan Bernstein *and* Francis Ford Coppola. *Starring* Frederic Forrest, Teri Garr, Raul Julia, Nastassja Kinski, Lainie Kazan, *and* Harry Dean Stanton.

THE IMPOSTURE OF IMMEDIACY

Translated by Patrick Camiller

Once the optical telegraph came into operation in 1794, the remotest battlefield could have an almost immediate impact on a country's internal life, turning upside down its social, political and economic field. The instantaneity of action over a distance was already an accomplished fact. Since then, as many people have noted, geographical space has been shrinking with every advance in speed, and strategic location has lost importance as ballistic systems have become more widespread and sophisticated. This technological development has carried us into a realm of factitious topology in which all the surfaces of the globe are directly present to one another.[1]

After the war of movement of mechanized forces, the time came for a strategy of Brownian movement, a geostrategic homogenization announced at the end of the last century in Mackinder's theory of the single "World Island" into which various continents are supposedly contracting. (One is reminded of the war in the Malvinas, whose remoteness did not dampen the British ardour for Antarctic contraction.) With the great universal or colonial exhibitions, it was no longer necessary for people to travel to distant lands; the faraway could be presented to them as such, on the spot, in the form of more or less obsolescent scale models. The transport revolution made itself felt less in the desire for exoticism than in a new endogeny. In breaking open one's normal surroundings through a lightening trip to dreamlands, one could conjure away the trip and not even know one was travelling.

The Disney Corporation (which the French have consulted for the ghostly Universal Exhibition of 1989) took over the idea of Disneyland and then for EPCOT (the Experimental Prototype of the Community of Tomorrow). Walt Disney, speaking on 15 November 1965 at a memorable press conference held in the great lounge of Orlando's Cherry Plaza, described EPCOT as "a new town of revolutionary design where we will try to solve *the communication and environmental problems posed for inhabitants of the cities of the future*." Disney died suddenly thirteen months later, after the bulldozers had begun work on the eleven thousand hectares of Florida swampland purchased in 1964, an area larger than that of San Francisco.

It is important that Disney's successors decided to solve the "communication problems" of the city of the future by erecting the "Showcase of the World." Here past, present and future are telescoped together, and the five continents, represented by assorted visual relics of monuments and real objects, lie overlapping on the narrow shoreline of an artificial lake. The buildings and the perfectly copied cars and trains are a fifth of the normal size—a scaling down that Disney saw as the essence of *dream creation*—and "cinema knowledge" here repeats the strategist's negation of dimensions.

When the offer of a trip "Around the World in Eighty Minutes" shone in lights outside cinemas in the thirties, it was already clear that film was superimposing itself on a geostrategy

---

[1] P. Virilio, *Vitesse et politique*, Paris, 1977.

which for a century or more had inexorably been leading to the direct substitution, and thus sooner or later the disintegration, of things and places. In 1926, in the Paramount "Hall of Nations" in New York, Adolf Zukor had the idea of bringing under one roof a collection of representative material from ruins around the world, as if to assemble the last witnesses of a physical universe that had vanished into the special effects of communication machines. Rich Americans like John D. Rockefeller Jr followed this example by incorporating genuine pieces of architecture from medieval churches or castles into modern architectural structures, while the funerary handprints of stars left in the concrete sidewalk of Grauman's Chinese Theatre in Hollywood already prefigured the "human negatives" of the atomic age.

Despite the massive accumulation of documents, publicity and films, young army recruits still say in response to questions that they cannot *imagine what a war would be like*. They are like that rookie in a fine chapter of Clausewitz's *On War* who, before facing the battlefield for the first time, looks at it from afar in astonishment and "for a moment still thinks he is at a show." The soldier then has to leave the calm of the surrounding countryside and to move ever closer to what might be regarded as the epicentre of battle, crossing one zone after another in which the intensity of danger continually increases. To the accompaniment of roaring cannons, whistling shells and quaking earth, more and more of his comrades collapse around him, dead or suddenly maimed … "beneath that steel storm in which the laws of nature appeared suspended, the midwinter air quivered as in the scorching days of summer and its flicker set stationary objects dancing to and fro."[2] Here the static sense of the world has come to an incomprehensible end. "Beyond a certain threshold," Clausewitz remarks, "the light of reason moves in a different medium and is reflected in a different manner."[3] Once his customary faculties of perception and reasoning have let him down, the soldier has to display that military virtue which consists in believing that he will come through it all. To be a survivor is to remain both actor and spectator of a living cinema, to continue being the target of subliminal audiovisual bombardment or, in the colloquial language of French soldiers, to "light up" (*allumer*) the enemy. It is also to try to postpone one's own death, that last technological accident or "final separation of sound and image" (William Burroughs).

During the Second World War, while still a child, I experienced firsthand the fierce flight of strategic bombing and, later, witnessed a series of land battles in the company of a former artillery liaison officer, a survivor from the '14–18 war who taught me how easily a tested mind could cut through such a subliminal barrage, could locate and materialize

---

[2] Ernst Jünger, *In Stahlgewittern* (translated here from the French edition, *Orages d'acier*, Paris 1970.)

[3] In *Cahiers du cinéma* (No. 311), Samuel Fuller argued that it was impossible to film the Normandy landing because you couldn't decently film yards of intestine on a beach. Apart from the fact that dead people do not take well to being photographed (see the pictures of assassinations or traffic accidents), Fuller's witticism suggests that military-industrial films cannot *decently* be horror films, since in one way or another they are intended to embellish death. Moreover, the Allied landing acutely re-posed the problem of documentary realism. Today everyone knows that there were not yards of intestine on the Normandy beaches and that the landing was a remarkable and technically difficult operation—not because of German resistance (which was virtually non-existent), but because of the adverse weather and the complicated Normandy countryside. Thus, *in order to make up the numbers*, the Allied commanders threw their men into operations like the storming of Hoc Point, which were as suicidal as they were spectacular. In 1962, when Zanuck made his fictional documentary with fifty stars, 20,000 extras and six directors, the action took place on the Ile de Ré or in Spain, where the beaches were "grander" than those of Arromanche. This immortalization of a battle that had never happened ensured that *The Longest Day* was a great box-office success.

in space the atmospheric dimensions of a battle, and could anticipate what the different parties intended to do. To cut a long story short, my old friend jubilantly described the *scenario* of battle which I, being a newcomer, saw only as its *special effects*. Young American GIs advancing to dangerous battlefield positions used the most eloquent expression: "We're off to the movies."

After 1945, this cinematic artifice of the war machine spread once more into new forms of spectacle. War museums opened all over liberated France at the sites of various landings and battles, many of them in old forts or bunkers. The first rooms usually exhibited relics of the last military-industrial conflict (outdated equipment, old uniforms and medals, yellowing photographs), while others had collections of military documents or screenings of period newsreels. It was not long, however, before the invariably large number of visitors were shown into huge, windowless rooms resembling a planetarium or a flight (or driving) simulator. In these *war simulators*, the public was supposed to feel like spectators—survivors of the recent battlefield. Standing in near-total darkness, they would see a distant, accurately curving coastline gradually light up behind the vast pane of a panoramic windscreen, which then displayed a rush of events indistinctly represented by dim flashes, rough silhouettes of aircraft and motor vehicles, and the glimmer of fires. It was as if newsreels had been too "realistic" to recapture the pressure of the abstract surprise movements of modern war; and so, the old diorama method, with its enhancement of the visual field, was brought into service to give people the illusion of being hurled into a virtually unlimited image. If one thinks of the cinema-mausoleums or atmospheric cinemas of the thirties, one can see in this a new outflanking of immediate reality by the cinematic paramnesia of the war machine. Shortly afterwards, in the 1950s, the grandson of the famous conjuror Robert Houdin invented the immediately popular "Son et Lumière," a kind of open-air museum in which the past is reinjected into real places (temples, castles, landscapes) by means of projectors, sound equipment, artificial mist and, more recently, laser graphics. Similarly, in the American "freedomlands" one can see "Old Chicago" collapse and rise again from the flames every twenty minutes, or join in the Civil War and escape by the skin of one's teeth through the gunsmoke as the opposing sides open fire. Because of their overexposure in time, the material supports thus lose out to artificial lighting and become no more than a crepuscular threshold. The audience itself no longer knows whether the ruins are actually there, whether the landscape is not merely simulated in kaleidoscopic images of general destruction.

The sites chosen for museums of the Second World War remind us that these fortress-tombs, dungeons and bunkers are first and foremost camerae obscurae, that their hollowed windows, narrow apertures and loopholes are designed to light up the outside while leaving the inside in semi-darkness. In his pencil-like embrasure, the look-out and later the gunner realized long before the easel painter, the photographer or the filmmaker how necessary is a preliminary sizing-up. "You can see hell much better through a narrow vent than if you could take it in with both eyes at once," wrote Barbey d'Aurevilly, evoking the sort of squint necessary in taking aim and firing. This action, like the seductive wink so fashionable in the thirties, increased the depth of the visual field while reducing its compass. As recent experiments in anarthoscopic perception have shown,

> It is not enough to know that one is looking through a crack; it is also necessary to see the crack and in certain circumstances the observer may even invent it. In any case, it

> has been proved that the form of the aperture influences the perceptual identification of objects, and that visual tracking is a constitutive element in anarthoscopic perception of a moving shape.

More simply, the soldier's obscene gaze, on his surroundings and on the world, his art of hiding from sight in order to see, is not just an ominous voyeurism but from the first imposes a long-term patterning on the chaos of vision, one which prefigures the synoptic machinations of architecture and the cinema screen. In the act of focusing, with its proper angles, blind spots and exposure times, the line of sight already heralds the perspectival vanishing-line of the easel painter who, as in the case of Dürer or Leonardo, might also be a military engineer or an expert in siege warfare.

The nineteenth-century development of viewfinders precisely allowed the view to be "found" and "snapped" for military purposes, within interpretative codes for fixing the three-dimensional identity of two-dimensional images. This introduced a new reading of the battlefield, but also considerably increased the impotence and obscenity of the military decision-maker, now in ever greater danger of being tracked down and eliminated. Thus, in order to escape two-dimensional observation from anchored reconnaissance balloons four or five hundred metres up, the army began to bury its strongholds and outworks in a third dimension, throwing the enemy into a frenzy of interpretation. Invisible in its sunken depths, the camera obscura also became deaf and blind, its relations with the rest of the country now depending entirely on the logistics of perception. Already, what I have called the problem of the "third window"—how to light the surrounding world without seeing it—posed itself in a most acute way.[4] From now on, strategy is concealed in the special effects of signals and communications:

> Located in deep shelters that open onto communication trenches, the projectors invented by General Mangin can send messages over a distance of more than eighty kilometres. The light from a powerful oil-lamp is concentrated in a telescope by means of a concave mirror. This telescope is fitted with a moveable shutter, so that one can obtain either a constant beam or a short burst or a long burst corresponding to the dot and dash of the Morse code (*Ecole du génie français*, 1887).

The inner walls of the central command posts became screens covered with gridded maps whose ceaseless animation abstractly logged the slightest movement of troops in what were still proximate theatres. About 1930, some countries, including Britain, wound down their conventional means of defence and concentrated on research into perception. This reorientation led to the development of cybernetics and radar, as well as advancing the sciences of goniometry, microphotography and, as we have seen, radio and telecommunications. Thus, during the Second World War, the military commands and war cabinets no longer needed to set up their bunkers near the field of battle, but were able to remain in Berlin or London, in command centres which bore a passable resemblance to huge theatre-halls, for a war which had already become a Space Opera.

[4] P. Virilio, *Bunker archéologie*, Paris, 1975.

No longer having any real extension in space, these centres of interaction received an endless mass of information and messages from the most scattered points and radiated it back into their own, defined universe. In a sense, they may be said to have taken over the inertia of the old *Kammerspiel*, with its subjection to the pressure of time. But in these aseptic chambers so overwhelming was the sense of *negative charge*, so bare the visual and acoustic representation, that Hitler decided to introduce sound effects into his control-room in Bruly-le-Pesch when he was planning Operation Sealion. For the miniaturization of technological power, reducing space and time to nothing, was incompatible with the expansive imagination of the Nazi *Lebensraum* and could only be countered with artificial depth and grandiosity.

SICUT PRIOR EST TEMPORE ITA QUO POTIOR IURE[1]

Translated by Patrick Camiller

Rest never comes for those transfigured in war. Their ghosts continue to haunt the screens or, most frequently, find reincarnation in an engine of war—usually ship, like the *Tirpitz*, which sank in a fjord in 1943 and whose technological metempsychosis was celebrated in a feature film. Admiral William Nimitz, the American commander-in-chief of naval aviation in the Pacific from 1942 to 1945, gave his name to a nuclear aircraft-carrier which featured in another recent film, Don Taylor's *The Final Countdown* (1980). In this work of science fiction, whose theme is war across time, the Japanese fleet is steaming towards Pearl Harbor when it is detected by the *Nimitz*, which has been carried back half a century by a disturbance in the space-time vortex. The ship's commander faces a dilemma: whether to let history take its course, or to block the attack on Pearl Harbor by using all the fire-power at his command.

The most interesting thing in this film is the new crisis of decision-making that results from the non-peaceful coexistence of different technologies. Where are the orders to come from? From the commander of Pacific forces who, in 1941, knows of no vessel by the name of *Nimitz*? Or from the commander of US Defense, in 1980? As with the planned film *Narvik*, we can see here a determination to extend military power on both sides of a hypothetical "time centre" by using relativity as a military manoeuvre. In the film, the nuclear carrier *Nimitz* acts as a watchtower across historical time: the means of communication and identification employed in modern warfare become ways of blocking history. The new media allow the viewer to sense the *differential time-span* borne by each technological object. The effect is a startling temporal relief, such that the engine of war restores the material war-time of military-industrial propaganda in which we are the involuntary protagonists.

The British, who had invented the "Fleet in Being" to rule the waves as well as vast continents, allocated enormous sums during the inter-war period for research into communications and detection, and were particularly receptive to this kind of retro-prospective effect. In 1930, the British actor Leslie Howard had made a strangely premonitory film, *Outward Bound*, in which a number of passengers find themselves on board an aeroplane without knowing the destination. Eventually it becomes clear to them that they are already dead and that the craft is simply transporting them into the next world. Thirteen years later, on June 1, 1943, a DC-3 Ibis on which Leslie Howard happened to be travelling also vanished without trace.

Back in October 1939 Howard had a hard time persuading Whitehall to help him make propaganda films in Britain. "Why don't you do that in the United States?" he was asked. "We're short of everything here." Instead, he was offered a liaison job similar to Noel Coward's

---

[1] "Priority in time gives priority in law." Roman adage.

work for the French government on the interpretation of Nazi propaganda.[2] Howard turned this down and submitted a proposal of his own:

> The first film that I want to make is a documentary of the British White Paper on the outbreak of war. I want to put it out as a film record, using some newsreel stuff, but acting the real parts. There is a theme I want to bring home. Let me explain—I am working on a simple principle: that the mind will always triumph over brute force in the long run.

When he was asked which role he would play, he replied:

> Oh, acting Hitler for a start, and then I want to play Sir Nevile Henderson myself. The last bid for peace against the tactics of Ribbentrop .... You see, nobody abroad wants to read official documents now. They won't buy your White Paper. But they will crowd into the cinemas to see an official documentary.[3]

Howard's attempts at persuasion ended in failure, but they led to the conception of Pimpernel Smith—the absent-minded professor who bamboozles the Nazis—which demonstrated Howard's ideas in a rather flippant style that he did not particularly like. Howard went on to make a number of propaganda films, including *The First of the Few* which featured some of the best pilots from the Battle of Britain (Townsend, Bader, Cunningham) in an account of the life of Spitfire designer R.J. Mitchell.

In 1943 Lubitsch presented *To Be or Not To Be* to American audiences—a film which, though largely inspired by Howard's misfortunes, aroused considerable indignation in the United States. For this was the year of Roosevelt's declaration of total war, and people preferred to see Hitler vanquished by Superman than by some unknown and rather shabby-looking Shakespearian actors. The film had an equally bad reception when it was shown in France in 1954, and yet this "disrespectful fantasy" was really a serious war film—disturbing, too, in its exposure of the philosophy of the Allied Special Services. British defence secrets, protected by a censor's office that was to remain in place for more than thirty years, really did reside as much in Shakespearian theatre as in the headquarters of the armed forces. For example, the plan for Montgomery's famous victory over Rommel at El-Alamein was drawn from *Macbeth* by a film director, Geoffrey Barkas, and a music-hall magician, Maskeline, the two men reproducing Malcolm's action at Birnham Wood. Over the hard sand of the desert, virtually devoid of landmarks, the British army moved so slowly that the enemy's sharpest look-outs, equipped with the best field-glasses, could detect no real advance.

---

[2] In January 1940 the British Ministry of Information published a memorandum on the state of the army's photography and film departments. In fact it wished to carry out a revolution by halting distribution of military documentaries that were considered too static and technical and therefore incapable of assisting the unprecedented war effort. The great photographer Cecil Beaton was to play a dominant role in implementing this reform. We should remember that in response to the nationalization of the Soviet cinema, an effective documentary school had been founded in 1928 with the support of men like Rudyard Kipling, the senior civil servant Stephen Tallents, and the film-maker John Grierson. This movement, which was conceived as a public service and enjoyed state subsidies, made a considerable international impact. It also led indirectly to the formation of the Crown Film Unit, the largest producer of British propaganda films during the war, which was based in the requisitioned Pinewood Studios. Cavalcanti was its director until 1940.

[3] Ian Goodhope Colvin, *Flight 777*, London 1957, pp. 48–49.

The British were soon to have another stroke of genius. Since the chronophotographic reconnaissance of the First World War, information had greatly depended upon central analysis and interpretation, and Whitehall well knew that German Intelligence, reconstituted in the thirties by Theo Rowehl, a close friend and ex-naval colleague of Admiral Canaris, had an insatiable appetite in such matters. The Luftwaffe's bombers and reconnaissance aircraft were at once engines of destruction and engines of cinema, movie producers, as it were, filming not only the battlefield but also the territory of the United Kingdom itself. Rather than attempt to interfere with this, the Allies therefore decided to take part in the *mise en scène* of Hitler's newsreel and intelligence films. Their main technique was not classical camouflage but, on the contrary, overexposure. Enemy cameras were offered sight of scenery, matériel, troop movements—all part of the almost limitless repertoire of visual illusions in real space.

At the crucial point when massive preparations were under way for the Normandy landings, the East Anglian countryside came to resemble an enormous film lot complete with Hollywood-style props. Men with imagination, such as the architecture professor Basil Spence, were assisted in their work of visual disinformation by a mass of painters, poets, theatre and cinema technicians. Famous studios like Shepperton near London went over to producing phoney armoured vehicles or landing ships.

> Smoke coiled from [the landing ships'] funnels, they were surrounded by oil patches, laundry hung from the rigging, motorboats left wakes from ship to ship, and intruding aircraft could see their crews—over-age or unfit soldiers of units such as the 10th Worcestershires and the 4th Northamptonshires. Thousands of carefully shielded truck lights indicated the presence of large convoys, and lights over "hards" gave the impression of intense loading activity after dark. And behind this "invasion fleet," which was large enough to "land" the entire 1st Canadian Army, which did not as yet exist, the fields of East Anglia and Kent were crowded with tanks, guns, half-tracks, ammunition dumps, field kitchens, hospitals, troop encampments and fuel lines. They, too, were fakes.[4]

The sound-track was also well worked out, with all the care of a film script. It contained various brief, misleading, dialogues that could be picked up by German radio-operators across the Channel—apparently part of the normal run of military signals. And to add a final touch of authenticity, public figures, including King George himself, and Generals Eisenhower and Montgomery, were invited to visit the spurious docks, ships and building-sites. At other key moments, look-alikes of Churchill and other military leaders embarked on aeroplanes to undertake bogus trips.

This relationship between actors and statesmen, like the grotesque substitution scenes of *To Be or Not To Be*, clearly reveals the kind of war strategems thought up by the Allies to mystify Hitler and the German high command about the real course of operations against the Third Reich, to leave the enemy bewildered as well as beaten.

After 1945, Britain's wartime services kept up their role of monitoring the varied scripts of international propaganda, with their attention now turned to the countries of the Eastern bloc. Technicians easily switched from special army measures to special cinema effects, and the old studios at Shepperton continued to house scale models and science-fiction devices.

---

[4] Cave Brown, *Bodyguard of Lies*, p. 603.

> During the summer and fall of 1978, a visitor to England's Shepperton Studios might have found that making the forty-five minute drive back to London would be easier than trying to get past the main gate. Four of Shepperton's massive sound-stages—one of them is amongst the largest in the world—were housing the sets for *Alien*. Twentieth Century Fox wanted to make sure that the sixteen weeks of principal shooting would only be witnessed by authorized eyes … The movie's biggest secret would be kept.

Roger Christian, the film's art director, adds: "Ridley showed us *Dr Strangelove* and he kept saying, 'That's what I want. Do you see? Not that it's a B-52 in outer space, but it's the military look.' I knew what he was saying because I had done it in *Star Wars*."[5] Like many cinema ships and vehicles before it, *Nostromo* in *Alien* contained a host of real features from World War Two battleships, tanks and bombers: "For instance, we made a control panel out of airplane junk and about a million switches."

On screen, science-fiction vessels become bright and sonorous plastic, a kind of thorough technological mix which, as with real military equipment, was designed to give the effect of synthesis to a variety of more or less anachronistic components. "Film criticism no longer has any meaning," Hans Zischler, one of Wim Wenders's actors, recently said to me; "it is *reality* that we have to analyse in a cinematic way." Evidently verisimilitude is no longer assured with the new engines of war: military technology has advanced too far out of our sight, its secrecy revives for us the attraction of faraway lands, and the wish for proximity is repeating the old imposture of immediacy. With its dreamlike design, its much-caressed contours, the machine's body pursues the derangement of its appearances. The most intense hope seems to have moulded its particular form—a hope in which aerodynamics suddenly loses its value as a science of air flow and becomes a logistical pantheism of time flow.

Back in the forties Orson Welles once said: "For me, everything that's been called direction is one big bluff. Editing is the only time when you can be in complete control of a film."[6]

Francis Coppola, a great admirer of Abel Gance, shared his passion for the techniques of military commanders and their way of eliminating random factors. After the seventies' vogue for electronic effects, which allowed a considerable reduction in the "natural," objective uncertainties of scenery and machinery, Coppola and quite a few others began to use the electronic prerecording of both sound and image to suppress any element of chance. Thus, shooting no longer involved the rigorous placement in time and space of the old *Kammerspiel*. As in radio productions, the actors played out their roles in the studio, and the director then worked ad lib on his editing table shuffling and inserting the various shots. "In this way," Coppola remarks, "he gets the most sophisticated possible result for the least price."[7]

Coppola has developed in an interesting direction since the partial disappointment of *Apocalypse Now*. In fact, the emotional *One from the Heart* is more of a war movie than *Apocalypse Now*, and it is quite clear that this new film art in which actors and sets vanish at will is an art of extermination. Coppola directly uses military equipment like the Xerox "Star" naval computer system, and his cost-benefit approach is like the attitude of the modern army

---

[5] Paul Scanlon and Michael Gross, *The Book of Alien*, London 1979, unpaginated.
[6] Quoted from "Made in USA," *Cahiers du cinéma*, April 1982.
[7] Ibid.

to miniaturization or automation, which is seen as "transferring the possibility of human error from the point of action to the design and development process."[8]

Thus, the last power left to the director, as to the army officer, is not so much to imagine as to foresee, simulate and memorize simulations. Having lost material space, the bunkered commander of total war suffers a loss of real time, a sudden cutting-off of any involvement in the ordinary world. Like the new opaque cockpits which prevent fighter pilots from looking outside, because "seeing is dangerous," war and its technologies have gradually eliminated theatrical and pictorial effects in processing the battle image, and total war followed by deterrence have tended to cancel the scenario effect itself in a permanent technological ambience devoid of any substratum. With the new composites, the world disappears in war, and war as a phenomenon disappears from the eyes of the world. Crew members on the aircraft carrier *Nimitz* recently told a journalist from *Libération*: "Our work is totally unreal. Every now and then, fiction and reality should get together and prove once and for all that we are really here."

Total war takes us from military secrecy (the second-hand, recorded truth of the battlefield) to the overexposure of live broadcast. For with the advent of strategic bombing everything is now brought home to the cities, and it is no longer just the few but a whole mass of spectator-survivors who are the surviving spectators of combat. Nuclear deterrence means that there are no longer strictly "foreign wars;" as the mayor of Philadelphia put it twenty years ago, frontiers now pass through the middle of cities. Berlin, Harlem, Belfast, Beirut, Warsaw and Lyon ... the streets themselves have now become a permanent film-set for army cameras or the tourist-reporters of global civil war. The West, after adjusting from the political illusions of the theatre-city (Athens, Rome, Venice) to those of the cinema-city (Hollywood, Cinecittà, Nuremberg), has now plunged into the transpolitical pan-cinema of the nuclear age, into an entirely cinematic vision of the world. Those American TV channels which broadcast news footage around the clock—without script or comment—have understood this point very well. Because in fact this isn't really news footage any longer, but *the raw material of vision*, the most trustworthy kind possible. The extraordinary commercialization of audiovisual technology is responding to the same demand. For videos and walkmans are reality and appearance in kit form: we use them not to watch films or listen to music, but to add vision and soundtracks, to make us directors of our own reality.

Even back in the fifties and sixties, when people were asked why they flocked to pop concerts or festivals like Woodstock, they used to say it was because they didn't want to hear themselves think, or because at such events there was no longer any real distinction between spectators and performers. Hundreds of thousands of actor-spectators went to stadium cycloramas, where the cameras and lasers illuminated not just the stars but also the wildly excited crowds. Those who came to watch also exhibited themselves, in a way heralding such spectacular actions of the seventies as the assassination of John Lennon.

Today, directors (and politicians) have lost all prominence, and are swallowed up in technical effects, rather like Nicholas Ray in Wim Wenders's *Lightning Over Water*. "We get our energy from chaos," the Rolling Stones once said. And from everyday terrorism to live-broadcast assassinations, the living pan-cinema is spreading before us that chaos which was once so well concealed by the *orderly* creation of war. Even if our actions are suddenly slipping out of their usual frames of reference, they are not *actes gratuits* but cinema-acts.

---

[8] Andrew Stratton, in Nigel Calder, ed., *Unless Peace Come*, Harmondsworth 1968, p. 98.

With the neutron bomb, urban populations have lost their ultimate value as nuclear hostages and have been abandoned by military planners. There are no more "immortals of the City." And cinema itself has lost its initiatory value and ceased to be the black mass of martial aboriginality which can offer cinematic Valhalla to the children of the fatherland in a communion of the quick and the dead. For the commercial distribution of video and audio equipment is destroying the extraordinary technical capacity of the old cinema to shape society through vision, to turn a thousand film-goers into a single spectator.

CHAPTER 40
GILLES DELEUZE

Gilles Deleuze (1925–1995) was a French philosopher and one of the central figures of French postmodernism. He is perhaps most famous for his collaborations with Félix Guattari and for his magnum opus, Difference and Repetition, *wherein the question of difference is centralized in Western thought. He is among the most important philosophers not only in the Continental tradition, but of the twentieth century, alongside (in the twentieth-century Continental tradition) figures such as Martin Heidegger, Jean-Paul Sartre, Michel Foucault, and Jacques Derrida. In addition, however, he is one of the foundational Continental philosophers of film—and certainly the one whose views on film are most well known—by way of his two-volume book,* Cinema I and II. *The text included here is the conclusion to* Cinema II: The Time-Image. *It was originally published in French (*Cinéma 2: L'image-temps*) by Éditions de Minuit in 1985.*

Contradicting many other Continental philosophers of film (especially those in or on the borderline of the traditions of semiology and semiotics, like Christian Metz or Umberto Eco), Deleuze argues from the very beginning that cinema is not a language. That said, he notes that cinema brings to light a necessary correlate of language—the unutterable movements and thought processes, and points of view on these, which underlie all linguistic signification. Cinema becomes, then, for Deleuze, a system of prelinguistic signs and images. On this basis, he argues that the difference between silent film and sound film—made so much of in discussions of the history and development of film—is actually not a fundamental difference. Rather, the fundamental difference in cinema is the difference between what Deleuze calls "movement-images" and "time-images." He devotes the first volume of Cinema *to elaborating the movement-image, and much of the second volume to explaining the difference between the movement-image and the time-image. As the selection here is from the conclusion to* Cinema II, *Deleuze presupposes as much as explains what he means by the movement-image.*

The movement-image, for Deleuze, is what we see in a film when we concentrate on the ways in which the film takes us from photographed object to object, from image to image. It is film understood as the "image" of the movement from image to image itself. Thus, the movement-image centralizes space and matter in our understanding of cinema—and presents us with a vision of the world that likewise focuses on the arrangements of objects: things and persons. The end product of the movement-image, Deleuze suggests, is the cinematic production of Leni Riefenstahl: a cinema that conceives of human beings as manipulable, organizable, deployable machines. It is a cinema that has a natural home in propaganda, and which dovetails with reconceptions of human society as itself a sort of machine. Thus, both individuals and groups are thought of as automata of movement (puppets, robots, zombies, or somnambulists)—all with a mysterious master or leader pulling the strings from a position of security and secrecy, behind the scenes. Deleuze makes clear that the movement-image meshes well with mass movements (which are always attempts to understand groups of human beings as sharing a single "soul" which moves them as a unit), and ultimately in Hitler—if we can think of Hitler as a certain sort of filmmaker. Because this relationship of master-automaton thinks of the soul as simply that which instills movement into the body, Deleuze calls such phenomena "spiritual automata." To conceive of film as movement-image, as spiritual automata, is to conceive of film as a body that moves.

One need not think of film in this way, or at least, not exclusively in this way, however. Deleuze suggests another possibility, the time-image, which does not focus on motion or objects, but on the phenomenon of projection. While we might see a film and think of the basic unit of cinema as the image of the object, in motion, we might alternatively think of the basic unit of film as transparent light projected onto a screen. Rethought in this way, film loses its central focus on space altogether: cinema becomes a question not of the arrangement of objects in space, but of the projection of information in time. The time-image centralizes data, whereas the movement-image centralized nature, and the difference in the conception of film unseats the soul (which, again, on this view is the principle of motion in the body) in favor of the mind. Spiritual automata are no longer at work; on this view, we are experiencing psychological automata.

The most straightforward instance of the psychological automaton is the computer-generated image which, at the time of Deleuze's writing, was even more obviously lacking in depth and materiality than it is today. Computer images are not images of anything, in the sense that they are not tied in any way to real objects in the material world: the opposite of the computer image is the photograph. While photography is essentially dependent upon the relationships between objects in space (and the spatial relationship of the camera to those objects-in-relationship), computer images lack spatiality altogether. They rely, ultimately, on the program—which is to say that computer imagery replaces movement at the heart of cinema with mere sequence. Space is decentralized in favor of time. Of course, as Deleuze notes, computer images are not required for the instantiation of the time-image: he sees the time-image in Robert Bresson's privileging of the speech act over motor actions, and in Alain Resnais' focus on speech and information instead of energy and movement. Ultimately, in conceiving of the time-image in terms of psychological automata, Deleuze is conceiving of something like a brain that could have a direct experience of time without the mediation of moving bodies.

Of course, in film as elsewhere, time and space are never entirely distinct from one another. Although the movement-image cannot give us the time-image, the movement-image is linked to an indirect representation of time—through the duration of motion. The only direct presentation of the time-image, Deleuze argues, is music, which is pure sequence and duration independent of any experience of motivity. Likewise, in the time-image, it is not that movement is missing—it is that movement is subordinated to time. He goes on to explain that, at the root of the movement-image is a sensorimotor link: perception and motion are inextricably intertwined. The time-image only results upon the dissolution (or abandonment) of this sensorimotor link; this, in turn, gives rise to situations in cinema to which we can no longer react: pure optical and sound situations. (Observing a sunset stimulates an affective response in the observer, as well as a movement of either attraction or aversion; observing orange alongside blue, however, whether by way of the presentation simply of adjoining colors or by way of an image of a sunset, stimulates thought but not motion, affective or otherwise.) Viewing a movement-image inspires the viewer to anticipate what is going to be shown in the next image; viewing a time-image inspires the viewer to contemplate what there is to be seen in this image at all. Put another way, the movement-image is important in a schema of motion, bodies moving from one position to another; the time-image, on the other hand, is important only in itself.

It is this difference which, for Deleuze, informs the difference between classical images and modern images—that is, classical and modern film images. In the classical image, time is presented (indirectly) as the measure of movement. In the images that constitute classic cinema, one is always expected to be asking oneself what is happening—and one experiences time as the framework within which whatever is happening happens. The modern cinematic image, however, is characterized by irrational cuts whereby development (and the impression of all movement) is thwarted. Whether this takes the form of unconventional shots, abstract montage, or something more experimental, the modern image undermines sequence itself. Whereas, in the classical image, the interval between shots was the unseen connective tissue that made the depiction of movement possible, in the modern image, the interval between shots serves no utilitarian purpose: it is set free. In this way, the interval becomes something irreducible, we begin to see the spaces between shots, and the interval stands on its own: time itself, presented in the cinema.

Filmography

- ***Das Kabinet des Dr. Caligari*** [*The Cabinet of Dr. Caligari*] (Germany, 1920). *Directed by* Robert Wiene. *Produced by* Rudolf Meinert *and* Erich Pommer. *Written by* Hans Janowitz *and* Carl Mayer. *Starring* Werner Krauss, Conrad Veidt, Friedrich Fehér, Lil Dagover, *and* Hans Twardowski.
- ***Metropolis*** (Germany, 1927). *Directed by* Fritz Lang. *Produced by* Erich Pommer. *Written by* Thea von Harbou. *Starring* Alfred Abel, Gustav Fröhlich, Rudolf Klein-Rogge, *and* Brigitte Helm.
- ***Vampyr—Der Traum des Allan Grey*** [*Vampyr: The Dream of Allan Grey*] (Germany–France, 1927). *Directed by* Carl Theodor Dreyer. *Produced by* Carl Theodor Dreyer *and* Julian West. *Written by* Christen Jul *and* Carl Theodor Dreyer. *Starring* Julian West, Maurice Schutz, Rena Mandel, Jan Hieronimko, Sybille Schmitz, *and* Henriette Gerard.
- ***Das Testament des Dr. Mabuse*** [*The Testament of Dr. Mabuse*] (Germany, 1933). *Directed by* Fritz Lang. *Produced by* Seymour Nebenzal. *Written by* Thea von Harbou *and* Fritz Lang. *Starring* Rudolf Klein-Rogge, Otto Wernicke, Oscar Beregi, Sr., *and* Gustav Diessl.
- ***L'Année dernière à Marienbad*** [*Last Year in Marienbad*] (France–Italy, 1961). *Directed by* Alain Resnais. *Produced by* Pierre Courau, Raymond Froment, Robert Dorfmann, *and* Anatole Dauman. *Written by* Alain Robbe-Grillet. *Starring* Delphine Seyrig, Giorgio Albertazzi, *and* Sacha Pitoëff.
- ***Une femme mariée*** [*A Married Woman*] (France, 1964). *Directed and Written by* Jean-Luc Godard. *Produced by* Anouchka Films *and* Orsay Films. *Starring* Bernard Noël *and* Macha Méril.
- ***Alphaville: une étrange aventure de Lemmy Caution*** [*Alphaville: A Strange Adventure of Lemmy Caution*] (France, 1965). *Directed and Written by* Jean-Luc Godard. *Produced by* André Michelin. *Starring* Eddie Constantine, Anna Karina, Akim Tamiroff, *and* Howard Vernon.
- ***Deux ou Trois Choses que je sais d'elle*** [*Two or Three Things I Know about Her*] (France, 1967). *Directed by* Jean-Luc Godard. *Produced by* Anatole Dauman *and* Raoul Lévy. *Written by* Catherine Vimenet *and* Jean-Luc Godard. *Starring* Joseph Gehrard, Marina Vlady, *and* Roger Montsoret.

- ***2001: A Space Odyssey*** (UK–USA, 1968). *Directed and Produced by* Stanley Kubrick. *Written by* Stanley Kubrick *and* Arthur C. Clarke. *Starring* Keir Dullea *and* Gary Lockwood.
- ***Je t'aime, je t'aime*** [*I Love You, I Love You*] (France, 1968). *Directed by* Alain Resnais. *Produced by* Mag Bodard. *Written by* Jacques Sternberg *and* Alain Resnais. *Starring* Claude Rich.
- ***La Région Centrale*** [*The Central Region*] (Canada, 1971). *Directed by* Michael Snow.
- ***Theodor Hierneis oder Wie man ehem. Hofkoch wird*** [*Theodor Hierneis or How to Become a Former Royal Chef/Le cuisinier du roi*] (West Germany, 1972). *Directed by* Hans-Jürgen Syberberg. *Produced by* TMS Film. *Written by* Hans-Jürgen Syberberg *and* Walter Sedlmayr. *Starring* Walter Sedlmayr.
- ***Karl May*** (West Germany, 1974). *Directed, Produced, and Written by* Hans-Jürgen Syberberg. *Starring* Helmut Käutner.
- ***Hitler, Ein Film aus Deutschland*** [*Hitler: A Film from Germany*] (France–UK–West Germany, 1977). *Directed and Written by* Hans-Jürgen Syberberg. *Produced by* Bernd Eichinger. *Starring* Heinz Schubert.
- ***Sauve qui peut (la vie)*** [*Every Man for Himself/Slow Motion*] (France, 1980). *Directed by* Jean-Luc Godard. *Produced by* Jean-Luc Godard *and* Alain Sarde. *Written by* Jean-Claude Carrière, Jean-Luc Godard, *and* Anne-Marie Miéville. *Starring* Jacques Dutronc, Isabelle Huppert, *and* Nathalie Baye.
- ***Parsifal*** (West Germany–France, 1982). *Directed by* Hans-Jürgen Syberberg. *Produced by* Annie Nap-Oleon. *Written by* Richard Wagner. *Starring* Armin Jordan.
- ***Passion*** (Switzerland–France, 1982). *Directed and Written by* Jean-Luc Godard. *Produced by* Armand Barbault, Catherine Lapoujade, *and* Martine Marignac. *Starring* Isabelle Huppert, Jerzy Radziwilowicz, Hanna Schygulla, Michel Piccoli, *and* Lázsló Szabó.
- ***Prénom: Carmen*** [*First Name: Carmen*] (France, 1983). *Directed by* Jean-Luc Godard. *Produced by* Alain Sarde. *Written by* Anne-Marie Miéville. *Starring* Maruschka Detmers *and* Jacques Bonnaffé.

THE TIME-IMAGE

Translated by Hugh Tomlinson and Robert Galeta

1

Cinema is not a universal or primitive language system [*langue*], nor a language [*langage*]. It brings to light an intelligible content which is like a presupposition, a condition, a necessary correlate through which language constructs its own "objects" (signifying units and operations). But this correlate, though inseparable, is specific: it consists of movements and thought-processes (pre-linguistic images), and of points of view on these movements and processes (pre-signifying signs). It constitutes a whole "psychomechanics," the spiritual automaton, the utterable of a language system which has its own logic. The language system takes utterances of language, with signifying units and operations from it, but the utterable itself, its images and signs, are of another nature. This would be what Hjelmslev calls non-linguistically formed "content," whilst the language system works through form and substance. Or rather, it is the first signifiable, anterior to all significance, which Gustave Guillaume made the condition of linguistics.[1] We can understand from this the ambiguity which runs through semiotics and semiology: semiology, which is of linguistic inspiration, tends to close the "signifier" in on itself, and cut language off from the images and signs which make up its raw material.[2] Semiotics, by contrast, is the discipline which considers language only in relation to this specific content, images and signs. Of course, when language takes over the content or the utterable it makes from them properly linguistic utterances which are no longer expressed in images and signs. But even the utterances are in turn reinvested in images and signs, and provide the utterable afresh. It seemed to us that cinema, precisely through its automatic or psychomechanical qualities, was the system of pre-linguistic images and signs, and that it took utterances up again in the images and signs proper to this system (the read image of the silent cinema, the sound components of the visual image in the first stage of the talkie, the sound image itself in the second stage of the talkie). This is why the break between the silent film and the talkie has never seemed fundamental in cinema's evolution. By contrast, what has seemed fundamental to us in this system of images and signs is the distinction between two kinds of images with their corresponding signs, movement-images and time-images which were only to appear and develop later. Kinostructures and chronogeneses are the two successive chapters of a pure semiotics.

Cinema considered as psychomechanics, or spiritual automaton, is reflected in its own content, its themes, situations and characters. But the relationship is complicated, because this reflection gives way to oppositions and inversions as well as to resolutions or reconciliations. The automaton has always had two coexistent, complementary senses, even when they were in conflict. On one

---

[1] An excellent general presentation of Guillaume's work in this connection will be found in Alain Rey, *Théories du signe et du sens*, Klincksieck, II, pp. 262–4. Ortigues gives a more detailed analysis in *Le discours et le symbole*, Aubier.

[2] On the tendency to eliminate the notion of sign, cf. Ducrot and Todorov, *Encyclopaedic Dictionary of the Sciences of Language*, pp. 349–65. Christian Metz shares this tendency (*Langage et cinéma*, Albatros, p. 146).

hand, the great spiritual automaton indicates the highest exercise of thought, the way in which thought thinks and itself thinks itself in the fantastic effort of an autonomy; it is in this sense that Jean-Louis Schefer can credit cinema with being a giant in the back of our heads, Cartesian diver, dummy or machine, mechanical man without birth who brings the world into suspense.[3] But, on the other hand, the automaton is also the psychological automaton who no longer depends on the outside because he is autonomous but because he is dispossessed of his own thought, and obeys an internal impression which develops solely in visions or rudimentary actions (from the dreamer to the somnambulist, and conversely through the intermediary of hypnosis, suggestion, hallucination, obsession, etc.).[4] Hence there is something specific to cinema which has nothing to do with theatre. If cinema is automatism become spiritual art—that is, initially movement-image—it confronts automata, not accidentally, but fundamentally. The French school never lost its taste for clockwork automata and clock-making characters, but also confronted machines with moving parts, like the American or Soviet schools. The man-machine assemblage varies from case to case, but always with the intention of posing the question of the future. And machines can take hold so fully on man that it awakens the most ancient powers, and the moving machine becomes one with the psychological automaton pure and simple, at the service of a frightening new order: this is the procession of somnambulists, the hallucinators, hypnotizers-hypnotized in expressionism, from *The Cabinet of Dr Caligari* to *Testament of Dr Mabuse* via *Metropolis* and its robot. German cinema summoned up primitive powers, but it was perhaps best placed to announce something new which was to change cinema, horribly to "realize" it and thus to modify its basic themes.

What is interesting in Krackauer's book *From Caligari to Hitler* is that it shows how expressionist cinema reflected the rise of the Hitlerian automaton in the German soul. But it still took an external viewpoint, whilst Walter Benjamin's article set itself inside cinema in order to show how the art of automatic movement (or, as he ambiguously said, the art of reproduction) was itself to coincide with the automization of the masses, state direction, politics become "art": Hitler as film-maker ... And it is true that up to the end Nazism thinks of itself in competition with Hollywood. The revolutionary courtship of the movement-image and an art of the masses become subject was broken off, giving way to the masses subjected as psychological automaton, and to their leader as great spiritual automaton. This is what compels Syberberg to say that the end-product of the movement-image is Leni Riefenstahl, and if Hitler is to be put on trial by cinema, it must be inside cinema, against Hitler the film-maker, in order to "defeat him cinematographically, turning his weapons against him."[5] It is as if Syberberg felt the need to add a second volume to Krackauer's book, but this second volume would be a film: not now from Caligari (or from a film from Germany) to Hitler, but from Hitler to *A Film from Germany*, the change taking place inside cinema, against Hitler, but also against Hollywood, against represented violence, against pornography, against business ... But at what price? A true psychomechanics will not be found unless it is based on *new associations*, by reconstituting the

---

[3] Jean-Louis Schefer, *L'homme ordinaire du cinéma*, Cahiers du cinéma/Gallimard.

[4] These are the two extreme states of thought, the spiritual automaton of logic, pointed to by Spinoza and Leibniz, and the psychological automaton of psychiatry, studied by Janet.

[5] Cf. Serge Daney, *La rampe*, 'L'Etat-Syberberg', p. 111 (and p. 172). Daney's analysis is based here on numerous declarations by Syberberg himself. Syberberg takes his cue from Benjamin, but goes further, launching the theme 'Hitler as film-maker'. Benjamin notes only that 'mass production' in the domain of art found its privileged object in 'the reproduction of the masses', grand processions, meetings, sporting gatherings, ultimately war ('The work of art in the era of mechanical reproduction', in *Illuminations*, trans. Harry Zohn, London: Fontana, 1973).

great mental automata whose place was taken by Hitler, by reviving the psychological automata that he enslaved. The movement-image, that is, the bond that cinema had introduced between movement and image from the outset, would have to be abandoned, in order to set free other powers that it kept subordinate, and which had not had the time to develop their effects: projection and back-projection.[6] There is also a more general problem: for projection and back-projection are only technical means which directly carry the time-image, which substitute the time-image for the movement-image. The film set is transformed, but in that "space here is born from time" (*Parsifal*). Is there a new regime of images like that of automatism?

A return to the extrinsic point of view obviously becomes necessary: the technological and social evolution of automata. Clockwork automata, but also motor automata, in short, automata of movement, made way for a new computer and cybernetic race, automata of computation and thought, automata with controls and feedback. The configuration of power was also inverted, and, instead of converging on a single, mysterious leader, inspirer of dreams, commander of actions, power was diluted in an information network where "decision-makers" managed control, processing and stock across intersections of insomniacs and seers (as in, for example, the world-conspiracy we saw in Rivette, or Godard's *Alphaville*, the listening and surveillance system in Lumet, but above all, the evolution of Lang's three Mabuses, the third Mabuse, the Mabuse of the return to Germany, after the war).[7] And, in frequently explicit forms, the new automata were to people cinema, for better and for worse (the better would be Kubrick's giant computer in *2001*), and restore to it, particularly through science fiction, the possibility of huge *mises-en-scènes* that the impasse in the movement-image had provisionally ruled out. But new automata did not invade content without a new automatism bringing about a mutation of form. The modern configuration of the automaton is the correlate of an electronic automatism. The electronic image, that is, the tele and video image, the numerical image coming into being, either had to transform cinema or to replace it, to mark its death. We do not claim to be producing an analysis of the new images, which would be beyond our aims, but only to indicate certain effects whose relation to the cinematographic image remains to be determined.[8] The new images no longer have any outside (out-of-field), any more than they are internalized in a whole; rather, they have a right side and a reverse, reversible and non-superimposable, like a power to turn back on themselves. They are the object of a perpetual reorganization, in which a new image can arise from any point whatever of the preceding image. The organization of space here loses its privileged directions, and first of all the privilege

---

[6] Syberberg does not begin like Benjamin from the idea of the reproductive arts, but from the idea of cinema as art of the movement-image: 'for a long time people have begun from the presupposition which let it be understood that to talk about cinema was to talk about movement', mobile image, mobile camera, and montage. He thinks that the culmination of this system is Leni Riefenstahl, and her 'master who was hiding there behind'. 'But it was forgotten that in the cradle of cinema there had also been something else, projection, transparency': another type of image, implying 'slow, controllable movements' capable of bringing contradiction into the system of movement, or of Hitler—film-maker. Cf. *Syberberg*, special number of *Cahiers du cinéma*, février 1980, p. 86.

[7] Cf. Pascal Kane, 'Mabuse et le pouvoir', *Cahiers du cinéma*, no. 309, mars 1980.

[8] On not only the technical but the phenomenological differences between the types of image, the reader is particularly referred to the studies of Jean-Paul Fargier in *Cahiers du cinéma* and of Dominique Belloir in the special number 'Video art explorations'. In an article in *Revue d'esthétique* ('Image puissance image', no. 7, 1984) Edmond Couchot defines certain characteristics of numerical or digital images, which he calls 'immedia', because there is no longer a medium properly speaking. The fundamental idea is that, already in television, there is no space or image either, but only electronic lines: 'the fundamental concept in television is time' (Nam June Paik, interview with Fargier, *Cahiers du cinéma*, no. 299, avril 1979).

of the vertical which the position of the screen still displays, in favour of an omni-directional space which constantly varies its angles and co-ordinates, to exchange the vertical and the horizontal. And the screen itself, even if it keeps a vertical position by convention, no longer seems to refer to the human posture, like a window or a painting, but rather constitutes a table of information, an opaque surface on which are inscribed "data," information replacing nature, and the brain-city, the third eye, replacing the eyes of nature. Finally, sound achieving an autonomy which increasingly lends it the status of image, the two images, sound and visual, enter into complex relations with neither subordination nor commensurability, and reach a common limit in so far as each reaches its own limit. In all these senses, the new spiritual automatism in turn refers to new psychological automata.

But we are all the time circling the question: cerebral creation or deficiency of the cerebellum? The new automatism is worthless in itself if it is not put to the service of a powerful, obscure, condensed will to art, aspiring to deploy itself through involuntary movements which none the less do not restrict it. An original will to art has already been defined by us in the change affecting the intelligible content of cinema itself: the substitution of the time-image for the movement-image. So that electronic images will have to be based on still another will to art, or on as yet unknown aspects of the time-image. The artist is always in the situation of saying simultaneously: I claim new methods, and I am afraid that the new methods may invalidate all will to art, or make it into a business, a pornography, a Hitlerism ...[9] What is important is that the cinematographic image was already achieving effects which were not like those of electronics, but which had autonomous anticipatory functions in the time-image as will to art. Thus Bresson's cinema has no need of computing or cybernetic machines; yet the "model" is a modern psychological automaton, because it is defined in relation to the speech-act, and no longer, as before, by motor action (Bresson was constantly thinking about automatism). Similarly Rohmer's puppet characters, Robbe-Grillet's hypnotized ones, and Resnais' zombies are defined in terms of speech or information, not of energy or motivity. In Resnais, there are no more flashbacks, but rather feedbacks and failed feedbacks, which, however, need no special machinery (except in the deliberately rudimentary case of *Je t'aime je t'aime*). In Ozu, it is the daring of the continuity shots at 180° that is enough to assemble an image "end to end with its obverse," and to make "the shot turn round."[10] Space muddles its directions, its orientations, and loses all primacy of the vertical axis that could determine them, as in Snow's *The Central Region*, using only a single camera and a rotary machine obeying electronic sounds. And the vertical of the screen now has only a conventional meaning when it ceases to make us see a world in movement, when it tends to become an opaque surface which receives, in order to disorder, and on which characters, objects and words are inscribed as "data." The readability of the image makes it as independent of the vertical human position as a newspaper can be. Bazin's alternative, either the screen acts as a frame of painting or as a mask (window), was never sufficient; for there was also the frame-mirror in the style of Ophüls, the wallpaper frame in the style of Hitchcock. But, when the frame or the screen functions as instrument

---

[9] Sometimes an artist, becoming aware of the death of the will to art in a particular medium, confronts the 'challenge' by a use which is apparently destructive of that medium: one might thus believe in negative goals in art, but it is rather a question of making up lost time, of converting a hostile area to art, with a certain violence, and of turning means against themselves. Cf. in regard to television, Wolf Vostell's attitude as analysed by Fargier ('The great trauma', *Cahiers du cinéma*, no. 332, février 1982).

[10] Noël Burch, *Pour un observateur lointain*, Cahiers du cinéma/Gallimard, p. 185.

panel, printing or computing table, the image is constantly being cut into another image, being printed through a visible mesh, sliding over other images in an "incessant stream of messages," and the shot itself is less like an eye than an overloaded brain endlessly absorbing information: it is the brain-information, brain-city couple which replaces that of eye-Nature.[11] Godard will move in this direction (*A Married Woman*, *Two or Three Things I Know about Her*), even before starting to use video methods. And, in the Straubs, and in Marguerite Duras, in Syberberg, the sound framing, the disjunction of the sound image and the visual image, use cinematographic methods, or simple video methods, instead of calling on new technologies. The reasons are not simply economic. The fact is that the new spiritual automatism and the new psychological automata depend on an aesthetic before depending on technology. It is the time-image which calls on an original regime of images and signs, before electronics spoils it or, in contrast, relaunches it. When Jean-Louis Schefer invokes the great spiritual automaton or the dummy at the back of our heads as principles of the cinema, he is right in defining it today by a brain which has a direct experience of time, anterior to all motivity of bodies (even if the apparatus invoked, the mill in Dreyer's *Vampyr*, still refers to a clockwork automaton).

The Straubs, Marguerite Duras and Syberberg have, with some justification, often been grouped together in the project of forming a whole audio-visual system, whatever the differences between these authors.[12] In Syberberg we effectively encounter the two great characteristics that we have tried to identify in the other cases. First, the disjunction of the sound and the visual appears clearly in *Le cuisinier du roi*, between the cook's flux of words and the deserted spaces, castles, shacks, sometimes an engraving. Similarly, in *Hitler* the visual space of the chancellery becomes deserted, while some children in a corner make heard the record of one of Hitler's speeches. This disjunction takes on aspects peculiar to Syberberg's style. Sometimes it is the objective dissociation of what is said and what is seen: front-projection and the frequent use of slides provide a visual space not only not seen by the actor himself, but with which he is associated without ever being a part of it, reduced to his words and a few accessories (for instance, in *Hitler* the giant furniture, the giant telephone, while the dwarf servant talks about the master's underpants). Sometimes it is the subjective dissociation of the voices and the body: the body is here replaced by a puppet, a jumping jack facing the voice of the actor or reciter; or as in *Parsifal* the playback is perfectly synchronized, but with a body which remains foreign to the voice it gives itself, a living puppet, whether a girl's body for a man's voice or two competing bodies for the same voice.[13] In other words, there is no

---

[11] Leo Steinberg ('Other criteria', lecture at the Museum of Modern Art, New York, 1968) was already refusing to define modern painting by the conquest of a pure optical space, and isolated two characteristics which, according to him, were complementary: the loss of reference to the vertical human carriage, and the treatment of the painting as surface of information; for instance, Mondrian, when he metamorphoses the sea and sky more or less into signs, but above all with reference to Rauschenberg. 'The painted surface no longer presents an analogy with a natural visual experience, but becomes related to operational processes...The plane of Rauschenberg's painting is the equivalent of consciousness plunged into the city's brain.' In the case of cinema, even for Snow who offers himself a 'fragment of nature in the wild state', nature and the machine 'inter-represent themselves': to the extent that visual determinations are information data 'caught in the machine's operations and passage': 'This is a film as concept where the eye has reached the point of not seeing' (Marie-Christine Questerbert, *Cahiers du cinéma*, no. 296, janvier 1979, pp. 36–7).

[12] Cf. especially Jean-Claude Bonnet, 'Trois cinéastes du texte', *Cinématographe*, no. 31, octobre 1977.

[13] On dissociation or disjunction, cf. the articles by Lardeau and by Comolli and Géré, in relation to Hitler, *Cahiers du cinéma*, no. 292, septembre 1978. For the definition of front-projection, and for the use of puppets, see the texts of Syberberg himself, in *Syberberg*, pp. 52–65. Bonitzer, in *Le champ aveugle*, draws out a whole conception of the complex shot in Syberberg.

whole: the regime of the "tear," where the division into body and voice forms a genesis of the image as "non-representable by a single individual," "appearance divided in itself and in a non-psychological way."[14] The puppet and the reciter, the body and the voice, constitute neither a whole nor an individual, but the automaton. This is the psychological automaton, in the sense of a profoundly divided essence of the psyche, even though it is not at all psychological in the sense that this division would be interpreted as a state of the non-machine individual. As in Kleist, or Japanese theatre, the soul is made from the "mechanical movement" of the puppet, in so far as the latter appoints itself an "internal voice." But, if the division is thus valid in itself, it is nevertheless not valid for itself. For, in the second place, a pure speech-act as creative story-telling or legend-making must extricate itself from all the spoken information (the most striking example is *Karl May* who must become a legend through his own lies and their exposure), but also the visual data must be organized in superimposed layers, endlessly mixed up, with variable outcrops, retro-active relations, heavings, sinkings, collapses, a rendering into muddle from which the speech-act will emerge, will rise up on the other side (these are the three layers of the history of Germany which correspond to the trilogy, Ludwig, Karl May, Hitler, and in each film the superimposition of slides like so many layers the last of which is the end of the world, "a frozen and murdered landscape"). As if it were necessary for the world to be broken and buried for the speech-act to rise up. Something similar to what we have seen in Straub and Duras happens with Syberberg: the visual and the sound do not reconstitute a whole, but enter into an "irrational" relation according to two dissymmetrical trajectories. The audio-visual image is not a whole, it is "a *fusion* of the tear."

But one of Syberberg's originalities is to stretch out a vast space of information, like a complex, heterogeneous, anarchic space where the trivial and the cultural, the public and the private, the historic and the anecdotal, the imaginary and the real are brought close together, and sometimes on the side of speech, discourses, commentaries, familiar or ancillary testimonies, sometimes on the side of sight, of existing or no longer existing settings, engravings, plans and projects, acts of seeing with acts of clairvoyance, all of equal importance and forming a network, in kinds of relationship which are never those of causality. The modern world is that in which information replaces nature. It is what Jean-Pierre Oudart calls the "media-effect" in Syberberg.[15] And it is an essential aspect of Syberberg's work, because the disjunction, the division of the visual and the sound, will be specifically entrusted with experiencing this *complexity* of informational space. This goes beyond the psychological individual just as it makes a whole impossible: a non-totalizable complexity, "non-representable by a single individual," and which finds its representation only in the automaton. Syberberg takes the image of Hitler as enemy, not Hitler the individual, who does not exist, but neither a totality which could produce him according to relations of causality. "Hitler in us" not only indicates that we made Hitler as much as he made us, or that we all have potential fascist elements, but that Hitler exists only through pieces of information which constitute his image in ourselves.[16] It could be said that the Nazi

---

[14] Cf. a crucial passage in Syberberg, *Parsifal*, Cahiers du cinéma/Gallimard, pp. 46–7.

[15] Jean-Pierre Oudart, *Cahiers du cinéma*, no. 294, novembre 1978, pp. 7–9. Syberberg has frequently emphasized his conception of 'documents' and the necessity of constituting a universal video school (*Syberberg*, p. 34); he suggests that the originality of cinema is defined in relation to information, rather than in relation to nature (Parsifal, p. 160). Sylvie Trosa and Alain Ménil have both underlined the non-hierarchic and non-causal character of the information system according to Syberberg (*Cinématographe*, no. 40, octobre 1978, p. 74, and no. 78, mai 1982, p. 20).

[16] Cf. in this connection Daney's commentaries, *La rampe*, pp. 110–11.

regime, the war, the concentration camps, were not images, and that Syberberg's position is not without ambiguity. But Syberberg's powerful idea is that *no information, whatever it might be, is sufficient to defeat Hitler.*[17] All the documents could be shown, all the testimonies could be heard, but in vain: what makes information all-powerful (the newspapers, and then the radio, and then the television), is its very nullity, its radical ineffectiveness. Information plays on its ineffectiveness in order to establish its power, its very power is to be ineffective, and thereby all the more dangerous. This is why it is necessary to go beyond information in order to defeat Hitler or turn the image over. Now, going beyond information is achieved on two sides at once, towards two questions: *what is the source and what is the addressee?* These are also the two questions of the Godardian pedagogy. Informatics replies to neither question, because the source of information is not a piece of information any more than is the person informed. If there is no debasement of information, it is because information itself is a debasement. It is thus necessary to go beyond all the pieces of spoken information; to extract from them a pure speech-act, creative story-telling which is as it were the obverse side of the dominant myths, of current words and their supporters; an act capable of creating the myth instead of drawing profit or business from it.[18] It is also necessary to go beyond all the visual layers; to set up a pure informed person capable of emerging from the debris, of surviving the end of the world, hence capable of receiving into his visible body the pure act of speech. In *Parsifal* the first aspect is taken up in the huge head of Wagner, which gives the speech-act as song its creative function, the power of a myth of which Ludwig, Karl May and Hitler are only the derisory, or perverse, putting to use, the debasement. The other aspect is taken up in Parsifal, who moves through all the visual spaces, themselves emerged from the great head, and who leaves the last end of world space divided in two, when the head itself divides, and the girl Parsifal does not utter, but receives into her whole being the redemptive voice.[19] The irrational cycle of the visual and the sound is related by Syberberg to information and its overcoming. Redemption, art beyond knowledge, is also creation beyond information. Redemption arrives too late (the point shared by Syberberg and Visconti); it appears when information has already gained control of speech-acts, and when Hitler has already captured the German myth or irrational.[20] But the too-late is not only negative; it is the sign of the time-image in the place where time makes visible the

[17] This is a constant theme of Syberberg's in his great text on irrationalism. 'L'art qui sauve de la misère allemande' in *Change*, no. 37. If there is none the less an ambiguity in Syberberg in relation to Hitler, it is Jean-Claude Biette who has most aptly expressed it: in 'the quantity of pieces of information' chosen, Syberberg emphasizes 'persecution against dead persons to the detriment of persecution against living ones', 'ostracism against Mahler' rather than 'ostracism against Schoenberg' (*Cahiers du cinéma*, no. 305, novembre 1979, p. 47).

[18] On myth as irrational story-telling function, and as constitutive relation with a people: 'L'art qui sauve...' What Syberberg reproaches Hitler for is having stolen the German irrational.

[19] Michel Chion analyses the paradox of the playback as it functions in *Parsifal*: synchronization no longer has the object of *making believe*, because the miming body 'apparently remains foreign to the voice it gives itself', whether because it is a girl's face over a man's voice, or because there are two people laying claim to it. The dissociation between the voice heard and the body seen is thus not overcome, but on the contrary strengthened, accentuated. So what is the purpose of synchronization? asks Michel Chion. It becomes part of the creative function of myth. It makes the visible body, not now something imitating the utterance of the voice but something constituting an absolute *receiver* or addressee. 'Through it the image says to the sound: stop floating everywhere and come and live in me; the body opens to welcome the voice'. Cf. 'L'aveu', *Cahiers du cinéma*, no. 338, juillet 1982.

[20] The question of redemption runs through Syberberg's book on *Parsifal*, on two axes: the source and the addressee (the great head of Wagner and the Parsifal couple), the visual and sound (the 'cephalic landscapes' and the spiritual speech-act). But the Parsifal couple forms no more of a totality than the rest: redemption comes too late, 'the world is dead, all that is left is a frozen and murdered landscape' (interview in *Cinématographe*, no. 78, pp. 13–15).

stratigraphy of space and audible the story-telling of the speech-act. The life or the afterlife of cinema depends on its internal struggle with informatics. It is necessary to set up against the latter the question which goes beyond it, that of its source and that of its addressee, the head of Wagner as spiritual automaton, the Parsifal couple as psychic automata.[21]

2

We can now summarize the constitution of this time-image in modern cinema, and the new signs that it implies or initiates. There are many possible transformations, almost imperceptible passages, and also combinations between the movement-image and the time-image. It cannot be said that one is more important than the other, whether more beautiful or more profound. All that can be said is that the movement-image does not give us a time-image. Nevertheless, it does give us many things in connection with it. On one hand, the movement-image constitutes time in its empirical form, the course of time: a successive present in an extrinsic relation of before and after, so that the past is a former present, and the future a present to come. Inadequate reflection would lead us to conclude from this that the cinematographic image is necessarily in the present. But this ready-made idea, disastrous for any understanding of cinema, is less the fault of the movement-image than of an over-hasty reflection. For, on the other hand, the movement-image gives rise to an image *of* time which is distinguished from it by excess or default, over or under the present as empirical progression: in this case, time is no longer measured by movement, but is itself the number or measure of movement (metaphysical representation). This number in turn has two aspects, which we saw in the first volume: it is the minimum unity of time as interval of movement or the totality of time as maximum of movement in the universe. The subtle and the sublime. But, from either aspect, time is distinguished in this way from movement only as indirect representation. Time as progression derives from the movement-image or from successive shots. But time as unity or as totality depends on montage which still relates it back to movement or to the succession of shots. This is why the movement-image is fundamentally linked to an indirect representation of time, and does not give us a direct presentation of it, that is, does not give us a time-image. The only direct presentation, then, appears in music. But in modern cinema, by contrast, the time-image is no longer empirical, nor metaphysical; it is "transcendental" in the sense that Kant gives this word: time is out of joint and presents itself in the pure state.[22] The time-image does not imply the absence of movement (even though it often includes its increased scarcity) but it implies the reversal of the subordination; it is no longer time which is subordinate to movement; it is movement which subordinates itself to time. It is no longer time which derives from movement, from its norm and its corrected aberrations; it is movement as *false movement*, as aberrant movement which now depends on time. The time-image has become direct, just

---

[21] This is what Raymond Ruyer has done philosophically in *La cybernétique et l'origine de l'information*, Flammarion. Taking into account the evolution of the automaton, he asks the question of the source and the addressee of information, and constructs a notion of 'framer' which has connections with the problems of cinematographic framing.

[22] Paul Schrader has spoken of a 'transcendental style' in certain cinema-authors. But he uses this word to indicate the sudden arrival of the transcendent, as he thinks he sees it in Ozu, Dreyer, or Bresson (*Transcendental Style in Film: Ozu, Dreyer, Bresson*, extracts in *Cahiers du cinéma*, no. 286, mars 1978). It is thus not the Kantian sense, which in contrast opposes the transcendental and the metaphysical or transcendent.

as time has discovered new aspects, as movement has become aberrant in essence and not by accident, as montage has taken on a new sense, and as a so-called modern cinema has been constituted post-war. However close its relations with classical cinema, modern cinema asks the question: what are the new forces at work in the image, and the new signs invading the screen?

The first factor is the break of the sensory-motor link. For the movement-image, as soon as it referred itself back to its interval, constituted the action-image: the latter, in its widest sense, comprised received movement (perception, situation), imprint (affection, the interval itself), and executed movement (action properly speaking and reaction). The sensory-motor link was thus the unity of movement and its interval, the specification of the movement-image or the action-image *par excellence*. There is no reason to talk of a narrative cinema which would correspond to this first moment, for narration results from the sensory-motor schema, and not the other way round. But precisely what brings this cinema of action into question after the war is the very break-up of the sensory-motor schema: the rise of situations to which one can no longer react, of environments with which there are now only chance relations, of empty or disconnected any-space-whatevers replacing qualified extended space. It is here that situations no longer extend into action or reaction in accordance with the requirements of the movement-image. These are pure optical and sound situations, in which the character does not know how to respond, abandoned spaces in which he ceases to experience and to act so that he enters into flight, goes on a trip, comes and goes, vaguely indifferent to what happens to him, undecided as to what must be done. But he has gained in an ability to see what he has lost in action or reaction: he SEES so that the viewer's problem becomes "What is there to see in the image?" (and not now "What are we going to see in the next image?"). The situation no longer extends into action through the intermediary of affections. It is cut off from all its extensions, it is now important only for itself, having absorbed all its affective intensities, all its active extensions. This is no longer a sensory-motor situation, but a purely optical and sound situation, where the seer [*voyant*] has replaced the agent [*actant*]: a "description." We call this type of image opsigns and sonsigns, they appear after the war, through all the external reasons we can point to (the calling into question of action, the necessity of seeing and hearing, the proliferation of empty, disconnected, abandoned spaces) but also through the internal push of a cinema being reborn, re-creating its conditions, neo-realism, new wave, new American cinema. Now, if it is true that the sensory-motor situation governed the indirect representation of time as consequence of the movement-image, the purely optical and sound situation opens onto a direct time-image. The time-image is the correlate of the opsign and the sonsign. It never appeared more clearly than in the author who anticipated modern cinema, from before the war and in the conditions of the silent film, Ozu: opsigns, empty or disconnected spaces, open on to still lifes as the pure form of time. Instead of "motor situation—indirect representation of time," we have "opsign or sonsign—direct presentation of time."

But what can purely optical and sound images link up with, since they no longer extend into action? We would like to reply: with recollection-images or dream-images. Yet, the former still come within the framework of the sensory-motor situation, whose interval they are content to fill, even though lengthening and distending it; they seize a former present in the past and thus respect the empirical progression of time, even though they introduce local regressions into it (the flashback as psychological memory). The latter, dream-images, rather affect the whole: they project the sensory-motor situation to infinity, sometimes by ensuring the constant metamorphosis of the situation, sometimes by replacing the action of characters with a movement of world. But we do not, in this way, leave behind an indirect representation, even though we come close, in certain exceptional cases, to doors of time that already belong to modern cinema (for instance, the flashback as revelation of a time which forks and frees itself in Mankiewicz, or the movement of world as the coupling of a pure description and dance in the American musical comedy). However, in these very cases, the recollection-image or the dream-image, the mnemosign or the onirosign, are gone beyond: for these images in themselves are virtual images, which are linked with the actual optical or sound image (description) but which are constantly being actualized on their own account, or the former in the latter to infinity. For the time-image to be born, on the contrary, the actual image must enter into relation with its *own* virtual image as such; from the outset pure description must divide in two, "repeat itself, take itself up again, fork, contradict itself." An image which is double-sided, mutual, both actual and virtual, must be constituted. We are no longer in the situation of a relationship between the actual image and other virtual images, recollections, or dreams, which thus become actual in turn: this is still a mode of linkage. We are in the situation of an actual image *and* its own virtual image, to the extent that there is no longer any linkage of the real with the imaginary, but *indiscernibility of the two*, a perpetual exchange. This is a progress in relation to the opsign: we saw how the crystal (the hyalosign) ensures the dividing in two of description, and brings about the exchange in the image which has become mutual, the exchange of the actual and the virtual, of the limpid and the opaque, of the seed and the surrounding.[23] By raising themselves to the indiscernibility of the real and the imaginary, the signs of the crystal go beyond all psychology of the recollection or dream, and all physics of action. What we see in the crystal is no longer the empirical progression of time as succession of presents, nor its indirect representation as interval or as whole; it is its direct presentation, its constitutive dividing in two into a present which is passing and a past which is preserved, the strict contemporaneity of the present with the past that it will be, of the past with the present that it has been. It is time itself which arises in the crystal, and which is constantly recommending its dividing in two without completing it, since the indiscernible exchange is always renewed and reproduced. The direct time-image or the transcendental form of time is what we see in the crystal; and hyalosigns, and crystalline signs, should therefore be called mirrors or seeds of time.

Thus we have the chronosigns which mark the various presentations of the direct time-image. The first concerns the *order of time*: this order is not made up of succession, nor is it the same thing as the interval or the whole of indirect representation. It is a matter of the internal relations of time, in a topological or quantic form. Thus the first chronosign has two figures: sometimes it is the coexistence of all the sheets of past, with the topological transformation of these sheets, and the overtaking of psychological memory towards a world-memory (this sign can be called sheet, aspect, or *facies*). Sometimes it is the simultaneity of points of present, these points breaking with all external succession, and carrying out quantic jumps between the presents which are doubled by the past, the future and the present itself (this sign can be called point or accent). We are no longer in an indiscernible distinction between the real and the imaginary, which would characterize the crystal image, but in undecidable alternatives

[23] More precisely, crystal-images are connected to the states of the crystal (the four states that we have distinguished), while crystalline signs or hyalosigns are connected to its properties (the three aspects of the exchange).

between sheets of past, or "inexplicable" differences between points of present, which now concern the direct time-image. What is in play is no longer the real and the imaginary, but the true and the false. And just as the real and the imaginary become indiscernible in certain very specific conditions of the image, the true and the false now become undecidable or inextricable: the impossible proceeds from the possible, and the past is not necessarily true. A new logic has to be invented, just as earlier a new psychology had to be. It seemed to us that Resnais went furthest in the direction of coexisting sheets of past, and Robbe-Grillet in that of simultaneous peaks of present: hence the paradox of *Last Year in Marienbad*, which participates in the double system. But, in any event, the time-image has arisen through direct or transcendental presentation, as a new element in post-war cinema, and Welles was master of the time-image …

There is still another type of chronosign which on this occasion constitutes *time as series*: the before and after are no longer themselves a matter of external empirical succession, but of the intrinsic quality of that which becomes in time. Becoming can in fact be defined as that which transforms an empirical sequence into a series: a burst of series. A series is a sequence of images, which tend in themselves in the direction of a limit, which orients and inspires the first sequence (the before), and gives way to another sequence organized as series which tends in turn towards another limit (the after). The before and the after are then no longer successive determinations of the course of time, but the two sides of the power, or the passage of the power to a higher power. The direct time-image here does not appear in an order of coexistences or simultaneities, but in a becoming as potentialization, as series of powers. This second type of chronosign, the genesign, has therefore also the property of bringing into question the notion of truth; for the false ceases to be a simple appearance or even a lie, in order to achieve that power of becoming which constitutes series or degrees, which crosses limits, carries out metamorphoses, and develops along its whole path an act of legend, or story-telling. Beyond the true or the false, becoming as power of the false. Genesigns present several figures in this sense. Sometimes, as in Welles, they are characters forming series as so many degrees of a "will to power" through which the world becomes a fable. Sometimes it is a character himself crossing a limit, and becoming another, in an act of story-telling which connects him to a people past or to come: we have seen the paradox by which this cinema was called "*cinéma-vérité*" at the moment that it brought every model of the true into question; and there is a double becoming superimposed for the author becomes another as much as his character does (as with Perrault who takes the character as "intercessor" or with Rouch who tends to become a black, in a quite different non-symmetrical way). It is perhaps here that the question of the author and the author's becoming, of his becoming-other, is already posed in its most acute form in Welles. Sometimes again, in the third place, characters dissolve of their own accord, and the author is effaced: there are now only attitudes of bodies, corporeal postures forming series, and a gest which connects them together as limit. It is a cinema of bodies which has broken all the more with the sensory-motor schema through action being replaced by attitude, and supposedly true linkage by the gest which produces legend or story-telling. Sometimes, finally, the series, their limits and transformations, the degrees of power, may be a matter of any kind of relation of the image: characters, states of one character, positions of the author, attitudes of bodies, as well as colours, aesthetic genres, psychological faculties, political powers, logical or metaphysical categories. Every sequence of images forms a series in that it moves in the direction of a category in which it is reflected, the passage of one category to another determining a change of power. What is said in the most simple terms about Boulez' music will also be said about Godard's cinema: having put everything in series, having brought about a generalized serialism. Everything which functions as limit between two series divided into two parts, the before and the after constituting the two sides of the limit, will also be called a category (a character, a gest, a word, a colour may be a category as easily as a genre, from the moment that they fulfill the conditions of reflection). If the organization of series generally takes place horizontally, as in *Slow Motion* with the imaginary, fear, business, music, it is possible that the limit or category in which a series is reflected itself forms another series of a higher power, henceforth superimposed on the first: as in the pictorial category in *Passion* or the musical one in *First Name Carmen*. There is in this case a vertical construction of series, which tends to return to coexistence or simultaneity, and to combine the two types of chronosigns.

The so-called classical image had to be considered on two axes. These two axes were the co-ordinates of the brain: on the one hand, the images were linked or extended according to laws of association, of continuity, resemblance, contrast, or opposition; on the other hand, associated images were internalized in a whole as concept (integration), which was in turn continually externalized in associable or extendable images (differentiation). This is why the whole remained open and changing, at the same time as a set of images was always taken from a larger set. This was the double aspect of the movement-image, defining the out-of-field: in the first place it was in touch with an exterior, in the second place it expressed a whole which changes. Movement in its extension was the immediate given, and the whole which changes, that is, time, was indirect or mediate representation. But there was a continual circulation of the two here, internalization in the whole, externalization in the image, circle or spiral which constituted for cinema, no less than for philosophy, the model of the True as totalization. This model inspired the noosigns of the classical image, and there were necessarily two kinds of noosign. In the first kind, the images were linked by rational cuts, and formed under this condition an extendable world: between two images or two sequences of images, the limit as interval is included as the end of the one *or* as the beginning of the other, as the last image of the first sequence or the first of the second. The other kind of noosign marked the integration of the sequences into a whole (self-awareness as internal representation), but also the differentiation of the whole into extended sequences (belief in the external world). And, from one to the other, the whole was constantly changing at the same time as the images were moving. Time as measure of movement thus ensured a general system of commensurability, in this double form of the interval and the whole. This was the splendor of the classical image.

The modern image initiates the reign of "incommensurables" or irrational cuts: this is to say that the cut no longer forms part of one or the other image, of one or the other sequence that it separates and divides. It is on this condition that the succession or sequence becomes a series, in the sense that we have just analysed. The interval is set free, the interstice becomes irreducible and stands on its own. The first consequence is that the images are no longer linked by rational cuts, but are relinked on to irrational cuts. We gave Godard's series as an example, but they can be found everywhere, notably in Resnais (the moment around which everything turns and repasses in *Je t'aime je t'aime*, is a typical irrational cut). By relinkage must be understood, not a second linkage which would come and add itself on, but a mode of original and specific linkage, or rather a specific connection between de-linked images. There are no longer grounds for talking about a real or possible extension capable of constituting an external world: we have ceased to believe in it, and the image is cut off from the external world. But the internalization or integration of self-awareness in a whole has no less disappeared: the relinkage takes place through parceling, whether it is a matter of the construction of series in Godard, or of the transformation of sheets in Resnais (relinked parcellings). This is why thought, as power which has not always existed, is born from an outside more distant than any external world, and, as power which does not yet exist, confronts an inside, an unthinkable or unthought, deeper than any internal world. In the second place, there is no longer any movement of internalization or externalization, integration or differentiation, but a confrontation of an outside and an inside independent of distance, this thought outside itself and this un-thought within thought. This is the unsummonable in Welles, the undecidable in Resnais, the inexplicable in the Straubs, the impossible in Marguerite Duras, the irrational in Syberberg. The brain has lost its Euclidean co-ordinates, and now emits other signs. The direct time-image effectively has as noosigns the irrational cut between non-linked (but always relinked) images, and the absolute contact between non-totalizable, asymmetrical outside and inside. We move with ease from one to the other, because the outside and the inside are the two sides of the limit as irrational cut, and because the latter, no longer forming part of any sequence, itself appears as an autonomous outside which necessarily provides itself with an inside.

The limit or interstice, the irrational cut, pass especially between the visual image and the sound image. This implies several novelties or changes. The sound must itself become image instead of being a component of the visual image; the creation of a sound framing is thus necessary, so that the cut passes between the two framings, sound and visual; hence even if the out-of-field survives in fact [*en fait*], it must lose all power by right [*de droit*] because the visual image ceases to extend beyond its own frame, in order to enter into a specific relation with the sound image which is itself framed (the interstice between the two framings replaces the out-of-field); the voice-off must also disappear, because there is no more out-of-field to inhabit, but two heautonomous images to be confronted, that of voices and that of views, each in itself, each for itself and in its frame. It is possible for the two kinds of images to touch and join up, but this is clearly not through flashback, as if a voice, more or less off, was evoking what the visual image was going to give back to us: modern cinema has killed flashback, like the voice-off and the out-of-field. It has been able to conquer the sound image only by imposing a dissociation between it and the visual image, a disjunction which must not be surmounted: irrational cut between the two. And yet there is a relation between them, a free indirect or incommensurable relation, for incommensurability denotes a new relation and not an absence. Hence the sound image frames a mass or a continuity from which the pure speech act is to be extracted, that is, an act of myth or story-telling which creates the event, which makes the event rise up into the air, and which rises itself in a spiritual ascension. And when the visual image for its part frames an any-space-whatever, an empty or disconnected space which takes on a new value, because it will bury the event under stratigraphic layers, and make it go down like an underground fire which is always covered over. The visual image will thus never show what the sound image utters. For example, in Marguerite Duras, the originary dance will never rise up again through flashback to totalize the two kinds of images. There will none the less be a relation between the two, a junction or a contact. This will be the contact independent of distance, between an outside where the speech-act rises, and an inside where the event is buried in the ground: a complementarity of the sound image, the speech-act as creative story-telling, and the visual image, stratigraphic or archaeological burying. And the irrational cut between the two, which forms the non-totalizable relation, the broken ring of their junction, the asymmetrical faces of their contact. This is a perpetual relinkage. Speech reaches its own limit which separates it from the visual; but the visual reaches its own limit which separates it from sound. So each one reaching its own limit which separates it from the other thus discovers the common limit which connects them to each other in the incommensurable relation of an irrational cut, the right side and its obverse, the outside and the inside. These new signs are lectosigns, which show the final aspect of the direct time-image, the common limit: the visual image become stratigraphic is for its part all the more readable in that the speech-act becomes an autonomous creator. Classical cinema was not short of lectosigns, but only to the extent that the speech-act was itself read in the silent film, or in the first stage of the talkie, making it possible to read the visual image, of which it was only one component. From classical to modern cinema, from the movement-image to the time-image, what changes are not only the chronosigns, but the noosigns and lectosigns, having said that it is always possible to multiply the passages from one regime to the other, just as to accentuate their irreducible differences.

3

The usefulness of theoretical books on cinema has been called into question (especially today, because the times are not right). Godard likes to recall that, when the future directors of the new wave were writing, they were not writing about cinema, they were not making a theory out of it, it was already their way of making films. However, this remark does not show a great understanding of what is called theory. For theory too is something which is made, no less than its object. For many people, philosophy is something which is not "made," but is pre-existent, ready-made in a prefabricated sky. However, philosophical theory is itself a practice, just as much as its object. It is no more abstract than its object. It is a practice of concepts, and it must be judged in the light of the other practices with which it interferes. A theory of cinema is not "about" cinema, but about the concepts that cinema gives rise to and which are themselves related to other concepts corresponding to other practices, the practice of concepts in general having no privilege over others, any more than one object has over others. It is at the level of the interference of many practices that things happen, beings, images, concepts, all the kinds of events. The theory of cinema does not bear on the cinema, but on the concepts of the cinema, which are no less practical, effective or existent than cinema itself. The great cinema authors are like the great painters or the great musicians: it is they who talk best about what they do. But, in talking, they become something else, they become philosophers or theoreticians—even Hawks who wanted no theories, even Godard when he pretends to distrust them. Cinema's concepts are not given in cinema. And yet they are cinema's concepts, not theories about cinema. So that there is always a time, midday-midnight, when we must no longer ask ourselves, "What is cinema?" but "What is philosophy?" Cinema itself is a new practice of images and signs, whose theory philosophy must produce as conceptual practice. For no technical determination, whether applied (psychoanalysis, linguistics) or reflexive, is sufficient to constitute the concepts of cinema itself.

CHAPTER 41
GIORGIO AGAMBEN

Giorgio Agamben (b. 1942) is an Italian philosopher deeply indebted in his thought and philosophical style to the major Continental thinkers of the mid-twentieth century: Heidegger, Foucault, Benjamin, Arendt, and others. He teaches in the Academy of Architecture at the Università della Svizzera Italiana. He is most famous for his work, Homo Sacer: Sovereign Power and Bare Life *(1995), and the research trajectory that has followed from it, wherein he brings notions of law, politics, and life into mutually constituting conceptual and sociopolitical relationships. The text included here is "Notes on Gesture," was originally published in French ("Notes sur la geste") in* Trafic *in 1992.*

Agamben famously begins the essay by asserting that the Western bourgeoisie "lost" its gestures in the late nineteenth century. He describes the detail with which Georges Gilles de la Tourette wrote his observations of the human gait, as well as the disorder that would eventually bear his name. Especially in his descriptions of gait, Tourette prefigured the detail possible in cinematographic depiction, Agamben suggests. By the early twentieth century, however, it is not only scientific observations of human movement such as Tourette's that cease to be made; there appear not to have been any cases of disorders such as Tourette syndrome to observe: atypical or disorderly bodily movements disappear from the record. One hypothesis, Agamben hazards—and it is the only hypothesis he mentions—is that, sometime in the late nineteenth or early twentieth centuries, everyone expressed and experienced the loss of control of their gestures. And Agamben gives us a clear account of what a world in which that had taken place would appear: the early silent cinema of the period, with its technical limitations, uniformly depicted movement in this way: jerky, sporadic, frequently interrupted, nonlinear, unmastered, uncontrolled.

Cinema, then, Agamben goes on to claim, tries to reclaim and record the loss of gestures. He argues that the age (the late nineteenth century) is obsessed with its lost gestures—and one can understand why, given that, according to Agamben, life becomes indecipherable without them. Interactions cease to take on meaning in the ways in which they used to do; in fact, they cease to be meaningful at all, at times, due to the loss of the ability to interpret bodily movements in a consistent way. Cut off from the world of bodily communication and interaction, one turns inward, and interiority trumps the outer world. In this way, psychology—the effort to explore and understand interiority—overcomes other critical approaches to human being. Agamben suggests that Nietzsche—and, specifically, Nietzsche's Thus Spoke Zarathustra*—stands at the climax of the loss of gestures in the West: both the last gasp of the gestural as well as a memorial to the loss. In an attempt to restore gestures to meaning, we see a flourishing of the gestural in art: in modern dance, in Proust and other modern writers, in art nouveau, and—importantly—in silent film. Despite their exaggerations (or, perhaps, because of them), one cannot help but think of the balletic movements of Charlie Chaplin or the broad expressiveness of the face of Buster Keaton as profound attempts to restore gesture to its place in both living and making sense of a meaningful human life.*

Agamben goes so far as to say that it is the gesture, and not the image, that is the basic element of cinema itself. He follows directly upon Deleuze's description of movement-images as images that present movement itself—not, as they are often understood, as snapshots of stilled motion. For Agamben, however, we must remove the image from the center of our understanding of film in order to see the significance of gesture there. This is not to say that cinema does not work in or contain images. But each image is, for Agamben, both the obliteration of a gesture and the presentation of the dynamic force of gesture: each image is, thus, the fragment of a gesture, a still from a lost film. He notes that a philosophical idea is really not a single thing, but a constellation, in which the phenomena in question are arranged as a gesture: the philosophical idea gestures more than it utters. Similarly, then, cinema brings images together into a constellation; cinema, that is, leads images back to gesture.

Gestures differ from images and speech, however, precisely to the extent that gestures interact with others in the world. While images and speech might express something to another, gestures implicate the other in one's own expression. It is this implication of the other that Agamben is referring to when he notes that, because it is rooted in the gesture, cinema is always ethical and political in addition to aesthetic. Gesture is, of course, neither action nor production, strictly speaking: it neither does nor makes anything. Gesture as such undermines the means/end dichotomy, privileging process, endurance, and support over accomplishment and production. Ultimately, in refusing to settle for either means or end, gesture prevents us from thinking past means directly to ends: that is to say, the gestural makes the means visible in their own right, as means, pausing their easy assumption into a discourse of ends. In so doing, gesture opens the ethical: the deliberation of means as means in light of but not understood exclusively in terms of the ends of action. In addition, in saying nothing, gesture pauses the movement of ethical judgment, as well. Gestures, essentially silent, open the ethical but do not close it.

Cinema, too, is essentially silent; according to Agamben, this has to do with its nature as gesture, and it is true whether we are considering silent or sound cinema. Even in its use of speech, cinema itself says nothing: it gestures, it opens the possibility of communication without communicating anything. In its silence, cinema is—like philosophy, Agamben adds—pure gesturality. Cinema and philosophy both are the appearance of what cannot be said. Agamben concludes the essay with the ambiguous but promising recognition that politics operates in the sphere of pure gesturality—noting a correspondence between cinema, philosophy, and politics, as well as the possibility of some union or overlap there. We might be able to see there some possible connections between the gesturalities of cinema and philosophy, and the questions and institutions of the political. But Agamben himself leaves the thought unexplored here.

NOTES ON GESTURE

Translated by Vincenzo Binetti and Cesare Casarino

1. *By the end of the nineteenth century, the Western bourgeoisie had definitely lost its gestures.*

In 1886, Gilles de la Tourette, "ancien interne des Hôpitaux de Paris et de la Salpêtrière," published with Delahaye et Lecrosnier the *Études cliniques et physiologiques sur la marche* [Clinical and physiological studies on the gait]. It was the first time that one of the most common human gestures was analyzed with strictly scientific methods. Fifty-three years earlier, when the bourgeoisie's good conscience was still intact, the plan of a general pathology of social life announced by Balzac had produced nothing more than the fifty rather disappointing pages of the *Théorie de la demarche* [Theory of bearing]. Nothing is more revealing of the distance (not only a temporal one) separating the two attempts than the description Gilles de la Tourette gives of a human step. Whereas Balzac saw only the expression of moral character, de la Tourette employed a gaze that is already a prophecy of what cinematography would later become:

> While the left leg acts as the fulcrum, the right foot is raised from the ground with a coiling motion that starts at the heel and reaches the tip of the toes, which leave the ground last; the whole leg is now brought forward and the foot touches the ground with the heel. At this very instant, the left foot—having ended its revolution and leaning only on the tip of the toes—leaves the ground; the left leg is brought forward, gets closer to and then passes the right leg, and the left foot touches the ground with the heel, while the right foot ends its own revolution.[1]

Only an eye gifted with such a vision could have perfected that footprint method of which Gilles de la Tourette was, with good reason, so proud. An approximately seven- or eight-meter-long and fifty-centimeter-wide roll of white wallpaper was nailed to the ground and then divided in half lengthwise by a pencil-drawn line. The soles of the experiment's subject were then smeared with iron sesquioxide powder, which stained them with a nice red rust color. The footprints that the patient left while walking along the dividing line allowed a perfect measurement of the gait according to various parameters (length of step, lateral swerve, angle of inclination, etc.).

If we observe the footprint reproductions published by Gilles de la Tourette, it is impossible not to think about the series of snapshots that Muybridge was producing in those same years at the University of Pennsylvania using a battery of twenty-four photographic lenses. "Man walking at normal speed," "running man with shotgun," "walking woman picking up a jug," "walking woman sending a kiss": these are the happy and visible twins of the unknown and suffering creatures that had left those traces.

[1] Gilles de la Tourette, *Études cliniques et physiologiques sur la marche* (Paris: Bureaux de progress, 1886).

The *Étude sur une affection nerveuse caractérisée par de l'incoordination motrice accompagnée d'écholalie et de coprolalie* [Study on a nervous condition characterized by lack of motor coordination accompanied by echolalia and coprolalia] was published a year before the studies on the gait came out. This book defined the clinical profile of what later would be called Gilles de la Tourette syndrome. On this occasion, the same distancing that the footprint method had enabled in the case of a most common gesture was applied to the description of an amazing proliferation of tics, spasmodic jerks, and mannerisms—a proliferation that cannot be defined in any way other than as a generalized catastrophe of the sphere of gestures. Patients can neither start nor complete the simplest of gestures. If they are able to start a movement, this is interrupted and broken up by shocks lacking any coordination and by tremors that give the impression that the whole musculature is engaged in a dance (*chorea*) that is completely independent of any ambulatory end. The equivalent of this disorder in the sphere of the gait is exemplarily described by Jean-Martin Charcot in his famous *Leçons du mardi*:

> He sets off—with his body bent forward and with his lower limbs rigidly and entirely adhering one to the other—by leaning on the tip of his toes. His feet then begin to slide on the ground somehow, and he proceeds through some sort of swift tremor.... When the patient hurls himself forward in such a way, it seems as if he might fall forward any minute; in any case, it is practically impossible for him to stop all by himself and often he needs to throw himself on an object nearby. He looks like an automaton that is being propelled by a spring: there is nothing in these rigid, jerky, and convulsive movements that resembles the nimbleness of the gait.... Finally, after several attempts, he sets off and—in conformity to the aforementioned mechanism—slides over the ground rather than walking: his legs are rigid, or, at least, they bend ever so slightly, while his steps are somehow substituted for as many abrupt tremors.[2]

What is most extraordinary is that these disorders, after having been observed in thousands of cases since 1885, practically cease to be recorded in the first years of the twentieth century, until the day when Oliver Sacks, in the winter of 1971, thought that he noticed three cases of Tourettism in the span of a few minutes while walking along the streets of New York City. One of the hypotheses that could be put forth in order to explain this disappearance is that in the meantime ataxia, tics, and dystonia had become the norm and that at some point everybody had lost control of their gestures and was walking and gesticulating frantically. This is the impression, at any rate, that one has when watching the films that Marey and Lumière began to shoot exactly in those years.

2. *In the cinema, a society that has lost its gestures tries at once to reclaim what it has lost and to record its loss.*

An age that has lost its gestures is, for this reason, obsessed by them. For human beings who have lost every sense of naturalness, each single gesture becomes a destiny. And the more gestures lose their ease under the action of invisible powers, the more life becomes indecipherable. In this phase the bourgeoisie, which just a few decades earlier was still firmly in possession of its symbols, succumbs to interiority and gives itself up to psychology.

---

[2] Jean-Martin Charcot, *Charcot, the Clinician: The Tuesday Lessons* (New York: Raven Press, 1987).

Nietzsche represents the specific moment in European culture when this polar tension between the obliteration and loss of gestures and their transfiguration into fate reaches its climax. The thought of the eternal return, in fact, is intelligible only as a gesture in which power and act, naturalness and manner, contingency and necessity become indiscernible (ultimately, in other words, only as theater). *Thus Spake Zarathustra* is the ballet of a humankind that has lost its gestures. And when the age realized this, it then began (but it was too late!) the precipitous attempt to recover the lost gestures in extremis. The dance of Isadora Duncan and Sergei Diaghilev, the novel of Proust, the great *Jugendstil* poetry from Pascoli to Rilke, and, finally and most exemplarily, the silent movie trace the magic circle in which humanity tried for the last time to evoke what was slipping through its fingers forever.

During the same years, Aby Warburg began those investigations that only the myopia of a psychologizing history of art could have defined as a "science of the image." The main focus of those investigations was, rather, the gesture intended as a crystal of historical memory, the process by which it stiffened and turned into a destiny, as well as the strenuous attempt of artists and philosophers (an attempt that, according to Warburg, was on the verge of insanity) to redeem the gesture from its destiny through a dynamic polarization. Because of the fact that this research was conducted through the medium of images, it was believed that the image was also its object. Warburg instead transformed the image into a decisively historical and dynamic element. (Likewise, the image will provide for Jung the model of the archetypes' metahistorical sphere.) In this sense, the atlas *Mnemosyne* that he left incomplete and that consists of almost a thousand photographs is not an immovable repertoire of images but rather a representation in virtual movement of Western humanity's gestures from classical Greece to Fascism (in other words, something that is closer to De Jorio than Panofsky). Inside each section, the single images should be considered more as film stills than as autonomous realities (at least in the same way in which Benjamin once compared the dialectical image to those little books, forerunners of cinematography, that gave the impression of movement when the pages were turned over rapidly).

3. *The element of cinema is gesture and not image.*

Gilles Deleuze has argued that cinema erases the fallacious psychological distinction between image as psychic reality and movement as physical reality. Cinematographic images are neither *poses éternelles* (such as the forms of the classical age) nor *coupes immobiles* of movement, but rather *coupes mobiles*, images themselves in movement, that Deleuze calls movement-images.[3]

It is necessary to extend Deleuze's argument and show how it relates to the status of the image in general within modernity. This implies, however, that the mythical rigidity of the image has been broken and that here, properly speaking, there are no images but only gestures. Every image, in fact, is animated by an antinomic polarity: on the one hand, images are the reification and obliteration of a gesture (it is the *imago* as death mask or as symbol); on the other hand, they preserve the *dynamis* intact (as in Muybridge's snapshots or in any sports photograph). The former corresponds to the recollection seized by voluntary memory, while the latter corresponds to the image flashing in the epiphany of involuntary memory. And while the former lives in magical isolation, the latter always refers beyond itself to a whole of which

[3] See Gilles Deleuze, *Cinema 1: The Movement-Image*, trans. Hugh Tomlinson and Barbara Habberjam (Minneapolis: University of Minnesota Press, 1986).

it is a part. Even the *Mona Lisa*, even *Las Meninas* could be seen not as immovable and eternal forms, but as fragments of a gesture or as stills of a lost film wherein only they would regain their true meaning. And that is so because a certain kind of *litigatio*, a paralyzing power whose spell we need to break, is continuously at work in every image; it is as if a silent invocation calling for the liberation of the image into gesture arose from the entire history of art. This is what in ancient Greece was expressed by the legends in which statues break the ties holding them and begin to move. But this is also the intention that philosophy entrusts to the idea, which is not at all an immobile archetype as common interpretations would have it, but rather a constellation in which phenomena arrange themselves in a gesture.

Cinema leads images back to the homeland of gesture. According to the beautiful definition implicit in Beckett's *Traum und Nacht*, it is the dream of a gesture. The duty of the director is to introduce into this dream the element of awakening.

4. *Because cinema has its center in the gesture and not in the image, it belongs essentially to the realm of ethics and politics (and not simply to that of aesthetics).*

What is a gesture? A remark of Varro contains a valuable indication. He inscribes the gesture into the sphere of action, but he clearly sets it apart from acting (*agere*) and from making (*facere*):

> The third stage of action is, they say, that in which they *faciunt* "make" something: in this, on account of the likeness among *agere* "to act" and *gerere* "to carry or carry on," a certain error is committed by those who think that it is only one thing. For a person can *facere* something and not *agere* it, as a poet *facit* "makes" a play and does not act it, and on the other hand the actor *agit* "acts" it and does not make it, and so a play *fit* "is made" by the poet, not acted, and *agitur* "is acted" by the actor, not made. On the other hand, the general [*imperator*], in that he is said to *gerere* "carry on" affairs, in this neither *facit* "makes" nor *agit* "acts," but *gerit* "carries on," that is, supports, a meaning transferred from those who *gerunt* "carry" burdens, because they support them. (VI VIII 77)[4]

What characterizes gesture is that in it nothing is being produced or acted, but rather something is being endured and supported. The gesture, in other words, opens the sphere of *ethos* as the more proper sphere of that which is human. But in what way is an action endured and supported? In what way does a *res* become a *res gesta*, that is, in what way does a simple fact become an event? The Varronian distinction between *facere* and *agere* is derived, in the end, from Aristotle. In a famous passage of the *Nicomachean Ethics*, he opposes the two terms as follows: "For production [*poiesis*] has an end other than itself, but action [*praxis*] does not: good action is itself an end" (VI 1140b).[5] What is new in Varro is the identification of a third type of action alongside the other two: if producing is a means in view of an end and praxis is an end without means, the gesture then breaks with the false alternative between ends and means that paralyzes morality and presents instead means that, *as such*, evade the orbit of mediality without becoming, for this reason, ends.

---

[4] Varro, *On the Latin Language*, trans. Roland G. Kent (Cambridge: Harvard University Press, 1977), p. 245.

[5] Aristotle, *Nicomachean Ethics*, trans. Martin Ostwald (Indianapolis: Bobbs-Merrill Educational Publishing, 1983), p. 153.

Nothing is more misleading for an understanding of gesture, therefore, than representing, on the one hand, a sphere of means as addressing a goal (for example, marching seen as a means of moving the body from point A to point B) and, on the other hand, a separate and superior sphere of gesture as a movement that has its end in itself (for example, dance seen as an aesthetic dimension). Finality without means is just as alienating as mediality that has meaning only with respect to an end. If dance is gesture, it is so, rather, because it is nothing more than the endurance and the exhibition of the media character of corporal movements. *The gesture is the exhibition of a mediality: it is the process of making a means visible as such.* It allows the emergence of the being-in-a-medium of human beings and thus it opens the ethical dimension for them. But, just as in a pornographic film, people caught in the act of performing a gesture that is simply a means addressed to the end of giving pleasure to others (or to themselves) are kept suspended in and by their own mediality—for the only reason of being shot and exhibited in their mediality—and can become the medium of a new pleasure for the audience (a pleasure that would otherwise be incomprehensible); or, just as in the case of the mime, when gestures addressed to the most familiar ends are exhibited as such and are thus kept suspended "entre le désir et l'accomplissement, la perpétration et son souvenir" [between desire and fulfillment, perpetration and its recollection]—in what Mallarmé calls a *milieu pur*, so what is relayed to human beings in gestures is not the sphere of an end in itself but rather the sphere of a pure and endless mediality.

It is only in this way that the obscure Kantian expression "purposiveness without purpose" acquires a concrete meaning. Such a finality in the realm of means is that power of the gesture that interrupts the gesture in its very being-means and only in this way can exhibit it, thereby transforming a *res* into a *res gesta*. In the same way, if we understand the "word" as the means of communication, then to show a word does not mean to have at one's disposal a higher level (a metalanguage, itself incommunicable within the first level), starting from which we could make that word an object of communication; it means, rather, to expose the word in its own mediality, in its own being a means, without any transcendence. The gesture is, in this sense, communication of a communicability. It has precisely nothing to say because what it shows is the being-in-language of human beings as pure mediality. However, because being-in-language is not something that could be said in sentences, the gesture is essentially always a gesture of not being able to figure something out in language; it is always a *gag* in the proper meaning of the term, indicating first of all something that could be put in your mouth to hinder speech, as well as in the sense of the actor's improvisation meant to compensate a loss of memory or an inability to speak. From this point derives not only the proximity between gesture and philosophy, but also the one between philosophy and cinema. Cinema's essential "silence" (which has nothing to do with the presence or absence of a sound track) is, just like the silence of philosophy, exposure of the being-in-language of human beings: pure gesturality. The Wittgensteinian definition of the mystic as the appearing of what cannot be said is literally a definition of the *gag*. And every great philosophical text is the *gag* exhibiting language itself, being-in-language itself as a gigantic loss of memory, as an incurable speech defect.

5. *Politics is the sphere of pure means, that is, of the absolute and complete gesturality of human beings.*

CHAPTER 42
JEAN-LUC NANCY

Jean-Luc Nancy (b. 1940) is a French philosopher and was a professor at the University of Strasbourg until his retirement in 2002. He is famous for his intensive (sometimes deconstructive) readings of significant philosophers in the history of Western thought (including Descartes, Kant, Hegel, Heidegger, and Lacan), his collaborations with Philippe Lacoue-Labarthe, and his innovative reconception of the notion of community (perhaps most evident in his work, The Inoperative Community [La Communauté désoeuvrée, *1983]). Nancy has made repeated contact with the world of cinema: he has had a work of his inspire the production of a film, has appeared in a small number of films himself, and has written on the nature and production of film. The text included here, "On Evidence:* Life and Nothing More, *by Abbas Kiarostami," was originally published in French in* Cinémathèque: revue semestrielle d'esthétique et d'histoire du cinéma *in 1995. It was later expanded into book form as* L'Évidence du film, Abbas Kiarostami/The Evidence of Film *(Klincksieck, 2001).*

Nancy's essay is an analysis of Abbas Kiarostami's 1992 film, Life and Nothing More, *although the ramifications for film theory seem to be broader than this relatively narrow focus might suggest. The film is set in 1990, after the devastating earthquake in Iran in that year, and serves as something of a sequel to Kiarostami's 1987 film,* Where Is the Friend's Home? *The plot of* Life and Nothing More *revolves around a filmmaker (Kiarostami) who, in the aftermath of the earthquake, searches for the child actors who starred in the 1987 film.* Life and Nothing More *is thus a semifiction: Kiarostami did in fact search for these actors after the earthquake, although many of the scenes in the film were staged reenactments, and some events transpiring in the film are outright fabrications. For its release in France, the film was given the French title,* Et la vie continue, *"And Life Goes On," and it is an analysis of this title and the ideas and sentiments it conveys which orients Nancy's overall approach to the film. He argues that the title connotes more than a simple statement about the fact that life goes on: it suggests that life must continue, and that it is good that it continues. Although the film is not indifferent to death—taking place in the aftermath of a grievous natural disaster, it depicts the catastrophic and the disastrous—but Kiarostami presents death in the film alongside the continuity of life, or, perhaps more accurately, for Nancy, presents even the catastrophic as* evidence *of life.*

The question of continuity is at the heart of Nancy's analysis of the film, and of what the film has to say about life. Ultimately, Nancy argues that, for Kiarostami, life itself is a perseverance of being—a sort of continuousness or continuation. Being goes on, or as he puts it, "it is that it continues." Even in the discontinuities themselves, life continues: it "discontinues continuously." Despite the fact that each moment ends, and that various elements or events within life also come to an end, and thus seem to break with life, life perseveres: it goes on. In this, Nancy points out, life is like film, which is simultaneously continuous (by way of motion) and discontinuous (by way of the gaps between the still frames), a continuous image of motion produced by a discontinuous series of still images. Not just despite its discontinuities, but by way of them, film continues: and so with life. Moving beyond the analogy, Nancy says that life continues in the continuation of cinema: the conception, recording, projection, and viewing of the film image is itself an instance of the continuation of life.

The image is not life, however, as the film image is always a deception. Nancy argues that there are two registers within which cinema operates: interrupted continuation, and passage through (or to) the image. The former is, as described above, the nature of film movement. The latter, on the other hand, is a consequence of the nature of cinematographic, if not also photographic, images: one cannot simply look at the surface of the projected image, one peers into it, through it, into the world of the film. By way of a series of still, two-dimensional images, a film produces the effect of time (the illusion of motion, and thus duration, created by the succession of images) and the effect of depth (the illusion of a third dimension, behind the screen onto which the film images are projected). With specific reference to Life and Nothing More, *Nancy notes that it is also a deception insofar as it is the fiction of a documentary: much of what the film appears to document Kiarostami has in fact created, or recreated. In addition, however, the film is a document about fiction: what it shows is not given in advance, it had to be invented. It is, in Nancy's sense of the term, evidence. Evidence, he notes, doesn't "fall into" meaning, it presents itself in the right way at the right time, at the right distance from that for which it serves as evidence. Getting the distance right is precisely what opens the continuity, allowing the relation between otherwise discontinuous elements (or moments) to take place.*

Nancy thinks that achieving the right distance is crucially important, and is something that characterizes Kiarostami's film, which manages the right distance between music and image, between image and noise, between the camera and the car which Kiarostami's character drives throughout the film, and between the film and life itself. To be just far enough away to see the continuity is, Nancy says, a matter of justice: the right distance is the just distance, the distance that does both the subject and the object justice. And justice is, first of all, a matter of taking the real into account. Thus, in Life and Nothing More *and everywhere else, to know death—to know catastrophe, and loss, and discontinuity's interruptions—is to do justice to the evidence of life. For Nancy, it is art that makes evidence visible as evidence, art that allows evidence to be seen as just. Cinema continues: it keeps going on its own, indefinitely, unveiling itself as it goes. And in this way we can see, Nancy thinks, how cinema is nothing but the linking of evidence: an art that, slowly, from film to film, produces meaning.*

Filmography

- ***Zendegi va digar hich*** [*Life and Nothing More*, French: *Et la vie continue*] (Iran, 1992). *Directed and Written by* Abbas Kiarostami. *Produced by* Ali Reza Zarrin. *Starring* Farhad Kheradmand *and* Buba Bayour.

ON EVIDENCE: *LIFE AND NOTHING MORE*, BY ABBAS KIAROSTAMI

Translated by Verena Andermatt Conley

And Life Goes On is, in its French translation ("I will come back to it"), the title of the film made in 1992 by Abbas Kiarostami.[1]

Among ordinary expressions, among current ways of speaking, that is to say, ways that have an immediately recognizable value and that can be exchanged without difficulty (that are exchanged for nothing, for their own echo and that, *therefore, are worth nothing*...), this one speaks of this constant and inevitable flow of life, which continues its course in spite of everything, in spite of mourning and catastrophe. In fact, the film tells us from the beginning, by means of a voice on the radio: "The magnitude of the disaster is enormous" (it's about the 1990 earthquake in Iran).

The expression says that it has to continue and it also says that it is good that it continues, that life is really, perhaps, also that: that it goes on. The expression says nothing about "life," its goal, its meaning, its quality; it does not say that it is the life of the species, or that of the universe that would unfold itself above that of individuals (no doubt, in the middle of the film, we will see a young couple getting married after the catastrophe, but we will not see the birth of a child); the expression does not imply an indifference to death, or to any form of completion or accomplishment. Quite the contrary, in a sense, the film is itself this accomplishment, it accomplishes, it shows that: the catastrophe, the continuity, and also something else, the image that the film both represents and designates at the same time—an image that is neither pure and simple "life" nor an imaginary. Neither a "realist" nor a "fictional" phantasm, but life *presented* or *offered* in its evidence.

(No doubt, I speak too quickly and say too much at a time. But that's how it goes with a film. It's about the simultaneity of succession: the paradox of what continues.)

The expression (or the title) says that in addition to accomplishments, in addition to discontinuous productions or revelations, in addition to, or by means of, them and in their center, or in their heart, as their very truth, there is the continuous (*le continu*), that it continues. In addition to what, at times, produces meaning or non-meaning, there is that which only moves on (*fait seulement du chemin*): that is, meaning in another way, the meaning of life as something "continuing" that is not even a direction (in the film people ceaselessly look for directions), that is not really a path, not really a journey, but a traversal without attributable borders, hence, without discontinuous markers, a traversal that only passes through (this is called an experience), a passing through (*un passer*) that only continues, a past that passes in fact (this is called mourning [*un deuil*]), a passage that continues and leads only to its own

[1] The English title of Abbas Kiarostami's film is *Life and Nothing More*. Jean-Luc Nancy plays on the French title, *Et la vie continue*, literally translated as "And Life Goes On" (Trans. note).

passing present, or else to its non present (this could be called an eternity)—and that which remains unseizable other than in passing, that which is life itself, its meaning and its salt, its truth that obeys no injunction, no destination.

And Life Goes On speaks of a perseverance of being, in being, that makes us think inevitably of Spinoza. But it is not necessary to stop at Spinoza. Rather, one must add this: this perseverance, this continuation—which is not simply a continuity—is nothing else but being itself. Being is not something; it is that something goes on. It is that it continues, neither above or below the moments, events, singularities and individuals that are discontinuous, but in a manner that is stranger yet: in discontinuity itself, and without fusing it into a *continuum*. It continues to discontinue, it discontinues continuously. Like the images of the film.

(On this point, it is of little importance that the original of the title in Persian says something slightly different: rather "*life and nothing more*," "*only life*," and therefore "I do not want (to show) anything else but life, simply life." Because this means: here, the film does nothing but continue, it shows a continuation, that of a story [before this film, there was another film, and they are looking for one of the young actors, they do not know if he survived], that of a journey [the search], that of the life of people after the earthquake, that of life in the film, and as film. It registers the continuation of several intertwined continuations, linked together or interlocking with one another.)

Cinema gathers itself here, it concentrates on its continuity and on its continuation. Quite deliberately, ostensibly and simply it gives itself to be seen as the uninterrupted movement of its shots and its cuts, not even interrupted at its beginning and end, continuing or straddling a space off, an outside of the film that is more than simply that, because it is yet another film that both precedes it and that will follow it (the latter in the form of a television broadcast that the child will watch). But the film outside the film, therefore, the film of the film, or the image of cinema itself is not projected into an imaginary consistency, it is not entrusted to an uncertain recalling; its continuation is assured only by the way in which the film interrupts itself at the beginning and at the end.

Before, after the film, there is life, to be sure. But life continues in the continuation of cinema, in the image and in its movement. It does not continue like an imaginary projection, as a substitute for a lack of life: on the contrary, the image is the continuation without which life would not live.

The image, here, is not a copy, a reflection, or a projection. It does not participate in the secondary, weakened, doubtful and dangerous reality that a heavy tradition bestows on it. It is not even that by means of which life would continue: it is in a much deeper way (but this depth is the very surface of the image) this, that life continues with the image, that is, that it stands on its own beyond itself, going forward, ahead, ahead of itself as ahead of that which, at the same time, invincibly, continuously, and evidently calls and resists it.

At the center of the film, there is an image, an image of an image and of the only image in the strict sense of the term (there is yet another, barely glimpsed: the photo of the young actor they look for, on the poster of the film in which he was acting): a kind of old, poor-quality color print affixed to the wall of a partially destroyed house. A crack in the wall crosses the image, tears it without undoing it. It's a traditional portrait of a man with a pipe, sitting near a table on which there is a glass and a pitcher. I don't know exactly what this image represents for an Iranian memory, and I do not try to find out (I want to remain this foreign spectator who I am, and whom the film, without explicating this image to me, lets me be). The filmmaker looks at this image. The filmmaker is the main character of the film (if one may say so: he is the gaze that moves through the film, the gaze that constitutes the film in the double sense of being its subject and object). There is, in the film, no commentary on this image in the film, which becomes, nonetheless, a kind of emblem for the entire film. The absence of commentary is filled only by the gaze of the filmmaker (actor) who looks at this image. The comment is simply: how does one pick up again the thread of images cut by the catastrophe.

And it is in relation to the image, and, more specifically, this time, to television, that the title of the film is enunciated inside the film itself, and rather late in the unfolding (*déroulement*) (around the 75th of 91 minutes). A few days, then, after the 1990 earthquake, a man installs a television antenna so that a group of refugees can watch the World Soccer Cup on television in their tents. The filmmaker (character) asks him: "*Do you find it appropriate to watch television these days?*" The man answers: "*Truthfully, I myself am in mourning. I lost my sister and three cousins. But what can we do? The Cup takes place every four years. Can't miss it. Life goes on.*" The Soccer Cup is for him, for them, pure image: television screens, as well as soccer imagery for all those who kick around bad balls on terrains of fortune, while dreaming vaguely of distant fame, of the kind achieved by Maradona. Kiarostami does not undertake to rehabilitate all this imagery that has been so much decried. He does not submit to it either (in fact, he will not show one single image of the Cup). But he does not decry it either with the chagrined and haughty minds of those who have nothing better to do than to denounce the "spectacle" *as if there were such a thing as a pure truth lodged in an "authentic" interiority*. He shows that life continues first of all in an exteriority, turned toward the outside of the world, turned toward those screens that do not function primarily as lures, but rather like eyes open onto the outside. The antenna searches the sky, searches for the air waves carrying these images that make people talk, bet, vibrate (children bet during the film on the outcome of the Cup), these images that are woven into social relations as much, if not more, than dreams (we learn that on the evening of the catastrophe many people had gone to the house of parents or friends to watch television, and that some have died there, while others have been saved; in that country, in order to watch television or a film, people often have to go elsewhere).

The entire film is thus inscribed in an avoidance of interiority. We do not know the thoughts of the filmmaker who is looking for his young actors who may have perished. We do not know anything about the meaning of his gaze (that could be mistaken for being too wise, too "interiorized," precisely, if it were *signified* by some discourse: but it never is, never). Interiority is avoided, it is voided: the locus of the gaze is not a subjectivity, it is the locus of the camera as *camera obscura* which is not, this time, an apparatus of reproduction, but a locus without a real *inside* (the tollbooth at the beginning and, then, the inside of the car, with the framing through its windows or windshield—or the inverse, the same car shot from the outside, be it from close up or far away). The image, then, is not the projection of a subject, it's neither its "representation," nor its "phantasm": but it is this outside of the world where the gaze loses itself in order to find itself as *gaze* (*regard*), that is, first and foremost as *respect* (*égard*) for what is there, for what takes place and continues to take place.

For once, sight is not the capturing of a subject; to the contrary, it is its deliverance, its sending forth ahead of itself (*envoi devant soi*), at times in extreme close up, thrown against large blocks of stone or rubble, heaps of ruins, the sides of trucks; at other times, in extreme long shot, thrown toward hazardous encampments, rocky hills; and always, toward the presence of the road, its unfolding ribbon, interrupted by faults, its unsteady shoulders, its bends and climbs the passage of which is in no way assured.

Here, cinema plays simultaneously, inextricably on two registers (but perhaps there is no cinema worthy of its name that does not play on these two registers):

- The first, is a register of interrupted continuation, of movement (after all, that is what *cinema* means: continuous movement, not representation animated with mobility, but mobility as essence of presence and presence as a coming, coming and passage), of displacement, of continuation, of perseverance, of the more or less errant and uncertain pursuit (the *automobile* as the central object and subject of the film, its character and its obscure box, its reference and its motor, the automobile gives back its full value to "automobile": it moves by itself, it moves ahead, outside of itself, it carries what presents itself, toilet seat or stove, occasional passengers, it links all these pedestrians who are walking along difficult and cut off roads, automobile pedestrians to whom a singular air of dignity has been restituted that makes of them *walking* more than *talking beings*). It's a register of permanent clearing: incessantly, one has to find, one has to reopen the road, one has to go back and stop, one has to pass alongside, climb, gather speed; one has to ask for directions but since the roads have been cut off, this does not make much sense: one has to evaluate distances that have been modified or lost: neighboring villages have been separated by faults. And there will be no end to this. The automobile carries around the screen or the lens, the screen-lens of its windshield, always further, and this screen is precisely not a screen—neither obstacle, nor wall of projection—but a *text* (*écrit*), a sinuous, steep and dusty trace.
- The other register is that of the passage through the image, or to the image: cinema itself, television, the soccer game on television, the image hanging on the wall, the gaze in general: not the gaze as point of view (no or little "point of view"; the image is always closer or further away than anything that could fix a "point of view"—and it is therefore not possible for the spectator of the film to identify with a certain point of view: it is a true model of what Brecht called *distanciation*, and that names nothing but the essence of the spectacle insofar as the spectacle is nothing "spectacular"), only the gaze as carrying forward, a forgetting of the self, or rather: (de-)monstration that there will never have been a *self* (*soi*) fixed in a position of spectator, because a subject is never but the acute and tenuous point of a forward movement (*avancée*) that precedes itself indefinitely. The subject has no *project*, it does not lead what is called a *quest* (there is no Grail here, not because there would be nothing to hope for, but because hope is something else than a draft drawn on a future that can be expected, hence imagined: to the contrary, hope is confidence in the image as that which precedes, always). That's why, besides, this "subject" is not really named. There is no subject as support of an intention, there is only tension and extreme attention of somebody—of numerous bodies (*nombreux quelques-uns*)—in the continuation of this: that it continues.

This continuation has nothing mechanical or haggard. Neither is it the brute and immanent force of the species that survives. It's everyone—*every one*—who goes to the end of the one.

Certainly, the image is not life. It is even, if necessary, shamelessly deceptive: we learn that for the film shot before the earthquake, they had used special effects. They have given one actor a false hump, another a false house. In a similar vein, the young couple who gets married the day after the catastrophe perhaps does so in an illusion, similar to that of the brilliant colors of their house, and the flowers and sheets that we see inside the house. And television remains television.

Just as the film remains a film, and never lets us forget it—precisely by means of its contrasts and its insistence on the framing—always the car, its windows, its doors and the sides of the road, always on the verge of being out of focus; but also and just as well the patient arrangement of everything, the scenes that are too sharp, too precise to have been taken from real-life situations: it all looks like reporting, but everything underscores (*indique à l'évidence*) that it is the fiction of a documentary (in fact, Kiarostami shot the film several months after the earthquake), and that it is rather a document about "fiction": not in the sense of imagining the unreal, but in the very specific and precise sense of the technique, of the *art* of constructing images. For the image by means of which, each time, each opens a world and precedes himself in it (*s'y précède*) is not pregiven (*donnée toute faite*) (as are those of dreams, phantasms or bad films): it is to be invented, cut and edited. Thus it is *evidence*, insofar as, if one day I happen to look at my street on which I walk up and down ten times a day, I construct for an instant a new *evidence* of my street.

The film is the continuous and intertwined movement of these two registers that run parallel to each other and that overlap at the same time. It is their simultaneous continuation and the continuation of each in the other: the road, the automobile, the image, the gaze; the search that moves forward, the image that presents itself; the uninterrupted movement, the rhythm of vision, the vast, permanent expanse of the countryside and its people, the interruption of lives and of contacts. The film registers the earthquake: precisely not in its terrifying imaginary—which could be only one of two things: either a reconstitution of a catastrophe-film (phantasm), or a camera really present and toppling over in the general ruin and tearing of all the images as well as of life. But the earthquake is present here as a limit of images, as the absolute real which is also the cut in the dark whence the film accedes to its first image, a cut (*coupe*) that is prolonged a little later by the crossing of a tunnel during which the credits appear: the film emerges slowly, little by little, it finds, or finds again, the possibility of the image that, at first, when it emerges from the tunnel, will consist of close ups of ruins, trucks, abandoned objects, mechanical shovels, dust, large rocks that had fallen onto the street. It is at the same time a question of getting out of the catastrophe, of finding the road leading to the villages that have been razed, and of getting out of the dark to find the image and its right distance.

Before the credits, during the first ten minutes, there will have been experimentation, and reference to what would not be the earthquake: the solidity of cement constructions opposed to those in terracotta that were wiped out; or emigration, evoked by means of a grasshopper; the little boy will have wanted to stop to relieve himself, and he just missed provoking an accident by putting the grasshopper in front of his father's eyes. The path of the image has not been set forward yet, even though the car is already posed as the frame of the image: the little boy pissing in the distance is shot from the inside of the car.

"To piss" will also be, in the film, a motif of life that goes on, of its evidence. The father in turn will also stop to piss, and nearby, he will find in a hammock a baby whose mother is off gathering wood. Later, they meet a man carrying a stone for a toilet (for what we call "a Turkish toilet"), they will take the man aboard and will put the stone on the roof rack. There will be a shot of the man's hand reaching through the window to hold on to the stone at each turn in the road. The father will say: "*You bought this on such a day?*" and the other will answer: "*The dead are dead. The living need this precious stone.*" (High angle shot of the roof of the car moving along with its toilet.)

The image is not given, it has to be approached: evidence is not what falls in any way whatever *into meaning* (*sous le sens*), as they say. Evidence is what presents itself at the right distance, or else, that in front of which one finds the right distance, the proximity that lets the relation take place, and that opens to continuity.

Similarly, we have to wait for the right moment for music to become possible: more than half an hour goes by before we hear Vivaldi's *Concerto for Two Horns*, while a high angle shot of the plain, accompanied by the father's gaze, shows in the distance people busy with a funeral. Until then, there had been only the heavy noises of cars, trucks, machinery and helicopters. These noises will persist until the end, together with that, more and more isolated and fragile, of the car that has difficulty in climbing the mountain roads ("*With this car you will not make it. There are dangerous turns.*"). But we will also hear an Iranian flute, while seeing images of a house painted bright blue, with flowers (color too emerges little by little, by discreet touches, a few flowers, a rug, the poor-quality color print on the wall, a red, yellow and blue ceramic rooster that the child finds, and these touches will be rare, isolated among the dominant spreads of ochre, brown, gray, sable, the pale blue and green). And the concerto will start up again, it will attempt to start up twice: the slow, suppressed movement eventually gives way to a slamming of car doors, before the final allegro accompanies the last climb of the car that loses itself among the steep heights. The final rejoicing of the music is not, however, a resolution of tension: the music remains at the same time at a distance from the image, and from the noise of the motor, just as the camera stays at a distance from the car that moves away, and that the film remains at a distance from life which it continues and which continues ahead of it.

The right distance of the image is not a matter of medium distance: the extreme close-up suits it just as well as the extreme long shot, or the most narrow frame (the windows of the car) just as well as the frameless shot that fills the entire screen, the immobile shots just as well as the tracking shots going at the speed of the car. The just distance (*distance juste*) is quite exactly a matter of *justice*. If life does not continue in any way whatever, in a kind of haggard, sleepwalking manner, but if it continues while exposing itself to the evidence of images, it is because it renders justice to the world, to itself.

The question of justice accompanies the entire film: if it is just that the houses of some resist while those of others do not; if it is just that one country suffers more from natural catastrophes than another; if it is just that there are catastrophes, if they are the will of God, or his punishment ("*I really do not know what crime this people has committed to be severely punished by God,*" says one man); if it is just that some have died and others not (those who went to watch the game, or others yet, the child of a family, and not his brothers or sisters). When the child asks his father if he can take a bottle of coke from an abandoned display shelf, the father answers: "*Yes, but put the money next to it.*" The coke is too warm, the child is going to pour it out, someone calls him from another car: "*Don't throw it away, give it to us for the baby.*" (We hear the baby cry.)

Justice is first of all to take the real into account. The child says to a woman whose daughter died: "*God does not like to kill his children.*" The woman: "*So, who does?*" The child: "*It is the earthquake.*" And the child goes on to tell the story of Abraham and Isaac, which is, in every tradition of the Book, the emblematic story for justice that springs forth and decides in the midst of injustice.

To say "it's the earthquake," is to speak at the level of the immediate real (*dire le réel nu*). It's to say too that, perhaps, there is no God who loves and protects his children, or else that this God has nothing to do with the real. It's to take the right distance from the belief in God. The image of life puts the imaginary at a distance.

It is not a question of rendering justice to injustice, that is to say, of submitting to it. We can build so as to reduce the effects of earthquakes. We can oppose reason to fatalistic belief.

First, we have to speak correctly: a girl says "*My father says it's the wilo of God*"; the father: "*The what of God?*", "*The wilo of God*", "*One does not say 'wilo,' but 'will'.*" But it's a question of doing justice to what interrupts meaning, to what cuts off the road, to what separates people from one another, and each one from himself. It's a question of rendering justice to life insofar as it knows death. To know death is to know that there will be an absolute point of arrest (*butée*) of which there is nothing to know. But to know *that* is to do justice to the evidence of life.

The man who had been endowed with a hump in the preceding film says: "*These men had put a hump on me to make me look older. I went along, but I did not like it. I thought it was unjust. What is this art that shows people older and uglier than they are? Art consists in showing people younger than they are.*" The father (the filmmaker) answers: "*Thanks to god you survived and you seem younger. The contrary is not art.*" The other: "*No one can appreciate youth as long as he is not old. No one can appreciate life as long as he has not seen death. If one could die and come back to life, one would live better.*"

There is no resurrection: there is only one life, and nothing but life, and that it continues and discontinues continuously. Old age is the continuation through which youth is what it is, that is, youth. Death is a suspended continuity by means of which life is what it is: a life that continues to the very end. Art makes up immediate reality, to make evidence visible—or, more precisely (because the film is not life), to make visible that *there is* (*il y a*) this evidence and this justice. Life goes all the way to the end—that's its right measure (*juste mesure*), and that's how it always keeps going beyond itself. Let's say: that's how it is an existence, and not only natural life, which would pass through catastrophes of the same name with indifference. Existence resists the indifference of life-and-death, it lives beyond mechanical "life," it is always its own mourning, and its own joy. It becomes figure, image. It does not become alienated in images, but it is presented there: the images are the evidence of its existence, the objectivity of its assertion. This thought—which, for me, is the very thought of this film—is a difficult thought, perhaps the most difficult. It's a slow thought, always under way, fraying a path so that the path itself becomes thought. It is that which frays images so that images become this thought, so that they become the evidence of this thought—and not in order to "represent" it.

Film may want to represent; it can also go in the direction of the phantasm, or of imagery; it may seek a "visionary" quality or to be formally "visual." But just as none of these orientations ever subsists in its pure and simple state (or else, it's a failure, a maniacal kind of cinema), in the same way, to be sure, there will always exist something of this dimension of evidence, which this film belabors for its own (*que ce film travaille pour elle-même*). The certainty not only of the accuracy (*justesse*) of an image (which can belong to the immobile image, to painting or photography), but of the accuracy and of the justice of a movement of approach of the image, of a movement that pertains at the same time to an uncovering, a revelation, a coming to, and keeping at, a distance: to see coming and passing by something true, not a truthful image, but the truth of life offering images to itself.

(A few more remarks: could it be that Abbas Kiarostami in a discreet homage to the culture of his people, and from the distance of a non-believer, thought of surās 98 and 99 of the Qur'ān, respectively entitled Evidence *and* The Earthquake*? The latter begins with these words: "When the earth will have experienced a violent trembling; when it will have expelled its burdens from its bosom, man will say: 'What may this mean?'—on that day, earth will tell what it knows.")*

Post-Scriptum (March 1994): I am reading in the *Cahiers du cinéma* an interview with Kiarostami who is making a new film, a sequel to *Life and Nothing More*, with a continuation of the story but also an uncovering of some of its artifices (for example, that the wedding celebrated a few days after the catastrophe was a fiction). Thus, cinema continues and Kiarostami continues to bring it to light as cinema. Cinema keeps going on its own, indefinitely, as if it were a virtually indefinite unveiling of itself: on the one hand, each new unveiling may conceal another artifice, and it conceals it by necessity; and on the other, what is to be unveiled is nothing "in itself." What would come back then to the proper of cinema, beyond narration and image, beyond editing and shooting, beyond script, actors or dialogues—all the elements that can be the concern of quasi literary, pictorial, even musical approaches—would be this singular manner of being nothing but the linking of evidence. Other arts can present evidence of a truth, of a presence, in brief, of a "thing in itself"—an evidence that, to mark the difference, I would rather call, a *patence* (thinking of truth according to Spinoza, that *se ipsam patefacit* that manifests itself *et nullo egeat signo*, and has no need for a sign). Cinema too takes up this gesture, this *presentation*. But what it adds as that which is its own, the most properly distinctive property of cinema, and, perhaps also that which can be least distinguished, the most indistinguishable property of the enormous flow of films throughout the world, is the linking, the indefinite sliding along of its presentation. Where does it slide to indefinitely? In a certain way, toward insignificance (*insignifiance*) (there where the other arts appeal to an excess of *signifiance*). Toward the insignificance of life that offers itself these images, always in movement, going toward no mystery, no revelation, only this sliding along by means of which it leads itself from one image to another (exemplary, subliminal, banal, grotesque or naive, tampered with, sketchy or overloaded). Life that invents its own cinema. What a strange story, this story of a civilization that has made this gift to itself, that has tied itself to it... An extreme giddiness, truly, a feverish intertwining of unveiling and of special effects, *as far as the eye can see* (*à perte de vue*), truly, an overload of effects and of semblance, all that is true. Cinema is marked by the heaviest and the most ambiguous of signs—myth, mass, power, money, vulgarity, circus games, exhibitionism and voyeurism. But all that is carried off in an endless movement (*défilement*) to such an extent that evidence becomes that of passage rather than some epiphany of meaning or presence. Cinema is truly the art—in any case the technique—of a world that suspends myths. Even if it has put itself in the service of myths, at the limit, it finishes by taking them away, it carries off all epiphanies of meaning and of immobile presence into the evidence of movement. A world that links by going from one film to the next, and that learns thus, very slowly, another way of producing meaning.

CHAPTER 43
ALAIN BADIOU

Alain Badiou (b. 1937) is a French philosopher, formerly of the École Normale Supérieure. He has often been associated (and sometimes worked) with postmodern thinkers such as Gilles Deleuze, Michel Foucault, and Jean-François Lyotard, but he claims himself that he is neither postmodern nor modern. His magnum opus is widely understood to be his book, Being and Event *(1988), in which he works across the lines dividing Continental and Analytic philosophies and mathematical and poetical thinking. As such, Badiou's thought is hard to classify among the Continental philosophers of film and, like Edgar Morin before him, he sits only somewhat uncomfortably among the postmodern thinkers in this section. He has written a number of essays on film over the course of his philosophical career, some of which he collected and published in the volume,* Cinema *(2010). The text included here, "The False Movements of Cinema," was originally published in French in his* Handbook of Inaesthetics *(*Petit manuel d'inesthétique*) in 1998.*

Badiou presents us with a vision of cinema that is essentially about absence and loss. He begins the essay by pointing out that film is always cut from the visible: It is never the presentation of a visible whole, but instead, some particular perspective, angle, or shot cut from the entirety of the visual field. In the cinema, for Badiou, cutting is more important than presence: Everything that we can see on the screen is the remnant of something we cannot see, something that was intentionally cut out of the visible frame. In addition, the film is constantly moving, constantly progressing toward its end, leaving each frame behind as it moves to the next with the viewer. In a film, every shot and every frame contributes to the whole, every frame matters: As a result, the viewing of a film is a lot more about having seen some things than it is about what one is seeing in the present moment. What has been seen lingers on, which has ramifications for every aspect and every moment of the film.

We have already seen that, for Badiou, the very nature of film has to do with movement, and in describing the cinema, Badiou relies very much on his account of movement. He asserts that there are three essential movements in film: global movement, local movement, and impure movement. Global movement is something like the movement of the world, or things in the world: It is typified by the movement of objects on the screen (constituents of the film world), and, thus, is characterized by the passage of objects out of existence. Film objects visit the viewer (or the characters in the film) only briefly, only temporarily, and then they are gone. That is the nature of the passage of time in film, and in particular, this notion of global movement. Local movement, on the other hand, is the movement we might ascribe to the camera or the editor: Its typical example is the cut, but whatever is demonstrated by local movement, it has to do with subtraction. Local movement sees the image subtract itself away from itself. Finally, impure movement is the arrangement of non-cinematic art forms within the film, such that a contrast—between the arts depicted, as well as between each of those arts and cinema itself—is developed. The fact that cinema links these three movements—global, local, and impure—together is what Badiou calls the "poetics of cinema," and it is what allows the idea to visit the sensible in film, to appear in the present moment and then pass into the past of the film.

Badiou reiterates each of the three movements briefly before attempting to show how each is, in fact, a false movement. Global movement, he says, expresses that the idea is just its passage; local movement, that the idea is also other than what it is; and impure movement, that the idea installs itself in relation to thoughts or ideas associated with other arts. With these summary views in mind, Badiou goes on. Global movement is false, he argues, because there is no measure adequate to it: The passage of objects into and then out of the frame, into and out of the spectator's grasp as they watch the film, is an unwinding of which no one keeps a count. It is only by way of not measuring the process that it can take place, the viewer attending to the passage itself rather than its length. In fact, global movement is really just the opening of a space within which things can be seen to move—and in this, it is precisely not the movement itself. It is a false movement.

Local movement is false, as well. Local movement is false because it is nothing but the effect that follows from the subtraction from the visible and audible or intelligible fields that is cutting, leaving the image or speech in the film to be seen or heard and understood. Local movement, then, is not the presentation of a movement at all—but the consequence or result of the movement of cutting or editing. Thus, in a way comparable to global movement, local movement isn't showing us what it seems to be showing us. Finally, impure movement is false—and the falsest of all, Badiou says—because there is no way to move from one art to another. Although cinema may suggest the movement of a theme or mood from visual imagery to spoken language to color to music and back again, such a movement is not possible, strictly speaking. Rather, the elements of the other arts appear throughout the film simultaneously, in relationship to one another, held together in a kind of constellation, but never such that the film transitions from image to sound or music to speech, and so on. Cinema itself, then, is something like the knot that binds these three false movements together into a single thing.

From the perspective of the viewer, for Badiou, there are similarly three ways in which to come to a judgment of a film. The first of these is the indistinct judgment, which is to judge the film as either something one liked or something one did not like. In making such a judgment, one is likely to talk about the actors, the special effects, the scenes, the plot, and so on. Another kind of judgment, however, the diacritical judgment, follows the indistinct judgment directly as opposition and contrast: the diacritical judgment claims that the film is trying to say or accomplish one task, principle, thought, etc. or another. In making a diacritical judgment, one talks about the author of the film exclusively, and this redescribes film as (its author's) style. Whereas the indistinct judgment seems to be exclusively about pleasure, the diacritical judgment is made as a way of arguing that a film should not just be enjoyed and forgotten. This judgment makes the attempt to distinguish between "quality film" and mere entertainment, but this distinction, Badiou argues, really has its origin in film criticism, not in film itself or filmmaking. The last kind of judgment we can make about a film, Badiou asserts, is the axiomatic judgment. The axiomatic judgment attempts to discern the effects of the film for thought. It is, thus, a non-normative judgment, unlike the indistinct (judging the film good or bad) and diacritical (judging a film superior or inferior) judgments.

Badiou's final point in the essay has to do with the nature of cinema as loss. Cinema summons its idea through the force of its loss, he argues, in precise contrast to painting, which presents its idea in what is given. In the end, a film is nothing but takes and editing—subtractions from the visible, and subtractions from those subtractions. More is unshot, unfilmed, cut out, or re-

edited than appears as it was initially conceived, and, thus, a film is always a reminiscence. As film is always moving (the motion *picture), something is always passing away in film. Only two possibilities exist: either something stops moving, and is passed by as the film progresses through time (which Badiou calls the "passage of an immobility"); or something remains front and center in the film precisely by maintaining itself in a movement that matches the film's development, but, in so doing, it remains unchanging in the spectator's vision of the film (which Badiou calls the "immobility of a passage"). Whatever the case, a film can only present one idea at a time, each passing into and then out of the frame. To conceive of film as a reminiscence means we always have a memory of the ideas that have passed before, and we experience film, thus, as a movement from idea to idea. Aware of film as movement and passing away, we can acknowledge that film is not about what we know, but what we* can *know—which is to say that film is about the possibilities of thought.*

Filmography

- ***Nosferatu, eine Symphonie des Grauens*** [*Nosferatu: A Symphony of Horror*] (Germany, 1922). *Directed by* F. W. Murnau. *Produced by* Enrico Dieckmann *and* Albin Grau. *Written by* Henrik Galeen. *Starring* Max Schreck, Gustav von Wagenheim, Greta Schröder, Alexander Granach, Ruth Landshoff, *and* Wolfgang Heinz.
- ***Touch of Evil*** (USA, 1958). *Directed and Written by* Orson Welles. *Produced by* Albert Zugsmith. *Starring* Charlton Heston, Janet Leigh, Orson Welles, Joseph Calleia, Akim Tamiroff, Marlene Dietrich, *and* Zsa Zsa Gabor.
- ***Film*** (USA, 1965). *Directed by* Alan Schneider. *Produced by* Evergreen. *Written by* Samuel Beckett. *Starring* Buster Keaton.
- ***Playtime*** (France, 1967). *Directed by and Starring* Jacques Tati. *Produced by* Bernard Maurice *and* René Silvera. *Written by* Jacques Tati *and* Jacques Lagrange.
- ***Morte a Venezia*** [*Death in Venice*] (Italy, 1971). *Directed and Produced by* Luchino Visconti. *Written by* Luchino Visconti *and* Nicola Badalucco. *Starring* Dirk Bogarde, Silvana Mangano, Romolo Valli, Mark Burns, *and* Björn Andrésen.
- ***Falsche Bewegung*** [*The Wrong Move/False Movement*] (West Germany, 1975). *Directed by* Wim Wenders. *Produced by* Albatros Produktion, Solaris Film, Westdeutscher Rundfunk, *and* Wim Wenders Stiftung. *Written by* Peter Handke. *Starring* Rüdiger Vogler, Hanna Schygulla, Ivan Desny, Marianne Hoppe, Peter Kern, Natassja Kinski, *and* Lisa Kreuzer.

THE FALSE MOVEMENTS OF CINEMA

Translated by Alberto Toscano

A film operates through what it withdraws from the visible. The image is first cut from the visible. Movement is held up, suspended, inverted, arrested. Cutting is more essential than presence—not only through the effect of editing, but already, from the start, both by framing and by the controlled purge of the visible. It is of absolute importance that the flowers cinema displays (as in one of Visconti's sequences) be Mallarméan flowers, that they be absent from every bouquet. I have seen them, these flowers, but the precise modality of their captivity to the cut brings forth, indivisibly, both their singularity and their ideality.

However, it is not by *seeing* these flowers that the Idea is grounded in thought, but rather by *having seen* them. Here lies the entire difference between cinema and painting. Cinema is an art of the perpetual past, in the sense that it institutes the past of the pass [*la passe*]. Cinema is visitation: The idea of what I will have seen or heard lingers on to the very extent that it passes. To organize within the visible the caress proffered by the passage of the idea, this is the operation of cinema. Each and every time, the possibility of cinema is reinvented by the operations proper to a particular artist.

In cinema, movement must therefore be thought in three different ways. First, it relates the idea to the paradoxical eternity of a passage, of a visitation. There is a street in Paris called the "Passage of the Visitation"—it could be called "Cinema Street." What is at stake here is cinema as a global movement. Second, movement is what, by means of complex operations, subtracts the image from itself. It is what makes it so that, albeit inscribed, the image is unpresented. It is in movement that the effects of the cut become incarnate. Even if, and, as we can see with Straub, especially, when it is the apparent arrest of local movement that exhibits the emptying out the visible. Or like in Murnau, when the progress of a tram organizes the segmented topology of a shady suburb. We could say that what we have here are the acts of local movement. Third and finally, movement is the impure circulation that obtains within the totality that comprises the other artistic practices. Movement installs the idea within a contrasting allusion (which is itself subtractive) to arts that are wrested from their proper destination.

It is effectively impossible to think cinema outside of something like a general space in which we could grasp its connection to the other arts. Cinema is the seventh art in a very particular sense. It does not add itself to the other six while remaining on the same level as them. Rather, it implies them—cinema is the "plus-one" of the arts. It operates on the other arts, using them as its starting point, in a movement that subtracts them from themselves.

Let us ask ourselves, for example, what Wim Wenders's *False Movement* owes to Goethe's *Wilhelm Meister*. We are dealing here with a film and a novel. We must indeed agree that the film would not exist, or would not have existed, without the novel. But what is the meaning of this condition? More precisely: Under what conditions pertaining to the cinema is this novelistic conditioning of a film possible? This is a difficult, even torturous question. It is clear that two operators are called for: that there be a story, or the shadow of a story, and that there be characters, or the allusions of characters. For example, something in Wenders's film operates a cinematic echo of the character of Mignon. However, the freedom of novelistic prose lies in not having to put bodies on display, bodies whose visible infinity evades even the finest of descriptions. Here instead, the actress offers us the body, but "actress" is a word of the theater, a word of representation. Here the film is already in the process of separating the novelistic from itself by something that we could refer to as a procedure of the theatrical sampling. It is evident that the filmic idea of Mignon is installed, in part, precisely through this extraction. The idea is placed between the theater and the novel, but also in a zone that is "neither the one nor the other." All of Wenders's art lies in being able to maintain this passage.

If I now ask what Visconti's *Death in Venice* owes to Thomas Mann's, I am suddenly transported in the direction of music. The temporality of the passage is dictated far less by Mann's prosodic rhythm than by the adagio of Mahler's *Fifth Symphony*. We need only recall the opening sequence. Let us suppose that, in this instance, the idea is the link between amorous melancholy, the genius of the place, and death. Visconti arranges (or "edits") the visitation of this idea in the space within the visible that is opened up by the melody. This takes place to the detriment of prose, since here nothing will be said, nothing textual. Movement subtracts the novelistic from language, keeping it on the moving edge between music and place. But music and place exchange their own values in turn, so that the music is annulled by pictorial allusions, while every pictorial stability is conversely dissolved into music. These transferences and dissolutions are the very thing that will have ultimately constituted the Real of the idea's passage.

We could call the link between these three acceptations of the word "movement" the "poetics of cinema." The entire effect of this poetics is to allow the Idea to visit the sensible. I insist on the fact that the Idea is not incarnated in the sensible. Cinema belies the classical thesis according to which art is the sensible form of the Idea. The visitation of the sensible by the Idea does not endow the latter with a body. The Idea is not separable—it exists only for cinema in its passage. The Idea itself is visitation.

Let us provide an example. It regards what happens in *False Movement* when a prominent character at long last reads his poem, a poem whose existence he had announced time and time again.

If we refer to the global movement, we will say that this reading is something like a section or a cut of the anarchic paths, the wanderings of the entire group. The poem is established as the idea of the poem by a margin effect, an effect of interruption. This is how the idea passes according to which every poem is an interruption of language, conceived as a mere tool for communication. The poem is an arrest of language upon itself. Save that in this instance, of course, language is cinematically nothing but the race, the pursuit, a kind of wild breathlessness.

If we refer instead to the local movement, we will observe that the bewilderment and visibility of the reader show that he is prey to his self-abolition in the text, to the anonymity that he becomes. Poem and poet reciprocally suppress one another. What remains is a sort of wonder at existing; a wonder at existing that is perhaps the true subject of this film.

Finally, if we turn to the impure movement of the arts, we see that the poetics of the film is really to be sought in the manner that the poetics supposed to underlie the poem is wrested from itself. What counts is precisely that an actor—himself an "impurification" of the novelistic aspect—reads a poem that is not a poem, so that the passage of an entirely other idea may be set up (or "edited"): the idea that, in spite of his boundless desire, this character will not, will never, be able to attach himself to the others and constitute, on the basis of this attachment, a stability within his own being. As is often the case in the first Wenders—before the angels, if I may put it this way—the wonder at existing is the solipsistic element, the one that, be it from a great distance, declares that a German cannot, in all tranquility, agree and link up with other Germans—for want of the (political) possibility that, today, one can speak of "being German" in an entirely transparent manner. Therefore, in the linkage of the three movements, the poetics of film is the passage of an idea that is not itself simple. At the cinema, as in Plato, genuine ideas are mixtures. Every attempt at univocity signals the defeat of the poetic. In our example, this reading of the poem allows the appearance or passage of the idea of a link among ideas: There is a (properly German) link between the being of the poem, the wonder at existing, and national uncertainty. This is the idea that visits the sequence in question. The linkage of the three movements is needed so that the mixed and complex nature of the idea may turn into what will have summoned us to thought. The three movements are: (1) the global movement, whereby the idea is never anything but its passage; (2) the local movement, whereby the idea is also other than what it is, other than its image; and (3) the impure movement, whereby the idea installs itself in the moving borders between deserted artistic suppositions.

Just as poetry is an arrest upon language, an effect of the coded artifice of linguistic manipulation, so the movements woven by the poetics of cinema are indeed false movements.

Global movement is false because no measure is adequate for it. The technical infrastructure governs a discrete and uniform unwinding, the entire art of which lies in never keeping count. The units of cutting, like the shots or the sequences, are ultimately composed not through a time measurement, but in accordance with a principle of proximity, recall, insistence, or rupture. The real thinking of this principle is in a topology rather than in a movement. As though filtered by the compositional space that is present as soon as filming begins, false movement, in which the idea is given only as passage, imposes itself. We could say that there is an idea because there is a compositional space, and that there is passage because this space offers or exposes itself as a global time. In *False Movement*, for instance, we can think of the sequence where the trains graze each other and grow distant as a metonymy for the entire space of composition. The movement of this sequence is the pure exposition of a site in which subjective proximity and distancing are indiscernible—this is effectively the idea of love in Wenders. The global movement is nothing but the pseudonarrative distension of this site.

The local movement is false because it is nothing but the effect that follows upon the subtraction of an image (or equally of speech) from itself. Here, too, there is no original movement, no movement in itself. What there is instead is a constrained visibility that, not being the reproduction of anything at all (let it be said in passing that cinema is the least mimetic of the arts), creates the temporal effect of a journey. On this basis, visibility may in turn be attested to "off-screen" [*hors image*], as it were, attested to by thought. I am thinking, for example, of the scene from Orson Welles's *Touch of Evil* in which the fat and crepuscular cop pays a visit to Marlene Dietrich. The local time is elicited here only because it really is Marlene Dietrich that Welles is visiting and because this idea does not at all coincide with the image, which should be that of a cop being entertained by an aging whore. The slow, almost ceremonial pace of the meeting derives from the fact that this apparent image must be traversed by thought up to the point at which, through an inversion of fictional values, we are dealing with Marlene Dietrich and Orson Welles, and not with a cop and a whore. The image is thereby wrested from itself so as to be restored to the Real of cinema. Besides, local movement is oriented here toward impure movement. The idea, that of a generation of artists coming to an end, establishes itself here at the border between film *as* film, on the one hand, and film as a configuration or art, on the other—at the border between cinema and itself or between cinema as effectiveness and cinema as a thing of the past.

Finally, the impure movement is the falsest of them all, for there really is no way of operating the movement from one art to another. The arts are closed. No painting will ever become music, no dance will ever turn into poem. All direct attempts of this sort are in vain. Nevertheless, cinema is effectively the organization of these impossible movements. Yet this is, once again, nothing but a subtraction. The allusive quotation of the other arts, which is constitutive of cinema, wrests these arts away from themselves. What remains is precisely the breached frontier where an idea will have passed, an idea whose visitation the cinema, and it alone, allows.

This is why cinema, as it exists in films, is like a knot that ties together three false movements. It is through this triplicate figure that cinema delivers the ideal impurity and admixture that seize us as pure passage.

Cinema is an impure art. Indeed, it is the "plus-one" of the arts, both parasitic and inconsistent. But its force as a contemporary art lies precisely in turning—for the duration of a passage [*passe*]—the impurity of every idea into an idea in its own right.

But does this impurity, like that of the Idea, not oblige us—if we wish simply to speak of a film—to undertake some strange detours, these same "long detours" whose necessity Plato established long ago? It is clear that film criticism is forever suspended between the chatter of empathy, on the one hand, and historical technicalities, on the other. Unless it is just a question of recounting the plot (the fatal novelistic impurity) or of singing the actors' praises (the theatrical impurity). Is it really so easy to speak about a film?

There is a first way of talking about a film that consists in saying things like "I liked it" or "It didn't grab me." This stance is indistinct, since the rule of "liking" leaves its norm hidden. With reference to what expectation is judgment passed? A crime novel can be liked or not liked. It can be good or bad. These questions do not turn that crime novel into a masterpiece of the art of literature. They simply designate the quality or tonality of the short time spent in its company. Afterward, we are overtaken by an indifferent loss of memory. Let us call this first phase of speech "the indistinct judgment." It concerns the indispensable exchange of opinions, which, like talk of the weather, is most often about what life promises or withdraws by way of pleasant or precarious moments.

There is a second way of talking about a film, which is precisely to defend it against the indistinct judgment. To show—which already requires the existence of some arguments—that the film in question cannot simply be placed in the space between pleasure and forgetting. It is not just that it's a good film—good in its genre—but that some Idea can be fixed, or at least foreseen, in its regard. One of the superficial signs of this change of register is that the author of the film is mentioned, as an author. On the contrary, indistinct judgment gives priority to mentions of the actors, of the effects, of a striking scene, or of the narrated plot. The second species of judgment aims to designate a singularity whose emblem is the author. This singularity is what resists the indistinct judgment. It tries to separate itself from what is said of the film within the general movement of opinion. This separation is also the one that isolates a spectator, who has both perceived and named the singularity, from the mass of the public. Let us call this judgment "the diacritical judgment." It argues for the consideration of film as style. Style is what stands opposed to the indistinct. Linking the style to the author, the diacritical judgment proposes that something be salvaged from cinema, that cinema not be consigned to the forgetfulness of pleasures. That some names, some figures of the cinema, be noted in time.

The diacritical judgment is really nothing other than the fragile negation of the indistinct judgment. Experience demonstrates that it salvages the films less than the proper names of the authors, the art of cinema less than some dispersed stylistic elements. I am tempted to say that the diacritical judgment stands to authors in the same relation that the indistinct judgment stands to actors: as the index of a temporary remembrance. When all is said and done, the diacritical judgment defines a sophistical or differential form of opinion. It designates or constitutes "quality" cinema. But in the long run, the history of "quality cinema" does not trace the contours of any artistic configuration. Rather, it outlines the (consistently surprising) history of film criticism. This is because, in all epochs, it is criticism that provides the reference points for diacritical judgment. But in so doing, it remains far too indistinct. Art is infinitely rarer than even the best criticism could ever suspect. This is already obvious if we read some bygone literary critics today, say Saint-Beuve. The vision of their century offered by their undeniable sense of quality and by their diacritical vigor is artistically absurd.

In actual fact, a second forgetting envelops the effects of diacritical judgment, in a duration that is certainly different from that of the forgetting provoked by indistinct judgment, but is ultimately just as peremptory. "Quality," that authors' graveyard, designates less the art of an epoch than its artistic ideology. Ideology, which is what true art has always pierced holes in.

It is therefore necessary to imagine a third way of talking about a film, neither indistinct nor diacritical. I see it as possessing two external traits.

First of all, it is indifferent to judgment. Every defensive position has been forsaken. That the film is good, that it was liked, that it should not be commensurable to the objects of indistinct judgment, that it must be set apart… all of this is tacitly presumed by the very fact that we are talking about it. In no way does it represent the sought-after goal. Is this not precisely the rule that we apply to the established artistic works of the past? Are we brazen enough to think that the fact that Aeschylus's *Oresteia* or Balzac's *Human Comedy* were "well liked" is at all significant? That "frankly, they're not bad"? In these instances, indistinct judgment becomes ridiculous. But the diacritical judgment fares no better. We are certainly not obliged to bend over backward to prove that the style of Mallarmé is superior to that of Sully Prudhomme—who in his day, incidentally, passed for a writer of the highest quality. We will therefore speak of film on the basis of an unconditional commitment, of an artistic conviction, not in order to establish its status as art, but to draw out all of its consequences. We could say that we thereby pass from the normative judgment—whether indistinct ("it's good") or diacritical ("it's superior")—to an axiomatic attitude that asks what are the effects for thought of such and such a film.

Let us then speak of axiomatic judgment.

If it is true that cinema treats the Idea in the guise of a visitation or a passage and that it does so in the element of an incurable impurity, to speak about a film axiomatically comes down to examining the consequences of the proper mode in which an Idea is treated thus by *this* particular film. Formal considerations—of cutting, shot, global or local movement, color, corporeal agents, sound, and so on—must be referred to only inasmuch as they contribute to the "touch" of the Idea and to the capture of its native impurity.

As an example, take the succession of shots in Murnau's *Nosferatu* that mark the approach to the site of the prince of the undead. Overexposure of the meadows, panicking horses, thunderous cuts, together unfold the Idea of a touch of imminence, of an anticipated visitation of the day by the night, of a no man's land between life and death. But there is also something mixed and impure in this visitation, something too manifestly poetic, a suspense that carries vision off toward waiting and disquiet, instead of allowing us to see the visitation in its definitive contours. Our thinking is not contemplative here, it is itself transported, traveling in the company of the Idea, rather than being able to take possession of it. The consequence that we draw from this is precisely that it is possible to think the thought-poem that traverses an Idea—less as a cut than as an apprehension through loss.

Speaking of a film will often mean showing how it summons us to such and such an Idea through the force of its loss, as opposed to painting, for example, which is *par excellence* the art of the Idea as meticulously and integrally given.

This contrast brings me to what I regard as the main difficulty facing any axiomatic discussion of a film. This difficulty is that of speaking about it qua *film*. When the film really does organize the visitation of an Idea—which is what we presuppose when we talk about it—it is always in a subtractive (or defective) relation to one or several among the other arts. To maintain the movement of defection, rather than the plenitude of its support, is the most delicate matter. Especially when the formalist path, which leads to supposedly "pure" filmic operations, presents us with an impasse. Let us repeat: In cinema, nothing is pure. Cinema is internally and integrally contaminated by its situation as the "plus-one" of arts.

For example, consider once again the long crossing of the canals at the beginning of Visconti's *Death in Venice*. The idea that passes here—and that the rest of the film both sutures and cancels—is that of a man who did what he had to do in his existence and who is consequently in suspense, awaiting either an end or another life. This idea is organized through the disparate convergence of a number of ingredients: There is the face of the actor Dirk Bogarde, the particular quality of opacity and interrogation carried by this face, a factor that really does belong to the art of the actor, whether we like it or not. There are the innumerable artistic echoes of the Venetian style, all of which are in fact connected to the theme of what is finished, settled, retired from history—pictorial themes already present in Guardi or Canaletto, literary themes from Rousseau to Proust. For us, in this type of visitor to the great European palaces there are echoes of the subtle uncertainty that is woven into the heroes of Henry James, for example. Finally, in Mahler's music there is also the distended and exasperated achievement, marked by an all-encompassing melancholy, that belongs to the tonal symphony and its use of timbre (here represented by the strings alone). Moreover, one can easily show how these ingredients both amplify and corrode one another in a sort of decomposition by excess that precisely serves to present the idea as both passage and impurity. But what here is, strictly speaking, the film?

After all, cinema is nothing but takes and editing. There is nothing else. What I mean is this: There is nothing else that would constitute "the film." It is therefore necessary to argue that, viewed from the vantage point of the axiomatic judgment, a film is what exposes the passage of the idea in accordance with the take and the editing. How does the idea come to its take [*prise*], how is it overtaken [*sur-prise*]? And how is it edited, assembled? But, above all, the question is the following: What singularity is revealed in the fact of being taken and edited in the disparate "plus-one" of the arts that we could not previously think or know about the idea?

In the example of Visconti's film it is clear that take and editing conspire to establish a duration. An excessive duration that is homogeneous with the empty perpetuation of Venice and the stagnation of Mahler's adagio, as well as with the performance of an immobile and inactive actor of whom only the face is, interminably, required. Consequently, in terms of the idea of a man whose being (or desire) is in a state of suspension, what this captures is that on his own, such a man is indeed immobile. The ancient resources have dried up. The new possibilities are absent. The filmic duration—composed from an assortment of several arts consigned to their shortcomings—is the visitation of a subjective immobility. This is what a man is when he is given over to the whim of an encounter. A man, as Samuel Beckett would say, "immobile in the dark," until the incalculable delight of his torturer, of his new desire, comes upon him—if indeed it does come.

Now, the fact that it is the immobile side of the idea that is brought forward here is precisely what makes for a passage. One could show that the other arts either deliver their idea as a donation (at the summit of these arts stands painting) or invent a pure time of the Idea, exploring the configurations that the influence of thinking may adopt (at the summit of these arts stands music). By means of the possibility that is proper to it—of amalgamating the other arts, through takes and montage, without presenting them—cinema can, and must, organize the passage of the immobile.

But cinema must also organize the immobility of passage. We could easily show this through the relation that some of Straub's shots entertain with the literary text, with its scansion and its progression. Alternatively, we could turn to the dialectic established at the beginning of Tati's *Playtime* between the movement of a crowd and the vacuity of what could be termed its atomic composition. That is how Tati treats space as a condition for the passage of the immobile. Speaking of a film axiomatically will always be potentially deceptive, since it will always be exposed to the risk of turning the film in question into nothing more than a chaotic rival of the primordial arts. But we can still hold on to the thread of our argument. The imperative remains that of demonstrating how a particular film lets us travel with a particular idea in such a way that we might discover what nothing else could lead us to discover: that, as Plato already thought, the impurity of the Idea is always tied to the passing of an immobility or to the immobility of a passage. Which is why we forget ideas.

Against forgetting, Plato invokes the myth of a first vision and a reminiscence. To speak of a film is always to speak of a reminiscence: What occurrence—what reminiscence—is a given idea capable of, capable of *for us*? This is the point treated by every true film, one idea at a time. Cinema treats the ties that bind together movement and rest, forgetting and reminiscence, the impure. Not so much what we know as what we *can* know. To speak of a film is less to speak of the resources of thought than of its possibilities—that is, once its resources, in the guise of the other arts, are guaranteed. To indicate what there could be, beyond what there is. Or again: How the "impurification" of the true clears the path for other purities.

That is how cinema inverts the literary imperative, which can be expressed as follows: To make it so that the purification of an impure language clears the path for unpredictable impurities. The risks involved are also opposite ones. Cinema, this great "impurifier," always risks being liked too much and thus becoming a figure of abasement. True literature, which is a rigorous purification, risks exaggeration by a proximity to the concept in which the effect of art is exhausted and prose (or the poem) is sutured to philosophy.

Samuel Beckett, who had a great love of cinema and who also wrote-directed a film (the very Platonic title of which is *Film—the* Film, that is), loved to gnaw at the edges of the peril to which all high literature exposes itself: no longer to produce unheard-of impurities, but to wallow in the apparent purity of the concept. In short, to philosophize. And therefore: to register truths, rather than producing them. Of this wandering at the edges, *Worstward Ho* remains the most accomplished witness.

- ***Espoir: Sierre de Teruel*** [*Days of Hope*] (Spain–France, 1945). *Directed by* André Malraux *and* Boris Peskine. *Produced by* Roland Tual *and* Édouard Corniglion-Molinier. *Written by* Max Aub, André Malraux, *and* Antonio del Amo. *Starring* Andrés Mejuto *and* Nicolás Rodríguez.
- ***Ghost Dance*** (UK, 1983). *Directed and Written by* Ken McMullen. *Produced by* Channel Four Films, Channel Four Television, Looseyard Productions, *and* Zweites Deutsches Fernsehen. *Starring* Leonie Mellinger, Pascale Ogier, Robbie Coltrane, Jacques Derrida, Dominique Pinon, John Annette, Stuart Brisley, *and* Barbara Coles.
- ***Shoah*** (France–UK, 1985). *Directed by* Claude Lanzmann. *Produced by the* BBC, Historia, Les Films Aleph, *and the* Ministère de la Culture de la Republique Française. *Starring* Simon Srebnik, Mordechai Podchlebnik, Motke Zaidl, Hanna Zaidl, Jan Piwonski, Richard Glazar, *and* Rudolf Vrba.
- ***D'ailleurs, Derrida*** [*Derrida's Elsewhere*] (Spain, 1999). *Directed by* Safaa Fathy. *Produced by* La Sept Art *and* Gloria Films. *Starring* Jacques Derrida.

CINEMA AND ITS GHOSTS

Interview conducted by Antoine de Baecque and Thierry Jousse
Translated by Peggy Kamuf

Interview conducted July 10, 1998 and November 6, 2000 in Paris. Transcribed and formatted by Stéphane Delorme.

When a philosopher admits to a "hypnotic fascination" with cinema, is it just chance that his thought leads him to encounter the ghosts haunting dark theaters?

—*Cahiers du cinéma*

It is not obvious that a journal such as *Cahiers du cinéma* would interview Jacques Derrida. Above all because, for a long time, Derrida seemed to be interested only in the phenomenon of writing, in its trace, in speech, in the voice. And then came several books: *Memoirs of the Blind*, around an exhibition at the Louvre, *Echographies of Television*, a conversation about that mass medium with Bernard Stiegler that affirmed a new interest in the image. And then too, a film, *Derrida's Elsewhere*, directed by Safaa Fathy, and a book *Tourner les mots*, co-written with the film's director, which finally tackled the experience of cinema. That's all we needed to go and ask some questions of a philosopher who, even though he admits he's not a cinephile, nevertheless has truly been thinking about the cinematographic apparatus, projection, and the ghosts that every normally constituted viewer feels an irresistible urge to encounter. Derrida's discourse, which resonates in the following interview, is thus that of neither a specialist nor a professor speaking from the height of commanding knowledge, but very simply that of a man who thinks and who goes back to the ontology of cinema while shedding new light on it.

Cahiers du cinéma: How did cinema enter your life?

Derrida: Very early. In Algiers, when I was ten or twelve years old, at the end of the war then right after the war. It was a vital way of getting out. I lived in a suburb of the city, El Biar. To go to the movies was an emancipation, getting away from the family. I remember well the names of all the movie houses in Algiers, I can see them still: The Vox, The Cameo, The Noon-Midnight, The Olympia… No doubt I went to the movies without being very selective. I saw everything, the French films made during the Occupation, and especially the American films that returned after 1942. I would be totally incapable of listing the titles of the films, but I remember the sort of films I saw. A *Tom Sawyer* for example, certain scenes of which came back to me recently: a cave where Tom is closed up with a little girl. A sexual emotion: I saw that a twelve-year-old boy could caress a little girl. I was about the same age. Of course a large part of one's sensual and erotic education comes from movies. You learn what a kiss is at the movies, before learning it in life. I remember that adolescent erotic thrill. I would be totally incapable of citing anything else. I have a passion for the cinema; it's a kind of hypnotic fascination, I could remain for hours and hours in a theater, even to watch mediocre things. But I have not the least memory for cinema. It's a culture that leaves no trace in me. It's virtually recorded, I've forgotten nothing, I also have notebooks where I keep reminders of the titles of films from which I don't remember a single image. I am not at all a cinephile in the classical sense of the term. Instead I'm a pathological case. During periods when I go to the movies a lot, particularly when I'm abroad in the United States where I spend my time in movie theaters, a constant repression erases the memory of these images that nonetheless fascinate me. In 1949, I arrived in Paris, for advanced preparatory school, and the rhythm continued, several shows a day sometimes, in the countless movie theaters of the Latin Quarter, especially the Champo.

Cahiers du cinéma: What is for you the first effect of film in the state of childhood? You mentioned the erotic dimension, which is certainly essential in the apprenticeship of images. But is it a relation to gestures, a relation to time, the body, space?

Derrida: If it wasn't the names of films, or the stories, or the actors that made an impression on something in me, it was surely another form of emotion that has its source in projection, in the very mechanism of projection. It is an emotion that is completely different from that of reading, which imprints a more present and active memory in me. Let's say that in the situation of a "voyeur," in the dark, I act out an incomparable liberation, a challenge to prohibitions of every sort. You are there, before the screen, invisible voyeur, permitted all possible projections, all identifications, without the least sanction and without the least work. Perhaps that's what I get from cinema: a way of freeing myself from prohibitions and especially a way of forgetting work. That's also why, no doubt, this cinematic emotion cannot, for me, take the form of knowledge, or even real memory. Because this emotion belongs to a totally different register, it must not be work, knowledge, or even memory. As for the impression cinema left in me, I would also underscore a more sociological or historical aspect: for a sedentary little kid from Algiers, cinema offered the extraordinary boon of travel. You could travel like crazy with the movies. Leaving aside American movies, which were exotic and familiar at the same time, French films spoke with a very particular voice, they bristled with recognizable scenery, they showed landscapes and interiors that were impressive for a young adolescent like me, who had never crossed the Mediterranean. So cinema was the scene of an intense learning experience at that time. Books didn't do the same thing for me. To go to the movies was immediately a guided tour. As for American film, for me who was born in 1930, it represented a sensual, free expedition that was hungry to conquer time and space. American movies arrived in Algiers in 1942, accompanied by what also made them powerful (including as a dream), music, dance, cigarettes… Cinema meant first of all "America." Cinema then followed me during my whole student life, which was difficult, anxious, tense. In this sense, it often acted on me like a drug, entertainment par excellence, uneducated escape, the right to wildness.

Cahier du cinéma: Doesn't cinema allow, more so than the other arts, for an "uncultured" relation between the spectator and the image?

Derrida: No doubt. One can say it's an art that remains popular, even if that is unfair to all those producers, directors, critics who practice it with great refinement or experimentation. It is even the only great popular art. As for me, as quite an avid spectator, I remain, I even plant myself on the side of the popular: cinema is a major art of entertainment. One really must let it have that distinction. Of the great number of films I saw as a student, while I was boarding at Louis-le-Grand, I really only remember Malraux's *L'Espoir*, at the film club at the Lycée Montaigne, so you see that's not very much by way of a "cultivated" relation to old films. Since then, my mode of life has taken me away a little from cinema, confining it to specific times when it plays the role of pure feeling of escape. When I'm in New York or California, I see countless American films, both ordinary fare and films that are talked about because I'm very easy to please. That is a time when I have the freedom and the chance to experience again the popular relation to cinema that's so indispensable for me.

Cahiers du cinéma: One can imagine that, when you are in a movie theater in New York or California, in a space unconnected to your life of academic knowledge, the screen continues to impress on you images that come straight from your childhood or adolescence…

Derrida: It's a privileged and original relation to the image that I maintain thanks to cinema. I know that there exists in me a type of emotion linked to images, which comes from far away. It does not get formulated in the manner of scholarly or philosophical culture. For me, the movies are a hidden, secret, avid, gluttonous joy—in other words, an infantile pleasure. This is what they must remain, and no doubt it is what bothers me a bit in talking to you because the space of *Cahiers* signifies a cultivated, theoretical relation to cinema.

Cahiers du cinéma: But what is interesting is that this relation to cinema, which is certainly different, often depends on the same kind of films. Traditionally, at the base of *Cahiers*, is American cinema, and not the most prestigious, but B movies, little films, Hollywood directors…

Derrida: I would say then that *Cahiers*, out of intellectual dandyism, out of cultivated nonconformism, finds agreement with a series of films to which I surrender out of more childish enjoyment. Everything is permitted at the movies, including this coming together of heterogeneous sorts of audiences and relations to the screen. Within the same person, moreover. There is for example a competition in me between at least two ways of looking at film or even at television. One comes from childhood, pure emotional pleasure; the other, which is more scholarly and strict, deciphers the signs emitted by the images in function of my more "philosophical" interests or questions.

Cahiers du cinéma: In *Echographies of Television*, you speak directly about cinema. About images more generally, specifically television, but also about cinema with regard to the film in which you had a role. You connect cinema to a particular experience, that of phantomality…

Derrida: The cinematic experience belongs thoroughly to spectrality, which I link to all that has been said about the specter in psychoanalysis—or to the very nature of the trace. The specter, which is neither living nor dead, is at the center of certain of my writings, and it's in this connection that, for me, a thinking of cinema would perhaps be possible. What's more, the links between spectrality and filmmaking occasion numerous reflections today. Cinema can stage phantomality almost head-on, to be sure, as in a tradition of fantasy film, vampire or ghost films, certain works of Hitchcock… This must be distinguished from the thoroughly spectral structure of the cinematic image. Every viewer, while watching a film, is in communication with some work of the unconscious that, by definition, can be compared with the work of haunting, according to Freud. He calls this the experience of what is "uncanny" (*unheimlich*). Psychoanalysis, psychoanalytic reading, is at home at the movies. First of all, psychoanalysis and filmmaking are really contemporaries; numerous phenomena linked to projection, to spectacle, to the perception of this spectacle, have psychoanalytic equivalents. Walter Benjamin realized this very quickly when he connected almost straightaway the two processes: film analysis and psychoanalysis. Even the seeing and perception of detail in a film are in direct relation with psychoanalytic procedure. Enlargement does not only enlarge; the detail gives access to another scene, a heterogeneous scene. Cinematic perception has no equivalent; it is alone in being able to make one understand through experience what a psychoanalytic practice is: hypnosis, fascination, identification, all these terms and procedures are common to film and to psychoanalysis, and this is the sign of a "thinking together" that seems primordial to me. What's more, a screening session or séance is only a little longer than an analytic one. You go to the movies to be analyzed, by letting all the ghosts appear and speak. You can, in an economical way (by comparison with a psychoanalytic séance), let the specters haunt you on the screen.

Cahiers du cinéma: You said that you could write about a very specific aspect of film, which is to say…

Derrida: If I were to write about film, what would interest me above all is its mode and system of *belief*. There is an altogether singular mode of *believing* in cinema: a century ago, an unprecedented experience of belief was invented. It would be fascinating to analyze the system of *credit* in all the arts: how one believes a novel, certain moments of a theatrical representation, what is inscribed in painting and, of course, which is something else altogether, what film shows and tells us. At the movies, you believe without believing, but this believing without believing remains a believing. On the screen, whether silent or not, one is dealing with apparitions that, as in Plato's cave, the spectator believes, apparitions that are sometimes idolized. Because the spectral dimension is that of neither the living nor the dead, of neither hallucination nor perception, the modality of believing that relates to it must be analyzed in an absolutely original manner. This particular phenomenology was not possible before the movie camera because this experience of believing is linked to a particular technique, that of cinema. It is historical through and through, with that supplementary aura, that particular memory that lets us project ourselves into films of the past. That is why the experience of seeing a film is so rich. It lets one see new specters appear while remembering (and then projecting them in turn onto the screen) the ghosts haunting films *already* seen.

Cahiers du cinéma: As if there were several levels of phantomality…

Derrida: Yes. And certain filmmakers try to play with these different temporalities of specters, like Ken McMullen, the director of a film, *Ghost Dance*, in which I had a role. There is elementary spectrality, which is tied to the technical definition of cinema; and within the fiction, McMullen puts on stage characters haunted by the history of revolutions, by those ghosts that rise up again from history and from texts (the Communards, Marx, etc.). Cinema thus allows one to cultivate what could be called "grafts" of spectrality; it inscribes traces of ghosts on a general framework, the projected film, which is itself a ghost. It's a captivating phenomenon and, theoretically, this is what would interest me in cinema as object of analysis. Spectral memory, cinema is a magnificent mourning, a magnified work of mourning. And it is ready to let itself be imprinted by all the memories in mourning, that is to say, by the tragic or epic moments of history. It is thus these successive periods of mourning, linked to history and to cinema, that today "put in motion" [*font marcher*] the most interesting characters. The grafted bodies of these ghosts are the very stuff of film plots. But what often comes back in these films, whether European or American, is the spectral memory of a time when there was as yet no cinema. These films are "fascinated" by the nineteenth century, for example, the legend of the West in Eastwood's Westerns, the invention of cinema in Coppola, or the Commune in Ken McMullen's film. In the same way, cinema is at work more and more frequently in the references made in books, paintings, or photographs. No art, no narrative can neglect cinema today. Nor can philosophy, moreover. Let's say that it weighs heavily with the weight of its ghosts. And these ghosts are, in very diverse and often very inventive ways, incorporated by the "competitors" of cinema.

Cahiers du cinéma: Why is cinema the most popular art form, and is it still?

Derrida: To answer this question—the great question—one must combine several types of analysis. First an "internal" analysis of the cinematic medium that would take into account the immediacy of emotions and apparitions such as they are imprinted on the screen and in the minds of spectators, in their memories, their bodies, their desires. Next an "ideological" analysis that notes how this spectral technique of apparitions was very quickly tied into a worldwide market of gazes that allowed any reel of printed film to be reproduced in thousands of copies liable to touch millions of viewers throughout the world, and to do this quasi simultaneously, collectively, since if cinema were a strictly individual or even domestic form of consumption, this wouldn't work. This conjunction is unprecedented because in a very brief time it unites the immediacy of apparitions and emotions (unlike what any other representation can propose) with a financial investment that no other art can equal. To understand cinema, one has to think the ghost together with capital, the latter being itself a spectral thing.

Cahiers du cinéma: Why does cinema "work" only thanks to the community of vision, the projection room? Why do specters appear to groups rather than to individuals?

Derrida: Let's begin by understanding this from the point of view of spectators, of perception and projection. Each viewer projects something private onto the screen, but all these personal "ghosts" combine into a collective representation. One must thus advance very cautiously with this idea of *community* of vision or of representation. Cinema, by its very definition—that of projection in a theater—calls up collectivity, communal spectacle and interpretation. But at the same time, there exists a fundamental disconnection: in the movie theater, each viewer is alone. That's the great difference from live theater, whose mode of spectacle and interior architecture thwart the solitude of the spectator. This is the profoundly political aspect of theater: the audience is one and expresses a militant, collective presence, and if the audience becomes divided, it's around some battles, conflicts, some intrusion of another into the heart of the public. This is what makes me often unhappy at the theater and happy at the movies: the power of being alone in the face of the spectacle, the disconnection that cinematic representation supposes.

Cahiers du cinéma: It's your problem with connection?

Derrida: I don't like to know that there is a viewer next to me, and I dream, at least, of finding myself alone, or almost, in a movie theater. So I wouldn't use the word "community" for the movie theater. I wouldn't use either the word "individuality," too solitary. The suitable expression is that of "singularity," which displaces, undoes the social bond, and replays it otherwise. It is for this reason that there exists in a movie theater a neutralization of the psychoanalytic sort: I am alone with myself, but delivered over to the play of all kinds of transference. And no doubt this is why I love the cinema so much, and that, even though I don't go often, in a certain way it is indispensable for me. There exists, at the root of the belief in cinema, an extraordinary conjunction between the masses—it's an art of the masses, which addresses the collectivity and receives collective representations—and the singular. This mass is dissociated, disconnected, neutralized. At the movies, I react "collectively," but I also learn to be alone: an experience of social dissociation that moreover probably owes a lot to America's mode of existence. This solitude in the face of the ghost is a major test of the cinematic experience. This experience was anticipated, dreamed of, hoped for by the other arts, literature, painting, theater, poetry, philosophy, well before the technical invention of cinema. Let's say that cinema needed to be invented to fulfill a certain desire for relation to ghosts. The dream preceded the invention.

Cahiers du cinéma: Speaking of film as imprint, what do you think of a film like Claude Lanzmann's *Shoah*?

Derrida: It is a testimony-film. But it confers on the acts of testimony a truly major role since it systematically refuses to use archival images so as to encounter the witnesses—their speech, their bodies, their gestures—in the present. It is thus also a great film of memory, which restores memory against representation and against, of course, reconstitution. The present prevents representation and, in this sense, I think that Lanzmann illustrates in the best way possible what the trace can be in film. *Shoah* is constantly seizing imprints, traces; the whole force of the film and its emotion depends on these ghostly traces without representation. The trace is the "that-took-place-there" of the film, what I call survivance. For all of these witnesses are survivors; they lived *that* and say so. Cinema is the absolute simulacrum of absolute survivance. It recounts to us what we cannot get over, it recounts death to us. By its own spectral miracle, it points out to us what ought not to leave any trace. It is thus doubly trace:

trace of the testimony itself, trace of the forgetting, trace of absolute death, trace of the without-trace, trace of the extermination. It is the rescue, by the film, of what remains without salvation, salvation for the without-salvation, the experience of pure survivance that testifies. I think that the viewer is seized hold of in the face of "that." This form that has been found for survivance is indisputable. It is certainly an illustrious illustration of the talking cinematograph.

Cahiers du cinéma: What is it in *Shoah* that seems to you specifically cinematographic?

Derrida: This presentation without representation of testimonial speech is striking because it is "film." *Shoah* would have been much less powerful and credible as a purely audible document. The presentation of the trace is not a simple presentation, a representation, or an image: it takes on a body, matches gesture with speech, recounts and inscribes itself in a landscape. The ghosts have survived, they are re-presentified, they appear in the whole of their speech, which is phenomenal and fantastic, that is, spectral (of the revenants-survivors). Before being historical, political, archival, the power of *Shoah* is thus essentially cinematographic. Because the cinematic image allows the thing itself (a witness who has spoken, one day, in some place) to be not reproduced but produced once again "itself there." This immediacy of the "itself there," but without representable presence, produced with each viewing, is the essence of cinema and of Lanzmann's film.

Cahiers du cinéma: This manner of presenting the unrepresentable, in *Shoah*, has likewise rendered suspect any reconstitution and any representation of the extermination. How do you explain that?

Derrida: What appears by disappearing in *Shoah*, this absence of direct or reconstituted images of what "it" was, of what is being spoken about, puts us into relation with the events of the Shoah, that is, the unrepresentable itself. Whereas all the films—whatever may otherwise be their strengths or their faults, which is not the question—that have represented the extermination can put us into relation only with something reproducible, reconstitutable, that is, with what the Shoah is not. This reproducibility is a terrible weakening of the intensity of memory. The Shoah must remain at once within the "it has taken place" and within the impossible that "it" has taken place and be representable.

Cahiers du cinéma: The force of *Shoah* has a lot to do with the recording of the voices. This is something to which you are very sensitive. You have, for example, recorded readings of texts, *Cinders* and *Circonfession*, where you participate entirely in your own voice.

Derrida: *Shoah* is much more than a recording of people speaking… But, to answer your question, yes, the recording of speech is one of the major phenomena of the twentieth century. It gives living presence a possibility, which has no equivalent and no precedent, of "being there" once again. The greatness of cinema, of course, is to have integrated voice recording at a certain moment of its history. This was not an addition, a supplementary element, but rather a return to the origins of cinema allowing it to be still more fully achieved. The voice, in cinema, does not add something: it is cinema because it is of the same nature as the recording of the world's movement. I don't believe at all in the idea that one must separate images—pure cinema—from speech: they are of the same essence, that of a "quasi presentation" of an "itself there" of the world whose past will be, forever, radically absent, unrepresentable in its living presence.

Cahiers du cinéma: Another specificity of cinema concerns montage. What do you think of this technique that allows one to assemble, reassemble, disassemble? In its very matter, cinema has no doubt gone furthest in the use of reflection on narrativity. Can one establish a link between the concept of "deconstruction" that you forged and the idea of montage in cinema?

Derrida: There is no real synchronization, but this comparison is important to me. Between writing of the deconstructive type that interests me and cinema, there is an essential link. It is the exploitation in writing, whether it be Plato's, Dante's, or Blanchot's, of all the possibilities of montage, that is, of plays with the rhythms, of grafts of quotations, insertions, changes in tone, changes in language, crossings between "disciplines" and the rules of art, the arts. Cinema, in this domain, has no equivalent, except perhaps music. But writing is, as it were, inspired and aspired by this "idea" of montage. Moreover, writing—or let us say discursivity—and cinema are drawn into the same technical and thus aesthetic evolution, that of the increasingly refined, rapid, accelerated possibilities offered by technological renewal (computers, Internet, synthetic images). There now exists, in a certain way, an unequaled offer or demand for deconstruction, in writing as well as in film. The thing is to know what to [do] with it. Cutting and pasting, recomposition of texts, the accelerating insertion of quotations, everything you can do with a computer, all this brings writing closer and closer to cinematic montage, and vice versa. The result is that, at a moment when "technicity" increases more and more, film is paradoxically becoming more "literary" and vice versa: it is obvious that writing, for some time now, has shared somewhat a certain cinematographic vision of the world. Deconstruction or not, a writer is always an editor [*monteur*]. Today he or she is that even more so.

Cahiers du cinéma: Do you yourself feel like a filmmaker as you write?

Derrida: I don't believe it's an exaggeration to say that, consciously, when I write a text I "project" a sort of film. That is my project and I project it. What interests me most about writing is less, as one might say, the "content" than the "form": the composition, the rhythm, the sketch of a particular narrativity. A parade of spectral powers producing certain effects that are fairly comparable to the progression of a film. It is accompanied by speech, which I elaborate as if on a separate track, however paradoxical that may seem. It is cinema, unquestionably. When and if I take pleasure in writing, that is what gives me pleasure. My pleasure is not, above all, to tell "the" truth or "the" meaning of the "truth"; it is in the mise en scène, whether that be through writing in books or through speech in teaching. And I am very envious of those filmmakers who, today, work on montage using hypersensitive machines that allow one to compose a film in an extremely precise way. That is what I am constantly looking for in writing or speech, even if, in my case, the work is more artisanal and even if it's my weakness to believe that the "effect" of meaning or the "effect" of truth still makes for the best cinema.

Cahiers du cinéma: I would like to talk about the film *Derrida's Elsewhere* by Safaa Fathy, in which you are both subject and actor. It seems to me that this experience led you to think about the functioning of the cinema machine (as concerns filming and montage) and about cinema in general.

Derrida: There were several periods in this experience, which I would be tempted to call an "apprenticeship film" the way one says an "apprenticeship novel" or "Bildungsroman." Beyond everything I was able to learn, understand, or approach indirectly, nothing equals this inflexible experience that leaves little room for the body to withdraw. I managed to understand many things about cinema in general, about the technology, the market (because there were some production problems between Arte and Gloria Films). In this sense, it was an "apprenticeship film." On the other hand, you alluded to *Tourner les mots* [the book Derrida drew from this experience of cinema, published by Éditions Galilée in 2000], where I refer to myself as the Actor. While writing this text, I played with capitalizing the words Actor and Author; it was a game, but a serious game; I had to play what was supposed to be my own character, who is himself but one character (each of us has several social characters). So, it was a matter for me of playing as Actor several of my characters, which had been chosen by the Author who made very many choices that I had to take into account. For example, the Author, Safaa Fathy, made the decision to remove me from French space; she deliberately chose to show me *elsewhere* by reconstituting some more or less fantasized genealogies—in Algeria, in Spain, in the United States. I had to learn to overcome my own inhibitions about exposing myself in front of the camera and to obey the Author's choices. In a final period, after the filming and editing (which I had nothing at all to do with), each of us separately wrote the texts that are collected in *Tourner les mots*. That allowed me to say a certain number of things that do not replace the film but that play with it.

Cahiers du cinéma: The text redistributes the film in another dimension and a different order; there is a connection inasmuch as the two concern and complete each other.

Derrida: The film and the book are at once connected to each other and radically independent. I try to show how, in a certain number of its image sequences, the film depends on some French idiom, some untranslatable idiom, as for example the word *ailleurs* ["elsewhere"]. In this text, I pose the question of the French language insofar as it determines, from within, the flow of images and insofar as it must cross the frontier, since we're talking about a film coproduced by Arte and destined immediately to be shown in non-French-speaking European countries. What was going to happen with the translation? In principle, words are translatable (although here the experience is daunting at every step), but what links images and words is not, and thus involves some stakes that are quite original. One must accept that, in its cinematic specificity, a film is linked to untranslatable idioms and that translation must take place without losing the cinematic idiom that links the word to the image.

Cahiers du cinéma: Is there not another problem that perhaps you felt, within the disjunction between seeing and speaking?

Derrida: Yes, this is one of the most interesting risks of the film. That is what the books' title stresses. "Tourner les mots" means to avoid words, to go around them, allow the cinematic to resist the authority of discourse; at the same time, it was a matter of turning words, that is, of finding sentences that were not sentences for interviews, courses, lectures, sentences already favorable for a cinematic frame; finally one has to hear "tourner," one has to understand how to "tourner" in the sense of shooting or filming words. And how to film words that become images which are inseparable from the body, not only from the body of the one who says them, but from the body, from the iconic ensemble, of what nevertheless remain words, with their sonority, tone, tempo of words? These words may sometimes be snatched up during an improvisation or else read out, because there are a few passages read by the actor or readable on a street sign. The places are never identified; they melt into each other; they share the common features of Southern California, Spain, Algeria, coastal, Mediterranean places; and the only moment when one can identify them by a proper name is something that is read silently on a street sign. It's an experience that seeks to be properly cinematic and yet does not sacrifice the discourse that obeys the law of film. It is often a question in this film of the theme of address, destination, the indetermination of the addressee. Who addresses what to whom? What counts in the image is not merely what is immediately visible, but also the words that inhabit the images, the invisibility that determines the logic of the images, that is, interruption, ellipsis, the whole zone of invisibility that presses on visibility. And the technique of interruption in this film is very savvy—in this regard, I often speak and so does Safaa Fathy of anacoluthon. This interruption of the image does not interrupt the effect of the image; it extends the force to which visibility gives momentum. The interrupted sequence either continues at another moment of the film or else it does not continue and it is up to the addressee, what is called the spectator, to orient him- or herself, to let things thread their way, to follow the stitches or not. Consequently, the body of the image qua image is shot through with invisibility. Not necessarily the sonorous invisibility of words, but another invisibility, and I believe that anacoluthon, ellipsis, interruption form perhaps what is proper to this film. What can be seen in the film has less importance no doubt than the unsaid, the invisible that is cast like a throw of the dice, relayed or not (it's up to the addressee to answer) by other texts, other films.

It's a film about mourning (the death of cats, the death of my mother), and it's a film in mourning for itself. In every work, there is such a sacrifice: nevertheless, in the writing of a text or a book, even though one must also throw out, sacrifice, exclude, the constraints are fewer, they are less external; when one writes a book, one does not have to obey, as is the case here, such a harsh, rigid commercial or mediatic law. That's why the book was a kind of breathing space.

Cahiers du cinéma: What you say about your experience of the film relates to more general concepts of cinema and television, such as the question of the specter.

Derrida: The theme of spectrality is presented as such in the film. As are mourning, sexual difference, addressing, inheritance. Spectrality came back regularly, even as an image, because one sees the specter of my mother, a phantom cat, a siamese cat who resembles the dead cat like a twin. This theme is treated both discursively and in images. And, elsewhere, in *Echographies of Television*, I had broached this question of the spectral dimension of the televisual or cinematic image, the question of virtualization. It has political stakes, which also shows up in *Specters of Marx*. All of this forms an inextricable network of motifs that are filmed the way one films cinema itself, since cinema is an example of what is in question here. In other words, it is as if spectral images came and said to you: we are spectral images (but without speculating on the academicism of authority, of the specular *self*-referentiality). How does one film a specter that says: I am a specter? Along with, naturally, the somewhat troubling or even sinister aspect of the afterlife. For one knows that an image can survive, like a text. One could see these images not only after the death of my little brother, my cat, my mother, and so on, but after my own death. And this would work in the same manner. It has to do with an effect of intrinsic virtualization that marks any technical reproducibility, as Benjamin would say. It is a film on technical reproducibility: one sees both nature in its wildest state, the ebb and flow of waves in California, Spain, or Algeria, and machines for reproducing, recording, archiving.

Cahiers du cinéma: The ghost was thought about at a certain moment in film theory but, today, this idea goes against the dominant conception of the image, namely, that there is supposedly a consistency of the visible in which one ought to believe.

Derrida: In a spontaneous ideology of the image, one often forgets two things: technicity and belief. Technicity, namely, where the image (news reporting or film) is supposed to put us face to face with the thing itself, without tricks or artifacts; people want to forget that technology can absolutely transform, recompose, artificialize the thing. And then there is the very strange phenomenon that is belief. Even in a fiction film, a phenomenon of belief, of "pretend as if," has a specificity that is very difficult to analyze: one "believes" a film more. One believes a novel less or in another way. As for music, that's something else again, it does not imply any belief. As soon as there is novelistic representation or cinematic fiction, a phenomenon of belief is carried by the representation. Spectrality is an element in which belief is neither assured nor disputed. That is why I believe one must connect the question of technicity with that of faith, in the religious and fiduciary sense, namely, the credit granted to an image. And to the phantasm. In Greek, and not only in Greek, *fantasma* designates the image and the revenant. The *fantasma* is a specter.

Cahiers du cinéma: What do you think of the filmed images of the liberation of the camps in relation to written texts?

Derrida: *Shoah* is a text of language as much as it is a corpus of images. They are "filmed words" [*mots tournés*], in a certain manner. Filmed speech is not speech captured as such on filmstock; it is speech that is interpreted, for example interrupted, restarted, repeated, put into a situation. To make a work (for the archive is also a work) accessible is to submit an interpretation to an interpretation.

Cahiers du cinéma: Was the power of the image greater than the text by Robert Antelme—*The Human Species*—which at the time did not have much impact?

Derrida: Or even now. It is a very important testimony but it did not have the power of distribution of a cinematic work. I don't want to have to choose between the two. I don't believe that one can take the place of the other. Moreover, there are many images in *The Human Species*. It is also a film-book in a certain way. *Shoah* is a text-film, a body of words, embodied speech. The time it takes to discover testimonies, the unconscious path that leads to the archives is something that deserves reflection. There is a (technical and psychic) time for the political lifting of repression. I was recently rereading (for something I would be talking about elsewhere) Sartre's *Reflections on the Jewish Question*, which was written after the war and some pages of which were written in 1944. The way he talks about the camps, very briefly, is rather strange. Did he know about them or not? After the war, there was no discussion of what happened at Auschwitz. The name Auschwitz (not to mention the name Shoah) were inaudible, unknown, or silenced. A psychoanalysis is necessary of the political field: of the impossible mourning, of repression. Benjamin is once again a necessary reference here: he linked the technical question of cinema and the question of psychoanalysis. Blowing up a detail is something both the movie camera and psychoanalysis do. By blowing up the detail one is doing something else besides enlarging it; one changes the perception of the thing itself. One accedes to another space, to a heterogeneous time. This is true for both the time of the archives and of testimony.

Cahiers du cinéma: Do you think the image is an inscription of memory or a confiscation of memory?

Derrida: Both. It is immediately an inscription, a preservation, either of the image itself at the moment it is taken, or of the memory act that the image speaks of. In the film, *Derrida's Elsewhere*, I evoke the past. There is both the moment *in which* I am speaking and the moment *of which* I am speaking. This already makes for two memories implicated in each other. But since this inscription is exposed to cutting, selection, interpretive choice, it is both a chance and a confiscation, a violent appropriation by both the Author *and* myself. When I speak about my past, whether voluntarily or not, I select, I inscribe, and I exclude. I don't believe there are archives that only preserve; this is something I try to point out in a short book, *Archive Fever*. The archive is a violent initiative taken by some authority, some power; it takes power for the future, it *pre-occupies* the future: it confiscates the past, the present, and the future. Everyone knows there is no such thing as innocent archives.

CHAPTER 45
BERNARD STIEGLER

Bernard Stiegler (b. 1952) is a French philosopher who created and presently serves as Director of the Institut de Recherche et d'Innovation du Centre Georges Pompidou. He is among the most prominent contemporary postmodern/post-structuralist/deconstructive philosophers, and is best known for his multivolume philosophical work, Technics and Time, *of which three volumes have so far been published (Stiegler appears to have in mind at least two additional volumes, as noted in the footnotes to the selection included here), and in which he argues (in part) that technical apparatuses are both an instantiation of memory and a sort of prosthetic for human beings. The text included here, "Cinematic Time," is the first chapter of* Technics *and* Time, 3: Cinematic Time and the Question of Malaise, *originally published in French* (La technique et le temps 3. Le Temps du cinéma et la question du mal-être) *by Éditions Galilée in 2001.*

Stiegler situates our love of the cinema in the context of the general human desire for stories as such. He notes that even in childhood, we exhibit a passion for fairy tales, and this passion holds out the promise of future stories to be told. In the contemporary West, the desire for narratives has been industrialized—in a manner Stiegler compares explicitly to that described by Horkheimer and Adorno in "The Culture Industry"—and he notes that the cultural industries are at the center of economic development today. This means, ultimately, that nothing today is independent of the desire for stories. The cinema has a unique place in the apparatus of contemporary storytelling, of course, given its unprecedented success at producing and disseminating stories globally, and to such profit. The extraordinary profits associated with the film industry only further demonstrate the popularity of film, which has its roots in the ease with which cinematic stories can be received by viewers: movies do not require moviegoers to work to get the story. And yet, even without any active input on the part of the viewer, a good movie can reinvigorate us, can bring us out of boredom back into the expectation that something might happen. Cinema thus both fulfills our desire for narrative while situating us, without any effort on our part, in time.

The time of our consciousness in viewing a film is totally passive, Stiegler argues, as the time we spend in movie watching is time outside of our real lives. At the same time, however, watching a film conjoins our experience of time to the time of the film, and cinema thus weaves itself into our time: even when we are aware of the passage of time in "real life," we are bound by the time of the film in sometimes startling ways. Cinematic time operates according to two fundamental principles, Stiegler suggests. First, cinematographic recording is ultimately photographic in nature, which produces the reality effect observed in photographs by Roland Barthes: when we view a photograph, we know that what we see really existed at some point in the past. Likewise, with cinematographic recording, we know that what we see on the screen did exist at some point in the past—despite the fact that we are only seeing it now, in the present. Second, film is also an instance of phonographic recording, and the recording of sound is always the recording of a fluid object. Like a melody, a film is a flux—and this flux is not unlike the fluidity of the spectator's stream of consciousness. From these two fundamental principles, then, Stiegler thinks we can derive two further coincidences: (1) the coincidence of the past and (the present) reality and (2) the coincidence of the film flow and the spectator's consciousness.

Drawing this distinction between the sorts of objects that can be photographed and those which must be filmed (or recorded phonographically), Stiegler introduces the notion of the temporal object, an object that not only exists in time but is also "woven of" time, that is, which depends essentially upon the passage of time to be observed or known. The primary example he gives is music, an example (and a notion) he borrows from Edmund Husserl. Temporal objects, like music or cinema, coincide as was noted above with consciousness itself: consciousness is also a flux.

For Stiegler, of importance in Husserl's account of temporal objects is their relationship to memory—and Husserl has a well-worked out conception of memory. Husserl makes a distinction between what he calls "primary retention" and "secondary retention" which Stiegler both relies upon and disputes, in different ways. For Husserl, primary retention is the series of past moments (prior "nows") which are retained in any given present moment of a temporal object. Taking a piece of music as our example, Husserl is saying that each moment of the melody only makes sense if the moment retains something of all the prior moments, all of the previous notes. Primary retention, then, is not memory per se, but is bound up with and grounded in perception itself: what it is to perceive the third note of a melody is to perceive the first two notes in the third, at the same time as the third. Stiegler notes here the famous "Kuleshov Effect," a cinematic phenomenon which shows that the same image of a man's face (in this case, an actor, Mozzhukhin) when preceded by differing scenes of differing emotional resonances will take on the appearance of differing affects for viewers.

For Husserl, secondary retention has to do with what happens when we recall a temporal object experienced in the past. We find that our memory of a melody heard yesterday, for example, is always reconstructed in the imagination: it is even condensed, as Stiegler notes later in the text, heavily edited by the one recalling it. That secondary retention takes place in the imagination, however, distances it absolutely from primary retention, as Stiegler understands the two: things imagined are not part of our experience, unlike things perceived. This is where Stiegler proposes the introduction of a third category, tertiary memory or tertiary retention, which is the capture and containment of a temporal object in a recording of the past—phonographic or cinematographic.

Recording technologies make it possible for me to hear the same melody—the very same performance of the very same melody—over and over again, responding to it each time anew, of course, thanks to my personal listening history, but nevertheless responding to the very same temporal object. While Husserl rejected what Stiegler calls "tertiary memory" as in any way exemplary of consciousness, Stiegler insists that the fact that we can come into relation with recorded temporal objects in different ways over time suggests that memory is not constructed solely out of imagination's relation to perceptual experience. Rather, in addition to the interplay of primary and secondary retentions, there is an additional interplay between primary and tertiary retentions. While the memory that is a painting or a photograph, a concerto or a film, is not the memory of anyone engaged in the viewing of it, that memory can nevertheless be interwoven with the consciousness of the spectator. In constructing such memories, the spectator ultimately must serve as editor, pasting together a montage of what the viewer takes to be the most significant elements of the whole. And this, Stiegler thinks, is how consciousness itself functions, as a sort of montage of temporal objects, sometimes music and cinema, more often lived experience in time. Nevertheless, these correspondences are enough for Stiegler to note that he takes the structure of consciousness itself to be cinematographic. And to see oneself as a self, according to Stiegler, to objectify oneself, is always already montage: self-reflection, self-awareness, self-consciousness—these are cinema.

Filmography

- ***The Man Who Knew Too Much*** (UK, 1934). *Directed by* Alfred Hitchcock. *Produced by* Michael Balcon. *Written by* Charles Bennett *and* D. B. Wyndham-Lewis. *Starring* Leslie Banks, Edna Best, Peter Lorre, Nova Pilbeam, *and* Frank Vosper.
- ***Gone with the Wind*** (USA, 1939). *Directed by* Victor Fleming. *Produced by* David O. Selznick. *Written by* Sidney Howard. *Starring* Clark Gable, Vivien Leigh, Leslie Howard, *and* Olivia de Havilland.
- ***A Streetcar Named Desire*** (USA, 1951). *Directed by* Elia Kazan. *Produced by* Charles K. Feldman. *Written by* Tennessee Williams. *Starring* Vivien Leigh, Marlon Brando, Kim Hunter, *and* Karl Malden.
- ***The Man Who Knew Too Much*** (USA, 1956). *Directed and Produced by* Alfred Hitchcock. *Written by* Angus MacPhail. *Starring* James Stewart *and* Doris Day.
- ***Four O'Clock*** (USA, 1957). *Directed by* Alfred Hitchcock. *Produced by* Shamley Productions. *Written by* Francis Cockrell. *Starring* Nancy Kelly, E. G. Marshall, Richard Long, Tom Pittman, *and* Harry Dean Stanton.
- ***La Dolce Vita*** (Italy, 1960). *Directed by* Federico Fellini. *Produced by* Giuseppe Amato *and* Angelo Rizzoli. *Written by* Federico Fellini, Ennio Flaiano, Tullio Pinelli, *and* Brunello Rondi. *Starring* Marcello Mastroianni, Anita Ekberg, Anouk Aimée, Yvonne Furneaux, Magali Noël, Alain Cuny, *and* Nadia Gray.
- ***L'Eclisse*** [*The Eclipse*] (Italy, 1962). *Directed by* Michelangelo Antonioni. *Produced by* Robert *and* Raymond Hakim. *Written by* Michelangelo Antonioni, Tonino Guerra, Elio Bartolini, *and* Ottiero Ottieri. *Starring* Alain Delon, Monica Vitti, Francisco Rabal, *and* Louis Seigner.
- ***America America*** (USA, 1963). *Directed, Produced, and Written by* Elia Kazan. *Starring* Stathis Giallelis.
- ***Mon oncle d'Amérique*** [*My American Uncle*] (France, 1980). *Directed by* Alain Resnais. *Produced by* Philippe Dussart. *Written by* Henri Laborit *and* Jean Gruault. *Starring* Gérard Depardieu, Nicole Garcia, *and* Roger Pierre.
- ***Intervista*** [*Interview*] (Italy, 1987). *Directed by* Federico Fellini. *Produced by* Ibrahim Moussa *and* Pietro Notarianni. *Written by* Federico Fellini *and* Gianfranco Angelucci. *Starring* Anita Ekberg, Marcello Mastroianni, Federico Fellini, *and* Sergio Rubini.

CINEMATIC TIME

Translated by Stephen Barker

Desire for Stories/Stories of Desire

The propensity to believe in stories and fables, the passion for fairy tales, just as satisfying in the old as in the very young, is perpetuated from generation to generation because it forges the link between the generations. Insatiable, they hold out the promise, to generations to come, of the writing of new episodes of future life, yet to be invented, to be fictionalized [*fabuler*].

This ancient desire for narrative(s) still orders modern society: it animates the most complex, and most secret, of social movements. But the conditions of this desire's satisfaction have been radically transformed; it has become the object of a global industry.

What Horkheimer and Adorno call "cultural industries" now constitute the very heart of economic development, whose most intimate power is clearly always the most ancient desire of all stories, and the key to (all contemporary) desire in general; but this desire is currently, in fact, increasingly subjugated to the developmental conditions of the technical transmission industries that by the end of the twentieth century and the beginning of the twenty-first have, in the sense that when we ponder the conditions of the very possibilities of transmission at least as an act of inheritance, succeeded in becoming both a genealogical connection and the *enunciation* of that connection between generations.

Global commerce now develops by mobilizing techniques of persuasion owing everything to the narrative arts. There is no event, no moment, independent of the desire for stories. Media networks and the programming industries exploit this fictionalizing *tendency* by systematizing the specific resources of audiovisual technics. And within the horizon of these immense technological and social issues, *cinema* occupies a unique place. Its technics of image and sound—now including informatics and telecommunications—re-invent our belief in stories that are now told with remarkable, unparalleled power. But at the same time, these technical powers cast doubt on and sow incredulity into the future of a world to whose disruption they have already greatly contributed.

If cinematic narratives' influence on the public results at its most fundamental level from a desire for the most ancient stories, and if this is a desire that can be found in every age, and if that underlies every era of the arts and all techniques for making such stories believable, it is all the more necessary that we analyze—and in detail—the *uniqueness* of the techniques that appeared specifically with cinema, techniques that more than any others in history have organized the programming industries' production practices, and we must do this in order to account for the incomparable efficacy of "the animated sound-image," to understand the extraordinary belief-effect it produces in the spectator: to explain how and why the cinema, in *becoming television* (i.e., the technical network as producer and diffuser of symbols through a global industry), combines the universal desire for fiction and, through it, conditions the entirety of humanity's evolution, though always at the risk of exhausting its desire for stories.

This analysis is all the more necessary since that cinematic singularity in turn reveals another singularity: that of the "human soul" as such; the cinematic techno-logically exhumes the "mechanism" of "hidden art" in its "depths."

Boredom

Which one of us, on a gloomy autumn Sunday afternoon, one of those afternoons when one feels like doing nothing, bored even with not wanting to do anything has not had the desire to watch some old film, no matter which, either at some nearby movie house, if it is in town and there are a few dollars to waste, or on video or DVD at home—or (last resort) just turning on the television where in the end there is no film but some very mediocre series, or indeed *anything*? Just to be lost in the flow of images.

Why don't we turn it off and pick up a book—a book, say, in which we could find a really good story, strong and well written? Why, on such a Sunday afternoon, do those moving images win out over written words in beautiful books?

The answer is that we need only look. And even if what we are looking at is completely inane but the filmmaker has somehow been able to exploit the video-cinematographic possibilities, the cinematic will attract our attention to the passing images, no matter what they are, and we will prefer to see them unfold before our eyes. We become immersed in the time of their flowing forth; we forget all about ourselves watching, perhaps "losing ourselves" (losing track of *time*), but however we define it, we will be sufficiently captured, not to say captivated, to stay with it to the very end.

During the passing ninety minutes or so (fifty-two in the case of the tele-visual "hour") of this *pastime*, the time of our consciousness will be totally passive within the thrall of those "moving" images that are linked together by noises, sounds, words, voices. Ninety or fifty-two minutes of our life will have passed by *outside* our "real" life, but *within* a life or the lives of people and events, real or fictive, to which we will have conjoined our time, adopting their events as though they were happening to us as they happened to them.

If by some lucky chance the film is a good one, we who are watching it in complete lethargy, the core validation of the animated sound-image by which we can leave everything behind and still be completely uninvolved—not even (as with a book) following written sentences and turning pages, careful not to lose the gist of the story; indeed, if the film is good, we come out of it less lazy, even re-invigorated, full of emotion and the desire to do something, or else infused with a new outlook on things: the cinematographic machine, taking charge of our boredom, will have transformed it into new energy, transubstantiated it, made something out of nothing—the nothing of that terrible, nearly fatal feeling of a Sunday afternoon of nothingness. The cinema will have brought back the expectation of *something*, something that must come that will come, and that will come to us from our own life: from this seemingly non-fictional life that we re-discover when, leaving the darkening room, we hide ourselves in the fading light of day.

Cinema's Two Fundamental Principles

In cinema we never have to be wary of losing a text's development: there is no text. And where there is none, it enters us without our having to look for it. Cinema weaves itself into our time; it becomes the temporal fabric of those ninety or fifty-two minutes of unconscious consciousness that is characteristic of a being, a film viewer, strangely immobilized by motion.

This is true because of cinema's two fundamental principles:

1. Cinematographic recording is an extension of photography; photography is an analog recording technique (which I analyze in *Technics and Time, 2* [12]), like the reality effect Roland Barthes describes in showing that a photograph's *noēme* is its "that-has-been":

> I call "photographic referent" not the *optimally* real thing to which an image or a sign refers but the *necessarily* real thing which has been placed before the lens, without which there would be no photograph. Painting can feign reality without having seen it.... In Photography, I can never deny that *the thing has been there*. There is a superimposition here: of reality and the past....
>
> Looking at a photograph, I inevitably include in my scrutiny the thought of that instant, however brief, in which a real thing happened to be motionless in front of the eye. I project the present photograph's immobility upon the past shot, and it is this arrest which constitutes the pose.[1]

The instant of the snap coincides with the instant of *what* is snapped, and it is in this co-incidence of two instants that the basis of the possibility of a conjunction of past and reality allowing for a "transfer" of the photograph's immobility in which the spectator's "present" coincides with the appearance of the spectrum.

2. The cinema adds sound by including *phono*-graphic recording. The phonogram, like the photo, results from an analogic technique of artificial memorization, which is why what is true of the photo is also, to a large extent, true of all phonograms: listening to a recorded concert, I must include in my listening experience the fact that the concert "has been," has already taken place. But the photo's truth is only the same as that of the phonogram to a certain point, since in the phonogram I am dealing with a fluid object, with an unfolding that changes the terms of analysis: the aural object is itself a flux in which it is impossible to isolate a moment of sound: it does not have a Barthesian "pose"; it emerges from the phenomenology of what Husserl calls "temporal objects."

Cinema can include sound because film, as a photographic recording technique capable of representing movement, is itself a temporal object susceptible to the phenomenological analysis proper to this kind of object. A film, like a melody, is essentially a flux: it consists of its unity in and as flow. The temporal object, as flux, coincides with the stream of consciousness of which it is the object: the spectator's.

The power of these two cinematic principles, and thus of the singularity of cinematic recording techniques, results from two other co-incident conjunctions:

- on the one hand, the phono-photographic coincidence of past and reality ("there is a double conjoint position: of reality and of the past," which induces this "reality effect"—believability—in which the spectator is located, in advance, by the technique itself);

[1] Barthes, *Camera Lucida*, 76, 78. Henceforth CL.

- on the other, the coincidence between the film's flow and that of the film spectator's consciousness, linked by phonographic flux, initiates the mechanics of a complete adoption of the film's time with that of the spectator's consciousness—which, since it is itself a flux, is captured and "channeled" by the flow of images. This movement, infused with every spectator's desire for stories, liberates the movements of consciousness typical of cinematic *emotion*.

Consciousness of "Cinematic Illusion"

In *The Movement Image*, Gilles Deleuze reverses what Henri Bergson in *Creative Evolution* calls the "cinematic illusion," which Deleuze summarizes thus:

> Cinema, in fact, works with two complementary givens: instantaneous sections which are called images; and a movement or a time which is impersonal, uniform, abstract invisible, or imperceptible, which is "in" the apparatus, and "with" which the images are made to pass consecutively. Cinema thus gives us a false movement—it is the typical example of false movement. But it is strange that Bergson should give the oldest illusion such a modern and recent name ("cinematographic").... Does this mean that for Bergson the cinema is only the projection, the reproduction of a constant, universal illusion? As though we had always had cinema without realizing it?[2]

Deleuze is certainly correct in objecting to Bergson's idea that the production of illusion is "also its correction, in a certain way." But he still does not draw out all of the consequences of his own argument—precisely because he does not take into account the specificity of this reproduction as a technique of analogico-photographic recording integrating the Barthesian "that-has-been," and as the fusion of instantaneous poses within the flux of a temporal object. Thus, it seems, he fails to explain what it means to have "always had cinema without realizing it," and thus to account for the power of the animated image.

It is Husserl who thinks through the temporal object. But to critique Bergson and Deleuze in Husserl's name is a delicate matter: Husserl himself completely neglects the phenomenon of recording in his analysis; in fact, he even excludes it. I have tried to show in the two previous volumes of *Technics and Time* that in so doing he commits a grave error,[3] which has led me to hypothesize an *essentially* cinemato-graphic structure for consciousness in general, as if it had "always had cinema without realizing it"—which explains the singular power of cinemato-graphic persuasion. This volume is dedicated to the development of that hypothesis. In order to accomplish this, in what follows I will have to summarize the essentials of what was established in the concluding chapter of *Technics and Time, 2*, "Temporal Object and Retentional Finitude"—but with regard to a new problemic: the "Kuleshov Effect."

---

[2] Deleuze, *The Movement Image*, 2, 3. Henceforth MI

[3] In the concluding chapter of *Technics and Time, 2*, "Temporal Object and Retentional Finitude." I also maintain that Husserl himself, later on partially "corrected" this position.

The Kuleshov Effect

Working through the concept of the temporal object in the fifth section of *Logical Investigations*, Husserl attempts to account for the temporality of all consciousness as a structure of flux. The question is thus to analyze the phenomenological conditions constituting this flux. But it is impossible for Husserlian phenomenology to engage in such an analysis of consciousness: its structure being intentional, consciousness is always consciousness *of* something; it is only possible to account for the temporality of consciousness by analyzing an "object" that is itself temporal.

Husserl discovers this object in 1905: melody. A melody is a temporal object in the sense that it is constituted only in its duration. As a temporal object its phenomenality is flow. A glass—say, a plain glass of water—is clearly a temporal object in the sense that it exists *in time* and is thus subject to universal physical laws and to entropy: it is temporal because it is not eternal. This is true of all "real" objects. But a properly temporal object is not simply "in time": it is *formed* temporally, woven in threads of time—as what appears in passing, what happens, what manifests itself in disappearing, as flux disappearing even as it appears. And the properly temporal object is the ideal object constituting the temporal fabric of the stream of consciousness itself, since the flux of the temporal object precisely coincides with the stream of consciousness of which it is the object. To account for the structure of the temporal object's flux is to account for the structure of the stream of consciousness of which it is the object.

In the temporal object as melody, Husserl discovers *primary retention*.

Primary retention is a kind of memory, but it is nonetheless not the aspect of memory involving recall. Husserl sometimes calls this "re-memory" sometimes "secondary memory."

Primary retention is what the *now* of an unfolding temporal object retains in itself from all of its previous *nows*. Even though they have passed, these preceding *nows* are maintained within the temporal object's current *now*, and, in this respect, they remain present even while perpetually becoming past; they remain present as having happened and in being sustained as having happened in the current *now*—they are maintained as *both* present and absent in the currently occurring *now* and insofar as the temporal object is not completely unfolded, completely past but still *passing* (i.e., temporal).

When I hear a melody, as a temporal object it presents itself to me as it unfolds. In the course of this process each note that is presented *now* retains in itself the preceding note, which itself retains the preceding one, etc. The current note contains within it all the preceding notes; it is the "now" as the maintainer of the object's presence: the temporal object's presence is its passing maintenance. This continuity is the temporal object's *unity*. Because the sonorous *now* retains all the notes preceding it, the present note can sound melodic, can be "musical," whether it is harmonic or unharmonic: it continues to be properly a *note* and not merely a sound or a noise.

Properly understood, for Husserl these primary retentions cannot be seen as memories in the sense that one can remember, for example, a melody one heard yesterday. That would only be a matter of recall, the recall of something that happened but is no longer present; primary retention, on the contrary, is an originary association between the *now* and what Husserl calls the "just-past," which remains present in the now. Maintaining the just-past in an ongoing present provides continuity to what is making itself present *now*, the most obvious example of which is melody in which a note can clearly only occur through an association with the notes that preceded and will follow it (those to follow being the ones that will resonate as a retention in the *current* note, which will be retained in its turn, but with which it will then share space as a protention concealed and sustained from preceding retentions). This is what has been called the "Kuleshov Effect,"[4] though it is considered by François Albera to be nothing more than a myth since Kuleshov himself never fully described it, and since the experience that catalyzes it can, as Albera emphasizes, be initially attributed to Pudovkin.[5] In any case, historically, the Kuleshov Effect consists of inserting the same image of the actor Mozzhukhin's face numerous times into a series of sequences constructed around the image, in which each time the actor's face appears it does so with three other quite different images. The image of Mozzhukhin's face, though it is always the same, is nonetheless perceived by viewers as three different images, each seeming to produce a different version of the same face.

In fact, it is this cinematic *effect* that ceaselessly produces a particular consciousness, projecting onto its objects everything that has preceded them within the sequence into which they have been inserted and that only they produce. And in fact this is the very principle of cinema: to connect disparate elements together into a single temporal flux.

Husserl's principle of primary retention is the most productive conceptual basis through which to analyze this "generalized cinema." Though Franz Brentano was the first to attempt to think through the primary retention of the just-past, according to Husserl he had failed, in that Brentano claimed that primary retention, as the past originarily engendered by the present now of perception, was a product of the *imagination*, originarily associated—as the past—with this perception. In Brentano's version, it is the imagination that both provides retention with the index of the past and that simultaneously connects the present now to its retentions in an out-flowing in which the passing temporal object finally disappears. But for Husserl such a viewpoint is inadmissible in that it amounts to saying that the time of a temporal object is *imagined*, not *perceived*—and that as a consequence, temporal objects are not realities but effects of the imagination: this would mean the negation of the reality of time itself.

However, in claiming that primary retention is not a product of the imagination but the phenomenon of the *perception* of time par excellence, Husserl must not only distinguish primary from secondary retention, which would obviously be necessary, but in fact *oppose* them.[6] Opposing primary memory to secondary memory, primary retentions of perception to re-memories, is to initiate an absolute difference between perception and imagination, to propose that perception owes nothing to the imagination, and that what is perceived is in no case imagined; further, this claim must absolutely not be contaminated by the persistent fictions produced by the imagination: life is perception, and perception is not imagination.

In other words, life is not cinema. Nor philosophy.

Life-as-perception of the living present, for Husserl, *does not tell us stories.*

---

[4] Xavier Lemarchand first compared this analysis to the Kuleshov Effect in his dissertation, *Différance et audiovisual numérique*, at the Université de technologie de Compiègne, 1998.

[5] Cf. Albera, Introduction to Lev Koulechov, *L'Art du cinéma et autres écrits*, 11. Henceforth FA.

[6] Jean-Michel Salanskis, in his very meticulous assessment of the first two volumes of *Technics and Time* ("Ecce faber," *Les temps modernes*, no. 608 [April-May 2000]), seems to me not to have understood this concluding chapter of volume 2, saying that in it I denounce Husserl's distinction between primary and secondary memories (that is, it must be noted, between perception and imagination). On the contrary, my goal there is precisely to reaffirm this distinction, asserting that it is weakened by the fact that Husserl himself understands it as an opposition. My claim is quite simply that a distinction is not an opposition, and further that this confusion is the origin of metaphysics—to which we will return at length. In this volume, and in volume 5 of *Technics and Time*, we will also return to a number of matters addressed in my good friend Salanskis' article.

Selections, Criteria, and Recordings

The Kuleshov Effect in particular and cinema in general nonetheless show that as an interdependence among just-past retentions is the ongoing present of a temporal object, and as the re-memory of the past in general, this primary/secondary opposition is a phantasm.

And if it were possible to demonstrate that lived reality is always a construct of the imagination and thus perceived only on condition of being fictional, irreducibly haunted by phantasms, then we would finally be forced to conclude that perception is subordinated to—is in a transductive relationship with—the imagination; that is, there would be no perception outside imagination, and vice versa, perception then being the imagination's projection screen. The relationship between the two would be constituted of previously nonexistent terms, and this in turn would mean that life is *always* cinema and that this is why "when one loves life one goes to the cinema" as though we go to the cinema in order to find life again—to be somehow resuscitated by it.

Philosophy would first have to ask: "Where do these phantasms come from?" And then: "What is a life that is in need of being constantly resuscitated?"

I have attempted to confront these questions in exploring the nature of a third kind of memory, not primary or secondary, but tertiary: a memory resulting from all forms of recordings—a memory Husserl designates as *consciousness of image*. Turning our attention to Freud later on,[7] we will see why these tertiary retentions are equally the support for the *protentions* constituting the expectation that animates a consciousness—built on archi-protentions: death, desire for reproduction and expenditure—whose core is the unconscious.

Primary retention, says Husserl, is grounded totally and uniquely on perception. The primary retentions constituting a temporal object are not the product of conscious selection, since if consciousness of time's unfolding were to select what it retained from that process, and if as a result it did not retain all of it, then it would no longer be a function purely and simply of perception, but already a kind of imagination, at least by default.

However, it is enough to have heard a melody twice through in order to be able to state that in these two hearings consciousness had not been listening with the same ears: that something happened between the first and second hearing. This is because each provides a new phenomenon, richer if the music is good, less rich if bad, that the melomane (the melody *maniac*) takes in heavy doses. This difference obviously results from an alteration in the phenomena of retention—i.e., from a variation in selection: consciousness does not retain everything.

From one hearing to another it is a matter of different ears, precisely because the ear involved in the second hearing has been affected by the first. The same melody, but not the same ears nor, thus, the same consciousness: consciousness has changed ears, having experienced the *event* of the melody's first hearing.

Consciousness is affected in general by phenomena presented to it, but this affect occurs in a special way with temporal objects. This is important to us in the current investigation because cinema, like melody, is a temporal object. Understanding the singular way in which temporal objects affect consciousness means beginning to understand what gives cinema its specificity,

---

[7] In Stiegler, *Technics and Time, 4: Symbols and Diabols, or the War of the Mind*, forthcoming.

its force, and its means of transforming life leading, for example, to the global adoption of "the American way of life." An inquiry such as this presupposes an analysis of the specifics and the specificity of the recording techniques producing cinematic flux and the effects it engenders in consciousness, especially in that consciousness is *already cinematographic* in its principles of selection for primary memories, a selection that relies on criteria furnished by the play of secondary memory and associated tertiary elements, the combination forming a montage through which a unified flux is constructed (as "stream of consciousness"), but which is identical in form to the cinematic flux of an actual film, as a temporal object and as the result of a constructed montage.

These are some of the preconditions for the association of primary, secondary, and tertiary retentions, of an associated-montage-of-retentions we will explore in this volume.

Consciousness has altered between two subsequent experiences of a melody, and this is why the same primary memories selected from the first hearing are not selected in the second, the object being the same, the phenomenon being different. But we must then ask how it is possible to say that "one consciousness can listen to the same temporal object twice." And this is in fact, and indeed, impossible without the existence of analog techniques for recording a melody phono-graphically. In other words, the fact of the consciousness's selection of primary retentions, and thus the intervention of the imagination at the heart of perception, is only made *obvious* by tertiary retention—by a phonogram, in that for the first time it makes possible the identical repetition of the same temporal object, within the context of a multiplicity of phenomena seen as so many diverse occurrences of one and the same object.

Let us examine this remarkable possibility more closely.

I hear, for the first time, a melody recorded on some mechanism, some phonographic support medium, analog or digital. Then later on I listen to the same melody again, from the same disc. Clearly in this new second hearing the sound just-past, insofar as it is now a primary retention into which other, previous primary retentions have been and are being incorporated, *in that it is past* and is no longer passing, yet in some fashion it did not happen *again* in precisely the same way as the first time. If this were not true, I would never hear anything other than what I had already heard. But the sound just-past, combining with other sounds just-past before it, and that pass each time differently from that first time, is absolutely new in its data, the phenomenon being a different phenomenon, the experience of the same piece of music giving me an *other*(ed) experience of that music despite my consciousness of the fact that it was the same music, played a second time, from which two different experiences occurred in me; at the same time, the passing of sound just-past, the primary retention constituting this unfolding in its original, unique construction—all of this "owes" something, in its very passage, to a previous passing that has disappeared, owes something to the preceding hearing: owes *that* hearing its modification.

In its passing, retention is modified and thus itself becomes past: retention-as-passage is essentially self-modification. But this modification is clearly *now* rooted in the secondary memory of the first hearing, even though on the other hand it precisely surpasses (is different from) that first hearing. In the melody's second hearing, what I hear results from the fact that I have previously heard it, yet it results from that previous hearing precisely and paradoxically in that I hear *something else* the second time: the first time, I never actually heard the melody; the second time, the already-known led me miraculously (back) to that unknown. In that second hearing, what is present is already known, but presents itself differently, such that the expected appears as unexpected.

Inscribed in my memory, the anteriority of the melody's first hearing arises from secondary memory, i.e., from the imagination and from fiction. What is strange is obviously that this already gives rise to the *not-yet*; that the already-heard gives way to the not-yet-heard, echoing a protentional expectation that has entered into a play of archi-protentions. Between the two hearings, consciousness has changed because a *clearing away* has taken place: primary retention is a selection process brought about through criteria that have been established during previous clearings away, which were themselves selections resulting from other, prior clearings. This occurs because as memorization, primary retention is also a primary memory *lapse*, a reduction of what *passes by* to a *past* that retains only what the criteria constituting the secondary retentions allow it to select: secondary retentions inhabit the process of primary retention in advance.

This is the case when I have already heard a melody and am hearing it again, but it is also the case when I have never heard it, since then I hear from the position of an expectation formed from everything that has already musically happened to me—I am responding to the Muses guarding the default-of-origin of my desire, within me. And this occurs because of a memory lapse, a *forgetting*, and because this forgetting occurs only as a function of certain criteria: my ability to construct the object of a critique. If "to memorize" did not mean already "to have forgotten," nothing could be retained, since nothing would have passed, nothing would have happened.

Imagine hypothetically that I have an infinite memory and that I can remember what happened yesterday. I thus remember every second and fraction of a second exactly identically. When I come to the end of the day, I remember that at that moment I am remembering the entire day, which I begin to do again in remembering myself remembering anew, each second exactly and identically, etc. There is no longer any difference, because there has been no selection: time has not *passed*. Nothing has happened nor can happen to me, neither present (in which something new always presents itself to me, including boredom with the absence of the new) nor past: the present no longer passing, no longer happening; no passage of time is possible. Time has ceased to exist.

In fact, remembering yesterday having a *past*, means reducing yesterday to less than today, diminishing yesterday, having no more than finite memories of it. This retentional finitude is the grounding condition of consciousness-as-temporal-flux. And what is true of secondary memory is true of all memory, including primary memory; thus primary retention can only be a selection, brought about according to criteria that are themselves the products of selections. However, in the case I have laid out here, i.e., understanding how we hear a melody recorded on any phonographic support mechanism, this secondary memory, indissociable (though different) from primary memory, is also indissociable from tertiary memory, "consciousness of image"—the phonogram as such.

And that is precisely what is at stake.

Phonographic Revelation

Husserl's examples of "consciousness of image," of what I call tertiary memory, are the painting or the bust. For Husserl, this "configuration through image," the object of a consciousness of image, plays absolutely no role in the constitution of a temporal object—nor, consequently, in the constitution of the flux of consciousness itself. Not only does such a memory type not appear to perception; it does not even appear to the past flow of consciousness, in contrast to secondary memory, which, though it no longer arises from perception, is inscribed in the flow of consciousness's past and appears to this living consciousness as its own past, since it was perceived.

For Husserl, the consciousness of image is not a *memory* of that consciousness; it is an artificial memory of what was not perceived nor lived by consciousness. A nineteenth-century painting is certainly a kind of memory, but one could not say, according to Husserl, that it is a memory of someone looking at it *now*. It is, rather, a memory trace of the painter, who has in some fashion exteriorized and frozen his memory, thus allowing, a century later, another consciousness to contemplate it as an image of the past—but in no case as a memory of his own lived past. In Husserlian phenomenology, only that which arises from conscious, *lived experience*, is, strictly speaking, unquestionable and should be taken into account in any analysis of the constituting conditions of phenomena. Husserl's phenomenological attitude consists of positioning consciousness as the constituter *of* the world, not something constituted *by* it. Since tertiary memory is a reality *in the world*, it cannot be constitutive of consciousness but must necessarily be derivative of a consciousness that has no real need of it.

However, since the unique event that is the advent of the technical possibility of analogic recording of a *temporal* musical object, and the ability to repeat it technically, the link between primary and secondary retentions has become obvious: clearly, even though each time it is repeated it is the same temporal object, it produces two different musical experiences. I *know* that it is the same temporal object, because I know that the melody was recorded by a technique producing a co-incidence between the stream of what was being recorded and that of the machine doing the recording. I know that the recording mechanism's time coincided with the melodic flux. And this co-incidence of machinic flux and that of the temporal object produces, for the flow of consciousness of both the object and its recording, a conjunction of past, reality, and this effect of the real that Barthes identifies in photography and that is replicated in the realm of sound, the difference being that as Barthes points out in the case of photography there is the *pose*, whereas in the case of phonography, of recorded sound (as in cinema), there is *flux*.

Consciousness of image, in the case of the phonogram (though it could also be said of cinematic recording), is what finally roots the primary and the secondary in one another, through the technical possibility of the temporal object's repetition (and it cannot be emphasized strongly enough that before the *phono*graph, as before the cinema, such repetitions were strictly impossible). At the same time it becomes obvious that the grounding of the *second primary* is in the memory of the *first primary*. It is obvious only because of the *fact* of recording: it is the phonographic *revelation* of the structure of *all* temporal objects.

Returning *to Intervista*

The consequences of this revelation are considerable: the criteria according to which consciousness selects primary retentions, passes them by consciousness, and distills them no longer applies solely to secondary retentions of lived, conscious memory, but equally to tertiary retentions; cinema shows us this most clearly.

To explore this point further, I must return to and extend the analysis I have already begun of a scene in Federico Fellini's *Intervista*.[8]

[8] This analysis was first presented in Rome in 1985 at the invitation of Jean Lauxerois and published in *La Revue Philosophique* in 1990 under the title "Mémoires gauches." I returned to it in the first chapter of *Technics and Time, 2*. Here I will extend those analyses, addressing their consequences for the temporal object, initiated in the last chapter of *Technics and Time, 2*, and whose principal results will be further explored within the context of this volume.

In the film, Fellini appears in a scene with Marcello Mastroianni, with whom he pays a visit to Anita Ekberg. In the course of the evening the three of them watch the Trevi Fountain scene [of Mastroianni and Ekberg] from *La Dolce Vita*. Thus, in *Intervista* we see an actress watching herself playing a character, and the scene's extreme tension results from its undecidability: Anita is appearing in a film by Fellini, but she is playing watching herself portraying a different character thirty years earlier, and no viewer of the second film, *Intervista*, could escape being certain that as she watches the earlier film—watches her *past* life, her *past* youth—Anita cannot simply play watching herself without knowing that this is a matter of the Quintessential Performance, the most serious one of all, the first and the last engagement, the play of all plays: no one looking at herself again, from thirty years later, having aged those thirty years, could not *not* feel the terrible reality of time passing through the photographic "that has been," through the "conjunction of reality and the past," the silvery co-incidence re-animated by cinema's temporal flux. *We* see an actress playing an actress watching an actress playing a "real" character in a fictional film, but we know that she is "playing" at watching herself *having been*, that what she is doing is no longer a simple portrayal, a pure performance any actor might be required to give (to play this or that character), but the absolutely tragic staging of *her own* existence, insofar as that existence is *passing by* irremediably and forever—*forever*, except for what concerns this silvery image she has left on a reel of film: an image in which she has been preserved.

Watching herself performing thirty years earlier, Anita must feel the future anterior so striking to Roland Barthes as he looks at the photograph of Lewis Payne taken several hours before Payne's hanging:

> In 1865, young Lewis Payne tried to assassinate Secretary of State W. H. Seward. Alexander Gardner photographed him in his cell, where he was waiting to be hanged. The photograph is handsome, as is the boy: that is the *studium*. But the *punctum* is: *he is going to die*. I read at the same time: *This will be* and *this has been*; I observe with horror an anterior future of which death is the stake. By giving me the absolute past of the pose (aorist), the photograph tells me death in the future. What *pricks* me is the discovery of this equivalence. In front of the photograph of my mother as a child, I tell myself: she is going to die: I shudder, like Winnicott's psychotic patient, *over a catastrophe which has already occurred*. Whether or not the subject is already dead, every photograph is this catastrophe. (CL, 96)

"Every photograph is this catastrophe"; every photograph declares this future anterior whose stakes are death—and the dramatic outcome of every narrative, every play, every cinematographic emotion.

In Anita's case, she is not merely *saying* this: as image, she is dead *and* she is going to die. She must say to herself: "I am going to die; I am dying." This *present participle* is *precisely that of flux*—that of her past life, of the film on which she has been recorded, and of her current consciousness of this film that, in unfolding, carries her along and makes her pass by, placing her in a time that leads toward the absence of time: non-passing, infinite memory that will no longer be special, where everything will be retained forever in its instant: "*The Instant of my Death*."

But all of that is, in this scene in *Intervista*, the result of the fact that film is a temporal object in which

> the actor's body is conflated with the character's; where the film's passing is necessarily also the actor's past, the moments of life of a character are instantly moments of the actor's past. That life is merged, in its being filmed, with that of its characters. (TT2, 22)

This confusion of the actor's life with the filmed one is that of primary, secondary, and tertiary retentions coinciding in a single event: the properly cinemato-graphic event. In this filmic coincidence, which Fellini stages in an extraordinary way by including the fact that, for any viewer of *Intervista* who has already seen *La Dolce Vita*, the latter necessarily also becomes part of the viewer's past, and a reference to the earlier film is not simply a reference made to one fiction in the course of another fiction, which would merely be a citation: this first fiction, *La Dolce Vita*, cited in the second fiction, *Intervista*, is simultaneously

1. a *tertiary retention* (an artificial memory presented in a support medium, of which an extract, a piece of film, is projected into another film and recorded on another piece of film);
2. a *temporal object* that has been seen and re-seen, and that is currently being seen by the viewer of *Intervista*; and further,
3. as a temporal object, the film is a secondary memory for this viewer, a part of his or her past stream of consciousness, then re-activated;
4. ninety minutes of the viewer's past life, the running time of *La Dolce Vita*, have been lived as the extended retention of primary retentions in the *now* of an elapsed narrative entitled (in its entirety) *La Dolce Vita*, and of which a particular sequence is then re-lived (i.e., the section included in *Intervista*); and
5. included in *Intervista*'s cinematic flux; that is, in Anita's passing stream of consciousness as well.

Additionally, *La Dolce Vita* is no longer simply a fiction for someone viewing *Intervista*: it has become its past, such that watching Anita watching herself perform the scene in *La Dolce Vita*, the viewer sees himself or herself passing by. This is true even if *La Dolce Vita* is not part of the viewer's past in the same way it is in Anita's, Mastroianni's, and Fellini's past; all three have actually lived what the spectator sees "in the cinema." *Intervista*, as a temporal object, is temporal in making the temporal object *La Dolce Vita*, lived by the characters in *Intervista* just as by its current viewers—each in a particular role—re-appear.

Consequently, the viewer (of *Intervista*) faced with the impossibility of distinguishing between reality and fiction, between perception and imagination, while (each in his or her particular role) *all* must also say to themselves, "*We* are passing by there."

We will see in the next chapter that this impossibility of distinguishing, this undecidability, also haunts Kant in the *Critique of Pure Reason*.

In Chapter 3 we will find that this indistinction is the fundamental condition for constituting a *We*—and that it nonetheless *must* be distinguished.

America, America

It would be a simple matter to show that this scenario could only result in the most general of structures, structures of haunting and phantasmatic spectrality already predicted by Socrates to the Athenians[9] regarding the immortality of the soul.

"The immortality of the soul" is the screen—confusing perception and imagination, *doxa* and *epistēmē*, sensible and intelligible, which must always be distinguished without ever being placed in opposition—onto which that structure will then be projected and dissimulated: as projection screen "the immortality of the soul" is the opening of a great "film," *metaphysics*, introducing the extravagant Socrates, played by Plato.

Fellini stages this spectacle's machinery most clearly at *Intervista*'s conclusion, showing how metaphysics "functions," and beyond that, the "consciousness" that is its product. This structure is *revealed* in its greatest force, the force of direct evidence, in cinema, and because cinema is a temporal object.

In a similar frame, we might *remember* the characters in Resnais's *My American Uncle*, in which memory is a dense fabric of cinematographic citations. As he set out on the project, Resnais had imagined making a film consisting entirely of citations but had to abandon the idea for economic reasons:

> The idea of only using extracts from existing films existed from the very first scenario. At one point we even thought of making a film exclusively based on scenes drawn from the millions of films that make up the history of cinema. The novel, the cinema, and the theater contain every possible behavior. With enough time and patience, perhaps it might happen. But financially it would be a mad undertaking.[10]

The great French actor Jean Gabin appears in the memory of René Ragueneau, being played by Gérard Depardieu. Gabin was a cinematic presence, "in the limelight" as would have been said before World War II. In that cinematic era there were "stars." Stars: inaccessible, untouchable, *impassive*, yet visible, perceptible beings; beings balanced between, on the one hand, the intelligible, where they seemed to be fabricated in the spirit of a Greek ideality (and in the pre-philosophic spirit of divinities), and on the other hand, the corruptible, sublunary world of the viewer's eye beholding them, an eye so fragile, so obviously predisposed to vanishing, so flawed: an eye merely passing by.

By the very fact of this juxtaposition of the cinematographic temporal object as between the real life of actors and that of their fictional characters, the Hollywood star could only *become* a star through a play of hauntings in which reality and fiction, perception and imagination become confused together—and along with them primary, secondary, and tertiary memory.

The great case in point that we still remember is Vivien Leigh's Blanche Dubois in *A Streetcar Named Desire*;[11] Blanche is a faded Southern belle who has lost the family house, a "house with colonnades," one of those residences that the Scarlett O'Hara of *Gone with the Wind*[12] would not abandon at any price. Watching Vivien Leigh playing Blanche, how could one avoid saying

---

[9] Cf. *Technics and Time, 4*, forthcoming.

[10] Resnais, *L'Avant-Scène Cinéma*, 7.

[11] Elia Kazan's 1951 film released in France with the title *Un tramway nommé Désir*.

[12] Victor Fleming, 1939; in French, *Autant en emporte le vent*.

to oneself that she, and director Elia Kazan, and all the viewers of *Streetcar*, are haunted by Scarlett: by her extraordinary beauty, her brilliant and unbearable coolness as a mad young Southern woman—how could one avoid it? Who has not seen, loved, and detested Scarlett? *Gone with the Wind* was made a dozen years before *A Streetcar Named Desire* and is, of course, among the greatest successes in cinema history; it is a film that has been seen—that has *passed by*, unfolded, been unrolled—literally everywhere, and with it, Scarlett O'Hara, as played by Vivien Leigh, loved and hated by the entire world. Kazan could neither ignore nor neglect this when he cast his later film. How not to shudder before such a psychotic, at the catastrophe that has unfolded when we see Blanche taken away forever from her "sanctuary" with Stella and Stanley? How not to feel insane ourselves, carried along by this exemplar of the great, mad American destiny—that never fails at the same time to sell us, through making us laugh and cry in the face of our own fate, the American Way of Life? *America, America!*

Repetition and the Unconscious

All of this is possible only because the structure of consciousness is thoroughly cinematographic, assuming that we can call "cinematographic" what unfolds through a montage of temporal objects—objects constituted through their movement.

If Husserl was unable to perceive the question posed by phonographic and cinematographic recordings and their identical repetition of the same temporal object, each time producing two different phenomena, he does nonetheless analyze the way in which secondary memory allows for the willful repetition, through the imagination, of a previously perceived temporal object. And Husserl further notes that in such a case (for example, I remember a melody I heard yesterday), consciousness possesses a freedom unavailable to perception since consciousness is within the imagination. For example, I can return to the memory of a concert I heard yesterday, speeding it up or slowing it down: "we can 'in all freedom' accommodate larger or smaller fragments of the process re-presented with its modes of flow, and thus experience it more quickly or more slowly."[13] Here Husserl addresses a remarkable phenomenon, recollection, in which "my past life is thus given to me, precisely and simply given as the 're-given' of life" (CIT, 60).

This means that in such a case secondary memory would be the repetition of the primary temporal object as it occurs, pure and simple. But in fact such recollection is impossible, because a temporal object consists not simply of retentions but also of *protentions*—anticipations—the second time I hear it, thanks to tertiary retention, or even if I reproduce it in my imagination, thanks to secondary memory. In both cases the anticipations that were blank during the first hearing are no longer blank: secondary memory can no more erase them than it can erase tertiary memory: it has already taken place, it "has been." Certainly, in the one case it is repeated objectively, as in analogic, photographic, or phonographic tertiary retention. But the conscious phenomenon (and the phenomenon is always that of consciousness) is different each time. In the other case, the repetition is subjective (i.e., in secondary memory): there is only the phenomenon of repetition but without objective repetition, and thus it is necessarily already different *as* phenomenon; were this not the case, it would contradict what Husserl says initially regarding the difference between imagination and perception, which for him is a

[13] Husserl, *On the Phenomenology of the Consciousness*, 66. Henceforth CIT.

principle, confirmed by the fact that in the imagination of secondary memory, anticipations or protentions have already occurred such that the imagining consciousness can no longer efface them. As Paul Ricoeur emphasizes,

> If the way in which memory presents the past differs fundamentally from the presence of the past in retention, how could a representation [a temporal object passing through secondary memory] be true to its object?[14]

"Recollection" is thus impossible. I have already pointed out why everything is inscribed in advance within the retentional finitude of consciousness: the fact that memory is originally selection and forgetting. But that in turn means that in all remembering of a past temporal object there is a necessary process of *dérushage*, of montage, a play of special effects, of slowing down, accelerating, etc.—and even freezing on an image: this is the time of reflection that Husserl analyzes precisely as such, a moment of the analysis of memory, of recollection's decomposition.

But given that we have also seen that this selection first of all affects primary retention itself, we would then have to say that consciousness is always in some fashion a montage of overlapping primary, secondary, and tertiary memories. Thus, we must mark as tertiary retentions all forms of "objective" memory: cinematogram, photogram, phonogram, writing, paintings, sculptures—but also monuments and objects in general, since they bear witness, for me, say, of a past that I enforcedly did not myself live.

Memory in all its forms would then always be a sort of rushing montage of frozen images, from the simplest juxtaposition to the greatest art of the scenarist, according to the quality of the consciousness and the nature of the object presented to it, and according to the criteria—the secondary memories, i.e., the experiences—it evokes from the object.

In one scene in *Mon oncle d'Amérique*, René Ragueneau "projects" a certain scene from a Jean Gabin film onto what is at that moment serving as the background and/or the projection screen. This is a projection that is clearly not a stranger to what Freud discusses in *Metapsychology*.

"Consciousness" would then be this post-production center, this control room assembling the montage, the staging, the *realization*, and the direction, of the flow of primary, secondary, and tertiary retentions, of which the *unconscious*, full of protentional possibilities (including the speculative), would be the producer. "Post-production" occurs when the "rushes" and the montage are out of sync: this is the phenomenon of the dream. Direct control occurs when consciousness "builds" such that it is "captured": this is the waking state. Cinema is of the order of the dream. The waking state is a sort of tele-vision. It is certainly always possible to think while awake; this would be tele-cinema.

The Protentions of *Four O'Clock*

Memory is originarily forgotten because it is necessarily a reduction of what *has* passed to the *fact* that it has passed, that it is in the past, and that it is thus *less* than the present. The

---

[14] Ricoeur, *Temps et récit III*, 55. Henceforth TR.

past is diminished in the present of its being remembered; if not, it would not have passed, it would not be passing. This is the normal structure of passage, of passing, in general, of time itself, which is why cinema and, more generally, all narratives can and must abridge and condense the time of what is being re-cited within the time of the story. In two hours I can tell a story that takes place over two millennia. The transmission of all knowledge (all "education"), in the family or in a school, rests on the originary law of condensation that occurs between the past (condensed) and the present (condensing). This condensation—what Bergson calls "contraction"—is a montage, a selection, an anthology of previous scenes, lived by me either through direct perceptions or through various images projected onto the support screen of the present. Cinema is a specific case of this, and one whose specificity results from the fact that it is a temporal object whose speed can be controlled, across a variety of production, post-production, projection, and reception machines, through what is now called a time-code.

Condensation-as-montage (Freud analyzes it in *On the Interpretation of Dreams*) is employed masterfully in Hitchcock's *Four O'Clock*,[15] as the most meticulous interactions between retentions and protentions, applied in direct connection with clock-time, providing a perfect opportunity to analyze in great detail the link between time-code and clock-time, as a demonstration of the condensation effect.

In *Four O'Clock*, a jealous husband, who is a watchmaker, has laid a trap for his wife, suspecting her of infidelity. He plans to leave home at four o'clock in the afternoon, at which point his wife's lover will sneak into the house. The watchmaker has devised a time bomb to explode when they are together. But just as he is preparing to leave, while activating the time bomb (the clock's alarm is the detonator), he surprises some robbers in the house. After a struggle they overpower him and tie him up in the basement, right next to the clock and the explosives—about which he has been unable to tell them. In the course of the final thirty-two minutes and twenty-three seconds of the film's running time—which last a total of forty-eight minute and twenty-three seconds—the cinema spectator participates in the growing anticipation of, and the growing terror provoked by, the explosion—*provoked in the spectator—via* the watchmaker. In this final section, the longest in the film, it is quite simple to measure Hitchcock's condensation effect since he shows the clock sixteen times.

The film is in three parts: the statistics of Hitchcock's condensation show this mounting terror: the film's first segment, introducing the watchmaker and his plan, takes place over approximately one full day; in the film it lasts nine minutes and eight seconds (9' 08").

The second part, as his growing resolve reaches the point at which he decides to go through with his plan, lasts 6' 52"; it covers two days in his life.

The third and last section, the countdown to the bomb's explosion, takes 32' 23" to show two hours of his life. But even during these 32' 23", the relation between the character's lived time and the film's elapsed time progressively compresses: it contracts as a function of the events controlling our anticipation. (Hitchcock articulates retentions and protentions in order to provoke suspense via a montage that lays out the nonlinear progression of the two time frames.)

The final minute before the anticipated explosion lasts *seventy-two seconds*: Hitchcock elongates and dilates time.

---

[15] Shown as an episode of the television series *Suspicion* in 1957.

In the end—no explosion. Yet what is astonishing is that when I watch the film again, I tremble again: I take on the character's anticipation, putting myself "in his skin." The protentional effect is not eliminated by the fact that the anticipation has already been dissipated—I know what is (not) going to happen. I am caught up in the flow of the cinematic action such that even if I notice something different *each time* I see it, I am compelled again, each time, to adopt the character's time, through abbreviation, condensation, contraction, of which the *de-contraction* of the "real time" final minute (60" expanded to 72") cancels the effect of all the preceding contracted, condensed, abridged minutes.

And yet, the emergence of all protentions occurs through the irreversible nature of their unfolding. This irreversibility is precisely the protention containing all protentions, the archi-protention: awareness of time as such, as it is woven through the "primitive scenes" that are the occult archival basis of all of Hitchcock's dramas, worked out as no one else has ever done.[16]

The Eclipse

In *The Eclipse* (1962), Michelangelo Antonioni shows the announcement, on the trading floor of the Stock Market, of a courier's death, then films a "minute of silence"—that actually lasts nearly a full minute (56 seconds, according to the timer on the VCR). The unfolding of this "real time" does not mean that the *cinematic* time is any more true or "realistic" when it coincides with "life-time." In fact, in this case it means a minute of death-time. And further, in that long, immobilized silence, on the contrary it becomes even clearer for the living consciousness of the spectator that time in every guise is always the time of contraction, condensation, abbreviation—the time of montage: it is always *cinematic time*, and there is a conjunction between the cinematic flux and that of the viewer's consciousness. The viewer can adopt the characters' time, grafted onto the viewer's own time as selection and contradiction, and as a montage of the viewer's own memories.

The minute-long hiatus that lasts nearly a minute is inserted into condensed cinematic time like an eclipse: it is a suspension in the face of death, a suspension of death, of death as complete de-contraction. Cinema—that is, movement; that is, life—is respected, made concessions to: the trading floor's frantic motion that had been nothing but rushing, shouting, buying, selling—all that is interrupted. The precise recording of the minute-long pause suspends life, as a *selection*.

"A minute here costs billions," says Piero (Alain Delon) in a low voice to Vittoria (Monica Vitti). And then trading roars into action again.

How much does a minute of film cost? Does "a minute" really cost "billions"? The coincidence of a minute with a minute indicates that *without* this coincidence there is cinema, and that cinema, which brings many such coincidences into juxtaposition, has no need of them—and that *everything*

[16] *The Man Who Knew Too Much* (filmed using two different scenarios) occupies a unique place in Hitchcock's cinema with regard to cinematic temporality, the unfolding of the spectator's and the film's stream of consciousness, but also of the sound track's connection to the images, and with regard to the resulting process of adoption: the pivotal moment is in "real time," during the performance of a piece of music on the screen. The song plays the role of the watch in *Four O'Clock*. A single cry from Dorothy, the heroine, at the crucial moment of an assassination attempt that must take place during the crash of cymbals simultaneously breaks the sequence's real time and that of the music: the concert is interrupted. Dorothy is also a singer.

has a price: the price of passing time, for example, and of the irreducibility and irreversibility of its selection. All cinema is "Hollywoodian"; every film waits for its "selection" and thus its price; especially *this* film, with its minute of silence lasting approximately a minute, an example of European neorealism in the age of the "New Wave," making a pure "time-image" visible.

The Time of the Other

My time is always that of others. Cinema reveals this cinemato-graphically. Stream of consciousness *is* the contraction of time, whose initiation process occurs in a cinema in which my time, within the film's time, becomes the time of an other and an other time.

My time is constructed by being laminated onto the time it takes from others—including giving itself to those others in interweaving flows, like sap.

This is why solitude is so difficult to withstand: in solitude, where the other is absent, there is no more time, "nothing is going on," "nothing happening," and I must face boredom, since I am encountering only the empty shell of a "me" that is no longer the time of the other.

If on some bleak Sunday afternoon cinematographic or tele-visual distraction can bring me a synthetic other, it is because cinematic flux makes my selections for me. It changes me and quenches my thirst, relaxes me, renews me like a tonic, *and* gives me access to the other who is (always) right next to me and who is only waiting to come to life (i.e., to cinema, to the image of the other) to be set in motion as a projection on a screen.

It is only possible to find the other in oneself. It is only possible to find in oneself—through the detour of an other, real or fictional—the other *of* oneself, the other as self, a new self following the story of (a) myself whose others consist of all the occasions and the possible graftings of a secondary story. I anticipate the other whom I expect will come into my film, my cinematic medium, by appearing on the screen—as co-producer, screenwriter, character, atmosphere, accessories, etc. I have more recently referred to this phenomenon[17] as the pre-textuality of the *I*, or the *I* that is already a *We*.

As Bergson says, the conscious present is the contraction of the entire past: "the present" for consciousness *is* memory, and because time, which is primary retention, consists of selection via secondary retention that is the cinema in/of accelerated life, I see, I remember everything that has been repressed/archived: images, sounds, smells, touches, contacts, caresses; I remember everything I forget *and* remember, everything I have abridged *and* condensed. This results in situations with characters: the very people onto whom I project a new scene and its visual images.

The other is not simply "others": I construct the documentary in specific—I can see the garden, the street, the mountain, the sea, the highway, the cars in front of me on the highway, those passing by, the crowds, the entire world of observation in which nothing happens to me but what happens to me holistically.

I can also see "myself" as an other; I can film "myself," project "myself," graft "myself" onto "myself," see "myself" as a tutor, as a support, a screen: writing, for example. That is, to "objectify," "exteriorize," "express" myself: to "tertiarize" myself.

And it is a montage, already cinema.

---

[17] In TT2. For more on this concept, see my "Ce qui fait défaut," *Césure*, no. 54 (1995).

Television

In the second half of the twentieth century, cinematic time overflowed into television. In 1954, 1% of French households had a television set. In 1960, 13.1%. In 1970, 70.4%. In 1980, 90.1%. In the world as a whole, it is estimated that today there are over a billion televisions: virtually the entire population of the world has been "converted."

The twentieth century, born of cinema, in the end manifested the astonishing domination of consciousness by audiovisual temporal objects broadcast over hundreds of channels and countless programs constructing a new social time, a new temporal orientation, in the area economists have named "the programming industry," reminding us of what in 1947 Horkheimer and Adorno called the *Kulturindustrie*.

Just as the cinema inherits photographic techniques and aligns itself with photography, televisual techniques add to cinema certain specific characteristics that produce an identifiable televisual effect.

We have seen that the objectivity of the camera lens, the "that-has-been" in which the viewer of the photograph believes instantly—believes that what is "in" the photograph "has been" because the viewer knows (intuitively) that the photons deposited on photosensitive paper were reflected from a real body that they apparently reproduce through the optico-chemical reconstitution of the associations and contrasts of the photonic emissions from the photographed body, as an analogic technique. Cinema adds the dimension of time, retinal persistence, and the succession of photograms, producing a *temporal* object composed of a pre-, a during-, and an after-movement, all moving within the viewer's consciousness, which itself moves as its visual object (cinematic flux) moves. But the chief characteristic of temporal objects is that their flux coincides "point-by-point"[18] with the stream of consciousness of which it is the object—which means that consciousness of a temporal object adopts the object's time: conscious-time *is* that of the object, in a process of adoption through which the familiar phenomenon of cinematic identification becomes possible.[19]

Television adds two new photographic and cinematic effects:

1. As a technique of tele-diffusion television enables a mass public simultaneously to watch the same temporal object from any location; further, it makes the construction of temporal mega-objects, the programming grid through which various audiovisual temporal objects are linked together to form a network (the "television network");
2. As a technique for "live" transmission, it enables this public collectively and universally to live *through* any event at the moment it is occurring, and thus the diffusion of a live temporal object. The World Cup Final, held in France on July 12, 1998, and broadcast live, is an exemplary case—it is the "immediate reception" of the event that makes it an event.

These two televisual effects simultaneously transform the nature of the event itself and the most intimate life of the population: the programming industries have initiated a

---

[18] This is Husserl's term, in CIT.

[19] And what Serge Daney and Jean-Michel Frodon call the cinematic "taming machine" and the "mechanical redemption" effect. Cf. Frodon, *La projection nationale*.

synchronization that suddenly contains all diachronies that now constitute *culture* and thus also *consciousnesses*. This is the process at the core of Horkheimer and Adorno's "cultural industries."

Works Cited

Albera, François. 1994. *L'art du cinéma et autres écrits*. Laussane: L'Âge d'homme.

Barthes, Roland. [1980] 1981. *Camera Lucida*. Trans. Richard Howard. New York: Hill and Wang.

Frodon, Jean-Michel. 1998. *La projection nationale. Cinéma et nation*. Paris: Odile Jacob.

Deleuze, Gilles. [1983] 1986. *The Movement Image*. Trans. Hugh Tomlinson and Barbara Habberjam. Minneapolis: University of Minnesota Press.

Husserl, Edmund. [1966] 1991. *On the Phenomenology of the Consciousness of Internal Time*. Trans. John B. Brough. Boston: Kluwer Academic Publishers.

Resnais, Alain. 1981. "La vie est un roman." *L'Avant-Scène Cinéma*, no. 263 (March).

Ricoeur, Paul. 1985. *Temps et récit III, Le temps raconté*. Paris: Seuil.

Stiegler, Bernard. [1996] 2008. *Technics and Time, 2: Disorientation*. Trans. Stephen Barker. Stanford, CA: Stanford University Press.

EPILOGUE
THE SIX MOST BEAUTIFUL MINUTES IN THE HISTORY OF CINEMA

Giorgio Agamben

Translated by Jeff Fort

Sancho Panza enters a cinema in a provincial city. He is looking for Don Quixote and finds him sitting off to the side, staring at the screen. The theater is almost full; the balcony—which is a sort of giant terrace—is packed with raucous children. After several unsuccessful attempts to reach Don Quixote, Sancho reluctantly sits down in one of the lower seats, next to a little girl (Dulcinea?), who offers him a lollipop. The screening has begun; it is a costume film: on the screen, knights in armor are riding along. Suddenly, a woman appears; she is in danger. Don Quixote abruptly rises, unsheathes his sword, rushes toward the screen, and, with several lunges, begins to shred the cloth. The woman and the knights are still visible on the screen, but the black slash opened by Don Quixote's sword grows ever larger, implacably devouring the images. In the end, nothing is left of the screen, and only the wooden structure supporting it remains visible. The outraged audience leaves the theater, but the children on the balcony continue their fanatical cheers for Don Quixote. Only the little girl down on the floor stares at him in disapproval.

What are we to do with our imaginations? Love them and believe in them to the point of having to destroy and falsify them (this is perhaps the meaning of Orson Welles's films). But when, in the end, they reveal themselves to be empty and unfulfilled, when they show the nullity of which they are made, only then can we pay the price for their truth and understand that Dulcinea—whom we have saved—cannot love us.

INDEX